ABNORMALITY

ABNORMALITY

Martin E. P. Seligman University of Pennsylvania

David L. Rosenhan Stanford University

W · W · NORTON & COMPANY
New York · London

Library of Congress Cataloging-in-Publication Data

Seligman, Martin E. P.
    Abnormality / Martin E. P. Seligman, David Rosenhan
        p.   cm.
    Includes bibliographical references and index.
    ISBN 0-393-97085-X (pbk.)
    1. Psychology, Pathological—Miscellanea.   I. Rosenhan, David.
II. Title.
RC454.4.S455   1997
616.89—dc21   97-24504
                                                                                              CIP

The text of this book is composed in Galliard,
with the display set in Futura Medium Condensed.
Composition by TSI Graphics.
Manufacturing by R.R. Donnelley, Roanoke.
Book design by Jack Meserole.

Cover Illustration: Photograph by Neil Ryder Hoos.

ISBN 0-393-97085-X (pbk.)

W. W. Norton & Company, Inc., 500 Fifth Avenue, New York, N.Y. 10110
                        http://www.wwnorton.com

W. W. Norton & Company, Ltd., 10 Coptic Street, London WC1A 1PU

1 2 3 4 5 6 7 8 9 0

This book is dedicated with love to the memory of Nina Rosenhan

CONTENTS IN BRIEF

Contents

PREFACE

This book was conceived in, of all places, a mental hospital. David Rosenhan was engaged in a study in which a diverse group of normal people went into mental hospitals pretending to have a single symptom: They heard voices that said "empty," "meaningless," and "thud." From the moment they were admitted, these pseudopatients abandoned that symptom and acted the way "normal" people do. But they were labeled as crazy and treated that way for reasons that will become clear as you read this book.

Martin Seligman heard about the study and wrote Rosenhan a fan letter, expressing his admiration for the courage it involved. To his surprise, Seligman received a phone call several days later inviting him to enter a hospital with Rosenhan. So it came about that in October 1973 both of us assumed false names (you figure out why) and wound up on the locked men's ward of a state mental hospital near Philadelphia.

We had never met before, but one can hardly think of a better place for two psychologists to become fast friends. In the hours and days that followed, the two of us talked over an enormous variety of topics: how we and our fellow patients were being treated, and why we were treated that way; our personal and academic lives; the legal rights of mental patients; how to choose a therapist; the dehumanizing effects of labeling; the diagnosis (and frequent misdiagnosis) of schizophrenia and depression; the causes of suicide; biological versus psychological causes and treatments for mental illness. And finally, teaching itself–how the experience of hospitalization, of psychopathology, of the richness of psychotherapy, the importance of diagnosis, and the panoramic range of psychological misery, could be conveyed to our students. We left the hospital good friends, and with the hope that we might some day attempt to do something to improve the teaching of abnormal psychology–above all with the hope that we would write a book together about mental illness.

Our talks on that locked men's ward of a psychiatric hospital ultimately led us to write *Abnormal Psychology*. We had written three editions of this book, when we decided to write a basic, concise version that could be used in conjunction with readings or in shorter courses or by students who are not psychology majors. This is the book you have before you. It is the result of almost twenty-five years of collaboration between us: research, clinical experience, delving into a vast and burgeoning literature, writing, rewriting and rewriting yet again, and teaching abnormal psychology to thousands of undergraduates.

During the lifetime of our collaboration, the progress that has been made in understanding and treating psychological disorders has been extraordinary. When we became psychologists, almost all disorders were wholly mysterious and untreatable, there was no agreement on nosology, and the search for causes of the mental illnesses was mired in a swamp of armchair theorizing. Today the schizophrenias, depression, anxiety disorders, and the sexual dysfunctions, can now be treated, often with considerable success. They are not yet fully understood, but neither are they entirely shrouded. The psychological and biological causes of all of these problems are coming to light. Indeed, we not only understand them better than ever before, but we are now enormously optimistic about the prospects of the immediate future. If the last twenty-five years were highly informative, the next twenty-five promise to be a time of extraordinary discovery.

Abnormal psychology is inherently interesting to anyone who is concerned with understanding people and what makes them tick. We have tried to augment that interest by using richly described case histories that convey the immediacy and drama of psychopathology. We hope, too, that we have sustained the reader's interest by writing clearly and directly, by treating research findings in a coherent manner, by avoiding shotgun citations, and by avoiding jargon. *Abnormality* is written for the intelligent reader, likely an undergraduate who has a quarter or semester to give to this effort. For that effort, we expect the reader will gain an informed grasp of, and sympathy for, the issues in abnormal psychology. We also hope that the reader will now be able to evaluate and appreciate the significance of new research and findings that will be made in the future, even after the course is completed.

This brief edition includes one historical chapter that also spells out the family resemblance approach to abnormality and the potential hazards of diagnosis. It now includes just two chapters on theories and approaches to abnormality and one combined chapter on assessment, diagnosis, and methodology, so as to get more quickly to the gist of abnormality: the various disorders themselves. It still has separate chapters for all the major disorders since these are the heart of abnormality. It also concludes with a chapter on the law and psychology, since we feel that how the law treats those diagnosed with mental disorders is a reflection of the society as a whole.

Abnormality stresses the diagnosis and treatment of mental disorders. It describes various approaches to abnormality and then goes into how psychologists use these approaches or a combination of these approaches to diagnose and treat patients. This edition includes the diagnostic criteria boxes for each major disorder from the fourth edition of the Diagnostic and Statistical Manual of Mental Disorders (DSM-IV). These are the criteria that we use for deciding whether someone can be considered to have a particular disorder. We also discuss DSM-IV within the text itself, but we do not blindly adhere to the classifications adopted by DSM-IV. Hence, we prefer to discuss obsessive-compulsive disorder with the somatoform and dissociative disorders rather than with phobia, panic disorder, and generalized anxiety disorder. We continue to call the chapter on depression by that name rather than calling it "the mood disorders" as DSM-IV labels these disorders because we believe that cognitive, somatic, and motivational symptoms are as important as are the emotional symptoms. We do not want to cloud students' understanding of the various disorders with material or names that may confuse rather than enlighten them.

Today, there is increasing concern with effective and affordable health care. There has been a sea change in people's insistence on receiving effective treatments for all sorts of psychological disorders. We want to know what works and what does not work. We therefore consult therapy outcome studies to discover whether a therapy has worked. Treatments change over time. New treatments arise and old ones fall by the wayside. A great deal is now known about how well different psychotherapies and different drugs work. So we evaluate the theories that best explain a disorder as well as the treatments that work. For every major disorder, we present a treatment table that compares the effectiveness of each major kind of psychotherapy used and the major drugs. We compare symptom relief, how well people do once treatment is discontinued, the side effects, the expense and duration of treatment, and then we hazard an overall rating on a scale from "useless" to "excellent."

This edition also goes into the applied work of therapists and researchers. It tries to present the story of how treatments are tested and used. It includes new "From the Clinician's Office" boxes and "From the Researcher's Laboratory" boxes to give students a sense of the process of discovery that goes on continually in this rapidly changing field.

One final point: The book emphasizes the science of abnormal psychology and, equally, the human suffering that abnormality spawns and its enormous social costs. We want to be clear about this joint emphasis. As we take up each disorder, the scientific theories that explain them and the therapies that best treat them, we have spared little effort in conveying the human side of this ongoing endeavor. Scientific explorations into diagnosis and treatment promise wholesale amelioration of human misery. Nothing else does with any kind of reliability. But the "science" of abnormality has no meaning unless human suffering is kept centrally in mind.

Acknowledgments

In the course of writing this book and *Abnormal Psychology*, we have accumulated intellectual and personal debts to colleagues, friends, students, and family. Many people have been more generous with time and critique than we had any right to anticipate. We are especially grateful to Don Fusting, who guided the first three editions and helped with the writing and organization of this brief edition. Don was passionately involved with this version, criticizing each chapter for its intellectual and educational message, offering conceptual and organizational suggestions, and writing, writing, writing. We learned to neglect Don's comments at the book's peril. Equally, we are grateful to our developmental editor, Sandra Lifland, whose efforts across the first three editions and this brief edition simply defy description. She took a collegial role throughout, raising theoretical questions and pressing relentlessly for answers. She ferreted out every instance of awkward and inelegant prose–there are none left, we now believe–and made handsome remedial suggestions. Much of what is visually attractive about the book grew from her hard work. We are greatly indebted to Paul Rozin (University of Pennsylvania), our friend and colleague and Norton's editorial adviser. He encouraged us when we flagged, and found merit when we seemed to be losing heart. He raised pointed questions in every draft of every chapter of the first edition, and continued to do so for the second and third editions and now for the brief edition.

We thank those at Norton who helped to make this edition possible. We are grateful to our new editor, John Byram, who stepped in and helped enormously in bringing this book to publication. We thank Jessica Elliott and Neil Hoos, who found many new photos to add to this edition, and Roy Tedoff, who made sure that all our efforts were carried successfully through the book production phase. We also thank Drake McFeely, the president of Norton, and Roby Harrington, head of the college department, whose vision of this edition made it happen.

We thank our colleagues who commented on material from the previous edition of *Abnormal Psychology*: Michael Bohn, University of Wisconsin; Irving Gottesman, University of Virginia; Will Grove, University of Minnesota; Janice Kiecolt-Glaser, Ohio State University; Gregory K. Lehne, Private Practice, Maryland; Sarnoff Mednick, University of Southern California; Patricia Minnes, Queen's University, Canada; John Monahan, University of Virginia.

We thank the teachers of courses in Abnormal Psychology on whom we came to rely for suggestions and changes: Raymond M. Bergner, Illinois State University; Ron Boykin, Salisbury State University; Enrico DiTommaso, University of New Brunswick; Mary Dozier, University of Delaware, Newark; Richard A. Gordon, Bard College; Charles Grunder, University of Maine; Laurie Heatherington, Williams College; Robert Hoff, Mercyhurst College; Mick Hunter, University of Newcastle, Australia; Gary G. Johnson, Normandale Community College; Carolin Keutzer, University of Oregon, Eugene; Steven Kubacki, University of Wyoming, Laramie; Mark Lenzenweger,

Cornell University; Stanley Lynch, Santa Fe Community College; Joanne Marrow, California State University, Sacramento; T. Mark Morey, SUNY, Oswego; E. George Nichols, Mount Allison University, Canada; Thomas Nielsen, Aarhus University, Denmark; J. Mitchell Noon, University of Sussex, United Kingdom; Demetrios Papageorgis, University of British Columbia, Canada; David Powley, Mobile College; Rena Repetti, University of California, Los Angeles; Georgina Rippon, University of Warwick, United Kingdom; Anita Rosenfield, California State University, Los Angeles; Jill A. Steinberg, San Jose State University; Laura Stephenson, Washburn University; Sherry Stewart, Dalhousie University, Halifax, Canada; Philip A. Street, Saint Mary's University, Canada; Carol Terry, University of Oklahoma; Steven Tiffany, Purdue University; Michael Wierzbicki, Marquette University.

This edition of the book also benefited enormously from the assistance of Scott Glassman, Paul Thomas, Chris Prokop, Shelly Zulman, Jennifer Ma, Midnight Toker, Shulamit Magnus, Justin Hayes, Anna Clarke, and Rebecca Kaplan. Administrative support came from Mary Tye, Elise McMahon, Carol McSorley, Jina Rhee, and Susan French. Our debt to these people is great.

M.E.P.S.
D.L.R.
May 1997

ABNORMALITY

CHAPTER

1

Abnormality: Past and Present

Detail from Hieronymus Bosch, *Garden of Earthly Delight: Hell.*

Throughout human history, there have been many different notions about what behaviors can be defined as abnormal. This is only to be expected, for as the elements of abnormality change relative to historical context, so do the notions of what is normal and abnormal. Behaviors that have been revered in one time or place may have been defined as clear examples of madness in others. The ancient Hebrews and the ancient Greeks held in awe those who claimed to be prophets and had "the gift of tongues." Yet, in the modern world, those who claim to see into the future generate suspicion, and those who speak in unknown words and rhythms are often classified as schizophrenics.

Consider the following excerpts, one from the Hebrew Bible, the other from a more modern source. Both involve "hearing voices." The source and meanings of those voices, however, are seen quite differently.

God put Abraham to the test. He said to him,
"Abraham."
And Abraham answered,
"Here I am."
And He said,
"Take your son, your favored one, Isaac, whom you love, and go to the land of Moriah, and offer him there as a burnt offering on one of the heights that I will point out to you."
So early next morning, Abraham saddled his ass and took with him two of his servants and his son Isaac. He split the wood for the burnt offering, and he set out for the place of which God had told him. On the third day Abraham looked up and saw the place from afar. Then Abraham said to his servants,
"You stay here with the ass. The boy and I will go up there; we will worship and we will return to you."

1

▲ *The Sacrifice of Isaac, c. 1490*, by Andrea Mantegna. Abraham believed he had heard God's voice telling him to sacrifice his son. In our time, "hearing voices" is considered to be a symptom of schizophrenia.

. . . They arrived at the place of which God had told him. Abraham built an altar there; he laid out the wood; he bound his son Isaac; he laid him on the altar, on top of the wood. And Abraham picked up the knife to slay his son. Then an angel of the Lord called to him from heaven:

"Abraham! Abraham!"

And he answered,

"Here I am."

And He said,

"Do not raise your hand against the boy, or do anything to him . . ." (Genesis: 22, 1–6; 9–12).

One effect of the illness was that I heard voices—numerous voices—chatting, arguing, and quarreling with me, telling me I should hurt myself or kill myself. I felt as if I was being put on a heavenly trial for misdeeds that I had done and was being held accountable by God. Other times I felt as if I was being pursued by the government for acts of disloyalty.

I thought the voices I heard were being transmitted through the walls of my apartment and through the washer and dryer, and that these machines were talking and telling me things. I felt that the government agencies had planted transmitters and receivers in my apartment so that I could hear what they were saying and they could hear what I was saying. I also felt as if the government had bugged my clothing, so that whenever I went outside my apartment I felt like I was being pursued. I felt like I was being followed and watched twenty-four hours a day.

I would like to point out that these were my feelings then, and in hindsight I hold nothing against these government agencies. I now know that this constant monitoring was either punishment at the hands of God's servants for deeds I committed earlier in my life . . . or alternatively, but less likely, that I just imagined these things (Anonymous, 1996).

Much as there have been remarkable differences in the ways in which such things as "hearing voices" have been interpreted, so have there been vastly contradictory theories about the causes of such behaviors. The English dramatist, William Shakespeare (1564–1616), portrayed Ophelia as driven "mad" by Hamlet's cruel rejection, implying to his Elizabethan audiences that Ophelia's withdrawal and eventual suicide were products of the social influences in her immediate environment. Yet, during the same period in history, other "mad" women were accused of having willfully made pacts with Satan. Clearly, a society's definitions of madness and perceptions of its causes have influenced whether the mad were revered, feared, pitied, or simply accepted. In turn, these perceptions have determined the ways in which those who were viewed as mad were treated: whether they were honored for their unique powers or incarcerated, treated or abandoned for their madness.

EARLY APPROACHES TO ABNORMALITY

There is very little about abnormality that tells what caused it, or that even provides clues about where to look for causes. Yet, because treatment and cure depend upon perceived cause, people find it difficult to resist attributing causes to abnormality. Thus, there were times when abnormality was attributed to the wrath of the gods or to possession by demons. At other times and in other places, earthquakes and tides, germs and illness, interpersonal conflict and bad blood were separately and together used to explain the origins of abnormality. Notions about abnormality arise from the culture's worldview. If the culture believes that animistic spirits cause events and behavior, abnormality will be viewed in animistic terms. If it believes in scientific and materialistic causes, abnormality will be viewed in scientific terms.

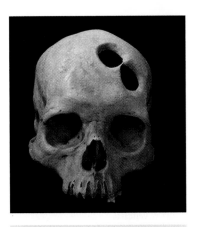

▲ Paleolithic cave dwellers are believed to have made holes, or trephines, in skulls to free those who were "possessed" by evil spirits.

Animistic Origins: Possession

In premodern societies, the belief in **animism**—that everyone and everything has a "soul"—was widespread, and mental disturbance was often ascribed to **animistic** causes. One of the most common explanations of madness was that evil spirits had taken possession of an individual and controlled that person's behavior. Much as a parasitic tapeworm lives in and weakens the body, so could a parasitic spirit inhabit and weaken the mind. Some skulls of Paleolithic cave dwellers have characteristic holes, called **trephines,** that appear to have been chipped out by stone instruments. It is thought that trephining was performed to provide an exit for demons or evil spirits trapped within the skull.

People could be possessed by many different kinds of spirits. The spirits of ancestors, animals, gods, and heroes, and of victims whose wrongs had not been redressed, were among those who could wreak madness. These spirits could enter a person through their own cunning, through the work of an evildoer with magical powers, or through a lack of faith on the part of the possessed individual. Not surprisingly, because possession was a result of invisible forces, freeing the possessed individual from these spirits required special techniques. Across time and place, there has been the widespread belief in the power of some individuals to use magic both to induce evil and expel it; shamans, witch doctors, sorcerers, and witches were all believed to be able to influence animistic forces (Douglas, 1970). In medieval Europe, for example, individuals from all levels of society resorted to sorcerers and witches for spells, potents, and prophecies.

By the middle of the fifteenth century, however, tolerance for bizarre behavior became strained. The perception of witches and the response to them changed radically—from respect to fear. As a result, thousands of suspected witches were put to death, both in Europe and later in America; this was believed to be the only fail-safe "cure" for their abnormality (see Box 1–1).

Physical Causes

While animistic beliefs served to explain psychological distress for centuries, an approach to abnormality that emphasizes **physical** causes can also be traced back to the ancient world. In fact, it is possible that the prehistoric peoples who practiced trephining were employing a primitive surgical technique to relieve the pain of severe headaches. One of the first psychological disorders thought to have arisen from physical causes was **hysteria.**

Papyri from early Egypt, as well as the writings of Greek physicians, record a remarkable disorder that was found mainly among women who were virgins or widows. Its symptoms included such complaints as epileptic-like fits, pains of all sorts in various parts of the body, aphonia (loss of voice), headaches, dizziness, paralysis, blindness, lameness, listlessness, and melancholia. The Greeks believed that all of these arose from a single source: a wandering uterus, which they believed had somehow dislodged itself from its normal place to rove around the body, perhaps in search of water and nourishment, but often enough, for no good reason, and which would attach itself here or there and create havoc. The Greek word for uterus is *hystera,* and the Greeks believed so deeply that the uterus was responsible for these difficulties that they named the entire disorder after it—hysteria (Veith, 1965).

This view of hysteria prevailed until the second century A.D., when it was challenged by physicians such as Galen, who recognized that the uterus was not a living animal. They believed that the *hystera* was a malfunctioning sexual organ. And they thought that there might be a similar organ in men

FOCUS QUESTIONS

1. What are the three perceived origins of abnormal behavior?
2. Describe each of the views of abnormality, and how they arose from the culture's worldview.
3. Describe both the physical and the psychological explanations of the causes of hysteria.

Box 1–1

EVIDENCE AT THE SALEM WITCH TRIALS

The famous Salem Witch Trials, and the witchcraft mania that grew up in that town, evidently arose from the antics of children. A group of young girls used to play imaginary games at the village minister's house. Ghosts, devils, witches, and the whole invisible world were the subjects of their games, borrowed in the manner that children today borrow space explorations from the adult world that surrounds them. Their games of imagination, however, came to the attention of the village elders who solemnly concluded that these children were "bewitched." The children, perhaps stimulated by the attention they were receiving and the excitement they had caused, became more involved in their imaginings, feeding the concern of the elders.

Pressed by the elders to name those who had been casting evil spells over them, they named one person, then another, then still others, until it appeared that nearly half of the people in the village had signed their souls over to the devil. Neighbors hurled wild accusations against each other. These accusations resulted in the arrest and trial of 250 persons in one year (1691-1692), of whom 50 were condemned, 19 executed, 2 died in prison, and 1 of torture.

It is important to remember that the elders of the community were "sane," sober, and intelligent people. Cotton Mather was a leading colonial figure, son of the president of Harvard University, and a founder of Yale. Deeply religious, he wanted to protect the community against dangers that, for him, were real. And precisely because he and other elders were so deeply convinced of the dangers, they were remarkably credulous in weighing the evidence. An example of their gullibility is seen in the interrogation of Sarah Carrier, age eight, whose mother, Martha, was subsequently hanged as a witch.

"How long hast thou been a witch?"
"Ever since I was six years old."
"How old are you now?"
"Nearly eight years old."
"Who made you a witch?"
"My mother. She made me set my hand to the book." "You said you saw a cat once. What did the cat say to you?"
"It said it would tear me to pieces if I would not set my hand to the book."
(Sarah is speaking here of the Devil's Book.)
"How did you know that it was your mother?"
"The cat told me so, that she was my mother."

SOURCE: Upham, 1876, cited in Deutsch, 1949, p. 35.

▲ As a result of the witchcraft mania and fear of satanic forces, 250 people were tried as witches in colonial Salem, Massachussets.

which, when malfunctioning, could cause men to have similar symptoms. Galen observed that both men and women suffer similar symptoms following periods of sexual abstinence, and therefore he argued that hysteria has a sexual basis, a view that is widely accepted today.

Attributing psychological distress to physical causes took a peculiar twist hundreds of years later with the belief in **animalism.** This belief asserted that there were remarkable similarities between animals and mad people. Like animals, the mad could not control themselves and therefore needed to be severely controlled. Like animals, the insane were capable of violence, often

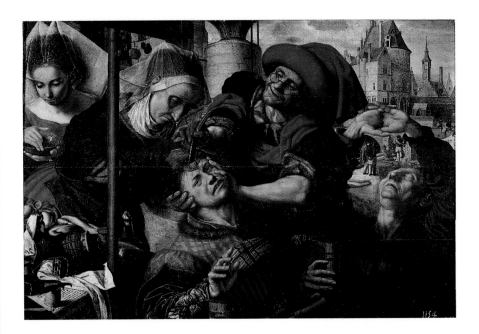

▶ This 1530 painting by Jan Sanders van Hemessen shows physicians trying to remove the "Stone of Folly" from a bound patient possessed with madness. However gruesome this procedure, the theory and treatment of mental illness as a disorder of the body has survived; we now know that tumors in the brain sometimes bring about abnormality.

▼ The Greek physician Galen (circa 130–201 A.D.) was one of the first to believe that some apparently physical disorders were psychological in origin.

suddenly and without provocation. Like animals, they could live without protest in miserable conditions, conditions under which normal people simply could not exist. One proponent of this view pointed to

> The ease with which certain of the insane of both sexes bear the most rigorous and prolonged cold. . . . On certain days when the thermometer indicated . . . as many as 16 degrees below freezing, a madman . . . could not endure his wool blanket, and remained sitting on the icy floor of his cell. In the morning, one no sooner opened his door than he ran in his shirt into the inner court, taking ice and snow by the fistful, applying it to his breast and letting it melt with a sort of delectation. (Foucault, 1965, pp. 74–75)

Much of the treatment of the insane followed from this view until the late eighteenth century (see Box 1–2).

The relatively primitive notions of physical cause that are captured in the early Greek views of hysteria, or in animalism, gradually yielded to more sophisticated approaches. With the development of modern medicine, many physicians came to consider madness to be a form of illness amenable to the same kinds of treatment as physical illness. Purges, bleeding, and forced vomiting were choice medical remedies of the seventeenth and eighteenth centuries, and these were administered to the infirm and the insane alike. Gradually, these views and treatments were replaced by approaches that characterize present-day medicine: surgery and pharmacology (see Chapter 2).

Psychogenic Origins

The quest for understanding psychological abnormality was pursued down still another path by the ancient Greeks and Romans, this time to its ***psychological*** origins. In addition to his observations about hysteria, Galen contributed important insights into the psychological causes of abnormality. In a particularly striking instance, Galen examined a woman who complained of sleeplessness, listlessness, and general malaise. He could find no direct evidence of physical illness and ultimately narrowed his inferences to two possibilities. Either she was suffering from melancholy, which was a physical

Box 1-2

TREATMENT OF THE INSANE

The beginning of the modern psychological era dates from the establishment of the psychiatric hospital. Both the medical hospital and the psychiatric hospital evolved from seventeenth-century institutions that were created to house and confine the poor, the homeless, the unemployed, and among them, the insane. In 1656, the Hôpital Général of Paris was founded for the poor "of both sexes, of all ages, and from all localities, of whatever breeding and birth, in whatever state they may be, able-bodied or invalid, sick or convalescent, curable or incurable" (Edict of 1656, cited in Foucault, 1965). From a strictly humane point of view, the Hôpital Général was surely an improvement over the conditions that preceded it. For the first time in France, the government took responsibility for feeding and housing its "undesirables." But in return, those social undesirables—the poor, the homeless, the mad—yielded up their personal liberty.

Although governments did not distinguish the insane from other unfortunates, within the hospital such distinctions were quickly made and were ultimately institutionalized. The insane were given much worse care, including brutal physical abuse, than were other residents. One eighteenth-century visitor to La Salpêtrière, a division of the Hôpital Général, commented that what made the place more miserable, and often fatal, was that in winter, "when the waters of the Seine rose, those cells situated at the level of the sewers became not only more unhealthy, but worse still, a refuge for a swarm of huge rats, which during the night attacked the unfortunates confined there and bit them wherever they could reach them; madwomen have been found with feet, hands, and face torn by bites which are often dangerous and from which several have died" (Desportes, cited in Foucault, 1965).

Paris was not unique. In St. Mary's of Bethlehem (which soon became known as Bedlam) in London, patients were chained to the walls or kept on long leashes. The United States established its first hospital, the Pennsylvania Hospital, in 1756. At the urging of Benjamin Franklin, the government set aside a section for "lunatics." They were consigned to the cellar and "their scalps were shaved and blistered; they were bled to a point of syncope, purged until the alimentary canal failed to yield anything but mucus, and in the intervals, they were chained by the waist or ankle to the cell wall. . . . It was not considered unusual or improper for the keeper to carry a whip and use it freely" (Morton, 1897, cited in Deutsch, 1949).

In the seventeenth and eighteenth centuries, it was believed that madness resulted from animalism, that the insane had lost the one capacity that distinguished humans from beasts: *reason*. Because the insane had lost that capacity, their behavior was disordered, unruly, and wild. The first mandate of treatment, then, was to restore reason. *Fear* was believed to be the emotion that was best suited to restoring the disordered mind.

By the end of the eighteenth century, however, the idea that the insane should be treated as animals was under attack. From a variety of respected sources, protest grew over the conditions of confinement, and especially over the shackles, the chains, the dungeons, and the whippings.

Hospitals began to unshackle their insane patients. The first hospital to remove the chains from psychiatric patients was St. Boniface in Florence, Italy. There, in 1774, Vincenzo Chiarugi introduced a radical reform in patient care: allowing patients freedom of movement. Later, in 1787, Joseph Dacquin initiated similar reforms in the Insane Department of the hospital at Chambery, France. Despite political opposition, Philippe Pinel, the newly appointed director of La Bicêtre, part of the Hôpital Général of Paris, unshackled the chains of the mental patients housed there in 1792, moved them from their cellar dungeons into sunny and airy rooms, and allowed them freedom of the hospital grounds. Pinel still believed in the need for control and coercion in psychiatric care, but he insisted that for coercion to be effective, it needed to be *psychological* rather than physical.

New models of treatment now were sought. One such model was found at Gheel, a religious Belgian community that had been accepting the insane for quite some time. There, consistent with a religious ethos, "cure" was achieved through prayer and in the "laying on of the hands." Those who prayed were treated in a special, and for the time, unusual way. The deeply troubled were shown habitual kindness, courtesy, and gentleness. The insane lived in a community, and apart from being forbidden alcohol, suffered few restrictions. Gheel was not a hospital, but rather a refuge for those who were fortunate enough to make their way there. Similarly, in England, reforms developed from religious concerns. Following the suspicious death of one Hannah Mills, a Quaker, who had been admitted to the Lunatick Asylum in 1791, William Tuke urged the Yorkshire Society of Friends to establish a humanitarian institution for the insane. Despite stiff political opposition, the Retreat of York was established in 1796. The Retreat's cornerstones were kindness, consideration, courtesy, and dignity. Also consistent with the Quaker philosophy was the emphasis on the value of work and the personal esteem that the patients, called guests, derived from it.

The ideas that led to the unshackling of the insane in Europe and to the founding and success of the community at Gheel and of Tuke's Retreat also spread quickly to the United States. This new form of treatment, called moral treatment, formed the basis of the Friends Asylum at Frankford, Pennsylvania, in 1817, and also of the Bloomingdale Asylum, which was established in 1821 in New York City by Quaker businessman Thomas Eddy. Although not yet especially effective, treatment became increasingly humane.

disorder of one of the four body "humors," or fluids, "or else she was troubled about something she was unwilling to confess," a psychological explanation. He concluded:

> After I had diagnosed that there was no bodily trouble, and that the woman was suffering from some mental uneasiness, it happened that at the very time I was examining her, this was confirmed. Somebody came from the theatre and said he had seen Pylades dancing. Then both her expression and the colour of her face changed. Seeing this, I applied my hand to her wrist, and noticed that her pulse had suddenly become extremely irregular. This kind of pulse indicates that the mind is disturbed; thus it occurs also in people who are disputing over any subject. So on the next day I said to one of my followers that, when I paid my visit to the woman, he was to come a little later and announce to me, "Morphus is dancing today." When he said this, I found that the pulse was unaffected. Similarly also on the next day, when I had an announcement made about the third member of the troupe, the pulse remained unchanged as before. On the fourth evening I kept very careful watch when it was announced that Pylades was dancing, and noticed that the pulse was very much disturbed. Thus I found out that the woman was in love with Pylades, and by careful watch on the succeeding days my discovery was confirmed. (Galen, cited in Veith, 1965, p. 36)

Galen's assessment of possible cause is the hallmark of the scientific method that was eventually to advance our understanding and treatment of psychological disorders. Rather than leaping to a conclusion, Galen tested two alternative hypotheses and decided which was correct according to the evidence. In this case, the evidence favored the hypothesis that stressed psychological experience rather than physiology.

Galen's observations on the psychological origins of abnormality were forgotten for centuries. Thus, until the middle of the eighteenth century, hysteria was believed to be a female neurological disorder that had its origins in genital illness. The recognition that mental disorders were psychological in origin and could be treated by psychological means did not arise again until the middle of the eighteenth century.

MESMERISM

To understand how the psychological view of abnormality returned in the eighteenth century, we first need to look at one of the most colorful people in the history of abnormal psychology, Franz Anton Mesmer (1734–1815). Mesmer is not only one of the most colorful, but surely one of the most maligned characters in the history of abnormal psychology. Variously called a genius and a charlatan, he proposed that many diseases, from epilepsy to hysteria, develop from the obstruction of the flow of an invisible and impalpable entity that he first called "universal magnetic fluid" and later animal magnetism. Very much a man of the Enlightenment, Mesmer was influenced by contemporary discoveries in electricity and proposed the existence of a physical magnetic fluid which, when unequally distributed, causes disease in the body. He theorized that magnetic fluid was influenced by the lunar cycle, the tides, the planets, and the stars. Mesmer believed that health could be restored by using certain techniques that induced "crises" in the body. These crises would be provoked again and again, but each time would be experienced as less severe, until they disappeared and the body was back in equilibrium.

Mesmer went to Paris from Vienna in 1778. He opened a clinic where patients suffering from the various symptoms of hysteria were seen in groups. In a heavily curtained room, patients were arranged around a large wooden tub, or baquet, which was filled with water and magnetized iron filings. Iron rods protruded from the tub and were pointed by the patients to

► Franz Anton Mesmer (1734–1815) and his patients around the baquet. The baquet was supposed to concentrate a patient's magnetic fluid and induce a crisis, which would eventually restore the body's equilibrium and the patient's health.

their ailing parts. The baquet was supposed to concentrate the magnetic fluid and induce the patient's crisis. Mesmer, dressed in a lavender cape, would pass among the patients to the accompaniment of gentle music, fixing his eye on them, and touching each with his iron wand. One patient would experience strange sensations, including trembling and convulsions. After the first succumbed, others were not long in having similar experiences, though there were always a few who were unaffected (Pattie, 1967).

Mesmer had departed from Vienna under a cloud: he had been accused of charlatanry. And, despite his therapeutic successes, it was not long before similar accusations were leveled against him in Paris. So heated and acrimonious were the charges and countercharges, that in 1783, Louis XVI appointed a Royal Commission to investigate animal magnetism. The Commission heard evidence and concluded that there was no such thing as animal magnetism and that Mesmer's cures were entirely due to "imagination." Crushingly defeated, Mesmer, a proud man, vanished into obscurity. But the *reality* of his "cures" remained. Animal magnetism, soon called **mesmerism,** continued to be practiced and in some cases succeeded in restoring people to health. It took the next generation of investigators to examine mesmerism and to conclude that it was not magnetized iron filings but rather "suggestion" and "suggestibility" that led to cures.

FROM HYPNOTISM TO PSYCHOANALYSIS

Cures derived from mesmerism continued to excite interest. The process now focused on the role of suggestion and came to be known as **hypnotism.** A major figure in the scientific study of hypnosis was Jean Martin Charcot (1825–1893), Medical Director of one of the largest sections at La Salpêtrière, where insane patients were treated in Paris. Charcot was widely regarded as a first-rate scientist, the most eminent neurologist of the nineteenth century, and an awesome and much-feared teacher. While Charcot was at La Salpêtrière, one of the wards in his charge housed women patients who suffered from convulsions. Using hypnosis, Charcot sought to distinguish hysterical convulsions from those brought on by epilepsy. If, for example, a patient who suffered a paralyzed arm was able to move her arm under hypnosis, then the diagnosis of hysteria could be given; otherwise, the appropriate diagnosis was a neurological disorder. Charcot also extended his study to male patients, demonstrating that the symptoms of traumatic paralysis in men were the same as those of hysterical paralysis (Ellenberger, 1970).

▶ Jean-Martin Charcot (1825–1893) demonstrating hypnosis to a class of medical students.

Hypnosis fascinated Charcot, and he quickly generated a neurological theory about it. His students, ever eager to please their teacher, tested his views and brought back confirmatory evidence. But Charcot himself never hypnotized his patients. Rather, his students "worked them up" and taught them how to perform, after which Charcot unwittingly used them as demonstration subjects. Other scientists, particularly Hyppolyte Bernheim in Nancy, were unable to replicate Charcot's findings, and quickly located the source of error.

Despite some initial setbacks, psychogenic theories about abnormal behavior began to gain credence. The emphasis turned to two explanations: first, that psychological distress could be an *illness*, not different in kind from other physical illnesses; and second, that mental disorder could be *psychological*, and *very* different in kind from physical illness.

Much of the excitement that was generated by the psychogenic viewpoint came about through the study of hysteria. With its paralyses, anesthesias, and convulsions, its loss of voice, sight, or hearing, and occasional loss of consciousness, hysteria seemed patently a *physical* disorder. Charcot used hypnosis to distinguish between symptoms that had an organic cause and symptoms that were hysterical in nature. Subsequent theorists proposed that the therapeutic effects of hypnosis resulted from psychological "suggestion" (Bernheim, 1886, cited in Pattie, 1967).

By the end of the nineteenth century, hypnosis was widely used in Europe and in the United States for treating hysterical disorders. It formed the basis for the development of modern forms of psychotherapy and was a significant milestone in the psychogenic approach to mental disorders.

One of the people who used hypnosis in his treatment of patients was Josef Breuer (1842–1925), a distinguished Viennese internist whose practice included a large number of hysterical patients. Breuer's treatment often consisted of inducing these patients to talk about their problems and fantasies under hypnosis. Frequently patients would become emotional under hypnosis, reliving painful experiences, experiencing a deep catharsis, or emotional release, and emerging from the hypnotic trance feeling much better. The patients, of course, were unaware of a relationship between what they discussed under hypnosis, how emotional they had become, and how they felt subsequently. But Breuer believed that because his patients had experienced a catharsis under hypnosis, their symptoms disappeared.

FOCUS QUESTIONS

1. Describe the rise of psychogenic treatments.
2. What was the cathartic method?

Just as Breuer was making these discoveries, Sigmund Freud (1856–1939), a Viennese neurologist who had just completed his studies with Charcot, began to work with Breuer. Together they utilized Breuer's "cathartic method," encouraging patients to report their experiences and fantasies under hypnosis. Freud, however, noticed that similar therapeutic effects could be obtained *without* hypnosis, so long as the patient reported everything that came to mind and experienced emotional catharsis. It was this discovery that led Freud to the theory and therapeutic technique called **psychoanalysis,** which is described in detail in Chapter 3. Freud's psychoanalytic theory made even more plausible the notion that abnormal behavior has a psychogenic origin. Although many of Freud's specific theories have subsequently been questioned and fallen into disrepute, the basic notion that the mind is at work influencing perceptions and behavior continues to hold great strength.

ABNORMALITY TODAY

Abnormality has always been perceived in the context of the times. Thus, how our understanding of abnormality is articulated depends on the beliefs that dominate in a culture and epoch. Historically, people have used animistic, physical, and psychogenic theories to explain disordered behavior. Today, both physical and psychological explanations continue to be offered to understand abnormality. But in our complex society, a more fundamental question has also been raised: What does it mean to say that someone is abnormal? In the past, hearing voices would be a sign of divine inspiration. Today, it would be a sign of madness. How do we *know* that a person's behavior is abnormal? How did it become that way? How can it be changed? The answers to these questions have implications for understanding the causes of mental distress and for organizing society's institutions for treating people with mental disorders.

The Elements of Abnormality

Abnormality is recognized everywhere, in every culture, by nearly everyone. Sometimes the impression of abnormality comes through clearly and unambiguously. At other times, reasonable people will disagree as to whether a particular person, action, or thought is or is not abnormal. The following clinical vignettes make this clear:

- Don is viewed by nearly everyone as a quiet, mild-mannered executive. But one day, gripped by a sudden seizure in the temporal lobe of the brain, he picks up his sales manager, chair and all, and hurls her to death through the eleventh floor window of an office building.
- Vanessa, a teenage girl, eats nothing at all for several days, then gorges herself on eight hot-fudge sundaes within two hours, vomits explosively, and then eats nothing more for three days.
- Carla's religious principles prohibit her from wearing makeup or drinking liquor. Her college friends do both. She is continually anxious when she is with them.

FOCUS QUESTIONS

1. How do we define "abnormality?"
2. What do we mean by "necessary" and "sufficient" conditions for applying the term "abnormality?"

Of these cases, two things can be said immediately. First, they involve different behaviors, which arise from sources as diverse as brain pathology and religious beliefs. And second, while some people will be quite confident that all of these instances represent abnormality, not everyone will agree. Everyone will judge the first case abnormal. Nearly everyone will

One of these images is by a commercial artist, one by a mental patient. Just as no single feature of the drawings sets them apart from each other, no single symptom or behavior is necessary or sufficient to define abnormality.

judge the second case abnormal. But there will be vigorous debate about the third.

The act of defining the word "abnormal" suggests that there is some single property that these three cases of abnormality, and all others, must share. This shared property is called a *necessary* condition for abnormality. But there is no common element among these three cases, for what is it that temporal lobe seizures, gorging oneself on hot-fudge sundaes, and conflict between religious conviction and social acceptance have in common? Moreover, a precise definition of "abnormal" requires that there be at least one distinguishing element that only cases of abnormality share and that no cases of "normality" share. This is called a *sufficient* condition of abnormality. But is there any one feature that separates all cases of abnormality from all those that we would call normal? Not any that we can find. In fact, as we will shortly see, there is no single element shared by all cases of abnormality, and no single element that distinguishes abnormality from normality.

In short, the word "abnormal" cannot be defined precisely. Indeed, few of the words we commonly use, and especially those that are used socially, are precisely defined, for the use of language often depends on flexible meanings. But the fact that abnormality cannot be defined "tightly" does not mean that abnormality does not exist or that it cannot be recognized at all. The determination of whether a behavior is abnormal is made by spelling out the properties of abnormality, the various *elements* that count toward defining a behavior as abnormal. The more such elements there are and the more clearly each one is present, the more likely it is that the behavior, thought, or person will be judged abnormal.

We will look at seven properties or elements that count toward deciding whether an action or a person is abnormal. Our analysis describes the way ordinary people and well-trained psychologists actually use the word. These elements or properties of abnormality are:

- Suffering
- Maladaptiveness
- Irrationality and incomprehensibility
- Unpredictability and loss of control
- Vividness and unconventionality
- Observer discomfort
- Violation of moral and ideal standards.

The more of these elements that are present, and the more clearly they can be seen, the more certain we are that the behavior or person is abnormal.

At least one of these elements *must* be present for abnormality to exist. But no one particular element must always be present, and only rarely will all of the elements be present. Let us examine these elements in greater detail.

SUFFERING

Abnormality hurts. A depressed student feels miserable. For her, the prospect of going through another day seems unbearable.

We are likely to call people abnormal if they are suffering psychologically, and the more they suffer, the more certain we are. But suffering is not a *necessary* condition of abnormality: it does not have to be present for us to label a behavior as abnormal. Someone who phones the President in the middle of the night, certain that the Chief Executive wants to hear all about his health-care plan, can feel exuberant, cheerful, and full of hope. Nevertheless, such a person is viewed as abnormal, since the other elements of abnormality override the absence of suffering and convince us that his behavior is abnormal.

Suffering, moreover, is not a *sufficient* condition for abnormality because suffering is commonplace in the normal course of life. A child will grieve for a dead pet, for example, much as all of us mourn the loss of loved ones. If no other elements of abnormality are present, however, grief and suffering will not be judged as abnormal.

Suffering, then, is an element that counts toward the perception of abnormality. But it is neither necessary nor sufficient. The context in which the suffering occurs counts heavily toward whether it is seen as abnormal.

MALADAPTIVENESS

Whether a behavior is functional and adaptive—how well it enables the individual to achieve certain goals—is a fundamental element in deciding whether the behavior is normal or abnormal. Behaviors that strongly interfere with individual well-being are maladaptive and would count as factors in assessing abnormality.

By individual well-being, we mean the ability to work and the ability to conduct satisfying relations with other people. Depression and anxiety interfere with love and work and, almost always, with an individual's sense of well-being. A fear of going out (agoraphobia) can be so strong that it keeps the sufferer locked inside an apartment, unable to fulfill any of the individual's goals. Such a fear grossly interferes with the enjoyment of life, the ability to work, and relations with others. The more there is such interference, the clearer the abnormality.

▶ Suffering. The person in this painting is obviously suffering, but a decision about the abnormality of her suffering would depend on whether other elements of abnormality were present. (*Melancholy, c.* 1874, by Edgar Degas)

FOCUS QUESTIONS

1. What are the seven elements of abnormality?
2. Explain when each of the elements is used to determine abnormality.

IRRATIONALITY AND INCOMPREHENSIBILITY

When a person's behavior seems to have no rational meaning, we are inclined to call that behavior and that person abnormal. One kind of incomprehensibility that counts very strongly for the designation of abnormality is thought disorder, a major symptom of schizophrenia. Beliefs that are patently absurd and bizarre, perceptions that have no basis in objective reality, and mental processes that ramble from one unrelated idea to another constitute thought disorders. A classic example of such thought disorganization occurred during a formal experiment. The patient's task consisted of sorting colored blocks of various shapes and colors into a number of groups. The patient was cooperative and earnest. But he also exhibited an irresistible tendency to sort objects on the desk and on the experimenter's person, as well as parts of the room, things he pulled from his pockets, and even the experimenter himself, whom the patient recommended be remade of wood and cut into blocks. Here is what he said:

> I've got to pick it out of the whole room, I can't confine myself to this game . . . Three blues (test blocks) . . . now, how about that green blotter? Put it there too. Green peas you eat. You can't eat them unless you write on it (pointing to green blotter). Like that wristwatch (on the experimenter's wrist, a foot from the subject)—don't see three meals coming off that watch . . . To do this trick *you'd* have to be made of wood. You've got a white shirt on—and the white blocks. You have to have them cut out of *you!* You've got a white shirt on—this (white hexagonal block) will hold you and never let you go. I've got a blue shirt on, but it can't be a blue shirt and still go together. And the room's got to be the same . . . (Excerpted from Cameron, 1947, p. 59)

UNPREDICTABILITY AND LOSS OF CONTROL

We expect people to be consistent from time to time, predictable from one occasion to the next, and very much in control of themselves. To be loved by someone one day but hated by the same person the next day is troubling. One hardly knows how to respond or what to expect. In a predictable world, we can maintain a sense of control. In an unpredictable one, we feel vulnerable and threatened. Don, the mild-mannered executive who adores his wife on Monday and pummels her brutally on Tuesday, is frightening in much the same way that Dr. Jekyll's alter ego, Mr. Hyde, is; both are unpredictable and out of control.

The judgment that behavior is out of control will be made under two conditions. The first occurs when the ordinary guides and inhibitors of behavior suddenly break down. Don exemplifies this judgment. The second condition occurs when we do not know what causes an action. Imagine coming upon someone who is angry—raging and screaming in the streets. There may be good and socially acceptable reasons for such an anger. But if we do not know those reasons and are unable to elicit them at the time, we are likely to consider that the person is out of control and to designate those actions as abnormal.

VIVIDNESS AND UNCONVENTIONALITY

Generally, people recognize as acceptable and conventional those actions that they themselves are willing to do. Those who accede to a request to walk around campus wearing a sandwich board that reads "EAT AT JOE'S" are likely to estimate that a healthy majority of their peers would make the same choice. On the other hand, those who are unwilling to wear such a sign estimate that relatively *few* people would be willing. Thus, with the exception of behaviors that require great skill or daring, we tend to judge the abnormality of others' behavior by our own. Would *you* wear a sign around campus? If you would, you would judge such behavior as conventional and

Behavior or appearances we consider vivid and unconventional—when measured against our own—we often also consider abnormal.

"Anything wrong?"

(Drawing by Sempé; © 1981, The New Yorker Magazine, Inc.)

normal. If you wouldn't, such behavior would stand out as unconventional and abnormal (Ross, Greene, and House, 1977).

The element of vividness is affected by whether an action is rare. Behaviors that are rare *and* undesirable seem quite vivid, and hence are often considered abnormal. It hardly matters whether the behavior actually *is* rare, so long as it is *perceived* to be rare. Thus, there are many varieties of sexual and aggressive fantasies that are quite common but that are perceived to be rare and therefore abnormal. Nor is rareness itself a necessary condition for abnormality. Depression is a common disorder, as are anxiety states, and both are considered to be abnormal. But behavior that is both rare and socially undesirable is seen as abnormal.

OBSERVER DISCOMFORT

People who are very dependent on others, or ingratiating, or hostile, create discomfort in observers. Their behaviors often enable them to feel more comfortable, but the psychological conflicts they create are painful for others. We are most likely to experience vague observer discomfort when someone violates his or her culture's unwritten *rules* of behavior (Scheff, 1966). Violation of those rules creates the kind of discomfort that leads to the designation "abnormal."

For example, in some cultures, there is an unwritten rule which states that, except when angry or making love, one's face should be at least ten inches away from that of one's partner. Should that invisible boundary be overstepped, a rule will be violated, and the partner will feel uncomfortable. Similarly, there are unwritten rules about clothing one's genital area which, when violated, contribute to the impression that the person is abnormal.

VIOLATION OF MORAL AND IDEAL STANDARDS

There are times when behavior is assessed, not against our judgments of what is common and conventional, but against moral standards and idealized norms that are believed to characterize all right-thinking and right-acting people. This view starts with the notion that people *ought* to behave in a certain way, whether they really do or not, and it concludes with the view that it is normal to behave in the way one ought, and abnormal to fail to behave properly. Thus, it is normal to work, and abnormal not to do so unless

▶ In the film, *Twelve Monkeys,* most of the psychiatrists believe that the character played by Bruce Willis is abnormal. It is ambiguous, however, whether his behavior really is abnormal.

wealth, the unavailability of job openings, or illness exonerate one. It is normal to love, to be loyal, and to be supportive, and abnormal not to—regardless of the fact that evidence for these dispositions is not widely found in modern society. It is abnormal to be too aggressive or too restrained, too shy or too forward, too ambitious or not sufficiently ambitious.

The Family Resemblance Approach

FOCUS QUESTIONS

1. What is the "family resemblance" approach to determining abnormality?
2. What are some of the pitfalls of psychological diagnosis?

Family members resemble each other across a fixed number of dimensions, such as height, hair and eye color, and shape of nose, mouth, and ears. How do we know, for example, that Ed Smith is the *biological* offspring of Bill and Jane Smith? Well, he *looks* like them. He has Bill's blue eyes and sandy hair, and Jane's upturned nose and easy smile. Even though Ed is six inches taller than his father and has a rounder face than his mother, we sense a *family resemblance* among them because they have many significant elements in common. (But careful now: Ed might just be the *adopted* son of Bill and Jane Smith. Such are the hazards of family resemblances!)

Abnormality is recognized in the same way, by determining whether the behavior, thought, or person bears a family resemblance to the behaviors, thoughts, and people we would all recognize as abnormal. Abnormality is assessed according to the match between an individual's characteristics and the seven elements of abnormality.

Examine the following case study with a view toward determining the "family resemblance" between the individual and the elements of abnormality.

Ralph, the seventeen-year-old son of a physician and a pharmacist, moved with his family from a small farming town to a large suburban community during the middle of his junior year in high school. The move was sudden: both his parents were offered jobs that were simply too good to turn down. The abruptness of the move generated no complaint from Ralph, nor did he acknowledge any difficulty. Nevertheless, he seemed to withdraw. At the outset, his family hardly noticed, but once the family settled down, his distant behavior became apparent. He made no friends in his new school, and when the summer came, he seemed to withdraw even further. He spent a good deal of the summer in his room, emerging only to take extended walks around the house. He often seemed preoccupied, and occasionally seemed to be listening to sounds that only he could hear.

Autumn approached and with it the time for Ralph to return to his senior year of high school. Ralph became even more withdrawn. He had difficulty sleeping, and he paced inside and outside the house. Shortly after he returned to school, his behavior deteriorated further. Sometimes, he seemed not to hear when called upon in class, while at other times his answers bore no relation to the questions. Both behaviors generated a good deal of mocking laughter in his classes, and his classmates actively avoided him. One day, he marched into class, stood up, and began to speak absolute gibberish. School authorities notified his parents, who came immediately to pick him up. When he saw them, he grimaced and began to roll a lock of hair between his fingers. He said nothing as he was brought to a psychiatric clinic. (Adapted from DSM-III Training Guide, 1981)

Is Ralph abnormal according to the preceding criteria? Even this brief vignette, which fails to describe fully the richness of Ralph's problem, leaves us convinced that Ralph is suffering some kind of psychological abnormality. Let us return to the elements of abnormality, and examine the extent to which Ralph's actions reflect those elements.

- *Suffering.* We have no information about whether, or to what degree, Ralph is suffering. His withdrawal from his family *might* reflect subjective distress. But then again, it might not.
- *Maladaptiveness.* Ralph's behavior is highly dysfunctional. Not only does he needlessly draw negative attention to himself, but he obviously fails to respond to the demands of school. Such behavior neither serves his own needs nor those of society.
- *Incomprehensibility and irrationality.* There can be little doubt that Ralph's behavior is incomprehensible to observers, and that his verbalizations seem irrational to them.
- *Unpredictability and loss of control.* There is little evidence for loss of control in the vignette, but Ralph's parents would presumably find his behavior unpredictable. So too might his schoolmates.
- *Vividness.* Ralph's behavior is quite vivid. His silent withdrawal stands out noticeably and his speeches in class make him the center of undesirable attention.
- *Observer discomfort.* It is not clear from the vignette whether *all* observers are made uncomfortable by Ralph's behavior, but it is a fair guess that his schoolmates are avoiding him because they feel uncomfortable.
- *Violation of moral and ideal standards.* There is no evidence that Ralph's behavior violates widely held moral standards.

In the main, then, Ralph's behavior is dysfunctional and incomprehensible. These elements alone would have qualified his behavior as abnormal in most people's judgment. Additionally, there is some evidence that his behavior is unpredictable, vivid, and creates discomfort in observers. These elements lend additional strength to the judgment that his behavior is abnormal.

What is the locus of Ralph's abnormality? His behavior is abnormal. His thought is abnormal. And because these problems of behavior and thought last for such a long time and occur across so many different situations, many would call Ralph himself abnormal. This is the convention; it invites us to generalize from the actions and thoughts of an individual to the individual himself. This linguistic convention is not without costs, however, for we can easily be misled into believing that a particular pattern of behavior or thought is much more disabling and pervasive than it really is. It is tragic enough that Ralph has the problems he is afflicted with. But it adds considerably to his tragedy to somehow infer that Ralph himself is flawed, rather than merely realizing that *sometimes* and in *some* situations Ralph's *behaviors and thoughts* are abnormal (see Box 1–3).

THE HAZARDS OF SELF-DIAGNOSIS

There is almost no one who has not harbored secret doubts about his or her normality. "Am I too afraid of speaking up in class?" "Do other people occasionally have fantasies about their parents dying in violent accidents?" "Why am I so down all the time?" A number of students show up in college counseling centers with such feelings.

After hearing and reading about various kinds of mental disorders in an abnormal psychology course, some students may find themselves prone to a phenomenon called "interns' syndrome." In the course of early training many years ago, a fledgling medical student reported finding in himself symptoms of almost every disease he studied.

I remember going to the British Museum one day to read up on the treatment for some slight ailment of which I had a touch—hay fever, I fancy it was. I got down the book, and read all I came to read; and then, in an unthinking moment, I idly turned the leaves, and began to indolently study diseases, generally. I forgot which was the first distemper I plunged into—some fearful, devastating scourge, I know—and, before I had glanced half down the list of "premonitory symptoms," it was borne in upon me that I had fairly got it.

I sat for a while frozen with horror, and then in the listlessness of despair, I again turned over the pages. I came to typhoid fever—read the symptoms—discovered that I had typhoid fever, must have had it for months without knowing it—wondered what else I had got; turned up St. Vitus's Dance—found, as I expected, that I had that too—began to get interested in my case, and determined to sift it to the bottom, and so started alphabetically—looked up ague, and learnt that I was sickening for it, and that the acute stage would commence in about another fortnight. Bright's disease, I was relieved to find, I had only in a modified form, and, so far as that was concerned, I might live for years. Cholera I had, with severe complications; and diphtheria I seemed to have been born with. I plodded conscientiously through the twenty-six letters, and the only malady I could conclude I had not got was housemaid's knee.

I felt rather hurt about this at first; it seemed somehow to be a sort of slight. Why hadn't I got housemaid's knee? Why this invidious reservation? After a while, however, less grasping feelings prevailed. I reflected that I had every other known malady in the pharmacology, and I grew less selfish, and determined to do without housemaid's knee. Gout, in its most malignant stage, it would appear, had seized me without my being aware of it; and zymosis I had evidently been suffering with from boyhood. There were no more diseases after zymosis, so I concluded there was nothing else the matter with me . . . I had walked into that reading-room a happy healthy man, I crawled out a decrepit wreck. (Jerome, 1880)

This description makes clear the hazards of self-diagnosis. As you read this book, you may encounter symptoms in yourself that may make you think that you have each disorder in turn. Be forewarned: It is a very unpleasant experience and one about which neither authors nor readers can really do much. In part, it arises from the privacy that surrounds our lives. Many of our thoughts, and some of our actions, strike us as private, if not secret—things about which no one should know. If they did know, people, even (perhaps particularly) friends, might think less of us, or be offended, or both. One consequence of this privacy is the development of an exaggerated sense of the uniqueness of our forbidden thoughts and behaviors. Seeing them suddenly alluded to on these pages and associated with certain syndromes (commonly in contexts that are quite different from the contexts of our own behaviors—but we

don't notice that) might make us believe that we have fallen prey to that problem too.

There are two things that can be done to combat the distress you may experience from reading this book and going to lectures. First, read carefully. You may, for example, be concerned when you read about depression: "Yes, I'm blue. I cry now more than I used to." But as you inquire deeply into the symptoms of depression, you will find that the absence of suicidal thoughts, your continued interest in sex or sports, your optimism about the future, all of these count against the diagnosis of depression.

Second, talk with your friends. Sometimes, merely mentioning that "when I read Chapter so-and-so, I get the feeling they're talking about me. Do you ever get that feeling?" will bring forth a chorus of "you bets," and relief for all.

Hazards of the "Family Resemblance" Approach to Abnormality

The virtue of a family resemblance approach to abnormality arises from the fact that, much as there is no *single* way in which all sons resemble all fathers, neither is there a *single* way in which all abnormal behaviors resemble each other. The notion that all abnormality must involve psychological suffering, or vividness, or observer discomfort is simply false, as we have seen. No single element exists that binds the behaviors of, say, a person who is deeply depressed, a person who is afraid to be alone, and a person who gorges herself and then vomits. Yet, we regard each of these people to be suffering an abnormality because their behaviors are members of the family of characteristics that we have come to regard as abnormal.

But there are some hazards to the family resemblance approach to abnormality. Let's look at three of these hazards: society's error, disagreement between observers, and disagreement between actor and observer.

SOCIETY MAY ERR IN WHOM IT CALLS ABNORMAL

Unlike the judgment of temperature, the judgment of abnormality is a social one. Look again at some of the elements: observer discomfort, vividness and unconventionality, and violation of moral and ideal standards. These all require the presence of other people, while the remaining elements of abnormality can also be interpreted socially. Social judgments, however, can easily be abused, and because the judgment of abnormality is so heavily social, it is even more susceptible to social abuse.

The notion of abnormality can easily and erroneously be applied to all manner of behavior that society presently finds objectionable. The very poor, who look so different from the rest of us, the deeply religious, whose values may seem idiosyncratic, these people march to their own drummers, and they create discomfort in the observers who disagree with them. Similarly, those who violate the ideal standards of others in the course of maintaining their *own* ideal standards risk being termed abnormal.

OBSERVERS WILL DISAGREE ABOUT PARTICULAR BEHAVIORS OR INDIVIDUALS

A family resemblance approach to abnormality is bound to generate some disagreements about whether or not a behavior qualifies as abnormal. Two observers might disagree that any given element was present. Moreover, they might disagree about whether enough elements were present, or whether they were present with sufficient intensity to constitute a clear case of abnormality.

Such an approach generates disagreement for the further reason that the elements of abnormality are neither so precise nor so quantifiable that everyone will agree that a behavior or person fits the category. The more dramatic the behaviors and the longer they are sustained, the more agreement there will be among observers. The problem of observer disagreement is a serious one. As we shall see in Chapter 4, the problem is dealt with, to some extent, by stipulating as clearly as one can, the kinds of behaviors that are associated with each element of abnormality. When this is done, wider agreement occurs.

OBSERVERS AND ACTORS WILL OCCASIONALLY DISAGREE

There will occasionally be different opinions as to whether a behavior or person should be judged as abnormal, according to who is doing the judging: the individuals who are generating the behaviors in question—we call them actors—or those who observe the behaviors. Generally, actors will be less inclined to judge their own behaviors as abnormal for three reasons: First, they have much more information available to them about their own behaviors than do observers. What seems unpredictable or incomprehensible to an observer may seem quite predictable and comprehensible to an actor, and what generates discomfort in an observer may, as we indicated, generate none in the actor. Second, people who are psychologically distressed are not distressed all the time. Distress comes and goes. People, therefore, may be "crazy" at one time, but not crazy at another. Actors are uniquely positioned to recognize changes in themselves. Observers, however, often assume a continuity of psychological state that does not exist. Third, people generally are inclined to see themselves in a more favorable light than observers see them. As a result, actors will tend to see themselves and their behaviors more favorably, and hence more normally, than observers.

Thus, the family resemblance approach to abnormality is not perfect; it has its pitfalls, some of which are worse than others. We might wish that this were not the case and that abnormality were a more objective judgment. But our present wishes are beside the point, though eventually abnormality may be assessed with considerably greater objectivity. We are not endorsing the way abnormality is presently judged. Nor are we prescribing how the word "abnormal" should be used. Rather, we are merely describing how the word is actually used by laymen and professionals alike with the hope that such a description will help in both diagnosis and treatment.

PROGNOSIS FOR CHANGE*

Even when observers can agree that a behavior is abnormal, they are not always able to agree as to what can be done to change that behavior. Most of us in the twentieth-century United States believe that we can improve in almost every way if we just identify what needs to be improved and work at changing. This includes the belief that we can change abnormal behavior. Yet, in fact, there are some things about ourselves that we can change and other things that we cannot change or that we can change only with extreme difficulty. We need to readdress the central questions about self-improvement and human plasticity and ask: What can we succeed in changing about ourselves? What can't we change about ourselves? When can we overcome our biology? When is our biology our destiny?

A great deal is now known about change. Much of this knowledge exists only in the technical literature and has often been obfuscated by vested commercial, therapeutic, and political interests. The behaviorists long ago told the world that everything can change—intelligence, sexuality, mood, masculinity, femininity. The psychoanalysts still claim that, with enough insight, all your personality traits can be "worked through." The "politically correct" movements of the 1980s and the self-help industry voiced their agreement. In contrast, the drug companies, the DNA mappers, and many biological psychiatrists tell us that our character is fixed and that we are prisoners of our genes and the chemicals bathing our brains. The latter assert that, short of powerful drugs, genetic engineering, or brain surgery, nothing basic can change: not mood or intelligence or sexuality.

Both the "everything changes" view and the "nothing changes" view are ideologically driven overstatements. In fact, some psychological problems change readily in therapy or with medications, and others resist change mightily. Here is a sampling of what can be changed:

- Panic can be easily unlearned in psychotherapy, but it has not been cured by drugs.
- The sexual "dysfunctions"—frigidity, impotence, premature ejaculation—are easily treated.
- Our moods, which can wreak havoc with our physical health, are readily controlled by both psychotherapy and medications.

*Adapted from M.E.P. Seligman, *What you can change and what you can't,* Chapter 1 (New York: Knopf, 1993).

- Depression can be relieved by changes in conscious thinking, and it can be helped by drugs but not by insight into childhood.

And here are some facts about what resists change:

- Dieting almost never works lastingly.
- No treatment is known to improve much on the natural course of recovery from alcoholism.
- Reliving childhood trauma does not undo adult personality problems.

This textbook not only discusses the diagnosis, theories, and etiology of disorders, but it attempts to provide an accurate and factual guide to what you can change and what you cannot change. To this end, we examine different models and treatments for abnormality and ask which work and which do not.

The methods of testing which therapies work for disorders have become very sophisticated, and there is now in our view an authoritative way of deciding which treatments work and which do not. Suppose for a moment that an epidemic of German measles is predicted. You are pregnant, and you know that German measles causes birth defects. Two vaccines, Measex and Pneuplox, are on the market. A famous Hollywood star on TV says that she was given Measex and didn't get German measles. An Olympic sprinter adds her testimonial. Your best friend has heard lots of good things about Measex. The manufacturer of Pneuplox, on the other hand, has not solicited testimonials nor is it advertising. Nonetheless, it has been testing Pneuplox in an outcome study, a study in which treatments, either biological or psychological, are compared to control treatment. In this particular case, five hundred people have been given Pneuplox, with two of them getting German measles, and five hundred people have been given a sham injection, with twenty-eight of them developing German measles. Measex has not been so tested. Which vaccine do you want? Pneuplox, of course, because it has passed a rigorous outcome test.

How should you make up your mind about whether to undergo psychotherapy and/or take drugs to treat various abnormal behaviors? The psychotherapeutic and pharmaceutical industries are enormous and profitable, and they try to sell themselves in any way they can, including using testimonials, case histories, word of mouth ("My doctor is the best specialist on X in the East"), and slick advertising. Just as these sales pitches should not affect your choice of which vaccine to have or your decision of whether to have chemotherapy or radiation to treat your cancer, you should not let them convince you to use a particular diet or to send your father to a particular alcohol treatment center or to take a particular drug for depression or to have a particular kind of psychotherapy. Rather, you should rely on much better evidence—outcome studies—to make such important decisions. Outcome studies come in two varieties: ***efficacy studies,*** which test a treatment under controlled laboratory conditions, and ***effectiveness studies,*** which test a treatment as it is actually delivered in the field. When these two kinds of evidence agree, we can feel most confident that the treatment works. In this text, we will rely heavily on the available evidence from outcome studies when we review which treatments work for each disorder.

MODELS OF ABNORMALITY

Once a behavior is judged to be abnormal, clinicians and researchers attempt to understand what makes it abnormal and from there to find treatments that will restore a patient to normal functioning. Modern approaches to ab-

FOCUS QUESTIONS

1. What are the three principal models of abnormality?

2. Describe what each model considers to be the cause of abnormality.

normality have, in part, grown out of earlier notions, profiting from both their successes and their failures. Over the past hundred years, researchers and clinicians have made their approaches to abnormality more formal, and now speak of these approaches as ***models of abnormality*** to mean the ways by which they seek to understand and treat mental disorders. Today, what model we follow and how we define the causes of abnormality both help to determine how we will treat abnormality. At present, there are three major models, which are sometimes complementary and often competing in their attempts to understand and cure abnormality. The ***biomedical model,*** discussed in Chapter 2, holds that abnormality is an illness of the body. The ***psychodynamic model,*** discussed in Chapter 3, holds that abnormality is driven by hidden conflicts within our personality. (Besides classical psychoanalysis, Chapter 3 discusses self theory and existential theory, which deal with questions of life's meaning, human potential, responsibility, and will.) The ***learning model,*** also discussed in Chapter 3, includes the behavioral approach, which holds that we learn to be abnormal through conditioning and that we can unlearn these maladaptive ways of behaving, and the cognitive approach, which holds that abnormality springs from disordered conscious thought about oneself and the world.

Believing in a particular model of abnormality is a matter of choice, and the choice always involves risk. For example, an investigator might believe that early childhood experiences are the primary influence on adult psychopathology. He could spend years studying his manic-depressive patient's past history and never cure him, for it might turn out that manic-depression is caused by a biological problem and cured by a chemical. His strict adherence to a particular model would have blinded him to this other possibility—in this case, a biological explanation of manic-depression. In sum, there is danger inherent in following any particular model of abnormality. By concentrating on one level of evidence, we might neglect some of the other, more crucial evidence. The kinds of abnormality vary so much that we do not believe that one particular model of abnormality will explain all mental disorders.

History—the many ways in which abnormality was perceived and used in the past—provides a special lens for examining abnormality today. What was once divine inspiration, even commands and commandments from the Lord, may be viewed as madness today. The fashions of the times change, and with them, the meanings and perceptions of abnormality. Similarly, the explanations for what causes abnormality also change, as clinicians and researchers learn more about the mind and body. In the next two chapters, we turn to an examination of the various models of abnormality and learn how abnormality is approached and studied and treated in the present.

SUMMARY

1. The times and culture in which individuals live and the general way in which they perceive the world influence how abnormality is understood and treated.

2. When the world is perceived in animistic terms, abnormality is likely to be viewed as a *supernatural* phenomenon. Prehistoric people attributed abnormality to *animism,* or possession by spirits trapped in the head, and chipped *trephines* in the skull to let the spirits out.

3. Some Greeks and Romans attributed abnormality to *physical* causes. For example, they believed that *hysteria* was caused by a wandering uterus that

created discomfort wherever it settled. They treated it by trying to draw the uterus back to its proper place. Galen challenged this idea and said that hysteria was caused by a malfunctioning sexual organ. Furthermore, Galen also contributed important insights into *psychological* causes of abnormality.

4. In the middle of the eighteenth century, it gradually was recognized that mental disorders were *psychological* in origin and could be treated by psychological means. Mesmer tried to induce crises to restore the flow of *animal magnetism.* Charcot treated mental disorders by *hypnosis,* after distinguishing hysterical convulsions from symptoms with an organic cause. Both Breuer and Freud used hypnosis to induce *catharsis* in hysterical patients.

5. There are no hard and fast definitions of normality and abnormality, for there is no single element that all instances of abnormality share, nor any single property that distinguishes normality from abnormality.

6. With regard to abnormality, there are seven properties or elements that count toward deciding whether a person or an action is abnormal: suffering, maladaptiveness, irrationality and incomprehensibility, unpredictability and loss of control, vividness and unconventionality, observer discomfort, and violation of moral and ideal standards. The more of these elements that are present, and the more visible each element is, the more likely are we to judge the person or the action as abnormal.

7. *Abnormality* is recognized the way members of a family are recognized: because they share a *family resemblance* in that they have many significant elements in common.

8. Because the judgment of abnormality is a social judgment, there is sometimes disagreement about who is abnormal, and about which thoughts and actions qualify as being considered abnormal. Society occasionally errs about whom it calls abnormal, as sometimes do observers, even those who are qualified diagnosticians. But the absence of complete agreement should not be taken to mean that abnormality is always or frequently a matter of dispute.

QUESTIONS FOR CRITICAL THINKING

1. Why was Mesmer able to cure patients of their ills despite the fact that animal magnetism actually did not exist?

2. How did people justify the cruel and inhumane treatment of the insane in the early hospitals?

3. What aspects of moral treatment were likely to help less severely afflicted psychiatric patients?

4. Why do you think that people may disagree as to whether a behavior or person should be judged as abnormal?

CHAPTER 2

The Biomedical Model

Frantisek Kupka, *Red and Blue Disks*, 1911.

Anthropologists study the root causes of culture by seeking out existing "primitive" peoples, untouched by modern society and technology. To do this, anthropologists travel to remote corners of the world. For biomedical researchers, the challenges of studying the root causes of mental illness have been even greater. How can we best study the genetic origins of the major disorders and personality traits? How can we separate out the contributions of child rearing, of trauma, and of culture from the contribution of genes? A few years ago, a group of researchers at the University of Minnesota studied a pair of identical twins, both named Jim, who had been raised apart since birth, unaware of each other's existence. The Jims' psychological similarities were extraordinary, and their discovery opened the floodgates to the study of many more such twin pairs. Here was one way of separating the vicissitudes of growing up from the contributions of genes.

The biomedical model not only explores the genetic origins of mental illness, it also explains abnormality as a physical malfunction, such as a chemical or anatomical defect. Thus, it explains such symptoms as memory loss for recent events, language disorders, inability to deal with new situations, loss of personal skills and abilities, and neglect of bodily functions in an older person as physical malfunctions rather than psychological problems. For example, it emphasizes the problems resulting from chemical abnormalities in the brain rather than considering poor adaptation to change or demoralization arising out of retirement and reduced income. Similarly, it explains depression or obsessive-compulsive disorder by concentrating on those symptoms that are related to the patient's biological processes rather than emphasizing distorted thinking or poor interpersonal relations. Note how the biomedical model differs from other models in assessment and treatment of this patient with obsessive-compulsive disorder:

An eighteen-year-old high school girl from a small town in Maine was brought to a psychiatrist by her mother because of her excessive showering and dressing rituals. Showers lasted two hours; it took a half hour to dress. Each act of dressing was counted and had to be repeated precisely seventeen times. These behaviors had begun gradually at age fifteen years, causing chronic tardiness at school; two months of counseling with the school psychologist was not helpful. When the psychiatrist was consulted, the patient's circle of friends and activities had narrowed, and she was missing school one or two times a week.

She had been an outgoing, popular girl, with average grades, who had not previously exhibited unusual concern for neatness, expressed odd thoughts or preoccupations, or presented any behavioral problems of note. When interviewed, she was embarrassed as she discussed her washing and counting behaviors. She said she "knew it was crazy" but said "I just have to do this—I don't know why." Her behavior was otherwise quite unremarkable; most striking was her claim that she struggled against the symptoms continually but without success. She had never heard of anyone else who had this problem.

The patient was referred to a psychologist for behavior therapy, but would not cooperate with treatment, insisting she *had* to continue these rituals. The psychiatrist applied for enrollment of the patient in a study involving a new drug protocol. After three months, the process was complete. Clomipramine hydrochloride was administered . . . for three months. After about three weeks of drug therapy, the urges to wash and to count had faded sufficiently so that the patient could cooperate with her family and psychologist in further reducing her strange behaviors. (Rapoport, 1988)

A biomedical scientist investigates the evidence that the chemistry of a depressed patient's brain changes when he is having depressed thoughts. The biomedical scientist will experiment with these biochemical factors in order to see if they are the cause of the depression. Also, in an attempt to treat the disorder, the biomedical investigator will be more likely to develop chemical therapies or drugs that will counteract biochemical factors. This approach lies at the core of the lively field of "Biological Psychiatry."

BIOLOGICAL CAUSES OF ABNORMALITY

Those who advocate the biomedical model typically approach abnormality as medical researchers approach an illness: They will group diverse, but co-occurring symptoms together into a coherent **syndrome.** Then they will

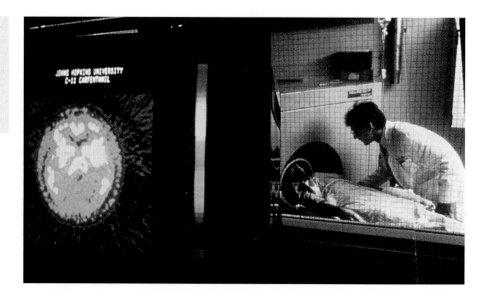

▶ The biomedical model uses tools such as the PET (Positron Emission Tomography) scan to study how the chemistry of a depressed patient's brain differs from that of the brain of a person who is not depressed.

FOCUS QUESTIONS

1. How do biomedical researchers approach a mental disorder?

2. What four possible causes of abnormality are examined by adherents of the biomedical model?

search for the *etiology,* or cause, of the syndrome, examining four possible causes: (1) *germs,* (2) *genes,* (3) the *biochemistry* of the patient's brain, and (4) the patient's *neuroanatomy.* Once an etiology has been discovered, some biological **treatment** that attacks the cause, usually a drug, will be sought to alleviate the abnormality. The major assumption of the biomedical model is that psychological disorders are really physical disorders. This was first demonstrated scientifically when the psychological disorder of general paresis was proved to be caused by the organic illness, syphilis.

Germs as Etiology: Syphilis and General Paresis

The worst epidemic of madness in recorded history began a few years after Christopher Columbus discovered the New World and continued with mounting ferocity until the early 1900s. We have come to call this disorder **general paresis.** Beginning with a weakness in the arms and legs, it proceeds to symptoms of eccentricity and then downright delusions of grandeur, the false notion that one is more important than the objective facts warrant. It finally progresses to global paralysis, stupor, and death.

As early as 1672, Thomas Willis (1621–1675), an English anatomist, observed that some of these patients exhibited dullness of the mind and forgetfulness that seemed to develop into downright stupidity and foolishness. Later in life, these same people would fall into paralysis. This was not a precise observation. Rather, it served loosely to differentiate one group of madmen from others, based on signs of developing stupidity and paralysis. In 1805, a French physician, Jean Esquirol (1772–1840), added another significant observation: the mental deterioration and paralysis observed in this group of patients quickly culminated in death.

There the matter stood until 1826, when Esquirol's student, A. L. J. Bayle, undertook the first major step necessary for a disorder to be understood as biomedical: organization of symptoms into a syndrome, which allowed precise description and diagnosis of the illness. He formalized the diagnosis by giving a complete and exact description of the physical and psychological symptoms, and arguing strongly that these constituted a separate disease, a different madness, if you will, from all others then known. He argued that mental deterioration, paralysis, and subsequent death, among others, were symptoms that clustered together and formed the distinct syndrome of general paresis.

Bayle's rigorous definition of the disorder led to considerable speculation about its etiology. Quite early, there had been some suspicion that it was caused by syphilis. But at the time, Wilhelm Griesinger (1817–1868), an eminent psychiatric authority of physiological bent, had dismissed that view on the seemingly sound basis that paresis occurred among people in whom no trace of syphilitic infection could be found. Reports of cases in which paretics were known to have had syphilis were clearly not sufficient, since these were contradicted by the paretics who adamantly denied they had ever had syphilis and who showed no evidence of syphilis.

Despite Griesinger's opinion and the support of his colleagues, evidence gradually emerged that syphilis was somehow implicated in general paresis. But that evidence was difficult to accumulate for three reasons. First, and perhaps most important, syphilis precedes paresis by as many as thirty years. The connection between the one and the other was difficult to see. Second, syphilis was then, as now, a disease about which there was considerable shame. People were often unable to admit to themselves, and surely not to others, that they had contracted the disease. Third, the diagnosis of syphilis was itself not an exact science. In the early part of the nineteenth century, techniques were still not available for ascertaining that someone had syphilis, because the overt symptoms that occur immediately after contracting it soon disappear. Not until there were improvements in microscopy was it ascertained that syphilitic organisms (spirochetes) remain in the body long after the overt symptoms vanish.

The evidence, then, accumulated slowly. By about 1860, it was possible to demonstrate that there was enormous destruction in the neural tissue of the brains of people who had died from general paresis. Later, in 1869, D. M. Argyll (1837–1909), a Scottish eye surgeon, demonstrated that the central nervous system was implicated in syphilis by showing that the eyes of syphilitics failed to show the standard pupillary reflex—the narrowing of the pupil to bright light. In 1884, Alfred Fournier (1832–1914), a French physician, provided highly suggestive *epidemiological* evidence (that is, evidence from many individuals) on the relation between syphilis and general paresis: some 65 percent of paretics had a demonstrable history of syphilis, compared to only 10 percent of nonparetics. That evidence, of course, was merely suggestive: it did not demonstrate cause since it did not show that 100 percent of paretics had prior histories of syphilis. But it added significantly to the mounting tide of data, turning belief away from Griesinger's view that strong spirits and cigars were the culprits, toward the syphilis-paresis link.

The overt symptoms of syphilis—the sores (chancres) on the genitals—may disappear in a few weeks, but the disease does not. It goes underground, attacking the central nervous system. Cures for syphilis were unknown then. Thus, not only was it true that if you had the disease you couldn't get rid of it, it was equally true and also known that *like measles, if you contracted syphilis once, you couldn't get it again.* More bluntly, if someone who has already become syphilitic (a paretic) comes in contact with another syphilitic germ, he will not develop sores on his genitals.

Consider the situation of those who believed that this psychological disorder (general paresis) was caused by the syphilitic germ. On the one hand, there was evidence that many paretics had syphilis. But some paretics claimed never to have contracted syphilis. The investigators had a hypothesis: perhaps those paretics who claimed not to have had syphilis actually had had the disease and did not know it or were too ashamed to admit it. If indeed these paretics were ignorant or not telling the truth, then the case for a biological cause of general paresis would be convincing. There was one means, but a risky one, of finding out by way of an experiment if these paretics had previously had syphilis. The investigators reasoned that if you inject these paretics with the syphilitic germ, one startling result would come about. The paretics would not contract the disease since you cannot get syphilis twice. Betting on this outcome, the German neurologist Richard von Krafft-Ebing (1840–1902) performed this critical experiment. In 1897, he inoculated nine paretics who had denied ever having had syphilis with material from syphilitic sores. None developed sores themselves, leading to the conclusion that they must have already been infected. The link between syphilis and general paresis was forged.

Once the syndrome was isolated and its etiology understood, it was only a matter of time before a German bacteriologist, Paul Ehrlich (1854–1915), discovered a drug that killed the syphilis germs in the bloodstream, thereby preventing the occurrence of paresis. It was not until the 1940s that penicillin, a drug that arrests syphilis almost at any point in its development, became the preferred treatment.

So successful was Krafft-Ebing's work and that of others who followed him that the most common mental illness of the nineteenth century was eradicated within a generation. But Krafft-Ebing, this scientist of courage and genius, accomplished more than just discovering that a particular germ

▲ The German neurologist Richard von Krafft-Ebing (1840–1902), an unsung hero of the biomedical model, performed the crucial experiment that forged the link between syphilis and general paresis.

STREPTOCOCCAL INFECTION AND SYDENHAM'S CHOREA AND TOURETTE'S SYNDROME

In order to develop the most effective treatment for a mental illness, we must often first discover what caused it. The connection between syphilis and general paresis, for example, remained unclear because people frequently contracted syphilis long before they developed paresis. Once it was proved that syphilis caused general paresis, treatments were developed to eliminate the disorder. Today, it has been proposed that two types of movement disorders and their related psychological symptoms may sometimes originate with exposure to strep infections. Further research is necessary to establish whether there is such a relationship and what the implications for treatment are.

"Faith" was a nine-year-old girl who came down with Sydenham's Chorea, a disorder in which the victim suffers from uncontrollable, jerking muscle movements. Over the two-week period before her hospital admission, Faith grew increasingly restless and clumsy. Her coordination gradually deteriorated to the point where she had trouble using eating utensils, writing, speaking, and walking. One month prior to that point, she had experienced nightmares and separation anxiety as well as mood swings, obsessions, and compulsions. She began to wash her hands up to fifteen times per hour and would no longer use public restrooms or pet the family dog. Faith's medical history revealed that she had had a mild respiratory infection three months before her hospitalization. Also around that time, several of her classmates had been diagnosed with streptococcal infections. Faith herself did not have "strep throat" when admitted, but she did show a high strep antibody level (Swedo, 1994).

There are now several striking case histories among children like Faith in which strep infections predate the deterioration of movement control and the development of obsessive-compulsive symptoms. In another case, a seven-year-old diagnosed with Tourette's syndrome (TS), a motor and verbal disorder in which the victim may cry out uncontrollably or make compulsive and often odd movements (tics), experienced a dramatic increase in tics after having the "flu." In one thirteen-year-old boy, both Tourette's and obsessive symptoms rapidly worsened following a strep infection (Kiessling, Marcotte, and Culpepper, 1993; Swedo, Leonard, Schapiro, et al., 1993; Swedo, 1994; Allen, Leonard, and Swedo, 1995).

These cases link Sydenham's Chorea, Tourette's syndrome, and obsessive-compulsive disorder (OCD) by pointing to strep infection as a common environmental trigger. Researchers speculate that the antibodies the immune system produces in reaction to the infection interfere with circuitry in the brain's frontal lobe, a region that regulates body movement. The connection between the virus and movement disorders has caused clinicians to change their treatment approach in cases where they suspect that an infection has occurred. Early results indicate that a treatment that reduces the amount of antibodies is more effective than one that treats the symptoms of the disorder alone.

Nevertheless, strep infection is at most just one contributor to movement disorders. Only a small number of children who have had strep infections develop movement problems, and many children with movement disorders have not had a strep infection.

---

was the cause of paresis. With this discovery, he convinced the medical world of something much more global: that mental illness could be just an illness of the body. This became the first principle, the rallying cry, and the agenda for the field of biological psychiatry. A century of research searching for biological foundations of schizophrenia, depression, Alzheimer's, and many other disorders ensued (see Box 2–1).

Genetics as Etiology

Genetics is the second biomedical etiology that may lead researchers to consider a psychological disorder as being a physical illness. A generation ago, few mental health professionals believed that inherited vulnerabilities could be central to the development of mental illness. Fearing that discovery of a genetic predisposition might cast a stigma on patients and lead to a questioning of the need for psychotherapy, clinical researchers strongly leaned toward social and developmental explanations of the inescapable fact that some mental illness can run in families. Gradually, however, the genetic evidence became too compelling to ignore. Consider schizophrenia, for example.

Schizophrenia is a severe psychotic condition that strikes approximately 1 percent of the world's population. Usually beginning in adolescence or early

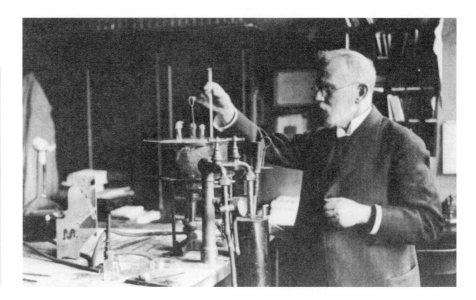

adulthood, it results in highly disordered thinking, perception, and language. Schizophrenic individuals function poorly in complex and primitive societies alike. What causes schizophrenia? The biomedical model holds that it is an illness passed on genetically. Investigators have approached schizophrenia by studying twins.

There are two kinds of twins: identical and fraternal. Identical twins (also known as **monozygotic,** since they developed from a single fertilized egg) have all the same genes, whereas fraternal twins (also known as **dizygotic,** since they developed from two different eggs) have an average of only half of their genes in common—exactly the same proportion of common genetic material as any two siblings share. Twins are an exquisite research tool for those who advocate the biomedical model because twins usually share very similar environments (same age, same social class, same food, similar social circles, etc.), while they differ systematically on how many genes they share, depending on whether they are identical or fraternal twins (see Box 2–2).

If there are genes that determine whether one will be schizophrenic or not, and if one twin becomes schizophrenic, what is the probability that the other twin will also be schizophrenic? If environment had no influence and only genes determined schizophrenia, then if one identical twin were schizophrenic, the other twin would also be schizophrenic, since they share all of their genes. This would not be so with fraternal twins, since they share only half their genes. Depending on the nature of the alleged gene, the prediction would be 50 percent or 25 percent for fraternal twins (McGue, Gottesman, and Rao, 1985). Those who hold the biomedical view use this method of observing identical and fraternal twins. If they find that one twin is schizophrenic, they will then find out if the other twin is also schizophrenic. When both twins are schizophrenic, they are called **concordant** for schizophrenia; when only one is schizophrenic, they are called **discordant.**

Many studies from Europe, Japan, and the U.S.A. have looked at hundreds of pairs of twins in this way. Overall, identical twins have a concordance rate for schizophrenia of about 50 percent, while fraternal twins have a concordance of about 10 percent. Keep in mind that the rate of schizophrenia in the population as a whole is about 1 percent. So when one of the identical twins is schizophrenic, the other is five times more likely to be schizophrenic than the fraternal twin of a schizophrenic, who is in turn ten times more likely than the average person to be schizophrenic. This suggests a causal influence of genes, but not genetic determination, since concordance for identical twins is only 50 percent, not 100 percent. And since the concor-

FOCUS QUESTIONS

1. Explain how studies of twins help to determine that there is a genetic component to schizophrenia.
2. How do adoptive studies tease apart the contribution to personality of child rearing versus genes?

GENES AND PERSONALITY

Over the last decade and a half, an iconoclastic group of University of Minnesota psychologists led by Tom Bouchard, David Lykken, and Auke Tellegen has studied the psychological profiles of twins. The researchers examined twins who were separated at birth and reared apart. By studying such twins, they were able to separate environmental and genetic influences. If twins who had been reared apart shared similar traits, it would seemingly indicate a large genetic contribution to the trait.

Bouchard and his colleagues started with the "Jim" twins (both were named Jim), identical twins whose reunion was covered in the press in the 1970s. The two Jims had not even known of each other's existence, but their psychological similarities were extraordinary: both had divorced a woman named Linda to marry a woman named Betty, one had named his son James Allen X while his co-twin named his son James Alan X. Could it just be coincidence? Unlikely. These "coincidences" did not seem to occur in the lives of fraternal twins reared apart. The Minnesota Twin Study has now accumulated 110 pairs of identical twins reared apart and 27 pairs of fraternal twins reared apart. Many of the twins' very first reunions took place in the Minnesota laboratory. Stories of spooky similarity repeat over and over.

The degree of heritability and the range of personality traits that are heritable are impressive. All of the following are *strongly* related in identical twins reared apart, and they are much less related in fraternal twins reared apart (Bouchard, Lykken, McGue, Segal, and Tellegen, 1990; Plomin, Corley, DeFries, and Fulker, 1990;

Waller, Kojetin, Bouchard, Lykken, and Tellegen, 1990; Bouchard and McGue, 1990; Edelbrock, Rende, Plomin, and Thompson, 1995; Bouchard, 1996):

IQ	danger seeking
mental speed	authoritarianism
perceptual speed	extraversion
and accuracy	neuroticism
religiosity	amount of television
traditionalism	viewing
alcohol and drug abuse	well-being
crime and conduct	self-acceptance
problems	self-control
job satisfaction	dominance
actual choice of jobs	pessimism
cheerfulness	hostility
depressiveness	cynicism

These findings have essentially been duplicated in another study carried out with 500 Swedish twins, identical and fraternal, reared apart and reared together, and now middle-aged (Pedersen, McClearn, Plomin, Nesselroade, Berg, and DeFaire, 1991; Plomin, Scheier, Bergeman, Pedersen, Nesselroade, and McClearn, 1992).

It is important to realize, however, that for every one of these heritable traits, the degree of heritability is much less than a perfect 1.00. Generally, heritability hovers a bit below .50. This means that genes do not determine at least half of any heritable personality traits, but it also means that genes do contribute much of what we are, normally and abnormally.

▲ Here is a set of twins separated at birth and reared apart. When they were reunited, they found out that both were fire chiefs and had the same mustache, sideburns, eyeglasses, drank the same beer, and used the same gestures.

FOCUS QUESTIONS

1. Describe how irregularities in an individual's biochemistry can lead to schizophrenic behavior.
2. How might disorders in the anatomy of the brain lead to psychopathology?

dance for identical twins is less than 100 percent, genes cannot be the whole etiological story. Environment also must have an influence on the cause of schizophrenia. This issue, the inheritance of schizophrenia, remains hotly debated. We will discuss it more fully in Chapter 9.

Biochemistry as Etiology: Dopamine and Schizophrenia

As we mentioned earlier, those believing in the biomedical model may also look for the cause of a disorder in a third category: irregularities in an individual's biochemistry. One hypothesis about schizophrenia is that it is caused by an unbalanced biochemistry. The "dopamine hypothesis," as it is called, states that schizophrenic behavior is caused by too much dopamine activity in the brain. Dopamine, like all neurotransmitters, is a chemical that is directly involved in transmitting nerve impulses from one nerve cell to the next. There is a considerable amount of evidence in favor of this hypothesis. But all of it is rather indirect, since it is still technically impossible to look into the brain of a living person and count how much of a given chemical is there. The most important evidence comes from the fact that drugs that usually relieve the symptoms of schizophrenia also lower the amount of usable dopamine in the brain. Such drugs do not completely cure schizophrenia, but they do reduce hallucinations and delusions, improve concentration, and make schizophrenic symptoms less bizarre. This action is called dopamine "blocking," and these drugs block dopamine activity by binding themselves to the nerve cells in the brain that receive dopamine, thus preventing naturally occurring dopamine from getting to these receptors. And the more dopamine that can be blocked by various drugs, the greater the ability of the drugs to relieve schizophrenic symptoms (Matthysse, 1973). Some investigators conclude that since these drugs decrease dopamine activity, an increase of dopamine activity causes schizophrenia (Krieckhaus, Donahoe, and Morgan, 1992; Heinz, Schmidt, and Reischies, 1994; Kapur and Remington, 1996).

Such evidence argues that the symptoms of schizophrenia are caused by too much dopamine activity in the brain. From the viewpoint of the biomedical school, evidence that shows that altering the biochemistry of the brain alters the symptoms of a disorder (for better or worse) suggests that the disorder is an illness. This further contributes to the notion—as we saw with both germs and general paresis, and genetics and schizophrenia—that psychological disorders are really physical disorders.

Neuroanatomy as Etiology: The Disordered Brain

Those who believe in the biomedical model also consider disorders in the anatomy of the brain as an explanation for psychopathology. Brain disorders may result from the malfunctioning of specific areas of the brain. Consider these two cases:

> A twenty-year-old man [Bob] was an excellent student, relatively conservative, and quite ambitious. He had enrolled in a university to become an engineer, and was doing well, a fact that pleased his wealthy family. Upon returning home from a summer job as a waiter at a resort, however, he seemed to have lost his purposefulness and motivation in general, and his behavior seemed more erratic. He announced to his family that he no longer wanted to study engineering, and wished to become a head waiter instead.

> A woman [Sylvia] had worked for years as a fish boner. One day, she began to experience difficulty in doing her job. She did not seem to know what to do with

▼The "dopamine hypothesis" states that schizophrenia may be caused by excess dopamine activity in the brain. Here is a PET scan of a schizophrenic patient's brain after it has been injected with a drug that reduces dopamine activity, allowing the brain to return to more normal activity.

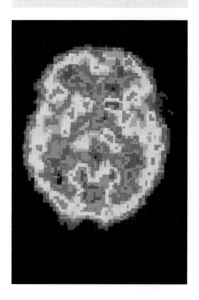

her knife. She would stick the point in the head of the fish, start the first stroke, then come to a stop. In her own mind, she knew how to fillet a fish, but yet she could not execute the maneuver. The foreman accused her of being drunk and sent her home for mutilating fish. (Critchley, 1966)

What do we make of these behaviors? Were these people shirking their responsibilities? Did they have psychological problems? Bob's parents, seeing that Bob's behavior was becoming more and more erratic—clearly abnormal for him—might well have encouraged Bob to see a psychotherapist to deal with his "motivational" problem. Sylvia's boss was clearly less sympathetic with her new and, for an experienced fish boner, abnormal approach to the task.

Bob's real problem came to light before having to spend months in psychotherapy working out his "motivational" problem. One day, he had an epileptic-like seizure, a clear sign of a problem in the anatomy of the brain. He underwent neurological tests that revealed a massive malformation of the blood vessels in the frontal area of his brain. Over the years, brain researchers have "mapped," that is, **localized,** anatomical areas of the brain according to which areas are related to which functions and behaviors. The activity in the frontal area of the brain has much to do with a person's motivation and sense of purpose. Bob had what we call an ***organic disorder.***

It turned out that Sylvia, too, had an organic disorder. She knew that she was not drunk on the job. Her abnormal behavior baffled her as much as it enraged her boss. She knew how to fillet a fish, but could not execute the appropriate movements. She underwent neurological testing, which revealed that she had damage to the area in the cortex that helps control movement.

So what looks to be a problem of personality, as in Bob's case, and a case of confusion to Sylvia (or a case of gross irresponsibility to Sylvia's boss) are really clear examples of organic disorders. Today, biomedical researchers are expending enormous energy trying to understand the relation between brain anatomy and behavior. They know that the brain is organized in a hierarchy from bottom to top, with the higher levels generally controlling more abstract, cognitive, and voluntary functions. These higher areas are more fragile. So the sequence of symptoms of senility—problems in coping with new situations, confusion about when events occurred, intermittent memory loss, loss of personal skills, abilities, and social habits, and eventually failures in ability to perform basic bodily functions—can be explained by the biomedical model, which says that higher levels of brain function will malfunction first, followed by malfunctioning of the lower systems.

Loss of other functions can also be explained by the biomedical model (see Chapter 11 for a discussion of some of the major organic disorders). Some functions of the brain are more vulnerable to damage than others; all parts of the brain are not equally resilient. A group of neurons may be more vulnerable because it has a relatively poor blood supply or because it has a higher requirement for oxygen or nutrients. Long-term memories, for example, are particularly vulnerable. They may be selectively damaged by general trauma (e.g., blows to the head), or by infections (e.g., the herpes simplex virus), or even by nutritional deficiencies (e.g., lack of vitamin B1, which is a critical component of metabolic processes in all cells of the body) (Hilton, 1994; Beers, Henkel, Kesner, and Stroop, 1995; Calingasan, Gandy, Baker, Sheu, Kim, Wisniewski, and Gibson, 1995).

TREATMENT

So the evidence that mental illness is at bottom physical illness comes from four sources: germs, genes, biochemical insufficiency, and anatomical malfunction. This has a straightforward implication for treatment: cure will follow only from getting rid of the physical illness. Kill the syphilitic spirochetes with penicillin and stop the mental deterioration. Restore the right biochemical balance in schizophrenia and restore healthy cognition. Those who adhere to the biomedical model believe that psychotherapy for a biological illness is at best cosmetic and that a therapist might, at most, help a paretic adjust to his deteriorating mental and physical state or help a schizophrenic not to talk about his delusions. Treatment in the biomedical model takes place, with minor exceptions, in a single modality: drugs (see Table 2–1).

Throughout the book, we will consider drug therapies for many disorders, including schizophrenia, major depressive disorder, bipolar disorder, anxiety, obsessive-compulsive disorder, and phobia. We will try to understand the

TABLE 2–1

DRUG TREATMENTS			
Disorder	Drug Treatment	Effectiveness	Side Effects
Schizophrenia	antipsychotics	majority show partial improvement	irregular heartbeat, low blood pressure, uncontrolled fidgeting, tardive dyskinesia, immobility of face
Depression	MAO inhibitors	majority show moderate improvement	toxicity
	tricyclics	majority show moderate improvement	cardiac problems, mania, confusion, memory loss, extreme fatigue
	serotonin reuptake inhibitors (e.g., Prozac)	majority show moderate improvement	nausea, nervousness, insomnia, possible preoccupation with suicide
Bipolar Disorder	lithium	large majority show substantial improvement	cardiac problems, gastrointestinal problems
Everyday Anxiety	anti-anxiety drugs (e.g., Miltown, Librium, Valium)	substantial majority show short-term improvement	less potent the longer you take them, may be addictive
Specific Phobias	anti-anxiety drugs	little relief	may be addictive
Social Phobia	MAO inhibitors	majority show improvement	toxicity
Panic	anti-anxiety drugs (e.g., Xanax)	half show improvement	less potent the longer you take them, may be addictive
Agoraphobia	tricyclics	majority show moderate improvement	cardiac problems, mania, confusion, memory loss, fatigue
	MAO inhibitors	majority show moderate improvement	toxicity
Generalized Anxiety Disorder	anti-anxiety drugs	little to no improvement	may be addictive

ways in which these drugs, really chemical compounds, act on the chemistry of the brain. And based on the latest outcome studies, we will look at the success rate of these drugs versus psychological therapies, and balance that rate against any unwanted side effects of the drugs.*

Schizophrenia and Antipsychotics

Horace shows up at his father's office one morning painted a dull brownish-red from head to toe, and daubed with slime. There is an enormous barbed fishhook sticking out of his cheek. He wears no clothes.

"I'm a worm!" he babbles as he crawls along the floor. The receptionist calls the police, and Horace is dragged off to the hospital.

In the hospital, Horace hallucinates floridly. He hears the sounds of fish in a feeding frenzy and believes he is the object of their frenzy. He has the unique delusion that he is a worm. ("You worm!" his girlfriend had shouted as she slammed the door and walked out of his life.) His mood gyrates from terror to giddiness to despair.

At Horace's case conference, there is a quarrel. The psychoanalysts advocate talking therapy. They believe that his delusion is a homosexual panic since all schizophrenia is "latent homosexuality." Drugging Horace will only be cosmetic and worse it may impede his gaining insight into the underlying conflict. But it is the summer of 1952 and one of the residents has just returned from a year in Paris, where a new drug treatment of psychosis was being tested. The resident argues doggedly, and Horace is injected with this drug, chlorpromazine. He relaxes right away. (The new drug is called a "major tranquilizer.") By the next weekend, the idea that he is a worm now seems as crazy to Horace as it does to those around him. Within three weeks, Horace is back at work as a delivery boy.

FOCUS QUESTIONS

1. Identify the four major categories of drug therapies and the disorders for which they are administered.
2. What are the side effects of the various drug treatments?
3. Why did the discovery of antipsychotic drugs produce a revolution in psychiatric treatment?

Until the mid-1950s, psychosis was untreatable. The back wards (called "snake pits") of mental hospitals were filled beyond their capacities with patients like Horace. Many of the inmates were hallucinating and unreachable, or mutely catatonic, or wild with delusions and straitjacketed. Everything was tried to treat these schizophrenics: electroconvulsive shock therapy, artificial hibernation, lobotomy, insulin shock, different combinations of drugs. Nothing worked very noticeably. The psychotics might have remissions, but their future was widely believed to be life in the back ward.

In Paris, Jean Delay and Pierre Deneker tried out a new antihistamine (chlorpromazine) that had been synthesized for hay fever two years earlier. Their patients became calm, their delusions dissolved, and their contact with the real world resumed. Soon, at every major hospital, chlorpromazine was tried and, by and large, it worked. Many patients got better in a few weeks—some were astonishingly better. Even patients who had vegetated in the back wards for many years recovered and could be discharged.

Outcome studies of the new antipsychotics were done, and people on the drugs usually did better than those in control groups. The antipsychotic drugs "work" about 60 percent of the time, although well-done outcome studies are scarce. A large minority of patients do not benefit. The most optimistic estimate we know of percentage effectiveness of the antipsychotics is: complete eradication of delusions and hallucinations, 22.5 percent; partial improvement, 60 percent; no improvement, 17.5 percent (Chandler and Winokur, 1989). Moreover, the antipsychotic drugs produce side effects, of which the most noticeable include: irregular heartbeat, low blood pressure, uncontrollable fidgeting, immobility of the face, tremor, and a shuffling gait. But the worst is **tardive dyskinesia**, brought on because the drugs destroy something, still

*Some of this chapter is based on M.E.P. Seligman, *What you can change and what you can't* (New York: Knopf, 1993), Chapter 3.

unknown, in the brain's control of movement. Victims suck and smack their lips uncontrollably like a frog catching an insect. Between one-quarter and one-third of patients who take antipsychotics develop tardive dyskinesia. The longer you take these drugs, the more likely it will develop, and once it starts, it is irreversible (ACNP-FDA Task Force, 1973; Wegner, Catalano, Gibralter, and Kane, 1985; Keck, Cohen, Baldessarini, and McElroy, 1989; Gualtieri, 1991; Dilip, Caligiuri, Paulsen, Heaton, Lacro, Harris, Bailey, Fell, and McAdams, 1995; Pourcher, Baruch, Bouchard, Filteau, and Bergeron, 1995).

Depression and the Antidepressants

As the drugs for psychotics showed promise, new drugs were tried on other disorders (Spiegel, 1989). The first antidepressant was discovered by accident. A new drug was tried on tuberculosis, and the patients improved. The patients were pleased, very pleased. They danced in the corridors and shouted in ecstasy. The drug—an MAO inhibitor called iproniazid—was an euphoriant, and it also relieved depression. Within its first year, 1957, 400,000 patients were treated with it (Kline, 1970). Unfortunately, iproniazid is toxic, even occasionally lethal. It was soon outsold by milder antidepressants, called tricyclics (Elavil, Trofranil, Sinequan). These also worked, and their side effects were less pronounced. A consensus figure is that about 65 percent of patients improve noticeably with tricyclics (Berger, 1977; Spiegel, 1989; White, Wykoff, Tynes, Schneider, et al., 1990; Montgomery, 1994). The newest antidepressant, Prozac (fluoxetine), works at just about the same rate as the old ones, but milder side effects were initially claimed (Hall, 1988). Like the antipsychotics, once you stop taking the antidepressants, you are just as likely to relapse or have a fresh attack of depression as you were before you took them.

Antidepressants, like antipsychotics, have side effects: the MAO inhibitors, like iproniazid, can be fatal. The tricyclics are milder, but they can produce cardiac problems, mania, confusion and memory loss, and extreme fatigue. At least 25 percent of patients can't tolerate them. Prozac produces less drowsiness, dry mouth, and sweating than tricyclics, but it also produces more nausea, nervousness, and insomnia. There are a few case histories accumulating about Prozac causing suicidal preoccupation, but no well-controlled study has yet been done (Wernicke, 1985; Cooper, 1988; Teicher, Glod, and Cole, 1990; Beaumont, 1990; Preskorn and Jerkovich, 1990; Greenberg, Bornstein, Zborowski, Fisher, and Greenberg, 1994; Orengo, Kunik, Molinari, and Workman, 1996).

Bipolar Disorder and Lithium

As we have seen, the antidepressants are moderately helpful. In contrast, strong relief for mania comes from lithium carbonate. In 1947, John Cade, an Australian physician working under primitive conditions, found that the urine of his manic patients caused guinea pigs to tremble, twitch violently, and die. He injected them with lithium, an element known to be a poison. The guinea pigs now became calm and survived injections of the manics' urine. Cade tried lithium on the manic humans whose urine was so lethal. Within days their euphoric excitement gave way to calm (Cade, 1970).

By 1970, biological psychiatrists prescribed lithium routinely for bipolar disorder. Before the use of lithium, bipolar disorder was a crippling illness: 15 percent of patients with bipolar disorder killed themselves, and most—many of whom were very talented—could not hold jobs. With lithium, this is no longer so. Roughly 80 percent of patients with bipolar disorder are helped, and most markedly.

▼Gerald Klerman (1928–1992) can be considered one of the driving forces of modern biological psychiatry. He was, until his untimely death, a professor of psychiatry and an active biomedical researcher specializing in the affective disorders. As head of the government agency in charge of mental health, he underwrote many therapy outcome studies to test which psychotherapies and drug therapies actually worked and he helped to launch the field of neuropsychology.

"AT THAT POINT THE MEETING BECAME CHAOTIC, AS EVERYONE'S MEDICATION SEEMED TO WEAR OFF AT THE SAME TIME."

Lithium is more effective for dampening manic episodes than it is for the depressive episodes in bipolar disorder. It can also prevent manic episodes if taken regularly between episodes. Its main problem is that many patients refuse to take it because they like the feeling of being manic (Sack and De Fraites, 1977; Johnson, Olafsson, Andersen, Plenge, et al., 1989). From the outset, lithium was a known poison, so its potentially toxic and even lethal side effects—cardiac and gastrointestinal—were monitored carefully. Unlike the rest of the drugs, lithium therefore generated few unpleasant surprises (Jefferson, 1990; Bowden, 1996).

Anxiety and Anti-Anxiety Drugs

In the mid-1950s, Miltown (meprobamate) was first used with anxious patients. Anxious patients relaxed profoundly in a few minutes, but they remained conscious and their troubles, which moments before had consumed them, now seemed far away. Sleep came more easily. Miltown was prescribed very widely. Librium (chlordiazepoxide) replaced Miltown and became the world's number one prescription drug. And Valium (diazepam), which is five times stronger, soon displaced Librium (Berger, 1970; Cohen, 1970).

Like the antidepressant and antipsychotic drugs, once you stop taking anxiolytics, anxiety usually returns in full force. When the anxiety stems from a real problem, you may find you have done nothing in the meantime to solve it. Anti-anxiety drugs do not have the *very* strong side effects that the antipsychotics and antidepressants have. They are probably not lethal, even in megadoses. But unlike the antipsychotic and antidepressant drugs, the anti-anxiety drugs become less potent the longer you take them, and they probably are addictive (Tinklenberg, 1977; Olivieri, Cantopher, and Edwards, 1986; Nagy, 1987; Roache, 1990). Nonetheless, Salzman claims that benzodiazepines, particularly alprazolam and clonazepam, have been used successfully for the treatment of panic disorder and agoraphobia (Salzman, 1993; Gold, Miller, Stennie, and Populla-Vardi, 1995).

Overall, then, drug treatments are often effective for several specific disorders. But like most useful agents, they have drawbacks. They only work for exactly as long as they are taken, and each can produce unwanted side effects, some of them crippling (see Table 2–1). Perhaps most importantly, when you take a drug you come to depend on an external agent for your well-being, rather than on your own skills and abilities.

EVALUATING THE BIOMEDICAL MODEL

Here are the bulwarks of the biomedical model: First, a large body of research in the last ten years has shown that some mental disorders are heritable. Second, some mental disorders are caused by germs, some by biochemical disturbances, and some by neuroanatomical problems. Third, drugs can change our emotions and moods. These three together form a powerful view of psychopathology: mental illness as physical illness. Let us now take a look at both the strengths and weaknesses of this model.

Strengths

The biomedical model is grounded in mature sciences. Its basic components, such as the dopamine hypothesis, heritability, and the central nervous system, seem measurable and objective. It has a well-defined sequence of methods: syndrome, etiology, and treatment. One hundred years of biomedical research, highlighted by such stunning successes as the eradication of general paresis, make it clear that its hypotheses are testable and, when correct, applicable.

Weaknesses

With all this, why don't we stop our search for models right here? Because the model also has several problems. The main bulwarks of the model are somewhat shakier than they first appear: First, that mental illness is physical illness has been demonstrated for only one mental illness—general paresis. The claim for schizophrenia, Alzheimer's disease, and manic-depression is plausible, but unproven—no biochemical cause has yet been isolated. The claim for depression, anxiety, sexual problems, and post-traumatic stress disorder is merely a research agenda, with little or no evidence to back it up.

Second, the claim that personality and mental disorder are inherited has strong evidence behind it. But personality is only *partly* genetic. Even by the most extreme estimates, about half of personality is not inherited. Much of the rest of the book is about how nongenetic influences can bring about mental illness and can relieve it.

The third bulwark, the claims about drug treatment, should be viewed with skepticism. Medications warrant only modest enthusiasm. There are indeed drugs that alter mood and psychopathology for some, but not for all people. But the risk of relapse is unchanged once the patient stops taking the drug. Further, all drugs produce unwanted side effects, some of which are ruinous. Because of this, many patients cannot tolerate the biomedical treatments.

Finally, there is a great deal to be said for psychological intervention without any biomedical intervention. As we will see throughout the book, psychological events sometimes cause psychopathology, and changing these events—without directly changing anything about the body—can indeed cure.

SUMMARY

1. The *biomedical model* holds that psychological disorders are illnesses of the body.

2. The biomedical school of thought dictates an ideal procedure for isolating a psychological disorder as an illness: grouping the symptoms into a coherent *syndrome* that can be diagnosed reliably; searching for an *etiology*, or cause, of the syndrome; and finding a *treatment* and *prevention* that follow from knowing the cause.

3. Four sorts of evidence about etiology of a disorder point toward a psychological disorder being considered a physical illness: discovery of a *germ* causing the illness, *genetic transmission* of the disorder, irregularities in the *biochemistry* of the brain leading to a disorder, or malfunctions in the *neuroanatomy* of the brain producing the disorder.

4. We discussed examples of each of these etiologies. The eradication of general paresis by the discovery that it was caused by the spirochete that caused syphilis exemplified the germ etiology. The evidence that schizophrenia is partly transmitted genetically exemplified the genetic etiology. The relationship between the blocking of dopamine and the alleviation of schizophrenia exemplified the biochemical etiology. The malfunctioning of higher and then lower levels of brain function illustrated the neuroanatomical etiology.

5. Biomedical therapy tries to correct disordered brain function with drugs and other agents. But these drugs only work while the patient continues to take them and may also have serious side effects.

6. The main strengths of the biomedical model are that it is grounded in well-established biological sciences, and that physical treatments are often able to bring relief.

7. The main weaknesses of the biomedical model are that the evidence about its central claims is incomplete, psychological treatments also are able to bring relief to individuals with psychological problems, and there are side effects to most biomedical treatments.

QUESTIONS FOR CRITICAL THINKING

1. How was the causal connection between syphilis and general paresis proven?

2. Why is there a causal influence of genes but not genetic determinism for schizophrenia?

3. How have biomedical researchers deduced the connection between levels of dopamine in the brain and schizophrenia?

4. What are the limitations of drug treatments?

CHAPTER 3

Psychological Approaches

Illustration by Eric Dinyer.

n this chapter, we will take up four approaches to abnormality that differ from the previous chapter's biomedical model in numerous ways. We categorize these four traditions—the psychodynamic, existential, behavioral, and cognitive—as *psychological approaches.* Each of these approaches seeks to explain our psyche by mental and behavioral principles underlying normal, as well as disordered behavior. We will consider each of these traditions and an example or two of the therapies that arise from them.

THE PSYCHODYNAMIC APPROACH

The psychodynamic theories of personality and abnormality are concerned with the psychological forces that—consciously or unconsciously—influence the mind. These inner forces, these desires and motives, often conflict. When these conflicts are well resolved, they produce growth, vigor. But when they are poorly resolved, or remain unresolved, conflicts generate anxiety and unhappiness, against which people try to defend themselves. In this chapter, we examine some of the causes and consequences of conflict and the conditions that lead to its resolution, for better or for worse.

The psychodynamic approach to personality and abnormality began with the work of a single towering genius—a Viennese physician named Sigmund Freud. Born in 1856, Freud produced some twenty-four volumes of theoretical observations and case histories before he died in 1939. His own methods of studying and changing personality, as well as those of his students, are called *psychoanalysis.*

▲ Sigmund Freud
(1856–1939) in 1909.

Throughout his life, Freud's consuming intellectual and clinical passion was with **psychic energy.** He assumed that people are endowed with a fixed amount of psychic energy. Why is it, then, that sometimes people seem to be vigorous and full of life, while at other times they seem listless? How is it that some people devote their energies to love and work, while others are largely concerned with their aches and pains?

The Three Processes of Personality

According to Freud, human personality is structured by three kinds of forces: the id, ego, and superego (see Table 3–1). These are neither objects nor places in the mind. Rather, they are dynamic and interactive processes, with their own origins and specific roles. The word "id" originates from the German "es," literally meaning "it," and connotes processes that seem to lie outside of an individual's control. "Ego" in German means "ich" or "I," and designates those capacities that enable a person to cope with reality, while "superego" (in German "Uberich" or "over I") describes those processes that are "above the self"—conscience, ideals, and morals.

The **id** represents raw and urgent biological drives. The id clamors for immediate gratification. It is guided by the **pleasure principle,** which demands immediate impulse gratification and tension reduction. The id is like a spoiled child. It wants what it wants when it wants it. When they seek external gratification, id drives know nothing of appropriateness, or even danger. Were people wholly dominated by id processes they would, like the spoiled child, eat any food when they were hungry, regardless of whether it was theirs, healthy, or even still alive.

Whereas the id seeks pleasure, the **ego** seeks reality. One function of the ego is to express and gratify the desires of the id but in accordance with the requirements of reality. While the id operates on the pleasure principle, the ego utilizes the **reality principle.** It tests reality to determine whether the expression of an impulse is safe or dangerous. It delays the impulses of the id until the time is right, and may even divert those impulses toward appropriate targets. The ego's success in enabling impulses to be realistically and safely gratified depends on its ability to use thought processes, like reasoning, remembering, evaluating, and planning. The ego is the executive of the personality, carrying out the demands of the id in such a way as to minimize negative consequences.

Lastly, the **superego** represents both conscience and idealistic striving. Yet, superego processes are just as irrational as id processes; neither cares or knows much about reality. Conscience can also be overly harsh, suppressing

TABLE 3–1

THREE PROCESSES OF PERSONALITY			
Process	Principle	Reality Concerns?	Characteristics
Id	Pleasure principle	No	Aims to achieve immediate gratification of biological drives
Ego	Reality principle	Yes	Directs impulses toward targets that are appropriate and that can be achieved
Superego	(Idealism)	No	Directs actions toward morality, religion, ideals

▲ The id is dominated by the pleasure principle. It demands immediate gratification.

not only permissible behaviors, but even the very thought of those behaviors. Whereas the person whose id processes are relatively uncontrolled seems impulse-ridden, the person who is overly dominated by his or her superego seems wooden and moralistic, unable to be comfortable with pleasure and overly sensitive to "Thou shalt not . . . ."

The processes that regulate normal personality and development are identical to those that regulate abnormal personality. What distinguishes normal from abnormal personality is the manner in which psychic energy is distributed between the three components of personality. In normal personality, psychic energy is strongly invested in ego processes, as well as those of the id and superego. In abnormal personality, psychic energy is distributed improperly, with the result that either the id or the superego is too strong, and ego processes are unable to control desire or conscience.

Freud believed that much of the interaction among id, ego, and superego goes on at an ***unconscious*** level, which includes both forgotten memories and repressed memories (those actively barred from consciousness). Certain personality processes operate more at the unconscious level than do others. Id impulses are entirely unconscious, as are many superego processes. In contrast, ego processes, because they must mediate between desire, conscience, and reality, are often conscious.

Anxiety and Defense Mechanisms

Conflicts among the id, ego, and superego regularly give rise to a kind of psychic pain that Freud termed ***anxiety.*** Anxiety can be conscious or unconscious, and its presence is always a signal that conflict is at hand. When the conflict causes the person to feel overwhelmed, helpless, and unable to cope, anxiety arises. The degree of experienced anxiety depends on the anticipated consequences to self.

The experience of anxiety, even the anticipation of anxiety, is an uncomfortable experience that people try to relieve immediately. Humans are particularly well-endowed with strategies for alleviating anxiety. Beyond "overcoming fear" as we do when we learn to ride a bicycle, or "fleeing the field" when pursued by strong enemies, humans can, in their own minds, alter the very meaning and significance of troublesome drives and impulses. They perform these alterations by using ***coping strategies,*** or ***defenses.*** The more common of these include such defenses as repression and projection, as well as identification and rationalization.

REPRESSION

Repression is the most fundamental and widely used means for altering psychological realities. It is a defense by which the individual unconsciously forces unwanted thoughts or prohibited desires out of mind. Memories that evoke shame, guilt, humiliation, or self-deprecation—in short, affective memories (Davis and Schwartz, 1987)—are often repressed. Repressed events live on, and all the more vigorously, because they are not subject to rational control. They reveal their potent identities in normal fantasies and dreams, in slips of the tongue and "motivated" forgetting, under hypnosis and in a variety of abnormal psychological conditions. By far, unconscious forces are the dominant ones in personality.

Ann was in love with two men, Michael and Jules. Both wanted to marry her, and she could not decide between them. Finally, after more than six months, she decided for Michael. The next night, she had the following dream:

"I was climbing the fire-escape outside my dormitory. It was a dark and rainy night, and I was carrying a big box under my raincoat. I came to the fifth floor,

FOCUS QUESTIONS

1. Describe the relations among the three processes of personality according to Freud.
2. What arises and on what levels as a result of conflicts among the three processes of personality?
3. Name some coping strategies, and describe their functions.
4. What is the most fundamental defense mechanism, and why is it so powerful and difficult to control?

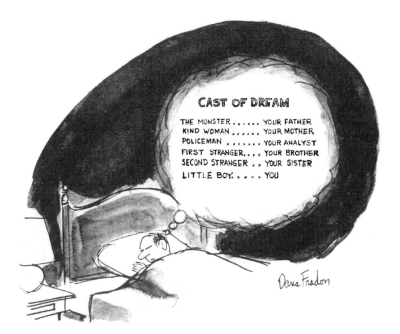

CAST OF DREAM

THE MONSTER . . . . . . YOUR FATHER
KIND WOMAN . . . . . . YOUR MOTHER
POLICEMAN . . . . YOUR ANALYST
FIRST STRANGER . . . . YOUR BROTHER
SECOND STRANGER . . YOUR SISTER
LITTLE BOY . . . . . YOU

Dana Fradon

▶ Freud seems best remembered by most people for his ideas on the expression of unconscious thoughts. (Drawing by Dana Fradon, © 1973, The New Yorker Magazine, Inc.)

opened the door silently, and tiptoed quickly to my room. Once inside, I double-locked the door, and put this box—it's a treasure chest—on my bed. I opened it and it was full of diamonds and rubies and emeralds."

Now, there is no evidence at all that dreams *regularly* mean anything. Yet it is hard to escape the possibility that in Ann's dream, "diamonds and rubies and emeralds" = jewels = Jules. Her dream reveals her continuing attachment to her former lover, and quite possibly her desire to maintain the relationship secretly. The mind's extraordinary capacity to play on Jules's name and to transform it into visual symbols is revealed in this dream.

Repression can be nearly complete, or it can be partial. When an idea or memory is partially repressed, some aspects may be consciously available, while others are not. For example, a person who had had a difficult relationship with a parent may recall crying at that parent's funeral but may not recall what he or she cried about or anything else about the event. The available evidence also suggests that it is *partially* repressed conflicts and memories that play a significant role in abnormal behavior (Perkins and Reyher, 1971; Reyher and Smyth, 1971; Burns and Reyher, 1976; Silverman, 1976). In **multiple personality,** for example, an individual has two or more personalities that are alien to each other. When one personality is dominant, the others are repressed.

The capacity of the mind to be "its own place" is not limited merely to its ability to repress, to reject images and memories from consciousness, as important as that ability is. Rather, the mind is an editor, deleting whole chapters of experience and reorganizing others. Ordinarily, even in the absence of conflict, both perception and memory are reconstructive (Anderson and Bower, 1973). This is to say that minds take direct experience, edit, and make something "new" of it, by adding to, or subtracting from perception, by embellishing memory in ways that range from innocent decoration to filling memorial gaps with new "memories." It is no surprise, therefore, that these enlivening capacities of the mind should be used in the coping process, when anxiety is experienced or when conflict occurs between self-image and impulse or behavior. Here, sometimes consciously, but more often unconsciously, editing processes are invoked to enable the individual to cope by making perception and memory more pleasant.

The notion that memories and experiences can be partially or wholly repressed has been widely, though not universally accepted among psychologists (see, for example, Holmes, 1990). But recently that acceptance has been questioned as people report the "return" of repressed memories, and on the basis of those newly returned memories, accuse others of sexual molestation, satanic behaviors, and even murder (Loftus, 1993). We examine this matter at greater length in Chapter 14, where we explore the legal implications of "forgotten memories."

PROJECTION

Projection consists in attributing to others those feelings and experiences that we personally *deny* having and that we usually repress. Think of the preacher who sees and decries sin everywhere but denies having a sinful impulse himself. Research has shown that people who deny or repress their own sexual impulses project them on others and rate others as more lustful than in fact they are (Halpern, 1977).

Projection plays a double role in psychological distress. First, it reduces distress by allowing a person to attribute an anxiety-provoking impulse to another person, rather than the self. Thus, if anger makes us feel anxious, then the anxiety that anger creates can be reduced by attributing that anger to someone else. Second, projection allows us to do something about anger. When someone is angry at us, we are permitted to take aggressive or retaliative action in our own defense. Thus, projection can provide the rationale for engaging in the behavior that would have been forbidden in the first place.

REACTION FORMATION

In *reaction formation,* an opposite reaction is formed to an initial impulse. Sometimes we say, "I hate her," when in fact we really mean "I love her." Reaction formation may be especially significant in mania. There, individuals behave as if they are full of joy and boundless energy, but one senses that their fundamental experience is one of sadness and depression, against which a reaction has been formed. Reaction formation is also seen in counterphobia, where individuals pursue precisely those activities that they deeply fear.

DISPLACEMENT

When the strategy of *displacement* is used, the individual edits the target of his or her emotions by replacing the true object with one that is more innocent and less threatening. People who are angry and frustrated at work, but who cannot vent those feelings at work, are unconsciously using displacement strategies when they return home and vent their feelings on innocent spouses and children.

IDENTIFICATION

Identification describes the process by which we internalize the characteristics of others—their ideas, values, mannerisms, status, and power. Identification is the opposite of projection. It is a fairly common strategy for overcoming fear and inadequacy.

People identify with those who have power and status, and they try to do many of the things that those they identify with do. Thus, some people are willing to spend considerably more money for a house in a "proper" neighborhood than they would spend for the identical house at a less fashionable address, feeling that if their home is in a better neighborhood, they must perforce be "better" people. Similarly, people often rate themselves and each other by the college they attended, where they buy their clothes, or by the car they drive, even though we are, all of us, precisely what we are, no more and no less, regardless of the neighborhood we live in, the status of our college, where we buy our clothes, or the car we drive.

Identification is a particularly useful strategy for coping with fear. Anna Freud tells of a little girl who was afraid to cross the hall in the dark lest she meet a ghost. She handled this fear by making peculiar gestures as she crossed the hall. "There's no need to be afraid in the hall," she explained to her little brother, "you just have to pretend that you're the ghost who might meet you" (A. Freud, 1936, p. 119). Incidentally, this example points out what has been stressed previously: coping strategies need not be unconscious.

DENIAL

If repression obliterates inner facts, **denial** does away with distressing external ones. Denial commonly occurs when our sense of security and of being loved is threatened. The fact that people generally find it difficult to perceive accurately negative feelings directed toward themselves suggests that the denial process is widespread (Taguiri, Bruner, and Blake, 1958). Denial is often used when people are threatened by death. The parents of a fatally ill child, much as the fatally ill themselves, often deny that anything is wrong, even though they have the diagnosis and prognosis in hand.

ISOLATION

Whereas in repression and denial, both the emotional and informational components of experience are deleted, in **isolation** only the emotional ones (which, after all, are the sources of distress) are repressed, while information is retained. People who have suffered great brutality and humiliation, such as those in the German death camps during World War II, or those who have been raped, may utilize isolation. They may be able to recount their experience precisely and in copious detail but be unable to recall the accompanying intense feelings. The very experiences that would ordinarily bring tears to a teller's eyes or make a listener wince in empathic pain, may be related blandly, suggesting that the feelings that were originally associated with the experience have been isolated.

Isolation can also be a constructive strategy. The parent who responsibly reprimands a child cannot be too sensitive to the hurt feelings the reprimand engenders, else the reprimand will fail. Neither can a surgeon allow herself to be overly sensitive to the fact that the tissue she is cutting is human flesh. Isolation constructively permits these emotional concerns to be withheld from consciousness.

INTELLECTUALIZATION

Related to denial and isolation, **intellectualization** consists of repressing the emotional component of experience, and restating the experience as an abstract intellectual analysis. Unable to deal with a particularly intense feeling, we sometimes seek to read all about it and to produce elaborate self-analyses that are all but devoid of feeling.

RATIONALIZATION

In recalling experiences and accounting for them, people commonly edit not only the facts of the experience but the motives as well. The process of assigning to behavior socially desirable motives that an impartial analysis would not substantiate is called **rationalization.** Late to a party that they didn't want to attend in the first place, some people will offer socially desirable excuses: the car broke down, or their watch stopped. Those excuses are rationalizations.

FOCUS QUESTIONS

1. Distinguish between psychosexual and psychosocial development.
2. In what ways did each neo-Freudian explore beyond Freud's original psychoanalytic theory?
3. Describe the core self, the subjective self, and the verbal self.

Rationalization plays a dramatic role in the development of **hypochondriasis,** which is the conviction in the absence of medical evidence that one is ill or about to become ill. "I can't do the job, not because I fear failure or because I fear it won't be done as well as the next guy, but because I'm not feeling well." Because illness evokes concern from others, the seemingly ill are encouraged to abandon the job and given a good measure of comfort to boot. Thus, the tendency to rationalize is often supported by the positive reactions it evokes from others.

SUBLIMATION

Sublimation is the process of rechanneling psychic energies from socially undesirable goals to constructive and socially desirable ones. Capacities for love, work, altruism, and even humor involve such rechanneling of raw sexual and aggressive impulses. According to Freud, love is an especially powerful form of sublimation because it allows people to achieve sexual gratification in a socially acceptable context. Simultaneously, however, loving leaves one vulnerable to rejection or the death of a loved one. Thus, the gratifications of loving and working are often matched by the anxieties to which they give rise. Sublimation, in Freud's view, is therefore as fragile as it is constructive.

Psychodynamic Theorists after Freud

Though they were rejected at first, Freud's ideas later came to attract a number of highly original thinkers, known as **neo-Freudians,** who elaborated on his views and often disagreed with them. Carl Jung (1875–1961), for example, placed greater emphasis on the **unconscious.** Jung felt that there was a **collective unconscious,** consisting of the memory traces of the experience of past generations and not just memories of early childhood as Freud thought. In Jung's view, we are born wiser than we think, already afraid of darkness and fire because our ancestors were, and already knowing of death because past generations have died. Jung called these universal ideas with which we are born **archetypes.** For Jung, these archetypes form the basis of personality, accounting for why people are not merely driven by their past experiences but also strive to grow and become something better. In essence, Jung saw the self as striving for wholeness.

Alfred Adler (1870–1937) placed less emphasis than Freud on the sexual and aggressive needs arising from the id and mediated by the ego. According to Adler, the self serves a more meaningful purpose. The self enables us to fulfill our lifestyle, to become more than the genes with which we are endowed and the environment that presses on us. The self creates something new, something unique, something that is not wholly determined by biological impulse or cultural press (Ansbacher and Ansbacher, 1956).

There was considerable difference in another area, that of psycho*sexual* versus psycho*social* development. Fundamentally, that difference reduced to whether people are fundamentally biological or social animals. For example, Karen Horney (1885–1952) saw basic anxiety as arising from social rather than biological needs. For her, basic anxiety consisted of "the feeling a child has of being isolated and helpless in a potentially hostile world" (Horney, 1945, p. 41).

Similarly, Harry Stack Sullivan (1892–1949) held that the very notion of personality is itself an illusion that cannot be separated from the social context in which it is seen and operates. According to Sullivan, psychological problems do not merely originate in faulty social development, they *consist* of faulty social relationships and need to be examined and treated as such. Sulli-

▲ Carl Jung (1875–1961).

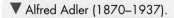

▼ Alfred Adler (1870–1937).

▶ *Left:* Karen Horney (1885–1952). *Right:* Harry Stack Sullivan (1892–1949).

van's concerns are mirrored in the modern emphasis on the social context in which personality operates (Nisbett and Ross, 1980; Gergen, 1982).

Erik Erikson (1902–1994) provided a broader theory of development, one that stresses the psycho*social* nature of people and the interrelations between individuals and society. Unlike Freud, who believed that the foundations of personality were essentially completed in childhood, Erikson saw human personality as developing and changing through eight stages, from infancy on through adulthood and old age.

Erich Fromm (1900–1980) saw personality as fundamentally social. At birth and with development, humans find themselves increasingly isolated from others. That isolation—the fundamental human condition—is painful, and however much people cherish their freedom, they also seek to terminate their isolation. They can do this either through love and shared work—a constructive mode—or through conformity and submission to authority, a very destructive mode.

As a group, the neo-Freudians brought refinements to basic Freudian theory. Since then, other theorists and practitioners have proposed further modifications. Today, there really is no single coherent theory of personality dynamics. Rather, the work that goes on in many clinics and laboratories sheds light on *aspects* of personality and human development, and it greatly revises Freud's notions and those of his immediate followers. The core of that revision has to do with the nature of the *self*—the processes and crises that shape it, the role of the defenses in shaping consciousness, and those aspects of the self that contribute to growth.

▶ *Left:* Erik Erikson (1902–1994). *Right:* Erich Fromm (1900–1980).

▲ Heinz Kohut (1913–1981).

Modern psychodynamic theorists ask what gives personality its unity. What leads individuals to believe that they are the same person across time and place, that they are not fractured and fragmented psychologically? How is it that even though they are *doing* different things at different times with different people, they remain the very same person? For some people, these questions have little meaning: they *are* the same person physically, and therefore psychologically. For others, however, especially those who have had a "shaky" self, or who see themselves as having undergone great change, such that they can say that "I am not the person that I was five years ago," these questions are significant and worth pursuing.

Modern psychodynamic theorists are concerned with the vast subjective psychological space that is the storehouse of personal experience within each of us. Central to their formulations is the *self* in all its senses, and especially the ways in which it *emerges,* is *experienced,* and often becomes embattled and *defended* (Winnicott, 1971; Kohut, 1971, 1977; Mahler, 1979; Stern, 1985). There are three aspects of self that arise sequentially and are especially important in modern psychodynamic theory: the core self, the subjective self, and the verbal self.

The ***core self*** arises sometime between the second and sixth months of an infant's life, when he becomes aware that he and his caregiver are *physically separate.* This is the "body self" and is pretty much taken for granted. Usually, people are unaware of their core self. Nevertheless, it serves a very important function. The core self gives each person his sense of separateness, coherence, and identity. Moreover, it is the core self that enables individuals to confer coherence and identity on *others.* So long as these features of the core self remain strong, personality remains strong. But if one develops the sense that "things are happening to me outside of my control" or that "I can control other people's minds," there is fertile ground for disruption.

At about seven to nine months of age, the ***subjective self*** emerges. It encourages the development of ***intersubjectivity***—the sense that we can empathize, that is understand each others' intentions and feelings, as well as share experiences about things and events (Kohut, 1978). Disturbances in the subjective self may result in difficulties in feeling connected to other people and in empathizing with them or with oneself. The sense of being out of touch with self and others is what may arise when there are disturbances in the subjective self.

At about fifteen to eighteen months of age, children begin to develop the third sense of self: the self as a storehouse of knowledge and experience. That ***verbal self*** develops by using symbols and language. The use of language, of course, opens a world of infinite variety and action for the infant. It permits rapid and direct communication. But language has a special down side, for it can distort the same reality that it might otherwise extend and enrich. Imagine a child who is visibly bored or tired, and whose parent says, "My! Aren't we having a wonderful time!"

The various selves are not sturdy and wholly independent structures. Much as they are formed by interactions between caregivers and infant, so they require support and sustenance from others throughout life. Those centrally important people who provide support for personality cohesiveness are called ***selfobjects,*** people and things that each of us requires to keep our personality functioning at its optimum level (Kohut, 1977). The notion of selfobjects underscores the importance of attachment and the environment for optimal personality functioning. It shows that we are, none of us, islands unto ourselves, free and independent of the contexts in which we are found. As we will see, problems with attachment are associated with anxiety, depression, and eating disorders, as well as being implicated in borderline personality disorder (Fonagy, Leigh, Steele, Steele, Kennedy, Mattoon, Target, and Gerber, 1996).

FOCUS QUESTIONS

1. How are brief psychoanalytically inspired treatments similar to classical psychoananlysis?
2. How does the case of Patty illustrate brief psychotherapy and the concepts of catharsis and transference?

Psychodynamic Treatment

Freud's own views and those of his disciples and descendants find expression in the modes of treatment that they have generated. Here, theory and practice come together, for it was from the clinic that Freud's most interesting ideas developed. We therefore turn to psychodynamic treatment in order to examine those views in practice. Much as psychoanalytic theory spawned a variety of psychodynamic theories, so did psychoanalysis as a mode of treatment give birth to numerous and varied treatment modes. Among these are a variety of brief psychoanalytically "inspired" treatments that alter classical treatment in a variety of important ways.

Brief psychoanalytically inspired treatments have much in common with classical psychoanalysis. Both seek to alter thought and behavior. Both do so by examining early conflicts in the context of present relationships, and by making conscious that which is repressed. Both examine free associations, dreams, and resistances. In so doing, psychic energy is freed for more constructive purposes, and the individual is able to find more constructive resolutions for conflict. Anxiety is reduced because impulses now find "safe" methods of expression. And coping strategies, where they are required, are now more mature. These matters become much clearer when we examine an actual case of psychodynamic psychotherapy.

It had been more than two years since Patty had had a moment's peace. Her problems were in her head, quite literally. There, continually pounding, intense headaches kept her in bed all day, every day, unable to sleep, unable to rise, clawing at the sheets. Patty had sought help for these headaches for well over a year. She had had several medical and neurological work-ups. She finally requested neurosurgery in the hope that the severing of nerve endings would alleviate the pain. Informed that nothing could be done surgically, she became exceedingly depressed. The situation by now seemed entirely hopeless to her. A burden to her husband, useless to her young children, there seemed little to do but end it all. It was then that she was referred for psychodynamic therapy.

The early part of her first meeting was spent describing the problem. With great pain, she described her headaches but quickly ran out of things to say. She didn't think that the problem was psychological, nor that anyone in their right mind would feel as she did under the circumstances. There being nothing more to say, she turned to the therapist and asked, "What should I talk about now?"

"Tell me about your childhood," he said.

She began slowly and then, with growing animation, described her father. (Indeed, during the remainder of that very long interview, Patty alluded to her mother only in passing.) Her father had come originally from a stretch of land that borders Greece and Turkey. He was a man of violent passions and frustrations, a

▶ Selfobjects are people and things that support and sustain the self throughout life.

man who had once angrily left his family for four years, only to return as suddenly as he had gone. In her earliest memory of him, he threatened to take a train to a far off place, never to return.

"Did you ever go to bed with your father?" The question came suddenly, without warning.* Patty paled. "How did you know?" she asked. And then, not waiting for the answer, she burst into tears.

"Yes, it was him. And I still hate him. He's an old man now. And I still hate him. On Sunday morning, my mother would clean the house. All of us, except my mother, slept late on Sunday. When she cleaned my room, I went into her bed. I would get under the covers, close my eyes, and go back to sleep. My father was there. He would touch me . . . rub . . . the rat. How could he do that to his own daughter?"

In anger, in sadness, and in shame, she cried as she tore furiously into incidents that had occurred more than a quarter century ago, when she was eight years old.

Suddenly, she stopped crying, even talking. Then smiling in disbelief, she said, "They're gone. The headaches are gone." She rose slowly and walked around the office, moving her head from side to side. For the first time in more than two years, she felt normal.

Before the session was over, those headaches would return again. But regardless, a connection had been made between her present suffering and her early memories of her father.

During subsequent sessions, Patty was able to retrieve from memory more experiences with her father. Her father, it appeared, had had another family, which he had left behind in Greece when he came to America and married her mother. Patty felt it was her responsibility to keep him in America by making him so happy that he would not want to return. The fear of abandonment ran deep in both Patty and her mother.

She could not recall what her father had done to her in bed, but she knew that it was bad and that even *he* must have thought so. Once, after an outing with a group of friends, her father spotted her on a subway platform. He pulled her roughly aside from her schoolmates, slapped her hard across the face, and called her "Whore."

Those recaptured events—relived, remembered, re-experienced during therapy—brought relief over longer and longer periods. But certain experiences and even thoughts brought on headaches suddenly and fiercely, as when:

- she was shopping for a brassiere;
- Phil, her husband, was bouncing their young daughters on his lap, and the three of them were laughing;
- friends suggested that they go to a movie;
- she had gone with the family to a Greek wedding celebration, and all the young people were dancing; and
- she was washing the children's laundry.

All of these scenes vaguely connoted sexuality and therefore brought pain. Talking about them was difficult. There was a tension between exploring the psychodynamics of her situation and risking disturbing a trouble-free day. But she pushed on, pursuing her mental and emotional associations to early experiences and memories, not only about father and mother, but also about husband, children, friends, and later even about the therapist.

To a psychodynamic therapist, this search into Patty's past suggested that her headaches resulted from severe sexual conflicts, which paralyzed her, rendering her unable to even initiate caregiving activities on behalf of her husband, children, and increasingly, even herself.

The headaches were themselves testimony to the power of the conflicts as well as the coping strategies. They symbolically suggested a conflict about rape. But since the conflict was going on in Patty's own mind, it suggested,

*Such questions are not usually asked so directly or so early in psychodynamic treatment. In this case, however, Patty's depression seemed so overwhelming that the therapist felt he had to quicken the therapeutic pace.

too, a conflict about her *own* sexual desires. By some process that is not yet understood, these conflicting desires were repressed and displaced, not outward to other people, but upward to her head.

Patty clearly projected much of this conflict onto her husband and even her children. Their horseplay was seen, not as an innocent rumpus, but as a highly sexualized event. Shopping for underclothes, weddings, Greek dancing, and the weekly laundry were all similarly sexualized. Ego processes that normally differentiate these events and allow people to share social perceptions of them were clearly defective here. The defects, psychodynamic therapists hold, arose because of the intense and poorly contained pressure that was generated from Patty's own sexual conflicts.

It was **catharsis,** the uncovering and reliving of early traumatic conflicts, that enabled Patty to remit her symptoms rapidly. But in psychodynamic theory, symptom remission is only part of the treatment, often the smallest part. Much more significant is the fact that enduring patterns of perceiving and reacting in adults are laid down in childhood and pervade all adult activities. They need to be altered because they are transferred from the people and impulses that originally stimulated the conflict to other significant people in one's life. Psychodynamic therapy seeks, therefore, not merely to relieve symptoms, but to alter personality—the very attitudes, perceptions, and behaviors that were misshaped by early experience.

How does psychodynamic treatment achieve personality changes? In practice, psychodynamic therapists must be nonreactive. They must listen calmly and intensely; they must not be shocked by the client's revelations, nor should they commonly offer opinions or judgments. They should act as blank screens, onto which clients can project their own expectations, imaginings, and attributions. Over time, therapists themselves become central in the lives of their clients. This centrality is of such therapeutic importance that it is given a technical name in psychodynamic theory: **transference.** Transference describes the fact that during psychodynamic therapy, clients come to transfer emotions, conflicts, and expectations from the diverse sources from which they were acquired, onto their therapists. Therapists become mother, father, son, daughter, spouse, lover, and even employer or stranger, to their clients. In this emotional climate, clients are encouraged to speak frankly, to let their minds ramble, to free associate to emotionally charged ideas, even if the resulting ideas seem silly, embarrassing, or meaningless. Under these conditions, what was formerly repressed and distorted becomes available to consciousness and therefore more controllable by ego processes, as can be seen from further examination of Patty's case.

In less than three months, Patty's symptoms had abated. Her attention turned away from her headaches to other matters. Her mother, for example, was a "pain." She had always been melancholy and merely obedient, surely no fun to live with. Patty quickly related the impression that "she was no fun to live with" to her own relationship with her father. He had already abandoned a family in Greece. Had she been trying to keep him in the family? Might he not abandon them? More important, could her own sexual involvement with her father have been little more than an attempt to keep him at home? That possibility cast her memories in a much more positive light, relieving her of the guilt that the memories evoked. Shortly thereafter, she could observe her husband and children playing together, without suffering from headaches and guilt.

Gradually, attention turned from her parents, even from her husband and children, to the therapist himself. His lack of reacting now provoked discomfort; his occasional lateness caused her to feel anxiety; and when her therapist took a week-long vacation, she experienced dread. In turn, these feelings led to long, blocked silences during the therapy sessions. What thoughts lay behind these silences? It was difficult for her to say, and nearly impossible for her to free associate. But finally, she was able to allude to the embarrassing sexual fantasies that attended these events, fantasies now about the therapist himself. This was transference, for it shortly became clear that she interpreted his silences, lateness, and absences as abandonment, and she was unconsciously motivated to do what she had wanted to do in the past to retain the affections of significant others. She was, of course, initially unaware of the unconscious connection between abandonment and sexuality, and she was therefore deeply embarrassed by the thoughts that assailed her. Once she understood the reasons for those thoughts, however, she was able to see her relationship to the therapist in more objective terms, to recognize that an occasional lateness or absence is not the same as abandonment, and to find less self-demeaning and guilt-provoking ways to express her affections.

At about this time, and seemingly for no good reason, Patty began to explore an entirely new matter: what to do with her life. Upon graduating high school, she had considered going to college, but had given up that idea as "simply ridiculous." She had also been attracted to dance, but had not acted on that interest either. Now both ideas returned, as well as the desire to take a job again, and she began to explore those ideas with great enthusiasm. In Freud's view, energies that had once been bound up in repression and other defensive maneuvers, were now freed for other activities.

A stronger and more mature identity resulted from achieving a greater understanding of herself and greater control over her impulses. Moreover, the more Patty probed, the less clear it became that she had actually had a sexual relationship with her father. Eventually, that "memory" came to be seen as a false one, reflecting her own desire to retain his affections, rather than his actual behavior. In this, Patty repeated the experience of many of Freud's clients, for the mind, Freud observed, is a powerfully inventive place in which even "memories" can arise from desires, conflicts, and defenses.

Evaluating Psychodynamic Theory

STRENGTHS OF PSYCHODYNAMIC THEORIES

FOCUS QUESTIONS

1. What are the strengths of psychodynamic theory?
2. What are the weaknesses of psychodynamic theory?

Psychodynamic theory is nothing less than a comprehensive description of human personality. This theory describes personality's development, the way personality functions, and every aspect of human thought, emotion, experience, and judgment—from dreams through slips of the tongue to normal and abnormal behavior.

Because of this, Freud is considered, along with Marx and Darwin, one of the great geniuses of the century. Perhaps the most important of his ideas is the view that the psychological processes that underlie normal and abnormal behaviors are fundamentally the same. Neither conflict, nor anxiety, nor defense, nor unconscious processes are the sole property of abnormal people. Rather, the *outcome* of conflict and the *nature* of defense will determine whether behavior will be normal or abnormal.

In addition, Freud developed a method for investigating psychodynamic processes and treating psychological distress. This was important for several reasons. First, his method of investigation shed light on abnormal processes and thus demystified them. By accounting for why they behaved as they did, Freud "rehumanized" the distressed, making their suffering more comprehensible to the rest of humankind. Second, by providing a method of treatment, Freud encouraged an optimism regarding psychological distress that had been sorely lacking before him. Finally, while Freudian psychoanalysis must be distinguished sharply from modern psychodynamic therapies, the former was the progenitor of the modern efforts, and the modern therapies have been found to be quite effective (Smith, Glass, and Miller, 1980; Crits-Christoph, 1992; Gabbard, 1992).

SHORTCOMINGS OF PSYCHODYNAMIC THEORIES

Any theory that aspires to be as comprehensive as psychodynamic theory inevitably has faults, and Freud's theories and those of his successors have been

TABLE 3-2

EVALUATING PSYCHODYNAMIC THEORY	
Strengths	*Weaknesses*
1. Provides a comprehensive description of human personality.	1. Difficult to disprove theories as behaviors are overdetermined and motives are inferred.
2. Psychological processes are the same in normal and abnormal behaviors.	2. Lack of scientific evidence.
3. Provides methodology for investigating and treating abnormal processes.	3. Underestimates role of situation and context, social class, and gender.

no exception (see Table 3–2). Central to the problems of psychodynamic theory and therapy are: (1) the theory is simply too difficult to prove or disprove; (2) when studies have been conducted, psychodynamic theories have often failed to be supported; and (3) in emphasizing the role of the person, these theories neglect the situation.

Some of the difficulty in supporting or disproving psychodynamic theories arises because they take complex views of personality and behavior. Many behaviors are held to be ***overdetermined,*** that is, determined by more than one force and with more than the required psychic energy. Altering a particular psychological force—for example, by recovering a crucial early memory—may have no visible effect on a particular trait or behavior because the latter are supported and sustained by many interrelated psychological forces.

Moreover, only rarely is it possible to confirm that a particular unconscious motive is really operating. Precisely because the motive is unconscious, it is invisible to the client and only ***inferred*** by the therapist. Even in Patty's case, where seeming confirmation was obtained because the headaches gradually disappeared, can we be sure that these changes were due to her increasing awareness of sexual motives and fears of abandonment? Might not the cure have arisen, with equal plausibility, from the fact that she had finally found someone whom she trusted and in whom she could confide?

Psychodynamic theories have been subjected to a variety of ingenious studies, many of which have failed to confirm the theories. Many aspects of psychodynamic theories have yet to accrue sufficient scientific support to merit belief.

Psychodynamic theories overwhelmingly emphasize the impact of traits and dispositions, those stable constellations of attitude and experience that are held to influence behavior. But what of situations? Because psychodynamic theories are derived mainly from information conveyed by clients during treatment, and because clients are encouraged to talk about their own reactions rather than the situation in which they find themselves, psychodynamic theory underestimates the role of situation and context. For example, it is much easier to infer that a person's continuing irritation with his employer results from unconscious and unresolved conflicts about authority when the employer's behavior has not been observed directly than when it has been. Similarly, it is easier to construe marital conflicts in terms of the traits of the spouse who has sought consultation precisely because one has no first-hand experience with that spouse's marital situation.

THE EXISTENTIAL APPROACH

Some theorists have sought to examine what is especially human in human experience, and particularly those aspects of human experience that

FOCUS QUESTIONS

1. What do existential theorists believe is most fundamental to the human experience?
2. Describe what existential psychologists believe is the central human fear and the strategies that people develop to cope with this fear.
3. Explain how existential therapists attempt to treat patients.
4. What are strengths and weaknesses of the existential approach?

contribute to growth or to abnormality. These ***existential theorists*** discuss the elements of freedom and choice—responsibility and willing—and the fundamental anxiety—the fear of dying.

Freedom and Choice

Existential theorists stress the importance of freedom and choice. They believe that individuals must use their freedom to make authentic choices based on their own desires and goals, not those of others. Existential theorists believe that growth will occur when people take responsibility for their actions and work toward their own freely chosen goals. Such authentic modes of thought and behavior will enable them to make the most of their potential.

RESPONSIBILITY

The assumption of personal ***responsibility*** is central to existential thinking. It says that we are responsible for the way we perceive the world and for the way we react to those perceptions. To be responsible "is to be aware that one has created one's own self, destiny, life, predicament, feelings and, if such be the case, one's own suffering" (Yalom, 1980).

Existential psychologists generally pay careful attention to language; they are especially sensitive to the use of such words as "can't" and "it." People often say, "I just can't study" or "I can't get up in the morning," implying that the behavior is somehow removed from their control. What they really mean is, "I won't do it." They bury an act over which they have control beneath the appearance of disability. Young children who break something are inclined to say, "it broke," not "I broke it." Similarly, for adults to say that "something happened" or "it happened" is to imply that one is passively influenced by a capricious world. In short, they do not want to be held responsible. Generally, the use of the passive rather than the active voice, the avoidance of first person pronouns, as well as the attributions of the causes of current events to historical sources (i.e., my upbringing, my parents, the things I did as a child), are seen as signs of avoidance of responsibility.

WILLING

The capacity to will is also a central feature of existential views. Yet, despite its centrality, will is difficult to define unambiguously. Will is used psychologically in at least two senses. First, there is will as in willpower: the will of gritted teeth, clenched jaw, and tensed muscle. This is ***exhortative will.*** It can be useful at times, as when we force ourselves to work when we would rather play.

▶ Existentialists believe that we are responsible for the way we perceive the world and for the way we react to those perceptions. This includes taking responsibility for those close to us when they cannot help themselves.

▲ Goal-directed will arises from hope, expectation, and free choice, rather than grim determination.

A second and more significant kind of will is associated with future goals. It is called **goal-directed will.** Much as memory is the organ of the past, goal-directed will has been called "the organ of the future" (Arendt, 1978). It is quite different from exhortative will, for it develops out of hope, expectation, and competence. Unlike exhortative will, it is not urged upon us but is rather a freely chosen arousal in the service of a future that is willingly embraced. This kind of will cannot be created: it can only be unleashed or disinhibited.

Fear of Dying

Existential psychologists assert that the central human fear and the one from which most psychopathology develops is the **fear of dying.** Anxiety about death is most prominent in, and best recalled from childhood. Perhaps because children are vulnerable, and because their worst imaginings are barely informed by reality, their fears are stark, vivid, and memorable. How do people deal with the fear of dying? Broadly speaking, there are two kinds of strategies: by believing themselves special, and by fusion (Yalom, 1980).

SPECIALNESS

One way through which some people protect themselves from death fears is by cultivating in themselves the notion that they are special. It is a peculiar notion in that it holds that the laws of nature apply to all mortals except oneself. The **notion of specialness** manifests itself in many ways. For example, the terminally ill simply cannot believe that it is they who are dying. They understand the laws of nature fully well, but they believe themselves somehow to be exempt from them. Similarly, people who smoke heavily, overeat, or fail to exercise sufficiently may also believe that somehow they are exempt from nature's laws.

The notion of specialness underlies many valued character traits. Physical courage may result from the belief that one is inviolable. So too may ambition and striving, and especially striving for power and control. But at the extreme, the unconscious belief in one's specialness may also lead to a spectrum of behavior disorders. The workaholic who compulsively strives to achieve success and power may also harbor the delusion that achieving that one kind of specialness may confer the other, immortal kind. Narcissistic people who devote enormous attention to themselves and are correspondingly insensitive to the requirements of others may believe that only that kind of self-indulgence will protect them from death and its associated anxieties.

FUSION

Protection against the fear of death or nonbeing can also be achieved by fusing with others. **Fusion** is an especially useful strategy for those whose death fears take the form of loneliness. By attaching themselves to, and making themselves indistinguishable from others, they hope that their lot is cast with them. They believe that much as these others continue to live, so will they. They also develop a fear of standing apart, as they believe that if they do stand apart, they will no longer be protected from death.

A well-trained, enormously presentable business executive had held seven positions in as many years, and he was now finding it difficult to gain employment. Each of his employers had been impressed both by his credentials and his industriousness. He was moved gradually into positions of greater responsibility. Oddly, however, just as he had begun to inspire faith in others, he would "foul up." His errors were as costly as they were inexcusable, and they led quickly to termination from the job. In the course of treatment with an existential therapist, it was found

▲ One defense against the fear of death has been the idea that people can have immortal qualities or talents, as shown in this Chinese painting of a "thunderbolt bearer."

that success had a powerfully unconscious meaning for him. He feared success, for it meant isolation, standing apart from others. For him, success was analogous to death, in that it destroyed fusion. He unconsciously felt that it was better to be indistinguishable from the mass of people than to stand alone, even successfully.

The fear of standing apart has socially valuable features. Why else would we marry and have children if not to create fusions? Why else would we form clubs, communities, and organizations? Such attachments protect against loneliness, against being separated from the flow of life. Yet, fusion may also lead to much unhappiness. A person may engage in inauthentic, or false, modes of behavior. He may say things to others that he hopes will please them, but that he does not really mean. For example, he may conform his opinions to theirs, bend his behaviors to suit them, do the things they do, even though his mind and body would rather believe and do something else. Gradually, he may come to lose sight of what *he* wants to do, while finding his conformity to others' opinions and behaviors only a pale pleasure. He may pay for a tenuous security against the fear of death by sacrificing his own authenticity.

Existential Treatment

Sometimes people need assistance in handling pain and risk. The existential movement has spawned therapies that focus on developing independence, goal-directed willing, and personal responsibility. Here, we see a patient who presents with major depression, which comes from not knowing what she wants to do with her life:

Susan was bright enough to do well in college but nevertheless was having a struggle. It was difficult for her to get up in the morning, difficult to crack the books, and difficult to put away the temptations that deflected her from achievement. She had no sense of what she wanted to study in college and, therefore, little motivation to work in her courses. After her mid-year grades were posted, she went to the counseling center to "try to get myself down to work."

Disorders of will are found among people who know what they should do, what they ought to do, and what they must do, but who have no notion of what they want to do. Lacking that knowledge of what they *want*, their goals seem apparently lusterless, and movement toward them is correspondingly difficult. People may fail to know what they want for three reasons. First, they may simply fear wanting. Wanting makes them vulnerable to failure and hurt, and that is especially difficult for those who wish to appear strong. Second, they may fail to know what they want because they fear rejection. They long ago learned that if their wishes departed from those of their friends or family, their wishes would infuriate and drive others away. Third, they may fail to know what they wish because they want others, magically, to discover their silent wishes and fulfill them.

During therapy sessions, the existential therapist who was counseling Susan helped her overcome depression by focusing on goal-directed willing. During several counseling sessions, Susan came to realize that although she had plenty of intelligence, she lacked confidence in her ability to do well in college and, as a result, found it difficult to commit herself to any career. Susan had had a difficult start in the primary grades, and in the counseling sessions she acknowledged that those bruises had remained with her. During one significant and productive session, Susan realized that grade school was far behind her and that she had achieved a great deal since those experiences.

Nearly simultaneously, a long-buried desire surfaced: to be a doctor. As her disorder of will was overcome, her depression lifted.

> At the next session, Susan reported that "her life had come together during the past week." No longer did she find it difficult to get up in the morning or to resist going to the movies. It was easy to study now, and indeed, she bounded out of bed and headed for the books effortlessly. "Now that I know what I want to do, everything else has fallen into place. I no longer have to force myself."

In another case, a student explored with an existential therapist why she was unable to motivate herself to do what was necessary to complete her graduate studies.

> Most graduate students complete a dissertation before receiving their doctoral degree, and the dissertation is often viewed by them as a significant hurdle in their graduate career. For some, however, that final hurdle is insurmountable. Such seemed to be the case for Cathy. She had done well until that point. Her course grades were excellent, and the research that she had completed while in graduate school had been quite interesting. But somehow she found it difficult to get down to the dissertation. In fact, she had begun three separate studies and had dropped each of them for no particular reason other than that she had lost interest. The fact of the matter was that she viewed the dissertation as a major undertaking, much bigger than anything she had undertaken before, and much beyond her abilities.

Cathy's fear of being criticized by her teachers or, worse, of failing her oral examination prevented her from finding a study that she really wanted to do. But there was more to her concerns than mere fear of criticism, or even fear of failure. Completing her degree meant no longer being a graduate student, and surprisingly, that was troublesome on at least two fronts. First, it meant leaving the cozy, comfortable place that had been hers for four years: the friends, the local haunts, the predictable professors as well as all the other *fusions* that had served her so well during her graduate career. Second, it meant becoming a full-fledged adult, being *responsible* for herself and her actions, choosing her life rather than having it chosen for her. Those two issues quickly formed the core of her treatment. As Cathy became comfortable with her own separateness and her freedom to live as she pleased, her fear of being criticized and of failing diminished correspondingly, and she got back to work on her dissertation, which she completed in record time.

▶ People may attempt to protect themselves against non-being by fusing with others. In an extreme case of fusion, these five people had plastic surgery to change their faces to those of rock stars Jim Croce, Linda Ronstadt, Kenny Rogers, Elvis Presley, and Buddy Holly, merging their identities with those of their favorite stars.

Evaluating the Existential Approach

The existential approach to personality and its disorders is very difficult to evaluate, in large measure because the approach is really a group of philosophical positions rather than a scientific theory. For example, whether people are capable of will or fully responsible for their acts are matters of belief rather than facts that can be proven or disproven. Because the approach is made up of a diverse collection of views and is based on beliefs rather than facts, it is difficult to know where to begin in evaluating the views and treatments derived from them.

Among the very attractive features of this approach, however, is the degree to which it accords with everyday notions of personality. People do behave as if they and others are responsible, as if they are free to do what they will, and as if their lives are not predetermined. Thus, the law, for example, holds people responsible for their behavior with fairly rare exceptions. It reflects the common belief that people act freely, for better or for worse, and that they should be held accountable for their actions. Rightly or wrongly, the existential approach reflects a great deal of common sense.

THE BEHAVIORAL MODEL

A single movement—*behaviorism*—dominated academic psychology in the United States and Soviet Russia for almost fifty years, roughly from 1920 until the mid-1960s. Behaviorism is an ambitious effort to discover in the laboratory the general laws of human and animal learning and to apply these laws to the classroom, the workplace, the penitentiary, and to society as a whole. Thus, behaviorism is not only a model for the study of abnormal behavior, it is a world view. Its first assumption is *environmentalism,* which states that all organisms, including humans, are shaped by the environment. We learn about the future through the associations of the past. This is why our behavior is subject to rewards and punishments. If our employers paid us twice as much per hour for working one Saturday, we would be more likely to work on future Saturdays.

The second assumption of behaviorism is *experimentalism,* which states that through an experiment, we can find out what aspect of the environment caused our behavior and how we can change it. If the crucial element is withheld, the present characteristic will disappear. If the crucial element is reinstated, the characteristic will reappear. For example, what causes us to work on Saturdays? Remove double-time pay, and work on Saturday will stop. Reinstate double-time pay, and work on Saturday will resume. This is the heart of the experimental method. From the experimental method, we can determine what causes people, in general, to forget, to be anxious, to fight, and we can then apply these general laws to individual cases.

The third assumption of behaviorism is *optimism* concerning change. If an individual is a product of the environment and if those parts of the environment that have molded him can be known by experimentation, he will be changed when the environment is changed.

These three assumptions apply directly to abnormal psychology. First, abnormal as well as normal behavior is learned from past experiences. Psychopathology consists of acquired habits that are maladaptive. Second, we can find out by experiment what aspects of the environment cause abnormal behavior. Third, if we change these aspects of the environment the individual will unlearn his old, maladaptive habits and will learn new, adaptive habits.

FOCUS QUESTIONS

1. What is behaviorism?
2. Explain each of these basic assumptions of behaviorism:
   - environmentalism
   - experimentalism
   - optimism

How do we learn and what is it we learn? For the behavioral psychologist, two basic learning processes exist, and it is from these two that all behaviors, both normal and abnormal, derive. We can learn what goes with what through *Pavlovian*, or *classical conditioning*. And we can learn what to do to obtain what we want and rid ourselves of what we do not want through *instrumental*, or *operant conditioning*.

Pavlovian Conditioning

Just after the turn of the century, the Russian physiologist Ivan Pavlov (1849–1936) began work on a phenomenon that would change the nature of psychology. Pavlov was studying the digestive system of dogs, specifically the salivary reflex. He received the Nobel Prize in 1904 for his studies of digestive physiology. During his experiments, he would put food powder in the dog's mouth, and he would then measure the drops of saliva by way of a tube surgically inserted into the dog's mouth. But in the course of his work, Pavlov noticed that dogs began to salivate merely when he walked into the room. This salivation could not be a reflex since it did not occur the first few times Pavlov walked in; it only occurred once the dog had learned that Pavlov's appearance signaled food. That is, Pavlov's appearance became associated with a future event: food. He called this a psychic reflex, or a conditional reflex, since it was conditional upon past experience. It has come to be called, through mistranslation, a *conditioned response*, or *CR*. A typical Pavlovian conditioning experiment goes as follows: we know that food (unconditioned stimulus, US) produces salivation (unconditioned response, UR)

$$\text{US (food)} \rightarrow \text{UR (salivation)}$$

We present a tone just prior to presenting the food. Because the tone itself does not produce salivation, it is a neutral stimulus. But after pairing the tone with the food several times we discover that salivation will occur upon presentation of the tone. The tone can now be called a conditioned stimulus (CS) because it produces salivation, the conditioned response (CR). In short:

$$\text{CS (tone)} \rightarrow \text{US (food)} \rightarrow \text{UR (salivation)}$$

After several pairings of CS and US:

$$\text{CS (tone)} \rightarrow \text{CR (salivation)}$$

This kind of experiment has been carried out using many species (Siamese fighting fish, rats, dogs, and humans), conditioned stimuli (tones, lights,

▶ Ivan Pavlov (1849–1936).

tastes), and unconditioned responses (salivation, fear, nausea). It also can be used in therapeutic situations to eliminate unsatisfactory behaviors. For example, Pavlovian conditioning might be used to treat a foot fetishist, as in the following case:

> Steven has been in trouble with the police for fondling strange women's shoes in public places. He is a foot fetishist with strong erotic attachment to women's feet and footwear. He agrees to undergo Pavlovian therapy rather than go to jail.
>
> In the therapist's office, Steven fondles women's shoes. He then drinks ipecac, a drug that causes him to become nauseated in a few minutes. He vomits. A week later, the same procedure is repeated. The shoes are the CS, the US is ipecac, and the UR is nausea and vomiting. After several sessions the pairing of shoes and vomiting produces a major change in Steven's sexual preferences. He is no longer aroused by women's shoes, and he throws away his collection of five thousand pictures of shoes.

THE BASIC PAVLOVIAN PHENOMENA

FOCUS QUESTIONS

1. Describe how the conditioned stimulus leads to the conditioned response in Pavlovian conditioning.
2. Explain the following basic Pavlovian processes:
   • acquisition
   • extinction
3. Describe how a phobia could result from Pavlovian conditioning.
4. Distinguish between flooding and systematic desensitization.

There are two processes in Pavlovian conditioning that occur time and time again, regardless of what species, what kind of CS or US, or what kind of a response is tested. Pavlov discovered both: acquisition and extinction.

Acquisition is the learning of a response based on the contingency between a CS and US. Depending on the response to be learned, acquisition usually takes from three to fifteen pairings. **Extinction** is the loss of the CS's power to produce the formerly acquired response. This is brought about by presenting the CS, and no longer following it with the US. For example, it is possible to condition fear in humans. Fear can be measured by increased heart rate, perspiration, and muscle tension. When mild shocks (US) are given to humans, these measures become evident, that is, pain (UR) is produced. After several pairings of tone (CS) and shock (US), the tone (CS) alone begins to elicit fear (CR). That is what we call acquisition. But if we now repeatedly present the tone (CS) no longer followed by the shock (US), the individual no longer shows signs of fear. The tone (CS) no longer signals a shock (US). We call this process extinction.

PAVLOVIAN CONDITIONING, EMOTIONS, AND PSYCHOPATHOLOGY

There are situations in the world that arouse strong emotions in us. Some of these arouse the emotion *unconditionally,* or from our very first encounter with them: a loud clap of thunder startles us the very first time we hear it. Other objects acquire emotional significance: the face of a person we love produces a sense of well-being; seeing a stranger in a dark alleyway arouses dread. Pavlovian conditioning provides a powerful account of how objects take on emotional significance; it is this account that makes conditioning of great interest to the student of abnormality.

According to the behavioral account, the basic mechanism for all acquired emotional states is the pairing of a neutral object (CS) with an unconditioned emotional state (US). With enough pairings, the neutral object will lose its neutrality, become a CS, and all by itself produce the emotional state (CR). Consider the case of a child who is continually beaten with a tan hairbrush by his father. Before the beatings, the child had no feelings about the brush whatsoever. But, after several beatings (US), the brush becomes a CS and merely seeing the tan brush produces fear (CR).

If normal emotions are acquired in this way, the same should be true of acquired emotional disorders. Several of the psychopathological disorders explored in the following chapters involve the acquisition of an exaggerated or unusual emotional state in regard to inappropriate objects (see Figure 3–1).

FIGURE 3–1

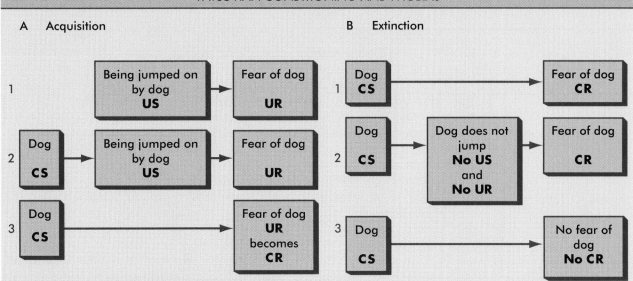

A   Acquisition

B   Extinction

A person who has a phobia has an exaggerated emotional reaction to an object. The person is terrified of the phobic object and unable to function in its presence. Pavlovian conditioning explains that the phobia is acquired when a neutral object (CS) is repeatedly paired with an unconditioned emotional state (US) until it loses its neutrality and evokes a conditioned fear response (CR) from the phobic person. Therapy consists of extinguishing the phobia by continuous pairing of the phobic object (CS) without the original trauma (US–UR) until the fear of the object (CR) is eliminated.

For example, phobias are said to be a result of Pavlovian conditioning. A *pho-bia* is a fear greatly out of proportion to how dangerous the phobic object actually is. For example, a cat phobic had a history of cats (CS) paired with painful events such as being scratched (US). As a result, cats became terrifying to the phobic individual, despite the fact that cats generally are not dangerous.

Here we can contrast the behavioral view of what causes emotional disorders with the biomedical model and the psychodynamic model. According to the behavioral view, the symptom of the disorder *is* the disorder. In the case above, the phobic individual's fear of cats is the disorder. There is no underlying pathological state that produces the symptoms. For the biomedical model, an underlying pathology such as a "virus," a disordered biochemistry, or a dysfunctional organ causes the symptoms. For the psychodynamic view, an intrapsychic conflict, usually sexual or aggressive in nature and stemming from childhood fixations, causes the symptoms.

The therapeutic optimism of the behavioral view follows directly from its view of the cause of the disorder. If the disorders are the symptoms and do not reflect an underlying pathology, eliminating the symptoms will cure the disorder. Since the symptoms of emotional disorders are emotional responses acquired by Pavlovian conditioning, it follows that those techniques that have been found experimentally to extinguish conditioned emotional responses will cure emotional disorders. This contrasts with the biomedical and psychodynamic views, which hold that eliminating symptoms is not enough, that cure consists of removing the underlying disorder. A strong test, then, of the behavioral view as opposed to the biomedical and psychodynamic views of emotional disorders would be whether the symptoms can be removed by extinction procedures, and whether other symptoms would then occur, reflecting an uncured underlying pathology (see Chapter 5).

In the chapters on phobias and sexual dysfunction, we will look in detail at the therapies involving Pavlovian extinction of emotional disorders. But some of the specific therapies should be briefly mentioned now.

Two Pavlovian therapies involving extinction have been applied to phobias and other anxiety disorders. In **_flooding,_** or **_exposure,_** the patient is immersed in the phobic situation (either real or imagined) for several consecutive hours. For example, a person with claustrophobia (a terror of being in small enclosed places) would be placed in a closet (CS); the original trauma (US) would not occur, and the fear of being enclosed would diminish (Stampfl and Levis, 1967; Marks, 1969). Or a rape victim with posttraumatic stress disorder would be told to imagine the rape and to narrate the story repeatedly, in detail, and with emotion, to the therapist. The CS's here are sex, men, and the place, all of which produce terror after the rape, but the original trauma (US) no longer occurs. This treatment diminishes anxiety symptoms (Foa, Rothbaum, Riggs, and Murdock, 1991; Bouchard, Gauthier, Benoit, French, Pelletier, and Godbout, 1996).

In another kind of Pavlovian therapy, **_systematic desensitization_** (developed by Joseph Wolpe, then a South African psychiatrist), the patient would imagine a set of gradually more frightening scenes involving the phobic object (CS), at the same time as he would be making a response incompatible with fear. Pavlovian extinction would occur with this exposure to the CS

▼ In this mild form of flooding, a child who had acquired a fear of dogs is gently prodded toward one. Upon learning that the dog no longer presents danger, the child's fear of dogs disappears.

▲ Edward L. Thorndike (1874–1949) studied animal intelligence and formulated the "law of effect."

(thoughts about and eventually the actual phobic object) without the US (original trauma) and the UR (terror) (Wolpe, 1969; Turner, Beidel, and Jacob, 1994; Nelissen, Muris, and Merckelbach, 1995).

Pavlovian conditioning, then, provides a theory of how we normally learn to feel a given emotion toward a given object. By applying its basic phenomena to emotional disorders, we can arrive at a theory of how emotional disorders come about, and we can deduce a set of therapies that should undo abnormal emotional responses.

Operant Conditioning

At about the same time that Pavlov discovered an objective way of studying how we learn "what goes with what," Edward L. Thorndike (1874–1949) began to study objectively how we learn "what to do to get what we want." Thorndike was studying animal intelligence. In one series of experiments he put hungry cats in puzzle boxes and observed how they learned to escape confinement and get food. He designed various boxes—some had levers to push, others had strings to pull, and some had shelves to jump on—and he left food—often fish—outside the box. The cat would have to make the correct response to escape from the puzzle box.

Thorndike's first major discovery was that learning what to do was gradual, not insightful. That is, the cat proceeded by trial and error. On the first few trials, the time to escape was very long; but with repeated success, the time gradually shortened to a few seconds. To explain his findings, Thorndike formulated the *law of effect.* Still a major principle, this holds that when, in a given stimulus situation, a response is made and followed by positive consequences, the response will tend to be repeated; when followed by negative consequences, it will tend not to be repeated. Thorndike's work, like Pavlov's, was an objective way of studying the properties of learning.

This tradition was refined, popularized, and applied to a range of real-life settings by B. F. Skinner (1904–1990), who worked largely with rats pressing levers for food and with pigeons pecking lighted discs for grain. It was Skinner who formulated the basic concepts of operant conditioning.

THE CONCEPTS OF OPERANT CONDITIONING

Through his basic concepts, Skinner defined the elements of the law of effect rigorously. His three basic concepts consist of the reinforcer (both positive and negative), the operant, and the discriminative stimulus.

A *positive reinforcer* is an event whose onset increases the probability that a response preceding it will occur again. In effect, a positive reinforcer rewards behavior. A *negative reinforcer* is an event whose removal increases the probability of recurrence of a response that precedes it. *Punishers,* on the other hand, are events whose onset will decrease the probability of recurrence of a response that precedes it. The same stimulus whose onset acts as a punisher will usually act as a negative reinforcer when removed.

An *operant* is a response whose probability can either be increased by positive reinforcement or by the removal of negative reinforcement. If a mother reinforces her twelve-month-old child with a hug every time he says "Daddy," the probability that he will say it again is increased. In this case, the operant is "saying Daddy." If the mother hugs the child for saying Daddy only when the child's father is in sight, and does not hug him for saying Daddy when the father is not around, she is teaching the child to respond to a discriminative stimulus. In this case, the father in sight is the *discriminative stimulus,* a signal that means that reinforcement is available if the operant is made.

▼ B. F. Skinner (1904–1990) formulated the basic concepts of operant conditioning.

FIGURE 3–2

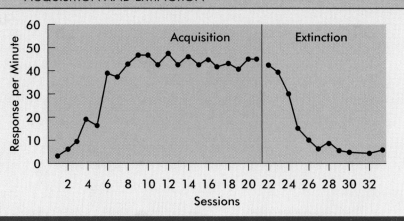

ACQUISITION AND EXTINCTION

This typical curve depicts the growth in the frequency of lever pressing over the course of a number of experimental sessions, followed by its extinction when reinforcement is discontinued. (SOURCE: Adapted from Schwartz, 1984)

The phenomena of *acquisition* and *extinction* in the operant conditioning of voluntary responses parallel the Pavlovian conditioning of involuntary responses. Consider a typical operant paradigm. A hungry rat is placed inside an operant chamber. The desired operant is the pressing of a lever. Each time the rat presses a lever, food is delivered down a chute. During this acquisition procedure, learning to lever press proceeds gradually, as shown in Figure 3–2. It takes about ten sessions for the rat to learn to press at a high and constant rate. Extinction is then begun (in session 22), and the reinforcer (food) is no longer delivered when the rat presses the lever. As a result, responding gradually diminishes back to zero.

THE OPERANT THERAPIES

The operant therapist uses operant principles in asking three essential questions: (1) What undesirable behavior or maladaptive operants does the patient engage in? (2) What reinforcers maintain these maladaptive responses? (3) What environmental changes, usually reinforcement or discriminative stimulus changes, can be made to change the maladaptive behavior into adaptive behavior (Ullmann and Krasner, 1965)? A variety of operant therapies have been employed for a variety of forms of psychopathology (see Table 3–3). We will look at a selection of them now; we will discuss others in more detail in the chapters that involve the specific disorders that these therapies treat.

Selective Positive Reinforcement In the technique of selective positive reinforcement, the therapist selects a *target behavior* or adaptive behavior that is to be increased in probability. By the systematic delivery of positive reinforcement contingent on the occurrence of the target behavior, this behavior becomes more frequent.

Anorexia nervosa is a life-threatening disorder that, for the most part, afflicts women in their teens and early twenties. They literally starve themselves to death. By engaging in bizarre eating habits, such as eating only three Cheerios a day, a person with anorexia will lose 25 to 30 percent of her body weight within a couple of months. When they are hospitalized, the first problem with these patients (who may weigh as little as seventy-five pounds) is not curing them, but just saving their lives. Such patients usually do not cooperate with regimes that attempt to force them to eat. One highly effective way of saving the life of a woman who is anorexic is selectively to reinforce her for eating by using a reinforcer that is more highly desired than is eating. But, if you ask her what would be a reward that would induce her to eat, she will probably not tell you. In order to discover what is positively re-

TABLE 3-3

	OPERANT THERAPY		
Maladaptive Behavior	Reinforcers That Maintain Behavior	Therapy	Response
Not eating by anorexic	Staying thin	Selective positive reinforcement (e.g., anorexic allowed to watch television after she has eaten)	Eating
Self-mutilation by autistic child	Self-stimulation	Selective punishment (e.g., pinches, spanking, cold water)	No self-mutilation
Hitting brother	Attention from parent	Selective punishment (e.g., television turned off)	No hitting brother
Patient disrupting nurses at nurses' station	Attention from nurses	Extinction (nurses ignore patient)	No disruptive visits

FOCUS QUESTIONS

1. Describe the basic concepts of operant conditioning:
   - positive reinforcer
   - negative reinforcer
   - punishers
   - operants
   - discriminative stimulus
2. Describe how the techniques of selective positive reinforcement and selective punishment can be used to treat maladaptive target behaviors.
3. What two relationships are learned in an avoidance situation?

inforcing, a therapist will look for a behavior that the patient engages in frequently and will only give her the opportunity to perform it if she first eats (Premack, 1959). If we observe and time what such a patient does during the day, we might find, for example, that she watches television for an hour and a half, spends forty-five minutes talking with fellow patients, and spends an hour pacing the halls. An operant therapist would then set up a regime such that in order to be allowed to do any one of these three activities, the patient would first have to eat a fixed amount. For example, if she first ate a tablespoon of custard, she would then be allowed to watch television for ten minutes; if she ate all of her steak, she would then be allowed to pace the halls for twenty minutes (Stunkard, 1976).

During thirty years of research, selective positive reinforcement has been shown to be an effective technique across a very wide range of behavioral disorders. When a discrete and specifiable instrumental response is missing from the adaptive repertoire of an individual, application of selective positive reinforcement will generally produce and maintain that response.

Selective Punishment   In *selective punishment,* the therapist selects a target behavior that is maladaptive. By applying an aversive event when this target behavior occurs, the therapist causes its probability of occurrence to decrease. An example might be eliminating or decreasing chronic nail-biting through applying mild aversion treatments (Allen, 1996).

Although we are not sure why, some autistic children engage in self-mutilation.* This maladaptive behavior is persistent, and most attempts at intervention on the part of a therapist will produce no, or only temporary, effects. In some of these cases, operant therapists have applied selective punishment. In one particular case, whenever the child hit himself, a shock was delivered to him. The child soon learned that his behavior brought punishment, and he engaged less often in self-mutilation (Lovaas and Simmons, 1969; Dorsey, Iwata, Ong, and McSween, 1980). This procedure did not cure the child's autism, but it did stop his maladaptive behavior.

Punishment in the form of pinches, spanks, and cold water is now widely used to curtail the self-destructive behavior of autistic children. Punishment in this form strikes some people as cruel, and in 1986 the Office for Children

*Autism is characterized by severe social withdrawal (see Chapter 10).

of the State of Massachusetts barred the use of such punishments in a school for autistic children. The children promptly regressed to their self-destructive behavior, and their parents went to court to overturn the ban, claiming that this was the only effective treatment their children had ever received. The court overturned the ban, charging that, out of sentimentalism, the Office of Children had played "Russian Roulette with the lives and safety of the students" by banning selective punishment (*New York Times,* June 5, 1986).

EXTINCTION

Extinction is another strategy for eliminating maladaptive behaviors: one can eliminate a behavior by merely omitting some highly desired event whenever the target behavior occurs. The most common use of extinction in behavior therapy is when the therapist suspects that some maladaptive target behavior is being performed in order to get some positive reinforcement. The therapist then arranges the contingencies so that this behavior no longer produces the reinforcement. If the behavior decreases in frequency, extinction has been successful. For example, there was a case of a female psychotic patient who would make numerous disruptive visits to the nurses' office on the ward. An operant therapist believed that the attention the patient received from the nurses when she barged into their office was a positive reinforcer that maintained the disruptive behavior. So the therapist instructed the nurses to ignore the patient completely when the patient entered their office, thereby eliminating what was believed to be positive reinforcement. After seven weeks of treatment, the patient's visits dropped from an average of sixteen per day to two per day (Ayllon and Michel, 1959).

Avoidance Learning

As we have seen, learning theorists regard human beings as capable of learning two sorts of relationships: the Pavlovian relationship—what goes with what—and the operant relationship—what to do in order to get what you want (see Table 3–4). There are many situations in which both sorts of learning go on at the same time. Prominent among such situations is learning to avoid aversive events. In an ***avoidance situation,*** two relationships have to be learned: (1) what predicts the aversive event, and (2) how to get away. The avoidance situation combines both a Pavlovian relationship and an operant relationship. To investigate avoidance, behavior theorists typically place a rat in a two-compartment chamber called a shuttlebox. After a while, a tone is turned on. Ten seconds after the tone has gone on, an electric shock is delivered through the floor of the apparatus. If the rat runs to the other side of the shuttlebox before the shock comes on, the tone terminates and the shock is prevented from occurring. Rats, dogs, and people usually learn to avoid shock altogether in these circumstances. In order to avoid the shock, the subject must learn two relationships (Mowrer, 1948; Rescorla and Solomon, 1967): (1) He must learn that the tone predicts shock, and he must become afraid of the tone. This is a Pavlovian relationship in which the CS is the tone, the US is the shock, and the CR is the fear. (2) Having learned to fear the tone, he must learn what to do about it—that running to the other side of the shuttlebox terminates the fearful tone and prevents the shock from occurring. This is an operant relationship in which the discriminative stimulus is the tone, the operant is running to the other side of the shuttlebox, and the reinforcer is the termination of fear and the prevention of shock.

An understanding of avoidance learning helps in the treatment of certain psychopathologies. The behavioral view of obsessive-compulsive disorders, for example, involves the concept of avoidance learning. According to this

TABLE 3–4

	Example of Problem	Origin	Therapy	Outcome
		PAVLOVIAN VS. OPERANT THERAPIES		
Pavlovian Therapies	Fear (CR) of closed spaces (CS)	CS (closed space) associated with US (abuse)/UR (terror)	CS (closed space) presented without US (abuse)/UR (terror) through flooding or systematic desensitization	CS (closed space) no longer produces CR (debilitating fear)
Operant Therapies	No social skills	Insufficient rewards for acquiring operant response (social skills)	Desired operant response (social skills) is rewarded through selective positive reinforcement (e.g., gets ice cream after interacting with others)	Operant response (social skills) is learned; patient interacts better with others

view, the obsessive-compulsive checker believes that by engaging in the compulsive behavior of checking the stove several hundred times a day, she can prevent disaster from befalling her family. In this case, the occurrence and persistence of the compulsion may be explained by avoidance learning. Moreover, the relief of obsessive-compulsive checking by flooding can be explained by the Pavlovian extinction of fear and the operant extinction of the ritual (Griest, 1994).

Behavior therapists often use both operant and Pavlovian procedures. Recall Steven, the foot fetishist who came to hate women's shoes after he received vomit-inducing ipecac. Whenever Steven made the operant response of reaching out to touch shoes, he felt queasy and withdrew his hand. By Pavlovian conditioning the sight and feel of shoes had become nauseating. By operant conditioning, Steven had learned that withdrawing his hand from the shoes would reduce his queasiness.

THE COGNITIVE MODEL

The cognitive model is an outgrowth and a reaction to the behavioral model. Cognitive psychologists believe that what a person thinks, believes, expects, attends to—in short, his or her mental life—influences how he or she behaves. Specifically, cognitive psychologists contend that disordered cognitive processes cause some psychological disorders and that by changing these cognitions, the disorder can be alleviated and perhaps even cured. The following case demonstrates the role that thoughts can play in producing anxiety:

Two individuals have the same speaking skills, but one is very anxious when giving a public speech, and the other speaks with ease in public. On different occasions, each gives a public speech and, as is common during the course of almost any speech, a few members of the audience walk out of the room during each speech. When these two people record what they were thinking when a member of the audience walked out, a very different pattern emerges. The anxious individual thinks, "I must be boring. How much longer do I have to speak? This speech is going to be a failure." In contrast, the low-anxiety person says to herself, "The person walking out must have a class to make. Gee, that's too bad, he will miss the best part of my talk." The same environmental event—people walking out of the room during the speech—produces a very different set of thoughts: the high-anxiety individual has depressing and tension-inducing thoughts, whereas the low-anxiety individual does not (Meichenbaum, 1977).

How do behavioral and cognitive therapists look at this? On the one hand, the behaviorist will focus on the particular environmental event—people walking out during a speech—and how this affects behavior. (In this example the environmental event is the same, but the consequences are different.) The cognitive therapist, on the other hand, will focus on the difference in the *thoughts* of the two speakers, on how the speaker *interprets* the event. For the cognitive therapist, a person's thoughts are of primary importance.

Cognitive Therapy

FOCUS QUESTIONS

1. Explain the importance of thoughts in the cognitive approach.
2. How does a cognitive therapist attempt to treat psychological disorders?
3. Describe cognitive therapeutic approaches to:
   - overcoming self-defeating expectations
   - modifying negative appraisals
   - changing attributions
   - overcoming irrational beliefs
4. What is multimodal therapy?

Underlying the cognitive model is the view that mental events—that is, expectations, beliefs, memories, and so on—can cause behavior. If these mental events are changed, behavior change will follow. Believing this, the cognitive therapist looks for the cause, or etiology, of psychological disorders in disordered mental events. For example, if someone is depressed, the cognitive therapist will look for the cause of the individual's depression in her beliefs or thoughts. Perhaps she believes that she has no control over the events of her life. Thinking that she has no control, the individual may well become passive, sad, and eventually clinically depressed. Successful therapy for such disorders will consist of changing these thoughts. In the case of the depressed individual, a cognitive therapist will draw out, analyze, and then help change the individual's thoughts, hoping to discover and then reverse the thoughts that caused the feeling of hopelessness.

To understand what a cognitive therapist does, let us return to the case study of the two speech givers. What if the high-anxiety speaker becomes increasingly depressed when he sees members of the audience walking out? He may label the speech, and himself, a failure. Perhaps he gets so depressed that he can no longer give a good speech, or worse, refuses to speak before an audience. Because of this problem, he may enter therapy. What will a cognitive therapist do?

Because a cognitive therapist is concerned primarily with what a person thinks and believes, he or she will inquire about the anxious speaker's thoughts. Upon finding out that the speaker thinks that he is boring his audience, the therapist will pursue two hypotheses. First, there is the hypothesis that the speaker in reality is boring. If, however, in the course of the therapy, the therapist learns that the person's speeches have in the past been received very well and that some have even been reprinted, the therapist will conclude that the first hypothesis is wrong.

After discarding the hypothesis that the speaker really is boring, the therapist will turn to the hypothesis that the speaker's thoughts are distorting reality. According to this hypothesis, the speaker is selecting negative evidence by focusing too narrowly on one event: he is thinking too much about those members of the audience who walked out. He believes that they think he is boring, that they dislike him, and so on. Here, the therapist gets the client to point out the contrary evidence. First, he has a fine speaking record. Second, only a very small number of people walked out; some probably had important appointments to catch and were glad to have heard at least part of the speech. Perhaps some of them were bored. But third, and most important, he minimized the fact that almost all of the audience remained, and he paid no attention to the fact that the audience applauded enthusiastically. The therapist's job is to draw out all of the distorted negative thoughts, to have the client confront the contrary evidence, and then to get the client to change these thoughts.

What kinds of mental events do cognitive therapists deal with? For the purposes of therapy, cognitive processes can be divided into short-term and long-term processes. The short-term processes are conscious. We are aware of them, or can become aware of them with practice. These include expectations, appraisals, and attributions. The long-term cognitive processes are not, generally speaking, available to consciousness. They are dispositions that show themselves in the way they govern the short-term processes. One long-term process involves beliefs. We will discuss the short-term processes first.

OVERCOMING SELF-DEFEATING EXPECTATIONS

Expectations are cognitions that explicitly anticipate future events. The speech giver who, upon seeing a few people walk out, thought "this is going to be a failure" is reporting an expectation. He anticipates future consequences—in this case, bad ones. There are two kinds of expectancies: an ***outcome expectation*** is a person's estimate that a given behavior will lead to a desired outcome, and an ***efficacy expectation*** is the belief that he can successfully execute the behavior that produces the desired outcome. Outcome and efficacy expectations are different because a person may be certain that a particular course of action will produce a given outcome, but he may doubt that he can perform this action. For example, he may realize that touching a snake will reduce his snake phobia, but he may still be unable to touch the snake. The cognitive psychologist Albert Bandura believes that the success of systematic desensitization and modeling therapies in curing phobias (see Chapter 5) is attributable to changes in efficacy expectations. In both situations, the patient learns that he can make those responses—relaxation and approach—which will overcome the phobia. A "micro-analysis" of efficacy expectations and behavioral change in snake phobics has confirmed this speculation. Successful therapy created high efficacy expectations for approaching a boa constrictor. The higher the level of efficacy expectations at the end of treatment, the better was the approach behavior to the snake (Bandura, 1977a, 1982, 1993; Bandura and Adams, 1977; Staats, 1978; Biran and Wilson, 1981; Rodgers and Brawley, 1996; Saigh, Mroueh, Zimmerman, and Fairbank, 1996).

▼Children's faces and gestures reflect their expectations of success or failure.

MODIFYING NEGATIVE APPRAISALS

We are constantly appraising and evaluating both what happens to us and what we do. These *appraisals* and evaluations are sometimes very obvious to us, but at other times we are unaware of them. For cognitive therapists, such automatic thoughts often precede and cause emotion (Beck, 1976). The speech giver becomes anxious and depressed once he thinks, "This is going to be a failure." He is not only expecting future consequences, he is also appraising his actions. He judges them to be failures, and this appraisal causes his negative emotions. This appraisal process is automatic. After a lifetime of practice, it occurs habitually and rapidly. The individual in therapy must be trained to slow down his thought process to become aware of such thoughts. Automatic thoughts are not vague and ill-formed, rather they are specific and discrete sentences. In addition, while they may seem implausible to the objective observer, they seem highly reasonable to the person who has them (see also Kanfer and Karoly, 1972; Mahoney and Thoresen, 1974; Lazarus, 1976; Rehm, 1978; Beck, Steer, and Epstein, 1992; Alden and Wallace, 1995).

One instrument for discovering the frequency of automatic thoughts is the *Automatic Thoughts Questionnaire* (Hollon and Kendall, 1980). In answering its questions, clients record the frequency with which they make the following sorts of automatic appraisals of themselves, "I'm no good," "I'm so weak," "My life is a mess," "No one understands me," "It's just not worth it." The results show that when people are depressed, they have many more frequent negative automatic thoughts than when they are not depressed, and further, that these thoughts are specific to depressives. Schizophrenics, substance abusers, and people with anxiety disorders do not record having frequent negative thoughts about themselves unless they are also depressed (Hollon, Kendall, and Lumry, 1986).

A major proponent of cognitive therapy, A. T. Beck (1976) argues that specific emotions are *always* preceded by discrete thoughts. Sadness is preceded by the thought "something of value has been lost." Anxiety is preceded by the thought "a threat of harm exists," and anger is preceded by the thought "my personal domain is being trespassed against." This is a sweeping and simple formulation of emotional life: the essence of sadness, anxiety, and anger consists of appraisals of loss, threat, and trespass, respectively. Thus, for cognitive therapists, modifying those thoughts will alter the emotion (Sokol, Beck, Greenberg, Wright, and Berchick, 1989; MacLeod and Cropley, 1995).

CHANGING ATTRIBUTIONS

Another kind of short-term mental event that cognitive therapists try to modify is attribution. An *attribution* is an individual's conception of *why* an event has befallen him. When a student fails an examination, he asks himself, "Why did I fail?" Depending on the causal analysis he makes, different consequences ensue. The student might make an *external* or *internal attribution* (Rotter, 1966). He might believe that the examination was unfair, an external cause. Alternatively, he might believe that he is stupid, an internal cause. A second dimension along which attributions for failure are made is *stable* or *unstable* (Weiner, 1974). A stable cause is one that persists in time; an unstable cause is one that is transient. For example, the student might believe that he failed because he did not get a good night's sleep, an unstable cause (which is also internal). Alternatively, the student might believe that he has no mathematical ability, a stable cause (which is also internal). Finally, an attribution for failure can be *global* or *specific* (Abramson, Seligman, and Teasdale, 1978; Seligman, 1991). An attribution to global factors means that failure must occur on many different tasks, and an attribution to specific factors means that failure must occur only on this task. For example, the student who

▶ Most observers would guess that these athletes' attributional styles are internal: they are taking personal responsibility for the outcome of the game.

fails might believe that he failed because he is stupid, a global cause (which is also stable and internal). Or he might believe that he failed because the form number of the test was 13, an unlucky number. This latter is a specific attribution (which is also external and stable). Table 3–5 presents these alternative attributions (Heider, 1958; Kelley, 1967; Weiner, 1972; Seligman, 1991).

Cognitive therapists try to change an individual's attributions. For example, women with low self-esteem usually make internal attributions when they fail. They believe that they have failed because they are stupid, incompetent, and unlovable. To deal with this attribution, each week the therapist has them record five different bad events that have occurred during each week and then he has them write down *external* attributions for the events. For example, one woman might write, "my boyfriend criticized my behavior at a party last night, not because I am socially unskilled, but rather because he was in a bad mood." The goal is to get the woman to shift from internal to external what she believes to be the causes of bad events. After a few

TABLE 3–5

ATTRIBUTIONS OF STUDENTS WHO DO POORLY ON THE GRADUATE RECORD EXAMINATION

| | Internal | | External | |
	Stable	Unstable	Stable	Unstable
Global	Lack of intelligence (Laziness)	Exhaustion (Having a cold makes me stupid.)	ETS gives unfair tests. (People are usually unlucky on the GRE.)	Today is Friday the 13th. (ETS gave experimental tests this time that were too hard for everyone.)
Specific	Lack of mathematical ability (Math always bores me.)	Fed up with math problems (Having a cold ruins my arithmetic.)	ETS gives unfair math tests. (People are usually unlucky on math tests.)	The math test was form No. 13. (Everyone's copy of the math test was blurred.)

NOTE: ETS = Educational Testing Service, the maker of graduate record examinations (GRE).
SOURCE: Abramson, Seligman, and Teasdale, 1978.

▲ Albert Ellis (1913–), founder of rational-emotive therapy, argues that psychological disorder stems largely from irrational beliefs.

weeks, clients begin to see that there are alternative causes for their failures, and the low self-esteem and depression brought about by the internal attributions begin to lift (Beck et al., 1979; Seligman, 1995).

CHANGING LONG-TERM BELIEFS

The short-term mental events that we have examined—expectations, appraisals, and attributions—are available to consciousness. Long-term cognitive processes are different. They are dispositions inferred to govern the mental events now in consciousness. One of these long-term cognitive processes is *belief.*

Albert Ellis, the founder of rational-emotive therapy, argues that psychological disorder stems largely from irrational beliefs. He gives an example of a client who, over the course of a lifetime, had had a set of destructive beliefs instilled in him by his parents and by society. Among these were the ideas that: (1) it is a dire necessity for an adult human being to be loved or approved by virtually every significant other person in his community; (2) one should be thoroughly competent, adequate, and achieving in all possible respects in order to be worthwhile; (3) it is awful and catastrophic when things are not the way one would very much like them to be; (4) human unhappiness is externally caused, and we have little or no ability to control our own sorrows; (5) our past history is an all-important determinant of our present behavior; if something once strongly affected our life, it should always have a similar effect; and (6) there is invariably a right, precise, and perfect solution to human problems, and it is catastrophic if this perfect solution is not found (Ellis, 1962).

These irrational and illogical beliefs shaped the short-term distorted expectations, appraisals, and attributions that produced psychological disorder. The client was afflicted with a "tyranny of shoulds," and the job of the therapist was to break the hold of these "shoulds." Once the patient abandoned the above beliefs, it was impossible for him to remain disturbed. The job of the therapist was to rid the individual of these beliefs. The therapy was an aggressive one. It made a concerted attack on the client's beliefs in two ways: (1) the therapist was a frank counter-propagandist who contradicted superstitions and self-defeating propaganda embodied in the irrational beliefs of the patient, and (2) the therapist encouraged, persuaded, cajoled, and occasionally insisted that the patient engage in behavior that would itself be forceful counter-propaganda against the irrational beliefs (Ellis, 1962; Kendall, Haaga, Ellis, and Bernard, 1995).

This particular brand of cognitive therapy is called rational-emotive therapy, and it is among the most active and aggressive of psychotherapeutic procedures. The following case illustrates the force of therapeutic persuasion:

During his therapy session, a twenty-three-year-old man said that he was very depressed and did not know why. A little questioning showed that this severely neurotic patient, whose main presenting problem was that he had been doing too much drinking during the last two years, had been putting off the inventory keeping he was required to do as part of his job as an apprentice glass-staining artist.

PATIENT: I know that I should do the inventory before it piles up to enormous proportions, but I just keep putting it off. To be honest, I guess it's because I resent doing it so much.
THERAPIST: But why do you resent it so much?
PATIENT: It's boring. I just don't like it.
THERAPIST: So it's boring. That's a good reason for disliking this work, but is it an equally good reason for resenting it?
PATIENT: Aren't the two the same thing?
THERAPIST: By no means. Dislike equals the sentence, "I don't enjoy doing

this thing, and therefore I don't want to do it." And that's a perfectly sane sentence in most instances. But resentment is the sentence, "*Because* I dislike doing this thing, I shouldn't *have* to do it." And that's invariably a very crazy sentence.

PATIENT: Why is it so crazy to resent something that you don't like to do?

THERAPIST: There are several reasons. First of all, from a purely logical standpoint, it just makes no sense at all to say to yourself, "Because I dislike doing this thing, I shouldn't *have* to do it." The second part of this sentence just doesn't follow in any way from the first part. Your reasoning goes something like this: "Because *I* dislike doing this thing, *other people* and the *universe* should be so considerate of me that they should never make me do what I dislike." But, of course, this doesn't make any sense. Why *should* other people and the universe be that considerate of you? It might be nice if they were. But why the devil *should* they be? In order for your reasoning to be true, the entire universe, and all the people in it, would really have to revolve around and be uniquely considerate of you. (Ellis, 1962)

Here the therapist directly attacks the client's belief, arguing that it is irrational. This is an important distinction between cognitive therapists, on the one hand, and behavioral or psychodynamic therapists on the other. Behavioral and psychodynamic therapists point out that a client's actions and beliefs are maladaptive and self-defeating. Cognitive therapists emphasize that, in addition, the beliefs are irrational and illogical.

Cognitive-Behavioral Therapy

Cognitive therapists, then, believe that distorted thinking causes disordered behavior and that correcting the distorted thinking will alleviate and even cure the disordered behavior. Behavior therapists, in contrast, view disordered behavior as learned from past experience, and they attempt to alleviate the disorders by training the patients to use new, more adaptive behaviors. These two positions are not incompatible, and many therapists try both to correct distorted cognitions and to train patients to engage in new behaviors. When therapists combine both techniques, it is called cognitive-behavioral therapy (CBT) (Ellis, 1962; Mahoney, 1974; Meichenbaum, 1977; Beck et al., 1979; Craske, Maidenberg, and Bystritsky, 1995).

Arnold Lazarus is one of the therapists who integrates cognitive and behavioral techniques in therapy (Lazarus, 1993). Lazarus argues that a disorder occurs in the same patient at seven different levels, and that there are levels of therapy appropriate to each level of disorder. The mnemonic device for these seven levels is BASIC ID, where B is behavior, A affect, S sensation, I imagery, C cognition, I interpersonal relations, D drugs. The job of the therapist using such ***multimodal therapy*** is to separate the disorder into its different levels and to choose appropriate techniques for each level. Lazarus is willing to use cognitive techniques, behavioral techniques, and even psychodynamic procedures. Table 3–6 shows the variety of treatments used in the course of the thirteen-month therapy for Mary Ann, a twenty-four-year-old woman diagnosed as having chronic undifferentiated schizophrenia with a very poor prognosis. She was overweight, apathetic, and withdrawn. She had been heavily medicated but with little effect. By the end of the thirteen months of the techniques shown in Table 3–6, she was functioning well and engaged to be married.

Combining Cognitive-Behavioral Therapy and Psychodynamics

There has been a movement among psychodynamically oriented therapists that augurs well for a fruitful combination of cognitively oriented concepts

TABLE 3–6

BASIC ID TECHNIQUES		
Modality	*Problem*	*Proposed Treatment*
Behavior	Inappropriate withdrawal responses Frequent crying Excessive eating	Assertiveness training Nonreinforcement Low-calorie regimen
Affect	Unable to express overt anger Frequent anxiety Absence of enthusiasm and spontaneous joy	Role playing Relaxation training and reassurance Positive imagery procedures
Sensation	Stomach spasms Out of touch with most sensual pleasures Tension in jaw and neck	Abdominal breathing and relaxing Sensate focus method Differential relaxation

Imagery	Distressing scenes of sister's funeral
	Recurring dreams about airplane
	  bombings
		Desensitization
		Vivid imagery evoking feelings of
		  being safe

Cognition	Irrational self-talk: "I am evil."
	  "I must suffer." "Sex is dirty."
	  "I am inferior."
	Overgeneralization
		Deliberate rational questioning
		  and corrective self-talk
		
		Critical analysis of irrational sentences

Interpersonal relationships	Childlike dependence Easily exploited and submissive Manipulative tendencies	Specific self-sufficiency assignments Assertiveness training Training in direct and confrontational behaviors
Drugs	Disordered biochemistry	Antipsychotic drugs

SOURCE: Adapted from Lazarus, 1976.

FOCUS QUESTIONS

1. What is the CCRT?
2. How can examining a patient's thoughts about three spheres of life reveal the CCRT and lead to positive therapeutic outcome?

and psychodynamic therapy. Lester Luborsky (1984) argues that what a patient consciously thinks about in three spheres of life reveals an underlying, and often unconscious, core conflictual relationship theme (CCRT). The three spheres are: (1) current in-treatment relationship (the relationship with the therapist), (2) current out-of-treatment relationships, and (3) past relationships. Common cognitions about these spheres, their recurrent overlap, point to the patient's basic conflicted theme about interpersonal relations (Luborsky, Popp, Luborsky, and Mark, 1994).

Ms. N. thinks, "I am trying to do well in my work," a thought about her current out-of-treatment relationships. She tells this to the therapist, and she begins to cry. The therapist then remarks, "You get tearful and cry when I refer to your attractiveness," a result of her thoughts about the in-treatment relationship. Ms. N. then spontaneously thinks about her past, "Father could never stand my being attractive." The content of these three conscious spheres reflects the main unconscious CCRT. By disentangling the cognitions involved in the three spheres, the therapist can discover the client's *wish:* "I wish I could find a suitable man to provide me with the physical and emotional support I need." The therapist can also discover (and attempt to alter) the negative *consequence*, or automatic thoughts, that follow from the wish: "But I shouldn't because I am independent, and I can't because I will be rejected, and the man will not be able to provide that kind of support."

By attending to the conscious automatic thoughts that cognitive therapists emphasize, psychodynamically oriented therapists are beginning to bring these two disparate models closer together (Horowitz, Stinson, Curtis, et al., 1993). Other integrations across models are likely in the future.

Evaluating the Behavioral and Cognitive Models

There are several virtues of behavior therapy and cognitive therapy: they are effective in a number of disorders; therapy is generally brief and inexpensive; they seem to be based on a science of behavioral and cognitive psychology; and their units of analysis—stimuli, responses, reinforcers, expectations, and attributions—can be measured. Behavioral and cognitive therapies, however, are not without problems. Perhaps the most serious allegation is that they are superficial.

FOCUS QUESTIONS

1. What are the strengths of the behavioral and cognitive models?
2. What are the problems with the behavioral and cognitive models?

Are humans more than just behavior and cognition? Are psychological disorders more than disordered behavior and disordered thinking? Must therapy, in order to be successful, do more than merely provide more adaptive behaviors and more rational ways of thinking? Because behavior therapists and cognitive therapists restrict themselves to an analysis of the discrete behaviors and cognitions of the human being, they miss the essence: that individuals are wholes, that individuals are free to choose. A patient with a cat phobia is more than a machine who happens to be afraid of cats. He is an individual whose symptoms are deeply rooted in his personality and psychodynamics. Alternatively, he is an individual who has made bad choices but who can still choose health. A child with autism who treats other human beings as if they were pieces of furniture may be taught by behaviorists to hug other people in order to receive food or to escape from shock. But in the end, all we have is a child with autism who hugs people. Merely changing how one behaves fails to change the underlying disorder.

Those who object to the behavioral and cognitive views feel that there are deeper disorders that produce symptoms. Because of this, seemingly superficial behavioral change may be short-lived, as in the case of what had been highly successful behavioral treatments of obesity. After one year and three years, obese individuals who had undergone behavior therapy had kept their weight down. But after five years, their weight returned (Seligman, 1993). Although behavior therapy had led to change by removing the symptom of obesity, the underlying problem, probably biological in nature, remained and ultimately sabotaged the therapy.

How might behavioral and cognitive therapists respond to these charges of superficiality? A militant response might be to deny the concept of the "whole person." To radical behaviorists such a concept is romantic; it makes sense in literature and in poetry, but not for human beings in distress and in need of relief. We would make a less militant reply. Removing symptoms—either behavioral or cognitive—at least helps. Symptom substitution has rarely, if ever, followed successful behavioral or cognitive therapy. Some disorders are highly specific, peripheral to the heart of an individual's being, and amenable to behavior and cognitive therapies. Phobias, obsessions, stuttering, and some sexual problems are such disorders. On the other hand, there may be deeper disorders left untouched by behavioral and cognitive therapy: schizophrenia and antisocial personality disorder, perhaps. For these disorders, change of personality, uncovering dynamics, and drugs are probably necessary.

Behavioral and cognitive theorists believe that human misery, including problems of psychological disorder, is sometimes, but not always, produced by an unfortunate set of environmental circumstances or by distorted cognition. To counteract such circumstances by applying behavioral and cognitive laws does not diminish or devalue human wholeness or freedom, but rather enlarges it. An individual who is so crippled by a phobia of leaving his apartment that he cannot work or see those he loves is not free. By applying behavioral and cognitive therapy to such an individual, one can remove this phobia. Such an individual will then be free to lead a rational life.

1. Psychodynamic theories are centrally concerned with conflict, anxiety, and defense. *Conflict* arises when desires cannot find immediate gratification because such gratification is not permitted by reality or conscience. Conflict generates *anxiety,* a form of psychic pain that arises when individuals feel they cannot cope. Anxiety can be either conscious or unconscious and gives rise to *defense mechanisms,* which are the mind's flexible editing mechanisms that allow individuals to alter or entirely obliterate painful stimuli that arise from either desire or reality.

2. Freud divided the personality into three kinds of processes: id, ego, and superego. The *id* is concerned with sexual and aggressive desires and is dominated by the *pleasure principle.* The *ego* is concerned with the individual's safety, allows desire to be expressed only when aversive consequences from other sources are minimal, and is dominated by the *reality principle.* The *superego* consists of the individual's conscience and ideals, and regardless of what reality permits, it either forbids individuals to express desires, or urges them toward the achievement of higher goals.

3. Many of our inner conflicts occur in the unconscious, which includes forgotten memories and repressed memories. Repressed memories live on because they are not subject to rational control; they are the dominant forces in personality.

4. Our inner conflicts can bring about much anxiety. To relieve anxiety, individuals use such coping strategies as repression, projection, reaction formation, displacement, identification, denial, isolation, intellectualization, rationalization, and sublimation.

5. The neo-Freudians, Jung, Adler, Horney, Sullivan, Erikson, and Fromm, generally found Freud's formulations too narrowly focused. Some stressed the impact of *social* relationships on psychological development. More recent theorists focus on the central role of ego processes in personality. These modern psychodynamic theorists stress the importance of the *self* as the repository of values and the source of continuity across time and place. There are at least three significant aspects of self: the core self, the subjective self, and the verbal self. Selfobjects are people and things that are especially important for maintaining the self.s

6. Psychodynamic therapies seek to make conscious that which is unconscious through encouraging the client to *free associate* and to examine dreams, resistances, and the *transference* that occurs between the client and therapist. Psychodynamic treatment aims to enable the client to reduce the amount of psychic energy that is invested in defensive maneuvers, and to achieve greater control over impulse expression.

7. Psychodynamic theories have demystified psychological processes and have offered the possibility of overcoming psychological distress. But critics cite difficulties of proof, their indifference to the scientific method, and their disregard of the situation.

8. Existential theorists hold that we are the authors of our experience. We determine what we perceive and what we experience; we are *responsible* for how we behave. Freedom and responsibility, however, may create anxiety. Responsibility avoidance is occasionally achieved through denying ownership of behavior and thought.

9. Existentialists often posit two kinds of will: *exhortative will* forces us to do what we know we should do, and *goal-directed will* is unleashed when we have freely chosen our goals and want to pursue and achieve them.

10. Existentialists believe that the fundamental anxiety is *fear of death.* Psychologically, death means nonbeing. Because the fear of death is so threatening, people attempt to endow themselves with immortality by becoming *special* or by *fusion* with others, which may lead to *inauthentic,* or false, modes of behavior.

11. The behavioral model aims to discover, by laboratory experiment, what aspect of the environment produces maladaptive learning, and it sees successful therapy as learning new and more adaptive ways of behaving.

12. Two kinds of basic learning processes exist: *Pavlovian* and *operant conditioning.* These have each generated a set of behavior therapies.

13. Pavlovian therapies begin with the assumption that emotional habits have been acquired by the contingency between a *conditioned stimulus* and an *unconditioned stimulus.* The formerly neutral conditioned stimulus now produces a *conditioned response,* which is the acquired emotion. Two Pavlovian therapies, *systematic desensitization* and *flooding,* extinguish some maladaptive emotional habits quite successfully.

14. Operant conditioning is based on three concepts: reinforcer, operant, and discriminative stimulus. Operant therapies are based on the assumption that people acquire voluntary habits by positive and negative reinforcement and punishment. Operant therapies provide new and more adaptive repertoires of voluntary responses and extinguish maladaptive voluntary responses. Among such therapies are *selective positive reinforcement, selective punishment,* and *extinction.* These have been applied with some success to such disorders as *anorexia nervosa* and *autism.*

15. The understanding of *avoidance learning* combines operant and Pavlovian theory, and helps in the treatment of obsessive-compulsive disorders.

16. The cognitive school holds that mental events can cause behavior. More particularly, disordered cognitions can cause disordered behavior, and changing these disordered cognitions can alleviate and sometimes cure psychopathology.

17. Cognitive therapy is carried out by attempting to change different sorts of mental events, which can be divided into short-term mental events and long-term mental events. Short-term mental events consist of expectations, including *outcome and efficacy expectations, appraisals* (mental evaluations of our experience), and *attributions* (the designation of causes concerning our experience).

18. Many therapists practice both cognitive and behavioral therapy and are called *cognitive-behavioral therapists. Multimodal therapy* is an example of the use of cognitive and behavioral techniques along with techniques from the other models.

19. The cognitive and behavioral models have been seriously criticized. The most important criticisms argue that human beings are more than their behaviors and cognitions, and that it is superficial to treat only the symptoms rather than the whole person. The cognitive and behavioral schools reply by arguing that many times it is helpful to the client merely to remove the symptoms, and that the disorder *is* often just the symptoms.

1. How does an overly strong id or superego lead to psychological problems?

2. What are the various ways that repressed thoughts can emerge in the conscious mind?

3. Give a Pavlovian explanation for how a child could develop a fear of the dark.

4. Give an explanation for compulsive gambling in terms of operant conditioning.

5. How do an individual's attributions affect whether he is able to bounce back quickly from a failed business or unhappy love affair?

4

Assessment, Diagnosis, and Methodology

Winold Reiss, Detail of Mural at Cincinnati Union Terminal.

S
ome people are terrified at the thought of entering an elevator; some feel sad all the time; some seem to act in a way that seems totally inappropriate, like laughing at a close friend's funeral; some complain of physical ailments that have no biological basis. People differ psychologically, and psychological assessment tells us how to measure the ways that they differ. Psychological diagnosis is a classification system for mental illness that permits us to group people according to their similarities. Scientific methodology enables us to discover how different people suffer similar kinds of psychopathology and how these problems can be cured and prevented.

In this chapter, we will concern ourselves with modern psychological assessment, diagnosis, and methodology. We will explore the assessment techniques that provide reliable understanding of human misery and lead to useful diagnosis. We will ask what diagnostic categories seem most promising for understanding and treating psychological distress and how to assess whether a diagnostic category is useful and reliable. We will then discuss different scientific methods that provide clues as to what causes the abnormal behavior that has been assessed and diagnosed. Finally, we will discuss how scientific methods have permitted us to discover treatments that will restore individuals to normal functioning.

PSYCHOLOGICAL ASSESSMENT

Psychologists seek to understand individuals through a variety of procedures. They talk to people, administer psychological tests, and assess their behavior in real-life situations. They use assessment to achieve a deep understanding of the client. That understanding may result in a diagnosis, but it commonly

FOCUS QUESTIONS

1. Describe how a structured interview differs from an unstructured interview.
2. What do the test items on the MMPI assess?
3. Describe what projective tests are used to assess and how they differ from objective psychological inventories like the MMPI.
4. Describe the techniques used to scan the brain and how they differ from each other.

also results in much more. Commonly, assessment yields a sense of a person's individuality, the forces that generate his or her uniqueness. Often, it will give a sense of why a person is in difficulty, and occasionally a clue as to how the difficulty can be resolved.

In order for an assessment device to generate meaningful understandings about people, it must possess two characteristics. First, it must be *reliable,* that is, it must generate the same findings on repeated use. Imagine a physical universe in which yardsticks are made of rubber. Each time you measured something, you would come up with different answers simply because of the nature of the rubber measuring instrument, which would stretch. Such an instrument would be *un*reliable, which is to say you could not depend on it to come up with the same measurement each time it was used. Second, a psychological test should be *stable,* yielding similar readings across time.

Third, an assessment device must be *valid.* It must be useful for the purposes for which it is intended. Even a good thermometer is useless for measuring a room. Similarly, a psychological test can be useful for one purpose and thoroughly invalid for others.

Psychological assessment techniques are divided into three processes: interviewing, testing, and observing. Each of these techniques can be used to gather information about a client's problems and disabilities.

The Clinical Interview

The *clinical interview* is the favorite instrument of clinical psychologists and psychiatrists, reflecting the widespread view that we don't know someone well until we've met and talked with him. Good interviewers get information, not only from what people say, but from how they say it: their manner, tone of voice, body postures, and degree of eye contact (Exline and Winters, 1965; Ellsworth and Carlsmith, 1968; Ekman, Friesen, and Ellsworth, 1972). Of course, in order to get this information, there must be a good rapport between the client and interviewer. One should not expect people to be honest if they feel that their statements are going to incriminate them or lead to aversive decisions about their future. For an interview to be maximally informative, the client needs to perceive the interviewer as being nonthreatening, supportive, and encouraging of self-disclosure (Jourard, 1974).

The clinical interview may range from an unstructured conversation to a quite structured encounter. Fundamentally, an *unstructured interview*

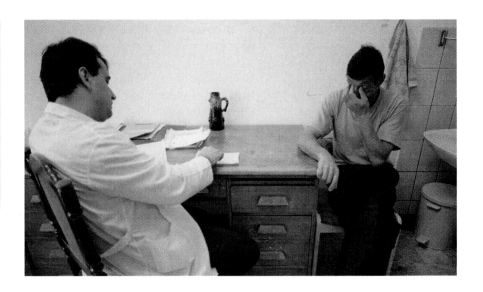

▶ Just as in everyday encounters with others, a patient speaks to a therapist in a clinical interview not only through words, but through her manner, posture, tone of voice, and degree of eye contact. This former front-line soldier weeps as he relates his war-related nightmares to a therapist at a psychiatric hospital in Tuzla, Bosnia.

allows the interviewer to change direction at a moment's notice. The client may want to talk about a particular problem, and right now, rather than later. The unstructured interview permits that. Similarly, the interviewer may want to inquire into a particular issue, perhaps related to his or her own theoretical bent. The unstructured interview, therefore, is very flexible, but it "pays a price" for that flexibility. Because they are unstructured, no two of these interviews are the same. They elicit different information and, therefore, the reliability and validity of the information that is elicited may be reduced (Fisher, Epstein, and Harris, 1967).

The ***structured interview*** is increasingly used to overcome the reliability and validity problems of the unstructured interview. The structured interview standardizes the questions that are asked by each interviewer. The amount of clinical judgment required in these interviews is substantially reduced, since the answers to the specific questions and probes lead automatically to the scoring of the symptoms, which can be processed by a computer. Such interviews remove much of the unreliability that is introduced by differences in the way clinicians elicit information in unstructured interviews (Matarazzo, 1983).

Psychological Testing

Additional psychological information about the nature of an individual's problems and disabilities comes from psychological testing. Some tests are specific, that is, designed to illuminate a single personality attribute, such as anxiety or depression, or to uncover a particular kind of brain damage. Others seek to describe a larger portion of personality and abnormality. Many tests are unstructured or projective, requiring the client to draw a person or persons or a series of designs, to determine abnormality through careful interviewing, while others aspire to the same goal through formal, structured examinations. Psychological tests fall into three categories: psychological inventories, "projective" tests, and intelligence tests.

PSYCHOLOGICAL INVENTORIES

Nearly everyone has taken an objective ***psychological inventory*** at one time or another for vocational guidance, or personal counseling, or in connection with a job. These tests are highly structured and contain a variety of statements that can be answered "true" or "false." The client is asked to indicate whether or not each statement applies to her. Inventories have enormous advantages, foremost among them, they are commonly highly reliable.

By far, the most widely used and studied personality inventory in clinical assessment is the ***Minnesota Multiphasic Personality Inventory (MMPI).*** The MMPI consists of 550 test items that inquire into a wide array of behaviors, thoughts, and feelings. Respondents are usually given the same test items, but the meaning of those items may not be identical for each respondent. Thus, a college student who responds "yes" to the statement "I usually feel fine" obviously means something quite different from the hospitalized person who responded "yes" without reading the statement. As a consequence, the meanings of the MMPI items are by no means self-evident, and they have had to be ascertained by empirical research (Hathaway and McKinley, 1943). Scales have been constructed by examining the responses of people with known characteristics, such as depressed versus nondepressed persons, manic versus nonmanic, introverted versus extraverted. All in all, the MMPI provides scores for the ten categories shown in Table 4–1. These categories have been validated against diagnostic judgments that arose from psychiatric interviews and other tests (Wrobel and Lochar, 1982).

Any paper-and-pencil inventory is subject to a variety of distortions, and the MMPI is no exception. One can simply lie. One can be evasive. Or one can try to put oneself in the best possible social light. And one can do these things intentionally or unintentionally. However, the MMPI contains four "validity" scales that are designed to alert the diagnostician to such distortions. Thus, if a person were to respond "true" to the following items: "I never tell lies," and "I read the newspaper editorials every day," it might be reasonable to surmise that the test-taker is trying to present herself as favorably as she can—since it is a rare person who never tells lies and who reads the editorials daily. Notice that these judgments about social desirability and lying are *not* absolutely foolproof. Rather they are "best guesses." Most (but not all) people who respond positively to the above items will be, wittingly or unwittingly, trying to improve their image. For all we know, however, there may well be some people who read every editorial every day and who never tell lies (bless 'em!).

The results of the MMPI are recorded in the form of a profile (Figure 4–1A). The profile tells a clinician more than the individual scores would. By utilizing a sourcebook of MMPI profiles (e.g., Gilberstadt and Duker, 1965; Greene, 1991), the profile of a particular person can be compared with similar profiles obtained from individuals about whom a great deal is known (Figure 4–1B). The resulting personality assessment is more than the sum of the individual's MMPI scores. This larger assessment can then be examined against inferences from other sources of information that the clinician has obtained, with the goal of noting consistencies and reconciling inconsistencies (Korchin, 1976).

TABLE 4–1

PERSONALITY CHARACTERISTICS ASSOCIATED WITH ELEVATIONS ON THE BASIC MMPI SCALES

Scale	Characteristics
1 (Hs), Hypochondriasis	High scorers are described as cynical, defeatist, preoccupied with self, complaining, hostile, and presenting numerous physical problems.
2 (D), Depression	High scorers are described as moody, shy, despondent, pessimistic, and distressed. This scale is one of the most frequently elevated in clinical patients.
3 (Hy), Hysteria	High scorers tend to be repressed, dependent, naive, outgoing, and to have multiple physical complaints. They express psychological conflict through vague and unbased physical complaints.
4 (Pd), Psychopathic Deviate	High scorers often are rebellious, impulsive, hedonistic, and antisocial. They often have difficulty in marital or family relationships and trouble with the law or authority in general.
5 (MF), Masculinity-Femininity	High-scoring males are described as sensitive, aesthetic, passive, or feminine. High-scoring females are described as aggressive, rebellious, and unrealistic.
6 (Pa), Paranoia	Elevations on this scale are often associated with being suspicious, aloof, shrewd, guarded, worrisome, and overly sensitive. High scorers may project or externalize blame.
7 (Pt), Psychasthenia	High scorers are tense, anxious, ruminative, preoccupied, obsessional, phobic, rigid. They frequently are self-condemning and feel inferior and inadequate.
8 (Sc), Schizophrenia	High scorers are often withdrawn, shy, unusual, or strange and have peculiar thoughts or ideas. They may have poor reality contact and in severe cases bizarre sensory experiences—delusions and hallucinations.
9 (Ma), Mania	High scorers are called sociable, outgoing, impulsive, overly energetic, optimistic, and in some cases amoral, flighty, confused, disoriented.
10 (Si), Social Introversion-Extraversion	High scorers tend to be modest, shy, withdrawn, self-effacing, inhibited. Low scorers are outgoing, spontaneous, sociable, confident.

SOURCE: Butcher, 1969.

FIGURE 4-1

THE MINNESOTA MULTIPHASIC PERSONALITY INVENTORY

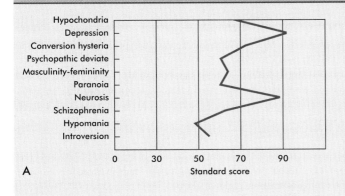

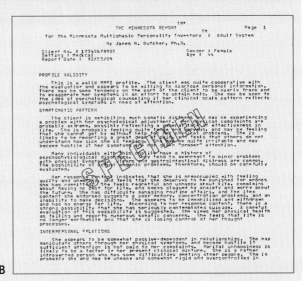

(A) An example of an MMPI profile. (B) An "automated" interpretation provided by a computer. The computer prints out statements that have been found to have some validity for other individuals with similar profiles. (SOURCES: Gleitman, 1981; NCS Interpretive Scoring Systems)

The MMPI is more than fifty years old. Times change. Language changes. And tests may need to change to accommodate to new circumstances and new ways of describing individuals in those changed times. The MMPI-2 was designed to do precisely that. It modernized language, changing such phrases as "acid stomach" to "upset stomach." And it attempted to assess modern psychological concerns, such as vulnerability to drug abuse and eating disorders, as well as poor adaptation to work (Butcher, Dahlstrom, Graham, Tellegen, and Kraemer, 1989; Greene, 1991).

Opinion regarding the MMPI-2 is divided. Many clinicians obviously appreciate the modernization, as well as the fact that it was standardized on a larger and more representative sample than was the MMPI. But others find the new test significantly flawed, perhaps irremediably so. For example, although the standardization sample for MMPI-2 is larger and more representative than for the original MMPI, it is still biased in the direction of respondents who have more education and higher professional achievements than the population at large. More significantly, it seems that the two versions of the MMPI can be inconsistent with each other on some occasions. One can get a score on one version that indicates substantial depression, and a score on the other that is quite within normal range. Finally, it appears that the enormous amount of detail in the form of "profiles" that has been accumulated on the MMPI for more than half a century will be inapplicable to the revised version—surely a major loss (Adler, 1989).

PROJECTIVE TESTS

For many psychologists, and especially those who are psychodynamically oriented, the focus of assessment is on unconscious conflicts, latent fears, sexual and aggressive impulses, and hidden anxieties. Structured inventories, because they inquire about *conscious* experience and feelings, obscure these deeper dynamics. But because **projective tests** utilize meaningless stimuli, such as inkblot forms, they minimize reality constraints, encourage imaginative processes, and maximize the opportunity for conflictual or unconscious concerns to emerge (Murray, 1951). Two of the most widely used projective tests are the Rorschach Test and the Thematic Apperception Test.

The Rorschach Test   Invented by Hermann Rorschach (1884–1922), a Swiss psychiatrist, the *Rorschach Test* consists of ten bilaterally symmetrical "inkblots," some in color, some in black, gray, and white, and each on an individual card. The respondent is shown each card separately and asked to tell the examiner everything she sees on the card, that is, everything the inkblot could resemble. Figure 4–2 shows two inkblots that are similar to such cards.

Here are the responses made by one person to the card on the left (Exner, 1978, p. 170):

PATIENT: I think it could be a woman standing in the middle there. . . . Should I try to find something else?
EXAMINER: Most people see more than one thing.
PATIENT: I suppose the entire thing could be a butterfly. . . . I don't see anything else.

Responses to these inkblots are scored in several ways. First, they are scored for the nature and quality of what has been seen. In this instance, the woman and the butterfly are well-formed percepts, indicative of someone whose view of the world is relatively clear. Second, whether the percept is commonly seen by others, or relatively rare (and if rare, whether creative or bizarre) is scored. Seeing a woman and a butterfly on this blot is a common occurrence. It suggests that this person is capable of seeing the world as others do. Additional scoring will examine whether the entire blot or only part of it was used, and whether color is used and integrated into the percept. These scores, as well as what is seen in the blot, are integrated to give an overall picture of the vitality of the respondent's inner life, his conflicts, the degree to which he can control sexual and aggressive urges, and the like.

Perusal of the inkblot on the left in Figure 4–2 will give some sense of the thinking that goes into Rorschach interpretation. Imagine someone who has responded to the bits of ink that surround the central percept, but who failed to respond to the main part of the blot. You might hypothesize (and it is *only* a hypothesis) that this individual has difficulty confronting "central" realities and perhaps, as a result, turns her attention to trivia, as if *they* were central. Using the responses to a single blot, of course, would be merely one clue to an individual's personality. There might, for example, be something about the central percept of this particular card that the respondent finds aversive. If so, the response would indicate little about generalized tendencies to avoid centralities. If, however, such responses occurred on several cards—if on each of them the respondent "missed" the central percept and

FIGURE 4–2

THE RORSCHACH TEST

Facsimiles of Rorschach Test cards. These projective instruments are composed of stimuli that seem like inkblots and that allow the respondent to project impressions of what those inkblots might be. (SOURCE: Gleitman, 1981, p. 635)

FIGURE 4–3

TAT pictures, such as this one, are designed to be sufficiently vague to allow respondents to project their own meaningful story onto it. (SOURCE: Gleitman, 1981, p. 685)

puttered about at the edges, an examiner might feel that the hunch was well-substantiated. This is the kind of thinking that is used to examine the use of color, of forms, of the popularity of the percept, and so on. A test record that reveals only commonly given percepts might be judged to be behaviorally conformist and cognitively banal, especially if all other indices are consistent with that view.

Interpreting the Rorschach requires enormous skill. It is a fascinating and complex process. But it is not without its hazards. Precisely because the interpretive logic is so compelling, there is a strong tendency to believe in it without validation, and to disregard contrary evidence.

The conflict between intuition (or common sense) on the one hand and validated data on the other pervades assessment, as it pervades psychological judgment in general. Time and again, it will seem to clinicians that a certain sign makes sense as an indicator of a larger behavior, so much so that it hardly seems worth the effort to assess the validity of the sign empirically. And time and again, when that assessment *is* made, it will be found that the correlation between sign and indicator is *illusory* (Chapman and Chapman, 1969), based merely on a commonly held view and not on reality.

As might be expected with an instrument that is so complex and that is predicated on ambiguity, neither the reliability nor the validity of the Rorschach has been high. Reliability of scoring is low despite the variety of manuals that are available to assist the clinician (e.g., Aronow and Reznikoff, 1976; Exner, 1993; Exner and Weiner, 1994; Wood, Nezworski, and Stejskal, 1996a, 1996b). One attempt to objectify and standardize scoring has resulted in another set of inkblots (Holtzman, 1961; Hill, 1972), which has been used mainly in research rather than in clinical practice.

Thematic Apperception Test   Another commonly used instrument is the ***Thematic Apperception Test,*** or the ***TAT*** (see Figure 4–3). It consists of a series of pictures that are not as ambiguous as Rorschach cards, but not as clear as photographs either. Respondents are asked to look at each picture and to make up a story about it. They are told to tell how the story began, what is happening now, and how it will end. As with the Rorschach, it is assumed that because the pictures are ambiguous, the stories will reflect the respondent's proclivity to see situations in a particular way. A respondent who repeatedly uses the same theme to describe several different pictures may be revealing personal psychodynamics (Bellak and Abrams, 1993).

The TAT has been used extensively as a research instrument to explore a variety of motives, particularly the need for achievement (McClelland et al., 1953; Atkinson, 1992). Its use in that context has been fruitful and provocative. But its use as a clinical instrument for assessing individual personality is prey to the same problems that beset the Rorschach. Although reliability of scoring is adequate (Harrison, 1965), the interpretations of TAT protocols by different clinicians is quite diverse (Murstein, 1965).

INTELLIGENCE TESTS

Perhaps the most reliable and, for many purposes, the most valid of all psychological tests are those that measure intelligence. Originally designed by Alfred Binet to differentiate "slow" schoolchildren from those who were mentally retarded, the test underwent many revisions, culminating in the Stanford-Binet Intelligence Test for Children. Somewhat later, David Wechsler standardized individually administered intelligence tests for both adults and children. These tests include the Wechsler Adult Intelligence Scale (WAIS), the Wechsler Intelligence Scale for Children (WISC), and the Wechsler Preschool and Primary Scale of Intelligence (WPPSI). The WAIS was revised and restandardized as the Wechsler Adult Intelligence Scale—Revised

"WE REALIZE YOU DO BETTER ON YOUR IQ TESTS THAN YOU DO IN ANYTHING ELSE, BUT YOU JUST CANNOT MAJOR IN IQ."

(WAIS-R) in 1981 to eliminate or modify items that were considered unfair to minority groups (Mishra and Brown, 1983), to update the test content, and to provide new norms. While there are high correlations between the WAIS and the WAIS-R, the overall scores on the latter tend to be substantially *lower* than those on the former (Urbina, Golden, and Ariel, 1982; Lippold and Claiborn, 1983; Mishra and Brown, 1983).

The Wechsler Scales provide a total IQ (Intelligence Quotient) which is composed of two subscores: Verbal IQ and Performance IQ. Verbal IQ comprises such matters as vocabulary, ability to comprehend verbal statements and problems, and general information. Performance IQ measures intelligence in ways that are less dependent upon verbal ability, such as the ability to copy designs and to associate symbols with numbers.

Intelligence tests play an important role in assessing mental retardation and brain damage. Moreover, they are the only psychological tests that are routinely administered to schoolchildren and that determine, in some measure, the kind of education that children will obtain. It is important, therefore, to understand what intelligence tests actually measure.

Intelligence itself is not directly knowable. It can only be inferred from behavior. Intelligence tests sample behaviors on certain standardized tasks, particularly those that predict success in school. Other behaviors, like the ability to make it "on the street" or the ability to appreciate classical music, are simply not measured. For that reason, intelligence has often been defined as what an intelligence test measures. That is not quite a satisfying definition, but it is accurate. If one's working definition of intelligence differs from the one that is implicit in a particular intelligence test, one should not be surprised that the test score fails to meet expectations. An intelligence test that measures verbal facility will not predict ability on psychomotor tasks well.

Observations

The assessment techniques reviewed so far—the interview, the standardized and projective tests, the intelligence test—have had one thing in common: all of them are verbal and all of them use words to portray psychological assets and liabilities. But words are often imprecise. Often they overstate the matter. Depressed people are wont to say that "My life is just miserable all the time," an expression that conveys the full sense of their feelings right now, but no sense at all of what the problem is, how often it occurs, and how to begin working on it. In marital conflict, for example, the following complaints are not uncommon.

HE: She never has a meal on the table on time.
SHE: He never takes me out.

Both clearly believe what they are saying, and their beliefs amplify their anger with each other. The beliefs, however, are false. When they begin to take notice of actual *behavior*, rather than accusations, they find that most (but not all) of the meals are on the table on time, and they go out with some frequency (but not as often as she would like). Already the gap between them has narrowed, creating a smaller disagreement out of what seemed to be a major conflict.

BEHAVIORAL ASSESSMENT

Behavioral assessment is commonly used in conjunction with treatment itself: to define the problem, to narrow it, to provide a record of what needs to be changed, and subsequently, of what progress has been made. The assessment does not stand apart from the treatment, nor is it an evaluation of the client for the therapist's use only. It is rather part and parcel of the treatment, a procedure of interest to both client and therapist, and one in which they fully share.

Behavioral assessment consists in keeping as accurate a record as possible of the behaviors and thoughts one wishes to change: when they occur (incidence), how long they last (duration), and where possible, how intense they are. A person might report, for example, that she becomes nervous when she has to speak in public. If a fairly precise measure of how nervous she becomes were required, she could be asked to deliver a speech publicly (Paul, 1966). One could then record, in good detail, not only how anxious she was—in blocks of thirty seconds throughout her speech—but what forms the anxiety took (e.g., trembling knees, rigid arms, lack of eye contact, quivering voice, flushed or pale face).

Behavioral assessment can also be done by clients themselves. People who desire to give up smoking are commonly asked to begin by recording when and under what conditions they smoke each cigarette. People who desire to lose weight are asked to record when, where, how much, and under what conditions they eat. Assessments by clients are not only useful for overt behaviors, but for private thoughts as well. Mahoney (1971), for example, asked a client to record each time she had a self-critical thought. Her record became the basis for evaluating whether subsequent interventions had any effect.

Sometimes behavioral assessment reveals causes for distress of which the respondent was unaware and that were not elicited in the interview (Mariotto, Paul, and Licht, 1995). Metcalfe (1956; cited in Mischel, 1976) asked a patient who was hospitalized for asthma but free to take leave from the hospital to keep a careful record of the incidence, duration, and the events surrounding her asthma attacks. Attacks occurred on fifteen of the eighty-five days during which records were kept. Nine of the attacks occurred after contact with her mother. Moreover, on 80 percent of the days in which she had no asthma attacks, she also had had no contact with her mother. But while "contact with mother" seemed to be a source of the attacks, attempts to induce an attack by *discussing* her mother during an interview, or by presenting the patient with mother-relevant TAT cards, were unsuccessful.

Because words, as symbols of experience, sometimes do not elicit the behaviors that the direct experiences themselves produce, interviews that rely heavily on words often fail to be fully diagnostic.

While behavioral assessment has clear advantages, it cannot be used with every psychological problem. Sometimes, tracking behavior in the required detail is simply too costly or time-consuming. Often, when the tracking is done by the client alone, the assessment fails for lack of motivation or precision. Finally, there are situations in which behavioral assessment may not work well: covert behaviors such as thoughts and feelings are not as amenable to reliable assessments as are overt behaviors.

PSYCHOPHYSIOLOGICAL ASSESSMENT

Some abnormal psychological states are reflected in physiological ones, while others grow directly out of physiological disorder. Careful diagnosis and treatment of abnormality therefore often require psychophysiological assessment, which has become increasingly sophisticated during the past decade. The treatment of physical tension has been enhanced by using psychophysiological assessment.

Anxiety, fear, and tension often have physiological correlates. When people are anxious, they may feel it in their muscles or in the way they breathe or perspire. Psychophysiological assessment not only confirms whether there is a physiological component to the anxiety, but how intense that component is, and whether treatment affects it. Indeed, some treatments can actually be pegged to psychophysiological changes. In a process called *biofeedback,* a client can be made attentive to small psychophysiological changes, and to the psychological states that bring them about. Tension headaches often arise from contraction of some of the facial muscles. During biofeedback, those contractions can be directly measured through the use of an *electromyagraph* (EMG) and communicated to the client. As the client is trained to relax, he can immediately see the effects of that relaxation on the EMG, and he can gradually eliminate muscle tension and headache by using the techniques he has learned (Budzynski, Stoyva, Adler, and Mullaney, 1973).

NEUROPSYCHOLOGICAL TESTING

Needless to say, the brain is exceedingly complex. Much of it remains to be mapped. But increasingly, we are able to see damage in certain parts of the brain that affect thought and behavior. Neuropsychological tests assess damage in the brain that appears to implicate thought and behavior. There are many widely used neuropsychological tests that attempt to fathom those kinds of difficulties, three of which will be discussed here.

▶ This client is being tested for psychophysiological changes through the use of an electromyagraph.

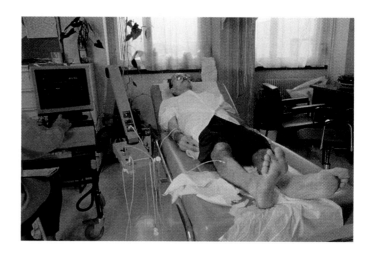

FIGURE 4–4

THE BENDER VISUAL-MOTOR GESTALT TEST

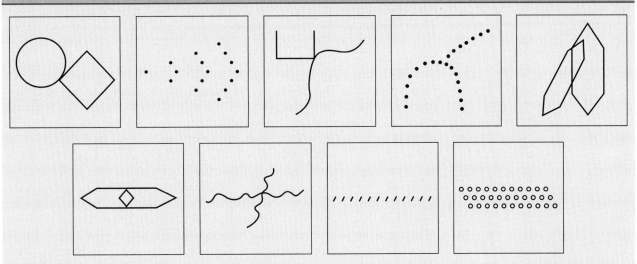

On the Bender Visual-Motor Gestalt Test, nine cards, each of which has a different design, are presented to clients. The clients must copy the designs and then draw them from memory.

The Bender Visual-Motor Gestalt Test   This is one of the oldest and most widely used neuropsychological tests, perhaps because it is also the simplest to administer. Consisting of nine cards, each of which shows a design, the client is asked first to copy the design, and then to draw those designs from memory (Figure 4–4). Errors either in direct reproduction or in recall may well reflect neurological impairment. The emphasis here is on the possibility that test results *may* reflect disorder, for difficulties on the test may arise from multiple sources, not all of which are neurological. Thus, a tremor that shows itself in an inability to draw a straight line or to copy small circles may indeed arise from brain impairment. But it may also arise from simple "test nervousness." Good examiners will be sensitive to the difference.

The Halstead-Reitan Neuropsychological Battery   One wants to know not only whether a person is "neurologically impaired," but if so, what the nature of the impairment is, and where it is located. The Halstead-Reitan (Reitan and Davison, 1974) enables intelligent speculation about the location of the neurological deficit. The test assesses, among other capacities, an individual's ability:

- to categorize a variety of items as either similar or different;
- to place blocks quickly into slots on a board, while blindfolded;
- to detect whether the rhythm of pairs of sounds is similar or different;
- to tap rapidly on a small lever;
- to grasp vigorously a "dynamometer," which measures strength of grip;
- to identify correctly aurally transmitted "nonsense" words.

Serious deficiencies in the ability to categorize often point to gross brain damage, while deficiencies in the ability to grasp the dynamometer sometimes point to the area in the brain that contains the lesion. Equally important, the Halstead-Reitan provides very useful information about cognitive and motor repertoires, information that is often overlooked in standard psychological examinations (Hartlage, Asken, and Hornsby, 1987).

The Halstead-Reitan, however, is a very time-consuming test, requiring as many as six hours to administer. It consists of six simple subtests, as well as a variety of optional tests, the scores on which are interpreted in light of what is presently known about brain structures, thought, and behavior. The administration time, as well as the scoring effort, has spurred the use of a different approach—the Luria-Nebraska tests.

Luria-Nebraska Neuropsychological Battery　Based on the work of the eminent Russian psychologist, Alexander Luria (1902–1977), this 269-item battery provides information about a broad spectrum of psychological functions. Among the data that emerge from such an examination are information about tactile and kinesthetic skills, verbal and spatial skills, fine and complex motor coordination, writing, reading, speech, and arithmetic skills, as well as intellectual and memory processes. The patterns of scores across the entire test are thought to reveal impairments in various parts of the brain (Golden, Hammeke, and Puriosch, 1980). A children's version of the test permits diagnosis of brain disorders among children from ages eight to twelve (Golden, 1981). One virtue of the test lies in the fact that it takes less time to administer than the Halstead-Reitan. Psychologists believe that the Luria-Nebraska is able to detect effects of brain damage that are not yet discernible on neurological examination. Finally, the Luria-Nebraska permits control for level of education, such that a person who is less educated does not receive a lower score simply because of that fact (Brickman, McManus, Grapentine, and Alessi, 1984).

SCANNING THE BRAIN

As you saw in Chapter 2, perhaps the most exciting assessment possibilities arise from recent technological innovations in **brain imaging.** These advances in capturing the way the brain looks and functions are likely to have obvious and important implications for the study of abnormality. Among the most promising at present are three such techniques.

Computerized Axial Tomography　Known as the **CAT** (or **CT**) **scan,** it relies on X-ray technology, sending a moving beam of X-rays across the brain. The beam is captured on the other side of the skull by an X-ray detector that measures the amount of radioactivity that penetrates through the brain. Differences in radioactivity reflect differences in tissue density. Information so obtained is computerized, generating a detailed two-dimensional view of a cross-section of the brain. By moving the beam around the patient's head, the machine scans yet another cross-section, ultimately generating images that show the locations of blood clots, tumors, and/or enlarged areas of the brain. Depending upon their location, those abnormalities could affect a person's emotions and/or behavior.

Positron Emission Tomography　The **PET scan** relies on the movement of radioisotopic substances that have been injected into the bloodstream. These substances emit particles that are called positrons. When the positrons arrive in the brain, they are detected by the electrons emitted by the scanner. Millions of such detections systematically occur and are recorded by a computer, which in turn converts them into a motion picture of the brain. These moving images can detect malignant and nonmalignant tumors in the brain, as well as the sites of damage from strokes or other injuries. Because the PET scan provides pictures of the brain *in motion*, it is a useful instrument for locating mental *processes*. Thus, because positron-carrying blood is conveyed to the areas of the brain in which there is heightened activity, one ought to be able to establish the locus in the brain for each of a variety of normal and disordered mental functions.

Magnetic Resonance Imaging (MRI) The newest of the computer-based recorders of brain and brain activity, **MRI** does not require radioactive substances injected into the bloodstream, and nevertheless produces pictures of very high quality. It does so by creating a magnetic field that organizes the hydrogen atoms in particular organs. When the magnet is shut down, those atoms return to their normal place, thereby creating a signal that is read by the scanner. Such signals are translated by computer into pictures of the brain. Because of the quality of MRI pictures, and the noninvasiveness of the technique, MRI is gradually replacing CAT scans as the technology of choice for brain assessment. In addition to providing information on the sites of tumors, lesions, and strokes, in the future it is likely to provide insight into mental processes involved in behavior, thought, and emotion.

DIAGNOSIS

The first hallmark of a good assessment instrument—whether it is a structured or unstructured interview, an objective or projective test, or a behavioral rating system—is its **reliability.** Will two skilled users obtain the same findings? And provided nothing changes, will the test impressions obtained at one time be similar to those obtained at a later date? These are the first issues with which one is concerned. But they are not the only issues. Equally important are the purposes for which the test is being used. The purpose of assessment is to understand people, and one form of understanding is categorization, or **diagnosis.** We turn now to an examination of the reasons for, and nature of, diagnosis.

Reasons for Diagnosis

FOCUS QUESTIONS

1. Give the five reasons why we diagnose.
2. What are the *Diagnostic and Statistical Manuals?*
3. How did DSM-II differ from DSM-III?
4. Describe the five axes on DSM-IV and why each individual is diagnosed on each of these axes.

Properly executed, diagnosis is a long and complicated procedure. What does one gain from careful diagnosis? There are five important reasons to make a diagnosis: (1) diagnosis is a communication shorthand, (2) it tells something about treatment, (3) it may communicate etiology, (4) it aids scientific investigations, and (5) it allows those who provide service to be paid for those services by third parties.

COMMUNICATION SHORTHAND

As we will shortly see, troubled people often have a host of symptoms. They may, for example, have trouble keeping their thoughts straight, often feel that people are out to get them, be unable to go to work, feel tense all the time, and have visual hallucinations. And they may be troubled by each of these symptoms simultaneously. A single diagnosis, in this case paranoid schizophrenia, incorporates all of these symptoms. Rather than going down an endless list of troubles, the diagnostician can merely indicate the **syndrome** (that is, the collection of symptoms that run together) in the single phrase: paranoid schizophrenia.

TREATMENT POSSIBILITIES

There is an ever-increasing fund of treatments available for psychological distress, and most are specific to certain disorders. Diagnosis enables the clinician to concentrate on the handful of treatments that might be useful in particular situations. Paranoid schizophrenia, for example, does not yield readily to verbal psychotherapies, nor is it effectively treated by Valium. But paranoid schizophrenics often respond well to a drug called chlorpromazine. A good diagnosis, then, suggests a small number of treatments that might alleviate the symptoms.

ETIOLOGY

People's problems arise from an infinity of sources, but certain problems are more reliably associated with particular causes or etiologies. For example, psychodynamic theorists believe that anxiety arises from poorly repressed conflicts and wishes. Knowing the diagnosis may tell something about the underlying cause.

AID TO SCIENTIFIC INVESTIGATIONS

Perhaps the main reason for psychological diagnosis is not clinical, but rather *scientific*. Abnormal psychology and psychiatry are developing sciences that have yet to discover all the causes and cures of human misery. By grouping together people with like symptoms, diagnosis allows psychological investigators to learn what those symptoms have in common by way of etiology and treatment. Indeed, for a developing science, this may be the single most important function of diagnosis.

ENABLING THIRD-PARTY PAYMENTS

The care and treatment of those with psychological disorders is funded mainly by third-party payers—insurance companies, Medicare, and the like. Those institutions that pay require patient diagnoses in order to be certain that the patient truly required care and occasionally to ascertain the quality of the care. Diagnosis, then, is essential for the economics of psychological treatment.

The Diagnostic and Statistical Manuals (DSM)

In 1952, the *Diagnostic and Statistical Manual of Mental Disorders* (DSM), a system of classification specifically designed to diagnose psychological problems, was developed in the United States. Approved by the American Psychiatric Association, it was refined and ultimately replaced by DSM-II in 1968. The diagnostic categories in DSM-II were premised on psychoanalytic theory, and the diagnoses that arose from that system were heavily influenced by *inferred traits*. The diagnoses that were made using DSM-II were problematical; when asked to diagnose a troubled person, diagnosticians had great difficulty agreeing with each other, and often they agreed no more than they would have by chance (Beck et al., 1962; Rosenhan, 1975; Spitzer, 1975). As a result of these concerns, DSM-III was published in 1980. The diagnostic categories in DSM-III were directly descriptive of *behaviors* rather than inferred traits. Moreover, the number of diagnostic categories was expanded, from fewer than one hundred in DSM-II to well over two hundred in DSM-III. Because of continuing reliability problems, however, DSM-III was replaced by DSM-III-R (for revised) in 1987. It began as an attempt to fine-tune DSM-III but ended up as a major revision. Finally, DSM-III-R was replaced by DSM-IV in 1994. While touted as being based on empirical efforts (Widiger, Frances, Pincus, Davis, and First, 1991; Blashfield and Livesley, 1991), well-informed authorities consider that it relies mainly on expert opinion (Spitzer, 1991) and may continue to have the same problems with diagnosis as did its predecessors. In any event, DSM-IV is likely to remain the "diagnostic bible" for the coming decade.

In DSM-IV, a **mental disorder** is defined as a behavioral or psychological pattern that either has *caused* the individual distress or *disabled* the individual in one or more significant areas of functioning. One must be able to infer that there is a genuine *dysfunction*, and not merely a disturbance between the individual and society. The latter is social deviance, and social deviance is not a mental disorder.

Beyond defining mental disorder, DSM-IV seeks to provide specific and operational diagnostic criteria for each mental disorder. To a substantial extent the shortcomings of previous diagnostic systems, especially DSM-II, arose from the fact that its definitions were vague and imprecise. For example, DSM-II described a depressive episode, but left it to the diagnostician to determine what precisely an "episode" consisted of. The definition left unresolved such practical questions as: Would a one-hour depressive experience qualify? Would depression that continued for a month be considered more than a single episode? The new diagnostic system takes some of the guesswork out of diagnosis by offering sharper definitions. With regard to a major depressive episode, for example, DSM-IV states that "At least five of the following symptoms have been present during the same two-week period . . . at least one of the symptoms is either (1) depressed mood, or (2) loss of interest or pleasure . . . ," and it lists nine different symptoms. It was hoped that the use of functional definitions would contribute to the reliability of diagnosis.

DSM-IV uses multidimensional diagnostic guides rather than a single classifying statement to make a diagnosis. All told, there are five dimensions or axes that should be used, not only to classify a disorder, but to help plan treatment and predict outcome. DSM-IV provides useful information for functional diagnoses on the following axes:

- *Axis I—Clinical Syndromes.* The traditional clinical labels are included here, among them such familiar diagnostic terms as paranoid schizophrenia, major depression, and the various anxiety disorders. Also included on this axis are conditions that are *not* mental disorders but that may nevertheless require treatment. Among the latter are school, marital, and occupational problems that do not arise from psychological sources.
- *Axis II—Personality Disorders.* The personality disorders are not listed on Axis I but often accompany Axis I disorders. Axis II disorders generally begin in childhood or adolescence and persist in stable form into adulthood. Often, such disorders are overlooked by the diagnostician. Listing them as a separate axis ensures that they will be attended to. Axes I and II, then, comprise all of the psychological diagnoses.
- *Axis III—General Medical Conditions.* All medical problems that may be relevant to the psychological ones are listed here.
- *Axis IV—Psychosocial and Environmental Problems.* Included here are sources of difficulty during the past year, or anticipated difficulties such as retirement, which may be contributing to the individual's present difficulties.
- *Axis V—Global Assessment of Functioning.* The level of adaptive functioning has powerful prognostic significance, since individuals commonly return to their highest level of functioning when their psychological difficulties become less intense. The assessment on Axis V considers three areas: social relations with family and friends, occupational functioning, and use of leisure time, and is noted on a scale that runs from 1 (very low) to 100.

Information gathered along all five axes can yield greater understanding about a person's difficulty than can a simple descriptive diagnosis based on Axis I (see Box 4–1).

The first two axes classify the disorders, with the other axes helping to get a fuller picture of the person, beyond the actual symptoms. A person's

BOX 4-1

IN THE CLINICIAN'S OFFICE

DIAGNOSING WITH DSM-IV

Done properly, psychological diagnosis is a complex matter. Troubles do not commonly come neatly packaged and often enough, the same behavior or "trouble" can reflect a whole variety of "disorders." The following case is rather different from those one commonly sees: the symptoms lead clearly and inexorably to the diagnosis. It serves, therefore, as a good vehicle for understanding how diagnosis should be done with DSM-IV.

> When Peggy was sixteen, she undertook a diet to lose six unwanted pounds. The diet was successful. Friends and family pointed out how much better she looked, and she herself felt better, too. Encouraged by the compliments and her own self-perceptions, she proceeded to lose another eight pounds. Over the next two years, she continued to diet and to exercise vigorously until her weight had declined to sixty-four pounds, and she stopped menstruating. She was admitted to a hospital, treated for peptic ulcer disease, and discharged only to be readmitted some three months later to the psychiatric unit of the same hospital. During that hospitalization, her weight rose to one hundred pounds, and she was able to go off to college.
>
> College brought with it increased academic and social demands. Peggy began to diet again. Her eating habits became quite ritualized, consisting of cutting her food into very small pieces, moving those pieces around her plate, and eating very slowly. She resisted eating food with high fat content or with carbohydrates. She worried about her figure, became much more anxious generally, ultimately left school and entered the hospital again. There she underwent a behavioral treatment program, where she was expected to gain two pounds each week and was restricted to bed rest if she failed to do so. It was a difficult program for her. She was slowly guided to discuss her feelings and to actually look at herself in the mirror.

A clinician would use DSM-IV to diagnose Peggy along the five axes. In addition to the diagnosis of an eating disorder, the clinician would decide whether to give Peggy another Axis I diagnosis, whether there was an Axis II personality disorder, whether there were Axis III medical conditions, any Axis IV psychosocial and environmental problems, and finally what her Axis V global assessment of functioning would be. Here is how Peggy would be diagnosed:

Axis I Clinical Disorder: *Anorexia Nervosa, severe*

Even in diagnosing so clear a case, there are troubling ambiguities. Recall that Peggy was given to cutting her food into very small pieces before eating it. Is that an indication of an Obsessive-Compulsive Disorder, perhaps as an additional diagnosis? And, during her treatment, Peggy suffered depression and panic. Should she additionally be accorded a Mood and/or Anxiety Disorder?

Axis II Personality Disorder: *None*

While there are some indications that Peggy was dependent for her self-evaluations on her friends and family,

there was no evidence that her dependence amounted to say, a Dependent Personality Disorder.

Axis III General Medical Conditions: *Peptic Ulcer, in remission*

Not all physical disorders qualify to be mentioned on Axis III, but those that might interact with the psychological disorder surely deserve mention. In Peggy's case, her early bouts of dieting had occurred concurrently with peptic ulcers.

Axis IV Psychosocial and Environmental Problems: *None*

There is no evidence that Peggy was suffering additionally from a social, vocational, or academic difficulty.

Axis V Global Assessment of Functioning: 50 (perhaps even 20)

While Peggy is quite responsive to treatment, she is nevertheless in substantial danger. Anorexia is a serious and often life-threatening disorder.

SOURCE: Adapted from the *DSM-IV Casebook: A Learning Companion to the Diagnostic and Statistical Manual of Mental Disorders.*

medical problems as well as any psychosocial and environmental stressors will certainly affect his condition. The level of the person's global functioning will be a factor in determining how well the individual can cope with his condition and the stressors in his life. DSM-IV describes the essential and associated features of each diagnosis. It then provides the research findings about such factors as age of onset, predisposing conditions, and prevalence of each disorder. Finally, it describes the specific criteria for each category, using symptoms and their duration, that would warrant such a diagnosis. Using the various assessment measures discussed earlier in the chapter, clinicians then determine which categories of DSM-IV best describe the individual and his condition.

EVALUATING PSYCHOLOGICAL DIAGNOSES

As we mentioned earlier, assessment devices and diagnoses must be both reliable and valid to be of use to psychologists. When they are reliable, they generate the same findings on repeated use. When they are valid, they are of use for the purposes for which they were intended.

Reliability

FOCUS QUESTIONS

1. Why is it important to have inter-judge reliability of diagnoses?
2. How did the compilers of DSM-III attempt to improve the reliability of diagnoses? Were they successful?
3. What are descriptive and predictive validity?
4. What conditions may bias diagnoses?

In order to arrive at a diagnosis, psychologists must use assessment devices that will give them a true picture of a patient and his or her problems. As mentioned earlier, they use clinical interviews, psychological tests, and observation. To arrive at a valid diagnosis, the tests must be reliable. Do two psychologists arrive at the same impression on the basis of psychological tests or interviews or observations? If they do, this is held to be evidence of *inter-judge reliability.* To what extent will a test administered today yield the same results when given a week or month from now *(test-retest reliability or test stability)*? Reliability refers to the extent to which an instrument—be it a test or an observer—yields the same result in repeated trials or with different observers. When a group of psychologists examines a patient, and all arrive at the same conclusion, that conclusion is said to have *high reliability.* When, however, they cannot agree, each proffered viewpoint is considered to have *low reliability.*

As anyone who has tried to measure a floor knows, even using physical yardsticks, one rarely gets perfect reliability. There are tiny measurement differences. Depending upon the purpose of the measurement, such differences may mean a great deal or nothing at all. A difference of an eighth of an inch means little to the height of an oak, but a lot to the diameter of a diamond. So it is with psychological measurement. How reliable an instrument needs to be depends upon many things, among them the purposes for which it is being used and the consequences of small and large errors (Cronbach et al., 1972). Generally, a high degree of reliability is required when individuals are being assessed, especially when the findings are to be used for individual care and treatment rather than, say, research. The human consequences of error in diagnosis and treatment are harsh: nothing less than individual well-being is at stake. Therefore, the reliability standards are stringent. A research diagnosis, however, is tentative until it is proven useful. Little harm is done with such diagnoses (Rosenhan, 1975).

FACTORS INFLUENCING RELIABILITY

Several factors influence both inter-judge reliability and test-retest reliability. Reliability determined after separate interviews (test-retest reliability) is commonly lower than after joint interviews (inter-judge reliability). These differences may arise from several sources: actual changes in the patient's condition between the interviews (occasion variance); different information obtained by each interviewer (information variance); and the absence of cues that are sometimes inadvertently provided by one observer to another in joint interview situations (Robins, 1985; Williams, Barefoot, and Shekelle, 1985).

THE RELIABILITY OF THE *DIAGNOSTIC AND STATISTICAL MANUALS*

The earliest *Diagnostic and Statistical Manuals* were badly flawed by problems of reliability. Experienced diagnosticians using DSM-II, for example, found they could not agree with each other. In some instances inter-judge reliability was so low as to make a diagnostic category functionally useless. Indeed, Spitzer and Fleiss (1974), in a review of all the reliability studies of DSM-II, found that only three broad categories were sufficiently reliable to be clinically useful: mental retardation, alcoholism, and organic brain syndrome. These are fairly broad categories, and when diagnosticians attempted to use finer categories—to distinguish the different kinds of alcoholism or brain damage, for example—diagnostic reliability fell further.

The compilers of DSM-III hoped to change all that. By making the categories more specific and precise, and by establishing criteria both for including and excluding behaviors in a particular diagnostic category, they hoped to increase reliability substantially.

Unfortunately, the reliability studies were quite disappointing, both for the manner in which they were conducted and in their actual outcome. Practicing clinicians were asked to examine patients and to arrive at independent diagnoses. They were asked not to confer before arriving at a diagnosis, and to submit their findings to a research committee even if they disagreed diagnostically. But because colleagues confer about diagnoses quite naturally, there needed to be a mechanism in place to prevent collaborative discussion. There was none. And because colleagues are likely to be more certain of efforts about which they agree than about those where they disagree, there needed to be some way to encourage submission of discrepant diagnostic findings. Again, there was none.

DSM-III encouraged clinicians to use multiple diagnoses, both within Axis I and Axis II, and between those axes. But multiple diagnoses, of course, *increase* the likelihood of agreement between clinicians. If clinician A makes six diagnoses and clinician B makes five, the likelihood that they will agree on *one of those diagnoses* is much higher than if each had only made a single diagnosis.

Thus, reliability studies on DSM-III were "stacked" in favor of inflated reliabilities. Despite the need to know the diagnostic reliabilities of *specific* diagnoses, reliabilities were established for *clusters* or classes of diagnosis. Thus, if two clinicians arrived at quite different diagnoses—if, for example, one found "agoraphobia with panic attacks" while the other found "obsessive-compulsive disorder"—diagnostic agreement would be considered "perfect" because the diagnoses were *in the same class,* even though there was no agreement on the specific diagnosis (Kirk and Kutchins, 1992). But no one is really interested in diagnostic classes. The central issue in diagnostic reliability is the reliability of the *specific* diagnoses. And when reliabilities were ultimately computed for *specific* diagnoses, they varied from quite reliable (for such diagnoses as panic disorder, agoraphobia, and obsessive-compulsive disorder) to utterly unreliable (for the simple phobias and for generalized anxiety disorder) (Mannuzza, Fyer, Martin, Gallops, Endicott, Gorman, Liebowitz, and Klein, 1989).

What of the current *Diagnostic and Statistical Manual* (DSM-IV)? How reliable is it? The answer depends on the way reliability is examined and on the diagnostic category. Obviously when reliability is computed on the basis of agreement of two raters who work at the same site it will be much higher than when it is made by people at different sites, because it it easier for people at the same site to confer with each other. Thus, with regard to the diagnosis of major depression, reliability is quite satisfactory when two judges diagnose at the same site, but it falls precipitously when they are at separate sites (Keller et al., 1995). With regard to the diagnosis of sleep disorders, within-site reliability is at best fair, and declines to poor and worse for specific sleep difficulties (Buysse et al., 1994). So, too, were reliabilities moderate for people whose problems consisted of mixed anxiety and depression (Zinbarg et al., 1994).

Why is the general reliability of the *Diagnostic and Statistical Manuals* so disappointing? Why should experienced psychologists and psychiatrists have such difficulty in agreeing on the diagnosis they accord individuals? To a certain extent, this dilemma was anticipated in Chapter 1, where we examined "family resemblances," that is, how people determine whether two individuals are members of the same family or not. Despite the fact that there are important differences between the individuals, the fact that they nevertheless "look the same" goes a long way toward enabling a good guess about family membership—not always correct, but surely better than chance. But in the diagnostic context, the question is a harder one, requiring a more careful discrimination and analogous to asking, not whether two people are members of the same family, but whether they are *first cousins*. Nearly all diagnostic categories have much in common, as we saw in Chapter 1: pain, suffering, observer discomfort, irrationality, unpredictability, and the like—so much so that their commonalities often seem to outweigh their differences. The *specific* diagnoses, in practice, are often so close together that differentiating among them is substantially more difficult than the scientists who compiled the *Diagnostic and Statistical Manuals* imagined. Often, the *context* in which the behavior occurs is of enormous importance in deciding the meaning of behavior (Rosenhan, 1973, 1975), and context is difficult to measure in the first place, and awfully hard to capture at the clinic, in the second.

Validity

The validity of an instrument is a measure of its ultimate usefulness, whether it does what it is supposed to do. People who obtain high scores on a good test of clerical ability, for example, should perform better at clerical tasks than those who obtain low scores. With regard to systems of diagnosis such as DSM-IV, we want to know whether the diagnostic categories satisfy the central functions of clinical diagnosis. Do they facilitate communication by describing patients, and particularly by differentiating patients in one category from those in another? This is called ***descriptive validity.*** Do diagnostic categories enable one to predict the course and especially the outcome of treatment? This is called ***outcome*** or ***predictive validity*** (Blashfield and Draguns, 1976). Of course, low reliability, as we have seen, undermines validity. To the extent that clinicians cannot agree about how the diagnostic categories should be applied, the usefulness of the diagnostic system is curtailed.

DESCRIPTIVE VALIDITY

To the extent that DSM-IV resembles its forebears, its descriptive validity is problematic. Most clinicians, when told that a patient is schizophrenic, for example, do not seem to get a rich sense of how that person will think, feel, and act. This failure has less to do with their imaginations and much more to do with the way clinical categories are used. A study by Zigler and Phillips (1961) exemplifies this problem. They investigated the relationship between the symptoms that patients presented to diagnosticians and the diagnoses that were made. In all, 793 patients were diagnosed in four broad categories: neurotic, manic-depressive, character disorder, and schizophrenic. Then the symptoms that these patients experienced were examined. A person whose symptom was "depressed" was likely to be diagnosed "manic-depressive." But he or she was also just as likely to be diagnosed "neurotic." Even of those diagnosed schizophrenic, better than one-quarter were likely to be depressed. Thus, the evidence from this study strongly suggests that diagnosis does not convey the kind of information about symptoms that might allow one to differentiate one patient from the other, or to have a reliable sense of what symptoms that patient has.

Perhaps that is the way it should be. After all, diagnosis does not proceed by simply listing symptoms and hoping they will *add* up to a particular diagnosis. Rather, a diagnosis emerges from a *pattern* of symptoms and from the current state of scientific understanding of abnormality. In the realm of physical disorder, "fever" yields a different diagnosis according to whether it is accompanied by a stuffed nose, swollen glands, or acute stomach pains. Similarly, symptoms such as "depressed" and "tense" mean different things when they are accompanied by other symptoms and form different patterns. Of course, this view of the diagnostic process only underscores the fact that summary diagnoses, such as schizophrenia and personality disorder, do not convey much information about a person.

PREDICTIVE VALIDITY

Predictive validity—demonstrating that the predictions that derive from a diagnosis are borne out by subsequent events—is especially crucial since it bears directly on the kind of treatment that is selected (Robins and Helzer, 1986). A diagnostic system with good outcome or predictive validity should also tell something about the future course of the disorder, and about what gave rise to the disorder. The validity of a system depends on the questions that are asked: Will the problem respond to particular kinds of treatment? Will the individual be violent or suicidal? What kinds of early childhood experiences may bring about the disorder? These are the kinds of questions that can be answered if a diagnostic system has high predictive validity.

Predictive validity is high when a diagnosis can lead to an effective treatment for a disorder. For example, the predictive validity for "Bipolar Affective Disorder" is quite high when the disorder is treated with a drug called lithium. Here, the diagnosis performs a fine predictive function, in that a specific treatment is mandated. So, too, does "Premature Ejaculation," in that the disorder responds well to specific behavioral and social learning treatments. In these instances, the diagnosis indicates a treatment that has a high probability of succeeding. Unfortunately, in most diagnostic situations, merely having a diagnosis is of limited use. Often, the diagnosis does not dictate a particular course of treatment, nor can the outcome of particular treatments be predicted. Moreover, the diagnosis does not say much about the causes of the disorder. When much more is learned about the nature of particular forms of abnormality, we may be able to say that a particular diagnostic scheme is valid. But right now, the predictive validity of many diagnostic categories of DSM-IV is still an open question.

Conditions That Bias Diagnoses

Psychological diagnoses are not at all like medical diagnoses. In the latter, there are physical data to support the final judgment. These include fever, X-ray results, and palpation. Often surgery and an array of laboratory reports back up the diagnosis. Psychological diagnosis is quite different. No evidence of psychological disorder can be found in feces, or blood, or on X-rays. You cannot palpate psychological disorder or see its physical presence. The evidence for psychological disorder is always transient, and highly subject to a variety of social and psychological considerations. Indeed, it is often those considerations that contribute to the unreliability of diagnoses. Three of the most important influences on diagnoses are context, expectation, and source credibility.

CONTEXT

The context in which a behavior is observed can dramatically affect the meaning that is ascribed to it (Asch, 1951; Gergen, 1982). In one study, a group of people who were free from major psychological symptoms *simulated* a particularly idiosyncratic symptom to the admitting doctors at general psychiatric hospitals. The "patients" alleged that they heard a voice—nothing particularly idiosyncratic about that—and that the voice said "dull," "empty," and "thud." Now *those* particular verbalizations were quite idiosyncratic, but nothing else about these people was unusual. Indeed, they had been carefully instructed to behave as they commonly behaved, and to give truthful answers to all questions, except those that dealt with their auditory hallucinations. Had they been outside of the hospital context, their simulation would have been detected, or at least suspected. Surely someone would have indicated that this single symptom with no accompanying symptoms was strange indeed. But that did not happen in the hospitals in which these patients sought admission. Rather, they were admitted mainly with the diagnosis of schizophrenia, and they were discharged with the diagnosis of schizophrenia in remission. The fact that most patients in hospitals who hallucinate are schizophrenics created a compelling context for these "pseudopatients" to be considered schizophrenics. Although their symptoms were not those of schizophrenia, the context of the symptoms mattered more in the diagnosis than did the symptoms themselves (Rosenhan, 1973).

Not only hospital settings, but the diagnoses themselves can constitute contexts that admit certain kinds of information and interpretations, bias other kinds, and disallow still others. For example, once the pseudopatients were admitted to the hospital, they of course began to observe their surroundings carefully and to take copious notes on their observations. Patients asked them what they were writing. Soon the patients concluded that the writers were not patients at all, but rather were journalists or college professors doing a study of the hospital. It was not an especially ingenious inference for the patients to make, since the pseudopatients did in fact behave quite differently than many of the real patients did. But the staff, on the other hand, made no such inference. They too noted that the pseudopatients often wrote. "Patient engages in writing behavior," the staff recorded about a particular patient. But they interpreted his writing within the context of the diagnosis itself, viewed the writing as yet another confirming bit of psychopathology, and closed off any explanation that lay outside of the diagnostic context.

Similar findings about the effects of contexts are demonstrated in a study in which clinicians were shown a videotape of a young man talking to an older, bearded man about his feelings and experiences in various jobs (Langer and Abelson, 1974). Some of the mental health professionals were told that the young man was a job applicant, while the others were told that he was a clinical patient. After seeing the videotape, all were asked for their observations about the young man. Those who saw the "job applicant" found him "attractive and conventional looking," "candid and innovative," an "upstanding middle-class citizen type." Those who saw the "patient" described him as a "tight, defensive person," "dependent, passive-aggressive," and "frightened of his own aggressive impulses."

In this study, the different labels—"job applicant" and "patient"—created not only a context for perceiving the person but also for explaining his behavior. The therapists were asked: "What do you think might explain Mr. Smith's outlook on life? Do you think he is realistic?" Those who saw the "patient" offered such observations as "Doesn't seem to be realistic because he seems to use denial (and rationalization and intellectualization) to center his problems in situations and other people . . . seems afraid of his own drives, motives . . . outlook not based on realities of objective world." But those who saw the "job applicant" explained the identical behavior in a quite different way. "His attitudes are consistent with a large subculture in the U.S. . . . the silent majority . . . he seems fairly realistic, fairly reality oriented: recognizes injustices of large systems but doesn't seem to think that he can individually do anything to change them." Context affected evaluations of adjustment, as well as the perception of the causes of the behavior.

EXPECTATION

Whether a diagnostician is expecting to see a person in distress or a normal person may heavily influence diagnostic judgment. For example, one hospital administrator, having heard how easily the pseudopatients described earlier had been diagnosed as schizophrenic and had gained admission to a hospital, insisted that "it can't happen here." As a result, a simple study was devised (Rosenhan, 1973). The hospital was informed that sometime during the following three months, one or more pseudopatients would appear at the admissions office. During this period, each staff member—attendants, nurses, psychiatrists, and psychologists—was asked to rate each patient who sought admission or who was already on the ward, using a scale that indicated how likely it was that the patient was, in fact, a pseudopatient. More than 20 percent of the patients who were admitted for psychiatric treatment were judged, with high confidence, to be pseudopatients by at least one staff member, and nearly 10 percent were thought to be pseudopatients by two staff members. Set in the direction of finding a pseudopatient, they found many. In fact, not a single pseudopatient ever presented himself for admission—at least not from this study!

SOURCE CREDIBILITY

Psychological diagnosis is particularly vulnerable to suggestions from "unimpeachable authorities." That vulnerability is demonstrated in a study in which groups of diagnosticians heard a taped interview of a man who seemed to be going through an especially happy and vigorous period in his life (Temerlin, 1970). His work was rewarding and going well, his relationships with others were cordial and gratifying, and he was happily married and enjoyed sexual relations. He was also entirely free of the symptoms that commonly generate a psychiatric diagnosis: depression, anxiety, psychosomatic symptoms, suspiciousness, hostility, and thought disturbance. After listening to the interview, one group of diagnosticians heard a respected authority say that the man seemed neurotic but was actually "quite psychotic." Other diagnosticians heard the same authority say that the person was quite healthy. Yet others heard someone on the tape say that it was an interview for a job. The results of this study are quite dramatic. Psychologically trained diagnosticians—psychiatrists, psychologists, and clinical psychology graduate students—were highly influenced by the assertions that this man might be quite disturbed. Indeed, they were somewhat more influenced by that assertion than were untrained diagnosticians, including law students and undergradu-

▲ The power of psychological diagnosis can make it as dangerous as it is indispensable. This is a Romanian boy considered "irrecoverable" by hospital staff, a diagnosis that meant he would spend the rest of his life in these conditions.

ates. Correspondingly, when a composite group of diagnosticians (including both trained and untrained ones) was told that the individual was "healthy," their diagnoses mentioned no evidence of disturbance.

Need for Categorization and Diagnosis

Thus we see that there are problems with the reliability and validity of the current assessment devices and the present diagnostic devices and that psychological diagnosis is vulnerable to context, expectation, and source credibility effects. But can we do without diagnosis? Absolutely not. There can be no science and no advance in understanding abnormality, without somehow segregating one kind of abnormality from another. That, you recall, is what initiated the understanding and, subsequently, the cure for general paresis (see Chapter 2). Diagnosing general paresis as something quite different from other mental disorders ultimately made the treatment breakthrough possible. Without diagnosis, that advance would not have been possible. On the other hand, Jacqueline Persons (1986) criticizes diagnostic systems such as those in the *Diagnostic and Statistical Manuals* precisely because they do not lend themselves sufficiently to scientific advance. She urges a closer examination of the symptoms of distress themselves, rather than the more global diagnoses. Such an approach has a number of attractive features, not the least of which is that it is likely to augment the reliability of classification, allowing us to study important phenomena that are buried in traditional classification. Jerome Wakefield also criticizes the *Diagnostic and Statistical Manuals* (1992a, 1992b, 1993), arguing that, as currently constituted, the definition of mental disorder in the various *Diagnostic and Statistical Manuals* fails to embrace the notion of harmful dysfunction, and fails also to provide a diagnostic scheme that is likely to be valid.

We cannot live without diagnosis, but this does not mean that every diagnosis is accurate, or that every diagnostic term in DSM-IV truly reflects illness or mental disorder. The accuracy and utility of any diagnosis needs to be demonstrated. Indeed, as scientific understanding progresses, we come to understand which diagnoses are useful and which are not. Some diagnoses have proven usefulness and precision. They are already reliable and valid. Most, however, are promising at best. Eventually, they may shed light on the nature and treatment of particular kinds of psychological distress. Meanwhile, however, they are necessary if research is to proceed, with their utility mainly residing in their promise as *research diagnoses* (i.e., hunches that may prove useful in communicating about people and in treating them). The difference between a research and clinical diagnosis is very important; it rests on the reliability and validity of the diagnosis (Rosenhan, 1975).

DISCOVERING CAUSES AND CURES

Psychologists and psychiatrists have sought to understand abnormal and normal behavior in order to diagnose and treat abnormal behavior. They use scientific methodology to search for the *etiology,* or cause, of abnormality as well as its cure. The *clinical case* method uses case histories as a source of hypotheses about the causes and cures of abnormality, although it does not enable psychologists to isolate the causal element. Another method involves using *experimental studies,* which manipulate possible causes in order to isolate the crucial elements. One powerful form of the experimental method that examines treatments of abnormality is *outcome studies,* which are experiments in which treatments, either biological or psychological, are compared to control treatments. Three alternate methods are used when for ethical or practical reasons, experiments cannot be carried out on people who have problems with psychopathology: correlational studies, experiments of nature, and laboratory models of psychopathology. *Effectiveness studies* are correlational studies that look at how well therapies work as they are actually performed in the real world as opposed to in controlled outcome studies. When several or all of the methods converge to form a woven fabric of evidence, psychologists can have confidence that they have truly arrived at an understanding of the etiology of a given behavior.

Before we begin our examination of method, a warning is in order. Sound method is a means, not an end. The end is becoming justifiably convinced that *A* is the cause of *B*, where *A* is a past event and *B* a form of abnormality, or where *A* is a therapy and *B* the relief of abnormality. Understanding can be arrived at by any of the methods discussed here; no one of them is the only road to truth. It is easy to become a slave to method, and to forget that the study of method describes how scientists or clinicians have attained understanding in the past. The study of method does not prescribe how this must be done in the future. Great thinkers have often developed (sometimes by accident) new methods at the same time as they discovered new truths.

The Clinical Case History

FOCUS QUESTIONS

1. What are the four advantages to studying the clinical case history?
2. Describe how each of the following is a limitation of clinical case histories:
   - selectivity
   - lack of repeatability
   - lack of generality
   - insufficient evidence of causality

If we keep in mind that the end point of any method is the discovery of evidence about cause, we will see that each of the methods we examine can lead toward this end. The first, the *clinical case history,* is the record of part of the life of an individual as seen during therapy. The clinician who is observing and recording the case history can not only make informed guesses or hypotheses, but sometimes he or she can test them and discover compelling evidence as to whether he or she is right or wrong about the cause of the problem. The following case of hysterical "anniversary blindness" is such an instance:

At age fifty, Jack went completely blind. For three months, he had been unable even to distinguish light from dark. His symptoms had begun, rather suddenly, at Christmas time. An exhaustive series of eye tests revealed nothing wrong physically. Medications and several types of psychotherapy had been tried, all to no avail.

Jack was conscious of no incident that might have precipitated the blindness, and nothing in Jack's narration of his life provided a clue. At this point, his therapist formulated an hypothesis: hysterical blindness. This was indicated by the total absence of physical cause plus the absence of psychological insight (almost to the point of indifference) concerning precipitating events. If this were classical hysteria, then some event, so traumatic that it had been driven out of the patient's consciousness and repressed, should be responsible. If this were so, Jack might have access to the event under hypnosis, and reliving the trauma might bring about a cure. The therapist therefore decided to hypnotize Jack. Under hypnosis, he instructed Jack to go back to any period of his life that he could not remember when he was awake. Jack then relived an astonishing event.

Twenty-five years ago, Jack had been deeply in love. Both he and an acquaintance, Ronald, were courting Sarah in open competition. One day—it was Christmas—she confronted Jack with bad news: she was in love with Ronald and would no longer see Jack. In a state of wild jealousy, he went to Ronald and told him a tragic lie: Sarah, Jack said, was not in love with either of them, but with a third party. Ronald became extremely upset, jumped into his car, and drove off at high speed. In a frenzy of rage, he tried to race a train to a crossing, but his car was hit, and he was killed. Sarah found out soon afterward that Ronald had been killed, and she suspected that Jack was involved. Sarah made Jack come with her to the scene of the accident, and as they arrived, the wreckage was being cleared and Ronald's mangled body was being taken away by ambulance. Sarah accused Jack of being directly responsible for Ronald's death. The whole incident was described under hypnosis with extreme emotion, and Jack climaxed the narrative by sobbing out, "She made me go up and *see* what I had done; that I had killed him!"

This was the buried trauma that the therapist had guessed was there. At this point, he reassured Jack that although he had some responsibility, he had not foreseen or intended Ronald's death, that it was an accident.

At this point yet another revelation occurred: every Christmas, Sarah, who had married someone else, called Jack to remind him of what he had done. This last Christmas had been the twenty-fifth anniversary and shortly after the call, the blindness had begun. The therapist inferred that Jack could no longer bear to *see* what he had done, and the memory of both the calls and the initial trauma had been repressed.

With the trauma relived under hypnosis, the therapist told Jack that upon waking, if he wanted to see, his sight would gradually return in the next few days, which, in fact, it did. (Stinnett, 1978)

Here then is an exemplary case history. A skilled therapist is presented with a syndrome: blindness with no physical cause. He then hypothesizes that it is hysterical blindness. Drawing on his knowledge of past case histories, theory, and therapeutic technique, he tests his hypothesis by finding under hypnosis a precipitating trauma of tragic proportions. Once the trauma is relived, the blindness disappears. Under hypnosis, two missing pieces—the accident and the anniversary phone calls—fall into place, and the etiology of the blindness becomes clear.

ADVANTAGES OF THE CLINICAL CASE HISTORY

As a method of inquiry, the study of the clinical case history has four advantages. First, it is not artificial. The investigation involves an actual person who has an actual problem. The reader can easily empathize with a well-reported case and understand the connection between past events and present problems, and between therapeutic actions and the patient's improvement.

Second, the clinical case history can document a phenomenon so rare or bizarre that it probably could not be explored by other standard forms of investigation. The origin of Jack's blindness is such a phenomenon.

Third, the clinical case history is a major source of hypotheses about the etiology and cure of abnormality. At the present state of knowledge, no other method equals it in the generation of ideas and insights that can then be tested in the laboratory and the clinic. Finally, a convincing clinical case history can provide disconfirming evidence against a generally accepted hypothesis.

DISADVANTAGES OF THE CLINICAL CASE HISTORY

There are four major disadvantages to clinical case histories: selectivity of memory, lack of repeatability, lack of generality, and insufficient evidence for causality.

- *Selectivity* The reported "evidence" may be distorted because it deals with incidents in the past, often in the distant past. The patient may have an axe to grind; he may, for example, want to absolve himself of blame or, conversely, emphasize his guilt. To accomplish this, he may select the evidence that serves these purposes, magnifying trivial events or ignoring important ones. Moreover, sometimes it is the therapist, not the patient, who has the axe to grind. A therapist might believe in a particular theory, which may influence what evidence she considers relevant and what evidence she ignores.

▼ The clinical case history of Bertha Pappenheim, known as Anna O. in *Studies on Hysteria,* helped Sigmund Freud to formulate his hypotheses on hysteria.

- **Lack of Repeatability** Because case histories are real, they are not repeatable. They are often "one of a kind," making it difficult to line up several clinical cases that point to a definite cause.
- **Lack of Generality** Even a convincing case history, like Jack's, is specific to one person. Does *all* hysterical blindness begin with an unconscious wish not to see, and conversely, do *all* such wishes result in hysterical blindness? A single case history can, at best, tell us only that one such case of hysterical blindness began in this way.
- **Insufficient Evidence for Causality** Single clinical case histories only rarely convince us about etiology. In cases like Jack's, the cause was clear, but usually cause is more ambiguous. In most cases, there are several incidents, each of which might be the cause, or there is no obvious incident at all. This is the most serious problem with clinical case histories. It is simply too difficult to isolate which possible incident might always cause the disorder.

Scientific Experimentation

The grand ambition of all scientific experiments is to provide understanding by answering the question of cause. The basic experimental method is simple: (1) you make a guess (hypothesis) at the cause of an event; (2) you remove the suspected cause, and see if the event fails to occur; (3) you put the suspected cause back in and see if the event now reoccurs.

An experiment, then, consists of a procedure in which the hypothesized cause is manipulated and the occurrence of the effect is measured. The hypothesized cause, which the experimenter manipulates, is called the ***independent variable.*** The effect, which the experimenter measures, is called the ***dependent variable,*** because its occurrence depends on whether the cause precedes it. Both independent and dependent variables are operationally defined. An ***operational definition*** is the set of measurable and repeatable conditions under which a phenomenon is said to occur. So, for example, obesity can be operationally defined as being 15 percent or more above the "ideal" weight for a given height as given in a table of weights, or depression can be defined as having greater than a given score on a checklist of depressive symptoms. When manipulating an independent variable produces changes in a dependent variable, an ***experimental effect*** has been obtained. Let's consider one particular experiment.

AN EXPERIMENT ON DREAM DEPRIVATION AND DEPRESSION

Several clinical case histories about sleep deprivation came to the attention of researchers looking for cures of depression. It appeared that, in a few instances, depressed individuals who for one reason or another missed several whole nights of sleep surprisingly became less depressed. Putting this together with the fact that two antidepressant drugs, tricyclics and MAO inhibitors, incidentally reduce the amount of dreaming, investigators hypothesized that dream deprivation itself might relieve depression (Vogel, 1975).

When we dream, our eyes move rapidly back and forth beneath our closed lids. Since we can monitor when an individual is dreaming, we can deprive him of dreams by waking him up every time these signs appear. Such dream deprivation, carried out in a sleep laboratory for several nights running, was the independent variable that was manipulated in this experiment. Individuals who had been hospitalized for depression were the subjects, and the dependent variables were changes in ratings of the severity of depression on a variety of symptoms. The investigators obtained the expected experi-

FOCUS QUESTIONS

1. Describe the basic experimental method, referring to the following:
- independent variable
- dependent variable
- operational definition
- experimental group
- control group

2. Explain how the following experimental confounds might lead to mistaken conclusions:
- nonrandom assignment
- experimenter bias
- subject bias
- demand characteristics

3. What are statistical inferences and when are effects statistically significant?

4. What are misses and false alarms?

mental effect: when the depressed people were deprived of dreaming over a period of three weeks, they became markedly less depressed. But not all the depressed people improved. Only the subgroup who suffered from a specific kind of depression (called depression with melancholia; see Chapter 8) showed signs of improvement.

Can we now conclude that dream deprivation causes relief from depression? Not yet. Perhaps it was not the dream deprivation that was effective, but some other aspect of what was done to the depressed patients. For example, the patients had electrodes strapped on them, got less total sleep than normal, and slept in a laboratory. Any one of these might have been effective, rather than the specific manipulation of preventing them from dreaming.

Factors other than the independent variable that might produce an experimental effect and that occur along with the independent variable are called **confounds.** In order to eliminate such confounds, experimenters use control procedures, the most typical of which is the **control group.** In principle, a control group is a group of subjects who are similar to those in the experimental group, who experience just the confounded factors that the experimental group had but who do not experience the hypothesized cause. In contrast, the **experimental group** experiences both the confounds and the independent variable. In general, whenever there is reason to suspect that some factor confounded with the independent variable might produce the effect, groups that control for that confounding factor must be run (see Figure 4–5).

In the dream deprivation study, the investigators ran an appropriate control group, which controlled for a number of confounds. Other depressed patients were put through exactly the same procedure as above. They spent three weeks sleeping in the laboratory, electrodes were taped on them, and they were awakened the same number of times during each night as were those in the experimental group. But there was one crucial difference: the awakenings occurred, not when the patients were dreaming, but during nondreaming phases of sleep. The patients in the control group did not become less depressed. Here we can conclude that dream deprivation alleviates depression in patients who have depression with melancholia. This study is a good example of a **therapy outcome study,** in which the effects of a therapy are observed as it attempts to alleviate a disorder. Therapy outcome studies come in two varieties: **efficacy studies** in which therapy is tested under laboratory conditions, and **effectiveness studies** in which the outcome of therapy is tested as it is delivered in the field. The dream deprivation study is an efficacy study and the *Consumer Reports* study (see Box 4–3) is an effectiveness study. Such studies allow us to determine which therapies work. When both kinds of outcome studies converge, we have the best evidence for the usefulness of a therapy..

EXPERIMENTAL CONFOUNDS

A well-done experiment can allow us to determine whether *A* causes *B*. Experimenters, however, must be on their guard against a variety of subtle confounds that might actually produce the experimental effect. Common among these are *nonrandom assignment, experimenter bias, subject bias,* and *demand characteristics.*

Nonrandom Assignment   In an experiment that includes an experimental group and a control group, it is important that subjects be assigned to groups on a random basis. Such **random assignment** means that each subject should have had an equal chance of being assigned to each group. If subjects are not assigned by random selection, disastrously mistaken inferences can sometimes occur.

FIGURE 4–5

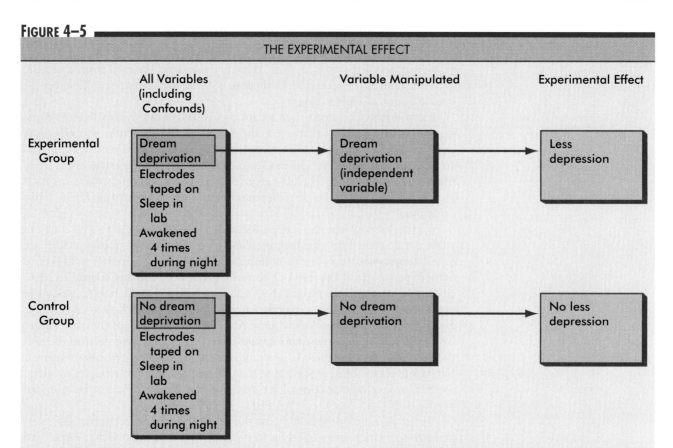

THE EXPERIMENTAL EFFECT

When manipulating an independent variable produces changes in a dependent variable, an experimental effect has been obtained. In the experiment above, the independent variable is dream deprivation, the dependent variable is depression, and the experimental effect is less depression as a result of the dream deprivation. To make sure that the experimental effect is not occurring because of the confounds (here, electrodes taped on, sleep in lab, awakened 4 times during the night), experimenters use control procedures. Control groups experience only the confounds; experimental groups experience both confounds and the hypothesized cause.

Experimenter and Subject Bias Another source of mistaken inference from experiments comes from *experimenter bias.* If an experimenter wants or expects a particular result, he can subtly influence his subjects to produce that result, sometimes without being aware of it. An even bigger problem than experimenter bias is *subject bias.* Human subjects routinely form beliefs about what they are expected to do. When someone believes that a drug that is actually useless is going to help him, he may still sometimes get better after taking the drug. For example, following major surgery, pain is frequent and severe. Yet, about 35 percent of patients report marked relief after taking a useless drug, or *placebo* (Beecher, 1959). Morphine, even in large doses, relieves pain only 75 percent of the time. We can conclude from this that suggestion probably provides some of the pain-killing benefits of morphine (Melzack, 1973). To deal with subject bias, investigators use an experimental group that receives a real drug and a control group that is given a placebo. Both groups are given identical instructions. The mere belief on the part of all subjects that any pill should work has powerful effects. For it to be considered effective, the investigators must then find the real drug to be more potent than the placebo alone.

If neither the experimenter nor the subject knows whether the subject is in the experimental or the placebo control group, the results cannot be affected by either experimenter or subject bias. This elegant design in which both subject and experimenter are "blind" as to which subjects have received a drug or placebo is called a **_double-blind experiment._** An experiment in which only the subject does not know whether he is receiving a drug or placebo is called a **_single-blind experiment._** The design in which only the experimenter is blind and the subject is not is an **_experimenter-blind design._**

Demand Characteristics   Other factors besides the independent variable may affect how subjects react in an experimental situation. Campus scuttlebutt, the advertisement to get subjects, the personality of the experimenter, the explicit statement of the instructions, implicit suggestions in the instructions, and the setting of the laboratory constitute **_demand characteristics_** that may produce an experimental effect. It may be the demand characteristic rather than the independent variable that produces a particular result.

Demand characteristics can be powerful cues that lead to grossly mistaken inferences. In the 1950s, the topic of sensory deprivation was fashionable. In studies of this phenomenon, college students were paid $20 for a twenty-four-hour day of lying on cots in darkened, sound-deadened rooms. They wore translucent goggles that made sight impossible, gloves and cuffs that made feeling impossible, and they listened to masking noise that blocked hearing (Bexton, Heron, and Scott, 1954). The investigators found that the subjects had hallucinations, and that they also felt highly stressed, nauseous, agitated, and fatigued. It was concluded that removing vision, touch, and hearing for normal human subjects produced stress-induced hallucinations.

But in reviewing these sensory deprivation experiments, Martin Orne and his associates noticed something fishy about their design. There seemed to be some powerful demand characteristics: subjects were first greeted by a doctor in a white coat; a sign "Sensory Deprivation Laboratory" was on the door; the subjects had to sign awesome release forms absolving the experimenter of responsibility should anything untoward happen; and they had a panic button that would release them from the experiment if "anything undesirable should happen." Could it be that these trappings communicated to the subject that he was expected to be stressed and perhaps to have hallucinations? This would mean that it was not the sensory deprivation but the demand characteristics that produced the experimental effect.

To test this, subjects were led into a room labeled "Memory Deprivation Laboratory," and they were greeted by a doctor in a white coat with a stethoscope. Awesome release forms were signed. Subjects were told that if the experiment proved to be too much for them, they could use the red panic button conspicuously installed in the wall of the experimental room. _No sensory deprivation whatsoever was imposed on the subjects._ Rather, they sat in a well-lighted room with two comfortable chairs, they were provided with ice water and sandwiches, and they were also given an optional task of adding numbers. In this situation, the subjects also reported stress-induced hallucinations, indicating that the demand characteristics and not the sensory deprivation may have caused the hallucinations (Orne, 1962).

STATISTICAL INFERENCE

Frequently there is room for doubt about whether an experimental manipulation really worked, even when experimental confounds have been ruled out. This is particularly true when there is an experimental and control group, each made up of several subjects. What happens when most, but not all subjects in the experimental group show an effect, and few, but not many subjects in the control group do not? How do we decide whether an effect is real, rather than due to chance?

Statistical inferences are the procedures we use to decide whether the **_sample,_** or particular observations we made, truly represents the **_population,_** or the entire set of potential observations we might have made.

▼ A subject participates in a sensory deprivation experiment. Will he have stress-induced hallucinations because of the isolation or because he _believes_ he should be having hallucinations during such an experience?

Suppose we try out a new drug therapy on a sample of ten schizophrenics, and at the end of a year, six of them recover from schizophrenia. Did the drug cure the disorder? To begin with, we need to compare the drug therapy group to a control group of schizophrenics who were given placebos. Let's say we have an excellent control group: there is a control group consisting of 100 wards, each of which contains ten schizophrenic individuals who have been given placebos and therefore are untreated. On the average, for all of these wards, three out of ten schizophrenics have recovered by the end of the year. Is the difference between six out of ten recoveries with the drug and an average of three out of ten recoveries with the placebo real? Or, could as many as six out of ten of the patients have recovered, untreated, by chance alone? If this were so, the new drug would be of little value. It is vital to decide this, for unless we can, we will not know if it is worthwhile to use the drug for the population of schizophrenics as a whole.

To decide if the difference between six out of ten and three out of ten could have occurred by chance, we need to know the **_frequency distribution_** of recoveries from ward to ward. A frequency distribution is the number of occurrences in each given class observed; in this case, the number of wards showing no recoveries, one recovery, two recoveries, and so on. This frequency distribution shows how different numbers of recoveries among the wards are distributed. We know that the **_mean,_** or total number of recoveries divided by the total number of schizophrenics, is three out of ten, but for how many of the other wards did six (or more) out of ten schizophrenics recover? With a mean of three out of ten, six could be a very infrequent occurrence. For example, if exactly three out of ten recovered in each and every ward, then six out of ten would be very unlikely to occur by chance. With a different distribution, it could be a very frequent occurrence, for example, if for 50 of the wards, six out of ten recovered, but for the other 50 wards, zero out of ten recovered. In the first case, we could be very confident that the drug produced a real effect; in the second case, we would have very little confidence that the drug worked, and we would assume that six out of ten recoveries was just a chance fluctuation in the recovery rate.

Scientists are generally quite conservative about making claims, and by convention, a real effect will be claimed only with at least 95 percent confidence that chance did not produce the result. When effects exceed this conventional confidence level, they are called **_statistically significant._**

Making inferences in this way, however, can result in two kinds of mistakes: **_misses_** (saying x is false when it is true) and **_false alarms_** (saying x is true when it is false). A miss can occur when, for example, confidence does not reach the 5 percent level: say we are only confident at the 10 percent level that the number of drug recoveries was not due to chance and so we reject the hypothesis that the drug causes recovery, and yet the drug really does cure schizophrenia. We have missed a real cure by our conservative procedure. On the other hand, a false alarm can occur when confidence does reach the 5 percent level: say we accept the hypothesis that the drug causes recovery, but this turns out to be one of the 5 percent of the wards in which six people would have recovered without treatment and the drug really does nothing. Here not being conservative enough caused us to adopt a therapy that was really ineffective.

EXPERIMENTS WITH A SINGLE SUBJECT

Most experiments involve an experimental group and a control group, each with several subjects. Several subjects, as opposed to one, increase our confidence in the causal inference made in an experiment because of two factors: (1) **_repeatability_**—the experimental manipulation is repeated and has its effect on several individuals; and (2) **_generality_**—several randomly chosen individuals, not just one, are affected, and this increases our confidence that any new individual, randomly chosen, would also be so affected.

But useful experiments can be carried out with just one subject, and a well-designed *single-subject experiment* can accomplish the goal of demonstrating repeatability. The demonstration of generality, however, always requires several subjects. An example of a single-subject experiment follows:

> Walter was a retarded ten-year-old, whose outbursts in his special education class were contagious, and therefore particularly disruptive. His teacher, in conjunction with several experimental and clinical psychologists, hypothesized that his outbursts, or "talk outs," were maintained by the teacher's attention to him when she reprimanded him, and that by ignoring the talk outs and giving attention to him for more constructive actions, the talk outs would extinguish. They designed what is called an "A-B-A-B" experiment to test this. In such a design untreated, or baseline, behavior is measured (A_1), then treatment is instituted (B_1), then there is a return to no treatment (A_2), then treatment is reinstituted (B_2). (You may notice, incidentally, that a clinical case history, like the case of Jack in which a therapeutic procedure is tried, is an A-B design: A_1, untreated, followed by B_1, treatment.)
>
> The experiment to change Walter's behavior was divided into four phases, during each of which the number of talk outs was counted. In the first five-day phase (A_1-untreated$_1$) the teacher handled the talk outs as she normally did, by reprimanding him. In the second five-day phase (B_1-treatment$_1$), the teacher ignored the talk outs and paid attention to Walter whenever he did anything constructive. The third phase (A_2-untreated$_2$) repeated the first phase: talk outs were again reprimanded. Finally, the fourth five-day phase (B_2-treatment$_2$) repeated the second phase: the talk outs were ignored, and the teacher only paid attention to him for constructive actions.

As you can see from Figure 4–6, the hypothesis proved correct. During A_1, there were about four outbursts in each session, but when contingent attention was instituted (B_1), Walter rapidly learned to produce no outbursts. The most important and convincing part of the experiments, however, were the repeated procedures, A_2 and B_2. These phases gave us evidence of

FIGURE 4–6

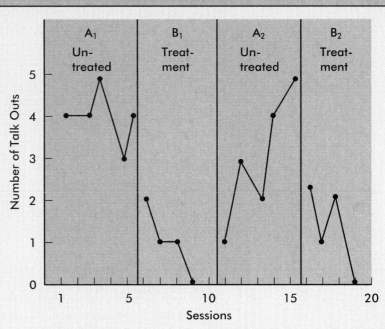

REPEATABILITY IN A SINGLE-SUBJECT EXPERIMENT

This record of talking-out behavior of a retarded student shows A_1 untreated—before experimental conditions; B_2 treatment—systematic ignoring of talking out and increased teacher attention to appropriate behavior; A_2 untreated—reinstatement of teacher attention to talking-out behavior; and B_2 treatment—return to systematic ignoring of talking out and increased attention to appropriate behavior. (SOURCE: Hall et al., 1971)

BOX 4–2 **IN THE RESEARCHER'S LABORATORY**

ETHICAL DIFFICULTIES OF EXPERIMENTATION

Very often we do not experiment for ethical reasons. In 1920, an experiment was performed on a healthy nine-month-old infant, Little Albert. Investigators experimentally instilled in him a phobia of small animals by pairing a startling loud noise with his playing with a white rat (Watson and Rayner, 1920). There are two sides to this ethical issue. Look at the experiment from Little Albert's point of view. An innocent and healthy child, with no say in the matter, was caused to be terrified of small, furry creatures. Should he have had to endure this suffering? Further, Albert was taken from the hospital by his mother, who was a wet nurse there, before curative procedures could be tried out, and he was never heard from again. Was he victimized by a lifelong phobia of rats? The moral climate has changed, and this experiment could not be undertaken today.

But now look at the Little Albert experiment from a real phobic's point of view. Forget, for a moment, Albert's suffering and the possibility that he became a phobic. As we shall see in the fear and phobia chapter, as a direct result of the Little Albert experiment, curative procedures were tried out in fearful children, experimental models of phobias were developed and refined in animals and then applied to human adults, and a cure for many phobias is now known. Thousands of phobic individuals today are free to lead normal lives because of a line of experimentation that began with Little Albert's suffering. There is a clear conflict of interest here, and it is very difficult to decide whose rights are more important: one innocent Albert made phobic through no choice of his own versus thousands of phobics who have been cured.

repeatability. By reinstituting reprimands and showing that talk outs again increased, the experimenters showed that the decrease in talk outs during treatment was unlikely to have been caused by chance; rather the high rate of outbursts probably was caused by the reprimands. Then, by reinstituting treatment and showing fewer outbursts once again, we can infer that treatment probably caused his quieter behavior rather than chance. In addition, since the two conditions (each repeated) differed only in the direction of the teacher's attention—to bad behavior or to constructive behavior—cause is isolated in the same way that a control group isolates cause in a multi-subject experiment. The control condition occurs within the same subject and therefore does not require a separate control *group*.

It could be, however, that only Walter in particular, rather than misbehaving, retarded boys in general, would improve with attention to constructive behavior. Only repeating the procedure with several subjects would show generality. When there is only one subject available, however, as in a rare disorder or unique therapy, single-subject designs are the only way of determining causality.

EVALUATION OF THE EXPERIMENTAL METHOD

The experimental method has three strengths and three weaknesses. The first strength is that it is the foremost method for isolating causal elements. Second, it is general to the population sampled, when group—as opposed to single-subject—experiments are done. Third, it is repeatable. The first weakness is that an experiment is artificial; it does not capture the full reality of a disorder. Second, inferences made are probabilistic, not certain. Finally, performing certain experiments sometimes may be unethical (see Box 4–2) or impractical. For example, a proposed experiment might be potentially dangerous to human or animal subjects, or it might simply be too expensive or time-consuming.

Correlation

Correlation is pure observation, without manipulating human or animal subjects with independent variables. An observer performing a correlation

FOCUS QUESTIONS

1. Explain the relationships between variables in the following:
   - positive correlation
   - negative correlation
   - lack of correlation
2. Explain how the relationship between two classes of events is determined.
3. When is a correlation generally considered to be statistically significant?
4. What are the advantages and disadvantages of correlational studies of abnormality?

measures two classes of events and records the relationship between them. There are three possible relationships: (1) As one increases, so does the other. This is called a ***positive correlation.*** Height, for example, correlates positively with weight, for the taller a person is, generally the more he weighs. This correlation is shown graphically in Figure 4–7A. (2) As one increases, the other decreases. This is called a ***negative correlation.*** Studying is, in general, negatively correlated with failure, for the more we study, the less likely we are to fail (Figure 4–7B). (3) As one changes, the other does not change in any systematic way. Two such events are said to be ***uncorrelated.*** Hair length is uncorrelated with failure on algebra exams, for how long our hair is, in general, makes no difference as to whether or not we fail (Figure 4–7C). The central point here is that in correlational studies, we are observers of the variables; we do not manipulate weight, height, hair length, studying, or failure. Instead, we look at the relationships among variables.

Let us now see how correlation can be applied to important issues of abnormal psychology by working through an example of a negative correlation. One investigator proposed an elegantly simple theory of human depression: that depression is caused by having too few rewards in daily life (Lewinsohn, 1975). Experimentation on this is limited by ethical considerations; we cannot take nondepressed people and withhold rewards in their daily lives to see if depression results. But we can perform relevant correlations: Does depth of depression correlate with the number of pleasant activities that different individuals engage in? The experimenter predicted a negative correlation: as pleasant activities decrease, the degree of depression increases. Both variables can be operationally defined: degree of depression by a self-report test (Beck Depression Inventory), which totals up the number and severity of mood, thought, motivational, and physical symptoms that an individual reports; and a Pleasant Events Scale, which totals up the number of pleasant events, such as going on a date, listening to music, watching TV, dancing, that the individual has recently engaged in. The predicted negative correlation has been found: the higher the degree of depression, the fewer pleasant events that have been engaged in.

CORRELATION COEFFICIENTS

The strength of the relationship between two classes of events can be expressed by a ***correlation coefficient,*** the symbol for which is r (representing the Pearson Product Moment Correlation Coefficient, which is named after its inventor, Karl Pearson). The range for r is as follows: r can be as great as

FIGURE 4–7

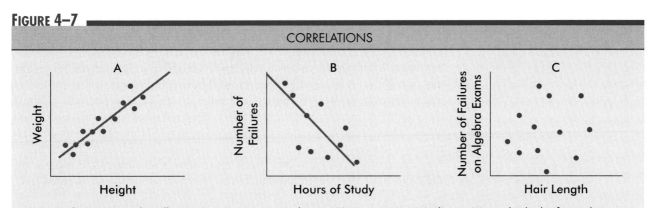

CORRELATIONS

Here are three scatterplots illustrating a positive correlation (A), a negative correlation (B), and a lack of correlation (C). The positive correlation indicates that taller individuals tend to weigh more. The negative correlation indicates that individuals who study less tend to fail more. The lack of correlation indicates no relationship between hair length and failure on algebra exams.

+1.00, for a perfect positive correlation; it can vary through 0.00, meaning no relationship at all; and it can go down to −1.00 for a perfect negative correlation. The *r* for our depression scores and pleasant activities turns out to be −.87, a strong negative correlation. The level of confidence that the relation did not occur by chance, or its ***statistical significance,*** can be determined for *r* by using logic similar to that used for deciding whether or not two groups really differ. In general, the farther the correlation coefficient is from .00, in either the positive or negative direction, and the more observations there are that contribute to the correlation, the higher is our confidence that the relationship did not occur by chance. Conventionally, the 95 percent level of confidence is chosen as statistically significant.

CORRELATION AND CAUSALITY

The main disadvantage of the correlational method as compared to the experimental method is that finding a strong correlation does not mean that we will discover a cause. There are really three causal possibilities for the negative correlation between pleasant events and depression: (1) engaging in only a few pleasant activities might cause depression; (2) depression itself might cause people to engage in fewer pleasant activities; for example, perhaps depression blunts the desire to be social; and (3) both depression and lower activity could be caused by some as yet unobserved third variable, such as some biochemical imbalance. In general, whether there is a correlation between X and Y, it can be either that X causes Y, that Y causes X, or that Z causes both X and Y.

Carrying out correlation studies, then, does not always lead us to discover cause. Correlations can, however, offer sound guidance for an investigator's next step. This next step might be further correlational studies, or it might be an experiment. For example, an experiment has actually been done to test causation for the depression example above. In this experiment, depressed students were induced to increase the number of pleasant events they engaged in each day. Depressed students who increased their activities did not become any less depressed than the control group of depressed students, who did not change their activity level; rather they became more depressed (Hammen and Glass, 1975). So the fact that activity and depression correlate negatively does not seem to reflect a causal relationship. Having few rewards probably does not cause depression, rather depression either causes individuals to engage in fewer rewarding activities, or both are caused by an unobserved third variable. We infer this because the number of pleasant activities has been experimentally manipulated, yet depression has not been alleviated.

Doing the relevant experiment is one way of determining the direction of causality that has been suggested, but not proven, by a correlation. A second way has to do with the order in which the variables occur in time. For example, positive correlations have been found between illness and the number of major life events, such as divorce and job loss, in the year preceding illness; the more life events before, the more illnesses after (Holmes and Rahe, 1967). Here, temporal sequence narrows the possibilities of cause from three to two: a hassled life could produce illness, or some third variable, like unstable personality, could produce both more illness and more life events, but the hypothesis that the illness causes the increases in life events is ruled out.

EPIDEMIOLOGICAL STUDIES

Since the advent of operational diagnostic criteria (as in DSM-III and DSM-IV), a concerted effort has taken place in the United States and Europe to determine just how much mental illness exists. These epidemiological studies represent some of the most productive uses of the correlational method. The initial purpose of these studies was practical: by determining how much of the different disorders existed, training and therapeutic resources could be allocated rationally. If there turned out to be a great deal of depression, for example, programs could be mounted to train more therapists to treat depressed patients, better antidepressant drugs could be developed, more money could be spent on research into the etiology of depression and to learn how to prevent depression.

In the best-done studies, such as the Epidemiologic Catchment Area (ECA) studies (Robins, Helzer, Weissman, et al., 1984) and the National Comorbidity Study (Kessler, McGonogle, Zhao, et al., 1994), trained diagnosticians went door-to-door to a representative sample of almost ten thousand individuals, and administered detailed structured diagnostic interviews. The disorders studied had clear operational definitions. The most important statistic they gathered was on the *lifetime prevalence* of each major disorder, the proportion of people in a sample who have ever experienced that particular disorder.

Table 4–2 presents the lifetime prevalence for the major disorders as discovered in three of the main sites of the Epidemiologic Catchment Area study. As you can see, the prevalence of mental disorder is alarmingly high—with around one-third of the people in America suffering at least one major disorder in their lifetime.

The National Comorbidity Study sampled 8,098 Americans and examined the influence of sex, race, income, education, and "urbanicity" on the various disorders. The data on relative risk were presented in "odds ratios" (OR), where 1.00 equaled no increased risk, numbers greater than 1.00 equaled increased risk, and numbers lower than 1.00 equaled decreased risk. Being female markedly increased risk for anxiety and depression, and markedly decreased risk for substance use. Being black lowered risk for anxiety and substance-use disorders. Being poor increased risk for all disorders, and living in a city increased risk for depression and substance abuse.

TABLE 4–2

LIFETIME PREVALENCE RATES (PERCENT) OF DISORDERS			
Disorders	New Haven (N = 3,058)	Baltimore (N = 3,481)	St. Louis (N = 3,004)
Any disorder	28.8	38.0	31.0
Substance use disorders	15.0	17.0	18.1
Alcohol use/dependence	11.5	13.7	15.7
Drug abuse/dependence	5.8	5.6	5.5
Schizophrenia	1.9	1.6	1.0
Affective disorders	9.5	6.1	8.0
Manic episode	1.1	0.6	1.1
Major depressive episode	6.7	3.7	5.5
Dysthymia	3.2	2.1	3.8
Anxiety/somatoform disorders	10.4	25.1	11.1
Phobia	7.8	23.3	9.4
Panic	1.4	1.4	1.5
Obsessive-compulsive	2.6	3.0	1.9
Somatization	0.1	0.1	0.1
Anorexia	0.0	0.1	0.1
Antisocial personality	2.1	2.6	3.3
Cognitive impairment (severe)	1.3	1.3	1.0

SOURCE: Robins, Helzer, Weissman, et al., 1984.

There are several advantages, and one major disadvantage, to correlational studies of abnormality. The use of correlations allows a quantitative and rigorous observation of relation between variables (see Box 4–3 to read about a sophisticated correlational study about therapy and major improvement in mental health and what specific variables produce improvement). Also, because the observations are on natural phenomena, correlational studies do not have the artificiality of laboratory studies. Further, correlational studies are an option when performing an experiment is not a possibility, whether for practical or for ethical reasons. Lastly, correlations are repeatable. On the negative side, the major disadvantage in performing correlational studies is that the cause of a particular phenomenon cannot be isolated. One can move closer to discovering the cause, but other methods, such as experimental tests, are needed to determine causation more definitively.

Experiments of Nature

Nature sometimes performs the experimental manipulation that scientists themselves could not do because of ethical or practical considerations. Sometimes a striking event occurs that changes the lives of individuals. An alert investigator can use such accidents to make inferences about what causes and cures abnormality. Such an occurrence is an *experiment of nature,* in short, a study in which the experimenter observes the effects of an unusual natural event.

An act of nature may permit us to study the effects of trauma on human behavior. We can go into villages to find survivors of earthquakes, volcano eruptions, and so on, and we can observe their behavior. Ethical considerations (if not practical ones) prevent scientists from intentionally subjecting humans to traumatic stress. But because knowledge about the effects of trauma is so important to the study of abnormality, scientists will occasionally visit the scenes of natural disasters to observe the effects of such experiments of nature. One such study looked at the effects of trauma on the survivors of a flood caused by the collapse of a dam in the Buffalo Creek area of Appalachia. For many months following the trauma, the survivors showed symptoms of terror, disturbed sleep, guilt over surviving, and reliving of the

▶ Experiments of nature are natural disasters, like the tornado that destroyed this little girl's home in Arkansas in March 1997.

Box 4-3 ━━━━━━━━━━━━━━━━━━━━━━━ **IN THE RESEARCHER'S LABORATORY**

THE CONSUMER REPORTS SURVEY

Consumer Reports (CR) included a supplementary survey about psychotherapy and drugs in one version of its 1994 annual questionnaire, along with its customary inquiries about appliances and services. CR asked readers to fill out the mental health section "if at any time over the past three years you experienced stress or other emotional problems for which you sought help from: friends, relatives, or a member of the clergy; a mental health professional like a psychologist or a psychiatrist; your family doctor; or a support group."

Twenty-six questions were asked about mental health professionals, and parallel, but less detailed, questions were asked about physicians, medications, and self-help groups. These questions included: What kind of therapist did you go to? How competent was the therapist? What was the presenting problem (e.g., general anxiety, panic, phobia, depression, low mood, alcohol or drugs, grief, weight, eating disorders, marital or sexual problems, children or family, work, stress)? What was your emotional state at the outset of therapy (from very poor to very good) and what is it now (from very poor to very good)? How frequently did you go for therapy and how long did it last? What was the cost of the therapy and was it covered by a health care plan? How much did the therapy help (from "made things a lot better" to "made things a lot worse") and in what areas (specific problem that led to therapy, relations to others, productivity, coping with stress, enjoying life more, growth and insight, self-esteem and confidence, raising low mood)? How satisfied were you with the therapy? Why did you terminate the therapy?

Twenty-two thousand readers responded to the survey. Of these, approximately 7,000 subscribers answered the mental health questions. Of these 7,000, about 3,000 had just talked to friends, relatives, or clergy; 4,100 had gone to some combination of mental health professionals, family doctors, and support groups; 1,300 had joined self-help groups; and about 1,000 had seen family physicians. Most were highly educated, predominantly middle class, had a median age of forty-six, and about half of them were women.

CR's analysts decided that no single measure of therapy effectiveness would provide useful information, and so they created a multivariate measure. This composite had three subscales consisting of: (a) specific improvement ("how much did treatment help with the specific problem that led you to therapy: made things a lot better; made things somewhat better; made no difference; made things somewhat worse; made things a lot worse; not sure"); (b) satisfaction ("overall how satisfied were you with this therapist's treatment of your problems: completely satisfied; very satisfied; fairly well satisfied; somewhat satisfied; very dissatisfied; completely dissatisfied"); and (c) global improvement (how respondents described their "overall emotional state" at the time of the survey compared to the start of treatment: "very poor: I barely managed to deal with things; fairly poor: Life was usually pretty tough for me; so-so: I had my ups and downs; quite good: I had no serious complaints; very good: Life was much the way I liked it to be"). Scores on each subscale were transformed and weighted equally on a 0–100 scale, resulting in a 0–300 scale for effectiveness. There were a number of clear-cut results, among them:

- Treatment by a mental health professional usually worked. Most respondents got a lot better. Of the 426 people who were feeling "very poor" when they began therapy, 87 percent were feeling very good, good, or at least so-so by the time of the survey. Of the 786 people who were feeling "fairly poor" at the outset, 92 percent were feeling very good, good, or so-so by the time of the survey.
- Long-term therapy produced more improvement than short-term therapy. This result was very robust, and held up over all statistical models.
- There was no difference between psychotherapy alone and psychotherapy plus medication for any disorder (very few respondents reported that they had medication with no psychotherapy at all).
- While all mental health professionals appeared to help their patients, psychologists, psychiatrists, and social workers did equally well and better than marriage counselors. Family doctors did just as well as mental health professionals in the short term, but worse in the long term. The advantages of long-term treatment by a mental health professional held not only for the specific problems, but for a variety of general functioning scores as well: ability to relate to others, coping with everyday stress, enjoying life more, personal growth and understanding, self-esteem, and confidence.
- No specific modality of psychotherapy (psychodynamic, behavioral, cognitive, feminist) did any better than any other for any problem. These results confirm the "dodo bird" hypothesis, that all forms of psychotherapy do about equally well (Luborsky, Singer, and Luborsky, 1975).

These survey results must be viewed with caution. Among the methodological problems: CR subscribers are an unusual sample of educated problem solvers and may not be representative of Americans generally. The sample might have been biased toward people who did well in therapy. The survey was self-report and retrospective without any diagnostician or therapist report, and it did not include a complete assessment battery to confirm its findings. These problems notwithstanding, the CR article finds robust benefits of long-term psychotherapy, and it pioneers observational methods of investigating the benefits of therapy.

SOURCE: Adapted from M.E.P. Seligman, The effectiveness of psychotherapy: The Consumer Reports study, *American Psychologist*, 50 (1995): 965–74.

FOCUS QUESTIONS

1. Describe some symptoms of survivors of natural disasters.
2. How are prospective longitudinal studies used to study genetic and environmental factors that may trigger schizophrenia?
3. What are the strengths and weaknesses of using experiments of nature to investigate abnormality?

events (Erikson, 1976). These symptoms characterize an anxiety disorder called "post-traumatic stress disorder" (see Chapter 5).

An experiment of nature is usually *retrospective,* with systematic observation beginning only after the precipitating event. But experiments of nature can also be *prospective,* with observation beginning before an expected outcome occurs. When prospective studies are *longitudinal* as well, looking at the same subjects on the same variables at different points over their lifetime, they are particularly powerful methods of investigation (Baltes, Reese, and Lipsitt, 1980). Consider the following prospective, longitudinal study of children vulnerable to schizophrenia by virtue of being born to a mother who was diagnosed with schizophrenia (Mednick, Parnas, and Schulsinger, 1987; Parnas, Cannon, Jacobsen, Schulsinger, Schulsinger, and Mednick, 1993). In this Copenhagen study, 207 children of schizophrenic mothers and 104 controls have been followed from 1962 until now. By 1972, 8.6 percent of the high-risk children had developed schizophrenia, but only 1 percent of the children of normal mothers. Which of the vulnerable children developed schizophrenia? Two factors emerge from this longitudinal study: (1) those high-risk children who had more traumatic births and birth complications tended to develop schizophrenia, and (2) those high-risk children who had more unstable parenting tended to develop schizophrenia.

EVALUATION OF EXPERIMENTS OF NATURE

Experiments of nature have three strengths as a method of inquiry: (1) like a case history, they document an actual happening and lack the artificiality of the laboratory experiment or the abstractness of a correlation; (2) no unethical manipulation is performed by the investigator since he merely observes an event produced by nature; and (3) the gross cause can be determined. In fact, the gross cause defines the investigation as an experiment of nature. However, the method also has three weaknesses: (1) we cannot isolate the elements in the gross cause that are active from those that are inactive; for example, we cannot know which aspects—the suddenness of the disaster or seeing others die or the uprooting of the community—of the Buffalo Creek Flood produced the stress disorder; (2) experiments of nature, as they are rare and conspicuous events, are not repeatable; and (3) like case histories, this method is also subject to retrospective bias by both victim and investigator. It is not irrelevant that the victims of the Buffalo Creek flood were suing the company that owned the dam for enormous sums.

The Laboratory Model

Correlations and experiments of nature are both used by investigators of abnormality when the road to experimentation is blocked. The final technique for getting around the impossibility of direct experimentation is the **laboratory model.** In the last decade, scientists have made considerable strides in understanding psychopathology by using such laboratory models.

A laboratory model is in essence the production, under controlled conditions, of phenomena analogous to naturally occurring mental disorders. That is, a particular symptom or constellation of symptoms is produced in miniature to test hypotheses about cause and cure. Confirmed hypotheses can then be further tested in situations outside the laboratory. Both human and animal subjects are utilized in laboratory models.

USING THE LABORATORY MODEL TO UNDERSTAND DEPRESSION

As an example of the use of the laboratory model, let us see how scientists have created an animal model of major depression. About twenty-five years

FOCUS QUESTIONS

1. Explain how scientists tested in the laboratory the hypothesis concerning the learned helplessness model of depression.
2. What are the strengths and weaknesses of the laboratory model of investigating abnormality?

ago, investigators noticed that animals who received electric shock that was *uncontrollable*—that went on and off regardless of what the animal was doing—later became very passive. Later on in a different situation, they failed even to try to escape shock that was actually escapable. They just sat and took the shock (Seligman and Maier, 1967; Maier and Seligman, 1976). Evidence soon began to accumulate that such "learned helplessness" had many of the same symptoms as depression in humans.

Learned helplessness has been systematically evaluated to find if it is a valid model of depression (Weiss, Simson, Ambrose, Webster, and Hoffman, 1985). For a person to meet the DSM-IV criteria for diagnosis of depression, at least five of these nine symptoms must be present: (1) loss of interest in usual activities, (2) weight loss and poor appetite, (3) insomnia, (4) psychomotor alterations, (5) fatigue or loss of energy, (6) diminished ability to think or attend, (7) depressed mood, (8) feelings of worthlessness, and (9) suicidal thoughts.

Animals who have experienced uncontrollable events show each of the first six symptoms. They would receive a diagnosis of depression if they were human. The last three symptoms (depressed mood, feelings of worthlessness, and suicidal thoughts) cannot be displayed by animals. But the argument can be carried further. When humans are given uncontrollable noise, they display depressed mood and feelings of worthlessness in addition to the hallmark symptoms above (Hiroto and Seligman, 1975; Abramson, 1978). This means that eight of the nine symptoms of depression can be produced in the laboratory by uncontrollable events. The ninth, suicidal thoughts, cannot be produced, but probably because the intensity of the uncontrollable events in the laboratory is very mild.

This mapping of symptoms has inspired investigators to look for the biochemical basis of learned helplessness and to discover drug treatments that cure learned helplessness in animals. The brain chemistry of those suffering from learned helplessness has been explored and looks quite similar to what is known about the brain chemistry of those suffering from depression (Weiss et al., 1985). In addition, the drugs that break up helplessness in animals also alleviate depression in humans (Sherman and Petty, 1980).

All of this seems to argue that learned helplessness in animals is a convincing laboratory model of depression in humans. This model may help us to understand the brain chemistry of human depression, to understand how drugs can relieve depression, and to find new treatments for depression. The brain chemistry and experimental drug treatment of depression cannot be ethically carried out on humans, but such animal models enable us to understand and relieve human suffering with experimental rigor and to do so with fewer ethical dilemmas (Miller, 1985).

EVALUATION OF THE LABORATORY MODEL

Laboratory models have three strengths: (1) as experiments, they can isolate the cause of the disorder; (2) they are repeatable; (3) they minimize unethical manipulation. Like all other methods, they also have several weaknesses: (1) as laboratory creations, they are not the natural phenomenon, only a *model* of it. Thus, they are *analogous* to but not identical with the real disorder itself; (2) since observers often use animal subjects in laboratory models, they must infer that humans and the species being investigated are similarly susceptible to the disorder.

As similarity of symptoms, cause, physiology, cure, and prevention mount, we become more convinced that the model is the actual disorder. In later chapters, we will see examples of models that have given insight into the cause and cure of such disorders as depression, stomach ulcers, and phobias. Sophisticated laboratory modeling is a new development in the field of

FOCUS QUESTIONS

1. Why is the best understanding of a disorder formed when all the methods of investigating abnormality converge on a theory?
2. For which disorders have the various methods converged on a theory about the disorder?

abnormality. The verdict is not entirely in on any one model, but the technique promises to add to our understanding of abnormality.

Combining Several Methods: A Woven Fabric

There is no single, most convincing way to understand abnormality. Each method has strengths and weaknesses (Table 4–3). But clinical case histories, experimental studies, correlational studies, experiments of nature, and laboratory models all can provide some insight. Each by itself can, on occasion, provide conclusive understanding. But most of the time, each taken in isolation resembles blind men groping at an elephant: one has hold of the tail, another the trunk, another a foot. Each captures only one aspect of being an elephant, but none captures the whole thing. Similarly, the clinical case, well done, best conveys the reality of a disorder, but it usually fails to isolate the cause. The experiment, well done, isolates the cause, but it remains artificial. The correlation, well done, picks out crucial relationships, but not necessarily causal ones. But when the methods together converge on a theory, a fabric of understanding is woven. In the particular disorders that we are close to understanding, case history evidence, experimental studies, correlations, experiments of nature, and laboratory models all play a role. A worthy scientific fabric of converging evidence has already been woven for phobias, for the genetics of schizophrenia, for depression, for certain kinds of brain damage, and for sexual identity. For some of the specific disorders that we will discuss in the ensuing chapters, the reader will realize that much still remains to be discovered before the disorder can be understood. For most others, the reader probably will feel that they are understood partially, but that pieces of

TABLE 4–3

	STRENGTHS AND WEAKNESSES OF VARIOUS METHODS	
Method	*Strengths*	*Weaknesses*
Single Clinical Case	1. Is not artificial. 2. Documents rare events. 3. Generates causal hypotheses.	1. Is selective and susceptible to retrospective bias. 2. Is not repeatable. 3. Is not general. 4. Does not isolate causal elements.
Experiments	1. Isolate causal elements. 2. Are general to population sampled (not true of single subject-experiments). 3. Are repeatable.	1. Are artificial; don't capture full reality of the disorder. 2. Inferences are probabilistic or statistical, rather than certain. 3. It is unethical or impractical to manipulate many crucial variables.
Correlations	1. Quantify and observe relationships. 2. Are not artificial. 3. Are repeatable.	1. Do not isolate causal elements.
Experiments of Nature	1. Are not artificial. 2. There is no unethical manipulation. 3. Isolate gross cause.	1. Do not isolate active elements of the cause. 2. Are not repeatable. 3. Are susceptible to retrospective bias.
Laboratory Models	1. Isolate causal elements. 2. Are repeatable. 3. Minimize unethical manipulation.	1. Are analogous to but not identical with the real disorder. 2. Make cross-species inferences (with animal models).

the puzzle are still missing. But for several others, the reader should feel the pleasure and excitement of discovery and understanding, because these are examples of the woven fabric.

SUMMARY

1. Personality assessment techniques may be divided into three processes: interviewing, testing, and observing. Assessment devices must be reliable and valid. *Reliability* refers to the stability of a measure, whether it yields the same findings with repeated use. *Validity* refers to how useful the device is, whether it can be used for the purposes for which it is intended.

2. The clinical interview may be structured and have standardized questions, or it may be unstructured and therefore more flexible.

3. Psychological tests fall into three categories: *psychological inventories* such as the MMPI and the MMPI-2; *projective tests,* including the Rorschach and the TAT; and *intelligence tests,* including the WAIS and the WISC. All of these are verbal tests and use words to portray psychological assets and liabilities.

4. *Behavioral assessment* is used in conjunction with treatment. It consists of a record of the patient's behavior and thoughts—their incidence, duration, and intensity.

5. *Psychophysiological assessment* attempts to link physiological states to psychological ones. *Neuropsychological testing* attempts to link neurological states to psychological ones. Some of these test batteries, such as the Luria-Nebraska and the Halstead-Reitan, assess a variety of cognitive and motor skills that have known loci in the brain. Other technologies, such as *CAT* (computerized axial tomography) scans, *PET* (positron emission tomography) scans, and *MRI* (magnetic resonance imaging), search directly in the brain for abnormalities that may be relevant to behavior.

6. *Diagnosis* is the categorization of psychological disorders according to behavioral or psychological patterns. Five reasons for making a diagnosis are: it indicates a syndrome, suggests treatments that may alleviate symptoms, suggests causes of the symptoms, is an aid to scientific investigation of symptoms, and enables third-party payments.

7. DSM-IV is a multidimensional diagnostic guide. It seeks to provide specific and operational diagnostic criteria for each mental disorder. Within DSM-IV, there are five dimensions, or axes, to classify a disorder and to help plan treatment and predict outcome.

8. When two psychologists arrive at the same assessment of a patient, there is said to be inter-judge *reliability.* The overall reliability of DSM-IV is unknown. The reliability of its progenitor, DSM-III, is only fair.

9. *Descriptive validity* refers to whether a diagnosis successfully differentiates patients in one category from those in another. *Outcome* or *predictive validity* refers to whether the diagnosis tells something about the future course of the disorder, what gave rise to the disorder, and whether the disorder will respond to treatment.

10. The accuracy and usefulness of a diagnosis may be compromised by the *context* in which it occurs and by the *expectations* and *credibility* of the diagnosticians and their informants.

11. Diagnosis and assessment are fundamental to treatment and necessary for scientific advancement. However, that does not mean that every assessment is useful or necessary. Some diagnoses may be useful for scientific purposes, but relatively useless for clinical ones.

12. The *clinical case history* is the record of part of the life of an individual as seen during therapy. Based on the patient's case history, the therapist will hypothesize about possible causes of a problem and then help the patient overcome his past.

13. A *scientific experiment* consists of a procedure in which the hypothesized cause (the *independent variable*) is manipulated and the occurrence of the effect (the *dependent variable*) is measured. Both independent and dependent variables are operationally defined. An *operational definition* is the set of measurable and repeatable conditions after which a phenomenon is said to occur. When manipulating an independent variable produces changes in a dependent variable, an *experimental effect* has been obtained.

14. *Confounds* are factors other than the independent variable that might produce an experimental effect. An *experimental group* experiences both the confounds and the hypothesized cause. The *control group* is similar to the experimental group, but the control group only experiences the confounds. Subtle confounds that might produce the experimental effect include nonrandom assignment, experimenter bias, subject bias, and demand characteristics.

15. *Statistical inferences* are the procedures used to determine whether the *sample* (the particular observations) truly represents the *population* (the entire set of potential observations). When effects exceed a conventional confidence level, they are called *statistically significant*.

16. If an hypothesis is rejected but it is really true, the mistake is called a *miss*. If an hypothesis is accepted but it is really false, the mistake is called a *false alarm*.

17. *Correlation* is pure observation without manipulation. In a correlation, two classes of events are measured and the relationship between them is recorded. In a *positive correlation*, as one variable increases, the other does too. In a *negative correlation*, as one variable increases, the other decreases. Events are *uncorrelated* when, as one variable changes, the other does not change in any systematic way.

18. A relationship is *statistically significant* if it is unlikely to have occurred by chance. Generally, the farther the correlation is from .00 in either the positive or negative direction and the more observations that are made, the higher the level of confidence and the greater the likelihood that the relationship did not occur by chance.

19. *Epidemiological* data concerning the lifetime prevalence of disorders can be used to make inferences about the etiology of the disorder as well.

20. *Experiments of nature* are studies in which the experimenter observes the effects of an unusual natural event. *Prospective longitudinal* studies are a powerful means of assessing the effects of events on the development of psychopathology.

21. In a *laboratory model*, investigators produce, under controlled conditions, phenomena that are analogous to naturally occurring mental disorders. This is done to test hypotheses about biological and psychological causes and cures of symptoms.

22. No one method alone will provide complete understanding of psychopathology. But each method may lead us to an understanding of various aspects of abnormality. When all these methods converge in confirmation of a theory, we can say that a fabric of understanding has been woven.

QUESTIONS FOR CRITICAL THINKING

1. Explain why psychological tests must be highly reliable when individuals are being assessed and diagnosed.

2. How would you design an experiment to determine if a diagnosis is being made because of a real problem or because the context suggests a particular diagnosis?

3. Why is the clinical case history method particularly susceptible to bias by patient and therapist?

4. Do you think that confidence levels for a new drug to treat schizophrenia should be set at more or less conservative levels?

CHAPTER

5

Phobia, Panic, and the Anxiety Disorders

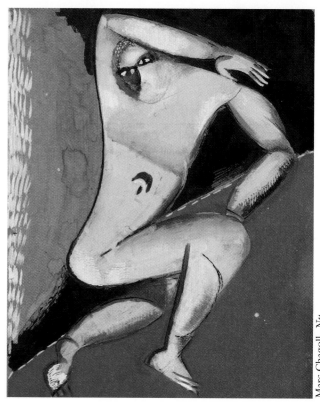

Marc Chagoll, *Nu.*

We now begin our discussion of the psychological disorders themselves. In this chapter and in Chapter 6, we discuss the disorders that were once known as the "neuroses." In this chapter, we consider the disorders in which fear and anxiety are actually felt. In Chapter 6, we will deal with the obsessive-compulsive, somatoform, and dissociative disorders, in which anxiety often is not felt, although its existence can be inferred from the individual's symptoms.

FEAR AND ANXIETY

There are five disorders in which fear and anxiety are actually felt by the individual, and these divide into two classes: the fear disorders and the anxiety disorders. Fear is distinguished from anxiety in that it is characterized by distress about a specific, dangerous object. Phobias and post-traumatic stress disorders constitute the fear disorders; in these disorders, a specified object causes the anxiety. In **phobic disorders,** the individual shows fear of an object (such as cats) which is out of all proportion to the reality of the danger that object presents. In **post-traumatic stress disorders,** the individual experiences anxiety, numbing, and repeated reliving of the trauma after experiencing an event that involves actual or threatened death or injury. For example, an undergraduate who was raped in her dormitory may subsequently relive the trauma repeatedly in memory and in her dreams, becoming numb to the world around her, avoiding men, and experiencing intense anxiety whenever she is alone with a man.

FOCUS QUESTIONS

1. Distinguish among the cognitive, somatic, emotional, and behavioral elements of fear.
2. Explain how the fear response can vary in different people and across different situations.
3. What is the difference between fear and anxiety?

Panic disorder, agoraphobia, and generalized anxiety disorder are the anxiety disorders. In these disorders, no specific object threatens the individual, yet he or she still feels very anxious. In *panic disorder,* an individual is suddenly and repeatedly overwhelmed with brief attacks of intense anxiety and terror. In *agoraphobia,* the individual fears going out to public places because he fears that he will experience a panic attack and that no one will come to his aid. In *generalized anxiety disorder,* the individual experiences pervasive anxiety and worry that can be more or less continually present for months on end.

All five of these disorders share in common a grossly exaggerated version of normal and adaptive fear that each of us has felt on many occasions. We begin our discussion of these disorders by examining what fear and anxiety are.

Fear

All of us have experienced fear. The degree of danger we encounter has to do in large part with our job, where we live, and so on. Being a member of a team responsible for constructing an oil rig in the wintry North Sea exposes one to more danger than being an accountant. But an accountant living in New York City may experience more danger than one working in De Kalb, Illinois. When the oilman experiences fear, it is directly related to the danger of his situation; his reactions will be appropriate and normal. Similarly, the accountant's heart has every reason to beat rapidly upon hearing a noise at the window at three o'clock in the morning. Normal fear and anxiety, unlike the disorders we will discuss in this chapter, are in keeping with the reality of the danger.

ELEMENTS OF FEAR

Fear may take several forms, and different elements may be involved. No two individuals need display the same elements of fear when they are afraid. Nor is there any particular element that must be present. Fear is identified according to the following logic: (1) all of the elements need not be present; (2) some of the elements must be present, although there need not be the same combination every time; (3) no one element must be present; (4) the more intense any element and the more elements present, the more confident are we in labeling the state as "fear."

When we experience danger, we undergo the various somatic and emotional changes that make up the fear response. There are four elements to

▶ The degree of danger we encounter often has to do with our jobs. Although most people would experience fear if they were close to tigers, this animal trainer does not look like he is afraid of the tigers behind him.

▶ Fear is a quickly recognizable state, as shown by Drew Barrymore in *Scream*.

the fear response: (1) cognitive elements—expectations of impending harm; (2) somatic elements—the body's emergency reaction to danger, as well as changes in our appearance; (3) emotional elements—feelings of dread and terror and panic; and (4) behavioral elements—fleeing and fighting (Lang, 1967; Rachman, 1978).

- **Cognitive elements.** These are expectations of specific impending harm, usually in the immediate future. A large doberman growls menacingly at you. You think, "He's going to bite me," and you feel a surge of fear. On a dark and lonely street, you sense a sudden movement behind you. You think, "It's a mugger," and you freeze. Notice that mental representations evoke the bodily reactions of fear (Lang, 1979; Foa and Kozak, 1986; Riskind, Moore, and Bowley, 1995; Thorpe and Salkovskis, 1995).

- **Somatic elements.** These include two classes of bodily reactions: external and internal changes. Outside, our skin becomes pale, goosebumps may form, beads of sweat appear on our forehead, the palms of our hands become clammy, our pupils dilate, our lips tremble, our muscles tense, and we show fear in our face. Inside, our body's resources are mobilized in the **emergency reaction,** wherein our heart rate increases, our spleen contracts and releases scores of red blood cells to carry more oxygen, our respiration accelerates and deepens, our air passages widen to take in more oxygen, adrenaline is secreted from the adrenal medulla into the bloodstream, the liver releases carbohydrates for use by the muscles, stomach acid is inhibited, and there is loss of bladder and sphincter control.

- **Emotional elements.** These may include a sense of dread, terror, panic, queasiness, the chills, creeping sensations, and a lump in the pit of the stomach. These elements are familiar to us because we talk about them when describing fear. We are generally more conscious of the emotional elements of fear than of our cognitions and the inner physiological workings that have been set off by fear.

- **Behavioral elements.** These include two kinds of fear behaviors: classically conditioned fear responses, which are involuntary reactions to being afraid, and instrumental responses, which are voluntary attempts to do something about the object we are afraid of.

In the world of elementary schoolchildren, bullies sometimes pick on a hapless child on his way home from school, perhaps in what was once a safe alley. After this occurs a few times, the child will become afraid when approaching the alley. He will display a number of involuntary fear reactions, like sweating and a faster heartbeat. This is an example of classical conditioning of fear. From Chapter 3, we know that classical fear conditioning takes place when a previously neutral signal is paired with a traumatic event. As a result of this pairing, the signal itself will cause fear reactions. In this case, the alley is the conditioned stimulus (CS), the encounter with the bullies is the unconditioned stimulus (US), and fear is the conditioned response (CR). Once conditioning has occurred, the signal alone causes the physiological emergency reaction to occur, profoundly changing other voluntary behavior. In our example, when the hapless child sees the alley, he will stop munching on potato chips and will cease reading his comic book.

Fleeing and fighting are the main instrumental behaviors in response to fear. There are two types of flight responses: escape and avoidance. In ***escape responding,*** the harmful event actually occurs and the subject leaves the scene. For example, the child who is being beaten up by his schoolmates will run out of the alley if given the chance. Similarly, a rat will jump across a hurdle to escape from and terminate an electric shock. In contrast, in ***avoidance responding,*** the subject will leave *before* the harmful event occurs. A signal will herald the bad event; the alley is a signal that some bullies might await the child, just as a tone might signal shock to a rat. The child will run out of the alley and take another route home, even if no bullies are beating him up. Responding to the tone, a rat will avoid the shock before it comes on, thereby preventing the shock from occurring at all. The signal, because of its previous pairing with shock (in early trials, in which the subject failed to make the avoidance response, shock occurred), produces fear, and the subject responds during the signal to remove itself from fear.

DEGREE OF FEAR

The degree of fear varies in different people and in different situations. Some people actually like to step inside a cage with a chair and whip to teach lions tricks. Lion tamers probably experience some fear, whereas most of us would be terrified. Hence, we do not go into cages. Instead, we go to the circus or the zoo. This is considered normal behavior.

There is a range of dangerous situations, as well as a range of fear responses. We accept our fear response when it is in proportion to the degree of danger in the situation. But when the fear response is out of proportion to the amount of danger, we label it abnormal, in short, a phobia. While fear is normal and a phobia is abnormal, they are both on the same continuum; they differ in degree, not in kind (see Figure 5–1).

▼ Symptoms of fear are normal or abnormal according to context. In these frightened reindeer or this firefighter, we would expect to find the somatic, emotional, cognitive, and behavioral symptoms of fear.

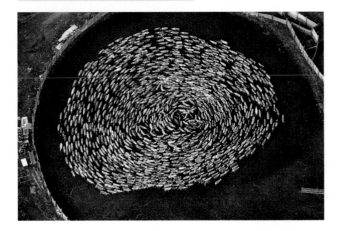

FIGURE 5–1

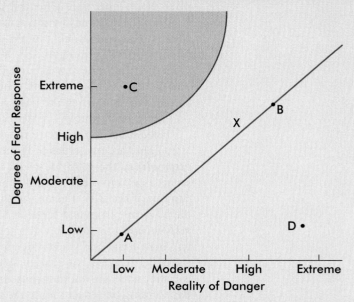

PHOBIA VERSUS NORMAL FEAR

This figure gives us a schematic way of distinguishing normal fear from a phobia. It plots the degree of the reality of the danger (as measured by societal consensus) against the degree of accompanying fear (as measured by the strength of the emergency reaction). The 45 degree line indicates normal fear. The area in red shows the phobic range. *A* plots an accountant at work, *B* plots an oil rig construction worker in the wintry North Sea. He probably feels more fear, but the level of fear is in proportion to what he should feel compared to an accountant. *C*, however, plots a phobic, whose reaction to the feared object is far out of proportion to the real danger. *D* plots decorated bomb disposers, who when placed in laboratory fear tasks, show a lack of reaction. Although these courageous individuals are in dangerous situations that would cause a high level of fear in most individuals, the bomb disposers display only a minimal emergency reaction (SOURCE: Based on Cox, Hallam, O'Connor, and Rachman, 1983).

Anxiety

Anxiety has the same four components as fear but with one crucial difference: the cognitive component of fear is the expectation of a clear and specific danger, whereas the cognitive component of anxiety is the expectation of a more diffuse danger. In phobia, a typical thought is, "A dog might bite me." In generalized anxiety disorder, in contrast, a typical thought is, "Something awful might happen to my child." The somatic component of anxiety is the same as that of fear: the elements of the emergency reaction. The emotional elements of anxiety are also the same as those of fear: dread, terror, apprehension, a lump in the pit of the stomach. Finally, the behavioral components of anxiety are also the same as those of fear: flight or fight is elicited. But the object that the afflicted individual should escape or avoid, or against which he should aggress, is less specific and sometimes shapeless. Thus, fear is based in reality, or an exaggeration of a real danger, whereas anxiety is based on a more formless danger.

We now turn to the specific disorders themselves. First, we will examine the two fear disorders: phobia and post-traumatic stress disorder. Then, we will discuss the anxiety disorders: panic disorder, agoraphobia, and generalized anxiety disorder. We begin with phobia.

A *phobia* is a persistent fear reaction that is strongly out of proportion to the reality of the danger. A cat phobic, for example, cannot even be in the same room with a house cat because of her extreme fear of cats. Although we can repeatedly tell the cat phobic that house cats rarely attack humans, the fear will persist nonetheless.

A fear reaction may interfere with a phobic's entire life. Consider the following case in which fear is so great that the woman is even afraid to leave her home:

> Anna was housebound. Six months ago, the house next door had become vacant and the grass had begun to grow long. Soon, the garden had become a rendezvous for the local cats. Now Anna was terrified that if she left her house, a cat would spring on her and attack her. Her fear of cats was of thirty years' status, having begun at age four when she remembered watching in horror as her father drowned a kitten. In spite of saying that she believed it was unlikely that her father actually did such a thing, she was haunted by fear. At the sight of a cat, she would panic and sometimes be completely overwhelmed with terror. She could think of nothing else but her fear of cats. She interpreted any unexpected movement, shadow, or noise as a cat.

FOCUS QUESTIONS

1. What is the difference between normal fear and phobia?
2. Describe the four classes of specific phobias.
3. What is a social phobia?
4. Explain how classical conditioning of fear can account for the onset and persistence of a phobia.

Anna is housebound because she is afraid that she might be attacked by a cat if she goes outside. Her fear is greatly out of proportion to the reality of the danger of actually being injured by a cat. The real danger is near zero, but her fear is extreme and irrational. Her problem is more than fear; it is a phobia.

There is little trouble diagnosing a phobia when it is present, since its symptoms are unambiguous: (1) persistent fear of a specific situation out of proportion to the reality of the danger, (2) great anxiety or even a panic attack produced by actual exposure to the situation, (3) recognition that the fear is excessive or unreasonable, (4) avoidance of the phobic situation, and (5) symptoms that are not due to another disorder (Marks, 1969; APA, 1994).

There is no question that phobias are abnormal. Many of the elements of abnormality are present. They cause the individual to suffer. They are maladaptive, since the individual's activities are greatly restricted. They are irrational, since the sense of danger is out of proportion to the reality of the danger. Phobics make others uncomfortable, and their behavior is considered socially unacceptable. Phobias are out of the individual's control, and phobics want to be rid of their fear.

Prevalence of Phobias

The most recent estimate of the prevalence of phobias puts the rate at 6.2 percent of the population with some phobic symptoms and about 1 percent of the population with severe phobias—phobias so strong that they keep the phobic housebound (Marks, 1986a; Regier, Narrow, and Rae, 1990; Fredrikson, Annas, Fischer, and Wik, 1996). *Prevalence* is defined as the percentage of population having a disorder at any given time and is contrasted with *incidence,* which is the rate of new cases of a disorder in a given time period. In clinical practice, about 5 percent of all psychiatric patients have phobias. Moreover, there may be a genetic predisposition to phobias. In seven of eight pairs of identical twins, both of the twins had phobic features, but in only five of thirteen fraternal twins did both have phobic features (Carey and Gottesman, 1981; Marks, 1986a; Neale, Walters, Eaves, Kessler, Heath, and Kendler, 1994).

Kinds of Phobias

While phobic symptoms are the same in all who suffer from phobia, the kinds of phobias vary greatly. Although there are reports of such unusual phobias as fear of flowers (anthophobia), the number 13 (triskaedekophobia), and snow (blanchophobia), these are very rare. The most common phobias in our society are social phobias and specific phobias (see Table 5–1).

THE SPECIFIC PHOBIAS

There are four classes of specific phobias: (1) fear of particular animals, usually cats, dogs, birds (most commonly pigeons), rats, snakes, and insects; (2) inanimate object phobias, including dirt, heights, closed spaces, darkness, and travel; (3) fear of illness, injury, or death; and (4) blood phobias. Together, these make up about half of all phobias (Boyd, Rae, Thompson, and Burns, 1990).

- **_Animal phobias._** Like Anna's cat phobia, these almost always begin in early childhood, and most are outgrown by adulthood. A dog phobia might develop after a child was bitten by a dog; a bird phobia might begin if a bird landed on a child's shoulder. Animal phobias are highly focused: Anna may be terrified of cats, but she is rather fond of dogs and birds. The vast majority (95 percent) of animal phobias are reported by women; the phobia is apt to be their only psychological problem (Marks, 1969; Bourdon, Boyd, Rae, and Burns, 1988; Fredrikson, Annas, Fischer, and Wik, 1996).

DSM-IV Criteria for Specific Phobia

A. Marked and persistent fear that is excessive or unreasonable, cued by the presence or anticipation of a specific object or situation (e.g., flying, heights, animals, receiving an injection, seeing blood).

B. Exposure to the phobic stimulus almost invariably provokes an immediate anxiety response, which may take the form of a situationally bound or situationally predisposed panic attack. (*Note:* In children, the anxiety may be expressed by crying, tantrums, freezing, or clinging.)

C. The person recognizes that the fear is excessive or unreasonable. (*Note:* In children, this feature may be absent.)

D. The phobic situation(s) is avoided or else is endured with intense anxiety or distress.

E. The avoidance, anxious anticipation, or distress in the feared situation(s) interferes significantly with the person's normal routine, occupational (or academic) functioning, or social activities or relationships, or there is marked distress about having the phobia.

F. In individuals under age 18 years, the duration is at least 6 months.

G. The anxiety, panic attacks, or phobic avoidance associated with the specific object or situation are not better accounted for by another mental disorder, such as Obsessive-Compulsive Disorder (e.g., fear of dirt in someone with an obsession about contamination), Post-traumatic Stress Disorder (e.g., avoidance of stimuli associated with a severe stressor), Separation Anxiety Disorder (e.g., avoidance of school), Social Phobia (e.g., avoidance of social situations because of fear of embarrassment), Panic Disorder with Agoraphobia, or Agoraphobia without History of Panic Disorder.

SOURCE: APA, DSM-IV, 1994.

TABLE 5–1

THE COMMON PHOBIAS			
Phobia		Sex Difference	Typical Age of Onset
Social Phobias (fear of being observed doing something humiliating)		majority are women	adolescence
Specific Phobias			
Animals		vast majority are women	childhood
Cats (ailurophobia)	Birds (avisophobia)		
Dogs (cynophobia)	Horses (equinophobia)		
Insects (insectophobia)	Snakes (ophidiophobia)		
Spiders (arachnophobia)	Rodents (rodentophobia)		
Inanimate Object Phobias		none	any age
Dirt (mysophobia)	Darkness (nyctophobia)		
Storms (brontophobia)	Closed places (claustrophobia)		
Heights (acrophobia)			
Illness-Injury (nosophobia)		none	middle age
Death phobia (thanatophobia)			
Cancer (cancerophobia)			
Venereal disease (venerophobia)			
Blood Phobia		probably more women	late childhood

SOURCE: Marks, 1969.

- *Inanimate object phobias.* Irrational fear of heights, closed spaces, storms, dirt, darkness, running water, travel, flying in airplanes, and wind make up the majority of these phobias. As in animal phobias, the symptoms are focused on one object, and the individuals are otherwise psychologically normal. Onset is sometimes embedded in a traumatic incident. For example, a nineteen-year-old develops an airplane phobia after a plane he has just gotten off crashes at its next stop. These phobias are somewhat more common than animal phobias, and they occur about equally in women and men. Unlike animal phobias, they can begin at any age.
- *Illness and injury phobias (nosophobias).* A person with such a phobia fears having one specific illness, although the kind of illness feared

▶ A specific childhood incident may set off a phobia. This child may grow up to be a person with a dog phobia.

has changed throughout the centuries. In the nineteenth century, nosophobics feared they had tuberculosis or perhaps syphilis and other venereal diseases. More recently, cancer, heart disease, stroke, and AIDS have been the terrors.

A nosophobic is usually perfectly healthy, but he worries endlessly that he may have or will soon contract a particular disease. He searches his body for the slightest sign of the disease, and since fear itself produces symptoms like tightness in the chest and stomach pain, he interprets these symptoms as further evidence that the disease is upon him. And so it spirals to more stomach or chest pain and to more certainty that he has the dreaded disease.

There are no sex differences in overall reports of nosophobia, although cancer phobias tend to occur more in females and phobias of venereal disease almost always occur in males. Other psychological problems accompany the disorder frequently, and it usually arises in middle age. Nosophobics often know someone who has the feared disease.

- **_Blood phobias._**   Such phobics become highly anxious in situations involving the sight of blood, injections, and injuries. They often avoid medical procedures because of their phobia. They cannot bear to watch gory films. About 4 percent of the normal population shows this phobia at least to a moderate extent (Agras, Sylvester, and Oliveau, 1969; Costello, 1982). It is probably somewhat more common in women than in men, and its onset is usually in late childhood (Öst, 1987; Kleinknecht and Lenz, 1989; Kleinknecht, 1994).

SOCIAL PHOBIAS

Social phobics fear being observed since they are afraid that they will act in a way that will be humiliating or embarrassing and that they will end up having a panic attack. Social phobics recognize that the fear is excessive or unreasonable, but they still avoid social situations that they think will provoke anxiety. Thus, for example, a social phobic may be unable to eat in a restaurant for fear of vomiting and being humiliated. A student may stop writing during an exam when watched by a teacher for fear of shaking violently. A factory

After 23 uneventful years at the zoo's snakehouse, curator Ernie Schwartz has a cumulative attack of the willies.

▲ Social phobics often crave companionship, but avoid it out of fear of embarrassment. The phobia may begin gradually or after a dramatic event that really was embarrassing.

worker may stop going to work because he fears that he will not be able to do his job if he is being observed. The fears are often unrealistic; individuals who fear they might shake, do not shake, nor do those who fear vomiting in public actually vomit in public.

Social phobias usually begin in adolescence, occasionally in childhood, and only rarely after age twenty-five (Schneier, Johnson, Hornig, et al., 1992). About 1 percent of adults have social phobias, and these phobias make up about 20 percent of all phobic cases. They are reported somewhat more often by women, and they are markedly more frequent among poor people. Unlike people with specific phobias, whose disorder is isolated, 70 percent of social phobics report other major disorders (Boyd, Rae, Thompson, and Burns, 1990; Schneier, Johnson, Hornig, et al., 1992).

Understanding Phobia

Many researchers and clinicians believe that phobias develop in people much the same way that conditioned responses develop in laboratory animals during classical conditioning (Seligman, 1970; Eysenck, 1979). This behavioral analysis of phobias begins by assuming that normal fear and phobia are learned in the same way. Both fear and phobia arise when a neutral signal happens to be around at the same time as a bad event. If the bad event is mild, the neutral signal becomes mildly fear provoking. If, however, the bad event is particularly traumatic, the signal becomes terrifying, and a phobia develops. Phobic conditioning is simply an instance of classical fear being conditioned by a particularly traumatic unconditioned stimulus.

CLASSICAL CONDITIONING OF FEAR

Recall that classical conditioning consists of a procedure in which a conditioned stimulus (CS)—or signal—happens to occur at the same time as an unconditioned stimulus (US)—or traumatic event in the case of fear conditioning—which evokes a strong unconditioned response (UR). Thereafter, the previously neutral CS produces a conditioned response (CR) that resembles the UR. The CR is the phobic response and the CS is the phobic object. This thinking originated with a pioneering, but in modern eyes, an ethically suspect experiment conducted in 1920 by John B. Watson and Rosalie Rayner. Little Albert B. was a normal, healthy eleven-month-old who, from birth, had been reared in the hospital in which his mother worked as a wet nurse. On the whole, he was big, stolid, and unemotional. One day, Albert was presented with a white rat, and he eagerly began to reach for it. Just as his hand touched the rat, the experimenters struck a metal bar suspended above Albert's head with a hammer. This produced such a loud and startling sound that Albert jerked violently, buried his head in the mattress, and whimpered. This pairing of the rat and the sound was repeated several times. When Albert was shown the rat later, he began to cry. He fell over on his side, and began to crawl away as rapidly as he could. A phobia had been conditioned.

Today, clinicians see numerous cases like this: A child might by mistake startle a dog while it is eating. The startled dog (CS) jumps on the child and bites him (US). The child becomes terrified (UR) and develops a phobia to dogs (CR). Every time he sees a dog (CS), the child is now terrified (CR) (see Figure 5–2).

THE PERSISTENCE OF PHOBIAS

Can the behavioral analysis also offer an account of persistence, a defining feature of phobias? After fear is classically conditioned in the laboratory by pairing a tone a few times with shock, extinction will occur rapidly when the tone is presented without the shock. Within ten or twenty presentations of the tone without shock, fear will always disappear (Annau and Kamin, 1961). Phobias, on the other hand, are very robust. They seem to resist extinction; some persist

▶ Classically conditioned fear of dogs would begin with the pairing of an unconditioned stimulus—dogs—with an unconditioned response—terror. A child who encountered dogs like these might develop a phobia (conditioned response) to all dogs (conditioned stimulus).

FIGURE 5–2

THE BEHAVIORAL ACCOUNT OF PHOBIA

When the signal (CS) is paired in time with the traumatic event (US), this elicits a reaction (UR). Later when the CS again occurs, it produces a phobia (CR).

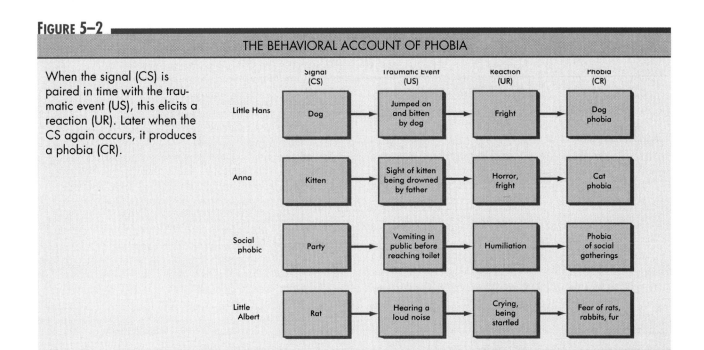

	Signal (CS)	Traumatic Event (US)	Reaction (UR)	Phobia (CR)
Little Hans	Dog	Jumped on and bitten by dog	Fright	Dog phobia
Anna	Kitten	Sight of kitten being drowned by father	Horror, fright	Cat phobia
Social phobic	Party	Vomiting in public before reaching toilet	Humiliation	Phobia of social gatherings
Little Albert	Rat	Hearing a loud noise	Crying, being startled	Fear of rats, rabbits, fur

for a lifetime (see Box 5–1). How can a model based on an ephemeral phenomenon, classical fear conditioning, capture phobias that last and last?

An *extinction trial* in fear conditioning occurs when the fear-evoking signal is presented to the subject, but the traumatic event no longer follows. For example, a rat is put into the box in which it has received shocks. A fear-evoking tone that has been paired with shock comes on but no shock is presented. The rat can do nothing to escape the tone and is exposed to the fact that the tone no longer predicts shock. Because the rat cannot escape, it *reality tests* and finds out that the trauma no longer follows the signal. Under these conditions, fear extinguishes rapidly.

In contrast, phobics rarely test the reality of their fears. When the phobic object is around, they rarely sit there waiting to be passively exposed to an extinction trial. Rather, they run away as quickly as possible. For example, Anna would avoid cats as best she could, but if she did happen across a cat, she would flee as fast as she could. She would not reality test by staying in the presence of the cat and finding out what would happen. We see a parallel situation in the animal laboratory: If given a chance to escape, a rat will do so upon hearing the tone (CS) that signals shock (US). This means that the rat will never stay long enough to discover that the shock is no longer being presented at all on subsequent trials (Rescorla and Solomon, 1967; Baum, 1969; Seligman and Johnston, 1973).

Consider the social phobic who no longer goes to parties because he was humiliated when he once vomited at a party. He avoids parties altogether, and if he must attend one, he escapes as quickly as he can. He is afraid that if he finds himself at a party (CS—the signal), he will again vomit (US—the trauma) and be publicly humiliated (UR—the reaction). His fear does not extinguish because he does not allow himself to be exposed to extinction trials—being at a party and finding out that he does not vomit and is not humiliated. He does not test the reality of the fact that parties (CS) no longer lead to vomiting (US) and humiliation (UR). The ability to avoid and escape the phobic object protects fear of the phobic object from being extinguished, just as allowing a rat to escape the signal and avoid the trauma protects fear from extinguishing.

Phobias occur almost entirely to a highly restricted set of objects, whereas ordinary classical conditioning of fear occurs to any object that happens to be around at the same time as trauma. Why are phobias of the dark so common but phobias of pillows nonexistent, although both are paired with nighttime trauma? Why are phobias of knives so rare even though knives are often paired with injury? Why have we never heard of a phobia of electric outlets? Why are there rat, dog, and spider phobias, but not lamb phobias?

Watson and Raynor had found it simple to condition Little Albert to fear rats, but E. L. Thorndike, the American learning theorist, had difficulty trying to train his children to stay away from sharp objects and to stay out of the street, even though such trespasses were paired with spankings. Apparently, phobic conditioning, both in and out of the laboratory, is highly selective.

It seems that the great majority of common phobias are of objects that were once actually dangerous to pre-technological man (De Silva, Rachman, and Seligman, 1977; Zafiropoulou and McPherson, 1986). Natural selection probably favored those of our ancestors who, once they had minimal exposure to trauma paired with such signals, were highly prepared to learn that strangers, crowds, heights, insects, large animals, and dirt were dangerous. Such primates would have had a clear reproductive and survival edge over others who learned only gradually about such real dangers. Thus, evolution seems to have selected a certain set of objects, all once dangerous to man, that are readily conditionable to trauma, and it seems to have left out other objects that are much more difficult to condition to fear (such as lambs, electric outlets, knives), either because they were never dangerous or because their origin is too recent to have been subject to natural selection.

Arne Öhman, Kenneth Hugdahl, and their collaborators at the University of Uppsala in Sweden created a close laboratory model of phobias (Öhman, Fredrikson, Hugdahl, and Rimmo, 1976). Fear was conditioned in student volunteers using a variety of prepared—once dangerous to Homo sapiens—or unprepared fear CSs: pictures of snakes or spiders (prepared) versus pictures of houses, faces, or flowers (unprepared). In a typical experiment, the "prepared" group was presented with pictures of snakes that signaled the occurrence of a brief, painful electric shock ten seconds later. In the "unprepared" group, pictures of houses signaled shock. Fear conditioning, as measured by galvanic skin response (akin to sweating), occurred much more rapidly to prepared signals than to unprepared ones when each was paired with shock. In fact, conditioning took place in one pairing with snakes or spiders, but it took four or five pairings with houses or flowers. Moreover, at the end of the conditioning, when the electrodes were removed and the subjects were told that shock would not be delivered anymore, fear extinguished immediately to houses and faces, but remained full-blown to snakes and spiders (Hugdahl and Öhman, 1977).

This study demonstrates that humans seem more prepared to learn to be afraid of certain objects than of others. Consider guns, therefore, as a potentially phobic object. Guns are too recent to have been prepared for fear conditioning by evolution, but guns have had voluminous cultural preparation: stories, TV shows, parental warnings. Does the fear of guns have the same properties as the fear of snakes and spiders, or the fear of houses and flowers? Guns turn out to resemble houses and flowers, not spiders and snakes, in their conditioning properties. This indicates that the preparedness to fear spiders and snakes is biological, not cultural.

One researcher tells the story of a four-year-old girl who saw a snake while walking through a park in England. She found the snake interesting, but she was not greatly frightened by it. A short time later, she returned to the family car, and her hand was smashed in the car door. She developed a lifelong phobia, not of cars or doors, but of snakes (Marks, 1977). So we see that phobias are selective, both in the laboratory and in real life.

The selectivity and irrationality of phobias suggest that phobias are not instances of ordinary classical conditioning; rather they are instances of **prepared classical conditioning.** Certain evolutionarily dangerous objects are prepared to become phobic objects when paired with trauma, but others are not and require more extensive and traumatic conditioning to become phobic objects (McNally, 1987; Menzies and Clark, 1995; Regan and Howard, 1995). Thus, it is utterly futile to try to convince a person with a cat phobia by arguing that cats aren't dangerous, while it is quite easy to convince the very same person that the building he works in has been effectively fireproofed.

Therapies for Phobias

The behavioral analysis can make direct predictions about therapy: those procedures that extinguish fear conditioning in the laboratory should also cure phobias. There are three behavioral therapies that have proven highly effective against phobias: systematic desensitization, flooding, and modeling. In addition, applied tension, a new therapy developed for blood phobia, has also been proven to be highly effective. All were developed within the framework of behavioral analysis.

FOCUS QUESTIONS

1. What are the three classical therapies for phobias?
2. How is blood phobia treated?
3. Evaluate the success of drug therapies for phobias.

SYSTEMATIC DESENSITIZATION

Developed in the 1950s by Joseph Wolpe, a South African psychiatrist, *systematic desensitization* involves three phases: training in relaxation, hierarchy construction, and counterconditioning. First the therapist trains the phobic patient in deep muscle relaxation, a technique in which the subject sits or lies with eyes closed, with all his muscles completely relaxed. This state of relaxation will be used in the third phase to neutralize fear, since individuals cannot be deeply relaxed and afraid at the same time (that is, fear and relaxation are incompatible responses). Second, with the aid of the therapist, the patient constructs a hierarchy of frightening situations, in which the most dreaded possible scene is on the highest rung and a scene evoking some, but minimal, fear is on the lowest rung. For example, a hierarchy constructed by a woman with a phobia of physical deformity (from Wolpe, 1969) might be as follows (from minimally feared situations to maximally feared situations):

1. Ambulances (minimally feared)
2. Hospitals
3. Wheelchairs
4. Nurses in uniform
5. Automobile accidents
6. The sight of somebody who is seriously ill
7. Someone in pain
8. The sight of physical deformity (maximally feared)

The third phase removes the fear of the phobic object by gradual counterconditioning; that is, causing a response that is incompatible with fear to occur at the same time as the feared CS. The patient goes into deep relaxation, and simultaneously imagines the first, least-arousing scene in the hierarchy. This serves two purposes. First, it pairs the CS, ambulances, with the absence of the original traumatic US. (You will recall that presenting the CS without the original US is an extinction procedure that will weaken the fear response to the CS.) Second, a new response, relaxation, which neutralizes the old response of fear, occurs in the presence of the CS. This is repeated until the patient can imagine scene 1 of the hierarchy without any fear at all. Then scene 2, which provokes a slightly greater fear than scene 1, is paired with relaxation. And so the patient progresses up the hierarchy by the graded extinction procedure until she reaches the most terrifying scene. Here the patient again relaxes and visualizes the final scene. When she can do this with no fear at all, the patient may be tested in real life by being confronted with

▶ Psychiatrist Joseph Wolpe conducts systematic desensitization with a patient. The patient imagines a fear-evoking scene while engaging in deep muscle relaxation. She will signal by lifting her forefinger if the fear becomes unbearable.

▲ Through flooding, this woman is gradually losing her fear of water.

an actual instance of something at the top of her hierarchy—in this case, with a real physical deformity. Therapy is considered successful when the patient can tolerate being in the actual presence of the most terrifying item on the hierarchy. Eighty to 90 percent of specific phobias improve greatly with such treatment. These gains are usually maintained over follow-ups of a year or two without new symptoms being substituted for those that have been eliminated (see Paul, 1967; Kazdin and Wilcoxon, 1976).

FLOODING

Recall that behaviorists believe that phobias persist because patients with phobia will avoid the phobic object if at all possible, and if forced into its presence, they will escape rapidly. This failure to find out that the phobic object no longer predicts the original traumatic event will protect the phobia from extinction.

What happens when a person with a phobia volunteers to be in the presence of a phobic object? What happens when rats, who avoid shock by escaping a tone, are forced to experience the tone and find out that shock no longer occurs? Such a *flooding,* or reality-testing procedure, in rats reliably brings a reduced amount of fear and eliminates future avoidance (Baum, 1969; Tryon, 1976). The success of eliminating fear in animals by a flooding procedure encouraged behavior therapists to try, with caution, flooding in real phobic patients (Stampfl and Levis, 1967).

In a flooding procedure, the phobic patient agrees, usually with great apprehension, to imagine the phobic situation or to stay in its presence without attempting to escape for a long period. For example, a person with claustrophobia will be put in a closet for four hours, or an individual with a fear of flying (aviaphobia) will take a course including a real, aborted jet takeoff and a real flight (Serling, 1986; McCarthy and Craig, 1995).

In general, flooding has proven to be equal, and sometimes even superior, to systematic desensitization in its therapeutic effects. By forcing a patient to reality test and to stay in the phobic situation, and thereby find out that catastrophe does not ensue, extinction of the phobia can usually be accomplished. This directly confirms the hypothesis that phobias are so persistent because the object is avoided in real life and therefore not extinguished by the discovery that it is harmless.

MODELING

The third effective therapy for phobias is modeling. In a typical modeling procedure, the phobic patient watches someone who does not have the phobia perform the behavior that the phobic patient is unable to do himself. For example, a person with a snake phobia will repeatedly watch a nonfearful model approach, pick up, and fondle a real snake (Bandura, Adams, and

▼ In modeling therapy for snake phobia, a phobic patient learns to handle snakes by watching another person handle them, and eventually loses her fear.

Beyer, 1977; Bandura, 1986). Seeing that the other person is not harmed, the phobic patient may become less fearful of the situation. The therapist will then gradually involve the phobic patient in the exercises. First, the phobic patient may be asked to describe aloud what he sees, then to approach the snake, and finally to touch it. The procedure will be repeated until the phobia diminishes.

Overall, modeling seems to work about as well as both desensitization and flooding in curing both mild and severe clinical phobias (Rachman, 1976; Moore, Geffken, and Royal, 1995). This therapy brings about cognitive change, as well as behavioral change. Once a patient has observed a model, the single best predictor of therapeutic progress is the extent to which he now expects that he will be able to perform the actions he formerly was unable to do (Bandura, Adams, and Beyer, 1977).

APPLIED TENSION

Another therapy for phobias is *applied tension,* and it is the therapy of choice for blood phobias. It derives from the same logic that Wolpe used when he created systematic desensitization. Wolpe reasoned that relaxation would countercondition fear because it mobilized the opposite biological system: relaxation was incompatible with the muscular tension and sympathetic arousal components of fear. So the phobic patient could not be fearful at the same time that he was relaxing. Lars-Goren Öst, a Swedish psychologist, noted that when confronted with the phobic stimulus of blood, people with a blood phobia have the opposite bodily reaction to that of people with other phobias when confronted with their phobic stimulus: people with blood phobia have a drop in blood pressure and heart rate and they often faint. Öst reasoned that making blood phobic patients tense their muscles would raise their blood pressure and heart rate, so that they could not have the phobic reaction of fainting at the sight of blood.

In the applied tension technique, the patient tenses the muscles of his arms, legs, and chest until he feels warmth suffusing his face. Then he lets the tension go. He practices this repeatedly so that he can use it when he encounters blood. In an outcome study involving thirty patients with blood phobia, Öst compared the applied tension technique to the relaxation technique and found that both helped considerably, but applied tension produced clinically meaningful improvement in 90 percent while relaxation produced meaningful improvement in only 60 percent (Öst, Sterner, and Fellenius, 1989; Öst, Fellenius, and Sterner, 1991).

A single underlying process—extinction—seems to be the operative element in all the effective therapies for phobias. In all four treatments, the patient is exposed, repeatedly and enduringly, to the phobic object in the absence of the original traumatic event. Each technique keeps the phobic patient in the presence of the phobic object by a different tactic so that extinction can take place: desensitization by having the patient relax and imagine the object, flooding by forcibly keeping the phobic patient in the phobic situation, modeling by encouraging the phobic patient to approach the phobic object as the model has done, and applied tension by preventing fainting in the presence of blood. The fact that each of these therapies works and employs classical fear extinction supports the view that the phobia was originally acquired by classical fear conditioning. Table 5–2 compares the use of extinction therapy and drugs to treat specific phobia and social phobia.

DRUGS

Drugs are not very useful with specific phobias. The anti-anxiety drugs produce calm and relaxation when the patient takes them in high doses during the phobic situation itself. The calm is accompanied by drowsiness and

TABLE 5–2

TREATMENT OF PHOBIA		
	Extinction Therapy	*Drugs*
Specific Phobia		
Improvement	60–80% markedly improved	probably better than placebo
Relapse*	10% or fewer relapse	high relapse
Side Effects	none	moderate
Cost	inexpensive	inexpensive
Time Scale	weeks/months	days/weeks
Overall	**excellent**	**marginal**
	Extinction Therapy	*Drugs (Tricyclics, MAO inhibitors)*
Social Phobia		
Improvement	60–80% markedly improved	60–80% markedly improved
Relapse*	10–20% relapse	high relapse
Side Effects	none	moderate
Cost	inexpensive	inexpensive
Time Scale	weeks/months	days/weeks
Overall	**very good**	**useful**

*Relapse after discontinuation of treatment.
SOURCE: Based on Martin E. P. Seligman, *What you can change and what you can't* (New York: Knopf, 1993), pp. 78–79.

lethargy. So for a flying phobic who *must* suddenly take a plane, a minor tranquilizer will often help, but only temporarily. The calm is cosmetic, however. Once the drug wears off, the phobia is still there undiminished (Noyes, Chaudry, and Domingo, 1986).

MAO inhibitors (a strong antidepressant) have been used with some success in treating patients with social phobia. From 60 to 80 percent of patients improve while on the drug. But the success is temporary, and the relapse rate is high once the drug is discontinued. Moreover, MAO inhibitors have dangerous side effects. Somewhat lower improvement (around 50 percent) occurs with the stronger anti-anxiety agents, like alprazolam (Xanax), and with beta-blockers. But again, the relapse rate is very high, and the drugs have marked side effects. A high relapse rate upon drug discontinuation suggests only a cosmetic effect on phobic anxiety (Versiani, Mundim, Nardi, et al., 1988; Levin, Scheier, and Liebowitz, 1989).

POST-TRAUMATIC STRESS DISORDER

Trauma used to be a part of everyone's life—the incorrigible human condition. Until this century, most people experienced life as a vale of tears. But modern technology, medicine, and a growing sense of social justice have created a world in which the experience of trauma is not inevitable. Bad things still happen all too frequently: we get disappointing grades; our stocks go down; we don't get the job we had hoped for; people we love reject us; we age and die. But we are usually prepared for many losses, or at least we know ways to soften the blow. Once in a while, however, the ancient human condition intrudes, and something irredeemably awful, something beyond routine disappointment and setback occurs.

So devastating and long-lasting are the effects of certain types of trauma and extraordinary loss, they have been given a name and a diagnostic category of their own: *post-traumatic stress disorder (PTSD)*. The following case shows an individual who is suffering from a delayed onset of post-traumatic stress disorder.

> Mr. A was raised as a Quaker until he was thirteen. In 1943 he was drafted into the Army and served as a machine gunner until the end of the war. A giant of a man, he could carry his fifty-five pound gun on his shoulder and run at full tilt. He was frequently in the center of combat and killed many enemy soldiers, often at close range. After the Battle of the Bulge, his sergeant and his assistant gunner were killed. For three days, he wandered the battlefield in a daze and cried, not noticing his own shrapnel wounds. There was one incident during the war of which he was ashamed. After machine-gunning a group of German attackers, he looked at the bodies and saw that many were teenage boys with imitation rifles. At the end of the war, only four of his original forty comrades remained alive, and Mr. A was awarded several of the nation's highest decorations for valor.
>
> Mr. A went on to become a very successful architect and remained in excellent health for the next twenty years. Aside from avoiding war movies, he seemed to show no immediate traces of his combat traumas. In 1975, thirty years after the war, because of diabetes and visual problems, he was forced to retire. At this point, he began to suffer nightmares about the war. In one recurring nightmare, his troop charged at and machine-gunned German teenagers, and he saw that they included his grandsons. When he revisited the battlefield as a guest of the German government in 1979, he broke down, distraught with anxiety about not being able to find the graves of his two comrades. He began to take many drugs to try to relieve his anxieties. (Van Dyke, Zilberg, and McKinnon, 1985)

Precipitants of Post-Traumatic Stress Disorder

The objects that set off a phobia are quite commonplace; for example, crowds, embarrassment, cats, and illness. But the precipitant of a post-traumatic stress disorder, in contrast, is unusual (see Table 5–3). There is debate about what kind of precipitating events should qualify for a diagnosis of PTSD. At the most extreme, some claim that the events must be catastrophic, beyond the usual range of human suffering: living through an earthquake, watching one's children being tortured, being in a concentration camp, being kidnapped, experiencing hand-to-hand combat. This was the criterion in DSM-III, which

TABLE 5–3

PHOBIA AND PTSD COMPARED			
	Origin	*Symptoms*	*Course*	*Therapy*
Single Phobia	Classical conditioning in which prepared (or occasionally unprepared) stimulus becomes a CS for fear reaction	Usually confined to phobic reaction to one object or situation; patient often functions well in other areas	Dissipates in most children, but unremitting if found in adults without therapy	Drugs ineffective; patient often responds well to brief behavioral/cognitive therapy
PTSD	Stressor outside normal range; confrontation with threat of death or injury responded to with horror or helplessness	Wide range of emotional, behavioral, and somatic symptoms; reliving of trauma, pervasive numbness, and anxiety are common	Symptoms may persist and interfere with many areas of functioning for decades	Drugs largely ineffective; early intervention with both stress inoculation and exposure therapy may work well

was used to diagnose many psychologically crippled veterans of the Vietnam War. But it is important to note that some people endured the Holocaust with no trace of PTSD, and that others in contrast show full-blown PTSD when their spouse dies or even when sued in court. A wider, but more specific, criterion has therefore been given in DSM-IV: having experienced, witnessed, or been confronted by an event or events that involved the threat of death, injury, or threat to the physical integrity of self or others. This would include rape, mugging, watching a bloody accident, committing an atrocity. What is crucial is the person's reaction to this "exceptional" stressor: intense fear, horror, helplessness, and a sense of ruination.

The criteria for the disorder are: (1) the person *relives* the trauma repeatedly, in dreams, in flashbacks, and in reverie; (2) the person becomes *numb* to the world, and avoids stimuli (for example, thoughts, feelings, places, people) that remind him of the trauma; (3) the person experiences symptoms of *anxiety* and arousal that were not present before the trauma, including trou-

---

DSM-IV Criteria for Post-Traumatic Stress Disorder

A. The person has been exposed to a traumatic event in which both of the following were present: (1) the person experienced, witnessed, or was confronted with an event or events that involved actual or threatened death or serious injury, or a threat to the physical integrity of self or others; (2) the person's response involved intense fear, helplessness, or horror. (*Note:* In children, this may be expressed instead by disorganized or agitated behavior.)

B. The traumatic event is persistently reexperienced in one (or more) of the following ways: (1) recurrent and intrusive distressing recollections of the event, including images, thoughts, or perceptions (*Note:* In young children, repetitive play may occur in which themes or aspects of the trauma are expressed.); (2) recurrent distressing dreams of the event (*Note:* In children, there may be frightening dreams without recognizable content.); (3) acting or feeling as if the traumatic event were recurring (includes a sense of reliving the experience, illusions, hallucinations, and dissociative flashback episodes, including those that occur on awakening or when intoxicated) (*Note:* In young children, trauma-specific reenactment may occur.); (4) intense psychological distress at exposure to internal or external cues that symbolize or resemble an aspect of the traumatic event; (5) physiological reactivity on exposure to internal or external cues that symbolize or resemble an aspect of the traumatic event.

C. Persistent avoidance of stimuli associated with the trauma and numbing of general responsiveness (not present before the trauma), as indicated by three (or more) of the following: (1) efforts to avoid thoughts, feelings, or conversations associated with the trauma; (2) efforts to avoid activities, places, or people that arouse recollections of the trauma; (3) inability to recall an important aspect of the trauma; (4) markedly diminished interest or participation in significant activities; (5) feeling of detachment or estrangement from others; (6) restricted range of affect (e.g., unable to have loving feelings); (7) sense of a foreshortened future (e.g, does not expect to have a career, marriage, children, or a normal life span).

D. Persistent symptoms of increased arousal (not present before the trauma), as indicated by two (or more) of the following: (1) difficulty falling or staying asleep; (2) irritability or outbursts of anger; (3) difficulty concentrating; (4) hypervigilance; (5) exaggerated startle response.

E. Duration of the disturbance (symptoms in Criteria B, C, and D) is more than 1 month.

F. The disturbance causes clinically significant distress or impairment in social, occupational, or other important areas of functioning.

SOURCE: APA, DSM-IV, 1994.

FOCUS QUESTIONS

1. What is the wider criterion diagnosing PTSD given in DSM-IV and who is likely to be most vulnerable to PTSD?
2. What are the six criteria for post-traumatic stress disorder?
3. Describe how rape trauma syndrome resembles post-traumatic stress disorder.
4. How successful have drug treatments and psychotherapy been for relieving PTSD?

ble sleeping, over-alertness, trouble concentrating, exaggerated startle, and outbursts of anger; (4) the person is unable to remember an important part of the traumatic event; (5) the person has less interest or participation in activities and feels detached from others, which significantly impairs his or her functioning; and (6) the symptoms last for more than a month.

It was once thought that victims of disaster recovered briskly. An early psychiatric study of the aftermath of disaster was of the relatives of the victims of a catastrophic nightclub fire during the 1940s. Interviews with the survivors and the families of the dead led to the the belief that an "uncomplicated grief reaction" would be gone in four to six weeks (Lindemann, 1944). Dr. Camille Wortman, a psychologist at the State University of New York at Stony Brook, found evidence that contradicted this assumption. She went through the microfilm records of every auto fatality in Michigan between 1976 and 1979. She randomly chose thirty-nine people who had lost a spouse and forty-one couples who had lost a child. She then interviewed them at length and compared them to matched controls.

Her interviews occurred four to seven years after the tragedy, and she found that the parents and spouses were still in decidedly poor shape. They were much more depressed than the controls. They were less optimistic about the future, and they did not feel good about their lives. They were more "worn out," "tense," and "unhappy." More of those who had lost a spouse or child had died than had the controls. While they did not differ on income before their child died, the bereaved parents now earned 25 percent less than did the controls. Twenty percent were now divorced (versus 2.5 percent of the controls). People were just as bad off seven years later as four years later, so there does not seem to be a noticeable natural healing process going on. Almost everyone asked "Why me?" Sixty percent could find no answer to this wrenching question (Lehman, Wortman, and Williams, 1987).

NATURALLY OCCURRING DISASTERS

The Los Angeles earthquake of 1994, the floods in the U. S. Midwest in 1993, and Hurricane Andrew in 1992 produced a large number of people with PTSD. Much of what we know about the suffering of these victims and the course of their problems begins with a study of a flood at Buffalo Creek, West Virginia, in 1972. This flood produced devastation and death in a small Appalachian community, setting off many cases of post-traumatic stress disorder among its survivors (Erikson, 1976; Green, Gleser, Lindy, et al., 1996). In the early morning of February 26, 1972, the dam on Buffalo Creek in the coal region of West Virginia collapsed, and within a few seconds, 132 million gallons of the sludge-filled black water roared upon the residents of the mountain hollows below. Wilbur, his wife Deborah, and their four children managed to survive. Here is how they describe what happened to them (Erikson, 1976, pp. 338–44):

> For some reason, I opened the inside door and looked up the road—and there it came. Just a big black cloud. It looked like 12 or 15 foot of water . . .
> Well, my neighbor's house was coming right up to where we live, coming down the creek . . . It was coming slow, but my wife was still asleep with the baby—she was about seven years old at the time—and the other kids were still asleep upstairs. I screamed for my wife in a bad tone of voice so I could get her attention real quick . . . I don't know how she got the girls downstairs so fast, but she run up there in her sliptail and she got the children out of bed and downstairs . . .
> We headed up the road . . . My wife and some of the children went up between the gons [railway gondolas]; me and my baby went under them because we didn't have much time . . . I looked around and our house was done gone. It didn't wash plumb away. It washed down about four or five house lots from where it was setting, tore all to pieces.

▲ While a specific object triggers the fear response in phobia, an unusually traumatic event—often a natural or man-made disaster—precipitates post-traumatic stress disorder. On the left, flood waters break a window during Hurricane Andrew in 1992; on the right, civilians and a U.N. soldier take cover during the war in Bosnia.

Two years after the disaster, Wilbur and Deborah describe their psychological scars, the defining symptoms of a post-traumatic stress disorder. First, Wilbur *relives* the trauma repeatedly in his dreams:

> What I went through on Buffalo Creek is the cause of my problem. The whole thing happens over to me even in my dreams, when I retire for the night. In my dreams, I run from water all the time, all the time. The whole thing just happens over and over again in my dreams . . .

Second, Wilbur and Deborah have become *numb* psychologically. Affect is blunted and they are emotionally anesthetized to the sorrows and joys of the world around them. Wilbur says:

> I didn't even go to the cemetery when my father died [about a year after the flood]. It didn't dawn on me that he was gone forever. And those people that dies around me now, it don't bother me like it did before the disaster . . . It just didn't bother me that my dad was dead and never would be back. I don't have the feeling I used to have about something like death. It just don't affect me like it used to.

And Deborah says:

> I'm neglecting my children. I've just completely quit cooking. I don't do no housework. I just won't do nothing. Can't sleep. Can't eat. I just want to take me a lot of pills and just go to bed and go to sleep and not wake up. I enjoyed my home and my family, but outside of them, to me, everything else in life that I had any interest in is destroyed. I loved to cook. I loved to sew. I loved to keep house. I was all the time working and making improvements on my home. But now I've just got to the point where it don't mean a thing in the world to me. I haven't cooked a hot meal and put it on the table for my children in almost three weeks.

Third, Wilbur experiences symptoms of *anxiety,* including hyper-alertness and phobic reactions to events that remind him of the flood, such as rain and impending bad weather:

> . . . I listen to the news, and if there is a storm warning out, why I don't go to bed that night. I sit up. I tell my wife, "Don't undress our little girls; just let them lay down like they are and go to bed and go to sleep and then if I see anything going to happen, I'll wake you in plenty of time to get you out of the house." I don't go to bed. I stay up.
> My nerves is a problem. Every time it rains, every time it storms, I just can't take it. I walk the floor. I get so nervous I break out in a rash. I am taking shots for it now . . .

Wilbur also suffers from ***survival guilt:***

> At that time, why, I heard somebody holler at me, and I looked around and saw Mrs. Constable. . . . She had a little baby in her arms and she was hollering, "Hey, Wilbur, come and help me; if you can't help me, come get my baby." . . . But I didn't give it a thought to go back and help her. I blame myself a whole lot for that yet. She had her baby in her arms and looked as though she were going to throw it to me. Well, I never thought to go help that lady. I was thinking about my own family. They all six got drowned in that house. She was standing in water up to her waist, and they all got drowned.

These symptoms persisted. Fourteen years after the Buffalo Creek Flood, 193 survivors were examined. Sixty percent had PTSD initially, and 25 percent still had it fourteen years later. Thirty-five percent had major depression initially, and 19 percent had it fourteen years after the flood (Green, Lindy, Grace, and Leonard, 1992).

MANMADE CATASTROPHES

The catastrophe that brings out a post-traumatic stress reaction need not be a naturally occurring one like the Buffalo Creek Flood. Human beings have made a hell of the lives of other human beings since time immemorial: concentration camps, war, and torture ruin lives long after the victims have ceased to experience the original trauma. Unfortunately, the disorders following these catastrophes may be even more severe and long-lasting than those following natural disasters; it may be easier for us to deal with the "acts of God" than with the acts of men.

The survivors of the Nazi concentration camps illustrate how long-lasting and severe the post-traumatic stress reaction can be. In a study of 149 camp survivors, 142 (or 97 percent) were still troubled with anxiety twenty years after they were freed from the camps (Krystal, 1968). Anxiety symptoms were marked: 31 percent were troubled with fears that something terrible would happen to their mates or their children whenever they were out of sight. Many of them were phobic about certain people whose appearance or behavior reminded them of their jailors; for example, the sight of a uniformed policeman or the inquisitive behavior of a doctor might be enough to set off panic. Seven percent had such severe panic attacks that the individual became confused and disoriented, entering a dreamlike state in which he believed himself to be back in the concentration camp.

The survivors relived the trauma in dreams for twenty years: 71 percent of these patients had anxiety dreams and nightmares, with 41 percent hav-

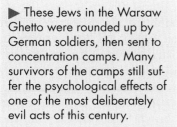
▶ These Jews in the Warsaw Ghetto were rounded up by German soldiers, then sent to concentration camps. Many survivors of the camps still suffer the psychological effects of one of the most deliberately evil acts of this century.

ing severe ones. These nightmares were usually of their persecution. Particularly terrifying were dreams in which only one detail was changed from the reality; for example, dreaming that their children who had not yet been born at the time of the camps had been imprisoned with them in the camps.

Eighty percent of the patients suffered survivor guilt, depression, and crying spells. Survival guilt was especially strong when the patient's children had been killed; those who were the most severely depressed had lost an only child or had lost all of their children, with no children being born since. Ninety-two percent expressed self-reproach for failing to save their relatives, and 14 percent wished they had been killed instead of their relatives (Krystal, 1968). One hundred and twenty-four Holocaust survivors were examined more than forty years after the war, and the findings were grim. Almost half were suffering PTSD, with sleep disturbance the most pervasive symptom. Survivors of Auschwitz were three times as likely to still have PTSD as survivors who had not been in concentration camps (Kuch and Cox, 1992).

Human inhumanity to other humans did not abate after World War II, and among its more awful consequences has been lasting PTSD. Fifty-five survivors of the Lockerbie air disaster of 1988 were examined, and the majority had PTSD, with victims over sixty-five, unlike younger victims, also having major depression (Livingston, Livingston, Brooks, and McKinlay, 1992; Brooks and McKinlay, 1992). Among evacuees of the SCUD missile attacks in Israel during the Gulf War of 1991, almost 80 percent met the criteria for PTSD. The more danger they encountered, the worse were their symptoms (Solomon, Laor, Weiler, and Muller, 1993). Pol Pot's murderous regime left a wake of PTSD among Cambodian children. A group of forty-six refugees to North America who were children at the time have been followed and subsequently examined. PTSD was found to persist in many through their adolescence and into their adulthood, but depression markedly decreased from adolescence to adulthood (Sack, Clarke, Him, and Dickason, 1993).

RAPE TRAUMA SYNDROME

The event that brings about a post-traumatic stress disorder need not be experienced en masse, as in flood, war, or concentration camps; it can also be solitary. Rape is, perhaps, the most common such trauma in modern American society. About 100,000 rapes are reported every year and possibly seven

▲ Rape trauma syndrome shares many symptoms with post-traumatic stress disorder, and as with PTSD, these symptoms are often profound and long-lasting.

times as many go unreported. A woman's reaction to rape looks very much like the post-traumatic stress disorder, and so has been called the ***rape trauma syndrome*** (Burgess and Holmstrom, 1979).

When a woman is raped, her first reaction is called the phase of "disorganization." In one study, researchers found that immediately following rape, a roughly equal number of women exhibited one of two emotional styles: *expressive*—showing fear, anger, anxiety, crying, sobbing, and tenseness—or *controlled*—showing a calm exterior. The symptoms of post-traumatic stress disorder were usually present as well. As many as 95 percent of the victims may show the symptoms of post-traumatic stress disorder within two weeks (Rothbaum, Foa, Riggs, Murdock, and Walsh, 1992). The victim relives the rape time and again, in waking life and in dreams. Sleep disturbance sets in, and there is both trouble getting to sleep and sudden awakening. Rape victims startle easily. Women who were suddenly awakened by the rapist ("blitz" rape) find that they awake each night at about the same time, screaming from rape nightmares. Normal sexual activity is difficult to resume, and a complete avoidance of sex sometimes develops.

Most victims get over the phase of "disorganization" in time and enter the "reorganization" phase. In the long-term process of reorganization, most women take action to ensure safety. Many change their telephone numbers, and half of the women make special trips home to seek support from family members. Half of the victims move. One victim who couldn't afford to move first stayed with relatives and then rearranged her home. As the rape had occurred in her bedroom, she did what she could to change that room: "Wouldn't sleep in my own bed. Stayed with friends for a while. Changed my bedroom around, and got a new bedroom set." Many of the victims begin to read about rape and to write about their experience. Some become active in rape crisis centers and assist other victims, and of these, 70 percent recover in a few months (Burgess and Holmstrom, 1979; Meyer and Taylor, 1986).

Four to six years after the rape, about 75 percent of rape victims said they had recovered. More than half of these recovered in the first three months, and the rest within two years. Victims with the least fear and the fewest flashbacks in the week following the rape recovered more quickly. The very distressed or numbed victims had a poor outcome. The violence of the assault and how life-threatening it was also predicted worse long-term outcome. Distressingly, 25 percent of rape victims said they had not recovered, even after four to six years. Seventeen years later, 16 percent still had post-traumatic stress disorder (Girelli, Resick, Marhoefer-Dvorak, and Hutter, 1986; Kilpatrick, Saunders, Veronen, Best, and Von, 1987; Kilpatrick, Saunders, Amick-McMullan, et al., 1989; Rothbaum, Foa, Riggs, Murdock, and Walsh, 1992).

Course of Post-Traumatic Stress Disorder

Not much is known about the specific course of the post-traumatic stress disorder. Sometimes the symptoms disappear within a few months, resembling recovery from a depressive disorder (see Chapter 8). DSM-IV labels PTSD as "acute" if the symptoms last for less than three months, as "chronic" if they last for more than three months, and as "delayed" if symptoms first occur six or more months after the trauma.

Overall, the prognosis for those who suffer from PTSD is probably bleak, particularly for the victims of very severe trauma. As we saw, a high percentage of concentration camp victims were still troubled with anxiety and guilt twenty years later, and people who lost a child or spouse in a motor accident were still more depressed and anxious four to seven years later (Lehman,

Wortman, and Williams, 1987). This also seems to be true of some veterans of combat. Sixty-two veterans of World War II who suffered chronic "combat fatigue," with symptoms of exaggerated jumpiness, recurrent nightmares, and irritability, were examined twenty years later. Irritability, depression, restlessness, difficulties in concentration and memory, blackouts, wakefulness, fatigability, and jumpiness persisted for twenty years. These symptoms were more prominent in the veterans suffering from combat fatigue than in noncombat patients or in healthy combat veterans (see Figure 5–3; Archibald and Tuddenham, 1965).

Years after the end of the Vietnam War, veterans still experienced post-traumatic stress disorder, particularly those who had seen buddies killed in action. Those who had seen, and particularly those who had participated in atrocities, have been shown to be at severe risk for post-traumatic stress disorder (Breslau and Davis, 1987). One group of Vietnam War veterans interviewed six to fifteen years after participating in violent combat had lives full of problems. They had more arrests and convictions, more drinking, more drug addiction, and more stress than veterans who had not seen combat (Yager, Laufer, and Gallops, 1984). Moreover, twenty years after the end of the war, Vietnam War veterans were found to be more likely to suffer from PTSD, generalized anxiety disorder, and depression than non-Vietnam War veterans (Boscarino, 1995).

Vulnerability to Post-Traumatic Stress Disorder

Who among us is particularly at risk? Psychologists comb over disasters looking for the people who survive them well (without signs of PTSD), and for those who crumble most readily. They then try to determine what factors protect or predispose some people to PTSD. Here is what they have found:

- A prior life history free of mental problems predicted who did best after a catastrophic factory explosion in Norway.
- Among 469 firefighters caught in a disastrous Australian brushfire, those most at risk for getting chronic PTSD scored high on neuroticism and had a family history of mental disorders. These were better predictors than even how much physical trauma each one had experienced.

▶ Men who have been through combat, such as these American soldiers in Vietnam, may later suffer from post-traumatic stress disorder.

FIGURE 5–3

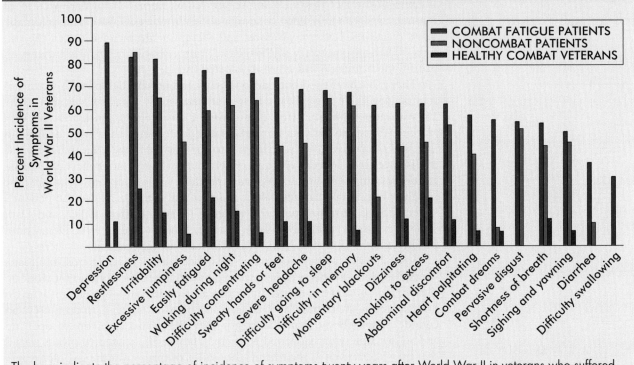

POST-TRAUMATIC STRESS DISORDER IN VETERANS

The bars indicate the percentage of incidence of symptoms twenty years after World War II in veterans who suffered combat fatigue in comparison to healthy combat veterans and noncombat patients. (SOURCE: Archibald and Tuddenham, 1965, p. 478)

- After fighting in Lebanon, Israeli combat casualty veterans who were the children of Holocaust survivors (called "second-generation casualties") had higher rates of PTSD than control casualties.
- Among Israeli combat veterans of two wars, those who experienced PTSD after the second war had had more combat stress reactions during the first war.

These findings indicate that people who are psychologically most healthy before the trauma are at least risk for PTSD. This may be of some consolation—if you happen to be psychologically healthy. But if the bad event is awful enough, previously good psychological health will not protect you (Solomon, Kotler, and Mikulincer, 1988; Weisaeth, 1989; McFarlane, 1989; Malt and Weisaeth, 1989; Solomon, Oppenheimer, Elizur, and Waysman, 1990; Rubonis and Bickman, 1991). A lack of social support when it is most needed may also cause previously healthy individuals to crumble under the stress of trauma and loss (Kaniasty and Norris, 1995).

Another possible factor contributing to vulnerability to PTSD is genetic predisposition. The sheer scale of the American participation in the Vietnam War has allowed the first major study of the heritability of PTSD. Over 4,000 twin pairs who were Vietnam veterans were examined after the war for PTSD symptoms and for how intense their combat experience had been. PTSD symptoms occurred in roughly half the veterans who saw intense combat. Identical twins showed more similar levels of PTSD symptoms than did fraternal twins, and identical twins also had more similar combat experience than did fraternal twins. But *both* genetics and the level of combat intensity contributed independently to PTSD. So PTSD has a heritable component *and* the more intense the combat experienced, the worse the PTSD (True, Rice, Eisen, et al., 1993).

Treatment

In spite of the fact that so many of our fellow human beings are victims of trauma, unfortunately little is known about how to alleviate post-traumatic stress reactions. Relatives, friends, and therapists are inclined to tell the victims of catastrophe to try to "forget it," but it should be apparent that such painful memories cannot be easily blotted out.

Therapists have tried both drug therapy and psychotherapy with victims of trauma (see Table 5–4). In the best controlled study, forty-six Vietnam veterans with post-traumatic stress disorder were given either antidepressants or a placebo. After the patients were given antidepressants, their nightmares and flashbacks decreased, but not down into the normal range. Numbing, a sense of distance from loved ones, and general anxiety were not relieved. Overall, antidepressants and anti-anxiety drugs produce some symptom relief for some patients, but drug treatment alone is never sufficient to relieve the patient's suffering in post-traumatic stress disorder (Frank, Kosten, Giller, and Dan, 1988; Friedman, 1988; Davidson, Kudler, Smith, et al., 1990; Demartino, Mollica, and Wilk, 1995; Marshall, Stein, Liebowitz, and Yehuda, 1996).

Several types of psychotherapy have been used to treat post-traumatic stress disorder. One takes its lead from Jamie Pennebaker's important work on silence. Pennebaker has found that Holocaust victims and rape victims who do not talk about the trauma later suffer worse physical health than do those who confide in somebody. Pennebaker got sixty Holocaust survivors to open up and to describe what happened to them. They finally related to others scenes that they had relived in their heads thousands of times over the last fifty years.

> They were throwing babies from the second floor window of the orphanage. I can still see the pools of blood, the screams, and hear the thuds of their bodies. I just stood there afraid to move. The Nazi soldiers faced us with their guns. (Pennebaker, 1990)

TABLE 5–4

TREATMENT OF POST-TRAUMATIC STRESS DISORDER		
	Exposure Therapy[*]	*Antidepressant and Anti-anxiety Drugs*[†]
Improvement	about 50% moderately improved	probably better than placebo
Relapse[‡]	infrequent relapse	moderate relapse
Side Effects	mild	moderate
Cost	inexpensive	inexpensive
Time Scale	weeks/months	weeks
Overall	**useful**	**marginal**

[*]Most data come from the exposure therapy of rape victims. Results with other traumas are uncharted. See also the promising, but preliminary findings for EMDR (Box 5-2).
[†]Based mainly on outcome studies of MAO-inhibitors, SSRI's, tricyclics, and minor tranquilizers.
[‡]Relapse after discontinuation of treatment.
SOURCE: Based on M.E.P. Seligman, *What you can change and what you can't* (New York: Knopf, 1993), Chapter 10, as well as T. Keane, Psychological and behavioral treatment of posttraumatic stress disorder, in P. Nathan and J. Gorman (eds.), *Treatments that work* (New York: Oxford, 1997), and on R. Yehuda, R. Marshall, and E. Giller, Psychopharmacological treatment of PTSD, in P. Nathan and J. Gorman (eds.), *Treatments that work* (New York: Oxford, 1997).

Ironically, the interviewers themselves had nightmares from hearing these long-buried stories, but the health of the disclosers improved. Similarly, Pennebaker had students write down their secret traumas: sexual abuse by a grandfather, death of a dog, a suicide attempt. The immediate consequence was increased depression. But in the long term, the number of physical illnesses of the students dropped—by 50 percent—and their immune systems became stronger (Pennebaker, 1990).

Prolonged exposure therapy, an extinction or habituation procedure like flooding in which individuals are repeatedly exposed to the feared stimulus, has also been used to treat post-traumatic stress disorder. In this kind of exposure treatment, victims relive the trauma in their imagination, while overcoming the tendency to dissociate from the experience. They describe it aloud to the therapist, in the present tense. This is repeated session after session. In the best controlled study of exposure treatment, Edna Foa and her colleagues treated forty-five rape victims who had post-traumatic stress disorder (Foa, Rothbaum, Riggs, and Murdock, 1991). They compared the exposure treatment to stress inoculation training, which included deep muscle relaxation, thought-stopping for countering ruminations, and cognitive restructuring. Another group received supportive counseling. The fourth group was a control group consisting of those put on a waiting list for future treatment.

All groups, including those in the wait-list control group, improved. Immediately after the five weeks of treatment, stress inoculation training relieved post-traumatic stress disorder symptoms the most. But after another four months, prolonged exposure treatment produced the most lasting effects (Foa, Rothbaum, Riggs, and Murdock, 1991; Foa and Riggs, 1995; see also Frank, Anderson, Stewart, Dacu, et al., 1988; Resick, Jordan, Girelli, Hutter, et al., 1988; Foa, Riggs, Massie, and Yarczower, 1995; Frueh, Turner, and Beidel, 1995).

In an ongoing study conducted by Edna Foa, the combination of stress inoculation and prolonged exposure produced very good results. After five weeks of treatment (9 sessions), 80 percent of the victims were no longer showing post-traumatic stress disorder and symptoms were markedly reduced. No significant relapse was found. These new findings are the best outcome yet for treatment of rape victims, who are usually quite reluctant to go for treatment because they want to avoid thinking about the rape.

Psychological treatment thus produces some relief, but as yet no cures, and future research in this domain is essential. Preliminary evidence seems to indicate that a new approach, Eye Movement Desensitization and Reprocessing (EMDR; see Box 5–2), has been useful in treating PTSD patients. Controlled outcome studies are being conducted to see whether these results hold up to scientific scrutiny.

DISORDERS OF ANXIETY

In our discussion so far, we have focused on phobia and post-traumatic stress disorders, which we consider ***fear disorders.*** Both are problems in which anxiety is felt. Also, the individual afflicted by either of them experiences the four elements of fear: expectations of danger (the cognitive element); the emergency reaction (the somatic element); feelings of terror, apprehension, and dread (the emotional element); and avoidance and escape (the behavioral element). Phobia and post-traumatic stress disorder are similar in that they both stem from a specific object: the phobic object (cat, etc.) in the case of phobias, and the precipitating situation (flood, etc.) in the cases of

Francine Shapiro came across EMDR (Eye Movement Desensitization and Reprocessing) therapy quite serendipitously. She was walking in a park in 1987, ruminating, when she noticed that the disturbing thoughts were markedly losing their hold. Paying close attention to what she had been doing, she noticed that her eyes had been moving spontaneously and rapidly back and forth in an upward diagonal. Eager to try this out as a therapeutic technique, she began asking colleagues and friends to concentrate on disturbing beliefs and simultaneously to move their eyes back and forth while holding on to the images. When people varied their eye movements—faster, slower, different trajectories—the disturbance caused by the image seemed to wane markedly (Shapiro, 1995).

From these simple observations developed one of the most widely used, and one of the most controversial, psychotherapies of the 1990s. Shapiro created the EMDR Institute, and she and her colleagues have trained 14,000 therapists in the technique.

The core technique is as follows: the patient and therapist select a target memory that causes distress, and the patient generates a negative verbal thought about the memory (e.g., "I am unlovable"). The patient also generates a positive thought designed to replace the negative one (e.g., "I am kind"). The therapist rapidly moves her finger back and forth in front of the patient's eyes, and the patient follows the moving finger with his eyes while concentrating on the disturbing image or memory. After a set of ten to twenty eye movements, the patient rates his distress and how strongly he believes in the positive thought. This is repeated until the image becomes less disturbing and the belief in the positive cognition is much stronger.

Many therapists have found strong and sudden improvement in patients with anxiety problems, and encouragingly so with patients suffering from post-traumatic stress syndrome, a disorder that has proved quite resistant to both psychotherapy and drugs. EMDR therapists were dispatched to Bosnia and to Oklahoma City in the wake of those traumas.

Based on the preliminary evidence and clinical enthusiasm, researchers have begun to carry out controlled outcome studies. In the best-done study to date, eighty participants who were "experiencing traumatic memories" received three ninety-minute sessions of EMDR, with half receiving treatment immediately and half acting as a control group with EMDR received later. The disturbing memories included physical and mental abuse, death of a loved one, health crises, sexual abuse, and the like. Forty-six percent of the participants were diagnosed as suffering from full-blown PTSD. Substantial and rapid improvement occurred for the treated group relative to the group yet-to-be-treated, and their improvement was maintained over a ninety-day follow-up. There was less subjective distress about the memory, as well as fewer symptoms of depression and anxiety (Wilson, Becker, and Tinker, 1996).

EMDR has been the subject of strong criticism. Why this treatment works remains a mystery, as do its active ingredients. It seems that the eye movements are not necessary to successful outcomes. Finally some clinicians have criticized Shapiro both for training so many people in the technique before controlled outcome studies were done and for the cultish secrecy surrounding the technique (McNally, 1996). At any rate, human desperation and invention have often produced relief from problems long before the mechanism of cure was discovered, and the preliminary findings on EMDR seem strong enough that thorough scientific exploration of the technique is in order.

---

post-traumatic stress disorder. In contrast, in the ***anxiety disorders*** (panic disorder, agoraphobia, and generalized anxiety disorder), although anxiety is felt, there is *no specific object* that is feared. In these disorders, the anxiety felt by the individual is not focused on a clear and specific object. Panic disorder and its close relative, agoraphobia, involve acute experiences of anxiety, whereas generalized anxiety disorder is the chronic experience of anxiety.

Panic Disorder

How many of us have at some time been suddenly overwhelmed by intense apprehension? Physically, we feel jumpy and tense. Cognitively, we expect that something bad—we don't know what—is going to happen. Such an attack comes out of nowhere; no specific object or event sets it off, and the attack gradually subsides. But some people have more severe attacks, and they have them frequently. These people suffer from ***panic disorder***. Panic disorder consists of recurrent panic attacks.

▶ Cognitive and physical symptoms of anxiety make the world a frightening place for people who suffer from panic attacks. Their own symptoms can be as unpredictable and threatening as these creatures of Wifredo Lam's *The Jungle*.

SYMPTOMS OF A PANIC ATTACK

A panic attack consists of the four elements of fear, with the emotional and physical elements most salient.

Emotionally, the individual is overwhelmed with intense apprehension, terror, or depersonalization.

> It was just like I was petrified with fear. If I were to meet a lion face to face, I couldn't be more scared. Everything got black, and I felt I would faint; but I didn't. I thought "I won't be able to hold on" . . . (Laughlin, 1967, p. 92)

Physically, a panic attack consists of an acute emergency reaction (including shortness of breath, dizziness, racing heart, trembling, chills, or chest pains).

> My heart was beating so hard and fast I thought it would jump out and hit my hand. I felt like I couldn't stand up—that my legs wouldn't support me. My hands got icy and my feet stung. There were horrible shooting pains in my forehead. My head felt tight, like someone had pulled the skin down too tight and I wanted to pull it away . . .
>
> I couldn't breathe; I was short of breath. I literally got out of breath and panted like I had run up and down the stairs. I felt like I had run an eight-mile race. I couldn't do anything. I felt all done in; weak, no strength. I couldn't even dial a telephone. . . . (Laughlin, 1967, p. 92)

Cognitively, the individual thinks he might have a heart attack and die, or go crazy, or lose control.

> Even then I can't be still when I am like this. I am restless and I pace up and down. I feel like I am just not responsible. I don't know what I'll do. These things are terrible. I can go along real calmly for awhile. Then, without any warning, this happens. I just blow my top. (Laughlin, 1967, p. 92)

Such an attack begins abruptly, usually peaks within ten minutes, and subsides gradually. Panic attacks come in two forms: *unexpected* ("out of the blue") and *situationally triggered*. Unexpected panic attacks are the defining symptom of panic disorder. After a few attacks, the individual is likely to worry persistently about having another one and about the consequences (e.g., going crazy or dying). Situationally triggered panic attacks may be set off by social situations or specific objects (e. g., cats). An occasional panic attack is quite common, with as many as 20 percent of students and about 5 percent of senior citizens reporting one episode of panic in the preceding week (Barlow, 1988). When panic attacks are frequent, however—three in three weeks or four in a month—the condition is severe enough to warrant a diagnosis of panic disorder. Panic disorder has a prevalence rate of around 0.5 percent and may be more common in females than males. The first attack typically occurs when the individual is in her early twenties (Barlow, 1986, 1988; Joyce, Bushnell, Oakley-Browne, and Wells, 1989; Regier, Narrow, and Rae, 1990).

UNDERSTANDING AND TREATING PANIC DISORDER

Biomedical Approach There are four questions that each bear on whether a mental problem is primarily biomedical: (1) Can it be induced biologically? (2) Is it heritable? (3) Are specific brain functions involved? and (4) Does a drug relieve it?

The answers to these four questions suggest that panic disorder may be a disease of the body. First, panic attacks can be induced chemically in the laboratory in patients who experience them frequently. Such patients are hooked up to an intravenous line that slowly infuses into their bloodstream sodium lactate, a chemical that normally produces rapid, shallow breathing and heart palpitations. Within a few minutes about 60 to 90 percent of these patients have a panic attack. Normal controls rarely have panic attacks when infused with sodium lactate (Liebowitz, Gorman, Fyer, et al., 1985; Liebowitz, Fyer, Gorman, et al., 1985).

Second, panic disorder may have a genetic origin. If one of two identical twins has panic disorder, 31 percent of the co-twins are also found to have the disorder. But if one of two fraternal twins has panic disorder, none of the co-twins are so afflicted. Panic runs in families, and more than half of panic disorder patients have close relatives who have some anxiety disorder or suffer from alcoholism (Torgersen, 1983; Crowe, 1990).

Third, there is some evidence that panic disorder patients may have a neurochemical abnormality. The efficiency of the circuits in the brain that dampen and shut down the emergency reaction may be impaired (Nesse, Cameron, Curtis, McCann, and Huber-Smith, 1984; Charney and

FOCUS QUESTIONS

1. What is panic disorder?
2. Explain the emotional, physical, and cognitive symptoms of panic disorder.
3. What four questions do proponents of the biomedical model ask in approaching the etiology and treatment of panic disorder?
4. How does the cognitive model answer these questions?

▲ David Clark (1954–) of Oxford University has designed and tested an effective form of cognitive therapy for panic disorder. Clark proposes that panic results from catastrophically misinterpreting bodily sensations of anxiety, such as a racing heart, as symptoms of a heart attack. He teaches people to correct these misinterpretations and to recognize that the symptoms signify anxiety, not physical catastrophe. This brief therapy eliminates panic disorder in more than 80 percent of patients.

Heninger, 1986). In addition, PET scans have shown that patients who have panic attacks after being infused with sodium lactate have higher blood flow and oxygen use in relevant areas of their brains than patients who don't panic after lactate infusions (Reiman, Raichle, Robins, et al., 1986).

Fourth, there are two kinds of drugs that relieve panic. Tricyclic antidepressant drugs and a potent anti-anxiety drug, Xanax (alprazolam), both work better than placebos (see Table 5–5). Panic attacks are dampened, and even sometimes eliminated. General anxiety and depression also decrease (Pecknold, Swinson, Kuch, and Lewis, 1988; Svebak, Cameron, and Levander, 1990; Tesar, 1990).

So by chemically inducing panic, by demonstrating some heritability, by finding biochemical abnormalities in the brain, and by relieving panic with drugs, a strong case can be made for viewing panic disorder as a disease of the body.

Cognitive Approach   Proponents of the cognitive approach offer an alternative view of panic disorder. Cognitive therapists claim that panic disorder results from *catastrophic misinterpretations* of bodily sensations (Beck and Emery, 1985; Clark, 1988, 1989). The patient with panic disorder misinterprets normal anxiety responses, such as racing heart, breathlessness, and dizziness, as indicating impending disaster. The patient interprets palpitations as meaning a heart attack is about to occur; dizziness as meaning insanity and loss of control. The cognitive view looks at each of the four pieces of evidence for the biomedical view in light of misinterpreting the meaning of bodily sensations: (1) Lactate induces panic because it makes your heart race. It then creates the first bodily sensations that you misinterpret as catastrophe. (2) Panic attacks are partially heritable because having a particularly noticeable bodily sensation, such as heart palpitations, is heritable, not because panic itself is directly heritable. (3) Brain areas that prevent the dampening of anxiety are active as a result of the panic attack, not as a cause of it. (4) Drugs relieve panic because they quiet the bodily sensations that get misinterpreted as catastrophe. When these drugs are no longer taken, panic attacks recur in full force.

In the past decade, the cognitive school has carried out a series of additional experiments and created a new therapy. David Clark and Paul Salkovskis compared panic disorder patients with patients who had other anxiety disorders and with normal people. Everyone was asked to read the following sentences aloud, but the last word presented was blurred. For example:

TABLE 5–5

TREATMENT OF PANIC DISORDER		
	Cognitive Therapy	*Medication*[*]
Improvement	more than 80% markedly improved	60–80% markedly improved
Relapse[†]	very infrequent relapse	moderate to high relapse
Side Effects	none	moderate
Cost	inexpensive	inexpensive
Time Scale	weeks	days/weeks
Overall	**excellent**	**useful**

[*]Based mainly on outcome studies of tricyclic antidepressants and alprazolam (Xanax).
[†]Relapse after discontinuation of treatment.
SOURCE: Based on M.E.P. Seligman, *What you can change and what you can't* (New York: Knopf, 1993), Chapter 5.

If I had palpitations I could be	*dying.*
	excited.
If I were breathless I could be	*choking.*
	unfit.

When the sentences were about bodily sensations, the panic patients, but no one else, saw the catastrophic endings fastest. This indicates that panic patients possess the habit of thinking catastrophically.

Next Clark and Salkovskis asked if words alone would activate this habit of catastrophic thinking, thereby inducing panic. Everyone read a series of word pairs aloud. When patients with panic disorder got to "breathlessness-suffocation" and "palpitations-dying," 75 percent had a full-blown panic attack—right there in the laboratory. No normal people had panic attacks, no patients who had recovered from panic disorder had panic attacks, and only 17 percent of other anxious patients had panic attacks.

Clark and Salkovskis reasoned that if catastrophic misinterpretations of bodily sensations are the cause of panic disorder, then changing the misinterpretation should cure the disorder. The therapy they developed to do this is straightforward and brief. Patients are told that panic results when they mistake normal symptoms of mounting anxiety for symptoms of heart attack, going crazy, or dying. Anxiety itself, they are informed, produces shortness of breath, chest pain, and sweating. Once you misinterpret these normal bodily sensations as an imminent heart attack, this makes the symptoms even more pronounced because it changes your anxiety into terror. A vicious circle has set in, culminating in a full-blown panic attack.

Patients are taught to reinterpret the symptoms realistically—as mere anxiety symptoms. Then they are given practice in dealing with the anxiety symptoms. First, the symptoms of anxiety are brought on right in the office. Patients are told to breathe rapidly into a paper bag. This will cause a buildup of carbon dioxide and shortness of breath, mimicking the bodily sensations that provoke a panic attack. The therapist will then point out that the symptoms the patient is now experiencing—shortness of breath and heart racing—are harmless. They are simply the result of overbreathing, not a sign of a heart attack. The patient will then learn to interpret the sensations correctly. The following case illustrates how a cognitive therapist would proceed:

> One patient upon feeling somewhat faint would have a panic attack. He became afraid that he would actually faint and collapse. He interpreted his anxiety as a further symptom of fainting. This escalated to panic in a few seconds.
> THERAPIST: Why are you afraid of fainting? Have you ever actually fainted?
> PATIENT: I always managed to avoid collapsing just in time by holding on to something.
> THERAPIST: That's one possibility. An alternative explanation is that the feeling of faintness that you get in a panic attack will never lead you to collapse, even if you don't control it. In order to decide which possibility is correct, we need to know what has to happen to your body for you to actually faint. Do you know?
> PATIENT: No.
> THERAPIST: Your blood pressure needs to drop. Do you know what happens to your blood pressure during a panic attack?
> PATIENT: Well, my pulse is racing. I guess my blood pressure must be up.
> THERAPIST: That's right. In anxiety, heart rate and blood pressure tend to go together. So you are actually *less* likely to faint when you are anxious than when you are not.
> PATIENT: But why do I feel so faint?
> THERAPIST: Your feeling of faintness is a sign that your body is reacting in a normal way to the perception of danger. When you perceive danger, more blood is sent to your muscles and less to your brain. This means that there is a small drop in oxygen to the brain and that is why you *feel* faint. However, this feeling is mislead-

TABLE 5–6

THE BIOMEDICAL AND COGNITIVE EXPLANATIONS OF PANIC DISORDER		
	Biomedical Explanation	*Cognitive Explanation*
Panic attacks can be induced by sodium lactate infusions.	Lactate causes panic attacks in people with the disorder because lactate produces panic directly in biochemically vulnerable people.	People with panic disorder panic to lactate because they misinterpret the drug-produced increases in heart rate and breathing; their cognitions produce acute anxiety, compounding those effects.
Concordance for panic disorder is higher in identical twins than in fraternal twins.	The biochemical vulnerability that produces panic is heritable because it is biochemical.	Vulnerability to panic disorder is heritable either because the tendency to misinterpret certain physical symptoms is heritable or because higher heart rate is heritable.
Patients with panic disorder enter the panic state and show less inhibition of the emergency reaction.	Lack of inhibition of the emergency reaction is caused by a heritable brain abnormality and is not under patient's control.	Lack of inhibition of the emergency reaction is a symptom of panic, caused ultimately by the patient's cognitions.
Antidepressants and anti-anxiety drugs alleviate panic.	Drugs block the biochemical process that produces panic.	Drugs block the symptoms that are misinterpreted in ways that induce panic.

ing because you will not actually faint since your blood pressure is up, not down.
PATIENT: That's very clear. So next time I feel faint, I can check out whether I am going to faint by taking my pulse. If it's normal or quicker than normal, I know I won't faint. (Clark, 1989)

How well does this simple therapy work? Eighty to 90 percent of the patients treated with this therapy are panic free at the end of therapy (Klosko, Barlow, Tassarini, and Cerny, 1988; Michelson and Marchione, 1989; Clark, Gelder, Saldovskis, Hackman, Middleton, and Anastasiades, 1990; Beck, Sokol, Clark, Berchick, and Wright, 1991; Öst, 1991; Margraf and Schneider, 1991; Margraf, Barlow, Clark, and Telch, 1993; Westling and Öst, 1995), and twenty-four months later (Brown, Barlow, and Liebowitz, 1994).

In summary, both the biomedical and the cognitive schools have made major contributions to the understanding of panic disorder (see Table 5–6). Both have produced therapies that appear to relieve panic, as well as theories of how it is caused. But the cognitive approach seems to explain all of the biomedical evidence (but not vice-versa), and it has created a therapy that the biomedical view cannot account for.

Agoraphobia

As the name **agoraphobia**, literally "fear of the marketplace," implies, this disorder was long thought to be a phobia. Two important facts gradually emerged, however, from careful study of many agoraphobic patients: (1) most cases begin with a panic attack, and (2) the individual is not afraid of the marketplace or of places of assembly in themselves, but of having an attack there, being helpless, and of no one coming to her aid. These facts strongly suggest that agoraphobia is not a true phobia, in the sense of fear of a specific situation, but rather it is a more global anxiety disorder. DSM-IV sensibly categorized agoraphobia as a subtype of panic disorder.

FOCUS QUESTIONS

1. What is agoraphobia and why is it now considered a subtype of panic disorder rather than a phobia?
2. What kinds of treatments have been effective for agoraphobia?
3. Describe generalized anxiety disorder.
4. What kinds of treatment are most effective in providing lasting relief of generalized anxiety disorder?

SYMPTOMS OF AGORAPHOBIA

People with agoraphobia are beset not only with a terror of being caught with panic in the marketplace, but they also fear open spaces, crowds, bridges, and streets, or being in any situation in which escape might be difficult or embarrassing, or in which help might not be available in the event of suddenly getting sick. They typically believe that some disaster, usually a panic attack, will befall them when they are traveling away from the security of their homes, and that no one will help them. They then go to great lengths to avoid such places. Agoraphobia is crippling because many people with agoraphobia are unable to leave their homes. Agoraphobia is not uncommon, having a prevalence of about 3 percent (Thompson, Burns, Bartko, et al., 1988; Regier, Narrow, and Rae, 1990; Boyd, Rae, Thompson, and Burns, 1990). The large majority of those with agoraphobia are women, and the first panic attack usually begins in late adolescence, followed shortly by avoidance of going out of the home as in the following case:

A girl of nineteen suddenly came home from her work as a shop assistant and screamed that she was going to die. While standing at her counter, she had experienced the worst sensations in her life. Her heart began to pound like a jackhammer, she could not catch her breath, she was gripped by panic and dread, she felt the ground underneath her was about to give way, and she was convinced she was having a stroke or a heart attack. She spent the next two weeks in bed and, thereafter, she refused to walk beyond the front gate. She did not improve after four months as a psychiatric in-patient. After her discharge, she left her home only twice in the following seven years.

People with agoraphobia dread a variety of objects connected with open space: smooth bodies of water, bleak landscapes, the street, train travel on clear days. These objects are much less terrifying when the space is more comfortably circumscribed, as by a snowstorm or trees, or when an enclosed space is easily within reach.

Agoraphobic patients are prone to panic attacks even when they are not in the agoraphobic situation. Moreover, they have more psychological problems—other than their disorder itself—than do those with true phobias. People with agoraphobia are often globally anxious and generally depressed. Seventy percent of fifty-five patients with agoraphobia and panic also suffered depression (Breier, Charney, and Heninger, 1986). Substance abuse is also a frequent complication of agoraphobia. Obsessive-compulsive disorders occasionally accompany agoraphobia as well, and the relatives of agoraphobic patients are at greater risk for the entire range of anxiety disorders (Harris, Noyes, Crowe, and Chaudry, 1983). Untreated, agoraphobia will sometimes remit spontaneously, and then return mysteriously, or it may be unabating (Marks, 1969; Zitrin, Klein, Woerner, and Ross, 1983).

TREATMENT FOR AGORAPHOBIA

Two kinds of treatments have been quite effective for agoraphobia: behavior therapy—particularly flooding—and antidepressant drugs (see Table 5–7). In a flooding procedure, the agoraphobic patient agrees, usually with great apprehension, to enter a crowded public setting and to stay there without attempting to escape for a long period. This can be done first in imagination and then in reality. When it is done in imagination, the agoraphobic patient will listen to a long and vivid tape recording that describes a scenario in which she goes to a shopping center, falls down, is trampled by crowds, and hears them laugh as they observe her vomiting all over herself. Usually she is terrified for the first hour or two of flooding, and then gradually the terror will subside as she realizes that nothing is really going to happen to her. When she is actually taken to a shopping center subsequently, she will usually be greatly improved, and the anxiety may be gone. Treatment gains are maintained: four years after flooding, 75 percent of a group of seventy agoraphobic patients remained improved (Marks, Boulougouris, and Marset, 1971; Crowe, Marks, Agras, and Leitenberg, 1972; Emmelkamp and Kuipers, 1979; Fava, Zielezny, Savron, and Grandi, 1995).

Antidepressant and anti-anxiety drugs may also be helpful in alleviating agoraphobia, either alone or when given in concert with behavior therapy and supportive therapy. But there is an important distinction between who will benefit from medication and who will not. The distinction is between agoraphobic patients who do and who do not have spontaneous panic attacks. There is a small minority of agoraphobic patients who do not have panic attacks, and they may be considered having true phobias rather than having a subtype of panic disorder. They do not seem to benefit from medication (Marks, Gray, Cohen, Hill, Mawson, Ramm, and Stern, 1983; Zitrin,

TABLE 5–7

TREATMENT OF AGORAPHOBIA		
Extinction Therapy	*Drugs (Tricyclics)*	*Combination*
Improvement — at least 50% moderately improved	at least 50% moderately improved	60–80% markedly improved
Relapse* — 10–20% relapse	high relapse	10–20% relapse
Side Effects — none	moderate	moderate
Cost — inexpensive	inexpensive	inexpensive
Time Scale — weeks/months	weeks	weeks/months
Overall — **useful**	**useful**	**very good**

*Relapse after discontinuation of treatment.
SOURCE: Based on Martin E. P. Seligman, *What you can change and what you can't* (New York: Knopf, 1993), pp. 78–79.

Klein, Woerner, and Ross, 1983; Charney and Heninger, 1985; Ballenger, 1986; Mavissakalian, Perel, Bowler, and Dealy, 1987; Pollard, Bronson, and Kenney, 1989; Mavissakalian and Perel, 1995).

The behavioral model suggests the following analysis of the acquisition of agoraphobia for those whose condition begins with a panic attack. The CS is the *agora* (a stimulus complex in which panic might occur and help not come), the US is the first panic attack, the UR is the panic response, the CR is fear and avoidance of the agora. Based on this analysis, one way to cure agoraphobia would be to remove the possibility of panic attacks by drugs and then to show the agoraphobic patient that panic no longer occurs. In fact, it appears that the antidepressant imipramine reduces and removes panic. Groups that receive both imipramine and exposure therapy show improvement in that they experience less panic and tend to avoid the agora less. In contrast, groups that receive only exposure therapy show no less panic and only partial improvement in avoidance of the agora (Klein, Ross, and Cohen, 1987). This suggests that imipramine works by quelling the agoraphobic patient's spontaneous panic attacks. Once the panic attack is so controlled, the agoraphobic patient need no longer fear going into the street because the panic attack had been the traumatic event (the US) that he had feared and that he now knows will no longer occur (Telch, Agras, Taylor, et al., 1985; Ballenger, 1986; Mavissakalian and Michelson, 1986; Mattick, Andrews, Hadzi-Pavlovic, and Christensen, 1990; De Beurs, Van Balkom, Lange, et al., 1995).

Generalized Anxiety Disorder

In contrast to a panic attack, which is sudden and acute, generalized anxiety is chronic, and may last for months on end, with the elements of anxiety more or less continually present. DSM-IV requires a period of six months during which most days are filled with worry and excessive anxiety for a diagnosis of ***generalized anxiety disorder (GAD).*** An individual with generalized anxiety disorder has trouble controlling the worry and anxiety. His symptoms cause him considerable distress and problems at work and in relationships. Emotionally, the individual feels restless, jittery and tense, vigilant, and constantly on edge.

> I feel tense and fearful much of the time. I don't know what it is. I can't put my finger on it. . . . I just get all nervous inside. . . . I act like I'm scared to death of something. I guess maybe I am. (Laughlin, 1967, p. 107)

Cognitively the individual expects something awful but doesn't know what.

> I am frightened, but don't know what I fear. I keep expecting something bad to happen. . . . I have thought I could tie it to definite things, but this isn't true. It varies, and is unpredictable. I can't tell when it will come on. If I could just put my finger on what it is. . . . (Laughlin, 1967, p. 107)

Physically, the individual experiences a mild chronic emergency reaction: he sweats, his heart races, his stomach is usually upset, he feels cold, light-headed, and his hands usually feel clammy. He tires easily, has difficulty concentrating, is irritable, tense, and has trouble sleeping.

Behaviorally, he is always ready to run away, flee, or hide.

> For the past week or so I don't want to get away from the house. I fear I might go all to pieces, maybe become hysterical . . .

DSM-IV Criteria for Generalized Anxiety Disorder

A. Excessive anxiety and worry (apprehensive expectation), occurring more days than not for at least 6 months, about a number of events or activities (such as work or school performance).

B. The person finds it difficult to control the worry.

C. The anxiety and worry are associated with three (or more) of the following six symptoms (with at least some symptoms present for more days than not for the past 6 months) (*Note:* Only one item is required in children): (1) restlessness or feeling keyed up or on edge; (2) being easily fatigued; (3) difficulty concentrating or mind going blank; (4) irritability; (5) muscle tension; (6) sleep disturbance (difficulty falling or staying asleep, or restless unsatisfying sleep)

D. The focus of the anxiety and worry is not confined to features of an Axis I disorder, e.g., the anxiety or worry is not about having a panic attack (as in Panic Disorder), being embarrassed in public (as in Social Phobia), being contaminated (as in Obsessive-Compulsive Disorder), being away from home or close relatives (as in Separation Anxiety Disorder), gaining weight (as in Anorexia Nervosa), having multiple physical complaints (as in Somatization Disorder), or having a serious illness (as in Hypochondriasis), and the anxiety and worry do not occur exclusively during Post-traumatic Stress Disorder.

E. The anxiety, worry, or physical symptoms cause clinically significant distress or impairment in social, occupational, or other important areas of functioning.

F. The disturbance is not due to the direct physiological effects of a substance (e.g., a drug of abuse, a medication) or a general medical condition (e.g., hyperthyroidism) and does not occur exclusively during a Mood Disorder, a Psychotic Disorder, or a Pervasive Developmental Disorder.

SOURCE: APA, DSM-IV, 1994.

> Sometimes I get fearful and tense when I am talking to people and I just want to run away. (Laughlin, 1967, p. 107)

Considerably less is known about GAD than about any other anxiety disorder. Indeed, there is controversy about whether it is a disorder at all, because there are doubts that it can be reliably distinguished from panic and obsessive-compulsive disorder on the one hand and from normal worrying and fretting on the other. Here are a few of the better-documented findings: with a prevalence of 2.3 percent, GAD is somewhat more prevalent than panic disorder; it is more frequent in females; and it is mildly heritable. Family studies suggest that it is separable from panic disorder since relatives of GAD patients have more GAD than panic disorder, and relatives of panic disorder patients have more panic disorder than GAD (Blazer, Hughes, and George, 1987; Noyes, Clarkson, Crowe, and Yates, 1987; Weissman, 1990; Rapee, 1991; Kendler, Neale, Kessler, and Heath, 1992).

Two kinds of treatment have been tested in controlled outcome studies of GAD: anti-anxiety drugs and cognitive-behavioral techniques (see Table 5–8). The drug evidence is consistent: anti-anxiety drugs produce clear reduction in anxiety symptoms for as long as the drug is taken (McLeod, Hoehn-Saric, Zimmerli, and de Souza, 1990; Schweizer, Rickels, Csanalosi, and London, 1990; Hunt and Singh, 1991; Enkelmann, 1991; Thompson, 1996). Because relapse is so likely once the drug is stopped and because the drugs have some potential for addiction, however, anti-anxiety agents are not an ideal treatment.

The range of cognitive and behavioral techniques have been tried on those with GAD, and there exist three well-done outcome studies. In one,

TABLE 5—8

TREATMENT OF GENERALIZED ANXIETY DISORDER		
	Cognitive-Behavioral Therapy	*Antidepressant and Anti-anxiety Drugs*
Improvement	about 50% moderately improved	better than placebo
Relapse*	moderate relapse	unknown relapse rate
Side Effects	mild	moderate
Cost	inexpensive	inexpensive
Time Scale	weeks/months	days/weeks
Overall	**useful**	**marginal**

*Relapse after discontinuation of treatment.
SOURCE: Based on D. Barlow, J. Esler, J., and A. Vitali, Panic disorders, phobias, and generalized anxiety disorders, in P. Nathan and J. Gorman (eds.), *Treatments that work* (New York: Oxford, 1997), and on P. Roy-Byrne, and D. Cowley, Psychopharmacologic treatment of panic, generalized anxiety, and phobic disorder, in P. Nathan and J. Gorman (eds.), *Treatments that work* (New York: Oxford, 1997).

fifty-seven GAD patients were randomly assigned to either cognitive-behavioral therapy (CBT), behavioral therapy alone, or wait-list control. Treatment lasted from four to twelve sessions and follow-up was continued for eighteen months. Cognitive-behavioral treatment fared best (Butler, Fennell, Robson, and Gelder, 1991). The second study compared cognitive-behavioral treatment to an anti-anxiety drug (diazepam) in 101 GAD patients. A six-month follow-up showed clear superiority for CBT, with the drug no more effective than a placebo (Power, Simpson, Swanson, and Wallace, 1990). The third study found both CBT and relaxation superior to nondirective therapy, and emphasized imagery as an active ingredient (Borkovec and Costello, 1993).

Overall, anti-anxiety drugs appear to produce temporary relief from GAD until the drug is discontinued, while cognitive-behavioral techniques seem to produce more lasting gains.

COPING WITH EVERYDAY ANXIETY

Let's say you do not fit the diagnostic criteria for phobia or PTSD or panic or agoraphobia or GAD. Does this mean that all is well in your emotional life? Hardly. Your everyday anxiety may be unacceptably high and debilitating.

▶ Even in the absence of a specific disorder, "everyday anxiety" can be chronically high, or sometimes overwhelming.

BOX 5–3 ═══════════════════════════ IN THE CLINICIAN'S OFFICE

ASSESSING ANXIETY

Is your life dominated by anxiety? Dr. Charles Spielberger, past President of the American Psychological Association, is also one of the world's foremost testers of emotion. He has developed well-validated scales for calibrating how severe anxiety and anger are. He divides these emotions into their "state" form ("How are you feeling right now?") and their "trait" form ("How do you generally feel?"). You can use the trait questions in his Self-Analysis Questionnaire below to evaluate whether your everyday anxiety is too high.

SELF-ANALYSIS QUESTIONNAIRE

Read each statement and then mark the appropriate number to indicate **how you generally feel.** There are no right or wrong answers. Do not spend too much time on any one statement but give the answer which seems to describe how you **generally** feel.

1. I am a steady person.

Almost Never	Sometimes	Often	Almost Always
4	3	2	1

2. I am satisfied with myself.

Almost Never	Sometimes	Often	Almost Always
4	3	2	1

3. I feel nervous and restless.

Almost Never	Sometimes	Often	Almost Always
1	2	3	4

4. I wish I could be as happy as others seem to be.

Almost Never	Sometimes	Often	Almost Always
1	2	3	4

5. I feel like a failure.

Almost Never	Sometimes	Often	Almost Always
1	2	3	4

6. I get in a state of tension and turmoil as I think over my recent concerns and interests.

Almost Never	Sometimes	Often	Almost Always
1	2	3	4

7. I feel secure.

Almost Never	Sometimes	Often	Almost Always
4	3	2	1

8. I have self-confidence.

Almost Never	Sometimes	Often	Almost Always
4	3	2	1

9. I feel inadequate.

Almost Never	Sometimes	Often	Almost Always
1	2	3	4

10. I worry too much over something that does not matter.

Almost Never	Sometimes	Often	Almost Always
1	2	3	4

Scoring. Simply add your numbers over the ten questions. Be careful to notice that some of the rows of numbers go up and others go down. The higher your total, the more the trait of anxiety dominates your life. Adult men and women have slightly different scores on average, with women being somewhat more anxious generally.

If you scored **10–11,** your anxiety level is in the lowest 10th percentile.

If you scored **13–14,** your anxiety level is in the lowest 25th percentile.

If you scored **16–17,** your anxiety level is about average.

If you scored **19–20,** your anxiety level is around the 75th percentile.

If you scored **22–24 and you are male,** your anxiety level is around the 90th percentile.

If you scored **24–26 and you are female,** your anxiety level is around the 90th percentile.

If you scored **25 and you are male,** your anxiety level is at the 95th percentile.

If you scored **27 and you are female,** your anxiety level is at the 95th percentile.

SOURCE: "Self-Analysis Questionnaire": developed by Charles Spielberger in collaboration with G. Jacobs, R. Crane, S. Russell, L. Westberry, L. Barker, E. Johnson, J. Knight, and E. Marks. We have selected the trait anxiety questions from the questionnaire, inverting some of the scoring of the negatively worded items for easy self-scoring.

Box 5–3 allows you to assess its intensity. Everyday anxiety level is not a category to which psychologists have devoted a lot of attention. The vast bulk of work on emotion is about "disorders."

There is enough research, however, for us to recommend two techniques that quite reliably lower everyday anxiety levels (see Table 5–9). Both techniques are cumulative, rather than quick fixes. They require devoting twenty to forty minutes a day of your time for them to work.

The first is *progressive relaxation* done once or twice a day (better) for at least ten minutes. In this technique, you tighten and then turn off each of the major muscle groups of your body until your muscles are wholly flaccid. Relaxation engages a response system that competes with anxious arousal (Öst, 1987).

The second technique is regular *meditation.* "Transcendental Meditation" (TM) is one useful, widely available version of this. Twice a day for twenty minutes, in a quiet setting, you close your eyes and repeat a "mantra" (a syllable whose "sonic properties are known") to yourself. Meditation works by blocking thoughts that produce anxiety. It complements relaxation, which blocks the motor components of anxiety but leaves the anxious

FOCUS QUESTIONS

1. What is progressive relaxation and how does it relieve anxiety?

2. How does meditation relieve everyday anxiety?

TABLE 5–9

	Meditation	Relaxation	Tranquilizers
TREATMENT OF EVERYDAY ANXIETY			
Improvement	60–80% markedly improved	at least 50% moderately improved	60–80% markedly improved
Relapse*	10–20% relapse	moderate relapse	high relapse
Side Effects	none	none	moderate
Cost	inexpensive	inexpensive	inexpensive
Time Scale	weeks/months	weeks	minutes
Overall	**very good**	**useful**	**marginal**

*Relapse after discontinuation of treatment.
SOURCE: Based on Martin E. P. Seligman, *What you can change and what you can't* (New York: Knopf, 1993), p. 58.

thoughts untouched. Done regularly, most meditators enter a peaceful state of mind. Anxiety at other times of the day goes down, and hyperarousal to bad events is dampened. Done regularly, TM probably works better than relaxation alone (Eppley, Abrams, and Shear, 1989; Butler, Fennell, Robson, and Gelder, 1991; Kabat-Zinn, Massion, Kristeller, et al., 1992).

We urge you to weigh your everyday anxiety. If it is mild and not irrational or paralyzing, live with it. Listen to its dictates, and change your outer life accordingly. If it is intense or irrational or paralyzing, act now to reduce it. Intense everyday anxiety is sometimes quite changeable. Meditation and progressive relaxation practiced regularly may change it—and lastingly so.

SUMMARY

1. Phobias and post-traumatic stress disorder are both disorders in which fear is felt and in which specific objects or events set them off. Panic disorder, agoraphobia, and generalized anxiety disorder are anxiety disorders in that the individual feels very anxious although the danger anticipated is less specific.

2. The state of fear consists of four elements: *cognitively,* the individual expects danger; *somatically,* the individual experiences the emergency reaction; *emotionally,* the individual feels apprehension, terror, or dread; and *behaviorally,* the individual tries to flee the feared situation. The elements of anxiety are identical to those of fear except for the cognitive element; the anxious individual does not expect a specific danger but simply that *something* bad will happen.

3. A *phobia* is a persistent fear of a specific object in which the fear is greatly out of proportion to the amount of danger actually present. There are social phobias and four specific phobias: phobias of particular animals and insects, phobias of inanimate objects, phobias of illness and injury (nosophobia), and blood phobia.

4. The behavioral school holds that phobias are merely instances of the normal classical conditioning of fear to an innocent object that happened to be around when a traumatic event occurred. The behavioral model is consistent with case histories and laboratory evidence, and it has generated four effective therapies based on classical fear extinction: systematic desensitization, flooding, modeling, and applied tension for blood phobia. This latter appears to be a virtual cure for blood phobia.

5. *Post-traumatic stress disorder* is a fear disorder that is set off by a specific event. In some cases, the specific event is a catastrophic happening such as natural disasters, combat, and imprisonment in a concentration camp. More commonplace adversities—death of a relative, divorce, and mugging—may also set off the symptoms of PTSD in some individuals. Following the event, symptoms of anxiety and avoidance, reliving the event in dreams and waking, and numbness toward the external world may develop. Also, the individual may experience survivor guilt. The symptoms may last a lifetime. Exposure therapy (extinction) shows some promise, particularly after rape, but medications do not. EMDR is a promising new therapy for PTSD.

6. *Panic attacks* come out of the blue, with no specific event or object setting them off. They last for only a few minutes and consist of the four elements of the anxiety reaction. *Panic disorder* consists of recurrent panic attacks. Panic disorders can be relieved by drugs and markedly relieved by learning to reinterpret frightening bodily sensations as resulting from stress and not impending doom. Both the biomedical and cognitive approaches have recently contributed to an understanding of panic, and the cognitive model may have developed a cure.

7. *Agoraphobia* is a subtype of panic disorder and not a true phobia. It consists of anxiety about venturing into public places lest a panic attack occur there, and it usually begins with a panic attack in a public place. The combination of antidepressant drugs and exposure therapy seems to be the treatment of choice.

8. *Generalized anxiety disorder* is similar to panic disorder in that there is no specific event that sets it off. In generalized anxiety disorder, however, the anxiety is milder and is chronic, with the elements of anxiety strongly present almost daily for months on end. Anti-anxiety drugs and cognitive-behavioral therapy both provide some relief.

9. Mild, *everyday anxiety* can be relieved by regular relaxation or meditation.

QUESTIONS FOR CRITICAL THINKING

1. Why do you think single phobias dissipate in most children but are unremitting in adults who are not in therapy?

2. How does prepared classical conditioning account for why humans seem more prepared to learn to be afraid of certain objects rather than others?

3. What is the reasoning behind the change from the criterion used by DSM-III to that used by DSM-IV to diagnose post-traumatic stress disorder?

4. Why is agoraphobia so debilitating, and how can it interfere with a person's whole life if it goes untreated?

6

Obsession, Conversion, and Dissociation

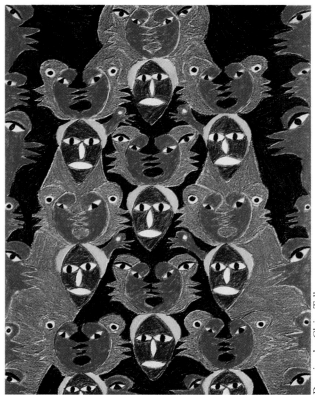

Drawing by Claire Teller

We have divided anxiety disorders into two classes: those in which anxiety is actually experienced by the sufferer, and those in which anxiety is not experienced but is inferred to explain the various symptoms. In the last chapter, we discussed those disorders in which anxiety is manifest: phobia, post-traumatic stress disorder, panic disorder, and generalized anxiety disorder. In this chapter, we will discuss those disorders in which underlying anxiety has often been inferred as the cause of symptoms.*

We will discuss three types of disorders. First is **obsessive-compulsive disorder (OCD),** in which the individual is plagued with uncontrollable, repulsive thoughts, and engages in seemingly senseless rituals. A person with OCD might think that he left the gas stove on and get out of bed to check it twenty times during the night. Another might have continual thoughts of killing her children and go to great lengths to keep all knives and sharp objects out of reach. The second disorder is the somatoform disorder called **conversion.** This disorder is characterized by a loss of physical functioning not due to any physical disorder but apparently resulting from psychological conflict. An individual might, for no biological reason, suddenly become blind, deaf, paralyzed, or suffer excruciating pain as a result of psychological stress. The third kind of disorder consists of **dissociative disorders,** in which the individual's very identity is fragmented. Among these are **dissociative amnesia,** in which an individual loses the memory of

*Note that in DSM-IV, obsessive-compulsive disorder is classified as an anxiety disorder, while the somatoform disorders and the dissociative disorders have their own separate classifications. This reflects the thinking of the committee that prepared DSM-IV. They believe that obsessive-compulsive disorder is more similar to phobia than to conversion or to dissociative amnesia. We still believe, however, that obsessive-compulsive disorder, the somatoform disorders, and the dissociative disorders should be discussed together because in each underlying anxiety is inferred by the theorist, rather than felt by the sufferer.

who he is, and *multiple personality disorder (dissociative identity disorder),* in which more than one identity exists in the same individual, each with a relatively rich and stable life of its own.

In contrast to the disorders in the last chapter, anxiety is not usually felt by the victims of these three types of disorders. Although people with obsessive-compulsive disorder often feel anxiety, they can ward off anxiety through quick and frequent rituals. Individuals with somatoform and dissociative disorders usually feel little anxiety. In fact, they may be surprisingly indifferent to their symptoms. But when psychoanalytic clinicians and researchers look at the conflicts that precede these disorders, they often infer that the symptoms are an attempt to control underlying anxiety that otherwise threatens to overwhelm the individual. For example, a man who believes he caused the paralysis of his friend may himself unconsciously assume the symptoms of paralysis; or a teenager who is plagued with unresolvable troubles at home and in school may forget who he is, wander to a new city, and assume a new identity. We begin our discussion of these disorders with obsessions and compulsions.

OBSESSIONS AND COMPULSIONS

All of us at least occasionally have distasteful and unacceptable thoughts. Many people at one time or another have had the following thoughts: "Might I do violence to someone I love?" "Am I absolutely sure that I've locked all the doors and windows?" "Have I left the gas in the stove on?" Most of us pay little attention to these thoughts when they occur; if we do, we soon dismiss them. Such is not the case in individuals with obsessive-compulsive disorders. An example of such an individual follows:

> A thirty-eight-year-old mother of one child had been obsessed by fears of contamination during her entire adult life. Literally hundreds of times a day, thoughts of being infected by germs would occur to her. Once she began to think that either she or her child might become infected, she could not dismiss the thought. This constant concern about infection resulted in a series of washing and cleaning rituals that took up most of her day. Her child was confined to one room only, which the woman tried to keep entirely free of germs by scrubbing it—floor to ceiling—several times a day. Moreover, she opened and closed all doors with her feet, in order to avoid contaminating her own hands. (Rachman and Hodgson, 1980)

FOCUS QUESTIONS

1. What is meant by anxiety felt and anxiety inferred?
2. Describe the two components of obsessive-compulsive disorder (OCD).
3. How does a person with obsessive-compulsive disorder attempt to ward off anxiety?
4. What characterizes an obsessive-compulsive personality?

Obsessive-compulsive disorder consists of the two components from which we derive its name: obsessions and compulsions. *Obsessions* are repetitive thoughts, images, or impulses that invade consciousness, are often abhorrent, and are very difficult to dismiss or control. These thoughts are not mere excessive worries about real-life problems. The person with an obsession recognizes that the thoughts are products of his mind rather than imposed from outside. He is also aware that his obsessions are excessive and unreasonable and inappropriate; and he attempts to suppress or neutralize them with another thought or action. In the case above, the mother is obsessed with repulsive thoughts and images of disease and infection that she cannot ward off.

Compulsions are the responses to obsessive thoughts. They consist of rigid rituals (such as handwashing or checking) or mental acts (such as counting or praying or silently repeating words) that the person feels driven to perform in response to the obsession or according to rigid rules. The compulsions are aimed at preventing or reducing distress or averting some dreaded event or situation; these actions, however, are not connected in a realistic way with what they are designed to prevent, and they are clearly excessive. The mother above, for example, reacts to her thoughts of germs by compulsively scrubbing her child's room. Consider, too, the case below:

> A twenty-seven-year-old veterinarian described his severe compulsive ritual. His compulsion required him to flush the toilet a multiple of three times whenever he entered a bathroom. Sometimes he was "satisfied" with three times only; but on other occasions, nine, twenty-seven, or even more were needed. He was at a loss to control his compulsive ritual which had sometimes embarrassed him socially and was professionally handicapping. (Laughlin, 1967, p. 351)

Obsessions and compulsions cause marked distress, are time-consuming (take more than one hour a day), and interfere with the person's normal routine, work, or social relations. Generally, individuals who are afflicted with obsessions also have compulsions (Rachman, 1978, 1994; Rachman and Hodgson, 1980; Ball, Baer, and Otto, 1996). The terms "obsessive" and "compulsive" are often used interchangeably in the popular press, but they refer to two essential and distinct phenomena: obsessions are intrusive, re-

---

DSM-IV Criteria for Obsessive-Compulsive Disorder

A. Either obsessions or compulsions:
Obsessions as defined by (1), (2), (3), and (4): (1) recurrent and persistent thoughts, impulses, or images that are experienced, at some time during the disturbance, as intrusive and inappropriate and that cause marked anxiety or distress; (2) the thoughts, impulses, or images are not simply excessive worries about real-life problems; (3) the person attempts to ignore or suppress such thoughts, impulses, or images, or to neutralize them with some other thought or action; (4) the person recognizes that the obsessional thoughts, impulses, or images are a product of his or her own mind (not imposed from without as in thought insertion).
Compulsions as defined by (1) and (2): (1) repetitive behaviors (e.g., hand washing, ordering, checking) or mental acts (e.g., praying, counting, repeating words silently) that the person feels driven to perform in response to an obsession, or according to rules that must be applied rigidly; (2) the behaviors or mental acts are aimed at preventing or reducing distress or preventing some dreaded event or situation; however, these behaviors or mental acts either are not connected in a realistic way with what they are designed to neutralize or prevent or are clearly excessive.
B. At some point during the course of the disorder, the person has recognized that the obsessions or compulsions are excessive or unreasonable. (*Note:* This does not apply to children.)
C. The obsessions or compulsions cause marked distress, are time consuming (take more than 1 hour a day), or significantly interfere with the person's normal routine, occupational (or academic) functioning, or usual social activities or relationships.
D. If another Axis I disorder is present, the content of the obsessions or compulsions is not restricted to it (e.g., preoccupation with food in the presence of an Eating Disorder; hair pulling in the presence of Trichotillomania; concern with appearance in the presence of Body Dysmorphic Disorder; preoccupation with drugs in the presence of a Substance Use Disorder; preoccupation with having a serious illness in the presence of Hypochondriasis; preoccupation with sexual urges or fantasies in the presence of a Paraphilia; or guilty ruminations [repeated thoughts] in the presence of Major Depressive Disorder).
E. The disturbance is not due to the direct physiological effects of a substance (e.g., a drug of abuse, a medication) or a general medical condition.
SOURCE: APA, DSM-IV, 1994.

---

current, anxiety-producing thoughts, while compulsions are the stereotyped physical or mental acts performed in order to rid oneself of the anxiety produced by an obsession. The two are usually found together.

What distinguishes obsessions of clinical proportions from more harmless recurring thoughts? There are three hallmarks: (1) obsessions are *distressing* and *unwelcome* and intrude on consciousness; an obsessive complains, "The thought that I might strangle my child keeps returning and prevents me from concentrating on my work," whereas mere recurring thoughts do not interfere with work; (2) obsessions arise *from within,* not from an external situation; and (3) obsessions are very *difficult to control.* Someone with merely recurring thoughts can readily distract himself and think of something else; someone with an obsession, in contrast, complains, "I can't help myself—I keep saying the numbers over and over again."

Anxiety, Depression, and Obsessions

What motivates a person with obsessive-compulsive disorder to perform such strange actions as flushing a toilet in multiples of three? How does he feel when he has obsessive thoughts and performs his compulsive rituals? The thoughts (the obsessive component) are very disturbing. Typically, the individual suffers considerable internal distress. A mild emergency reaction of the type described in the previous chapter is often present; he feels foreboding and dread. If the ritual is performed frequently and fast enough in response to the thoughts, he can reduce or even ward off the ensuing anxiety. This is why obsessions and compulsions are put in the anxiety-inferred category. The patient finds ways of dealing with the anxiety—by acting out his compulsions. But if his compulsive ritual is prevented, he will first feel tension similar to what we would feel if someone prevented us from answering a ringing telephone. If the barrier persists, intense distress will sweep over the patient. Here, of course, the anxiety will be felt. The individual's distress then can only be alleviated by carrying out the compulsion, thereby neutralizing the anxiety evoked by the obsessive thoughts and images. The next case illustrates this.

> A middle-aged woman complained of an obsession concerning colors and heat. "The main problem is colors. I cannot look at any of the colors that are in the fire, red, orange or pink."
>
> She believed the colors blue, green, brown, white, and gray were neutral, and she used these colors to "neutralize" the fiery colors. "If I happen to see a fire color, I've got to immediately look at some other color to cancel it out. I've got to look at a tree or flowers out on the grounds, something brown or white, to neutralize it." She used to walk around with a small piece of green carpet in order to neutralize the effects of any orange colors she might happen upon and see or imagine.
>
> She described the traumatic feelings that images of colored stimuli (or hot stimuli) evoked:
>
> It starts in my mind, and when I look at the color, I start to tremble and I go hot all over, just as though I'm on fire. I cannot stand up; I've got to sit down or else I'll fall. I feel sick, and all I can say is that it is a traumatic feeling, that's the only word I can think of to describe it. If it is the last color I look at before I get into bed, I just won't sleep all night. . . .
>
> I try to fight it, and get into bed and tell myself it is ridiculous. I know it can't hurt me physically, although it does harm me mentally. I lie there and this hot feeling comes over me, and I start to tremble. If that happens, I have to get up, put all my clothes on again and start once more, as though I am getting into bed. Sometimes I have to do this four or five times before finally getting to sleep. (Rachman and Hodgson, 1980)

Anxiety is in some way always there. And it is not the only negative affect associated with obsessions. Depression bears an intimate relationship as well. Obsessions and clinical depression appear frequently in the same person; as such, they are called **comorbid.** In fact, from 10 to 35 percent of depressed patients may have obsessions as well (Gittleson, 1966; Sakai, 1967; Beech and Vaughan, 1979; Ricciardi, 1995). During their periods of depression, the incidence of obsessions triples over the rate before and after the depression (Videbech, 1975). Not only do depressed patients tend to develop obsessions, but obsessional patients are prone to develop depression as well (Wilner, Reich, Robins, Fishman, and Van Doren, 1976; Teasdale and Rezin, 1978).

Vulnerability to Obsessive-Compulsive Disorder

Obsessive-compulsive disorders are not uncommon. Between 2 and 3 percent of adults are diagnosed as obsessive-compulsive. Women are probably more vulnerable than men (Robins et al., 1984). The problem may be somewhat heritable, since identical twins show higher concordance than fraternal twins (Carey and Gottesman, 1981). Relatives of OCD patients often do not have obsessive-compulsive disorders themselves, but they do often suffer from other anxiety disorders as well as subclinical obsessions and compulsions (Black, Noyes, Goldstein, and Blum, 1992). The disorder usually comes on gradually, beginning in adolescence or early adulthood. Our patient with color obsession describes the typically vague and gradual onset of her disorder:

> It is hard to say exactly when the obsession started. It was gradual. My obsession about colors must have been coming on for a couple of years very, very gradually. I only noticed it fully during the past twelve years when it got worse and worse. I can't look at certain colors, can't bathe, can't do any cooking, have to repeat many activities over and over again. . . .
>
> I think it all began some years ago when I had a sort of nervous breakdown. At the onset, I went very hot; it seemed to happen overnight somehow. I was in bed, and woke up feeling very hot. It was connected with an obsession that I had about my ailing mother at the time. I feared for her safety, and when I got a horrible thought that she might have an accident or a serious illness, this horrible hot feeling came over me. (Rachman and Hodgson, 1980)

Is there a specific type of personality that is vulnerable to an obsessive-compulsive disorder? Here we should make an important distinction between OCD and **obsessive-compulsive personality.** The popular notion is that a person with an obsessive-compulsive personality is methodical and leads a very well-ordered life. He is always on time. He is meticulous in how he dresses and what he says. He pays exasperatingly close attention to detail, and he strongly dislikes dirt. He may have a distinct cognitive style, showing intellectual rigidity and focusing on details. He is deliberate in thought and action, and often highly moralistic. He is preoccupied with rules, lists, order, organization, or schedules to the point where he cannot see the forest through the trees. His perfectionism interferes with completing a task. He works so devotedly that he has no leisure and few friends. He is not a warm individual. In addition, he is reluctant to delegate tasks or to work with others (Sandler and Hazari, 1960; Shapiro, 1965; Pollack, 1979; DSM-III-R; DSM-IV Options Book; Sachdev and Hay, 1995).

The crucial difference between having an obsessive-compulsive personality and having an obsessive-compulsive disorder has to do with how much the person *likes* having the symptoms. An obsessive-compulsive person views his meticulousness and love of detail with pride and self-esteem. For an individual with an obsessive-compulsive disorder, however, these characteristics are abhorrent, unwanted, and tormenting. They are "ego-alien."

When one actually looks at the personality of individuals with obsessive-compulsive disorders, little evidence emerges showing that they also have an obsessive-compulsive personality. A majority of OCD patients have no history of an obsessional personality, and few people with an obsessional personality develop OCD. What they do have are excessive concerns about cleanliness, checking, and conscience (see Box 6–1).

Theories of Obsessive-Compulsive Disorder

What causes an obsessive-compulsive disorder? There are three major theoretical views: psychodynamic, cognitive-behavioral, and biomedical (see Table 6–1). Their strengths complement each other well. The psychodynamic view wrestles with the question of the genesis of the obsession—who gets it and why it takes a particular form—but is less illuminating about why it persists for years once it has started. The cognitive-behavioral view illuminates its persistence, but leaves us in the dark as to who gets it and what its content will be. The biomedical view points to the brain structures underlying OCD.

THE PSYCHODYNAMIC VIEW OF THE OBSESSIVE-COMPULSIVE DISORDER

The questions "Who will get an obsessive-compulsive disorder?" and "What form will it take?" lie at the heart of the psychodynamic view of obsessive thoughts. According to this view, an obsessive thought is seen as a *defense* against an even more unwelcome and unconscious thought. This defensive process involves *displacement* and *substitution* (see Chapter 3). What happens

---

Box 6–1 ━━ **IN THE CLINICIAN'S OFFICE**

TESTING FOR OCD

Among the tools that are useful to clinicians are questionnaires, or inventories, that reliably aid in diagnosis. S. J. Rachman and Ray Hodgson of the Maudsley Hospital in London developed a questionnaire that helps determine who might have OCD. The questionnaire isolates three major components of obsessive-compulsive disorders: cleaning, checking, and doubting. The answers are those typically given by OCD patients.

SAMPLE QUESTIONS FROM THE MAUDSLEY OBSESSIVE-COMPULSIVE INVENTORY

Components of Obsessive-Compulsive Disorder	Obsessive-Compulsive Disorder Answer
Cleaning	
1. I am not excessively concerned about cleanliness.	False
2. I avoid using public telephones because of possible contamination.	True
3. I can use well-kept toilets without any hesitation.	False
4. I take a rather long time to complete my washing in the morning.	True
Checking	
1. I frequently have to check things (gas or water taps, doors) more than once.	True
2. I do not check letters over and over again before mailing them.	False
3. I frequently get nasty thoughts and have difficulty getting rid of them.	True
Doubting-Conscience	
1. I have a very strict conscience.	True
2. I usually have serious doubts about the simple everyday things I do.	True
3. Neither of my parents was very strict during my childhood.	False

SOURCE: Rachman and Hodgson, 1980.

FOCUS QUESTIONS

1. Describe the three theories that explain the etiology of OCD.
2. What are the strengths of each of these explanations?
3. What are the neurological and brain abnormalities that have been found in many OCD patients?
4. Describe the therapies for OCD.

is that an unconscious dangerous thought, such as "my mother might die of a fever" in the previously mentioned case of the woman with color and heat obsession, threatens to break into the individual's consciousness. This arouses anxiety. To defend against this anxiety, the individual unconsciously displaces this anxiety from the original terrifying thought onto a less unwelcome substitute, like hot and fiery colors. The defense has a powerful internal logic, and the thoughts that are substituting for the underlying thought are not arbitrary. Fiery and hot colors symbolize the fever that her ailing mother might die of.

Psychodynamic theory explains *who* will develop an obsession in response to underlying conflict-arousing anxiety, and *what content* the obsession will take on to symbolize the underlying conflict. The following case of obsession about infanticide illustrates why the particular individual would be susceptible to the particular form of obsession she developed:

A thirty-two-year-old mother of two had obsessional thoughts of injuring and murdering her children and more infrequently, her husband. These thoughts were almost as threatening and as guilt-provoking as the very act itself. Therapy uncovered even more threatening impulses from her childhood which had been displaced onto her children. She had been the eldest of three siblings and while very young had been given undue responsibility for their care. She felt deprived of affection from her parents and was greatly resentful of her younger sister and brother. She entertained murderous fantasies about them, which were accompanied by tremendous guilt and anxiety. As a result, these fantasies had been completely driven from consciousness. When she became an adult, her children symbolically stood for her siblings, whose destruction would make her the sole object of parental love and relieve her of her childhood burden. Her own mother's occa-

TABLE 6-1

VIEWS OF OBSESSIVE-COMPULSIVE DISORDER				
Theoretical view	Who develops OCD?	What happens?	How is it sustained?	How is it cured?
Psychodynamic view	People with specific unconscious conflicts (e.g., thoughts of injuring or murdering one's child or mother)	Obsessive thought begins as a defense against a more unacceptable thought.	Obsession and accompanying compulsion are maintained because they successfully defend against anxiety.	Unconscious conflict is recognized and worked through.
Cognitive-behavioral view	People who cannot distract themselves easily from troubling thoughts, often combined with depression	Obsessive thoughts (present in normals also) become frequent and persistent, while depression simultaneously weakens ability to distract oneself.	Patient discovers a ritual that temporarily relieves anxiety, which is then reinforced through repetition.	Response blocking of compulsion extinguishes obsession.
Biomedical view	People with overactive cortical-striatal-thalamic circuit	Repetitive behavior may be poorly inhibited; anxiety may be inadequately dampened; filtering of irrelevant information may be inadequate.	Obsessive thoughts and compulsive behaviors are directed toward objects and situations evolution has prepared us to see as threatening.	Drugs (e.g., clomipramine) down-regulate overactive cortical-striatal-thalamic circuit.

▲ S.J. Rachman has formulated a comprehensive cognitive–behavioral theory of obsessions.

sional visits triggered the obsessions. She was particularly susceptible because she had unresolved and anxiety-provoking resentment against her own parents and siblings. Her obsession had the content of death as it symbolized the death of her siblings, which would have solved her childhood problem. (Adapted from Laughlin, 1967, pp. 324–26)

Thus, the psychodynamic view of obsessions claims that powerful, abhorrent wishes and conflicts that have been repressed and threaten to break into consciousness put an individual at risk for obsessions, and that adopting the defense of displacement and substitution provides the immediate mechanism for relief (Wegner and Zanakos, 1994). In addition, the particular content of the obsessions these individuals acquire will be a symbol for the underlying conflict.

COGNITIVE-BEHAVIORAL VIEW OF THE OBSESSIVE-COMPULSIVE DISORDER

S. J. Rachman and Ray Hodgson have formulated the most comprehensive cognitive-behavioral theory of obsessions (Rachman, 1978; Rachman and Hodgson, 1980). The theory begins with the assumption that we all experience obsessional thoughts occasionally. The thought "Step on a crack and you'll break your mother's back" followed by an avoidance of sidewalk cracks is a common obsessive-compulsive ritual in children. For others, memories of radio jingles often intrude, unbidden, into consciousness. But most of us outgrow the sidewalk ritual, and we easily are able to distract ourselves from or habituate to the radio jingles. We can also dismiss the more awful thoughts that occasionally run through our heads. Individuals with obsessive-compulsive disorders, however, differ from the rest of us in that they are unable to habituate, dismiss, and distract themselves from such intrusive thoughts.

The more anxiety-provoking and depressing the content of the obsession, the more difficult it is for anyone—obsessive or nonobsessive—to dismiss the thought or distract himself from it. When normal individuals are shown a brief but stressful film, most of them have intrusive and repetitive thoughts. For example, a stressful film depicting a gruesome woodshop accident brought about anxiety and repetitive thoughts about the accident. The more emotionally upset an individual was made by the film, the more intrusive and repetitive the thoughts (Horowitz, 1975). Furthermore, anxious individuals find threatening words more intrusive than normal controls

▶ Drawing by W. Miller, © 1992 The New Yorker Magazine, Inc.

(Matthews and MacLeod, 1986; MacLeod and McLaughlin, 1995; Matthews, Mogg, Kentish, and Eysenck, 1995). This supports two of the assumptions of the cognitive-behavioral view of obsession: (1) we all have unwanted and repetitive thoughts; and (2) the more stressed we are, the more frequent and intense are these thoughts.

Recall now the link between depression and obsession. To the extent that an individual is depressed beforehand, obsessive thoughts will be more disturbing and therefore more difficult to dismiss. In addition, as we will see in Chapter 8, depressed individuals display more helplessness (Seligman, 1975). This means that they are less able to initiate voluntary responses to relieve their own distress. The act of distracting oneself is a voluntary cognitive response, and like other such responses, it will be weakened by depression. A background of depression is therefore fertile soil for an obsessive-compulsive disorder.

Here, then, is the chain of events that distinguishes a person with obsessive-compulsive disorder from a nonobsessive person, according to the cognitive-behavioral view. For a nonobsessive person, some initiating event, either internal or external, leads to a disturbing image or thought. A nonobsessive person may find this thought unacceptable but will not be made anxious by it. If he is not in a state of depression, he will easily dismiss the thought or distract himself from it. In contrast, the person with obsessive-compulsive disorder will be made anxious by the thought, and the anxiety and depression will reduce his ability to dismiss it. The thought will persist, and the person's inability to turn the thought off will lead to further anxiety, helplessness, and depression, which will increase his susceptibility to the intrusive thought.

The cognitive-behavioral view also attempts to explain compulsive rituals. The rituals are reinforced by the temporary relief from anxiety that they bring. Since the person with obsessive-compulsive disorder cannot remove the thoughts by the distraction and dismissal techniques that the rest of us readily use, he resorts to other tactics. He attempts to neutralize the bad thought, often by substituting a "good" action. The person with the fiery color obsession neutralized the color orange by looking at a swatch of green carpet. Individuals who are obsessively afraid that their doors are not locked check them dozens of times a night. These compulsive rituals produce temporary relief, but they also produce a stronger tendency to check, wash, or seek reassurance, since they are followed by anxiety reduction and are therefore strengthened or reinforced. But the rituals can only be cosmetic; the relief they provide is only temporary. The obsessions are left intact, and they return with increased frequency and intensity. Each time a thought recurs, the ritual must be performed in order to produce any relief.

The strength of the cognitive-behavioral view is that it provides an account of why obsessions and compulsions, once started, might be maintained. The strength of the psychoanalytic view is that it tries to explain both the content of the obsessions and who is vulnerable. The next view we turn to, the biomedical view, can claim to be the most basic of the three: it looks for the brain structures underlying OCD.

THE BIOMEDICAL THEORY OF THE OBSESSIVE-COMPULSIVE DISORDER

Biomedical researchers claim that OCD is a brain disease. There are four lines of evidence for this view: (1) neurological signs, (2) brain scan abnormalities, (3) the primitive content of obsessions and compulsions, and (4) an effective drug (which we will discuss in more detail in the treatment section).

Neurological Signs OCD has been known to develop right after a brain trauma. On neurological examination, many OCD patients are said to show a number of abnormalities: poor fine motor coordination, more involuntary jerks, and poor visual-motor performance. The more pronounced such "soft signs" are, the more severe the obsessions (Hollander, Schiffman, Cohen, et al., 1990; Tien, Pearlson, Machlin, et al., 1992). This is consistent with the presence of an underlying, but subtle, neurological disorder.

> Jacob, eight years old, was playing football in the backyard. He collapsed and went into a coma with a brain hemorrhage. When he came out of brain surgery, which went very well, he was now plagued by numbers. He had to touch everything in 7's. He swallowed in 7's and asked 7 times for everything. (Rapoport, 1990)

OCD is also comorbid with neurological disorders such as epilepsy. After the great sleeping sickness epidemic (a viral brain infection in Europe from 1916 to 1918) there was an apparent rise in the number of OCD patients (Rapoport, 1990). Tourette's syndrome is a compulsive-like disorder of motor tics and uncontrollable verbal outbursts, apparently of neurological origin. There is a high concordance between OCD and Tourette's syndrome in identical twins, and many patients who have Tourette's syndrome also have OCD (Robertson, Trimble, and Lees, 1988; Leonard, Lenane, Swedo, et al., 1992; George, Trimble, Ring, et al., 1993; Swedo and Kiessling, 1994; Allen, Leonard, and Swedo, 1995).

Brain Scan Abnormalities   The second line of biomedical evidence comes from brain scan studies of patients with OCD. Several areas of the brain show high activity in OCD patients: the caudate nucleus, the orbito-frontal cortex, and the cingulate cortex (part of the striatum). Together, they constitute a "cortical-striatal-thalamic" circuit (see Figure 6–1). These areas are related to filtering out of irrelevant information and perseveration (or repetition) of behavior. In fact, inability to turn off distracting thoughts and perseveration of behavior seem like central problems in obsessions and compulsions. When these patients are treated successfully with drugs, these brain areas decrease their activity.

Unfortunately, different brain scan studies conflict on which brain areas increase and decrease in activity (Insel, 1992; Baxter, Schwartz, Bergman, Szuba, et al., 1992; Rubin, Villanueva-Meyer, Ananth, et al., 1992; Swedo, Pietrini, Leonard, et al., 1992; Robinson, Wu, Munne, et al., 1995). The remainder of the decade promises exciting research in this field, with the possibility of tracking down how the hyperactive cortical-striatal-thalamic circuit actually works and how drugs and behavior therapy affect this circuit. Consistent with this hypothesis is the finding that surgical interruption of this circuit produced substantial reduction in OCD symptoms in about one-third of thirty-three patients (Jenike, Baer, Ballantine, et al., 1991).

Primitive Content of Obsessions and Compulsions   The third line of evidence for a biological view concerns the specific content of OCD. The content of obsessions and compulsions is not arbitrary. Like the content of phobias, consisting mostly of objects that were once dangerous to the human species, the content of obsessions and of compulsive rituals is also narrow and selective. The vast majority of OCD patients are obsessed with germs or with violence, and they wash or they check in response. Why such a specific focus? Why not obsessions about particular shapes, like triangles, or about socializing only with people of the same height? Why no compulsions about push-ups, or about hand-clapping, or about crossword puzzles? Why germs and violence? Why washing and checking?

Across evolution, washing and checking have been very important. The grooming and physical security of oneself and one's children are central

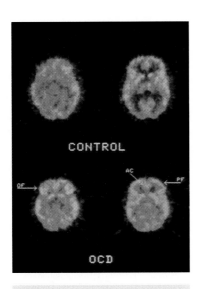

▲ PET scans of an OCD patient (bottom) and a normal control (top) reveal the differences in metabolic activity between OCD patients and normal controls. Blue indicates the lowest level of metabolic activity, with green and then yellow showing increasing activity.

FIGURE 6-1

THE CORTICAL-STRIATAL-THALAMIC CIRCUIT AND OCD

Several areas of the brain are implicated in patients with obsessive-compulsive disorder. The caudate nucleus, the frontal cortex, and the cingulate cortex (part of the striatum) together constitute the "cortical-striatal-thalamic circuit" (shown in red). These areas are related to filtering out irrelevant information and disengaging attention. Malfunction of the circuit may lead to the symptoms of OCD whereby the patient is unable to filter out irrelevant information and unable to disengage attention.

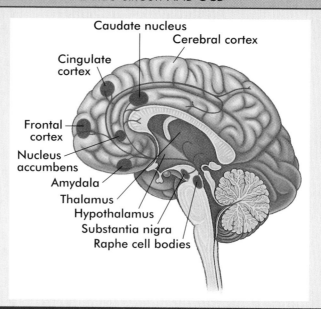

primate concerns. Perhaps the brain areas that kept our ancestors grooming and checking are the very areas gone awry in OCD. Perhaps the recurrent thoughts and the rituals in OCD are deep vestiges of primate habits run amok (Rapoport, 1990; Marks and Tobena, 1990).

Drug Therapy   Useful drug therapy is the final line of evidence for the biological theory. The drug clomipramine has been found to alleviate the symptoms of obsessions and compulsions in many OCD patients. We will discuss clomipramine in more detail as we examine the range of therapies available for OCD.

Treatment for Obsessive-Compulsive Disorder

Until recently, the prognosis for those with obsessive-compulsive disorders, either treated or untreated, was not particularly promising. But at present, three kinds of treatments are being used for those with OCD—psychoanalytic therapy, behavior therapy, and drug therapy—with varying results.

PSYCHOANALYTIC THERAPY

In psychoanalytic therapy for obsessions, the central issue is to enable the patient to recognize the underlying conflict by undoing repression of this unconscious conflict. The mother with thoughts of infanticide must gain insight into her impulse to do away with her siblings during childhood and understand the connection of this conflict to her present problems. The psychodynamic treatment of the patient with obsessive-compulsive disorder involves a thorough analysis of the patient's defenses and can be expected to take several years (Fenichel, 1945; Laughlin, 1967). Because there has been no controlled study of psychoanalytic treatment of obsessive-compulsive disorders, however, we can conclude little about its effectiveness.

BEHAVIOR THERAPIES

Behavior therapies for obsessive-compulsive disorders have shown promise, but so far these therapies have not usually resulted in complete cures. A combination of the three basic techniques of behavior therapy—response prevention, flooding, and modeling—are used in treating obsessive-compulsive disorders (Marks and Rachman, 1978; Griest, 1994). These three procedures all encourage and persuade but do not force the patient to endure disturbing situations. For example, these techniques were used to treat a patient who had obsessive thoughts that he might be contaminated with germs and who as a result spent four hours a day washing himself. In therapy, he first watched the therapist contaminate himself with dirt (modeling). He then was urged to rub dirt and dust all over himself (flooding) and endure it without washing it off (response prevention). After a dozen sessions of covering himself with dirt and just sitting there without washing it off, the thoughts of contamination diminished and the washing rituals no longer occurred in his daily life.

In this case, flooding the patient and preventing him from washing off the dirt cured the compulsion. In addition to such case histories, there have been six controlled studies of response prevention, flooding, and modeling in obsessive-compulsive patients (Rachman, Hodgson, and Marks, 1971; Hodgson, Rachman, and Marks, 1972; Rachman, Marks, and Hodgson, 1973; Roper, Rachman, and Marks, 1975; Marks and Rachman, 1978; Salzman and Thaler, 1981). These studies indicated marked improvement in about two-thirds of the patients; follow-up for as long as six years indicates that improvement is maintained in all but about 10 percent of respondents (Emmelkamp, Hoekstra, and Visser, 1985; O'Sullivan, Noshirvani, Marks, et al., 1991; Foa and Kozak, 1993). Moreover, in a summary of sixteen studies involving more than 300 OCD patients who were given behavior therapy, an average of 83 percent were judged "improved" by the end of therapy, and 76 percent were still improved over an average of two-and-one-half years of follow-up. The behavior therapies are specific in their effects: obsessive thoughts, compulsive rituals, and anxiety all decrease, but depression, sexual adjustment, and family harmony are not clearly helped. These results are not conclusive, however, since very few patients lose all their symptoms completely or are functioning well in all areas of life at follow-up. In addition, roughly 20 to 30 percent fail to improve at all (Meyer, 1966; Hackmann and McLean, 1975; Rabavilos, Boulougouris, and Stefanis, 1976; Beech and Vaughan, 1979; Rachman, Cobb, Grey, MacDonald, Mawson, Sartory, and Stern, 1979; Dominguez and Mestre, 1994).

Why do flooding, response prevention, and modeling often work, and what are their critical elements? Reconsider the man who washed himself for four hours a day. He had the obsession that some terrible illness would strike him if he did not wash. When he was persuaded to endure being dirty without washing, his obsessive thoughts of illness waned, and his compulsive rituals of washing vanished. What had he learned during flooding and response prevention? By covering himself with dirt and then not washing, his fear that dirt would lead to illness extinguished. The conditioned stimulus (CS) was the dirt, and the anticipated unconditioned stimulus (US) was illness. He received stark exposure to being dirty without getting sick, and Pavlovian extinction occurred. In addition, he learned that illness did not happen even though he did not wash. This was an instrumental extinction procedure for the compulsive ritual of washing. So flooding and response prevention may work for two reasons: (1) by showing the patient that the dreaded event does not occur in the feared situation (Pavlovian extinction), and (2) by showing the patient that no dreaded event occurs even though the compulsive ritual is not performed (instrumental extinction of the compulsion).

DRUG THERAPY

There is a drug that works markedly better on OCD than do placebos. Clomipramine (trade name: Anafranil) has been used with thousands of

▲ The American behavior therapist Edna Foa, of the Medical College of Pennsylvania, has pioneered the use of exposure therapy for post–traumatic stress disorder following rape and contributed to the evaluation of behavior therapy for obsessive–compulsive disorder.

TABLE 6–2

TREATMENT OF OBSESSIVE-COMPULSIVE DISORDER		
	Behavior Therapy	*Clomipramine*
Improvement[*]	50–60% moderate-marked improvement	50–60% moderate-marked improvement
Relapse[†]	10–20% relapse	moderate relapse
Side Effects	none	moderate
Cost	inexpensive	inexpensive
Time Scale	weeks/months	weeks
Overall	**very useful**	**quite useful**

[*]There is insufficient evidence as yet about the *combined* effects of clomipramine and behavior therapy to know if it is superior to either alone. See I. Marks, P. Lelliott, M. Basoglu, et al., Clomipramine, self-exposure, and therapy-aided exposure for obsessive-compulsive rituals, *British Journal of Psychiatry 152* (1988): 522–34.

[†]Relapse after discontinuation of treatment.

SOURCE: Based on Martin E. P. Seligman, *What you can change and what you can't* (New York: Knopf, 1993), p. 93.

OCD sufferers in more than a dozen controlled studies. Clomipramine is a potent antidepressant drug, a serotonin reuptake inhibitor. When OCD sufferers take clomipramine, obsessions wane and compulsions can be more easily resisted (Jenike, Baer, Summergrad, et al., 1989; Katz, DeVeaugh-Geiss, and Landau, 1990a, 1990b; Mavissakalian, Jones, Olson, and Perel, 1990; Trimble, 1990; Pato, Piggott, Hill, et al., 1991; Clomipramine Collaborative Study Group, 1991; Leonard, Swedo, Lenane, et al., 1991, 1993; Griest, Jefferson, Kobak, et al., 1995; Jefferson and Griest, 1996). An average of between 50 to 60 percent of OCD patients have shown improvement when treated with clomipramine (Foa and Kozak, 1993).

Clomipramine, however, is not a perfect drug. A large minority of patients (almost half) do not get better, or they will not take it because of its side effects, which include drowsiness, constipation, and loss of sexual interest. Those who benefit are rarely cured; their symptoms are dampened, but traces of the obsessive thoughts usually remain and the temptation to ritualize is still present. When those who do benefit stop taking the drug, many—perhaps most—of them relapse completely. But clomipramine is decidedly better than nothing (Pato, Zohar-Kadouch, Zohar, and Murphy, 1988; Piggott, Pato, Bernstein, et al., 1990; Griest, 1990; O'Sullivan, Noshirvani, Marks, et al., 1991). See Table 6–2 for a comparison of behavior therapy and clomipramine in the treatment of OCD.

SOMATOFORM DISORDERS

A woman is brought into a clinician's office. She cannot move her legs. And curiously, she seems little concerned about her seemingly paralyzed state. Following an initial interview with the patient, the clinician calls in a neurologist. After several neurological tests, the patient goes back to the clinician with a sealed report indicating "no neurological problem." Having seen this before, the clinician must now try to discover the psychological problem underlying the woman's paralysis. Such disorders are called ***somatoform disorders,*** and they have fascinated clinicians and researchers from Jean Charcot and Sigmund Freud to our contemporaries.

The Types of Somatoform Disorders

There are five factors to consider when diagnosing a patient suspected of having a somatoform disorder: First, the patient has lost or altered physical functioning. She may present with symptoms of deafness or paralysis. Second, the symptom cannot be explained by a known physical or neurological condition. There is no evidence of neurological damage to produce the deafness or the paralysis. Third, there is positive evidence that psychological factors are related to the symptom. Fourth, the patient is often, but not always, indifferent to the physical loss. More specifically, she does not feel anxiety about the symptoms. Finally, the symptoms are not under voluntary control. Conversion, somatization disorder, and pain disorder are all categorized as somatoform disorders in DSM-IV.

CONVERSION

Conversion, once known as hysterical conversion, is a disorder in which psychological stress is converted into physical symptoms. Consider this very curious case:

> Bear was a burly twenty-five-year-old construction worker who was paralyzed from the waist down—totally without movement or feeling—and had been so for three weeks. What's more, he was not particularly upset by his paralysis; that is, he was a bit concerned that he could not walk, but he was not emotional nor excessively anxious.
>
> After three days of tests that failed to show anything, the neurologist examining Bear had decided that there was nothing wrong with him physically and had sent him to Psychiatry.
>
> In Psychiatry, there was the same frustration as that experienced by the neurologist. Bear's recent life seemed uneventful to him, and he recalled no precipitating incident. He had used drugs occasionally, and he drank a bit, but he had no previous psychiatric history. Mystified, groping for any lead, one of the residents asked him if he knew anybody else who was paralyzed. At first, Bear couldn't think of anyone, but after a minute or so, he mumbled, without any show of emotion:
>
> "Yeah, come to think of it, Tom, a good friend of mine, is paralyzed from the waist down. Broke his neck."
>
> "How did that happen?"
>
> "It was really sad, and, you know, I guess it was pretty much my fault. Tom's a

---

DSM-IV Criteria for Conversion Disorder

A. One or more symptoms or deficits affecting voluntary motor or sensory function that suggest a neurological or other general medical condition.

B. Psychological factors are judged to be associated with the symptom or deficit because the initiation or exacerbation of the symptom or deficit is preceded by conflicts or other stressors.

C. The symptom or deficit is not intentionally produced or feigned (as in Factitious Disorder or Malingering).

D. The symptom or deficit cannot, after appropriate investigation, be fully explained by a general medical condition, or by the direct effects of a substance, or as a culturally sanctioned behavior or experience.

E. The symptom or deficit causes clinically significant distress or impairment in social, occupational, or other important areas of functioning or warrants medical evaluation.

F. The symptom or deficit is not limited to pain or sexual dysfunction, does not occur exclusively during the course of Somatization Disorder, and is not better accounted for by another mental disorder.

SOURCE: APA, DSM-IV, 1994.

virgin, like in every way possible. Doesn't even drink or smoke. Well, we were together at a party about a month ago, and I was riding him. I thought he should live a little, try some LSD. I guess he couldn't take it, so he gave in.

"Well, we downed a couple of tabs, and within a few minutes he was flying. Seeing all sorts of weird things. He ran out of the apartment, and I followed, a little afraid for him. God, it was awful! He was running away from something in his head. Next thing I knew, he jumped off the bridge. You know, the one over the tracks at 30th Street Station. He was still alive when the rescue squad got him down from the high tension lines. They say he'll never walk, or anything, again."

"Bear, tell me again when your problem started."

"Out of nowhere. About three weeks ago. I was at work, driving my forklift down at the station. As I crossed over the tracks under the high tension lines, suddenly I was all dead down there. I shouted for help, and my buddies took me off to. . . . Oh, my God! Don't you see what I've done!"

And within a few days, Bear walked home. (Stinnett, 1978)

Bear's paralysis has the five symptoms of somatoform disorder. First, he has lost physical functioning: he is paralyzed. Second, physical damage cannot explain the paralysis, since he is neurologically sound. Third, the paralysis is not under voluntary control. Fourth, Bear seems remarkably indifferent to his paralysis; he feels no anxiety about his paralysis. And fifth, there is good evidence that psychological factors are certainly related to, and probably caused the symptoms: (1) he has a friend with paralysis caused partly by his actions; (2) the paralysis began at the same site that his friend's paralysis occurred; (3) Bear did not easily remember the incident when his friend was paralyzed, nor did he relate it to his own paralysis; and (4) Bear could not control his paralysis, but when he gained insight into this, his paralysis remitted.

SOMATIZATION DISORDER (BRIQUET'S SYNDROME)

In *somatization disorder,* also called ***Briquet's disorder,*** the person has had many physical complaints that began before age thirty, resulting in a complicated history of medical treatment. These complaints involve many different organs and cannot be fully explained from known physical causes nor are they under voluntary control. The symptoms include a history of pain related to at least four different areas, such as the head, stomach, back, joints, arms and legs, rectum, chest, or pain on sexual intercourse, menstruation, or urination. In addition, the patient has at least two gastrointestinal symptoms other than pain, such as nausea, diarrhea, vomiting, or food allergies. The patient also has a history of at least one sexual or reproductive symptom other than pain, such as indifference to sex, problems with having an erection or ejaculation, irregular periods, excessive menstrual bleeding, or vomiting all through pregnancy. The patient also has a history of at least one "pseudoneurological" or conversion symptom that is not limited to pain, such as impaired coordination, paralysis, blindness, deafness, or loss of the sensation of touch. Unnecessary surgery, addiction to prescription medicines, depression, and attempted suicide are common complications of this syndrome. The fundamental difference between somatization and conversion is that the somatizer will suffer from many physical problems; the conversion patient generally has only one complaint.

PAIN DISORDER (PSYCHALGIA)

In addition to conversion and somatization, ***pain disorder (psychalgia)*** is also a somatoform disorder. In pain disorder, pain in one or more parts of the body, which causes marked distress or impairment, is the central symptom. Psychological factors account for its onset, or how severe it is, or its undue persistence, or for the worsening of the pain. The symptom is not

---

DSM-IV Criteria for Pain Disorder

A. Pain in one or more anatomical sites is the predominant focus of the clinical presentation and is of sufficient severity to warrant clinical attention.

B. The pain causes clinically significant distress or impairment in social, occupational, or other important areas of functioning.

C. Psychological factors are judged to have an important role in the onset, severity, exacerbation, or maintenance of the pain.

D. The symptom or deficit is not intentionally produced or feigned (as in Factitious Disorder or Malingering).

E. The pain is not better accounted for by a Mood, Anxiety, or Psychotic Disorder and does not meet criteria for Dyspareunia.

SOURCE: APA, DSM-IV, 1994.

DSM-IV Criteria for Somatization Disorder

A. A history of many physical complaints beginning before age 30 years that occur over a period of several years and result in treatment being sought or significant impairment in social, occupational, or other important areas of functioning.

B. Each of the following criteria must have been met, with individual symptoms occurring at any time during the course of the disturbance: (1) *four pain symptoms:* a history of pain related to at least four different sites or functions (e.g., head, abdomen, back, joints, extremities, chest, rectum, during menstruation, during sexual intercourse, or during urination); (2) *two gastrointestinal symptoms:* a history of at least two gastrointestinal symptoms other than pain (e.g., nausea, bloating, vomiting other than during pregnancy, diarrhea, or intolerance of several different foods); (3) *one sexual symptom:* a history of at least one sexual or reproductive symptom other than pain (e.g., sexual indifference, erectile or ejaculatory dysfunction, irregular menses, excessive menstrual bleeding, vomiting throughout pregnancy); (4) *one pseudoneurological symptom:* a history of at least one symptom or deficit suggesting a neurological condition not limited to pain (conversion symptoms such as impaired coordination or balance, paralysis or localized weakness, difficulty swallowing or lump in throat, aphonia [loss of voice], urinary retention, hallucinations, loss of touch or pain sensation, double vision, blindness, deafness, seizures; dissociative symptoms such as amnesia; or loss of consciousness other than fainting).

C. Either (1) or (2): (1) after appropriate investigation, each of the symptoms in Criterion B cannot be fully explained by a known general medical condition or the direct effects of a substance (e.g., a drug of abuse, a medication); (2) when there is a related general medical condition, the physical complaints or resulting social or occupational impairment are in excess of what would be expected from the history, physical examination, or laboratory findings.

D. The symptoms are not intentionally feigned or produced (as in Factitious Disorder or Malingering).

SOURCE: APA, DSM-IV, 1994.

under voluntary control. Statistically, it may be the most frequent of the somatoform disorders (Watson and Buranen, 1979; Drossman, 1982). The following case illustrates an individual suffering from psychalgia:

> Harry, a forty-one-year-old man, suffered a sudden onset of severe abdominal pain. Emergency surgery was about to be performed, but there was no elevated white cell count, and other physical symptoms were normal. In addition, Harry seemed emotionally indifferent to the pain and the fact of impending surgery. He was obviously in pain, but not anxious about it.
>
> Upon consultation, it was decided to abandon urgent preparations for surgery, and to explore for a possible psychological basis. It emerged that Harry had had a childhood that predisposed him to psychalgia. His parents had been materially wealthy, but they had given him very little love and affection. The one break in this emotional barrenness in his childhood had been his appendectomy. The love he had received during this period was meaningful, real, and what he had "always longed for."
>
> The present abdominal pain was set off by an incident of domestic deceit. His wife had become infatuated with another man and had threatened to go off with him. At this very point, the abdominal pain had begun. (Adapted from Laughlin, 1967, pp. 667–68)

The hypothesis in Harry's case is that whenever he is under serious stress, he will suffer pain in his abdomen. This pain becomes a somatic excuse for not suffering the anxiety brought on by the stressful events.

Diagnosing Somatoform Disorder

A somatoform disorder is one of the most difficult disorders to diagnose correctly. In the case study discussed earlier, how can we tell if Bear was faking paralysis or if he had some obscure physical illness that was as yet undiagnosed?

In an attempt to make diagnosis clearer, let us distinguish somatoform disorders from four other disorders with which it can be confused, sometimes tragically. These disorders are malingering, psychosomatic disorders, factitious disorder, and undiagnosed physical illness. In principle, there are two differences between *malingering* (faking) and an authentic somatoform disorder—neither of which is easy to pin down in practice. First, the symptoms of a malingerer are under his voluntary control, whereas they are not under the voluntary control of an individual with a somatoform disorder. A malingerer can turn the paralysis on and off, although it may be difficult indeed to induce him to display this voluntary control for you. The individual suffering conversion cannot. For example, even if we had offered Bear an irresistibly large amount of money to get up out of his wheelchair and walk away, he would not have been able to do so. Second, the malingerer acquires an obvious environmental goal as a result of his symptom (e.g., getting out of the army by feigning paralysis), whereas an individual with a conversion disorder does not necessarily achieve anything obvious by his symptom (see Box 6–2).

Malingering itself should be distinguished from *secondary gain.* Secondary gain consists of deriving benefits from one's environment as a consequence of having abnormal symptoms. Individuals with somatoform disorders frequently get secondary gains. So, for example, a person with pain disorder may get more love and attention from his family when he is in pain. The use of secondary gain seems to be part of the universal human trait of making the best of a bad situation. A person with a somatoform disorder who derives secondary gain, however, differs from a malingerer. The malingerer is faking the initial symptoms and then may, in addition, use them to benefit. The individual with the somatoform disorder, in contrast, is not faking the symptoms but may well derive benefit from having them. The pattern of symptoms sometimes distinguishes malingering from somatoform disorders. Hysterically blind patients do not crash into objects, but malingerers may.

Psychosomatic disorders, which are taken up in Chapter 11, also resemble somatoform disorders. What distinguishes psychosomatic disorders from somatoform disorders is the existence of a physical basis that can explain the symptom. Although some individuals who have a peptic ulcer or high blood pressure may have these conditions exaggerated or even initiated by psychological factors, the ulcers and hypertension are actually being caused by specific known physical mechanisms. In contrast, *glove anesthesia,* a conversion symptom in which nothing can be felt in the hand and fingers, but in which sensation is intact from the wrist up, cannot be induced by any known pattern of damage to the nerves controlling the hand.

The third disorder from which somatoform disorder must be distinguished is *factitious disorder,* also called "Münchhausen syndrome." This disorder is characterized by multiple hospitalizations and operations in which the individual voluntarily produces the signs of illness, not through underlying anxiety, but by physiological tampering (Pope, Jonas, and Jones, 1982; Folks, 1995). There was one documented case of a thirty-four-year-old man who, over a decade, had made 200 visits to physicians under dozens of aliases at more than sixty-eight hospitals and who had cost Britain's health service $2,000,000. In contrast to malingering, a factitious disorder has no obvious goal other than gaining medical attention. It is crucially different from so-

Box 6–2

IN THE CLINICIAN'S OFFICE

SIGHT LOSS AS CONVERSION DISORDER?

Under the regime of Cambodian leader Pol Pot, it is estimated that at least one million people (out of a total population of only seven million) were killed. Many were exiled from their homes in the city to the countryside, and there abused and even tortured. It became common for relatives to see the murder and torture of family members.

Clinicians have treated and studied the survivors of these atrocities. One woman, they report, watched as her three-month-old nephew was clubbed to death against a tree by Khmer Rouge soldiers. Soon after, she saw three other nephews and nieces beaten to death, and then her brother and his wife were murdered in front of her. She eventually emigrated to the United States and reacted to her Cambodian experiences by becoming blind. Two researchers have studied 150 cases of this sort just in the Long Beach, California, area. After finding no evidence of neurophysiological damage to the visual system, Gretchen Van Boehmel, an electrophysiologist, and Patrick Rozee, a psychologist, interviewed thirty of these women, aged fifty-one to seventy. They became convinced that the visual problems were conversion symptoms.

Unlike malingerers, these women had little to gain from blindness. Malingerers "play up" their symptoms by walking with exaggerated tripping motions and pretending they are not able to touch their nose with their fingers. But these women do not. Further, the longer the women spent under the Khmer Rouge and in Thai refugee camps, the worse their visual problems were.

Using a skill building and group therapy intervention with ten of the women, Van Boehmel and Rozee reported improved vision in four of them.

These could possibly be cases of conversion on a massive scale in which the women no longer "wanted" to see. Alternatively, however, undiagnosed physical illness must be considered. Undetected neurological damage resulting from years of malnutrition and abuse might be the cause.

SOURCE: DeAngelis, 1990.

▲ These civilian survivors of the atrocities perpetuated by Pol Pot's political party, the Khmer Rouge, were forcibly marched 160 miles across the Cambodian-Thai border. Many watched countless others die on the march, weakened by starvation and exhaustion.

matoform disorders because the symptoms are voluntarily produced by the person who has them and they are physically based.

Finally, a somatoform disorder may be misdiagnosed and actually result from an ***undiagnosed physical illness.*** The diagnosis of a somatoform disorder is for many people degrading, as the patient and his family are told that the disease is in his mind, not in his body. Current medical diagnosis is far from perfect, and occasionally an individual who has been diagnosed as having a somatoform disorder will eventually develop a full-blown physical disease, such as multiple sclerosis, which in fact had caused the earlier symptoms. This is one reason the diagnosis must be made with caution.

Table 6–3 summarizes the distinctions among conversion, malingering, psychosomatic disorders, factitious disorders, and undiagnosed physical illness.

Vulnerability to Somatoform Disorders

Conversion disorders are not common. Estimates vary widely, but probably not more than 5 percent of all nonpsychotic patients (or much less than 1 percent of the entire American population) have conversion disorders (Laughlin, 1967; Woodruff, Clayton, and Guze, 1971; Rogers, Weinshenker, Warshaw, et al., 1996). Conversion symptoms usually are displayed from late adolescence to middle adulthood; they occur in children and old people, but rarely (Kotsopoulos and Snow, 1986; Lemkuhl, Blanz, Lemkuhl, and Braun-Scharm, 1989). Although the large majority of patients with conversion disorder are women, between 20 and 40 percent of conversion disorders occur in men (Chodoff, 1974; Tomasson, Kent, and Coryell, 1991).

Somatization disorder, in which the patient has a complicated medical history before the age of thirty-five, with a large number of symptoms ranging across many organ systems, and with no known medical explanations, is more common. As many as 2 to 10 percent of all adult women may display this disorder, and it is rarely diagnosed in men (Woodruff, Clayton, and Guze, 1971; Cloninger et al., 1984).

There is marginal evidence that somatoform disorders may run in families (Torgersen, 1986). Somatization disorder probably does run in families. The sisters, mothers, and daughters of women with this disorder are ten times more likely to develop it than women in the general population (Woodruff, Clayton, and Guze, 1971). Nothing is presently known about family patterns of pain disorder.

TABLE 6–3

CRITERIA FOR DIFFERENTIAL DIAGNOSIS OF SYMPTOMS SUGGESTING PHYSICAL ILLNESS

Classification	Can a known physical mechanism explain the symptom?	Are the symptoms linked to psychological causes?	Is the symptom under voluntary control?	Is there an obvious goal?
Conversion	Never	Always	Never	Sometimes
Malingering	Sometimes	Sometimes	Always	Always
Psychosomatic Disorders	Always	Always	Never	Sometimes
Factitious Disorder	Sometimes	Always	Always	Never (other than medical attention)
Undiagnosed Physical Illness	Sometimes	Sometimes	Never	Never

SOURCE: Based on Hyler and Spitzer, 1978.

FOCUS QUESTIONS

1. What five symptoms characterize somatoform disorders?
2. Describe conversion, somatization disorder (Briquet's syndrome), and pain disorder (psychalgia).
3. Distinguish somatoform disorders from malingering, psychosomatic disorders, and factitious disorder.
4. Describe the psychoanalytic, communicative, and percept blocking views of somatoform disorders.
5. Explain how suggestion, insight, advice, drug treatment, and family therapy are used to treat somatoform disorders.

The Etiology of Somatoform Disorders

What causes the loss of the function of a bodily organ in the absence of any underlying physiological basis? This remains one of the great questions of psychopathology.

THE PSYCHOANALYTIC VIEW

The psychoanalytic view was put forth by Sigmund Freud in 1894 and remains a pillar of psychoanalytic thinking today. Freud believed that the physical symptom was a defense that absorbed and neutralized the anxiety generated by an unacceptable unconscious conflict (Freud, 1894/1976, p. 63). Today, the psychodynamic explanation of conversion still revolves around this notion, and postulates three distinct processes: First, the individual is made anxious by some unacceptable idea, and the conversion is a defense against this anxiety. Second, psychic energy is transmuted into a somatic loss. The anxiety is detached from the idea, rendering it neutral. Because anxiety is psychic energy it must go someplace, and in this case it is used to debilitate a physical organ. Third, the particular somatic loss symbolizes the underlying conflict. For Bear, the three processes seem to play a role: Bear is unconsciously anxious and guilty about causing Tom's paralysis, and he walls off these feelings from consciousness by transmuting the guilt and anxiety into his own paralysis. The particular symptom—paralysis—obviously symbolizes the real paralysis suffered by his friend.

This theory is just about the only idea that can explain one of the strangest symptoms of conversion: "la belle indifference." Unlike patients with actual physical loss due to injury, conversion patients are often strangely indifferent to their physical symptoms. For example, a patient with conversion paralysis may show much more concern over a minor skin irritation on his legs than the fact that he cannot move them (Laughlin, 1967, pp. 673–74). In the psychoanalytic view, a conversion symptom may absorb anxiety so well by transmuting it into a physical loss that the patient can actually be calm about being crippled, blind, deaf, or insensate.

While no complete behavioral view of somatoform disorders has been put forward, the psychoanalytic view gives a hint of what the behavioral view might look like. If conversion symptoms do, in fact, absorb anxiety, anxiety reduction reinforces the patient for having a symptom.

THE COMMUNICATIVE VIEW

There are negative emotions other than anxiety: sadness, anger, guilt, awe, bewilderment, and shame are all elements of the human experience. People with phobias or obsessive-compulsive disorders experience these emotions as well as anxiety, particularly sadness and anger. Moreover, patients with conversions—if they are defending at all—might not be defending against anxiety but against depression, guilt, or anger. This possibility has spawned another theory of conversion, which emphasizes the *communicative,* rather than the defensive, function of the symptom. The communicative model claims that the patient uses the disorder to deal with a variety of distressing emotions—not only anxiety—and to negotiate difficult interpersonal transactions. He expresses his underlying distress to himself in terms of physical illness, thereby distracting himself from his distress. He then communicates the fact that he is distressed to others with his physical loss. He unconsciously chooses his symptoms according to his own conception of a physical illness—which will derive in part from the illnesses that important people in his life have had—and according to what does and doesn't count as an illness in his time. His particular symptoms will then simulate physical illness either expertly or crudely, depending on how much he knows (Ziegler and Imboden, 1962).

The communicative model views the case study of Bear in the following way: Bear is depressed, anxious, and guilty over his role in paralyzing his friend. In addition, he cannot *talk* about his distress because he is not verbal about his troubles. By paralyzing himself he is able to distract himself from these emotions, so he *shows* his distress to others by his paralysis. Bear's particular symptom derives directly from identification with his friend's paralysis. Bear is alexithymic. The term **alexithymia** (literally, no words for feelings) has been coined to categorize such people who cannot easily express their feelings (Sifneos, 1973). When asked about how they feel about highly charged events, such as the death of a spouse, they describe their physical symptoms or simply fail to understand the question. For example, they may say, "My headaches got worse . . . it was like a band around my head . . . that's all I felt" (Lesser, 1985; Bach and Bach, 1995). Alexithymic people are particularly susceptible to somatoform disorders and the psychosomatic problems discussed in Chapter 11.

Experiencing a trauma but not talking about it may precede physical health problems. In a survey of 2,020 respondents, 367 reported having at one time experienced a sexual trauma. These people had higher rates of virtually all physical diseases inquired about than did those who had not experienced a trauma (Rubenstein, 1982; Pennebaker, 1985). In another study, 115 students were classified into a group that had not experienced a trauma, that had experienced a trauma but had confided in others, and a group that had experienced a trauma but had not told anybody. Those in the trauma/no confide group had more diseases, symptoms, and took more medication. Among nineteen people whose spouses had died by accident or suicide, the illness rate was substantially greater in those who did not talk to their friends about the death (Pennebaker, 1985). In a study of Hmong refugees in the United States who were originally from Southeast Asia, considerable somatization was observed. Somatization was strongly associated with depression. Those who were most acculturated to America (had American friends, used the mass media, owned a car) were less likely to somatize (Westermeyer, Bouafuely, Neider, and Callies, 1989). This suggests that those refugees least able to communicate mental distress in their new world expressed it through bodily distress. While these studies are not definitive, the possibility that silence hurts is intriguing and important. The mechanism by which silence hurts may be rumination; the less people talk to others about tragedy or distress, the more they ruminate, and there may be some as yet unknown way in which rumination undermines physical health (Rachman and Hodgson, 1980).

The communicative model holds that conversion reactions "talk." They are a cry for help, particularly among individuals who are reluctant or unable to *talk* about their emotional distress. Such people may be forced to rely on physical symptoms to tell the people they love and their physicians that all is not well in their emotional lives.

THE PERCEPT BLOCKING VIEW

There is a third view of somatoform disorders compatible with either the psychoanalytic or communicative views. It focuses on how a perception can be blocked from conscious experience. This view is best illustrated by hysterical blindness, a conversion disorder in which blindness is the physical loss. Surprisingly, in spite of the claim that he is aware of no visual input at all, the behavior of a hysterically blind person is often controlled by visual input. Such individuals usually avoid walking in front of cars and tripping over furniture, even though they report no awareness of actually seeing anything. In the laboratory, they also give evidence that some visual material is getting through. When given discrimination tasks that can only be solved by visual cues, such as "pick the side—left or right—that has the square, as opposed to the circle, on it," they perform significantly *below* chance. They do worse than if they were guessing at random, and they systematically pick the side that has the circle. In order to be so wrong, the patient must be right—the square of which he is not aware must register at some level of his mind, and then be reacted to by choosing the circle (Theodor and Mandelcorn, 1978; see also Brady and Lind, 1961; Gross and Zimmerman, 1965; Bryant and McConkey, 1989).

What are we to make of this? If we assume that the hysterically blind individual is not lying when he says he is not aware of anything visual, then we are led to the following model: visual input can register in the sensory system and directly affect behavior (hence the avoidance of furniture and below-chance performance), while being blocked from conscious awareness (hence the report "I see nothing"). The conversion process consists in the blocking of the percept from awareness (Hilgard, 1977; Sackeim, Nordlie, and Gur, 1979). This is compatible with both the psychoanalytic and communicative models since it makes no claims about what motivations can cause blocking—a need to defend against anxiety or a desire to distract oneself from inner distress. This model is also physiologically possible. When some parts of the brain that control vision are destroyed, individuals report that they can see nothing at all in specific regions of their visual field. But in spite of consistent reports of blindness, such patients perform above chance on visual discrimination problems. When confronted with this fact, the patients, like the hysterically blind, insist they saw nothing at all and were merely guessing (Weiskrantz, Warrington, Sanders, and Marshall, 1974). So we conclude that the mechanism of hysterical blindness may be the blocking of a visual percept from awareness. The blocking could be motivated either by anxiety (as Freud held), by a need to communicate distress, or it might be reinforced by anxiety reduction (as a behaviorist would hold).

Treatment of Somatoform Disorder

There is an ancient Persian legend about a physician named Rhazes who was called into the palace for the purpose of diagnosing and treating a young prince. Apparently, the prince could not walk. After the usual examination of the day, Rhazes determined that there was nothing wrong with the prince's legs, at least not physically. With little more than a hunch, Rhazes set out to treat what may be the first recorded case of conversion. In doing so, he took a risk: Rhazes unexpectedly walked into the prince's bathroom brandishing a dagger and threatened to kill him. Upon seeing him, "the startled prince abruptly fled, leaving his clothes, his dignity, his symptom, and undoubtedly part of his self-esteem behind" (Laughlin, 1967, p. 678).

CONFRONTATION

Modern clinicians tend to approach their "princes" brandishing a less drastic treatment. They will sometimes confront a conversion patient and try to force him out of his symptom. For example, therapists may tell hysterically blind patients that they are performing significantly below or above chance on visual tasks in spite of seeing nothing, which may cause visual awareness gradually to return in the patient (Brady and Lind, 1961; but see also Gross and Zimmerman, 1965). But these recoveries are usually temporary, and they may produce conflict and loss of self-esteem in the patient. They also may make the patient feel that the therapist is unsympathetic, and so they may ultimately undermine therapy.

Simple suggestion, merely telling a patient in a convincing manner that the symptoms will go away, may fare somewhat better than confrontation does. Conversion patients are particularly suggestible, and certain therapists have found improvement by directly telling the patient, in an authoritative sounding way, that the symptom will go away. In an account of 100 cases of patients with conversion symptoms, one investigator found that following strong suggestion 75 percent of the patients were either symptom-free or much improved four to six years later (Carter, 1949). But since there was no comparison group that might have controlled for the spontaneous disappearance of conversion without suggestion, we cannot be sure that suggestion had any real effect (Bird, 1979).

INSIGHT

Insight, or coming to recognize the underlying conflict producing the physical loss, is psychoanalysts' therapy of choice for conversion disorders. According to these therapists, when the patient comes to see, and emotionally appreciate, that there is an underlying conflict that is producing a conversion disorder, the symptom should disappear. A number of dramatic case histories confirm this. For example, when Bear realized that his paralysis expressed his guilt over his friend's paralysis, the symptom remitted. Unfortunately, there does not exist a well-controlled study that tests whether psychoanalytic insight has any effect over and above suggestion, confrontation, spontaneous remission, or the mere formation of a helping alliance with a therapist.

OTHER THERAPIES

There are suggestions of promising effects from a variety of other approaches. Amitriptyline, an antidepressant with pain-killing effects, seems to have some beneficial effects on a minority of pain disorder patients, although its biochemical mechanism is unknown (Van Kempen, Zitman, Linssen, and Edelbroek, 1992). Sensible advice also helps pain disorder: telling the patient that the treatment goal is not to cure the pain, but to help him achieve a sense of control over pain and improve his functioning in life (Lipowski, 1990). Family therapy also may help. In a study of eighty-nine youngsters with conversion disorders, family therapy approaches produced recovery within two weeks for half the patients (Turgay, 1990). Because suggestion is such a strong factor in conversion, however, skepticism is in order. Placebo-controlled studies of therapy for somatoform disorders are *still* very much needed—more than one hundred years after the first cures were claimed by the very people who founded abnormal psychology as we know it.

DISSOCIATIVE DISORDERS

All of us have at one time or another awakened in the middle of the night and being somewhat befuddled, wondered, "Where am I?" Sometimes the disorientation is more profound. "Who is the person sleeping next to me?" "Who am I, anyway?" When such an event happens—most commonly following fatigue, travel, or drinking—it usually wears off in a few seconds or minutes, and knowledge of our identity returns. But for others it is different. Such a loss of memory about identity sometimes occurs in people who have suffered a strong psychological trauma. It is then more profound, extends over a longer time, and is at the heart of the ***dissociative disorders.*** They are called "dissociative" because two or more mental processes co-exist or alternate

FOCUS QUESTIONS

1. What lies at the heart of dissociative disorders?
2. Describe how dissociation can be experienced as amnesia, depersonalization, derealization, identity confusion, and identity alteration.
3. What is a fugue state?
4. Distinguish between generalized amnesia and retrograde amnesia.

without becoming connected or influencing each other (Gregory, 1987). Some area of memory is split off or dissociated from conscious awareness.

The dissociative disorders have much in common with our last topic, the somatoform disorders, particularly conversion. In conversion disorder, anxiety is not experienced by the victim; in fact, complete indifference is common. Rather, the symptom can be seen as a way to prevent underlying anxiety from surfacing. So it is with dissociative disorders. For example, when an individual suddenly loses his memory following an unbearable trauma, he is not necessarily overtly anxious. Rather, theorists infer that the loss of memory allows him to escape from intolerable anxiety brought on by the trauma (Spiegel and Cardena, 1991).

The experience of dissociation consists of either: (1) *amnesia,* in which a substantial block of time in one's life is forgotten—after the catastrophic collapse of the Hyatt Hotel skywalks in Nevada, 28 percent of the survivors had memory deficits (Wilkinson, 1983); (2) *depersonalization,* in which one feels detachment from oneself—as if one is just going through the motions or looking at oneself from the outside; 57 percent of survivors of a series of deadly tornadoes reported such detachment (Madakasira and O'Brien, 1987); (3) *derealization,* in which the world, not the self, seems unreal; 72 percent of survivors of life-threatening dangers reported feeling as if space and time had altered (Noyes and Kletti, 1977); (4) *identity confusion,* in which one is confused or uncertain about who one is; (5) *identity alteration,* in which one displays a surprising skill—e.g., speaking Flemish or tightrope walking—that one did not know one had (Steinberg, Rounsaville, and Cicchetti, 1990). Dissociative states are not rare, with only 3 percent of the Dutch and Flemish population, mostly male, reporting serious dissociative experiences (Vanderlinden, Van Dyck, Vandereycken, and Vertommen, 1991).

We will discuss two dissociative disorders: *dissociative amnesia,* a loss of personal memory caused by severe trauma such as the death of a child or the dashing of a career; and *multiple personality disorder* (dissociative identity disorder), in which two or more distinct identities exist within the same individual and each leads a rather full life.

Dissociative Amnesia

> Timmy was fifteen years old and attending high school in upstate New York. He was teased mercilessly by his fellow students and was doing poorly in his schoolwork. In addition, he fought constantly with his parents. He was very upset about his problems, and it seemed to him that they had become absolutely unsolvable. One spring afternoon, he went home from school extremely distressed and threw his books down on the porch in disgust.
>
> At that moment, Timmy became a victim of amnesia. This was his last memory for a year, and we will never know exactly what happened next. The next thing we know with certainty is that a year later, a young soldier was admitted to an army hospital after a year of military service. He had severe stomach cramps and convulsions of no apparent physical origin. The following morning, he was better, calm and mentally clear. Astonishingly, he was at a total loss to explain where he was or how he got there. He asked how he came to be in the hospital, what town he was in, and who the people around him were. He was Timmy, all right, awake and in a military hospital with his last memory that of throwing his books down on the porch in disgust. Timmy's father was phoned, and he corroborated the story. At his father's request, Timmy was discharged from the service as underage. (Adapted from Laughlin, 1967, pp. 862–63)

Timmy was the victim of amnesia (the loss of memory of one's identity). As in many cases of amnesia, Timmy wandered and took up a new life

▶ In the movie *The English Patient,* the burned and broken Count Almasy suffers from amnesia as to who he is and is mistakenly believed to be an English pilot.

by joining the army. Such unexpected travel away from home during amnesia is called a ***fugue state,*** from the Latin *fuga,* meaning flight. Timmy's loss of memory and fugue are understandable as a flight from intolerable anxiety caused by his problems at home and at school. Timmy adopted the most extreme defense against a painful situation: he became amnesic, not only for the situation, but for his very identity, and he took up a new identity. By becoming amnesic, he was able to escape from his anxiety. During his army life, he remembered nothing about his previous painful life and following recovery of his earlier memories, he was totally amnesic for his year in the army.

KINDS OF DISSOCIATIVE AMNESIA

What happened to Timmy was a ***global*** or ***generalized amnesia:*** all the details of his personal life had vanished when he joined the army. Amnesia can be less global than this. ***Retrograde amnesia*** is a more localized amnesia, in which all events immediately before some trauma are forgotten. For example, an uninjured survivor of an automobile accident may be unable to recall anything that happened during the twenty-four hours up to and including the accident that killed the rest of her family. ***Post-traumatic amnesia*** is the inability to recall events *after* the episode. Rarest is ***anterograde amnesia,*** in which there is difficulty remembering new material. This form of amnesia almost always has an organic cause, like a stroke. Finally, there exists ***selective*** or ***categorical amnesia,*** in which only events related to a particular theme vanish (Hirst, 1982; Roediger, Weldon, and Challis, 1989).

DISSOCIATIVE VERSUS ORGANIC AMNESIA

Amnesia can also be caused by physical trauma, such as a blow to the head or a gunshot wound to the brain, alcoholism, Alzheimer's disease, and stroke (see Chapter 11). Such organically caused amnesia should be distinguished from dissociative amnesia. Aside from its physical basis, organic amnesia differs from dissociative amnesia in several ways. First, a dissociative amnesic is usually sorely troubled by marital, financial, or career stress before the amnesia, whereas an individual who suffers organic amnesia need not be (Coons, Bowman, Pellow, and Schneider, 1989). Second, dissociative amnesia does not result from any known neural damage.

DSM-IV Criteria for Dissociative Amnesia

A. The predominant disturbance is one or more episodes of inability to recall important personal information, usually of a traumatic or stressful nature, that is too extensive to be explained by ordinary forgetfulness.

B. The disturbance does not occur exclusively during the course of Dissociative Identity Disorder, Dissociative Fugue, Post-traumatic Stress Disorder, Acute Stress Disorder, or Somatization Disorder and is not due to the direct physiological effects of a substance (e.g., a drug of abuse, a medication) or a neurological or other general medical condition (e.g., Amnestic Disorder Due to Head Trauma).

C. The symptoms cause clinically significant distress or impairment in social, occupational, or other important areas of functioning.

SOURCE: APA, DSM-IV, 1994.

A person with dissociative amnesia shows a fourfold pattern of memory loss that no one with organic amnesia has ever shown. First, the person with dissociative amnesia loses his past, both recent and remote—he cannot remember how many brothers and sisters he has; he cannot remember a well-learned fact from the distant past, nor can he remember what he had for breakfast right before the amnesia started. Those with organic amnesia, on the other hand, remember the distant past well—after a blow to the head, they can tell you perfectly well who taught them Sunday school when they were six years old, or the starting lineup of the 1964 Phillies—but they remember the recent past poorly. Second, an individual with dissociative amnesia loses his personal identity—name, address, occupation, and the like—but his store of general knowledge remains intact. He still remembers who the President is, what the date is, and what the capital of Saskatchewan is (Regina). People with organic amnesia, in contrast, tend to lose both personal and general knowledge.

Third, those with psychogenic amnesia have no anterograde loss; they remember well events that happen after the moment amnesia starts. In contrast, patients with organic amnesia have severe anterograde amnesia, and this is their primary symptom; they remember very little about episodes that happen after the organic damage (like the name of the doctor treating them for the blow to the head). Finally, dissociative amnesia often reverses abruptly. Dissociative amnesia often ends within a few hours or days, and within twenty-four hours of the return of his memory the individual may even recall the traumatic episode that set off the memory loss. In organic amnesia, memory only gradually returns for retrograde memories and hardly ever returns for anterograde memories following organic treatment, and memory of trauma is never revived (Suarez and Pittluck, 1976).

VULNERABILITY AND CAUSE OF DISSOCIATIVE AMNESIA

Only a few other facts about dissociative amnesia are known, and they tell us a bit more about vulnerability to this disorder. Dissociative amnesia and fugue states (assuming a new identity) are rare disorders in peacetime, but in times of war and natural disaster they are much more common. They apparently occur in men more than in women and in younger people more than in old people.

The cause of dissociative amnesia is a mystery, more shrouded even than the causes of the somatoform disorders, which it resembles. We can speculate on how it might be caused, however. If we take the symptoms of conversion at face value, we assume that the mind sometimes can deal with emotionally distressing conflicts by producing physical losses. So, Bear, anxious and guilty about causing his friend's paralysis, converts his distress into his own paralysis. We do not know the mechanism of this conversion, but whatever it is, it might also be working in the amnesic. What happens when a vulnerable individual faces an even more traumatic conflict, such as occurs during war? What happens when one's physical existence is suddenly threatened, or when one's entire life plans are shattered? Enormous anxiety should be generated. Perhaps we have one ultimate psychological escape hatch—to forget who we are and thereby neutralize our anxiety about our possible death, our shattered future, or our insoluble problems. Both the psychoanalytic model and behavioral model are compatible with this explanation. For the psychoanalyst, the painful memory of who we are is repressed, and this defends successfully against anxiety. For the behaviorist, anxiety reduction reinforces the symptom of taking on a new identity. In short, amnesia may be the most global of defenses against anxiety produced by very traumatic and unacceptable circumstances.

We will now take up the final disorder in this chapter, multiple personality (dissociative identity), in which amnesia plays a major role. Here it will be quite clear that the multiple identities and their attendant amnesia for each other function to minimize unbearable anxiety.

Multiple Personality Disorder (Dissociative Identity Disorder)

Multiple personality disorder (MPD), which is called **dissociative identity disorder (DID)** by DSM-IV, is defined as the occurrence of two or more distinct identities* in the same individual, each of which is sufficiently integrated to have a relatively stable life of its own and recurrently to take full control of the person's behavior (DSM-IV). It is as astonishing a form of psychopathology as exists. Multiple personality disorder was formerly thought of as a very rare disorder—only 200 cases had been reported—but now that clinicians are looking for it, much more of it seems to be around. Very few cases were reported before 1970. But one researcher, Eugene Bliss, saw 14 cases of it in the late 1970s, just in Utah (Bliss, 1980; Bliss and Jeppsen, 1985), and 100 other cases were reviewed by another group in the 1980s (Putnam, Guroff, Silberman, et al., 1986). At present, the rate of diagnosed multiple personality disorder may run as high as 5 percent of inpatient psychiatric admissions in some clinics (Ross, 1991; Ross, Anderson, Fleisher, and Norton, 1991).

The upsurge in the number of cases may be more than just a diagnostic fad. There seem to be three basic reasons for why multiple personality disorder is seen so often. First, the diagnostic probe for amnesia is crucial ("Are there large swaths of the week that you can't remember?"). If the answer to the question turns out to be "yes" many times, there is a possibility that other distinct identities may exist. Thus, amnesia is now part of the diagnosis, with "inability to recall important personal information that is too extensive to be explained by ordinary forgetfulness" a hallmark.

Second, multiple personality disorder fits the psychoanalytic model to a T, and so psychodynamic therapists are highly prepared to diagnose it. As we shall see, the disorder begins with childhood trauma that is repressed, and other identities are generated as a defense against the trauma (Loewenstein and Ross, 1992). Treatment consists of cathartic reintegration of the identities. It is not an exaggeration to say that multiple personality disorder has breathed new life into the psychodynamic movement.

Third, diagnosis of multiple personality disorder has surged with the new and highly visible awareness of child abuse. As we will see, child abuse—often sexual abuse—is generally claimed to be the trigger for the disorder. The immensely popular "Recovery Movement" sees such adult problems as depression, anxiety, eating disorders, and sexual dysfunction as resulting from child abuse (Bradshaw, 1990). Adherents of this movement believe that only by coming to grips with this early, and often unrecognized abuse, can an adult regain mental health. Multiple personality disorder is perhaps the best-documented example of the claims that child abuse has effects that last into adulthood. All these claims, however, are speculative and controversial.

MULTIPLE PERSONALITY DISORDER DESCRIBED

Eugene Bliss, who is the pioneer of modern work on multiple personality disorder, had his first introduction to the disorder in 1978 when he received a call

---

DSM-IV Criteria for Dissociative Identity Disorder (formerly Multiple Personality Disorder)

A. The presence of two or more distinct identities or personality states (each with its own relatively enduring pattern of perceiving, relating to, and thinking about the environment and self).

B. At least two of these identities or personality states recurrently take control of the person's behavior.

C. Inability to recall important personal information that is too extensive to be explained by ordinary forgetfulness.

D. The disturbance is not due to the direct physiological effects of a substance (e.g., blackouts or chaotic behavior during Alcohol Intoxication) or a general medical condition (e.g., complex partial seizures). (*Note:* In children, the symptoms are not attributable to imaginary playmates or other fantasy play.)

SOURCE: APA, DSM-IV, 1994.

---

*Historically, these identities have been referred to as "personalities" by researchers. DSM-IV calls them "distinct identities" or "personality states," but we believe that a "personality state" is a contradiction in terms, as a state is not a trait. Therefore we choose not to use the terminology "personality states," but will instead refer to different "identities" in patients with multiple personality disorder.

FOCUS QUESTIONS

1. What is multiple personality disorder (MPD)?
2. Describe the development (etiology) of multiple personality disorder.
3. What therapy is used for those with multiple personality disorder?

from a distressed supervisor of nurses at a Salt Lake City hospital. The supervisor suspected that one of her nurses had been secretly injecting herself with Demerol. The supervisor and Bliss called the nurse into the office and accused her of improper conduct. They asked the nurse to roll up her sleeves because they wanted to examine her arms for needle marks. The nurse complied, and the telltale marks were there. But in the process of complying, the nurse underwent a remarkable transformation. Her facial expression, her manner, and her voice all changed, claiming that she was not Lois, the demure nurse, but Lucy, the brazen drug addict. Almost everyone has heard of other famous multiple personalities, as in "The Three Faces of Eve" (Thigpen and Cleckley, 1954), Sybil (Schreiber, 1974), or Dr. Jekyll and Mr. Hyde. Among these cases is that of Julie-Jenny-Jerrie (Davis and Osherson, 1977):

> Julie came to therapy through her son, Adam, age nine, who had been referred for counseling because of very poor school performance, poor relations with peers, and aggressive behavior at home. Eventually it was decided to see his thirty-six-year-old mother, Julie, in hope that she could help in the therapeutic process.
>
> Julie was highly cooperative, sophisticated, and concerned about Adam. She seemed to have a good understanding of herself, and her general style of solving interpersonal problems was discussion and compromise. She felt that she had trouble setting limits for her son, and she worried that she sometimes behaved too rigidly toward him.
>
> During a session in the sixth week of discussions with Julie, she suddenly announced that she wanted to introduce someone to the therapist. The therapist assumed there was someone out in the waiting room, but to his astonishment he witnessed the following: Julie closed her eyes for a few seconds, frowned, and then raised her eyelids slowly. Putting out her cigarette, she said, "I wish Julie would stop smoking. I hate the taste of tobacco." She introduced herself as Jerrie, and later in the hour and in the same way, she introduced Jenny, yet a third personality.
>
> Jenny revealed that she was the original personality and said that she created Jerrie at age three and subsequently created Julie at age eight. Both times Jenny created the new personalities to cope with her disturbed family life. Jerrie emerged as the outer personality when Jenny was recovering from a severe case of measles, and Jerrie became a buffer who allowed Jenny to keep her distance from seven rejecting siblings and two frightening parents. Jenny said that observing Jerrie was like observing a character in a play.
>
> Between the ages of three and eight, Jenny remembers that her physical welfare was neglected, that she was sexually molested by a neighbor, and was given away for permanent adoption at age eight, with her parents telling her she was "incorrigible." At this time, Jenny created Julie, a gentle personality who was better able to

▶ The distinct identities in a person with multiple personality disorder may or may not know of each other's existence. When they do, they may conflict bitterly.

cope with rejection and not as vulnerable to cruelty as either Jerrie or Jenny. Remarkably, while Julie was allowed to know about Jenny, the original personality, Julie was kept unaware of the existence of Jerrie. Julie did not find out about Jerrie until age thirty-four, two years before therapy began.

At age eighteen, Julie-Jenny-Jerrie left home for good. Jerrie and Julie by this time were always the alternating outer personalities, and Jenny was always inside. In fact, Jenny had been "out" only twice since age seven. At age twenty-six, Jerrie married, and the couple adopted Adam, who was the husband's son by a woman with whom he was having an affair while he and Jerrie were married. Jerrie soon divorced him, but she kept Adam.

The three personalities were strikingly different. Jenny—the original—was a frightened person, very shy and vulnerable. She was the most insecure and child-like of the three and felt "exposed" whenever she was out. Jenny felt she had created two Frankensteins who were now out of her control. She liked Julie better, but she was put off by Julie's stubbornness and strong individuality. She felt Jerrie was tougher than Julie and better able to cope with the world, but she didn't like her as well. Jenny's main hope in therapy was that Julie and Jerrie would come to get along better with each other and therefore be better mothers to Adam.

Julie seemed to be the most integrated of the three personalities. Julie was heterosexual, and emotionally invested in being a good mother—this in spite of the fact that it was Jerrie who had adopted Adam.

Jerrie was the opposite of Julie. Jerrie was homosexual, dressed in masculine fashion, sophisticated, and sure of herself. She was accomplished and proficient in the business world, and she enjoyed it. Jerrie didn't smoke, whereas Julie was a heavy smoker, and Jerrie's blood pressure was a consistent twenty points higher than Julie's.

Jerrie had known about Julie since Julie was "born" at age eight, but she had been in touch with her only in the past two years. She wanted to have nothing to do with Julie because she was afraid Julie would have a mental breakdown. Julie and Jerrie did not get along. When one of them was out and having a good time, she would resist relinquishing her position. But when a crisis was at hand, the personality who was out would duck in, leaving the inner personality to face the problem. For example, Julie took LSD and then let Jerrie out so that Jerrie would be the victim of the hallucinations.

Ultimately Jerrie was able to tell Adam that there were two personalities who had been contributing to his misery, and Adam's immediate response was amusement and curiosity. He was able to accept the explanation that "Mother is two people who keep going in and out, but both of them love me." Adam appeared relieved rather than disturbed. Soon thereafter, Jerrie terminated therapy. Julie, in a suicidal depression, had gotten herself admitted to a state hospital against Jerrie's will, but Jerrie had gained control and talked her way out of the hospital. Julie wrote the therapist that she wanted to come to therapy, but Jerrie would not allow it and refused to come anymore. And this was the last that was seen of Julie-Jenny-Jerrie. (Adapted from Davis and Osherson, 1977)

This fascinating case exemplifies much of what is known about multiple personality disorder. Amnesia of some kind or other almost always exists. It is common for one of the identities to be aware of the experience of the other identities (Jenny knew of both Julie and Jerrie, and Jerrie knew of Julie), and for one of the identities to be amnesic about the others (Julie did not know of Jerrie). The presence of unexplained amnesia—hours or days each week that are missing—is a crucial clue to the undetected presence of multiple personality disorder.

In the history of a person with multiple personality disorder, the distinct identities within an individual—like Julie-Jenny-Jerrie—differ along many dimensions. Not only do they differ in their memories, but also in their wishes, attitudes, interests, learning ability, knowledge, morals, sexual orientation, age, rate of speech, personality test scores, and physiological indices such as heart rate, blood pressure, and EEG (Lester, 1977). In a systematic study of the autonomic patterns of nine patients with multiple personality disorder compared to five hypnotized controls at the National Institute of Mental Health, the distinct identities in the patients with multiple personality disorder showed highly distinct patterns of breathing, sweating, heart rate, and habituation (Putnam, Zahn, and Post, 1990). Remarkably, some women with multiple personality disorder report that they menstruate much of the month because each identity has her own cycle (Jens and Evans, 1983). Most patients with multiple personality disorder are women.

The identities also differ in psychological health. Often, the dominant identity is the healthier identity. One patient, a proper Southern lady, was publicly accused of wanton sexuality, including intercourse with strangers. She made a clumsy attempt at a self-induced abortion, but she could not remember it. Her submerged identity said, "I did it because I suspected a pregnancy. I took a sharp stick and shoved it inside, then I started to bleed badly" (Bliss, 1980). The dominant identity, however, is not always the healthiest, and a submerged identity may actually sympathize with an unhealthy dominant identity and try to help. In one case, the submerged identity wrote to the dominant identity giving her helpful information to try to make her healthier (Taylor and Martin, 1944).

THE ETIOLOGY OF MULTIPLE PERSONALITY DISORDER

Where does multiple personality disorder come from? The fourteen cases of multiple personality disorder that were seen by Bliss shared some important common features, and provide us with some clues as to how multiple

▶ A patient with multiple personality disorder produced this handwriting sample, showing seventeen distinct identities—each with distinct handwriting which emerged when that identity was dominant.

personality disorder begins and how it develops. Bliss's hypothesis about how multiple personality disorder proceeds has three steps. First, an individual between ages four and six experiences a traumatic emotional problem. Indeed, multiple personality disorder has much in common with post-traumatic stress disorder (Spiegel, 1984), and the rate of claims of child abuse experienced by those who develop multiple personality disorder may be as high as 97 percent (Putnam, Guroff, Silberman, et al., 1986; Ross, Miller, Reagor, Bjornson, et al., 1990; Coons, 1994; Keaney and Farley, 1996). She copes with the trauma by creating another distinct identity to take the brunt of the problem. Second, the individual is particularly vulnerable because she is highly susceptible to self-hypnosis, a process by which one is able to put oneself at will into trance states that have the properties of formal hypnotic inductions. Third, the individual finds out that creating another distinct identity by self-hypnosis relieves her of her emotional burden, so that in the future, when she confronts other emotional problems, she creates new distinct identities to take the brunt (see also Kluft, 1984; 1991).

There is some evidence for each of these three steps. First, all fourteen of the patients that Bliss saw did, in fact, create their first alternative identity between the ages of four and six, and each seemed to be created in order to cope with very difficult emotional circumstances. Roberta, for example, created the first of her eighteen distinct identities when her mother held her under water and tried to drown her. This personality had the purpose of controlling and feeling Roberta's anger and of handling Roberta's homicidal rage without Roberta having to do so. Another patient was molested at age four by an adult man; she created her first alternative identity in order to handle the molestation and thereafter used this identity to handle all sexual encounters.

Second, there is evidence that these patients are extraordinarily good at self-hypnosis (see Box 6–3). All fourteen of Bliss's patients were excellent hypnotic subjects. When Bliss hypnotized them, they went rapidly into a trance on the first induction. During the hypnosis, when he instructed them to have amnesia for what happened during hypnosis, they did this as well. In addition, when these patients reported the way in which they created the identities, they described a process that sounds like hypnotic induction. One of the identities of a patient said, "She creates personalities by blocking everything from her head, mentally relaxes, concentrates very hard and wishes." Another said, "She lies down, but can do it sitting up, concentrates very hard, clears her mind, blocks everything out and then wishes for the person, but she isn't aware of what she is doing." Once these patients were introduced to formal hypnosis in therapy, most reported that this experience was identical to experiences they had had dating back to their childhood, and that an inordinate amount of their lives had been spent in this altered state of consciousness. One patient said, "I spent an awful lot of time in hypnosis when I was young. . . . I've always lived in a dream world. Now that I know what hypnosis is, I can say that I was in a trance often. There was a little place where I could sit, close my eyes and imagine, until I felt very relaxed, just like hypnosis—and it could be very deep."

Third, patients used new identities to defend against distress later in life. Jenny, you will recall, created Julie, a gentle identity, to cope with her parents' putting her up for adoption at age eight. Most of the patients reported instances in which they created new identities to cope with new stresses even when they were adults.

PSYCHOTHERAPY FOR MULTIPLE PERSONALITY DISORDER

As in the case of Julie-Jenny-Jerrie, the treatment of patients with multiple personality disorder is difficult and frustrating. Therapy for multiple personality disorder has been conceptualized both in psychodynamic terms and as

Box 6–3

MULTIPLE PERSONALITY DISORDER AND MEMORIES OF CHILD ABUSE

Researchers believe that a central element in the etiology of multiple personality disorder is physical and sexual abuse in childhood. Most studies of patients with multiple personality disorder are based on the adult patient's uncorroborated memory that abuse occurred when she was a small child. Some psychologists have been concerned about the veracity of the adult patients' memories of child abuse (Ganaway, 1989). As a result, some investigators have begun to look at children who are known to have been abused to see how these children use dissociation as a way of dealing with the trauma of the abuse (Putnam, 1989).

Society has become much more willing to listen to buried family secrets and to "believe the children." As a result, in the early 1990s, following the explosion in the diagnosis of multiple personality disorder, "memory retrieval" therapy became quite fashionable. In such a treatment, the therapist strongly encourages the patient to explore for and find long-buried memories of abuse, usually sexual, that might be at the root of the patient's adult problems. There has been a trend toward facile acceptance of extensive, incredible, and contradictory accounts of abuse. This has placed the hard-won scientific credibility of the field of multiple personality disorder into jeopardy. Memory retrieval therapy is now highly controversial, and there is evidence that it may sometimes be based on false memories and may sometimes make patients worse, whether the memories are true or false.

In discussing dissociation and multiple personality disorder, David Spiegel (1990) points to the existence of the "grade 5" hypnotizable person. Only 5 percent of the population falls into this category. Grade 5's are extremely hypnotizable, very suggestible, show pathological compliance with their therapists, and give up critical judgment. They report vivid, rich, detailed "memories" from trance states—that are without factual foundation. Virtually all patients with multiple personality disorder are grade 5's (Ganaway, 1989).

The reports of patients with multiple personality disorder must be considered at high risk for contamination by such pseudo-memories. Ganaway's many patients have told him in vivid detail of encounters with demons, angels, lobsters, chickens, tigers, God, and a unicorn. In one case, Sarah, a fifty-year-old woman diagnosed with multiple personality disorder, was shocked when Carrie, a five-year-old "alter" (jargon for one of the distinct identities), relived in vivid detail the brutal rape and murder of twelve girls from her Sunday school class. Carrie was spared by the cult leader because she was unlucky number 13. On further exploration, Sherry, another alter, revealed that she had created Carrie to absorb the terror she had felt when her grandmother read grisly murder stories to her (Ganaway, 1989).

Besides examining the veracity of childhood memories of abuse, some psychologists have begun to study the usefulness of memory retrieval therapy in improving the quality of patients' lives. In 1990, Washington State let people have treatment under the Crime Victims Act if they claimed repressed memory of childhood sexual abuse. So in 1996 the Washington Department of Labor and Industries gathered preliminary statistics on the outcome of treatment for thirty randomly selected patients (Loftus, Grant, Franklin, Parr, and Brown, 1996). Before the repressed memories were retrieved in therapy, 10 percent had suicidal ideation, 7 percent had been hospitalized, and 3 percent had self-mutilated. After the memories were recovered, 67 percent had suicidal ideation, 37 percent had been hospitalized, and 27 percent had self-mutilated. Ninety-seven percent claimed they had been abused by parents or family members in satanic rituals, with the abuse beginning at seven months of age on average. The patients, it was noted, saw master's level therapists (87 percent). They were well-educated, and 83 percent had jobs before therapy. Three years later, only 10 percent were employed, half of them had been separated or divorced from their spouses, and all of them were estranged from their extended families. It cannot be known if the memories were true, but recovering them made many of their lives dramatically worse.

At this point, we should remain skeptical about the validity of some of the patients' tales of abuse, particularly the more outlandish ones, and about whether memory retrieval therapy actually benefits all patients. Some of the memories may be true, and some may be false; some of the therapy may help patients, and some may actually make them worse. The truth or falsity of the memories, however, does not matter nearly as much as the fact of their telling, the needs that such telling reveal about the patient, and the usefulness of such material for healing. Therapists must take care in encouraging patients to talk about such memories and in helping them to work through their problems as adults so that their emotional lives can become richer rather than more impoverished.

"tactical integration," a cognitive therapy approach (Fine, 1991). In the cognitive approach, the therapist collects the automatic thoughts of the patient, teaches skills of disputing and challenging irrational thoughts, and tries to find the basis for why these irrational thoughts were credible to the patient. Hypnosis is used in both the cognitive treatment and the more widely used psychodynamic treatment.

In the psychodynamic treatment, the first step is to make the patient aware of the problem. Although she may have lived in this strange state for many years, had amnesia, and been told by others about her bizarre behavior, she may not yet have confronted the fact of other identities. Under hypnosis, the therapist calls up the alter-egos and allows them to speak freely. In addition, the patient herself is asked to listen and then is introduced to some of these identities. She is told to remember the experience when she emerges from hypnosis. Enormous distress and turmoil often follow this discovery, but it is important for her to keep hold of the facts of many identities. At this point, she may display one of the most troublesome problems for therapy—dodging back into a self-hypnotic state and so avoiding the unpleasant reality. The therapist may then try to enlist the aid of various identities (Kluft, 1987).

After the patient is made fully aware of her many distinct identities, the therapist explains to her that they are products of self-hypnosis induced at an early age and without any conscious or malicious intent. The patient is told that now she is an adult, strong and capable, and that if she has the courage, she can flush these specters out and defeat them. The other identities may object, or want to continue their own life, but she is the only real person here. There is only one body and one head, and the other identities are her creations. She will have the privilege of deciding what aspects of the identities she will retain. In one study of thirty-four patients treated by an experienced therapist, 94 percent apparently showed strong improvement, with a two-year follow-up (Kluft, 1987).

In a survey of 305 clinicians who treat multiple personality disorder, Putnam and Loewenstein (1993) found that the average patient is in treatment for almost four years. Individual therapy (both psychodynamic and cognitive) and hypnosis were most widely used. Antidepressant and anti-anxiety drugs were also used by two-thirds of the clinicians with "moderate" relief reported. The remainder of the decade promises more systematic outcome studies of the effectiveness of psychotherapy and drugs for patients with multiple personality disorder.

Overall, multiple personality disorder, like somatoform disorders and dissociative amnesia, can be seen as an attempt to defend against severe emotional distress. A child of four to six who is unusually capable of self-hypnosis creates a new identity—an imaginary companion and ally—to help her deal with the anxiety generated by a possible traumatic experience. This innocent, childhood ploy inadvertently becomes an adult disaster as the patient repeatedly uses this technique to cope with the stresses she encounters as she grows up.

THE NEUROSES AND ANXIETY

In this chapter and Chapter 5, we have examined disorders that appear, on the surface, to be quite varied: phobia, post-traumatic stress disorder, panic disorder, generalized anxiety disorder, obsessive-compulsive disorder, somatoform disorders, dissociative amnesia, and multiple personality disorder. In the past, these disorders looked more like a coherent whole than they do today. Historically, they were all viewed as "neuroses" and all were thought to involve anxiety as the central process. In the case of phobia and post-traumatic stress disorder, fear is on the surface; in panic disorder and generalized anxiety disorder, anxiety (fear without a specific object) is also on the surface. The individual with one of these problems feels anxiety, apprehension, fear, terror, and dread in his daily life. In obsessive-compulsive disorders, on the other hand, anxiety is sometimes felt, but not if the compulsion is frequent and effective. In contrast, in the somatoform disorders and the dissociative disorders, anxiety is not usually observed. But in order to explain the bizarre symptoms of these disorders, theorists have inferred that, with his symptoms, the individual is defending against underlying anxiety. To the extent that the defense is successful, the symptoms will appear, and anxiety will not be felt.

The last twenty years have witnessed a sea change in the field of psychopathology: our categories have become more descriptive and less theoretical. DSM-IV disavows a common process—defending against anxiety—as the mechanism of these disorders. The dissociative disorders and somatoform disorders no longer fall under the larger class "Anxiety Disorders." Rather, DSM-IV includes as anxiety disorders only those disorders in which anxiety is observed: phobia, panic disorder, generalized anxiety disorder, post-traumatic stress disorder, and obsessive-compulsive disorder. Descriptively it makes good sense to segregate those disorders in which anxiety is observed from those in which anxiety is only inferred by a theory. But at a theoretical level, these disorders cry out for a common explanation.

For phobia and post-traumatic stress disorder, theories that come out of behavioral models seem appropriate. In both of these disorders we can postulate a trauma that imbued parts of the environment with terror, and the symptoms, the course, and the therapies roughly follow known behavioral laws. Obsessive-compulsive disorder is not as easy to handle in this way. How obsessions stay around once they have been acquired fits reasonably well within behavioral views, as do therapies that alleviate obsessions. But this is only part of the story. The questions of who is vulnerable to obsessions and what content obsessions will take are not answered by the behavioral school, nor is there even a useful theory from this tradition. These questions may be best viewed within a psychodynamic tradition, in which emotional distress lurks beneath the surface. Finally, we have somatoform disorders, dissociative amnesia, and multiple personality disorder. Here theories of surface anxiety are useless, nor does there exist an adequate behavioral theory of these three disorders. Anxiety, or some other unpleasant emotion that lies beneath the surface and is being defended against, seems to make more sense of the symptoms of these disorders, but the details of their etiology and which therapy is best for them remain a mystery.

Overall, then, we find that when fear and anxiety are on the surface, behavioral models serve us well. As fear and anxiety tend to disappear from the surface, however, we find ourselves in need of models to attempt to explain what we do observe. It seems likely that for the present we still need, at least for disorders like conversion, amnesia, and multiple personality disorder, theories such as the psychodynamic model, which postulates deep, unobserved emotional conflict and psychological defenses that are so rich as to inspire awe in those who study these disorders closely.

SUMMARY

1. This chapter examined the disorders in which anxiety is inferred to exist as opposed to being observed. Three kinds of disorders were considered: obsessive-compulsive disorders, somatoform disorders, and dissociative disorders.

2. *Obsessive-compulsive disorders* (OCD) consist of *obsessions,* which are repetitive thoughts, images, or impulses that invade consciousness, are often abhorrent, and are very difficult to dismiss or control. In addition, most obsessions are associated with *compulsions,* which are repetitive, stereotyped, and unwanted thoughts or actions to counter the obsession. Compulsions can be resisted only with difficulty.

3. An obsessive-compulsive individual displays anxiety when his or her rituals are blocked. In addition, depression is associated with this disorder. When such an individual is depressed, obsessions occur much more frequently, and such individuals are more prone to depression than the normal population. There is no personality type that seems predisposed to obsessive-compulsive disorders. Individuals who are obsessive-compulsive in their daily life and concerned with order are not more vulnerable to obsessive-compulsive disorder. What distinguishes these individuals from individuals with the disorder is that individuals with the obsessive-compulsive personality are proud of their meticulousness and love of detail, whereas individuals who have the disorder are tormented by their symptoms.

4. Psychoanalytic theory explains who is vulnerable to the disorder and why it has the particular content it does. It claims that the obsessive thought is a *defense* against an even more unwelcome unconscious thought. The anxiety the unconscious thought arouses is displaced onto a less unwelcome substitute that symbolically stands for the underlying conflict.

5. Cognitive-behavioral theory explains why the disorder and its rituals are maintained. The theory claims that individuals with the disorder are unable to habituate, dismiss, or distract themselves from disturbing thoughts. Behavior therapies for obsessive-compulsive disorders include *flooding*, forcing the patient to endure the aversive situation, *response blocking*, preventing the individual from engaging in the ritual, and *modeling*, watching another person refrain from the ritual. These therapies bring about marked improvement in about two-thirds of the patients with obsessive-compulsive disorders.

6. The biomedical view holds that OCD is a disorder of the brain. Neurological signs, brain scan findings, the evolutionarily primitive content of obsessions and compulsions, and the success of clomipramine, an antidepressant drug, are all evidence for this view.

7. Clomipramine produces improvement in 50 to 60 percent of OCD patients, but relapse is almost universal when the drug is stopped.

8. The *somatoform disorders* have five symptoms: (1) lost or altered physical functioning, (2) the absence of a known physical cause, (3) positive evidence that psychological factors are associated with the symptom, (4) indifference to the physical loss, and (5) the absence of voluntary control over the symptom.

9. Three kinds of somatoform disorders are: (1) *conversion*, in which one physical function is lost or altered, (2) *somatization disorder*, in which there is a dramatic and complicated medical history for multiple and recurrent bodily complaints in many organs, although the symptoms are not physically caused, and (3) *pain disorder*, in which the onset, severity, or persistence of pain is not attributed to physical cause. Pain disorder is the most common somatoform disorder today. Somatoform disorders should be distinguished from malingering, psychosomatic disorders, factitious disorder, and undiagnosed physical illness.

10. Psychoanalytic theory holds that somatoform disorders are a defense against anxiety, that psychic energy is transmuted into somatic loss, and that the particular somatic loss symbolizes the underlying conflict. The communication view of somatoform disorder holds that the disorder is the alexithymic's way of saying she is distressed psychologically. The percept blocking view focuses on how a perception can be blocked from conscious experience and makes no claims about the motivation causing this blocking.

11. The experience of dissociation consists of either: (1) *amnesia,* in which a substantial block of one's life is forgotten, (2) *depersonalization,* in which one feels detachment from oneself, (3) *derealization,* in which the world, not the self, seems unreal, (4) *identity confusion,* in which one is confused or uncertain about who one is, or (5) *identity alteration,* in which a surprising skill, like speaking a novel language, is displayed. In *dissociative disorders,* some area of memory is split off or dissociated from conscious awareness.

12. *Dissociative amnesia* is a loss of memory for important personal information caused by unbearable trauma and can either be general or highly specific. *Retrograde amnesia* is a specific amnesia in which events immediately *before* some trauma are forgotten. *Anterograde amnesia* is difficulty remembering anything that occurs *after* a trauma.

13. *Multiple personality disorder* (MPD), or *dissociative identity disorder* (DID), is the existence of two or more distinct identities in the same individual, each identity being sufficiently integrated to have a relatively stable life of its own and to be able recurrently to take full control over the person's behavior. This disorder is more frequent than previously believed and seems to involve individuals who are highly susceptible to self-hypnosis, who claim to have experienced a serious trauma between ages four and six, and who use the creation of alternative identities to bear this trauma, which they are unable to cope with in any other way.

QUESTIONS FOR CRITICAL THINKING

1. Explain why obsessions and depression often occur in the same person.

2. Why do you think women are more likely to develop somatoform disorders than are men?

3. Why is it possible that an undiagnosed physical disorder may be misdiagnosed as a somatoform disorder?

4. Do you think that someone with multiple personality disorder should be held accountable for the actions or crimes of each of his or her distinct identities?

CHAPTER

7

Personality Disorders

Painting by Jean-Marie Heyligen.

People who cheat needlessly and lie without reason are a diagnostic dilemma. So are those who are always suspicious of others' intentions. And so too are people who always respond passively to all provocation, regardless of source or intensity. Such people are hardly psychotic, for they have a good grip on reality. Nor are they necessarily dominated by unwarranted fears, sexual difficulties, addictions, and the like. Nevertheless, their behaviors strike observers as odd, as deviant, or as abnormal. Theirs seems to be a disorder of personality, which impairs their ability to function across many domains (Herbert, Hope, and Bellack, 1992), and does so for a substantial part of their lives. Their characteristic ways of perceiving and thinking about themselves and their environment are inflexible, and a source of social and occupational maladjustment. In addition, their behaviors may well be a source of distress for themselves and others. Their disorders are called **personality disorders.** According to DSM-IV, these behaviors form an enduring pattern of long duration that deviates considerably from that expected by the individual's culture. The pattern appears in at least two of these four areas: cognitive, emotional, interpersonal, or impulse control.

The personality disorders have provided a fascinating source of psychological study across the decades because they ascribe a stability and sturdiness to personality and behavior that extends across time and context. The personality disorders are fundamentally disorders of **traits,** that is, disorders that are reflected in the individual's tendency to perceive and respond to the environment in broad and maladaptive ways. Perhaps the most fascinating of these disorders is the **antisocial personality disorder.** Known also as **sociopathy** and **psychopathy,** this disorder has been studied extensively and is the best understood of the personality disorders.

198

THE ANTISOCIAL PERSONALITY DISORDER

People who suffer from the psychological disorders that were examined in earlier chapters create distress for their families and friends, but mainly they themselves are the ones who suffer. In contrast, the suffering in an individual with the antisocial personality disorder is muted. The hallmark of the disorder is a rapacious attitude toward others, a chronic insensitivity and indifference to the rights of other people that is marked by lying, stealing, cheating, and worse. Whereas those who suffer other psychological difficulties may be unpleasant, contact with people diagnosed with antisocial personality disorder may be downright dangerous, for many of them are outright criminals. Because their numbers are not small, they constitute a major social and legal problem, as well as a psychological one.

The prevalence of antisocial behavior is roughly 2 to 3 percent, with men accorded the diagnosis of antisocial personality disorder as much as four times more often than women (Warner, 1978; Regier, Myers, Kramer, Robins, Blayer, Hough, Easton, and Locke, 1984; Cadoret, 1986). But does this difference reflect a sex bias in the eyes of diagnosticians, or a true base-rate difference in the prevalence of this disorder? Present evidence strongly supports a sex bias generated by the stereotypic expectations of the diagnostician, especially about women, rather than by substantive differences among the clients themselves (Warner, 1978; Ford and Widiger, 1989).

Characterizing the Antisocial Personality Disorder

To be diagnosed as having antisocial personality disorder, a person must exhibit antisocial behaviors that meet two primary criteria. First, the behavior has to be longstanding. Although the diagnosis cannot be applied to a person who is under eighteen, current diagnostic criteria require substantial evidence of a conduct disorder before the age of fifteen. Such evidence can include habitual lying, early and aggressive sexual behavior, destructiveness, theft, vandalism, and chronic rule violation at home and at school. Second, the present antisocial behavior must be manifested in at least three classes of

FOCUS QUESTIONS

1. What are the three areas that encompass the characteristics of a person with an antisocial personality disorder?
2. Describe the role of the family and social context as possible causes of antisocial personality disorder.
3. What defects in learning may underlie antisocial behavior?

TABLE 7–1

THE ANTISOCIAL PERSONALITY DISORDER			
Definition	*Childhood Antecedents*	*Adult Behaviors*	*Influencing Factors*
Longstanding antisocial behavior manifested across a spectrum of activities, among which are aggressiveness, irresponsibility, recklessly endangering others, failure to honor financial obligations	Habitual lying Theft Aggressive sexuality Vandalism Truancy Impulsivity	Deceitfulness Irritability Repeated aggressiveness Criminal behavior Failure to plan ahead Lack of remorse	Deficiencies in social learning abilities, especially in avoidance learning Emotional underarousal Genetic predisposition to criminality Brain abnormalities

behavior, among which are: repeated aggressiveness; recklessness that endangers others; deceitfulness, lack of remorse, and consistent irresponsibility as evidenced by such behaviors; and failure to honor financial obligations. The antisocial personality disorder then is defined by sustained antisocial behaviors that, having begun by adolescence, continue in a variety of areas during adulthood (see Table 7–1).

What personality characteristics are reflected in such behaviors? In 1964, Hervey Cleckley described some of them in *The Mask of Sanity* (see Box 7–1). They can be grouped in three broad categories: (1) inadequately motivated antisocial behavior, (2) the absence of a conscience and sense of responsibility to others, and (3) emotional poverty.

INADEQUATELY MOTIVATED ANTISOCIAL BEHAVIOR

Crime "makes sense" for normal criminals. We understand what they are doing and why, and so do they. They want to get rich—quick—and they may want status. But the crimes of those with antisocial personality disorder often seem aimless, random, and impulsive. We do not understand why they did what they did, and neither do they understand it. They seem not to be motivated by any rational purpose, but rather seem perversely impulsive, as shown in the following case:

▼ Convicted killer Gary Gilmore was examined in 1976 and found to be suffering an antisocial personality disorder. He would have been accorded the same diagnosis under DSM-IV.

> On October 7, 1976, Gary Gilmore was sentenced to death by a Utah court after a seemingly purposeless crime spree, and on January 7, 1977, he became the first person to be executed in the United States since 1966. During a psychological evaluation to determine whether Gilmore was competent to stand trial, it was determined that he suffered an antisocial personality disorder. Gilmore's activities provide an interesting example of crime without understandable motives.
>
> Gilmore had been released from prison only six months earlier, after serving time for armed robbery. He promptly violated parole by leaving the state. His probation officer gave him another chance. But shortly thereafter, following a heated argument with his girlfriend, Gilmore stole a stereo. Once again, he persuaded the police not to bring charges. Gilmore himself described the next events: "I pulled up near a gas station. I told the service station guy to give me all his money. I then took him to the bathroom and told him to kneel down and then I shot him in the head twice. The guy didn't give me any trouble but I just felt like I had to do it."
>
> The very next morning, Gilmore left his car at another service station for minor repairs and walked to a motel. "I went in and told the guy to give me the money. I told him to lay on the floor and then I shot him. I then walked out and was carrying the cash drawer with me. I took the money and threw the cash drawer in a bush and I tried to push the gun in the bush too. But as I was pushing it in the bush, it went off and that's how come I was shot in the arm. It seems like things have always gone bad for me. It seems like I've always done dumb things that just caused trouble for me."

A CASE OF ANTISOCIAL PERSONALITY DISORDER

Hervey Cleckley (1905–1984) spent his entire professional career studying psychopathy, which is called the Antisocial Personality Disorder in DSM-IV. What captured him most was the paradox between the good impression he frequently had of such people, and their often disturbing behavioral record. What follows is an abbreviation of one of Cleckley's classic cases, as fresh and striking today as it was when it was first published nearly half a century ago. Some things don't change very much.

From all outward appearances, one thing was clear. Tom neither looked like a criminal or shifty delinquent, nor did he behave like one. His manner and appearance pleased. He was poised. There was no evidence that he was trying to fake an attitude, or put on an appearance. At twenty-one, he was good-looking and clearly in robust physical health. In the small town in which he grew up and now resided, there would seem to be few more presentable young men than Tom.

So it was odd, to say the least, that his family and the legal authorities should have hoped to find some "mental disorder" that might account for his errant behavior on the one hand, and enable him to escape a jail sentence for stealing on the other.

As far back as childhood, Tom *appeared* to be reliable, yet he couldn't be counted upon to complete a task or to give a straight answer about his whereabouts. He was given a generous allowance, but he nevertheless was caught stealing some of his father's chickens. He was often truant from high school, and he would loiter around town, hanging out at the pool room, throwing rocks at squirrels, perpetrating small thefts, and charging various items to his father's account. He lied so plausibly, devised such ingenious alibis, and provided such convincing appearances of candor that the magnitude of his career in petty thefts and crimes was always underestimated.

Tom learned to drive at fourteen and began to steal cars with some regularity. After he tried to sell a stolen car, his father consulted some advisers who proposed that Tom might have a special craving for cars and that his father should buy him one as a therapeutic measure. His father did. Yet, shortly thereafter, Tom deliberately parked his own car and stole a car that was an inferior model, driving it out of town and leaving it there slightly damaged. And during the same period, he regularly forged his father's name on small checks and stole small items at school and elsewhere.

Ultimately, he was arrested and sent to a federal institution that had a well-organized program of rehabili-

tation and guidance. He impressed the authorities there with his appropriate attitude, and especially the way he discussed his past errors and his plans for a different future.

On discharge, Tom took a job in the drydock of a nearby port. There, he talked modestly and convincingly about the course he would not follow. His employers found him energetic and enthusiastic about his work. But soon, evidence of inexplicable irresponsibility emerged and accumulated. Sometimes he missed several days of work, and provided simple (but convincing) excuses of illness. These occasions, however, multiplied inexplicably. Later, he sometimes simply left the job and stayed away for hours, providing no account of his behavior except that he didn't feel like working at the time.

Reliable information indicated that Tom had been arrested and imprisoned 50 or 60 times, and that he would have been jailed on roughly 150 other occasions if his family had not made good on his thefts and damages and paid his fines. Occasionally, he'd be arrested for fighting, sometimes for striking others with dangerous objects.

Tom's mother complained over the years about his sudden and unexplained absences. He'd kiss her goodbye, say that he was going downtown for a Coke or to a movie, and stay away for several days or even a couple of weeks!

Ultimately, Tom married a girl who had been the local prostitute and who had a colorful reputation. But he left her shortly after they were married, without showing the slightest bit of chagrin about her character, remorse over the marriage, or any shred of responsibility toward her.

Tom illustrates all of the features required for the DSM-IV diagnosis of Antisocial Personality Disorder:

- Current age over eighteen.
- Evidence of a Conduct Disorder (stealing, lying, truancy, vandalism, delinquency, chronic violations of rules) before age fifteen.
- Since age nineteen, a pervasive pattern of irresponsible behavior and disregard for and violation of the rights of others.
- Lack of remorse.

SOURCE: Abbreviated and modified from Cleckley, H., *The Mask of Sanity*, 5th Edition, 1976.

ABSENCE OF A CONSCIENCE AND A SENSE OF RESPONSIBILITY TO OTHERS

The absence of shame or remorse for past misdeeds, of any sense of humiliation for egregious ones, is one of the most common characteristics of those with antisocial personality disorder. They lack conscience, and with it, any deep capacity to care about other people (Hare, 1980; Williamson, Hare, and Wong, 1987). Their relationships, therefore, tend to be quite shallow and exploitative. They lack a capacity for love and sustained attachment and are unresponsive to trust, kindness, or affection. They lie shamelessly and can mercilessly abuse those who have trusted them. Gary Gilmore did not have a serious relationship until several weeks before he committed the two murders. He was then thirty-six years old. Describing the affair, he said that it was "probably the first close relationship that I ever had with anyone. I just didn't know how to respond to her for any length of time. I was very insensitive to her . . . I was thoughtless in the way I treated her. . . . [H]er two children bugged me and sometimes I would get angry at them and slap them because they were so noisy."

EMOTIONAL POVERTY

One of the major differences between the normal person who is a criminal and the individual with an antisocial personality disorder lies in the depth of experienced emotion. Ordinary criminals presumably experience the same emotions as other normal people. But people with antisocial personality disorder experience very shallow emotions. They seem to lack the capacity for sustained love, anger, grief, joy, or despair. During a psychiatric interview, Gilmore observed that "I don't remember any real emotional event in all my life. . . . When you're in the joint, you stay pretty even all the time . . . I'm not really excitable you know. I don't get emotional." Indeed, their incapacity to experience emotion may be significantly related to their lack of conscience and to the ease with which they violate the expectations of others (Hare, Williamson, and Harpur, 1988; Patrick, Bradley, and Cuthbert, 1990; Patrick, Cuthbert, and Lang, 1990).

The Sources of Antisocial Personality Disorder

Personality disorders are long-lived. The antisocial personality disorder originates in childhood or early adolescence as a conduct disorder and then continues into adulthood (see Box 7–2). Once again, Gary Gilmore is a case in point. Examining his childhood, we find that he had been suspended from school on several occasions for truancy and for alleged thefts from his classmates. When he was fourteen, he was sent to a correctional youth facility for

---

DSM-IV Criteria for Antisocial Personality Disorder

A. There is a pervasive pattern of disregard for and violation of the rights of others occurring since age 15 years, as indicated by three (or more) of the following: (1) failure to conform to social norms with respect to lawful behaviors as indicated by repeatedly performing acts that are grounds for arrest; (2) deceitfulness, as indicated by repeated lying, use of aliases, or conning others for personal profit or pleasure; (3) impulsivity or failure to plan ahead; (4) irritability and aggressiveness, as indicated by repeated physical fights or assaults; (5) reckless disregard for safety of self or others; (6) consistent irresponsibility, as indicated by repeated failure to sustain consistent work behavior or honor financial obligations; (7) lack of remorse, as indicated by being indifferent to or rationalizing having hurt, mistreated, or stolen from another.
B. The individual is at least age 18 years.
C. There is evidence of Conduct Disorder with onset before age 15 years.
D. The occurrence of antisocial behavior is not exclusively during the course of Schizophrenia or a manic episode.
SOURCE: APA, DSM-IV, 1994.

WHO ARE THE FLEDGLING PSYCHOPATHS?

The terms "Antisocial Personality Disorder" and "Psychopathy" generally describe the same phenomena, the latter being "common parlance" for the former. Regardless of what you call them, the people who bear those appellations are the meanies and baddies of psychopathology. Psychopathic offenders are more prolific and versatile offenders than ordinary criminals. They are much more violent (Hare and McPherson, 1984; Rice, Harris, and Quinsey, 1990). They recidivate, that is, they repeat their offenses, much more often than nonpsychopathic people. And they are quite recalcitrant to treatment (Ogloff, Wong, and Greenwood, 1990).

As you might well imagine, such people are of interest not only to psychologists, but also to sociologists, criminologists, police, and law enforcement personnel. There is a vast literature describing the behavior and antecedents of psychopaths. Donald Lynam (1996) has attempted to provide a coherent framework for organizing this literature, and especially for understanding the antecedents of the antisocial personality disorder.

We have always understood that the antisocial personality disorder had childhood antecedents and indeed, the DSM-IV symptoms make that clear. But *which* antecedents? Children can suffer emotional problems, problems with their conduct, hyperactivity and attentional difficulties, to name but a few. Are all these problems antecedent to the adult antisocial personality disorder? If not, which are?

The evidence is strong that children with the cluster of problems that is denoted by hyperactivity, impulsivity, and attentional difficulties (HIA)—as opposed to those with mainly emotional difficulties—are those who develop antisocial personality disorders later in life. Several longitudinal studies support this view. For example, Satterfield, Hoppe, and Schell (1982) found that children who were diagnosed HIA were, as adolescents and adults some ten years later, arrested for more serious offenses and sent to jail or prison substantially more often than controls (25 percent versus 1 percent).

But that's not the entire story. While HIA powerfully predicts adult psychopathy, an even more powerful predictor arises in the mixture of HIA and Conduct Problems (CP). Several longitudinal studies (e.g. Moffitt, 1990; Farrington, Loeber, and Van Kammen, 1990; Magnussen, 1988) have shown that the group of children most likely to engage in antisocial behavior as adults, are those who both have HIA and conduct problems. These are the fledgling psychopaths.

---

auto theft. By the time of his last arrest, Gilmore had spent fifteen of his sixteen adult years behind bars.

What factors give rise to such continuously antisocial behavior? Four potential sources have been given considerable attention: (1) the family and social context, (2) defects in learning, (3) genetics, and (4) physiological dysfunctions in the central nervous system.

THE FAMILY AND SOCIAL CONTEXT

Because the person with antisocial personality disorder seems not to have internalized the moral standards of the larger society, it is natural to examine the agents of socialization, particularly the family and social context, for clues about sociopathy. There is evidence, for example, that people with antisocial personality disorder who grew up in the lower social classes experienced more difficult childhoods than other people from those same social strata. A number of studies indicate that losing a parent through desertion, divorce, or separation (rather than through death or chronic hospitalization) is highly correlated with the later development of antisocial behavior (Gregory, 1958; Greer, 1964; Oltman and Friedman, 1967). Moreover, the more severe the antisocial behavior, the more likely it is that the person with antisocial personality disorder experienced parental deprivation. Most writers believe, however, that it is not the parental deprivation per se that promotes antisocial personality disorder—otherwise the findings would include deprivation through death and hospitalization. Rather it is the emotional climate that precedes the divorce—the arguments and violent fights, the blatant promiscuity, alcoholism, parental instability, the neglectful or antisocial father—which is implicated in socialization for antisocial personality disorder (Robins, 1966; Smith, 1978). Again taking Gary Gilmore's life as an example, we find that although Gilmore's parents were never formally separated, his father spent so much of his time away from home that Gilmore considered himself to have been raised by "a single parent." During some of that time, his father was in prison, serving eighteen months on a bad check charge. His mother was simultaneously overindulgent and neglectful: Gilmore was often left to fend for himself. Reflecting on his family, he described it as "typical" and noted that "there wasn't much closeness in it."

Children who later develop antisocial personality disorder often find themselves in juvenile court. If they are sent to correctional institutions, they very likely pick up some of the habits of their antisocial peers. These findings, however, should not be interpreted to mean that *all* punishment for juvenile offenses is necessarily harmful to the child. Indeed, one study revealed that children who were apprehended and *moderately* punished for juvenile crimes have a lower recidivism rate than those who were apprehended and released without punishment (McCord, 1980). In order for children to be deterred from further crime, they must be given a clear message that what they did was wrong. The message is clearest when it comes as punishment. *Too* clear a message—one that results in sending children to penal institutions—may teach that crime is wrong, but it may also put them in an environment where they can learn from their peers how to pursue a criminal career successfully.

Longitudinal studies underscore the relationship of the home environment and subsequent criminality in delinquent boys. Once again, whether the father was absent or present was not a key determinant of subsequent criminality. The factors that did influence whether delinquent boys became criminal adults were maternal affection and self-esteem, parental supervision, harmony within the household, and the father's deviance. Indeed, separation and divorce do not lead to criminal behavior so long as the mother is affectionate and self-confident, the child is supervised, the level of discord between the parents is minimal, and the father is nondeviant (McCord, 1979).

DEFECTS IN LEARNING

Many clinicians have been struck by the seeming inability of those with antisocial personality disorder to learn from experience. Prichard (1837) called them "moral imbeciles." Cleckley (1964) observed that they failed especially to learn from punishing experiences, and as a result, had poor judgment. But they are often "savvy" and intelligent. If they suffer a defect in learning, it must be a fairly subtle one. What form might such a defect take?

Cleckley's observations, in particular, suggested that sociopaths were especially deficient in *avoidance* learning. Ordinary people rapidly learn to anticipate and avoid punitive situations. But those with antisocial personality disorder, perhaps because they are underaroused and underanxious, fail to do so. To examine this possibility, people with antisocial personality disorder and those without it were taken into the laboratory to test their ability to master a certain task (Lykken, 1957). The task involved learning to press a "correct" lever, but the idea was to find out which group learned to avoid punishment.

Participants sat in front of a panel that had four levers. Immediately above each lever was a red light and a green light. The subject's task was to find and press the lever that turned on the green light on each of a series of twenty trials. Since the correct lever changed on each trial, the subjects had to remember their sequence of responses from the first trial to the one they were now working on. A certain pattern had to be learned, and it was quite a complicated task, a veritable mental maze.

On each trial, the subject had four choices, only one of which turned on the green light. Two of the levers turned on a red light—clearly a wrong response—while the third delivered electric shock. Having two kinds of wrong responses, one that simply says "wrong" and the other that delivers physical punishment, enabled the investigator to answer a telling question. Is it that people with antisocial personality disorder cannot learn from negative experi-

▼ Hannibal Lecter (played by Anthony Hopkins) in the 1991 film *Silence of the Lambs* showed no remorse for his crimes, seemed to lack a conscience, and to be incapable of deep emotional feeling. This serial killer would probably have been diagnosed as having an antisocial personality disorder.

ence, or are there particular negative experiences, namely *avoidance* experiences, from which they cannot learn?

As expected, there were no differences in the total number of mistakes made by those with or without antisocial personality disorder. But whereas people who did not have the disorder quickly learned to avoid the electrified levers, those who had the disorder made the most errors that led to shock, suggesting that their particular learning defect was an inability to learn from painful experiences (Lykken, 1957). In effect, punishment or threat of punishment does not seem to influence the behavior of a person with antisocial personality disorder.

Why should people with antisocial personality disorder be deficient in avoidance learning? One possibility is that individuals with the disorder do not avoid shock because they do not find shock as noxious as do normal people, and they do not find shock as noxious because they are chronically *underaroused* (Hare, 1965). Put differently, people with the disorder may actually seek stimulation in order to elevate arousal to an optimal level. Indeed, it has often seemed to clinical observers that that is the case (Cleckley, 1964). Gary Gilmore may well have experienced underarousal and the need for stimulation as a child. Gilmore said, "I remember when I was a boy I would feel like I had to do things like sit on a railroad track until just before the train came and then I would dash off. Or I would put my finger over the end of a BB gun and pull the trigger to see if a BB was really in it. Sometimes I would stick my finger in water and then put my finger in a light socket to see if it would really shock me."

Because they are underaroused in general, the emotions that ordinarily inhibit criminal behavior are not sufficiently aroused in people with antisocial personality disorder (Williamson, Harpur, and Hare, 1990). At the same time, the emotions that propel people into crimes of passion are also absent. Individuals with antisocial personality disorder are mainly responsible for "cool" crimes such as burglary, forgery, and con games. When they are involved in violence, as Gilmore was, it tends to be impulsive and irrational violence, and perverse because it so lacks in feeling.

There are several kinds of punishment. There is *physical* punishment to which people with antisocial personality disorder do not respond as the above experiments suggest. But there is also *tangible* punishment such as the loss of money, and *social* punishment such as disapproval. Are people with antisocial personality disorder as unresponsive to the latter kinds of punishment as they are to physical punishment? The same "mental maze" was used to examine this question. But this time, if one of the wrong levers was pressed, the subject lost a quarter. If another was pressed, the subject received social disapproval, and the third wrong lever brought electric shock. Once again, those with antisocial personality disorder learned the task as quickly as those without the disorder. And again, those with the disorder were considerably less responsive to physical punishment than were those without the disorder. They were also less responsive to social disapproval. But they quickly learned to avoid the lever that would cost them a quarter. Indeed, they avoided this lever somewhat more than normals, indicating that people with antisocial personality disorder can learn to avoid punishment provided that the punishment is noxious to *them* (Schmauk, 1970). Even so, in the real world, they seem undeterred by the criminal justice system, nor do they *anticipate* that their actions will lead them to it.

GENETICS AND CRIMINALITY

The possibility that antisocial personality disorder has a genetic basis has long interested researchers. In the popular imagination, sociopathy and antisocial behavior have long been associated with the "bad seed," and particularly the bad seed that came from a family of bad seeds. That view, however, is hard to

FOCUS QUESTIONS

1. Describe how adoption studies have been used to determine whether there is a genetic component to criminal behavior.
2. What physiological differences between sociopaths and normals have been found?

assess. The problems of sorting environmental from genetic influences are as difficult here as elsewhere. But the task here is further compounded by the fact that it is *criminals*—those who have been apprehended and convicted of a crime—who come to our attention, not those who have eluded apprehension. Not all criminals have antisocial personality disorder, of course, nor are all who have the disorder criminals.

The data on the biology of sociopathy are fascinating for, though they are complex, they appear to indicate that both genetics and the environment play strong roles in the development of antisocial personality disorder. For particular insight, we will now examine adoption studies. When children are raised by their natural parents, it is impossible to separate the effects of genetics from those of environment on their development. But studies of children who have been adopted at an early age allow these influences to be separated. These studies also provide evidence for the influence of heredity in both criminality and antisocial personality disorder. One study examined the criminal records of adopted persons in Denmark (Hutchings and Mednick, 1977; Mednick, Gabrielli, and Hutchings, 1984). Their names were drawn from the Danish Population Register, which records the names of both the adoptive and the biological parents of these adoptees. Thus, it is possible to compare the criminal records of the adopted children with those of both sets of parents. These comparative data are shown in Table 7–2. The incidence of crime among these offspring was lowest when neither the biological nor the adoptive fathers had been convicted of a criminal offense. Nearly indistinguishable from that low rate was the rate among adoptees whose adoptive fathers had been convicted, but whose biological fathers were "clean." The incidence of criminal conviction among adoptees jumped dramatically, however, when the natural father had a criminal record, but the adoptive father had none, providing clear support for the view that the tendency to engage in criminal acts is hereditary. But highest of all was the incidence of criminality among adoptees when both their natural *and* adoptive fathers had criminal records, underscoring again the combined influence of heredity and environment on criminality. These individuals probably inherited a tendency toward criminality from their biological fathers and learned criminal behavior from their adoptive fathers (Cloninger and Gottesman, 1987). As we mentioned, however, criminality is not identical with antisocial personality disorder. But when a measure of sociopathy rather than criminality was used, similar findings were obtained (Schulsinger, 1972).

TABLE 7–2

CRIMINALITY OF ADOPTED SONS ACCORDING TO THE CRIMINALITY OF THEIR ADOPTIVE AND BIOLOGICAL FATHERS

Father		Percentage of sons who are criminal offenders	Number
Biological	Adoptive		
No registered offense	No registered offense	10.5	333
No registered offense	Criminal offense	11.5	52
Criminal offense	No registered offense	22.0	219
Criminal offense	Criminal offense	36.2	58
Total			662

SOURCE: Modified from Hutchings and Mednick, 1977, p. 132.

PHYSIOLOGICAL DYSFUNCTIONS

A number of investigators have sought to discover physiological differences between people with and without antisocial personality disorder. And a good number of such differences have been discovered. For example, a substantial proportion of those with antisocial personality disorder have abnormal electroencephalograms (EEG's). This is especially true of those who are most violent and aggressive. The abnormalities are of two kinds. First, people with antisocial personality disorder show the slow brain waves that are characteristic of children and that suggest brain immaturity—in effect, a lack of development in those parts of the brain responsible for moral understanding and behavior. Second, a sizable proportion of those with antisocial personality disorder show positive spiking in their brain waves. Positive spikes are sudden and brief bursts of brain wave activity. These spikes occur in the EEG's of 40 to 45 percent of those with antisocial personality disorder as compared to about 1 to 2 percent of the general population (Kurland, Yeager, and Arthur, 1963). Positive spiking is itself associated with impulsive, aggressive behavior. Most individuals who commit aggressive acts and who also manifest positive spiking report no guilt or anxiety about their actions.

These findings are of interest for several reasons. First, the possibility that people with antisocial personality disorder suffer cortical immaturity (Hare, 1978) suggests that as they get older and their cortexes become more mature, they should engage in less antisocial behavior. That is precisely what has been found. Particularly between the ages of thirty and forty, a substantial proportion of those with antisocial personality disorder show marked behavioral improvements (Robins, 1966).

Second, those positive spikes—the sudden and brief bursts of brain wave activity—appear to reflect a dysfunction in the brain's limbic system, precisely the system that controls emotion and motivation. And what emotion might be affected by this physiological dysfunction? Some theorists speculate that it is *fear*, the very emotion that is thought to be implicated in the phenomena of socialization and self-control (Cleckley, 1964). The inability of the person with antisocial personality disorder to inhibit behaviors and delay gratifications is generally thought to be similar to that of animals who have suffered lesions in the brain's septal region (Gorenstein and Newman, 1980). Thus, the failure to learn from punishing experiences may be the product of faulty physiology. Biology, rather than malice, may be the wellspring of the antisocial personality disorder.

OTHER PERSONALITY DISORDERS

The antisocial personality disorder is the best known and best studied of the personality disorders, but it is not the only one. People who are characteristically suspicious and distrustful, or passive, or inappropriately emotional, or overly dependent upon others, or enormously compulsive and orderly may also be suffering from a personality disorder.

Paranoid Personality Disorder

After his wife died, Seymour moved to a retirement community in Florida. Healthy and attractive, he immediately joined a folk dancing group, a current events discussion group, and a ceramics class. Within six weeks, however, he had dropped out of all the programs, complaining to his children that other residents were talking about him behind his back, that he was unable to find a dancing partner, was ignored in the current events group, and had been given improper instruction in ceramics.

Before his retirement, Seymour had been a physicist. He had always been close-mouthed about his work. His home study had always been locked. He had not permitted anyone to clean it, and he had become angry if anyone entered it without his permission. His son reported that his parents had been extremely close and affectionate, but that his father had had few other friends. He had been wary of new faces and concerned about the motives of strangers.

A hard worker throughout his life, he was now gripped by fear. He spent much of his time overseeing his investments, fearful that his broker would give him poor advice, or neglect to tell him when to buy and when to sell.

The prominent characteristics of the ***paranoid personality disorder*** are a pervasive and longstanding distrust and suspiciousness of others; hypersensitivity to slight; and a tendency to scan the environment for, and to perceive selectively, cues that validate prejudicial ideas and attitudes. Those who suffer from the paranoid personality disorder are often argumentative, tense, and humorless. They seem ready to attack. They tend to exaggerate, to make mountains out of molehills, and to find hidden motives and special meanings in the innocuous behavior of others. They tend to blame others for whatever difficulties they experience, and they cannot themselves accept any blame or responsibility for failure. Some evidence suggests that relatives of those with a schizophrenic disorder may be somewhat more likely to be diagnosed with paranoid personality disorder than would people without a schizophrenic relative (Kendler and Gruenberg, 1982; Siever et al., 1990a).

Because such people tend to externalize blame and guilt, they are rarely seen in clinics or psychiatric hospitals. Thus, it is difficult to estimate how prevalent this problem is. Generally, however, it is felt to be a problem that tends to afflict men more than women (Kass, Spitzer, and Williams, 1983). The prognosis for this disorder is guarded indeed.

Histrionic Personality Disorder

People who have long histories of drawing attention to themselves and of engaging in excited emotional displays that are caused by insignificant events are captured in the diagnosis of ***histrionic personality disorder.*** Such people are apt to be superficially charming, warm, and gregarious, but they are often viewed by others as insincere and shallow. They seem to be seeking admiration by playing continually to unknown audiences. Once they form relationships, they become demanding and inconsiderate, egocentric, and self-absorbed. They can be enormously flirtatious or coquettish, yet their sexual adjustment is as often naive or frigid, suggesting that their flirtatious behavior serves the ends of attention-getting much more than those of sexuality. Women have been perceived by diagnosticians as being more likely to have histrionic traits than men (Ford and Widiger, 1989). Yet, recent epidemiological studies indicate that men and women under age forty-five are as likely to have the disorder, although it is more common in women over forty-five (Nestadt et al., 1990; Weissman, 1993).

> At forty-two, Michael entered therapy after his second marriage failed. He strikes you as every bit the college professor: pipe-smoking, tweedy, facile with words, and somewhat theatrical. His difficulties are gripping, and they extend beyond his marriage. He has been the victim of muggings and robberies, of badly diagnosed ailments, and wrongly prescribed drugs. His scholarly papers are often rejected by journal editors, and his colleagues seem not to appreciate his genius. For all of this, he seems clearly a charming man, though one who is more interested in the therapist's reactions than in understanding his own plight.
>
> Michael reports that he has an interesting social life, though he complains in passing that people often do not invite him to dinner a second time. Nor do they lend him money or allow him to borrow their car. Some probing reveals that Michael has frequently failed to repay loans, and that he has often been involved in accidents with other people's cars ("well, they're insured . . ."). He is prone to cancel social engagements at the last minute if something more interesting comes up. Indeed, he calls often to change his scheduled therapy sessions and is upset when those changes cannot be arranged.

If, upon perusing Michael's history, you have the sense that the diagnosis is not entirely clear, that it seems to overlap with other personality disorders, perhaps especially with the borderline personality (see below), or even the antisocial personality disorder—you may well be right. There seems to be considerable overlap between the histrionic personality disorder and other disorders (Pfohl, 1991; Grueneich, 1992).

Narcissistic Personality Disorder

FOCUS QUESTIONS

1. How is the paranoid personality disorder best characterized?
2. Describe people who have a histrionic personality disorder.
3. What is the central feature of the narcissistic personality disorder and how does this lead to disturbances in interpersonal relationships?
4. Describe the vicious cycle that characterizes the lives of those with avoidant personality disorder.

The central feature of the *narcissistic personality disorder* is an outlandish sense of self-importance. It is characterized by continuous self-absorption, by fantasies of unlimited success, power or ideal love; beauty, brilliance, by exhibitionistic needs for constant admiration, and by the use of a substantially more benign standard for evaluating self than for judging others (Kernberg, 1975; Tangney, Wagner, and Gramzow, 1992). Criticism, the indifference of others, and threats to esteem characteristically receive exaggerated responses of rage, shame, humiliation, or emptiness. Of course, the near-total preoccupation with self massively disturbs interpersonal relationships in a variety of ways. Such people may simply lack the ability to recognize how others feel. They may have an exaggerated sense of "entitlement," expecting that the world owes them a living without assuming reciprocal responsibilities. They may simply be exploitative, taking advantage of others to indulge their own desires. When they are able to establish a relationship, they may vacillate between the extremes of overidealization and enormous devaluation of the other person.

There is reason to believe that, perhaps as a result of parental training, those who suffer the narcissistic personality disorder simply *expect* too much from others (Benjamin, 1987). And self theorists (see Chapter 3) would suggest that these expectations arise because empathic relationships with caregivers failed to develop (Kohut, 1971, 1977, 1978), resulting in a fragmented sense of self that is especially vulnerable to feelings of emptiness and low self-esteem, and the compensatory behaviors that these generate, as the following case illustrates.

> Marion is a bit player who, at twenty-four, has not had a major theatrical role since her high school play. She has just been turned down for the lead in a new musical. Plagued with self-doubt, she is simultaneously furious with the casting director, a man with whom she has studied acting for the past three years. In her view, she should have gotten the part—both because she was every bit as good as the young woman who ultimately did get it, and because she was owed the support of the director who encouraged her and took her money for years. Marion is certain that the other actress got the part because she slept with the director. But her own time will come, Marion believes, and when it does, her own name will be displayed on the theater marquee.
>
> Beyond her vocational difficulties, Marion also has difficulty in establishing and maintaining friendships. Slender, beautifully dressed, and seemingly self-assured,

▶ Histrionic personalities seem to live their lives as elaborate emotional shows played continuously to unknown audiences.

she has no trouble attracting men. At first, she enthusiastically envisions great times with them. But shortly thereafter she drops them, terming them "duds," "sexually unexciting," or "just plain boring." Women seem to fare no better. Marion gave a friend a ticket to see her in a play. Instead, her friend visited a hospitalized aunt. Marion fumed and viewed her friend's absence as a "betrayal."

Avoidant Personality Disorder

At the core of the ***avoidant personality disorder*** is a *turning away:* from people, from new experiences, and even from old ones. The disorder often combines a fear of appearing foolish with an equally strong desire for acceptance and affection. Individuals who experience this disorder want very much to enter into social relationships or new activities, but they may find themselves unwilling to take even small risks unless they are given strong guarantees of uncritical acceptance.

Elaine became quite distraught when her co-worker and close friend left to train as a nurse-practitioner. Her replacement was "nice enough," but Elaine feared the new woman would find her boring. At twenty-one, Elaine has only one other friend, her married sister. But her sister is "too busy with her family right now," and so Elaine spends very little time with her. Her social life in high school was quite restricted, and at present, she has no social life at all. At work, she eats lunch alone and is viewed by other workers as unfriendly.

People with avoidant personality disorder are shy (Zimbardo, 1977). The slightest hint of disapproval by others and the slightest whiff of potential failure lead them to withdraw. They may interpret apparently innocuous events as ridicule. People suffering from this disorder are likely to be distressed by their relative inability to relate comfortably to others, which adds to their low self-esteem, which in turn makes them even more sensitive to criticism and humiliation—an especially vicious cycle. But is the avoidant personality disorder truly a separate disorder, or is it indistinguishable from generalized social phobia, which we examined in Chapter 5? The available evidence suggests that, by and large, the diagnosis of avoidant personality disorder tells us little more than is told by the Axis I diagnosis of social phobia (Herbert, Hope, and Bellack, 1992; Holt, Heimberg, and Hope, 1992; Turner, Beidel, and Townsley, 1992). To the extent that there is a difference between those two diagnoses, it may lie in the possibility that those with the avoidant personality disorder are more anxious in social situations and possess inferior social skills to cope with them (Turner, Beidel, Dancu, and Keys, 1986; Widiger, 1992).

DSM-IV Criteria for Avoidant Personality Disorder

A pervasive pattern of social inhibition, feelings of inadequacy, and hypersensitivity to negative evaluation, beginning by early adulthood and present in a variety of contexts, as indicated by four (or more) of the following: (1) avoids occupational activities that involve significant interpersonal contact, because of fears of criticism, disapproval, or rejection; (2) is unwilling to get involved with people unless certain of being liked; (3) shows restraint within intimate relationships because of the fear of being shamed or ridiculed; (4) is preoccupied with being criticized or rejected in social situations; (5) is inhibited in new interpersonal situations because of feelings of inadequacy; (6) views self as socially inept, personally unappealing, or inferior to others; (7) is unusually reluctant to take personal risks or to engage in any new activities because they may prove embarrassing.

SOURCE: APA, DSM-IV, 1994.

▲ Deference and fearfulness characterize the dependent personality disorder.

Dependent Personality Disorder

The central characteristic of the **dependent personality disorder** involves allowing others to make the major decisions, to initiate the important actions, and to assume responsibility for significant areas of one's life. People with this disorder often defer to spouse, parent, or friend regarding where they should live, the kind of job they should have, and who their friends should be. They also have trouble disagreeing with others for fear of losing their support or approval. They subordinate their own needs to the needs of the people upon whom they are dependent, feeling that any assertion of their own needs may jeopardize the relationship. Such people will often tolerate enormous physical and/or psychological abuse for fear that they will be abandoned. Correspondingly, when they are alone even for brief periods of time, they may experience intense discomfort and helplessness. Thus, they often seek companionship at great cost. They lack self-esteem, and they often refer to themselves as stupid or helpless. The disorder may have its origin in parental behavior that is both overprotective and authoritarian. Such behavior may well be synergistic. Overprotective parents encourage dependency in children, and such dependent behavior brings forth comforting protectiveness from parents (Hunt, Browning, and Nave, 1982; Bornstein, 1992).

The mother of two small children, Joyce was brought to the emergency room with multiple facial abrasions and a fractured jaw. She was no stranger to the hospital staff. Eight months earlier, she had been treated for two broken ribs and assorted bruises. Joyce was reluctant to give the details of her injuries. But the neighbor who brought her to the hospital reported that Joyce had been physically assaulted by her husband. According to the neighbor, Joyce's husband frequently abused her verbally and "slapped her around" on a number of occasions. Although Joyce feared for her own safety and that of her children, she was unresponsive to suggestions that she move out and separate from her husband.

The middle child of three, Joyce was given neither great responsibility nor great attention during her childhood. Her father was a man of strong opinions and made all the decisions in the family. He believed adamantly that women belonged at home, and joked often and coarsely about "buns in the oven and bums in bed." He controlled the family finances, and delegated no responsibility in that area.

Apart from a course in typing, Joyce learned no vocational skills in high school,

---

DSM-IV Criteria for Dependent Personality Disorder

A pervasive and excessive need to be taken care of that leads to submissive and clinging behavior and fears of separation, beginning by early adulthood and present in a variety of contexts, as indicated by five (or more) of the following: (1) has difficulty making everyday decisions without an excessive amount of advice and reassurance from others; (2) needs others to assume responsibility for most major areas of his or her life; (3) has difficulty expressing disagreement with others because of fear of loss of support or approval (*Note:* do not include realistic fears of retribution.); (4) has difficulty initiating projects or doing things on his or her own (because of a lack of self-confidence in judgment or abilities rather than a lack of motivation or energy); (5) goes to excessive lengths to obtain nurturance and support from others, to the point of volunteering to do things that are unpleasant; (6) feels uncomfortable or helpless when alone because of exaggerated fears of being unable to care for himself or herself; (7) urgently seeks another relationship as a source of care and support when a close relationship ends; (8) is unrealistically preoccupied with fears of being left to take care of himself or herself.

SOURCE: APA, DSM-IV, 1994.

and dropped out to get married. Indeed, other than baby-sitting and summer jobs as a mother's helper, Joyce had no work experience at all.

During the five years of her marriage, Joyce left all decisions to her husband, even to the point of agreeing to the purchase of a sofa that she really disliked. Her husband was intensely jealous of her friendships, and she therefore abandoned all of them. Indeed, except for visits to her mother who lived in the neighborhood, she went nowhere without her husband.

It was generally believed that the dependent personality disorder occurred more frequently among women than among men (Kass, Spitzer, and Williams, 1983), but research now seems to indicate that it is as prevalent in men as in women (Reich, 1990; Nestadt et al., 1990). Pregnant women who suffer this disorder are much more anxious at the time of birth if their husbands are not in the delivery room, whereas women who do not suffer the disorder seem unaffected by their husbands' absence during delivery (Keinan and Hobfoll, 1989; Bornstein, 1992). Moreover, the disorder impairs occupational functioning if the nature of the job requires independent decision making. Social relations may be restricted to the few people upon whom the person is dependent. And when the dependent relationship is threatened, vast depression may ensue (Bornstein, 1992).

Obsessive-Compulsive Personality Disorder

FOCUS QUESTIONS

1. Describe the central characteristic of the dependent personality disorder and how it may originate.
2. Why do those with the obsessive-compulsive personality disorder often procrastinate and have trouble making decisions?
3. What is the central feature of the schizoid personality disorder?
4. Describe what may cause the instability and unpredictability that characterize borderline personality disorder.

The *obsessive-compulsive personality disorder* is characterized by a pervasive pattern of striving for perfection, order, and control. Those with the disorder demand perfection in themselves as well as others. Nothing they do seems to please them, however excellent the outcome. And because they anticipate being unable to meet their own unattainable standards, they often procrastinate in important matters, allocating their time poorly and leaving the things that mean most to them to the very last. While they prize work and productivity over pleasure and interpersonal relationships, they get overly involved in details, in lists and rules and schedules. They have great trouble making work-related decisions and are excellent at postponing pleasure-related ones. People who suffer this disorder tend to have difficulty expressing emotion, and they are often seen by others as formal, stiff, overly conscientious, and moralistic. The disorder is commonly made for both men and women, although men seem to be diagnosed with it more often. Those men who are diagnosed with the disorder are generally white, educated, married, and holding down a job (Nestadt et al., 1991). Obsessive-compulsive personality disorder should not be confused with obsessive-compulsive disorder, an unrelated problem (Chapter 6).

Laura and Steve began to see a marriage counselor because Steve insisted on it. He had become extremely distressed by Laura's unavailability and perfectionism. At thirty-seven, Laura was a partner in one of the nation's largest accounting firms. She worked long hours at the office, brought work home, was unwilling to go out more than once a week, and resisted taking vacations. At home, she snapped out orders to the children about housework and schoolwork. She could not tolerate an unwashed dish or a jacket on the sofa and was critical and demanding of household help. Much of the time, Steve found her sexually unresponsive.

Laura did not believe she had a "marriage problem," though she freely acknowledged feeling harassed at work and at home. She attributed her long hours at work to the demands of her profession. Snapping at the children and nit-picking about domestic order were, she insisted, the result of being the person who had to clean up after everyone else. Laura did not consider herself sexually unresponsive, but she did think she was often tense and fatigued. The only child of upwardly striving immigrant parents, Laura had been encouraged to excel. She was valedictorian of her high school class and among the top ten of her college graduating class. The social milieu in which she grew up put great stress on the value of close family relationships. Laura never doubted that she would be a wife and mother, and she married soon after graduating college.

Schizoid Personality Disorder

The central feature of the *schizoid personality disorder* is a defect in the capacity to form social relationships, as reflected in the absence of desire for social involvements, indifference to both praise and criticism, insensitivity to the feelings of others, and/or lack of social skills. Such people have few, if any, close friends. They are withdrawn, reserved, and seclusive. Others see them as "in a fog" and absent-minded. In short, they are extreme introverts. Their feelings tend to be bland and constricted; they seem to lack warm feelings or the capacity for emotional display and are therefore perceived as cold, aloof, or distant. Sometimes, and especially in jobs that require a good deal of social isolation, these characteristics can be assets. But more often, the very poverty of social skills restricts occupational and social success.

A thirty-eight-year-old chemical engineer, Homer was forced into marriage counseling by his wife who complained of his failure to join in family activities or to take an interest in the children, his general lack of affection and responsiveness, and his disinterest in sex. His failure to relate socially to others extended also to his job, where colleagues characterized him as either shy and reticent, or as cold and aloof.

Homer's history revealed longstanding social indifference and little emotional responsiveness. He recalled that he was indifferent to the idea of marrying, but did so to please his parents. His wife tried repeatedly to arrange social situations that might be of interest to him, but to no avail.

Schizotypal Personality Disorder

The *schizotypal personality disorder* is described mainly by longstanding oddities in thinking, perceiving, communicating, and behaving—oddities that are severe enough to be noticed, but not serious enough to warrant the more serious diagnosis of schizophrenia (McGlashan, 1987). Odd thinking can be manifest in extreme superstitiousness, or in the sense that one is especially noticed by others. The latter sense, which is technically called an *idea of reference,* can also be a fertile breeding ground for suspiciousness and paranoia. Depersonalization—a sense of estrangement from oneself and from one's environment—may be present. Communication may be odd, but not downright peculiar. It may be tangential, digressive, vague, or overly elaborate, but it is not loose or incoherent. Finally, people suffering from this disorder may also experience constricted or inappropriate feelings, with the result that they are unable to maintain rapport in face-to-face interactions.

The schizotypal personality disorder seems genetically related to schizophrenia (Kety, 1974; Kendler and Gruenberg, 1984; Baron, Gruen, Kane, and Amis, 1985; Siever et al., 1990b). Indeed, many of the disturbances described here are similar to those seen among people with chronic schizophrenia, but here the disturbances appear in milder forms. It is an error, however, to identify this disorder wholly with the schizophrenias because differences of degree are very important differences as far as psychological distress and prognosis are concerned (McGlashan, 1986b). As we do not confuse the poor and the rich, even though both have some money, so must the schizotypal personality disorder be distinguished from its more intense relatives, the schizophrenias.

At twenty-one, Mark complains that he feels "spaced out" and "creepy" much of the time. Unemployed, he lives with his parents and spends much of his time watching television or staring into space. He says that he often feels as if he is outside himself, watching himself through a TV screen, or running through a script that someone else has written. Mark has had several jobs, but none has lasted more than a month. He was fired from his last position as a toy salesman after several customers had complained that he had talked to them in vague terms about irrelevant things.

Mark is convinced that people do not like him, but he does not understand why. He is certain that people change their seats on buses to avoid sitting next to him. He is unhappy about his loneliness and isolation, but he has made no attempt to reestablish old relationships.

Several months ago, Mark learned that one of his parents' friends planned to open a chain of athletic shoe discount stores. Although he has no experience or training in business, Mark is "waiting" for an offer to manage one of these stores.

DSM-IV Criteria for Schizotypal Personality Disorder

A. A pervasive pattern of social and interpersonal deficits marked by acute discomfort with, and reduced capacity for, close relationships as well as by cognitive or perceptual distortions and eccentricities of behavior, beginning by early adulthood and present in a variety of contexts, as indicated by five (or more) of the following: (1) ideas of reference (excluding delusions of reference); (2) odd beliefs or magical thinking that influences behavior and is inconsistent with subcultural norms (e.g., superstitiousness, belief in clairvoyance, telepathy, or "sixth sense"; in children and adolescents, bizarre fantasies or preoccupations); (3) unusual perceptual experiences, including bodily illusions; (4) odd thinking and speech (e.g., vague circumstantial, metaphorical, overelaborate, or stereotyped); (5) suspiciousness or paranoid ideation; (6) inappropriate or constricted affect; (7) behavior or appearance that is odd, eccentric, or peculiar; (8) lack of close friends or confidants other than first-degree relatives; (9) excessive social anxiety that does not diminish with familiarity and tends to be associated with paranoid fears rather than negative judgments about self.

B. Does not occur exclusively during the course of Schizophrenia, a Mood Disorder with Psychotic Features, another Psychotic Disorder, or a Pervasive Developmental Disorder.

SOURCE: APA, DSM-IV, 1994.

Borderline Personality Disorder

Borderline personality disorder is a very broad category whose essential feature is *instability* in a variety of personality areas, including interpersonal relationships, behavior, mood, and self-image. These areas are not necessarily related and, indeed, are themselves so broad that people with quite different problems are likely to be considered for this diagnosis.

The borderline personality disorder diagnosis is, by far, the most prevalent of the personality disorder diagnoses in both inpatient and outpatient settings (Grueneich, 1992). About 75 percent of patients with a diagnosis of borderline personality disorder are women (APA, 1994). Any diagnosis that is so broad and potentially inclusive, however, runs the risk of becoming a "kitchen sink" diagnosis. In order to increase the validity of the borderline diagnosis, as well as limit its use to a restricted range of people, DSM-IV requires evidence for instability in at least five of nine areas: frantic efforts to avoid abandonment, unstable interpersonal relationships, unstable self-image, self-damaging impulsivity (in spending, sexual behavior, substance abuse, reckless driving, or bingeing), suicidal behavior or self-mutilating behavior, emotional instability, chronic feelings of emptiness, lack of control over anger, stress-related paranoid thoughts or severe dissociative symptoms.

What causes the instability and unpredictability that is so characteristic of the borderline personality disorder? Both empirical evidence and intelligent speculation suggest that the person who suffers borderline personality disorder is, to begin with, a *gifted* person. She is gifted with unusual perceptiveness about, and insight into, the feelings that other people have (Park, Imboden, Park, Hulse, and Unger, 1992). She is, moreover, particularly empathic (Ladisich and Feil, 1988) and quite sensitive to nonverbal nuances (Frank and Hoffman, 1986). Such gifts would ordinarily augur well for her social development were it not for the fact that she has regularly been exposed to psychological abuse in the form of devaluation and blame (Zanarini, Gunderson, Marina, Schwartz, and Frankenberg, 1989; Stone, 1990), and often to sexual and physical abuse (Paris and Zweig-Frank, 1992; Weaver and Clum, 1993). It is her intuitive brilliance that is assaulted, rather than vaunted, by the abusive parent (Park, Imboden, Park, Hulse, and Unger, 1992). In order to maintain a "secure" emotional base, she rejects herself and her gifts, while absolving the abusive parent (Bowlby, 1988; Crittenden and Ainsworth, 1989).

Moreover, modern self theorists (see Chapter 3) speculate that it is a failed self-object relationship in childhood that leads to adult instability of this sort (Kohut, 1977). In particular, the self is especially sensitive to failures in the growth of esteem, as well as failures in the development of the sense of agency. These result in protracted fragmentation of the self, and with it the sense that one is losing control or "coming apart." Moreover, self injuries may arise out of destructive impulses turned inward, with the borderline patient directing his or her anger and aggressive impulses toward an unintegrated part of the self (Kernberg, 1992; Wagner and Linehan, 1994). The following case illustrates some of the difficulties of the borderline personality:

▼ Thomas Wolfe (1900–1938).

Thomas Wolfe was a writer whose first work was published in 1929 and who died less than ten years later, before he was forty. In that brief decade, he was a literary sensation, hailed by the greatest novelists of his time. He was enormously productive and driven. And he was painfully unhappy. Wolfe was described as nervous, surly, suspicious, given to brooding, to drinking, to violent outbursts, and sometimes even to fears that he was going mad. He was rude and dislikable. He said of himself that he was afraid of people and that he sometimes concealed his fear by being arrogant and by sneering magnificently.

It was hard for him to begin writing on any particular day, but once he began it was harder still for him to stop. The words would simply pour out of him. He would sleep late, gulp down cup after cup of black coffee, smoke innumerable cigarettes, pace up and down—and write endlessly. He would scrawl down the words on sheet after sheet of yellow paper, so hastily and hugely that the pages often contained only twenty words apiece, and those in abbreviated scrawl. At night, he would prowl the streets, drinking heavily, or spending hours in a phone booth, calling friends, and accusing them of having betrayed him. The next day, overcome with remorse, he would call again and apologize.

For all his writing, he had difficulty putting together a second book after *Look Homeward Angel.* Although he had written a million words, ten times that of an average novel, it still was not a book. He was fortunate to have as his editor Maxwell Perkins, who had discovered his talent and who cared to nurture it. Wolfe wrote: "I was sustained by one piece of inestimable good fortune. I had for a friend a man of immense wisdom and a gentle but unyielding fortitude. I think that if I was not destroyed at this time by the sense of hopelessness . . . it was largely because of . . . Perkins . . . I did not give in because he would not let me give in." Perkins recognized that Wolfe was a driven man, and feared that he would suffer either a psychological or physical breakdown, or both. He proposed to Wolfe that, having written a million words, his work was finished: it only remained for both of them to sit down and make a book out of his effort.

That collaboration was difficult. A million words do not automatically make a book. Wolfe was reluctant to cut. Most of the editing, therefore, fell to Perkins. And as Perkins slowly made a book out of Wolfe's words, Wolfe's resentment of Perkins increased. The work was not perfect, Wolfe felt. And it upset him to bring forth a book that did not meet his standards.

Until the book was published, Wolfe believed it would be a colossal failure. The reviews were magnificent, however. But although Wolfe was at first heartened by the reviews, he gradually began to feel again that the book was less than perfect, a matter for which he held Perkins responsible. His relationship with Perkins deteriorated. He became suspicious, even paranoid. Yet, apart from Perkins, he had no close friends. He became increasingly unpredictable, yielding easily to incensed anger, unable to control it. Ultimately, he broke with Perkins. Rosenthal (1979) has suggested that Wolfe's emotional liability, his inability to control his anger, the difficulties he had in being alone, his many self-damaging acts, as well as his identity problems point to the diagnosis of a borderline personality disorder. At the same time, Wolfe also had personality features that were consistent with the schizotypal personality disorder, especially his ideas of reference that made him so suspicious and paranoid.

Today, various treatments are being used to help those with borderline personality disorder. Psychodynamic therapy has been found to be useful, although relapse rates when therapy is discontinued are relatively high. Behavioral therapy is also useful although relapse rates and side effects are still under study. Several drug therapies have been tried as well, with varying success, but more outcome studies are needed before definite conclusions can be drawn as to their effectiveness, relapse rates, and side effects (see Table 7–3).

TABLE 7–3

	TREATMENT OF BORDERLINE PERSONALITY DISORDER				
	Individual Psychodynamic Therapy	Behavior Therapy	Serotonergic Agents	Lithium	Noradrenergic Agents
Improvement	about 50% moderately improved	probably better than placebo	probably better than placebo	about 50% moderately improved	about 50% moderately improved
Relapse*	moderate to high relapse	unclear	unclear	unclear	unclear
Side Effects	unclear	unclear	mild	mild	severe
Cost	expensive	moderately expensive	inexpensive	inexpensive	inexpensive
Time Scale	years	months	weeks/months	weeks/months	weeks/months
Overall	**useful**	**useful**	**useful**	**useful**	**marginal**

*Relapse after discontinuation of treatment.
SOURCE: Based on P. Crits-Cristoph, Psychological treatment for personality disorders, in P. Nathan and J. Gorman (eds.), *Treatments that work* (New York: Oxford, 1997).

Laboratory experiments, naturalistic studies, and longitudinal surveys all converge to support the existence of the antisocial personality disorder. On a variety of specific criteria, individuals with the disorder are demonstrably different from those who do not have it. However, the legitimacy of the other personality disorders is far more problematic. No matter how convincing the descriptions of these disorders seem to be, the documentation for their existence as reliable and valid syndromes is often, at bottom, anecdotal. It has grown out of clinical lore, and while it is not to be lightly dismissed for that reason, neither can it be easily accepted. For despite the effort that has gone into tightening the various categories of personality disorders they are still particularly prone to a variety of errors that easily erode their usefulness.

Alternative Views of the Personality Disorders

FOCUS QUESTIONS

1. Why do the personality disorders present diagnostic and therapeutic challenges to researchers and clinicians?
2. What are potential sources of error in making diagnoses of personality disorders?

Because personality disorders are characterized by the presence of enduring *traits* that often originate in childhood or early adolescence, evidence for their existence needs to be accumulated across a considerable period of time. As a result, distortions of memory and failure to obtain and properly assess facts are powerful potential sources of error for these diagnoses. Consider Seymour, who was held to be suffering from a paranoid personality disorder. The behavioral facts relating to his difficulties were quite accurate. But subsequently, a careful investigation of the sources of his difficulties yielded a quite different picture. It turned out that Seymour had been experiencing a marked hearing loss. He had not mentioned it during his early interviews both because he underestimated its extent and because he dreaded wearing a hearing aid. He had difficulty getting dancing partners because, while he heard the music, he often missed the instructor's calls and was commonly out-of-step. In the discussion group, he often repeated comments that had already been made by others or, worse, misheard others' comments, such that his own were inappropriate and disruptive. Similar difficulties pervaded his experience in the ceramics class. Moreover, his seeming distrust of others, which had been manifested in the locking of his study and in not talking about his work, takes on a somewhat different meaning when one learns that as a physicist, he had spent his entire career working on classified military problems. In addition, like many professionals of the 1950s and 1960s, Seymour had moved a great deal. Making new friends in each new location required a heavy expenditure of time and energy. Precisely because he had a close relationship with his wife and because he was deeply involved in his work, Seymour was simply unwilling to invest himself in new, but transient, relationships.

Thus, the possibility of misinterpreting lifelong behaviors is potentially dangerous because the contexts in which those behaviors developed may not be readily retrievable now. But even when considerable information *is* available, therapists of different theoretical persuasions may arrive at different diagnostic conclusions as far as the personality disorders are concerned. Consider Laura, who appeared to have all of the characteristics of an obsessive-compulsive personality disorder. Might not a feminist therapist who is sensitive to the conflicts that arise from the competing demands of gender and work roles, see the case differently? Laura, who was traditional in her attitudes toward family and home, was simultaneously ambitious in her professional life. In attempting to fulfill both roles with excellence, she unwittingly aspired to the impossible: to be a "superwoman." She wanted her house neat, her children at the top of their class, and herself at the top of her male-dominated profession. Her carping and her insistence that the house be spotless reflected this competition between roles, for if the house was not spotless, to whom would it fall to clean it up? Similarly, in her refusal to take holidays and her long working hours, she was behaving like the ambitious men in her profession.

Finally, there are theorists who question whether the psychological predispositions that presumably underlie the personality disorders really exist and, therefore, whether the personality disorders themselves are real (Mischel, 1973; Mischel and Peake, 1982). Although the notion that traits exist is nearly as old as the notion of personality itself, it has proved quite difficult to obtain evidence that people are consistent in their dispositions and perceptions across different situations. To say that someone suffers a dependent personality disorder, for example, is to say that she manifests the traits of passivity and dependence in a variety of different contexts. Evidence for that assertion is, in fact, very hard to find. Nearly all studies that have attempted to verify the cross-situational assumptions behind the notion of traits have failed. If the notion of traits has little merit, then the personality disorders that are built upon them have shaky foundations indeed. It is no wonder then that, in DSM-IV, with the exception of the antisocial personality disorder, whose reliability (see Chapter 4) ranges between .38 and .56 for nonhospitalized groups (Widiger and Corbitt, 1995), inter-judge reliability of the remaining personality disorders is uncertain, often plummeting as low as .26. Some attempts to improve the reliability and validity of personality disorder diagnoses, however, are promising (Stangl, Pfohl, Zimmerman, Bowers, and Corenthal, 1985; Loranger, Susman, Oldham, and Russakoff, 1987).

SUMMARY

1. The personality disorders are fundamentally disorders of *traits,* that is, disorders that are reflected in the individual's tendency to perceive and respond to the environment in broad and maladaptive ways. The notion of a personality disorder assumes that people respond consistently across different kinds of situations.

2. Of all of the personality disorders, the *antisocial personality disorder* is the most widely studied. It is a disorder that is characterized clinically by inadequately motivated antisocial behavior, the apparent lack of conscience or shame, and emotional poverty.

3. The antisocial personality disorder originates in childhood or early adolescence. As children, those who suffer the disorder often come from emotionally deprived backgrounds and marginal economic circumstances. Moreover, there is evidence that their antisocial behaviors have a genetic basis that may be manifested in a constitutional brain defect. This defect makes them underaroused emotionally, and therefore less able to learn from punishment or to control their impulses.

4. While severe punishment in childhood, such as sending a boy to a penal institution, increases the likelihood that the boy will subsequently engage in criminal activities, so too does no punishment at all. Moderate punishment—enough to make the boy take the consequences seriously, but not so much as to send him to places where he can learn to be a criminal—has a genuine deterrent effect.

5. The remaining personality disorders each center on a striking personality trait. *Paranoia, dependency, narcissism, avoidance,* and *obsessive-compulsiveness*

are traits that have become so dominant that they merit the personality disorder designation. In addition, some personality disorders, such as *schizotypal*, reflect many of the symptoms that are found in the corresponding Axis I disorder, but in lesser degree and without the florid thought disorder.

6. With the exception of the antisocial personality disorder, there is genuine disagreement regarding whether the personality disorders truly and reliably exist. To some extent, the disagreement arises from the low reliability of the personality disorder diagnoses. But to a larger degree, the disagreement is rooted in the scientific debate about the existence of personality traits. If traits play a relatively minor role in personality organization, then the personality disorders cannot play a large role in abnormal psychology, for they are based on the notion of traits.

QUESTIONS FOR CRITICAL THINKING

1. How may underarousal lead to antisocial behavior and what kind of punishment is most effective with people diagnosed with antisocial personality disorder?

2. Why do you think that some of the disorders (e.g., histrionic personality disorder and dependent personality disorder) that were once believed to be more prevalent in women are now considered as likely to be diagnosed in men as in women?

3. What distinguishes the schizotypal personality disorder from the schizophrenias, and why is this distinction so important?

4. Why may people be misdiagnosed as suffering from personality disorders when their behavior is viewed out of context?

8

Depression and Suicide

Depression is the most widespread psychological disorder. And it has been strongly on the rise recently. If you were born after 1970, you are ten times more likely to become depressed than were your grandparents. If you are a teenager today, your risk for becoming depressed in the next year has never been higher.

Depression is the common cold of mental illness. Almost everyone has felt depression, at least in its mild forms. Loss and pain are inevitable parts of growing up and growing older. Sometimes people we care for reject us, we write bad papers, our stocks go down, we fail to get the job we want, people we love die. When these losses occur we go into mourning, and then emerge, our lives poorer, but with hope for the future. Almost everyone reacts to loss with some of the symptoms of depression. We become sad and discouraged, apathetic and passive, the future looks bleak, some of the zest goes out of living. Such a reaction is normal—and we have repeatedly found that at any given moment 25 to 30 percent of college undergraduates will have such symptoms, at least to some extent (Seligman, unpublished). In the following case, Nancy's depression is mild and within the normal range of reaction to loss.

Within a two-day period, Nancy got a C on her Abnormal Psychology midterm and found out that the boy she had loved in her home town during high school had become engaged. The week that followed was awful; her future looked empty since she believed she would now not get into graduate school in clinical psychology and that she would never find anyone she could deeply love again. She blamed herself for these failures in the two most important arenas of her life. For the first few days she had trouble getting out of bed to go to class. She burst into tears over dinner one evening and had to leave the table. Missing dinner didn't much matter anyway since she wasn't hungry. After one week, the world started to look better. The instructor said that because the grades were so low on the mid-term, everyone had the option of writing a paper to cancel out their mid-term grade, and Nancy found herself looking forward to a blind date that her roommate had arranged for the weekend. Her usual bounce and enthusiasm for life began to return, and with it her appetite. She thought, "It will be an uphill battle, but I'm basically O.K. and I think I may find love and success."

How does such "normal depression" relate to clinical depression? Normal depression differs in degree from clinical disorder. Both are characterized by the same kinds of symptoms, but the person with clinical depression has more symptoms, more severely, more frequently, and for a longer time. The line between a "normal" depressive disturbance and a clinically significant depressive disorder is blurry.

In this chapter, we shall discuss the symptoms, causes, and treatment for depression in its various aspects. We shall first discuss how DSM-IV classifies these disorders (which it refers to as the ***mood disorders***, but which we will refer to as the affective disorders), and then we will go on to discuss in turn the two major subdivisions: the depressive disorders and the bipolar disorders. We will conclude the chapter by examining the most catastrophic outcome of both depressive disorders and bipolar disorders: suicide.

CLASSIFYING THE AFFECTIVE DISORDERS

FOCUS QUESTIONS

1. What is the difference between normal and clinical depression?
2. How do the depressive disorders differ from the bipolar disorders?
3. Distinguish between depression with and without melancholia.
4. Describe the two chronic affective disorders: dysthymic disorder and cyclothymic disorder.

DSM-IV divides the "mood disorders" into the depressive disorders and the bipolar disorders, thus using the most reliable and basic distinction in depression: the unipolar-bipolar distinction. In ***major depressive episode*** (or ***unipolar depression***), the individual suffers only depressive symptoms without ever experiencing mania. In ***bipolar disorder*** (or ***manic-depression***), the individual experiences both depression and mania. ***Mania*** is defined by excessive elation, expansiveness, irritability, talkativeness, inflated self-esteem, and flight of ideas.

A major depressive episode generally lasts at least two weeks. The patient experiences five or more emotional, cognitive, motivational, and somatic symptoms (see pp. 224–28), with one of the symptoms being depressed mood or loss of interest or pleasure. Such episodic depression lasts for less than two years and has a clear beginning, which distinguishes it from previous nondepressed functioning. In contrast, ***dysthymic disorder*** is chronic depression in which the individual has been depressed (experiencing two or more symptoms, such as poor sleep, low energy, low self-esteem, poor appetite, hopelessness, indecisiveness) for at least two years without more than a two-month remission (or return) to normality. It is much less common than episodic depression. Some unfortunate people have ***double depression,*** consisting of a depressive episode on top of an underlying dysthymic disorder. Those suffering from double depression have more severe symptoms and a low rate of remission (Keller and Shapiro, 1982; Wells, Burnam, Rogers, and Hays, 1992).

DSM-IV also distinguishes between depression with melancholia and depression without melancholia. The distinction is an attempt to separate biologically based (endogenous—coming from within the body) depressive episodes from psychologically based (exogenous—coming from outside the body) depressive episodes. DSM-IV defines "melancholic features" as loss of pleasure in all activities and numbing or general lack of reaction to pleasurable events, which is worse in the morning; early morning awakening; lethargy; weight loss; and guilt.

Two fairly reliable symptom clusters have been found for the two kinds of episodes. Those experiencing a melancholic depressive episode have slow speech and movement, more severe symptoms, a lack of reaction to environmental changes during the episode, loss of interest in life, and somatic symptoms. Those undergoing a nonmelancholic depressive episode have fewer of these characteristics. In addition, early morning awakening, guilt, and suicidal behavior may be more associated with a melancholic depressive episode (Mendels and Cochran, 1968; Haslam and Beck, 1994).

The distinction between depression with melancholia and depression without melancholia has treatment implications since melancholic depressive episodes may respond better to antidepressant drugs and electroconvulsive shock, while nonmelancholic depressions may fare better with psychotherapy alone. The results of differential treatment studies have not been uniform, however, and the distinction must be viewed with caution (Fowles and Gersh, 1979; Nelson, Mazure, and Jatlow, 1990; Abrams and Vedak, 1991; Parker and Hazdi-Pavlovic, 1993; Rush and Weissenburger, 1994; Sackeim and Rush, 1995).

Bipolar disorders are clearly distinguishable from normal and major depressive disorders. They involve swings between episodes of mania and episodes of depression, and as we will see, they probably have a genetic component. DSM-IV distinguishes between two kinds of bipolar disorders, depending on whether the depression alternates with full manic episodes or hypomanic episodes (manic episodes that are not as extreme as full manic episodes). DSM-IV calls a milder but chronic form of bipolar disorder *cyclothymic disorder*, in which the individual experiences depressive and hypomanic symptoms for at least two years (with occasional remissions to normal functioning that last no more than two months). Bipolar disorders develop at a younger age than depressive disorders, and are often more crippling to the individual. Fortunately, a specific drug, lithium carbonate, seems to help those with bipolar disorders considerably.

DEPRESSIVE DISORDERS

Symptoms of Depression

Depression is widely regarded as a disorder of mood (in fact, DSM-IV classifies it as a "mood disorder"), but this is an oversimplification. There are actually four sets of symptoms in depression. In addition to mood or emotional symptoms, there are thought or cognitive symptoms, motivational symptoms, and physical or somatic symptoms. An individual does not have to have all these symptoms to be correctly diagnosed as "depressed," but the more symptoms he or she has and the more intense is each set, the more confident we can be that the individual is suffering from depression (see Box 8–1).

EMOTIONAL SYMPTOMS

When a depressed patient is asked how she feels, the most common adjectives she uses are: "sad, blue, miserable, helpless, hopeless, lonely, unhappy, downhearted, worthless, humiliated, ashamed, worried, useless, guilty."

Sadness is the most salient and widespread emotional symptom in depressed people. A few are so depressed that they are unable to carry on a social conversation without excessive crying. This melancholic mood varies with time of day. Most commonly, depressed people feel worse in the morning, but the mood seems to lighten a bit as the day goes on. Along with feelings of sadness, feelings of anxiety are very often present in depression (Fowles and Gersh, 1979).

Lenore Radloff at the Center for Epidemiological Studies of the National Institutes of Mental Health has developed a widely used inventory of depressive symptoms. Each of the questions describes one of the symptoms of depression, and each question provides a severity score of 0 through 3 for that symptom. The person circles the answer that best describes how he or she feels right now. The symptoms divide into mood, thought, motivational, and physical sets. The statements below show responses to eight of the twenty questions of the CES–D (Center for Epidemiological Studies–Depression).

This test is designed, not as a way of diagnosing depression, but as a way of knowing how many symptoms are present and how severe they are once depression is clinically diagnosed. A high score alone is not diagnostic of clinical depression or mental illness. Generally speaking, research has shown that the average score (for the total of the numbers from the eight questions) in a North American college population is about 3 or 4, and students who score below this can be considered nondepressed. Mildly depressed students typically have scores from about 5 to 9, and scores of 10 or higher suggest moderate to severe depression. If an individual scores 10 or more for a period of one or two weeks, it would probably be in his best interest to seek help. If he has serious or persistent thoughts of suicide, regardless of his score, it is imperative that he seek aid.

CENTER FOR EPIDEMIOLOGICAL STUDIES-DEPRESSION INVENTORY

Mood A (Sadness)
I felt sad.
0   Rarely or none of the time (less than 1 day)
1   Some or a little of the time (1–2 days)
2   Occasionally or a moderate amount of time (3–4 days)
3   Most or all of the time (5–7 days)

Mood B (Enjoyment of life)
I did not enjoy life.
0   Rarely or none of the time (less than 1 day)
1   Some or a little of the time (1–2 days)
2   Occasionally or a moderate amount of time (3–4 days)
3   Most or all of the time (5–7 days)

Thought C (Pessimism)
I felt hopeless about the future.
0   Rarely or none of the time (less than 1 day)
1   Some or a little of the time (1–2 days)
2   Occasionally or a moderate amount of time (3–4 days)
3   Most or all of the time (5–7 days)

Thought D (Failure)
I thought my life had been a failure.
0   Rarely or none of the time (less than 1 day)
1   Some or a little of the time (1–2 days)
2   Occasionally or a moderate amount of time (3–4 days)
3   Most or all of the time (5–7 days)

Motivation E (Work initiation)
I felt that everything I did was an effort.
0   Rarely or none of the time (less than 1 day)
1   Some or a little of the time (1–2 days)
2   Occasionally or a moderate amount of time (3–4 days)
3   Most or all of the time (5–7 days)

Motivation F (Sociability)
I talked less than usual.
0   Rarely or none of the time (less than 1 day)
1   Some or a little of the time (1–2 days)
2   Occasionally or a moderate amount of time (3–4 days)
3   Most or all of the time (5–7 days)

Physical G (Appetite)
I did not feel like eating; my appetite was poor.
0   Rarely or none of the time (less than 1 day)
1   Some or a little of the time (1–2 days)
2   Occasionally or a moderate amount of time (3–4 days)
3   Most or all of the time (5–7 days)

Physical H (Sleep loss)
My sleep was restless.
0   Rarely or none of the time (less than 1 day)
1   Some or a little of the time (1–2 days)
2   Occasionally or a moderate amount of time (3–4 days)
3   Most or all of the time (5–7 days)

SOURCE: Seligman, 1993.

Almost as pervasive as sadness in depression is loss of gratification, the numbing of the joy of living. Activities that used to bring satisfaction feel dull and flat. Loss of interest usually starts in only a few activities, such as work. But as depression increases in severity, it spreads through practically everything the individual does. The pleasure derived from hobbies, recreation, and family diminishes. Gregarious individuals who used to enjoy partygoing avoid social gatherings. Finally, even biological functions, such as eating and sex, lose their appeal. Ninety-two percent of depressed patients no longer derive gratification from some major interests in their life, and 64 percent of depressed patients lose their feeling for other people (Beck, 1967; Clark, Beck, and Beck, 1994).

COGNITIVE SYMPTOMS

A depressed person thinks of himself in a very negative light. These negative thoughts color his view of himself and of the future. A depressed individual

▲ *The Old Guitarist* by Pablo Picasso, shows a man who may be undergoing a major depressive episode.

often has low self-esteem. He believes he has failed and that he is the cause of his own failures. He believes he is inferior, inadequate, and incompetent. But these views of failure and incompetence are often distortions. One patient managed to wallpaper a kitchen although very depressed. Here is how he distorted this achievement into a failure:

> THERAPIST: Why didn't you rate wallpapering the kitchen as a mastery experience?
> PATIENT: Because the flowers didn't line up.
> THERAPIST: You did in fact complete the job?
> PATIENT: Yes.
> THERAPIST: Your kitchen?
> PATIENT: No. I helped a neighbor do his kitchen.
> THERAPIST: Did he do most of the work?
> PATIENT: No, I really did almost all of it. He hadn't wallpapered before.
> THERAPIST: Did anything else go wrong? Did you spill the paste all over? Ruin a lot of wallpaper? Leave a big mess?
> PATIENT: No, no, the only problem was that the flowers did not line up.
> THERAPIST: So, since it was not perfect, you get no credit at all.
> PATIENT: Well . . . yes.
> THERAPIST: Just how far off was the alignment of the flowers?
> PATIENT: (holds out fingers about 1/8 of an inch apart) About that much.
> THERAPIST: On each strip of paper?
> PATIENT: No . . . on two or three pieces.
> THERAPIST: Out of how many?
> PATIENT: About 20–30.
> THERAPIST: Did anyone else notice it?
> PATIENT: No. In fact, my neighbor thought it was great.
> THERAPIST: Did your wife see it?
> PATIENT: Yeah, she admired the job.
> THERAPIST: Could you see the defect when you stood back and looked at the whole wall?
> PATIENT: Well . . . not really.
> THERAPIST: So you've selectively attended to a real but very small flaw in your effort to wallpaper. Is it logical that such a small defect should entirely cancel the credit you deserve?
> PATIENT: Well, it wasn't as good as it should have been.
> THERAPIST: If your neighbor had done the same quality job in your kitchen, what would you say?
> PATIENT: . . . pretty good job!
>
> (Beck et al., 1979)

Depressed people not only have low self-esteem, but they blame themselves and feel guilty for the troubles that afflict them. When failure occurs, depressed individuals tend to take the responsibility on themselves.

In addition to negative beliefs and guilt about the self, the depressed individual almost always views the future with great pessimism and hopelessness. A depressed individual believes that his actions, even if he could undertake them, are doomed. For example, when a middle-aged, depressed woman was told by her therapist that it would be a good idea for her to get a job, she replied, "I just couldn't possibly do it. How would I find the number of an employment agency? Even if I found the phone number, no one would want to hire me because I'm unqualified." Upon being reminded that she held a Ph.D. she replied, "Well, they might hire me, but they will surely fire me because I'm incompetent; and even if they kept me on it wouldn't be because of competence, but only because I'm so pathetic" (Seligman, unpublished). The depressed individual is equipped with a host of reasons for future failure, and no reasons at all for why success might occur.

Depressed patients show low self-esteem and pessimism about the future.

MOTIVATIONAL SYMPTOMS

Depressed individuals have great trouble getting up in the morning, going to work, beginning projects, and even entertaining themselves and others. An advertising executive loses his initiative in planning a major sales campaign; a college professor cannot bring herself to prepare her lectures; a student loses the desire to study.

One depressed man who was hospitalized after a suicide attempt merely sat motionless day after day in the lounge. His therapist decided to prepare a schedule of activities to get the patient engaged:

> THERAPIST: I understand that you spend most of your day in the lounge. Is that true?
> PATIENT: Yes, being quiet gives me the peace of mind I need.
> THERAPIST: When you sit here, how's your mood?
> PATIENT: I feel awful all the time. I just wish I could fall in a hole somewhere and die.
> THERAPIST: Do you feel better after sitting for two or three hours?
> PATIENT: No, the same.
> THERAPIST: So you're sitting in the hope that you'll find peace of mind, but it doesn't sound like your depression improves.
> PATIENT: I get so bored.
> THERAPIST: Would you consider being more active? There are a number of reasons why I think increasing your activity level might help.
> PATIENT: There's nothing to do around here.
> THERAPIST: Would you consider trying some activities if I could come up with a list?
> PATIENT: If you think it will help, but I think you're wasting your time. I don't have any interests.
>
> (Beck et al., 1979)

In extreme form, lack of response initiation is "paralysis of the will." Such a patient cannot bring himself to do even those things that are necessary to life. He has to be pushed and prodded out of bed, clothed, and fed. In severe depression, there may be *psychomotor retardation* in which movements slow down and the patient walks and talks excruciatingly slowly.

Difficulty in making a decision also seems to be a common symptom of depression (Hammen and Padesky, 1977). The following case illustrates how indecisiveness can overwhelm a depressed individual:

> Sylvia is a very bright college student whose life is being ruined by her depression. She finds it increasingly difficult to get on with routine studying because she can't take the initial steps. Now a major life decision has paralyzed her for the last three weeks. She has been accepted to two good graduate schools and has to make up her mind which to accept. One school offers a large scholarship, the other is more prestigious. She constantly ruminates over being selfish if she chooses the prestigious one without money, versus the cowardliness of giving in to her parents by choosing the other. Sylvia has managed to turn a can't-lose situation into a can't-win situation. (After Beck et al., 1979)

For a depressed individual, making a decision may be overwhelming and frightening. Every decision seems momentous, of make or break significance, and the fear of the wrong decision can be paralyzing.

SOMATIC SYMPTOMS

Perhaps the most insidious symptoms in depression are the physical changes. As depression worsens, every biological and psychological joy that makes life worth living is eroded.

FOCUS QUESTIONS

1. List and describe the four main categories of symptoms of depression.
2. What roles do a negative view of self and belief in a hopeless future play in depression?
3. What are some of the physical changes that occur in a depressed individual?

Loss of appetite is common. A gourmet finds that food does not taste good to her anymore. Weight loss occurs in moderate and severe depression, although in mild depression weight gain sometimes occurs. Sleep disturbance occurs as well. Depressed individuals may experience trouble getting to sleep at night, or they may experience early morning awakening, with great difficulty getting back to sleep for the rest of the night. Sleep disturbance and weight loss both lead to weakness and fatigue. A depressed individual also may lose interest in sex. Erectile difficulties in men and lack of arousal in women are common side effects of depression.

A depressed individual is often self-absorbed and focused on the present. His body absorbs his attention, and increased worry about aches and pains can occur. In addition to more worrying about health, depressed individuals may, in fact, be more susceptible to physical illness, since depression as it becomes severe may erode basic biological drives. For example, when a flu swept through an Army base, those individuals who had been depressed took significantly longer to recover (Imboden, Cantor, and Cluff, 1961).

Vulnerability to Depression

How specific can we be about this "common cold of mental illness"? At this very moment about one out of twenty Americans is severely depressed, and chances are one in ten—or higher—of having a depressive episode of clinical proportions at least once in your lifetime (Myers et al., 1984; Robins et al., 1984; Angst, 1992).

There is growing evidence that we now live in an Age of Melancholy. At least two lines of evidence point this way: (1) epidemiological studies of large groups of Americans, randomly sampled, show that people born earlier in this century have experienced less depression in their lifetime than people born later (Robins et al., 1984); and (2) diagnostic studies of relatives of people who have clinically severe depression show that older relatives are less susceptible than younger relatives (Klerman, Lavori, Rice, et al., 1985).

Who, among our population, is *vulnerable* to depression? Everyone. No group—not blacks or whites, not women or men, not young or old, not rich or poor—is wholly spared. While depression is found among all segments of mankind, some groups, however, are more susceptible than others.

SEX DIFFERENCES IN DEPRESSION

Women seem to have twice the risk for depression as men (Nolen-Hoeksema, 1988; Weissman and Olfson, 1995). Both studies of patients undergoing therapy and community studies indicate that females are significantly more depressed than males, with a mean ratio of 2:1 (Nolen-Hoeksema, 1987, 1990). But why this is so is not clear. Several hypotheses have been advanced. First, women may be more willing to express depressive symptoms than men are in Western society. When they confront loss, women are more reinforced for passivity and crying, while men are more reinforced for anger or indifference (Weissman and Paykel, 1974; Nolen-Hoeksema and Girgus, 1994). Second, biological hypotheses suggest that vulnerability to depression in women may be related to chemical enzyme activity, genetic proneness, and a monthly bout of premenstrual depression given a tentative classification of "premenstrual dysphoric disorder" by DSM-IV and characterized by such symptoms as emotional lability [feeling suddenly sad or tearful or oversensitive], anger, tension, depression, low interest, fatigability, a feeling of being overwhelmed, difficulty concentrating, appetite changes,

DSM-IV Criteria for Major Depressive Episode

A. Five (or more) of the following symptoms have been present during the same 2-week period and represent a change from previous functioning; at least one of the symptoms is either (1) depressed mood or (2) loss of interest or pleasure. (*Note:* Do not include symptoms that are clearly due to a general medical condition, or mood-incongruent delusions or hallucinations.) (1) depressed mood most of the day, nearly every day, as indicated by either subjective report (e.g., feels sad or empty) or observation made by others (e.g., appears tearful) (*Note:* In children and adolescents, can be irritable mood.); (2) markedly diminished interest or pleasure in all, or almost all, activities most of the day, nearly every day (as indicated by either subjective account or observation made by others); (3) significant weight loss when not dieting or weight gain (e.g., a change of more than 5% of body weight in a month), or decrease or increase in appetite nearly every day (*Note:* In children, consider failure to make expected weight gains.); (4) insomnia or hypersomnia [excessive sleeping] nearly every day; (5) psychomotor agitation or retardation nearly every day (observable by others, not merely subjective feelings of restlessness or being slowed down); (6) fatigue or loss of energy nearly every day; (7) feelings of worthlessness or excessive or inappropriate guilt (which may be delusional) nearly every day (not merely self-reproach or guilt about being sick); (8) diminished ability to think or concentrate, or indecisiveness, nearly every day (either by subjective account or as observed by others); (9) recurrent thoughts of death (not just fear of dying), recurrent suicidal ideation without a specific plan, or a suicide attempt or a specific plan for committing suicide.
B. The symptoms do not meet criteria for a Mixed Episode.
C. The symptoms cause clinically significant distress or impairment in social, occupational, or other important areas of functioning.
D. The symptoms are not due to the direct physiological effects of a substance (e.g., a drug of abuse, a medication) or a general medical condition (e.g., hypothyroidism).
E. The symptoms are not better accounted for by bereavement, i.e., after the loss of a loved one, the symptoms persist for longer than 2 months or are characterized by marked functional impairment, morbid preoccupation with worthlessness, suicidal ideation, psychotic symptoms, or psychomotor retardation.

SOURCE: APA, DSM-IV, 1994.

---

oversensitivity to rejection, sleep changes, or physical symptoms). Also there is the possibility that female carriers of a depressive gene become depressed, whereas male carriers of the same gene become alcoholic (Robinson, Davis, Nies, Ravaris, and Sylvester, 1971; Winokur, 1972). A third hypothesis grows out of the learned helplessness theory of depression (see pp. 244–48). If depression is related to helplessness, then to the extent that women learn to be more helpless than men, depression will appear more frequently in women than in men. A society that rewards women for brooding and becoming passive in the face of loss while rewarding men for active coping attempts may pay a heavy price in later female depression (Radloff, 1975). Fourth, women are *more state-oriented* than men, and so are inclined to ruminate (worry about) and focus on bad life events (foremost among them, depression itself), whereas men are inclined to more *action* and less thought (Nolen-Hoeksema, 1987, 1991). State-orientation about depression will amplify depression (Zullow and Seligman, 1985), whereas action-orientation may dampen or distract from a depressive mood and bring about the resolution of the life problems. The fifth hypothesis has to do with body image and the pursuit of thinness through dieting common to women in developed nations. As we will see, one root cause of depression is failure and helplessness. Dieting sets up a cycle of failure and helplessness: pitting the goal of slimming to an almost unattainable "ideal" weight against untiring biological defenses. At first, dieters lose weight, and with it, the depression about being overweight. Ultimately, however, dieters become dismayed as the pounds come back, as they do in 95 percent of dieters. Repeated failure and all the daily reminders of being overweight again bring depression in their wake (Wadden, Stunkard, and Smoller, 1986; Seligman, 1993). On the other hand, about 5 percent of dieters keep the weight from coming back, but they have to stay indefinitely on an unsatisfying low-calorie diet to do so. A side effect of prolonged malnutrition is depression. Either way, the pursuit of thinness makes people vulnerable to depression (Garner and Wooley, 1991). Moreover, it has been found that eating disorders—anorexia nervosa and bulimia—arise in the cultures—among them, white America, Sweden, Great Britain, the Czech Republic—that have a thin ideal for women and that these cultures have roughly twice as much depression in women as in men (Jeffrey, Adlis, and Forster, 1991). Women in the cultures—among them, Egypt, Iran, India, Uganda—without the thin ideal are not known to have eating disorders, and the amount of depression in women and men is roughly the same in these cultures. These findings suggest that around the world the thin ideal and dieting not only cause eating disorders, they also cause women to be more depressed than men (McCarthy, 1990; Stice, 1994).

AGE AND DEPRESSION

As we saw earlier, severe depression is more common in the 1990s than it was earlier in the century. It also attacks its victims when they are much younger. Peter Lewinsohn and his colleagues gave diagnostic interviews to 1,710 randomly selected western Oregon adolescents. By age fourteen, 7.2 percent of the youngest adolescents, born in 1972–1974, had had a severe depression; in contrast, 4.5 percent of the older adolescents, born in 1968–1971, had had a severe depression (Lewinsohn, Rohde, Seeley, and Fischer, 1993). In a study of over 3,000 twelve- to fourteen-year-olds in the southeastern United States, 9 percent had experienced major depressive disorder (Garrison, Addy, Jackson, McKeown, and Waller, 1992). This high a percentage of children suffering severe depression and at such a young age is dismaying (see Box 8–2). Whether children will become severely depressed may depend on inherited characteristics as well as the type of environment in which they grow up (Tharpar and McGuffin, 1994; Murray and Sines, 1996).

The earliest psychological state that may be related to depression was described by the American psychiatrist René Spitz in 1946 and was called **anaclitic depression.** Spitz observed that when infants between the ages of six and eighteen months were separated from their mothers for prolonged periods of time, a state of unresponsive apathy, listlessness, weight loss, increased susceptibility to serious childhood illness, and even death occurred. The mothers' return, or the substitution of a different, permanent mother, reversed these effects (Spitz, 1946).

Childhood depression is a controversial issue (Schulterbrand and Raven, 1977). It was formerly alleged that depression in childhood, with the core symptoms of passivity, negative cognitions, resigned behavior, sadness, and inhibition in working and loving, was relatively rare. Instead, reaction to loss was thought to take other forms, such as hyperactivity, aggression, and delinquency (Cytryn and McKnew, 1972). More sensitive tests of depression in childhood have been developed, however, and have revealed as high a rate of depressive symptoms in children as among adults, along with accompanying intellectual deficits (Kovacs and Beck, 1977; Kaslow,

THE EPIDEMIC OF DEPRESSION AND THE SELF-ESTEEM MOVEMENT

Depression is a disorder of individual helplessness and individual failure. When a person finds himself helpless to achieve his goals, he suffers depression. Why then is there an epidemic of depression, particularly among young people in America today?

First, in contemporary America, individualism has become rampant and the self all-important, while at the same time the old spiritual consolations that buffer against depression—God, nation, community, family—have lost their powers. Second, for the last thirty years, America has had a movement in parenting and education that has stressed self-esteem in children. Paradoxically, the doctrine of raising our children to feel good and enjoy high self-esteem at all times, may have contributed to the epidemic of feeling bad. For, the more that a child believes that he is all that matters and that his goals, his successes, and his pleasures are of paramount importance, the more hurtful the blows when life brings its inevitable failures. In attempting to cushion bad feeling, the self-esteem movement has minimized the three good uses of feeling bad.

The first good use of strong negative emotions, such as anxiety, depression, and anger, is to galvanize you into action to change yourself or the world, and by doing so to terminate the negative emotion. The states of dysphoria—anxiety, depression, and anger—each bear a message. Anxiety warns you that danger is around. Sadness informs you that a loss threatens. Anger alerts you that someone is trespassing on your domain. All these messages, of necessity, carry pain, and it is this very pain that makes it impossible to ignore what is going wrong and goads you to act to remove the threat.

Bad feeling as an alarm system is far from flawless. Many, perhaps even most, of its messages are false alarms—the kid who elbowed you is not a bully but just clumsy, and the bad grade does not mean your teacher thinks you're stupid. When bad feelings become chronic and paralyzing, and when they set off too many false alarms, we call this state "emotional illness," and we try to dampen it with drugs or correct it with psychotherapy. But dysphoria's primary virtue is that most of the time, the system is your first line of defense against danger, loss, and trespass.

The second good use of bad feeling is overcoming boredom and achieving "flow." Flow is a state in which time seems to stop for you, when you feel truly at home, wanting to be nowhere else—perhaps when you are playing a sport, listening to a CD, speaking to a group, writing a poem, painting a fence or picture, making love, or engaging in conversation about a favorite topic. Flow is one of the highest states of positive emotion, a state that makes life worth living. Researchers have been studying it—who experiences it, when it occurs, what impedes it—for two decades. Flow occurs when your skills are used to their utmost—matched against a challenge just barely within your grasp. Too little challenge produces boredom. Too much challenge or too little skill produces helplessness and depression. Success after success—unbroken by failure, regrouping, and trying again—will not produce flow. Rather, overcoming frustration, working through anxiety, and confronting the highest challenges are needed to achieve flow (Csikszentmihalyi, 1990).

The third good use of bad feeling concerns overcoming helplessness. Any complicated task you undertake consists of several steps, each of which is more or less easy to fail at. If you falter at any step, try again, and then succeed at that step, you get to go on to the next step. If the steps are not too numerous, and no one of them is insurmountable, you will succeed—but only if you keep trying after each small failure.

Every small failure, as well as every big failure, produces bad feeling—some admixture of anxiety, sadness, and anger. These emotions, when moderate, are galvanizing, but they are also daunting. But sometimes, in order to experience mastery, it is necessary for you to fail, to feel bad, and to try again repeatedly until success occurs. Failure and feeling bad can be building blocks for ultimate success and feeling good.

Children need to fail sometimes. When we always protect our children from failure as the "feel good" society suggests, we deprive them of learning persistence. When they encounter obstacles and we leap in to bolster their self-esteem and to soften the blows, we make it harder for them to achieve mastery. And if we deprive them of mastery, we weaken their self-esteem just as certainly as if we had belittled, humiliated, and physically thwarted them at every turn.

So it is possible that the self-esteem movement in particular, and the "feel good" ethic, in general, have had the untoward consequence of producing low self-esteem on a massive scale. By cushioning feeling bad, it has made it harder for our children to feel good and to experience flow. By circumventing feelings of failure, it has made it more difficult for our children to feel mastery. By blunting warranted sadness and anxiety, it has created children at high risk for unwarranted depression. By encouraging cheap success, it may have produced a generation at risk for depression.

SOURCE: Adapted from Seligman, Reivich, Jaycox, and Gillham, 1995.

Tanenbaum, Abramson, Peterson, and Seligman, 1983; Blumberg and Izard, 1985). While the rate of major depressive disorder among children is less than 3 percent, at puberty the prevalence rises markedly to at least 6.4 percent (DuBois, Felner, Bartels, and Silverman, 1995).

Another form of loss for a child is divorce and separation, as well as its precursor, parental turmoil. In a longitudinal study of 400 children who were followed as they went from third grade through sixth grade, 20 percent developed moderate to severe depressive symptoms (Nolen-Hoeksema, Girgus, and Seligman, 1986, 1992). Among the most salient precipitants of depression was parental turmoil—the report that parents had been fighting more lately. Parents' fighting probably undermines the child's sense of security and often leads to a string of bad life events, such as separation and economic problems, and so increases a child's risk for depression. Finally, when divorce occurs, and the child "loses" the parent through the divorce, the child may start to exhibit depressive symptoms, as in the following case:

> Peter, age nine, had not seen his father, who lived nearby, more than once every two to three months. We expected that he would be troubled, but we were entirely unprepared for the extent of this child's misery. The interviewer observed: "I asked Peter when he had last seen his dad. The child looked at me blankly and his thinking became confused, his speech halting. Just then, a police car went by with its siren screaming. The child stared into space and seemed lost in reverie. As this continued for a few minutes, I gently suggested that the police car had reminded him of his father, a police officer. Peter began to cry and sobbed without stopping for 35 minutes. (Wallerstein and Kelly, 1980)

In adolescents, depression has all the symptoms that we saw for depression in adults. In addition to the core symptoms, depressed adolescents, particularly boys, are commonly negativistic and even antisocial. Restlessness, grouchiness, aggression, and strong desire to leave home are also common symptoms; and sulkiness, uncooperativeness in family activities, school difficulties, alcohol and drug abuse can also be symptoms.

Depression among adults does not increase in frequency and in severity with age as used to be believed (Myers et al., 1984; Robins et al., 1984). Although depression in old age is compounded by the helplessness induced by increasing physical and mental incapacities, as a visit to any nursing home will dramatically confirm, the frequency of depression among old people is at present much lower than among younger people.

▼ Children show as high a rate of depressive symptoms as do adults.

RACE AND SOCIAL CLASS

The National Comorbidity Study of 8,098 Americans shows that the rate of affective disorder among blacks is about two-thirds that of whites and Hispanics, and that poorer people have somewhat more affective disorder (Kessler, McGonagle, Zhao, et al., 1994). Caution should be used, however, in interpreting any study of cross-racial, cross-age, cross-sex, or cross-cultural psychological disorders. Since diagnosis is, for the most part, made by middle-class white psychiatrists and psychologists, insensitivity to symptoms of depression within another culture or elicitation of greater hostility among the patients may contaminate the results (Tonks, Paykel, and Klerman, 1970).

No strong differences occur in depression among social classes. Unlike schizophrenia, which is less frequent in middle and upper classes, depression is democratic. Again, however, it is possible that depression may have different manifestations according to the patient's social class: lower-class patients may show more feelings of powerlessness and hopelessness, middle-class patients stronger feelings of loneliness and rejection, and upper-class patients greater pessimism and social withdrawal (Schwab, Bialow, Holzer, Brown, and Stevenson, 1967). At any rate, the similarities in the occurrence of depression between black people and white people and between rich people and poor people far outweigh the differences.

EFFECTS OF LIFE EVENTS

Are the lives of depressed people, before the onset of their depression, different from the lives of people who do not become depressed? Depressed individuals have experienced more early childhood losses than nondepressed individuals and more frequent stressful losses within a year or two before the onset of depression. Yet, many individuals suffer both early childhood loss and recent loss without becoming depressed, and a substantial number of depressed individuals do not suffer early childhood loss or recent loss. So we are far from saying that such life events *cause* depression, but some events do seem to increase the risk of depression.

The death of a person's mother before the child is eleven years old may predispose an individual to depression in adulthood. One study found that the rate of depression was almost three times higher among women who, before age eleven, had lost their mother and also had experienced a severe recent loss, than among women who, before age eleven, had not lost their mother but had experienced a similar recent loss. Death of the mother after the child reached age eleven had no effect on risk for depression according to this study (Brown and Harris, 1978). Death of the father while the child is young is also probably associated with later depression (Barnes and Prosin, 1985).

Most depressions are preceded by a recent stressful loss. Failure at work, marital separation, failure at school, loss of a job, rejection by a loved one, death of a child, illness of a family member, and physical illness are common precipitants of depression. Individuals who become depressed show more such losses preceding their depression than matched controls (Leff, Roatch, and Bunney, 1970; Paykel, 1973; Brown and Harris, 1978; Littlefield and Rushton, 1986; Breslau and Davis, 1986).

But such losses do not always bring on depressions, by any means. Only about 10 percent of those persons who experience losses equivalent in severity to those of an average depressed person become depressed themselves. Why is it that the other 90 percent do *not* become depressed? Only half the women who, before age eleven, had lost their mother and also had suffered a recent loss became depressed. What about the other half? Brown and Harris proposed that there are four invulnerability factors that can help prevent

If a woman has more than three young children at home, she may be more vulnerable to depression after a stressful loss.

depression from occurring, even in the presence of the predisposing factors and recent loss. The invulnerable women had either (1) an intimate relationship with a spouse or a lover, or (2) a part-time or full-time job away from home, or (3) fewer than three children still at home, or (4) a serious religious commitment. So intimacy, employment, a life not overburdened by child care, and strong religious belief may protect against depression. Perhaps what these four invulnerability factors have in common is that they contribute self-esteem and a sense of mastery, while undercutting the formation of an outlook pervaded by hopelessness. All of these, in effect, help to ward off depression.

The Course of Depression

When a vulnerable individual becomes depressed, what is likely to happen if the individual fails to seek out treatment? If anything good about depression can be said, it is that it usually dissipates in time. After the initial attack, which comes on suddenly about three-quarters of the time, depression seems to last an average of about three months in outpatients. Among inpatients, who are usually more severely depressed, it lasts about six months on the average. At first, the depression gets progressively worse, eventually reaching the bottom, but then the depressed individual begins to recover gradually to the state that existed before the onset (Beck, 1967; Robins and Guze, 1972). What our grandmothers told us about our own personal tragedies—time heals all wounds—is certainly true for depression. The mind, or the body, seems incapable of sustaining a dark mood forever, and unknown homeostatic mechanisms take over and, in time, correct the disorder.

The time that a depressive episode lasts, however, is painfully long, and to an individual suffering from it, it seems like forever. For this reason, a therapist will always emphasize that the depressive episode will go away in time. Without minimizing the suffering the patient is feeling now, the therapist should tell the patient that complete recovery from the episode occurs in 70 to 95 percent of the cases. For some, this ray of hope may speed the time when the depression will lift.

Once a depressive episode has occurred, one of three patterns may develop. The first is *recovery without recurrence*. **Recurrence** is defined as the return of symptoms following at least six months without significant symptoms of depression. This should be differentiated from ***relapse*** into the same episode, which may occur when drug therapy or psychotherapy relieves symptoms for only a short while. If the patient goes for six months free of symptoms, however, it is generally believed that the episode has run its course. About half the patients who have had a depressive episode will not have another one, at least during the following ten years. Generally, the more stable a person is before the episode, the less likely depression will recur. On the other hand, half of depressed individuals will show the second pattern: *recovery with recurrence*.

The second depressive episode, if it occurs, will tend to be of about the same duration as the first attack. On the average, however, most individuals who have recurrent episodes of depression can expect an average symptom-free interval of more than three years before the next episode. But the interval between episodes in recurrent depression tends to become shorter over the years. The period of greatest risk for recurrence is in the first six months after recovery. And substance abuse increases the risk for recurrence (NIMH, 1984). For some individuals, a third pattern will develop: *chronic depression*, or ***dysthymic disorder***. Roughly 10 percent of those individuals who have a major depressive episode

DSM-IV Criteria for Major Dysthymic Disorder
A. Depressed mood for most of the day, for more days than not, as indicated either by subjective account or observation by others, for at least 2 years. (*Note:* In children and adolescents, mood can be irritable and duration must be at least 1 year.)
B. Presence, while depressed, of two (or more) of the following: (1) poor appetite or overeating; (2) insomnia or hypersomnia [excessive sleeping]; (3) low energy or fatigue; (4) low self-esteem; (5) poor concentration or difficulty making decisions; (6) feelings of hopelessness.
C. During the 2-year period (1 year for children or adolescents) of the disturbance, the person has never been without the symptoms in Criteria A and B for more than 2 months at a time.
D. No Major Depressive Episode has been present during the first 2 years of the disturbance (1 year for children and adolescents); i.e., the disturbance is not better accounted for by chronic Major Depressive Disorder, or major Depressive Disorder, In Partial Remission. (*Note:* There may have been a previous Major Depressive Episode provided there was a full remission (no significant signs or symptoms for 2 months) before development of the Dysthymic Disorder. In addition, after the initial 2 years (1 year in children or adolescents) of Dysthymic Disorder, there may be superimposed episodes of Major Depressive Disorder, in which case both diagnoses may be given when the criteria are met for a Major Depressive Episode.
E. There has never been a Manic Episode, a Mixed Episode, or a Hypomanic Episode, and criteria have never been met for Cyclothymic Disorder.
F. The disturbance does not occur exclusively during the course of a chronic Psychotic Disorder, such as Schizophrenia or Delusional Disorder.
G. The symptoms are not due to the direct physiological effects of a substance (e.g., a drug of abuse, a medication) or a general medical condition (e.g., hypothyroidism).
H. The symptoms cause clinically significant distress or impairment in social, occupational, or other important areas of functioning.
SOURCE: APA, DSM-IV, 1994.

will not recover and will remain chronically depressed (Perris, 1968; Kerr, Roth, Schapira, and Gurney, 1972; Schuyler, 1974; Angst and Wicki, 1991; Keller, Lavori, Mueller, and Endicott, 1992). Therapy for depression usually attempts to make the current episode shorter or to postpone the time at which another episode might strike. The therapies for depression derive from three different theories, and it is to these theories and therapies that we now turn.

THEORIES AND THERAPIES OF THE DEPRESSIVE DISORDERS

What causes depression, and how is depression most effectively treated? Although several theories, with substantial research support, have emerged to explain the origins of depression, we still cannot say with certainty what the cause of depression is or how it can best be treated. Even so, between 80 and 90 percent of severe depressions can now be markedly alleviated with a brief course of therapy. There are three main theories and therapies for depression: the biological model, the psychodynamic model, and the cognitive model. These theories overlap, and there is also a good deal of overlap in the therapies each recommends, but each tends to focus on one aspect of depression. At the end of this section, we will attempt a synthesis of these models.

The Biological Model of Depression

FOCUS QUESTIONS

1. What are the four clues that indicate that there is a biological basis of depression?
2. Describe the neurochemical mechanisms that might explain depression
3. How do certain drugs alter this neurochemical mechanism?
4. What is electroconvulsive shock therapy (ECT)?

According to the biological model, depression is a disorder of the body. Proponents of this view have focused almost entirely on the brain, and in particular on depletion of a class of chemicals in the brain (biogenic amines) that help transmit nerve impulses across the gaps (synapses) between nerve cells (neurons). There are four indications that there is a biological basis of depression (Schuyler, 1974). First of all, depression occurs with some frequency following periods of natural physiological change in women: after giving birth to a child, at menopause, and just before menstruation. Second, there is considerable similarity of symptoms across cultures, sexes, ages, and races, indicating an underlying biological process. Third, somatic therapies, in particular drugs like tricyclic antidepressants, serotonin reuptake inhibitors, and MAO inhibitors, and electroconvulsive shock, are effective treatments of depression. Fourth, depression is occasionally induced in normal individuals as a side effect of medications; in particular, depression may be induced by reserpine, a high-blood-pressure-reducing drug (Schuyler, 1974).

GENETICS AND UNIPOLAR DEPRESSION

There is some evidence that genetics is implicated in depression. First-degree relatives of patients with depressive disorders are between two and five times more at risk for depression than are those in the general population (Weissman, Kidd, and Prusoff, 1982; Keller, Beardslee, Dorer, Lavori, Samuelson, and Klerman, 1986). If the depressed patient is alcoholic as well, the risk for the first-degree relative developing both depression and alcoholism increases; but if the depressed patient is not alcoholic, there is increased risk for the first-degree relative to develop only depression (Merikangas, Leckman, Prusoff, Pauls, and Weissman, 1985; Winokur and Coryell, 1992). Moreover, genetic factors may make relatives of those with depressive disorders more sensitive to negative life events, doubling their risk for developing major depression when they experience severe stressors such as marital problems or physical abuse (Kendler, Kessler, Walters, et al., 1995).

While there is evidence that bipolar disorder can be strongly inherited, unipolar depression is only weakly inherited (Torgersen, 1986a). Only 28 percent of identical twins are discordant for bipolar disorder, but at least 60 percent of identical twins are discordant for unipolar depression (Allen, 1976; McGuffin, Katz, Watkins, and Rutherford, 1996). Further evidence comes from studies of adoptive versus biological relatives of depressed patients. Biological relatives had an eightfold increased risk for unipolar depression relative to adoptive relatives (Wender, Kety, Rosenthal, Schulsinger, Ortmann, and Lunde, 1986). So having a depressed family member confers risk for depression, but whether this risk is genetic awaits more evidence. Thus, the genetic evidence gives some support for a biomedical approach to unipolar depression. The drug and biochemical evidence is even stronger.

THE NEUROCHEMICAL BASIS OF DEPRESSION

The biological model holds that depression is a disorder of motivation caused by insufficiencies of the biogenic amines. The **biogenic amines** are neurochemicals that facilitate neural transmission. They divide into two groups with different chemical structures: the **catecholamines,** which include norepinephrine, epinephrine, and dopamine; and the **indoleamines,** which include serotonin and histamine. Speculation about the neurochemical basis of depression has centered primarily around decreased availability of one of the catecholamines, **norepinephrine (NE)** (Schildkraut, 1965), and one of the indoleamines, *serotonin* (Maas, 1975; McNeal and Cimbolic, 1986; Potter and Manji, 1994).

Figure 8–1 depicts the hypothesized mode of action of norepinephrine in transmission of a nerve impulse from one neuron across the synapse to a second neuron. When a nerve impulse occurs in neuron 1, norepinephrine is discharged into the synapse (the gap between neuron 1 and neuron 2). This stimulates neuron 2 to fire when the NE makes contact with the receptors on the membrane of neuron 2. Norepinephrine is now sitting in the synapse and on the membrane of neuron 2. Neuron 2 will continue to fire until the NE is inactivated. There are two relevant ways that norepinephrine can now be inactivated. The first way is by *reuptake,* in which neuron 1 reabsorbs norepinephrine, thereby decreasing the amount of norepinephrine at the receptors. The second is by *breakdown,* in which norepinephrine is broken down chemically and rendered inactive. As we said above, norepinephrine is a catecholamine, which is one of two classes of biogenic amines. The biogenic amines affect our motivation. And when we decrease the amount of biogenic amines (in this case, norepinephrine), we will have less motivation. The catecholamine hypothesis claims that when reuptake and/or breakdown are doing their job too well, our norepinephrine level drops too low, and we become highly unmotivated, in short, depressed.

Two groups of drugs use these routes to treat depression: tricyclic antidepressants (which block reuptake of norepinephrine) and MAO inhibitors (which break down norepinephrine). Each increases the availability of NE in the brain, and with this change in the level of NE comes relief from depression. Moreover, research with laboratory animals has shown that administering tricyclic antidepressants over long periods reduces the number of "5-HT$_2$ receptors," which participate in the reuptake of serotonin. The reduction of these receptors may be responsible for the effectiveness of tricyclic antidepressants in clinical trials (Taylor, Carter, Eison, et al., 1995).

FIGURE 8–1

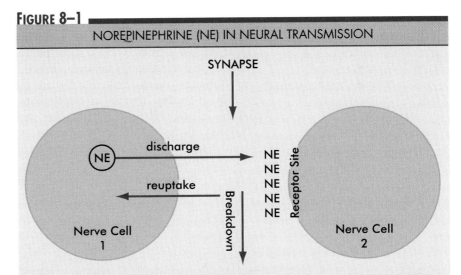

NE produced in nerve cell 1 is discharged into the synapse, where it stimulates nerve cell 2 to fire. In order to stop the NE from stimulating nerve cell 2, NE can be inactivated either by being reabsorbed back into nerve cell 1 (reuptake) or by being broken down and excreted out of the synapse (breakdown). Antidepressant drugs keep NE available in the synapse by blocking its reuptake (tricyclics) or slowing its breakdown (MAO inhibitors). The same logic holds for the serotonin model, with drugs like fluoxetine (Prozac) blocking the reuptake of serotonin.

Despite the favorable evidence supporting the catecholamine hypothesis based on the action of these drugs, advocates of the hypothesis are appropriately cautious. The reason is that the tricyclics and the MAO inhibitors all have a large number of effects other than their effect on norepinephrine. Because of this, it is very possible that their effects might be due to some other properties of the drugs and not necessarily to their effect on norepinephrine.

While the catecholamine hypothesis of depression claims that unavailability of NE is the cause, the indoleamine hypothesis claims that unavailability of serotonin is the cause. With this in mind, scientists set out to find a drug that would affect the availability of serotonin. In 1974, chemists reported that the chemical compound fluoxetine specifically inhibits the reuptake of serotonin (Wong, Horng, et al., 1974). Dubbed Prozac, this drug was released in 1987 and has become enormously popular.

In severe depression, Prozac has about the same efficacy as the tricyclics and MAO inhibitors, producing relief in 60 to 70 percent of cases. It produces less drowsiness, dry mouth, sweating, and risk of overdose than the NE drugs, but it produces more nausea, nervousness, and insomnia (Wernicke, 1985; Cooper, 1988; Beaumont, 1990; Henry, 1992; Boulos, Kutcher, Gardner, and Young, 1992).

THE NEUROANATOMICAL BASIS OF DEPRESSION

There is also an anatomical theory of depression that claims that overactivity of the right frontal lobes in the brain produces depression. This is based on two lines of evidence. First, normal subjects express more negativity about pictures of faces presented to the right hemisphere (left visual field) than about pictures presented to the left hemisphere (right visual field). This is particularly accentuated in depressed people (Davidson, Schaffer, and Saron, 1985). And second, brain damage to the left hemisphere due to stroke (oxygen starvation in part of the brain) more often results in depression than does damage to the right hemisphere (Sackeim, Greenberg, et al., 1982).

One brain-imaging study showed that the blood flow to the left frontal lobe decreased in patients with major depression. The blood supply to the same region increased when these patients recovered from their depression following drug therapy (Bench, Friston, Brown, Frackowiak, and Dolan, 1993; Bench, Frackowiak, and Dolan, 1995).

Other studies have linked depression to the underactivity of specific parts of the left frontal lobe. In unipolar depressed patients, these spots appear "cooler," or less active on brain scans, when compared to the same areas in nondepressed controls. Researchers believe that this underactivity leads to the apathy related symptoms of depression. Indeed, patients who have permanent damage in these locations often show blunted emotions, low arousal, decreased motivation, and lack of interest (Biver, Goldman, Delvenne, et al., 1994).

A new technique using very powerful magnetic fields to disable specific areas of the brain for brief periods of time has provided additional evidence for the anatomical basis of depression. The procedure, known as transcranial magnetic stimulation (T.M.S.), made it possible for Dr. Alvarel Pascual-Leone to produce temporary mood changes in normal people. Applying repeated magnetic pulses to the brain area above the left eyebrow caused subjects to feel sad and apathetic, while applying the pulses to the area above the right eyebrow caused subjects to feel happier and more energetic. Moreover, magnetic pulses can increase the activity of specific regions, and when used to stimulate the left frontal lobe, severely depressed patients feel better. T.M.S. may one day replace electroconvulsive therapy; currently, however, not everyone responds to the treatment and the effects tend to wear off (George, Wasserman, Williams, et al., 1995).

FIGURE 8–2

DRUG TREATMENTS FOR DEPRESSION

Norepinephrine is discharged into the synapse when a nerve impulse from neuron 1 to neuron 2 fires. Generally, the norepinephrine is inactivated by either reuptake, whereby neuron 1 reabsorbs the norepinephrine, or breakdown of the norepinephrine by the enzyme MAO. In a depressed person, breakdown or reuptake or both of either norepinephrine (indicated by the blue part of the arrow) or serotonin (indicated by the red part of the arrow) removes the norepinephrine or serotonin, leaving the person depressed. MAO inhibitors work by preventing the breakdown of norepinephrine; tricyclic antidepressants work by preventing the reuptake of norepinephrine; fluoxetine works by preventing the reuptake of serotonin.

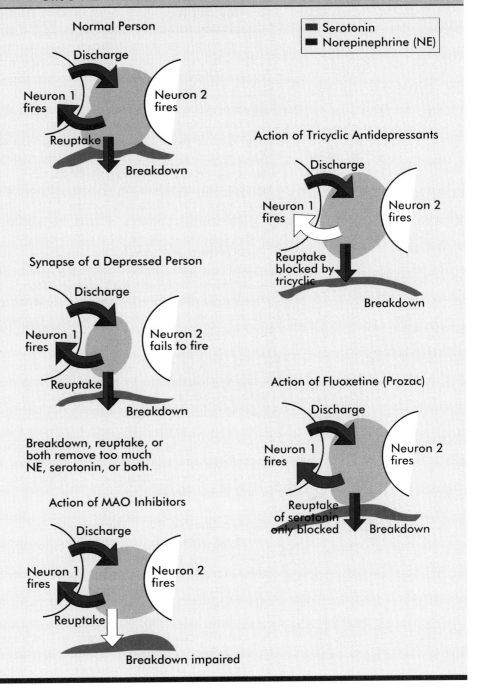

SOMATIC THERAPIES FOR DEPRESSION

Advocates of the biological model approach the treatment of unipolar depression, particularly when it is severe, in two ways. The first is to treat the patient with drugs; fluoxetine (Prozac), the tricyclics, and the MAO inhibitors may be used (see Figure 8–2). Relief is moderate, but the relapse rate is high when the drugs are stopped. The second approach is to administer electroconvulsive shock (ECT). There is marked improvement, but the relapse rate is high as in treatment with drugs.

Drug Treatment   Fluoxetine (Prozac) is currently widely prescribed, particularly for less severe depressions. As we saw, it specifically inhibits only the reuptake of serotonin. It produces relief in 60 to 70 percent of those who have major depressions, with low risk of overdose. But it produces nausea, nervousness, and insomnia in some patients (Beaumont, 1990; Henry, 1992; Gram, 1994). It may also produce preoccupation with suicide (Teicher, Glod, and Cole, 1990; Beasley, Dornseif, Bosomworth, et al., 1992). Having a patient with recurrent depression continue to take fluoxetine reduces the occurrence of relapses (Lonnqvist, Shihvo, Syvälahti, et al., 1995).

Tricyclic antidepressants, you will recall, block the reuptake of norepinephrine. As a result, NE is available and the patient becomes less depressed. On average, between 63 and 75 percent of depressed patients given tricyclics show significant clinical improvement (Beck, 1973). Further, maintaining a patient with recurrent depression on tricyclics between attacks also reduces recurrence (Gelenberg and Klerman, 1978; NIMH, 1984).

The MAO inhibitors prevent the breakdown of norepinephrine by inhibiting the enzyme MAO. With more NE available, the patient becomes less depressed. But MAO inhibitors are now prescribed less often than fluoxetine or tricyclics, largely because the MAO inhibitors can have lethal side effects. When combined with cheese, alcohol, pickled herring, narcotics, or high-blood-pressure-reducing drugs, MAO inhibitors can be fatal. Most studies show MAO inhibitors to be superior to placebos in alleviating depression, however, and if fluoxetine or the tricyclics fail, the MAO inhibitors should be tried.

What all of the drug therapies for depression have in common is that while the relief produced is moderate to good, relapse and recurrence rates are high once the drug is stopped. Patients who respond well to drugs may have to take the drug indefinitely to prevent recurrence (Kupfer, Frank, Perel, et al., 1992). It has been suggested that drug treatments work better than psychotherapy for depression, particularly when depression is severe (Schulberg and Rush, 1994). Comparisons of psychotherapy and drugs, however, reveal an equal effect for severe depression (Munoz, Hollon, McGrath, et al., 1994).

Electroconvulsive Shock (ECT)   Electroconvulsive shock is, to the layman, the scariest of the antidepressant treatments. In the two decades following ECT's discovery as a psychotherapeutic treatment in 1938, enthusiasm was high, and it was promiscuously prescribed for a very broad range of disorders. The treatment, particularly in its less refined forms, can have very serious side effects, however, and it has come to be regarded by the general public as "barbaric" and "punitive." But strong evidence exists that ECT, when given to severely depressed unipolar depressive patients, is a highly effective antidepressant therapy. Modern techniques have greatly reduced the common and severe side effects of yesteryear, and about 80 percent of patients with major depression respond to ECT (Fink, 1979; Malitz et al., 1984; Devanand, Sackeim, and Prudic, 1991).

Typically, ECT is administered by a medical team consisting of a psychiatrist, an anesthesiologist, and a nurse. Metal electrodes are taped to either side of the patient's forehead, and the patient is anesthetized. The patient is given drugs to induce muscular relaxation in order to prevent the breaking of bones during the convulsion. A high current is then passed through the brain (sometimes through only half of the brain) for approximately a half second. This is followed by convulsions that last for almost one minute. As the anesthetic wears off, the patient wakens and will not remember the period of treatment. Within twenty minutes, the patient is functioning reason-

A patient is prepared for electroconvulsive shock treatment. The object in her mouth is to prevent her from swallowing her tongue when the electric current passes through her body.

ably well and has little, if any, physical discomfort. A course of electroconvulsive shock therapy usually consists of a half dozen treatments, one every other day (Schuyler, 1974).

Exactly how ECT works is unknown, but it probably increases available norepinephrine and other biogenic amines. Isolating the effective ingredient in ECT is quite difficult, however, as it is such a gross technique—shocking half, sometimes the entire brain—and has so many other effects, including memory loss and motivational changes (Squire, 1986; Devanand, Fitzsimons, Prudic, and Sackeim, 1995; Philibert, Richards, Lynch, and Winokur, 1995).

The Psychodynamic Model of Depression

Psychodynamic theorists have stressed three causes of depression: anger turned against the self, excessive dependence on others for self-esteem, and helplessness at achieving one's goals.

ANGER TURNED UPON THE SELF

The first contributions of the psychodynamic model to the understanding of depression came from the early psychoanalysts. Karl Abraham (1911) and Sigmund Freud (1917) in his classic paper, "Mourning and Melancholia," both stressed the importance of anger turned inward upon the self in producing depression.

On the surface, depressed individuals often seem drained of anger, and this leads to the suspicion that their anger may be bound up inside them. For Freud, the main clue to their inner state came from the difference between normal bereavement (mourning) and depression (melancholia). The non-depressed individual and the depressed individual have two strikingly different reactions to the loss of a person they love. For the mourner, the world now seems empty, but his self-esteem is not threatened. The mourner will survive the loss. In contrast, according to Freud, the depressive will begin to feel a powerful sense of worthlessness and self-blame. He will feel rotten and guilty; he will accuse himself of being a failure. This self-reproach is usually moral, grossly unjustified, and most remarkable, publicly and shamelessly declared. It provides the clue that anger turned against the self is actively motivated and generates the low self-esteem of depression.

On the surface, depressed individuals may seem drained of anger, but they may bind up anger and turn it against themselves.

FOCUS QUESTIONS

1. Describe the anger-turned-inward view of psychodynamic theorists.
2. Describe the depressive personality.
3. How might perceived helplessness lead to loss of self-esteem and depression?

THE DEPRESSIVE PERSONALITY

Psychodynamic theorists since Freud have emphasized a personality style that may make individuals especially vulnerable to depression: the depressed person depends excessively on others for his self-esteem. The depressed patient desperately needs to be showered with love and admiration. He goes through the world in a state of perpetual greediness for love, and when his need for love is not satisfied, his self-esteem plummets. When he is disappointed he has difficulty tolerating frustration, and even trivial losses upset his self-regard and result in immediate and frantic efforts to relieve discomfort. So depressed patients are seen as love addicts, who have become exquisitely skilled at producing demonstrations of love from others and who insist on a constant flow of love. Beyond receiving such love, however, the depressed individual cares little for the actual personality of the person he loves (Rado, 1928; Fenichel, 1945; Arieti and Bemporad, 1978).

HELPLESSNESS AT ACHIEVING ONE'S GOALS

The third major strand in psychodynamic theorizing about depression comes from the psychoanalyst Edward Bibring's (1953) claim that depression results when the ego feels helpless before its aspirations. Perceived helplessness at achieving the ego's high goals produces loss of self-esteem, the central feature in depression. The depression-prone individual has extremely high standards, and this increases his vulnerability to feeling helpless in the face of his goals. The combination of strongly held goals to be worthy, to be strong, and to be good, along with the ego's acute awareness of its helplessness and incapacity to live up to these goals, is for Bibring the mechanism of depression.

PSYCHODYNAMIC THERAPY FOR DEPRESSION

In general, psychodynamic theory emphasizes the long-term predisposition to depression, rather than the losses that happen to set it off in the short term. Psychodynamic therapies similarly are directed toward long-term change, rather than short-term alleviation of depression. Several therapeutic strategies follow from the three strands of psychodynamic theorizing about depression. First, psychodynamic therapists inclined toward the anger-turned-inward theory of depression will attempt to make the patient conscious of his misdirected anger and the early conflicts that produced it. Learning to come to terms with the anger that loss and rejection produce and to direct it toward more appropriate objects should prevent and relieve depression. Second, psychodynamic therapists who deal with the depressed patient's strong dependence on others for self-esteem will attempt to get the patient to discover and then resolve the conflicts that make him perpetually greedy for love and esteem from others. Such a patient must learn that true self-esteem comes only from within. And third, therapists who work within Bibring's helplessness approach try to end the patient's depression by getting him to perceive his goals as being within reach, to modify his goals so that they can now be realized, or to give up these goals altogether.

INTERPERSONAL THERAPY

Although interpersonal therapy (IPT) originated in the psychoanalytic treatments of Harry Stack Sullivan and Frieda Fromm-Reichman, it does not deal with childhood or defense mechanisms. Rather, it focuses on social relations in the present and specifically deals with current interpersonal problems. Ongoing disputes, frustrations, anxieties, and disappointments are the main material of therapy.

Interpersonal therapy looks at four problem areas: grief, fights, role transitions, and social deficits. When dealing with grief, IPT looks at abnormal grief reactions. It brings out the delayed mourning process and helps the patient find new social relationships that can substitute. When dealing with fights, the IPT therapist helps determine where the disrupted relationship is going: Does it need renegotiation? Is it at an impasse? Is it irretrievably lost? Communication, negotiation, and assertiveness skills are taught. When dealing with role transitions, including retirement, divorce, and leaving home, the IPT therapist gets the patient to reevaluate the lost role, to express emotions about the loss, to develop social skills suitable for the new role, and to establish new social supports. When dealing with social deficits, the IPT therapist looks for recurrent patterns in past relationships. Emotional expression is encouraged. Role playing and enhanced communication skills are used to overcome recurrent weaknesses in social relationships.

The main virtues of this approach are that it is brief, sensible, and inexpensive (a few months). It has no known bad side effects, and it has been shown to be quite effective against depression, bringing relief in around 70 percent of cases. A manual for it exists (Klerman, Weissman, Rounsaville, and Chevron, 1984). Its main problem is that it has not been widely practiced, so little research has been done to discover how it works.

Cognitive Models of Depression

The two cognitive models of depression view particular thoughts as the crucial cause of depressive symptoms. The first, developed by Aaron T. Beck, derives mainly from extensive therapeutic experience with depressed patients, and it views depression as caused by negative thoughts about the self, about ongoing experience, and about the future. The second, developed by Martin E. P. Seligman, derives mainly from experiments with dogs, rats, and mildly depressed people, and it views depression as caused by the expectation of future helplessness. A depressed person expects bad events to occur and believes that there is nothing he or she can do to prevent them from occurring.

BECK'S COGNITIVE THEORY OF DEPRESSION

Aaron T. Beck (along with Albert Ellis) founded a type of therapy called cognitive therapy. According to Beck, two mechanisms, the **cognitive triad** and **errors in logic,** produce depression.

▼ Aaron T. Beck has developed cognitive treatments for depression.

The Cognitive Triad The cognitive triad consists of negative thoughts about the self, about ongoing experience, and about the future. The negative thoughts about the self consist of the depressed person's belief that he is defective, worthless, and inadequate. The symptom of low self-esteem derives from his belief that he is defective. When he has unpleasant experiences, he attributes them to personal unworthiness. Since he believes he is defective, he believes that he will never attain happiness.

The depressed person's negative thoughts about experience consist of his interpretation that what happens to him is bad. He misinterprets small obstacles as impassable barriers. Even when there are more plausible positive views of his experience, he is drawn to the most negative possible interpretation of what has happened to him. Finally, the depressed person's negative view of the future is one of helplessness. When he thinks of the future, he believes the negative things that are happening to him now will continue unabated because of his personal defects.

FOCUS QUESTIONS

1. According to Aaron Beck, how do the mechanisms of the cognitive triad and errors in logic produce depression?
2. Explain the four specific cognitive therapy techniques: detection of automatic thoughts, reality testing automatic thoughts, reattribution training, and changing depressogenic assumptions.

Errors in Logic Beck believes that systematic errors in logic are the second mechanism of depression. According to Beck, the depressed person makes five different logical errors in thinking, and each of these darkens his experiences: arbitrary inference, selective abstraction, overgeneralization, magnification and minimization, and personalization.

Arbitrary inference refers to drawing a conclusion when there is little or no evidence to support it. For example, an intern became discouraged when she received an announcement which said that in the future all patients worked on by interns would be reexamined by residents. She thought, incorrectly, "The chief doesn't have any faith in my work." *Selective abstraction* consists of focusing on one insignificant detail while ignoring the more important features of a situation. In one case, an employer praised an employee at length about his secretarial work. Midway through the conversation, the boss suggested that he need not make extra carbon copies of her letters anymore. The employee's selective abstraction was, "The boss is dissatisfied with my work." In spite of all the good things said, only this was remembered.

Overgeneralization refers to drawing global conclusions about worth, ability, or performance on the basis of a single fact. Consider a man who fails to fix a leaky faucet in his house. Most husbands would call a plumber and then forget it. But a depressed patient will overgeneralize and may go so far as to believe that he is a poor husband. *Magnification and minimization* are gross errors of evaluation, in which small bad events are magnified and large good events are minimized. The inability to find the right color shirt is considered a disaster, but a large raise and praise for good work are considered trivial. And lastly, *personalization* refers to incorrectly taking responsibility for bad events in the world. A neighbor slips and falls on her own icy walk, but the depressed next-door neighbor blames himself unremittingly for not having alerted her to her icy walk and for not insisting that she shovel it.

THE LEARNED HELPLESSNESS MODEL OF DEPRESSION

The second cognitive model of depression is the *learned helplessness model.* It is cognitive because it holds that the basic cause of depression is an expectation: the individual expects that bad events will happen to him and that there is nothing he can do to prevent their occurrence. We will discuss the phenomenon and theory of learned helplessness, and then we will discuss the relationship between learned helplessness and depression.

Causes of Learned Helplessness Learned helplessness theory argues that the basic cause of deficits observed in helpless animals and humans after uncontrollable events is the expectation of future noncontigency (unrelatedness) between responding and outcomes. Thus dogs given inescapable shock will be profoundly passive later on when they are given escapable shock, and will be unable to learn later that responding could terminate shock (Overmier and Seligman, 1967; Miller and Seligman, 1976). Similarly, humans given inescapable noise over several trials, when later given an opportunity to escape the noise, will still sit there passively without trying to escape (Hiroto, 1974). This expectation that future responding will be futile causes the two helplessness deficits: (1) it produces deficits in responding by undermining the motivation to respond, and (2) it produces later difficulty in seeing that outcomes are contingent upon responding when they are. The experience of shock, noise, or problems in themselves does not produce the motivational and cognitive deficits, only *uncontrollable* shock, noise, and problems produce these deficits. This strongly suggests that both animals and humans learn during uncontrollable events that their responding is futile and come to expect this in future situations.

When a human being experiences inescapable noise or unsolvable problems and perceives that his responding is ineffective, he goes on to ask an important question: What causes my present helplessness? The causal attribution (explanation) that a person makes is a crucial determinant of when and where expectancies for future failure will recur. There are three attributional dimensions that govern when and where future helplessness deficits will be displayed (Abramson, Seligman, and Teasdale, 1978).

The first dimension is ***internal-external.*** Consider an individual who has received unsolvable problems in an experiment. When he discovers that responding is ineffective, he can either decide that he is stupid (internal) and the problem is solvable, or that the problems are rigged to be unsolvable (external) and he is not stupid. In addition to deciding whether or not the cause of failure is internal or external, an individual who has failed also considers the ***stable-unstable*** dimension: "Is the cause of my failure something permanent or transient?" An individual who has failed may decide that the cause of the failure is stable and that it will persist into the future. Examples of such stable factors are stupidity (which is internal as well as stable), or the difficulty of the task (which is stable but external). In contrast, an individual may decide that the cause of his failure is unstable. An individual who has failed an exam can believe that the cause was his bad night's sleep the night before, an unstable cause that is internal. Alternatively, he might decide that he failed because it was an unlucky day, an unstable cause that is external. The attributional theory of helplessness postulates that when the cause of failure is attributed to a stable factor, the helplessness deficits will persist in time. Conversely, if the individual believes that the cause of his failure is unstable, he will not necessarily fail again when he encounters the task months hence. According to the attributional model of learned helplessness, stable explanations lead to permanent deficits, and unstable explanations to transient deficits.

The third and final dimension is ***global-specific*** (see Figure 8–3). When an individual finds that he has failed, he must ask himself whether or not the cause of his failure is global—a factor that will produce failure in a wide variety of circumstances—or specific—a factor that will produce failure only in similar circumstances. For example, an individual who has failed to solve a laboratory problem may decide that he is unskilled at solving laboratory problems and probably unskilled at other tasks as well. In this instance, being unskilled is global and the expectation of failure will recur in a wide variety of other situations. It is also a stable and internal factor. Alternatively, he might decide that these particular laboratory problems are too hard. The difficulty of laboratory problems is a specific factor, since it will only produce the expectation that future responding will be ineffective in other laboratory problems and not in real life. This factor, aside from being specific, is stable and external. The attributional model of helplessness holds that when individuals

▼ (A) Someone with an external, unstable, and specific explanatory style may blame Hurricane Andrew for the damage to his life but may be able to pull his life together more quickly than a person (B) with an internal, stable, and global explanatory style, who may feel helpless and hopeless in the face of a natural disaster.

A

B

FIGURE 8–3

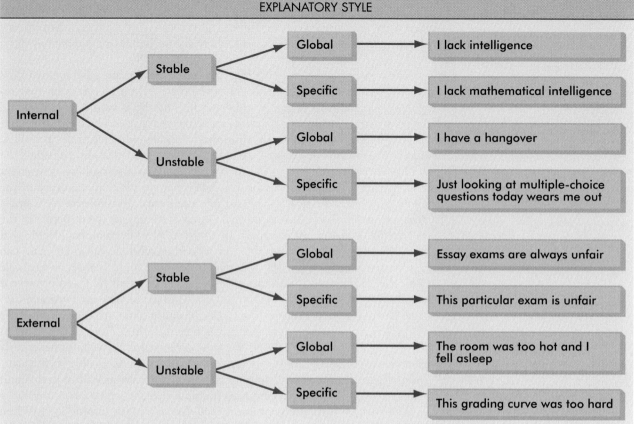

EXPLANATORY STYLE

Depressed individuals would attribute their failing a test to internal, global, and stable factors and their doing well on a test to external, unstable, and specific factors.

make global explanations for their failure, helplessness deficits will occur in a wide variety of situations. When individuals believe that specific factors cause their failures, the expectation of response ineffectiveness will be narrow, and only a narrow band of situations will produce helplessness.

The helplessness model, then, suggests that an insidious explanatory or attributional style (attributing failure to internal, global, and stable factors; attributing success to external, unstable, and specific factors) predisposes an individual to depression. A variation is the ***hopelessness theory of depression*** (Abramson, Metalsky, and Alloy, 1989; Alloy, Lipman, and Abramson, 1992). This theory emphasizes the stable and global dimensions for negative events as determinants of hopelessness, and proposes a subtype of depression, ***hopelessness depression.***

Parallels between Depression and Learned Helplessness   There are notable similarities in symptoms, cause, cure, prevention, and predisposition between learned helplessness in the laboratory and major depression as it occurs in real life (see Table 8–1; Seligman, 1975; Weiss, Simson, et al., 1985).

The failure to escape noise and to solve problems after experience with uncontrollable events is the basic *passivity deficit* of learned helplessness. This passivity seems similar to the *motivational deficits* of depression (Miller and Seligman, 1975, 1976; Price, Tryon, and Raps, 1978). Nondepressed individuals given inescapable noise or unsolvable problems show the *cognitive deficit* of learned helplessness: they have difficulty learning that responding is successful, even when it is. Depressed individuals show exactly the same defi-

FOCUS QUESTIONS

1. What is the learned helplessness model of depression?
2. What roles do attributions and explanatory style play in unipolar depression?
3. Describe the parallels between the symptoms, cause, and therapies for learned helplessness and those for depression.
4. What are three problems with the cognitive model of depression?

cit. Nondepressed human beings made helpless fail to see patterns in anagrams and fail to change expectancy for future success when they succeed and fail in skill tasks. Depressed students and patients show these same deficits in the laboratory (Miller and Seligman, 1975, 1976; Abramson, Garber, Edwards, and Seligman, 1978).

When individuals are made helpless by inescapable noise and attribute their failure to their own shortcomings as opposed to external causes, not only are the motivational and cognitive deficits of helplessness and depression observed, but *self-esteem* drops as well. This parallels the low self-esteem that occurs in depressed individuals, particularly among those who blame themselves for their troubles (Abramson, 1978).

Parallel *mood changes* occur both in learned helplessness and depression. When nondepressed subjects are made helpless by inescapable noise or unsolvable problems, they become sadder, more hostile, and more anxious. These reports parallel the emotional changes in depression: more sadness, anxiety, and perhaps more hostility.

In the laboratory, rats who receive inescapable shock eat less food, lose more weight, aggress less against other rats, and lose out in competition for food with rats who had received either escapable shock or no shock. This *loss of appetite* and *loss of aggression* produced by helplessness in the laboratory parallel the somatic symptoms of depressed individuals: they lose weight, eat less, lose sleep, their social desires and status drop, and they become less aggressive. Finally, learned helplessness in the rat is accompanied by *norepinephrine depletion*. Jay Weiss has demonstrated that the brains of rats who have received inescapable shock have less available norepinephrine than the brains of animals who receive no shock or escapable shock (Weiss, Glazer, and Pohoresky, 1976).

The learned helplessness hypothesis says that depressive deficits, which parallel the learned helplessness deficits, are produced when an individual expects that bad events may occur and that they will be independent of his responding. When this is attributed to internal factors, self-esteem will drop; to

TABLE 8–1

	SIMILARITY OF LEARNED HELPLESSNESS AND DEPRESSION	
	Learned Helplessness	*Depression*
Symptoms	Passivity	Passivity
	Cognitive deficits	Negative cognitive triad
	Self-esteem deficits	Low self-esteem
	Sadness, hostility, anxiety	Sadness, hostility, anxiety
	Loss of appetite	Loss of appetite
	Loss of aggression	Loss of aggression
	Sleep loss	Sleep loss
	Norepinephrine and serotonin depletion	Norepinephrine and serotonin depletion
Cause	Learned belief that responding is independent of important outcomes (plus attributions to internal, global, and stable factors)	Generalized belief that responding will be ineffective
Therapy	Change belief in response futility to belief in response effectiveness	Cognitive and behavioral antidepressant therapy
	ECT, MAO-I, tricyclics, fluoxetine	ECT, MAO-I, tricyclics, fluoxetine
	REM deprivation	REM deprivation
	Time	Time
Prevention	Immunization	Optimism training
Predisposition	Insidious explanatory style	Insidious explanatory style

stable factors, the depression will be long-lived; and to global factors, the depression will be general. The experimental evidence confirms this. This insidious attributional style has been found in depressed students, children, and patients. Depressed patients, moreover, believe that the important goals in their life are less under their control than do other psychiatric patients (Eidelson, 1977; Seligman et al., 1979; Raps, Reinhard, and Seligman, 1980). Most important, individuals who have this explanatory style but are not depressed, become depressed when they later encounter bad events (Peterson and Seligman, 1984; Seligman, 1991).

COGNITIVE THERAPY

In cognitive therapy, the patient is taught to conquer problems and master situations that he previously believed were insuperable. Cognitive therapy differs from most other forms of psychotherapy. In contrast to the psychoanalyst, the cognitive therapist actively guides the patient into reorganizing his thinking and his actions, not about the past, but primarily about the present. The cognitive therapist talks a lot and is directive. She argues with the patient. She persuades; she cajoles; she leads.

Beck's Cognitive Therapy   Beck's cognitive therapy attempts to counter negative thoughts and errors in logic (Beck, 1967; Beck, Rush, Shaw, and Emery, 1979). There are four specific cognitive therapy techniques that are used: detecting automatic thoughts, reality testing automatic thoughts, reattribution training, and changing depressogenic (depression causing) assumptions.

Beck argues that there are discrete, negative sentences that depressed patients say to themselves quickly and habitually. These automatic thoughts maintain depression. Cognitive therapy helps patients to identify such automatic thoughts. Once the patient has learned to identify such thoughts, the cognitive therapist engages in a dialogue with the patient in which evidence for and against the thoughts is scrutinized. This is not an attempt to induce spurious optimism, rather to encourage the patient to use the reasonable standards of self-evaluation that nondepressed people use (see Box 8–3). A young student despondent over the belief that she would not get into a particular college would be taught to criticize her automatic negative thoughts.

THERAPIST: Why do you think you won't be able to get into the university of your choice?
PATIENT: Because my grades were really not so hot.
THERAPIST: Well, was your grade average?
PATIENT: Well, pretty good up until the last semester in high school.
THERAPIST: What was your grade average in general?
PATIENT: A's and B's.
THERAPIST: Well, how many of each?
PATIENT: Well, I guess almost all of my grades were A's, but I got terrible grades in my last semester.
THERAPIST: What were your grades then?
PATIENT: I got two A's and two B's.
THERAPIST: So your grade average would seem to me to come to almost all A's. Why don't you think you'll be able to get into the university?
PATIENT: Because of competition being so tough.
THERAPIST: Have you found out what the average grades are for admission to the college?
PATIENT: Well, somebody told me that a B+ average should suffice.
THERAPIST: Isn't your average better than that?
PATIENT: I guess so.

(Beck et al., 1979)

FLEXIBLE OPTIMISM

People who have the skill of making unstable, specific, and external explanations for the bad events that occur to them do better in several realms of life. Seligman (1991) calls them "optimists." They fight off depression better, achieve more in school, sports, and the workplace, and enjoy better physical health than do "pessimists," people who see bad events as stable, global, and internal.

Optimism is no panacea. For one thing, it may sometimes keep us from seeing reality with necessary clarity. For another, it may help us to evade responsibility for failure by blaming it on others. But these limits are just that, limits. They do not nullify the benefits of optimism; rather they put it in perspective.

Until the development of cognitive therapy, if you were a pessimist, you had no choice but to live with the pessimism. You would endure frequent depressions; your work and your health would suffer. In exchange for this you might have a keener sense of reality and a stronger sense of responsibility.

You now have a choice. If you undergo cognitive therapy and learn to make unstable, specific, and external explanations for failures more readily, you can choose to use its techniques whenever you need them—without becoming a slave to them.

For example, let's say you are now able to curtail depression by disputing the catastrophic thoughts that used to plague you. Along comes a new setback. You fail your Psychology and your English mid-terms. You are not a brilliant student, *and* you didn't study enough for them. You might, if you choose, launch into all the disputations that would let you continue thinking that you are so smart you don't need to study: the exam was unfair, the grading was too hard, the professor is a poor teacher, the curve was too stringent. But you can also choose not to dispute. You can say to yourself that this is one of those moments that call for seeing yourself with merciless clarity, not one of those moments that call

for warding off your own depression. Your academic future is at stake. The cost of being wrong here outweighs the importance of fighting off demoralization. Rather it is the time to take stock and appreciate your need to study hard more clearly. You can choose *not* to dispute the pessimistic thoughts.

What you now have is more freedom—an additional choice. You can choose to use optimism when you judge less depression is the issue, or more achievement, or better health. But you can also choose not to use it, when you judge that clear sight or taking responsibility are called for. Learning optimism does not erode your sense of values or your judgment. Rather it frees you to use cognitive techniques as a tool to achieve the goals you set.

What criteria should guide you when deciding whether to use optimism or pessimism? The fundamental guideline for *not* deploying the skills of optimism and cognitive therapy is to ask what the *cost of failure* is in the particular situation. If the cost is high, optimism is the wrong strategy. In the cases of the pilot in the cockpit deciding whether to de-ice the plane one more time, the partygoer deciding whether to drive home after drinking, the student deciding to go skiing for the weekend rather than studying for the critical final exams, the costs of failure are, respectively, death, an auto accident, failing. Using techniques that minimize those costs are a disservice. On the other hand, if the cost of failure is low, use optimism. The sales agent deciding whether to make one more call only loses her time if she fails. The shy person deciding whether to attempt to open a conversation only risks rejection. The teenager contemplating learning a new sport only risks frustration. The disgruntled executive, passed over for promotion, only risks some refusals if he quietly puts out feelers for a new position. All should use optimism.

SOURCE: Adapted from Seligman, 1991.

By learning to scrutinize and criticize her automatic thoughts and marshaling evidence against them, the patient would undermine her negative automatic thoughts, and they would wane.

Depressed patients tend to blame themselves for bad events for which they are not, in fact, responsible. To counteract such irrational blame, the therapist and the patient review the events, applying the standards of nondepressed individuals in order to come up with an assignment of blame. This is not to absolve the patient of blame, but to let him see that there may be other factors besides his own incompetence that contribute to a bad event.

The final technique of Beck's cognitive therapy is the explicit change of assumptions (Ellis, 1962). Beck outlines six assumptions that depressed individuals base their life upon, thereby predisposing themselves to sadness, despair, and disappointment: (1) in order to be happy, I have to be successful in whatever I undertake; (2) to be happy, I must be accepted by all people at all times; (3) if I make a mistake, it means I am inept; (4) I can't live without love; (5) if somebody disagrees with me, it means he doesn't like me; and

(6) my value as a person depends on what others think of me. When the patient and therapist identify one of these assumptions, it is vigorously attacked. The validity of the assumption is examined, counterarguments are marshaled, plausible alternative assumptions are presented, and the disastrous consequences of holding the assumption are exposed.

Therapy for Learned Helplessness   Since the cause of learned helplessness and depression is hypothesized to be the expectation that responding will be ineffective in controlling future events, the basic therapeutic theme should be to change this belief to one in which the individual will be effective and anticipated bad events will be avoided. The attributional theory of learned helplessness suggests some basic strategies for doing this. So, for example, learned helplessness theory suggests that therapies such as teaching social skills and assertiveness training should be antidepressive because they teach the individual that he can control affection and the esteem of other people by his own actions. Further techniques such as criticizing automatic thoughts (it's not that I'm an unfit mother, rather I'm grouchy at 7 A.M.) help alleviate depression because they change attributions for failure from internal, stable, and global (unfit mother) to external, unstable, and specific (7 A.M.). These strategies are similar to the techniques of cognitive and behavioral therapies that we have just reviewed.

Cognitive Therapies and Prevention   Cognitive therapies have been used to try to prevent both learned helplessness and depression in vulnerable individuals. Thus, parents can help prevent helplessness in their children by encouraging them to master difficult tasks or solve frustrating problems on their own (Nolen-Hoeksema, Mumme, Wolfson, and Guskin, 1995). Learned helplessness in animals can be prevented by prior experience with mastery and immunization. If an animal first controls important events, such as shock and food, helplessness will not occur later. In effect, it will be prevented. Such immunization seems to be lifelong: rats who learn to escape shock as weanlings do not become helpless when as adults they are given inescapable shock. Conversely, lifelong vulnerability to helplessness is produced by early experience with inescapable shock: rats who receive inescapable shock as weanlings become helpless adults (Hannum, Rosellini, and Seligman, 1976). This parallels the data on the prevention of and vulnerability to depression. Individuals whose mother dies before the child is eleven years old are more vulnerable to depression than those whose mother does not. There are, however, invulnerability factors that prevent depression from occurring in such individuals: a job, an intimate relationship with a spouse or lover, not having life burdened with child care, and religious belief (Brown and Harris, 1978). These invulnerability factors may all increase the expectation of future control, and vitiate the expectations of future helplessness.

One of the controlled studies that has been performed to study factors that might prevent depression is the Pennsylvania Prevention Project. In this study, researchers from the University of Pennsylvania used principles of cognitive therapy with normal children to see if depressive symptoms could be prevented in advance (see Figure 8–4; Jaycox, Reivich, Gillham, and Seligman, 1994; Gillham, Reivich, Jaycox, and Seligman, 1995). Children were chosen because they were at risk for depression by one of two criteria: either they had mild symptoms of depression already, or their parents were fighting.

At-risk ten- to thirteen-year-olds learned the cognitive and problem-solving skills that patients who were already diagnosed with depression were taught during cognitive therapy. The results showed that depressive symptoms were markedly reduced in the prevention groups as compared to the control groups. A six-month follow-up showed prevention of de-

FOCUS QUESTIONS

1. Explain how each theory of depression contributes to our understanding of depression.
2. Describe how drugs, cognitive therapy, and interpersonal therapy are used to treat depression.

FIGURE 8–4

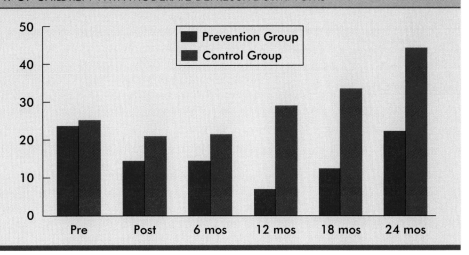

PERCENT OF CHILDREN WITH MODERATE DEPRESSIVE SYMPTOMS

Preventive intervention cuts the percentage of children suffering moderate or severe depression in half and its effect grows in time after treatment has stopped. (SOURCE: Gillham et al., 1995)

pressive symptoms as well as significantly fewer behavioral problems in the treated children than in the controls. The most unusual findings began to show up in the one-year follow-up. It is a universal finding in therapy outcome studies that even "successful" effects wane. Surprisingly, the Pennsylvania Prevention Project found that the prevention effects got larger over time. One-year, eighteen-month, and two-year follow-ups showed increasing gains and increasing separation between the treated groups and control groups on depressive symptoms. At the eighteen-month point, 33.3 percent of the control children had moderate or severe depressive symptoms, but only 12.2 percent of the treated children showed such symptoms. In addition, prevention was most effective in the children who were most at risk.

The researchers may have found a critical age to teach skills to guard against depression. The skills become incorporated into the child's repertoire; as the child goes into puberty, and depression becomes commonplace, he or she can use these skills repeatedly and increasingly to navigate the shoals of adolescence.

PROBLEMS OF THE COGNITIVE MODEL OF DEPRESSION

The cognitive model of depression has three main problems. First, it is vague on what kind of depression is modeled (Depue and Monroe, 1978). It is probably not an especially good model of the subclasses of major depression that are "melancholic." Biological depressions may be better treated by somatic therapy than by cognitive-behavioral therapies, although this has yet to be tested.

Second, cognitive theory is weak in accounting for the somatic symptoms of depression; these seem better explained by the biological model. Similarly, although the cognitive model does not predict that somatic therapy would be effective, the effective somatic therapies, including ECT, MAO inhibitors, tricyclics, serotonin enhancers (e.g., fluoxetine), and dream deprivation, do succeed in breaking up learned helplessness in animals, as well as depression in humans (Porsolt et al., 1978; Brett, Burling, and Pavlik, 1981; Peterson, Maier, and Seligman, 1993).

Third, experimental controversy still rages over many of the major points of the learned helplessness model of depression. Some critics doubt whether learned helplessness in animals is produced by an expectation, believing it to be either learned inactivity or norepinephrine depletion (Glazer and Weiss, 1976; Weiss, Glazer, and Pohoresky, 1976; Anisman, 1978). Others have argued that the learned helplessness deficits seen in human beings do not follow closely from the theory (Costello, 1972; Buchwald, Coyne, and Cole, 1978). There also has been difficulty in replicating some of the basic human phenomena (McNitt and Thornton, 1978; Willis and Blaney, 1978). Finally, it is still controversial whether helplessness and depressive explanatory style are consequences or causes of depression (Peterson and Seligman, 1984).

Comparing Therapies for Major Depression

The National Institutes of Mental Health (NIMH) sponsored a landmark collaborative study on the effectiveness of cognitive therapy, interpersonal therapy (IPT), and tricyclic antidepressants for overcoming major depression (Elkin, Shea, Imber, Pilkonis, Sotsky, Glass, Watkins, Leber, and Collins, 1986; Elkin, Shea, Watkins, Imber, et al., 1989; Imber, Pilkonis, Sotsky, and Elkin, 1990; Shea, Elkin, Imber, and Sotsky, 1992). This study is the most extensive and thorough trial of any psychotherapy ever done (see Table 8–2).

Two hundred and fifty patients with major depression were randomly assigned to one of four groups, and the design was carried out at three different treatment centers. The patients were moderately to severely depressed, and 70 percent were female. Twenty-eight trained therapists were used. Cognitive therapy focused on detecting and changing negative thoughts and assumptions. IPT focused on interpersonal problems; these therapists taught depressed patients better techniques for resolving conflicts with others (Klerman, Weissman, Rounsaville, and Chevron, 1984). The drug group was given tricyclic antidepressant drugs, and a fourth group was given a placebo. Therapy was brief: sixteen weeks. Recovery from depression was carefully assessed by a battery of tests and interviews.

More than 50 percent of the patients recovered in the two psychotherapy groups (cognitive therapy and interpersonal therapy) and in the drug group. Only 29 percent recovered in the placebo group. The drug treatment produced faster improvement, but by the end of the sixteen weeks patients in the two psychotherapies had caught up.

Relapse data from the collaborative study were unclear. While most treated subjects were improved, only 25 percent both recovered and remained well across all follow-ups (Shea, Elkin, Imber, and Sotsky, 1992).

TABLE 8–2

	TREATMENT OF DEPRESSION			
	Cognitive Therapy	Interpersonal Therapy	Drugs*	Electroconvulsive Shock Therapy
Improvement	60–80% markedly improved	60–80% markedly improved	60–80% markedly improved	80% markedly improved
Relapse†	moderate relapse	moderate relapse	high relapse	high relapse
Side Effects	none	none	moderate	sometimes severe
Cost	inexpensive	inexpensive	inexpensive	inexpensive
Time Scale	one month	months	weeks	days
Overall	**very good**	**very good**	**very good**	**very good**

*Drugs include tricyclics, MAO inhibitors, and serotonin reuptake inhibitors.
†Relapse after discontinuation of treatment.
SOURCE: Adapted from Martin E. P. Seligman, *What you can change and what you can't* (New York: Knopf, 1993), p. 114.

THE TREATMENT OF SEVERE DEPRESSION: DRUG THERAPY OR PSYCHOTHERAPY?

Despite hundreds of well-controlled studies supporting the effectiveness of drug therapy and psychotherapy for depression, researchers continue to disagree about when antidepressant drugs as opposed to psychotherapy should be used to treat depression. Guidelines issued by the American Psychiatric Association (1993) and Agency for Health Care Policy and Research (1993) suggest that clinicians should use drug therapy instead of psychotherapy to treat severe depression. These recommendations have sparked a debate over the effectiveness of drug therapy and that of interpersonal and cognitive-behavioral psychotherapies (Munoz, Hollon, McGrath, et al., 1994) when depression is severe and when it is mild. After carefully reanalyzing the results of treatment outcome studies, researchers still reach different conclusions about which treatment works best.

Some evidence indicates that drug therapy may not be as effective for mild depression as it is for severe depression. The Treatment of Depression Collaborative Research Project (TDCRP; Elkin, Parloff, Hadley, and Autry, 1985), one of the largest and most ambitious outcome studies ever conducted, found that medication did not help mildly depressed patients any more than did placebos. In addition, the side effects and risk factors of drug therapy may make it an unsuitable approach for these kinds of cases. Indeed, many researchers believe that psychotherapies, especially cognitive-behavioral and interpersonal therapies, better fit the needs of mildly to moderately depressed patients. Cognitive-behavioral therapy combats depression by trying to change patients' distorted beliefs and damaging behaviors. Interpersonal therapy aims to reduce depressive symptoms by improving interpersonal relationships and social skills.

But how effective is psychotherapy as opposed to drug treatment in severe depression? One side argues that drug therapy is better than psychotherapeutic approaches while the other claims that cognitive-behavioral therapy is as good as medication in treating severe depression. The TDCRP project showed that severely depressed patients assigned to the cognitive-behavioral treatment did worse than those assigned to the drug condition. The difference, however, did not prove to be strong at every treatment site and no other study has produced similar results (Jacobson and Hollon, 1996). Also, regardless of severity, those treated with drug therapy as opposed to psychotherapy did not have a significantly better prognosis in terms of long-term outcome. Klein (1996) criticizes these studies for not using a placebo control. Jacobson and Hollon (1996) do not consider this to be a major problem; they conclude that the studies provide reliable results without the control.

Taken together, the data suggest that cognitive-behavioral and interpersonal therapies offer a viable alternative to antidepressants even when used to treat severe depression, although it is quite possible that the most severely depressed patients will have a better outcome if they have antidepressants rather than interpersonal or cognitive-behavioral therapies (Frank and Spanier, 1995).

This suggests that the sixteen weeks of psychotherapy were insufficient for maintained antidepressant effects. There is evidence from other studies, however, which suggests that patients in cognitive therapy have learned a skill to cope with depression that the patients given drugs have not, and that this results in lower relapse of those treated with cognitive therapy (see Box 8–4). For example, in one study, forty-four depressed outpatients were randomly assigned for twelve weeks either to individual cognitive therapy or to therapy with tricyclic antidepressants (Rush, Beck, Kovacs, and Hollon, 1977; Kovacs, Rush, Beck, and Hollon, 1981). Their depressions were quite severe: on the average, the current episode of depression had lasted for twelve months, and patients had already been unsuccessfully treated by two previous therapists. During the course of therapy, the patients in the cognitive therapy group had a maximum of twenty sessions, and the patients in the drug group were given a tricyclic daily, plus twelve brief sessions with the therapist who had prescribed the drugs.

By the end of treatment, both groups had improved according to both self-report and therapist ratings of depression. Only one of the nineteen patients assigned to cognitive therapy had dropped out, whereas eight of the twenty-five assigned to drug therapy had dropped out. This is not surprising since there is usually notable attrition due to side effects and reluctance to take drugs in drug treatment. Of the cognitive therapy patients, 79 percent showed marked improvement or complete remission, but only 20 percent of the drug patients showed such a strong response. Follow-up at three months, six months, and twelve months after treatment indicated that both groups maintained their improvement. The group that had received cognitive therapy, however, continued to be less depressed than the group that had received drug therapy. In addition, the cognitive group had half the relapse rate of the drug group (see also Reynolds and Coats, 1986).

Overall then two systematic psychotherapies—cognitive therapy and interpersonal therapy—work about as well as tricyclic antidepressant drugs against major depression. And all three treatments work better than placebos. Tricyclics work faster, but the psychotherapies may produce more lasting relief.

BIPOLAR DISORDER (MANIC-DEPRESSION)

We have now explored the great majority of depressions: 80 to 95 percent of depressions are unipolar and occur without mania. This leaves between 5 and 20 percent of depressions that occur as part of *manic-depression.* These are called *bipolar disorders.*

We classify bipolar disorders in the following way: Given the presence of manic symptoms, an individual is judged to be manic-depressive if he has had one or more depressive episodes in the past. On the other hand, he is diagnosed as having experienced only a *manic episode* if he has never had a depressive episode. Mania itself can occur without depression, although this is very rare. Usually, a depressive episode will occur eventually, once a manic episode has happened. Another form of bipolar disorder occurs when depression is regularly set off by the approach of winter. This is called *seasonal affective disorder (SAD).*

Since the symptoms of the depressive component of bipolar disorder are similar to what we described for unipolar depression, we need only describe mania here in order to have a clear picture of bipolar disorder. Here is what it feels like to be in the manic state of a manic-depressive disorder:

> When I start going into a high, I no longer feel like an ordinary housewife. Instead, I feel organized and accomplished, and I begin to feel I am my most creative self. I can write poetry easily, I can compose melodies without effort. I can paint. My mind feels facile and absorbs everything. I have countless ideas about improving the conditions of mentally retarded children, how a hospital for these children should be run, what they should have around them to keep them happy and calm and unafraid. I see myself as being able to accomplish a great deal for the good of people. I have countless ideas about how the environmental problem could inspire a crusade for the health and betterment of everyone. I feel able to accomplish a great deal for the good of my family and others. I feel pleasure, a sense of euphoria or elation. I want it to last forever. I don't seem to need much sleep. I've lost weight and feel healthy, and I like myself. I've just bought six new dresses, in fact, and they look quite good on me. I feel sexy and men stare at me. Maybe I'll have an affair, or perhaps several. I feel capable of speaking and doing good in politics. I would like to help people with problems similar to mine so they won't feel hopeless. (Fieve, 1975, p. 17)

Symptoms of Mania

The onset of a manic episode usually occurs fairly suddenly, and the euphoric mood, racing thoughts, frenetic acts, and resulting insomnia stand in marked contrast to the person's usual functioning. Mania presents four sets of symptoms: emotional, cognitive, motivational, and somatic.

MOOD OR EMOTIONAL SYMPTOMS

The mood of an individual in a manic state is euphoric, expansive, and elevated. A highly successful manic artist describes his mood:

> I feel no sense of restriction or censorship whatsoever. I'm afraid of nothing and no one. During this elated state, when no inhibition is present, I feel I can race a car with my foot on the floorboard, fly a plane when I have never flown a plane before, and speak languages I hardly know. Above all, as an artist, I feel I can write poems and paint paintings that I could never dream of when just my normal self. I don't want others to restrict me during this period of complete and utter freedom. (Fieve, 1975)

Grandiose euphoria is not universal in mania, however. Often the dominant mood is irritability, and this is particularly so when a manic individual is thwarted in his ambitions. People with mania, even when high, are peculiarly close to tears, and when frustrated may burst out crying. This is one reason to believe that mania is not wholly the opposite state of depression, but that a strong depressive element coexists with it.

THOUGHT OR COGNITIVE SYMPTOMS

The manic cognitions are appropriate to the mood. They are grandiose. The manic patient does not believe in limits to his ability, and worse, he does not recognize the painful consequences that will ensue when he carries out his plans. A manic patient who spends $100,000 buying three automobiles in a week does not recognize that he will have a great deal of trouble trying to pay for them over the coming years; a manic patient who calls the President in the middle of the night to tell him about her latest health care proposal does not recognize that this call may bring the police down on her; the manic patient who enters one sexual affair after another does not realize the permanent damage to her reputation that may ensue.

A person in a manic state may have thoughts or ideas racing through his mind faster than he can write them down or say them. This *flight of ideas* easily becomes derailed because the manic patient is highly distractible. In some extreme cases, the manic patient has delusional ideas about himself. He may believe that he is a special messenger of God; he may believe that he is an intimate friend of famous political and show business figures. The manic patient's thinking about other people is black and white: the individuals he knows are either all good or all bad; they are his best friends or his sworn enemies. The following is a case showing a manic flight of ideas:

> "I went mad at the winter Olympics in Innsbruck. My brain got cloudy, as if a fog from the Alps had enveloped it. In that condition I came face to face with one gentleman—the Devil. He looked the part! He had hooves, fur, horns, and rotten teeth that looked hundreds of years old. With this figure in mind I climbed the hills above Innsbruck and torched a farm building. I was convinced that only a brilliant bonfire could burn off that fog. As I was leading the cows and horses from the barn, the Austrian police arrived. They handcuffed me and took me down into the valley . . . Back over the border I was delivered to the doctors in Prague . . .
>
> "Then the bad times began. The doctors, with their pills, got me into a state in which I realized I was mad. That is sadness, when you know that you are no Christ but a wretch whose brain, which makes a man a man, is sick . . .
>
> ". . . I know I suffered terribly. There are no words to describe it. And if there were such words, people would not believe them because they do not want to hear about madness. It frightens them.
>
> "When I felt better, I tried to remember what had been beautiful in my life. I did not think about love or how I had wandered all over the world . . . I remembered most the river I had loved most in my life. Before I could fish in it again I

would take its water in the shell of my hands and kiss it as I would kiss a woman. . . Sometimes, when I sat at the barred window and fished in memory, the pain was almost unbearable. I had to block it out, the beauty, and I had to remind myself that dirt, foulness, and muddy waters also ran the world. When I succeeded in this, I did not long so much for my freedom . . .

"I wanted to kill myself a hundred times when I felt I couldn't go on, but I never did. Maybe my desire to kiss the river and catch the silver fish again kept me going. Fishing taught me patience and my memories helped me go on." (Pavel, 1990)

MOTIVATIONAL SYMPTOMS

Manic behavior is hyperactive. The manic patient engages in frenetic activity, be it in his occupation, in political or religious circles, in sexual relationships, or elsewhere. Describing the mania of a woman, one author wrote:

Her friends noticed that she was going out every night, dating many new men, attending church meetings, language classes, and dances, and showing a rather frenetic emotional state. Her seductiveness at the office resulted in her going to bed with two of the available married men, who didn't realize she was ill. She burst into tears on several occasions without provocation and told risqué jokes that were quite out of character. She became more talkative and restless, stopped eating and didn't seem to need any sleep. She began to talk with religious feeling about being in contact with God and insisted that several things were now necessary to carry out God's wishes. This included giving herself sexually to all who needed her. When she was admitted to the hospital, she asked the resident psychiatrist on call to kiss her. Because he refused to do so, she became suddenly silent. Later, she talked incessantly, accusing the doctor of trying to seduce her and began to talk about how God knew every sexual thought that she or the doctor might have. (Fieve, 1975, pp. 22–23)

The activity of the manic patient has an intrusive, demanding, and domineering quality to it. People in a manic state sometimes make us uncomfortable because of this. It is difficult to spend much time with an individual who delivers a rapid succession of thoughts and who behaves in a frenetic way almost in disregard of those around him. Other behaviors that commonly occur during mania are compulsive gambling, reckless driving, poor financial investments, and flamboyant dress and makeup.

PHYSICAL OR SOMATIC SYMPTOMS

With all this flurry of activity comes a greatly lessened need for sleep. Such hyposomnia virtually always occurs during mania. After a couple of days of this, exhaustion inevitably sets in and the mania slows down.

Course and Characteristics of Bipolar Disorder

Between .6 and 1.1 percent of the population of the United States will have bipolar disorder in their lifetime (Robins et al., 1984; Keller and Baker, 1991). Unlike unipolar depression, which affects more women than men, bipolar disorder affects both sexes equally. The onset of bipolar disorder is sudden, usually a matter of hours or days, and typically no precipitating event is obvious. The first episode is usually manic, not depressive, and it generally appears between the ages of twenty and thirty. This first attack occurs somewhat earlier than a first attack in unipolar depression. (Ninety percent of people with bipolar disorder will have had their first attack before they are fifty years old.)

FOCUS QUESTIONS

1. Give general definitions of bipolar disorder (manic-depression) and manic episodes.
2. What are the four broad symptoms of mania?
3. Describe the evidence for a genetic predisposition to bipolar disorder.
4. How is bipolar disorder treated?
5. What is seasonal affective disorder (SAD) and how is it treated?

DSM-IV Criteria for Manic Episode

A. A distinct period of abnormally and persistently elevated, expansive, or irritable mood, lasting at least 1 week (or any duration if hospitalization is necessary).

B. During the period of mood disturbance, three (or more) of the following symptoms have persisted (four if the mood is only irritable) and have been present to a significant degree: (1) inflated self-esteem or grandiosity; (2) decreased need for sleep (e.g., feels rested after only 3 hours of sleep); (3) more talkative than usual or pressure to keep talking; (4) flight of ideas or subjective experience that thoughts are racing; (5) distractibility (i.e., attention too easily drawn to unimportant or irrelevant external stimuli); (6) increase in goal-directed activity (either socially, at work or school, or sexually) or psychomotor agitation; (7) excessive involvement in pleasurable activities that have a high potential for painful consequences (e.g., engaging in unrestrained buying sprees, sexual indiscretions, or foolish business investments).

C. The symptoms do not meet criteria for a Mixed Episode.

D. The mood disturbance is sufficiently severe to cause marked impairment in occupational functioning or in usual social activities or relationships with others, or to necessitate hospitalization to prevent harm to self or others, or there are psychotic features.

E. The symptoms are not due to the direct physiological effects of a substance (e.g., a drug of abuse, a medication, or other treatment) or a general medical condition (e.g., hyperthyroidism). (*Note:* Manic-like episodes that are clearly caused by somatic antidepressant treatment (e.g., medication, electroconvulsive therapy, light therapy) should not count toward a diagnosis of Bipolar I Disorder.)

SOURCE: APA, DSM-IV, 1994.

Bipolar disorder tends to recur, and each episode lasts from several days to several months. Over the first ten years of the disorder, the frequency and intensity of the episodes tend to worsen. Surprisingly, however, not many episodes occur twenty years after the initial onset. Both manic and depressive episodes occur in the disorder, but regular cycling (e.g., three months manic, followed by three months depressive, and so on) is rare. The depressive component of bipolar disorder is similar in kind to that of unipolar depression, but it is often more severe (Angst, Baastrup, Grof, Hippius, Poldinger, and Weiss, 1973; Depue and Monroe, 1978; Loranger and Levine, 1978; Fogarty, Russell, Newman, and Bland, 1994).

Bipolar disorder is not a benign, remitting disorder. For some, extreme manic episodes may bring about much hardship. Their hyperactivity and bizarre behavior may be self-defeating. Employers may become annoyed at their behavior, and some people with bipolar disorder may then find themselves without a job. For others, entire careers may be lost. In addition, their social relationships tend to break down. The manic person is hard to deal with. A much higher percentage of married manic-depressive patients divorce than do married unipolar depressive patients. Alcohol abuse, either in attempted self-medication or due to poor judgment and impulsiveness, is very high in bipolar disorder. The more severe the mania, the more frequent the alcoholism (Maier, Lichtermann, Minges, Delmo, and Heun, 1995). In all, between 20 and 50 percent of people with bipolar disorder suffer chronic social and occupational impairment. In most extreme cases, hospitalization is required. And for a few, suicide is a constant threat. The rate of attempted and successful suicides is also higher in bipolar than in unipolar depressions. As many as 15 percent of those with bipolar disorder may end their life by suicide (Brodie and Leff, 1971; Carlson, Kotin, Davenport, and Adland,

▲ There is evidence that Theodore Roosevelt had a manic-depressive disorder, and that the mania contributed to his political success.

1974; Reich, Davies, and Himmelhoch, 1974; Dunner, Gershom, and Goodwin, 1976; Sharma and Markar, 1994).

When the mania is more moderate and the depressions are not too debilitating, however, the manic-depressive patient's ambition, hyperactivity, talkativeness, and grandiosity may lead to great achievements. This behavior is conducive to success in our society. It is no surprise that many creative people, leaders of industry, entertainment, politics, and religion may have been able to use and control their less severe levels of bipolar disorder. Abraham Lincoln, Winston Churchill, and Theodore Roosevelt probably all suffered from bipolar disorder.

Cause of Bipolar Disorder

The cause of bipolar disorder is unknown. On the surface, with its euphoria and hyperactivity, it looks like the opposite state of depression. But as we have seen, feelings of depression are close at hand during the mania. The bipolar individual, when manic, is close to tears; he voices more hopelessness and has more suicidal thoughts than is normal. This has led some theorists to believe that mania is a defense against an underlying depression, that the individual in a manic episode is experiencing a brittle euphoria that is warding off more fundamental sadness.

Other theorists believe that bipolar disorder results from self-correcting biological processes that have become ungoverned. Generally, when an individual becomes depressed, the depression is allegedly ended by switching in an opposite, euphoric state that cancels it out. Conversely, when an individual becomes euphoric, this state is kept from spiraling out of bounds by switching in a depressive state that neutralizes the euphoria. Investigations of the biochemistry of this switching process seem to indicate that it is a disturbance in the balance of mania and depression, with the reaction to either overshooting its mark, that may actually be responsible for the bipolar disorder.

One theory about the underlying biological basis for bipolar disorder identifies three separate systems in the brain that may become unbalanced and cause different groups of symptoms. First, the switching from the lack of interest and lack of enjoyment of the depressed phase to the excessive pleasure-seeking activity of the manic phase may involve disturbances in the brain's reward system, with an excess or a lack of pleasure "inhibition" determining whether the individual is overenthusiastic or apathetic. Second, high sensitivity to pain and negative events in depression and low sensitivity to them in mania may result from a separate disinhibition-inhibition process. Third, the shift from hyperactivity to retarded motor activity seen in a bipolar cycle may stem from an unregulated movement processing system. Different neurotransmitters are thought to control the switching processes within each of these three systems (Carroll, 1994).

Individuals are genetically vulnerable to bipolar disorder. Manic-depressive individuals are more often found in families in which successive generations have experienced depression or manic-depression. Relatives of manic-depressive patients have five times the normal 1 percent risk for developing the disorder (Rice, Reich, Andreasen, Endicott, Van Eerdewegh, Fishman, Hirschfeld, and Klerman, 1987). Identical twins have five times the concordance for bipolar disorder than do fraternal twins. Thus, the familial risk is probably genetic, at least in part for manic-depression, but less so for unipolar depression (Allen, 1976; McGuffin and Katz, 1989; Carroll, 1994).

TABLE 8–3

	Psychosocial Treatment*	Medications[†]
Improvement	marginal	80% marked relief from mania; 60–80% moderate relief from depression
Relapse[‡]	unknown	high relapse rate
Side Effects	none	moderate to severe
Cost	inexpensive	moderately expensive
Time Scale	months/weeks	weeks/months
Overall	**marginal**	**very good**

*Psychosocial treatment is given an adjunct of medication only. Both family interventions and cognitive-behavioral therapy have been used coupled with medication in several controlled trials.
[†]Medications include lithium for bipolar disorder, as well as valproate and carbamazepine for acute mania.
[‡]Relapse after discontinuation of treatment.
SOURCE: Based on E. Craighead, D. Miklowitz, and F. Vajk, Psychosocial treatments for bipolar disorder, in P. Nathan and J. Gorman (eds.), *Treatments that work* (New York: Oxford, 1997). P. Keck, and S. McElroy, Bipolar disorders, in P. Nathan and J. Gorman (eds.), *Treatments that work* (New York: Oxford, 1997).

Treatment

By and large, bipolar disorder can be successfully treated with lithium salts (see Table 8–3). Lithium was originally used as a table salt substitute. In 1949, John Cade, an Australian physician, having found that lithium made guinea pigs lethargic, tried it to dampen mania in humans and found that lithium ended severe manic attacks. Since that time, lithium carbonate has been shown to be an effective treatment both for mania and for the depressive aspects of bipolar disorder. Approximately 80 percent of manic-depressive patients will show a full or partial alleviation of symptoms during lithium administration. It is also clear, however, that the other 20 percent of bipolar depressive patients do not respond to the lithium (Depue, 1979; Manji, Potter, and Lenox, 1995; Solomon, Keitner, Miller, Shea, and Keller, 1995).

While lithium can be viewed as a miracle drug for bipolar disorder, its side effects, particularly its cardiovascular, digestive, and central nervous system effects, can be quite serious. Close medical supervision should always accompany the administration of lithium. Both the evidence on the effectiveness of lithium as well as the evidence on genetic vulnerability suggest that bipolar disorder is best understood within the framework of the biological model.

Seasonal Affective Disorder (SAD)

The most recent addition to the bipolar family has been dubbed ***seasonal affective disorder (SAD).*** For millennia, human activity in the temperate zones has been strongly influenced by the seasons, with highly active behavior occurring during spring and summer, and withdrawal from the frenzy of life tending to occur during fall and winter. This may be the evolutionary basis for SAD.

When John moved to Washington, D.C., from Florida at age twenty-one, he experienced his first depression. He went there to attend medical school, and for each of the next four winters the depression recurred. He was hospitalized and became hopeless about his goal of becoming a physician because of his depression problem. He plodded on through his internship in Maryland, with the depressions continuing yearly.

He noticed that each year his depression remitted in the spring. The depression started around the first of December, when the days were getting short, and it lifted by the first of April. In some years, the depressions came on gradually, but in other years a bad event, like a patient dying, precipitated the depression. His mood was worse in the morning; he had trouble sleeping; he craved carbohydrates and gained weight. He was apathetic, irritable, and felt pessimistic.

After reading about SAD, he entered light therapy treatment at the National Institutes of Mental Health. He found that brilliant grow lights, on for two hours before dawn, markedly relieved his depression. Finally, he treated himself. He moved, and opened a practice in San Diego. He has not experienced a winter depression since. (Adapted from Spitzer, Gibbon, Skodol, Williams, and First, 1989, pp. 19–21)

SAD is characterized by depression beginning each year in October or November and fully remitting, sometimes switching toward mania, when the days start to lengthen (March and April). Patients complain of fatigue, oversleeping, and carbohydrate craving as well as the more typical symptoms of depression. Women outnumber men, and young children show the problem as well. In a nationwide Japanese survey, only 1 percent of the over 5,000 depressed outpatients were identified as having SAD (Sakamoto, Kamo, Nakadaira, and Tamura, 1993). In contrast, among a random sample of 283 Alaskans, who have less sunlight, twenty-six (9.2 percent) had SAD (Booker and Hellekson, 1992). In one of the first major studies, twenty-nine SAD patients reported their clinical history of depression by month. Depressive episodes were yoked to the sunlight and temperature of each month, with greatest depression in the winter months and least in the summer (see Figure 8–5). Not only is depression governed by the amount of sunlight where these patients live, but when they travel the depression changes. When they travel south in the winter, depression remits in a few days and when they travel north in the winter it tends to worsen (Rosenthal, Sack, Gillin, et al.,

FIGURE 8–5

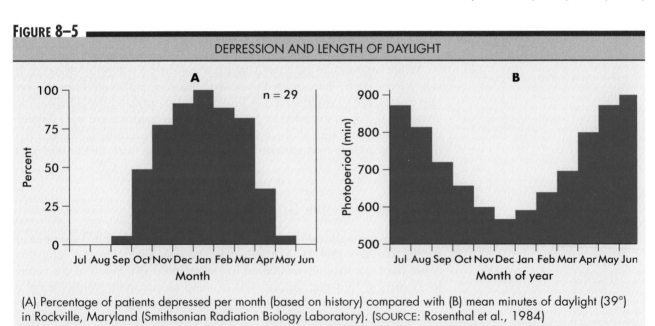

(A) Percentage of patients depressed per month (based on history) compared with (B) mean minutes of daylight (39°) in Rockville, Maryland (Smithsonian Radiation Biology Laboratory). (SOURCE: Rosenthal et al., 1984)

DSM-IV Criteria for Seasonal Pattern Specifier

DSM-IV suggests criteria for describing recurrent episodes of mood disorders with Seasonal Pattern (can be applied to the pattern of Major Depressive Episodes in Bipolar I Disorder, Bipolar II Disorder, or Major Depressive Disorder, Recurrent):

A. There has been a regular temporal relationship [occurring at the same time] between the onset of Major Depressive Episodes in Bipolar I or Bipolar II Disorder or Major Depressive Disorder, Recurrent, and a particular time of the year (e.g., regular appearance of the major Depressive Episode in the fall or winter). (*Note:* Do not include cases in which there is an obvious effect of seasonal-related psychosocial stressors; e.g., regularly being unemployed every winter.)

B. Full remission (or a change from depression to mania or hypomania) also occur at a charateristic time of the year (e.g., depression disappears in the spring).

C. In the last 2 years, two Major Depressive Episodes have occurred that demonstrate the temporal seasonal relationships defined in Criteria A and B, and no nonseasonal major Depressive Episodes have occurred during that same period.

D. Seasonal Major Depressive Episodes substantially outnumber the nonseasonal Major Depressive Episodes that may have occurred over the individual's lifetime.

SOURCE: APA, DSM-IV, 1994.

1984; Rosenthal, Carpenter, James, et al., 1986; Molin, Mellerup, Bolwik, Scheike, and Dam, 1996).

These findings led to the use of artificial light as therapy. Bright "grow-lights" are strategically located in the homes of the patients and come on very early in the morning and after sunset to lengthen daylight hours artificially. Prompt relief of depressive symptoms, particularly with the morning lights, has been reported, and relapse has been reported when light is withdrawn (Hellekson, Kline, and Rosenthal, 1986; Lewy, Sack, Miller, and Hoban, 1987; Rosenthal, Moul, Hellekson, and Oren, 1993). Exposure to natural light in the morning also seems to reduce depressive symptoms (Wirz-Justice, Graw, Krauchi, et al., 1996).

SUICIDE

Suicide is the most disastrous consequence of depression, bipolar or unipolar. Depression is the precursor of a vast majority of suicides. Death only rarely results directly from other psychological disorders: the anorexic patient who refuses food; the hallucinating schizophrenic, who believing he is Christ, attempts to walk on water; the heroin addict who administers an overdose. But it is depression that most frequently results in irreversible harm: death, by suicide.

Suicide is the second most frequent cause of death, after accidents, among high school and college students (U.S. Department of Health and Human Services, 1987). Further, it is on the rise in this age group. The death of a young person, because of all his unfulfilled promise, is a keenly felt tragedy. As a young man, Beethoven almost took his own life before composing his second symphony. What held him back was the thought that he had not yet produced the best that might be inside him.

Suicide is an act that most societies forbid. Many religions regard it as a sin; and it is, ironically, a crime in several states. No act leaves such a bitter

▲ Kurt Cobain committed suicide at the height of his popularity. Unlike Beethoven, who considered suicide after writing his first symphony but did not kill himself, we will never know what other music Cobain might have written had he not taken his life.

and lasting legacy among friends and relatives. It leaves in its wake bewilderment, guilt, shame, and stigma that relatives may carry to their own graves.

The individual who is deciding whether or not to take his own life is usually strongly ambivalent about the decision. One vote can tip the balance, as in a declaration of war (see Table 8–4). For example, when a physician canceled an appointment with a patient, this last straw in a series of disappointments tipped the balance toward suicidal death.

The ethical quandaries of suicide are immensely difficult. Does an individual have a right to take his own life, not interfered with by others, just as he has a right to dispose, unimpeded, of his own property (Szasz, 1974)?

Who Is at Risk for Suicide?

At the very least, 25,000 people end their lives by suicide every year in the United States. There are also estimated to be at least ten times as many suicide attempts as successful suicides, and it has been estimated that in the United States today, five million people are alive who have attempted suicide.

Suicide may run in families, and to the extent that depressive disorders are heritable, suicide itself may be heritable. In a study of the Amish, a highly insular group of people who tend to marry within the group and to live in Lancaster County, Pennsylvania, all twenty-six suicides over the last hundred years were analyzed. Twenty-four of these individuals had had major affective disorders; 16 percent of the families accounted for 73 percent of the suicides (Egeland and Sussex, 1985).

Suicide may even have a biochemistry. Among depressed patients, suicide attempts were most frequent in those having low serotonin levels, and when low-serotonin patients attempted suicide, they used more violent means (Asberg, Traskman, and Thoren, 1976). The brains of suicide victims have

TABLE 8–4

FABLES AND FACTS ABOUT SUICIDE	
Fable	*Fact*
Individuals who talk about killing themselves do not kill themselves.	Of every ten persons who have killed themselves, eight gave definite warnings of their intentions.
Suicidal individuals have made a clear decision to die.	Most are undecided about living or dying. They often gamble with death, leaving it to others to save them.
Once an individual is suicidal, he is forever suicidal.	Usually individuals who wish to kill themselves are suicidal only for a limited period. Suicidal wishes are often linked to depression, and depression usually dissipates in time.
The suicidal risk is over when improvement occurs following a suicidal crisis.	Most suicides occur while the individual is still depressed, but within about three months after the beginning of "improvement." It is at that time that the individual has better access to weapons and more energy to put his suicidal plans into effect than when he is in the hospital or at the lowest point in his depression.
Suicide occurs more often among the rich.	Suicide is equally frequent at all levels of society.
The suicidal act is the act of a sick person.	While the suicidal person is almost always extremely unhappy, he is not necessarily "mentally ill." Suicide can be a rational act.

SOURCE: Adapted from Shneidman, 1976.

FOCUS QUESTIONS

1. Which group is most vulnerable to suicide?
2. Describe the sex and age differences regarding suicide.
3. Describe the surcease and manipulation motivations for suicide.
4. What steps can be taken to prevent suicide?

lower serotonin in their brainstem and cerebrospinal fluid, but not in their frontal cortex (Mann, Arango, and Underwood, 1990; Bourgeois, 1991; Traskman-Bendz, Alling, Alsen, et al., 1993).

DEPRESSION AND SUICIDE

Depressed individuals are the single group most at risk for suicide. While suicide occasionally occurs in the absence of depression and the large majority of depressed people do not commit suicide, depression is a strong predisposing factor to suicide. An estimated 80 percent of suicidal patients are significantly depressed. Depressed patients ultimately commit suicide at a rate that is at least twenty-five times as high as control populations (Pokorny, 1964; Flood and Seager, 1968; Robins and Guze, 1972).

SEX DIFFERENCES AND SUICIDE

Women make roughly three times as many suicide attempts as men, but men actually succeed in killing themselves three times more often than women. These discrepancies seem to have diminished a bit over the last few years. The greater rate of suicide attempts in women is probably related to the fact that more depression occurs in women, whereas the greater completed suicide rate in men probably has to do with choice of methods: women tend to choose less lethal means, such as cutting their wrists and overdosing on sleeping pills; whereas men tend to shoot themselves and jump off buildings. The suicide rate for both men and women is higher among individuals who have been divorced and widowed; loneliness as well as a sense of failure in interpersonal affairs surely contributes to this statistic. Men who kill themselves tend to be motivated by failure at work, and women who kill themselves tend to be motivated by failure at love (Mendels, 1970; Linden and Breed, 1976; Shneidman, 1976). As one female patient who tried to find surcease in suicide after being rejected by her lover said, "There's no sense in living. There's nothing here for me. I need love and I don't have it anymore. I can't be happy without love—only miserable. It will just be the same misery, day in and day out. It's senseless to go on" (Beck, 1976).

CULTURAL DIFFERENCES AND SUICIDE

Race, religion, and nationality contribute somewhat to vulnerability to suicide. The suicide rate of young black and white men is approximately the same (Hendin, 1969; Linden and Breed, 1976; McIntosh, 1989), but black women and older black men probably kill themselves less often than whites (Swanson and Breed, 1976; McIntosh, 1989). There is some evidence that American Indians may have a higher suicide rate than the rest of the population (Frederick, 1978). Religion, at least in the United States, does not offer any protection against suicide in spite of varyingly strong strictures against it. The rate of suicide is roughly the same whether the individual is nonreligious, or Catholic, Protestant, or Jewish.

Suicide occurs in all cultures, but it seems to be more common in industrialized countries. At the present time, the countries of central Europe (Hungary, Austria, and the former Czechoslovakia) and northern Europe (Finland and Denmark) seem to have the highest suicide rate. The suicide rate in the former Soviet Union almost doubled over the period from 1965 to 1984. Then during the period of democratization from 1984–1988, the suicide rate halved again. In regions of strong political antagonism (Baltic States) and of forced social changes (Russia) the rate was high, but in regions where families and religious faith were strong, the rate was low (Varnik and Wasserman, 1992). Ireland and Egypt have very low suicide rates, perhaps because suicide is considered a mortal sin in these cultures. The United States has, on the world scale, an average suicide rate. Sweden has a middling high rate of suicide. Some have blamed this on the lack of incentive provided by its social welfare system, but its suicide rate has remained the same since about 1910, before the introduction of social welfare (Shneidman, 1976; Department of International Economic and Social Affairs, 1985).

AGE AND SUICIDE

Among children, suicide is rare, with probably fewer than 200 suicides committed in a year in the United States by children who are under the age of fourteen. But among those preschoolers who are suicidal, they tend to be more impulsive and hyperactive, show less pain and crying when hurt, and have parents who abuse and neglect them (Rosenthal and Rosenthal, 1984).

Discussing her wish to die, Michelle, age nine, talks with Joaquim Puig-Antich, a leading expert on childhood depression:

> JOAQUIM PUIG-ANTICH: Do you feel you should be punished?
> MICHELLE: Yes.
> JPA: Why?
> M: I don't know.
> JPA: Have you ever had the thought that you might want to hurt yourself?
> M: Yes.
> JPA: How would you hurt yourself?
> M: By drinking a lot of alcohol, or jumping off the balcony.
> JPA: Have you ever tried to jump?
> M: I once stood on the edge of the terrace and put one leg over the railing, but my mother caught me.
> JPA: Did you really want to jump?
> M: Yes.
> JPA: What would have happened if you had jumped?
> M: I would have killed myself.
> JPA: Did you want to get killed?
> M: Uh-huh.
> JPA: Why?
> M: Because I don't like the life I live.
> JPA: What kind of life do you live?
> M: A sad and miserable life.

(Jerome, 1979)

▼ Richard Bosman's *Witness*, 1983, shows people watching a man jump to his death.

Suicide among young people is on the rise. In the past thirty-five years, the suicide rate among college-age groups has tripled. Males between the ages of twenty and twenty-four are hardest hit, with a rate of about 28 per 100,000 compared to a rate of 12 per 100,000 in the general population. Studies of the psychological "autopsies" of young suicides have strongly implicated substance abuse and untreated depression as precursors (Holden, 1986b).

Suicide rate rises dramatically through middle age and into old age. Increasing depression, loneliness, moving to a strange setting, loss of a meaningful role in family and society, and loss of people they love all surely contribute to the high rate of suicide among old people. In cultures and communities in which the aged are revered and remain important in the life of the family, suicide is infrequent.

The Motivation for Suicide

In the first major modern study of suicide, the French sociologist Émile Durkheim (1858–1917) distinguished three motivations for suicide, all of them intimately related to the way an individual sees his place in society. He called these motives anomic, egoistic, and altruistic. ***Anomic suicide*** is pre-

▲ Buddhist monks in Vietnam burned themselves to death to protest their government's policies in the late 1960s and early 1970s.

cipitated by a shattering break in an individual's relationship to his society: the loss of a job, economic depression, even sudden wealth. ***Egoistic suicide*** occurs when the individual has too few ties to his fellow humans. Societal demands, principal among them the demand to live, do not reach the egoistic individual. Finally, ***altruistic suicide*** is required by the society. The individual takes his own life in order to benefit his community. Hara-kiri is an altruistic suicide. The Buddhist monks who burned themselves to death to protest the injustices of the Vietnam War are recent reminders of individuals who committed altruistic suicide.

Modern thinkers see two more fundamental motivations for suicide: ***surcease*** and ***manipulation.*** Those who wish surcease have simply given up. Their emotional distress is intolerable, and they see no alternative solution. In death, they see an end to their problems. Fifty-six percent of the suicide attempts observed in a systematic study were classified as individuals trying to achieve surcease. These suicide attempts involved more depression, more hopelessness, and they tended to be more lethal than the remaining suicide attempts (Beck, 1976).

The other motivation for suicide is the wish to manipulate other people by a suicide attempt. Some wish to manipulate the world that remains by dying: to have the final word in an argument, to have revenge on a rejecting lover, to ruin the life of another person. More commonly in manipulative suicide, the individual intends to remain alive, but by showing the seriousness of his dilemma, he is crying for help from those who are important to him. Trying to prevent a lover from leaving, getting into the hospital and having a temporary respite from problems, and being taken seriously are all manipulative motives for suicide with intent to live.

Thirteen percent of suicide attempts were found to be manipulative; these involved less depression, less hopelessness, and less lethal means than did the surcease attempts (Beck, 1976). Those suicides that are manipulative are clearly cries for help, but it should be apparent that not all suicides are cries for help (see Box 8–5). The individual who wishes to escape because life is not worth living is not crying out for help, but for an end to his troubles. The remaining 31 percent of suicide attempts combine surcease and manipulative motivation. Here the individual is not at all sure whether he wishes to live or die, whether he wishes surcease or a change in the world. In this undecided group, the more hopeless and the more depressed the individual is, the stronger are the surcease reasons for the suicide attempt (Beck, Rush, Shaw, and Emery, 1979).

Prevention and Treatment

In the initial therapeutic interview with a depressed individual, suicide is the overriding question in the back of the therapist's mind. If clear suicidal intent and hopelessness are pervading themes, crisis intervention, close observation, and hospitalization will probably ensue. If they are not, therapy will proceed at a somewhat more leisurely pace, directed toward careful understanding of the other depressive problems.

In the late 1960s, a network of more than 300 suicide prevention centers was established in the United States to deal with suicidal crises. In addition, hospitals and outpatient units set up hot-lines to deal with the crises of acutely suicidal individuals. It was believed that if someone was available for the suicidal individual to talk to, the suicide could be prevented.

In terms of prevention of suicide, once the suicidal person makes contact with a telephone hot-line volunteer, a psychologist, a psychiatrist, a family physician, a pastor, or emergency room doctor, evaluation of the

BOX 8–5 ━━━━━━━━━━━━━━━━━━━━━━━━━━━━━ IN THE CLINICIAN'S OFFICE

SUICIDE NOTES

About one-sixth of those individuals who die by their own hand leave suicide notes. A romantic view would lead us to expect that these final words, like those that are supposed to be uttered on the deathbed, would be masterful summaries of a life that preceded them and of the reasons for dying. Only occasionally are they:

"There should be little sadness, and no searching for who is at fault; for the act and result are not sad, and no one is at fault.

"My only sorrow is for my parents who will not easily be able to accept that this is so much better for me. Please, folks, it's all right, really it is.

"I wanted to be too many things, and greatness besides—it was a hopeless task. I never managed to really love another person—only to make the sounds of it. I never could believe what my society taught me to believe, yet I could never manage to quite find the truth.

"Two-fifteen p.m.—I'm about to will myself to stop my heartbeat and respiration. This is a very mystical experience. I have no fear. That surprises me. I thought I would be terrified. Soon I will know what death is like—how many people out there can say that?"

But much more often the notes are commonplace. Creative, unique, and expansive pieces of writing are rare in suicide notes. The individual is usually constricted, his field of consciousness has narrowed, and he is in despair. This is not a state conducive to creativity.

"Dearest darling I want you to know that you are the only one in my life I love you so much I could not do without you please forgive me I drove myself sick honey please believe me I love you you again and the baby honey don't be mean with me please I've lived 50 years since I met you, I love you—I love you. Dearest darling I love you, I love you. Please don't discriminate me darling I know that I will die don't be mean with me please I love you more than you will ever know. Darling please and honey, Tom, I don't tell Tom why his daddy said goodbye honey. Can't stand it anymore. Darling I love you. Darling I love you."

A good number of suicide notes merely contain instructions and directions:

"Dear Mary. I am writing you, as our divorce is not final, and will not be til next month, so the way things stand now you are still my wife, which makes you entitled to the things which belong to me, and I want you to have them. Don't let anyone take them from you as they are yours. Please see a lawyer and get them as soon as you can. I am listing some of the things, they are: a blue davenport and chair, a Magic Chef Stove, a large mattress, an electrolux cleaner, a 9 x 12 rug, reddish flower design and pad. All the things listed above are almost new. Then there is my 30-30 rifle, books, typewriter, tools and a hand contract for a house in Chicago, a savings account in Boston, Massachusetts. Your husband."

And some are simple and starkly practical. A workman before hanging himself in an abandoned house chalked his suicide note on the wall outside.

"Sorry about this. There's a corpse in here. Inform police."

SOURCE: Adapted from Shneidman, 1976.

suicidal risk takes first priority. Does the individual have a clear plan? Does he have access to a weapon? Does he have a past history of suicidal acts? Does he live alone? Once suicidal risk in a crisis is assessed, a treatment decision must be hastily made: home visit, hospitalization, medication, the police, or outpatient psychotherapy. In some cases, merely holding the person on the phone may be the appropriate action. Long-term follow-up and after-care must then occur.

To assess the success of the suicide prevention centers, the total number of prevention centers in each state was tabulated, and the number of suicides in that state over the next decade was compared to the rates that existed before the prevention centers were started. The more suicide centers that had been established, the larger the drop in suicide rate. The effect, however, was not large, and whether the centers caused the drop, or some other demographic variable did, was unclear (Diekstra, 1992; Hazell and Lewin, 1993; Lester, 1993).

In addition to suicide prevention, psychological intervention in the lives of the surviving relatives is also important (Hazell and Lewin, 1993). As we have seen, the survivors are themselves more vulnerable to later depression and suicide. They are faced with shame, guilt, bewilderment, and stigma. This is a group that has been neglected and that might benefit greatly from systematic care.

1. The *affective disorders* consist of major depressive disorder (unipolar depression) and bipolar disorder (manic-depression). *Unipolar depression (major depressive episode)* consists of depressive symptoms only and involves no symptoms of mania. It is by far the most common of the depressive disorders, and has become much more frequent since World War II. *Dysthymic disorder* consists of chronic (more than two years) depressive symptoms. *Bipolar disorder* occurs in individuals who have both periods of depression and periods of mania as well. *Cyclothymic disorder* is a chronic form of bipolar disorder.

2. There are four basic symptoms of unipolar depression: emotional symptoms, largely sadness; motivational symptoms, largely passivity; cognitive symptoms, largely hopelessness and pessimism; and somatic symptoms, including loss of weight and loss of appetite. Untreated, these symptoms will usually dissipate within about three months.

3. Women are more at risk than men for unipolar depression.

4. Three theories—biological, psychodynamic, and cognitive—have all shed light on unipolar depression.

5. Biological models have generated four effective therapies: *tricyclic antidepressant drugs, MAO inhibitors, serotonin reuptake inhibitors,* and *electroconvulsive therapy* (ECT). The biomedical school holds that depression is due to depletions in certain central nervous system neurotransmitters, *serotonin* or *norepinephrine.*

6. Psychodynamic theories concentrate on the personality that predisposes one to depression. These theories hold that depression stems from *anger turned upon the self,* and that individuals who are predisposed to depression are overdependent on other people for their self-esteem and that they feel helpless to achieve their goals.

7. Cognitive models concentrate on particular ways of thinking and how these cause and sustain depression. There are two prominent cognitive models: the view of Aaron Beck, which holds that depression stems from a *negative cognitive triad,* and Seligman's *learned helplessness model* of depression.

8. A pessimistic explanatory style predicts risk for depression. Changing this attribution style to optimistic may relieve and prevent depression.

9. Unipolar depression can now be effectively treated: nine out of ten people who suffer a severe unipolar depressive episode can be markedly helped either by drugs, ECT, cognitive therapy, or interpersonal therapy.

10. Depressive symptoms can be prevented among pre-teenagers. Learning social and cognitive antidepressant skills reduced symptoms of depression over two-year follow-up.

11. *Bipolar disorder* (manic-depression) is the most crippling of the affective disorders. It results in ruined marriages, irreparable damage to reputation, and not uncommonly, suicide. Mania consists of four sets of symptoms: euphoric mood, grandiose thoughts, frenetic activity, and lack of sleep.

12. Eighty percent of bipolar depressions can now be greatly helped by *lithium.* This disorder is best viewed within the biomedical model.

13. *Seasonal affective disorder* is characterized by depression that begins each year in October or November and ends in the early spring. Light therapy has been shown to be effective.

14. *Suicide* is the most disastrous consequence of depression. Its frequency is rising among young people, and it is the second most frequent cause of death among college students. Women make more suicide attempts than men, but men actually succeed in killing themselves more often than women. There are two fundamental motivations for suicide: *surcease,* or desire to end it all, and *manipulation,* or desire to change the world or other individuals by a suicide attempt.

QUESTIONS FOR CRITICAL THINKING

1. Describe ways of helping individuals to deal with loss and the consequences of being unable to cope with loss and disappointment.

2. Why do you think depressed individuals have difficulty initiating responses and making decisions?

3. Describe how Prozac works and its side effects. Do you think the benefits of Prozac outweigh its side effects?

4. How do you think creative people are able to use and control their manic-depression? What can happen when manic episodes get out of control?

CHAPTER

9

The Schizophrenias

There is no more puzzling and profound psychological disorder than schizophrenia. Many theories try to account for it, but a complete understanding of this complex disorder continues to elude us. Briefly, **schizophrenia** is a disorder of thinking and troubled mood. This thought disorder is manifested by difficulties in maintaining and focusing attention and in forming concepts. It can result in false perceptions and beliefs, in enormous difficulties in understanding reality, and in corresponding difficulties with language and emotional expression.

"Schizophrenia" is not a single disorder but rather a group of psychoses. As such, we often refer to these disorders as "the schizophrenias." We will try to understand the schizophrenic disorders by examining the symptoms that are part of them, and the psychological and biological determinants that promote them. Then we will examine the various treatments that are available for the schizophrenias.

DIAGNOSING SCHIZOPHRENIA

What schizophrenia is, as well as who is and who is not schizophrenic, has generated heated debate since German psychiatrist Emil Kraepelin described the symptoms of **dementia praecox,** literally, early or premature deterioration, in his *Psychiatrie* in 1896 (see Box 9–1). For Kraepelin, the diagnosis of *dementia praecox* was indicated when individuals displayed certain unusual symptoms and showed a deteriorating course thereafter. Included among these were inappropriate emotional responses such as laughter at a funeral; stereotyped motor behavior such as bowing repeatedly before entering a room; attentional difficulties such as inability to read because of shifting

269

BOX 9–1 ▬▬▬▬▬▬▬▬▬▬▬▬▬▬▬▬▬▬▬▬▬▬▬▬▬▬▬▬▬ IN THE CLINICIAN'S OFFICE

SOME MYTHS ABOUT SCHIZOPHRENIA

People with schizophrenia have been called lunatics, madmen, raving maniacs, unhinged, deranged, and demented. These words suggest that those with schizophrenia are dangerous, unpredictable, impossible to understand, and completely out of control. But clinicians see a different picture. To them, these notations say more about non-schizophrenics' fear and ignorance than they do about the nature of schizophrenia itself.

- Myth #1, *Dangerousness.* Rather than being raving maniacs on the rampage, people with schizophrenia are often withdrawn and preoccupied with their own problems. Sometimes they yell and scream, and occasionally they strike someone. But it is by no means clear whether these behaviors arise from the actual disorder, or from the way schizophrenic people are treated. Like others, schizophrenic individuals often mirror their treatment. When the treatment is civilized, so are the patients. The mistaken notion that criminals are less dangerous than those with schizophrenia, and that one would be better off living near a prison than near a hospital, rests squarely on ignorance and fear.
- Myth #2, *Split Personality.* Another common misconception about schizophrenia is that it involves a split personality of the Dr. Jekyll and Mr. Hyde sort, with

its attendant unpredictability and potential for violence. This error arises from the origins of the word schizophrenia (*schizo* = split, *phreno* = mind). When Eugen Bleuler coined the term, he intended to suggest that certain psychological functions were divided in those with schizophrenia, not that there were two or more alternating personalities residing in the schizophrenic person. Although Bleuler's view is no longer as widely accepted as it once was, the misconception that arose from his view continues to exist, fostered by Hollywood and television.
- Myth #3, *Schizophrenic Forever.* A third myth about schizophrenia is that once a person is found to have schizophrenia, he or she will always have schizophrenia. But in fact, the schizophrenic disorders are not necessarily durable, and surely not always lifelong. Often, a single episode will occur and then disappear, never to recur. Sometimes, after a long period in which the individual has been symptom-free, another episode may occur. Many people who have suffered a schizophrenic disorder engage in athletics, read newspapers and novels, watch television, obtain college degrees, and relate to their friends and families in much the same way that others do. Long stretches of time can pass without evidence of their distress.

---

shadows; sensory experiences in the absence of appropriate stimuli such as seeing people when none are present; and beliefs sustained in spite of overwhelming contrary evidence such as insisting that one is an historical personage like Napoleon.

The diagnosis of schizophrenia remains controversial today because each of its symptoms is quite similar to the symptoms that may arise from other mental or physical illnesses, traumatic stress, prescription medications, street drugs, and brain injury (Gottesman, 1991). The most recent definition was offered in 1994 in DSM-IV. For a diagnosis of schizophrenia, the symptoms must last for at least six months, and those symptoms must have induced a marked deterioration from the individual's previous level of functioning at work, in social relations, and in self-care. Those are the *temporal* criteria.

FOCUS QUESTIONS

1. What are the substantive criteria used by DSM-IV for a diagnosis of schizophrenia?

2. What are the temporal criteria used by DSM-IV to diagnose schizophrenia?

3. Who is most at risk for schizophrenia?

There are also two *substantive* criteria for the diagnosis: (1) There must be a gross impairment of reality testing, that is, the individual must evaluate the accuracy of his or her thoughts incorrectly and, as a consequence, must make obviously incorrect inferences about reality. Such an impairment in reality testing is called a **psychosis.** Psychoses reflect major disruptions of contact with reality. Minor impairments, such as a tendency to undervalue one's abilities or attractiveness, do not qualify. (2) The disturbance typically must affect several psychological processes, including thought, perception, emotion, communication, and psychomotor behavior. Disturbances of thought characteristically take the form of delusions and hallucinations.

Delusions are false beliefs that resist all argument and are sustained in the face of evidence that normally would be sufficient to destroy them. An individual who believes that he has drunk of the Fountain of Youth and is therefore immortal suffers a delusion.

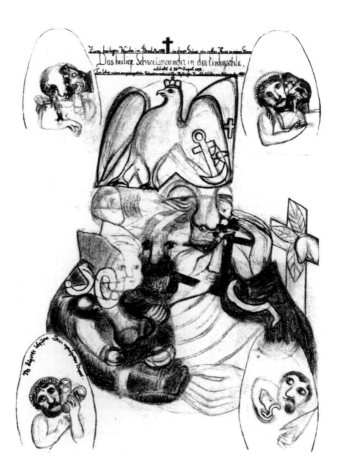

▶ Entitled "Holy Sweat Miracle on the Insole," this drawing was done by a schizophrenic patient suffering from a systematic delusion. According to the patient, the Holy Ghost arose from a "miracle in the insole of the victim ruthlessly sacrificed, disinherited, declared dead, by the secret violent poisoning and brain crushing of assassins possessed by Satan and mentally disturbed. . ."

Hallucinations are false sensory perceptions that have a compelling sense of reality, even in the absence of external stimuli that ordinarily provoke such perceptions. Individuals with schizophrenia hear voices that are not there, or see people or things not really present.

Consider the case of Carl whom we shall follow throughout the chapter:

Carl was twenty-seven years old when he was first admitted to a psychiatric facility. Gangling and intensely shy, he was so incommunicative at the outset that his family had to supply initial information about him. They, it seemed, had been unhappy and uncomfortable with him for quite some time. His father dated the trouble from "sometime in high school." He reported, "Carl turned inward, spent a lot of time alone, had no friends and did no schoolwork." His mother was especially troubled about his untidiness. "He was really an embarrassment to us then, and things haven't improved since. You could never take him anywhere without an argument about washing up. And once he was there, he wouldn't say anything to anyone." His twin sisters, six years younger than Carl, said very little during the family interview, but rather passively agreed with their parents.

One would hardly have guessed from their report that Carl graduated high school in the upper quarter of his class and had gone on to college where he studied engineering for three years. Though he had always been shy, he had had one close friend, John Winters, throughout high school and college. John had been killed in a car accident a year earlier. (Asked about Winters, his father said, "Oh, him. We don't consider him much of anything at all. He didn't go to church either. And he didn't do any schoolwork.")

Carl and John were unusually close. They went through high school together, served in the army at the same time and when discharged, began college together and roomed in the same house. Both left college before graduating, much to the chagrin of Carl's parents, took jobs as machinists in the same firm, and moved into a nearby apartment.

They lived together for three years until John was killed. Two months later the company for which they worked went out of business. John's death left Carl enormously distraught. When the company closed, he found himself without the energy and motivation to look for a job. He moved back home. Disagreements between Carl and his family became more frequent and intense. He became more reclusive, as well as sloppy and bizarre; they, more irritable and isolating. Finally they could bear his behavior no longer and took him to the hospital. He went without any resistance.

After ten days in the hospital, Carl told the psychologist who was working with him: "I am an unreal person. I am made of stone, or else I am made of glass. I am wired precisely wrong, precisely. But you will not find my key. I have tried to lose the key to me. You can look at me closely if you wish, but you can see more from far away."

Shortly thereafter, the psychologist noted that Carl ". . . smiles when he is uncomfortable, and smiles more when in pain. He cries during television comedies. He seems angry when justice is done, frightened when someone compliments him, and roars with laughter on reading that a young child was burned in a tragic fire. He grimaces often. He eats very little but always carries food away."

▲ "I am an unreal person. I am made of stone. . ." *The Song of the Violet*, a painting by Magritte.

FOCUS QUESTIONS

1. What are five subtypes of schizophrenia?
2. What are the salient features of each type of schizophrenia?

After two weeks, the psychologist said to him: "You hide a lot. As you say, you are wired precisely wrong. But why won't you let me see the diagram?"

Carl answered: "Never, ever will you find the lever, the eternalever that will sever me forever with my real, seal, deal, heel. It is not on my shoe, not even on the sole. It walks away."

Incidence and Prevalence of Schizophrenia

Over the course of a lifetime, 1 in 100 people will develop symptoms of schizophrenia. And 1.85 million Americans over age sixteen have had an episode of schizophrenia (Gottesman, 1991). Compared to incidence among the wealthy, the incidence of the schizophrenias among the poor is three times greater, while its prevalence (the proportion of people in the population diagnosed with schizophrenia at any one time) is eight times as high, mainly due to downward social drift (Dohrenwend et al., 1992). It especially affects the urban poor.

The first episode of schizophrenia can occur anytime from puberty and adolescence up through the late forties. The episode, if untreated, may last for as little as a few weeks or may extend for several years. Although many treated schizophrenic patients return to a level of functioning called "social recovery," they may recover only to the bare level tolerated by society or, at worst, recover enough to leave the hospital while continuing in a chronic condition of disability as homeless people, or living in "SROs," or living in geriatric hostels, even though they are young (Gottesman, 1991).

There are substantial sex differences in the time of first occurrence: men are at risk for schizophrenia when they are younger, mainly before age twenty-five, with peak incidence occurring at age twenty-four. Women are at risk after age twenty-five (Lewine, 1981; Zigler and Levine, 1981; Sartorius, Jablensky, Korten, Ernberg, Anker, Cooper, and Day, 1986; Saugstad, 1989). Moreover, these sex differences persist. Women are hospitalized less often than men, and for shorter periods (Goldstein, 1988). The long-term prognosis for women is better than it is for men (Nyman and Jonsson, 1983), perhaps because women seem to have better social skills (Mueser, Bellack, Morrison, and Wade, 1990).

Types of Schizophrenia

Although we speak of schizophrenia as if this is a unitary disorder, the differences between the various types of schizophrenia overwhelm their similarities. The clinical heterogeneity of schizophrenia is so vast that some believe that the schizophrenias may even represent a number of potentially separable diagnostic entities (Fenton and McGlashan, 1991). We will focus on five subtypes of schizophrenia: paranoid, disorganized, catatonic, residual, and undifferentiated (see Table 9–1).

PARANOID SCHIZOPHRENIA

The presence of systematized delusions or extensive auditory hallucinations marks this subtype. The individual with ***paranoid schizophrenia*** suffers delusions of persecution or grandeur that are remarkably systematized and complex, often like the plots of dark mysteries. This complexity provides a schizophrenic individual with a way of understanding his or her experiences—a matter of no small importance to which we will return—while simultaneously making the experiences impenetrable to the outsider.

Beyond experiencing delusions of persecution and/or grandeur, those with paranoid schizophrenia may also experience delusional jealousy, the deep belief that their sexual partner is unfaithful. But despite the intensity of

TABLE 9–1

	THOUGHT AND EMOTION IN THE SCHIZOPHRENIAS	
Type	*Thought*	*Emotion*
Paranoid	Delusions of persecution are complex and coherent	Either intensely emotional or very formal
Disorganized	Less coherent delusions, often centered on own body	Inappropriate and voluble
Catatonic	Delusions often centered on death and destruction	Very inappropriate, either very excited or "frozen" behavior
Residual	No delusions	May be flattened; may show impairment of hygiene or peculiar behavior

their feelings, they seldom display severely disorganized behavior, incoherence, or loose associations. Nor do they experience flat or inappropriate emotion. Rather, their demeanor tends to be extremely formal or quite intense.

DISORGANIZED SCHIZOPHRENIA

The most striking behavioral characteristic of those with ***disorganized schizophrenia*** is apparent silliness and incoherence. They burst into laughter, grimaces, or giggles without an appropriate stimulus. Their behavior is jovial, but quite bizarre and absurd, suggesting extreme sensitivity to internal cues and extreme insensitivity to external ones. Correspondingly, they are voluble, bursting into meaningless conversation for long periods of time.

People with disorganized schizophrenia may experience delusions and hallucinations that tend to be more disorganized and diffused than those experienced by people with paranoid schizophrenia and that often center on their own bodies. For example, people with disorganized schizophrenia may complain that their intestines are congealed or that their brains have been removed. Sometimes, however, the delusions may be quite pleasant and contribute to the silliness of their behavior.

Individuals with disorganized schizophrenia often disregard bathing and grooming. They may not only become incontinent but also frequently eat their own body products, as well as other dirt. Again, a marked insensitivity is found here, similar to their insensitivity to social surroundings.

CATATONIC SCHIZOPHRENIA

The salient feature of ***catatonic schizophrenia*** is motor behavior that is either enormously excited or strikingly frozen, and that may occasionally alternate between the two states. The onset of the disorder is sudden. When behavior is excited, the individual may seem quite agitated, even wild, vigorously resisting all attempts at control, and dangerous to self and others. Affect is quite inappropriate, while agitation is enormously energetic and surprisingly prolonged, commonly yielding only to strong medication.

Stuporous or frozen behavior is also quite striking in this subtype of schizophrenia. Individuals may be entirely immobile, often adopting quite uncomfortable postures and maintaining them for long periods. If someone moves them, they will freeze in a new position. A kind of statuesque "waxy flexibility" is characteristic. After emerging from such a stuporous episode, patients sometimes report that they had been experiencing hallucinations or

▶ Catatonic schizophrenics may be entirely immobile, sometimes maintaining uncomfortable positions for hours.

delusions. These sometimes center on death and destruction, conveying the sense that any movement will provoke an enormous catastrophe.

Negativism—the apparently motiveless resistance to all instructions or attempts to be moved—is a common characteristic of catatonic schizophrenia, so much so that, in addition to the excited and stuporous behaviors, some theorists take negativism to define the category (Maher, 1966). Forbidden to sit, the catatonic individual will sit. Told to sit, the catatonic individual will insist on standing. Today this subtype is rare, possibly because the behavior is being controlled with antipsychotic drugs (Jablensky, Sartorius, Ernberg, Anker, Korten, Cooper, Day, and Bertelsen, 1992).

RESIDUAL SCHIZOPHRENIA

This form of schizophrenia is characterized by the *absence* of prominent symptoms, such as delusions, hallucinations, incoherence, or grossly disorganized behavior. Rather, continuing evidence of the disorder is indicated by the presence of two or more symptoms which, though they are *relatively* minor, are nevertheless very distressing. These symptoms include: (a) marked social isolation or withdrawal; (b) marked impairment in role functioning; (c) very peculiar behavior; (d) serious impairment of personal hygiene and grooming; (e) blunt, flat, or inappropriate emotional expression; (f) odd, magical, or bizarre thinking; (g) unusual perceptual experiences; or (h) apathy or lack of initiative (DSM-IV, 1994).

UNDIFFERENTIATED SCHIZOPHRENIA

This designation is used to categorize individuals who do not otherwise fit neatly into other classifications. It is a diagnosis for disturbed individuals who present evidence of thought disorder, as well as behavioral and affective anomalies, but who are not classifiable under the other subtypes.

SYMPTOMS OF SCHIZOPHRENIA

In the case history presented earlier, Carl exhibited many of the characteristics associated with schizophrenia: lack of interest in life, withdrawal from social activity, seemingly bizarre behavior, incomprehensible communications, and increasing preoccupation with private matters. These symptoms, like many of the others that are common in schizophrenia, involve three areas of psychological functioning: perception, thought, and emotion (see Box 9–2).

The police were asked to hospitalize Miriam because her mother feared that Miriam might harm both of them. When she arrived at the hospital, Miriam claimed that she was fifty-six years old, and that she lived with her seventy-six-year-old "assumed" mother, Esther, and her own twelve-year-old daughter, Alice. Miriam described Esther as a family friend who had given her and Alice a room some years ago, but who had increasingly angered Miriam by acting as a mother and a grandmother, invading her privacy, attacking her in her sleep, and jealously turning Alice against her.

According to Miriam, she and Esther had squabbled on the night that she was admitted to the hospital in a manner that had threatened to turn violent. For her part, Miriam expected to leave the hospital just as soon as the social worker could relocate her and Alice to a "condominium or other suitable environment in which to rear my own child, who is coming of age as a young lady." In the course of her intake interview, she acknowledged a sense of confusion and described a "whooshing" sound in her "cranium" that she felt resulted from fluid in her ear.

Miriam said that she was born in Italy fifty-six years ago. Her "biologic parents," as she put it, were Louise and William, wealthy New Yorkers who brought her up in their country house. She had lived in Europe and in North Africa, and was present in Hiroshima when the atom bomb was dropped, an event that left her with a steel plate in her head and an "atom brain." She lived with Louise and William from 1957 to 1968, after which she had three husbands and seven children. Her youngest, Alice, was fathered by her last husband and was born in 1968, some four years after his death. Asked how this could be, she explained that a "tubal infection" had delayed the baby's conception in a "technical way."

Miriam's mother, however, related quite a different history, which was corroborated by other family members. Miriam was actually thirty, while Esther was fifty-six. When Miriam was seven, her father abandoned the family. The following year, Miriam and her older sister were sent to live with Esther's middle-class Aunt Louise and Uncle William. Miriam was a good student, though she had few friends and mainly kept to herself. When she was seventeen, she became pregnant by a cousin whom she never saw again. Ashamed, she returned to her mother's home to have the baby. Esther cared for them both and took responsibility for rearing her granddaughter, Alice, while Miriam attended night classes in business, doing poorly. Miriam worked for a year and then quit, feeling that people were against her. At that point, she began to hear voices that were commenting on her behavior. Admitted to a psychiatric hospital, she improved on medication. Ultimately, the voices ceased. Once discharged, she lived at home, working occasionally as a secretary.

But all did not go well. Some months after she returned from the hospital, her mother rented an apartment for her. Miriam mismanaged her money, however, and was evicted. The stress proved too much. She became psychotic again, and moved back to her mother's apartment, improving greatly on antipsychotic medication. During the following year, she worked intermittently, but then stopped taking her medication and quit working entirely. At about this point, she began to call her mother "Esther," saying that she was not her real mother. She was friendless, and spent most of her time in her room alone, venturing out only for shopping trips during which she would purchase very expensive clothes. She became unkempt and unwilling to help with household chores. She was belligerent, especially to her mother. She began yelling at imaginary people to leave her alone and not to touch her. The police were summoned on several occasions, but by the time they arrived, Miriam would calm down. On the night she was admitted to the hospital, however, she was clearly out of control, threatening to throw herself and her mother out of the window. She needed to be handcuffed, forcibly.

During her admissions interview, the psychologist characterized her social behavior as calm and appropriate. He noted that while she was obese and rather homely, she was tastefully dressed. Her speech and movement were normal in tempo. Her emotions were constricted. At times she seemed pedantic and haughty, and during her interview with her mother, she seemed to be containing her anger and sarcasm. Her thought processes seemed vague. But the most striking thing about her was her language. She invented new words (technically, these are called neologisms), and found new contexts for old words. Among those neologisms were the following:

"Medicine makes me incognizant. . ."
"I am not correlative enough. . ."
"My mother does not accreditize me. . ."
"The hospital will have my records if they are consortive. . ."
"My cousin was a devasive schizoid. . ."

The intake staff concluded that no medical condition or evidence of substance abuse could account for these symptoms. Rather, the deterioration in functioning over several years, the bizarre delusions (that the conception of her child was delayed several years, that she had been in Hiroshima, that she had a steel plate in her head) and hallucinations (the "whooshing" sounds, the imaginary antagonists) strongly argued for a diagnosis of schizophrenia. Her intense preoccupation with several of these delusions, as well as the absence of disorganized speech or flat affect, suggested that the type of schizophrenia was paranoid.

SOURCE: Modified from the *DSM-IV Casebook,* 1994.

Perceptual Difficulties

Perceptual anomalies often accompany schizophrenia. Patients sometimes report spatial distortions, such that a room may seem much smaller and more constricting than it really is. Controlled laboratory studies indicate that compared to non-schizophrenic individuals, people with schizophrenia are less able to discriminate faces and, more interesting, less able to decode the emotions that are being facially communicated (Feinberg, Rifkin, Schaffer, and Walker, 1986). Moreover, they are less able to estimate sizes accurately (Strauss, Foureman, and Parwatikar, 1974) and less able to judge the passage of time (Petzel and Johnson, 1972).

Generally, upon admission to a hospital, schizophrenic patients report a great number of perceptual difficulties, such as difficulties in understanding others' speech or identifying them, or overly acute auditory perception. These perceptual difficulties may provide a fertile soil for hallucinations. Other people, as well as the self, may be described and apparently experienced as hollow, flat, or two-dimensional. Carl, for example, feels that he is made of steel or of glass.

As we noted earlier, hallucinations are false sensory experiences that have a compelling sense of reality. In fact, PET scans of schizophrenic patients' brains show that the visual cortex is energized during visual hallucinations, and that hallucinations may be related to the failure to activate areas of the brain that are concerned with monitoring inner speech (Buchsbaum and Heier, 1987; McGuire, Silbersweig, Wright, Murray, David, Frackowiak, and Frith, 1995). Hallucinations are often gripping, and they are sometimes terrifying. Everyone knows what a visual hallucination is because everyone dreams. But for most people, dreams occur only during a certain portion of sleep, called "rapid eye movement," or REM sleep. They do not occur when we are awake, presumably because there is a neurotransmitter-mediated mechanism that inhibits them. Some researchers believe that this mechanism has failed in schizophrenic patients who hallucinate (Assad and Shapiro, 1986).

Auditory hallucinations are the most common hallucinations in schizophrenia (Heilbrun, 1993). One finds their origins in ordinary thought, where it is common enough to conduct a private dialogue by imagining oneself talking to others and others talking back. And it is quite common for people actually to talk to themselves, or to talk with deities whose presence

▶ A person with schizophrenia may have visual and auditory hallucinations that have a compelling sense of reality.

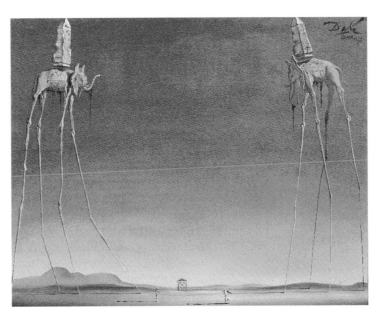

can only be presumed. (The psychiatrist Thomas Szasz [1970] observes that it is quite normal to talk with God, and that when we do so it is called prayer. Only when God responds is it called an hallucination!) Of course, the non-schizophrenic individual has considerably greater control over the internal dialogue than does the schizophrenic individual. The latter, when experiencing an auditory hallucination, does not believe that the voices originate within the self, or that she has the ability to begin or end the talk. The inability to distinguish between external and internal, real and imagined, controllable and imposed, is central to the schizophrenic experience.

Thought Disorders

Insofar as their speech reflects their thought, those with schizophrenia can have a variety of ways in which their thought may be disordered. Sometimes the *process* of thinking is disordered, and sometimes it is the *content* of thought that is peculiar.

THE DISORDERED PROCESS OF THOUGHT

When the process of thinking is disturbed, the train of thought seems moved by the *sound* of words rather than by their meaning. ***Clang associations,*** that is, associations produced by the rhyme of words, such as ". . . my real, seal, deal, heel," abound. There may be ***neologisms,*** new words like "eternalever" that have only private meaning. In addition, the use of vague, overly abstract or overly concrete, repetitive, or stereotyped words can impoverish the content of schizophrenic patients' speech, such that little information is communicated. These communication disturbances seem not to arise from lack of education or low intelligence but apparently from the disorder itself. Finally, some of the most interesting evidence about schizophrenic thought arises from studies of attention and distractibility.

Attentional Deficits   Everyone at one time or another has had trouble paying attention or concentrating, in spite of trying hard to do both. Tired or upset, we find our attention roaming, and we cannot direct it. What we have experienced briefly and in microcosm, people with acute schizophrenia experience profoundly. One patient explains his problem with attention in this way:

> I can't concentrate. It's diversion of attention that troubles me . . . The sounds are coming through to me, but I feel my mind cannot cope with everything. It's difficult to concentrate on any one sound. It's like trying to do two or three different things at one time. (McGhie and Chapman, 1961, p. 104)

Consider for a moment what normal attention involves. We are continuously bombarded by an enormous number of stimuli, much more than our limited channel capacity can absorb. So we need some mechanism for sorting out stimuli to determine which ones will be admitted and which ones barred. That mechanism has been referred to metaphorically as a ***cognitive*** or ***selective filter*** (Broadbent, 1958). Normally, that filter is flexible, sensitive, and sturdy. Sometimes it permits several different stimuli to enter simultaneously, and other times it bars some of those same stimuli. When you drive a car on a clear road, for example, you usually can conduct a conversation with a passenger, often while listening to background music. But when the roads are treacherous, and below you is a several hundred foot drop, attention narrows: it becomes impossible to conduct a conversation and what was formerly soothing music is now quite an irritant. All of the mind's energy, as it were, is directed to one thing and one thing only: driving safely. Everything else is filtered out.

▶ Among schizophrenic individuals, the attentional filter appears to have broken down, so that the mind is invaded by stimuli. The person shown in the sketch seems besieged by a multitude of motifs and patterns.

Among schizophrenic individuals, something seems wrong with the attentional filter, so wrong, in fact, that attentional deficits have long been thought to be at the heart of the thought disorder that characterizes schizophrenia (Kraepelin, 1919; Bleuler, 1924; Chapman and Chapman, 1973; Garmezy, 1977b; Place and Gilmore, 1980). The sense that there is a breakdown of the filter, that the world's hodgepodge has simply invaded the mind, that one cannot control one's attention and therefore one's thoughts or speech, that it is difficult to focus the mind or sustain that focus once it is achieved—all of these experiences are said to be central to schizophrenia. A former patient puts it well:

> Each of us is capable of coping with a large number of stimuli, invading our being through any one of the senses. We could hear every sound within earshot and see every object, line and colour within the field of vision, and so on. It's obvious that we would be incapable of carrying on any of our daily activities if even one-hundredth of all these available stimuli invade us at once. So the mind must have a filter which functions without our conscious thought, sorting stimuli and allowing only those which are relevant to the situation in hand to disturb consciousness. And this filter must be working at maximum efficiency at all times, particularly when a high degree of concentration is required. What happened to me . . . was a breakdown in the filter, and a hodge-podge of unrelated stimuli were distracting me from things which should have had my undivided attention. (MacDonald, 1960, p. 218)

Some people with schizophrenia seem to suffer generalized attentional deficits; they seem not to be attending to anything at all. Others pay too much attention to some stimuli, and not enough to others. For example, someone who is experiencing hallucinations is likely to be hyperattentive to the hallucinations and correspondingly insensitive to external social stimuli.

Overinclusiveness   Schizophrenic thinking generally also tends to be overinclusive (Cameron, 1938, 1947; Chapman and Taylor, 1957; Payne, 1966; Yates, 1966; Marengo, Harrow, and Edell, 1993). *Overinclusiveness* refers to the tendency to form concepts from both relevant and irrelevant information. This thought defect arises from an impaired capacity to resist distracting information, and it strongly suggests a defect in cognitive filtering.

Generally, then, those with schizophrenia may be processing much more information than non-schizophrenic individuals, by virtue of overinclusiveness. Evidence from other research indicates that psychotic states generally tax and deplete information processing, slowing and straining a system that is already quite limited, and impairing performance for tasks that require full use of processing capabilities (Braff and Saccuzzo, 1985; Grove and Andreasen, 1985; Ohman, Nordby, and d'Elia, 1986; Patterson, Spohn, Bogia, and Hayes, 1986; Saccuzzo and Braff, 1986).

Cognitive Distractibility   The notion of a defective filter that gives rise to overinclusiveness in schizophrenic thinking merits further examination. Are there rules that determine what is relevant information and what irrelevant? Of course not. Very likely all of us differ with regard to the kind of information that we attend to and exclude, even on simple tasks. In what ways, then, may the thought and attentional processes of schizophrenics be different from those of normals?

The difference between schizophrenic and non-schizophrenic thinking is unlikely to be a qualitative one, since all of us have associations to stimuli that may or may not prove to be relevant. The difference lies in the number of associative intrusions, the context in which they arise, and in how they are integrated conceptually. Imagine yourself writing a New Year's greeting to a friend. You wish her a happy and healthy year and then refer to the pleasures and sadnesses of the previous year. Compare your greeting to that written by a schizophrenic patient:

> I wish you then a good, happy, joyful, healthy, blessed and fruitful year, and many good wine-years to come, as well as a healthy and good apple-year, and sauerkraut and cabbage and squash and seed year. (Bleuler, 1950, cited in Martin, 1977)

Here, there are many more associations than are found in normal greetings. These associations, moreover, arise in chains that appear to be generated by specific words that seem to distract the patient from his ultimate goal and impair the overall meaning of the greeting. The word fruitful seems to evoke associations to wine, apple, sauerkraut, cabbage, squash, and the like. Moreover, in this context, wine and sauerkraut are not normally the domi-

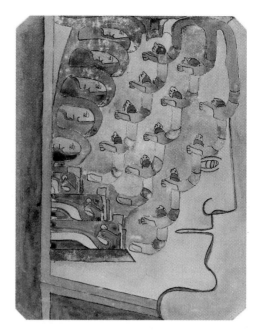

▶ Hospitalized in a mental asylum and labeled as schizophrenic, August Klotz spent his time drawing such pictures as this. Here he depicts a person's hair as a combination of worms, fingers with nails, and heads of caterpillars, describing the drawing through free association: "Worm holes (bath faces), worm paths (pianomusicstickteeth), worm strings (spitbathlife of the archlyregallery-tin-timeler-reflections: ad mothersugarmoon in the sevensaltnose water . . ."

nant associations of the word fruitful; abundance is. But the patient seems to have centered on "fruit" and to have generated associations that are appropriate for that word but not for "fruitfulness."

THE DISORDERED CONTENT OF THOUGHT

Evidence for disordered thought is as commonly found in the content as in the process of thinking. Sometimes the schizophrenic person develops the belief that certain events and people have special significance for him—that television newscasters are speaking to him, for example, or that strangers in the street are looking at him. These beliefs are called *ideas of reference.* When such beliefs become organized into a larger and coherent framework, they are called delusions.

Earlier we noted that a *delusion* is a private theory, deeply held, that often persists despite sound contradictory evidence, and that often does not fit with the individual's level of knowledge or cultural group. These beliefs are so deeply held that psychological lore tells of a delusional patient who was once wired to a lie detector and asked if she were the Virgin Mary. "No," she replied. But the detector indicated that she was lying!

Delusions are common in a variety of psychoses. What differentiates schizophrenic delusions from those of, say, depressives, is their mood incongruence. Unlike depressed patients, whose delusions bear a strong relationship to their moods, schizophrenic patients have delusions that seem incongruent with their present feelings (Winokur, Scharfetter, and Angst, 1985; Farmer, McGuffin, and Gottesman, 1987; Junginger, Barker, and Coe, 1992).

There are five prominent kinds of schizophrenic delusions: delusions of grandeur, delusions of control, delusions of persecution, delusions of reference, and somatic delusions. *Delusions of grandeur* consist of convictions that one is especially important. The belief that one is Jesus Christ or fourth in line to the throne of Denmark would indicate a delusion of grandeur.

Delusions of control are characterized by beliefs that one's thoughts or behaviors are being controlled from without. The patient attributes the source of angry, sexual, or otherwise sinful thoughts to external agents. For example, someone who believes that beings from another universe are giving him instructions is suffering from a delusion of control.

Delusions of persecution consist of fears that individuals, groups, or the government have bad intentions and are "out to get me." The focus of the

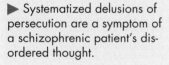

▶ Systematized delusions of persecution are a symptom of a schizophrenic patient's disordered thought.

delusion may be quite specific: a neighbor, one's boss, the FBI, or a rather vague "they." When these delusions combine with hallucinations so that the subject "sees" and "hears" evidence of a plot, they can induce continual panic. Confirmation for these imaginings can often be found in misinterpretations of everyday experience, as shown in the following case:

> Arthur, who had been insecure and shy for as long as he could remember, took a job in a large office. Unsure of his clerical abilities, he worked long and hard at his job, rejecting invitations to have lunch or coffee with his colleagues. Gradually they stopped inviting him, going off merrily by themselves, and returning full of laughter and cheer.
>
> One day Arthur's supervisor found a substantial error in his work. Although it was his first error and the supervisor would easily have forgiven it, Arthur simply could not forget it. It seemed to underscore his own perception of his abilities, a perception that he was quite anxious to conceal. He came to believe that his supervisor knew of other mistakes he had made, and that his colleagues and supervisor were collaboratively examining his work daily. He "knew" that they were excluding him and talking about him, and that their lunchtime laughter was entirely at his expense. Moreover, he felt that their interest in his performance gradually overflowed into an interest in his personal life. When he encountered his co-workers after hours or on the weekend he felt certain that they were following him.
>
> Six weeks after his error had been discovered, he began to "sense" that people had been through his drawers, both at home and in the office. Moreover, certain papers that were necessary for his work were missing, leading him to believe that others were now actively plotting his vocational downfall. Their failure to invite him to lunch was taken as further evidence of the plot.
>
> He became very fearful and disorganized. Continually preoccupied with his troubles, he found it difficult to sleep, eat, or concentrate. His work deteriorated both in quality and in output. When his supervisor finally asked him what was wrong, he blurted out, "You know what's wrong. You and they have made it wrong ever since I came here." He then ran out of the office, never to return. Within the year, Arthur's behavior had so deteriorated that he was hospitalized with the diagnosis of paranoid schizophrenia.

Arthur's sense that others were actively seeking his errors and taking his papers constituted a delusion of persecution. But the continual misinterpretation of others' laughter, as well as their failure to invite him to lunch, constituted the fourth kind of delusion: a **_delusion of reference._** Such delusions rest on the incorrect assumption that the casual remarks or behaviors of others apply to oneself, and can extend to how others act in the street or subway, as well as to the behavior of actors on television. Depending on what they refer to, referential delusions can make a person miserably unhappy, as in the above instance, or quite joyful.

Finally, **_somatic delusions_** are characterized by the unverified belief that something is drastically wrong with one's body. A schizophrenic patient who suffers somatic delusions might believe, for example, that something is rotting inside her body.

▼ The schizophrenic may avoid social contacts, withdrawing behind a blank mask.

Affective Disturbances

Emotions, or affects, are jointly a function of perception, cognition, and physiological arousal. _Perceiving_ a mad dog quickly generates some worrisome _cognitions_ (or thoughts) that in turn generate an _emotion,_ fear. Because schizophrenia arises from disorders of perception and cognition, it follows that there should be affective disturbances also.

For some schizophrenic individuals, affect is characteristically flat or bland. Their voice may be monotonous and their face immobile. They seem entirely unresponsive emotionally. The apparent inability of some schizophrenic individuals to display affect should not, however, be mistaken for absence of *any* affective experience. People with schizophrenia are deeply emotional and deeply responsive to cognitions (Arieti, 1974). But the cognitions that affect them are not the ones that are evocative for most of us, and vice versa. In one respect, the schizophrenic experience is like our own when we visit unfamiliar places. For example, American guests at a Thai wedding, not knowing what all of the symbols mean, would hardly know how to act or what to feel. Shared symbolic meanings allow feelings to arise, be expressed, and be understood by others. Because people with schizophrenia have lost contact with the socially shared domain of symbols and meanings, their affective responses to those stimuli are likely to be blunted.

Sometimes, schizophrenic affect is best characterized as inappropriate. Carl's affect seemed to take that form:

> He smiles when he is uncomfortable, and smiles more when in pain. He cries during television comedies. He seems angry when justice is done . . . and roars with laughter on reading that a young child was burned in a tragic fire.

Affective disturbance can take yet another form: intense ambivalence. A person or situation may arouse opposite feelings simultaneously. Such ambivalence may lead to behavioral paralysis, or to seemingly bizarre attempts to resolve the situation by expressing one affect overwhelmingly and suppressing the other entirely.

Finally, those with schizophrenia often experience recurrent depression, a depression so intense that it may result in suicide. In fact, suicide is the most frequent cause of mortality among people with schizophrenia, far surpassing any other cause (Gottesman, 1991). Because more than 10 percent of those with schizophrenia end their lives through suicide, battling depression is often as important in helping schizophrenic patients as dealing with other symptoms of the schizophrenic disorder.

Meaning in Schizophrenia

Most people who read Carl's words are struck and upset by their incomprehensibility. "I am made of stone," he says, "or else I am made of glass. I am wired precisely wrong, precisely . . ." Anxious communications evoke understanding. If you are told "I'm afraid to go outside," you have little difficulty comprehending the communication, even empathizing with the speaker. But schizophrenic communications often seem to be gibberish; they seem to result in word salads and syllabic stews. Ideas are not transmitted. Unable to understand, people often turn away from those with schizophrenia, treating what they say as part of the symptomatology of the disorder, and not as communication.

Do people with schizophrenia attempt to communicate? Is what they say gibberish? Was Carl saying anything that was meaningful? It appears that he was. But from the listener's viewpoint, it was difficult to find the communication in the thicket of strange verbalization.

> I am an unreal person. . . . I am wired precisely wrong, precisely. But you will not find my key. . . . You can look at me closely if you wish, but you see more from far away.

Carl is hiding. That is, he is trying "precisely" to mislead his observers. When angry, he pretends friendship; when sad, happiness. He wants to maintain privacy, and he may also feel in danger of being exposed. He is, therefore, all the more in need of concealment. When hiding by means of transparent opposites fails—as when he is asked an intrusive question—he hides more energetically. Or, he hides in more bizarre ways: by generating neologisms, by using clang associations to speak—in short, by talking a lot and saying little, by conveying his need to hide in his talk.

The divided self is a self that operates at two levels (Laing, 1965b). On one level, there is the silent self—clearly active but vulnerable and afraid to emerge. There is also a smoke-screen self, a mask, a disguise, designed to conceal and protect that silent self. There is no strong evidence for this two-self view, but many psychologists and psychiatrists who have worked with schizophrenic patients find merit in it. For example, later in his treatment, when his need to hide had abated, Carl had this to say of himself:

> When it's all over, it's hard to remember what you said and how you said it. I wouldn't want to talk that way now even if I could. I was putting people off almost consciously by talking that way. It would have been impossible for me to let on how I really felt. It's still hard. . . . But at the same time, while I was putting you off, I really wanted you to know. But I couldn't come out with it—that was too risky. Sometimes I would say things in a special way, hoping you'd take special notice. When I said I'm not angry. . . . I wagged my hand back and forth, making a "no" sign—telling but not saying that I'm angry. I don't know why I wanted someone to know. After all, I was hiding. But it was a prison I had made for myself. I didn't know how to get out myself. So I kept throwing out little keys, hoping someone would get at the lock.

DIMENSIONS OF SCHIZOPHRENIA

In DSM-IV, patients with schizophrenia are categorized according to their symptoms. But they can also be categorized according to the onset of schizophrenia, the way the symptoms develop, and the ways in which they respond to treatment. The most common clinical dimension for categorizing schizophrenia is acute versus chronic, while a research mode of characterizing this set of disorders is Type I versus Type II.

Acute and Chronic

The distinction between acute and chronic conditions is based on how quickly the symptoms have developed and how long they have been present. *Acute schizophrenia* is characterized by rapid and sudden onset of very florid symptoms. Quite frequently, one can point to a specific precipitating incident that led to the difficulties: a reactive crisis that was precipitated by a severe social or emotional upset, often an upset from which the individual perceives no escape (Zigler and Phillips, 1961; Arieti, 1974). For some schizophrenic individuals, that crisis may involve leaving home, leaving school for a job, their first sexual experience, the loss of a parent or sibling, or marriage. Prior to that upset, their history seems well within normal bounds.

In contrast, *chronic schizophrenia* is characterized by rather gradual and prolonged withdrawal. No single crisis or identifiable stresses trigger the disorder. Rather, early history gives evidence of familial and peer rejection, inferior school and social adjustment, and intense shyness and social withdrawal, such that peer relations are impaired over a long period of time.

In clinical practice, the acute-chronic distinction rests on how many episodes a person has had and how long she has been hospitalized. First

FOCUS QUESTIONS

1. What criteria are used to distinguish between acute and chronic schizophrenia?
2. How does Type I schizophrenia differ from Type II schizophrenia?
3. What are the positive and negative symptoms of schizophrenia?

▶ Representations of irrationality. Left: Plate from *Urizen* by William Blake; right: *Agony-Raving Madness* by Richard Dadd, a nineteenth-century English artist who was hospitalized as a schizophrenic patient after he killed his father.

episodes that result in hospitalization for less than a year, or several episodes that lead to a series of very brief hospitalizations, qualify a person for an acute designation. Hospitalization that extends for more than two years invariably results in a chronic classification. When a person has been hospitalized from roughly eighteen to twenty-eight months, it is difficult to distinguish between acute and chronic conditions. That fact alone largely accounts for the low reliability of the classification.

Type I and Type II

The dimensions of the schizophrenias can be examined not only from the precipitants, but also from the symptoms that are generated, the response to certain kinds of treatment, and the long-term outcome. ***Type I*** schizophrenia is characterized by a sudden onset of disorder in a person who seemed to be functioning well before the episode (Fenton and McGlashan, 1991), and by such symptoms as delusions, hallucinations, and prominent thought disorder. These are called "positive symptoms" because they reflect marked departures from ordinary cognition. Such positive symptoms are reversible. They are thought to arise from a disturbance in brain chemistry, specifically the neurotransmission of dopamine, an important matter that we will examine shortly. And they are thought to be responsive to a class of medications called ***neuroleptics,*** which alter brain chemistry.

The ***Type II*** syndrome is characterized by such symptoms as flat affect, poverty of speech, and loss of volition. These "negative symptoms" are more difficult to define because they reflect the absence or diminution of normal everyday functions, and "absence" is often more difficult to define and more elusive to measure. Negative symptoms are occasionally found in disorders other than schizophrenia. But they are a central and common aspect of schizophrenia and may even represent a distinct pathological process within schizophrenia (McGlashan and Fenton, 1992). Negative symptoms seem much more difficult to reverse than positive symptoms, and they are more closely associated with poor long-term outcome. The symptoms are unrelated to dopamine transmission, but may well be associated with structural changes in the brain, as well as intellectual impairment. Type II symptoms have a much poorer prognosis.

While the schizophrenias have been studied for more than a century, progress in understanding them has been painfully slow. We know less about the origins and treatment of the schizophrenias than we do about some other disorders. In the following sections, we will outline the dominant approaches currently used in the search for the causes and treatment of the schizophrenias.

Knowledge about the origins of schizophrenia is concentrated in four major areas: genetics, neurochemistry, the role of the family, and the role of society. Research on the schizophrenias, like that on other psychological questions, is two-pronged, involving both biological and social questions. Some consider schizophrenia to be rooted in nature; others say that it is the product of social experience. Still others are convinced that nature-nurture interactions are involved, and that these interactions of genetic, biochemical, familial, and social factors predispose a person to schizophrenia (Zubin and Spring, 1977).

The Genetics of Schizophrenia

Various researchers have examined the notion of a genetic vulnerability to schizophrenia. Twin studies, family studies, and adoption studies have demonstrated a strong basis for the genetic component in schizophrenia (Gottesman, 1993).

CONCORDANCE FOR SCHIZOPHRENIA IN TWINS

FOCUS QUESTIONS

1. What is the genetic evidence for schizophrenia?
2. What is the dopamine hypothesis?
3. What brain abnormalities may lead to Type II schizophrenia?
4. What environmental factors may foster schizophrenia?

MZ and DZ Twins We can best understand a possible genetic contribution to behavior by examining the similarities and differences between twins. As we discussed in Chapter 2, twins are of two kinds: identical and fraternal. Both kinds descend from the zygote, the fertilized egg from which all life begins. Identical twins are *monozygotic* (MZ), which means that both individuals developed from a single egg fertilized by a single sperm that divided and produced two individuals. Because all of the cells of these two individuals derived from a single egg, the genes and chromosomes—in short, the heredity—of these individuals is identical. They will, of course, have the identical physical makeup: genes, blood type, and eye color will be the same. There may be differences between them, but such differences will be entirely attributable to different life experiences: one may be thinner because of nutritional differences, or the other may limp because of an accident.

Fraternal, or *dizygotic* (DZ) twins develop from two different eggs and two different sperm. Except for the fact that they are born at the same time, DZ twins are like ordinary siblings. Their heredity makeup is quite different. They may be of different gender; they may have different eye color. They have different fingerprints. They can be accurately distinguished from MZ twins on the basis of these characteristics alone, and certainty can be increased by DNA "fingerprinting" as used in paternity testing or by the FBI.

The logic of a genetic study is really quite simple: if all other things are equal, the more similar people are in their genetic makeup, the more traits they will have in common if those traits are genetically influenced. MZ twins should resemble each other more than DZ twins or ordinary siblings. And DZ twins and siblings should have more in common than unrelated individuals. If both members of a twin set have a trait in common, we say that that twin set is *concordant* for that particular trait. If, however, one member has the trait and one does not, we call the twin set **discordant** for the trait. For quantitative differences, correlations are examined.

MZ twins are wholly identical in their genes and chromosomes. If the traits that subsequently develop are entirely determined by their genetic makeup, there should be 100 percent concordance. If one twin has the trait, the other should have it too. Anything less than 100 percent concordance (but more than the percentage found in DZ twins) will suggest that heredity *influences,* but does not actually determine, the presence of the trait. What is more, that influence depends on the assumption that all other possible influences, such as nutrition, physical health, and psychological environment, are themselves about the same. If one twin's physical and social environment diverges from the other's, that difference could explain any discrepancy between the pair.

Linking Genetics and Schizophrenia   Although genetic studies of schizophrenia have been conducted for over seventy-five years, Irving Gottesman and James Shields (1972) conducted one of the very few studies that were planned in advance. From 1948 through 1964, every patient admitted for treatment to the psychiatric unit at the Maudsley and Bethlem Royal Hospital in London was routinely asked if he or she was a twin. Over these sixteen years, the investigators located 55 patients (out of more than 45,000 admitted) who were twins and whose twin could be located and would cooperate in the study. For analytic purposes, the twin who was first seen at the psychiatric clinic is called the **index case** or **proband.** The other twin, who will be examined for the presence or absence of schizophrenia, is called the **co-twin.**

Of these fifty-five sets of twins, it was determined that twenty-two were MZ twins and thirty-three were DZ twins. The twins ranged in age from nineteen to sixty-four, with a median age of thirty-seven initially. Concordance for schizophrenia, where it was already present in the co-twin at the time the proband was admitted to the hospital, could of course be determined immediately. Discordant pairs were followed for at least thirteen and as long as twenty-six years to determine if schizophrenia subsequently developed in the co-twin (Gottesman, McGuffin, and Farmer, 1987).

Such a lengthy study examines more than simple diagnosis. In analyzing an enormous variety of psychological, medical, and social data for each twin pair, Gottesman and Shields observed two findings of special relevance to our own investigation into the genetic causes of schizophrenia. First, they found strict concordance when the proband's co-twin had been hospitalized and diagnosed with schizophrenia: 50 percent of MZ twins and 9 percent of DZ twins were concordant for schizophrenia, a ratio of roughly 4:1. Despite the small sample, this is a very significant finding, one consistent with other genetic studies.

Second, using length of hospitalization to indicate severity of schizophrenia, Gottesman and Shields found substantial differences in the rates of concordance between MZ twins whose probands had been hospitalized for more than two years and those whose probands had been hospitalized for less than two years. Hospitalization for more than two years is critical to a diagnosis of chronic schizophrenia. It is therefore of enormous interest that concordance rates rose to 77 percent in this sample. For those who were hospitalized less than two years (very likely people with acute, reactive schizophrenia), the concordance rate was only 27 percent (Gottesman and Shields, 1972). What this finding means practically is that severity of schizophrenia in a proband also increases the chances that the co-twin will become disabled (Torrey, 1992).

The evidence from the many studies summarized in Table 9–2 is strong: concordance rates for MZ twins are higher than they are for DZ twins;

TABLE 9-2

	MZ		DZ	
Study	Pairs	Rate	Pairs	Rate
Finland 1963, 1971	17	35	20	13
Norway 1967	55	45	90	15
Denmark 1973	21	56	41	27
United Kingdom 1966, 1987	22	58	33	15
Norway 1991	31	48	28	4
United States 1969, 1983	164	31	268	6
Pooled concordance (excluding U.S.)				
Median	146	48	212	15
Weighted mean		48		16
Pooled concordance (all studies)				
Median	310	46	480	14
Weighted mean		39		10

CONCORDANCE RATES FOR SCHIZOPHRENIA IN TWIN STUDIES

SOURCE: Adapted from Gottesman, 1991.

concordance rates for DZ twins are higher than the rate for unrelated persons in the general population (about 1 percent). Concordance, however, is never 100 percent because the genetic component of schizophrenia does not guarantee occurrence. Genetics only makes one vulnerable to schizophrenia; it does not guarantee that it will occur. Indeed, 89 percent of people diagnosed with schizophrenia have no known relative who has schizophrenia (Cromwell, 1993).

CONCORDANCE FOR SCHIZOPHRENIA IN FAMILIES

Family studies begin from the same premise as twin studies: individuals who have a similar heredity are more likely to possess a particular trait than those who are unrelated. Parents and siblings of a schizophrenic proband should be more likely to have or to develop schizophrenia than remote relatives, who in turn are more prone to schizophrenia than are those who are not related. The data from more than a dozen studies support this conclusion (Rosenthal, 1970a). As can be seen in Figure 9–1, the likelihood that ordinary siblings of a proband will also have schizophrenia is about 9 percent—much higher than the 1 percent one finds among the general population, but much lower than the 48 percent we find among identical twins. Similarly, the child of two schizophrenic parents has about a 46 percent chance of developing schizophrenia. The evidence clearly supports genetic vulnerability—but only vulnerability. In no study do concordance and risk rise to 100 percent. Once again, it takes more than genetic vulnerability to produce schizophrenia.

BUT IS IT REALLY GENETIC?

We have assumed that if all other things are equal, the more similar people are in their genetic makeup, the more traits they will have in common if those traits are genetically influenced. But are all other things equal? Consider the finding that children of two schizophrenic parents stand a 46 percent chance of developing schizophrenia themselves. Is that because they share a common gene pool, or is it because schizophrenic parents may be terrible parents, fully capable of inducing schizophrenia in their children, regardless of their common gene pool? Or consider again the twin studies. We know that MZ twins share a unique environment with each other. They tend to mature and to develop language more slowly than other children. They

FIGURE 9–1

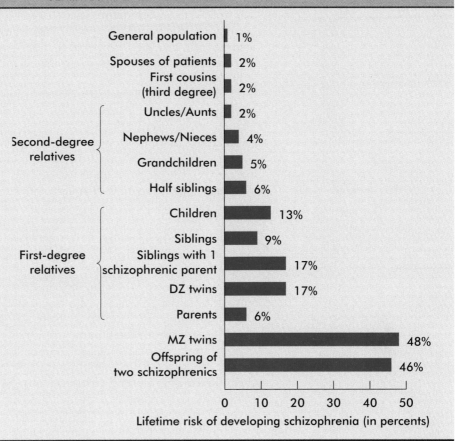

GENETICS AND SCHIZOPHRENIA

The graph shows risk estimates for developing schizophrenia as a function of relationship to a schizophrenic proband (SOURCE: Gottesman, 1991, p. 96).

tend to be mistaken for one another and therefore to suffer identity problems of indeterminate magnitude. Could not these environmental problems, rather than genetics, be a major factor in their eventual schizophrenia?

Behavior geneticists have responded to these questions in three ways. First, they have tried to locate probands and co-siblings who have been reared apart. Studies of this kind are called **adoption studies.** Second, they have conducted studies of people who are presumed to be at risk for schizophrenia because other members of their families have schizophrenia. These high-risk studies seek to map the development of behavior before schizophrenia occurs, in the hope of relating causative, correlative, and especially preventive factors. Finally, there are studies of non-schizophrenic twins which bear on this question.

Adoption Studies Leonard Heston (1966) studied forty-seven children of schizophrenic mothers who had been placed in adoptive or foster homes less than one month after birth. He compared them to fifty control offspring. The environments for both groups were similar, and they were not environments produced by the schizophrenic mothers. All forty-seven offspring took intelligence tests and psychological tests. Each was interviewed by a psychiatrist. Then two other psychiatrists not previously involved in the experiment came in to evaluate the offspring's dossiers and, if necessary, to diagnose them. Neither psychiatrist knew the offspring's origins, or the nature of the mothers' illness. Even so, the two evaluating psychiatrists diagnosed five of the children of schizophrenic mothers as having schizophrenia. None of those from the control group were so diagnosed. Moreover, thirty-seven of the forty-seven children of schizophrenic mothers were given some kind of psychiatric diagnosis, as compared with nine of the fifty offspring from the control group. Considering that the environments were matched for both groups and the very early age at which the children were placed, the much higher incidence of disordered behavior among the children of schizophrenic mothers points to a strong genetic component in the origins of schizophrenia.

Seymour Kety, David Rosenthal, Paul Wender, and Fini Schulsinger (1968) in the Copenhagen Adoption Study examined the records of all children born between 1924 and 1947 in Copenhagen, Denmark, who were adopted when quite young. From this large group, they selected those adoptees who were subsequently admitted to a psychiatric hospital and diagnosed as having schizophrenia. Thirty-three such probands were compared with a control group drawn from the same population but lacking any psychiatric history. The family histories of biological (but not adoptive) relatives of the schizophrenic index cases revealed a higher incidence of disturbance (which included schizophrenia, uncertain schizophrenia, and inadequate personality) than did those of the controls (8.7 percent to 1.9 percent). A replication in Finland of the Copenhagen Adoption Study yielded roughly the same findings, and provided further evidence for a genetic vulnerability to schizophrenia (Tienari, 1991). Thus, genes contribute to *vulnerability* to schizophrenia, although they do not in themselves completely explain its presence.

Although most schizophrenia researchers agree that genetics remains a central etiologic factor in schizophrenia, debate continues regarding the magnitude of the genetic contribution. Torrey, for example, tends to minimize the contribution of genetics. He reviewed concordance rates for eight twin studies of schizophrenia which used representative samples of twins and determined whether they were MZ or DZ twins with reasonable certainty through using such techniques as DNA and red cell typing. (A representative sample is one that, for example, uses a population in which birth registers have recorded every twin.) The eight studies showed a pairwise concordance rate for schizophrenia that is 28 percent for MZ twins and 6 percent for DZ twins. The pairwise concordance rates support a lower genetic contribution to schizophrenia (Torrey, 1992). Others set those estimates much higher (Gottesman, 1991; McGue, 1992).

The Twin Factor   MZ twins grow up sharing a common environment that often treats them as if they were a single person. They are often dressed alike, confused for one another, compared to one another, and generally scrutinized more closely than are DZ twins or mere siblings. These experiences collectively create a distinct environment for MZ twins in addition to their identical genetic makeup. Could that environment account for the greater probability of schizophrenia in the co-twin when the proband has schizophrenia? Probably not. If the special environment and psychological factors common to MZ twins were the factors that produced schizophrenia, then the rate of schizophrenia among MZ twins would be higher than that of the general population. But that is not the case. MZ twins are not more likely to develop schizophrenia than are non-twins. A co-twin is more likely to develop schizophrenia if, and only if, the proband has schizophrenia, and not otherwise (Rosenthal, 1970b). Thus, the identical environment in which MZ twins develop has no bearing on whether the twins develop schizophrenia.

Children at Risk for Schizophrenia   At-risk studies are important because they can identify those children who are most likely to develop schizophrenia, and the investigators can then observe the effects of specific influences on such children in order to reduce the incidence of schizophrenia. At-risk children are more vulnerable to schizophrenia than are other children. Their vulnerability may derive from several factors. Often, at-risk children are defined as those with schizophrenic parents or siblings. As we will see later, other factors also make children vulnerable; these are factors that relate to environment and to social class: poverty, broken homes, families where the **_double-bind_** reigns. (This latter hypothesis, formulated by Gregory Bateson, refers to two mutually exclusive messages from one person, which can neither be satisfied nor avoided.) All of these sources contribute to a child's vulnerability, or high risk for schizophrenia, and all can be studied in an at-risk program (Watt, Anthony, Wynne, and Rolf, 1984).

Perhaps the most extensive at-risk study of schizophrenia was a Danish study begun in 1962 by Sarnoff Mednick and Fini Schulsinger (Mednick, Cudeck, Griffith, Talovic, and Schulsinger, 1984; Parnas, Cannon, Jacobsen, Schulsinger, Schulsinger, and Mednick, 1993). These investigators isolated 207 subjects who were at significant risk for schizophrenia (they had schizophrenic mothers) and 104 low-risk people who were matched on such variables as age, gender, years of education, father's occupation, and place of residence. When the study began, the average age of the subjects was about fifteen years, and none of them were diagnosed with schizophrenia. Ten years later, 17 of the high-risk (and only 1 of the low-risk) people were diagnosed with schizophrenia. The mothers of these schizophrenic individuals were distinguished from the rest of the sample on a variety of characteristics. Most striking among these were the facts that the mothers' own psychotic episodes were precipitated by the childbirth, and that more generally, the mothers were unstable in their relations with men, and were not emotionally attached to the father when pregnancy occurred. Moreover, the fathers themselves were unstable at work and often addicted to drugs or alcohol (Talovic, Mednick, Schulsinger, and Falloon, 1981). The mothers of these disturbed offspring, moreover, were quite temperamental and tended to direct their emotions outward in highly aggressive forms (Mednick, 1973).

Although the Danish at-risk study confirms the genetic hypothesis, its primary importance resides in understanding the influence of nongenetic factors—nutrition, psychophysiology, family, social and academic history, personal skills and liabilities—on the development of schizophrenia. Moreover, similar studies may point to other, positive factors that may be derived from a genetic predisposition to schizophrenia; the genes that produce schizophrenia in some people may also lead to creativity (see Box 9–3). Ultimately, it is hoped that at-risk studies will suggest biological and social interventions that can break the chain that leads to schizophrenia, and enable more of those with a genetic predisposition to schizophrenia to achieve creative solutions to problems rather than the debilitating, negative manifestations of schizophrenic symptoms.

The Biology of the Schizophrenias

Over the past decade, enormous progress has been made in understanding the biology of the schizophrenias. Two lines of research have been particularly illuminating. The first has looked at irregularities in the neurochemistry of the schizophrenias, the second at differences in brain structure between schizophrenic and non-schizophrenic individuals. Both lines of investigation have important consequences for understanding Type I and Type II schizophrenia.

THE NEUROCHEMISTRY OF THE SCHIZOPHRENIAS: THE DOPAMINE HYPOTHESIS

The idea that there may be biochemical antecedents to schizophrenia is not new. Researchers have frequently tried to find the biochemical differences

BOX 9–3 ━━━━━━━━━━━━━━━━━━━━━━━━━━━━━━ IN THE CLINICIAN'S OFFICE

SCHIZOPHRENIA AND CREATIVITY

John Nash was a child prodigy. No, he was not a straight A student (prodigies rarely are). But he read constantly, played chess, whistled entire melodies from Bach, invented things, and conducted experiments. He graduated high school at seventeen, went on to Carnegie Tech (now known as Carnegie Mellon), where he majored in mathematics, and graduated in three years. He went to Princeton University for graduate work in mathematics, and once again, showed himself to be brilliant. He took his Ph.D on his twenty-second birthday. His Ph.D. thesis was a mere twenty-seven pages, but it was long enough for him to win the Nobel Prize in Economics in 1994.

Between the time he took his Ph.D. and the day he won the Nobel Prize, however, Nash's life had not been sweet at all. By the time he was thirty—by then, teaching at M.I.T., married, and soon to become a father—Nash had succumbed to paranoid schizophrenia. His speech rambled and became disjointed. His lectures no longer made sense. He resigned from M.I.T. and went to Europe, where he traveled from city to city. He feared he was being spied upon and pursued. He tried to give up his U.S. citizenship. He was hospitalized many times. Nothing availed. He and his wife were divorced, although he remained in their Princeton home, and she continued to support him and their child.

As difficult and peculiar as his behavior seemed, Nash was ultimately more at home in Princeton, and especially among its mathematicians, than he might have been anywhere else in the world. According to Nash's sister, "Being in Princeton was good for him. In a place like Princeton, if you act strange, you're special. In Roanoke [where Nash grew up], if you act strange, you're just different. They didn't know who he was here."

Then, some two decades after paranoid schizophrenia had descended upon him as suddenly as a terrible wind, John Nash's symptoms remitted. And much as we do not understand why he developed schizophrenia in the first place, we don't understand his remission, for neither drugs nor treatment appeared to have made a difference.

Various studies seem to indicate that there may be a relationship between schizophrenia and creativity. This may be true in some people who later develop schizophrenia, as did John Nash, or in some people who are related to those with schizophrenia but do not have schizophrenia themselves. Reporting on a follow-up study of children born to schizophrenic mothers and placed in adoptive or foster homes shortly after birth, Leonard Heston and Duane Denney noted that the children who did not develop schizophrenia were more "spontaneous, had more colorful life histories, held more creative jobs, and followed the more imaginative hobbies. . . ." than non-schizophrenic individuals (Heston and Denney, 1968, p. 371). Moreover, another study reported that non-paranoid schizophrenic patients scored higher on a test of creativity than either paranoid schizophrenic individuals or non-paranoid controls (Keefe and Magaro, 1980; Magaro, 1981).

A study of genetics and schizophrenics in Iceland by Karlsson (1972) further supports the connection between creativity and schizophrenia. Karlsson observed that the "genetic carriers" of schizophrenia often exhibit "unusual ability" and display "a superior capacity for associative thinking" (Karlsson, 1972, p. 61). Fascinated by this finding, Karlsson proposed that society may even depend upon "persons with a schizophrenic constitution" for its social and scientific progress. He remarked that a disproportionate number of the most creative people in philosophy, physics, music, literature, mathematics, and the fine arts often developed psychiatric disorders. *Superphrenic* is Karlsson's term for these people who are both related to schizophrenic individuals and recognizably outstanding in politics, science, and the arts.

SOURCE: Adapted from Sylvia Nasar, The Lost Years of a Nobel Laureate, *New York Times*, November 13, 1994.

---

between schizophrenic and non-schizophrenic individuals, but with little luck. Reports of vast differences in the chemistry of blood or urine of non-schizophrenic individuals as opposed to hospitalized schizophrenic patients have turned out merely to reflect differences in the diets of hospitalized and non-hospitalized people, or bad lab technique, or the absence of control groups, or experimenter bias.

More recently, the strategy has shifted. Instead of looking for biochemical substances that differentiate schizophrenic from non-schizophrenic individuals, scientists are now searching for abnormalities in neurochemical functioning. Specifically, they are looking at special chemicals in the brain, called **neurotransmitters.** The way these chemicals function, and how increases or decreases in the available quantities of neurotransmitters affect behavior and perhaps influence the development of schizophrenia—these are presently the dominant research concerns. By focusing on these chemicals and by drawing connections between schizophrenia, amphetamine psychosis, and Parkinson's disease, scientists have constructed what is now called the ***dopamine hypothesis*** (as we first mentioned in Chapter 2).

First, consider the similarities between the symptoms of schizophrenia and the effects of the amphetamines, or "speed." Large doses of amphetamines can create a psychosis, with symptoms indistinguishable from those of acute paranoid schizophrenia. Patients suffering amphetamine psychosis have, in fact, been wrongly diagnosed as having schizophrenia (Snyder, 1974b). What is more, a very low dose of a drug related to the amphetamines, methylphenidate, will exacerbate the symptoms of schizophrenia almost immediately: people with paranoid schizophrenia, for example, become increasingly paranoid. Finally, the drugs most helpful in treating the symptoms of schizophrenia—the neuroleptics—are also the best antidotes for amphetamine psychosis and for the exacerbated schizophrenic symptoms induced by amphetamines (Snyder, 1981; Snyder, Banerjee, Yamamura, and Greenberg, 1974).

These neuroleptics produce varying effects on schizophrenia. One class of neuroleptic, the phenothiazines, blocks the brain's receptors for a neurotransmitter called dopamine. Neurotransmitters are chemicals that facilitate the transmission of electrical impulses between the brain's nerve endings. There are perhaps twenty different neurotransmitters, of which dopamine is particularly important. Since the phenothiazines both decrease the amount of available dopamine and also relieve the symptoms of schizophrenia, it seems to follow that schizophrenia results from excess dopamine. These findings have opened the door for the dopamine hypothesis, with the connection between Parkinson's disease and dopamine offering more support for the hypothesis.

Characterized by growing stiffness in the arms and legs, Parkinson's disease is particularly noticeable because it renders facial expressions flat and dull, and causes tremors, especially in the hands. It happens that the main pathway in the brain for dopamine is an area that helps coordinate motor activity. This pathway deteriorates in Parkinson's disease, thus explaining the patient's inability to move and tendency to shake. When victims of Parkinson's disease are treated with L-DOPA, a drug that increases the amount of dopamine available in the brain, their symptoms are relieved. Curiously, when individuals suffering from schizophrenia are treated with heavy doses of phenothiazines for a prolonged period of time, they display symptoms very much like those associated with Parkinson's disease. They, too, develop motor difficulties: they have tremors in their extremities and problems in controlling their body movements in general. While there is no direct proof of a connection, it is thus possible that the neurotransmitter, dopamine, is involved in schizophrenia. In Parkinson's disease, L-DOPA is given to overcome the insufficiency of dopamine. In schizophrenia, the phenothiazines seem to calm disordered behavior by reducing the amount of dopamine available in the brain. Over time, however, they seem to cause an insufficiency of dopamine, and bring about symptoms of Parkinson's disease. That an excess of dopamine is one of the roots of schizophrenia has been shown in the PET (Positron Emission Tomography) scans, which show that there is increased dopamine receptor density in a schizophrenic patient's brain, and which suggest that an excess of cells sensitive to dopamine may be the crucial biochemical deficit in schizophrenia.

There is now mounting evidence that confirms the dopamine hypothesis. Post-mortem examination of the brains of schizophrenic patients confirms what PET scans reveal: a marked increase in the number of dopamine receptor sites. While the precise cause of this increase is not yet known, it is clearly *not* the result of drug treatment. Patients who had been drug-free for at least a year before death also showed a greater number of dopamine receptors (Crow, 1980, 1982; Mackay, 1980).

Increased production of dopamine was once thought to be characteristic of all forms of schizophrenia. But recent thinking limits the dopamine hypothesis to Type I schizophrenia (see the discussion of Types I and II on p. 285). Type I is associated with the dramatic positive symptoms of the disorder: delusions, hallucinations, and thought disorders. Those are the symptoms that are alleviated by the phenothiazines, which decrease the amount of dopamine in the brain. Type II schizophrenia is characterized by the "negative" or deficit symptoms of the disorder, such as flat affect, loss of motivation, and poverty of speech. Those symptoms seem unrelated to dopamine and are unaffected by the phenothiazines. Indeed, they seem presently to have no consistent neuroendocrinological basis (Lieberman and Koreen, 1993). Instead, they seem to arise from a wholly different source—peculiarly abnormal structures in the brain.

BRAIN STRUCTURE IN SCHIZOPHRENICS

Over the past two decades there has been growing evidence that schizophrenic patients who manifest Type II symptoms—particularly flat emotion, loss of motivation, and poverty of speech—may be suffering from one or several abnormalities in the structure of the brain. So far, three kinds of abnormalities seem to have been located. The first relates to the ***frontal lobes,*** which are known to be important in attention, motivation, and in planning and organizing behavior. People with Type II schizophrenia may have smaller frontal lobes (as well as smaller cerebrums and craniums) than do non-schizophrenic individuals (Andreasen, Nasrallah, Dunn, Olson, Grove, Ehrhardt, Coffman, and Crossett, 1986). PET scans and other cerebral blood flow studies have confirmed considerably reduced function, as well as decreased metabolism, in the frontal regions of the brains of schizophrenic patients (Buchsbaum, 1990), as well as reduced thalamic activity and size (Buchsbaum, Someya, Teng, Abel, Chin, Najafi, Heier, Wu, and Bunney, 1996). Disturbances in gait, posture, and eye movements, which are important neurological signs in schizophrenia, often arise from frontal-lobe dysfunction (Weinberger, 1988; Robbins, 1990; Sweeney, Haas, and Li, 1992). Indeed, such a high proportion of schizophrenic patients show abnormalities in certain kinds of eye movements, that this has become a genetic marker for schizophrenia (Clementz, Sweeney, Hirt, and Haas, 1990; Iacono, Moreau, Beiser, Fleming, and Lin, 1992). Finally,

▶ PET scans showing the brain of a non-schizophrenic person (left) and the brain of a patient with schizophrenia (right). Red indicates greatest metabolic activity. In the schizophrenic patient, there is low activity in the frontal lobes and basal ganglia.

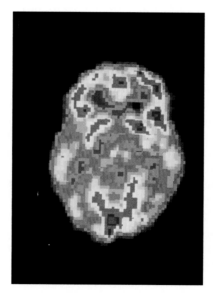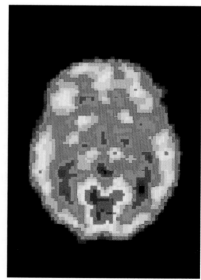

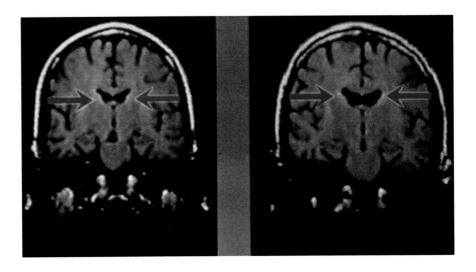

▶ MRIs of the brains of non-schizophrenic and schizophrenic twins have revealed that the ventricles (cavities filled with fluid) of schizophrenic patients (indicated in the right MRI) are larger than those of non-schizophrenic individuals (indicated in the left MRI).

the reduction of memory capacity in schizophrenia has been found to be consistent with frontal-lobe abnormalities (Gold, Randolph, Carpenter, Goldberg, and Weinberger, 1992).

The second type of abnormality relates to the size and proportion of the **brain ventricles.** Ventricles are cavities in the brain, spaces that are filled with fluid. The ventricles of schizophrenic patients are substantially larger than those of non-schizophrenic people (Nopoulos, Torres, Flaum, Andreasen, Ehrhardt, and Yuh, 1995). Moreover, the ventricles on the left side of the schizophrenic brain appear to be substantially larger than those on the right side (Losonczy et al., 1986). Ventricular enlargement suggests a process of deterioration or atrophy in brain tissue whose precise effects can only be speculated upon (Brown, Colter, Corsellis, Crow, Frith, Jagoe, Johnstone, and Marsh, 1986; Bogerts, 1993; Gur, Mozley, Shtasel, Cannon, Gallacher, Turetsky, Grossman, and Gur, 1994). But whether such atrophy is the cause or the consequence of schizophrenia is still an open question (Suddath, Christison, Torrey, Casanova, and Weinberger, 1990).

Finally, there is mounting evidence of **neuronal degeneration,** especially in the cortex of schizophrenic patients (Benes, Davidson, and Bird, 1986), as well as evidence for decreased blood flow in that region (Weinberger, Berman, and Zec, 1986).

While the evidence for differences in brain structure mounts daily, just how those differences are related to schizophrenic symptoms—especially Type II symptoms—remains unclear. But the emerging picture seems to support the view that there are at least two forms of schizophrenia. Type I results from difficulties in **neurotransmission,** and particularly from an overabundance of dopamine receptors. That form of schizophrenia seems to be quite responsive to neuroleptic medications. Type II schizophrenia, on the other hand, results from abnormalities in **brain anatomy,** and is largely unaffected by neuroleptic treatment.

The Schizophrenogenic Family

The above evidence convinces us that heredity and biology play a role in the development of schizophrenia. But other factors—family and society—contribute in as yet unknown ways and proportions to one's vulnerability to schizophrenia. Heredity tells us about a biological component of schizophrenia. It can suggest, perhaps, that an individual will be prone to attentional difficulties, to overinclusive thinking, to delusions, and to hallucinations. But heredity does not assure that a propensity will become a certainty.

Nor does heredity specify the content of disordered thought and the social reaction it will elicit. In all likelihood, the family plays some role in the development of schizophrenia, although establishing the nature of its contribution with precision is difficult. Families that seem to foster the emergence of schizophrenia in one or more family members are called *schizophrenogenic families.* Such families may be disordered in the way they communicate and in the family structure itself.

Since schizophrenia is centrally marked by a thought disorder and since we are examining the families from which schizophrenic individuals come, it follows that we should look at communication within the family as a correlate or cause of such thought disorder. Many researchers believe that the parents of those diagnosed with schizophrenia distort their children's perceptions in two principal ways: by encouraging them to doubt their own feelings, perceptions, and experiences and by catching them in double-binds, wherein the parent sends out contradictory messages to which there is no appropriate response (Bateson, Jackson, Haley, and Weakland, 1956; Laing and Esterson, 1964). Whatever one calls it, this "effort to drive the other person crazy" (Searles, 1959) involves distorting the child's reality both verbally and nonverbally.

Investigations of familial influences have centered mainly on expressed emotion—attitudes of cynicism, hostility, or overinvolvement expressed by an important relative toward a schizophrenic person. When criticism and hostility are directed at an offspring, the offspring is more likely to develop the spectrum of symptoms associated with schizophrenia (Rodnick, Goldstein, Lewis, and Doane, 1984). Correspondingly, living in an environment where expressed emotion is low calms those already diagnosed with schizophrenia and contributes to their remission (Falloon, 1988). Moreover, the rate of relapse among those who are returning home after hospitalization for a schizophrenic episode is more than twice as high among people who are returning to families that are high rather than low in expressed emotion (Goldstein, Strachan, and Wynne, 1994; Miklowitz, 1994).

Society and Schizophrenia

Whether we are schizophrenic or non-schizophrenic, we are all members of a society that, in many ways, exerts its influence upon us. In approaching any mental disorder, scientists will take society into account.

Schizophrenia can afflict anyone, in any society or socioeconomic class. But it happens that, particularly in large urban areas, rates of mental disturbance, and especially of schizophrenia, are significantly and inversely related to social class: the lower the class, the higher the rate of schizophrenia (see Figure 9–2). The larger the city, the more powerful the relationship; in small cities, the relationship between schizophrenia and social class disappears (Clausen and Kohn, 1959). In the United States, the highest rates of schizophrenia occur in the centers of cities that, in turn, are inhabited by people of lower socioeconomic status (Faris and Dunham, 1939; Hollingshead and Redlich, 1958; Srole, Langner, Michael, Opler, and Rennie, 1962; Saugstad, 1989). Similar findings relate to occupation: rates of schizophrenia are highest in the lowest status occupations (Clark, 1948). Moreover, some Finnish researchers have found that among subjects with schizophrenia there is a constant downward drift in socioeconomic status, especially to unemployment, as well as a marked decline from parents' social status (Aro, Aro, and Keskimaki, 1995).

Not only social class but also culture affects rates of schizophrenia. Although the incidence of schizophrenia throughout the world is about the

FIGURE 9–2

THE PREVALENCE OF SCHIZOPHRENIA IN A CITY

In this map of Chicago in 1934, the center zone is the business and amusement section, which is uninhabited, except for transients and vagabonds. Surrounding the center, there is a slum area, largely made up of unskilled workers of low socioeconomic status, and having the highest rate of schizophrenia. The next circle is occupied by skilled workers and has a lower rate of schizophrenia than the slum. The next zone is inhabited by middle-class and upper-middle-class people. The last circle is populated by upper-middle-class commuters and shows the lowest rate of schizophrenia. (SOURCE: Gleitman, 1991, p. 762, based on data from Faris and Dunham, 1939)

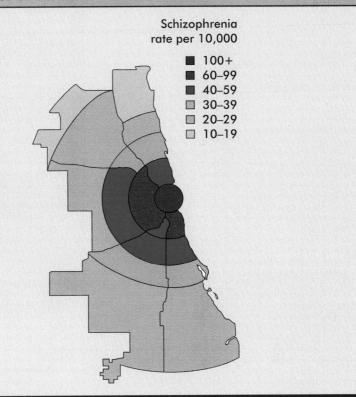

Schizophrenia
rate per 10,000

■ 100+
■ 60–99
■ 40–59
□ 30–39
□ 20–29
□ 10–19

same—1 percent—culture may affect the *outcome* of schizophrenia. Across more than two decades, the World Health Organization has been conducting cross-cultural epidemiological studies of a variety of disorders, including schizophrenia. Its most recent collaborative study examined the determinants of severe mental disorders in ten countries. Well over thirteen hundred patients were examined, the majority of whom came from urban areas and from socioeconomic circumstances that are best described as average. And while the study confirmed the ubiquitousness of schizophrenia and its similar clinical features across cultures, it provided quite a surprise with regard to outcome, with schizophrenic individuals from *developing* nations (for example, India, China) faring far better than those from developed countries (for example, the United States, Great Britain). The symptoms of 63 percent of participants in developing countries remitted over the course of the two-year follow-up, while those of only 37 percent in developed nations did so. Thirty-eight percent of those in developing nations were wholly symptom-free during much of the course of the follow-up, while only 22 percent of those in developed countries were symptom-free. Finally, 38 percent of those from developed countries fell into the category termed "worst possible outcome," while only 22 percent of those from developing nations were in that category (Sartorius, Jablensky, Korten, Ernberg, Anker, Cooper, and Day, 1986; Jablensky, Sartorius, Ernberg, Anker, Korten, Cooper, Day, and Bertelsen, 1992).

Society's values are often contradictory, and many people may find these contradictions difficult, even impossible, to live with. This may be especially true in developed countries, certainly in inner cities, where violence and poverty are facts of life. Life events can trigger schizophrenic episodes, and the modern world may cause people to experience a greater number of stressful life events. In one study, schizophrenic individuals who had relapsed were compared to those who had not relapsed. Shortly before their relapse,

the former were found to have experienced more stressful life events over which they had no control (Ventura, Neuchterlein, Lukoff, and Hardesty, 1989).

Searching for some meaningful purpose in life in the developed world, people are often confronted with meaninglessness on every level, from the personal to the global. Many people find themselves running in place so as not to fall behind, working at unfulfilling jobs, often for minimal pay, simply to keep up with the body's demands for food, clothing, and shelter. Rich nations are riddled with unemployment, inflation, and other economic ills. Many are precluded from enjoying material comforts, yet materialist dreams are instilled in all. Such stresses of modern living may lead people with genetic predispositions to schizophrenia to be unable to cope and thus more vulnerable to schizophrenia.

All of the theories about the causes of schizophrenia that we have surveyed are fascinating but unsatisfactory in that they provide only part of the explanation for the emergence of schizophrenia in any one individual. Studies of twins lend credence to a fundamental genetic propensity to schizophrenia. But since perfect concordance does not exist even among MZ twins, it is likely that additional variables, particularly overproduction of neurotransmitters like dopamine and peculiarities of brain structure, play a role in vulnerability to schizophrenia. Moreover, an individual's vulnerability to schizophrenia may be heightened by social and environmental factors. While schizophrenia may "run in the family" because of a common genetic background, "schizophrenogenic" families may also create a stressful and disordered environment that may induce schizophrenia among the vulnerable (Lewis, Rodnick, and Goldstein, 1981; Roff and Knight, 1981). Similarly, very poor people whose lives are filled with the stress of maintaining a marginal subsistence may be particularly vulnerable to schizophrenia.

Nowhere is the interrelation between symptoms, biology, and family more clear than it is in a study of the conditions that predict the outcome of an episode of schizophrenia. For the first decade after the episode, premorbid functioning—that is, the individual's capacity to cope with his or her life stresses before succumbing to schizophrenia—was the most influential predictor. In the second decade, family functioning was as important as premorbid coping. Long-term outcome—twenty or more years after the episode—was best predicted by family genetics (McGlashan, 1986a).

THE TREATMENT OF SCHIZOPHRENIA

Until the mid-1950s, treatment of schizophrenic patients was primarily custodial or downright barbaric. Patients were warehoused for long periods of time in environments that were both boring and hopeless. Often their disorder and the hospital environment interacted to bring about behavior that required physical restraint. In 1952, however, a lucky accident changed this bleak situation, and led to a revolution in the treatment of schizophrenia.

Drug Therapy

FOCUS QUESTIONS

1. How do the neuroleptics treat the positive symptoms of schizophrenia?

2. What are side effects of chlorpromazine?

3. Why does milieu therapy reduce relapse rates of schizophrenic patients?

4. How are schizophrenic patients treated in therapeutic communities?

While synthesizing new drugs called *antihistamines* that benefit asthmatics and those with allergies, researchers noticed the strong calming effects of these drugs. In fact, one of the drugs, promethazine, was so tranquilizing that the French surgeon Henri Laborit gave it to his patients as a prelude to anesthesia. Using a close relative of promethazine with even stronger sedative effects, French psychiatrists Jean Delay and Pierre Deniker treated various mentally disordered patients with varying results. Those who improved had a common diagnosis: schizophrenia. The drug they took was chlorpromazine. Now a prominent member of a class of drugs variously called *neuroleptics, psychotropics,* or *tranquilizing agents,* chlorpromazine revolutionized the treatment of schizophrenia. In 1955, there were about 560,000 patients in American psychiatric hospitals. One out of every two hospital beds was devoted to psychiatric care. It was then estimated that by 1971, 750,000 beds would be required to care for growing psychiatric populations. In fact, there were only 308,000 patients in psychiatric hospitals in 1971, less than half the projected estimate, and about 40 percent fewer than were hospitalized in 1955. By 1986, that number had declined further to 161,000, of

▶ Until chlorpromazine was used to treat schizophrenic patients, they generally spent their lives in back wards such as this one.

TABLE 9–3

	Neuroleptics	Neuroleptics and Anti-Parkinson Agents	Neuroleptics and Lithium or Anti-Convulsants	Beta Blockers	Megavitamins
PHARMACOLOGICAL TREATMENTS OF SCHIZOPHRENIA					
Improvement	about 50% moderately improved	about 50% moderately improved	about 50% moderately improved	somewhat better than placebo	none
Relapse*	high relapse	high relapse	high relapse	high relapse	high relapse
Side Effects	severe	moderate	severe	mild	mild
Cost	moderately expensive	moderately expensive	moderately expensive	inexpensive	inexpensive
Time Scale	months/years	months/years	months/years	month	months/years
Overall	**good**	**good**	**useful**	**probably useless**	**probably useless**

*Relapse after discontinuation of treatment.
SOURCE: Based on R.W. Buchanan, Clozapine: Efficacy and safety, *Schizophrenia Bulletin*, 21, no. 4 (1995), 579–91; L. B. Dixon, A. F. Lehman, and J. Levine, Conventional antipsychotic medications for schizophrenia. *Schizophrenia Bulletin*, 21, no. 4 (1995), 567–77.

which less than half carried the diagnosis of schizophrenia, as there had been a major shift in the administration of psychiatric service. More than 1.4 million clients (of which more than 300,000 were schizophrenic) were being seen as outpatients, and an additional 133,000, roughly half of whom were schizophrenic, were being treated in the community (Rosenstein, Milazzo-Sayre, and Manderscheid, 1990). Community-based treatment is now growing quickly. But neither it nor outpatient clinic care could have occurred without the advent of neuroleptic medications.

ANTIPSYCHOTIC EFFECTS OF DRUG THERAPY

Of the major tranquilizers, chlorpromazine, haloperidol, and clozapine are three of the most commonly used. Their most striking effect is the degree to which they "tranquilize," make peaceful, even sedate. Could it be that these antipsychotics are no different from barbiturates, whose sedative action produces no greater improvements for schizophrenia than placebos? Some evidence suggests that this is not the case. Beyond their sedative effects and even beyond their impact on anxiety, the antipsychotic drugs seem to have specific ameliorating effects on thought disorders and hallucinations (see Table 9–3). Subjective emotional experiences, such as guilt and depression, however, continue unabated despite a course of drug treatment.

The chief mode of action of neuroleptic drugs is in binding to dopamine receptors, thereby preventing dopamine itself from binding to those receptors. Once the dopamine is blocked, the positive symptoms of schizophrenia are also blocked, resulting in marked cognitive and behavioral improvement. While chlorpromazine and haloperidol seem to affect only the positive symptoms of schizophrenia, clozapine may treat the negative symptoms as well and appears to be effective where other treatments fail (Breslin, 1992; Buchanan, 1995; Dixon, Lehman, and Levine, 1995).

The antipsychotic drugs have been so successful in treating patients that the average hospital stay for a schizophrenic patient has declined to fewer than thirteen days, when formerly it was months, years, even a lifetime. Phenothiazines, nearly alone, have been responsible for a revolution in psychiatric care.

The antipsychotic drugs have a variety of unpleasant side effects that often lead patients to discontinue using them. Side effects of chlorpromazine (Thorazine), for example, frequently include dryness of mouth and throat, drowsiness, visual disturbances, weight gain or loss, menstrual disturbances, constipation, and depression. For most patients, these are relatively minor problems, but annoying enough to induce them to discontinue medications on discharge.

But there are two classes of side effects that are extremely serious. Chlorpromazine produces extrapyramidal or Parkinson-like effects, which appear to arise because, as we have seen, antipsychotic medications affect the dopamine receptors, which are in turn implicated in Parkinson's disease. (These drugs do not cause Parkinson's disease, but they do induce analogous symptoms.) These symptoms include stiffness of muscles and difficulty in moving, freezing of facial muscles, which results in a glum or sour look, as well as an inability to smile, tremors at the extremities as well as spasms of limbs and body, and **akathisia**—a peculiar "itchiness" in the muscles which results in an inability to sit still, and an urge to pace the halls continuously and energetically (Snyder, 1974a). Other drugs can control these side effects, however.

Even more serious is a neurological disorder called **tardive dyskinesia.** Its symptoms consist of sucking, lip-smacking, and tongue movements that seem like fly-catching. Tardive dyskinesia is not reversible. Conservatively, it affects 24 percent of schizophrenics after seven years of cumulative neuroleptic exposure (Wegner, Catalano, Gibralter, and Kane, 1985; Jeste and Caligiuri, 1993). The prevalence and severity of tardive dyskinesia increase with age. And there may well be a relationship between the severity of a person's *negative* symptoms of schizophrenia and the risk of developing tardive dyskinesia (Barnes and Braude, 1985).

Clozapine often improves a patient where other neuroleptics fail and does not produce either extrapyramidal side effects or tardive dyskinesia. Indeed, clozapine would be the treatment of choice for schizophrenia were it not for the fact that it sometimes produces a condition called **agranulocytosis,** a deficiency in granulocytes, which are produced in the bone marrow and combat infection. Because such a condition can ultimately be toxic, clozapine needs to be administered very carefully, which at present, contributes greatly to its cost (Kane and Marder, 1993).

Psychological Treatment

The treatment of patients diagnosed with schizophrenia cannot be confined to drugs. Antipsychotic drugs help ameliorate the symptoms of schizophrenia, but the symptoms are by no means the entire problem. Indeed, the very fact that these drugs alter symptoms and only symptoms raises profound questions about what is meant by treatment, recovery, and cure. Psychological as well as pharmacological interventions are needed to treat patients successfully, for although the hospital population of schizophrenic patients has declined radically since 1955, readmission rates have soared. One study found a 79 percent relapse rate within two years of discharge (Hogarty, Anderson, Reiss, Kornblith, Greenwald, Javna, and Madonia, 1986). Studies have shown that only 15 to 40 percent of people diagnosed with schizophrenia are able to work or care for themselves (Keith, Gunderson, Reifman, Buchsbaum, and Mosher, 1976), that many released patients return to aversive environments (Leff, 1976) and to communities that are less than welcoming, that many lack work skills (Gunderson and Mosher, 1975) and

THE CONSEQUENCES OF DEINSTITUTIONALIZATION

Not all political and therapeutic processes that begin well, end well. Deinstitutionalization, unfortunately, is a case in point.

In 1955, there was some 558,000 patients in public mental hospitals, while the population of the United States was roughly 160 million. By 1994, the population had grown to 260 million, and if the proportions remained the same, there should have been some 885,000 people in public hospitals. But in fact, there were only 71,619, roughly 8 percent of what might be expected. Why? The reason was deinstitutionalization, the policy of moving large numbers of severely disturbed people out of mental hospitals.

It's hard to say when the policy of deinstitutionalization began, but surely one of the signal events that launched that policy was the ways in which hospitalized psychiatric patients had been treated. In 1943, a group of pacifists who were conscientious objectors to participating in the Second World War, were assigned to work in psychiatric hospitals in lieu of military service. They were shocked by what they found. At Cleveland State Hospital, they discovered that psychiatric patients were frequently shackled and beaten, provided with inadequate and commonly revolting food, little treatment, and overcrowded quarters. Four women, for example, had been placed in seclusion rooms, and simply abandoned. They were found unconscious and close to death.

The pacifists detailed their observations to a newspaper reporter who wrote a series of scathing articles in the *Cleveland Press*. The hospital and the state mental health authorities vigorously denied these allegations. In 1944, the Governor convened a grand jury to investigate the situation. The jury's report not only substantiated the allegations, it added some new ones

. . . the Grand Jury is shocked beyond words that a so-called civilized society would allow fellow human beings to be mistreated as they are at the Cleveland State Hospital. No enlightened community dare tolerate the conditions that exist at this institution. . . .

Cleveland State Hospital is not a hospital; it is a custodial institution in which we have incarcerated the sick. It presents a case history of brutality and social criminal neglect. Patients have died shortly after receiving violent attacks from the hands of attendants or other patients, made possible only by the lack of proper supervision. In other cases patients have died under circumstances which are highly suspicious.

Frequent active assaults have resulted in broken bones, lacerations, bruises and a consequent deterioration of the mind. Favorite weapons have been the buckles of heavy straps, the loaded end of heavy key-rings, metal plated shoes and wet towels which leave no marks after choking. . .

As a direct consequence of the grand jury investigation and the publicity surrounding these findings, the superintendent of the hospital was fired and monies were added to the hospital budget. At the end of the war, such investigations spread to other hospitals in other states, and a national movement for psychiatric hospital reform was established. However, it proved rather costly to reform psychiatric care in hospitals. Moreover, the impetus to do so diminished markedly as the public became relatively inured to the lurid headlines. Some ten years later, with the advent of Thorazine, the first antipsychotic drug, the effort on behalf of psychiatric patients became less concerned with reform of hospitals than it was with deinstitutionalization. If hospitals were that bad, and indeed they were, patients were better off outside them than locked up within, and the hospitals ought best be shut down—which they were. The policy of deinstitutionalization was greeted warmly by many in the psychological and psychiatric communities, and especially among those who were concerned with patients' rights.

Some forty years later, in 1994, the outcome of deinstitutionalization seemed less rosy. There were, for example, about 150,000 seriously disturbed people who, but for deinstitutionalization, would be hospitalized, but constituted about a third of the growing cadre of homeless people. In addition, on any given day, there were about 160,000 seriously disturbed people in public jails and prisons, who really ought to have been elsewhere. Among those apprehended for violent crimes, a substantial number were seriously disturbed and, but for deinstitutionalization, might have been out of harm's way. And countless others remained at home, often without treatment, their lasting afflictions burdens not only to themselves but to their hapless families.

How then, E. Fuller Torrey (1997) asks, do we adjudicate between the rights of the disturbed and the rights of the people around them? Surely a civilized society cannot remand them once again to the snake pits of yore. But neither can it afford to let better than three-quarters of a million of them loose on society. In this instance, civility, charity, and necessity dictate the same solution: humane institutions—well-funded, thoughtfully appointed, and with well-trained staff. There seems to be no other alternative.

SOURCE: Torrey, E.F. (1997). *Out of the shadows: Confronting America's mental illness crisis.* New York: Wiley.

social skills, and that many stop taking medications on discharge because of the drugs' aversive effects (see Box 9–4). Some of these problems can be addressed by teaching patients work and social skills and finding interventions that work outside the hospital setting.

TABLE 9–4

	Group Therapy	Family Therapy	Social Skills Training	Token Economy (Inpatient)	Cognitive Therapy
			PSYCHOSOCIAL TREATMENTS* OF SCHIZOPHRENIA		
Improvement	about 50% moderately improved	about 50% moderately improved	about 50% moderately improved	about 50% moderately improved	unclear
Relapse[†]	high	moderate	high	high	high
Side Effects	unclear	unclear	unclear	unclear	moderate
Cost	inexpensive	inexpensive	inexpensive	expensive	inexpensive
Time Scale	months/years	years	months/years	month	months/years
Overall	**useful**	**good**	**useful**	**useful**	**marginal**

*Used in combination with pharmacological treatments.
[†]Relapse after discontinuation of treatment.
SOURCE: Based on A. Kopelowicz and R. P. Liberman, Psychological and behavioral treatments for schizophrenia, in P. Nathan and J. Gorman (eds.), *Treatments that work* (New York: Oxford, 1997); J. A. Mattes, Risperidone: How good is the evidence for efficacy? *Schizophrenia Bulletin, 23,* no. 1 (1997), 155–62.

Because schizophrenia arises mainly between the ages of eighteen and thirty-five, it disrupts educational and vocational training, social skills, friendships, and marriages. In addition, because the seeds of the disorder are sown before the disorder appears, both in the individual and in the family, it is a safe bet that there are problems in communication and self-esteem—in short, *psychological problems*—that the antipsychotic drugs simply do not touch. Given that psychological problems exist and that drugs do not alleviate them, a variety of psychological approaches to schizophrenia have been tried across the decades.

Although many psychological treatments have had unimpressive outcomes, several approaches have shown promising results (see Table 9–4). For example, when schizophrenic patients are given social skills training, and their families are trained to become more proficient in "family problem solving," the relapse rate among such patients declines markedly—though it doesn't disappear by any means (Hogarty et al., 1986). Another approach that seems to deal successfully with schizophrenic patients' psychological problems is a relatively structured treatment called Interpersonal Therapy (IPT; already discussed in Chapter 8 as a treatment for depression). IPT is a set of structured intervention programs that are derived from cognitive and behavioral principles and that attempt to remedy the cognitive and behavioral dysfunctions that are characteristic of schizophrenia. Evaluative studies of IPT suggest that as a result of the program schizophrenic patients show improvement in such elementary cognitive processes as attention, abstraction, and concept formation (Brenner, Hodel, Roder, and Corrigan, 1992; Liberman and Green, 1992). Moreover, there is reason to believe that such treatment, as well as treatments that are designed to improve social skills among schizophrenic individuals (Liberman, Nuechterlein, and Wallace, 1982), works especially well in conjunction with drug therapy (Morrison and Bellack, 1984; Bellack, 1992). Nonetheless, the combination of these psychotherapies with drug therapies does not raise improvement rates to better than 50 percent moderately improved.

Another successful psychological treatment for schizophrenic patients is *milieu therapy.* Patients are provided with training in social communication, in work, and in recreation—in effect, skills that help them cope with the world (Hogarty et al., 1986; Liberman, Mueser, and Wallace,

1986). Hospitals that have incorporated such milieu treatments have successfully decreased their relapse rate. Moreover, families that have been trained to cope better with stress through greater understanding of the schizophrenic individual's problems and more efficacious family problem solving appear to improve the emotional quality of the home environment and to reduce the rate of relapse once patients have left hospitals (Vaughn, Snyder, Jones, Freeman, and Falloon, 1984; Doane, Falloon, Goldstein, and Mintz, 1985).

The ideal treatment for schizophrenia involves carefully monitored psychopharmacological interventions that are combined with psychological ones. Such treatment is now being administered in two ways: by bringing treatment to patients outside the hospital or clinic, and in group residences.

Because medication is sometimes aversive, patients may stop taking their "meds" as soon as they are discharged from the hospital. But they generally need medication to stabilize their personalities; without it, patients will often decline psychologically and be forced to return to the hospital. One way to abort this cycle of hospitalization requires that the treatment go to the patient rather than vice versa. In New York and Michigan, for example, teams of psychologists, psychiatrists, and social workers visit with, counsel, and treat former inpatients and outpatients who are struggling with unemployment and homelessness, in addition to not taking their medications. Such programs are achieving enormous success in enabling people to stay out of psychiatric hospitals (*New York Times,* April 24, 1994).

A second form of treatment involves ***group residences*** (also known as group homes). Today, there are thousands of group homes and apartments across the United States, so many in fact that in some states, more patients are accommodated in group homes and apartments than in state mental hospitals. Group homes house small numbers of people. They blend pharmacological interventions with a warm, understanding approach to people who are occasionally greatly distressed. Because entry and exit in these homes is voluntary, such centers cannot use coercion to compel obedient behaviors. As a result, many of the distressing problems that arise in psychiatric hospitals are avoided. At the same time, the homes enable individuals to make significant progress toward living outside the hospital and being fully independent and productive (Winerip, 1994). These homes are located in residential neighborhoods, and upscale communities often fight to keep them out. But the overwhelming experience with such homes has been quite positive, with community fears and prejudice generally unfounded.

SUMMARY

1. The schizophrenias are marked by a *thought disorder* that is often combined with affective and behavioral anomalies. There are five clinical subtypes of schizophrenia: *paranoid, disorganized, catatonic, residual,* and *undifferentiated.* Schizophrenic patients can be differentiated according to whether their condition is *acute* or *chronic.* They can also be differentiated according to the kinds of symptoms they present. *Type I schizophrenia* is associated with the *positive* symptoms of the disorder, such as hallucinations, delusions, and bizarre thoughts. *Type II schizophrenia* is identified with the *negative* symptoms of the syndrome, such as withdrawal, blunted affect, and reduced motivation.

2. The schizophrenic individual's subjective experience is often one of being invaded by the world's stimuli, crowded by them, and unable to process them. We find this experience rooted in what appears to be a defective *cognitive filter*, itself related to serious *attentional difficulties*. The incapacity to focus attention, as well as the sense that too many stimuli are invading and capturing attention, is characteristic of many schizophrenic patients' experience.

3. In the cognitive domain, schizophrenic patients make the same errors of association that non-schizophrenic individuals make, but they make many more of them. They seem especially attracted to the *dominant associations* or connotations of words, regardless of the context in which they are found. Often, their attentional difficulties seem to distract them from the ultimate goal of thought and speech. Thinking may therefore be *overinclusive*, and speech dotted with *clang associations* and *neologisms*.

4. Many schizophrenic individuals appear to experience flattened or restricted emotion, which may make it difficult for them to experience reality meaningfully.

5. Schizophrenic individuals seem to experience perceptual intensities or deficits that lead them to experience the world differently from others. Delusional, hallucinatory, or other cognitive experiences often bring grief or a sense of uniqueness.

6. Vulnerability to schizophrenia is a highly individual matter, but there seem to be five significant factors that promote it. First, there seems little doubt that the schizophrenias are in part a *genetic* disorder. The schizophrenias occur much more often among MZ than DZ twins, and among biological than adoptive relatives of schizophrenics. Second, there is reason to believe that the schizophrenias are *biological* disorders. People diagnosed with Type I schizophrenia appear to be suffering a *neurotransmission* disorder, especially involving *dopamine*. People diagnosed with Type II schizophrenia seem to have *structural brain deficits*, including smaller frontal lobes, enlarged brain ventricles, neuronal degeneration, and reduced blood flow in the cortex. Third, faulty communications within the *family* may well promote the development of schizophrenia. Fourth, schizophrenia is a disorder that affects the *poor* more than the rich, and whose outcome seems to depend on the culture in which it occurs. Schizophrenia in well-developed countries appears to have a worse prognosis than the same disorder in developing nations. The stresses of modern living may negatively impact those who become schizophrenic.

7. Treatment of the schizophrenias has been revolutionized by the invention of strong antipsychotic drugs that seem to work directly on symptoms of schizophrenia. Hospitalization has become briefer, and there is a greater probability that the schizophrenic person will return to society. The effectiveness of the antipsychotic drugs, however, is limited.

8. Because schizophrenia is a psychological as well as a biological disorder, there have been increasing attempts to discover nonpharmaceutical methods for treating the schizophrenias. Two of these methods are Interpersonal Therapy and milieu therapy. Increasingly, schizophrenic individuals are being treated in the community, either in group residences or by bringing treatment personnel to patients, rather than requiring patients to go to the hospital or clinic.

1. Why does a breakdown in the attentional filter cause untreated schizophrenic individuals to have problems leading normal lives?

2. Why do you think that one identical twin may have schizophrenia while his or her co-twin will not have it?

3. Why are schizophrenic patients in developed countries less likely to recover from schizophrenia than are those in developing countries?

4. Do you think that the side effects of schizophrenia are so bad that drug treatment of schizophrenic individuals should be discontinued?

CHAPTER

10

Childhood
Disorders*

I n this chapter, we turn to the problems of children and adolescents. For several reasons, these problems are often more difficult to understand than those of adults. First, children's problems occur in the context of growing up. But normal psychological development proceeds at different rates for different children. As a result, it is often difficult to distinguish a genuine psychological problem that requires attention from one that merely reflects a developmental lag. For example, it is normal for children to learn at different speeds, so it is difficult to know if a particular child has a learning disorder or is temporarily slower than other children. Second, children often cannot communicate a problem directly through language. Instead, their distress is frequently manifested indirectly through maladaptive behaviors, and it is then up to parents and teachers to identify behaviors in children that might indicate severe problems. But adults might mislabel a child's behavior as a "psychological problem" when it is merely something that will pass with time. Or they might ignore children's problem behaviors, believing the child will grow out of these behaviors, when the child really does need adult intervention. Finally, children's problems are often quite specific to particular situations and contexts. Children may be aggressive at home, but not at school. Even overactivity—a common complaint of teachers—depends on the circumstances and situations. One study found that 75 percent of children who were allegedly overactive in school were not overactive at home or in the clinic (Klein and Gittelman-Klein, 1975).

We will examine several kinds of children's problems. All are considered psychological disorders, not only because the child deviates from what is expected of a particular age and sociocultural context, but also for two other reasons: (1) the problem is persistent and severe, and (2) it impairs the child or others. Either the child must be suffering, as when a child with an animal

*This chapter is a revision and abridgment of a chapter written by Susan Nolen-Hoeksema for *Abnormal Psychology,* 3rd ed. (Norton, 1995).

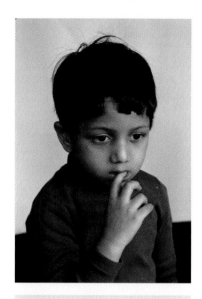

▲ Young children may not be able to communicate problems through language, but show distress through behavior. This boy may be in a pensive mood, or he may be withdrawn because of an anxiety he cannot express in words.

phobia is paralyzed with fear, or the child is making others suffer, as when the child's aggression is turned on schoolmates or pets.

How common are DSM-type psychological disorders in children? Several large-scale epidemiological studies conducted in the United States, Europe, and Australia have sought to answer this question by administering a clinical interview to children from the general population (see Brandenburg, Friedman, and Silver, 1990). On the basis of information from these clinical interviews, researchers estimate that between 14 and 20 percent of children suffer from moderate to severe psychological problems.

What distinguishes a childhood disorder from normal variation in development is often only a matter of degree. With few exceptions, these disorders are not qualitatively different from normal, and minor variations on these problems can be found in many essentially normal children (Rutter, 1985). Thus, the temper tantrums that occur in most children once a month would hardly be labeled a psychological disorder. But if the tantrums were much more frequent, or they occurred in peculiar circumstances, or for a very long time, then the behavior might be considered abnormal. The timing during development of behavior problems also is important. For example, most preschoolers show anxiety about separating from their parents, particularly just before they are to begin school. This separation anxiety is seldom persistent or predictive of future problems. But separation anxiety occurring much later in childhood is more likely to be persistent and associated with more severe malfunctioning in a child (Rutter, 1985). Before going into the specifics of any one disorder, let's look at the system by which all childhood disorders are broadly classified.

CLASSIFYING CHILDREN'S DISORDERS

As a road map for viewing the scope of childhood disorders, consider Table 10–1. The disorders can be divided into four categories. **Disruptive behavior disorders** are characterized by symptoms such as hyperactivity, inattention, aggressiveness, destructiveness, and defiance of authorities. **Emotional**

TABLE 10–1

MAJOR CLUSTERS OF CHILDHOOD DISORDERS	
Disruptive behavior disorders	Attention-deficit hyperactivity disorder Conduct disorder Oppositional defiant disorder
Emotional disorders	Separation anxiety disorder Reactive attachment disorder Childhood depression Phobias
Habit and eating disorders	Elimination disorders (e.g., bed-wetting) Speech disorders (e.g., stuttering) Tic disorders Anorexia nervosa Bulimia nervosa
Developmental disorders	Mental retardation Learning disorders Autistic disorder

SOURCE: Adapted from DSM-IV.

FOCUS QUESTIONS

1. What are the four categories of childhood disorders?
2. Briefly describe each of them.

disorders are those in which symptoms of fear, anxiety, sadness, poor attachment, and even depression predominate. *Habit and eating disorders* include a rather wide variety of disorders that are characterized by the repetitive acting out of maladaptive or nonfunctional behaviors. Examples include bed-wetting, stuttering, motor tics, and eating large quantities of food and then forcing oneself to vomit. *Developmental disorders* are characterized by marked deficiencies in the child's development of important intellectual capabilities and social skills. This category includes the several levels of mental retardation as well as less severe learning disorders (such as developmental reading disorder). The category also includes autistic disorder, which is characterized by severe deficits in communication skills and social responsiveness.

DISRUPTIVE BEHAVIOR DISORDERS

There are three types of disruptive behavior disorders. *Conduct disorders* are characterized by persistent behaviors that seriously violate the rights of others and basic societal norms. Children with conduct disorders often get in trouble with the law and become career criminals. *Attention-deficit hyperactivity disorder* is characterized by marked impulsivity, inattention, and hyperactivity. Children with this disorder are often very disruptive at school and at home. A third disorder in this category is *oppositional defiant disorder.* Children with this disorder show a pattern of negativistic, hostile, and defiant behavior, but do not show serious violations of other's rights.

Conduct Disorders

Most children, at one time or another, transgress important rules of conduct. A survey of 1,425 British boys aged thirteen to sixteen years, from all socioeconomic groupings, found that 98 percent of them admitted to keeping something, often of little value, that did not belong to them (Belson, 1975). But there are some children whose conduct persistently violates very basic norms for interpersonal behavior. These children are often physically aggressive and cruel to others. They habitually lie and cheat. When adolescents, they may engage in muggings, armed robberies, and even rapes and homicides. When a child chronically shows such behavior, he or she may be diagnosed as having a conduct disorder. The following case is representative of a child with one type of conduct disorder:

> Alan is the sort of teenager who makes all caring professionals despair. He has been in and out of trouble since he was six years old. At that early age, he truanted from school, and by the time he was twelve Alan had been excluded from ordinary schools and had been brought into juvenile court for persistent stealing. Within his neighborhood gang, he was popular with both boys and girls, and he was sexually active before he was fourteen. But he was quick to pick fights with boys who did not belong to his gang.
>
> At fourteen his criminal career seemed set. He had been sentenced several times for stealing cars, and no end of this activity was in sight. His probation officer had the sense of standing by impotently until either maturation or a heavy prison sentence altered Alan's behavior.
>
> Alan seemed to have all the cards stacked against him. He was the youngest of a large family. His father had himself been in and out of prison before finally deserting his mother when Alan was four. The mother struggled to keep the family together, but she frequently became depressed, during which times Alan spent long periods in foster homes. School was no refuge from these difficulties. Despite being of near-average ability, Alan had experienced considerable difficulty learning to read and spell. At fourteen, he could scarcely write a letter home.

▶ Children with conduct disorders have chronic and consistent behavior problems that often persist into adulthood. Three times as many boys as girls are diagnosed with conduct disorders.

The persistence of antisocial and aggressive tendencies from childhood into early adulthood that Alan shows is common in children with conduct disorders (Olweus, 1979; Huesmann, Eron, Lefkowitz, and Walder, 1984). Indeed, conduct disturbances and aggressivity are unusually stable characteristics across childhood and adolescence, particularly among boys (Offord et al., 1992). Approximately 35 to 40 percent of children with conduct disorder develop antisocial personality disorder as adults, and about 75 to 85 per-

---

DSM-IV Criteria for Conduct Disorder

A. A repetitive and persistent pattern of behavior in which the basic rights of others or major age-appropriate societal norms or rules are violated, as manifested by the presence of three (or more) of the following criteria in the past 12 months, with at least one criterion present in the past 6 months: *Aggression to people and animals*—(1) often bullies, threatens, or intimidates others; (2) often initiates physical fights; (3) has used a weapon that can cause serious physical harm to others (e.g., a bat, brick, broken bottle, knife, gun); (4) has been physically cruel to people; (5) has been physically cruel to animals; (6) has stolen while confronting a victim (e.g., mugging, purse snatching, extortion, armed robbery); (7) has forced someone into sexual activity. *Destruction of property*—(8) has deliberately engaged in fire setting with the intention of causing serious damage; (9) has deliberately destroyed others' property (other than by fire setting). *Deceitfulness or theft*—(10) has broken into someone else's house, building, or car; (11) often lies to obtain goods or favors or to avoid obligations (i.e., "cons" others); (12) has stolen items of nontrivial value without confronting a victim (e.g., shoplifting, but without breaking and entering; forgery). *Serious violations of rules*—(13) often stays out at night despite parental prohibitions, beginning before age 13 years; (14) has run away from home overnight at least twice while living in parental or parental surrogate home (or once without returning for a lengthy period); (15) is often truant from school, beginning before age 13 years.
B. The disturbance in behavior causes clinically significant impairment in social, academic, or occupational functioning.
C. If the individual is age 18 years or older, criteria are not met for Antisocial Personality Disorder.
SOURCE: APA, DSM-IV, 1994.

cent of these children experience as adults significant problems in social functioning, such as chronic unemployment, unstable personal relationships, impulsive physical aggression, and spouse abuse (Zoccolillo, Pickles, Quinton, and Rutter, 1992).

Alan's criminal behavior is typical of children with conduct disorders. Although many children will show minor, transient conduct disturbances, only between 3 and 7 percent will be as disturbed as Alan and will qualify for a diagnosis of conduct disorder (Robins, 1991). The disorder is over three times more common in boys than in girls. About half of the children diagnosed with conduct disorders are eventually classified as juvenile delinquents in adolescence. And over half of juvenile delinquents commit serious crimes by the age of twenty-five (Ross and Wirt, 1984). Some of the strongest predictors of which disruptive children will go on to engage in serious criminal behavior are: (1) high frequency of deviant acts as a child, (2) greater variety of deviant acts, (3) deviant acts performed across multiple settings, and (4) early onset of deviant acts (Loeber, 1990).

POSSIBLE ORIGINS OF CONDUCT DISORDERS

What causes a child to develop patterns of aggressivity and criminal behavior? First we shall consider the influence of the social environment on the development of conduct disturbances. Then we shall investigate the possible genetic origins of these disorders.

Sources of Conduct Disorders   Children with aggressive disorders often come from unpleasant social environments (see Box 10–1). They come from families with lower socioeconomic status, and frequently have a parent who can be characterized as having an antisocial personality disorder (Lahey, Piacentini, McBurnett, Stone, Hartdagen, and Hind, 1988). Their families tend to be those in which affection is lacking and discord is rampant, where discipline is harsh and inconsistent, where prosocial behaviors are not reinforced, where children's activities are poorly supervised, where the parents have parted through divorce or separation, or where the children have been placed outside the home during times of family crisis (Rutter, 1975; Farrington, 1978; Hetherington and Martin, 1979; Loeber and Dishion, 1983; Patterson, DeBaryshe, and Ramsey, 1989; Loeber, 1990). In turn, children with conduct disorders are often rejected by their peers (Coie and Kupersmidt, 1983; Dodge, 1983) or become members of deviant peer groups (gangs) that reinforce them for delinquent acts (Elliott, Hulzinga, and Ageton, 1985; Patterson, DeBaryshe, and Ramsey, 1989). Moreover, verbal intelligence plays a substantial role in the conduct disorders. Those with conduct disorders display significantly less verbal intelligence than children who do not suffer such disorders (Lahey, Loeber, Hart, Frick, Applegate, Zhang, Green, and Russo, 1995). Many of the children also have problems maintaining attention (Quay, 1986; Anderson, Williams, McGee, and Silva, 1987). Thus, they also do poorly in school, rendering them not only restless in the classroom during the long school day but also unavailable to the kinds of self-esteem socialization and feelings of competence that proper school performance engenders.

Genetic Influences on the Development of Conduct Disorders   Genetic factors may also play a role in determining which children have conduct problems and which do not. Most genetic studies have examined rates of criminal behavior rather than diagnoses of conduct disorders. Twin studies find the concordance rate for criminality to be 26 to 51 percent in MZ twins versus 13 to 22 percent in DZ twins (Rutter, Quinton, and Hill, 1990). Studies comparing the criminal records (rather than the clinical diagnoses) of adopted children with those of their natural and adoptive fathers have found that the criminal records of adopted sons

FOCUS QUESTIONS

1. Describe conduct that would lead to a diagnosis of a conduct disorder.
2. What are the strongest predictors of which disruptive children will go on to engage in serious criminal behavior?
3. Explain the possible origins of conduct disorders.
4. Describe the goals and interventions derived from social learning theory that are used to treat children diagnosed with conduct disorders.

Box10-1 **IN THE RESEARCHER'S LABORATORY**

YOUTHFUL VICTIMS OF VIOLENCE

Children with conduct disorders are often subjected to abuse as children. What are the consequences of being exposed to violent parents, and sometimes even parents diagnosed with antisocial personality disorder? Is exposure to violence merely a passing matter in a child's life, or are there long-term sequelae?

There is reason to believe that violence is on the rise in Western society. But nowhere does violence occur more often than it does to the young. Among youths who are ten to sixteen, more than a third reported that they had been victims of violence. Their victimization was no passing matter. Many found themselves left with behavioral and psychological symptoms that endured well after the victimization period.

Boney-McCoy and Finkelhor (1995) interviewed a representative sample of 2,000 males and females between the ages of ten and sixteen. They identified these young people as having been victimized if they had experienced such events as *aggravated assault* (physical assault involving either a weapon or physical injury); *simple assault* (without a weapon and without injury) by a nonfamily member; physical assault by a *parent*; physical assault by a *family member* other than a parent; *attempted or completed kidnapping;* or *sexual assault*. In addition, *violence to genitals,* commonly by a kick or a punch, was assessed for boys.

While these young people were not diagnosed formally, they were asked how often in the past week they had experienced symptoms that are often associated with post-traumatic stress syndrome, such as "trouble falling asleep," "thoughts and images that are frightening," and "temper outbursts that you could not control." They were also asked how often in the past month they had felt sad, or experienced trouble with a teacher.

Some 35 percent of the sample reported a victimization experience at some time in their lives. An additional 5.4 percent reported either an attempted kidnapping or an attempted sexual assault. Thus, better than 40 percent of the entire sample reported having been a victim. For females, the most common form of victimization was sexual assault (15.3 percent); for males, it was aggravated assault by a nonfamily member. The median time that had elapsed since the last victimization was seven months.

Boys and girls who had been sexually assaulted manifested symptoms associated with post-traumatic stress. They reported greater difficulty with teachers. In addition, sexually assaulted girls manifested substantial sadness. Moreover, it hardly mattered whether the sexual assault had merely been attempted, or had actually been completed. Even the least invasive sexual assault was associated with greater subsequent symptomatology.

But lest you believe that sexual assault is the only serious form of child trauma, nearly all of the other forms of victimization produced equally serious consequences. For example, the effects of parental violence equaled or exceeded those of sexual assault. So, too, did aggravated assault and genital violence. Only the effects of nonparental violence were weaker than those of sexual assault.

bear stronger resemblance to those of their biological fathers, with whom they never lived, than to the records of their adoptive fathers (Crowe, 1983; Cloninger and Gottesman, 1987; Mednick, Gabriella, and Hutchings, 1987).

What may be inherited and what may influence subsequent criminality is the failure to experience high emotional arousal (see Chapter 7). Because of such failure, boys with conduct disorders are less responsive than others to praise and encouragement (Patterson, 1975; Robins, 1991). Psychophysiologically they manifest low arousal and show a learning deficit in fear avoidance situations (Davies and Maliphant, 1971; Trasler, 1973)—precisely those situations that encourage stabilization and that discourage social rule violation. Conversely, genetic inheritance may account for the fact that some children from very difficult circumstances fail to become delinquents. Because they have inherited the capacity to be aroused by social stimuli, they avoid delinquency by becoming socialized.

Yet, several studies suggest that children who are genetically at risk to develop conduct disorder, or more specifically to become criminals, are unlikely to do so unless they are also exposed to environments that promote antisocial behavior (Cadoret, 1986; Cloninger and Gottesman, 1987; Rutter, Quinton, and Hill, 1990; Rutter et al., 1990). This suggests that even children who are genetically predisposed to conduct disorder might be successfully treated with environmental interventions.

Historically, treatment of conduct disorders has focused on interventions derived from social learning theory (see Lochman, White, and Wayland, 1991). Goals of such interventions include: (1) teaching a child how to identify situations that trigger aggressive or antisocial behavior, (2) teaching the child how to take the perspective of others and care about this perspective, (3) reducing the aggressive child's tendency to overattribute hostility in others, and (4) teaching the child adaptive ways of solving conflicts with others, such as negotiation. Each of these goals is accomplished by reinforcing positive behaviors and punishing negative behaviors in the child and by modeling and observational learning procedures (see Chapter 3). Often a child's family will be involved in treatment, since the dynamics of the family may actually be supporting the child's conduct disorder. Interventions such as these have proven promising in outcome research (see Table 10–2), although it may be crucial for these interventions to take place soon after the child begins to exhibit antisocial behavior, and to include the child's parents or family, for the interventions to have long-term positive effects (Lochman, White, and Wayland, 1991).

As an example of the application of these interventions, especially behavioral contracting, consider John, whose conduct disorder stemmed from communication problems with his parents:

> John was fourteen when he was referred to a treatment center because he had been stealing from his mother. He frequently stole large sums of money, often in excess of twenty dollars. His mother, however, knew precisely how much money she had, and there was no way in which John could pretend that his stealing would go unnoticed.
>
> Interestingly, during early discussions with the therapist, it became clear that John respected his parents, and that they loved him. The problem was that they could no longer discuss things together. John's stealing had driven a wedge of distrust between them, such that his parents could think of nothing else, yet John resented not being trusted.

TABLE 10–2

	TREATMENT OF CONDUCT DISORDER			
	Problem-Solving Skills Training	Parent Management Training	Family Therapy	Lithium
Improvement	about 50% moderately improved	about 50% moderately improved	about 50% moderately improved	unclear
Relapse*	moderate	moderate	moderate	unclear
Side Effects	unclear	unclear	unclear	mild
Cost	moderately expensive	moderately expensive	moderately expensive	moderately expensive
Time Scale	months	months	months/years	weeks/months
Overall	**good**	**marginal**	**marginal**	**probably useless**

*Relapse after discontinuation of treatments.
SOURCE: Based on M. Campbell, and J. Cueva, Psychopharmacology in child and adolescent psychiatry: A review of the past seven years, Part 2, *Journal of the American Academy of Child and Adolescent Psychiatry*, 34 (1995), 10; C. A. Kaplan and S. Hussain, Use of drugs in child and adolescent psychiatry, *British Journal of Psychiatry*, 166, no. 3 (1995), 291–98; A. E. Kazdin, Treatments of conduct disorder in children, in P. Nathan and J. Gorman (eds.), *Treatments that work* (New York: Oxford, 1997); D. Offord and K. Bennett, Conduct disorder: long-term outcomes and intervention effectiveness. *Journal of the American Academy of Child and Adolescent Psychiatry*, 33 (1994), 8.

In fact, stealing was simply the most irritating of a group of problems that typically arise during adolescence and that neither John nor his parents knew how to discuss and resolve. Among these problems were conflicts over curfew, neatness, personal cleanliness, and table manners.

Recognizing that these conflicts were by no means trivial irritants, the therapist arranged a series of contracts between John and his parents, whereby the rewards and penalties for meeting or violating explicit agreements were clear to both sides. In these contracts, John acknowledged that his lateness might be a source of great concern to his parents, while they recognized that his room was his own "space" which, subject only to fundamental rules of sanitation, was his to do with as he pleased. At the same time, the therapist encouraged John and his father to role-play how they might settle differences of opinion at home. After the first meeting, stealing was never discussed nor was it targeted as an area for contract or discussion. Nevertheless, it stopped altogether and long before the eight-week treatment terminated.

Sometimes a child's behavior is so disruptive, or his family environment is so dysfunctional, that he or she will be sent to a treatment home such as Achievement Place. At Achievement Place, which began at the University of Kansas and is now in several locations around the country, two professionally trained "teaching parents" live together in a family-style arrangement with six to eight delinquent adolescent children. Often the children's homes are in the same community, and they can continue to attend their regular school and visit in their own homes.

The aim of Achievement Place is to teach prosocial behaviors. The teaching parents develop a mutually reinforcing relationship with their charges and model, role-play, and reinforce the kinds of social skills they want the children to acquire. They emphasize skills such as responding appropriately to criticism, as well as the academic skills that are necessary to make school interesting and to obtain employment afterwards. Moreover, Achievement Place emphasizes self-government, whereby the children take increasing responsibility for their own behavior and for helping their housemates (Wolf, Phillips, and Fixsen, 1975; Kirigin, Wolf, Braukmann, Fixsen, and Phillips, 1979).

Attention-Deficit Hyperactivity Disorder (ADHD)

Parents and teachers often complain that children are overactive and restless, that they won't sit still and cannot concentrate for long. What they usually mean is that the children won't concentrate for as long as *adults* would like, forgetting that attention span and concentration increase with age. But there are cases in which children do show gross overactivity, both at home and at school, and these children can truly be regarded as having an ***attention-deficit hyperactivity disorder (ADHD)***. Their behavior is marked by developmentally inappropriate inattention, impulsiveness, and motor hyperactivity (see Box 10–2). In the classroom, their attentional difficulties are manifested in their inability to stay with a specific task. They have difficulty organizing and completing work. They often give the impression that they are not listening or that they have not heard what they have been told, and they seem unable to sit still. These children do not appear to have specific problems with processing information (such as reading deficits); instead their problems lie in self-regulation (Henker and Whalen, 1989). In interactions with peers, these children are hapless and disorganized, often rejected by others as annoying and intrusive. Similarly, at home they are described as failing to follow through on parental requests and instructions and failing to sustain activities, including play, for periods of time that are appropriate for their age. A good example of an attention-deficit hyperactivity disorder is provided in the following case:

BOX 10–2　　　　　　　　　　　　　　　　　　　　IN THE CLINICIAN'S OFFICE

DIAGNOSING ATTENTION-DEFICIT HYPERACTIVITY DISORDER

Nine-year-old Joshua is embroiled in a very special set of classroom difficulties. He is so restless that neither he nor his classmates are able to concentrate on their schoolwork. He is hardly ever in his seat. Instead, he roams the classroom, talking with other students, occasionally poking them, and surely interfering with their work. On those rare occasions when his teacher is able to nail him to his seat, Joshua fidgets constantly, dropping things on the floor. He never seems quite to know what he is going to do next and, indeed, may do something quite outrageous. His most recent suspension occurred for swinging from the fluorescent light fixture over the blackboard. He was unable to get down. The class roared.

According to his mother, Joshua has been difficult since he was a toddler, if not earlier. As a three-year-old he was unbearably restless and demanding. He required little sleep, and woke up before everyone else. He got into everything, particularly in the early morning when he would go downstairs by himself. His parents would awaken to find the kitchen or living room "demolished." By the time he was four, he could unlock the apartment door and wander off. He was rescued from the oncoming traffic on a busy street by a passerby. Rejected by a preschool program because his behavior was so difficult, and after a troublesome year in kindergarten, he was placed in a special behavior program for first- and second-graders.

Psychological testing reveals that Joshua is a boy with average *ability*, an assessment that, given his restlessness, probably underestimates his natural ability. His *achievements*, however, are only slightly below his expected level—which is to say that, for all his classroom difficulties, Joshua is learning. His attention span is virtually nonexistent. He has no interest in TV, dislikes games or toys that require any concentration or patience, and is not invited to participate in group games because he simply cannot wait his turn.

Joshua's behavior classically demonstrates the characteristic inattention, impulsivity, and hyperactivity of the attention-deficit hyperactivity disorder (ADHD) in DSM-IV. Nevertheless, it is a diagnosis that must be given with care. ADHD requires that the symptoms of the disorder be present in at least two different kinds of environments, such as *school* and *home*, and that the onset of the symptoms occur before age seven, in order to avoid giving the diagnosis in cases where the behavior is specific to a situation. For example, if a child is bored in school, or if the teacher is simply offering up boring material, the ensuing fidgeting and restlessness should not be seen as ADHD. Unfortunately, it is widely believed that many more children are being diagnosed with ADHD than is warranted.

SOURCE: Modified from the *DSM-IV Casebook.*

James was four years old when he was first admitted to a children's psychiatric ward as a day patient. Ever since infancy he had made life difficult for his elderly parents. As soon as he could crawl, he got into everything. He had no sense of danger. He slept very little at night and was difficult to pacify when upset. It was only because he was their only child and they could devote all of their time to him that his parents managed to maintain him at home.

His problems were noticed by others just as soon as James began preschool at age three. He made no friends among the other children. Every interaction ended in trouble. He rushed around all day, and could not even sit still at story time. His flitting from one activity to another completely exhausted his teachers. After some eighteen months of trying, his teachers suggested that he be referred to the hospital for assessment and treatment.

On examination, no gross physical damage could be found in his central nervous system. Psychological examinations revealed that James had a nearly average intelligence. In the hospital, he was just as hyperactive as he had been in school and at home. He climbed dangerously to the top of the outdoor swings. He ran from one plaything to another and showed no consideration for other children who were using them. Left to his own devices, he was constantly on the move, tearing up paper, messing with paints—all in a nonconstructive manner.

James was placed in a highly structured classroom, with two teachers and five other children. There his behavior was gradually brought under control. He was given small tasks that were well within his ability, and he was carefully shown how to perform them. His successes were met with lavish praise. Moreover, patience and reward gradually increased the length of time he would spend seated at the table.

Ultimately, James was placed in a small, structured, residential school. By age sixteen, he had settled down a great deal. He was no longer physically overactive, but his conversation still flitted from one subject to another. He had no friends

DSM-IV Criteria for Attention-Deficit/Hyperactivity Disorder

A. Either (1) or (2): (1) *inattention:* six (or more) of the following symptoms of inattention have persisted for at least 6 months to a degree that is maladaptive and inconsistent with developmental level: (a) often fails to give close attention to details or makes careless mistakes in schoolwork, work, or other activities; (b) often has difficulty sustaining attention in tasks or play activities; (c) often does not seem to listen when spoken to directly; (d) often does not follow through on instructions and fails to finish schoolwork, chores, or duties in the workplace (not due to oppositional behavior or failure to understand instructions); (e) often has difficulty organizing tasks and activities; (f) often avoids, dislikes, or is reluctant to engage in tasks that require sustained mental effort (such as schoolwork or homework); (g) often loses things necessary for tasks or activities (e.g., toys, school assignments, pencils, books, or tools); (h) is often easily distracted by extraneous stimuli; (i) is often forgetful in daily activities. (2) *hyperactivity-impulsivity:* six (or more) of the following symptoms of hyperactivity-impulsivity have persisted for at least 6 months to a degree that is maladaptive and inconsistent with developmental level: *Hyperactivity*—(a) often fidgets with hands or feet or squirms in seat; (b) often leaves seat in classroom or in other situations in which remaining seated is expected; (c) often runs about or climbs excessively in situations in which it is inappropriate (in adolescents or adults, may be limited to subjective feelings of restlessness); (d) often has difficulty playing or engaging in leisure activities quietly; (e) is often "on the go" or often acts as if "driven by a motor"; (f) often talks excessively. *Impulsivity*—(g) often blurts out answers before questions have been completed; (h) often has difficulty awaiting turn; (i) often interrupts or intrudes on others (e.g., butts into conversations or games).

B. Some hyperactive-impulsive or inattentive symptoms that caused impairment were present before age 7 years.

C. Some impairment from the symptoms is present in two or more settings (e.g., at school [or work] and at home).

D. There must be clear evidence of clinically significant impairment in social, academic, or occupational functioning.

E. The symptoms do not occur exclusively during the course of a Pervasive Developmental Disorder, Schizophrenia, or other Psychotic Disorder and are not better accounted for by another mental disorder (e.g., Mood Disorder, Anxiety Disorder, Dissociative Disorder, or a Personality Disorder).

SOURCE: APA, DSM-IV, 1994.

among his peers, although he could relate reasonably well to adults. He showed little initiative in matters concerning his own life, and his prospects for gaining employment were not good.

FOCUS QUESTIONS

1. Describe the usual behavior of a child diagnosed with attention-deficit hyperactivity disorder (ADHD).
2. What are some possible causes of ADHD?
3. Describe the two main therapies for treating children with ADHD.

James's behavior is typical of children with attention-deficit hyperactivity disorder. He is hyperactive, always on the go, with apparently boundless energy. He is impulsive, doing whatever comes to mind, often without regard to physical danger. And he has problems maintaining his attention on any one task without a great deal of support from teachers. As with James, children with ADHD often show these problems in very early childhood. The prevalence of attention-deficit disorders in preadolescents is about 6.7 percent, with over five times more boys than girls having this diagnosis (Anderson et al., 1987). Some children "grow out" of the symptoms, but as many as 50 to 80 percent continue to show symptoms into adolescence (Barkley, Fischer, Edelbrock, and Smallish, 1990; Fischer, Barkley, Fletcher, and Smallish, 1993). Hyperactive children tend to do very poorly in school, and as adults, are prone to interpersonal disharmony, frequent job changes, traffic accidents, marital disruptions, and legal infractions (Henker and Whalen, 1989).

Most theories of the etiology of attention-deficit hyperactivity disorder have focused on mechanisms in the central nervous system that control arousal (Douglas, 1983). Researchers have suggested that hyperactive children suffer from chronic *underarousal*, which makes it more difficult for them to maintain attention (Zentall and Zentall, 1983). Some studies find that hyperactive children have been exposed to more disruptions in their families, such as frequent changes in residence or parental divorce, than control groups. Whether these family disruptions are causes or merely correlates of ADHD is unclear. The fathers of ADHD children are more prone to irresponsible and antisocial behavior, but it is unclear whether these fathers influenced their children's behavior through genetic or environmental routes (Barkley, Fischer, Edelbrock, and Smallish, 1990).

TREATMENT

When they are very young, children with ADHD are very difficult to deal with. They quickly exhaust their teachers and parents, and they often cannot be taught in ordinary school classes. The two main therapeutic approaches are drug therapy and behavior management (see Table 10–3).

Drug Therapy Paradoxically, hyperactive children are made worse by tranquilizers. Instead, most hyperactive children show decreases in hyperactive behavior when given stimulant drugs. The most common stimulant is an amphetamine whose trade name is Ritalin. Children taking this drug show decreases in demanding, disruptive, and noncompliant behavior, plus increases in interpersonal responsiveness and goal-directed efforts. There are side effects of Ritalin, however, such as insomnia, headaches, and nausea. In addition, the gains ADHD children make when taking stimulants are short-lived, and children who receive these medications do not have a better long-term prognosis than children who do not (Henker and Whalen, 1989). Moreover, there are large differences between children in their responses to these drugs. Some children respond rapidly to small doses of Ritalin, whereas others respond only to large doses.

TABLE 10–3

TREATMENT OF ATTENTION-DEFICIT HYPERACTIVITY DISORDER (ADHD)

	Stimulants	Antidepressants	Behavior Therapy
Improvement	about 50% moderately improved	about 50% moderately improved	about 50% moderately improved
Relapse*	high	high	high
Side Effects	moderate	mild	unclear
Cost	inexpensive	inexpensive	expensive
Time Scale	weeks/months	weeks	weeks/months
Overall	**good**	**marginal**	**marginal**

*Relapse after discontinuation of treatment.
SOURCE: Based on M. Campbell, and J. Cueva, Psychopharmacology in child and adolescent psychiatry: A review of the past seven years, Part 2, *Journal of the American Academy of Child and Adolescent Psychiatry*, 34 (1995), 10; L. Greenhill, Childhood attention-deficit hyperactivity disorder: Pharmacological treatments, in P. Nathan and J. Gorman (eds.), *Treatments that work* (New York, Oxford, 1997); S. Hinshaw, R. Klein, and H. Abikoff, Childhood ADHD: Nonpharmacologic and combination treatments. In P. Nathan and J. Gorman (eds.), *Treatments that work* (New York, Oxford, 1997).

Behavior Management Operant conditioning programs have been relatively effective in treating overactivity and its associated attentional deficits, particularly in the short run. Several investigators have used these techniques to extinguish the hyperactive child's problem behaviors—for example, distracting others—while simultaneously extending the amount of time the child attends. In one case, for example, after carefully establishing how overactive a nine-year-old boy was—that is, his base rate of overactive behavior—the boy was rewarded for sitting still. For every ten seconds that he sat quietly, he earned a penny. The first experimental session lasted only five minutes. But by the eighth session, the boy's overactivity had virtually ceased and, at follow-up four months later, his teacher reported that not only was he much quieter but he was also progressing in reading and making friends. Thus, the straightforward use of attention and tangible reinforcers can produce significant and rapid changes when they are systematically applied (Pelham, 1989; Barkley, 1990).

Several researchers have argued that the most effective treatment for ADHD is a combination of drug therapy and behavioral therapy (Pelham, 1989; Rapport, 1987; DuPaul and Barkley, 1993). Medications may make it easier for children to learn from behavioral interventions. It is clear, however, that children's responses to both stimulant medications and behavior therapy are highly idiosyncratic. An effective dose of either stimulant medications or behavior therapy for one child may be an ineffective dose for another. Thus, clinicians must carefully monitor children's responses to these interventions and vary dosage levels and techniques to meet an individual child's needs.

EMOTIONAL DISORDERS

The symptoms of childhood emotional disorders are frequently similar to those seen in adult emotional disorders (see Chapters 5, 6, and 8)—feelings of inferiority, self-consciousness, social withdrawal, shyness, fear, overattachment, chronic sadness, and the like. These complaints result in diagnoses that include anxiety states, depressive disorders, obsessive-compulsive conditions, phobias, and hypochondriasis.

But there are several important differences between childhood emotional disorders and adult emotional disorders. For example, adult emotional disorders are more common among women, while many childhood emotional disorders occur equally among boys and girls and only begin to be more common among girls at the onset of adolescence. In addition, many childhood emotional disorders are age-specific, that is, they occur or terminate at particular ages. Animal phobias, for example, always begin in early childhood, while agoraphobia is rarely experienced before adulthood.

Because the emotional disorders of childhood do bear a strong resemblance to those of adulthood, we do not review all of the emotional disorders here. Rather, we shall discuss what appear to be the most common childhood emotional disorders. First, we review two disorders that are characterized by heightened levels of anxiety in children: separation anxiety and phobias. Then we review the emerging literature on childhood depression. Finally, we discuss the treatments that are currently used for emotional disorders in children.

Separation Anxiety Disorder

Most of us can remember an incident sometime in our childhood in which we suddenly realized we had been separated from our parents and could not

FOCUS QUESTIONS

1. Describe the symptoms of separation anxiety.
2. What is school phobia?
3. What are the risk factors for depression in children?
4. Describe the therapies used for treating each of the childhood emotional disorders.
5. What are some of the effects of childhood sexual abuse, and what is the focus of treatment for those who have been abused?

find them. We felt terror about being alone; we wondered if they would ever return. Eventually we were reunited with our parents, with great relief. For a short period after the incident, we were somewhat anxious about again being separated from our parents, and tried to stay close to them when in stores or other big places. But for the most part, the separation was an isolated incident that we soon forgot.

There are some children who live every minute of the day with terror that they might be separated from their families. They worry that terrible things will happen to their parents, siblings, or other loved ones. They refuse to be separated from loved ones, and become panicked if they must be separated. They have nightmares with themes of separation. They cling to loved ones and follow them around the house constantly. They may show continual physical symptoms of anxiety, such as headaches, stomachaches, and nausea, particularly on days that they must be separated from parents (such as school days). Children who show such symptoms for at least two continuous weeks may be suffering from *separation anxiety.*

Separation anxiety appears to be the most common of childhood emotional disorders, with a prevalence of 3.5 percent among preadolescents (Anderson et al., 1987). It is nearly twice as common in girls as in boys. In its severe form, separation anxiety can be incapacitating for children, preventing them from attending school or extracurricular activities. Also, these children often undergo repeated physical examinations as a result of their frequent complaints of aches and pains (APA, 1987). Episodes of separation anxiety often occur repeatedly over childhood and adolescence for children with this diagnosis.

A first episode of separation anxiety often occurs after some traumatic event in the child's life, such as the death of a relative or pet, being hospitalized, or moving to a new town. Children whose parents suffer from an anxiety disorder, particularly agoraphobia, are at an increased risk for separation anxiety (Gittelman and Klein, 1984). In addition, children with this disorder tend to come from very close-knit families.

Phobias

Fears are very common throughout childhood, much more so than adults realize or remember from their own early years. The nature of those fears often varies with age. Preschool children tend to be afraid of tangible objects, such as animals and insects. Tangible fears can continue throughout childhood and into adulthood, but they rarely begin after age five. As children grow older, so grow their fears of imaginary creatures, of disastrous events, and of the dark. Ghosts, murderers, and hidden dangers populate their imaginations. School-connected fears begin at age five or six when children are first enrolled in school, and they increase markedly between the ages of nine and twelve. From about age twelve and on through adolescence, children's fears begin to resemble those of adults, including fears about social relationships and anxieties about identity.

Fears become phobias when, as we saw in Chapter 5, the fear is out of proportion to the reality of the danger that an object presents. The prevalence of simple phobias in preadolescents is about 2.4 to 9 percent, with twice as many girls as boys showing the disorder (Anderson et al., 1987; Rutter, 1989). In many children, phobias are often associated with general anxiety or emotional disturbance, and with having parents who are phobic (see Rutter and Garmezy, 1983).

A phobia that creates significant distress in both children and their parents is *school phobia.* Such phobias are seen in about 5 percent of all clinic-referred children and 1 percent of children in the general population (Burke and Silverman, 1987). Adolescents who refuse to go to school tend to be more severely impaired and less responsive to treatment than younger children. Adults who, as children or adolescents, refused to go to school are at risk for several problems, including agoraphobia, job difficulties, and personality disorders.

Children suffering from school phobia generally achieve very well at school, say that they want to return to school, but describe all manner of anxiety symptoms whenever they set out to attend school. For example, they need to go to the toilet frequently and often feel sick and sweat profusely when the topic of school is brought up. Unlike truants, whose parents are often unaware that their offspring are not at school, children with school phobia are at home during their prolonged absences, and their parents know exactly where they are. Consider the following case:

Richard was a twelve-year-old who had been out of school almost continuously for five months. The previous summer he had won a scholarship to a well-known private school. He did exceedingly well in his first term. Then, just after the beginning of the second term, he contracted severe influenza which left him feeling very weak. He was worried that he would lose ground academically, and his anxious parents shared that concern. He tried to go back to school, but once in the classroom, he had a panic attack and ran home. Thereafter, he worried increasingly about what to say to the other boys and how to explain his flight and long absence. He was brought to a therapist for help in overcoming his fear.

Richard was given some training in relaxation and was accompanied to his school in graded stages during the summer vacation. He and his therapist rehearsed what he would say to his friends when he returned in the fall. The therapist accompanied him to school for the first three mornings, but thereafter, he was on his own. Follow-up during the next two years revealed no further difficulty. (Yule, Hersov, and Treseder, 1980)

School phobia presents a serious challenge because it is so puzzling to teachers, to parents, and to the child who suffers from it. The situation is made more tragic by the fact that the child previously was a good attender and was doing well in school when, suddenly and for no apparent reason, he stopped going to school. Careful investigation often reveals many reasons for school refusal. In Richard's case and in most others, threats to self-esteem and an unrealistically high level of aspiration play significant roles in refusal. To a child who regularly receives straight A's, the threat of even a "B" can be highly aversive and anxiety-producing.

Childhood Depression

Clinicians formerly assumed that prepubescent children would be unlikely to develop depression, because their sense of self and of the future was too immature for them to develop low self-esteem, guilt, or hopelessness (Rie, 1966). Research over the last two decades has shown, however, that prepubescent children can and do develop the symptoms that make up the syndrome of depression (Kovacs, Gatsonis, Paulauskas, and Richards, 1989). Certainly, the prevalence of major depression in children is lower than in adults; most studies find a prevalence of less than 3 percent in the general population of children (Fleming and Offord, 1990). This prevalence increases sharply in adolescence, however, to about double that in childhood.

The risk factors for depression in children are similar to those for adults: low self-esteem, pessimistic attitudes, and family dysfunction (Kovacs, Gatsonis, Paulauskas, and Richards, 1989; Fleming and Offord, 1990; Angold, 1994; see Chapter 8). Family dysfunction may be an especially potent source of depression for children. And indeed, there is accumulating evidence that childhood depression is related to parental, and especially maternal, depression (Hammen, 1991; Tisher, Tonge, and Horne, 1994). As a result, many clinicians believe that they cannot treat depression in children without treating the family as a whole.

Although many children who become depressed recover quickly when positive changes in their environment are made, a substantial minority of them

▶ A nine-year-old painted this picture to describe a recurring nightmare she had of being trapped in a hole. The milder forms of depression are as common in children as they are in adults, although major depression appears less often in children.

remain depressed for months, perhaps years (Nolen-Hoeksema, Girgus, and Seligman, 1992). In some children, a "kindling phenomenon" may occur, by which each depressive episode becomes longer and more severe and less related to specific stresses (Cytryn and McKnew, 1996). A substantial proportion of these depressed children will be at risk for subsequent suicide (Rao, Weissman, Martin, and Hammond, 1993). A bout of depression in childhood may so affect a child's functioning during critical periods in the development of skills and self-concept as to leave long-lasting scars on his or her beliefs about the self and the world. Thus, depression may lead to deficits in social competence and problem solving that have far-reaching effects on the individual, both as a child and as an adult (Levendosky, Okun, and Parker, 1995).

Treatment of Emotional Disorders

Increasingly, biologically oriented clinicians are using psychotropic drugs, usually antidepressants, to treat emotional disorders in children. Outcome studies on the effectiveness of these drugs have shown mixed results, however (Harrington, 1992). Some studies suggest that tricyclic antidepressants can be helpful for separation anxiety and depression, but others find them no more helpful than placebos. The possible toxic side effects of these drugs in children and adolescents are causes of concern.

Phobias in children, like those in adults, respond best to behavioral treatments, especially modeling (Bandura, 1969; Gelfand, 1978; Rosenthal and Bandura, 1979). In these treatments, children are exposed to, and encouraged to imitate, models who are both attractive and relatively fearless. The use of such models enables children to overcome their fears quickly. Specific fears, such as fear of animals, respond best to such treatment.

Treatment of school refusal also often follows a behavioral approach (Burke and Silverman, 1987). Sometimes this disorder is treated like a simple phobia, with systematic desensitization and modeling techniques (see Chapter 5). In other cases, school refusal is seen as the result of secondary reinforcements from parents, and interventions focus on reducing the reinforcements parents give children for avoiding school and more generally improving parents' skills at managing positive behaviors in their children.

Cognitive therapies like those designed by Aaron Beck (see Chapter 8) are increasingly being used to treat emotional disorders in older children and adolescents (Meyers and Craighead, 1984). Obviously, cognitive therapy must be adapted to the language level of the child being treated. Outcome studies of cognitive therapies for depressed children and adolescents have indicated that these therapies can be effective (e.g., Reynolds and Coats, 1986; Lewinsohn, Clarke, Hops, and Andrews, 1990; Stark, 1990). Again, however, many clinicians believe that children with emotional disorders such as depression need to be treated in the context of their entire family, since family stress or dysfunction is so frequently related to the child's disorder.

Childhood Sexual Abuse

We pause here to consider not a specific disorder, but a potential source of a range of disorders in children and adults: childhood sexual abuse. Children who are the victims of inappropriate sexual interactions with adults (e.g., fondling of genitals, intercourse) are at increased risk of developing emotional disorders, including anxiety disorders, depression, and post-traumatic stress disorder, and behavioral disorders such as conduct disorder and substance abuse (Kilpatrick, Resnick, and Veronen, 1981; Stein et al., 1988;

Cutler and Nolen-Hoeksema, 1991; Boney-McCoy and Finkelhor, 1995). Childhood sexual abuse is associated with long-lasting poor psychological health. Many victims continue to suffer from severe emotional or behavioral problems long into adulthood. For example, in a large study of adults in the general population of Los Angeles, Burman and colleagues (1988) found that 18 percent of those who had been sexually abused as children were suffering from major depression and 20 percent were suffering from drug abuse as adults. Women who had been abused were most likely to develop an emotional disorder such as depression, whereas men who had been abused were most likely to develop a behavioral problem such as drug abuse.

Treatments for children, or adults, who have been abused tend to focus on the survivor's self-evaluations and understanding of the abuse experience. The therapist looks for signs that the abuse survivor is blaming herself or himself for the abuse, or more generally, has developed a negative view of the self as a result of the abuse. Then, the therapist works to help the survivor develop a more realistic and positive view of the self. Therapists also often work with survivors to help them recognize, express, and understand the range of feelings they have about the abuser. When children have been abused by a family member, especially a parent, obviously the therapist must ensure that the abuser cannot harm the child further. Sometimes the child must be removed from his or her home. Sometimes the entire family enters therapy, often in the form of group therapy.

HABIT DISORDERS AND EATING DISORDERS

The habit disorders and eating disorders comprise a group of diagnoses that are united by a single fact: the troublesome behavior has a habitual physical component. They include the elimination disorders (enuresis and encopresis), speech disorders (stammering and stuttering), motor tics, and eating disorders (anorexia and bulimia). While the causes of these disorders are not entirely clear, their psychological consequences are dramatic. To be a bedwetter or a stutterer in Western society is to be stigmatized and to have to deal regularly with the taunts of others and assaults on one's self-esteem. Below we shall discuss in detail one of the elimination disorders, enuresis, and then the eating disorders.

Enuresis

Enuresis is arbitrarily defined as involuntary voiding of urine at least twice a month for children between five and six, and once a month for those who are older. Most children gain bladder control between eighteen months and four years of age. Thereafter, the proportion of children who have difficulty containing urine, either during the day or while in bed, drops markedly. At age twelve, 8 percent of boys and 4 percent of girls are enuretic (Friman and Warzak, 1990).

As with the other physical disorders, the problems of the enuretic are compounded by the social consequences of the disorder. Parents object to soiled clothes and bedding and commonly stigmatize the enuretic as immature. Schoolmates and friends are likely to tease the child who has an occasional "accident," the more so when those accidents are regular occurrences. Enuretics find it nearly impossible to accept overnight invitations from friends or go to camp. These social consequences may create a fertile ground for other more serious psychological problems.

FOCUS QUESTIONS

1. What are causes and treatments for enuresis?
2. What are the main symptoms and causes of anorexia and bulimia?
3. Describe some treatments for the eating disorders.

TABLE 10–4

	Behavior Therapy	Desmopressin*
TREATMENT OF ENURESIS		
Improvement	about 50% moderately improved	about 50% moderately improved
Relapse[†]	low	moderate
Side Effects	unclear	moderate
Cost	inexpensive	inexpensive
Time Scale	months	weeks
Overall	**good**	**useful**

*An antidiuretic drug used to treat enuresis.
[†]Relapse after discontinuation of treatment.
SOURCE: Based on S. Thompson and J. M. Rey, Functional enuresis: Is desmopressin the answer: *Journal of the American Academy of Child and Adolescent Psychiatry*, 34, no. 3 (1995), 266–71.

CAUSES OF ENURESIS

The social consequences of enuresis are especially unfortunate because little is known about its causes. A distinction is made between primary enuresis, which is caused by a biological abnormality, and secondary enuresis, which has psychological causes such as anxiety. There is evidence that the predisposition to enuresis often is inherited. Approximately 75 percent of enuretic children have first-degree relatives who are or were enuretic, and the concordance for enuresis is higher in identical (MZ) than in fraternal (DZ) twins. That is, the more similar a person's genetic blueprint is to an enuretic's, the more likely the individual will also be enuretic (APA, 1980).

TREATMENT

Some drugs, such as the antidiuretics (for example, desmopressin) or imipramine, suppress bed-wetting temporarily (see Table 10–4). Usually children begin to bed wet again once the drug is stopped. However, even so, a few dry nights can be an enormous morale-booster to an enuretic child, particularly if it allows the child to visit friends overnight or go to camp without fear of embarrassment. But these drugs may have significant side effects that may outweigh their usefulness, including water retention, dry mouth, cognitive impairment, and even toxic death (Thompson and Rey, 1995).

Behavioral treatments have been quite successful with enuresis, far more successful than drug treatment (Houts, 1991). Most common is a procedure that was first described over fifty years ago (Mowrer and Mowrer, 1938). The child sleeps in his or her own bed. Beneath the sheets or attached to a belt that the child wears is a special pad which, when moistened by urine, completes a harmless electric circuit that sounds a bell and awakens the child, who then goes to the toilet. A number of studies have shown that approximately 75 percent of children treated by the "bell and pad" method gain bladder control during the two-week treatment period. There is a relapse rate of up to 35 percent, but that can be reduced to 15 to 25 percent by giving a longer treatment period or by offering an additional dose of treatment (Lovibond and Coote, 1970; Shaffer, 1976; Doleys, 1979; Houts, 1991).

Eating Disorders: Anorexia and Bulimia

There are two primary types of eating disorders, anorexia and bulimia. Although these two disorders have distinct features, they share some common

---

DSM-IV Criteria for Enuresis

A. Repeated voiding of urine into bed or clothes (whether involuntary or intentional).
B. The behavior is clinically significant as manifested by either a frequency of twice a week for at least 3 consecutive months or the presence of clinically significant distress or impairment in social, academic (occupational), or other important areas of functioning.
C. Chronological age is at least 5 years (or equivalent developmental level).
D. The behavior is not due exclusively to the direct physiological effect of a substance (e.g., diuretic) or a general medical condition (e.g., diabetes, spina bifida, a seizure disorder).

SOURCE: APA, DSM-IV, 1994.

▶ Anorexics are preoccupied with body image, as illustrated in this painting made by an anorexic during the severest stage of her illness.

symptoms, and to some degree, possibly common etiologies.

The main symptoms of ***anorexia nervosa*** are the refusal to maintain body weight at or above a minimally normal weight for one's age and height, an intense fear of gaining weight despite being much underweight, and a distorted body image. Even when they are emaciated, anorexics often feel fat. There appear to be two subtypes of anorexics: restricters and purgers. Restricters are thin primarily because they refuse to eat. Purgers also refuse to eat much of the time, but when they do eat, use vomiting and laxatives to purge what they have eaten. Often, the disorder is accompanied by a variety of other physical changes. Amenorrhea, the absence of menstrual periods, is common among female anorexics. Blood pressure may be lowered, life-threatening cardiac arrhythmias (irregular heart beating) may occur, body temperature is low, bone growth is retarded, and anemia is common.

About 95 percent of anorexics are female. The prevalence of this disorder appears to be rising, such that about 1 in 100 females succumb (Fairburn, Welch, and Hay, 1993). The reason anorexia is considered a disorder of childhood is that its onset is usually in early to late adolescence, although it can begin at any age.

The following case illustrates some of the common features of anorexia:

DSM-IV Criteria for Anorexia Nervosa

A. Refusal to maintain body weight at or above a minimally normal weight for age and height (e.g., weight loss leading to maintenance of body weight less than 85% of that expected; or failure to make expected weight gain during period of growth, leading to body weight less than 85% of that expected).

B. Intense fear of gaining weight or becoming fat, even though underweight.

C. Disturbance in the way in which one's body weight or shape is experienced, undue influence of body weight or shape on self-evaluation, or denial of the seriousness of the current low body weight.

D. In postmenarcheal females, amenorrhea, i.e., the absence of at least three consecutive menstrual cycles. (A woman is considered to have amenorrhea if her periods occur only following hormone, e.g., estrogen, administration.)

SOURCE: APA, DSM-IV, 1994.

Frieda had always been a shy, sensitive girl who gave little cause for concern at home or in school. She was bright and did well academically, although she had few friends. In early adolescence, she had been somewhat overweight and had been teased by her family that she would never get a boyfriend unless she lost some weight. She reacted to this teasing by withdrawing and becoming very touchy. Her parents had to be careful about what they said. If offended, Frieda would throw a tantrum and march off to her room—hardly the behavior they expected from their bright and sensitive fifteen-year-old.

Frieda began dieting. Initially, her family was pleased, but gradually her parents sensed that all was not well. Mealtimes became battletimes. Frieda hardly ate at all. Under pressure, she would take her meals to her room and later, having said that she had eaten everything, her mother would find food hidden away untouched. When her mother caught her deliberately inducing vomiting after a meal, she insisted they go to the family physician. He found that Frieda had stopped menstruating a few months earlier. Not fooled by the loose, floppy clothes that Frieda was wearing, he insisted on carrying out a full physical examination. Her emaciated body told him as much as he needed to know, and he arranged for Frieda's immediate hospitalization.

People with *bulimia* often wish they could restrict their food intake better, and many were on highly restrictive diets before they developed bulimia. But people with this disorder find themselves bingeing, often on large quantities of food, with a sense that they completely lack control over their eating. Now, everyone binges occasionally. As many as 30 percent of college students say they binge at least twice a month, and 16 to 20 percent say they binge once per week (Schotte and Stunkard, 1987). People with bulimia, however, are excessively self-critical about their binges, and more generally about their physical appearance. As a result, they attempt to purge after a binge, by self-induced vomiting, by misusing laxatives, diuretics, or other medications, by fasting, or by excessive exercising. Often the binge/purge episodes take hours out of each day of a bulimic's life, and begin to control her life. The sense of shame, distress, and helplessness that follows these episodes is often overwhelming. Many bulimics also suffer from severe depression.

As with anorexia, most people who suffer from bulimia are women. Although poor eating patterns may be rampant among adolescents and young adults, only about 1 percent of patients in this age range will qualify for a diagnosis of bulimia (Schotte and Stunkard, 1987; Drewnowski, Hopkins, and Kessler, 1988; Fairburn and Wilson, 1993; Heebink, Sunday, and Halmi, 1995). Some bulimics are excessively thin, but many are of normal weight. Bulimia is still a very dangerous disorder physically, however. Frequent vomiting and other types of purging can lead to severe loss of body fluids and electrolytes, and the stomach acid vomited up can lead to severe tooth decay (Fairburn and Wilson, 1993). Many bulimic women also experience menstrual problems.

THEORIES OF ANOREXIA AND BULIMIA

Some researchers believe that both anorexia and bulimia are variants of a mood disorder (see Agras and Kirkley, 1986). Dysphoria and depression are common among both anorexics and bulimics, and the families of people with eating disorders often have histories of affective disorders (Hudson, Pope, Jonas, and Yurgelun-Todd, 1987). Whether depression is a cause or consequence of eating disorders is unclear, however. Similarly, although the metabolic changes that occur in anorexia have led some researchers to suggest that a malfunction of the hypothalamus causes this disorder, it is unclear whether changes in hypothalamic functioning precede or follow self-starvation by anorexics (Mitchell, 1986).

There are a number of psychosocial theories of the eating disorders. The facts that both anorexia and bulimia have increased in prevalance in recent decades and are more common in developed countries than underdeveloped countries have led some researchers to argue that modern cultural norms play a role in the etiology of these disorders (Garfinkel and Garner, 1982; McCarthy, 1990). The "thin ideal" of Western-oriented societies (see Chapter 8) may lead some people to go on extremely restrictive diets, which are chronically stressful and frustrating. These people, when they break their dietary rules, may lose their sense of control over their eating and end up bingeing. Then the guilt and fear of fatness that follow the bingeing may lead them to purge (Polivy, 1976; Rosen and Leitenberg, 1982; Garner, 1993). Stress reduction models of bulimia suggest that bingers eat when faced with stressful circumstances to escape anxiety and distress (Heatherton and Baumeister, 1991). They focus on the short-term gratification of food in lieu of their long-term goals for weight control, and end up eating large amounts of food even though they are not hungry. Purging is then a way of reducing the distress that the binge has caused.

Most of the psychosocial theories of anorexia suggest that it arises from a deep need for autonomy, which comes from being in an overcontrolling family (Minuchin, Rosman, and Baker, 1980; Bruch, 1982). These families also tend to restrict shows of emotion or conflict and to demand perfection from their children, so that the adolescent girl is not allowed to express her needs or her anger at her parents. Eventually, the adolescent girl may discover that she can control at least one aspect of her life—her eating. Gaining complete control over her food intake becomes all important, the way the girl defines her self-esteem and gets attention. Some females who develop eating disorders have a history of sexual abuse, usually by a family member (Kanter, Williams, and Cummings, 1992). In these cases, the eating disorder may develop as a result of a distorted body image or low self-esteem caused by the abuse, or out of a need to control some aspect of their lives.

TREATMENT FOR EATING DISORDERS

Antidepressant drugs have been helpful for some people with eating disorders (Mitchell and de Zwaan, 1993). Whether these drugs relieve an underlying biological dysfunction that is the cause of the eating disorder, or simply make it easier for the woman to participate in psychotherapy and to change her eating habits is unclear.

TABLE 10–5

	Interpersonal Therapy	Behavioral Therapy	Cognitive-Behavioral Therapy	Cognitive-Behavioral Therapy and Antidepressant Drugs	Antidepressant Drugs Alone
TREATMENT OF BULIMIA					
Improvement	about 50% moderately improved	about 50% moderately improved	better than 50% moderately improved	about 60% moderately improved	about 50% moderately improved
Relapse*	moderate	moderate	low to moderate	low to moderate	high relapse
Side Effects	unclear	unclear	mild	moderate	moderate
Cost	moderately expensive	moderately expensive	moderately expensive	moderately expensive	moderately expensive
Time Scale	months	months	weeks/months	weeks/months	weeks/months
Overall	**useful**	**useful**	**good**	**good**	**useful**

*Relapse after discontinuation of treatment.
SOURCE: Based on A. Yates, Current perspectives on eating disorders, Part 2, Treatment, outcomes, and research directions. *Journal of the American Academy of Child and Adolescent Psychiatry,* 29 (1990), 1; J. E. Mitchell, N. Raymond, and S. Specker, A review of the controlled trials of pharmacotherapy in the treatment of bulimia nervosa. *International Journal of Eating Disorders,* 14, no. 3 (1993), 229–247; M. E. P. Seligman, *What you can change and what you can't* (New York: Knopf, 1993), Chapter 12; G. T. Wilson and C. Fairburn, Treatment of eating disorders, in P. Nathan and J. Gorman (eds.), *Treatments that work* (New York: Oxford, 1997).

Most clinicians agree that psychotherapy is necessary for eating disorders, even for people who are taking antidepressant drugs (see Table 10–5). Cognitive-behavioral therapies have proven effective for eating disorders, especially bulimia (Agras, 1993). They teach patients to identify environmental triggers for bingeing, to introduce feared foods into their diets while controlling the amount they eat, and to identify and change distorted cognitions about food intake, weight, and body shape. One study found that 56 percent of bulimic patients ceased bingeing and purging by the end of treatment with a cognitive-behavioral therapy (Agras, Schneider, Arnow, Raeburn, and Telch, 1989a, 1989b).

There are over a dozen outcome studies of the cognitive-behavioral approach to bulimia and the results are good. Better than 50 percent of the patients experienced a substantial reduction in binging and purging (somewhat better than when antidepressant drugs are used). But, unlike drugs, there is little relapse after treatment. Attitudes toward weight and shape relax, and dieting withers. Several studies explicitly compared drugs and cognitive-behavioral treatment, and by-and-large, drugs did worse, particularly because of the high relapse rate for drugs when they are discontinued. Combining both cognitive-behavioral therapy and antidepressant drugs may be superior to either alone (Wilson and Fairburn, 1997; Mitchell, Pyle, Eckert et al., 1990; Agras, Rossiter, Arnow et al., 1992).

Family therapies (see Table 10–6) focusing on the ways family members control each other and express conflict are often recommended for anorexia (Minuchin, Rosman, and Baker, 1980). Unfortunately, however, families with an anorexic member often do not enter therapy until the anorexia reaches a crisis point, at which time the anorexic is dangerously ill. It may be necessary to hospitalize the anorexic patient to stabilize her health. Even then, some anorexics will protest that they have no problem, and as many as 30 percent will refuse treatment (Crisp, 1980). Obviously, force-feeding an anorexic patient in the hospital can tap into the very autonomy issues that are supporting her anorexia. The family may also deny that there is anything wrong within the family, identifying the anorexic as their only "problem."

TABLE 10–6

	Outpatient: Family Therapy	Outpatient: Behavior Therapy	Outpatient: Cognitive Therapy	Outpatient: Dietary Advice	Inpatient: Behavior Therapy and Dietary Advice
	TREATMENT OF ANOREXIA NERVOSA				
Improvement	about 50% moderately improved	about 50% moderately improved	about 50% moderately improved	about 50% moderately improved	about 50% moderately improved
Relapse*	moderate	moderate	moderate	moderate	moderate
Side Effects	unclear	unclear	unclear	unclear	unclear
Cost	inexpensive	inexpensive	inexpensive	inexpensive	very expensive
Time Scale	months	months	months	weeks/months	weeks/months
Overall	**good**	**good**	**good**	**good**	**useful**

*Relapse after discontinuation of treatment.
SOURCE: Based on A. Yates, Current perspectives on eating disorders, Part 2, Treatment, outcomes, and research directions. *Journal of the American Academy of Child and Adolescent Psychiatry,* 29 (1990), 1; G. T. Wilson and C. Fairburn, Treatment of eating disorders, in P. Nathan and J. Gorman (eds.), Treatments that work (New York: Oxford, 1997).

Thus, anorexia can be a difficult disorder to treat. Clinicians and researchers are continuing to explore combinations of drug and psychological therapies that will be most effective.

DEVELOPMENTAL DISORDERS

According to DSM-IV, the essential feature of developmental disorders is that the predominant disturbance is in the acquisition of cognitive, language, motor, or social skills. Moreover, the course of developmental disorders tends to be chronic, with some signs of the disorder persisting in a stable form into adult life. However, in many mild cases, adaptation or full recovery may occur.

Mental Retardation

FOCUS QUESTIONS

1. What two criteria are necessary to make a diagnosis of mental retardation?
2. Distinguish among mild, moderate, severe, and profound mental retardation.
3. What are some of the causes of mental retardation?
4. Describe how mentally retarded children can be treated so that they are able to function more effectively in school and in society.

Mental retardation is a disorder that afflicts three out of every hundred children, two-thirds of them boys. Thus, it is a widely prevalent disorder, often heartbreaking in its emotional costs to families and in the lifelong economic burdens it imposes on them and on society. For all of its prevalence, however, and despite the fact that everyone feels they know what mental retardation is, it is a difficult disorder to define precisely and to diagnose accurately. In part, the difficulty arises from the stereotypes that people have about mental retardation. But in larger measure, the difficulty occurs because the notion of intelligence is at the heart of mental retardation, and intelligence is very difficult to define (Kamin, 1974; Gould, 1981).

The definition of mental retardation most used in the United States is the one provided by the American Association on Mental Retardation (AAMR): "Mental Retardation refers to substantial limitations in present functioning. It is characterized by significantly subaverage intellectual functioning, existing concurrently with related limitations in two or more of the following applicable adaptive skill areas: communication, self-care, home living, social skills, community use, self-direction, health and safety, functional academics, leisure, and work. Mental retardation manifests before age eighteen" (Luckasson, Coulter, Polloway, Reiss, Schalock, Snell, Spitalnik, and Stark, 1992). This definition has been incorporated into the DSM-IV as criteria for diagnosing mental retardation. In general, the diagnosis of mental retardation can only be made when low IQ is accompanied by deficits in ability to cope with the demands of daily life. Adaptive behavior scales assess the degree to which an individual meets the standards of personal independence and social responsibility expected for a child's age or cultural group (Grossman, 1983). One difficulty with this type of assessment is that standards of behavior and achievement are determined by an individual's society. However, the skills typically assessed by adaptive behavior scales are based on standards that are relatively universal, such as toilet training, control of aggression, and respect for authority figures. An IQ score of less than 70 remains the long accepted criterion of mental retardation. Though not without its problems, the Wechsler Intelligence Scale for Children, Revised (WISC-R) and other intelligence tests continue to be regarded as acceptable measures to provide a meaningful criterion of mental retardation.

LEVELS OF RETARDATION

The various levels of mental retardation and their associated IQ scores on a standard test of intelligence are shown in Table 10–7. What do these levels of retardation mean?

Mild Mental Retardation   The largest group of retarded children, about 85 percent of them, fall into this category. These children develop social and communication skills just like all others and at quite the same times. In fact, their retardation is often not noticed until they are in the third or fourth grade, when they begin to have academic difficulties. Without help, they can acquire academic skills through the sixth grade; with help, they can go beyond that level. In all other respects, their needs and abilities are indistinguishable from those of other children. Special education programs often enable these children to acquire the vocational skills that are necessary for minimal self-support. When under social or economic stress, they may need guidance and supervision, but otherwise they are able to function quite adequately in unskilled and semiskilled jobs.

Moderate Mental Retardation   Children in this category make up 10 percent of the mentally retarded. Like other children, they learn to talk and communicate during the preschool period. But unlike other children, the moderately retarded have difficulty learning social conventions. During the school-age period, they can profit from training in social and occupational skills, but they are unlikely to go beyond the second-grade level in academic subjects. Physically, they may be clumsy and occasionally they may suffer from poor motor coordination. They may learn to travel alone in familiar places and can often contribute to their own support by working at semiskilled or unskilled tasks in protected settings.

TABLE 10–7

SEVERITY LEVELS OF MENTAL RETARDATION		
Level	Percent of Retarded People	Wechsler IQ
Mild	85	50–70
Moderate	10	35–49
Severe	4	20–34
Profound	>1	below 20

DSM-IV Criteria for Mental Retardation

A. Significantly subaverage intellectual functioning: an IQ of approximately 70 or below on an individually administered IQ test (for infants, a clinical judgment of significantly subaverage intellectual functioning).

B. Concurrent deficits or impairments in present adaptive functioning (i.e., the person's effectiveness in meeting the standards expected for his or her age by his or her cultural group) in at least two of the following areas: communication, self-care, home living, social/interpersonal skills, use of community resources, self-direction, functional academic skills, work, leisure, health, and safety.

C. The onset is before age 18 years.

SOURCE: APA, DSM-IV, 1994.

Severe Mental Retardation Before they are five, the severely retarded provide considerable evidence of poor motor development, and they develop little or no communicative speech. At special schools, they may learn to talk and can be trained in elementary hygiene. Generally, they are unable to profit from vocational training, though as adults they may be able to perform simple and unskilled job tasks under supervision.

Profound Mental Retardation Children in this category are severely handicapped in adaptive behavior and are unable to master any but the simplest motor tasks during the preschool years. During the school years, some development in motor skills may occur, and the child may respond in a limited way to training in self-care. Severe physical deformity, central nervous system difficulties, and retarded growth are not uncommon. Health and resistance to disease are poor, and life expectancy is shorter than normal. These children require custodial care.

CAUSES OF MENTAL RETARDATION

Our knowledge of the causes of mental retardation is ever expanding. Mental retardation is a symptom, not a specific disease, and there are a multitude of causes. The more severely impaired an individual, the more likely a cause can be found. Mental retardation may result from infections and intoxications, physical trauma leading to brain damage, metabolism or nutrition problems, gross brain disease, unknown prenatal influences, chromosomal disorders, gestational disorders, and psychosocial disadvantages. Table 10–8 presents some common causes of mental retardation.

TABLE 10–8

PHYSICAL CAUSES OF MENTAL RETARDATION

Genetic abnormalities	Infectious conditions	Traumatic conditions
Down Syndrome	Rubella	Rh Factor
Phenylketonuria (PKU)	Syphilis	Malnutrition
Tay-Sachs Disease	Toxoplasmosis	Lead Poisoning
Klinefelter's Syndrome	Encephalitis	Irradiation
Fragile X Syndrome	Meningitis	Anoxia
	Herpes Simplex	Head Injuries
		Drugs

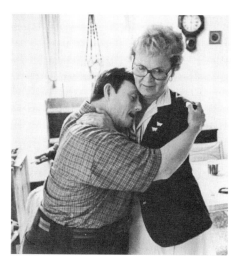

▶ Down syndrome is a form of moderate to severe mental retardation.

A major cause of mental retardation is a chromosomal disorder known as **Down syndrome,** named for Langdon Down, a physician who first recognized it in 1886. While the most common form of Down syndrome is not inherited, it occurs at conception and immediately affects the development of the fetus. It arises because there are forty-seven chromosomes, rather than the usual forty-six, in the cells of the children born with the disorder, although the reason for this chromosomal abnormality is not presently known. Interestingly, while the risk for the disorder is about 1 in 1,500 for children born to mothers in their twenties, it increases to 1 in 40 when the mother is over forty. Many babies born with Down syndrome suffer from physical anomalies as well as cognitive delay. Fortunately, with the advent of infant heart surgery, advanced surgical skills, and the development of better antibiotics, most of these defects are readily correctable or treatable. Most of the data previously gathered about Down syndrome are very suspect as they were based on a population that faced both early death due to physical problems that were not treatable as well as institutionalization.

Other chromosomal abnormalities associated with mental retardation include Fragile X syndrome, trisomy 13, and trisomy 18. Fragile X syndrome is caused when a tip of the X chromosome breaks off. The syndrome is characterized by severe to profound mental retardation, autistic behaviors (see pp. 335–340), and speech defects. In addition, males with Fragile X syndrome have large ears, long faces, and enlarged testes. Trisomy 13 and trisomy 18 are caused when chromosomes 13 and 18 are present in triplicate rather than in pairs. Both disorders cause more severe retardation than Down syndrome, and a shorter life expectancy.

It is possible to detect chromosomal problems through **amniocentesis,** a test that is administered to the mother after the thirteenth week of pregnancy. In this procedure, a small amount of amniotic fluid (the fluid that surrounds the fetus) is drawn off and examined for the presence of abnormal chromosomes. When abnormalities are found, mothers have the option of continuing the pregnancy or undergoing an abortion. A newer test, known as **chorionic villus sampling (CVS),** can be done earlier in a pregnancy, between the eighth and twelfth weeks, to test for Down syndrome and other chromosomal abnormalities. A sampling of cells is taken via the mother's vagina and cervix, or through her abdominal wall. The advantage of CVS is that earlier detection of birth defects is possible, allowing for an earlier and perhaps less complicated abortion, if the mother chooses one. The disadvantage of CVS is that it is somewhat less accurate than amniocentesis.

There are a number of metabolic diseases that are associated with mental retardation, including Tay-Sachs disease, Nieman-Pick disease, and phenylketonuria (Carter, 1970). A child affected by Tay-Sachs disease appears normal until age three to six months, when mental and physical deterioration begins. Tay-Sachs disease is uniformly fatal within the first six years of life, and no effective treatment has been developed.

Phenylketonuria (PKU) is a rare metabolic disease that occurs in roughly 1 out of 20,000 births. PKU results from the action of a recessive gene that is inherited from each parent. The infant cannot metabolize phenylalanine, an amino acid that is an essential component of proteins. As a result, phenylalanine and its derivative, phenyl pyruvic acid, build up in the body and rapidly poison the central nervous system, causing irreversible brain damage. About a third of such children cannot walk; nearly two-thirds never learn to talk; and more than half have IQs that are below 20.

Carriers of PKU can be identified through biochemical tests and receive genetic counseling (Stern, 1981). In addition, affected babies can be identified by a simple test of their urine about three weeks after birth. Provided they are kept on a diet that controls the level of phenylalanine in their system until age six, when the brain is nearly fully developed, their chances of surviving with good health and intelligence are fairly high.

For approximately two-thirds of children with mental retardation, there is no clear injury or disease that caused their retardation. Rather, there seem to be factors in their genetic backgrounds that have contributed to their condition.

Cognitive ability (as measured by the IQ) appears, to some extent, to be passed through the genes. The IQs of identical (MZ) twins reared together correlate between .80 and .95, whereas the IQs of fraternal (DZ) twins correlate much lower, from .40 to .70 (Schwartz and Johnson, 1985). Even MZ twins reared apart have more similar IQs than DZ twins reared together (Scarr, 1975). The IQs of adopted children correlate more powerfully with the IQs of their biological parents (.48) than their adoptive parents (.19) (Munzinger, 1975). These data suggest intelligence is substantially inherited.

Recent studies indicate that many disorders in intellectual functioning, including mental retardation and autism, co-occur in families at a high rate (Quay, Routh, and Shapiro, 1987). But there may not be a genetic predisposition specifically to mental retardation. Rather, it may be intellectual ability in general that is partially influenced by genetics.

Environment also appears to play an important role in the development of intelligence. The prenatal environment to which the fetus is exposed can have a profound effect on intellectual development. Some chronic medical conditions in the mother, such as high blood pressure or diabetes, if untreated, can interfere with fetal brain development. In addition, drugs that the mother takes while pregnant can affect fetal development. Fetal alcohol syndrome (FAS) is a condition involving a variety of physical defects and deformities and mental retardation in fetuses exposed to alcohol through the mother's drinking during pregnancy. Children whose mothers severely abused alcohol during pregnancy have an average IQ in the 60s (Streissguth, Grant, and Barr, 1991). It is unclear whether there is a safe amount of alcohol mothers can ingest during pregnancy.

One of the tragedies of the emergence of crack cocaine in recent decades is "crack babies," infants born to mothers who took crack while pregnant. Crack, or any form of cocaine, constricts the mother's blood vessels, leading to reduced oxygen and blood flow to the fetus. Crack babies are born with a variety of neurological deficits, and are irritable and difficult to soothe.

Lower-class mothers are more likely to give birth to premature infants with low birth weights, and low birth weight is a risk factor for retardation

(Kiely, Paneth, and Susser, 1981). Children from impoverished backgrounds also face a number of postnatal environmental challenges to intellectual growth. Some of these children ingest toxic levels of lead by eating fragments of lead-based paint that peel off the walls of the old buildings in which they live. In turn, exposure to lead is associated with retarded intellectual growth. In addition, children from lower-class families are more likely than upper-class children to be malnourished, to receive poor health care, and to suffer from a variety of illnesses across childhood. Such an environment inhibits the full development of the intellectual abilities a child does have.

Physical abuse of children and accidental falls or blows to the head can also cause brain damage and mental retardation. Brain trauma can occur if an infant is simply shaken hard, because the infant's head is large and heavy compared to her body, and her neck muscles are too weak to control her head movements. The infant's soft brain literally bangs against the inside of the skull, causing bruising.

TREATMENT

Mentally retarded children often have defects in language skills that manifest themselves even before the child enters school. Training in language necessitates that the required sounds be demonstrated, and that the child be rewarded for closer and closer approximations to normal speech. Such training, whether conducted by professionals (Baer and Guess, 1971; Garcia, Guess, and Brynes, 1973), or by parents who have been trained to do such teaching (Cheseldine and McConkey, 1979), can be very useful in helping the child communicate more effectively. Behavioral training methods have also been used successfully to teach self-care skills (Watson and Uzzell, 1981).

As we indicated earlier, many children, particularly those who are mildly handicapped, are not identified as requiring assistance until they enter school. There is considerable controversy about the kind of remedial help they need once they are in school. One view holds that they should be "mainstreamed," that is, educated with other children, in the same classes and with the same teachers, since the vast majority of them will ultimately live with their "normal" peers. Another view holds that the needs of the retarded are so different that they need to be educated separately, with separate teaching methods and different schedules and curricula. According to this view, the education of mentally retarded children proceeds best when they are segregated in different institutions, or at least in separate classes. The fact is that neither mainstreaming nor segregation has proven particularly effective in training mentally retarded children (Cegelka and Tyler, 1970; MacMillan and Semmel, 1977).

Learning Disorders

FOCUS QUESTIONS

1. What distinguishes children with learning disabilities?
2. Describe the treatment that has proven to be effective for many children with reading disabilities.

Much more common than mental retardation are the *learning disorders,* difficulties that reflect enormous developmental tardiness and mainly affect the development of language and academic skills. Learning disorders occur frequently in combination with other difficulties, and in fact, may spawn them.

To survive in the modern world, people must be able to learn a language, to learn to read, and to do simple arithmetic. Because of this, most modern industrial societies make education compulsory for about ten years of a child's life. As in most developmental matters, children progress in their education at different speeds. A certain amount of lagging behind is to be expected of some children some of the time. But when a child is significantly below the expected level, as indexed by the child's schooling, age, and IQ, then the matter is viewed as a psychological problem. For children between the ages of eight and thirteen—the critical ages for the acquisition and

▲ Children's rates of development naturally vary, but if a child lags more than two years behind his age group, an underlying disorder may be the cause. Learning disorders such as reading difficulties are associated not only with poor school performance but with low self-esteem and other psychological problems.

FOCUS QUESTIONS

1. What is the central feature of autism?
2. Describe the difficulties that autistic children have with communication, including their problems with language.
3. Explain the psychogenic and biological theories of the causes of autism.
4. How is autism treated?

implementation of academic skills—a significant problem may exist if a child is more than two years behind his or her age level.

Of all the learning disorders, reading difficulties have been studied most. As a group, poor readers are late in acquiring language, and they have more of a history of reading difficulty in their families. Most children who have reading difficulties also have trouble with other domains of learning. More than three times as many boys as girls suffer serious reading difficulties. Children with severe reading difficulties at age ten have an increased risk of other psychological disorders, particularly behavior disorders.

A combination of training in reading skills and behavior therapy designed to maintain a child's interest in learning has proven effective for many children with reading disabilities. This training must start early in a child's school career and be maintained throughout the school years for the child to sustain the gains that have been made and to continue to improve. Unfortunately, children's reading difficulties often are not detected until quite late in childhood.

The social implications of serious reading problems are alarming. Poor readers who are of average intelligence rarely read books or newspapers. They aspire to little that involves reading and, therefore, they often fail to graduate from high school. Poor readers emerge from the school system handicapped educationally, socially, and economically, in the sense that their employment opportunities have been significantly constricted (Yule and Rutter, 1976).

Autism

Pervasive developmental disorders are all-encompassing, involving difficulties of such magnitude and across so many modalities—language, attention, responsiveness, perception, motor development—that little doubt remains about the psychological devastation they create. The primary type of pervasive developmental disorder is autism.

The total number of children suffering from autism is considerable. It occurs in about 4 cases per 10,000, about as frequently as deafness occurs among children, and twice as commonly as blindness (Ritvo et al., 1989). With regard to sex differences, boys outnumber girls by about three to one. The disorder does not appear to be related to socioeconomic status or race. The prevalence of autism appears to be similar across several different countries (Ritvo et al., 1989).

The essential feature of ***autism*** is that the child's ability to respond to others does not develop within the first thirty months of life. Even at that early age, gross impairment of communicative skills is already quite noticeable, as are the bizarre responses many of these children make to their environment. Most autistic children lack interest in and responsiveness to people and fail to develop normal attachments. In infancy, these characteristics are manifested by their failure to cuddle, by lack of eye contact, or by downright aversion to physical contact and affection. These children may fail entirely to develop language. Such children also react very poorly to change, either in their routines or in their environments. These symptoms will be taken up at greater length momentarily. But first, some of the difficulties created by autism can be seen in the following case:

Looking at family photographs of John, one sees a good-looking, well-built, sandy-haired ten-year-old. He looks like thousands of other ten-year-olds—but he's not. If one saw a movie of John it would be immediately obvious that his *be-havior* is far from normal. His social relationships seem peculiar. He seems distant, aloof. He seldom makes eye contact. He rarely plays with other children, and when he does, he plays like a three-year-old, not like someone who is ten.

Some things fascinate him, and his most recent fascination has been with shiny leather belts. He carries one around with him nearly always and at times whirls it furiously, becoming more and more excited in the process. At the height of his excitement, he lets out high-pitched, bird-like noises, jumps up and down on the spot, and flaps his hands at eye level. At other times, John appears to be living in a world of his own, entirely impervious to what is happening around him. A car can backfire near him, but he doesn't flinch. He stares into space, gazing at nothing in particular, occasionally flicking his fingers at something in the periphery of his vision.

In addition to the peculiar squeaks, John's speech is most unusual. He can follow a few simple instructions, but only if he is in familiar surroundings. He will say, "Do you want a drink?," and his parents will know that he means *he* wants a drink. Often, he will repeat complex phrases that he has heard a few days before; television commercials particularly feature in this sort of meaningless speech.

John's parents are both intelligent, articulate, professional people who, right from the early months after John was born, were convinced that something was wrong with him. They brought John to child specialists. Finally, he was formally tested by a psychologist, and a surprising fact emerged. Although he was grossly retarded in language development, he was advanced for his age on nonverbal puzzles. Difficulties with hearing were ruled out, and it was during these investigations that autism was first suggested.

John's parents managed to get him into a small class in a school for children with learning handicaps. The teacher took a special interest in John and, encouraged by his parents, she adopted a firm, structured approach to teaching him. To everyone's surprise, he took to some aspects of schoolwork readily. He loved counting things and could add, subtract, multiply, and divide by the time he was seven. Moreover, he learned to read fluently—except that he could not understand a single word of what he read. This was brought home to his parents when he picked up a foreign language journal of his father's and read a whole page in phonic French—without, of course, understanding a word! At about this time, he began talking. He referred to himself as "John," got his personal pronouns in a dreadful muddle, and learned to say "no." He used telegraphic sentences of a sort more appropriate to a boy many years younger than he, but at least he was beginning to make himself understood.

He seemed to cherish all kinds of monotonous routines. His diet consisted of a very restricted selection of foods, and he could not be induced to try new foods. He went to school by a prescribed and invariable route, watched television from the same armchair, and strenuously resisted change. Taking him outside was a nightmare, for there was no anticipating when he might throw an embarrassing tantrum. Try as she might, his mother could not help but be hurt by the glares and comments from passersby as she struggled to get John out of the supermarket or into their car. "If only he looked *abnormal*," she often said, "people would be more understanding."

SYMPTOMS OF AUTISM

The central feature of autism, according to Leo Kanner, a child psychiatrist who was the first to recognize this disorder as a distinct syndrome, is the "inability to relate . . . in the ordinary way to people and situations . . . an *extreme autistic aloneness* that, whenever possible, disregards, ignores, shuts out anything that comes to the child from outside" (Kanner, 1943). This striking aloneness takes a variety of forms in the areas of language, behavior, intellectual and cognitive development, and in social relationships (see Box 10–3).

Language Development　One of the striking features of autistic children is how poorly their understanding and use of spoken language develops. Most parents report that the language of autistic children is delayed and deviant right from the beginning. Toward the end of the second year, when normal children are babbling in a characteristically varied way, autistic children frequently show decidedly abnormal and idiosyncratic patterns. Speech falters badly in these children because they fail to imitate or to initiate imaginative

DIAGNOSING AUTISTIC DISORDER

Stanley is a good-looking three-and-a-half-year-old, whose parents have been worried about him ever since he was a few months old. He seems quite self-sufficient and well-coordinated physically. But socially, he is aloof, to say the least. He won't greet his mother in the morning or his father when he comes home from work. He has no interest in other children. He ignores his younger brother, and screams endlessly when left with a baby-sitter. He babbles without either conversational intonation or meaning. He echoes phrases and words he has heard in the past, often with the speaker's original intonation. And he uses some of those phrases to indicate his own needs. For example, he will say "Do you want a drink?" to indicate that he is thirsty. He does not communicate by facial expression, gesture, or words, except that he will pull you along and place your hand on the object he wants.

Bright lights and spinning objects fascinate him. He stares at them, flaps his hands, laughs, and dances. He does the same when he hears music, and he has loved music from infancy. He *always* carries his miniature car in his hand, but he never plays imaginatively with it or any other toy. He assembles jigsaw puzzles with re-markable speed—and with one hand, since his car is always in the other.

Ever since he was two years old, Stanley has collected kitchen untensils and arranged them in repetitive patterns all over the floor of his house. That, and a bit of aimless running around, constitutes his entire repertoire of spontaneous activities. Any attempt to change or extend his interests meets with intense resistance. Removing his toy car, disturbing his puzzles or patterns, trying to get him to look at a picture book—any of this will precipitate a temper tantrum that can last for an hour or more, replete with kicking, screaming, or biting himself or others.

His stereotyped and restricted interests, his social aloofness, and his tendency to echo the words and phrases of others, are characteristic of autistic disorder (a pervasive developmental disorder) in DSM-IV.

SOURCE: Abbreviated from the *DSM-IV Casebook.*

---

play, both of which are crucial for early language development. For example, they show little skill in such simple social imitations as "waving bye-bye." And their later use of small toys in imaginative play is severely limited if, indeed, it ever develops. Unlike deaf children, who understand the ideas of communication and who have developed nonverbal skills for communicating, autistic children do not use gestures and mime to make their needs known. They may point to objects they need, but if the object is not immediately present, their ability to communicate about it is very much restricted.

It is in their very peculiar use of sounds and words that autistic children's difficulties are most noticeable. About half of the autistic children never learn to use simple words. Those who do show many characteristic abnormalities. For example, in the early stages, the child often uses a high-pitched, bird-like squeaking voice, as John did. Again, like John, the autistic child latches on to a phrase from, say, a television commercial, and echoes it for weeks on end. Even the small proportion of autistic children who do learn to talk continue to use language in a noticeably peculiar way. Often it is *too perfect,* too grammatical, rather like a person using a foreign language learned artificially. There is a lack of colloquialism. Conversation is stilted. These children can maintain a concrete question-and-answer interchange, but the subtleties of emotional tone are lost on them. They seem to know the formal rules of language, but they do not comprehend the idea of communication. This defect extends to the nonverbal aspects of communication as well.

Insistence on Sameness   Many normal children react badly to changes in their environment, particularly if those changes are sudden. But for reasons that are not at all clear, autistic children show this trait in greatly exaggerated form. For example, some autistic children will have severe temper tantrums if the furniture in the house is moved around. Others insist on being driven to school over the same route every day. Parents find that what begins as a harmless routine becomes so rigid that it seriously interferes with everyday life.

▼ Autistic children often have severe temper tantrums, particularly when their environments change suddenly.

▲ An autistic boy.

Insistence on sameness is seen in other ways. Autistic children frequently use toys and other objects to make long lines or complex patterns. They seem more interested in the pattern than in the functional or imaginative play qualities of the objects. Frequently, these children become intensely attached to one or more objects. John, you recall, carried around a long belt and gyrated it. Other children may refuse to part from a grubby piece of toweling.

Social Development One other striking characteristic of the autistic child is aloofness, a physical and emotional distance from others that is especially troublesome to parents and quite noticeable by others. John was clearly aloof, and his mother particularly was troubled by it. This aloofness reflects a fundamental failure to develop social attachments. Some evidence suggests that autistic children have fundamental problems in understanding expressions of emotions in others and in using their own faces, voices, and gestures to communicate their own emotions (Hobson, 1986; Volkmar, Carter, Sparrow, and Cicchetti, 1993). Other research indicates that some autistic children can show emotion and form secure attachment to their mothers, but that they may have problems in the areas of joint attention and social referencing (Sigman, Arbelle, and Dissanayake, 1995).

Many autistic children gradually improve in their social relationships beginning at about age five, provided that they have not been institutionalized in unstimulating surroundings. Ultimately, however, the relationships these children establish are difficult at best. Their social skills show themselves in their lack of cooperative group play with other children, in their failure to make personal friendships, and in the enormous difficulty they have in recognizing and responding appropriately to other people's feelings.

Intellectual Development While autistic children do poorly on tests that require verbal ability, they may perform far above average on tests that involve rote memory or spatial tasks. Moreover, they may be quite talented in music or drawing. But despite evidence of islands of intelligence, autistic children function quite poorly in the cognitive domain. Only about 25 to 40 percent of them have IQ scores above 70, and those scores appear to be quite stable over a ten-year period (Ritvo et al., 1989). In fact, the child's measured IQ is one of the best predictors of later progress: those with higher IQ scores do better in a variety of educational and remedial settings (Mittler, Gillies, and Jukes, 1966; Gittleman and Birch, 1967; Lockyer and Rutter, 1969; DeMeyer, Barton, Alpern, Kimberlin, Allen, Yang, and Steel, 1974).

CAUSES OF AUTISM

The sorts of behavior associated with autism are so far removed from people's expectations of normal development that most now believe that there must be some biological abnormality underlying the syndrome. During adolescence, nearly 30 percent of autistic children develop epileptic seizures even though they had shown no clear evidence of neurological disorder when they were younger. Furthermore, electroencephalographic (EEG) studies—that is, studies that examine the electrical activity of the brain—reveal that autistic children have a higher rate of abnormal brain waves than do normal children. A variety of other structural and functional differences between the central nervous systems of autistic and nonautistic children have been found, suggesting that there are multiple biological causes of autism, or several subtypes of autism, each with different causes (Prior, 1987).

Another focus for biological studies of autism involves whether there is a genetic component to the disorder. Because autism is a relatively rare condition, however, it is difficult to gather extensive data on the genetics of this disorder. But one study found that about 10 percent of families with one autistic

DSM-IV Criteria for Autistic Disorder

A. A total of six (or more) items from (1), (2), and (3), with at least two from (1), and one each from (2) and (3): (1) qualitative impairment in social interaction, as manifested by at least two of the following: (a) marked impairment in the use of multiple nonverbal behaviors such as eye-to-eye gaze, facial expression, body postures, and gestures to regulate social interaction; (b) failure to develop peer relationships appropriate to developmental level; (c) a lack of spontaneous seeking to share enjoyment, interests, or achievements with other peope (e.g., by a lack of showing, bringing, or pointing out objects of interest); (d) lack of social or emotional reciprocity. (2) qualitative impairments in communication as manifested by at least one of the following: (a) delay in, or total lack of, the development of spoken language (not accompanied by an attempt to compensate through alternative modes of communication such as gesture or mime); (b) in individuals with adequate speech, marked impairment in the ability to initiate or sustain a conversation with others; (c) stereotyped and repetitive use of language or idiosyncratic language; (d) lack of varied, spontaneous make-believe play or social imitative play appropriate to developmental level. (3) restricted repetitive and stereotyped patterns of behavior, interests, and activities, as manifested by at least one of the following: (a) encompassing preoccupation with one or more stereotyped and restricted patterns of interest that is abnormal either in intensity or focus; (b) apparently inflexible adherence to specific, nonfunctional routines or rituals; (c) stereotyped and repetitive motor mannerisms (e.g., hand or finger flapping or twisting, or complex whole-body movements); (d) persistent preoccupation with parts of objects.

B. Delays or abnormal functioning in at least one of the following areas, with onset prior to age 3 years: (1) social interaction, (2) language as used in social communication, or (3) symbolic or imaginative play.

C. The disturbance is not better accounted for by Rett's Disorder or Childhood Disintegrative Disorder.

SOURCE: APA, DSM-IV, 1994.

child have at least one other autistic child (Ritvo et al., 1989). The specific syndrome of autism may be only weakly transmitted genetically. Instead, a more general vulnerability to several types of cognitive impairment, only one of which is manifested as autism, seems to run in autistic children's families, and specifically their identical twins (Quay, Routh, and Shapiro, 1987). A significant percentage of autistic children also experience other severe, sometimes chromosome-linked, biological disorders, such as Fragile X syndrome, phenylketonuria, rubella, encephalitis, and epilepsy (Prior, 1987). Finally, autism is associated with a higher rate of obstetric and neonatal complications (Goodman, 1990). Whether these other disorders are causes of autism or simply caused by another underlying biological abnormality that also causes autism is unknown (Gilberg, 1991).

TREATING AUTISM

Drug treatments have been used with mixed results in autistic children (Gilberg, 1991). Instead, current treatment efforts arise mainly from behavioral sources that focus on the specific deficits that are engendered by autism. Considerable effort, for example, has focused on language development, on the grounds that the inability to communicate properly is so central to this disorder. In these treatments, children's vocalizations are reinforced by the therapist until they occur very frequently. Next, the children are rewarded for imitating the sounds produced by the therapist, and simultaneously punished for producing meaningless sounds. When imitation is established, children are taught to label everyday objects. And finally, the same techniques

▲ From a very early age, many autistic children avoid physical affection and seem unable to form attachments to people.

are used to teach them to ask questions (Lovaas, 1966; Risley and Wolf, 1967). Early studies of the effectiveness of these methods engendered considerable optimism that these behavioral techniques might enable children to overcome the deficits associated with autism. But this optimism was tempered somewhat by the studies showing that gains made during treatment often disappear when the children are returned to institutional care (Lovaas, 1973). One study, however, suggests that if autistic children are given intensive behavioral treatment for a significant period of time (i.e., forty hours per week for at least two years) at an early age, long-term prognosis can be good (Lovaas, 1987). In this study, 47 percent of the autistic children receiving such intensive treatment achieved normal intellectual and educational functioning by age six to seven, compared to only 2 percent of autistic children who received minimal, institutional care. Furthermore, when parents participate in treatment programs, both their behaviors and those of the children undergo change. And the more the parents are involved in the treatment program, the more likely are the language gains to be maintained (Hemsley, Howlin, Berger, Hersov, Holbrook, Rutter, and Yule, 1978).

In conjunction with behavioral approaches, direct structured educational approaches have also proven beneficial to autistic children (Hung, Rotman, Consentino, and MacMillan, 1983). These approaches zero in on the specific cognitive, motor, and perceptual handicaps of these children. A carefully designed educational program minimizes the kinds of distractions that accompany ordinary teaching, making it possible for these children to concentrate. For example, when normal children are taught to read, some texts and teaching materials print vowels in one color and consonants in another. While this helps normal children differentiate between vowels and consonants, it confuses children with pervasive developmental difficulties (Schreibman, 1975). Generally, structured education aimed at overcoming the specific handicaps of the disorder seems to be the best method presently available for helping these children. Again, including parents in these treatments, teaching them how to overcome their child's specific deficits, increases the effectiveness of the treatments.

Despite the gains associated with treatment, long-term follow-up studies of autistic children indicate that the prognosis for them is still not favorable. Close to 60 percent will be unable to lead an independent life as adults (Gilberg, 1991). Only about 4 percent will eventually recover to a point where they are indistinguishable from normal children. The remaining children will make some progress in developing skills but will still manifest a host of odd behaviors.

▶ Behavioral techniques may successfully treat specific deficits caused by autism. These autistic children receive positive reinforcement for hugging each other.

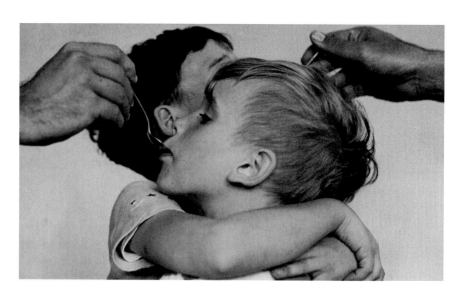

There are at least three broad sets of questions about childhood psychopathology in general that need to be addressed over the next few years. First, does the current DSM-IV classification system for childhood disorders accurately represent the breakdown of childhood syndromes? Children's problems are extremely difficult to translate into specific syndromes with clear-cut criteria for diagnosis. This is because the symptom configuration of any disorder may change with the child's development. Also, some symptoms, such as aggressive behavior, are associated with many different disorders. The classification of children's disorders is one area that experts expect to undergo much revision in the next decade.

The second question is related to the first: How can we better identify children who have serious psychological problems and how can we assess their particular problems? We must rely on the adults in a troubled child's life to bring that child to the attention of clinicians. In addition, children's underdeveloped language skills make it difficult to obtain information from them about their condition. We need to know how to ask better questions of parents, teachers, and children that will provide the information clinicians need to assess children's psychological health.

The final question is about the long-term prognosis for children who have a psychological problem. We mentioned that children with autism or a conduct disorder appear to be at high risk for psychological disturbance in adulthood. We know very little about the long-term prognosis of many of the other disorders, however. There have just been too few studies that follow children all the way into adulthood. We also know very little about the long-term effects of different types of therapy for children, especially drug therapies. Longitudinal studies of the outcome of children with different types of problems, who undergo different types of therapy, will be expensive, but the need for them is obvious.

FOCUS QUESTIONS

1. Why are children's psychological problems so difficult to classify?

2. Why is it so difficult to identify children who have serious psychological problems?

3. Why is there a need for longitudinal studies of children with psychological problems?

SUMMARY

1. Children's psychological disorders are often difficult to distinguish from the relatively common problems of growing up because they occur in a developmental context, because children cannot communicate a problem directly through language, and because children's problems are often specific to particular situations and contexts.

2. On the whole, children's problems can be divided into four areas: disruptive behavior disorders, emotional disorders, habit and eating disorders, and developmental disorders.

3. The disruptive behavior disorders, including conduct disorder, oppositional defiant disorder, and attention-deficit hyperactivity disorder, appear to be quite persistent from childhood into adulthood. Children with these disorders often show criminal behavior, drug abuse, and low educational and occupational attainment.

4. The most common emotional disorder in children is separation anxiety disorder. Children with this disorder have a marked fear of separation from loved ones. Phobias, such as school phobia, are also common among children.

5. The habit disorders and eating disorders include bed-wetting, stuttering, tics, and two eating disorders, anorexia and bulimia. The prevalence of the two eating disorders appears to be increasing.

6. The developmental disorders range from learning disabilities in specific areas such as reading or math to various levels of mental retardation to autism. Autism is the most severe of these because it involves both intellectual retardation and severe disturbances in the abilities to have social and emotional experiences. The developmental disorders are more likely than any other class of disorders to persist into adulthood.

QUESTIONS FOR CRITICAL THINKING

1. What are the indications that children with conduct disorder or attention-deficit hyperactivity disorder may be suffering from chronic underarousal?

2. Describe some reasons for school refusal and why children who suffer from school phobia may be at risk for agoraphobia, job difficulties, and personality disorders as adults.

3. How do genes and environment interact to produce more or less severely retarded children?

4. Why should involving parents in treatment strategies for mental retardation and autism increase the effectiveness of the treatments?

11

Montage by David McGlynn

Psychosomatic and Organic Disorders: The Psychology of Health

What we think and what we feel change our physical well-being. We learned from our discussion of emotion in Chapters 5 and 6 that our thoughts and emotions can modify how our body reacts. One of our bodily reactions is, of course, disease, and we do not usually think of physical disease—stomach ulcers, coronary heart disease, cancer, tuberculosis, asthma—as reactions that can be influenced by thoughts and feelings. But there is a good deal of evidence that the course, and perhaps the very occurrence, of such illnesses can be influenced by the psychological states of their victims.

Conversely, the condition of our body can influence and even cause a disorder of the mind. Here the evidence is strong, especially regarding damage to the brain from within, as in Alzheimer's disease, dementia, and stroke, or from without, as in a blow to the head or an attack of a virus.

This chapter takes up several disorders that arise from mind-body interactions. Clearly, such interactions can occur in other disorders discussed in this book. But here we focus on the direct links, of influence or of cause, between our physical and mental selves. In such cases where mind seems to influence body, we are speaking of ***psychosomatic disorders.*** Where body alters mind, we are investigating ***organic disorders.***

PSYCHOSOMATIC DISORDERS

Many people believe that some ulcers, heart attacks, and other physical problems are partly caused by an adverse psychological state. But how does a clinician know this, and when there is evidence, how does the clinician classify it?

The diagnosis of psychosomatic disorder is made if (1) there is a disorder of known physical pathology present, *and* (2) psychologically meaningful events preceded and are judged to contribute to the onset or worsening of the disorder. When psychological factors influence physical illness, the individual commonly denies that he is ill, refuses to take medication, and may ignore the presence of risk factors that will likely worsen the physical condition (DSM-IV).

These two defining criteria of psychosomatic disorder have been incorporated into a particular model: the ***diathesis-stress model.*** "Diathesis" refers to the constitutional weakness that underlies the physical pathology, and "stress" to the psychological disturbance to meaningful events. According to this model, an individual develops a psychosomatic disorder when he both has some physical vulnerability (diathesis) and experiences psychological disturbance (stress). If an individual is extremely weak constitutionally, very little stress will be needed to trigger the illness; if, on the other hand, extreme stress occurs, even individuals who are constitutionally strong may fall ill. In effect, the model suggests that individuals who develop coronary heart disease are both constitutionally vulnerable to cardiovascular problems and experience sufficient stress to trigger the pathology.

Psychological factors can affect many physical conditions in a large number of organ systems: the skin, the skeletal-musculature, the respiratory, the cardiovascular, the blood and lymphatic, the gastrointestinal, the genitourinary, the endocrine systems, or the sense organs (Looney, Lipp, and Spitzer, 1978). There is no evidence, however, that the process causing psychosomatic effects is different for each different organ, although any given individual may be especially vulnerable to psychosomatic influence in only one organ system. Some of us react to stress with the stomach, others by sweating, some by muscle tension, and still others with a racing heart. For this reason, DSM-IV does not have separate categories for each psychosomatic problem. Rather it has only one, "Psychological factors affecting medical condition." The diagnostician fills in which psychological factors (for example, a stressful divorce) affect which medical condition (for example, a heart attack).

FOCUS QUESTIONS

1. What are stigmata?
2. How do stigmata exemplify a psychosomatic disorder?

Stigmata

One of the most dramatic examples of psychosomatic disorders is the rare phenomenon of ***stigmata.*** Stigmata are marks on the skin—usually bleeding or bruises—often of high religious or personal significance, brought on by an emotional state. About 300 instances of stigmata, many of them called miracles,

▲ Steven's right forearm shows indented weals, resembling rope marks. They appeared when he relived, under a hypnotic drug, an earlier traumatic experience.

have been reported in the last 2,000 years. Most are found in religious histories, but only a handful of these are documented well enough to take seriously scientifically. This handful provides the quintessential demonstration of a psychosomatic phenomenon: a mental state causing the body to react in a way usually thought of as being purely physical. Consider the following case history:

> Since childhood, Steven had suffered from nightmares and sleepwalking. His sleepwalking became a particular problem when, in 1935, he was hospitalized because of an infection. To prevent him from sleepwalking about the ward in the middle of the night, he was restrained physically while he slept; his hands were tightly bound behind his back when he went to sleep. On one such occasion he awoke, and in a half-conscious state, found himself tied down. Although he could not untie his hands, he was still able to evade his bodyguard and escape into the surrounding countryside, from which he returned a few hours later.
>
> Some ten years later, at age thirty-five, Steven was again admitted to a hospital—this time in an attempt to cure his recurrent sleepwalking. One evening at about midnight the nurse saw him struggling violently on his bed, apparently having a nightmare. He was holding his hands behind his back and seemed to be trying to free them from some imaginary bond. After carrying on in this way for about an hour, he crept out of bed still holding his hands behind his back, and disappeared into the hospital grounds. He returned twenty minutes later in a state of normal consciousness. As the nurse put him into bed, she noted deep weals like rope marks on each arm, but until then Steven seemed unaware of their presence. The next day the marks were still visible and were observed by the hospital staff. Three nights later the marks had disappeared.
>
> His physician believed that the marks were stigmata caused by reliving the traumatic event of a decade earlier. To test this, he caused Steven to relive the experience of ten years before under a hypnotic drug. While reliving the experience, Steven writhed violently on the couch for about three-quarters of an hour. After a few minutes weals appeared on both forearms. Gradually these became deeply indented and finally blood appeared along their course. Next morning the marks were still clearly visible. (Moody, 1946)

Here is a clear example of an essentially psychosomatic phenomenon. A process that we usually believe to be strictly physical—the appearance of rope marks and bleeding—is induced by the mental state of recalling a traumatic incident with high emotion. The patient was carefully observed during the development of the rope marks, and there is no ready explanation other than emotional state influencing a physical state.

Coronary Heart Disease

In the last century, Sir William Osler (1849–1919), a famous Canadian physician, prefigured what was to be learned in our century about personality and heart attacks:

> A man who has early risen and late taken rest, who has eaten the bread of carefulness, striving for success in commercial, professional, or political life, after twenty-five or thirty years of incessant toil, reaches the point where he can say, perhaps with just satisfaction, "Soul, thou has much goods laid up for many years; take thine ease," all unconscious that the fell sergeant has already issued the warrant. (Osler, 1897)

Coronary heart disease (CHD) kills more people than any other disease in the Western world. In the United States, over half the deaths of individuals over forty-five are caused by some form of heart or circulatory problem (Lachman, 1972; Weiner, 1977; Gillum, 1994; Eriksson, 1995). The underlying condition in most instances of heart attack and sudden death is *arteriosclerosis,* a building up of fat on the inner walls of the coronary arteries. Such clogging blocks blood from reaching the heart muscle; heart attack and sudden death can result (Diamond, 1982).

Epidemiologists have thoroughly studied risk factors for CHD. There are seven major physical risk factors: (1) growing old, (2) being male, (3) smoking cigarettes, (4) having high blood pressure (hypertension), (5) having high serum cholesterol, (6) physical inactivity, and (7) genetics. A psychological risk factor now joins the list: the Type A personality, which we will consider here.

CORONARY HEART DISEASE AND THE TYPE A PERSONALITY

Type A personality was said to have been discovered by an upholsterer. When he came to reupholster the chairs in the office of a physician who specialized in seeing patients who had had heart attacks, he noticed that the chairs in the waiting rooms were worn in the front of the seat, not the back. Type A's sit on the edge of their chair. They are defined by (1) an exaggerated sense of time urgency, (2) competitiveness and ambition, and (3) aggressiveness and hostility, particularly when things get in their way. They contrast to *Type B personalities,* who are relaxed, serene, and have no sense of time urgency. When Type A's miss a bus, they become upset. When Type B's miss a bus, they say to themselves, "Why worry? There will always be another bus coming along." The Type A sees the environment as threatening, and seems to be engaged in prolonged emergency reactions. Type A characteristics may begin when a person is as young as three or four years old (Steinberg, 1986).

Classifying individuals into Type A's and Type B's is done either by a standard stress interview or by a self-administered questionnaire (Jenkins, Rosenman, and Friedman, 1967; Glass, 1977; Yarnold and Bryant, 1994; Bryant and Yarnold, 1995). Typical questions are:

1. "Has your spouse or friend ever told you that you eat too fast?" Type A's say, "yes, often." Type B's say, "yes, once or twice" or "no."
2. "How would your spouse (or best friend) rate your general level of activity?" Type A's say, "too active, need to slow down." Type B's say, "too slow, should be more active."
3. "Do you ever set deadlines or quotas for yourself at work or at home?" Type A's say, "yes, once a week or more often." Type B's say, "no" or "only occasionally."
4. "When you are in the midst of doing a job and someone (not your boss) interrupts you, how do you feel inside?" Type A's say, "I really feel irritated because most such interruptions are unnecessary." Type B's say, "I feel O.K. because I work better after an occasional break."

Several excellent prospective studies exist of the Type A personality as a risk factor for CHD in the population at large:

- *The Western Collaborative Study.* Beginning in 1960, 3,200 working men who had no history of CHD were followed in a longitudinal study. Men who had been judged Type A by the structured interview had 2.2 times as much CHD as Type B's. When the physical risk factors were statistically controlled, Type A's still had double the risk for CHD (Rosenman, Brand, Jenkins, Friedman, Straus, and Wurm, 1975; Hecker, Chesney, Black, and Frautschi, 1988; Carmelli, Dame, Swan, and Rosenman, 1991).
- *The Framingham Heart Study.* More than 1,600 men and women, who were classified Type A or B by a questionnaire and who were free of any CHD, were followed for eight years. White-collar Type A men had almost three times the risk of CHD as white-collar Type B's (Haynes, Feinleib, and Kannel, 1980; Eaker, Haynes, and Feinleib, 1983).

FOCUS QUESTIONS

1. Distinguish between Type A and Type B personalities.
2. What components of Type A may lead to coronary heart disease?
3. What role might helplessness play in CHD, and why might a Type A's reaction to helplessness predispose him to CHD?
4. Why might Type A's have prolonged emergency reactions, and why might this make them at greater risk for CHD?

FIGURE 11-1

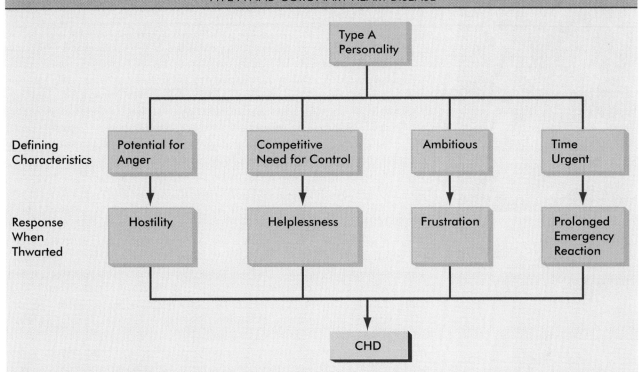

TYPE A AND CORONARY HEART DISEASE

When Type A personalities are not able to exercise control, they may experience hostility, helplessness, frustration, and a prolonged emergency reaction, all of which may contribute to a high risk for coronary heart disease.

- *The Belgian Heart Disease Prevention Trial.* Two thousand men, having demonstrated good health by passing a strenuous exercise test, were rated along the Type A–B continuum and followed for five years. The upper third (those nearer to the Type A part of the continuum) had 1.9 times the risk for CHD as the lower third (Kittel, Kornitzer, deBacker, and Dramaix, 1982).

- *The Cardiovascular Risk in Young Finns Study.* Lifestyle risk factors for CHD were studied in 3,596 Finnish children and young adults over six years. Male adolescents classified as Type A's were shown to have a high level of aggressiveness, which was significantly associated with the presence of multiple risk habits such as smoking, alcohol use, and physical inactivity. High aggressiveness also predicted an increase in metabolic factors that contribute to heart disease, including obesity and hypertension (Raitakari, Leino, Räikkönen, et al., 1995; Ravaja, Keltikangas-Järvinen, and Keskivaara, 1996).

Although the idea has not gone unchallenged (Cohen and Reed, 1985; Shekelle, Hulley, Neaton, et al., 1985), many studies conclude that Type A confers extra risk for CHD in the general population (see Figure 11–1).

HOSTILITY AND CORONARY HEART DISEASE

Hypertensives (people with high blood pressure) are particularly sensitive to hostility and respond with blood pressure elevation to threat in general and anger toward the threat in particular (Wolf, Cardon, Shepard, and Wolff, 1955; Kaplan, Gottschalk, Magliocco, Rohobit, and Ross, 1960; Diamond, 1982; Miller, Smith, Turner, et al., 1996). Other studies have shown that opportunities to vent hostility lower blood pressure, and that the failure to

▲ Hostility and anger may lead to hypertension, although the opportunity to vent hostility may lower blood pressure.

release hostility may keep blood pressure high (Hokanson, 1961; Hokanson and Burgess, 1962; Hokanson, Willers, and Koropsak, 1968; Dimsdale, Pierce, Schoenfeld, Brown, Zusman, and Graham, 1986; Scheier and Bridges, 1995). Moreover, two very long-term studies directly relate hostility to CHD. Two hundred and fifty-five physicians were given the MMPI in medical school and were followed for twenty-five years (see Figure 11–2). One component of the MMPI is the Cook-Medley hostility score (Cook and Medley, 1954). High hostility scores strongly predicted CHD (Barefoot, Dahlstrom, and Williams, 1983; Williams, Barefoot, and Shekelle, 1985; Barefoot, Larson, Von der Lieth, and Schroll, 1995). This relationship was replicated in the Western Electric Study of 1,877 men followed for ten years. The high hostility men had five times the incidence of CHD (Shekelle, Gale, Ostfeld, and Paul, 1983).

In an exploration of the mechanism by which hostility might damage the heart, eighteen men angrily recounted incidents from their lives that had annoyed them. As they spoke, the pumping efficiency of their heart dropped by 5 percent on average, suggesting a drop in blood flow to the heart itself. Pumping efficiency was not changed by other stressors (Ironson, Taylor, Boltwood, et al., 1992; see also Krantz, Helmers, Bairey, et al., 1991). It has been speculated that hormonal changes during anger may provide a link from anger to CHD. To test this, the blood of 90 newlywed couples was monitored for hormonal changes during conflict. Hostile behavior was associated with significant changes in five different hormones (Williams, Lane, Kuhn, et al., 1982; Malarkey, Kiecolt-Glaser, Pearl, and Glaser, 1994). Whether it is expressing anger, damming up anger, or just underlying anger that produces CHD, and how the link from anger to hormonal changes to coronary changes actually works remain two of the most intriguing questions in health psychology today.

HELPLESSNESS AND CORONARY HEART DISEASE

Helplessness may correlate highly with Type A personality and coronary heart disease. People who are ambitious, competitive, and time urgent may get themselves into and react more strongly to situations that produce more frustration, failure, and helplessness. Type A individuals seem to be engaged in a lifelong struggle to control a world they see as threatening. David Glass suggests that it is this struggle for control that crucially distinguishes a Type A from a Type B personality. Glass postulates that a cycle of desperate efforts to control the environment, alternating with profound giving up when the environment proves uncontrollable, is repeated over and over again during the lifetime of the Type A individual. This struggle may result in high blood pressure and other physiological changes that in turn cause heart attacks.

FIGURE 11–2

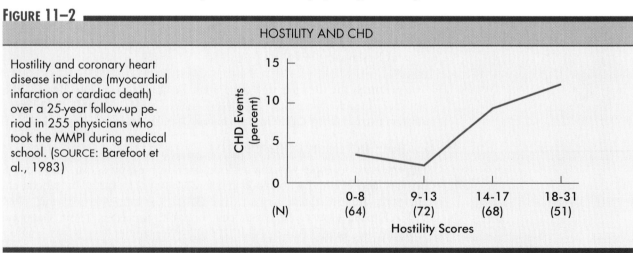

Hostility and coronary heart disease incidence (myocardial infarction or cardiac death) over a 25-year follow-up period in 255 physicians who took the MMPI during medical school. (SOURCE: Barefoot et al., 1983)

A second line of evidence comes from a study of "inhibited need for power" and hypertension. Seventy-eight Harvard juniors were tested in the late 1930s and early 1940s for high blood pressure and various personality characteristics. Ten years later, these individuals were given a projective test in which they told stories about five pictures from the TAT (see Chapter 4). The themes of the stories they told were used as indications of what their personalities were like. Twenty years later, in the early 1970s, these men were tested for high blood pressure. The findings were remarkable.

Men who had a high need for power (which was greater than their need for affiliation), but who showed high inhibition, were more likely to develop high blood pressure. Twenty-three of the men fell into this group at approximately age thirty. By the time these men were in their fifties, 61 percent had shown definite signs of hypertensive pathology, whereas only 23 percent of the remaining forty-seven men showed hypertensive pathology. These findings become even more remarkable when we realize that they are unrelated to the blood pressure of these men when they were in their thirties. In other words, at age thirty the need for power combined with its inhibition predicted that individuals would be at risk for severe high blood pressure at age fifty, irrespective of what their blood pressure was when they were thirty years old (McClelland, 1979). We can view the inhibited need for power as a sign of the repeated helplessness in these individuals' lives.

THE EMERGENCY REACTION AND CORONARY HEART DISEASE

Continuing threat leads to a ***continual emergency reaction.*** Consider the heart as a glorified pump. As a pump breaks after some fixed number of uses, so the heart fails after it has exceeded its genetically allotted number of beats. The more beats you use up, the earlier your heart will fail. Being a Type A, continually viewing the world as a hostile and threatening place, will lead to the beats being used up earlier. We saw in Chapter 5 that when we are threatened we go into an emergency reaction that involves increased heart rate and increased blood pressure (Southard, Coates, Kolodner, Parker, Padgett, and Kennedy, 1986; Bystritsky, Craske, Maidenberg, Vapnik, and Shapiro, 1995). As such, those who view the world as threatening may experience a sustained emergency reaction, which on average will use up their allotted beats more quickly.

Data on ***overload*** at work are compatible with this simple hypothesis (Jenkins, 1982; Steptoe, Roy, Evans, and Snashall, 1995). In the Western Collaborative Study, men who carried two jobs were at greater risk for CHD. In a particularly elegant analysis, job demand and decision latitude were related to CHD (Karasek, Baker, Marxer, Ahlbom, and Theorell, 1981; Alterman, Shekelle, Vernon, and Burau, 1994). Among over 1,500 Swedish workers, a hectic and demanding job increased the risk for CHD, as did low amount of choice (see Figure 11–3). We might infer from this that workers whose jobs create the most frequent emergency reactions (high demand, low choice) use up their beats faster than those with other kinds of jobs, and such workers are at greater CHD risk.

Further evidence for the possibility that people who have prolonged emergency reactions are at greater risk for CHD comes from a prospective, longitudinal study of 126 alumni from the Harvard classes of 1952–1954. As students, these men were given an experimental stress test in which there was persistent criticism and harassment from the experimenter. Thirty-five years later, the amount of CHD was 2.5 times as great in those who experienced severe anxiety during the stress test than in those who did not (Russek, King, Russek, and Russek, 1990).

Physical activity and exercise lower the risk for CHD. In a review of forty-three studies, inactivity presented a consistent risk for CHD of about the same size as high blood pressure, smoking, or high cholesterol

FIGURE 11–3

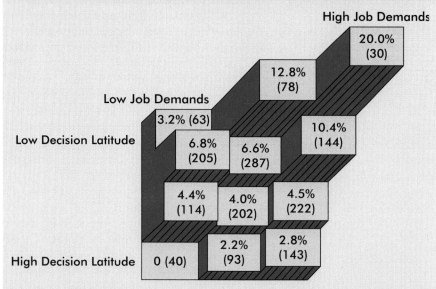

PREVALENCE OF CORONARY HEART DISEASE

The risk for coronary heart disease is increased where job characteristics include high demands and low decision latitude. The vertical bars indicate the percent of people developing CHD according to whether their job characteristics include high, medium, or low job demands and high, medium, or low decision latitude. There was a grand total of 1,621 men who at the beginning of the study in 1968 did not have CHD. The numbers in parentheses are the number of people in each subgroup, and the percentage is the percent of those people in the subgroup who developed symptoms of CHD over the six-year course of the study. (SOURCE: Adapted from Karasek, Baker, Marxer, Ahlbom, and Theorell, 1981)

(Powell, Thompson, Caspersen, and Kendrick, 1987). The practical importance of this study is that in prevention programs, regular exercise should be promoted strongly. The theoretical importance concerns the emergency reaction: While vigorous exercise increases heart rate and blood pressure when you are engaged in it, its long-term consequences are to lower resting heart rate and blood pressure, thereby conserving the pump.

PSYCHONEUROIMMUNOLOGY (PNI)

Psychological factors, in particular hostility and pessimism, can increase the risk of coronary heart disease. Can psychological factors increase the risk of infectious disease, allergy, auto-immune disease, cancer, and even death? There is a field of health psychology, called *psychoneuroimmunology (PNI)*, which studies how psychological factors change the immune system and ultimately increase the risk for disease. The basic findings in this field are that personality, behavior, emotion, and cognition can all change the body's immune response, and thereby change risk for these diseases. The hope of this field is that psychotherapy can be used to prevent, and perhaps to cure, such physical illnesses. First, we will examine how the immune system works under optimal conditions, then we will go into the mechanisms whereby the immune system breaks down.

The Immune System

FOCUS QUESTIONS

1. What is psychoneuroimmunology?
2. How does our body's immune system destroy antigens?
3. Which psychological states might cause lowered immunocompetence in humans?
4. Describe the chain of events that may lead from loss to cancer.

The immune system has two basic tasks. First it must recognize foreign invaders, called antigens, and then it must inactivate them and remove them from the body (Maier, Laudenslager, and Ryan, 1985; Borysenko, 1987; Gold and Matsuuch, 1995). A group of cells, called lymphocytes, recognizes foreign cells. There are four main types of lymphocytes: B-cells (which come from bone marrow), K-cells, T-cells (which come from the thymus gland), and Natural Killer (NK) cells. B-cells and T-cells have receptors on their surface that recognize antigens. This recognition is very specific, and any given lymphocyte recognizes only a small number of foreign invaders, so that at any time there are a large number of different lymphocytes surveying the body for different antigens.

What happens when antigens are spotted? They are destroyed in four main ways (see Figure 11–4). First, the B-cells that are specific to that antigen multiply and produce antibodies (or they activate K-cells that work to destroy the antigen). Antigens often simply bind to the antibody and form a complex that is inactive and can do no further harm. Second, some T-cells, once activated by recognizing their specific antigen, multiply rapidly and can directly kill their antigens by lysing (breaking down) the cell membrane of the target. Third, some T-cells attract macrophages (big eaters) and neutrophils. Macrophages eat the antigens, and neutrophils eat the antigen-antibody complexes. Fourth, when the antigen is a tumor, Natural Killer cells rapidly lyse the cells of the tumor.

It is important that the second time the body is challenged by a specific invader, the immune system does a better job of destroying it than it did the first time. This is called *immunologic memory.* The T-cells and B-cells that took on the antigen the first time will multiply more rapidly the second time this antigen is spotted. This memory is responsible for *immunization. Immunocompetence,* the degree to which these events proceed efficiently to protect the organism, is measured in several ways: assessing the amount of immunoglobulin (antibodies formed after immunization) in the blood or

FIGURE 11–4

SCHEMA OF THE IMMUNE RESPONSE

Once the immune system recognizes an antigen such as a tumor, it takes action to inactivate and remove it. B-cells specific to the antigen multiply and produce antibodies that activate K-cells that work to destroy the antigen. T-cells multiply and either directly kill the antigen or activate macrophages and NK cells that work to destroy the antigen.

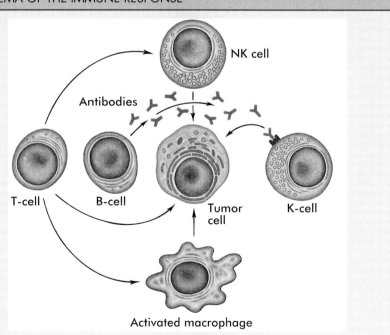

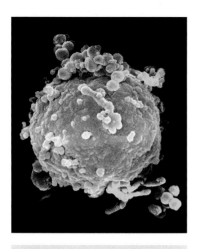

▲ B-cells are lymphocytes that are specific to a particular antigen and that can make antibodies only against that antigen. Pictured here is a B-lymphocyte (the large round body) and chlamydia bacteria (the clusters of small, round bodies). The photograph has a magnification of 14,000 times the actual size.

saliva, assessing the amount of T-cell multiplication when antigens are challenged, assessing the ability of Natural Killer cells to kill tumors, and measuring how much the skin reddens and swells when injected with an antigen (the greater the reaction, the better the immune system is working) through the delayed hypersensitivity test.

Lowered Immunocompetence in Humans

Evidence is accumulating that psychological states produce immune and disease changes in humans (see Box 11–1). There are several examples of how depression, helplessness, hopelessness, and stressful life events seem linked to immune change in people. Infectious illnesses and number of doctor visits were counted for undergraduates who had either an optimistic or pessimistic explanatory style. You will recall from Chapter 3 that individuals who habitually see the causes of bad events as internal, stable, and global ("it's me," "it's going to last forever," "it's going to undermine everything") are said to have a pessimistic explanatory style. In the year following the test for explanatory style, pessimists had about twice as many infectious illnesses and made about twice as many visits to doctors as optimists (Peterson and Seligman, 1987). In another study, twenty-six spouses whose mates had died were followed for six weeks after the death of their spouses; the bereaved group showed depressed T-cell multiplication to antigens (Bartrop, Luckhurst, Lazarus, Kiloh, and Penny, 1977). In a different study of senior citizens, blood was drawn after explanatory style had been measured. Antigens were placed in the blood samples, and the efficiency of the immune reaction was measured. Pessimists had poorer T-cell function than optimists (Kamen-Siegel, Rodin, Seligman, and Dwyer, 1991). Moreover, in a study of healthy male college students, those with more pessimistic explanatory style for bad events also showed lower T-cell responses to antigens placed in their blood samples (Zorilla, Redei, and DeRubeis, 1994).

Natural Killer cell activity was found to be lower in women who had recently experienced major life events like the death of their spouse; the more depressed the woman, the more both NK and T-cell functions were impaired (Irwin, Daniels, Bloom, Smith, and Weiner, 1987). In a similar sample of widows, women who were diagnosed with major depression had lower NK-cell activity than did those who did not meet the criteria for major depression (Zisook, Shuchter, Irwin, et al., 1994). In another study, blood was drawn twice from seventy-five first-year medical students, one month before and then on the day of final exams. NK activity was lower just at finals time; the more loneliness and the more stressful life events reported, the lower the NK activity (Kiecolt-Glaser, Garner, Speicher, Penn, Holliday, and Glaser, 1984; Kiecolt-Glaser and Glaser, 1987).

As the population ages, more people are suffering from senile dementia (Alzheimer's disease), and many relatives have now become caregivers of Alzheimer's patients. Taking care of such a patient is a difficult and helplessness-inducing, full-time task. In a longitudinal study of the consequences of taking care of such relatives, sixty-nine spouses of Alzheimer's patients were followed for thirteen months. They were compared to a matched control group of non-caregivers. Caregivers had more days of infectious illness, primarily colds. They had more depression, and the functioning of their immune system, as measured by multiplication of cells to antigen challenge, was poorer than that of controls (Kiecolt-Glaser, Dura, Speicher, Trask, and Glaser, 1991; Castle, Wilkins, Heck, Tanzy, and Fahey, 1995; Esterling, Kiecolt-Glaser, and Glaser, 1996).

Susceptibility to the common cold is now being investigated in the laboratory to determine the effects of psychological factors on the immune-

PSYCHOLOGICAL FACTORS AND CANCER

One of the most insidious of all illnesses influenced by psychological factors is cancer. There is mounting evidence that hopelessness may play a role in susceptibility to cancer. Fifty-one women who had previously been shown to have possibly cancerous cells in the cervix entered a clinic for a cancer test. Upon their arrival, they were interviewed by investigators, who found that eighteen of these fifty-one women had experienced significant losses in the last six months to which they reacted with feelings of hopelessness and helplessness. The others had experienced no such life event. Of the eighteen who had experienced hopelessness, eleven were found to have cancer. Of the thirty-three in the other group, only eight had cancer. The difference between the two groups was statistically significant (Schmale and Iker, 1966).

Psychological distress may increase the rate of negative outcomes among women at risk for breast cancer by interfering with their personal health decisions. Distressed women may be less likely to seek predictive genetic testing, volunteer for prevention trials, or obtain regular breast examinations. The results of one randomized trial indicate that breast cancer risk counseling can significantly reduce breast-cancer-specific stress and improve health-related behavior (Lerman, Schwartz, Miller, et al., 1996).

Lack of meaning in one's life, job instability, and no plans for the future predict who has lung cancer better than does the amount of smoking (Horne and Picard, 1979). Conversely, breast cancer patients who re-sponded with a fighting spirit rather than stoic acceptance had a better chance of recurrence-free survival five years later (Greer, Morris, and Pettingale, 1979).

David Spiegel and his colleagues followed a group of eighty-six women for ten years who had been referred to them for psychotherapy after the diagnosis of metastatic breast cancer (Spiegel, Bloom, Kraemer, and Gottheil, 1989). The women were randomly assigned either to therapy or to be controls without psychotherapy. Psychotherapy lasted for a year, while routine physical treatment for breast cancer continued. Therapy focused on expressing their feelings about their illness and talking about the effect of the illness on their lives. Self-hypnosis for pain control was also taught. At no time were patients led to expect that psychotherapy would affect the course of the illness.

Ten years later, Spiegel looked at survival rates of the women in the two groups. On average, women in the psychotherapy group lived twice as long as women in the control group. The figure below represents the survival curves for the two groups of women.

Although the mechanism by which psychotherapy prolongs survival is a matter of sheer speculation, this and other studies (e.g., Fawzy, Fawzy, Hyun, et al., 1993; Fawzy, Fawzy, Arndt, and Pasnau, 1995; McDaniel, Musselman, Porter, et al., 1995) give us hope that the next decade will see the development of psychological interventions that may treat and even prevent such illnesses as cancer and heart attack.

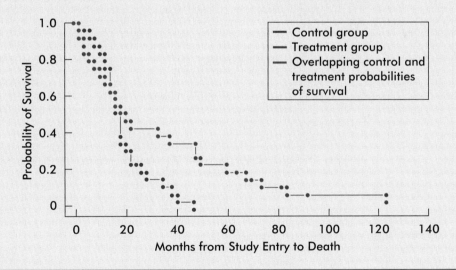

disease link. In one study, 394 healthy volunteers were given controlled amounts of cold virus in a nasal spray, and the severity of the ensuing cold was measured. Subjects who had recently had more negative events in their lives, who had felt more negative affect, and who had had more perceived stress came down with worse colds (Cohen, Tyrrell, and Smith, 1993; Stone, Neale, Cox, et al., 1994).

These studies indicate that one's explanatory style, depression, helplessness, hopelessness, and stressful life events can lower immunocompetence. Various researchers have speculated on how they do so (Maier, Watkins, and Fleshner, 1994; Evans, Leserman, Perkins, et al., 1995; Kiecolt-Glaser and Glaser, 1995). Consider how the experience of a loss might bring about lung cancer: (1) The individual whose husband has died perceives that she has lost something valuable. (2) She believes she is helpless to do anything about it, and if she has a pessimistic explanatory style she becomes severely depressed. (3) Depression and helplessness, as we saw in Chapter 8, are accompanied by depletion of certain neurotransmitters in the brain, as well as by an increase in endorphins, internal morphine-like substances that block pain. (4) The immune system has receptors for endorphins that may then lower immunocompetence. (5) If there are pathogens in the body, say the beginnings of a tumor in the uterus, NK cells and T-cells may be too inactivated to kill it. (6) A tumor that would ordinarily have been lysed in its early stages can now grow to life-threatening size.

We do not know if this schema is correct, but there is now evidence for each stage of this chain. If such a chain illuminates how tragedy can make us physically ill, there are important implications for prevention and therapy. Procedures that intervene at each of the steps might prevent or even reverse such illnesses. So, for example, cognitive therapy might be used to prevent the perception of helplessness or the depressive response, thereby interrupting the chain. Or drug therapy that breaks the catecholamine-endorphin link or blocks the immune receptors to endorphin stimulation might also interrupt the chain. We believe major advances will be made in this area.

THEORIES OF PSYCHOSOMATIC ILLNESS

We have now had a detailed look at two physical problems that are influenced by psychological factors: coronary heart disease and a weakened immune system. In addition to these two, many other diseases are often thought to have psychosomatic components: peptic ulcers, migraine headaches, arthritis, chronic pain, and asthma, among others (see Box 11–2).

Let us now look at the different principles that recur through explanations of the cause and the alleviation of these psychosomatic disorders. There are four theories, and they correspond to four of the schools of abnormality: biomedical, psychodynamic, behavioral, and cognitive. All are compatible with the diathesis-stress perspective.

The Biomedical Model of Psychosomatic Disorders

FOCUS QUESTIONS

1. How does the biomedical model explain psychosomatic disorders through genetics, specific organ vulnerability, evolution, and stress?
2. What is the psychodynamic explanation of psychosomatic disorder?
3. What roles do conditioning, cognitions, life events (controllable vs. uncontrollable), and lifestyle play in psychosomatic disorders?

The biomedical model emphasizes the diathesis underlying psychosomatic illness. There are four components that fall under the biomedical view: genetic, specific organ vulnerability, evolutionary selection, and the general adaptation syndrome. These components do not all exclude one another, and most biomedical theorists emphasize more than one of them when explaining psychosomatic disorders.

Is the predisposition to psychosomatic disorders genetically inherited? This seems to be the case for coronary heart diseases. If one identical twin has CHD, then his co-twin is more likely to have CHD than is the case between fraternal twins. All the genes of two identical twins are the same, but only half the genes of fraternal twins are the same. The higher concordance of identical twins is most likely explained by genetics.

A variant of the genetic view holds that it is weakness in a specific organ that is inherited. That is, when an individual is stressed, the weakest link in his bodily chain snaps. The hypothesis that a greater propensity to build up fat in

BOX 11–2 ━━━━━━━━━━━━━━━━━━━━━━━━━━━━━━ IN THE CLINICIAN'S OFFICE

ASTHMA IN CHILDREN AND FAMILY SEPARATION

Asthma is a condition in which the air passages of the bronchia narrow, swell, and secrete excess fluid to a variety of stimuli. This results in wheezing, which in its worst form can be severe and can produce a convulsive struggle for breath. Asthma can be caused by infection, by allergy, or by psychological factors. It has been estimated that each of these plays the dominant role in about a third of the cases (Weiner, 1977). Put differently, asthma stems from psychological sources in only a minority of cases. In this minority, the personal relations between parents and the asthmatic child have long been suspected to be the major source of psychological disturbance.

Anecdotes indicated that when European children with asthma were sent off by their parents to spas "to take the waters" they cheerfully ignored their parents' long lists of instructions, showed few signs of asthma, and seemed to be psychologically improved as well. To test the possibility that separation from parents might alleviate asthma, Dennis Purcell and his colleagues chose twenty-five chronically asthmatic schoolchildren who lived with their families (Purcell, Brady, Chai, Muser, Molk, Gordon, and Means, 1969). They divided these children into two groups—those in whom emotional factors had usually preceded past attacks of asthma at home, and those in whom emotional factors seemed irrelevant to the onset of past attacks. The first group was expected to benefit from separation, but not the second.

The parents and siblings were removed from the home and sent to a motel for two weeks, while the child continued to live in his home environment. A surrogate parent was provided, and the child continued normal attendance at school and normal play activities. After two weeks of not seeing their child, the parents returned to the home and life went on as usual.

As predicted, the effects were beneficial for the group suspected of emotionally induced asthma. Their medication during separation was reduced by half during daily physician checks, and on top of this the number of asthma attacks and amount of wheezing were reduced by half as well. When the parents returned, wheezing, number of attacks, and amount of necessary medication all increased. Beneficial effects of separation on asthma did not appear for the group in which emotional factors had been judged unimportant.

So, for some children, emotional factors are probably irrelevant to asthma. For others, however, family stresses may set off or worsen asthmatic attacks. In a prospective study of 100 infants with a family history of allergy, the researchers examined the relationship between family-related emotional distress and asthma. Children who came from families with low cohesiveness and a poor ability to adapt to stress were no more likely to develop wheezing problems than children from more functional family environments. However, once the child developed wheezing problems, there was a significantly greater chance for the initiation or maintenance of dysfunctional interaction patterns. Thus, asthma in children may be a cause rather than a result of family-related stress (Gustafsson, Bjorksten, and Kjellman, 1994).

In cases in which emotional factors are related to asthmatic attacks, if the family members learn more effective and less stressful ways of dealing with each other, the child's asthma may get better.

---

one's arteries is an inherited cause of CHD is an instance of the specific organ vulnerability hypothesis. Organ specificity is confirmed by the fact that individuals tend to react to stress with one characteristic part of the body. Some of us usually react to stress with a queasy stomach, others with headache, others with sweating, and still others with a racing heart. Patients with ulcers react with harmful gastric secretion, and patients with recurrent headaches tend to react with increased muscle tension (Malmo and Shagass, 1949; Lacey, 1950).

Evolution may have actually favored the development of certain psychosomatic disorders. Consider the emergency reaction for which evolution has clearly selected. In a generally threatening environment, individuals who tended to perceive the world as hostile and responded crisply with elevation of blood pressure, muscle tension, and the like, would be those most likely to survive and reproduce. Only under modern conditions, in which the level of physical threat has been reduced from the days of the cave and the jungle, is hypertension considered a disorder rather than a strength. Notice that hypertension does not kill young persons; it is deadly to individuals who are many years past the prime age of reproduction. This seems to suggest that tendencies to various psychosomatic disorders are inherited because at one time in history these "diseases" actually favored survival and reproduction.

Hans Selye (1907–1983) integrated the emergency reaction of the sympathetic nervous system into the major theory of reaction to stress. He

▶ Disasters like the nuclear accidents at Chernobyl and Three Mile Island have allowed researchers to develop more sophisticated theories of stress. This family living near Chernobyl was forced to move.

emphasized the stress side of the diathesis-stress model. Selye believed that the general adaptation syndrome is nonspecific, that one and the same stress reaction will occur to the whole gamut of disturbing events. He held that when a human being or an animal is stressed, a sequence of three stages called the *general adaptation syndrome* ensues. The first stage is the *alarm reaction*. After an initial phase of lowered resistance, the system goes into *counter shock*—the pituitary gland releases ACTH (adrenocorticotrophic hormone) into the bloodstream, which stimulates the adrenal cortex. This throws the organism into the emergency reaction. If the alarm reaction stage is successful, it restores bodily balance. The alarm reaction is followed by a second stage—the stage of *resistance,* in which defense and adaptation are sustained and optimal. If the stressor persists, the final stage, *exhaustion,* ensues, and adaptive responding ceases. Illness and, in some cases, death may follow (Selye, 1956).

From the point of view of this theory, symptoms such as high blood pressure and stomach ulcer may indicate that the individual is in an alarm reaction to stress. The theory postulates that psychosomatic symptoms are general stress reactions underlying the general adaptation syndrome (Selye, 1975; but see Mason, 1971, 1975).

Stress theorists traditionally rely on three basic concepts—stress, life events, and social support. Each of these concepts, however, has proven to be too global: stressors produce both good as well as the expected bad effects, life events produce illness as expected but also sometimes spurts of growth, and social support sometimes bolsters but sometimes undermines adaptive functioning (Veiel, 1993). Modern stress theorists now attempt to decompose these global notions into their constituent parts and their mechanisms. So, for example, Andrew Baum has proposed that one mechanism by which stress produces illness is by setting off intrusive thoughts—ruminations, automatic thoughts, and traumatic memories. Baum and his colleagues have followed the residents of Three Mile Island, who lived near the site of a nuclear power plant where a radioactive accident occurred in March 1979. They find that the more intrusive memories an individual has, the greater the number of symptoms of somatic distress (Baum, Cohen, and Hall, 1993). Stress theory now shows promise of increasing sophistication.

The Psychodynamic Model

Diathesis and other biological considerations play a large role in the predisposition to psychosomatic disorders, but there is also evidence that personality and psychodynamics play a role as well. These factors contribute to the stress side of the diathesis-stress model.

Franz Alexander (1950) was the most influential psychoanalytic theorist of psychosomatic disorders. According to Alexander, a vulnerable organ system, an underlying dynamic conflict, and a precipitating life situation, all interact to produce a disorder. The essence of the personality constellation for an individual who will develop peptic ulcer is conflict over dependent needs versus independent self-assertion. Alexander postulates other conflicts for asthma, arthritis, and skin disorders.

Some evidence supports this theory: from the psychological profile alone, researchers have been able to pick out which male patients have ulcers well beyond the level of chance. Further, gastric secretion occurs when the relevant emotions are aroused in individuals who have ulcers (Freeman, Schweizer, and Rickels, 1995). Some evidence contradicts this theory as well, however. In a thirty-year longitudinal study of ninety-five men, fifty developed one of the classic psychosomatic illnesses. But the locus of physical symptoms under stress did not predict which psychosomatic illness would develop. So the eleven men who eventually developed ulcers were not the same men who had earlier reported abdominal pain under stress (Vaillant, 1978).

Behavioral and Cognitive Models

Theories that stem from behavioral and cognitive views hold that learning or cognition produces psychosomatic disorders, and they emphasize the stress side of diathesis-stress. The stress can be produced by conditioning, by cognitions, or by life events.

CONDITIONING

The conditioning view of psychosomatic disorders maintains that the symptoms are a conditioned response acquired when a neutral stimulus was paired with an unconditioned stimulus that produced the disorder. In one experiment with healthy adult women, red and blue colors were repeatedly paired with an arithmetic task that produced stress-related airway resistance. When presented without the task later, red and blue caused a greater level of muscle tightening in the throats of participants than did a control color, suggesting that classical conditioning occurred (Miller and Kotses, 1995). Another example of asthma conditioned in the laboratory is the following:

> A thirty-seven-year-old shop assistant suffered from severe bronchial asthma that could be reliably set off by house dust. In the laboratory, she was sprayed with an aerosol having a neutral solvent; the aerosol was to be the conditioned stimulus. Following being sprayed with the aerosol, she inhaled house dust (unconditioned stimulus), and an asthma attack (unconditioned response) followed. Thereafter, upon inhaling from the aerosol, asthma attacks ensued. (Dekker, Pelse, and Groen, 1957)

Since individuals who suffer from asthma sometimes have attacks following exposure to highly specific events, such as experiencing a family argument or other emotional conflicts, this is an appealing model of psychosomatic illness (see again Box 11–2). It has, however, only been demonstrated under limited laboratory conditions and only some patients can be so conditioned.

COGNITIONS AND PSYCHOSOMATIC DISORDERS

Could it be that specific thoughts set off physical symptoms? William Grace and David Graham argue that an individual's perception of the world and what he thinks about threat predicts what psychosomatic disorder will develop. This argument antedates, but is wholly compatible with the cognitive

▲ Uncontrollable life events like the death of a close relative can be a factor in psychosomatic problems. This boy is attending his father's funeral in Bosnia.

model of abnormality. Grace and Graham interviewed 128 patients with a variety of diseases to find out what situations immediately preceded the onset of the symptoms and how the individual perceived what was happening to him. They found specific thoughts associated with specific illnesses. For example, individuals with high blood pressure were in a state of constant preparation to meet all threats, and when confronted with threat they thought, "Nobody is ever going to beat me. I'm ready for everything." Table 11–1 lists other illnesses that have specific thoughts associated with them (Grace and Graham, 1952). The modern cognitive school has yet to put forward a more articulate, research-supported view. Meanwhile, Baum seems to be moving stress theory toward an integration with cognitive theory (Baum, 1990; Breslin, Hayward, and Baum, 1994).

LIFE EVENTS

Another behavioral theory of psychological influence on illness involves life stressors. It holds that stressful life events set off disease. If our reaction to stress makes us susceptible to physical disease, then frequent stressful life events should correlate with frequent disease. In the early pioneering research on this question, Thomas Holmes and Richard Rahe devised a life events scale, the Social Readjustment Rating Scale, by having individuals rank the amount of stress different life events would cause them. Based on these rankings, Holmes and Rahe assigned a number to each stressful event (see Table 11–2). Death of a spouse was the most stressful life event; divorce and separation were near the top; taking a new job in the middle; holidays, vacations, minor violations of the law were considered the least stressful. Some of the life events are positive *entrances*, such as item 25, outstanding personal achievement, while others are negative *exits*, like item 1, the death of a spouse. Losses or exits seem to produce more problems than do entrances (Paykel, 1974a, 1974b).

The basic idea states that the more life events an individual experiences, the more likely he or she is to get sick from a variety of disorders. For example, individuals who had heart attacks had more total significant life events in the

TABLE 11–1

	COGNITIONS AND PSYCHOSOMATIC DISORDERS	
Illness	Cognition	Examples of thoughts during illness-producing event
1. Hives	Perception of mistreatment.	"My fiance knocked me down and walked all over me, but what could I do?"
2. Eczema	Being prevented from doing something and helpless to deal with the frustration.	"I want to make my mother understand but I can't."
3. Asthma	Wishing the situation would go away or someone else would take over the responsibility for it.	"I just couldn't face it."
4. Diarrhea	Wishing to be done with the situation and have it over with.	"If the war was only over with."
5. Constipation	Grim determination to carry on when faced with an unsolvable problem.	"This marriage is never going to be any better but I won't quit."
6. Ulcer	Revenge seeking.	"He hurt me, so I wanted to hurt him."
7. Migraine headache	Engaged in an intense effort to carry out a definite plan.	"I had a million things to do before lunch."

SOURCE: Based on Grace and Graham, 1952.

TABLE 11–2

	SOCIAL READJUSTMENT RATING SCALE		
Rank	*Life event*	*Rank*	*Life event*
1	Death of spouse	22	Change in responsibilities at work
2	Divorce	23	Son or daughter leaving home
3	Marital separation	24	Trouble with in-laws
4	Jail term	25	Outstanding personal achievement
5	Death of close family member	26	Wife begins or stops work
6	Personal injury or illness	27	Begin or end school
7	Marriage	28	Change in living conditions
8	Fired at work	29	Revision of personal habits
9	Marital reconciliation	30	Trouble with boss
10	Retirement	31	Change in work hours or conditions
11	Change in health of family member	32	Change in residence
12	Pregnancy	33	Change in schools
13	Sex difficulties	34	Change in recreation
14	Gain of new family member	35	Change in church activities
15	Business readjustment	36	Change in social activities
16	Change in financial state	37	Small mortgage
17	Death of close friend	38	Change in sleeping habits
18	Change to different line of work	39	Change in number of family get-togethers
19	Change in number of arguments with spouse	40	Change in eating habits
20	Large mortgage	41	Vacation
21	Foreclosure of mortgage or loan	42	Christmas
		43	Minor violations of the law

SOURCE: Adapted from Holmes and Rahe, 1967.

six months prior to their heart attack than in the year before. Similarly, individuals who became depressed had a larger number of life events, particularly losses, than those who did not (Holmes and Rahe, 1967; Paykel, Meyers, Dienelt, Klerman, Lindenthal, and Pfeffer, 1969; Theorell and Rahe, 1971).

This idea has spawned some refinements: First, and curiously, it may be that the repetitive, daily hassles of life are better predictors of illness than major life events. Losing your wallet, a price rise in the weekly food bill, and the breaking of a window may ultimately push health around more than deaths, divorces, and pregnancies (Kanner, Coyne, Schaefer, and Lazarus, 1981; Dohrenwend and Shrout, 1985). The gradual chipping away at an individual by stresses may wear him down to a point where susceptibility to illness jumps dramatically (Depue and Monroe, 1986).

Second, it might not be life events themselves but ***uncontrollable life events*** that precede heart attacks, especially among Type A's. Death of a close family member, death of a best friend, and being laid off from work are considered uncontrollable losses, but divorce, separation, and changes in eating habits are believed to be controllable life events (Dohrenwend and Martin, 1978). David Glass identified three groups of patients who had experienced the same total number of life events in the preceding year. Those who had had heart attacks (who tended to be Type A's) and those who had been hospitalized for noncoronary illnesses experienced more helplessness-inducing life events than did the healthy controls. This suggests that a combination of being a Type A and experiencing uncontrollable life events—as opposed to a large number of life events per se—may be a formula for heart attack (Glass, 1977).

Third, it might be personality and social supports, and not the number or ranking of the life events, that most influence resistance to physical disease. Personality can modify what the response to life events is. In one study, two

groups of executives had comparable numbers of life events over the previous three years, but only one group tended to become ill. The *hardy* group, characterized by a strong sense of self, a strong sense of meaning, and vigor, resisted illness (Garrity, Somes, and Marx, 1977; Kobasa, 1979). Similarly, people who were pessimists tended to suffer more illness and die younger than people who were optimists (Peterson, Seligman, and Vaillant, 1988; Buchanan, 1994). Social support can similarly buffer the effects of life events. Individuals who are isolated from friends and relatives are at higher risk for illness and death (Berkman, 1984, 1986).

VOLUNTARY BEHAVIOR

Most of the classic work on psychosomatic disorders from the psychodynamic and biomedical models focused on behaviors over which we have little or no voluntary control. Specific organ vulnerability and unconscious conflicts happen to us; we do not make them happen. The behavioral and cognitive models have shifted the focus onto behaviors that we can control voluntarily. A major part of health psychology emphasizes that we choose lifestyles and particular actions that can produce illness, and that by knowing this we can choose to lead healthier lives.

In our discussion of CHD, we emphasized that some of the risk factors are chosen: lack of exercise, eating cholesterol-laden foods, and smoking. We can choose not to engage in these behaviors. Others, like the time urgency component of the Type A personality, we can learn to change with counseling. From the behavioral and cognitive point of view, a major part of the cause, the cure, and the prevention of psychosomatic disorders comes from the choices we make every day about how we will lead our lives.

ORGANIC DISORDERS*

We have reviewed evidence and theories that suggest that one's psychological makeup, personality, and reaction to stress can all influence our body's immune system and the course, even the cause, of physical diseases, among them, coronary heart disease. Because researchers are discovering more and more about how the mind affects the body, we can develop interventions to thwart the harmful effects of our minds on our bodies.

*The remainder of this chapter is a much abbreviated version of a chapter written by Morris Moscovitch and Paul Rozin for our *Abnormal Psychology*, third edition.

The disorders we take up now have more to do with how mind, personality, and behavior are affected by physical problems or assaults on the body, particularly the nervous system. These *organic disorders* are particularly devastating. Unlike psychosomatic disorders, which can be treated by changing personality, explanatory style, and level of stress, the organic disorders, which bring about such mental disorganization and social disruption, often cannot be directly treated. Once damaged, the nervous system generally does not return to its original working state.

In the following section, we consider some major disorders of the nervous system. We have selected these disorders because they are common and well-studied. We begin with the disorders of language.

The Aphasias: Disorders of Language

FOCUS QUESTIONS

1. What are the symptoms and cause of expressive aphasia?
2. What are the symptoms and cause of receptive aphasia?
3. Describe developmental dyslexia.
4. Describe the three routes from print to meaning and relate those to phonological dyslexia and surface dyslexia.

Language is a uniquely human activity, and of vital importance to thought, communication, and social life. Hence, disturbances in language are particularly upsetting. Most major disorders of language have a well-defined neurological basis, and are called *aphasias.*

Language functions are generally localized in the left side of the brain (the left hemisphere of right-handers); hence, aphasias in 95 to 98 percent of right-handers are almost always the result of damage to the left hemisphere. Often, such damage is caused by a stroke, a condition in which blood vessels are clogged and unable to deliver oxygen to parts of the brain. Speech is controlled primarily by neurons located in the part of the frontal lobe designated Broca's area, in honor of the nineteenth-century neurologist, Paul Broca, who first described this syndrome (see Figure 11–5). Damage in this area leads to difficulties in expression.

While perception and comprehension of language are often more or less intact, speech is halting, labored, and ungrammatical. Many of the common small words are omitted. This pattern of symptoms is described as an *expressive aphasia,* as in this case:

> This fifty-five-year-old, right-handed housewife . . . suddenly developed a weakness on her right side and was unable to speak. Apparently, the right-sided weakness mainly affected her face and arm since she was still able to walk. Neurological examination revealed the following: The patient was alert. She had no spontaneous speech and could not use speech to answer questions and could not even use yes or no answers. She could not repeat words. The patient was, however,

FIGURE 11–5

BROCA'S APHASIA

CAT scan and diagram of a patient with Broca's aphasia. Note the darker area in the upper left (left frontal area) indicating brain damage. In describing a picture of a boy flying a kite, this patient says, "Waving and uh . . . the . . . oh dear . . . and the kite and boy and . . . and eeth . . . uh barking and a . . . a lil boy and a bigs. . . ." (SOURCE: Kertesz, 1982, p. 35)

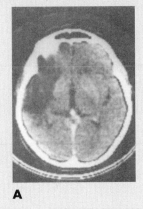

A

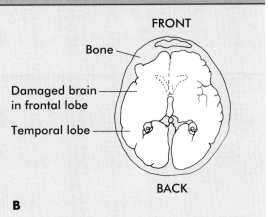

B

FRONT

Bone

Damaged brain in frontal lobe

Temporal lobe

BACK

able to indicate answers to questions by nodding or shaking her head if questions were posed in a multiple-choice situation. In this manner, it was possible to determine that she was grossly oriented for time, place, and person. The patient was able to carry out spoken commands and simple written commands. There was greater loss of strength in the right arm, which suggested that the damage was in the left hemisphere. The fact that all of the symptoms were in action, as opposed to sensation, suggested a forward location of the lesion, as did the fact that the language problem was in expression, rather than in comprehension of speech. (Curtis, Jacobson, and Marcus, 1972, pp. 526–28)

The *perception* of speech is accomplished primarily in a part of the left temporal lobe called Wernicke's area (see Figure 11–6). Damage to this area results in a **receptive aphasia.** The patient has difficulties in perceiving and/or comprehending speech, and so has difficulty following instructions. Speech is also disordered in a manner that is consistent with a comprehension deficit: although there is fluent and grammatical speech, it consists of many empty words, circumlocutions, paraphasias (word or sound substitutions), and neologisms (new, made-up words). This damage is also usually caused by a stroke. Consider the following case of Wernicke's aphasia:

A patient suddenly developed severe comprehension problems. She was unable to comprehend the simplest words or sentences. When addressed, she responded with grammatically correct but meaningless sentences spoken in a pleasant manner with the intonation and inflection of someone recounting a story to friends over coffee. She was unaware that what she was saying was often gibberish, nor was she sensitive to the responses of the person to whom she addressed her remarks. For example, when asked to describe a picture, she replied, "Yeh, about . . . mmmm . . . that is all. It's a bramblejite. I was at work at soler baks and baks. I did a lot of litins in England. . . . Well, kurly re retin han just the han junikin saddle. We'd nothin to sigh in England, tenah we'd come off the durlin a lot." (Case history courtesy of the Communication Department, Baycrest Hospital, Toronto, Ontario)

Aphasias can be devastating to a person's day-to-day existence. Depending upon the degree of brain damage and the resulting deficit, victims often cannot return to work, cannot participate in the most basic of conversations, and may require constant caregiving from others (Karbe, Kessler, Herholz, Fink, and Heiss, 1995). There are no treatments that can "repair"

FIGURE 11–6

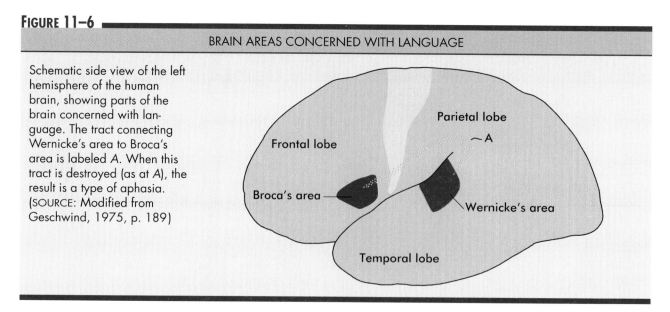

BRAIN AREAS CONCERNED WITH LANGUAGE

Schematic side view of the left hemisphere of the human brain, showing parts of the brain concerned with language. The tract connecting Wernicke's area to Broca's area is labeled A. When this tract is destroyed (as at A), the result is a type of aphasia. (SOURCE: Modified from Geschwind, 1975, p. 189) the damage that led to the aphasia. Although rehabilitation therapy or compensatory methods may enable the patient to work around the problem, there is generally not a return to the level of functioning that existed before the damage to the brain occurred.

Dyslexia: The Reading Disorder

Learning disabilities are a common disorder of childhood. One subtype, ***developmental dyslexia,*** consists of a difficulty in learning to read that is out of proportion to the child's intellectual and emotional development. The incidence of dyslexia varies greatly as a function of both the precise definition employed and the country or locality in question. Estimates vary from about 1 percent to over 10 percent. About 75 percent of dyslexics are male (Rutter, 1978). Because literacy is so important in our society, a great deal of attention has been paid to this problem.

Many beginning readers sound out a written word that they have never seen before, recognize this sound as a familiar word, and then have access to all of its meanings. As readers become more fluent, the sounding-out process seems to recede. Some very common words may be recognized directly by their overall shapes. More importantly, readers seem able to convert written letter sequences directly into meanings, as if they had created an internal dictionary (or lexicon). The lexicon has information about both the meaning and pronunciation of all letter sequences that are entered in it. Readers learn about regularities in the sequences of letters: *u* regularly follows *q*, *w* never follows *v*. Knowledge of these regularities allows for rapid perception of words.

For adult English readers, there seem to be three routes from print to meaning: one via conversion to sound and then to meaning, a second via direct conversion from letter sequence to meaning, and a third from word shape to meaning. Indeed, some children learn to read without going through direct training in sounding out words; they may directly learn the letter sequences that correspond to meanings, though they almost always also learn to sound out words even if they weren't so instructed. There are reading disorders corresponding to damage in two of these pathways.

In ***phonological dyslexia,*** there is damage to the system involved in reading by sound. Because the visual route is available, such a patient may not make too many mistakes reading aloud. But these patients are unable to pronounce a written word that they have never seen even if it corresponds to a spoken word they know. Lacking the ability to convert even familiar written words to their sound directly, such patients will also be unable to determine whether visually presented non-words rhyme with each other. Asked to choose which two of the following three words rhyme ("rite," "kight," and "rit") they are likely to guess that the first and third rhyme, because they resemble each other visually (Beauvais and Derouesne, 1979; Coltheart, 1985; Hanley and Gard, 1995).

Patients with ***surface dyslexia*** cannot read words by sight; they read the words only by sounding them out. Although they can sound out words they have never seen before, there are many familiar words that they cannot read correctly; these are the words that violate standard rules of pronunciation, such as "have," "yacht," "bread," "sew," and "sword."

Children with dyslexia face enormous challenges. Since much of early learning depends on reading, the dyslexic child can easily fall behind at school. Often the dyslexia is not noticed or diagnosed, and the child will proceed through school barely keeping up. The child might then be seen as "slow" by teachers and called "stupid" by peers, and he or she will suffer the loss of self-esteem that follows such labeling. If a child's problem is caught early on, however, he can be taught some skills to overcome the deficit.

The Amnesic Syndrome: A Disorder of Memory

We have considered the varieties of pathology that can cause disorders in language and reading. We now turn to one specific and common disorder, *the amnesic syndrome.*

We are now at what will be, in but a moment, a memory. It is this memory of our past experiences, the idea that it is "me" who has passed through all of these experiences, the yesterdays and years ago, that gives continuity to the self. Amnesia strikes at this junction between the present and the past (see Rozin, 1976; Moscovitch, 1982a; Squire, 1987; Squire and Butters, 1992, for more detailed reviews of amnesia).

To convey the character of this syndrome, we will describe the case of H.M., which is probably the most studied neurological case in history (Scoville and Milner, 1957; Milner, 1970). His case is an example of as "pure" an amnesic syndrome as has ever been described.

> H.M. was a blue-collar worker suffering from severe epileptic seizures. They became progressively worse, and by age twenty-seven he was unable to work. Neurosurgeons removed parts of both temporal lobes (the source of the seizures) to control the seizures in 1953. H.M. was carefully evaluated prior to the operation, and had a normal memory and an I.Q. of 112. On the return of consciousness following surgery, he could no longer recognize the hospital staff, apart from Dr. Scoville, whom he had known for many years. He could not remember or learn his way around the hospital. He could not remember important events that occurred in the few years before the surgery, such as the death of his uncle, but his early memories appeared clear and vivid. His short-term memory appeared normal, and he could carry on a normal conversation. However, he could not remember any events that occurred after the operation, once they passed out of his direct attention (short-term memory). He did the same puzzles day after day and reread the same newspapers and magazines. Each time he learned of the death of his uncle, he became very moved, treating it as a new occurrence. H.M. is still alive. His epilepsy is under control, but he still shows the same amnesic syndrome. He is dimly aware of his father's death, which occurred some years ago. He has aged normally in appearance, but is surprised whenever he sees himself in a mirror, since he remembers himself as he was at twenty-seven. [In 1997, he is now about sixty-nine.] Remarkably, H.M.'s "intelligence" remained intact; over many years his I.Q. did not decrease. He has some realization that he has a memory deficit. He says: "Every day is alone in itself, whatever enjoyment I've had, and whatever sorrow I've had. . . . Right now, I'm wondering, have I done or said anything amiss? You see, at this moment everything looks clear to me, but what happened just before? That's what worries me. It's like waking from a dream. I just don't remember." As you might expect, H.M. is able to remember something if he can keep it "in mind." He can retain a number, say 584, by constantly repeating it to himself, or repeatedly adding up the three digits. However, after being interrupted with another task for less than a minute, he is unable to recall either the number or the fact that he had been rehearsing it for some minutes. (Adapted from Milner, 1970)

CAUSES OF AMNESIA

The range of pathological agents that can produce amnesia is astounding. In addition to the usual causes of specific neurological syndromes such as strokes and tumors, a variety of generally harmful agents can cause amnesia (see Box 11–3). For example, infections can produce amnesia: when the herpes simplex virus attacks the nervous system, it seems to have a predilection for a few structures, including the hippocampus, an area critical for memory. Toxins and nutritional deficiencies can also cause amnesia. Chronic alcoholics get a good portion of their calories from alcohol, an essentially vitamin-free food source. They sometimes develop a deficiency in vitamin B1 (thiamine), a critical component of metabolic processes in all cells of the body. It is believed that, for some reason, a few groups of cells in the memory system are particularly vulnerable to

A CASE OF RETROGRADE AND ANTEROGRADE AMNESIA

In severe cases, a person with amnesia cannot remember a large part of his past or form memories of recent events. As a result, he lives in a "present" that often lacks meaning and continuity. Greg F., a twenty-five-year-old former hippie and Hare Krishna, was suffering from such a condition when he entered a hospital for long-term care in 1977. Doctors had removed an enormous tumor that had permanently damaged several areas of his brain, causing blindness, movement difficulties, and memory deficits.

Greg, however, seemed unaware that he had any problems and did not know why he was in the hospital. Experiencing retrograde amnesia, he did not remember spending six years at a Hare Krishna temple in New Orleans before his hospitalization. He could recall events from the mid- to late sixties, but he had almost no memory of events that took place after 1970. When asked to name the current president, he replied, "Jimi Hendrix," demonstrating his time-related confusion. Moreover, he only became excited when he spoke about rock bands and songs from the sixties.

Damage to the hippocampus, a structure in the brain involved in the creation of new memories, appeared to limit Greg mostly to the thoughts, emotions, and beliefs that he associated with the sixties. If given a list of words or told a story, he would forget what he saw or heard within a few minutes. The poor functioning of his short-term memory forced him to live in the moment. Unlike normal individuals, he lacked a sense of "next," and consequently, he felt indifferent most of the time. The tumor did not completely destroy Greg's ability to record new experiences, though, for he could become familiar with sounds, people's faces, and locations after frequent contact with them. For example, within three months of being at the hospital, he could find his way to his favorite places. In addition, he held on to his ability to play the guitar and successfully learned how to play new songs. He also remembered theorems he had learned in school, indicating that he had an intact semantic, or meaning-oriented, memory.

SOURCE: Adapted from Oliver Sacks, *An Anthropologist on Mars* (New York: Knopf, 1995).

this deficiency. They are the first to be destroyed, leading to the amnesia of Korsakoff's syndrome. Moreover, a concussion or other severe blows to the skull, as often happens in automobile accidents, and occasionally in sports and other activities, can produce an amnesic syndrome that is usually transient but can last for years. Amnesia rarely occurs unless there was loss of consciousness. Finally, memory failures are among the most common features of aging.

Although we don't understand the process of memory formation, there are clear relations between a set of interconnected brain structures that make up the limbic system and amnesic syndromes (Victor, Adams, and Collins, 1971; Mishkin and Appenzeller, 1987). In most cases of Korsakoff's syndrome, there is bilateral (both sides) damage to the mammillary bodies and/or the dorsomedial nucleus of the thalamus (see Figure 11–7). In cases resulting from surgery, viral attacks, and other sources, there is

---

DSM-IV Criteria for Amnestic Disorder Due to . . . [Indicate the General Medical Condition]

A. The development of memory impairment as manifested by impairment in the ability to learn new information or the inability to recall previously learned information.

B. The memory disturbance causes significant impairment in social or occupational functioning and represents a significant decline from a previous level of functioning.

C. The memory disturbance does not occur exclusively during the course of a delirium or a dementia.

D. There is evidence from the history, physical examination, or laboratory findings that the disturbance is the direct physiological consequence of a general medical condition (including physical trauma).

SOURCE: APA, DSM-IV, 1994.

FIGURE 11-7

THE LIMBIC SYSTEM AND MEMORY

The structures of the limbic system are involved in memory. Damage to the mammillary bodies, to the dorsomedial nucleus of the thalamus, and to cells in the hippocampus can lead to amnesic syndromes. (SOURCE: Adapted from Bloom, Lazerson, and Hofstadter, 1985)

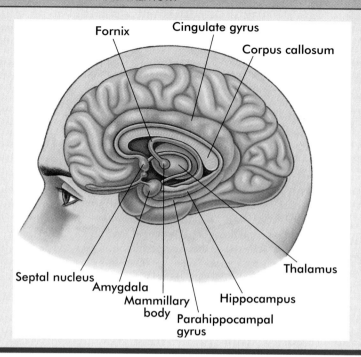

Fornix Cingulate gyrus Corpus callosum

Septal nucleus Amygdala Mammillary body Parahippocampal gyrus Hippocampus Thalamus

bilateral damage to the hippocampus, in the temporal lobe. Damage to a layer of cells in the hippocampus is sufficient to produce a full-blown amnesic syndrome (Zola-Morgan, Squire, and Amaral, 1986; Squire, 1992), but in cases of damage to the temporal lobes where there is no bilateral damage to the hippocampus, memory loss is minimal (Milner, 1972).

Bilateral damage must occur to produce the full syndrome. It is usually caused by general insults to the brain, such as traumatic accidents, poisoning, vitamin deficiencies, infections, or degenerative processes. In contrast, tumors, strokes, and externally induced wounds almost always occur in one continuous spatial location, and hence they are likely to affect only one side.

Careful analysis of patients with unilateral damage to the critical memory structures reveals a more limited memory deficit, of just the type one would predict given the specialized functions of the two hemispheres. Left temporal damage (in right-handers, of course) leads to a memory impairment primarily for verbal materials, and right temporal damage leads to deficits in memory for visual and other forms of "nonverbal" memory (Milner, 1972).

Let's look more closely at the nature of the memory defect in the amnesic syndrome (reviewed in Milner, 1972; Rozin, 1976; Moscovitch, 1982a; Squire, 1987). Short-term memory, that is, memory for that which is currently at the forefront of one's consciousness (e.g., a telephone number after it has just been given by an operator) seems not to be greatly affected. But there may be severe deficits in recall and recognition of events experienced since the onset of the disease *(anterograde amnesia)*. Or there may be loss of recall and recognition for events that occurred for a period of time *prior* to the onset of the syndrome *(retrograde amnesia)*. The retrograde amnesia typically runs back in time from the onset of the illness or accident, and covers recent events (days, months, years) but not usually early events of life. In most accident cases, the retrograde amnesia is eventually reduced to a period of seconds or minutes preceding the injury (Russell, 1959). One professional quarterback, following a head injury on the field, returned to the huddle and called plays that came from his previous team; he showed temporary retrograde amnesia for the period in which he had learned his new team's plays.

The amnesic syndrome is characterized by a lack of a sense of familiarity ("I've seen it before") when re-presented with recently experienced events. Nonetheless, some specific types of learning and memory are preserved in amnesics (Moscovitch, Vriezen, and Goshen-Gottstein, 1994). Thus, amnesics can be taught new perceptuo-motor skills, such as making drawings while looking in a mirror (Milner, 1972). Generally, the preserved skills are described as ***implicit learning.***

Severely amnesic patients have no recall or recognition of events that occurred even a few minutes ago, but they have some type of record of them. That record can be revived if the patient is cued in particular ways and encouraged to respond without reflecting on the past. The procedure that elicits this performance is called ***priming.*** For example, when asked to remember a series of words, like "metal" or "carpet," after a brief delay, amnesics failed miserably. When prompted with partial cues (e.g., "met" or "car"), however, and encouraged to say the first word that came to mind, they guessed the words quite accurately, though claiming no sense of familiarity with the words they had uttered (Warrington and Weiskrantz, 1973; Diamond and Rozin, 1984; Schacter, 1992; Moscovitch, Vriezen, and Goshen-Gottstein, 1994).

THE COURSE AND TREATMENT OF AMNESIA

Patients with amnesias produced by head trauma typically recover completely, and the main function of medical treatment is to maintain the health of the patient in the acute phase of the illness. Occasionally, cases caused by tumors or infections may be treated surgically or with drugs, with possible alleviation of some symptoms. At this time, there is no treatment that will arrest or slow down the degeneration of neurons that causes the amnesias associated with senile dementia (see discussion of Alzheimer's disease, below). Although neural structures cannot be repaired, treatment programs can be designed that use the structures that remain intact.

Memory disorders can also be treated as problems in living. Family members can accommodate to and compensate for some of the problems. Adjustments in living and working conditions can be made. Sometimes, memory tricks such as simply writing notes on a pad can help. We must remember that there is a little memory loss in all of us. As we grow older, it becomes more severe in most people. Intelligent people compensate in their lifestyle and in the memory support or crutches they develop for themselves. This is graphically illustrated by a study that compared memory in University of Toronto students and sixty- to seventy-year-old alumni (Moscovitch, 1982b). Subjects from each age group were told they were in a study of memory, and that the task was simply to remember to call a particular phone number on a particular day and at a particular time (some weeks ahead), simply leaving their name. All agreed to do it. About half of the students failed to call, whereas almost all of the older group remembered to call. It appears that at least part of the result is due to different approaches to remembering. The student subjects, interviewed after the study, said they were confident they would remember the task, and they made no special effort to remind themselves. The older people thought they would forget, wrote the date down in their date books, put notes by the phone, and so on. Old age would be a lot less tolerable if these compensations did not occur.

Alzheimer's Disease: A Form of Dementia

FOCUS QUESTIONS

1. What are the symptoms of Alzheimer's disease?
2. Describe the dysfunctional brain pathology found in Alzheimer's patients.
3. What are some of the hypotheses about the causes of Alzheimer's disease?
4. What are early symptoms of AIDS dementia?

Dementia is a progressive loss of a variety of higher mental functions usually occurring in old age. Alzheimer's disease, which is one form of dementia, is a disease of major proportions. About 5 percent of American adults over sixty-four years of age suffer from this disorder, and about one-third of these people are severely handicapped (Terry and Davies, 1980). The beginning of the decline in mental functioning is sometimes seen in people in their fifties. About half of all old people diagnosed as demented probably have Alzheimer's disease. There is accumulating evidence that Alzheimer's disease is inherited in a small proportion of people. The risk of Alzheimer's disease in first-degree relatives (immediate family) of patients with the disease converges on 50 percent by age ninety compared to a risk of about 25 percent in the population at large in this age range (Mohs, Breitner, Silverman, and Davis, 1987; Silverman, Zaccario, Smith, et al., 1994; Heun and Maier, 1995). Controlling for known risk factors, it has been found that depression in individuals over the age of sixty moderately increases their chances of developing dementia, particularly Alzheimer's disease. It is possible, though, that depression merely signals Alzheimer's disease or relates to another unidentified risk factor (Devanand, Sano, Tang, et al., 1996). Here is a case of Alzheimer's disease:

> For two or three years, Mary's memory was slipping, but she compensated by writing things down. At first, she found herself groping for a word she had always known, and noticed that she often lost the thread of a conversation. Though she worried that her mind might be slipping away, she didn't want to think about getting old and, most important, she didn't want to be treated as if she were senile. She was still enjoying life and able to manage.
>
> Then Mary got pneumonia and had to be taken to the hospital. In those strange surroundings, she could no longer compensate for her forgetfulness. People told her where she was, but she forgot. She complained that her daughter-in-law never visited her, though she had been there in the morning.
>
> Although the fever and infection passed, the illness had focused attention on the seriousness of her condition. Her family realized she could no longer live alone. She was taken to live with her son's family where she was given a room. Because only some of her things were there, she thought that perhaps the rest were stolen while she was sick even though she had been told many times where her things were. She got lost in the neighborhood and often could not find her way around the house. . . .
>
> Mary continued to deteriorate. Dressing became an insurmountable ordeal. . . . she no longer knew how to button buttons, to unzip zippers. Mary gradually lost the ability to interpret what she saw and heard. Words and objects began to lose their meaning. Sometimes she would react with terror and panic, or with anger. Her things were gone, her life seemed gone. She could not understand the explanations that were offered or, if she understood, she could not remember them. . . . However, Mary's social skills remained so that when she finally relaxed she was personable and engaging. She also loved music and sang old familiar songs. Music seemed to be embedded in a part of her mind that she retained long after much else was lost.
>
> The time finally came when the physical and emotional burden of caring for Mary became too much for her family, and she went to live in a nursing home. After the initial days of confusion and panic passed, the reliability of the routine comforted her and gave her a measure of security.
>
> Mary was glad when her family came to visit. Sometimes she remembered their names; more often she did not. . . . (Source: Adapted from Mace and Robins, 1981)

Alzheimer's disease may have early onset, but generally it begins gradually in old age. Its initial symptoms include loss of initiative, forgetfulness, naming disability, apraxia (impairment in the ability to plan or sequence movements), and spatial disorientation. Different symptoms predominate in different patients. In many patients, an amnesic syndrome will be the prominent symptom; in other patients, naming or spatial disorders are the primary symptoms (Martin, 1987; Schwartz, Baron, and Moscovitch, 1990). With time, the nervous system in Alzheimer's patients deteriorates further. In many patients, sleep is severely disturbed, wandering occurs, maintaining basic hygiene and cleanliness becomes problematic. People with Alzheimer's disease may be incontinent of urine and feces; other unmanageable behaviors, such as screaming, aggression, and refusal to eat or drink, may appear. There are problems in walking and balance that lead to falls and injuries. As the disease progresses, more and more severe deficits appear, in more and more systems. Thus, over a period ranging from a few to ten years, it leads to severe deterioration of intellectual and basic maintenance functions. In the final stages, the person may be confined to bed, incontinent and inert. The immediate cause of death is often a complicating condition such as pneumonia, malnutrition, dehydration, or infection.

Patients with Alzheimer's disease have been shown to have a loss of cells as well as malformed neurons, especially in the hippocampus, which may be due to an accumulation of the protein beta amyloid (Hardy and Higgins, 1992). They may also have a neurotransmitter deficit, wherein the enzyme that is crucial in the synthesis of acetylcholine (which is important in memory) may be at an abnormally low level (Coyle, Price, and DeLong, 1983; Sherif and Ahmed, 1995; Sisoda and Price, 1995). Another hypothesis is that Alzheimer's disease may be caused by one or more chromosomal abnormalities (St. George-Hyslop et al., 1987; St. George-Hyslop, Haines, Rogaev, et al., 1992; Corder, Saunders, Strittmatter, et al., 1993; Saunders, Strittmatter, Schmechel, et al., 1993).

DSM-IV Criteria for Dementia of the Alzheimer's Type

A. The development of multiple cognitive deficits manifested by both: (1) memory impairment (impaired ability to learn new information or to recall previously learned information), and (2) one (or more) of the following cognitive disturbances: (a) aphasia (language disturbance); (b) apraxia (impaired ability to carry out motor activities despite intact motor function); (c) agnosia (failure to recognize or identify objects despite intact sensory function); (d) disturbance in executive functioning (i.e., planning, organizing, sequencing, abstracting).

B. The cognitive deficits in Critera A1 and A2 each cause significant impairment in social or occupational functioning and represent a significant decline from a previous level of functioning.

C. The course is characterized by gradual onset and continuing cognitive decline.

D. The cognitive deficits in Criteria A1 and A2 are not due to any of the following: (1) other central nervous system conditions that cause progressive deficits in memory and cognition (e.g., cerebrovascular disease, Parkinson's disease, Huntington's disease, subdural hematoma, normal-pressure hydrocephalus, brain tumor); (2) systemic conditions that are known to cause dementia (e.g., hypothyroidism, vitamin B_{12} or folic acid deficiency, niacin deficiency, hypercalcemia, neurosyphilis, HIV infection); (3) substance-induced conditions.

E. The deficits do not occur exclusively during the course of a delirium.

F. The disturbance is not better accounted for by another Axis I disorder (e.g., Major Depressive Disorder, Schizophrenia).

SOURCE: APA, DSM-IV, 1994.

> ### DSM-IV Criteria for Dementia Due to HIV Disease
>
> **A.** The development of multiple cognitive deficits manifested by both: (1) memory impairment (impaired ability to learn new information or to recall previously learned information), and (2) one (or more) of the following cognitive disturbances: (a) aphasia (language disturbance); (b) apraxia (impaired ability to carry out motor activities despite intact motor function); (c) agnosia (failure to recognize or identify objects despite intact sensory function); (d) disturbance in executive functioning (i.e., planning, organizing, sequencing, abstracting).
> **B.** The cognitive deficits in Critera A1 and A2 each cause significant impairment in social or occupational functioning and represent a significant decline from a previous level of functioning.
> **C.** There is evidence from the history, physical examination, or laboratory findings that the disturbance is the direct physiological consequence of HIV disease.
> **D.** The deficits do not occur exclusively during the course of a delirium.
> SOURCE: APA, DSM-IV, 1994.

AIDS Dementia

It is now recognized that clinically observable neurological disorders occur in about 40 percent of adult AIDS patients, and pathological changes in the nervous system have been noted in 80 to 90 percent of cases that have come to autopsy (Snyder, Simpson, Nielson, et al., 1983). Some of the changes may be caused by tumors or bacterial infections that accompany AIDS. In a significant number of cases, however, there is a syndrome of acquired dementia, called ***AIDS dementia complex,*** that cannot be explained as secondary to tumor growth or bacterial infection.

The early symptoms of AIDS dementia complex include word-finding difficulty, verbal memory deficits, psychomotor slowing, impaired problem-solving ability, and poor fine motor control. AIDS was first recognized as a syndrome in 1981, and the dementia that sometimes accompanies it was not noted until a few years later. It is therefore too early to know exactly which brain regions are affected. But consistent with the behavioral symptomatology, the affected region is initially subcortical; later, there is cortical involvement, particularly in the region of the frontal lobes (Price, Brew, Sidtis, et al., 1988; Gray, Huag, Chimelli, et al., 1991; Brew, Rosenblum, Cronin, and Price, 1995).

More controversial is whether there are any cognitive deficits in individuals who are HIV positive but who show no clinical symptoms of AIDS. Early reports of extensive deficits have been disconfirmed (Horter, 1989; Janssen, Saykin, Cannon, et al., 1989; McArthur, Cohen, Selnes, et al., 1989; Law, Martin, Mapou, et al., 1994). The consensus now is that these individuals are normal except for some psychomotor slowing on reaction-time tests, which may be indicative of subtle central nervous system involvement (Martin, Heyes, Salazar, Law, and Williams, 1993).

Disorders Related to the Frontal Lobes

The frontal lobes comprise about one-third of the cortex in humans. They probably constitute the areas of the human cerebral cortex that are most different in size and structure from comparable areas in nonhuman primates. The frontal lobe is not a homogeneous structure but consists of a number of distinct regions that together receive a variety of inputs from other cortical areas as well as from many subcortical structures (Goldman-Rakic, 1987; Pandya and Barnes, 1987). Given the strong connections so many regions

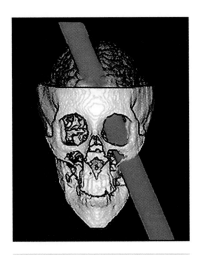

▲ Skull of Phineas Gage showing the hole in the frontal bone made by the iron rod blown through his head; the bar entered below the left eye and passed through the skull. A reconstruction of the injury to Phineas Gage's brain was made using careful measurements of the surviving skull, reconstruction of the path of the rod through the brain, and computer simulation.

FOCUS QUESTIONS

1. What are some disorders whose symptoms indicate frontal-lobe dysfunction?
2. Describe how damage to the frontal lobes can alter personality.
3. Why do some patients with frontal-lobe damage confabulate?

have with the frontal lobes, it should not be surprising to learn that symptoms indicative of frontal-lobe dysfunction are associated with many disorders that do not affect the frontal lobes directly, such as Parkinson's and Huntington's disease, as well as obsessive-compulsive disorder and attention-deficit hyperactivity disorder.

THE FRONTAL LOBES, PERSONALITY, AND SOCIAL CONDUCT

A classical case that gives the flavor of frontal damage on an entire personality is that of Phineas Gage (Harlow, 1868; Damasio, Grabowski, Frank, Galaburda, and Damasio, 1994).

> Phineas Gage was the twenty-five-year-old foreman of a group of men working on railroad track in Vermont in 1848. An explosion caused an iron bar, over an inch in diameter, to pass through the front of his skull, damaging a large part of the frontal area of his brain. Miraculously, Gage survived, with no more than a few moments of loss of consciousness. After recovery, he reapplied for his job as foreman. His contractors, who had regarded him as the most efficient and capable foreman in their employ previous to his injury, considered the change in his mind so marked that they could not give him his place again. The equilibrium or balance, so to speak, between his intellectual faculties and animal propensities, seemed to have been destroyed. He was fitful, irreverent, indulging at times in the grossest profanity (which was not previously his custom), manifesting but little deference for his fellows, impatient of restraint or advice when it conflicted with his desires, at times perniciously obstinate, yet capricious and vacillating, devising many plans of future operations, which are no sooner arranged than they are abandoned in turn for others. . . . his mind was radically changed, so decidedly that his friends and acquaintances said he was "no longer Gage." (Harlow, 1868, pp. 339–40)

Such reports of changes in personality and difficulties in interpersonal relationships after frontal lesions are not uncommon. Aberrant social behavior and altered personality may appear in the absence of the cognitive deficits that are indicative of frontal-lobe damage (Eslinger and Damasio, 1985; Shallice and Burgess, 1991), though typically cognitive and personality changes occur together. The social disorder may be so severe in some patients that it complies with the DSM-IV diagnostic criteria for antisocial personality disorder. Here is a description of such a patient:

> By age thirty-five, E.V.R. was a successful professional, happily married, and the father of two. He led an impeccable social life, and was a role model to younger siblings. Because a meningioma (tumor of the meninges, the covering of the brain) was found on the ventromedial frontal lobes, a bilateral excision (removal) of the region was necessary.
>
> E.V.R.'s intelligence, memory, and other cognitive functions were not compromised by the surgery. In stark contrast, E.V.R.'s social conduct was profoundly affected. Over a brief period of time, he entered disastrous business ventures (one of which led to predictable bankruptcy), and was divorced twice. (The second marriage, which was to a prostitute, lasted only six months.) He has been unable to hold any paying job since the time of surgery, and his plans for future activity are defective. He now lives in a sheltered environment, unable to support himself or his family. (Damasio, Tranel, and Damasio, 1990, pp. 81–82)

When this type of damage is sustained in childhood, significant changes in personality and disturbances in social behavior occur and persist, and even worsen over time (Hogan, 1969; Hawley, 1988; Grattan and Eslinger, 1992; Tucker, Luu, and Pribaum, 1995). Children who were good-natured and even-tempered become moody, surly, and given to uncontrollable rage. Despite average or superior intelligence, these children have behavioral and academic problems in school and later have erratic work histories. In the social realm, adolescence is marked by noncooperative relationships and alienation from peers. This condition continues into adulthood, manifested as a failure to establish lasting, meaningful relationships.

Like other people who display sociopathic behavior, people with frontal-lobe lesions have full knowledge of what constitutes normal social behavior and are aware of the consequences of violating laws or social conventions (Saver and Damasio, 1991). Yet they seem unwilling or unable to act on their knowledge. Even their autonomic responses to social stimuli, such as pictures of mutilated bodies or nude people, are deficient (Damasio, Tranel, and Damasio, 1990). Although the link between frontal-lobe damage and disorders of personality and social behavior is now being established, the processes that lead to these disorders are still poorly understood.

THE FRONTAL LOBES AND MEMORY IMPAIRMENT

The frontal lobes' role in memory is similar to their role in other domains. People with frontal-lobe damage or dysfunction are impaired in memory sequencing, that is, they have difficulty placing remembered events in the proper temporal order with respect to one another, even though memory for the events themselves is preserved. They also have difficulty in organizing information so that they will remember it better, and in devising and implementing proper retrieval strategies. For example, if asked to search their memory for a personal event associated with the cue "letter" or "broken" or a historical event having to do with "a battle," people with frontal-lobe damage often draw a blank unless they are given more specific, direct cues to guide them (e.g., did you ever have any broken bones or teeth or did you break something valuable as a child?). People with frontal-lobe damage also do not monitor or evaluate their memories normally to determine whether they are genuine or appropriate.

The most extreme example of the failure of frontal function with respect to memory is noted in some patients who **confabulate,** that is, make up stories. They do not distort the truth deliberately, but instead they are "honest liars" in the sense that they are trying to tell the truth as best they can but miss the mark without any awareness that they have done so. Confabulations are not pure fabrications. Rather, they consist of disorganized memories that the patients have recovered. Accurately remembered elements of one event are combined with those of another without regard to their internal consistency or even plausibility. Sometimes events are recalled but placed in inappropriate context or in impaired temporal order, as in this case:

> Mr. W. is sixty-one years old and has had frontal damage caused by an aneurysm (an expanded blood vessel) of the anterior communicating artery. He has been married for over thirty years to the same woman and has four children ranging in age from twenty-seven to thirty-four years.

> Clinician: How long have you been married?
> Patient: About four months.
> Clinician: What is your wife's name?
> Patient: Martha.
> Clinician: How many children do you have?
> Patient: Four. (He laughs.) Not bad for four months.
> Clinician: How old are your children?
> Patient: The eldest is thirty-two; his name is Bob. The youngest is twenty-two; his name is Joe.
> Clinician: How did you get these children in four months?
> Patient: They're adopted. (He laughs again.)

Mr. W. responds correctly, or nearly so, regarding his wife's name and the age of his children. Yet he confabulates about how long he's been married. Then to make sense of the inconsistencies, he concocts a story about adoption. Failure to search for a proper reply, monitor the answer, and evaluate it to make sure it is consistent with his other knowledge accounts for confabulation.

The frontal lobes have been termed "working-with-memory" structures (Moscovitch, 1992; Moscovitch and Winokur, 1992). They operate on the information encoded in memory and recovered from it. The frontal lobes are necessary for converting remembering from a stupid, reflexive act triggered by a cue to an intelligent, reflective, goal-directed activity that is under voluntary control, much like solving a problem. In trying to place a person that looks familiar or to determine where you were during the last week of July, the appropriate memory does not emerge automatically but must be ferreted out, often laboriously, by retrieval strategies, and the output must be monitored and evaluated. As the confabulating patient demonstrated, even a simple question, such as how long have you been married, may involve the "working-with-memory" functions of the frontal lobes.

THE TREATMENT OF ORGANIC DISORDERS

FOCUS QUESTIONS

1. What are the factors that affect the course and effectiveness of treatment of neurological disorders?
2. What medical measures can be taken while the nervous system repairs itself or when cure is impossible?
3. How can people with neurological damage restructure their patterns of living?

The prognosis and treatment of organic disorders are determined in large part by the body's very limited ability to make new neurons but also by the possibility that damaged neurons may sometimes recover or that new connections may be formed. The course and effectiveness of treatment depend on the nature of the disorder, the spatial extent of the pathology (generalized or highly localized), and the specific location of the pathology (whether it is accessible to surgery, for example) (Adams, 1989; McDowell, 1994).

Age can also be a factor. For some disorders, the younger one is, the better the prognosis. Even so, organic disorders are among the most debilitating and for many, the situation can only be reversed if there is damage to, but not destruction of, neurons. Such reversible damage might be produced by lowered oxygen and nutrient supply resulting from stroke or lung disease, or it might be produced by acute pressure caused by swelling of the brain after head trauma, infection, or a tumor that impedes circulation of cerebrospinal fluid. Since damaged or nutrient-deprived neurons can recover, intervention can produce a cure. This would be the case for infections, which can be treated with antibiotics, for acute cases of high intracranial pressure, which can be relieved by draining some of the fluid, or for certain tumors, which can be removed. Since the nervous system has some ability to repair itself, a large part of the treatment of some acute disorders consists in maintaining the patient's health to allow his nervous system to recover from the shock of trauma. Partial recovery from strokes occurs for this reason. For most of the degenerative diseases, however, as well as many of the cases of stroke or hemorrhage, there is little that can be done that would constitute a cure.

Nonetheless, medical measures might be taken to contain the problem or to treat the symptoms. The use of L-DOPA to replace the deficiency in neurotransmitters in someone with Parkinson's disease is an example of this. The L-DOPA does not cure the disease, but it reduces symptoms such as tremor and rigidity.

The situation of many people with neurological damage can also be improved by restructuring their patterns of living. Family members can compensate for deficits, by taking over or assisting in those functions that are

▲ Stephen Hawking, a distinguished British physicist, suffers from a neurological disorder called amyotrophic lateral sclerosis (ALS) and is almost completely paralyzed. Even so, Hawking is able to produce scientific writings of major import through the use of a personal computer.

compromised. It is sometimes possible to teach them ways around their deficit: Braille for the blind, memo pads for those with bad memories, or personal computers for those who are paralyzed.

For the moment, the triumph of neurology is in diagnosis. It is a frustration to the neurologist that she can understand many disease processes and disorders, but she cannot cure them. Although neurologists know a lot about the nervous system, they still have only limited abilities to repair it, and none to replace it. Dramatic cures of neurological disorders sometimes can be produced by neurosurgery, and many symptoms can be relieved with drugs. It is much more common, however, to have understanding without successful treatment in neurology than in psychology. Our present ability to treat the psychosomatic disorders discussed in the first part of the chapter is probably better than our ability to repair the organic disorders arising from assaults on our nervous system.

SUMMARY

1. Psychological factors can influence the course, and even the beginning, of a physical illness. *Psychosomatic disorders* are defined as physical illnesses whose course or onset can be influenced by psychological factors.

2. Psychosomatic disorders can be viewed within a *diathesis-stress model.* In this view, psychosomatic disorder occurs when an individual is both constitutionally vulnerable to a particular physical problem and experiences life stress.

3. Coronary heart disease (CHD) is the leading cause of death in the Western world. The Type A personality—characterized by aggressiveness, time urgency, and competitiveness—is a risk factor for CHD. But hostility may be the active, insidious component of Type A. Also, helplessness in the face of uncontrollable events might be another insidious component of the Type A personality. Frequent engagement in the emergency

reaction may be the process by which Type A's, hostile people, and overloaded people are at greater risk for CHD.

4. The immune system recognizes and destroys antigens, and its activity can be influenced by psychological states. Psychoneuroimmunology, a field that studies this process, has learned that depression, stressful life events, and helplessness decrease immunocompetence and increase immune-related diseases.

5. The biomedical view emphasizes the "diathesis" of the diathesis-stress model, and it argues that genetic inheritance and vulnerability in a specific organ contribute to psychosomatic disorders.

6. The psychodynamic view emphasizes the personality types in whom underlying dynamic conflicts, a vulnerable organ system, and a precipitating life situation interact to produce psychosomatic disorders.

7. The behavioral and cognitive views emphasize the "stress" of the diathesis-stress model. They hold that the way individuals learn to cope with threat, think about threat, and the actual stressful and uncontrollable life events that they experience play the major role in the way psychological factors cause and aggravate physical illness. They emphasize that choice and voluntary behavior are central to the cause and prevention of psychosomatic disorders.

8. One major group of illnesses can be traced to specific defects in the structure and function of the nervous system. This group, called the *organic disorders*, falls in the domain of neuropsychologists and neurologists.

9. The *aphasias*, disorders of language, can be subdivided in terms of whether reception, comprehension, or production of language is primarily affected. The specific deficit depends on where the brain is damaged.

10. The symptoms of *dyslexia* will vary depending on which reading processes are disturbed. *Phonological dyslexics* are impaired at sounding out words, whereas *surface dyslexics* have a deficit in identifying words by their visual form.

11. The most common disorder of memory, the *amnesic syndrome*, most frequently results from aging (senile dementia, such as Alzheimer's disease), head trauma, or chronic alcoholism (Korsakoff's psychosis). The major feature of the amnesic syndrome is the inability to recall or recognize recent events, although new information can be "acquired" and retained without any awareness of these new memories.

12. *Alzheimer's disease* is a degenerative disorder associated with old age. It is characterized by progressive loss of mental functions, with memory disorders and problems in spatial relations often the most prominent early symptoms. A distinctive pathology of neurons is associated with this disorder, especially in the hippocampus.

13. Frontal-lobe functions are apparent in social and emotional behavior. As a result, *frontal-lobe damage* or dysfunction may lead to changes in personality, and to memory impairment.

14. Because new neurons rarely, if ever, arise in adult humans, the prospects for treatment of neurological illness are limited. But recovery sometimes occurs because damaged neurons can recover. In addition, symptoms can be treated by drugs and by teaching the patient strategies that help him to minimize deficits. These strategies often involve enlisting the help of friends or family, and/or special devices such as computers.

1. Describe the characteristics of Type A individuals that cause them to engage in a lifelong struggle to control a world they see as threatening. Why does this make them at risk for CHD?

2. Explain why hopelessness and helplessness contribute to susceptibility to death during bereavement, after a stroke, or after a heart attack.

3. What physical, mental, and social symptoms may indicate frontal-lobe damage?

4. Where cure is impossible, what medical measures can be taken to contain an organic disorder or treat its symptoms? Take one disorder and indicate the possible benefits (and problems, if any) of using medical measures to treat it.

12

Psychoactive Substance Use Disorders*

Melissa Miller, *Smokey Spirits*, 1986.

Humans have used drugs for thousands of years, to cure diseases, alleviate pain, and relieve mental suffering. People have often sought, in the words of Shakespeare, "some sweet oblivious antidote" to the hardships of living *(Macbeth)*. Through the ages, people have used drugs to alter their mental states—to improve mood, experience euphoria, alter perception, or reduce anxiety. But the role of psychoactive drugs in our present society is very complex and often associated with highly charged, emotional debate. Although explanations and theories of drug use have emerged from many fields of study, including medicine, psychiatry, psychology, law, and biology (Babor, 1990), there are many aspects of drug-taking behavior that we do not understand despite considerable research efforts.

Substance abuse is *the* major health problem in the United States today. The costs to society in terms of death, disease, and injury attributable to alcohol and nicotine abuse alone are enormous, and the emotional toll on the lives of abusers and their families is immeasurable. Abuse of alcohol, cigarettes, and other drugs results in nearly $200 billion annually in economic costs to society, a truly staggering number. Yet, paradoxically, our society tacitly condones drug use, since the two drugs that cause the most suffering, alcohol and nicotine, are the ones that are legal. Why do people risk their lives to abuse these substances and what makes society seemingly blind to these problems? In this chapter, we will explore these questions and examine the powerful motivating properties of drugs.

*This chapter is an abbreviated version of a chapter originally written by Ann E. Kelley for *Abnormal Psychology,* third edition.

In the context of abnormal behavior, it is important to focus our discussion on the abnormal or *excessive* use of drugs. In our society, the use of certain psychoactive substances, such as coffee or moderate amounts of alcohol, is considered normal and appropriate behavior. When does drug taking become inappropriate and maladaptive? How do we actually define drug abuse? These are difficult questions that have posed a considerable challenge to mental health professionals, and the definitions and diagnoses have changed over the decades. Like many psychiatric disorders for which there is no obvious physical abnormality or laboratory diagnostic test, what actually constitutes dependence is somewhat a matter of opinion, and often controversial.

Historical Concepts of Drug Use and Dependence

FOCUS QUESTIONS

1. What does it mean to say that drug-taking behavior can best be understood in terms of "drugs, set, and setting"?
2. Describe the three characteristics of the DSM-IV criteria for psychoactive substance dependence.
3. How does the World Health Organization define the dependence syndrome?

Consideration of the historical and cultural aspects of drug use provides a useful framework for current concepts of substance use disorders. How a society views use of a particular drug has an important influence on how we might attempt to define addiction or dependence. For centuries, people have used mind-altering drugs for social, religious, medicinal, and recreational purposes. For example, opium has been used in various societies for over 3,000 years. In the nineteenth century in this country and in England, various opium preparations were widely available and used, even for children. Middle-class consumption of opium was very common, and it was not considered a major social problem or an "addiction." It was only later in this century that use of opiates came to be associated with addiction, crime, and moral degeneration. Hallucinogenic drugs, too, have been viewed in different ways depending on the societal context. Plants containing powerful hallucinogens have been used for religious, ritual, or ceremonial purposes by many primitive societies (Schultes, 1987). Alcohol has also had mixed reviews, depending on the culture or the historical period. During Prohibition in this country, in the 1920s, manufacture and sale of alcohol was illegal. It was widely believed at that time that alcohol was associated with debauchery and weak moral character. Today alcohol is not only legal and widely available, but also associated with many positive features as displayed in many beer and wine commercials. These examples illustrate the point that the social and cultural context of drug use is an important part of understanding addiction. Addiction researcher Norman Zinberg emphasized that drug-taking behavior can best be understood in terms of "drugs, set, and setting," meaning that it is the *interactions* between the chemical substance, personality or individual characteristics, and social setting that determine controlled use or compulsive, destructive use of a drug (Zinberg, 1984).

The concept of addiction has undergone considerable evolution throughout recent history. Central to the development of this notion has been the role of volition or "will" of the addicted individual and personal responsibility. Before the nineteenth century, addictions were generally considered as vice, sin, or moral failings. It was generally thought that drinking was something over which the individual had final control; that is, that drinking to excess was an individual choice.

The notion that alcoholism (and eventually, drug addiction) was more like a disease than willful immoral behavior has its roots in the nineteenth century. Thomas Trotter wrote in 1804 that "the habit of drunkenness is a disease of the mind." In 1791, Benjamin Rush argued that drunkenness began as an act of free will but descended into a disease or "derangement of the will" (cited in Berridge, 1990).

DSM-IV Criteria for Substance Dependence

A maladaptive pattern of substance use, leading to clinically significant impairment or distress, as manifested by three (or more) of the following, occurring at any time in the same twelve-month period:

(1) tolerance, as defined by either of the following: (a) a need for markedly increased amounts of the substance to achieve intoxication or desired effect; (b) markedly diminished effect with continued use of the same amount of the substance;

(2) withdrawal, as manifested by either: (a) the characteristic withdrawal syndrome for the substance (refer to Criteria A and B or the criteria sets for withdrawal from the specific substances); (b) the same (or a closely related) substance is taken to relieve or avoid withdrawal symptoms;

(3) the substance is often taken in larger amounts or over a longer period than was intended;

(4) there is a persistent desire or unsuccessful efforts to cut down or control substance use;

(5) a great deal of time is spent in activities necessary to obtain the substance (e.g., visiting multiple doctors or driving long distances), use the substance (e.g., chain-smoking), or recover from its effects;

(6) important social, occupational, or recreational activities are given up or reduced because of substance use;

(7) the substance use is continued despite knowledge of having a persistent or recurrent physical or psychological problem that is likely to have been caused or exacerbated by the substance (e.g., current cocaine use despite recognition of cocaine-induced depression, or continued drinking despite recognition that an ulcer was made worse by alcohol consumption).

SOURCE: APA, DSM-IV, 1994.

In this century, the ***medical model*** of alcoholism and other drug addictions has been most influential. The addict is viewed as a victim or patient with a disease, in need of medical or psychiatric treatment. It should be noted that the disease theory of dependence has its detractors. For example, Stanton Peele has argued that the disease concept has actually caused addictive behavior to increase because it excuses uncontrolled behaviors and allows people to interpret their lack of control as the expression of a disease they can do nothing about (Peele, 1985).

DSM-IV Criteria for Drug Dependence and Abuse

Traditionally, the appearance of a physical withdrawal syndrome was essential in determining if someone was "addicted" to a substance. For example, some years ago cocaine was not thought to be addictive because users experienced no apparent withdrawal syndrome during abstinence from the drug. Today, physical signs of addiction are still important but not necessary for diagnosis. The DSM-IV criteria for psychoactive substance dependence emphasize clusters of symptoms or behavioral *manifestations* that clearly indicate distress or disability. These criteria reflect behavioral changes that would be considered as extremely undesirable in all cultures. There are three basic characteristics to this set of criteria: (1) loss of control over the use of the substance; (2) impairment in daily functioning and continued use of the substance despite adverse consequences; and (3) physical or emotional adaptation to the drug, such as in the development of tolerance or a withdrawal syndrome. It is sometimes helpful to think of the essentials of drug dependence being defined by the "three C's": loss of Control regarding drug use, Continued use in the face of adverse consequences, and **C**ompulsion (or need) to use the drug (Shaffer and Jones, 1985). The criteria for *substance abuse* reflect a maladaptive, harmful pattern of drug use but do not include physical dependence or compulsive use.

Basic Effects of Drugs

It is useful to consider what we mean by the term "drug." A drug is any chemical substance that has the ability to alter a biological system. The drugs we discuss in this chapter are psychoactive drugs, which affect brain function, mood, and behavior. Although different drugs often have very different effects on the brain, they also share many common properties and characteristics. Thus, the effectiveness and potency (the amount of a drug that must be given in order to obtain a particular response) of all drugs are influenced by: (1) the route of administration, (2) the ability of the drug to cross membranes and to enter the brain, (3) how well a drug interacts with receptors in the brain, and (4) how quickly the drug is deactivated.

ROUTE OF ADMINISTRATION

For a drug to affect mental states, it must first reach the brain. All drugs are carried into the brain via the circulatory system, or blood supply to the brain. There are different ways that people deliver or administer drugs to achieve this purpose. Understanding these different routes is important because very often the route of administration determines how much of the drug reaches the brain, how quickly a drug effect occurs, and in some cases, the actual subjective response to the drug. For example, in smokers, nicotine enters the body through inhalation. The surface area of the lungs is great and in close contact with the circulatory system. Thus, relatively large amounts of nicotine enter the blood and hence the brain rather quickly. Direct injection of a drug into a vein (known as "mainlining" in street jargon) results in the drug reaching the brain quite quickly. This is a route preferred by many heroin addicts. Other routes of administration include intranasal and intraoral delivery, in which the drug is absorbed through the lining of these tissues into the circulatory system. An example of intraoral drug delivery is that of chewing tobacco.

LIPID SOLUBILITY AND THE BLOOD-BRAIN BARRIER

All drugs must cross several biological membranes (for example, the stomach lining or the capillaries in the lungs) before reaching their target, the brain. The most important membrane or "barrier" that a drug must cross to exert a psychoactive effect is the ***blood-brain barrier***. This barrier is composed of specialized cells that stop certain compounds in the circulatory system from entering the brain. It allows certain drugs to pass through and affect brain cells, and excludes others, depending on the size and chemical characteristics of the drug molecule. ***Lipid (fat) solubility*** is an important factor in whether and how fast a drug reaches the brain. Since cell membranes are composed primarily of fatty substances, a relatively more lipid soluble drug will be absorbed more quickly. For example, a small chemical modification of morphine results in heroin, which is considerably more lipid than morphine. Heroin is preferred to morphine by opiate addicts because it reaches the brain more quickly and in higher concentrations. Certain general anesthetics are highly lipid soluble, reaching the brain and causing loss of consciousness within a matter of seconds.

DRUGS AND NEUROTRANSMITTERS

All psychoactive drugs have various effects upon neurotransmitter systems in the brain. Normally, receptors help to conduct messages by recognizing specific neurotransmitters, much the way a lock fits a certain key. Drugs can mimic neurotransmitters by interacting with the brain's receptor molecules. There are a number of ways that drugs can do this, and different drugs have different effects at the synapse, which is the gap between two communicating neurons. Drugs can affect the synthesis of the neurotransmitter, affect the vehicles that store the neurotransmitter, block the release of the neurotransmitter, prevent the reuptake or deactivation of the neurotransmitter after its release into the synapse, or bind to postsynaptic receptors (see Figure 12–1).

ADAPTATION TO DRUGS: TOLERANCE AND PHYSICAL DEPENDENCE

Neuroadaptation refers to the complex biological changes that occur in the brain with repeated or chronic exposure to a drug. Drugs by their very definition induce some change in the neurochemical environment of the brain;

FIGURE 12–1

SYNAPTIC SITES OF ACTION OF PSYCHOACTIVE DRUGS

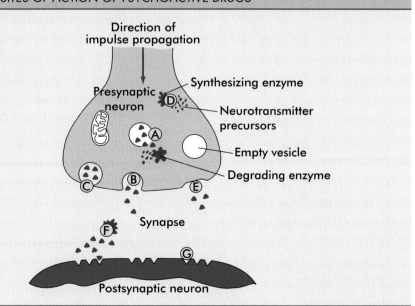

Drugs can cause neurotransmitter molecules to leak out of vesicles (A); crowd neurotransmitters out of storage vesicles (B); block release of neurotransmitter into the synapse (C); inhibit enzymes that synthesize the neurotransmitter (D); block neurotransmitter reuptake (E); block enzymes that degrade neurotransmitters (F); bind to postsynaptic receptors and either mimic or block the action of the neurotransmitter (G). (SOURCE: Snyder, 1986, p. 15)

one exposure to a particular drug will cause a specific effect (for example, increased levels of a particular neurotransmitter). One such effect is ***intoxication,*** an acute, maladaptive psychological change such as impaired thinking or judgment, that develops soon after ingestion and goes away in time. However, with repeated exposure, the body and brain often adapt to the presence of the drug. Through self-corrective mechanisms, the nervous system attempts to compensate for the effects of the drug. ***Tolerance*** is one form of this adaptation. Tolerance refers to a state of decreased response to a drug following prior or repeated exposure to that drug. Progressively more drug is needed in order to obtain the same effect. Compared with inexperienced drinkers, people who regularly consume alcohol often show a high degree of tolerance to its behavioral effects. Tolerance may be accompanied (although not necessarily) by ***physical dependence.*** Physical dependence is characterized by the need for the presence of the drug in order to function normally, and by the appearance of a withdrawal syndrome upon cessation of the drug. The ***withdrawal syndrome*** (also called abstinence syndrome) is usually characterized by observable, physical signs such as marked changes in body temperature or heart rate, seizures, tremors, or vomiting. Such a syndrome may occur, for example, following abrupt cessation of chronic heavy drinking. In some forms of dependence, such as those associated with cocaine or nicotine, the so-called withdrawal syndrome may not be easily observable; it may take the form of severe depression, irritability, or craving.

Theories of Drug Dependence

There are many approaches, ideas, and theories pertaining to drug addiction. Here, we offer only an overview of a few theories or models. The most important point to keep in mind is that drug dependence is a complex phenomenon that results from an interaction of many factors. The goal is not to develop a unitary theory of dependence, but rather to understand as much as possible the psychological, social, and biological conditions that contribute to substance use disorders.

PERSONALITY AND PSYCHOLOGICAL MODELS

For many years, it was believed that a so-called "addictive" personality existed. It was thought that substance abusers had some personality flaw that made them vulnerable to use and become addicted to drugs. Attempts to demonstrate an addictive personality empirically have not been successful. However, considerable research has examined the comorbidity of specific psychiatric disorders with substance abuse disorders. Antisocial personality disorder is the most prevalent coexisting psychiatric disorder among males with substance abuse disorder (Hesselbrock, Meyer, and Hesselbrock, 1992). Antisocial personality disorder is characterized by a pattern of irresponsible, destructive, antisocial behaviors beginning in childhood or early adolescence and continuing to adulthood. While the prevalence of this diagnosis is 2 to 3 percent in the general population, it ranges from 16 to 49 percent in studies of alcoholics, cocaine, and heroin addicts (Gerstley, Alterman, McLellan, and Woody, 1990; Cottler, Price, Compton, and Mager, 1995; Kokkevi and Stefanis, 1995). It is likely that antisocial personality disorder is a risk factor for the development of alcoholism and other addictive disorders. Why this might be so is uncertain, but it may be that such individuals are more likely to be exposed to drugs, to experiment more, and to ignore their adverse consequences (see Chapter 7).

Psychodynamic views have also contributed to psychological perspectives of drug dependence. The general notion here is that drug use is seen as a

FOCUS QUESTIONS

1. Describe some psychological and biological factors that may put people at risk for developing substance dependence.
2. Explain opponent-process theory.
3. How do positive reinforcement models explain drug use?
4. Explain how psychoactive drugs may activate neurotransmitters and receptors that play a fundamental role in natural rewards.
5. What are "drug cues" and how do they induce craving for the drug and trigger relapse?

means to compensate for defective ego functions (Treece and Khantzian, 1986). Drugs are used to reduce painful emotional states or as a defense mechanism in relation to an internal conflict. According to one user's view, "Cocaine was a way of numbing out feelings. . . . Being stoned is like having a layer between me and reality, like doing things with gloves on. I dealt with emotions by avoiding them" (Shaffer and Jones, 1985). The use of drugs to cope with the anxiety associated with intimacy, especially during adolescence, has been noted by several theorists (Hendin, 1974).

BIOLOGICAL VULNERABILITY

People may be at risk for developing substance dependence because of biological factors that may be inherited. Most of the evidence for this viewpoint comes from research on alcoholism. Children of alcoholics are four times more likely to become alcohol-dependent than people in the general population. This risk factor is true even for children who were adopted away from the alcoholic family into nondependent families, suggesting that some genetic predisposition may be at work. Of course, these findings do not mean that there are "alcoholic genes" but rather that certain complex genetic factors may contribute to a person's biological response to alcohol. We do not yet know what these factors are; but they may involve deficits or dysfunctions in certain neurochemical systems. In fact, one view of substance abuse is that it is a form of "self-medication"; people take drugs to correct (unknowingly) some predisposing biochemical imbalance in the brain. Certain psychoactive drugs might alleviate the emotional distress associated with such states.

OPPONENT-PROCESS THEORY

The opponent-process theory of acquired motivation has strongly influenced notions of addictive behavior (Solomon and Corbit, 1974). The idea of opponent process is based on the theory that systems react and adapt to stimuli by opposing their initial effects. Although the theory was meant to explain many types of acquired motives such as love, social attachments, thrill seeking, and food craving, it is particularly relevant to drug addictions. The theory is best introduced with an example, that of eating a potato chip. As we all know, it's difficult to "eat just one." After consuming one chip, the motivation to eat more increases. If the bag is taken away, the craving for more chips remains for a period of time and gradually dissipates. It is as though the pleasurable experience with one chip sensitizes feelings or needs that were not there before tasting the chip. The same phenomenon is true for psychoactive drugs. A desire or craving for a drug, which clearly did not exist before experience with the substance, increases with exposure to it.

The opponent-process theory attempts to explain this increased motivation to continue drug use. It is based on three important phenomena that are common to all drugs that produce dependence. First, the pharmacological effect of drugs following initial use results in a hedonic (emotional) state known as ***affective pleasure.*** Different drugs arouse different subjective states, but overall these states are associated with positive affect. For example, alcohol may provide a sense of relaxation and relief from stress while cocaine results in feelings of arousal and energy. Second, with repeated exposure, ***affective tolerance*** develops. As we saw earlier, tolerance refers to the diminution of a drug effect with repeated exposure. In the present case, tolerance develops to the affective, euphoriant effects of the drug. The rush or pleasurable feelings are not as intense as they were with initial administration. In order to achieve the same subjective effect, the user needs to take progressively higher doses of the drug. The third phenomenon, which is related to tolerance, is known as ***affective withdrawal.*** It is proposed that this state, which arises upon removal of the drug reinforcer, is the hedonic opposite of affective pleasure. For example, heroin produces feelings of euphoria and calmness, while withdrawal from heroin is associated with dysphoria (discomfort), panic, and anxiety.

POSITIVE REINFORCEMENT MODELS

The positive reinforcement models focus on the pleasurable, euphoriant effects of drugs and posit that these powerful rewarding effects are the primary explanation for drug use. These models were developed in the tradition of behaviorism and operant psychology. Many years ago, it was found that animals would make an operant response, such as lever pressing, to obtain an intravenous injection of a drug. In 1964, Thompson and Shuster showed that monkeys would reliably give themselves morphine. This was a landmark experiment because until that time it was thought that drug taking was a uniquely human behavior, indicative of psychological or social stress. Soon after, it was observed that monkeys would self-administer many of the drugs abused by humans: morphine, codeine, cocaine, amphetamine, pentobarbital, ethanol, and caffeine (Deneau, Yanagita, and Seevers, 1969). Most importantly, in that experiment it was shown that physical dependence was not a necessary condition for the animals to self-administer drugs. Such observations suggest that drugs are powerful reinforcers and that a preexisting psychopathology or addictive vulnerability is not necessary for initial or continued drug taking (Jaffe, 1985; White, 1996). Researchers have found that many of the brain regions and neurotransmitters that are involved in natural rewards (food, sex) are also those affected by reinforcing drugs (Koob and Bloom, 1988; Parada, Puig de Parada, and Hoebel, 1995; Salamone, Kurth, McCullough, and Sokolowski, 1995; Weiss, Parsons, Schulteis, et al., 1996). Both receptors for dopamine and for endogenous opioids (naturally occurring morphine-like substances) may be affected by drugs and lead to positive reinforcement effects (Gianoulakis, 1996).

CONDITIONING AND LEARNING MODELS

The pleasurable states that drugs induce and the relief they bring to aversive withdrawal states are important factors underlying drug-seeking behavior. However, the greatest problem in substance abuse treatment is keeping the individual abstinent. Weeks, months, or even years following successful detoxification, the patient may yield to uncontrollable drug cravings and may relapse (see Figure 12–2). The conditioning and learning models provide a framework for understanding this aspect of substance dependence. These models embrace the notion that a drug is an unconditioned stimulus that becomes associated with many signals in the user's environment: sights, sounds, feelings, situations. These signals become powerful conditioned stimuli through their repeated pairing with the drug state, and may contribute to the reinstatement of drug-seeking behavior.

The acknowledged father of conditioning models is Abraham Wikler (1973). At the Public Health Service Hospital in Lexington, Kentucky, Wikler was observing opiate addicts in a group therapy session. These particular patients had been free of drugs for several months, and there were certainly no signs of opiate withdrawal. However, when the patients began talking about drugs, Wikler noticed that some of them began to show signs of withdrawal, such as tearing eyes, runny nose, sweating, and yawning. He labeled this phenomenon "conditioned withdrawal" and also noted its occurrence when the former addicts returned to neighborhoods where they had previously used drugs. Wikler suggested that through classical conditioning, environmental stimuli acquire the ability to elicit the signs of withdrawal. Moreover, these *drug cues,* or drug "reminders," induced craving for the drug as well and played an important role in triggering relapse.

FIGURE 12–2

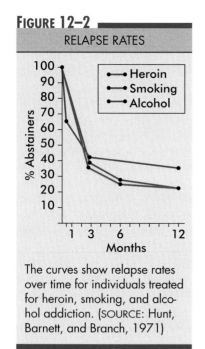

RELAPSE RATES

The curves show relapse rates over time for individuals treated for heroin, smoking, and alcohol addiction. (SOURCE: Hunt, Barnett, and Branch, 1971)

There is much evidence, both from human studies and animal research, to support Wikler's theories. Charles O'Brien and his colleagues at the Addiction Research Center at the University of Pennsylvania have shown in the laboratory setting that presentation of drug-related stimuli to patients in treatment induces strong signs of physiological arousal and self-reports of drug craving (O'Brien, Childress, McLellan, and Ehrman, 1992; Droungas, Ehrman, Childress, and O'Brien, 1995). Their research suggests that conditioned cues elicit "drug-opposite" responses that reinstate the overwhelming need for the drug. This may be true for a variety of psychoactive substances and situations. For example, passing a bar or arriving at a cocktail party may induce a strong desire for a drink (even in a social, moderate drinker), and the smell of smoke or sight of cigarettes can induce a strong craving in smokers trying to quit.

ALCOHOL

For reasons that are probably social or cultural, we often do not classify alcohol as a drug. For example, people often speak of "drugs and alcohol," and the term "substance abuse" is used to include both drug abuse and alcoholism. However, alcohol is indeed a psychoactive drug with many of the characteristics of other drugs of abuse; it causes effects on the brain and behavior, and it has considerable potential for addiction and adverse consequences. In fact, if one excludes cigarette smoking, alcoholism is by far the most serious drug problem in the United States. At the same time, our society accepts and even condones its controlled use. Alcohol has a long history of this "love-hate" relationship with human society (Ray and Ksir, 1987).

Effects of Alcohol

FOCUS QUESTIONS

1. Describe the behavioral and central nervous system effects of alcohol.
2. What are three kinds of tolerance to alcohol?
3. What factors predispose an individual to alcoholism?

Alcohol is somewhat unusual in comparison with many other psychoactive drugs. It is not very potent, requiring several grams to exert measurable effects (most psychoactive drugs are effective in milligram quantities). A blood alcohol content (BAC) of approximately 20 to 50 mg of ethanol per 100 milliliters of blood is necessary for alcohol to have noticeable effects in most individuals. This would be equivalent to a BAC of 0.025 to 0.05 percent. A BAC of 0.1 percent is considered to be legally intoxicating in most states. Alcohol is consumed as a beverage and is absorbed from the stomach and small intestine. The concentration of alcohol is the primary factor in determining the rate of absorption, but other factors can influence the rate, such as food in the stomach or whether the alcohol is dissolved in a carbonated beverage. Food slows absorption of alcohol, and carbonation increases it. The amount of alcohol required to reach a particular blood alcohol concentration very much depends on the weight of the person and proportion of body fat. Alcohol is excreted in very small amounts in breath, urine, sweat, and feces, but over 90 percent is metabolized by the liver. Chronic users often suffer from liver damage, because the liver spends so much time trying to metabolize the alcohol.

BEHAVIORAL EFFECTS

People have used alcohol for millennia to stimulate feelings of pleasure and relaxation, to quell anxieties and worries, and to increase their sense of self-confidence and power. From the psychopharmacological point of view, the effects of alcohol on human behavior and performance are complex and very

▲ Psychoanalytic views of drug and alcohol use consider it a defense against painful internal conflicts. Perhaps Degas meant to suggest the same view in his painting *The Absinthe Drinker.*

much dependent on a number of factors, such as dose and previous experience with alcohol. At low to moderate doses of alcohol, most people experience a sense of relaxation and mild euphoria. Although alcohol is classified as a sedative-hypnotic drug, because of its obvious depressant properties, in low doses it can act as a stimulant. People become more talkative, more outgoing, and less constrained by social inhibitions. These effects are in large part due to **disinhibition.** Disinhibition refers to a state in which people do things they wouldn't normally do for fear of adverse consequences. The behaviors that are released from inhibition depend on the history or personality of the individual. For example, a shy, reserved person may become gregarious, or a normally passive person may become aggressive or belligerent. As some of us unfortunately might know from experience, people may do or say things under the influence of alcohol that they would never do when sober. There is a close relationship between the blood alcohol level and the nature of the behavioral effects of alcohol. A colorful description of this relationship is provided by Bogen (as cited in Ray and Ksir, 1987):

At less than 0.03%, the individual is dull and dignified
At 0.05%, he is dashing and debonair
At 0.1%, he may become dangerous and devilish
At 0.2%, he is likely to be dizzy and disturbing
At 0.25%, he may be disgusting and disheveled
At 0.3%, he is delirious and disoriented and surely drunk
At 0.35%, he is dead drunk
At 0.6%, the chances are he is dead

Higher doses of alcohol are associated with depressant effects and considerable impairment of sensory and motor functions. There are decreases in visual acuity and in sensitivity to taste and smell. Reflexes are slowed, and movement and speech may be sluggish. Reaction time is slowed by blood alcohol levels of 0.08 to 0.1 percent; complex reaction time tests, which require the subject to integrate information from several sources before responding, show that even at lower doses, both speed and accuracy are decreased (McKim, 1986). Memory processes are also disrupted by alcohol. Attention to stimuli, ability to encode new information, and short-term memory are all decreased. In heavy drinkers, "blackouts" may occur during periods of high consumption. As the name may suggest, these are periods when the individual has no recollection of events surrounding the drinking episode.

CENTRAL NERVOUS SYSTEM EFFECTS

Alcohol produces a variety of complex effects on brain function. In contrast to most psychoactive drugs that have relatively specific effects at the synapse,

DSM-IV Criteria for Alcohol Intoxication
A. Recent ingestion of alcohol.
B. Clinically significant maladaptive behavioral or psychological changes (e.g., inappropriate sexual or aggressive behavior, mood lability, impaired judgment, impaired social or occupational functioning) that developed during, or shortly after, alcohol ingestion.
C. One (or more) of the following signs, developing during, or shortly after, alcohol use: (1) slurred speech; (2) incoordination; (3) unsteady gait; (4) nystagmus; (5) impairment in attention or memory; (6) stupor or coma.
D. The symptoms are not due to a general medical condition and are not better accounted for by another mental disorder.
SOURCE: APA, DSM-IV, 1994.

High doses of alcohol debilitate sensory and motor functions, and severe withdrawal can be life-threatening.

alcohol affects many neurotransmitter systems and many aspects of neuronal function. It has long been known that one of the principal effects of alcohol is a nonspecific interaction with neuronal membranes (Chin and Goldstein, 1977). The alcohol "dissolves" in the membrane and alters the physical state of the membrane lipids by making them more fluid. This in turn interferes with the ability of the neuron to conduct action potentials, thus reducing neuronal activity. The debilitating effects of high doses of alcohol on sensory and motor functions are largely due to this general depressant action. However, alcohol also affects a number of neurotransmitter systems, in particular norepinephrine, dopamine, serotonin, and gamma-aminobutyric acid (GABA). Alcohol's influence on these systems may be related to its mood-altering, reinforcing, and anxiety-reducing effects.

ALCOHOL TOLERANCE AND PHYSICAL DEPENDENCE

Tolerance develops to many of the effects of alcohol. In colloquial terms, someone who is able to "hold his liquor" is displaying tolerance to alcohol. There are several phenomena associated with tolerance to alcohol. The first is *metabolic* tolerance, in which the liver produces more metabolizing enzymes and breaks down alcohol at a faster rate. This mechanism does not account for most of the tolerance observed with chronic alcohol use, although it certainly contributes to liver damage. Behavioral tolerance and cellular tolerance are probably more important. *Behavioral* tolerance occurs when the individual learns to function under the influence of the drug. For example, there are some alcoholics who appear to work and perform activities normally at blood alcohol levels that would seriously impair most individuals. *Cellular* tolerance, in which neurons adapt to the presence of the drug, can also be demonstrated. In the cerebellum, a region implicated in the motor-intoxicating effects of alcohol, neurons respond to intravenous alcohol by increasing their firing rate. However, this pattern of activation returns to normal following long-term exposure to alcohol (Rogers, Siggins, Schulman, and Bloom, 1980). During withdrawal from alcohol, there is a marked decrease in the firing rate.

Physical dependence develops quite rapidly with alcohol. In fact, anyone who has experienced a hangover after a bout of binge drinking has experienced a form of alcohol withdrawal. For this reason, there is actually some truth in the saying that drinking will cure a hangover. True physical dependence, however, develops with prolonged heavy use of alcohol, and the severity of the withdrawal syndrome varies with the level and duration of drinking. As is true with most depressant drugs, the withdrawal syndrome can be quite severe and sometimes life-threatening if not treated. Symptoms usually appear eight to twelve hours following the last drinking bout. Early symptoms may include nausea, weakness, anxiety, tremors, rapid heartbeat, and disturbed sleep. In severe cases, the syndrome progresses to include hallucinations, disorientation, confusion, and agitation. In the worst cases, tremors, seizures, and severe delirium—known as delirium tremens, or the "D.T.s"—may develop within two to four days. If left untreated, the syndrome will subside in about seven to ten days (Jaffe, 1985; Daryanani, Santolaria, Reimers, et al., 1994). However, in most cases, alcohol withdrawal is treated pharmacologically to reduce the mortality rate and ease the symptoms. Several treatments, most prominently with the benzodiazepine drugs, are very successful in this regard (Bohn, 1993; Miller, 1995). Naltrexone is also extremely effective in reducing alcohol use by reducing craving. Clinical trials have shown that it helps relieve withdrawal symptoms with few side effects, making it an attractive alternative to benzodiazepine drugs (Volpicelli, Clay, Watson, and O'Brien, 1995). Alcohol also relieves the withdrawal state at any stage. The obviously aversive physical and emotional aspects of withdrawal are strong motivation for the dependent individual to resume drinking, thus setting in motion the addictive cycle.

Etiology of Alcoholism

In general, the individual diagnosed as an alcoholic has been drinking heavily over an extended period of time, and has consequently suffered from many major life problems. There is often compulsive drinking and an inability to stop, despite repeated efforts. Consumption is often high, exceeding a fifth of liquor or its equivalent in wine or beer. Alcohol dependence can range from mild to severe. If there is recurrent drinking with adverse consequences, but the symptoms have not met the criteria for dependence (for example, no evidence of withdrawal or compulsive use), a diagnosis of alcohol abuse may be given.

Who becomes an alcoholic? Well over half the adult U.S. population uses alcohol regularly, but only a small fraction of those people become dependent. There are many theories concerning the etiology of alcoholism. We can begin with the caveat that there is no one environment, upbringing, personality, or gene that causes alcoholism. Alcoholism is found in all socioeconomic classes and in all walks of life. As in all substance dependence, the development of pathological alcohol-related behavior is the result of the interaction of many factors. Research focuses on vulnerability factors—the factors that predispose an individual to alcoholism.

BIOLOGICAL VULNERABILITY TO ALCOHOLISM

There is strong evidence that alcoholism is a genetically influenced disorder (Schuckit, 1984, 1987; Goldman, 1995). Alcoholism is three to five times as frequent in the parents, siblings, and children of alcoholics as in the general population (Cotton, 1979). Twin studies provide evidence of the concordance rate being much higher in identical twins than in fraternal twins, although it never reaches 100 percent, suggesting that the heritability factor cannot be explained by simple genetic mechanisms (Kaij, 1960; Hrubec and Omenn, 1981; Kendler, Neale, Heath, Kessler, and Eaves, 1994). Adoption studies put any genetic hypothesis to the most stringent test, and here too the evidence is quite convincing. A study of Danish adopted-away sons of alcoholics revealed a rate of alcoholism at the age of thirty of 18 percent, compared with a rate of 5 percent in adopted-away control subjects (Goodwin, Schulsinger, Hermansen, Guze, and Winokur, 1973), and the amount of alcoholism in the adopted children of alcoholics does not vary with whether the adoptive parent is alcoholic or not (Goodwin, Schulsinger, Moller, Hermansen, and Winokur, 1974). A fourfold higher rate of alcoholism was shown in adopted-away daughters of alcoholic mothers (10.3 percent) than in controls (2.8 percent) (Bohman and Sigvardsson, 1981). In another study, the rate of alcoholism was twice as high in males with alcoholic biological fathers (60.6 percent) as in adoptees from "clean" biological backgrounds (32.7 percent) (Cadoret, Yates, Troughton, Woodworth, and Stewart, 1995).

PERSONALITY AND PSYCHOLOGICAL FACTORS

Psychological theories of alcoholism tend to emphasize associations between psychological or environmental variables and the development of alcoholism. As is true for substance abuse in general, a specific type of personality disorder has been frequently found to be associated with alcoholism. A diagnosis of antisocial personality disorder is a risk factor for the development of alcoholism, independent of having a family history of the disorder (Drake and Vaillant, 1988; Cadoret, O'Gorman, Troughton, and Heywood, 1985; Hesselbrock, Meyer, and Hesselbrock, 1992; Cadoret, Yates, Troughton, Woodworth, and Stewart, 1995, 1996).

Tension reduction has also been suggested to account for alcoholism. People drink to reduce anxiety or stress, and in some cases progress to abuse or dependence. Perhaps people who drink to excess suffer from high levels of anxiety or tension. Since alcohol has clear anti-anxiety effects, this hypothesis has much intuitive appeal. For example, clinical observations reveal a strong association between anxiety and alcoholism, and phobic patients report that they use alcohol to cope with their phobias (Mullaney and Trippet, 1982). Moreover, stressful life events are often associated with relapse to drinking (Marlatt and Gordon, 1985; Linsky, Straus, and Colby, 1985). However, the relationship between tension reduction and alcohol is complex. Although alcoholics and social drinkers report that alcohol helps them to relax and boosts their confidence, actual observation of the behavior of alcoholics while drinking reveals them to be anxious, depressed, and nervous (Tamerin and Mendelson, 1970).

Treating Alcoholism

The goal of treatment of alcoholism, as is true for treatment of any drug addiction, is prevention of relapse. Most alcoholics have tried to stop drinking and have remained abstinent for periods of time, but eventually relapse. Detoxification (the reduction and removal of alcohol from the body) is important initially in severely dependent people, in order to treat the alcohol withdrawal syndrome. This is usually done in a hospital or treatment center under medical supervision. Following detoxification there is an active treatment phase. In general, rehabilitation for alcoholism utilizes the strategies employed to treat other behavioral or psychological disorders. These techniques may include psychotherapy, counseling, or behavioral therapy, often carried out in groups. Many programs emphasize development of coping skills, enhancement of self-esteem, behavior change, and finding strategies to cope with the possibility of relapse.

COGNITIVE-BEHAVIORAL TREATMENT

The cognitive-behavioral model of treatment emphasizes three main strategies (Marlatt and Gordon, 1985): skill training, cognitive restructuring, and lifestyle intervention (see Figure 12–3). Skill-training techniques include teaching the patient to identify and cope effectively with "high-risk" situations in which the loss of control or threat of relapse is increased. Examples of such situations are negative emotional states (depression, frustration, anxiety), social pressure, or interpersonal conflict. The therapist's aim is to instill a sense of mastery or perception of self-control in these situations. This notion of self-efficacy is described as a kind of "I know I can handle it" feeling. Cognitive restructuring involves changing the individual's perception of violation of abstinence, or a "slip." If a relapse does occur, instead of reacting to the lapse as a personal failure characterized by guilt and internal attributions, the individual is taught "to reconceptualize the episode as a single, independent event and to see it as a mistake rather than a disaster that can never be undone" (Marlatt and Gordon, 1985, p. 59). The principal goal of lifestyle intervention is to develop activities that offset sources of stress in daily life, or to replace negative addictions with "positive addictions," such as exercise, relaxation, or meditation.

FIGURE 12–3

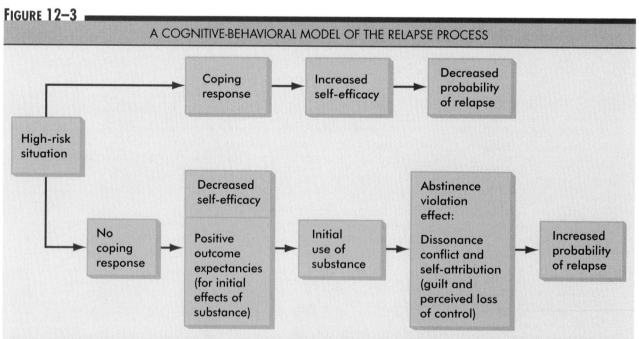

A COGNITIVE-BEHAVIORAL MODEL OF THE RELAPSE PROCESS

The cognitive-behavioral model for treatment of alcoholism emphasizes strategies that enable the patient to cope with high-risk situations. These include skill training, cognitive restructuring, and lifestyle intervention. When the patient uses these coping strategies, he is less likely to relapse than he would be if he had no strategies for dealing with high-risk situations. (SOURCE: Marlatt and Gordon, 1985)

FOCUS QUESTIONS

1. What are the cognitive-behavioral model's three main strategies for treating alcoholism?
2. What is AA and what is its philosophy?
3. How can therapeutic drugs be used to treat alcoholics?
4. Describe four factors that may contribute to a positive outcome and recovery from alcoholism.

Some alcoholics seek the support of the organization known as Alcoholics Anonymous (AA). AA is a self-help program that was started in 1936 by two recovering alcoholic men, and it has grown to be the world's largest self-help network. An estimated 800,000 alcoholics attend meetings of 23,000 groups in ninety countries (Goodwin, 1988). Its philosophy is based not upon scientific research but rather on experience gained through extensive work with alcoholics. AA views alcoholism as a progressive disease that cannot be controlled without the help of a higher being and the support of fellow members, and it believes that complete abstinence is required to deal with the disease. Education about alcohol and its consequences is provided, and testimonials of individuals with alcohol problems are shared.

DRUG TREATMENT

Alcoholism can also be treated with therapeutic drugs. Disulfiram (Antabuse) is a drug that inhibits the enzyme that aids the metabolism of alcohol. If alcohol is drunk in the presence of this drug, there is a buildup of acetaldehyde in the body and the person will feel very sick. The rationale underlying this treatment is that the fear of or prior experience with this unpleasant result will deter the individual from drinking further. It is frequently prescribed in treatment programs as an adjunct to therapy, although there is little evidence that abstinence is increased by disulfiram over the long term. However, disulfiram may lower the frequency of drinking in patients who have difficulty remaining abstinent (Bohn, 1993).

Recent clinical trials suggest that treatment with another drug, naltrexone, may be effective in reducing craving and preventing relapse (Volpicelli, Alterman, Hayashida, and O'Brien, 1992; Volpicelli, Clay, Watson, and O'Brien, 1995). Naltrexone is an opiate antagonist that blocks or reduces opioid transmission in the brain. Naltrexone may actually reduce the motivation to drink since it was particularly effective in subjects who sampled alcohol or had one "slip"; that is, naltrexone helped to stop the resumption of binge drinking typically seen in placebo-treated subjects.

PROGNOSIS

How effective is treatment? What are the chances of recovering from alcoholism? Unfortunately, not very good. No single inpatient, outpatient, counseling, self-help, or drug treatment has been shown to reduce relapse rates significantly over the long term. When researchers evaluate treatment over a short period, like six months, they are likely to see positive results. Approximately 65 percent of people are still abstinent for this long after treatment (Seligman, 1993). Long-term studies reveal a different picture, however. A survey of hundreds of studies done on thousands of patients indicates that no one type of treatment is more effective than another, and most surprisingly, that treatment is not superior to no treatment (Emrick, 1982; Goodwin, 1988; Seligman, 1993). The most extensive studies of alcoholism and its course throughout the life cycle have been conducted by George Vaillant, a Harvard researcher who has followed 700 individuals over fifty years (Vaillant, 1983, 1992). He has consistently found, as have other researchers, that about one-third of alcoholics recover whether or not treatment programs are followed. He states a "one-third" rule for alcoholism: by age sixty-five, one-third are dead or in awful shape, one-third are abstinent or drinking socially, and one-third are still trying to quit (cited in Seligman, 1993). However, Vaillant has also found that certain factors are strongly predictive of a positive outcome and recovery from alcoholism. These four factors are: (1) experiencing a strongly aversive experience related to drinking (e.g., having a serious medical emergency or condition), (2) finding a substitute dependency to compete with alcohol use (e.g., meditation, overeating, exercise), (3) obtaining new social supports (e.g., an appreciative employer or new marriage), and (4) joining an inspirational group (e.g., a religious group or AA). Vaillant finds a strong association between these factors and relapse prevention.

Medical and Social Complications

The medical and social complications of alcohol use and alcoholism are extensive. Measured in terms of accidents, lost productivity, crime, death, or damaged health, the economic cost of problem drinking in the United States is over 100 billion dollars annually (Jaffe, 1985). Drunken driving accounts for many motor vehicle deaths and injuries in this country. Alcohol intoxication is present in nearly half of all suicides, homicides, and accidents, and about 40 percent of all hospital admissions are alcohol related. Medical costs of alcohol and detriments to health form a long list. Cirrhosis of the liver, damage to the nervous system, heart, and digestive system, and cancer are all associated with chronic alcohol use. Chronic use of alcohol in pregnancy can also result in *fetal alcohol syndrome,* in which the offspring of the alcoholic person has distinct physical and mental abnormalities. Sadly, fetal alcohol syndrome carries the costs of alcohol abuse to the next generation.

STIMULANTS

FOCUS QUESTIONS

1. Describe the effects of the stimulants on physiology and behavior.
2. How does cocaine affect the brain?
3. What are the phases of cocaine use and dependence?
4. Describe some successful treatment programs for cocaine abusers.

Although cocaine and amphetamine are the prototypical illicit stimulants, stimulating drugs are also found in coffee, tea, soft drinks, cigarettes, chocolate, and many nonprescription medicines. If one includes all of these sources, stimulants are by far the most widely used psychoactive drug. Cocaine and amphetamine are the most commonly used illegal stimulants. Since cocaine is the drug most associated with medical problems and addiction, our discussion will focus mainly on this drug. In the mid-1980s, the National Institute on Drug Abuse declared it was the greatest drug problem facing this country. From 1976 to 1986, there was a fifteen-fold increase in the number of emergency room visits attributed to cocaine, in cocaine-related deaths, and in the number of people seeking treatment for cocaine addiction (Gawin and Ellinwood, 1988).

Cocaine is prepared from the leaves of the coca plant, which grows wild and has been cultivated in South America for thousands of years. The custom of chewing the leaves by the native peoples of the Peruvian Andes dates back at least 5,000 years. The plant played an integral role in the Incan religious and social system, where it was considered a divine and highly prized plant. Incan corpses would have their cheeks stuffed with leaves, to "ease their journey to the next world" (Grinspoon and Bakalar, 1976). Cocaine was introduced into mainstream Western society in the last two decades of the nineteenth century, in various tonics, patent medicines, and remedies.

Amphetamine is a synthetic drug that was developed in the early part of this century as a treatment for asthma. In fact, it was a synthetic substitute for a drug called ephedrine, which was an extract of a plant used in ancient Chinese remedies. It was available for many years under the brand name of Benzedrine, in inhalant form for asthma. It was not until 1959 that the FDA banned the use of amphetamine in inhalants. By that time, however, the stimulant and euphoriant properties of the drug had become widely known. Various forms of amphetamines, known as "speed" in street jargon, became very popular in the 1960s hippie drug culture. With the rising popularity of cocaine in the 1970s and 1980s, however, that drug became the preferred "upper" among drug abusers, and amphetamine use decreased.

Effects of Stimulants

Cocaine induces profound changes in behavior and psychological state as well as alterations in bodily physiology. It is administered in a variety of ways, but most commonly it is injected intravenously, snorted intranasally, or smoked in its solid, free-base form ("crack"). Cocaine induces changes in mood and emotional state. In general, cocaine produces feelings of stimulation, well-being, vigor, and euphoria. Enhanced alertness, increased sexuality, heightened energy, and deepening of emotions may accompany the cocaine high. In contrast to some drugs, cocaine does not appear to alter perceptual processes or distort reality. It has been said that cocaine and other stimulants produce a neurochemical magnification of the pleasure experienced in most activities (Gawin and Ellinwood, 1988).

It is clearly these positive properties that attract people to cocaine and underlie its addictive properties. However, cocaine can also induce negative emotional states and severe disruptions of behavior. High doses of stimulants can cause dysphoria and intense anxiety, and chronic use can result in hyperaggressiveness, complete insomnia, serious weight loss, irritability, attention and concentration problems, impulsiveness, and panic. Cocaine intoxication in extreme cases is characterized by paranoid psychosis and violent behavior; it may also cause cardiac arrhythmias or cerebral hemorrhages that may lead to death.

COCAINE AND REINFORCEMENT

Cocaine is a potent, reinforcing drug. In fact, of all the drugs that are self-administered by animals and humans, it may well be the most reinforcing. The cocaine addict will engage in behavior that entails extraordinary risks to health and social stability. The extreme desire to obtain the drug has been shown in animal studies of cocaine use. Rats and monkeys rapidly acquire self-administration behavior when given access to intravenous cocaine via a lever-press. In fact, the pattern of drug-taking strongly resembles the bingeing behavior in human cocaine addicts. In a classic study by Aigner and Balster (1978), monkeys who had previously self-injected cocaine were given a choice between food and cocaine every fifteen minutes for eight days. The animals almost exclusively chose cocaine, resulting in weight loss and other signs of toxicity.

DSM-IV Criteria for Cocaine Intoxication

A. Recent use of cocaine.
B. Clinically significant maladaptive behavioral or psychological changes (e.g., euphoria or affective blunting; changes in sociability; hypervigilance; interpersonal sensitivity; anxiety, tension, or anger; stereotyped behaviors; impaired judgment; or impaired social or occupational functioning) that developed during, or shortly after, use of cocaine.
C. Two (or more) of the following, developing during, or shortly after, cocaine use: (1) tachycardia or bradycardia; (2) pupillary dilation; (3) elevated or lowered blood pressure; (4) perspiration or chills; (5) nausea or vomiting; (6) evidence of weight loss; (7) psychomotor agitation or retardation; (8) muscular weakness, respiratory depression, chest pain, or cardiac arrhythmias; (9) confusion, seizures, dyskinesias, dystonias, or coma.
D. The symptoms are not due to a general medical condition and are not better accounted for by another mental disorder.
SOURCE: APA, DSM-IV, 1994.

Since the cocaine epidemic reached its peak in the 1980s, researchers have confronted a fundamental question: What is it about cocaine's effects on the brain that makes it so rewarding and so addictive? Research suggests that cocaine and amphetamine are powerful activators of the brain's central reinforcement system. It seems that all drugs of abuse that are self-administered by humans and animals share an ability to activate dopaminergic synapses. However, most of these drugs, such as alcohol, nicotine, and opiates, have many other significant pharmacological effects. With psychostimulants, activation of the dopamine system is the *primary* pharmacological effect.

Cocaine Dependence

With the spread of "crack" (solid, free-base cocaine) in the 1980s, cocaine dependence was recognized as a substance abuse disorder, as compulsive use, loss of control, and a withdrawal syndrome were seen in addicts. Crack was much cheaper than powdered cocaine and became widely available, particularly to the poor. The smoking of the drug leads to a rapid, short-lasting but profound euphoria that is extremely addictive. Although cocaine dependence can occur with intravenous and (less frequently) with intranasal administration, it was the widespread practice of smoking crack that led to the cocaine epidemic.

There are distinct phases of cocaine use and dependence. Early experiences with the drug result in increased pleasure in many daily activities, and include heightened energy and alertness, increased self-esteem and confidence, and magnified positive social interactions. The positive affective state induced by cocaine, combined with the relative lack of negative consequences, makes such early cocaine experiences extremely seductive. With repeated use, the dose of cocaine is often increased and the drug experience is intensified. Eventually, the user focuses on the intense euphoric, physical sensations produced by cocaine intoxication, rather than the enhancement of normal, external activities. Pursuit of this state becomes so dominant that the user begins to ignore signs of mounting personal problems. A number of factors may contribute to the development of compulsive "bingeing" behavior, in which the individual repeatedly administers high doses of cocaine. Increased availability and a switch in the route of administration (from intranasal to smoking) increase likelihood of dependence. The pattern of use at this stage is most often characterized by continuous bingeing followed by several days of abstinence. There is a complete preoccupation with the cocaine high and with obtaining more cocaine, and ". . . nourishment, sleep, survival, money, loved ones, and responsibility all lose significance" (Gawin and Ellinwood, 1989).

A "triphasic" abstinence pattern generally follows a cocaine binge (Gawin and Ellinwood, 1988). The first phase is termed the "crash," which lasts from hours to days. The crash is characterized by a sharp decrease in mood and energy, as well as by agitation, anxiety, depression, and craving for cocaine. There is an extreme need for sleep, which is usually met by the ingestion of sedatives, alcohol, or opiates. The next phase, "withdrawal," can last for many weeks and is characterized primarily by an intense dysphoric syndrome. Depression and anhedonia (inability to experience pleasure) contrast with memories of stimulant-induced euphoria and often lead to a repetition of the bingeing cycle. If the user continues to be abstinent, the third phase emerges, "extinction." During this phase, normal mood and energy are restored. However, the user may experience occasional cravings for cocaine for months or even years after the last binge. The cravings are usually invoked by stimuli or memories associated with the cocaine experience.

DSM-IV Criteria for Cocaine Withdrawal

A. Cessation of (or reduction in) cocaine use that has been heavy and prolonged.

B. Dysphoric mood and two (or more) of the following physiological changes, developing within a few hours to several days after Criterion A: (1) fatigue; (2) vivid, unpleasant dreams; (3) insomnia or hypersomnia; (4) increased appetite; (5) psychomotor retardation or agitation.

C. The symptoms in Criterion B cause clinically significant distress or impairment in social, occupational, or other important areas of functioning.

D. The symptoms are not due to a general medical condition and are not better accounted for by another mental disorder.

SOURCE: APA, DSM-IV, 1994.

Treating Cocaine Dependence

The obstacles to successful treatment of cocaine dependence are similar to those for other drug addictions. Although motivation to quit cocaine may be very high initially, relapse is a major problem, particularly in the period when depression and anhedonia are present. A number of different strategies have been tried in treatment programs, with varying outcomes. These strategies include a range of psychotherapeutic techniques as well as pharmacotherapies. Pharmacological strategies, especially the antidepressant drug desmethyimpramine, are sometimes useful in achieving initial cocaine abstinence, but counseling and intensive psychotherapy are important for long-term success. One promising clinical study reported marked success with a behavioral therapy treatment approach over a twenty-four week period (Higgins, Budney, Bickel, Hughes, Foerg, and Badger, 1993). Cocaine-dependent patients in an outpatient treatment program were divided into two groups. One group received behavioral therapy based on the contengency-management approach. Several times a week, patients' urine was screened for cocaine metabolites. If the urine was negative, the subject received points that were recorded as vouchers for future purchase of retail items in the community. The number of points increased with each consecutive negative urine specimen, or decreased if a positive specimen was noted. Individuals who remained abstinent for a twelve-week period could obtain nearly $1,000 worth of retail goods. This system was supplemented with the community reinforcement approach, in which a spouse, friend, or family member participates in counseling. The control group received standard drug abuse counseling based on the disease model of dependence. There was a marked difference in cocaine abstinence in these two groups (see Figure 12–4). The percentages of subjects in the behavioral and standard counseling groups who achieved at least eight and sixteen weeks of continuous abstinence, respectively, were 68 percent versus 11 percent, and 42 percent versus 5 percent. These results suggest that availability

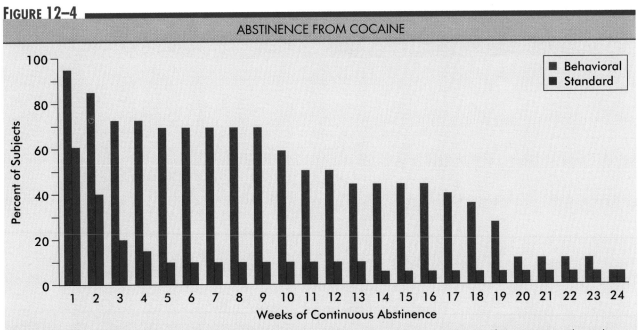

FIGURE 12–4

ABSTINENCE FROM COCAINE

The bars represent the percentage of cocaine-dependent outpatients who achieve abstinence from cocaine. The red bars are for patients given behavioral therapy based on the contingency-management approach. The blue bars are for patients given standard drug abuse counseling. (SOURCE: Higgins, Budney, Bickel, Hughes, Foerg, and Badger, 1993)

▲ Crack cocaine's low price and easy availability have contributed to a wide range of social problems, including affecting the fetuses of pregnant women who continue to smoke crack while pregnant. This woman gave birth to twins, who were taken into a state agency's custody because the addicted mother was unable to care for them.

and emphasis of alternative rewards can increase the motivation of the user to abstain from cocaine.

Another treatment approach is based on the learning model of addiction. As discussed earlier, exposure to drug-related cues in the environment can trigger cravings and induce relapse even in long-abstinent individuals. These powerful drug-associated stimuli can elicit clear changes in physiological responses, such as in heart rate or skin conductance. When recovering addicts were exposed to cocaine-associated stimuli, an involuntary physiological response (lowered skin temperature) was induced. The aim of the treatment based on the learning model is to eliminate these conditioned responses through repeated exposure to drug-related stimuli in a safe, controlled setting. By repeatedly exposing the patient to cocaine "reminders" without cocaine, it should be possible to extinguish the conditioned responses (arousal, craving) that could lead to relapse (O'Brien, Childress, McLellan, and Ehrman, 1992; O'Brien, 1994). These researchers treated patients in the course of fifteen extinction sessions in which the subjects were exposed to audiotapes and videotapes of cocaine-related stimuli (e.g., drug paraphernalia, someone shooting up) and engaged in a simulated cocaine ritual (preparation of drug, handling of syringe). Over the course of the extinction sessions, the craving for cocaine was reduced. Although the physiological responses were also somewhat reduced by the last session, they were surprisingly resistant to extinction. There was also a higher number of patients continuing with outpatient treatment and a higher proportion of clean urines in the extinction group compared with control groups (standard psychotherapy or drug abuse counseling).

In summary, for successful treatment of cocaine addiction, the cycle of dependence must first be broken. During the withdrawal phase, relief of depression may be aided by antidepressants or dopamine agonists. Behavioral therapeutic approaches may increase the motivation of the patient to stay abstinent. Extinction of the conditioned craving and physical responses elicited by drug reminders may be very important for avoidance of relapse.

OPIATES

The *opiate* drugs consist of a class of compounds that are extracted from the poppy plant *(Papaver somniferum)*, including opium, morphine, and codeine, as well as synthetic derivatives such as heroin and meperidine (Demerol). Like many of the psychoactive compounds, opiates have long been used in human society. In fact, use of the extracts of the poppy plant for its psychological and medicinal properties may date back over 5,000 years. These substances have been known for their ability to relieve pain and suffering, and they have played an important role in many ancient cultures. References to opium use are found in the writings of early Egyptian, Greek, Roman, Arabic, and Chinese cultures. In the nineteenth century, opium became an important part of the pharmacopeia in England and America.

While the pain-relieving effects of opiates were much appreciated, the dangers and addictive properties also became clear as their use spread throughout society. In the early part of this century in the United States, opiate drugs became illegal except through prescription. Heroin, the most commonly used illicit opiate, is not available even by prescription in this country (it is in Britain in certain circumstances).

Today, heroin addiction remains a major drug problem, although heroin use is far more rare than marijuana or cocaine use. The number of addicts who use heroin regularly in the United States is estimated at approximately

500,000. This number has remained stable in recent years. In the 1980s, drug users sometimes combined intravenous heroin and cocaine (the so-called "speedball"). Moreover, a recent phenomenon has been documented that suggests that highly pure, smokable heroin is making its way through certain middle- and upper-class circles associated with the film, rock, and fashion industries (Gabriel, 1994). It has been suggested that this is now the "chic" drug among such people, much as cocaine was the cocktail of choice for the affluent in the early 1980s.

Effects of Opiates

FOCUS QUESTIONS

1. Describe the behavioral and physical effects of the opiates.
2. What are the stages that characterize heroin withdrawal?
3. Give an example of how environment can affect drug use.
4. What is maintenance therapy and how effective is it in treating heroin addicts?

The primary active ingredient of opium is morphine, named after the Greek god Morpheus, the god of dreams. Morphine is widely used for pain relief in medicine. Heroin is a semisynthetic opiate made by altering the morphine molecule. It was first made and promoted by Bayer Laboratories (the same company that makes Bayer aspirin) in 1898. It originally was marketed as a nonaddictive substitute for codeine. However, as use spread, it soon became apparent that heroin was the most addictive of all the opiates. The minor chemical modification makes heroin much more potent than morphine, because it reaches the brain more quickly and in higher concentrations. Among the opiate addict population, heroin is the drug of choice. It is usually injected into the veins (intravenously), although it is also injected beneath the skin, which is known as "skin-popping." When injected intravenously, heroin is absorbed very rapidly and reaches the brain in a matter of seconds. Subjective accounts by addicts of the heroin high or "rush" describe a warm flushing of the skin and sensations described in intensity and quality as a "whole-body orgasm" (Jaffe, 1985). This initial effect lasts for less than a minute. Tolerance often develops to this euphoric effect of the drug. Opiates also can induce general feelings of well-being, calmness, and a sleepy dream-like state known as "twilight sleep." Feelings of anxiety, hostility, and aggression are reduced by opiates. Indeed, in addition to the pleasurable feelings they induce, the ability to blunt psychological pain may be an important motivation for taking these drugs.

PHYSIOLOGICAL EFFECTS

A number of physiological symptoms result from opiate administration as a consequence of the drug acting in several brain regions. The main physical effect these drugs have is to reduce pain perception. Opiates commonly cause nausea and vomiting, particularly with initial use. They also cause a marked constriction of the pupils, known as "pinpoint pupil." This sign is commonly seen in heroin addicts. Opiates slow the movement of food through the digestive tract and thus cause constipation. They lower blood pressure and cause sweating. Although the initial subjective effect of heroin is likened to sexual orgasm, chronic use is associated with decreased sexual drive and sexual dysfunction. The most serious direct physiological effect is respiratory depression; respiratory arrest is the most common cause of death from overdose. Indirectly, opiate use puts addicts at great risk for Acquired Immunodeficiency Syndrome (AIDS) because they often share needles when administering the drug. The HIV virus that causes AIDS can contaminate needles, thereby transferring the virus from one user to another.

PHARMACOLOGICAL EFFECTS AND SITES OF ACTION

One of the most interesting aspects of opiate drugs is the fact that the brain contains a system of neurotransmitters and corresponding receptors that are remarkably similar to the opiate drugs. The diverse effects of these drugs on

A. Recent use of opioid.
B. Clinically significant maladaptive behavioral or psychological changes (e.g., initial euphoria followed by apathy, dysphoria, psychomotor agitation or retardation, impaired judgment, or impaired social or occupational functioning) that developed during, or shortly after, opioid use.
C. Pupillary constriction (or pupillary dilation due to anoxia from severe overdose) and one (or more) of the following signs, developing during, or shortly after, opioid use: (1) drowsiness or coma; (2) slurred speech; (3) impairment in attention or memory.
D. The symptoms are not due to a general medical condition and are not better accounted for by another mental disorder.

SOURCE: APA, DSM-IV, 1994.

psychological and physiological functions are likely due to direct stimulation of opiate receptors in areas of the brain that mediate emotion and mood, as well as pain transmission. The subjective, pleasurable effects of opiates may be caused by stimulation of such opiate receptors.

Opiate Dependence

Opiate dependence may develop in susceptible individuals in a number of situations. One pattern of drug use begins with recreational or experimental use, usually with intravenous heroin. First use is often introduced or encouraged by a drug-using friend, and with continued use a compulsive habit may develop. In this case the addict may need three to four injections per day, and obviously must obtain the heroin from illegal sources. Consequently, a great deal of time is spent trying to procure the drug. By far the most common users in this category are young males in poor, urban environments. There are several other patterns of use that are less common. There is a small subgroup of addicts whose dependence began with medically prescribed oral painkillers, and who continue to obtain them somehow. Moreover, the incidence of opiate dependence among physicians, nurses, and other health professionals is higher than in people of similar background in other occupations (Jaffe, 1985; Centrella, 1994). Such individuals have easier access to the drugs and may start using them for a variety of reasons, such as relief of a physical ailment or to alleviate depression.

Opiate dependence may be associated with a high degree of tolerance and physical dependence. With repeated use, the dose taken by the user gradually becomes higher. After continued use of fairly high doses, some users can administer doses up to fifty times what would kill a nontolerant individual (Grilly, 1989). However, tolerance develops to some effects of opiates and not to others. For example, a remarkable degree of tolerance may be exhibited to the respiratory depressant, sedative, analgesic, nauseating, and euphoric effects while little tolerance is seen to the constipating and pupil-decreasing effects.

There are several stages that characterize heroin withdrawal, which consists of clearly observable signs and symptoms that are in general opposite to those that are produced by the drug. It starts approximately eight to twelve hours after the last dose, reaches its peak at about forty-eight to seventy-two hours, and completely subsides in seven to ten days. At first, the addict experiences restless sleep, followed by dilated pupils, irritability, loss of appetite, and tremor. At peak intensity, the individual experiences insomnia, violent yawning, excessive tearing, and sneezing. Muscle weakness and depression

▲ River Phoenix died young as a result of drug use.

may be pronounced. Piloerection, resulting in "goosebumps," gives the skin the appearance of a plucked turkey; hence the expression "cold turkey" given to signify abrupt withdrawal. Gastrointestinal distress, characterized by cramps and diarrhea, is also apparent. Dehydration and weight loss may result from the failure to take food and fluids and from vomiting, sweating, and diarrhea. The syndrome can be immediately reversed at any stage by readministration of an opiate. Gradually, the acute phase subsides, although mild physiological alterations may be present for weeks. A common misperception is that the syndrome is always very severe and aversive; in fact, in most cases it is rarely life-threatening and seldom more disruptive than a bad case of the flu. Nevertheless, avoidance of the dysphoria that accompanies this state is an important motivating factor for continuing opiate use, although it cannot account for initial use nor for relapse long after the syndrome has subsided.

Treating Opiate Addiction

The problem of treatment for opiate addiction has challenged researchers and clinicians for many years. Although some compulsive opiate users eventually stop drug use on their own, most chronic users need some form of treatment or therapy in order to overcome dependence. In the 1960s, a number of therapeutic communities were established, sometimes by former addicts. Programs such as Synanon, Phoenix House, or Odyssey House are meant to provide a community of support while helping the individual to stay free of drugs. The philosophy of many of these communities is complete abstinence from all psychotropic drugs and, like AA, they believe that there is no "cure," just control of an illness. There is little evidence, though, that long-term abstinence is achieved by these programs.

For the past thirty years, the primary treatment for opiate addiction has been pharmacological. Maintenance or substitution therapy has involved substituting an oral synthetic opiate, usually methadone, for the intravenous heroin. There are a number of reasons why methadone is preferable to heroin (see Table 12–1). First, it can be taken orally and thus intravenous injection is avoided. Second, methadone is longer acting than heroin and prevents the onset of withdrawal symptoms for twenty-four to thirty-six hours, with withdrawal from methadone less severe in intensity than withdrawal from heroin. Third, little or no euphoria is produced by methadone or by heroin while the individual is on methadone, as methadone is already occupying the opiate receptors in the brain (Kreek, 1992). Fourth, to obtain methadone, patients must come to the local clinic daily, which provides

TABLE 12-1

	Heroin	Methadone
HEROIN VERSUS METHADONE		
Route of administration	Intravenous	Oral
Onset of action	Immediate	30 minutes
Duration of action	3–6 hours	24–36 hours
Euphoria	First 1–2 hours	None (with appropriate dose)
Withdrawal symptoms	After 3–4 hours	After 24 hours

SOURCE: Kreek, 1992.

social support and structure to the addict's daily life, and helps in limiting or removing drug-related, illegal activities. Since the reinforcing effects of heroin are diminished and the unpleasant withdrawal state is avoided, methadone therapy is successful in getting users off heroin. But on a more pessimistic note, the relapse to illicit opiate use among former methadone patients is 70 to 80 percent (Ball and Ross, 1991). In other words, once methadone is stopped, the chances of long-term abstinence are very low (Zanis, McLellan, Alterman, and Cnaan, 1996). These rather dismal figures once again underscore the extreme difficulty in remaining completely drug-free. Many methadone patients choose to remain on methadone indefinitely, which is certainly medically possible.

HALLUCINOGENS

Hallucinogens consist of a number of different drugs with varying chemical structures and behavioral effects. The feature that distinguishes these drugs from other classes of drugs is their ability markedly to alter sensory perception, awareness, and thoughts. Drugs such as LSD, mescaline, and psilocybin are examples of such compounds. Use of hallucinogens is relatively low according to the National Household Survey. In 1991, 8 percent of the population reported using hallucinogens at some point in their lifetime, while 0.3 percent reported use in the past month.

Effects of Hallucinogens

Most of the hallucinogens are derived from plant substances and are very similar in chemical structure to certain neurotransmitters in the brain (serotonin, norepinephrine, dopamine). Because of their remarkable effects upon the mind, these substances were used in religious ceremonies and folk medicine by the early cultures that discovered them. Mescaline is derived from the cactus plant peyote, and has been used for centuries in the mystical religious practices of the Mexican Indians; the Aztecs regarded the plant as sacred. Psilocybin is found in several species of mushroom, popularly known as the "magic mushroom." Stone sculptures of psychoactive mushrooms found in Central America date well before 500 B.C. (Snyder, 1986). Its Indian name meant "food of the gods," and it was used in secret religious rituals among the Indians.

LSD (D-lysergic acid diethylamide) is a synthetic drug, but it is related chemically to a number of compounds found in the ergot fungus that infects grains, especially rye. In the 1940s, the chemist Albert Hofmann at Sandoz

FOCUS QUESTIONS

1. What are common psychological effects of LSD?
2. What is PCP and what are its effects?
3. Describe the effects of MDMA.

Drug Company in Basel, Switzerland, was experimenting with various derivatives of ergot compounds in hopes of finding new medicines. He synthesized a series of compounds, one of which was LSD.

Reports on LSD eventually found their way into the scientific literature. Although pharmacologists and psychologists were very interested in its effects, research indicated that there was little therapeutic value to the compound. In the early 1960s, the drug became illegal, although soon after, in the late 1960s and early 1970s, its use in the "hippie" subculture reached its peak.

The psychological effects of the hallucinogenic drugs are difficult to describe because they are so subjective, varying with the individual and the person's expectations and experience with the drug. One of the most common reports is that of profound changes in sensory perception, including visual, tactile, or auditory distortions. Images and sounds may be remarkably vivid or bizarre. Aesthetic experiences, such as viewing art or listening to music, can be enhanced. The sense of time is also extremely altered. The neuropharmacologist Solomon Snyder, upon having ingested LSD, noted that "two hours after having taken the drug, I felt as if I had been under the influence for thousands of years. The remainder of my life on the planet Earth seemed to stretch ahead into infinity, and at the same time I felt infinitely old" (Snyder, 1986). Sensations may be transposed from one mode to another, a phenomenon known as synesthesia. Snyder wrote: "I clapped my hands and saw sound waves passing before my eyes." Emotions and the sense of self are often affected, with a feeling of depersonalization or loss of ego boundaries. In many cases, users report that they develop special insights into themselves or the world. In some instances, this feeling is experienced as positive; for others, it can be quite disturbing and result in profound dysphoria.

There are a number of important differences between hallucinogens and other drugs of abuse. Unlike drugs such as cocaine, amphetamine, or heroin, hallucinogens do not cause a rush or strong feeling of pleasure. People seem to desire these drugs uniquely for their complex effects on the mind, rather than for euphoriant or relaxing properties. It is possible that the hallucinogens do not affect the brain reward system the way most other drugs of abuse do. Animals cannot be taught to self-administer these compounds; hallucinogens seem to lack true reinforcing effects in both animals and humans. Use of hallucinogens is not continual or chronic; people generally take these compounds on infrequent occasions. Moreover, people do not develop physical dependence or become addicted to them. Although they are illegal, hallucinogens do not induce cravings or compulsions.

▲ Effects of LSD may include a feeling of depersonalization or loss of ego boundaries, which some users welcome and others find deeply disturbing.

DSM-IV Criteria for Hallucinogen Intoxication

A. Recent use of a hallucinogen.

B. Clinically significant maladaptive behavioral or psychological changes (e.g., marked anxiety or depression, ideas of reference, fear of losing one's mind, paranoid ideation, impaired judgment, or impaired social or occupational functioning) that developed during, or shortly after, hallucinogen use.

C. Perceptual changes occurring in a state of full wakefulness and alertness (e.g., subjective intensification of perceptions, depersonalization, derealization, illusions, hallucinations, synesthesias) that developed during, or shortly after, hallucinogen use.

D. Two (or more) of the following signs, developing during, or shortly after, hallucinogen use: (1) pupillary dilation; (2) tachycardia; (3) sweating; (4) palpitations; (5) blurring of vision; (6) tremors; (7) incoordination.

E. The symptoms are not due to a general medical condition and are not better accounted for by another mental disorder.

SOURCE: APA, DSM-IV, 1994.

DSM-IV Criteria for Hallucinogen Persisting Perception Disorder (Flashbacks)

A. The reexperiencing, following cessation of use of a hallucinogen, of one or more of the perceptual symptoms that were experienced while intoxicated with the hallucinogen (e.g., geometric hallucinations, false perceptions of movement in the peripheral visual fields, flashes of color, intensified colors, trails of images of moving objects, positive afterimages, halos around objects, macropsia, and micropsia).

B. The symptoms in Criterion A cause clinically significant distress or impairment in social, occupational, or other important areas of functioning.

C. The symptoms are not due to a general medical condition (e.g., anatomical lesions and infections of the brain, visual epilepsies) and are not better accounted for by another mental disorder (e.g., delirium, dementia, Schizophrenia) or hypnopompic hallucinations.

SOURCE: APA, DSM-IV, 1994.

Consumption of hallucinogens is not without potential adverse consequences, however. Most common is an acute psychotic reaction or "bad trip," in which the user experiences a severe panic reaction due to the feeling that he or she is going insane. In rare but tragic cases, the perceptual alterations may cause suicide; in the 1960s, stories appeared about young LSD users jumping out of windows because they believed they could fly. Another disturbing side effect is a phenomenon known as "flashbacks," brief episodes of drug effects that occur long after the last exposure. No one knows what causes flashbacks, which happen in approximately 15 percent of users, but they can recur intermittently even for years after LSD exposure.

PCP and MDMA

Several other drugs in this class deserve mention because of their increasing abuse in recent years. **PCP** (phencyclidine, also known as "angel dust") and the related drug ketamine were originally developed in the 1950s as anesthetics. People anesthetized with these drugs were awake but appeared disconnected from their environment. For this reason, they are classified as **dissociative anesthetics.** However, it was soon discovered that they had similar properties to hallucinogens, and their use was discontinued in humans. PCP was synthesized illicitly in the 1970s, when its use as a recreational drug was popular. The drug is smoked, snorted, or injected intravenously. Ingestion

DSM-IV Criteria for Phencyclidine Intoxication

A. Recent use of a phencyclidine (or a related substance).

B. Clinically significant maladaptive behavioral changes (e.g., belligerence, assaultiveness, impulsiveness, unpredictability, psychomotor agitation, impaired judgment, or impaired social or occupational functioning) that developed during, or shortly after, phencyclidine use.

C. Within an hour (less when smoked, "snorted," or used intravenously), two (or more) of the following signs: (1) vertical or horizontal nystagmus; (2) hypertension or tachycardia; (3) numbness or diminished responsiveness to pain; (4) ataxia; (5) dysarthria; (6) muscle rigidity; (7) seizures or coma; (8) hyperacusis.

D. The symptoms are not due to a general medical condition and are not better accounted for by another mental disorder.

SOURCE: APA, DSM-IV, 1994.

results in subjective feelings of intoxication, warmth, a tingling feeling, and a sense of numbness in the extremities. Unlike the visual hallucinations that characterize LSD intoxication, distortions in body image and feelings of extreme depersonalization are typical of the PCP state. With increasing doses, confused, excited intoxication may develop or there may be stupor or coma. In some people a schizophrenia-like psychosis appears, which may persist for weeks or months. Although its use has declined sharply in recent years, there is still cause for concern because its use has been linked to violence and aggressive behavior, suicides, and depression.

MDMA (3,4-methylenedioxymethamphetamine), known as "Ecstasy" in street language, is a drug chemically related to amphetamine. However, it is principally classified as a hallucinogen and not a stimulant because it causes changes in perceptual awareness. Recreational users say that MDMA causes feelings of euphoria, tingling, and a sense of increased sociability. Users claim that even after the acute effects of the drug have subsided, they feel more insightful, empathetic, and aware. Unfortunately, it is also now known that MDMA has neurotoxic effects on the brain, most notably on the central serotonin neurons (Stone, Merchant, Hanson, and Gibb, 1987; Green, Cross, and Goodwin, 1995).

MARIJUANA

In contrast to the hallucinogens, marijuana continues to be a relatively popular illicit drug. As of 1991, about one-third of the target population in the National Household Survey reported that they had used marijuana one or more times in their lifetime; about 10 percent had used it within the last year. These figures translate into nearly 70 million people who have used marijuana at least once. Among teenagers and young adults, use is more prevalent; nearly 25 percent of this age group reported having used it within the past year and 50 percent reported use in their lifetime. However, as is true for other illicit drugs, use is markedly down from the late 1970s, when marijuana use peaked.

Marijuana is a preparation of the leaves from the hemp plant, or *Cannabis sativa*. It is not known where the plant originated, but it is likely that it was somewhere in central Asia. It is now cultivated in many areas of

FOCUS QUESTIONS

1. Differentiate between marijuana and hashish.
2. Describe the behavioral and cognitive effects of marijuana on experienced users.
3. What is the abstinence syndrome that may occur following abrupt cessation of chronic high doses of THC?

the world. Use of cannabis in human societies predates recorded history. It was used in China as an intoxicant as early as 6,000 years ago. In the Western world, the hemp plant was grown for its medicinal properties and fiber (for making rope), without its intoxicating effects being widely recognized. In the nineteenth century, European physicians expounded the usefulness of hemp as an appetite stimulant and anticonvulsant, and in treating a wide variety of ills such as migraine, asthma, and painful menstruation. It is believed that marijuana smoking for recreational purposes was introduced into this country by Mexican laborers in the early twentieth century (McKim, 1986). Use spread slowly and eventually stirred the concerns of people who thought that its use was associated with moral degeneration and violent crime. By the end of the 1930s, marijuana was illegal in most states.

Effects of Marijuana

The psychoactive ingredient in cannabis is delta-9-tetrahydrocannabinol (THC), which is concentrated in the resin of the plant. Marijuana is a preparation of the leaves and buds; hashish is almost pure resin and therefore much more potent. Marijuana and hashish are usually smoked, and as we know, this is a very efficient way of delivering the drug to the brain. Psychoactive effects begin after a few minutes and reach their peak after about thirty minutes. People sometimes take this drug orally, baked in cookies or brownies. Since absorption through the GI tract is much slower, effects are not felt before two to three hours. THC is highly lipid soluble. It is taken up and stored in the fatty tissues of the body. This characteristic results in THC remaining in the body for long periods of time, for as long as one month following one dose of THC.

PSYCHOLOGICAL EFFECTS

Knowledge of the behavioral and cognitive effects of marijuana is based on both reports of users and a considerable amount of laboratory research in both animals and humans. It is difficult to describe precisely the psychological changes caused by marijuana because individuals may have differing reactions depending on dose, experience with the drug, expectations, and so on. In an experienced user, marijuana typically elicits feelings of well-being and mild euphoria, usually referred to as "being high." An initial stimulating effect may be replaced by feelings of tranquility and dreaminess. Rapid mood changes or exaggerated emotions may occur. Often, when marijuana is consumed socially, there is frequent laughter and hilarity. Perceptual and sensory changes may occur, but generally these are mild exaggerations of pleasurable experiences. For example, music or tastes may be enhanced. However, following very high doses of THC, hallucinations and feelings of paranoia may occur.

DSM-IV Criteria for Cannabis Intoxication

A. Recent use of cannabis.
B. Clinically significant maladaptive behavioral or psychological changes (e.g., impaired motor coordination, euphoria, anxiety, sensation of slowed time, impaired judgment, social withdrawal) that developed during, or shortly after, cannabis use.
C. Two (or more) of the following signs, developing within 2 hours of cannabis use: (1) conjunctival (eye) infection; (2) increased appetite; (3) dry mouth; (4) tachycardia.
D. The symptoms are not due to a general medical condition and are not better accounted for by another mental disorder.

SOURCE: APA, DSM-IV, 1994.

▲ About half of teenagers and young adults, as of 1991, reported that they had tried marijuana at least once.

The cognitive deficits induced by smoking marijuana are also variable, but there is general agreement that there are rather striking deficits in short-term memory, in which information is held actively in the brain for short periods. Following cannabis intoxication, users may show what has been called temporal disintegration; that is, they may lose the ability to retain and coordinate information for a purpose (McKim, 1986). It is common, for example, for people to start a sentence and fail to finish it because they forgot what they started to say. It is thought that this may be due to the intrusion of irrelevant associations (Hooker and Jones, 1987). Moreover, as with hallucinogens, there is a distortion in the sense of time, which seems to pass much more slowly.

TOLERANCE AND DEPENDENCE

Tolerance occurs to some of the effects of marijuana, although users often claim that there is a reverse tolerance, or sensitization to the drug. In one laboratory study in which subjects were given oral doses of THC every four hours for several weeks, tolerance developed to the effects on heart rate, to the subjective effects, and to the disruptive effects on cognitive and motor performance (Jones and Benowitz, 1976). It is likely that high, chronic doses of marijuana are needed for tolerance to develop. The impression of sensitization in experienced users may result primarily from learning to inhale and thus to increase more effectively blood concentrations of THC, as well as from learning what to expect from the drug-induced subjective state.

Physical dependence is very unlikely with marijuana. The majority of social users smoke it occasionally, not daily. Even smoking one marijuana cigarette a day for twenty-eight days does not cause withdrawal symptoms (Frank, Lessin, Tyrrel, Hahn, and Szara, 1976). However, it is now recognized that following abrupt cessation of chronic high doses of THC, an abstinence syndrome can occur. This syndrome is characterized by irritability, restlessness, weight loss, insomnia, tremor, and increased body temperature (Jones and Benowitz, 1976). Psychological dependence is more common with marijuana, although even here most experts would agree that compulsive use and craving are considerably less than those associated with other drugs such as cocaine, opiates, and alcohol. Nevertheless, certain individuals may meet the DSM-IV criteria for Cannabis Dependence, in which they use very potent cannabis for months or years and spend considerable time acquiring and using the substance.

PHYSIOLOGICAL AND NEUROCHEMICAL EFFECTS

THC is absorbed by all tissues. It affects nearly all biological systems and has a "fluidizing" effect on biomembranes (similar to the effects of alcohol). Therefore, for many years, it was thought to be "nonspecific" pharmacologically. However, recently a unique receptor that binds cannabinoids was characterized and localized in specific brain structures (Herkenham, Lynn, Little, Johnson, Melvin, de Costa, and Rice, 1990; Romero, Garcia, Fernandez-Ruiz, Cebeira, and Ramos, 1995), so this may be a specific site where THC acts. There is also speculation that THC has anticholinergic activity (disrupting functions of the neurotransmitter acetylcholine), which may underlie the memory deficits induced by the drug and some of the physiological effects such as dry mouth (Miller and Branconnier, 1983). Recent studies suggest that the hippocampus, an area of the brain involved in memory function, contains a large number of cannabinoid receptors. Altered activity in this area may explain the memory deficits induced by the drug (Molina-Holgado, Gonzalez, and Leret, 1995). In addition, researchers speculate that THC acts on certain genes that affect the production of dopamine and other neurotransmitters (Mailleux, Verslype, Preud'homme, and Vanderhaeghen, 1994).

Tobacco has been used by humans for several thousand years. Native peoples in North and South America were the first to grow the tobacco plant and smoked its leaves for its psychoactive effects. New World explorers first observed tobacco smoking in the time of Columbus, and it was introduced into Western cultures and other parts of the world in the sixteenth century. The plant was named *Nicotiana tabacum* after the French ambassador Jean Nicot, who promoted its development and believed that it had medicinal values. In colonial times, tobacco was smoked in pipes, chewed, or ground into a powder and used as snuff. In the mid-nineteenth century, the cigarette was developed, which produced a smoke so mild (compared to cigars or pipes) that it could be inhaled.

In our present society, smoking is a common and legal form of psychoactive drug consumption. Although there are over 3,000 chemical components in cigarette smoke, it is now believed that nicotine is the active and addictive ingredient. Thus, nicotine is one of the most widely consumed psychoactive drugs in the world. A one pack-per-day smoker will administer hundreds of nicotine doses to himself daily (about 200 puffs), which amounts to over 70,000 doses of nicotine per year. Levels of smoking in the population have declined in recent years; the National Household Survey reports that smoking has decreased from about 40 percent of the target population to 27 percent over the past twenty years. Although these are encouraging figures, people continue to smoke despite current widespread knowledge of the adverse health consequences of smoking. In fact, most people who smoke would like to quit. It is paradoxical that in a society that condemns drug use, nicotine consumption is a legal activity and a $30 billion a year industry. However, it is important to realize that a major difference between cigarette smoking and other drugs such as cocaine or alcohol is that chronic use of nicotine, even in high quantities, does not result in impairment of mental functioning. Although nicotine is certainly a "psychoactive" drug, its effects on the brain and behavior are subtle.

▶ Roy Carruthers' *Three Smokers.*

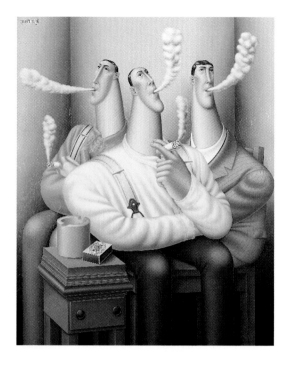

Effects of Nicotine

FOCUS QUESTIONS

1. What are the effects of nicotine?
2. What are three motives for smoking?
3. Describe the withdrawal syndrome that occurs when someone tries to give up smoking.
4. Why is nicotine replacement an effective treatment for those who wish to quit smoking?

Nicotine can be administered in a variety of ways, but smoking is by far the most common route of administration. As smoke is drawn into the lungs via particles of "tar" (condensate), nicotine is absorbed rapidly into the circulatory system. Blood concentrations rise rapidly, and it is estimated that nicotine enters the brain in approximately seven seconds. Ingestion of nicotine via oral routes (chewing tobacco, nicotine gum, oral snuff) results in a much slower rise in blood nicotine concentrations, and levels persist for longer periods. Nicotine has a variety of complex effects on the peripheral and central nervous systems. It can act as both a stimulant and a depressant. In studies of subjective effects of smoking, people say that they smoke for both its arousing and relaxation effects.

Tolerance develops to many of the effects of nicotine. The first smoke one experiences as a teenager often produces nausea, vomiting, pallor, and dizziness. Tolerance rapidly occurs to these aversive effects with continued smoking. A certain degree of tolerance also develops to the arousing and subjective effects of nicotine. Presumably, at least in susceptible individuals, the positive effects of smoking outweigh the unpleasant side effects, such that smoking behavior is repeated. Physical dependence may then develop.

Why do people smoke? Social factors are probably very important in the teenage years, when smoking dependence most often develops. Peer pressure, parental modeling, and experimentation may contribute to initiation of the behavior. When the habit is well established, it is likely that other factors related to the biological effects of nicotine contribute to the maintenance of the behavior. Perhaps most important of these are nicotine's positive reinforcing effects. Like all drugs of abuse, nicotine affects mood, emotion, and cognitive functions. Self-administration tests in animals have shown that rats and monkeys will press a lever to deliver intravenous nicotine (Henningfield and Goldberg, 1983; Corrigall and Coen, 1991). Nicotine presumably has pleasurable properties for people who smoke; laboratory studies in humans have shown this to be the case (Henningfield and Jasinski, 1983). One study in England found that subjects rated smoking as an activity with both "pleasurable-relaxation" and "pleasurable-stimulation" effects (Warburton, 1988). However, it does not appear that nicotine produces the powerful euphoria or "rush" that is experienced with other drugs that are smoked or delivered intravenously, such as heroin or cocaine.

A further important model of smoking behavior is the coping model. This notion is related to the idea that people take drugs to relieve distress, or to help them cope with the stresses or challenges of daily life. Many studies have found that people smoke more when worried, nervous, or anxious, and that they find smoking helps to relieve these feelings. For example, a study of students found that they smoked more and inhaled more strongly during examination periods (Warburton, 1988). Other work has found that autonomic responsivity, such as skin conductance, is blunted by smoking, thus providing evidence that smoking is able to reduce the stress response (Gilbert and Hagen, 1980).

The "functional" model focuses on nicotine's ability to improve performance, and emphasizes that people smoke to control their psychological state and to gain optimal mental functioning. It appears that the mild stimulant properties of nicotine indeed can improve performance. In tests of vigilance, attention, memory, or information processing, smoking or oral nicotine results in improved scores. These effects are present even in nonsmokers given oral nicotine (Warburton and Wesnes, 1978; Wesnes and Warburton, 1984a, 1984b). Thus, people may smoke because of the beneficial effects nicotine provides to performance of the many tasks of everyday life.

▼ The coping model holds that people use smoking to combat the difficulties and anxieties of everyday life.

It is important to remember that there are many motives for smoking. The three models discussed are not mutually exclusive; many people smoke for a combination of factors, principally because of the mild pleasurable effects produced by nicotine, the alleviation of negative psychological states, and the improvement in daily functioning.

Nicotine Dependence

As recently as 1994, executives of tobacco companies claimed that smoking and nicotine were not addictive (Hilts, 1994). A vast amount of scientific evidence suggests otherwise. Two of the leading experts in drug research compared nicotine to five other drugs; both ranked nicotine low as far as the level of intoxication it produces, but highest as far as dependence (see Table 12–2). Of those smokers trying to quit, approximately 70 percent relapse within three months. Figure 12–2 shows that relapse to smoking follows a similar pattern to relapse to other drugs such as heroin and alcohol. The Surgeon General has proclaimed nicotine as addictive as heroin, which might seem shocking given that nicotine is a legal drug. However, it comes as no surprise to people who have tried numerous times to quit. As Mark Twain quipped, "I can quit smoking if I tried; I've done it a thousand times" (cited in Volpicelli, 1989). What is nicotine dependence, and why is it so difficult to give up, often despite high levels of motivation?

TABLE 12–2

NICOTINE COMPARED TO OTHER DRUGS

Withdrawal Presence and severity of characteristic withdrawal symptoms.

Reinforcement A measure of the substance's ability, in human and animal tests, to get users to take it again and again, and in preference to other substances.

Tolerance How much of the substance is needed to satisfy increasing cravings for it, and the level of stable need that is eventually reached.

Dependence How difficult it is for the user to quit, the relapse rate, the percentage of people who eventually become dependent, the rating users give their own need for the substance, and the degree to which the substance will be used in the face of evidence that it causes harm.

Intoxication Though not usually counted as a measure of addiction in itself, the level of intoxication is associated with addiction and increases the personal and social damage a substance may do.

Dr. Jack E. Henningfield of the National Institute on Drug Abuse and Dr. Neal L. Benowitz of the University of California at San Francisco ranked six substances based on five problem areas.

1 = Most serious   6 = Least serious

HENNINGFIELD RATINGS

Substance	Withdrawal	Reinforcement	Tolerance	Dependence	Intoxication
Nicotine	3	4	2	1	5
Heroin	2	2	1	2	2
Cocaine	4	1	4	3	3
Alcohol	1	3	3	4	1
Caffeine	5	6	5	5	6
Marijuana	6	5	6	6	4

BENOWITZ RATINGS

Substance	Withdrawal	Reinforcement	Tolerance	Dependence	Intoxication
Nicotine	3*	4	4	1	6
Heroin	2	2	2	2	2
Cocaine	3*	1	1	3	3
Alcohol	1	3	4	4	1
Caffeine	4	5	3	5	5
Marijuana	5	6	5	6	4

*Equal ratings
SOURCE: Philip J. Hilts, Is Nicotine Addictive? It Depends on Whose Criteria You Use. *New York Times*, August 2, 1994, p. C3.

DSM-IV Criteria for Nicotine Withdrawal
A. Daily use of nicotine for at least several weeks.
B. Abrupt cessation of nicotine use, or reduction in the amount of nicotine used, followed within 24 hours by four (or more) of the following signs: (1) dysphoric or depressed mood; (2) insomnia; (3) irritability, frustration, or anger; (4) anxiety; (5) difficulty concentrating; (6) restlessness; (7) decreased heart rate; (8) increased appetite or weight gain.
C. The symptoms in Criterion B cause clinically significant distress or impairment in social, occupational, or other important areas of functioning.
D. The symptoms are not due to a general medical condition and are not better accounted for by another mental disorder.
SOURCE: APA, DSM-IV, 1994.

If we review some of the major criteria for drug dependence disorder, we find that cigarette smoking meets these criteria in most individuals who smoke: compulsive drug use, overwhelming involvement with the use of the drug, concern with the securing of its supply, and a high tendency to relapse after its withdrawal. Of course, some people smoke very little or only occasionally, but that situation is relatively rare. Smoking cessation often results in a distinct withdrawal syndrome, although it may vary from person to person in its intensity and specific symptoms. The most common signs and symptoms are irritability, anxiety, restlessness, impaired concentration, and a strong craving for tobacco. Headaches, drowsiness, insomnia, and gastrointestinal complaints are also common. Neuropsychological tests in smokers undergoing withdrawal show decreases in vigilance, attention, and psychomotor performance, and increases in hostility. The syndrome gradually subsides within days or weeks, but the craving and desire for a cigarette often far outlast the physical complaints. Increased appetite and weight gain are extremely common problems associated with smoking cessation. (Smokers as a group weigh less than nonsmokers.) Research in animals and humans has shown this to be due to a number of metabolic changes, although the strong desire for a "substitute" oral behavior may also contribute. The fear of gaining weight after stopping smoking may contribute to a lowered motivation to quit, particularly among women.

Treatment

Most smokers who successfully quit do so without assistance from counseling programs, groups, or pharmacotherapies (Fiore, Novotny, Pierce, Giovino, Hatziandrev, Newcomb, Surawicz, and Davis, 1990). About two-thirds of smokers make serious attempts to quit each year, but most relapse within weeks or months. Although behavioral therapy, group counseling, or physician advice may be helpful in some cases, there is little evidence that these strategies work in the absence of nicotine replacement therapy. Nicotine replacement, via nicotine gum or transdermal patch (a patch placed on the skin that slowly releases nicotine, which is then absorbed by the skin into the body), has been shown to be effective in smokers unable to quit by alternative methods. The rationale underlying this approach is similar to that used in treating opiate addiction with methadone. The aim is to eliminate smoking behavior while still making nicotine available for a limited period of time. Nicotine delivered this way does not result in the same blood levels or psychoactive effects of smoking but does reduce the severity of the withdrawal symptoms and craving. The transdermal nicotine patch is a recent development that shows much promise. It is easier to use, causes fewer side effects than nicotine gum, and has been shown to help smokers remain abstinent (Fiore, Smith, Jorenby, and Baker, 1994; Dale, Hurt, Offord, et al., 1995; Stapleton, Russell, Feyerabend, et al., 1995).

SEDATIVE-HYPNOTICS AND TRANQUILIZERS (BARBITURATES, BENZODIAZEPINES)

Barbiturates and benzodiazepines are *sedative-hypnotic drugs* ("downers"); that is, their principal effects are to depress the activity of the central nervous system. In this way, they are similar to alcohol, which is also a sedative-hypnotic, but there are some important differences as well. In contrast to many of the abused drugs that have been used for thousands of years, barbiturates and benzodiazepines are drugs that were developed in this century for therapeutic purposes. The barbiturates were first synthesized in Germany in the early 1900s, and many of them are still prescribed today for anesthesia, sedation, and control of seizure disorders. Examples of barbiturates are pentobarbital (Nembutal), secobarbital (Seconal), amobarbital (Amytal), and phenobarbital (Luminal). These compounds differ slightly in chemical structure and duration of action. Benzodiazepines were introduced in the 1960s as safer alternatives to the barbiturates, particularly in the treatment of anxiety states and insomnia. Well-known benzodiazepines include alprazolam (Xanax), diazepam (Valium), chlordiazepoxide (Librium), triazolam (Halcion), and oxazepam (Tranxene). Valium is one of the most commonly prescribed drugs in the United States. Although both the barbiturates and benzodiazepines have important medical uses, they are also abused drugs.

Effects of Sedatives

FOCUS QUESTIONS

1. What are the psychological and physical effects of the barbiturates?
2. Describe the psychological and physical effects of the benzodiazepines and how they differ from those of the barbiturates.
3. Describe the withdrawal syndrome that can occur when chronic use of barbiturates is stopped.

The psychological and physical effects of barbiturates are very similar to those of alcohol. At low or moderate doses, barbiturates cause mild euphoria, light-headedness, and loss of motor coordination. Higher doses may cause severe intoxication characterized by difficulty in thinking, slurred speech, poor comprehension and memory, emotional lability, and aggressive behavior. Loss of consciousness may occur, and breathing is slowed. With large enough doses, as in accidental or intentional overdose, breathing ceases altogether. Indeed, barbiturates are the favored drug for committing suicide. More than 15,000 deaths per year result from overdose, and the majority of these are suicides. Unintentional deaths may result from combining alcohol with barbiturates or benzodiazepines, since the effects of these drugs are additive.

Psychological and physical effects of benzodiazepines share some characteristics with those of the barbiturates, but in general they have milder effects and much lower toxicity. In therapeutic doses they have anxiolytic (anxiety-relieving) effects, although at these doses there are few discernible effects in non-anxious individuals. At moderate doses, they can cause mild pleasurable feelings and paradoxical stimulant effects, similar to low doses of alcohol. In fact, both benzodiazepines and barbiturates are self-administered by animals, indicating their reinforcing effects. High doses of benzodiazepines cause sedation and sleep, but respiration rate is not nearly as affected as with the barbiturates. Since the margin of safety is very high with these drugs, these are the preferred drugs for treatment of anxiety and insomnia. Death from overdose of benzodiazepines is virtually unheard of, although the combination of these drugs with alcohol is dangerous.

Several potential side effects of the benzodiazepines are of considerable concern. Memory deficits may be associated with benzodiazepine use, and

> ## DSM-IV Criteria for Sedative, Hypnotic, or Anxiolytic Intoxication
>
> **A.** Recent use of a sedative, hypnotic, or anxiolytic.
> **B.** Clinically significant maladaptive behavioral or psychological changes (e.g., inappropriate sexual or aggressive behavior, mood lability, impaired judgment, impaired social or occupational functioning) that developed during, or shortly after, sedative, hypnotic, or anxiolytic use.
> **C.** One (or more) of the following signs, developing during, or shortly after, sedative, hypnotic, or anxiolytic use: (1) slurred speech; (2) incoordination; (3) unsteady gait; (4) nystagmus; (5) impairment in attention or memory; (6) stupor or coma.
> **D.** The symptoms are not due to a general medical condition and are not better accounted for by another mental disorder.
>
> SOURCE: APA, DSM-IV, 1994.

cases of complete amnesia induced by the short-acting benzodiazepines such as triazolam have been reported (Lister, 1985; Vgontzas, Kales, and Bixler, 1995). Increased hostility or aggression can occur in some individuals who take these drugs chronically.

Researchers have made considerable progress in understanding the neural mechanisms underlying the psychoactive effects of barbiturates and benzodiazepines. These studies are particularly interesting because they provide insight into the neural basis of anxiety and anxiety disorders. Although these compounds interact with many neurotransmitter systems, the one most affected is GABA, the principal inhibitory neurotransmitter in the brain. It is thought that the anxiety-relieving effects of these drugs are due to direct effects on the GABA receptor complex.

Sedative Dependence

While abuse and dependence on sedatives have decreased in recent years, they are nevertheless significant problems. In 1991, about 5 percent of the population reported nonmedical use of sedatives or tranquilizers at some point in their lives. People dependent on other drugs, such as opiates or alcohol, sometimes use sedatives as well. Although sedatives can be obtained through illicit sources, often the first contact is through a physician's prescription. In these individuals, the development of the problem may be gradual, beginning with habitual use for insomnia or anxiety, and progressing to increased dosage several times a day (Jaffe, 1985).

Tolerance and dependence develop with both classes of sedatives. Barbiturate dependence and its corresponding withdrawal syndrome have been problems since the drugs were first developed. The symptoms are similar to those of alcohol withdrawal and can be life-threatening in extreme cases. Tremors, anxiety, insomnia, delirium, and seizures can occur following cessation of chronic use of barbiturates. After the benzodiazepines were developed it was thought for many years that chronic use of these compounds, at least in therapeutic doses, was not associated with a withdrawal syndrome. All the benzodiazepines have less addiction potential than the barbiturates, but in recent years it has been recognized that an abstinence syndrome can result from withdrawal. Even at relatively low doses, benzodiazepine withdrawal is associated with increases in anxiety and sleep disturbances, heightened sensitivity to stimuli, and EEG changes (Petursson and Lader, 1981; Lader, 1988; Petursson, 1994). Treatment of barbiturate or benzodiazepine dependence consists primarily of management of the withdrawal syndrome, usually through a gradual reduction of dosage over a period of weeks or months, combined with supportive psychotherapy.

DSM-IV Criteria for Sedative, Hypnotic, or Anxiolytic Withdrawal

A. Cessation of (or reduction in) sedative, hypnotic, or anxiolytic use that has been heavy and prolonged.
B. Two (or more) of the following, developing within several hours to a few days after Criterion A: (1) autonomic hyperactivity (e.g., sweating or pulse rate greater than 100); (2) increased hand tremor; (3) insomnia; (4) nausea or vomiting; (5) transient visual, tactile, or auditory hallucinations or illusions; (6) psychomotor agitation; (7) anxiety; (8) grand mal seizures.
C. The symptoms in Criterion B cause clinically significant distress or impairment in social, occupational, or other important areas of functioning.
D. The symptoms are not due to a general medical condition and are not better accounted for by another mental disorder.
SOURCE: APA, DSM-IV, 1994.

FUTURE DIRECTIONS IN TREATMENT AND PREVENTION OF SUBSTANCE ABUSE

FOCUS QUESTIONS

1. Describe the association between availability and addiction to drugs.
2. How can drug education programs reduce drug use?
3. What kind of research is needed to improve long-term outcome in recovering addicts?

Although there has been a substantial and significant decline in drug use in recent years, drug abuse remains one of the most critical problems facing the United States. Drug abuse is linked to neglect of children, family violence, crime, homelessness, AIDS, enormous health care and economic costs, urban decay, and many other social problems (Kleber, 1994). Herbert Kleber, an expert on drug abuse and treatment, observes that most people are poor judges of their own susceptibility to addiction. In the thirty years he has treated drug addicts, he notes that few anticipated addiction when they started using drugs. Most believed they had the will power to use drugs occasionally or casually. Although many people do use drugs or alcohol in a controlled or socially acceptable manner, many others become entrapped in a destructive cycle of dependence. The disease model of dependence has fostered a sense of social obligation to help dependent individuals, and on a larger scale, to reduce or prevent addiction in our society. But what should be the goals and philosophy of drug abuse prevention? How should government funds be distributed among law enforcement, drug abuse education, and treatment programs and research?

- *Limiting Drug Availability* Limiting drug availability is one approach to combating drug dependence. If there were no drugs, there would be no drug dependence. If there were no alcohol, as is true in some Islamic societies, there would be no alcoholism. Use of legal drugs—alcohol, nicotine, caffeine—is by far greater than use of illicit drugs. In general, as availability of a substance increases, so does the substance use disorder. Nevertheless, despite the clear association between availability and addiction, our society does not seem prepared to do away with drugs altogether. After all, laws could be enacted that make alcohol and cigarettes illegal, but that scenario seems unlikely. Rather, policies that reduce consumption (and therefore addiction) are needed. For example, the federal tax on alcohol and cigarettes could be greatly increased, which would likely cut consumption and the number of deaths related to these substances.
- *Drug Education and Prevention* It is now recognized that one of the most effective deterrents to drug use is education and dissemination of knowledge about drugs, alcohol, and their effects. This is particularly important for children and adolescents. The 1995 National Household Survey on Drug Abuse found increases in drug use among young

people aged twelve to seventeen; this included increased use of marijuana, cocaine, and hallucinogens. Broad-based community programs, in schools, or in youth services, or in religious organizations, as well as media campaigns and parent programs are critical for providing information to combat drug use. Many public schools, even at the elementary level, have drug education programs, and many have the "drug-free zone" symbol posted on the school property. Although such initiatives increase awareness of the drug problem at a very young age, warning about the dangers of drug use is a necessary, but not sufficient, component of prevention (Kleber, 1994; Epstein, Botvin, Diaz, Toth, and Schinke, 1995). Teaching adolescents decision-making skills and techniques for confronting peer pressure to use drugs is also thought to be very important (Ellickson, 1994; Donaldson, Graham, Piccinin, and Hansen, 1995).

- ***Improved Treatment and Research*** There is a critical need for more effective and expanded treatment programs. Both the number of treatment programs and their effectiveness remain woefully inadequate. Currently, approximately 1.7 million addicts are in treatment programs, but 2.5 to 3 million need treatment. Thus, more funding is needed from federal and state governments to expand resources and the number of treatment centers. Treatment methods and research on improving treatment must also be expanded. We need much more research about the determinants of successful treatment and the factors involved in relapse. Basic biological research, for example, may lead to development of better drug therapies for reducing craving in the recovering addict. Further research into behavioral and cognitive treatment methods could result in improved long-term outcome.

SUMMARY

1. Substance abuse is *the* major health problem in the United States. The costs to society are enormous, and yet our society continues to have an ambivalent attitude about psychoactive drugs.

2. The diagnosis of drug dependence is made if the person exhibits: (1) loss of control over the use of the substance, (2) impairment in psychological and social functioning, and (3) physical or emotional adaptation to the drug.

3. The effectiveness of psychoactive drugs depends on several important factors, such as the route of administration, the ability of the drug to enter the brain, how well the drug interacts with the brain's receptors, and how quickly the drug is deactivated.

4. Psychological, social, and biological factors contribute to the development of substance use disorders. A diagnosis of antisocial personality disorder is a risk factor for drug and alcohol addiction. Genetic factors may also influence vulnerability to addiction.

5. The opponent-process theory suggests that drugs may cause *affective pleasure*, which diminishes with *affective tolerance* (lessened response to the drug). *Affective withdrawal*, the opposite of affective pleasure, results when the drug is removed, and avoidance of this negative state may explain continued drug taking.

6. Positive reinforcement models of addiction posit that the powerful rewarding effects of drugs are the primary explanation for their use.

Research using these models shows that animals self-administer many of the drugs abused by humans. There are several brain systems thought to play a critical role in drug reinforcement, including the dopamine and opioid systems.

7. The conditioning and learning models of addiction postulate that a drug state is an unconditioned stimulus that becomes associated with many signals in the user's environment. These signals become powerful conditioned stimuli and may contribute to the reinstatement of drug-seeking behavior.

8. Alcohol dependence is a very common mental disorder. Chronic use of alcohol results in impaired mental functioning and physical damage to organs. Physical dependence develops rapidly with excessive alcohol use. There is convincing evidence that alcoholism is a genetically influenced disorder. Most alcoholics do not recover; however, certain factors such as membership in a supportive group have positive influences on outcome.

9. Amphetamine and cocaine are the most commonly used illegal stimulants, and cocaine dependence is a serious problem in the United States. Cocaine (particularly its more potent form crack), produces profound euphoria and is extremely addictive. Cocaine use is associated with many medical and social problems. Chronic use can cause psychosis and paranoia, and withdrawal from cocaine is accompanied by dysphoria and depression.

10. Opiate drugs produce pharmacological effects by binding to opiate receptors in the brain. Opiate use is associated with a high degree of tolerance and physical dependence. Maintenance therapy with a synthetic opiate, methadone, is the primary treatment for opiate addiction.

11. Hallucinogens distort reality and alter self-perception. LSD is the prototypical hallucinogen. People take hallucinogens for their complex sensory and perceptual effects, rather than for euphoric or relaxing properties. Physical dependence does not develop with hallucinogens.

12. Marijuana is a commonly used illicit drug and causes mild perceptual changes and feelings of well-being.

13. People smoke cigarettes for the mild pleasurable effects produced by nicotine, for stress reduction, and for improvement in cognitive functioning. Nicotine is highly addictive, and the majority of smokers are not able to stop smoking permanently.

14. Barbiturates and benzodiazepines are depressants of the central nervous system. People take them to relieve anxiety and insomnia. Abuse of barbiturates has decreased in recent years, but benzodiazepine abuse and dependence have been increasingly recognized as a problem. The benzodiazepines increase the effectiveness of GABA, the principal inhibitory neurotransmitter in the brain.

15. Drug education, prevention programs, widespread media campaigns, expanded treatment programs, and more research can all contribute to reducing drug abuse in our society. Limiting drug availability can also lower rates of drug use and dependence.

QUESTIONS FOR CRITICAL THINKING

1. Explain why the social and cultural context of drug use affects whether drug users are considered "addicts" and how they are treated.

2. Does disruption of early life development and/or genetic predisposition to alcoholism inevitably lead to alcoholism? Why or why not?

3. What has led to the crack epidemic and how does crack use affect the user, the family, and society?

4. Do you think that more government funds should be used for law enforcement, for education, for treatment, or for research on drug use and abuse?

CHAPTER 13

Sexual Dysfunction and Sexual Disorder

Isabel Bishop, *The Encounter,* 1940.

otions of what is sexually normal and what is sexually abnormal change with time and place. What one society labels as deviant may well be labeled as normal by another. Although premarital sex, masturbation, oral sex, and homosexuality were all condemned by our puritanical society in the past, today most people consider these behaviors to be quite normal.

In the past, what constituted "normal sexual order" and "normal sexual function" was clearer than it is today. Ordinary sexual practices among men and women in our society seem to be more diverse today than they were in the past. And so, our concept of what sexual order is has broadened and our concept of what sexual disorder and dysfunction are has narrowed.

In this chapter, we will discuss the scientific study of sexual problems and their treatment. Despite changing attitudes and more permissiveness in our society, we still find many instances of sexual "disorder" and sexual "dysfunction." The sexual "disorders" are problems of *sexual identity, sexual orientation,* and *sexual interest.* The main disorder of sexual identity is transsexualism, in which a man believes he is a woman trapped in the body of a man, or a woman believes she is a man trapped in the body of a woman. Egodystonic homosexuality, in which the person's homosexual orientation is unwanted and distressful, is a disorder of sexual orientation. Disordered sexual interest manifests itself through sexual arousal to the unusual or bizarre, such as fetishes for panties, masochism, and exhibitionism. These are the paraphilias. The sexual "dysfunctions" are *low desire, low arousal,* or *problems with orgasm.* Both the sexual dysfunctions and the sexual disorders grossly impair affectionate, erotic relations between human beings, and as such, we consider them abnormal.*

*There have been long-standing controversies about what to call these sexual behaviors. Some prefer to call them "variations" and "preferences"; others label them "deviations," or even "diseases." We adopt the term "dysfunction" to refer to the sexual inabilities. We adopt the term "disorder" to refer to the paraphilias and transsexualism.

Our erotic life is organized into five layers, each grown around the layer beneath it. Sexual disorders, as well as sexual problems, can occur at each layer. At the core is sexual identity,* our awareness of being male or female. The next layer is sexual orientation, followed by sexual interest, sex role, and sexual performance.

Sexual identity is almost always consistent with our genitals. If we have a penis, we feel ourselves to be male; if we have a vagina, we feel ourselves to be female. Scientists know that sexual identity has a separate existence of its own because of the rare and astonishing dissociation of sexual identity and sexual organs. Some men (we call them men because they have penises and a pair of XY chromosomes) feel that they are women trapped in men's bodies, and some women (who have vaginas and a pair of XX chromosomes) feel that they are men trapped in women's bodies.[†] These individuals with the disorder "transsexualism" provide the key to understanding this deepest layer of normal sexual identity.

The stratum directly over the core sexual identity is our basic **sexual orientation.**[‡] Do you fall in love with men or women or both? Are you heterosexual, homosexual, or bisexual? Our erotic fantasies indicate to us our sexual orientation. If you have had erotic fantasies only about the opposite sex, you are exclusively heterosexual. If you have had erotic fantasies only about members of your own sex, you are exclusively homosexual. If you have often masturbated to both kinds of fantasies, you should consider yourself bisexual. The only problem that can occur at this level is when your orientation causes you distress and confusion and you want to be rid of it. (In DSM-III this was known as "ego-dystonic homosexuality," but this category was eliminated in DSM-III-R and DSM-IV.)

The third layer is **sexual interest:** the types of persons, parts of the body, and situations that are the objects of your sexual fantasies and arousal. What parts of the body and what situations turn you on? What scenes do you masturbate about? What is on your mind at the moment of orgasm? For most men, the female face, breasts, buttocks, and legs are most arousing. For most women, the male chest and shoulders, arms, buttocks, and face are most arousing.

But these are not universal sexual interests by any means. Many people crave nonstandard objects and situations, such as feet, hair, ears, belly buttons; silk or rubbery textures; panties, stockings, or jeans; peeping, flashing, receiving or inflicting pain. When these or other more bizarre sexual turn-ons get in the way of an affectionate, erotic relationship with another consenting human being, a line has been crossed into disorder.

The fourth layer, the one next to the surface, is our **sex role.** This is the public expression of sexual identity, what an individual says or does to indicate that he is a man or she is a woman. Most people who feel that they are male adopt male sex roles, and most females adopt female sex roles. But we

▲ Gustav Klimt's *The Kiss.*

---

*Sexologists universally refer to these layers as gender identity, gender role, and the like (e.g., Money and Ehrhardt, 1972). We find the word "gender" in such usage unpalatable. Pronouns, but little else, can be properly said to have gender.

†There are 23 pairs of chromosomes in both males and females. The twenty-third pair normally determines the individual's sex. In males, the two chromosomes of this pair differ—one is an X chromosome, the other is a Y chromosome. In females, both are X chromosomes.

‡Sexologists lump the homosexual versus heterosexual choice into the same category ("sexual object choice") as the choice of body parts, fetishistic objects, and erotic situations (sadomasochism, pedophilia, flashing, etc.). We break these into two separate categories, sexual orientation and sexual interest, because we think they are different in kind. The homosexual/heterosexual "choice" is deeper, dictated earlier in life, and more inflexible than the sexual preferences for body parts, inanimate objects, and arousing situations.

FOCUS QUESTIONS

1. List the five layers of erotic life.
2. What is sexual identity?
3. What are the three possible kinds of sexual orientation?
4. When are sexual interests considered sexual disorders?
5. What are sex roles?
6. What is the surface layer of erotic life?

know of the separate existence of sex roles because men and women do not always adopt the usual male and female sex roles; some women behave aggressively and like to dominate, and some men are passive and submissive. There are no defined categories of "disorder" at this level.

The surface layer is ***sexual performance***—how adequately you perform when you are with a suitable person in a suitable erotic setting. Do desire, arousal, and orgasm occur? There is a set of problems common to this stage, and these are called the sexual "dysfunctions" or "inabilities."

We have organized erotic life into these five layers for one basic purpose—to order how easily problems at each layer will change in the natural course of life and in therapy. The deeper the layer, the harder it is to change. In this view of human sexuality, transsexuality is a problem at the core level and simply will not change; sexual orientation, the next deepest layer, very strongly resists change; sexual interests, once acquired, are strong, but some change can be wrought; sex role can change quite a bit; correcting sexual performance is not trivial, but because performance problems are at the surface layer, they can be changed.

SEXUAL IDENTITY AND TRANSSEXUALISM: LAYER I

Few things are more basic to what we are than our sense of what sex we are, and it is this sense that has gone awry in transsexualism. The therapy for most sexual disorders is psychologically based, but the therapy for transsexualism does not consist of changing the psychosexual identity. So basic is identity that the therapy of choice is a matter of actually changing the body to conform to the disordered identity.

Characteristics of Transsexuals

A male-to-female ***transsexual*** is a man who feels as if he is a woman trapped in a man's body, wants to be rid of his genitals, wants female sexual characteristics, and wants to live as a woman. A female-to-male transsexual is a woman who feels as if she is a man trapped in a woman's body, wants to acquire male characteristics, and wants to live as a man. Transsexuals feel, from early in life, that they were given the wrong kind of body. This body often disgusts them and the prospect of having to remain in it all their days makes

▶ Sexual identity is the most basic level of erotic life.

them hopeless, depressed, and sometimes suicidal. They will sometimes mutilate their genitals. By their early twenties, many transsexuals will cross-dress, that is, masquerade in the clothes of the opposite sex. In effect, transsexuals often do everything they can to pass for members of the opposite sex. Unlike transvestites, such actions, particularly the cross-dressing, are not sexually exciting to them. Rather, they are the means of leading the life compatible with their sexual identity. Transvestites are decidedly not transsexual and would be horrified at the idea of changing their sex.

Before this century, transsexuals were doomed to live out their lives in a body that repelled them. In the last twenty-five years, medical procedures have been developed—although they have not been perfected—which allow transsexuals to acquire the anatomy they desire. The case of Allen-Allison shows the transsexual's problems with sexual identity:

For the last four years, Allen has been passing as a female, but he is in reality an anatomically normal twenty-three-year-old male. He takes female hormones, and has had his facial and chest hair removed. Six months ago, he had his first operation: plastic surgery to enlarge his breasts. He expects in the next two years to undergo sex reassignment surgery to construct a vagina from his penis and scrotum.

Allen says that "As early as I can recall I never had any boyish interests and always wanted to become a girl and change my name to Allison." He loved to dress in his mother's clothes and always preferred to play with "feminine" things. On one occasion, when he was given a fire engine, he threw a tantrum insisting that he wanted a doll. From about kindergarten on, he demanded acceptance from his parents as a girl and this made for constant conflict. Finally, in the fourth grade, he persuaded his parents to allow him to "be" a girl at home, except that he had to wear boys' clothes to school. For the next few years he led a double life, attending school dressed as a boy and then returning home to dress and live as a girl. By eighth grade, he began to feel very uncomfortable around people. He began to avoid school and spent a great deal of time alone.

At fifteen, both school life and family life had become unbearable, and he ran away to San Francisco, where he experimented with homosexuality. He found he could not tolerate homosexual males and left after only a month. While he was attracted to men as sexual partners, only those normal heterosexual men who had accepted him as a female aroused him sexually. Soon, thereafter, he began the odyssey of physical transformation.

Allen is now becoming Allison. (Adapted from Pauly, 1969)

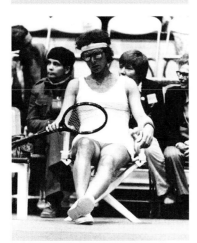

▼ Renee Richards, a tennis player and male-to-female transsexual whose name before sex-reassignment surgery was Dr. Richard Raskin.

Allen-Allison is an adult male transsexual. By age three or four, his identity as a female was well on its way to being fixed. Before puberty, most transsexual boys will play almost exclusively with girls, will act like girls, prefer to play with dolls, sew and embroider, and help their mothers with housework. They refuse to climb trees, play cowboys and Indians, or roughhouse. By puberty, they feel completely like females, and they want to be accepted by society as females. Transsexualism is chronic: once it has developed, it does not spontaneously disappear. When transsexuals come to know sex-reassignment operations exist they desperately want one (Walinder, 1967; Pauly, 1969; Stoller, 1969; Money and Ehrhardt, 1972; Doorn, Poortinga, and Verschoor, 1994; Tiefer and Kring, 1995).

Transsexualism is rare. Perhaps somewhat more than 1 in 100,000 people is transsexual (Walinder, 1967; Pauly, 1974). In the Netherlands, which has quite a supportive climate for transsexuals, a prevalence of 1:11,900 for male-to-female transsexuals and 1:30,400 for female-to-male transsexuals was found (Bakker, Van Kesteren, Gooren, and Bezemer, 1993). The best estimate of the male-to-female ratio is about 2.5 to 1.

DSM-IV Criteria for Gender Identity Disorder (formerly Transsexualism)

A. A strong and persistent cross-gender identification (not merely a desire for any perceived cultural advantages of being the other sex). In children, the disturbance is manifested by four (or more) of the following: (1) repeatedly stated desire to be, or insistence that he or she is, the other sex; (2) in boys, preference for cross-dressing or simulating female attire; in girls, insistence on wearing only stereotypical masculine clothing; (3) strong and persistent preferences for cross-sex roles in make-believe play or persistent fantasies of being the other sex; (4) intense desire to participate in the stereotypical games and pastimes of the other sex; (5) strong preference for playmates of the other sex. In adolescents and adults, the disturbance is manifested by symptoms such as a stated desire to be the other sex, frequent passing as the other sex, desire to live or be treated as the other sex, or the conviction that he or she has the typical feelings and reactions of the other sex.

B. Persistent discomfort with his or her sex or sense of inappropriateness in the gender role of that sex. In children, the disturbance is manifested by any of the following: in boys, assertion that his penis or testes are disgusting or will disappear or assertion that it would be better not to have a penis, or aversion toward rough-and-tumble play and rejection of male stereotypical toys, games, and activities; in girls, rejection of urinating in a sitting position, assertion that she has or will grow a penis, or assertion that she does not want to grow breasts or menstruate, or marked aversion toward normative feminine clothing. In adolescents and adults, the disturbance is manifested by symptoms such as preoccupation with getting rid of primary and secondary sex characteristics (e.g., request for hormones, surgery, or other procedures to physically alter sexual characteristics to simulate the other sex) or belief that he or she was born the wrong sex.

C. The disturbance is not concurrent with a physical intersex condition.

D. The disturbance causes clinically significant distress or impairment in social, occupational, or other important areas of functioning.

SOURCE: APA, DSM-IV, 1994.

The Etiology of Transsexualism

Where does such a deep disorder come from?* What sorts of events must conspire in order for a physically normal girl to feel that she is really a boy, or a boy to feel that he is a girl? We hypothesize that most of sexual identity—both normal and transsexual—comes from an unknown hormonal process in the second to fourth month of pregnancy.

We begin with a simplified version of how a fetus becomes a male or female. The embryo has both potentials. Very early, testes or ovaries appear, but this does not set the sex of the fetus. Both sets of internal organs—male and female—are still present. The fetus goes on to become female unless the next, crucial step occurs: in male fetuses, two masculinizing hormones are secreted from the testes. The female internal organs then shrivel up, the male internal organs grow, and the external male organs develop. In the absence of the masculinizing hormones at this stage, the male internal organs shrivel up, and female internal and external organs develop. All this happens roughly at the end of the first three months of pregnancy.

PSYCHOLOGICAL EFFECTS OF FETAL HORMONES

Besides the physical effects, the masculinizing hormones also have a psychological effect on the brain. They produce male sexual identity, or in their ab-

*This theory and much else in this chapter are derived from M. Seligman, *What you can change and what you can't*, Chapter 11 (New York: Knopf, 1993).

FIGURE 13–1

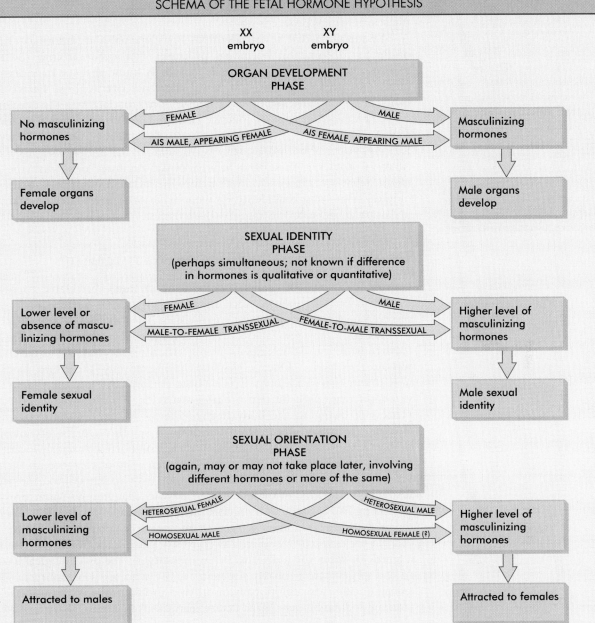

SCHEMA OF THE FETAL HORMONE HYPOTHESIS

XX embryo   XY embryo

ORGAN DEVELOPMENT PHASE

FEMALE — No masculinizing hormones
MALE — Masculinizing hormones
AIS MALE, APPEARING FEMALE
AIS FEMALE, APPEARING MALE

Female organs develop   Male organs develop

SEXUAL IDENTITY PHASE
(perhaps simultaneous; not known if difference in hormones is qualitative or quantitative)

FEMALE — Lower level or absence of masculinizing hormones
MALE — Higher level of masculinizing hormones
MALE-TO-FEMALE TRANSSEXUAL
FEMALE-TO-MALE TRANSSEXUAL

Female sexual identity   Male sexual identity

SEXUAL ORIENTATION PHASE
(again, may or may not take place later, involving different hormones or more of the same)

HETEROSEXUAL FEMALE — Lower level of masculinizing hormones
HETEROSEXUAL MALE — Higher level of masculinizing hormones
HOMOSEXUAL MALE
HOMOSEXUAL FEMALE (?)

Attracted to males   Attracted to females

This diagram represents a schema of how disruption of a hormonal process in the second to fourth month of pregnancy may affect organ development, sexual identity, and sexual orientation. According to this hypothesis, masculinizing hormones lead to male sexual organs, male sexual identity, and attraction to females; a lower level or even absence of the masculinizing hormones leads to female sexual organs, female sexual identity, and attraction to males. Disruptions can occur during each phase, although the different hormones involved and the timing of the process are presumably much more complex than can be shown here, and their relationship with environmental factors of childhood and adolescence cannot be predicted. The theory is not meant to suggest that homosexuality is determined solely by events taking place before birth, only that fetal hormones contribute to it.

sence, female sexual identity. In this view, the brain components of sexual identity are present in the fetus. In transsexuals, however, some as yet unknown disruption of only the sexual identity phase, but not the organ development phase, takes place (see Figure 13–1). Thus, for the male-to-female transsexual, the identity phase of masculinization does not occur, but the

FOCUS QUESTIONS

1. Describe how a transsexual's sexual identity fails to correspond to his or her body.
2. Explain how a fetus becomes male or female, and what might go wrong in the womb to lead to transsexualism.
3. Describe the therapy for treating transsexuals.
4. What does follow-up of patients who have undergone sex-reassignment surgery reveal?

masculinization of the sexual organs proceeds normally. For the female-to-male transsexual, masculinization of identity occurs, but the feminization of the sexual organs proceeds normally.

We speculate that sexual identity—both normal and abnormal—has its origin in fundamental hormonal processes that occur around the third month of fetal development. One recent study found that the hypothalamus of six male-to-female transsexuals was the same size as those found in females, supporting the hypothesis that hormones interact with the developing brain to determine gender identity (Zhou, Hofman, Gooren, and Swaab, 1995). But fetal hormones are not the only influence on sexual identity. Rearing, pubertal hormones, sex organs, and stigmatization also play a role. At most, however, these later influences can reinforce or disturb the core identity that starts to develop well before the moment of birth. The early, biological origin of sexual identity is what makes it so hard to shake, and what makes psychotherapy for transsexualism useless.

Therapy for Transsexualism: Sex Reassignment

Conventional psychotherapies have only very rarely been able to reverse transsexualism (see Barlow, Abel, and Blanchard, 1979, for the single report of reversal of transsexualism—by exorcism). Nevertheless, there is hope for transsexuals today (see Table 13–1). Sex-change operations (now called "sex reassignment") give transsexuals the opportunity to acquire the sexual characteristics they desire. Once a headline-making novelty, these operations are now routine; tens of thousands have been performed. Once the patient convinces the diagnosticians that the transsexual identity is unshakable, the long process of changing the body begins. Therapy for transsexuals consists of changing the physical characteristics of one's sex through surgery and hormones. This biological transformation is then supported by social, vocational, domestic, and secondary bodily changes in an attempt to shore up the new sex status. For example, in the more common male-to-female case, the person first lives for a period of time in the female role, changing his name, dressing, and acting like a woman. Often, therapists treating a transsexual who is a candidate for sex-reassignment surgery require that the person first live for two years in the new sex role. If after two years of passing for and being treated as a female or male, the individual still wants surgery, the psychological hazards of the surgery are probably lessened. Those who are schizophrenic, delusional, or otherwise emotionally disordered should probably not undertake it (Money and Ambinder, 1978; Petersen and Dickey, 1995).

TABLE 13–1

TREATMENT OF TRANSSEXUALISM		
	Psychosocial Treatments	*Sex-Reassignment Surgery*
Improvement	none	60–80% markedly improved
Relapse*	high relapse	low to moderate relapse
Side Effects	none	severe
Cost	inexpensive	expensive
Time Scale	weeks/months	years
Overall	**useless**	**good**

*Relapse after discontinuation of treatment.
SOURCE: Based on M.E.P. Seligman, *What you can change and what you can't* (New York: Knopf, 1993), Chapter 11.

Bodily changes are a prerequisite for sex-reassignment surgery. In male-to-female sex changes, there is a combination of hormonal treatment to make the breasts grow, electrolysis to remove facial hair, and surgery to transform the penis into a vagina. Because the skin of the penis is used to line the vagina, sexual intercourse—when the surgery is successful—is erotically pleasurable. Orgasm is a warm, sometimes spasmodic, glow through the body.

In female-to-male sex-reassignment operations, the surgery is much more complicated and extensive. It involves multiple operations that take place over several years. First, hormonal treatment suppresses menstruation, deepens the voice, and causes growth of facial and body hair. Then surgery is performed to remove the breasts, the ovaries, and, rarely, to construct a penis. The capacity of orgasm is always retained, but such a penis cannot become erect, and a prosthetic device has to be used for sexual intercourse.

Follow-up of patients who have undergone sex-reassignment surgery reveals mixed results. What is clear is that when the two-year trial period in the role of the desired sex precedes the operations, patients tend to have better results. But in a follow-up of fourteen patients operated on at UCLA, almost all of the patients had had surgical complications (Stoller, 1976). In a six- to twenty-five-year follow-up of thirteen male-to-female transsexuals, only one-third remained sexually active after surgery and only one-third had fair to good sexual "adjustment." Only half could reach orgasm. Four regretted having had the surgery (Lindemalm, Korlin, and Uddenberg, 1986). As radical as sex-reassignment surgery is, however, long-term follow-up of hundreds of patients suggests that, while far from ideal, it is the best hope for transsexuals. Although the transsexual must cope with new problems of adjustment, the operation has become more satisfactory as surgical techniques have improved. Most patients are much happier and adapt fairly well to their new lives, living comfortably in their new bodies, dating, having intercourse, and marrying.

SEXUAL ORIENTATION: LAYER II

Sexologists, overly fond of jargon, use the word "object choice" to denote how we come to love what we love. Gay activist groups, on the other hand, say we have no choice at all. The truth is most probably in between, although much closer to the gay activists than to the sexologists. We therefore label this layer sexual "orientation," rather than sexual "object choice." The basic sexual orientation is homosexual or heterosexual. We will focus on male homosexuality as an example of human sexual orientation as a whole. We want to emphasize that we do not view homosexuality as a disorder. Rather we discuss it now because its origins shed light on the deep roots of all human sexual orientation.

Origins of Male Homosexuality

When does a male become heterosexual or homosexual? How does it happen? Once sexually active, can he change if he wants to? We must distinguish between "exclusive" homosexuals on the one hand and bisexuals on the other. Most men who have sex with other men are bisexuals. A minority of men who are homosexual are exclusively homosexual; as far back as they can remember, they have been erotically interested only in males. They have sexual fantasies only about males. They fall in love only with males. When they masturbate or

FOCUS QUESTIONS

1. What defines a person as an exclusive male homosexual?
2. Describe the hypothesis that says that hormonal events in the womb may create a strong predisposition to homosexuality or heterosexuality.
3. What differences in brain structure have been found in homosexual men, heterosexual men, and women?
4. What is the concordance for homosexuality in identical twins, fraternal twins, and nontwin brothers, and what do these rates seem to indicate about a genetic contribution to homosexuality?

have wet dreams, the objects are always males. The orientation of the exclusive male homosexual—and of the exclusive heterosexual—is firmly made.

FETAL DISRUPTION

A major theory of the origin of homosexuality holds that the tendency is laid down before birth by a combination of genetic, hormonal, and neurological processes, and that this orientation is activated by hormonal changes at the onset of puberty (Ellis and Ames, 1987). Learning only alters how, when, and where homosexuality will be expressed. According to the Ellis-Ames fetal disruption theory, the crucial neurochemical events that control masculinization occur during the second to fourth months of pregnancy. This sequence of events is delicate and exquisitely timed and if it is disrupted, incomplete masculinization of the fetus will occur. The fetus is masculinized enough, however, to have a male identity and to have male external organs. The main effect is to change in utero just one aspect of his erotic life: sexual attraction to men rather than to women (see Figure 13–1).

This view does not assert that sexual orientation is *determined* in the womb. Rearing, role models, pubertal hormones, genes, the content of late childhood fantasies and dreams, and early sexual experiences all probably also play a role in whether one becomes homosexual or heterosexual. The view does assert, however, that hormonal events in the womb can create a strong predisposition to homosexuality or heterosexuality.

TIMING OF MATURATION

In late childhood and early adolescence, the content of masturbatory fantasies and nocturnal emission both probably play a role in the acquisition of a homosexual orientation. One theory proposes that the timing of the maturation of sex drive is critical. It hypothesizes that if most of your social group are of the same sex as you when you come into puberty, you will tend to become homosexual; if most are of the opposite sex when you come into puberty, you will tend toward heterosexuality. This theory predicts that early maturing males and individuals with same-sex siblings will have a higher rate of homosexuality, and this may be so (Storms, 1981).

ANATOMICAL BASIS FOR SEXUAL ORIENTATION

Human sexual orientation may even have a basis in the anatomy of the brain (Swaab and Hofman, 1995; Swaab, Gooren, and Hofman, 1995). Brain researcher Simon LeVay (1991) examined the brains of dead homosexual men, heterosexual men, and heterosexual women. Most were AIDS victims. He focused his autopsy on one small area, the medial anterior hypothalamus. This area is implicated in male sexual behavior, and men usually have more tissue here than women. He found a remarkably large difference in the amount of tissue: heterosexual men have twice as much as homosexual men, who have about the same amount of tissue as women. Moreover, the anterior hypothalamus is just the area that controls male sexual behavior in rats. Also, this area develops when the brains of male rats are hormonally masculinized before birth.

Too little research has been done on lesbians to know if the same theories might apply to female homosexuals. It is unknown if a slight masculinization of a chromosomally female fetus (XX) produces lesbians. It is possible, but still uncertain, that lesbianism is the mirror image of male homosexuality. Lesbians, unlike exclusive male homosexuals, however, commonly report choosing homosexuality after adolescence.

TWIN DATA

It is relevant that identical twins are more concordant for homosexuality than fraternal twins and that fraternal twins are more concordant than nontwin brothers. In one study of fifty-six pairs of identical twins in which one twin was known to be homosexual, in 52 percent of the identical twins the co-twin was also found to be homosexual, as opposed to 22 percent of fraternal twins. Only 9 percent of nontwin brothers were concordant for homosexuality. The difference between the identical twins and the fraternal twins suggests a genetic component to homosexuality. But nontwin brothers and male fraternal twins share on average the same percentage (50 percent) of genes. The fact that fraternal twins, who share the same uterine world, are more concordant than nontwin brothers points to fetal hormones as an additional cause. It has also been suggested that they might be concordant for a small medial anterior hypothalamus (Ellis and Ames, 1987; Haynes, 1995; Turner, 1995).

There is evidence for a sizable genetic contribution to female homosexuality; out of a sample of over 100 twins, one of whom was lesbian, the co-twin was homosexual in 51 percent of the identical twins, but only in 10 percent of the fraternal twins (Bailey, Pillard, and Agyei, 1993; Pillard and Bailey, 1995).

Thus there is evidence for four different sources of homosexual versus heterosexual orientation: (1) *genetic*—identical twins are more concordant than fraternal twins for homosexuality; (2) *anatomical*—the medial anterior hypothalamus is smaller in homosexual men than in heterosexual men; (3) *fetal*—homosexuality may involve incomplete hormonal masculinization of the fetus during the first three months of pregnancy; (4) *experience*—whether one's first sexual encounters are homosexual or heterosexual as one enters puberty may contribute, as well as the content of masturbatory fantasy and nocturnal emission early in puberty, which may reflect and consolidate sexual orientation.

Disordered Sexual Orientation: Ego-Dystonic Homosexuality

Up until the 1980s, the topic of homosexuality was listed in textbooks as a paraphilia or a "sexual deviation." Sexual "disorders" used to be defined as conditions that grossly impaired affectionate sexual relations between a man and a woman, and so homosexuality was, by definition, a disorder. Now there is good reason not to classify homosexuality as a disorder. DSM-IV, in fact, does not consider homosexuality a disorder. Sexual disorders are now

▶ Homosexuality is no longer classified as abnormal, as it does not impair affectionate relations between consenting people.

viewed as conditions that grossly impair affectionate sexual relations between two *human beings*. Homosexuality, while it may impair such relations between men and women, does not, of course, impair them between a man and a man, or a woman and a woman, and hence is not considered a disorder.

Most homosexuals are satisfied with their sexual orientation, do not show signs of psychopathology, and function quite effectively at love, at work, and at play. Yet, there is a small group, which we call ego-dystonic homosexuals, who are dissatisfied and distressed by their sexual orientation. They are depressed, anxious, ashamed, guilty, and lonely. They are also manifestly impaired in their capacity to love. On the one hand, they feel ashamed of their attraction to members of their own sex, but on the other, they are not sexually aroused by members of the opposite sex.

SOURCES OF EGO-DYSTONICITY

Part of the dissatisfaction of ego-dystonic homosexuals stems from their desire to have children and a conventional family life. Another source of dissatisfaction comes from the pressures that our society puts on individuals to conform to its sexual norms. A major source of the distress felt by ego-dystonic homosexuals stems from rejection and disapproval by their families, their friends, and their co-workers. Moreover, they also feel distress because of their images of "normality."

Some writers believe that the suffering that society's oppression inflicts on homosexuals raises serious ethical questions about whether a therapist should ever consent to treat homosexuality. When an ego-dystonic homosexual comes into therapy with a request that the therapist help him to change his sexual orientation, these writers believe that the therapist should refuse. They believe that because the self-loathing and the desire to become heterosexual are products of the oppression of homosexuals by society, the desire of the ego-dystonic homosexual to change his orientation has been coerced and is not "voluntary," and so should be disregarded (Davison, 1976, 1978). Others disagree. They believe that individual suffering is often the product of societal disapproval and rejection. Exactly how the suffering comes about is theoretical and speculative, but what is not speculative is that another human being comes into the therapist's office and voices a desire to change. The expressed desire to change is, for some, the bottom line of therapeutic decision. The therapist is first and foremost an agent of the patient. When a patient, in obvious distress, asks for help, he or she has called on the therapist's primary duties. The essence of trust between patient and therapist, just as between any two human beings, is that the expression of desires is taken seriously and, if possible, acted upon.

TREATMENT OF EGO-DYSTONIC HOMOSEXUALITY

There are two aspects of ego-dystonic homosexuality that might be treated: the dystonicity and/or the homosexuality. The anxiety, depression, guilt, shame, and loneliness that make up the dystonicity may be amenable to the treatments for anxiety and depression outlined in the anxiety and depression chapters (see Chapters 5 and 8). Cognitive therapy, assumption challenging, and progressive relaxation should each allay the sadness and fears that make up the distress.

Traditional psychotherapy does not seem to hold much promise for changes of sexual orientation, but behavior therapy may. In two controlled studies involving seventy-one male homosexuals, a group of British behavior therapists found that sexual orientation could be changed in nearly 60 percent of the cases by using aversion therapy of the sort described below for the paraphilias (Feldman and MacCulloch, 1971; McConaghy, Armstrong, and Blaszczynski, 1981). They defined "change" as the absence of homosex-

FOCUS QUESTIONS

1. Describe ego-dystonic homosexuality.
2. What are some of the sources of distress for ego-dystonic homosexuals?
3. Describe treatments that may help ego-dystonic homosexuals.

ual behavior, plus only occasional homosexual fantasy, plus strong heterosexual fantasy, and some overt heterosexual behavior one year after treatment.

The fetal disruption theory (Ellis and Ames, 1987) claims that exclusive homosexuality should be almost unchangeable by therapy, since it has its origins before birth. The data are consistent with this view, since individuals who had had some heterosexual experience before therapy showed more change than exclusive homosexuals who had had no prior pleasurable heterosexual history (Mendelsohn and Ross, 1959; Marciano, 1982; Schwartz and Masters, 1984; Haldeman, 1994). When treatment concentrates on additional targets, such as intimacy and social skills, more change occurs (Adams and Sturgis, 1977).

SEXUAL INTEREST: LAYER III

Sometime in the first fifteen years of life, individuals acquire their sexual interests, the objects of their erotic interest, and these objects and situations are likely to be sexually arousing to them for the rest of their lives. Most men are aroused by the female body; most women are aroused by the male body. There is a very large range of situations that men and women find sexually arousing: seductive conversation, holding a member of the opposite sex in their arms, or seeing the person naked. But other more unusual objects or situations may also be sources of sexual arousal, and it is to these that we now turn.

Types of Paraphilias

When sexual interest is so disordered that it impairs the capacity for affectionate erotic relations between human beings, it is called a ***paraphilia*** (from the Greek "love of [philia] what is beyond [para]"). The paraphilias comprise an array of unusual objects and situations that are sexually arousing to some individuals. Among the more common paraphilias are female underwear, shoes, inflicting or receiving pain, and "peeping."

The paraphilias divide into three categories: (1) sexual arousal and preference for nonhuman *objects,* including fetishes and transvestism; (2) sexual arousal and preference for *situations* that involve suffering and humiliation, including sadism and masochism; and (3) sexual arousal and preference for *nonconsenting partners,* including exhibitionism, voyeurism, telephone scatologia, and child molesting.

For some paraphilics, fantasies or the object itself is always included in sexual activity. For others, the paraphilia occurs only episodically, for example, during difficult periods of life. Paraphilic fantasies are common in people who do not have a paraphilia. Panties, peeping, and spanking, for example, are sexually exciting fantasies for many men. The hallmarks of crossing the line to paraphilia are when the person acts on it, when the object becomes necessary for arousal, when the person is markedly distressed by his or her actions, or when the object displaces his human partner.*

Often paraphilics are happy with their sex lives, and their only problem is the reaction of others to their sexual interests. Many other paraphilics are guilt-ridden, full of shame, and depressed by their actions, which they regard as disgusting and immoral. Sexual dysfunctions frequently accompany paraphilia, particularly when the object is absent.

FOCUS QUESTIONS

1. What are the paraphilias?
2. Describe the three categories of paraphilias.
3. Define fetishes, transvestism, and sadomasochism.
4. Describe the paraphilias that involve sexual arousal with nonconsenting partners.

To have a *fetish* is to be sexually aroused by a nonliving object (e.g., underwear, shoes, feet, hair, rubber, silk). In many cases, it is harmless. For example, women's panties are sexually arousing to many men. When a man fantasizes and talks erotically about panties during sexual intercourse with a mutually consenting partner, the paraphilia may be playful and lead to heightened arousal. More typically, however, his partner feels excluded; when the underwear a woman wears displaces the woman, and her partner cannot be sexually aroused unless she is wearing it, the object is no longer a means to arousal but the end of arousal. Here is an example of a foot fetish:

> At the age of seven Leo was taught to masturbate by his older half sister. In the course of the lesson she accidentally touched his penis with her slipper. From that time on, the mere sight of a woman's shoe was enough to induce sexual excitement and erection. Now twenty-four, virtually all his masturbation occurred while looking at women's shoes or fantasizing about them. When he was at school he was unable to keep himself from grasping his teacher's shoes and in spite of punishment continued to attack her shoes. He found an acceptable way of adapting his life to his fetish. When he was eighteen, he took a job in a shop which sold ladies' shoes and was excited sexually by fitting shoes onto his customers. He was absolutely unable to have intercourse with his pretty wife unless he was looking at, touching, or thinking about her shoes at the same time. (Krafft-Ebing, 1931, case 114)

As in Leo's case, it is typical that a fetish is acquired during childhood. The object that will become the fetish accompanies early erotic play. The fetish grows in strength when it is repeatedly fantasized about and rehearsed, especially during masturbation. The fetishist often masturbates while holding, rubbing, or smelling the object, or may ask his partner to wear or hold the object during sex. A fetish may reveal itself when adult interpersonal relationships are unsatisfactory. At this point, one's childhood experience may take over and the fetishist may seek comfort in the simpler sexual pleasures of childhood instead of dealing with the complexity of another human being.

Interestingly, virtually all cases of fetishes and the vast majority of all paraphilias occur among men. Such a man is usually full of shame and guilt about his fetish, which isolates him from sexual activity with other people. Erectile dysfunction is the regular consequence of fetishism when the fetish is absent. Depression, anxiety, and loneliness often accompany the fetish. In addition to such individual problems, fetishists are occasionally in trouble with the

▶ A scene from the film *The Balcony*, based on Jean Genet's play, suggests an especially passionate foot fetish.

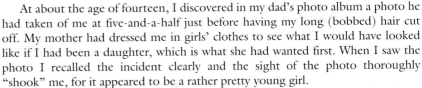

law. They may steal objects of the fetish, lunge for the objects in public, and they may masturbate on the objects. Some will frequently acquire a collection of the objects. One young shoe fetishist was discovered with a collection of 15,000 to 20,000 pictures of shoes.

TRANSVESTISM

Transvestism occurs when a man persistently dresses in women's clothes to achieve sexual arousal. He usually has a collection of women's clothes, and while masturbating he frequently imagines that he is done up as a woman and wearing women's clothes. Transvestism is usually carried on in secret, although a transvestite's wife may share the secret and cooperate by having intercourse with him when he is dressed as a woman. The secrecy of the act makes its prevalence difficult to estimate, but it is probably rare—occurring in fewer than 1 percent of adult men. There have been virtually no reports of transvestism in women.

Transvestism usually begins with cross-dressing in childhood, as here:

▲ A transvestite, Edward Hyde, Lord Cornbury, governed the colonies of New York and New Jersey.

> At about the age of fourteen, I discovered in my dad's photo album a photo he had taken of me at five-and-a-half just before having my long (bobbed) hair cut off. My mother had dressed me in girls' clothes to see what I would have looked like if I had been a daughter, which is what she had wanted first. When I saw the photo I recalled the incident clearly and the sight of the photo thoroughly "shook" me, for it appeared to be a rather pretty young girl.
>
> The emotional result was twofold. It aroused my first interest in girls and also an interest in girls' clothes. I found myself compelled to go back to look at the photo again and again.
>
> One winter my wife and I were living alone. Our marital relations were good. We were spending New Year's Eve entirely alone and for some reason my wife, not knowing of my mere leanings (at the time) toward transvestism (a word I did not know then), decided to put one of her dresses on me and make up my face just as a sort of New Year's Eve prank. When she finished we sat around for a while and she asked me how I liked it. When I answered in the affirmative she became resentful and very anxious for me to take off the clothes she had put on me voluntarily. (Adapted from Stoller, 1969)

When cross-dressing begins, only one or two items of clothing, such as panties, may be used. This item of clothing may become a fetish habitually used in masturbation and in intercourse with a cooperating partner. Such a man may wear these panties under his daily masculine garb. Cross-dressing sometimes progresses from a single item to a total costume. It may be done alone or as part of a whole group of transvestites. When dressed as a woman, the transvestite feels considerable pleasure and relaxation; he is intensely frustrated if circumstances block his cross-dressing. Sometimes sexual arousal by wearing women's clothes disappears, but the transvestite continues to dress up to relieve anxiety and depression.

A transvestite may believe he has two personalities: one male, which dominates his daily life, and the other female, which comes out when he is dressed up. In other respects, the transvestite is unremarkably masculine in appearance and conventional in his behavior.

Transvestism is often mistakenly confused with homosexuality on the one hand and with transsexuality on the other. Transvestites are decidedly not homosexual: almost three-quarters of them are married and have children, and on the average they have had less homosexual experience than the average American man (Benjamin, 1966; McCary, 1978). Further, a transvestite is aroused by his fetish, whereas a homosexual is obviously aroused by another person. While a male homosexual will occasionally dress in female clothes in order to attract another man, a homosexual, unlike a transvestite, is not sexually aroused by the fact that he is in "drag."

Since most transvestites merely want to be left alone in order to pursue their habit secretly, we must ask why it is considered a problem. Depression, anxiety, shame, and guilt often occur in transvestites; and while sexual arousal is intense during cross-dressing, affectionate sexuality is often impaired by transvestism. A transvestite will commonly be impotent unless he is wearing some female clothing, and this is often not possible when his partner objects.

SADOMASOCHISM

The second class of paraphilias involves inflicting or receiving suffering as a means of sexual excitement, and it consists of two distinct disorders that complement each other. In *sadism* the individual becomes sexually aroused by inflicting physical or psychological suffering or humiliation on another human being, while in *masochism* the individual becomes sexually aroused by having suffering or humiliation inflicted on him. These terms are greatly overused in ordinary language. We often hear individuals who cheerfully put up with suffering or hardship called masochists, and individuals who are aggressive and domineering called sadists. Much more than this is required for sadism or masochism. A sadist *repeatedly* and *intentionally* inflicts suffering on his partner, sometimes a nonconsenting partner, in order to produce sexual excitement. And a masochist repeatedly and intentionally participates in activity in which he is physically harmed, his life is threatened, or he is otherwise made to suffer in order to feel sexual excitement. Not uncommonly, the masochist and sadist will seek each other out and marry in order to engage in mutually desirable sadomasochism. Both disorders are accompanied by persistent and insistent fantasies in which torture, beating, binding, and raping are common themes producing high sexual arousal. Consider this case:

Thomas, a masochist, and his wife enact a periodic sadomasochistic ritual, in which about once every six weeks Thomas has himself beaten by his wife. She punishes him for his "weak" and "feminine" behavior. In his daily life he is an aggres-

DSM-IV Criteria for Sexual Masochism

A. Over a period of at least 6 months, recurrent, intense sexually arousing fantasies, sexual urges, or behaviors involving acts (real, not simulated) of being humiliated, beaten, bound, or otherwise made to suffer.

B. The fantasies, sexual urges, or behaviors cause clinically significant distress or impairment in social, occupational, or other important areas of functioning.

SOURCE: APA, DSM-IV, 1994.

sive and controlling executive, but underneath he deeply longs to be controlled. He feels he should be punished because it is wrong for him to have feelings of needing to be dominated, and so he has his wife tie him to a rack in their cellar and beat him. (Adapted from Gagnon, 1977)

Many individuals who are neither sadists nor masochists have occasional sexual fantasies about humiliation and suffering. But such fantasies are not necessary for sexual arousal or orgasm in the great majority of individuals, and this differentiates them from sadomasochists (Gagnon, 1977; McCary, 1978). In addition to fantasies, overt acts involving suffering and humiliation in order to produce arousal must occur for sadism or masochism to be diagnosed. Nor are all overt acts that produce pain during sex play considered sadomasochistic: lightly biting a partner's earlobe or leaving scratch marks or bruises on a partner's back are common elements of sex play. The true sadist or masochist both has the relevant fantasies and engages in acts that sexually arouse him, causing more than minimal pain.

EXHIBITIONISM, VOYEURISM, AND PEDOPHILIA

The final category of paraphilias involves sexual arousal with nonconsenting partners. Unlike the foregoing, all of these paraphilias are crimes in our society. The criminal aspect derives from the fact that they violate the freedom of others to make unconstrained sexual decisions. *Exhibitionism* involves exposing the genitals to unwitting, and usually unwilling, strangers. *Voyeurism* involves observing the naked body, the disrobing, or the sexual activity of an unsuspecting victim. *Telephone scatologia* consists of recurrent and intense sexual urges to make obscene calls to a nonconsenting individual. *Pedophilia* involves sexual relations with children below the age of puberty, the age at which we consider it reasonable for a person to be able to give mature consent.

Rape—the sexual violation of one person by another—is the most heinous instance of sex involving nonconsenting partners. We shall not discuss rape in this section for two reasons: First, it is not clearly a paraphilia. To be a paraphilia, the act must be the individual's exclusive, or vastly preferred, mode of sexual release. The shoe fetishist does not become erect or have an orgasm unless he is fantasizing about, seeing, or touching shoes. In contrast, the vast majority of rapists, most of the time, can and do become sexually aroused and achieve sexual release in activities other than rape. Second, rape is a major crime, an act for which it is imperative that society hold the individual responsible, punishing him accordingly. If we were to include rape as a *disorder* in the nosology of paraphilias, there would be some tendency to excuse the act and lighten the burden of the rapist's individual responsibility— even if there was not a shred of evidence other than the rape itself that indicated psychological abnormality. The acts of murder, assault, and theft are not automatically thought of as psychological disorders unless there is additional evidence of abnormality, nor should rape be thought of as a psychological disorder. The expression "Only a crazy man could have done that," when applied to bad action, seems to us deeply and insidiously confused. To call an evil person crazy or an evil act insane is not only a sloppy use of language, but it blackens the character of all the good, crazy people in the world—the fine people to whom our field is dedicated.

The distinction between "evil" and "crazy" is deeply entrenched in our language and our moral codes. Distinguishing between them is central to being able to excuse people occasionally for bad actions when they are not responsible by reason of insanity (see Chapter 14). We must not blur this distinction any further.

Exhibitionism   *Exhibitionism* consists of exposing the genitals to an unwitting stranger, on repeated occasions, in order to produce sexual excitement. The exposure itself is the final sexual act, and the exhibitionist does not go on to attempt sexual relations with his victim after exhibiting himself. A "flasher," or "flagwaver," as he is called in prison slang, typically approaches a woman or a child with his genitals exposed. He usually has an erection, but sometimes he is flaccid. Sometimes he will ejaculate while exhibiting himself or, more commonly, he will masturbate when he is alone afterwards (Katchadourian and Lunde, 1972).

Exhibitionism is the most common sexual crime in the United States, with roughly one-third of sexual offenders arrested for it (Gebhard, Gagnon, Pomeroy, and Christenson, 1965). Surprisingly enough, exhibitionism is very rare outside the United States and Europe and nonexistent in cultures such as India and Burma.

Exhibitionists are usually not dangerous although they wish to shock and horrify their victims, and this is essential for the act to be gratifying. The act usually takes place six to sixty feet from the victim; very rarely is the victim touched or molested. The exhibitionist is more of a nuisance than a menace, and it is uncommon for exhibitionists to become child molesters (Gagnon, 1977; McCary, 1978).

The settings in which exhibitionists expose themselves vary. The most common are in front of girls' schools or churches, in crowds, and in parks; and in these settings, the exhibitionist may pretend he is urinating. Among the more imaginative scenarios are wearing only a raincoat in a department store, taking out a whistle and blowing it, and as the female shoppers look in the direction of the whistler, opening the raincoat; rapping on the window of a house with one's erect penis; sitting down near women in darkened movie theaters and masturbating. All these situations have one important element in common: they are public and it is very unlikely that sexual intercourse could possibly take place. These points provide clues to the dynamics of an exhibitionist: The exhibitionist needs to display his masculinity without the threat of having to perform in an adequate sexual role (Kaplan, 1974).

Voyeurism   In the eleventh century Leofric, the Lord of Coventry, agreed to lower taxes if his wife, Lady Godiva, would ride unclothed on a white horse through the town. As a friend of the poor, Lady Godiva consented, and everyone in town shuttered their windows and hid their eyes out of respect and gratitude. Only Tom, the tailor, peeked; and he went blind, becoming our legendary Peeping Tom, the "original" voyeur.

Voyeurs are individuals who repeatedly seek out situations in which they can look at unsuspecting women who are naked, disrobing, or engaged in sexual activity. The acts of a Peeping Tom are secret. The voyeur will masturbate during these acts or while fantasizing about the memory of these encounters. Watching an unsuspecting stranger is the final act, and the voyeur almost never approaches his victim for sexual contact. Visual stimulation is commonly erotic both to men and women, but merely being aroused by seeing a naked woman or a sexual act is not equivalent to voyeurism. In normal individuals, visual stimulation is usually a prelude to further sexual activity. In contrast to voyeurs, normal men do not need to watch an unsuspecting stranger in order to become aroused. The illegal, secretive nature of his peeping is itself arousing to the voyeur.

Almost all information about voyeurs comes from those cases in which they are caught. The act is a crime, and many of the problems—such as shame and danger to reputation—that it produces come only in the aftermath of the arrest and exposure. In addition to shame, voyeurs sometimes fall off window ledges, are shot as burglars, and are assaulted by couples who catch them peeping.

Pedophilia   The *pedophile,* sometimes called the child molester, prefers sexual activity with prepubescent children and acts out his preference repeatedly. The child molester may just undress the child and look, exposing himself, masturbating in front of the child, or gently touching and fondling the child. Some go further and have oral, anal, or vaginal sex with the child, sometimes using force. Penetration probably occurs in only about 10 percent of the cases of child molestation. Society feels a special sense of horror and reserves special fury for the child molester. Other than lust murder, pedophilia is the most heavily punished crime of the paraphilias. About 30 percent of all convictions for sex offenses are for child molesting, but it is probably even more common than generally supposed. Between one-quarter and one-third of all adults *report* that when they were children they had been approached sexually by an adult (Kinsey et al., 1948; MCConaghy, 1969; McCary, 1978; Erickson, Walbek, and Seely, 1988).

There are probably two reasons society consigns pedophiles to a special hell. First, we do not consider a child capable of consenting to sexual activity in the same way a mature adult can, and so the child's freedom is seen as being grossly violated in such circumstances. Second, there is a common, but unsubstantiated, belief in sexual imprinting; the child's attitude toward future sexuality may be warped by these early sexual contacts.

Society's image of the child molester as a dirty stranger lurking in the shadows is far from the truth. Most acts of convicted pedophiles take place between the child and a family acquaintance, neighbor, or relative. The acts usually occur in the child's own home or during a voluntary visit of the child to the home of the pedophile. The relationship is not usually particularly intimate, nor is it prolonged. It typically ends when the child begins to protest or reports it to the parents.

Molesters are often beset with conflicts about religious piety versus sexuality, are guilt-ridden, and feel doomed. They often lack ordinary adult social skills (Overholser and Beck, 1986), lack confidence, and may be uneasy in adult social and sexual relations and feel more comfortable with children than adults (Levin and Stava, 1987). The disorder is usually chronic, especially in those attracted to boys. For habitual child molesters, the frequency of paraphilic behavior often fluctuates with psychosocial stress. Occasionally, isolated acts of sexual behavior with children by nonpedophilic individuals will be precipitated by a stressor, most commonly upon discovering that one's wife or girlfriend has been unfaithful. In other cases, child molesters may be substituting child contact for adult contact that they have been unable to get (Gagnon, 1977).

DSM-IV Criteria for Pedophilia

A. Over a period of at least 6 months, recurrent, intense sexually arousing fantasies, sexual urges, or behaviors involving sexual activity with a prepubescent child or children (generally age 13 years or younger).

B. The fantasies, sexual urges, or behaviors cause clinically significant distress or impairment in social, occupational, or other important areas of functioning.

C. The person is at least age 16 years and at least 5 years older than the child or children in Criterion A. *Note:* Do not include an individual in late adolescence involved in an ongoing sexual relationship with a 12- or 13-year-old.

SOURCE: APA, DSM-IV, 1994.

The Causes of Paraphilias

Two schools of thought, the psychodynamic and the behavioral, have wrestled with the problem of the origin of paraphilias. While neither has been completely successful, both have contributed to our understanding.

THE PSYCHODYNAMIC VIEW OF PARAPHILIAS

FOCUS QUESTIONS

1. What is the psychodynamic view of the paraphilias?
2. Describe the behavioral view of the paraphilias in terms of CS, US, UR, and CR.
3. How do learning theories explain the persistence of the paraphilias?
4. Describe aversion therapy and explain how it is used to treat the paraphilias.

According to Freud, the concepts of "fixation," "object-cathexis," and "sexual object choice" are attempts to describe and explain how certain objects become imbued with erotic attraction for certain individuals as they grow up. ***Cathexis*** refers to the charging of a neutral object with psychical energy, either positive or negative. In the case of a "positive cathexis," the libido, or the sexual drive, attaches to the object, and it becomes loved. In the case of a "negative cathexis," the object becomes feared. Cathected paraphilias have the same three properties as other objects of sexual interest: (1) they have their beginnings in childhood experience; (2) they resist change, particularly rational change; and (3) they last and last—usually remaining for a lifetime.

Freud described the case of the typical foot fetishist who recalled that when he was six, his governess, wearing a velvet slipper, stretched her foot out on a cushion. Although it was decently concealed, this kind of foot, thin and scraggy though it was, thereafter became his only sexual interest (Freud, 1917/1976, p. 348). The fetishist had cathected onto this kind of foot. Freud considered this cathexis to be a concentration of very high psychical energy, bounded and protected by a shield of dead layers. This protection against external stimuli allowed the cathected object to retain its erotic power through life, and only traumatic experiences could breach the protective gates.

While the concept of cathexis is useful descriptively, it is not a satisfactory explanation, for as Freud acknowledged, it is unknown why it strikes one individual rather than another. And this is the main question that concerns us here. The psychodynamic view is content to describe as an acquired cathexis the origins of passion for the fetishist, the transvestite, the sadist, the masochist, the exhibitionist, the voyeur, and the pedophile. But it only describes the fact that for all of these individuals their sexual object choice is not a means to an end but an end in itself, that it is persistent, and that it does not yield to reason. Cathexis does not explain how this happens.

THE BEHAVIORAL VIEW OF PARAPHILIAS

The learning theories, too, have wrestled with the problem of erotic attachment. The most common account is Pavlovian. Recall the case of Leo, whose foot fetish began when, as a seven-year-old, his half sister's slipper touched his penis. The conditioned stimulus (CS) here is the sight of the slipper. It is paired with the unconditioned stimulus (US) of genital stimulation and the unconditioned response (UR) of sexual pleasure. As a result, in the future slippers come to produce the conditioned response (CR) of sexual arousal. Such an account explains how cathexis might occur to odd objects in childhood, and it supplements the Freudian account by providing a mechanism.

Why do paraphilias persist, once they are conditioned? Once the fetishistic object has been paired with erotic stimulation and the paraphilic masturbates in the presence of the fantasy of the object or in the presence of the very object itself, he provides himself with additional Pavlovian conditioning trials, thereby greatly strengthening the connection between the object and the unconditioned response of sexual pleasure. So an adolescent who experienced the sight of panties originally paired with sexual teasing by the girl next door may greatly strengthen his attachment to panties when he masturbates to orgasm while fantasizing about panties (McGuire, Carlisle, and Young, 1965; Storms, 1981).

There is another factor, ***preparedness,*** which was brought up in explaining phobias (see Chapter 5) and which might also help to account for the irrationality and resistance to extinction of fetishes. As for phobias, there is a limited set of objects that actually become paraphilic. Why are paraphilias about parts of the body and about dominance and submission common, but paraphilias about windows, pillows, or yellow walls nonexistent, despite the fact that such objects are often paired with sexual stimulation in childhood? If there is a special class of objects that are *prepared* to take on an erotic character once the objects have been paired with unconditioned sexual stimuli, then the other properties of preparedness should follow. Such objects, once conditioned, should be irrational, robust, and easily learned. These facts describe both the paraphilias and phobias.

Changing Sexual Interest

Sexual interests, which rarely die of their own accord, can—with explicit therapy—sometimes be altered. There are extensive studies of therapy to change sexual interest, but they come mostly from atypical men: sex offenders. An exhibitionist (flasher) or a pedophile (child molester) may be arrested and then have therapy mandated in addition to, or instead of, jail. So, our knowledge of therapy outcomes for changing sexual interest, unlike most areas of therapy, comes only from people who are under strong external pressure to change (see Table 13–2).

Behavior therapists have reported some favorable results in changing the paraphilias, but the success rate is far from perfect (Maletzky, 1974; Rooth and Marks, 1974; Blair and Lanyon, 1981). If paraphilias arise by conditioning during fantasy and masturbation, it might be sufficient for ***aversion therapy*** to concentrate on fantasy. The use of imagined sexual stimuli followed by aversive US's is called ***covert sensitization*** (Cautela, 1967; LaMontagne and LeSage, 1986). The treatment of exhibitionists is typical, and all of the following are used extensively, alone or in combination: (1) Electric shock or chemical nauseants—The patient reads aloud, in the first person, an exciting sequence of vignettes about flashing. When he gets to the climax of exposing his erect penis, painful shock or chemical nauseants are delivered. As the climactic act becomes aversive, the aversive stimulus is now delivered earlier and

TABLE 13–2

	TREATMENT OF PARAPHILIAS	
	*Psychosocial Treatments**	*Chemical Castration*[†]
Improvement	more than 50% markedly improved	more than 90% markedly improved
Relapse[‡]	low to moderate relapse	high relapse
Side Effects	none	moderate to severe
Cost	inexpensive	inexpensive
Time scale	weeks/months	weeks
Overall	**good**	**very good**

*These are treatments for the entire range of paraphilias.
[†]This is a treatment for brutal rape and pedophilia only.
[‡]Relapse after discontinuation of treatment.
SOURCE: Based on M.E.P. Seligman, *What you can change and what you can't* (New York: Knopf, 1993), Chapter 11, and a conservative reading of B.M. Maletzky, The paraphilias: Research and treatment, in P. Nathan & J. Gorman (eds.), *Treatments that work* (New York: Oxford, 1997), which awaits widespread replication.

earlier in the sequence. (2) Orgasmic reconditioning—The man masturbates, narrating his fantasies aloud. As he reaches climax, he substitutes a more acceptable scene for the flashing fantasy. (3) Masturbatory satiation—He continues to masturbate for half an hour after ejaculation—a deadly task—while rehearsing every variation of flashing aloud. These treatments are mildly effective. In one study with a six-year follow-up, only 40 percent of treated men continued to flash, whereas 60 percent of untreated men reoffended.

Behavior therapists also have used social skills training and imagery-stopping techniques to modify paraphilias. Although some success has been reported using these techniques with exhibitionists (Maletzky, 1974), these procedures have also been known to fail (McConaghy, 1969).

More recently, therapists have started to treat this problem cognitively. For example, the patient carries cards with exciting vignettes about flashing. On the back of each card is a horrible consequence of flashing and getting caught. Whenever he is tempted to flash, the patient is instructed to read the sequence, turn the cards over, and then ruminate on the awful consequences. This may reduce the rate of reoffending to about 25 percent (Marshall, Eccles, and Barbaree, 1991).

Much more promising results have now been reported by Maletzky (1997) using cognitive-behavioral techniques. In a report on 4,000 offenders who were followed over an average of nine years, reoffense rates dropped to 4 percent for molesters of little girls, 4 percent for exhibitionists, 6 percent for voyeurs, 6 percent for fetishists, 22 percent for transvestites, and 25 percent for rapists. If these findings are replicated widely, they will provide new hope for those suffering from the paraphilias.

What is changing here? Patients report changes both in their overt behavior and in their desire to flash as well. What they do is substantially changed. We believe, however, that what they want is largely unchanged. It is very much in the interest of the offender to tell the therapist, the judge, the probation officer, and the world that he no longer wants to flash, and so his reports about desire are not completely reliable. Nevertheless, the behavioral record documents that he actually does flash less. We suspect the offender learns in therapy to restrain himself from acting on his desires, which are unchanged. While not a cure, this is all to the good. It also suggests that some change—perhaps not in desire but in action—can occur with sexual interests (Hall, 1995).

It should not go unnoted that there is a substantially more effective way to curtail brutal sex offenders: castration. It is used in Europe for very serious offenses—brutal rape and child molestation. Castration is done surgically—cutting off the testicles—or, more commonly, with drugs that neutralize the hormone that the testicles produce. In four studies of over 2,000 offenders followed for many years, the reoffense rate dropped from around 70 percent to around 3 percent. Drug castration, which unlike surgery is reversible, works as well as surgical castration (Bradford, 1988; Kravitz, Haywood, Kelly, Wahlstrom, Liles, and Cavanaugh, 1995). In America, castration is considered "cruel and unusual punishment," and is thus not performed. When we consider all the wasted years in prison, the high likelihood of repeated offense, and the special hell that other prisoners reserve for child molesters, however, castration seem to us less cruel than the "usual" punishment.

SEX ROLE: LAYER IV

Sex role is the public expression of sexual identity—what one says and what one does to indicate being a man or a woman. In today's more tolerant world there are no "disorders" of sex role. Compassionate men and tough women, male nurses and female construction workers are not deemed to suffer from any sexual problem. We discuss the issue of sex role now—in spite of there being no sex role disorders—because sex role fills out and illuminates the layers of our sexual existence. What role we adopt is elaborated around our sexual identity, our sexual orientation, and our sexual interests.

The word "role" is misleading. As a term of the theater, it makes it sound as if sex role is a costume we can take off or put on at will—an arbitrary convention of how we are socialized. While sex role is partly learned and is more plastic or changeable than sexual interest, which is in turn more plastic than orientation and identity, it is not arbitrary.

There are huge sex-role dissimilarities between very young boys and girls (Maccoby and Jacklin, 1974; Huston, 1985; Sedney, 1987; Levy, 1995; Martin, Eisenbud, and Rose, 1995; Zucker, Wilson-Smith, Kurita, and Stern, 1995):

- By age 2 boys want to play with trucks and girls want to play with dolls.
- By age 3 children know the sex stereotypes for dress, toys, jobs, games, tools, and interests.
- By age 3 children want to play with peers of their own sex.
- By age 4 most girls want to be teachers, nurses, secretaries, and mothers, while most boys want to have "masculine" jobs.

In most cultures, young children categorize the world according to sex and organize their lives around these categories. No one has to teach them sex-role stereotypes: they spontaneously invent them. The usual explanation is that they learn sex roles from their parents. After all, parents decorate the rooms of girls in pink and put dolls in their cribs, while boys get blue cribs and toy guns.

What is surprising is that children reared "androgynously" (from the Greek for "both male and female") display their stereotypes as strongly as children not so reared. Young children's stereotypes bear no relationship to their parents' attitudes or to their parents' education, class, employment, or sexual politics. Children's play is strongly sex-stereotyped, even when their parents are androgynous in politics and behavior.

It is not that boys are merely indifferent to lessons about "androgyny." Boys don't just ignore being told it's okay to play with dolls; they actively resist. Having a teacher try to persuade a child to give up a "sex-appropriate" toy produces resistance, anxiety, and backlash, particularly among boys. Watching videotapes of other kids playing joyfully with sex-inappropriate toys doesn't work either. Intensive home programs incorporating androgynous toys, songs, and books with mother as the teacher produce no changes. Extensive classroom intervention produces no changes in androgyny—outside the classroom (Huston, 1985; Sedney, 1987).

These findings seem to disprove the belief that social pressure creates sex roles in the first place. If social pressure creates it, intense social pressure by committed parents and teachers should diminish it. But it has not been demonstrated to do so.

Since social pressure does not play a measurable role in creating sex roles, one determinant could, at least in part, be fetal hormones. There are two lines of evidence for this: In one study, seventy-four mothers had taken prescription drugs to prevent miscarriage during their pregnancies in the 1970s. These drugs had the common property of disrupting the masculinizing hormone, androgen. When the children were ten years old, the games they liked to play were compared to the games enjoyed by matched controls. The boys' games were less masculine, and the girls' games were more feminine.

FOCUS QUESTIONS

1. Describe some of the sex-role dissimilarities between very young boys and girls.
2. What are the two lines of evidence that indicate that fetal hormones may play a role in creating sex roles?
3. Why may sex-role stereotypes diminish as children mature?

A second line of evidence is a disease (Congenital Adrenal Hyperplasia, or CAH) that bathes female fetuses with extra androgen. As young children, CAH girls like male-stereotyped toys and rough and tumble play, and they are more tomboyish than matched controls. These findings suggest that one source of boys' wanting to play with guns and girls' wanting to play house originates in the womb (Money and Ehrhardt, 1972; Meyer-Bahlburg, Feldman, Cohen, and Ehrhardt, 1988; Berenbaum and Hines, 1992; Kuhnle, Bullinger, and Schwarz, 1995).

In light of this evidence, one might be tempted to leap to the conclusion that sex roles are biologically deep and unchangeable. This, however, is not true. As children grow up, the stereotypes get weaker and easier to defy. In late childhood, children begin to have stereotypes about crying, dominance, independence, and kindness, but they are much weaker than the toy and job stereotypes of early childhood.

Although pressuring kids to become androgynous does not work immediately, it may have a "sleeper" effect. As children mature into adults, sex-role stereotypes start to melt away. When children grow up, the ones who were raised by androgynous parents tend to become androgynous themselves. Supporting intellectual interests for daughters and warmth and compassion for sons, exposing children to a range of roles, may work after all—but only in the long run (Reinisch, 1992).

This is important, and it makes sense. Young children see the world in black and white terms. "I'm either a boy or a girl. There's nothing in between. If I like dolls, I'm a sissy." These are deeply held convictions. Young children seem to have a drive to conform which may have its roots in the fetal brain. As a child matures, however, considerations of morality, of justice, of fairness enter. Tolerance starts to displace blind conformity. He or she now chooses how to behave. Decisions about androgyny, about unconventionality, about rebellion are conscious choices based on a sense of what is right and what the adolescent individual wants for his or her own future. As such, the choice of androgyny requires a mature mind and a conscience; it is not a product of mechanical childhood socialization.

SEXUAL PERFORMANCE: LAYER V

Assume that the first four layers of your sexuality are in good order. You have a clear sexual identity and orientation, you have clear sexual interests, and a well-entrenched sex role. You are alone with an appropriate, consenting partner. What can now go wrong? In what ways can the surface layer of erotic life—sexual performance—be impaired?

The Physiology of the Human Sexual Response

In both men and women, the sexual response consists of three phases: the first is *erotic desire and arousal,* in which a variety of stimuli—tactile, visual, and more subtle ones such as fantasy—produce arousal. The second phase, *physical excitement,* consists of penile erection in the male and vaginal lubrication and swelling in the genital area of the female. The third phase is *orgasm.* We shall review these phases in some detail because sexual dysfunction can disrupt any of them.

MALE SEXUAL RESPONSE

In men, erotic arousal results from a wide variety of events. Being touched on the genitals or looking and touching a sexually responsive partner are

FOCUS QUESTIONS

1. What are the three phases of the human sexual response?
2. What is sexual dysfunction and in what areas of the sexual response can it occur?
3. Describe the subjective and physiological symptoms of sexual unresponsiveness in women.
4. Describe the different possible kinds of erectile dysfunctions and orgasmic dysfunctions in men.

probably the most compelling stimuli. In addition, visual stimuli, smells, a seductive voice, and erotic fantasies, among many others, all produce arousal.

The second phase of excitement is intertwined with the first phase of erotic arousal. In the male, it consists of penile erection. Sexual excitement stimulates parasympathetic nerves in the spinal cord, and these nerves control the blood vessels of the penis. These vessels widen dramatically and highly oxygen-rich blood streams in, producing erection. The blood is prevented from leaving by a system of valves in the veins. When the parasympathetic fibers are inhibited, the vessels empty, and rapid loss of erection occurs.

Orgasm in men consists of two stages that follow each other very rapidly—emission and ejaculation. Unlike arousal and erection, orgasm is controlled by the sympathetic nervous system, as opposed to the parasympathetic nervous system. When sufficient rhythmic pressure on the head and shaft of the penis occur, the stage of orgasmic inevitability is reached and orgasm arrives. Orgasm is engineered to deposit sperm deep into the vagina near the head of the uterus, maximizing the possibility of fertilization. Emission (the discharge of semen) occurs when the reproductive organs all contract. This is followed very rapidly by ejaculation, in which powerful muscles at the base of the penis contract vigorously, ejecting sperm from the penis. During ejaculation, these muscles contract by reflex at intervals of 0.8 seconds. This phase of orgasm is accompanied by intense pleasure. After orgasm has occurred, a man, unlike a woman, is "refractory," or unresponsive to further sexual stimulation for some interval. This interval varies from a few minutes to a few hours, and it lengthens as the man gets older.

FEMALE SEXUAL RESPONSE

The sexual response of a woman transforms the normally tight and dry vagina into a lubricated, perfectly fitting receptacle for the erect penis. The stimuli that produce arousal in women are similar to those that produce arousal in men. Kissing and caressing, visual stimuli, and a whole host of subtle cues are usually effective as sexually arousing stimuli. In our culture, at least, there appear to be some gender differences in what is arousing, with subtle stimuli and gentle touch more initially arousing to women than direct stimulation.

Once a woman is aroused, the excitement or "lubrication-swelling" phase begins. When at rest, the vagina is collapsed, pale in color, and rather dry. When arousal occurs, the vagina balloons exactly enough to "glove" an erect penis, regardless of its size. At the same time, the clitoris, a small knob of tissue located forward of the vagina, swells. Lubrication occurs on the walls of the vagina, making penile insertion easier. As excitement continues, the walls of the uterus fill with blood, and the uterus enlarges. This engorgement of blood and swelling greatly add to erotic pleasure and set the stage for orgasm.

Orgasm in women consists of a series of reflexive contractions of the muscles surrounding the vagina. These contract rhythmically at 0.8 second intervals against the engorged tissue around the vagina, producing the ecstatic sensation of orgasm. Both the clitoris and the vagina itself play a role: orgasm is triggered by stimulation of the clitoris, and then expressed by contraction of the vagina.

Thus, similar stimuli produce erotic arousal in both sexes. Blood flow under the control of the parasympathetic nervous system produces physical excitement and penile erection and both the lubrication and swelling phases of the vagina. Orgasm consists of powerful muscular contractions at 0.8 second intervals, produced by rhythmic pressure on the head and shaft of the penis in the man and of the clitoris of the woman. These parallels are lovely and deep. Before they were known, it was easy to fall prey to the belief that chasms separated the experience of sex between men and women. To learn that one's partner is probably experiencing the same kind of joys that you are is powerful and binding knowledge.

Impairment of Sexual Performance

When the normal mechanism of desire, arousal, or orgasm goes awry, we say an individual suffers a sexual dysfunction. Dysfunction can occur in any or all of the three areas of sexual response: (1) Erotic arousal may be dysfunctional if fantasies about and interest in sexual activity are low or nonexistent. (2) When in an appropriate sexual situation, failure to have or maintain an erection in men and lack of vaginal lubrication and genital swelling in women may occur. (3) In women, orgasm may fail to occur altogether; in men, ejaculation may be premature, occurring with minimal sexual stimulation, or retarded, occurring only after prolonged, continual stimulation, if at all.

Impairment may occur in only one of these three areas of sexuality, or in all three in the same individual. The impairment may be lifelong or acquired, it may be limited to only one situation or occur in all situations, and it may occur infrequently or all the time. For example, the failure to maintain an erection can develop after years of satisfactory intercourse, or it can occur from the very first attempt at sexual intercourse. It can occur only with one partner or with all women. It can occur only once in a while or it can occur every time the individual tries to have intercourse.

SEXUAL UNRESPONSIVENESS IN WOMEN

Because erotic desire and physical excitement are so intertwined, we will treat them together. In women, lack of sexual desire and impairment of physical excitement in appropriate situations are called **sexual unresponsiveness** (formerly "frigidity"). Some of the symptoms are subjective: the woman may not have sexual fantasies, she may not enjoy sexual intercourse or stimulation, or she may consider sex an ordeal. Other symptoms are physiological: when she is sexually stimulated, her vagina does not lubricate, her clitoris does not enlarge, her uterus does not swell, and her nipples do not become erect. Frequently, she becomes a spectator rather than losing herself in the erotic act. The woman may be unresponsive in all situations or only in specific ones. For example, if the problem is situational, she may be enraged or nauseated by the sexual advances of her husband, but she may feel instantly aroused and may lubricate when an attractive, unavailable man touches her hand. Such a woman may have problems with orgasm as well, but it is not uncommon for a "sexually unresponsive" woman—whose arousal and excitement are impaired—to have orgasm easily once intercourse takes place.

Women's reactions to this problem vary. Some patiently endure unexciting sexual intercourse, using their bodies mechanically and hoping that their partner will ejaculate quickly. But this is often a formula for resentment. Watching her husband derive great pleasure from sex over and over while she feels little pleasure may be frustrating and alienating for a woman. And eventually some women may attempt to avoid sex, pleading illness or deliberately provoking a quarrel before bedtime (Kaplan, 1974).

ERECTILE DYSFUNCTION IN MEN

In men, global impairment of desire (DSM-IV calls it "hypoactive sexual desire" or "sexual aversion") occurs, but it is much rarer than in women. Rather, the most common dysfunction in men is one of excitement, called **erectile dysfunction** (formerly "impotence"). It is defined as a recurrent in-

---

DSM-IV Criteria for Female Sexual Arousal Disorder

A. Persistent or recurrent inability to attain, or to maintain until completion of the sexual activity, an adequate lubrication-swelling response of sexual excitement.

B. The disturbance causes marked distress or interpersonal difficulty.

C. The sexual dysfunction is not better accounted for by another Axis I disorder (except another Sexual Dysfunction) and is not due exclusively to the direct physiological effects of a substance (e.g., a drug of abuse, a medication) or a general medical condition.

SOURCE: APA, DSM-IV, 1994.

ability to have or maintain an erection for intercourse. This condition can be humiliating, frustrating, and devastating since male self-esteem across most cultures involves good sexual performance. When erection fails, feelings of worthlessness and depression often ensue.

Erectile dysfunction in the male can be either primary or secondary, situation specific or global. Men who have had ***primary erectile dysfunction*** have never been able to achieve or maintain an erection sufficient for intercourse; whereas men who have ***secondary erectile dysfunction*** have lost this ability. When the dysfunction is situation specific, a man may be able to maintain an erection with one partner, but not with another. Some men may become erect during foreplay, but not during intercourse. When the dysfunction is global, a man cannot achieve an erection with any partner under any circumstances. It is important and reassuring for a man to know that a single failure in no way implies "erectile dysfunction," which is, by definition, recurrent. Virtually every man on one occasion or another—particularly when upset or fatigued—cannot get an erection or keep it long enough for intercourse.

Here is a case of primary impotence that begins with a particularly sordid circumstance surrounding the man's first attempt at intercourse:

Sheldon was nineteen when his teammates from the freshman football team dragged him along to visit a prostitute. The prostitute's bedroom was squalid; she seemed to be in her mid-fifties, and had an unattractive face, a fat body, and foul-smelling breath. He was to be the last of a group of five friends scheduled to perform with her. Sheldon had never had intercourse before and had been anxious to begin with. His anxiety increased as his teammates returned one by one to describe in detail their heroic successes. When his turn arrived, the other four decided to watch and cheer him on, and Sheldon could not get an erection. His teammates shouted that he should hurry up and the prostitute was obviously impatient. He was pressured beyond any ability to perform and ran out of the room.

After this incident, he avoided all erotic contact with women for five years, fearing that he would fail again. At age twenty-four, when his fiancée pressured him to have sex, he was overwhelmed with fears that he would fail, remembering his humiliating failure with the prostitute. This brought Sheldon into therapy for primary erectile dysfunction. (Adapted from Masters and Johnson, 1970)

ORGASMIC DYSFUNCTION IN WOMEN

Some women do not achieve the third phase of sexual response: orgasm. How easily different women can achieve orgasm lies on a continuum. At one extreme are the rare women who can have an orgasm merely by having an intense erotic fantasy, without any physical stimulation at all. Then there are women who climax merely from intense foreplay, women who have orgasm during intercourse, and women who need long and intense clitoral stimulation in order to climax. At the other extreme are approximately 10 percent of adult women who have never had an orgasm in spite of having been exposed to a reasonable amount of stimulation.

Nonorgasmic women frequently have a strong sexual drive (Andersen, 1983). They may enjoy foreplay, lubricate copiously, and love the sensation of phallic penetration. But as they approach climax, the woman may become self-conscious; she may stand apart and judge herself. She may ask herself, "I wonder if I'll climax." "This is taking too long; he's getting sick of it." Frustration, resentment, and the persistent erosion of a couple's erotic and affectionate relationship bring nonorgasmic women into therapy (Kaplan, 1974; McCary, 1978).

Failure to have an orgasm may be primary, with orgasm never having occurred, or secondary, with loss of orgasm. It may be situation specific, with orgasm occurring, for example, in masturbation when alone but not in intercourse, or it may be global.

ORGASMIC DYSFUNCTION IN MEN

In men, there are two kinds of orgasmic difficulties and they are opposite problems: premature ejaculation and retarded ejaculation.

Premature Ejaculation   Most men have ejaculated occasionally more quickly than their partner would like, but this is not equivalent to premature ejaculation. ***Premature ejaculation*** is the recurrent inability to exert any control over ejaculation such that once sexually aroused, the man reaches orgasm very quickly. This is probably the most common of male sexual problems.

Premature ejaculation can wreak havoc with a couple's sex life. A man who is worrying about ejaculating as soon as he becomes aroused may have trouble being sensitive and responsive to his lover. He may be self-conscious, and his partner may feel rejected and perceive him as cold and insensitive. Not uncommonly, secondary erectile dysfunction often follows untreated premature ejaculation.

Retarded Ejaculation   ***Retarded ejaculation,*** which is less common than premature ejaculation, is defined by great difficulty reaching orgasm during sexual intercourse. Frequently, the man may be able to ejaculate easily during masturbation or foreplay, but intercourse may last for a half hour or more with no ejaculation. Contrary to popular myth, the staying power of the retarded ejaculator does not place him in an enviable position. His partner may feel rejected and unskilled. He may feign orgasm, and he may have high anxiety accompanied by self-conscious thoughts like, "She must think something is wrong with me." The retarded ejaculator finds his own touch most arousing, and he may be numb to his partner's touch on his penis. His psychological

---

DSM-IV Criteria for Premature Ejaculation

A. Persistent or recurrent ejaculation with minimal sexual stimulation before, on, or shortly after penetration and before the person wishes it. The clinician must take into account factors that affect duration of the excitement phase, such as age, novelty of the sexual partner or situation, and recent frequency of sexual activity.
B. The disturbance causes marked distress or interpersonal difficulty.
C. The premature ejaculation is not due exclusively to the direct effects of a substance (e.g., withdrawal from opioids).

SOURCE: APA, DSM-IV, 1994.

arousal does not keep pace with his physiological arousal (Apfelbaum, 1980). Secondary erectile dysfunction sometimes follows.

It is unwise to attach time numbers to both retarded ejaculation and premature ejaculation, saying, for example, that premature ejaculation occurs whenever ejaculation persistently takes less than thirty seconds and retarded ejaculation occurs whenever ejaculation persistently takes more than half an hour. This misses the important point that the definition of the sexual problem, both orgasmic and arousal, is always relative to your own and your partner's expectations. Many couples are able to work out quite satisfactory erotic relationships even when one partner climaxes very quickly or very slowly, and it would be inappropriate to label these individuals as having sexual dysfunction.

The Causes of Sexual Dysfunction

PHYSICAL CAUSES

Impairment of sexual desire in both men and women can stem from aging, drug use that impairs sexual hormones (e.g., alcohol, barbiturates, narcotics, and marijuana), and prescription drugs (e.g., antihypertensives, major and minor tranquilizers, MAO inhibitors, and antihistamines) (Schiavi et al., 1984; Gitlin, 1994; Schiavi and Rehman, 1995). A woman's capacity for sexual arousal may be impaired by injuries, physical anomalies of the genitals, hormonal imbalances, neurological disorders, and inflammations (Kaplan, 1974; McCary, 1978). Male sexual dysfunctions may be caused by excessive alcohol or drugs, vascular problems, aging, exhaustion, or anatomical defect. Poor circulation resulting in insufficient oxygen in the blood in the penis and low testosterone may be responsible for some erectile dysfunction problems (Benet and Melman, 1995). Out of 105 patients, 35 percent had disorders of the pituitary-hypothalamic-gonadal axis, and 90 percent of these had potency restored with biological therapy (Spark, White, and Connelly, 1980).

Nevertheless, physical causes probably account for a minority of the problems of sexual dysfunction in both men and women. There is a useful way of distinguishing between which men are physically and which men are psychologically unable to have erections. All of us dream approximately 100 minutes a night. In the male, dreaming is almost invariably accompanied by an erection (in the female, by vaginal lubrication). We are not certain why this occurs, but it does tell us if a man is physically capable of erection. If a man who is otherwise "impotent" gets erections during dreaming or has an erection upon waking in the morning, the problem is of psychological, not physical, origin.

FOCUS QUESTIONS

1. What are some of the physical causes of sexual dysfunction in men and women?

2. Describe the psychodynamic view of the causes of sexual dysfunction.

3. Describe the behavioral view of the causes of sexual dysfunction.

4. What are some cognitions that may interfere with sexual performance?

5. Describe how direct sexual therapy is used to treat sexually dysfunctional patients.

Psychological problems probably cause the clear majority of the sexual dysfunctions. Negative emotional states impair sexual responsiveness. Earlier, we spoke of the sensitive interplay of physiological and psychological factors. The physiological part of the sexual response is autonomic and visceral; essentially it is produced by increased blood flow to the genitals under the control of the autonomic nervous system. But certain autonomic responses, sexual arousal among them, are inhibited by negative emotions. If a woman is frightened or angry during sex, visceral responding will be impaired. Similarly, if a man is frightened or feeling pressured during sex, there may not be sufficient blood flow to cause erection.

The Psychodynamic View What are the sources of the anxiety and anger that might cause sexual unresponsiveness in women or men? Psychodynamic theorists consider several possibilities: A woman may fear that she will not reach orgasm, or she may feel helpless or exploited. Some men and women feel unconscious conflict, shame, or guilt, or they may believe that sex is a sin; they may have grown up in situations where sex was seen as dirty and bad, and they may have trouble ridding themselves of feelings of shame and guilt even in the shelter of marriage. Some women may expect physical pain in intercourse and therefore dread it. Many men fear rejection and become self-conscious, thereby inhibiting an otherwise normal physiological potential. And often there is the fear of pregnancy.

Negative emotions arising in relationships must not be overlooked either. Relationships do not always progress well. People change, sometimes developing different living habits and preferences. Their partner may not change accordingly, and conflict may then ensue, bringing about negative feelings between the couple. Understandably, it is often difficult to discard these feelings when the couple enters the bedroom. In such cases, one or both partners may develop a sexual dysfunction, probably specific in nature.

The Behavioral View The behavioral school offers an explanation of the causes of sexual dysfunction based on learning theory. For men, erectile dysfunction may result from an early sexual experience. A particularly traumatic first sexual experience will condition strong fear to sexual encounters. Recall Sheldon's first and formative sexual encounter. Heterosexual activity was the conditioned stimulus (CS), which resulted in a humiliating, public failure to have an erection (US) and an unconditioned response (UR) of ensuing shame and anxiety. Future exposures to the CS of sexual encounters produced the conditioned response (CR) of anxiety, which in turn blocked erection. This formulation fits many of the instances in which there is an early traumatic experience, and it also explains the success of direct sexual therapy with erectile dysfunction. It fails to account for those cases in which no traumatic experience can be discovered, and it also does not account for why certain individuals are more susceptible to sexually traumatic experiences than others. For every individual who undergoes an initial sexual experience that is a failure (such as Sheldon's) and develops erectile dysfunctions, there are many who encounter similar initial failures but do not develop such dysfunctions.

The Cognitive View In addition to psychodynamic and behavioral accounts of sexual dysfunctions, the cognitive view suggests other important considerations as well (see Table 13–3). For both the orgasmic and the arousal dysfunctions, what an individual thinks can greatly interfere with performance. Men and women with orgasm difficulties become "orgasm watchers." They may say to themselves, "I wonder if I'll climax this time." "This is taking much too long; he must think I'm frigid." Individuals who have arousal dysfunctions may say

TABLE 13–3

	VIEWS OF ERECTILE AND ORGASMIC DYSFUNCTION		
	Psychodynamic View	*Behavioral View*	*Cognitive View*
Origin	Unconscious conflict, shame, or guilt about sex	Traumatic early sexual experience	Traumatic sexual experience in someone with a certain cognitive style
Process	Unconscious conflict produces anxiety during sex	Conditioned fear of failure produces anxiety during sex	Person observes and judges him- or herself during sex, interfering with enjoyment and producing anxiety
Result	Anxiety leads to sexual unresponsiveness	Anxiety blocks erection or orgasm	Anxiety blocks erection or orgasm

to themselves, "If I don't get an erection, she'll laugh at me." "I'm not going to get aroused this time either." These thoughts produce anxiety, which in turn blocks the parasympathetic responding that is the basis of the human sexual response. Such thoughts get in the way of abandoning oneself to erotic feelings. Thus, therapy for the sexual dysfunctions can deal with problems at four levels: physical, behavioral, psychodynamic, and cognitive, for difficulties at any of these levels can produce human sexual dysfunction.

Treatment of Sexual Dysfunctions

It has been estimated that half of American marriages are flawed by some kind of sexual problem (Masters and Johnson, 1970; Frank, Anderson, and Rubenstein, 1978; Oggins, Leber, and Veroff, 1993). Sexual problems usually occur in the whole context of a relationship between two human beings. When sex goes badly, many other aspects of the relationship may go badly, and vice versa. Sex—often, but not always—mirrors the way two people feel about and act toward each other overall. Sex therapists often find that underneath the sexual problems are more basic problems of a relationship—love, tenderness, respect, honesty—and that when these are overcome, a fuller sexual relationship may follow (Jacobson, 1992; Speckens, Hengeveld, Lycklama a Nijeholt, Van Hemert, and Hawton, 1995). Let's look at one case:

> When they came to therapy, Carol, age twenty-nine, and Ed, age thirty-eight, had been married for three-and-a-half years and had one child. When they were first married, Carol had achieved orgasm almost every time they made love, but now orgasm was rare for her. She was feeling more and more reluctant to have intercourse with Ed. Ed had a strong sex drive and wanted to have intercourse every day. But Carol had made rules about sex, stating what Ed could and could not do.
>
> As time went on, Carol found it more and more difficult to keep her part of the bargain. Carol's headaches, fatigue, and quarrels deferred Ed's effective initiation of lovemaking. When he did make love to her, Carol would complain about his lovemaking technique. This effectively ended the encounter.
>
> When they first sought out sexual therapy, they were having intercourse once every two weeks, but Carol was becoming progressively more reluctant and intercourse was becoming even more of a dreaded ordeal for her. (Adapted from Kaplan, 1974, case 22)

DIRECT SEXUAL THERAPY

William Masters and Virginia Johnson, researchers who brought the study of sexual behavior into the laboratory and who have worked to discover the nature and treatment of sexual dysfunction, founded ***direct sexual therapy*** with sexually dysfunctional patients like Ed and Carol. Such therapy differs in three important ways from previous sexual therapy. First, it defines the problem differently: sexual problems are not labeled as "neuroses" or "diseases" but rather as "limited dysfunctions." Direct sexual therapy formulates the problem as local rather than global. A woman like Carol is not labeled as "hysterical," defending against deep intrapsychic conflicts by "freezing" her sexual response, as psychodynamic therapists claim. Rather, she is said to suffer from "inhibition of arousal." Second, and most dramatic, through direct sexual therapy, the clients explicitly practice sexual behavior with the systematic guidance of the therapists. A couple like Carol and Ed first receives education and instruction about their problem, then an authoritative prescription from Masters and Johnson about how to solve it, and most importantly, accompanying sexual practice sessions together. Their third major departure is that people are treated not as individual patients but as couples. In treating individuals, Masters and Johnson had often found that sexual problems do not reside in one individual, but in the interaction of the couple. Carol's lack of interest in sex is not only her problem. Her husband's increasing demands, rage, and frustration contribute to her waning interest in sex. By treating the couple together, Ed and Carol's deteriorating sexual interaction could be reversed.

Sensate focus is the major strategy of direct sexual therapy for impaired excitement in females and erectile dysfunction in males. The basic premise of sensate focus is that anxiety occurring during intercourse blocks sexual excitement and pleasure. In the female, anxiety blocks the lubrication and swelling phase; in the male, it blocks erection. The overriding objectives of treatment are to reduce this anxiety and to restore confidence. The immediate goal is to bring about one successful experience with intercourse. This is accomplished, however, in a way in which the demands associated with arousal and orgasm are minimized. Sensate focus has three phases: "pleasuring," genital stimulation, and nondemand intercourse (Masters and Johnson, 1970; Kaplan, 1974; Rosen and Leiblum, 1995). Let us look at the sensate focus treatment for Carol and Ed.

In the "pleasuring" phase, Carol and Ed were instructed not to have sexual intercourse and not to have orgasm during these exercises. Erotic activity was limited to gently touching and caressing each other's body. Carol was instructed to caress Ed first, and then the roles were to be reversed and Ed was to stroke Carol. This was done to permit Carol to concentrate on the sensations later evoked by Ed's caresses without being distracted by guilt over her own selfishness. It also allowed her to relax knowing that intercourse was not going to be demanded of her.

After three sessions of pleasuring, Carol's response was quite dramatic. She felt freed from pressure to have an orgasm and to serve her husband, and she experienced deeply erotic sensations for the first time in her life. Further, she felt that she had taken responsibility for her own pleasure, and she discovered that she was not rejected by her husband when she asserted herself. They then went on to phase two of sensate focus—"genital stimulation." In this phase, light and teasing genital play is added to pleasuring, but the husband is cautioned not to make orgasm-oriented caresses. Orgasm and intercourse are still forbidden. The woman sets the pace of the exercises and directs the husband both verbally and nonverbally, and then the roles are reversed.

The couple's response was also very positive here. Both felt deep pleasure and were aroused and eager to go on to the next step, "nondemand intercourse." In this final phase, after Carol had reached high arousal through pleasuring and genital stimulation, she was instructed to initiate intercourse. Ed and Carol were further instructed that there was to be no pressure for Carol to have an orgasm.

In spite of—or because of—the instruction, Carol had her first orgasm in months. At this point, Ed and Carol were able to work out a mutually arousing and satisfactory style of lovemaking. Carol and Ed's improvement was typical: only about 25 percent of patients fail to improve with sensate focus for female sexual unresponsiveness or for male erectile dysfunction (Masters and Johnson, 1970; Kaplan, 1974; McCary, 1978; Segraves and Althof, 1997).

Evaluation of Sexual Therapy

Direct sexual therapy seems to be quite effective in alleviating the dysfunctions of arousal and orgasm in both men and women (Marks, 1981; Heiman and LoPiccolo, 1983; see Table 13–4). There is more than 75 percent marked improvement in cases of premature ejaculation, and more than 75 percent marked improvement in cases of female orgasmic dysfunction (Segraves and Althof, 1997). Moreover, systematic desensitization may also be effective in enhancing desire and orgasm, particularly in women with sexual anxiety (Andersen, 1983). Caution is required in two respects, however. First, the Masters and Johnson reports of success are not as well documented as many would like. Masters and Johnson do not report percentages of *successes,* but rather they report percentages of *failures.* So, for example, they report that only 24 percent of females "failed to improve" following sensate focus training for arousal dysfunction. This is not equivalent to a 75 percent *cure* rate. What "failure to improve" means is not well defined. Moreover, the percentage of patients showing only mild improvement, great improvement, or complete cure is not reported. While direct sex therapy techniques are far superior to what preceded them, well-controlled replications with explicit criteria for sampling and for improvement will be needed before they can be considered definitive (Zilbergeld and Evans, 1980).

The second caution is that while the therapeutic techniques seem effective, the reasons for their good effects are not wholly clear. As has often been

TABLE 13–4

TREATMENT OF SEXUAL DYSFUNCTIONS BY DIRECT SEXUAL THERAPY		
	Female Arousal and Desire Disorders	*Male Erectile Disorder*
Improvement	more than 65% markedly improved	more than 65% markedly improved
Relapse*	moderate to high relapse	moderate relapse
Side Effects	none	none
Cost	inexpensive	inexpensive
Time Scale	weeks	weeks
Overall	**good**	**very good**
	Female Orgasmic Dysfunction	*Male Premature Ejaculation*
Improvement	more than 75% markedly improved	more than 75% markedly improved
Relapse*	low to moderate relapse	low relapse
Side Effects	none	none
Cost	inexpensive	inexpensive
Time Scale	weeks	weeks
Overall	**very good**	**excellent**

*Relapse after discontinuation of treatment.
SOURCE: Based on M.E.P. Seligman, *What you can change and what you can't* (New York: Knopf, 1993), Chapter 11, and R. Segraves & S. Althof, Psychotherapy and pharmacotherapy of sexual dysfunctions, in P. Nathan and J. Gorman (eds.), *Treatments that work* (New York: Oxford, 1997).

the case in psychology and in medicine, effective cure often precedes understanding, and this seems to be the case for sexual dysfunctions as well.

CONCLUSION

We can see that the idea of *increasingly deep layers* organizes our erotic life and how changeable it is. Sexual identity and sexual orientation are very deep and don't change much, if at all. Thus, lack of change in therapy, lifelong fantasies of one sex only, small anterior hypothalamus, high concordance for homosexuality of identical twins, and fetal development all point to an almost inflexible process. Homosexuality is not quite as unchangeable as transsexualism. Male transsexuals never lose the feeling that they are women. They rarely marry and have natural children, whereas homosexual men sometimes marry and have children. They manage this feat by a trick of fantasy. During sex with their wives, they manage to stay aroused and climax by having fantasies about homosexual sex (just as heterosexual men restricted to homosexual release in prison do). Some measure of flexibility is thus available to exclusively homosexual men—they can choose whom they perform with sexually, but they cannot choose whom they want to perform with.

Sexual interest and sex role are of middling depth and accordingly change somewhat. Once identity and orientation are dictated largely by biology, the sexual interests are elaborated around them largely by environmental stimuli: breasts or bottoms, peeping, lace panties, calves or feet, rubber textures, the missionary position or oral sex, sadism, blond hair, bisexuality, spanking, or high-heeled shoes. These interests are not easily shelved once acquired. Unlike exclusive heterosexuality or homosexuality, however, they surely do not arise in the womb. Rather our sexual interests have their beginnings in late childhood as the first hormones of puberty awaken the dormant brain structures that were laid down in the womb and the child has encounters with potential sexual objects. With repeated masturbation and fantasy, these biologically prepared objects become strong but not wholly unchangeable life goals.

Finally, sexual dysfunction is a surface problem, and with proper treatment it can change quite readily.

SUMMARY

1. Human sexuality is composed of five layers, each grown around the layer beneath it. This five-layer organization corresponds to depth. The deeper the layer, the harder it is to change.

2. The first and deepest layer of erotic life is *sexual identity*, the awareness of being male or female. This layer has its origin in fetal hormones. *Transsexualism*, a disorder of sexual identity, occurs in men who believe they are really women trapped in men's bodies and in women who feel that they are really men trapped in women's bodies. These individuals seek to get rid of their genitals and live in the opposite sex role. *Sex-reassignment operations* provide some relief for this most distressing condition.

3. The second deepest layer is *sexual orientation*, that is, whether you are sexually attracted to men or women. One's erotic and masturbatory fantasies reveal one's sexual orientation. Ego-dystonic homosexuality may occur when an individual's homosexuality causes him intense distress.

4. *Sexual interest* is the next layer of human sexuality, dealing with the types of persons, parts of the body, and situations that are the objects of sexual fantasy and arousal. When the object of a person's arousal impairs an affectionate erotic relationship with another consenting human being, the line between normal and disordered sexual interest has been crossed. The *paraphilia*s consist of sexual desire for unusual and bizarre objects. Three categories are: sexual arousal to nonhuman objects—most commonly *fetishes* and *transvestism;* sexual arousal in situations that produce suffering and humiliation—*sadomasochism;* and sexual arousal with nonconsenting partners—*exhibitionism, voyeurism, telephone scatologia,* and *pedophilia.* The paraphilias are often lifelong, and they may have their origin in *cathexes,* or emotional bonding, which is then reinforced and potentiated by masturbatory fantasies about the object. It is difficult to change the paraphilias in therapy, but recent behavior therapy techniques have had some success.

5. *Sex role* comprises the fourth layer. This is the public expression of sexual identity, what an individual does to indicate that he is a man or she is a woman. There are no disorders of sex role. Although sex-role stereotypes are rigid in young children, they weaken with age.

6. The layer closest to the surface is *sexual performance,* how adequately an individual performs with a suitable person in a suitable erotic setting. The human sexual response is similar in both men and women and consists of three phases: *erotic desire and arousal; excitement,* which consists of penile erection or vaginal lubrication; and *orgasm.* The *sexual dysfunctions* consist of impairment of desire, excitement, or orgasm. In women, these are manifested by insufficient desire, lack of excitement in sexual intercourse, and infrequent or absent orgasm. In men, there is lack of erection, *premature ejaculation,* and *retarded ejaculation.* All these conditions are quite treatable. The *direct sexual therapy* of Masters and Johnson, which uses *sensate focus* to treat couples, suggests that many, if not most of these sexual dysfunctions may be curable or greatly improved in a short period of time.

QUESTIONS FOR CRITICAL THINKING

1. Why do you think sex reassignment is the only therapy that is effective for treating transsexuals? Do you think that those who undergo such surgery are ultimately happier and more adjusted after the surgery?

2. What are the implications of LeVay's study of the brains of homosexual men, heterosexual men, and heterosexual women for societal attitudes toward homosexuality?

3. Describe how the notion of preparedness can be applied to the paraphilias.

4. Why do you think young children categorize the world according to sex and organize their lives around these categories? Why do rigid sex-role stereotypes often weaken with maturity?

14

Law and Abnormality

Giorgio de Chirico, *The Enigma of a Day*, 1914.

T here are two perspectives from which psychological distress can be examined. The first is the perspective of the individual who is suffering: how he or she might have acquired the disorder, what the present experience is like, and what remedies are available to ameliorate that condition. Until now, that has been the perspective of this book.

But there is another way to examine abnormality, and that is from the viewpoint of society. In this chapter, we examine the ways in which society protects its members from the consequences of psychological suffering. The conditions under which society moves to protect and the forms that such protection takes often involve options that are costly in terms of human rights as well as monetarily. In choosing between public protection and the civil liberties of the mentally ill, as exemplified in laws concerning civil and criminal commitment, society must make difficult and often painful choices (Steadman, 1981). After discussing the issues associated with involuntary and criminal commitment, we will then examine other areas in which abnormal psychology and the law intersect.

INVOLUNTARY COMMITMENT AND TREATMENT

No societal response to psychological suffering has received more attention during the past several decades than has ***involuntary commitment,*** the process whereby the state hospitalizes people for their own good, and even over their vigorous protest. In effect, the state acts as parent to those who have "lost their senses," doing for them what they might do for themselves if they had their wits about them, and uses its police power to protect the public from the foreseeable and avoidable danger that the mentally disordered may present.

Involuntary Commitment and Perceptions of Abnormality

Consider the following situations in which the state might seek to commit an individual involuntarily, and in which most people would agree that the state is right in doing so:

- As a result of a toxic psychosis, a young man wants to throw himself from the roof of a very tall building. In twenty-four hours, both the impulse and the psychosis will have passed—if he remains restrained now.
- A young man is despondent over the termination of his first love. To him, there is currently no alternative to suicide. A month from now, he may think differently.
- An attorney is overcome by irrational guilt. She calls two of her clients and informs them that she has not handled their cases properly, and that she has stolen from them. Of course, this is untrue. She would have called the rest of her clients had the state, through her family, not intervened and hospitalized her against her will.
- Following the birth of two previous children, a woman suffered a postpartum depression, and attempted to murder the infants. She is about to give birth again, and is experiencing the same impulse. To protect those young lives, the state hospitalizes the mother involuntarily.

FOCUS QUESTIONS

1. What is involuntary commitment?
2. Describe the definition of "mental disorder" as given by DSM-IV.
3. What are two problems that arise from the notion of dangerousness of an individual to self or others?
4. Describe what is meant by "grave disability" and explain why this criterion may lead to errors.

For most people, these cases are compelling arguments for involuntary hospitalization. Where there is clear-cut danger to self or to others, most people agree that some intervention is necessary. But most cases are not nearly so clear-cut. The informal social conventions that regulate who should and who should not be hospitalized because they are dangerous to themselves are sometimes inconsistent and ambiguous. People who seem to be experiencing similar degrees of danger to themselves may be seen as good candidates for commitment in one case but not in another. Many cases test the very meaning of normality and abnormality that we discussed in Chapter 1. Abnormal by whose standard? Recall that some people believe themselves depressed for good reason, but "society" finds them "mentally ill" and in need of treatment. Others radically alter their lifestyles on discovering a "true religion," but society may designate that discovery as psychotic and commit the discoverer to a psychiatric facility. *Mayock* v. *Martin** illustrated this issue well:

> Mr. Mayock was hospitalized in July 1944 after he had removed his right eye. He was subsequently diagnosed having paranoid schizophrenia, eventually released on probation, and finally discharged three years later. Three days after discharge, Mayock removed his right hand, and was committed once again to the state hospital. At the time of trial, some twenty years later, Mayock was still confined involuntarily to the state hospital with the diagnosis of paranoid schizophrenia.
>
> At his trial, Mayock insisted that there was nothing mysterious or crazy about his self-maiming. Rather, he is a deeply religious man who believes that society's attempts to establish peace by force are entirely misguided. God's way, he says, is to encourage peace through love. If society continues on its present path, many lives will be lost through war. Mayock believes that one man has been chosen to make a peace offering to God: that he, Mayock, is that man, and that it is better for one person to accept a message from God to sacrifice an eye or a hand than it is for society to suffer a great loss of human life.
>
> During the twenty years that he had been hospitalized, Mayock had had complete freedom of the hospital grounds. He had not once maimed himself. Yet, he acknowledged that he would gladly do so again either as a significant freewill offering or in response to divine revelation.

*Mayock v. Martin, 157 Conn, 56, 245A. 2d 574 (1968).

Beyond this single symptom, there was no further evidence that Mayock was disturbed. He had risen to a position of considerable responsibility in the hospital, running the recreation center for parole-privileged patients, as well as the hospital newsstand. There was ample evidence that he could handle financial matters and take care of himself in all other respects.

Psychiatrists at the hospital contended that his prophetic view of himself was "grandiose," that his religious beliefs were "grossly false," and that the diagnosis of paranoid schizophrenia was entirely warranted by the facts. Mayock contended that he is religious, not mentally ill, and that his First Amendment constitutional rights ("Congress shall make no law respecting an establishment of religion or prohibiting the free exercise thereof . . .") had been violated.

Mayock lost. Some will feel that he should have lost, for only the truly mad would gouge out their eyes and chop off their arms. Others will feel that Mayock's loss is tragic, for he was acting with courage upon deeply held religious beliefs and harming no one but himself. Perhaps the tragedy lies in that ambiguity, for Mayock can be seen as quite abnormal by some standards, and not abnormal at all by others.

The use of involuntary hospitalization of people who are believed to be dangerous to themselves is usually guided by the "thank you" test (Stone, 1975). This test asks: Will the person, once recovered, be grateful for that hospitalization, however much it was protested? The test would likely be passed by people who are severely depressed and suicidal and who, once the depression lifted, would be grateful to be alive.

But the informal social conventions that regulate who should and who should not be hospitalized because they are dangerous to themselves are sometimes inconsistent and ambiguous. People who seem to be experiencing similar degrees of danger to themselves may be seen as good candidates for commitment in one case but not in another, as the following two cases demonstrate:

Case 1: Emma Lake. At sixty, Emma Lake was involuntarily committed to St. Elizabeth's Hospital after she was found wandering the streets of Washington, D.C. At the commitment hearing, two psychiatrists testified that she was unable to care adequately for herself. At a subsequent hearing, she was held to be suffering from "chronic brain syndrome with arteriosclerosis (hardening of the arteries). . ." She was prone to "wandering away and being out exposed at night or any time that she is out." On one occasion, it was related, Mrs. Lake left the hospital and was missing for about thirty-two hours. She was brought back after midnight by a policeman who found her wandering the streets. She thought she had only been gone for a few hours, could not tell where she had been, and suffered a minor injury, that she attributed to having been chased by boys.

Mrs. Lake acknowledged that there were times when she lost track of things. Nevertheless, she felt able to be at liberty and willing to run the requisite risks. Her husband and sister were eager for her release and willing to provide a home for her. Moreover, she was willing to endure some form of confinement at home rather than the total confinement of a psychiatric hospital.

Ultimately the court concurred with her psychiatrist and required that she be hospitalized. She spent the last five years of her life in a psychiatric hospital, during the last year of which she received no visitors (Chambers, 1972). Often, family that would willingly provide a home for a patient are unable or unwilling to visit a psychiatric hospital regularly.

Case 2: Robert Jackson. At the age of sixty-two, Justice Robert Jackson suffered a severe heart attack while serving on the United States Supreme Court. The Court's work is arduous and taxing. His doctors gave him the choice between years of comparative (though not, by any means, total) inactivity off the Court, and the risk of death at any time by continuing his work on the Court. Jackson chose to remain on the Court. He suffered a fatal heart attack shortly thereafter.

No court interfered with the Justice's decision, nor was it ever suggested that he was dangerous to himself and therefore in need of psychiatric care. Quite the contrary: his decision to continue the work of the Court was widely praised. Many people would choose to do the same: take their chances with the things they enjoy doing rather than be cooped up, inactively, for the rest of their lives.

What distinguishes Mrs. Lake's case from Justice Jackson's? For both, the choices jeopardized their lives, Jackson's even more than Lake's. Why was Lake involuntarily committed and Jackson never questioned? The major difference between Mrs. Lake's case and Justice Jackson's is that Mrs. Lake's request to live out her years at home, and with people who loved her, was "psychiatrized." That is, her choice was believed to arise from mental illness ("chronic brain syndrome"), while Justice Jackson's was not. The fact that she suffered "chronic brain syndrome" obscured the similarities between her choice and others. If Mrs. Lake's case serves to teach anything, it is that once behavior is described or "explained" in terms of psychological abnormality, it encourages people to think of a different set of "solutions" than they would if it had been explained as the product of rational decision making. Now, it is clearly the case that some psychologically distressed persons suffer thought disorders of such magnitude that they are rarely, if ever, lucid. But that was not the case with Mrs. Lake, nor is it the case for most psychiatric patients, all of whom enjoy long periods of clarity during which they are as capable as others of making significant choices between the risks of liberty and the security of incarceration (Dershowitz, 1968).

In order to understand the thousands of commitments that occur involuntarily, be they cases like that of Mr. Mayock or Mrs. Lake or cases that appear to be more clear-cut instances of mental disorder, we need to know something about the laws that regulate commitment procedures. Our focus will be on laws in the United States.

Procedures to Commit

The issues associated with civil commitment have been dominated by intense controversy historically. Commitment procedures have varied through the years and from state to state. There is no simple federal law concerning commitment procedures, and states differ enormously in the procedures that are used to commit people, and in the safeguards those procedures provide.

COMMITMENT CRITERIA

Three elements remain the same across statutes in all states: In order to be committed, an individual must be (1) mentally disordered, (2) dangerous to self or others, and (3) gravely disabled. In addition, the American Psychiatric Association has proposed a fourth criterion, "likely to suffer substantial mental or physical deterioration," and has been trying to convince state legislatures to include such a criterion in their commitment procedures (American Psychiatric Association, 1983; Monahan and Shah, 1989). This criterion is fundamentally a predictive one that encourages civil commitment when, as evidenced by recent behavior, if not treated, a person will "suffer or continue to suffer severe and abnormal mental, emotional, or physical distress [which] . . . is associated with significant impairment of judgment, reason, or behavior causing a substantial deterioration of his previous ability to function on his own" (APA, 1983, p. 673).

Mental Disorder All states require that an individual be ***mentally disordered,*** that is, suffering from a psychological disability. But definitions of mental disorder vary widely across the states. Perhaps the most thoughtful is that

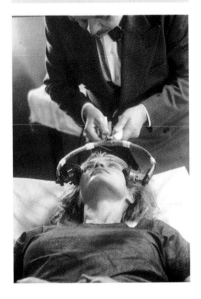

▼ In the movie *Frances*, Jessica Lange plays Frances Farmer, whose involuntary commitment was based on "impaired judgment."

offered by the American Psychiatric Association, which would restrict civil commitment only to those with *severe* mental disorders. A severe mental disorder is defined as "an illness, disease, organic brain disorder, or other condition that (1) substantially impairs the person's thought, perception of reality, emotional process, or judgment, or (2) substantially impairs behavior as manifested by recent disturbed behavior." Roughly speaking, a severe mental disorder corresponds to a psychotic disorder.

Dangerousness to Self or Others   Many states require that there be some evidence that the individual is dangerous, either to himself or to others. And indeed, more involuntary hospitalizations are justified on these grounds than on any others. But here, too, the definition of dangerousness is vague, and regardless of how carefully it is defined, two serious problems arise, one legal and the other scientific. The legal problem is straightforward. Incarcerating people because they are *predicted* to be dangerous creates a dilemma because Western legal traditions generally mandate the deprivation of liberty only *after* a crime has been committed, not before. The mere fact that someone is expected to violate the law is not sufficient reason for incarceration.

The scientific problem is whether dangerousness can ever be predicted so precisely that only the dangerous will be hospitalized, while the not dangerous will not be. Clearly, the ability to predict dangerous behavior lies at the very heart of civilized and rational civil commitment procedures. Yet, over the past two decades scientists have thought the capacity to predict dangerousness more elusive than real (Diamond, 1974; Ennis and Litwack, 1974; Stone, 1975). One of the most interesting of these studies arose out of the case of *Baxstrom* v. *Herold** (Steadman and Keveles, 1972, 1978).

> After serving more than two years for second-degree assault, Johnnie K. Baxstrom was certified as insane by a prison physician and transferred to a prison-hospital. Baxstrom's sentence was about to end, however, but because he was still in need of psychiatric care, the director of the prison-hospital petitioned that Baxstrom be committed involuntarily to an ordinary psychiatric hospital. That petition was denied for administrative reasons. Baxstrom, therefore, was forced to remain where he was.
>
> Baxstrom went to court with the following contention: If he was sane, he deserved to be discharged as soon as he completed his sentence. And if he was not sane, he should be transferred to an ordinary psychiatric hospital. Thus, he argued, his constitutional rights were being violated insofar as he was required to remain in prison beyond the termination of his sentence.

▼ A person society considers dangerous to himself or others may be involuntarily committed. But the definition of "dangerous" may be vague, based on the prediction that a mental patient may behave dangerously in the future, rather than on an act he has already committed.

The United States Supreme Court agreed. And as a result, "Operation Baxstrom," which was designed to effect the rapid release of 967 similarly confined patients from New York State's prison-hospitals, was launched. These people were not merely predicted to be dangerous to others on the basis of their "insanity." They were considered to be ***criminally insane,*** held to be violent now and in the future because they had been violent in the past and because, additionally, they were psychologically distressed. Would those predictions hold up?

In fact, there were abundant false positives—individuals who did not act out violently—as well as false negatives—individuals released as nonviolent who later committed violent crimes. After four years, Steadman and Keveles (1972) reported that only 2.7 percent of those released patients had behaved dangerously and were either in a correctional facility or back in a hospital for the criminally insane. Careful examination of those who were dangerous revealed no "set of factors that could have selected these returnees from all the

*Baxstrom v. Herold, 383 U.S. 107 (1966).

Baxstrom patients without a very large number of false positives" (Steadman, 1973, p. 318).

Recently, however, there have been some improvements in our ability to predict violent behavior (Monahan, 1992). Although past violent behavior may not be an indicator of future violent behavior, many of the mentally disordered who are currently experiencing psychotic symptoms may be dangerous to others (Link, Andrews, and Cullen, 1992; Monahan, 1992). Moreover, some studies have indicated that clinicians, even inexperienced ones, can detect which male patients will become violent toward others, much better than chance and substantially better than they might have predicted had they relied only on the actuarial characteristics (e.g., age, race, and sex) of the patients (Lidz, Mulvey, and Gardner, 1993). (Unfortunately, they did not fare nearly as well in predicting female violent behavior.) Thus, it is not unreasonable for society to ask mental health professionals to attend to those who are believed to be dangerous to others. But such a request makes sense if, and only if, mental health professionals are truly able to predict who will become violent. Until such predictions become much more accurate, involuntary commitment on the basis of dangerousness to others will necessarily be a questionable procedure (Melton, Petrila, Poythress, and Slobogin, 1987; Teplin, Abram, and McClelland, 1994).

Grave Disability   Many states permit commitment of distressed individuals when, as the result of their mental state (and for no other reason), they are unable to provide for their basic needs for food, shelter, clothing, health, and safety. Thus incapacitated, they become "passively dangerous," that is, dangerous to themselves, not because they might actively attempt suicide or mutilation, but because they will not do those things that seem necessary to stay alive and healthy. But where those needs can be met through the willing assistance of relatives, as in the case of Emma Lake (see p. 452), should we deprive people of their liberty?

DUE PROCESS OF LAW

Involuntary commitments are not entirely unlike imprisonment insofar as deprivation of liberty is concerned. Yet, few of the procedures that protect an alleged criminal defendant have been available to the psychologically distressed. They can be involuntarily hospitalized on an emergency basis for as little as twenty-four hours (in Georgia) to as long as twenty-eight days (in Oklahoma), entirely without a trial or judge, and often on the allegation of a spouse or friend. In some jurisdictions, hospitalizations can be extended indefinitely, simply on the word of a physician who deems the individual in need of further observation or treatment. And even when the matter is subjected to judicial review, the courts often rubber-stamp the physician's view, on the grounds that the hospitalization is being undertaken with the patient's best interests in mind. Thus, at many such judicial reviews, the patient need not be present, and commonly is not afforded an attorney. Many writers, and especially psychiatrist Thomas Szasz (1963), see in the involuntary commitment process an enormous and needless abuse of constitutional protection. Yet, no "plot" to deprive patients of their rights is intended in these procedures. Rather, because patients are held to be "sick," and because they are being sent to a hospital, the ordinary protections that are accorded to those who have been accused of committing a crime have not been deemed necessary.

It seems only reasonable, however, to provide the psychologically distressed with the same privileges that are given to anyone whose liberty is threatened by state action—to criminal defendants, for example. These rights and privileges are collectively called "due process of law" and include:

- The right to be notified of trial in a timely manner
- The right to trial by jury
- The right to be present at one's own trial
- The right to legal counsel and the appointment of counsel in a timely manner
- The right to exclude unreliable evidence, such as hearsay evidence, from the testimony
- The right to challenge witnesses
- The privilege against self-incrimination
- The right to counsel at all interviews, including psychiatric interviews
- The right to know, with considerable precision, which laws one has violated and under which laws one stands accused.

STANDARD OF PROOF

FOCUS QUESTIONS

1. What are the three standards of proof available in law and which standard did the Supreme Court decide should be used in cases of involuntary commitment?
2. What rights do the courts believe should be accorded to patients who have been involuntarily committed?
3. What is the usual duration of civil commitment and what are the alternatives to hospitalization of those who are mentally disordered?
4. Describe the patients' rights movement.

In order to commit an individual involuntarily, and so restrict a person's freedom, one must prove that, in accord with the law, he or she belongs in a psychiatric hospital. Mere allegation is insufficient. What standard of proof should be required? Generally speaking, three standards of proof are available in law: preponderance of evidence, beyond a reasonable doubt, and clear and convincing proof.

Often called the 51 percent standard, the ***preponderance of evidence*** standard requires just enough proof to shift the weight of evidence to one side. This is the standard used in civil cases, where penalties are often monetary and do not involve deprivation of liberty.

Beyond a reasonable doubt is the most severe standard of proof and requires that the evidence be so compelling as to convince a reasonable listener beyond a reasonable doubt. This standard is used in criminal law, where the presumption of a defendant's innocence is very strong, and the cost of wrongful incarceration of an innocent person high indeed. It is often termed the 90 percent or 99 percent standard, implying that the weight of evidence must be such that people would be willing to stake high odds on the guilt of the defendant.

Clear and convincing proof is an intermediate standard that is not quite so severe as that requiring proof beyond a reasonable doubt, but not as lenient as the 51 percent standard that requires the mere preponderance of evidence. Consider it the 75 percent standard. In *Addington* v. *Texas,** the U.S. Supreme Court decided in 1979 that the presentation of clear and convincing evidence is the minimum standard for involuntary commitment and that states may not commit below this minimum standard (though they are free to fix standards that are higher than this required minimum).

The Right to Treatment

What rights do people have after they have been committed? Is there a "right to treatment" for those who have been deprived of their liberty, presumably because they required psychiatric treatment? Oddly, and with few exceptions, the courts have been very cautious on this matter. They are understandably reluctant to invent new "rights." Yet, deprivation of liberty is a serious matter in a democratic society, and the courts have occasionally been responsive to cases in which hospitalization has occurred without the person receiving adequate treatment. Thus, in *Rouse* v. *Cameron,*† Judge David Bazelon clearly enunciated a right to treatment that was rooted in federal statute. He wrote:

*Addington v. Texas, 99 S. Ct. 1804 (1979).
†Rouse v. Cameron, 373 F. 2d 451 (D.C. Cir. 1966).

▲ Conditions such as the starkness of this environment caused the courts to stipulate minimal objective standards of care in psychiatric hospitals.

The purpose of involuntary hospitalization is treatment, not punishment . . . absent treatment, the hospital is transform[ed] . . . into a penitentiary where one could be held indefinitely for no convicted offense. . . . The hospital need not show that the treatment will cure or improve him but only that there is a bona fide effort to do so. This requires the hospital to show that initial and periodic inquiries are made into the needs and conditions of the patient with a view to providing suitable treatment for him. . . . Treatment that has therapeutic value for some may not have such value for others. For example, it may not be assumed that confinement in a hospital is beneficial "environment therapy" for all. (*Rouse v. Cameron*, 1966, pp. 453, 456)

In *Wyatt v. Stickney,** Judge Frank Johnson insisted that the constitutional right to treatment is accorded to every person who has been involuntarily hospitalized. He therefore stipulated minimal objective standards of care, standards, by the way, that were far below those recommended by the American Psychiatric Association. Thus, he required that for every 250 patients, there should be at least two psychiatrists, three additional physicians, twelve registered nurses, ninety attendants, four psychologists, and seven social workers. While these may seem a large number of personnel for every 250 patients, remember that patients are in the hospital twenty-four hours a day, seven days a week, and that personnel are needed to take care of them on a continuous basis. Johnson also made clear that patients have a right to privacy and dignity and that each patient is entitled to an individual treatment plan, and to periodic review of his or her plan and progress.

Judge Bazelon's and Judge Johnson's opinions have been hailed by civil libertarians and mental health professionals alike as major steps forward in the treatment of the psychologically distressed. Although other courts have not concurred that there is a right to treatment, these opinions have had far-reaching effects (see Box 14–1).

Opinions written in such cases as *Rouse* v. *Cameron* and *Wyatt* v. *Stickney* have alerted people to the plight of psychiatric patients, and promise to improve their fate. But unfortunately, they have also had a major unintended consequence. Faced with the prospect of pouring more money into psychiatric care, many states have taken the least expensive route and have simply discharged patients from psychiatric hospitals, and closed the hospitals. During the seventies, for example, California closed a majority of its psychiatric hospitals and cut back severely on funding of mental health programs. Other states followed suit. As a result, thousands of people who were formerly housed in psychiatric hospitals were shunted to "board and care" homes in local communities. The new visibility of these people has frequently created a harsh and angry community reaction. The powerful stigma associated with those labeled mentally ill, and particularly the violence and unpredictability that is often erroneously attributed to mental patients, creates enormous community fear and backlash.

The Patients' Rights Movement

The wholesale release of patients into the community has had some positive effects. In many communities, former psychiatric patients have established self-help organizations which, in addition to providing social networks and employment opportunities, also have given the mentally ill a political base. A Presidential Commission on Mental Health, appointed by President Carter in 1978, led to the passage of Section 501 of the Mental

*Wyatt v. Stickney, 344 F. Supp. 343 (M.D. Ala. 1972).

Box 14-1

IN THE JURIST'S NOTEBOOK

KENNETH DONALDSON'S SAGA

Perhaps Kenneth Donaldson needed treatment. But did he get it?

Kenneth Donaldson was already forty-eight years old when his parents, themselves in their seventies, petitioned for his commitment to Florida State Hospital at Chattahoochee. His life had not been an easy one until then, Donaldson frankly points out in his book, *Insanity Inside Out* (1976). He had had one psychiatric hospitalization of three-months' duration some thirteen years earlier. It was a hospitalization that followed him, and marred his life subsequently. Afterwards, his marriage had failed, his relationship with his children had cooled, he had had difficulty holding a job, and sometimes he had felt that people were out to get him. But he was not dangerous to himself, had never been dangerous to others (although his father had alleged he was in order to get him committed), and he emphatically did not want to be committed to Chattahoochee. One hospitalization was more than enough.

The judge who committed Donaldson told him that he would be in the hospital for "a few weeks." A progress note written less than three months after he was admitted indicated that he appeared to be in remission. And because his first hospitalization had been brief, there was every reason to expect this one to be brief too. Nevertheless, Donaldson remained in Florida State Hospital for fourteen-and-a-half years.

Donaldson is a Christian Scientist. Medication and electric shock treatments were both offered to him, but he refused them on religious grounds. What care and treatment did he get then? None. He rarely saw Drs. O'Connor or Gumanis, his physicians, and then only

▲ Kenneth Donaldson after the Supreme Court ruled in his favor.

briefly. Grounds privileges and occupational therapy were denied him during the first ten years of his hospitalization. Some six years after he had been hospitalized, Helping Hands, Inc., a reputable organization that operates halfway houses for mental patients, offered to care for Donaldson. But his psychiatrist, Dr. O'Connor, refused to release him to anyone but his parents. By this time, his parents were too old and infirm to accept that responsibility, and presumably Dr. O'Connor knew that. Finally, a college friend made four separate attempts to have Donaldson released in his custody. His requests were either refused outright or frustrated.

During this period, Donaldson smuggled letters out of the hospital to anyone who might help. Often, however, mail sent through hospital channels would be opened or simply thrown out. Donaldson's teenage daughter wrote, "Daddy, I know you are not sick. But why don't you write?" "I was writing," Donaldson says. "Then her letters stopped" (Donaldson, 1976, p. 84). As a result, he acquired a reputation for being a difficult person. But he had much to be difficult about. Day after day was spent in a locked crowded room with sixty other people, nearly one-third of whom had undergone criminal commitments. At night, some of the patients would have fits. It was frightening. Some of the beds in this crowded room were so close together that they touched. Donaldson lived in constant fear that someone would jump him during the night.

Donaldson sought the help of the Mental Health Law Project, a Washington, D.C., group of lawyers who serve the legal needs of the mentally distressed. And, finally, in 1971, Donaldson sued for his release and for damages from Drs. O'Connor and Gumanis, alleging "intentional, malicious, and reckless disregard of Donaldson's constitutional rights." The jury awarded Donaldson compensatory and punitive damages from both physicians. The physicians appealed, and the case went up to the Supreme Court, where many of the justices were simply outraged over Donaldson's incarceration (Woodward and Armstrong, 1979). On January 26, 1975, the Court unanimously wrote in *O'Connor* v. *Donaldson*:

A state cannot constitutionally confine . . . a nondangerous individual who is capable of surviving safely in freedom by himself or with the help of willing and responsible family members or friends.*

*O'Connor v. Donaldson, 422 U.S. 563, 95 S.Ct 2486 (1975).

Health Systems Act of 1980, otherwise known as the Patients' Bill of Rights (see Box 14-2). While this law is only advisory in nature, most states provide at least some of those rights, and some states provide all of them.

Box 14–2

SUMMARY OF THE PATIENTS' BILL OF RIGHTS

The right to appropriate treatment and related services in a setting which is most supportive and least restrictive of a person's liberty.

The right to an individualized, written treatment or service plan.

The right, consistent with one's capabilities, to participate in and receive a reasonable explanation of the care and treatment process.

The right not to receive treatment without informed, voluntary, written consent, except in a documented emergency or as permitted under applicable law for someone who has been civilly committed.

The right not to participate in experimentation in the absence of informed, voluntary, written consent.

The right to be free from restraint or seclusion except in an emergency situation pursuant to a contemporaneous written order by a responsible mental health professional.

The right to a humane treatment environment that affords reasonable protection from harm and appropriate privacy.

The right to confidentiality of personal records.

The right to have access to personal mental health records and have a lawyer or legal representative have reasonable access to records if the patient provides written authorization.

The right to private conversations, to reasonable access to telephones and mail, and to visitation during regular visiting hours.

The right to timely and meaningful information about one's rights at the time of and after admission.

The right to assert grievances with regard to the infringement of rights.

The right to have a fair, timely, and impartial grievance procedure provided.

The right of access to, including private communications with, any available rights protection service or qualified advocate.

The right to exercise other rights without reprisal, including denial of appropriate treatment.

The right to referral as appropriate to other providers of mental health services upon discharge.

The right to confidentiality of and access to records continues following one's discharge.

The patient has a right that his attorney or legal representative has reasonable access to the patient/client, the facility at which the patient resides, and, with written authorization, the patient's medical and service records.

SOURCE: Adapted from the Mental Health Systems Act, 1980.

To assure that the rights of the mentally ill are protected, former patients, their families, and others have joined to form a network of patients' rights advocates, such as NAMI (National Alliance for the Mentally Ill) or CAMI (California Alliance for the Mentally Ill). These advocates work for changes in state laws, monitor mental health facilities, and in some cases, provide legal representation for patients. Their efforts have resulted in considerable improvement in the conditions under which patients are housed and treated.

CRIMINAL COMMITMENT

Involuntary commitment is sometimes called *civil commitment,* the process used to hospitalize people who have committed no crime. *Criminal commitment,* on the other hand, refers to the coerced psychiatric hospitalization of people who have acted harmfully but are not legally responsible because they lack a "guilty mind" or *mens rea.* "Where there is no *mens* (i.e., mind) there can be no *mens rea*" the legal maxim goes (Fingarette and Hasse,

1979, p. 200). In the eyes of the law, such people are insane, and the legal defense used in their cases is called the ***insanity defense.***

The Insanity Defense

The insanity defense requires that the defendant was wholly or partially irrational *when the crime took place,* and that this irrationality affected his or her behavior. The psychologist or psychiatrist who serves as an expert witness in this matter is required to reconstruct the defendant's state of mind as it was before and during the crime. This is not a simple task. If diagnostic opinions are often unreliable for *present* behavior, as we saw in Chapter 4, how much more unreliable are they for speculative reconstructions of the past? No wonder, then, that experts for the defense are often contradicted by equally capable experts for the prosecution, and that judges and jurors will disagree on the defendant's state of mind when he committed the crime (Low, Jeffries, and Bonnie, 1986).

Popular opinion notwithstanding, the insanity defense is not widely used. It is invoked in fewer than 1 out of 400 homicide cases that come to trial, even more rarely in nonhomicide trials. And it is successful in many fewer cases than that, mainly by agreement between the prosecutor and defense attorneys. Even when successful, it usually leads to long-term incarceration in an institution for the criminally insane, a fate sometimes worse than incarceration in prison. Nevertheless the role and meaning of the insanity defense is one of the most hotly debated issues in criminal law. Why should that be?

The insanity defense is the exception that proves the rule: the notion that each of us is responsible for his or her behavior is strengthened by the recognition that some of us patently are not (Stone, 1975; Rosenhan, 1983). Below are three cases in which the insanity defense has been used (adapted from Livermore and Meehl, 1967). Is there *mens rea* in each of these defendants?*

Case 1: The Pigtail Snipper. Victor Weiner, a hair fetishist, was charged with assault for snipping off a girl's pigtail while standing on a crowded bus. His experience before cutting off the pigtail (which was corroborated by psychiatric testi-

*51 Minn L. Rev. 789, 833–55 (1967).

mony and by an acquaintance with whom he had discussed this problem several days earlier) was one of mounting tension, accompanied by a feeling that was close to anxiety and erotic excitement. He made various efforts to distract himself and place himself in situations where he would be safe from performing this act, but finally he gave in to the impulse and boarded the bus with a pair of scissors in his pocket. Victor was diagnosed "sociopathic personality disturbance, sexual deviation, fetishism."

Case 2: The Axe-handle Murderer. Arthur Wolff, a fifteen-year-old, was charged with murdering his mother.* During the year preceding the crime, Wolff "spent a lot of time thinking about sex." He made a list of the names and addresses of seven girls in his community whom he planned to anesthetize and then either rape or photograph nude. One night, about three weeks before the murder, he took a container of ether and attempted to enter the house of one of these girls through the chimney. But he became wedged in and had to be rescued. In the ensuing weeks, Wolff apparently decided that he would have to bring the girls to his house to achieve his sexual purposes, and that it would therefore be necessary to get his mother (and possibly his brother) out of the way first.

On the Friday or Saturday before he murdered his mother, Wolff obtained an axe handle from the family garage and hid it under the mattress of his bed. On Sunday, he took the axe handle from its hiding place and approached his mother from behind, raising the weapon to strike her. She sensed his presence and asked him what he was doing; he answered that it was "nothing," and returned to his room and hid the axe handle under his mattress again. The following morning, Wolff ate the breakfast that his mother had prepared, went to his room, and took the axe handle from its hiding place. He returned to the kitchen, approached his mother from behind, and struck her on the back of the head. She turned around screaming. He hit her several more times, and they fell to the floor fighting. He got up to turn off the water running in the sink, and she fled through the dining room. He gave chase, caught her in the front room, and choked her to death with his hands.

Wolff then took off his shirt and hung it by the fire, washed the blood off his face and hands, read a few lines from the Bible or prayer book lying upon the dining room table, and walked down to the police station to turn himself in. He told the desk officer, "I have something I wish to report . . . I just killed my mother with an axe handle." The officer testified that Wolff spoke in a quiet voice and that "his conversation was quite coherent in what he was saying and he answered everything I asked him right to a T."

At his trial, four expert witnesses testified that Arthur Wolff had been suffering from schizophrenia when he murdered his mother.

Case 3: The Delusional Informer. Calvin Ellery was a paranoid schizophrenic who experienced delusions and hallucinations, and who believed that the Masons were plotting to take over the government. He believed, moreover, that the Masons had learned that he was aware of their intentions, and that because he was a potential informer, the Masons had determined to do away with him.

As a result of delusional misinterpretation of certain things he had heard on a news broadcast, Ellery believed that "today is the day for his execution." When a salesman with a Masonic button on his lapel came to the front door, he was sure that the salesman had been sent to kill him. When the salesman reached into his pocket for his business card, Ellery was convinced that he was reaching for a revolver. Ellery drew his own weapon and shot first in self-defense.

What determines if the insanity defense can be used (see Table 14–1)? When is a person considered to be so insane that criminal law does not apply? Because the answer to these questions is crucial to the very meaning of criminal law, the questions themselves have generated hot dispute. Historically, there have been three views of the insanity defense: the M'Naghten

*People v. Wolff, 61 Cal. 2d 795, 800.

TABLE 14–1

			ACQUITTAL UNDER THE VARIOUS INSANITY DEFENSES			
Case	Diagnosis	M'Naghten "right-wrong" test	Durham "product of mental disease" test	American Law Institute (ALI) "appreciate and conform" test	Guilty but mentally ill	Insanity Defense Reform Act
Victor Weiner (Pigtail snipper)	Fetishist	Guilty—he knew it was wrong.	Not guilty—fetishism is a mental disease according to DSM-IV.	Maybe—depends on court's assessment of his ability to conform his conduct to law.	Guilty	Guilty
Arthur Wolff (Axe-handle murderer)	Schizophrenic	Guilty—he knew it was wrong.	Probably acquitted—if he were not schizophrenic, he probably would not have murdered.	Probably guilty if *affectively*, he knew murder was wrong.	Guilty	Guilty
Calvin Ellery (Delusional informer)	Paranoid schizophrenic	Not guilty—he thought he was shooting in self-defense.	Not guilty—the killing was clearly the product of his delusions.	Not guilty—he could not appreciate the criminality of his conduct.	Guilty	Not guilty

rule, the Durham test, and the American Law Institute rule. And recently, under the Insanity Defense Reform Act, another standard has been introduced (see Figure 14–1).

M'NAGHTEN: THE "COGNITIVE" FORMULA

In 1843, Daniel M'Naghten came to London for the purpose of killing Sir Robert Peel, the British Prime Minister. In so doing, M'Naghten was responding to a "voice of God," which had instructed him to kill the Prime Minister. Peel, however, was traveling with Queen Victoria on that day, and Edward Drummond, Peel's secretary, was in the Prime Minister's carriage. Drummond caught M'Naghten's bullet and was killed.

The trial was remarkable in that M'Naghten's defense counsel relied heavily on *Medical Jurisprudence of Insanity* (1838), a recently published work by Dr. Isaac Ray. M'Naghten, the defense counsel argued, was clearly deranged, in that he suffered delusions of persecution (and, in modern terms, command hallucinations). It was one of the first times that psychiatric testimony had been permitted in a murder trial, and the judges were so impressed that the Lord Chief Justice practically directed a verdict for M'Naghten. But subsequently, Queen Victoria, who had been subject to attempted assassination three times in the preceding two years, called in the Lord Chief Justice, as well as the other fourteen justices, and reproved them. They buckled quickly and wrote what has since been known as the **M'Naghten rule,** under which Daniel M'Naghten would clearly have been convicted! According to that rule,

FIGURE 14–1

QUESTIONS IN AN INSANITY-DEFENSE TRIAL

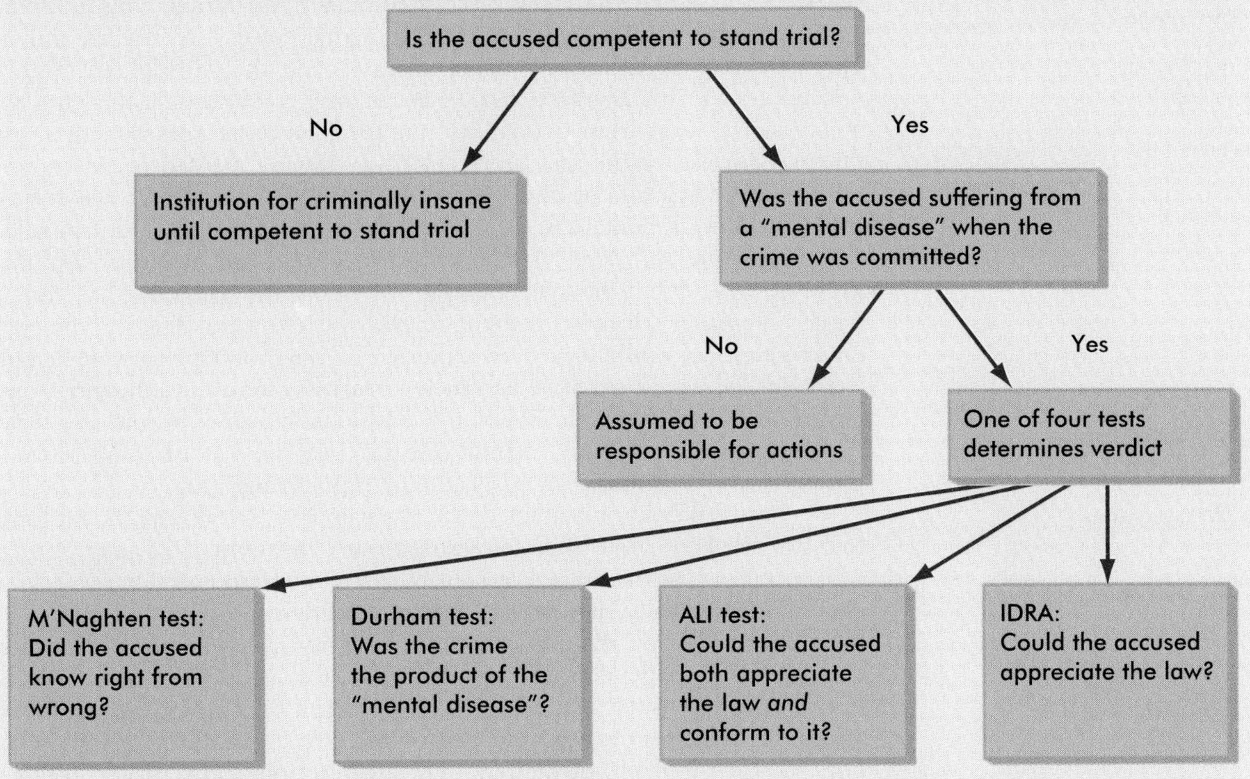

Is the accused competent to stand trial?

No

Institution for criminally insane until competent to stand trial

Yes

Was the accused suffering from a "mental disease" when the crime was committed?

No

Assumed to be responsible for actions

Yes

One of four tests determines verdict

M'Naghten test:
Did the accused know right from wrong?

Durham test:
Was the crime the product of the "mental disease"?

ALI test:
Could the accused both appreciate the law *and* conform to it?

IDRA:
Could the accused appreciate the law?

There are four standards that determine if an insanity defense can be used. The M'Naghten, Durham, and ALI (American Law Institute) tests are used by different states; IDRA (the Insanity Defense Reform Act) is the current federal standard and is being advocated by many as the standard for the states.

It must be clearly proved that, at the time of the committing of the act, the party accused was laboring under such a defect of reason, from disease of the mind, as not to know the nature and quality of the act he was doing; or, if he did know it, that he did not know he was doing what was wrong.

The M'Naghten test is widely used in the United States. Nearly half of the states use it alone as the yardstick for insanity, while other states use the M'Naghten rule in conjunction with other rules. It is a relatively narrow test, which relies merely on whether the accused suffered "a disease of the mind," what he understood about the nature of his actions, and whether he understood that those actions were wrong. But while the test is narrow, it taxes everything we have learned about abnormal psychology. What, for example, are diseases of the mind? Do they really exist, or are they simply metaphoric? And how do we know whether someone understood his actions when he attempted murder, and whether he knew that murder was "wrong"?

Under the M'Naghten rule, only Calvin Ellery, the delusional informer, would be acquitted, for only he clearly did not "know the nature and quality of the act he was doing," believing that he was acting in justifiable self-defense. The axe-handle murderer's behavior was clearly bizarre, yet because there was no evidence that he failed to distinguish right from wrong, he could not be acquitted according to the M'Naghten rule. Similarly, Weiner, the pigtail snipper, though clearly disturbed and seemingly caught up in an impulse that ultimately overcame his best efforts at suppression, could not be acquitted under the M'Naghten rule. He, too, knew right from wrong.

In *Durham* v. *United States*,* Judge David Bazelon broadened the insanity defense to state that "an accused is not criminally responsible if his unlawful act was the product of mental disease or mental defect." Notice the difference between the Durham "mental disease" and the M'Naghten "right-wrong" test. In the **Durham test,** incapacitating conditions, such as the inability to tell right from wrong, are not specified. One goes directly from "mental disease" to the act (Brooks, 1974a), leaving it to advanced knowledge in psychiatry and psychology to determine whether the act was or was not a product of mental disease or mental defect. Under the Durham rule, the axe-handle murderer would probably have been acquitted on the grounds that, absent his schizophrenic condition, he would not have murdered his mother. Likewise, defining fetishism as a "mental disease," the pig-tail snipper, too, would have been acquitted on the grounds that were he not a fetishist, he would not have had such a prurient interest in little girls' pigtails. And of course, Calvin Ellery, the delusional informer, would also have been acquitted under the "mental disease" test (he was paranoid schizophrenic), as well as under the M'Naghten "right-wrong" test.

As Justice Bazelon maintained, the Durham rule was an experiment, one that extended for some eighteen years, from 1954 until 1972, and during which time, a view of criminal responsibility and nonresponsibility was developed. Fundamentally, the Durham rule was withdrawn for two reasons: (1) it relied too heavily on the expert testimony of psychiatrists, rendering judge and jury wholly dependent upon psychiatric testimony for the determination of criminal responsibility, and (2) it was as difficult then as it is now to know and attain agreement about what constituted a "mental disease." The metaphor itself left much to be desired, implying a distinct and verifiable organic state. Moreover, one could never be sure which of the disorders listed in the *Diagnostic and Statistical Manual of Mental Disorders* qualified. Should stuttering, tobacco dependence, and sociopathy all be considered mental diseases that can produce unlawful acts? The seeming breadth of the Durham rule created problems that were difficult to adjudicate and that ultimately led to its near demise. Only one state, New Hampshire, still uses the Durham test.

THE AMERICAN LAW INSTITUTE (ALI) RULE: "APPRECIATE AND CONFORM"

In *United States* v. *Brawner*,† some eighteen years after the *Durham* case, the Durham mental disease test was succeeded by a modification of the insanity defense that had earlier been propounded by the American Law Institute (ALI). That rule is considerably more specific than the Durham rule, and yet not so narrow as the M'Naghten rule. It states:

1. A person is not responsible for criminal conduct if, at the time of such conduct, as a result of mental disease or defect, he lacks substantial capacity either to appreciate the criminality (wrongfulness) of his conduct or to conform his conduct to the requirements of law.
2. As used in the Article, the terms "mental disease or defect" do not include an abnormality manifested only by repeated criminal or otherwise antisocial conduct. (American Law Institute, 1985, p. 62)

In the *Brawner* case, the court tried to narrow the meaning of "mental disease." Citing an earlier case,‡ it wrote:

---

*Durham v. United States, 214 F. 2d 862 (D.C. Cir. 1954).
†United States v. Brawner, 471 F. 2d 969 (D.C. Dir. 1972).
‡McDonald v. United States, 312 F. 3d 847 (D.C. Cir. 1962).

[A] mental disease or defect includes any abnormal condition of the mind which substantially affects mental or emotional processes and substantially impairs behavior controls.

The **ALI rule,** as modified in the *Brawner* case, is used in twenty-one state courts. Under that standard, Calvin Ellery would, of course, be acquitted. Convinced that the Masons were plotting both to take over the government and assassinate him, Ellery clearly lacked "substantial capacity . . . to appreciate the criminality (wrongfulness) of his conduct." The verdict with regard to Victor Weiner, the pigtail snipper, would depend on whether the court was willing and able to assess the strength of Weiner's desire and, therefore, his ability "to conform his conduct to the requirements of law."

The outcome of the case of Arthur Wolff, who murdered his mother because she seemed in the way of his sexual schemes, depends wholly on how a jury would interpret the word *appreciate* in the section of the ALI rule that says ". . . he lacks substantial capacity . . . to appreciate the criminality (wrongfulness) of his conduct. . . ." Wolff "knew" he did wrong in killing his mother, for he confessed immediately at the police station. But did he really *appreciate* that this was wrong? Did he "feel it in his heart" affectively, or did he merely "know" cognitively? If the latter, he would be acquitted under the ALI rule. If the former, he would be convicted of murdering his mother.

THE INSANITY DEFENSE REFORM ACT

On June 21, 1982, a federal jury found John W. Hinckley, Jr., not guilty by reason of insanity in his attempted assassination of President Reagan. The jury's verdict was based on its perception that Hinckley was unable "to conform his conduct to the requirements of the law," which is the "volitional" standard of the ALI rule. But the public was outraged about that verdict. Only three days after the jury acquitted Hinckley, the Subcommittee on Criminal Law of the Committee of the Judiciary of the United States Senate began hearings on limiting the insanity defense. And over the next two and a half years, similar hearings were conducted in the legislative hearing rooms of many states.

At issue was the volitional prong (whether the criminal impulse could be resisted) of the ALI standard. Was it truly an *irresistible* impulse, or simply an impulse not resisted? Whether volition itself was a useful notion was a matter about which psychologists and psychiatrists could not agree, raising serious

▶ John Hinckley, Jr., successfully used the insanity defense at his trial for the attempted assassination of former President Ronald Reagan.

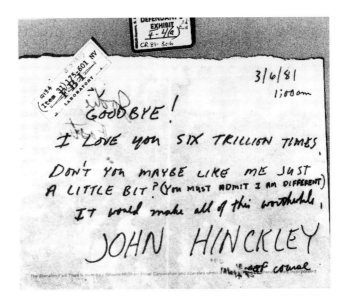

questions about whether the law should even include it. Ultimately, in 1984, President Reagan signed the Insanity Defense Reform Act, which eliminated the volitional prong of the insanity defense in federal courts. The new federal standard states that:

> It is an affirmative defense to a prosecution under any federal statute that, at the time of the commission of the acts constituting the offense, the defendant, as a result of a severe mental disease or defect, was unable to appreciate the nature and quality or the wrongfulness of his acts. Mental disease or defect does not otherwise constitute a defense.

It had previously been the task of the prosecution to prove sanity, and sanity of course is very difficult to prove. With the new federal standard, the burden of proving by clear and convincing evidence that the defendant was insane, and hence not responsible for his actions, was placed on the defendant.

GUILTY BUT MENTALLY ILL (GBMI)

Perhaps as the result of public perceptions that defendants are "beating the rap" by entering insanity pleas, some states have abolished the "not guilty by reason of insanity" verdict, replacing it with the verdict of "guilty but mentally ill" (GBMI). A finding that a defendant is guilty but mentally ill results in commitment to a mental institution rather than to a prison.

The GBMI verdict is an instance of a legislative rush to action, and it is mistaken on at least two counts. In the first place, the insanity defense is rarely invoked and much more rarely successful. The public impression of its usefulness arises nearly wholly from sensational news stories, not from accurate estimates of incidence. Moreover, the GBMI verdict is a contradiction in its own terms. In order to be guilty, one needs to have been able to form a morally coherent intent to harm. But mental illness exonerates one precisely because one is held to be *unable* to form such an intent. How then can one be simultaneously guilty and mentally ill?

Clearly, enormous effort has gone into defining the meaning of insanity and limiting its effects in criminal trials. But that effort has not yet paid off in terms of outcome. Regardless of which definition of insanity is used, people seem to convict and acquit in pretty much the same proportions (James, 1959; Finkel, 1989; Steadman, McGreevy, Morrissey, Callahan, Robbins, and Cirincione, 1993). One possible reason for this disappointing outcome is that the law typically gives jurors only two choices: guilty (for whatever reason), or not guilty (for whatever reason). But when jurors in simulated trials were permitted to distinguish among several shades and types of insanity, they were considerably more able to tailor their verdicts to the requirements of law (Finkel, 1990, 1991).

Competence to Stand Trial

For every defendant found not guilty by reason of insanity, at least a hundred defendants are found incompetent to stand trial and are sent to institutions for the criminally insane until they are able to be tried (Bacon, 1969). The average confinement of people committed as incompetent is 6.4 months (Steadman, Monahan, Hartstone, Davis, and Robbins, 1982). Yet, it occasionally happens that people alleged to be incompetent to stand trial are remanded to institutions for the criminally insane for decades, and simply forgotten. At one such institution, three people were incarcerated for forty-two, thirty-nine, and seventeen years respectively—this, before any determination of their guilt had been made (McGarry and Bendt, 1969)! In the case below, the man was locked up for sixty-eight years:

▲ Junius Wilson, declared insane and incarcerated for 68 years for a crime of which he was never convicted, after his release at the age of 96.

Black and deaf, Junius Wilson was confined for sixty-eight years to the locked ward of Cherry Hospital, a psychiatric institution located in Goldsboro, NC. In 1925, when he was twenty-eight years old, he was charged with assault with the intent to commit rape. He was never convicted of that (or any other) criminal offense. In fact, the charge was eventually dropped. Moreover, there is no evidence that he was ever insane. Nevertheless, he was declared insane and committed to what was then the state insane asylum for black people. Before he entered the hospital, the State had him castrated.

In 1970, hospital authorities realized that Mr. Wilson was perfectly sane and that he did not belong in the hospital. But by then, he had lived in Cherry Hospital for more than forty years. His family could not be found. And it was by no means clear that freeing him then would have improved his life. Living in a psychiatric hospital is not ideal preparation for living outside of it. So he remained on the locked ward, although he was given "privileges."

In 1991, John Wasson was appointed Wilson's legal guardian and social worker. Once he learned that Wilson was not insane, Wasson worked to get Wilson out of the locked ward of the hospital. Wasson threatened to sue the state for Wilson's release. It took three years, but in February 1994, North Carolina renovated a cottage on hospital grounds, and the ninety-six-year-old Wilson occupied it. A free man at last, Wilson could pass the rest of his life outside the locked psychiatric ward.

What does "incompetent to stand trial" mean? Most statutory definitions are similar to New York's, which defines an "incompetent person" as one "who as a result of mental disease or defect lacks capacity to understand the proceedings against him or to assist in his own defense."* The intent of the statute is noble, growing out of the English common law tradition that forbids a trial in absentia. While the defendant may be physically present, when he is judged incompetent to stand trial, he is believed to be *psychologically absent,* and the trial is delayed until he can participate in his own defense.

Until 1972, there were no limits on *how long* people could be committed until judged competent to stand trial. What if they would *never* be competent to stand trial? Such a dilemma arose tragically in *Jackson* v. *Indiana.*†

Theon Jackson was a mentally defective deaf-mute. He could not read, write, or otherwise communicate except through limited sign language. In May, 1968, at the age of twenty-seven, Jackson was charged with separate robberies of two women, both of which robberies were alleged to have occurred in the previous July. The first robbery involved a purse and its contents; the total value was four dollars. The second concerned five dollars in cash. Jackson entered a plea of not guilty through his attorney.

Had he been convicted, Jackson would likely have received a sentence of sixty days. But he could not be tried because, in accord with Indiana law, Jackson was examined by two psychiatrists who found that he lacked the intellectual and communicative skills to participate in his own defense, and that the prognosis for acquiring them was dim indeed. Moreover, Jackson's interpreter testified that Indiana had no facilities that could help someone as badly off as Jackson to learn minimal communication skills. The trial court, therefore, found that Jackson "lack[ed] comprehension sufficient to make his defense," and ordered him committed until the Indiana Department of Mental Health certified that the "defendant is sane."

Jackson's attorney filed for a new trial, contending that Jackson was not insane, but that because his mental retardation was so severe, he could never attain competence to stand trial. Jackson's commitment under these circumstances amounted to a life sentence without his ever having been convicted of a crime! By the time the case reached the U. S. Supreme Court, Jackson had already been "hospitalized"

*New York Criminal Code S730.10(1) (1993).
†Jackson v. Indiana, 406 U.S. 715 (1972).

for three and a half years. Justice Blackmun, writing for a unanimous court, concurred with Jackson's attorney that Indiana's rule was unconstitutional. Jackson was freed.

Theon Jackson's case resolved one issue—that a person who would never be competent to stand trial could not be detained indefinitely. Many others are still unresolved. What of a person who might some day be competent to stand trial? How long may he or she be held? Some states set no limits. Other states limit the duration of hospitalization to the time of the maximum sentence the individual would have received if he had been competent to stand trial and found guilty. Others, like New York, limit incarceration, depending upon the charge. Federal courts require release after eighteen months. But do even those limited periods violate a person's right to bail and to a speedy trial? And should they count against time served if convicted? Can a person be required to take medications against his or her will in order to be competent to stand trial? Practices in these matters vary enormously across states and are unlikely to be systematically resolved in the near future because such defendants, by definition, often lack the resources to press their claims vigorously.

As a result, some have urged that the notion of incompetence to stand trial be abolished on the grounds that even if impaired, the defendant is better off tried. "Withholding trial often results in an endless prolongation of the incompetent defendant's accused status, and his virtually automatic civil commitment. This is a cruelly ironic way by which to ensure that the permanently incompetent defendant is fairly treated" (Burt and Morris, 1972, p. 75). This view, however, violates the Supreme Court's dictum in *Pate* v. *Robinson* that "the conviction of an accused person while he is legally incompetent violated due process . . ."*

PSYCHOLOGICAL ISSUES AND THE LAW

Commitment proceedings and the insanity defense are not the only areas in which the law and abnormal psychology intersect. Questions about the nature of responsibility and about the validity of evidence can arise in cases involving multiple personality disorder as well as those involving "recovered memories." The legal system can easily be abused by individuals trying to fake diagnoses to avoid punishment. Moreover, experts can be used by families or companies or political leaders to make psychological diagnoses that support their needs, perhaps for inheritance purposes or for the control of dissidents. This neither invalidates the legal system nor psychological assessment, but it does require us to take special care to evaluate evidence, recognize inconsistencies, and try to avoid error.

Multiple Personality Disorder and the Courts

Ordinarily, when someone is accused of a crime, at issue is whether the person committed the crime or not. But consider the following case, where the accused person claimed to have multiple personality disorder (now called dissociative identity disorder):

James Carlson stood trial for rape, theft, forgery and kidnapping. He claimed that he had eleven different personalities and was suffering from a multiple personality

*Pate v. Robinson, 383 U.S. 375, 378 (1966).

James Carlson took the witness stand dressed as a woman during his 1994 trial in Arizona. He pleaded not guilty on the grounds that he suffered from multiple personality disorder and that his other personalities had committed his crimes. He was later found to be faking MPD.

FOCUS QUESTIONS

1. What are the problems that arise when a person who claims to have multiple personalities is on trial for a crime?
2. What are recovered memories?
3. What is the delayed discovery doctrine?
4. What are some of the legal problems surrounding the recovery of repressed memories?

disorder. Among those personalities were Jim, who committed the rape; Woofie, a fifteen-year-old boy; Jimmy, a seven-year-old; and Laurie Burke, a seventeen-year-old lesbian prostitute. In fact, at one point during the trial, Carlson took the witness stand as Laurie, wearing a skirt, black tights, pink sweater, high-heel shoes, press-on nails, and a wedding band.

In her summation, Carlson's lawyer put the issue to the jury as follows. "James Carlson's body committed the crimes. But James was not in control of the body when any of the acts occurred." The prosecutor put the matter differently. "Your Honor, the statements [Carlson's confession] were made by a human being, sitting here today. The charges are not brought against any one [personality]. They are brought against the human being."

As is commonly the case in such trials, there was a battle of experts. One psychologist testified that Carlson suffered a multiple personality disorder that developed after Carlson had been molested in kindergarten. Another psychologist thought Carlson was faking, and faking badly.

The jury convicted Carlson. After the trial, Carlson acknowledged that he had read about multiple personalities in a psychology textbook and faked his performance, both because he wanted to avoid prison, and because he had fallen in love with his attorney. She "would see more of me when I was a multiple than if I was just myself." (*Arizona Republic*, 1994)

Carlson's case raises three very dramatic questions. First, does the multiple personality disorder really exist? Is it possible for an individual to have separate identities, but not be aware of them. Second, if this disorder does exist, how can we distinguish real cases from malingering? And third, assuming the defendant is convicted, how can we punish a person for the acts committed by one identity when the other identities may have had no knowledge or control over those acts? Is this different from other psychological or organic conditions involving uncontrollable behavior and subsequent amnesia? Fortunately, none of these questions had to be answered in Carlson's case.

Recovered Memories

The idea of repression is central to many views of personality, and especially to psychodynamic views (cf. Chapter 3). Experiences and memories that evoke shame, guilt, humiliation, or self-deprecation are often repressed, especially when those experiences conflict with one's self-image. When a memory is repressed, however, that memory does not disappear. It continues to exist and is simply inaccessible to consciousness, at least for the present. When psychological conditions change, the memory may reappear and the individual may become aware again of experiences long forgotten (Loftus, 1993, 1994).

The renewed awareness, however, is quite problematic. First, when you recover the memory of an event that transpired, say, twenty years ago, how can you be sure what you are recalling actually occurred? For some memories, that's hardly a problem. If you suddenly remember that you were lost in a department store when you were five years old, you can often find confirmation (or disconfirmation) by turning to your parents or siblings. But what if the event recalled occurred privately and to your shame? What if the event concerned sexual molestation, for which there was no witness? How, then, do we determine whether what is "recalled" occurred? The conviction with which the belief is held is, unfortunately, no sure guide. A person who now vividly "recalls" having been sexually abused by her father may well have a father who, just as vividly, has absolutely no recollection of the alleged events. That person may confuse an event that was only imagined or suggested with a true one, incorporating elements of the truth, such that this imagined memory has the feeling of authenticity (see Box 14–3).

RECOVERED MEMORIES AND SUGGESTIBILITY

Paul Ingram had been widely respected in Olympia, Washington, and not without reason. He was chairman of the local Republican party, chief civil deputy in the sheriff's department, and an active member of his church. His personnel file was filled with commendations from ordinary citizens who thanked him for his courtesy. Across seventeen years, no letter of complaint had ever been received about him. His wife Sandy operated a day-care center out of their home. Neighbors described them as strict but loving parents to their children.

But on November 28, 1988, fifteen minutes after he arrived at work, Sheriff Gary Edwards summoned Ingram to his office and relieved him of his automatic pistol. Ericka and Julie Ingram, then twenty-two and eighteen respectively, had accused their father of sexual molestation. While Ingram could not remember ever having molested his daughters, he added, "There may be a dark side of me that I don't know about." By the end of the day, Ingram confessed. "I really believe that the allegations did occur and that I did violate them and abuse them and probably for a long period of time. I've repressed it." Asked why he was confessing if he couldn't remember the violations, Ingram replied, "Well, number one, my daughters know me. They wouldn't lie about something like this."

Ingram's daughters' allegations had first surfaced some three months earlier. They were at a religious retreat when the leader told the sixty girls in attendance that she had a vision of someone in the audience who had been molested by a relative. There are a number of conflicting stories concerning how this occurred, but according to the leader, she simply prayed over Ericka and felt herself prompted by the Lord to say, "You have been abused as a child, sexually abused." Ericka wept quietly. The leader received another divine prompting, and said, "It's by her father, and it's been happening for years." Ericka then began to sob hysterically. The leader urged her to obtain counselling in order to work through the memories that were causing her so much

pain. Later, Ericka's memories included her brothers, as well as her father's friends among those who had molested her. Later still, her mother and brothers were included, not only in sexual abuse, but in satanic rituals that involved, among other things, sacrificing a baby.

After each of these allegations, Paul Ingram would go into a trancelike state, and would retrieve vivid recollections of these events. Encouraged by his pastor and detectives in his own department, Ingram found more and more to confess to. Nearly everyone, except his accused friends and one social psychologist, seemed convinced that Ingram was precisely as his children had described him: utterly corrupt.

The psychologist, Dr. Richard Ofshe, was intrigued by Ingram's ability to imagine scenes of abuse, and then come to feel, with great confidence, that they had actually occurred. This seemed to Ofshe more like suggestibility than anything else, and that hypothesis was worth testing. Ofshe told Ingram that one of his sons and one of his daughters had reported that Ingram had made them have sex together. At first, Ingram, quite correctly, couldn't remember having done that. Then he closed his eyes and acknowledged that he could see his son and daughter. The next time Ofshe visited, Ingram said he now had clear memories of his children having sex. And at their third meeting, Ingram proudly produced a three-page confession that described how he had directed his children to have sex with each other, and what they had done.

Of course, none of this was true. By the time Mr. Ingram realized that his visualizations had been fantasies, not real memories, he obtained a new lawyer and filed to retract his confessions on the grounds that they had been coerced by his investigators. But it was too late to stop the legal process, and Ingram was convicted. And in a sad footnote to a painful case, Ericka Ingram appeared at her father's leniency hearing, to demand that the judge give him the most severe sentence possible. Paul Ingram was sentenced to twenty years.

Second, the recovery of long-buried memories creates significant problems for the statute of limitations, which requires that claims for injuries must be instituted promptly. That requirement insures that memories remain fresh, and that witnesses can be examined. But where the incidents have been forgotten, how can one institute legal proceedings if one can't remember the harmful events?

Because there has been a rise in the incidence of recovered memories where the alleged crime consists of physical and sexual abuse, a substantial number of states have made an exception to the statute of limitations for such cases, much as they do for certain medical malpractice cases. If, for example, a surgeon left a roll of tape in a patient's stomach, but the tape was not discovered until many years later when the patient had a physical examination, the doctor can nevertheless be sued for malpractice under the *delayed discovery doctrine,* which holds that the statute of limitations does not begin to toll until all the facts that are essential to the complaint have been discovered. Similarly, when memories of sexual abuse have been repressed, no cause of action can be filed until they are recovered. The statute of limitations begins to toll from that point.

Those problems aside, it is clear that recovered memories are not merely a "family affair," but rather touch on many lives and on the nature of psychological treatment, as the following case indicates:

> Holly Ramona was nineteen years old when she consulted Marche Isabella for treatment. Holly's problem was bulimia and depression. Ms. Isabella suggested that bulimia might be rooted in childhood sexual abuse. Soon, Holly had terrifying flashbacks in which she recalled her father repeatedly molesting her between the ages of five and sixteen. In order to confirm her own memory, she undertook a "truth serum" interview. Reassured of the accuracy of her memory, she instituted legal proceedings against her father.
>
> Holly's father, Gary, was just as convinced that the sexual abuse had never occurred, but was rather suggested to Holly by her therapist. He sued the therapist, contending that Holly's allegation had caused his wife to seek a divorce, alienated him from his other children, and led directly to the loss of his job as an executive. The jury returned a verdict in his favor.
>
> According to the jury's foreman, the jury had not explored the efficacy of recovered memories, but had concentrated on the therapist's alleged negligence. Holly Ramona, however, remains convinced of the truth of her memories and feels that she benefited greatly from her therapy. And Gary Ramona remains equally convinced that "Holly's supposed memories are the result of the [therapist's] drugs and quackery, not anything I did." (*New York Times*, 1994)

Expert Opinion and the Potential for Abuse

Both clinical psychologists and lawyers want to help people, but there are times when both the law and psychology may be misused and end up hurting rather than helping people. Sometimes this is because of deliberate manipulation. Sometimes it happens because of carelessness or incompetence. But often it is the result of difficulties inherent both in diagnosis and in discovering the truth. The potential for abuse arises from the very definition of abnormality that we discussed in Chapter 1. There we suggested that whether or not people are seen as abnormal depends on whether they possess a "family resemblance" to other abnormal people. There need not be a perfect match between the behaviors of those people and the behaviors of abnormal people. So long as *some* elements are similar, individuals might be considered abnormal by society. The many sane political dissidents who were forced into psychiatric hospitals—really, psychoprisons—should be a constant reminder of the potential abuse of psychology and psychiatry. The ruined lives of individuals subsequently proven not to have committed sexual abuse must be seen as a caution toward accepting all recovered memories without outside verification.

Potential for abuse can arise from the fact that society endows psychologists and psychiatrists with enormous power. Perry London (1986) says they constitute a "secular priesthood"; Thomas Szasz (1963) sees (and decries) the rise of the "therapeutic state." But any general reservations we might have about psychiatry and psychology often dissolve when our own lives are touched by psychological distress. We tend to rely on the judgments and recommendations of psychologists and psychiatrists even though they are as human and as prone to error as the rest of us. Ultimately, however, they are our best hope for help in overcoming psychological disintegration and achieving psychological health.

1. The constitutional privileges that are available to ordinary citizens are not extended to the severely distressed, who can be deprived of liberty through *involuntary commitment,* often without trial.

2. There is no one federal standard for involuntary commitment, but all state statutes require that individuals who are committed must be mentally disordered, dangerous to themselves or others, or suffering from a "grave disability." The notion of dangerousness, especially, is rife with scientific, legal, and moral problems.

3. Involuntary commitment deprives a person of liberty. Before it occurs, *clear and convincing* evidence must be marshaled that indicates that the person requires hospitalization.

4. Several significant court decisions have held that those committed to psychiatric hospitals have a *right to treatment* that includes individual diagnosis and the preparation of a treatment plan that is periodically reviewed. One negative consequence of right-to-treatment decisions has been the decline in support for mental health programs. A positive result of deinstitutionalization, however, has been the growth of the patients' rights movement, including self-help organizations and patients' rights advocates.

5. *Criminal commitment* can occur either because a person was "insane" at the time of the crime, or because he or she is presently psychologically incompetent to stand trial.

6. The *insanity defense* requires that the defendant was wholly or partially irrational when the crime took place, and that this irrationality affected his or her behavior. While the insanity defense seemingly protects those who commit crimes while distressed, such people are commonly sent to prison-hospitals, where care is worse than in prisons themselves, and incarceration longer. Because being indefinitely committed to a psychiatric hospital is often worse than going to prison, the insanity defense is rarely used.

7. Historically, there have been three views of the insanity defense: the M'Naghten "right-wrong" test, the Durham "product of mental disease" test, and the American Law Institute (ALI) "appreciate and conform" rule. The modern standard, which is now used in all federal courts, was instituted in 1984 as the *Insanity Defense Reform Act.* It requires only that the defendant "was unable to appreciate the nature and quality or the wrongfulness of his acts." Yet another standard, termed *guilty but mentally ill,* is used in some states, but is a contradiction in terms.

8. The notion of *competence to stand trial* is rooted in the right of every person to defend himself against accusations. A person judged incompetent to stand trial is sent to an institution for the criminally insane until he is able to be tried, which often means a long incarceration.

9. Multiple personality (dissociative identity) disorders constitute a perplexing problem for the legal system. If one identity has no knowledge, or control, of the perpetrating identity, who is to be punished? Moreover, if one identity is guilty, are *all* identities to be punished? Fortunately, proving that one suffers a multiple personality disorder has been sufficiently difficult that the courts have not had to deal with the issues of guilt and punishment.

10. Memories that were once repressed and are now available raise difficult issues of proof, mainly because the events often transpired decades before the memory of those events was recovered. Juries have been willing to convict on the basis of such recollections, though recent testimony has increasingly come under scrutiny.

11. Psychiatry and psychology remain particularly prone to social and political abuses. But this neither invalidates the legal system nor psychological diagnosis.

QUESTIONS FOR CRITICAL THINKING

1. What does it mean to "psychiatrize" a case, and how does this cause people to come up with different solutions than they might have if the case had not been psychiatrized?

2. What are the problems of committing an individual based on the criterion of dangerousness to self and others and on the grave disability criterion?

3. Do you think those who are guilty and able to form an intent to commit a crime should be excused for their actions?

4. What procedures might be set up to ensure that a person judged incompetent to stand trial doesn't remain hospitalized indefinitely without any redress?

GLOSSARY

acquisition In Pavlovian conditioning, the learning of a response based on the contingency between a conditioned stimulus and an unconditioned stimulus.

acute schizophrenia A condition characterized by the rapid and sudden onset of very florid symptoms of schizophrenia.

addiction Dependence on a drug, resulting in tolerance and withdrawal symptoms when the addict is deprived of the drug. *See also* tolerance, withdrawal syndrome.

adoptive study The study of offspring and biological and adoptive parents to see whether the occurrence of a trait is related to genes or environment. This method is one of two widely used methods (the other is the twin study) for quantifying the relative contribution of genetic to nongenetic determinants of psychological traits.

affective disorders A class of mental disorders characterized by a disturbance of mood. Includes unipolar depression, bipolar depression, and mania.

affective pleasure An effect of drug use in the opponent-process model of addiction. Affective pleasure is the pleasant emotional state that is the initial pharmacological effect produced by the drug.

affective tolerance An effect of drug use in the opponent-process model of addiction. With continued use, the addictive drug tends to lose its affective pleasure.

affective withdrawal An effect of drug use in the opponent-process model of addiction. The sudden termination of narcotic use often produces the opposite affective state of the initial pleasant one.

agoraphobia An anxiety disorder characterized by fear of situations in which one might be trapped and unable to acquire help, especially in the event of a panic attack. Agoraphobics will avoid crowds, enclosed spaces (such as elevators and buses), or large open spaces. From the Greek "fear of the marketplace."

akathisia A side effect of chlorpromazine in which an itchiness in the muscles occurs and results in an inability to sit still.

alexithymia The word literally means "no words for feelings" and is used to describe people who have difficulty expressing their feelings.

altruistic suicide Suicide required by the society (as defined by Durkheim; for example, hari-kari).

Alzheimer's disease Degenerative disease of late middle or old age, in which mental functions deteriorate. An amnesic syndrome is often the major feature of this disorder. Its initial symptoms include loss of initiative, extreme forgetfulness, memory disability, and spatial disorders. It progresses to severe deteriorations of intellect and basic maintenance functions that lead to death.

amenorrhea Loss of the menstrual period. A common occurrence in women anorexics.

American Law Institute (ALI) rule A legal test for insanity that holds that a person is not responsible for his criminal conduct if, at the time of the crime and as a result of mental disease or defect, he lacks substantial capacity to appreciate the criminality of the conduct or to conform his conduct to the law.

amnesia A dissociative disorder characterized by loss of memory of happenings during a certain time period, or loss of memory of personal identity. Includes generalized amnesia, retrograde amnesia, post-traumatic amnesia, anterograde amnesia, and selective amnesia.

amnesic syndrome A disorder of memory, of organic origin, in which memory for recent events (events occurring after the brain damage) is very poor or completely absent.

amphetamine A stimulant that causes agitation, increase in energy and activity, hyper-responsiveness to the environment, euphoria, and a number of physiological signs of hyperactivation.

anaclitic depression A depression experienced by some infants between the ages of six and eighteen months who have been separated from their mothers for prolonged periods. This disorder is characterized by apathy, listlessness, weight loss, susceptibility to illness, and sometimes death.

androgen A hormone that is principally responsible for the morphological development of the external genitals of the male.

androgen insensitivity syndrome A syndrome in which the fetus lacks the receptors for the sex hormone, androgen, and which produces neurological females in male fetuses.

animism The belief in premodern societies that everyone and everything has a "soul" and that mental disturbance was due to animistic causes, e.g., an evil spirit had taken control of an individual and was controlling that individual's behavior.

animal phobias Specific phobias in which an individual has a fear of a particular animal, usually cats, dogs, birds, rats, snakes, and insects.

anomic suicide Suicide precipitated by a shattering break in an individual's relationship to his society (as defined by Durkheim).

anorexia nervosa A disorder in which the individual has an intense fear of becoming fat, eats far too little to sustain herself, and has a distorted body image.

anterograde amnesia Difficulty learning new material after a traumatic event.

antigens Invaders of the immune system.

antisocial personality disorder (or psychopathy, sociopathy) A personality disorder in which the individual has a rapacious attitude toward others and a chronic insensitivity and indifference to the rights of other people. The behavior must be longstanding and must be manifested in at least three classes of behavior, among which are: repeated aggressiveness; recklessness that endangers others; deceitfulness, lack of remorse, and consistent irresponsibility; failure to honor financial obligations.

anxiety Fear characterized by the expectation of an unspecified danger, dread, terror, or apprehension, often leading to an emergency reaction and "flight or fight" behavior. As used in psychoanalytic theory, the psychic pain that results from conflicts among the various personality processes.

anxiety disorders A class of mental disorders characterized by chronic and debilitating anxiety. Include agoraphobia, generalized anxiety disorder, panic disorder, phobias, and post-traumatic stress disorder.

aphasia Disorders of language resulting from damage to certain areas of the cerebral cortex.

applied tension A technique in which, upon seeing blood, blood phobics tense the muscles of their arms, legs, and chest, thereby raising their blood pressure and heart rate, which prevents them from fainting at the sight of blood.

appraisal Evaluation of short-term mental events, a target of cognitive therapy.

apraxia A disorder of movement in the absence of muscle weakness or inability to perform any specific movement.

arbitrary inference Reaching a conclusion for which there is little or no evidence. According to Beck, depressives are prone to making arbitrary inferences.

archetypes As used by Jung, universal ideas about which we are knowledgeable even at birth.

arteriosclerosis A building up of fat on the inner walls of the coronary arteries; this clogging blocks blood from reaching the heart muscle, and heart attack and sudden death can result.

attention-deficit hyperactivity disorder A disorder characterized by marked impulsivity, inattention, and hyperactivity.

attribution An assignment of cause for an event; a short-term mental event, and a target of cognitive therapy.

autism A childhood disorder whose central feature is the failure to develop the ability to respond to others within the first thirty months of life.

automatic thoughts Discrete sentences, negative in character, that a person says to himself, quickly and habitually. According to Beck, depressives typically engage in automatic thoughts.

aversion therapy A behavior therapy that seeks to rid a client of undesired behavior by pairing that behavior with aversive consequences.

avoidance-approach conflict   A conflict between a desire to approach an object or situation that has some positive value, and a desire to avoid that object or situation because it has been associated with harm. According to traditional learning theory, this conflict is a root of anxiety.

avoidance responding   The act of getting out of a situation that has been previously associated with an aversive event, thereby preventing the aversive event. Differs from escape responding, which is getting out of the aversive event itself.

avoidant personality disorder   A disorder whose central feature is social withdrawal combined with hypersensitivity to rejection.

barbiturates   A class of drugs depressing the central nervous system, decreasing anxiety and blunting sensitivity to the environment. Includes phenobarbital, pentobarbital, secobarbital, and benzodiapines.

behavior therapy   A therapy that is rooted in the view that psychological distress results from learned behavior that can be unlearned; the therapy seeks to replace the distressing behavior with more constructive modes of coping and adaptation.

behavioral assessment   A record of behaviors and thoughts one wishes to change, including their time of occurrence, duration, and intensity.

behavioral disorder   A disorder in which something behavioral, rather than emotional, is amiss, such as hyperactivity, attentional problems, and aggressive, destructive, and dishonest behaviors.

behavioral school   The school of abnormal psychology that claims that behavior is shaped by the environment, and that behavior can be changed by changing the environment. According to the behavioral theorists, the symptomatic behavior of a mental disorder is the disorder, and is that which should be treated.

benzodiazepines   A group of mild tranquilizers producing muscle relaxation, decreased anxiety, and sedation. Includes Librium, Valium, and Dalmane.

beta cells   Lymphocytes that come from bone marrow and that have receptors on their surface for specific antigens.

beta-endorphins   Large proteins that are produced in the body and that are opiate-like compounds.

biofeedback   Therapeutic technique in which the individual is given electronically amplified information on certain (somewhat) controllable physiological systems (such as heart rate and blood pressure) and trained to control that response system.

biogenic amines   Neurochemicals that facilitate neural transmission, including catecholamines and indoleamines.

biological psychiatry   The area of psychiatry specializing in the drug treatment, the biochemistry, neuroanatomy, and genetics of mental disorder.

biomedical model of abnormality   The school of abnormal psychology that claims that mental disorders are illnesses of the body resulting from an underlying physiological pathology such as a virus, disordered biochemistry or genes, or a dysfunctional organ.

bipolar disorder (or manic-depressive)   An affective disorder characterized by alternating periods of depression and mania.

bisexuality   Desire for sexual relations with members of both sexes.

blitz rape   Sudden and unexpected rape, as contrasted to acquaintance rape, often leading to PTSD.

blood-brain barrier   A barrier in the brain composed of specialized cells that prevent certain compounds in the circulatory system from entering the brain.

blood phobia   A specific phobia in which the individual becomes highly anxious in situations involving the sight of blood, injections, and injuries.

borderline personality disorder   A broad Axis-II diagnostic category that designates people whose salient characteristic is instability in a variety of personality areas, including interpersonal relationships, behavior, mood, and self-image.

brain imaging   Techniques such as PET scans and CAT scans that capture the way that the brain looks and functions.

breakdown   One of the ways in which norepinephrine is reduced during neural transmission; the enzyme monoamine oxidase (MAO) and other enzymes chemically break down the norepinephrine in the synaptic gap and render it inactive.

Briquet's syndrome   *See* somatization disorder.

bulimia   A disorder in which people alternately gorge themselves with enormous quantities of food, and then purge themselves of that food by vomiting, or using laxatives or diuretics.

caffeine   A drug that stimulates the central nervous system and the skeletal muscles, lengthening the time it takes to fall asleep, decreasing fatigue, and aiding the individual in doing physical work.

catecholamines   Hormones involved in neural transmission in the brain. Includes norepinephrine, epinephrine, and dopamine.

categorical amnesia   *See* selective amnesia.

catharsis   In psychoanalytic theory, the uncovering and reliving of early traumatic conflicts.

CAT scan   *See* computerized axial tomography.

central nervous system (CNS)   That part of the nervous system that coordinates all of the activity of the nervous system. In vertebrates, the CNS is made up of the brain and the spinal cord. All sensory inputs are transmitted to the CNS and all motor impulses are transmitted from the CNS.

cerebral cortex   The outermost layer (gray matter) of the cerebral hemispheres.

cerebrospinal fluid   A clear fluid, like blood plasma, that accounts for some of the circulation in the brain and spinal cord.

cholinergic   A descriptive term for the nerve cells that use acetylcholine as a chemical transmitter. The parasympathetic nervous system is a cholinergic system.

civil commitment   The process used to hospitalize mentally disordered people who have committed no crime.

clang associations   Associations produced by the rhyme of words. Commonly found in schizophrenics.

classical conditioning   *See* Pavlovian conditioning.

clinical case history   The record of part of the life of an individual seen in therapy.

cocaine   The psychoactive agent in the coca plant. Cocaine increases energy, combats fatigue and boredom, and enhances the individual's responsiveness to things in his environment.

cognitions   Beliefs, thoughts, attitudes, expectations, and other mental events.

cognitive-behavioral therapy   A therapeutic technique in which therapists attempt to alter both the maladaptive thoughts and maladaptive behaviors of a client through restructuring of maladaptive belief systems and re-training behavior.

cognitive (or selective) filter   A mechanism for sorting out stimuli to determine which ones will be admitted and which ones barred; something seems wrong with this filter in schizophrenics.

cognitive model   The school of abnormal psychology that claims that many disorders result from maladaptive beliefs or thought styles.

cognitive restructuring   Treatments that are predicated on the assumption that irrational thoughts create irrational behaviors, which can be eliminated by changing the underlying thoughts.

cognitive therapy   Used primarily in the treatment of depression, this therapy seeks to change the cognitive triad of (a) self-devaluation, (b) a negative view of life experience, and (c) the pessimistic view of the future, as the determining cognitions for depression.

cognitive triad   According to Beck, a group of cognitions characterizing depressives. These cognitions include (a) negative thoughts about the self, (b) negative thoughts about ongoing experience, and (c) negative thoughts about the future.

collective unconscious   As used by Jung, the memory traces of the experience of past generations.

compulsion   A repetitive, stereotyped, and unwanted action that can be resisted only with difficulty. It is usually associated with obsessions.

compulsive personality disorder   A disorder that is characterized by the long-term inability to express warm emotions, combined with an inappropriate preoccupation with trivial rules and details.

computerized axial tomography (CAT or CT scan)   An X-ray technique, used in neurological diagnosis, for constructing three-dimensional representations of the X-ray density of different areas of the brain.

concordant   When both of two twins have a disorder such as schizophrenia, they are called concordant for that disorder. *See also* discordant.

conditioned response (CR) A response that is evoked by a certain stimulus (conditioned stimulus) once that stimulus has become associated with some other stimulus (unconditioned stimulus) that naturally evokes the unconditioned response. *See also* Pavlovian conditioning.

conditioned stimulus (CS) A stimulus that, because of its having been paired with another stimulus (unconditioned stimulus) that naturally provokes an unconditioned response, is eventually able to evoke that response. *See also* Pavlovian conditioning.

conduct disorders A cluster of children's behavioral disorders consisting mainly of aggressive and rule-breaking behaviors.

confabulation Making up stories based on recovered but disorganized memories.

confound A factor other than the experimentally controlled independent variable that might produce an experimental effect.

congenital adrenal hyperplasia (CAH) A disease that bathes female fetuses with extra androgen. As young children, CAH girls like male-stereotyped toys, rough and tumble play, and are more tomboyish than matched controls.

contingency A conditional relationship between two objects or events, describable by the probability of event A given event B, along with the probability of event A in the absence of event B. A positive contingency between A and B obtains when A is more likely in the presence of B than in the absence of B. *See also* Pavlovian conditioning.

control group A group of subjects similar to those in an experimental group, who experience everything the experimental group does, except the independent variable.

conversion A somatoform disorder characterized by the loss of functioning of some part of the body not due to any physical disorder, but apparently due to psychological conflicts. The loss is not under voluntary control.

coping strategies As used by psychoanalytic theorists, the process by which people alter the meaning and significance of troublesome drives and impulses in order to eliminate anxiety.

core self The self that develops first, between the second and sixth month of an infant's life. It embraces the infant's awareness that she and her caregiver are *physically separate*.

coronary heart disease (CHD) Heart or circulatory problems often caused by arteriosclerosis; it can often lead to heart attack and sudden death.

correlation Pure observation without manipulation to determine the relationship between two classes of events.

correlation coefficient A statistic indicating the degree of contingency between two variables.

cosmetic psychopharmacology A change in personality, rather than mere change in mood, that is brought about by drugs.

co-twin As used in psychological research, one of a pair of twins whose sibling is seen at a psychiatric clinic in order to diagnose a psychological problem.

counterconditioning A therapeutic technique for phobias in which a phobic patient is helped to relax while imagining fear-provoking situations (usually the least fear-provoking situation first, then gradually more and more fear-provoking situations). The relaxation response to the imagined situation is incompatible with the fear the patient has previously associated with the situation, and the fear is thus extinguished.

counterphobia The pursuit of precisely those activities that are deeply feared.

covert sensitization A behavioral therapy for changing sexual interest; it uses imaged sexual stimuli followed by aversive US's to treat such paraphilias as exhibitionism.

criminal commitment The coerced psychiatric hospitalization of mentally disordered people who have acted harmfully but are not legally responsible because they lack *mens rea*, or a "guilty mind."

cross tolerance When tolerance to one drug produces tolerance to other drugs.

cyclothymic disorder A mild but chronic form of bipolar disorder in which the patient experiences depressive and hypomanic symptoms for at least two years.

defense mechanisms *See* coping strategies.

delirium tremens A dangerous syndrome of withdrawal from alcohol, which is characterized by psychomotor agitation, hyper-activity of the autonomic nervous system, anxiety, loss of appetite, delusions, amnesia, and convulsions.

delusions False beliefs that resist all argument and are sustained in the face of evidence that normally would be sufficient to destroy them.

delusions of control Beliefs that one's thoughts or behaviors are being controlled from without.

delusions of grandeur Unsubstantiable convictions that one is especially important.

delusions of persecution Groundless fears that individuals, groups, or the government has malevolent intentions and is "out to get me."

delusions of reference Incorrect beliefs that the casual remarks or behaviors of others apply to oneself.

demand characteristics Aspects of the experimental setting that induce the subject to invent and act on a hypothesis about how one should behave.

dementia A more or less general deterioration of mental function, found most commonly in old people. Alzheimer's disease is a common form of dementia.

denial As used in psychoanalytic theory, the process by which distressing external facts are eliminated.

dependent personality disorder A disorder wherein people allow others to make major decisions, to initiate important actions, and to assume responsibility for the significant areas of their life.

dependent variable The factor that the experimenter expects will be affected by changes in the independent variable.

depersonalization Feeling detachment from oneself; just going through the motions or looking at oneself from the outside.

depression An affective disorder characterized by (a) sad affect and loss of interest in usually satisfying activities, (b) a negative view of the self and hopelessness, (c) passivity, indecisiveness, and suicidal intentions, and (d) loss of appetite, weight loss, sleep disturbances, and other physical symptoms.

derealization Feeling as if the world, not the self, seems unreal.

descriptive validity The ability of a system of diagnosis to facilitate communication by accurately describing patients and differentiating patients in one category from another.

developmental disorders A cluster of disorders of childhood that may consist of deficits in language comprehension, speech, and responses to others that can result in such serious disorders as autism or childhood schizophrenia.

developmental dyslexia Difficulty in learning to read out of proportion to intellectual and emotional development.

diathesis Physical vulnerability or predisposition to a particular disorder.

diathesis-stress model A general model of disorders that postulates that an individual develops a disorder when he both has some constitutional vulnerability (diathesis) and when he experiences psychological disturbance (stress).

direct sexual therapy A therapeutic method developed by Masters and Johnson, in which (a) sexual dysfunctions are clearly and simply defined, (b) clients explicitly practice sexual behavior under the systematic guidance of therapists, and (c) clients are treated as couples, not as individuals.

discordant When only one of two twins has a disorder such as schizophrenia, they are called discordant for that disorder. *See also* concordant.

disinhibition An increase in some reaction resulting from release of inhibition.

disorganized schizophrenia A schizophrenic disorder whose most striking behavioral characteristic is apparent silliness and incoherence. Behavior is jovial but quite bizarre and absurd, suggesting extreme sensitivity to internal cues and extreme insensitivity to external ones, but without systematic delusions or hallucinations.

displacement A cognitive alteration of reality that involves replacing the true object of one's emotions with one that is more innocent and less threatening.

disruptive behavior disorders A cluster of disorders characterized by symptoms such as hyperactivity, inattention, aggressiveness, destructiveness, and defiance of authority.

dissociation A situation in which two or more mental processes co-exist or alternate without being connected or influencing each other, with some area of memory split off or dissociated from conscious awareness.

dissociative amnesia   A loss of personal memory caused by severe trauma such as the death of a child or the dashing of a career. (Formerly known as psychogenic amnesia.)

dissociative disorders   A group of mental disorders characterized by fragmentation of an individual's identity. Dissociative disorders include amnesia, fugue, multiple personality, and depersonalization disorder.

dissociative identity disorder (or multiple personality disorder)   The occurrence of two or more identities in the same individual, each of which is sufficiently integrated to have a relatively stable life of its own and recurrently to take full control of the person's behavior.

dizygotic twins   Fraternal twins, or twins who developed from separate eggs, and whose genes are no more alike than are those of any pair of non-identical-twin siblings.

dopamine   A catecholamine that facilitates neural transmission.

dopamine hypothesis   The theory that schizophrenia results from an excess of the neurotransmitter dopamine.

double-blind experiment   An experiment in which both the subject and experimenter do not know whether the subject has received an experimental treatment or a placebo.

double depression   A major depressive episode superimposed on an underlying chronic depression.

Down syndrome   A disorder that results from the fact that an individual has forty-seven rather than the usual forty-six chromosomes in his or her cells.

drug cues   Drug reminders, such as settings in which drugs were taken, that induce craving for the drug and can trigger relapse in those who have been free of drugs.

drug dependence   The regular use of drugs acting on the brain that leads to maladaptive behavioral changes that would be seen as maladaptive in any culture. Three criteria characterize the disorder: (a) a pattern of pathological use of a drug, (b) impairment in occupational, social, physical, or emotional functioning, and (c) evidence of affective or physical adaptation to the drug.

drug tolerance   The need to use increased amounts of the drug to get the desired effect.

drug withdrawal   Characteristic affective and physical symptoms that follow drug use after the drug is discontinued.

DSM-IV   Published in 1994, this is the fourth edition of the *Diagnostic and Statistical Manual of Mental Disorders* of the American Psychiatric Association.

Durham test   A legal test for insanity which provides that an accused is not criminally responsible if his unlawful act was the product of mental disease or mental defect.

dysfunction   Impairment of functioning.

dyslexia   *See* developmental dyslexia, phonological dyslexia, surface dyslexia.

dysphoria   An unpleasant emotional state experienced during drug withdrawal; the opposite of euphoria.

dysthymic disorder   Chronic depression in which the individual has been depressed for at least two years without having had a remission to normality that lasted more than two months.

effectiveness studies   Research studies in which the outcome of therapy is tested as it is delivered in the field.

efficacy expectation   According to Bandura, a person's belief that he can successfully execute the behavior that will produce a desired outcome.

efficacy studies   Research studies in which a therapy is tested under laboratory conditions.

ego   The self.

ego-dystonic homosexuality   Homosexuality that is incongruent with the individual's desire for sexual preference, and which the individual wants to change.

ego-syntonic homosexuality   Homosexuality that is congruent with the individual's desire for sexual preference, and which the individual does not want to change.

egoistic suicide   Suicide resulting when the individual has too few ties to his fellow humans (as defined by Durkheim).

electroconvulsive shock treatment (ECT)   A therapeutic treatment for depression, in which metal electrodes are taped to either side of the patient's head, and the patient is anesthetized. A high current is passed through the brain for a half second, followed by convulsions lasting almost one minute.

electroencephalogram (EEG)   A record of the electrical activity of cells in the brain (primarily the cortex) obtained from wires placed on the skull, and used in neurological diagnosis.

EMDR (Eye Movement Desensitization and Reprocessing)   A therapy used to treat patients with post-traumatic stress disorder in which the patient follows the rapidly moving finger of the therapist while concentrating on a disturbing image or memory; patients come to replace negative thoughts with positive thoughts and to experience less distress.

emergency reaction   A reaction to threat in which the sympathetic nervous system mobilizes the body for action. The blood pressure rises, heart rate increases, breathing becomes deeper, perspiration increases, and the liver releases sugar for use by the muscles.

emotional disorders   A cluster of disorders in which symptoms of fear, anxiety, inhibition, shyness, and overattachment predominate.

empiricism   The school of philosophy that claims that all that people are and all that they know are the result of experiences.

endogenous depression   A depression resulting from disordered biology. From the Greek "arising from within."

endorphins   Endogenous morphine-like substances.

enkephalins   Small amino acid compounds that are endogenous opioids.

enuresis (or bed-wetting)   A disorder that is manifested by regular and involuntary voiding of urine.

environmentalism   The first assumption of behaviorism; it states that all organisms, including humans, are shaped by the environment.

epidemiological evidence   Evidence from many individuals.

episodic depression   Depression that has a clear onset and that lasts less than two years.

erectile dysfunction (or impotence)   In males, recurrent inability to have or to maintain an erection for intercourse.

erotic arousal   Excitement of sexual desire.

escape responding   The act of getting out of an ongoing harmful situation. *See also* avoidance responding.

etiology   Causal description of the development of a disorder.

exhibitionism   A psychosexual disorder in which the individual is sexually aroused primarily by exposing his genitals to unwitting strangers.

exhortative will   The will whereby we force ourselves to work.

existential theory   A theory that holds that mental disorders result when an individual fails to confront the basic questions of life successfully. Three issues are particularly important: fear of dying, personal responsibility, and will.

existential therapy   A therapy that encourages clients to view their psychological problems as being of their own making.

exogenous depression   A depression precipitated by a life stressor. From the Greek "arising from without."

expectations   Cognitions that extrapolate the present to the anticipation of future events.

experiment   A procedure in which a hypothesized cause (independent variable) is manipulated and the occurrence of an effect (dependent variable) is measured.

experimental effect   The change in the dependent variable as a result of the manipulation of the independent variable.

experimental group   A group of subjects who are given experience with an independent variable.

experimentalism   The behaviorist view that experiments can reveal what aspects of the environment cause behavior.

experimenter bias   The exertion of subtle influences by the experimenter on subjects' responses in an experiment.

experimenter-blind design   An experiment in which the experimenter, but not the subject, is blind as to whether a subject is receiving a drug or placebo.

experiments of nature   Studies in which the experimenter observes the effects of an unusual natural event.

exposure therapy   A behavioral form of treatment for phobia and PTSD in which the patient repeatedly endures the phobic object or original trauma in vivo or in imagination. *See also* extinction, flooding.

expressive aphasia   A language disorder that manifests itself primarily as a deficit in speech or the organization of spoken language.

external attribution   An assignment of cause for an event to a factor that is outside oneself (i.e., other people or circumstances).

extinction In Pavlovian conditioning, cessation of a previously conditioned response to a conditioned stimulus, due to having learned that the conditioned stimulus no longer signals the onset of an aversive or desirable event. In instrumental learning, cessation of acquired operant responses due to reinforcement being discontinued. Modern theorists believe that extinction occurs when there is a negative contingency between the conditioned stimulus and the unconditioned stimulus. *See also* contingency.

factitious disorder (or **Munchhausen syndrome**) A mental disorder characterized by multiple hospitalizations and operations precipitated by the individual's having self-inflicted signs of illness.

false alarm In experimental analysis, accepting the hypothesis that independent and dependent variables are related, when they really are not. *See also* miss.

family resemblance approach Assessing abnormality based on the match between an individual's characteristics and the seven elements of abnormality: suffering, maladaptiveness, incomprehensibility and irrationality, unpredictability and loss of control, vividness, observer discomfort, and violation of moral and ideal standards.

family therapy A group of diverse psychotherapies that treat the couple or family, rather than the individual alone.

fat solubility *See* lipid solubility.

fetish A psychosexual disorder characterized by a need to have an inanimate object close by in order to become sexually aroused.

flooding A method used by behavioral therapists to treat phobias. The phobic individual is exposed to the situations or objects most feared for an extended length of time without the opportunity to escape. *See also* response prevention.

fluoxetine (Prozac) A serotonin reuptake inhibitor prescribed for depression.

free association A psychoanalytic instruction to say whatever comes to mind, regardless of how ridiculous or embarrassing it is, and without attempting to censor.

frequency distribution The number of observations in each given class observed.

frontal lobe A lobe in each cerebral hemisphere that includes control and organization of motor function.

fugue state A dissociative disorder in which an individual, in an amnesic state, travels away from home and assumes a new identity.

fusion Protecting oneself against the fear of death or nonbeing by fusing with others such that one becomes attached to and indistinguishable from the others.

gender identity Awareness of being male or being female.

gender identity disorder A class of mental disorders in which the essential feature is an incongruence between anatomic sex and gender identity. Includes transsexualism.

gender role Public expression of gender identity; what an individual does and says to indicate that he is a man or she is a woman.

general adaptation syndrome According to Selye, a sequence of three stages that ensues when an individual is stressed: (a) the somatic emergency reaction is initiated, (b) the individual engages in defensive behaviors, and (c) eventually the individual's adaptative actions are exhausted.

generalized anxiety disorder An anxiety disorder characterized by chronic tenseness and vigilance, beliefs that something bad will happen, mild emergency reactions, and feelings of wanting to run away.

general paresis A disorder characterized by mental deterioration, paralysis, then death. This disorder is caused by a spirochete involved in syphilis.

Gestalt therapy A therapy that emphasizes taking responsibility for one's life by living in the present.

global attribution An individual's assignment of cause for an event to a factor that will affect a number of different areas of his life.

glove anesthesia A conversion symptom in which nothing can be felt in the hand and fingers, but sensation is intact from the wrist up.

goal-directed will The will that develops out of hope, expectation, and competence, wherein we are able to work toward future goals.

grade 5 hypnotizable person That fraction of the population (5 percent) that is extremely hypnotizable, very suggestible, showing pathological compliance with their therapists and giving up critical judgment. Most MPD's are grade 5.

grave disability A legal phrase that describes an individual's psychological inability to provide food or shelter for herself, which places her in imminent danger.

group residences Group homes for patients discharged from psychiatric hospitals in which the patients live together and run the household, shop, and work.

habit disorders A collection of childhood disorders in which the prominent symptoms include difficulties associated with eating, movement disorders, or tics. These disorders consist of a diverse group of problems with physical manifestations such as bedwetting, stuttering, sleepwalking and epilepsy.

half-life The length of time it takes for the level of a drug in the blood to be decreased by 50 percent.

hallucination A perception that occurs in the absence of an identifiable stimulus.

hallucinogens Chemicals that cause perceptual disorientation, depersonalization, illusions, hallucinations, and physiological symptoms such as tachycardia, palpitations, and tremors. Includes LSD, PCP, and MDMA.

health psychology The field that deals with disorders that stand at the border of psychology and medicine.

heritability coefficient The quantitative estimate of the contribution of genetic factors to a trait, relative to nongenetic factors. It can be calculated as $2 \times$ (correlation of MZ twins − the correlation of DZ twins).

heterosexuality Preference for sexual partners of the opposite sex.

histrionic personality disorder A personality disorder in which people are shallow, egocentric, and self-absorbed and have long histories of drawing attention to themselves and engaging in excited emotional displays caused by insignificant events.

homosexuality Preference for sexual partners of one's own sex.

hopelessness theory of depression A theory that emphasizes the stable and global dimensions for negative events as determinants of hopelessness.

hormones Genes that modulate physical growth, bodily differentiation, and psychological growth.

hypertension High blood pressure.

hypomanic personality A chronic form of mania involving an unbroken two-year-long manic state. *See also* mania.

hyposomnia Greatly lessened need for sleep.

hyperactivity A disorder that is marked by developmentally inappropriate impulsiveness, inattentiveness, and excessive motor behavior. *See also* attention-deficit hyperactivity disorder.

hypochondriasis The sustained conviction, in the absence of medical evidence, that one is ill or about to become ill.

hysterical conversion *See* conversion.

id In psychoanalytic theory, the mental representation of biological drives.

ideas of reference The belief that certain events and people have special significance for the patient (e.g., that newscasters are speaking to him or that strangers in the street are looking at him).

identity alteration A dissociative experience in which one displays a skill that one did not know one had.

identity confusion A dissociative state in which one is confused or uncertain about who one is.

illness and injury phobias (or **nosophobias**) Specific phobias in which an individual fears having one specific illness or injury or death.

immunocompetence The degree to which the immune system is able to protect the organism efficiently.

immunologic memory The factor that enables those T-cells and B-cells that initially combated an antigen to multiply more rapidly the second time the antigen is spotted, such that the immune system is able to do a better job of destroying the antigen than it did the first time.

inanimate object phobias Specific phobias in which the symptoms are focused on one object, including dirt, heights, darkness, closed spaces, and travel.

incidence The rate of new cases of a disorder in a given time period.

independent variable   The hypothesized cause of some effect, manipulated by the experimenter in an experiment.

index case (or **proband)**   In psychological research, one of a pair of twins who is first seen at a psychiatric clinic.

indoleamines   Hormones involved in neural transmission. Indoleamines include serotonin and histamine.

inhibition   An active process through which the excitability of a particular neuron or center (group of neurons) is decreased.

insanity defense   A defense for a crime that requires that the individual was wholly or partially irrational when the crime took place, and that this irrationality affected his or her behavior.

Insanity Defense Reform Act (IDRA)   A federal standard for determining whether the insanity defense can be used; it eliminates the volitional prong of the ALI standard and states that the insanity defense can be used if at the time of the crime the defendant, as a result of severe mental disease or defect, was unable to appreciate the nature and quality or wrongfulness of his act.

instrumental learning (or **instrumental conditioning)**   A technique in which an organism must learn to perform some voluntary behavior in order to acquire a desired outcome, or to stop an undesirable event.

instrumental response   A response whose probability can be modified by reinforcement; a response that an organism has learned will bring about a desired outcome, or will stop an undesired event. *See also* operant.

intellectualization   A coping strategy that takes the form of repressing the emotional component of experience, and restating that experience as an abstract intellectual analysis.

inter-judge reliability   When two psychologists arrive at the same impression on the basis of psychological tests and observation.

internal attribution   An individual's assignment of cause for an event to a factor that is an aspect of himself.

interpersonal therapy (IPT)   A therapy that deals with depression as it results from interpersonal difficulties.

intersubjectivity   The sense that we understand each others' intentions and feelings, as well as the sharing of experience about things and events.

intoxication   An acute, maladaptive psychological change, such as impaired thinking or judgment, that develops after ingestion of alcohol or a drug and that goes away in time.

involuntary commitment   The process whereby the state hospitalizes people for their own good, and even over their vigorous protest.

isolation   A coping strategy in which only the affective component of an unpleasant experience is repressed while the information is retained.

Korsakoff's syndrome   A particular form of the amnesic syndrome caused by alcoholism.

laboratory model   The production, under controlled conditions, of phenomena analogous to naturally occurring mental disorders.

learned helplessness   A condition characterized by an expectation that bad events will occur, and that there is nothing one can do to prevent their occurrence. Results in passivity, cognitive deficits, and other symptoms that resemble depression.

learning disorders   Difficulties that reflect enormous developmental tardiness and mainly affect the development of language and academic skills, including reading difficulties.

learning model   The model that includes the behavioral approach, which holds that we learn abnormal behavior through conditioning and that we can unlearn these maladaptive ways of behaving, and the cognitive approach, which holds that abnormality springs from disordered conscious thought about oneself and the world.

lifetime prevalence   The proportion of people in a sample who have ever experienced a particular disorder.

lipid (or **fat) solubility**   Ability of a drug to be stored in fat cells; this is an important factor in whether or how fast a drug reaches the brain; more lipid soluble drugs will be absorbed more quickly.

LSD (lysergic acid diethylamide)   An hallucinogenic drug that causes changes in body sensations (dizziness, weakness, nausea), perception (distorted time sense), emotion, and cognitive processes.

lymphocytes   Cells in the immune system that recognize foreign cells.

macrophages   Cells in the immune system that "eat" antigens.

magnetic resonance imaging (MRI)   A brain-imaging technique in which each type of atom behaves like a tiny spinning magnet, wobbling at a characteristic frequency in the magnetic field. An MRI shows the elemental composition of cells and surrounding tissue. Damaged areas of the brain have a different concentration of elements than normal areas and appear differently on an MRI.

magnification   Overestimating the impact of a small bad event; error of logic made by those who are depressed.

malingering   A disorder in which the individual reports somatic symptoms, but these symptoms are under the individual's control, and the individual has an obvious motive for the somatic complaints. *See also* conversion.

mania   An affective disorder characterized by excessive elation, expansiveness, irritability, talkativeness, inflated self-esteem, and flight of ideas.

manic-depression   *See* bipolar disorder.

MAO (monoamine oxidase)   An enzyme that helps to break down catecholamines and indoleamines. MAO inhibitors are used to treat depression.

marijuana   A psychoactive drug that, when used chronically and heavily, causes impairment of ability to focus on a task, impulsive and compulsive behavior, delusions, sensory-perceptual distortions, and sometimes panic reactions.

masochism   A psychosexual disorder in which the individual prefers to become sexually aroused by having suffering or humiliation inflicted upon him.

mean   Average value of a set of values.

meditation   A relaxation technique in which one closes one's eyes and silently repeats a mantra; it works by blocking thoughts that produce anxiety.

melancholia   Depression characterized chiefly by loss of pleasure in most activities and by somatic symptoms, including sleep loss and loss of appetite.

mental disorder   In DSM-IV, a behavioral or psychological pattern that is genuinely dysfunctional and that either distresses or disables the individual in one or more significant areas of functioning.

mental retardation   Substantial limitations in present functioning; characterized by significantly subaverage intellectual functioning and limitations in two or more skill areas such as communication, self-care, home living, social skills, community use, self-direction, health and safety, functional academics, leisure, and work.

methadone   A narcotic used in heroin treatment programs. Methadone acts as a substitute for heroin, and prevents the heroin addict from experiencing withdrawal.

milieu therapy   Therapy in which patients are provided with training in social communication, work, and recreation.

Minnesota Multiphasic Personality Inventory (MMPI)   A widely used personality inventory consisting of 550 test items that inquire into a wide array of behaviors, thoughts, and feelings.

minimization   Downplaying good events; an error of logic in depression.

miss   Rejecting a hypothesis that the independent variable and dependent variable are related, when they really are.

M'Naghten test   A legal test for insanity which provides that a person cannot be found guilty of a crime if, at the time of committing the offense, due to "disease of the mind," the individual did not know the nature and quality of the act or that the act was wrong.

modeling   The observation and gradual imitation of a model who exhibits behavior that the client seeks to adopt in place of an undesirable behavior.

monozygotic (MZ) twins   Identical twins, or twins who developed from a single egg fertilized by a single sperm, which divided and produced two individuals who have identical genes and chromosomes.

moral treatment   The humane, nonthreatening treatment of the insane.

MRI   *See* magnetic resonance imaging.

multiple personality disorder   A dissociative disorder in which more than one distinct identity exists in the same individual, and each identity is relatively stable and recurrently takes full control of the person's behavior.

mystification   A process in which people are encouraged to doubt their own feelings, perceptions, and experiences.

narcissistic personality disorder   A personality disorder whose salient characteristics are an outlandish sense of self-importance, continual self-absorption, fantasies of unlimited success, power and/or beauty, and need for constant admiration.

narcotics   A class of psychoactive drugs blocking emotional response to pain and producing euphoria, dysphoria, apathy, psychomotor retardation, drowsiness, slurred speech, and maladaptive behavior. Includes opium, morphine, heroin, and methadone.

natural killer cells   Cells in the immune system that lyse cells of a tumor.

nature-nurture issue   A major debate in psychology, concerning the relative roles of environment and heredity in the development of personality and behavior.

negative correlation   A relationship between two classes of events wherein as one increases, the other decreases.

negative reinforcer   An event whose removal increases the probability of a response that precedes it. *See also* punishment.

Neo-Freudians   Psychodynamic theorists who modified and expanded upon Freud's views.

neuroadaptation   The complex biological changes that occur in the brain with repeated or chronic exposure to a drug.

neurology   The clinical discipline that studies the diseases of the nervous system.

neurosis   Formerly, a category for disorders in which the individual experienced (a) emotionally distressing symptoms, (b) an unwelcome psychological state, (c) reasonably good reality testing, and (d) behavior that was reasonably within social norms. A neurotic disorder was not considered a transient reaction to stress or the result of organic brain damage.

neurotransmitter   A chemical that facilitates the transmission of electrical impulses among nerve endings in the brain.

neutrophils   Cells in the immune system that "eat" an antigen-antibody complex.

nicotine   The active ingredient in tobacco that produces psychoactive effects.

norepinephrine   A neurochemical involved in neural transmission. Disturbances of the availability of norepinephrine in the brain have been associated with affective disorders.

nosophobias   *See* illness and injury phobias.

obsessions   Repetitive thoughts, images, or impulses that invade consciousness, are abhorrent, and are very difficult to dismiss or control; usually associated with compulsions.

obsessive-compulsive disorder   An anxiety disorder in which the individual is plagued with uncontrollable, repulsive thoughts (obsessions) and engages in seemingly senseless rituals (compulsive behaviors).

obsessive-compulsive personality disorder   A personality disorder characterized by a pervasive pattern of striving for perfection in oneself and others.

operant   A response whose probability can be increased by positive reinforcement, or decreased by negative reinforcement.

operant conditioning   Training the organism to perform some instrumental response in order to escape punishment or gain reward.

operational definition   A set of observable and measurable conditions under which a phenomenon is defined to occur.

opiates (or narcotics)   Drugs that produce euphoria or dysphoria, apathy, psychomotor retardation, pupillary constriction, drowsiness, slurred speech, and impairment in attention and memory. Includes codeine, opium, morphine, heroin, and methadone.

opponent-process model of addiction   A model developed by Richard Solomon which explains the increased motivation to use a drug which occurs with continued use of that drug. According to the model, all drugs that produce dependence have three properties: affective pleasure, affective tolerance, and affective withdrawal.

oppositional defiant disorder   A disruptive behavior disorder in which children show a pattern of negativistic, hostile, and defiant behavior, but do not show the more serious violations of others' rights as do children with conduct disorders.

organic syndromes   Abnormal behaviors caused by known pathology in structure or function of the nervous system. Neurology and neuropsychology concentrate on the study of these syndromes.

outcome expectation   A person's estimate that a given behavior will lead to the desired outcome. *See also* efficacy expectation.

outcome studies   Research studies in which the effects of a therapy are observed as it attempts to alleviate a disorder. Therapy outcome studies can be either efficacy studies or effectiveness studies. *See also* effectiveness studies, efficacy studies.

outcome validity   *See* predictive validity.

overdetermination   Behaviors that are caused or determined by more than one psychological force and with more than the requisite psychic energy.

overgeneralization   Drawing global conclusions on the basis of a single fact; an error of logic made by those who are depressed.

overinclusiveness   The tendency to form concepts from both relevant and irrelevant information; this thought defect, which is generally present in schizophrenics, arises from an impaired capacity to resist distracting information.

pain disorder (or psychalgia)   A somatoform disorder in which the individual experiences pain, not attributable to a physical cause, but to psychological conflict.

panic disorder   An anxiety disorder characterized by severe attacks of panic, in which the person (a) is overwhelmed with intense apprehension, dread, or terror, (b) experiences an acute emergency reaction, (c) thinks he might go crazy or die, and (d) engages in fight or flight behavior.

paranoid personality disorder   A personality disorder in which the person has a pervasive and longstanding distrust and suspiciousness of others; hypersensitivity to slight; and a tendency to look for hidden motives for innocuous behavior.

paranoid schizophrenia   A form of schizophrenia in which delusions of persecution or grandeur are systematized and complex.

paraphilias   A group of psychosexual disorders in which bizarre sexual acts or imagery are needed to produce sexual arousal. Includes fetishes, masochism, exhibitionism, voyeurism, transvestism, sadism, zoophilia, and pedophilia.

passive-aggressive personality disorder   A disorder that is characterized by resistance to social and occupational performance demands through procrastination, dawdling, stubbornness, inefficiency, and forgetfulness that seem to border on the intentional.

Pavlovian conditioning (or classical conditioning)   Training in which an organism is exposed to one neutral stimulus (conditioned stimulus) and a stimulus (unconditioned stimulus) that naturally provokes a certain response (unconditioned response). Through the learned association between the conditioned stimulus and the unconditioned stimulus, the conditioned stimulus is able to evoke the conditioned response. Modern theorists believe that acquisition occurs when there is a positive contingency between the conditioned stimulus and the unconditioned stimulus. *See also* contingency.

PCP (phencyclidine)   An hallucinogen that causes sensitization to all sensory inputs, depersonalization, diminished awareness of self and the environment, disorientation, muddled thinking, and impaired attention and memory.

pedophilia   A psychosexual disorder in which the individual needs to engage in sexual relations with children below the age of mature consent in order to be sexually aroused.

personality disorders   Disorders in which characteristic ways of perceiving and thinking about oneself and one's environment are inflexible and a source of social and occupational maladjustment. *See also* antisocial personality disorder, avoidant personality disorder, dependent personality disorder, histrionic personality disorder, narcissistic personality disorder, obsessive-compulsive personality disorder, paranoid personality disorder, schizoid personality disorder, schizotypal personality disorder.

personalization   Incorrectly taking responsibility for bad events; an error of logic in those who are depressed.

pervasive learning disorders   Disorders that are all-encompassing, involving difficulties of great magnitude and across many modalities, including language attention, responsiveness, perception, and motor development. *See also* autism.

PET scan *See* positron emission tomography.

pharmacology The study of drugs and their actions in cells and physiological processes.

phenylalanine An amino acid that is an essential component of proteins. Children with phenylketonuria cannot metabolize phenylalanine.

phenylketonuria (PKU) A rare metabolic disease that prevents digestion of an essential amino acid called phenylalanine. As a result of this disease, phenopyruvic acid, a derivative of phenylalanine, builds up in and poisons the nervous system, causing irreversible damage.

phobia An anxiety disorder characterized by (a) persistent fear of a specific situation out of proportion to the reality of the danger, (b) compelling desire to avoid and escape the situation, (c) recognition that the fear is unreasonably excessive, and (d) the fact that it is not due to any other disorder.

phonological dyslexia Inability to pronounce a written word that has never been seen before even if it corresponds to a known spoken word.

physical dependence The need for the presence of a drug to function normally, and the appearance of the withdrawal syndrome upon cessation of the drug.

physiological Having to do with the body.

placebo A neutral stimulus that produces some response because the subject believes it should produce that response.

placebo effect A positive treatment outcome that results from the administration of placebos.

pleasure principle As used in psychodynamic theory, biological drives that clamor for immediate gratification.

population The entire set of potential observations.

positive correlation A relationship between two classes of events wherein when one increases so does the other.

positive reinforcer An event that increases the probability of a response when made contingent upon it. *See also* instrumental learning, operant.

positron emission tomography (PET) scan A brain-imaging technique that produces a three-dimensional image of the brain. A radioactive substance, usually glucose or oxygen, is incorporated directly into the neuron in proportion to the metabolic rate. With the aid of a computer, a representation of metabolic rate in different brain regions can be shown.

post-traumatic amnesia The inability to recall events *after* the traumatic episode

post-traumatic stress disorder (PTSD) An anxiety disorder resulting from having witnessed or been confronted by the threat of death, injury, or threat to the physical integrity of self or others, including rape, mugging, watching a bloody accident, or watching or committing an atrocity; the three symptoms defining the disorder are: (a) numbness to the world, (b) reliving of the trauma in dreams, flashbacks, and memories, and (c) symptoms of anxiety and arousal not present before the trauma.

predictive (or outcome) validity The ability of the diagnostic categories in a system of diagnosis to predict the course and outcome of treatment.

premature ejaculation The recurrent inability to exert any control over ejaculation, resulting in rapid ejaculation after penetration.

premenstrual dysphoric disorder A tentative DSM-IV classification of premenstrual symptoms into a disorder characterized by a combination of some or all of the following symptoms: emotional lability, anger, tension, depression, low interest, fatigue, a feeling of being overwhelmed, difficulty concentrating, oversensitivity to rejection, and appetite and sleep changes.

prepared classical conditioning In learning theory, the concept of the organism as being biologically predisposed to learning about relationships between certain stimuli, and therefore learning the relationship very easily.

prevalence The percentage of a population having a certain disorder at a given time.

primary erectile dysfunction A disorder in which the male has never been able to achieve or maintain an erection sufficient for intercourse.

proband *See* index case.

prognosis Outlook for the future of a disorder.

progressive relaxation A technique for reducing anxiety in which one tightens and then turns off each of the major muscle groups of one's body, until the muscles are wholly flaccid; the resulting relaxation engages a response system that competes with anxious arousal.

projection Attributing private understandings and meanings to others; substituting "you" for "I."

psychalgia *See* pain disorder.

psychic energy The energies that fuel psychological life.

psychoactive drugs Drugs that affect consciousness, mood, and behavior.

psychoanalysis The psychological theory that claims that disorders are the result of intrapsychic conflicts, usually sexual or aggressive in nature, stemming from childhood fixations. Psychoanalysis is also a therapeutic method in which the therapist helps the patient gain insight into those intrapsychic conflicts behind his or her symptoms.

psychodynamic Dealing with the psychological forces that influence mind and behavior.

psychodynamic approach An approach whose theorists believe that abnormality is driven by hidden conflicts within the personality.

psychogenic amnesia *See* dissociative amnesia.

psychological inventory A highly structured test containing a variety of statements that the client can answer true or false as to whether or not they apply to her; used for vocational guidance, personal counseling, or in connection with a job.

psychomotor retardation Slowing down of movement and speech; prominent in severe depression.

psychoneuroimmunology (PNI) The study of how mental state and behavior influence the immune system.

psychopharmacology That branch of pharmacology that studies drug effects on the cells of the brain and drug actions affecting consciousness, mood, and behavior.

psychosexual disorders A class of mental disorders in which psychological factors impair sexual functioning.

psychosis A mental state characterized by profound disturbances in reality testing, thought, and emotion. *See also* schizophrenia.

psychosomatic disorders A group of disorders in which actual physical illness is caused or influenced by psychological factors. The diagnosis of a psychosomatic disorder requires that the physical symptoms represent a known physical pathology and that psychologically meaningful events preceded and are judged to have contributed to the onset or worsening of the physical disorder.

punishment In psychology experiments, inflicting aversive stimuli on an organism, which reduces the probability of recurrence of certain behaviors by that organism. *See also* negative reinforcement.

random assignment Assigning subjects to groups in an experiment such that each subject has an equal chance of being assigned to each group.

rape The sexual violation of one person by another.

rape trauma syndrome A woman's reaction to rape in which symptoms similar to those of post-traumatic stress disorder occur.

rational-emotive therapy A therapy in which the therapist challenges the irrational beliefs of the client, and encourages the client to engage in behavior that will counteract his irrational beliefs.

rationalization The process of assigning to behavior socially desirable motives, which an impartial analysis would not substantiate.

reaction formation The process of substituting an opposite reaction for a given impulse.

reactive schizophrenia A schizophrenic condition precipitated by a severe social or emotional upset from which the individual perceives no escape.

realistic anxiety As used in psychoanalytic theory, the fear that arises from the expectation that real world events may be harmful to the self.

reality principle In psychodynamic theory, the way in which the ego expresses and gratifies the desires of the id in accordance with the requirements of reality.

receptive aphasia An aphasia (disorder of language) where the primary deficit is in the perception of speech.

recovered memories Memories that were repressed because of shame, guilt, humiliation, or self-deprecation but that reappear and become accessible to consciousness years later.

recurrence The return of depressive symptoms following at least six months without significant symptoms of depression.

reinforcement An event that, when made contingent on a response, increases its probability. A reward or punishment.

relapse The return of depressive symptoms after drugs or psychotherapy have relieved the depression for less than six months.

relaxation response Physiological response regulated by the parasympathetic nervous system (PNS), which counteracts the emergency reaction to threat. In the relaxation response, the PNS inhibits heart action, constricts respiratory passages, and causes secretion of digestive fluids.

reliability The characteristic whereby an assessment device generates the same findings on repeated use.

repeatability The chance that, if an experimental manipulation is repeated, it will produce similar results.

repression A coping strategy by which the individual forces unwanted thoughts or prohibited desires out of consciousness and into the unconscious mind.

research diagnoses Hunches that may prove useful in communicating about people and treating them; not as reliable or valid as clinical diagnoses.

reserpine A powerful sedative given to lower high blood pressure. Reserpine occasionally induces depression.

residual rules Unwritten rules of behavior that no one ever teaches but that we know intuitively and that we use to guide our behavior.

residual schizophrenia A form of schizophrenia characterized by the absence of such prominent symptoms as delusions, hallucinations, incoherence or grossly disorganized behavior, but in which there is continuing evidence of the presence of two or more relatively minor but distressing symptoms.

response prevention A therapeutic technique in which a therapist prevents the individual from engaging in a behavior that the therapist wishes to extinguish. *See also* flooding.

retarded ejaculation In men, great difficulty reaching orgasm during sexual intercourse.

retrograde amnesia Loss of memory of events predating some disease or trauma. The loss is often confined to a period seconds or minutes prior to a trauma.

reuptake One of the ways in which norepinephrine is inactivated during neural transmission, wherein neuron 1 reabsorbs the norepinephrine in the synaptic gap, thereby decreasing the amount of norepinephrine at the receptors of neuron 2.

reward In psychology experiments, giving the organism positive stimuli, which increases the probability of recurrence of certain behaviors by the organism. *See also* positive reinforcer.

role construct repertory test (Rep test) A personality inventory that examines the constructs that a person uses in interpreting significant events.

Rorschach test A personality test consisting of ten bilaterally symmetrical "inkblots," some in color, some in black, gray, and white, each on an individual card. The respondent is shown each card separately and asked to name everything the inkblot could resemble. The test is supposed to elicit unconscious conflicts, latent fears, sexual and aggressive impulses, and hidden anxieties.

sadism A psychosexual disorder in which the individual becomes sexually aroused only by inflicting physical and psychological suffering and humiliation on another human being.

sample A selection of items or people, from the entire population of similar items or people.

schizoid personality disorder A disorder that is characterized by the inability to form social relationships, the absence of desire for social involvements, indifference to both praise and criticism, insensitivity to feelings of others, and by lack of social skills.

schizophrenia A group of disorders characterized by incoherence of speech and thought, hallucinations, delusions, blunted or inappropriate emotion, deterioration in social and occupational functioning, and lack of self-care.

schizophrenogenic families Families that seem to foster schizophrenia in one or more family members.

schizotypal personality disorder A personality disorder characterized by longstanding oddities in thinking, perceiving, communicating, and behaving.

school phobia A persistent and irrational fear of going to school.

seasonal affective disorder (SAD) Characterized by depression beginning each year in the fall and remitting or switching to mania in the spring.

secondary erectile dysfunction Loss of the ability in a male to achieve or maintain an erection.

selective abstraction Focusing on one insignificant detail while ignoring the more important features of a situation; an error of logic in those who are depressed.

selective amnesia (or categorical amnesia) Loss of memory of all events related to a particular theme.

selective positive reinforcement Therapeutic technique in which the therapist delivers positive reinforcement contingent on the occurrence of one particular behavior.

selective punishment Therapeutic technique in which the therapist negatively reinforces a certain target event, causing it to decrease in probability.

selfobject Those people and things that are critically significant for personality cohesiveness.

self theory A personality theory that addresses the fact that people feel *whole* and *unified* rather than fragmented into ego, superego, behaviors, etc. Wholeness is thought to be endowed by the *self*.

sensate focus A strategy of direct sexual therapy that involves (a) a "pleasuring" phase during which the couple engages in nongenital erotic activity, but restrains from intercourse, then (b) a phase of "genital stimulation" in which the couple engages in genital play, but without intercourse, then (c) the phase of "nondemand intercourse" in which the couple engages in intercourse, but without making demands on each other.

separation anxiety disorder A disorder characterized by a very strong fear of being separated from one's family. Children with this disorder become panicked if they must separate from loved ones, and they often show continual physical symptoms of anxiety.

sex role The public expression of sexual identity, what an individual says or does to indicate that he is a man or she is a woman.

sexual dysfunction Disorders in which adequate sexual arousal, desire, or orgasm are inhibited.

sexual identity Generally consistent with one's genitals; feeling that one is male if one has a penis; feeling that one is female if one has a vagina.

sexual interest The types of persons, parts of the body, and situations that are the objects of sexual fantasies, arousal, and preferences.

sexual orientation Attraction to and erotic fantasies about men, women, or both.

sexual unresponsiveness (or frigidity) In women, lack of sexual desire and impairment of physical excitement in appropriate situations.

single-blind experiment An experiment in which the subject, but not the experimenter, does not know whether the subject has received an experimental treatment or a placebo.

social phobias Unreasonable fear of and desire to avoid situations in which one might be humiliated in front of other people.

somatic Having to do with the body.

somatization disorder (or Briquet's syndrome) A somatoform disorder characterized by the experience of a large number and variety of physical symptoms for which there are no medical explanations. These symptoms are not under the voluntary control of the individual.

somatoform disorders A group of mental disorders characterized by (a) loss or alteration in physical functioning, for which there is no physiological explanation, (b) evidence that psychological factors have caused the physical symptoms, (c) lack of voluntary control over physical symptoms, and (d) indifference by the patient to the physical loss. Includes conversion, pain disorder, somatization disorder.

specific attribution An individual's assignment of cause for an event to a factor that is relevant only to that situation.

specific phobias There are four classes of specific phobias: animal phobias are unreasonable fears of and desires to avoid or escape specific animals. Illness and injury phobias (nosophobias) are unreasonable fears of and desires to avoid or escape a specific illness or injury. Inanimate objects phobias are unreasonable fears of and desires to avoid certain situations or objects other than social situations, crowds, animals, illness, or injuries. Blood phobias are an unreasonable fear of blood.

stable attribution An individual's assignment of cause for an event to a factor that persists in time.

statistical inferences Procedures used to decide whether a sample or a set of observations is truly representative of the population.

statistically significant effect An effect that is highly unlikely (typically less than one time in twenty) to occur solely by chance.

stigmata Marks on the skin, usually bleeding or bruises, and often of high religious or personal significance, brought on by an emotional state.

stimulants A class of psychoactive drugs that induces psychomotor agitation, physiological hyperactivity, elation, grandiosity, loquacity, and hypervigilance. Includes amphetamines and cocaine.

subclinical The property of being symptomatic, but more mild than a full-blown disorder.

subject bias The influence of a subject's beliefs about what he is expected to do in an experiment on his responses in the experiment.

subjective self The second sense of self, which develops between the age of seven and nine months. It gives rise to the sense that we understand each others' feelings and intentions.

sublimation In psychoanalytic theory, the transfer of libidinal energies from relatively narcissistic gratifications to those which gratify others and are highly socialized. More generally, the process of rechanneling psychic energy from socially undesirable goals to constructive and socially desirable ones.

superego Those psychological processes that are "above the self," i.e., conscience, ideals, and morals.

surface dyslexia Someone with surface dyslexia can only read words by sounding them out.

symptom A sign of disorder.

syndrome A set of symptoms that tend to co-occur.

systematic desensitization A behavior therapy primarily used to treat phobias and specific anxieties. The phobic is first given training in deep muscle relaxation and is then progressively exposed to increasingly anxiety-evoking situations (real or imagined). Because relaxation and fear are mutually exclusive, stimuli that formerly induced panic are now greeted calmly.

tardive dyskinesia A nonreversible neurological side effect of antipsychotic drug treatment, whose symptoms consist of sucking, lip smacking, and peculiar tongue movements.

T cells Cells in the immune system that are produced in the thymus gland. They have receptors on their surfaces for specific antigens.

telephone scatologia A paraphilia that consists of recurrent and intense sexual urges to make obscene telephone calls to a nonconsenting individual.

temporal lobe A lobe in each cerebral hemisphere that includes the auditory projection area and is particularly involved in memory.

tension reduction hypothesis A hypothesis that states that people drink alcohol to reduce tension.

Thematic Apperception Test (TAT) A personality test that consists of a series of pictures that are not as ambiguous as Rorschach cards, but not as clear as photographs either. Respondents look at each picture and make up a story about it. The test is supposed to elicit underlying psychological dynamics.

therapeutic alliance An agreement between therapist and patient on the goals of therapy and how they can best be achieved.

tolerance The state of drug addiction in which, after repeated use of a drug, the addict needs more and more of the drug to produce the desired reaction, and there is great diminution of the effect of a given dose.

Tourette's syndrome A disorder characterized by motor tics and uncontrollable verbal outbursts, usually beginning in childhood.

transsexuality A psychosexual disorder characterized by the belief that one is a woman trapped in the body of a man, or a man trapped in the body of a woman.

transvestism (or transvestic fetishism) A psychosexual disorder in which a man often dresses in the clothes of a woman in order to achieve sexual arousal.

tricyclic antidepressants Antidepressant drugs that block uptake of norepinephrine, thus increasing the availability of norepinephrine.

tumor An abnormal tissue that grows by cell multiplication more rapidly than is normal.

twin study The study of the degree of concordance of a trait in identical versus fraternal twins. This method allows the quantification of the heritability of psychological traits. *See also* adoptive study.

Type A behavior pattern A personality type characterized by (a) an exaggerated sense of time urgency, (b) competitiveness and ambition, and (c) aggressiveness and hostility when thwarted.

unconditioned stimulus (US) A stimulus that will provoke an unconditioned response without training. For example, a loud noise will naturally provoke a startle response in humans.

unconscious In psychoanalytic theory, the large mass of hidden memories, experiences, and impulses.

undifferentiated schizophrenia A category of schizophrenia used to describe disturbed individuals who present evidence of thought disorder, as well as behavioral and affective anomalies, but who are not classifiable under the other subtypes.

unipolar depression A disorder characterized by depression, in the absence of a history of mania.

unstable attribution An individual's assignment of cause for an event to a factor that is transient.

validity The extent to which a test of something is actually measuring that something.

verbal self The third sense of self, which develops between fifteen and eighteen months of age. It is the verbal and symbolic storehouse of experience and knowledge.

voyeurism A psychosexual disorder in which the individual habitually gains sexual arousal only by observing the naked body, the disrobing, or the sexual activity of an unsuspecting victim.

withdrawal syndrome (or abstinence syndrome) A substance-specific syndrome that follows cessation of the intake of a substance that has been regularly used by the individual to induce intoxication; usually characterized by observable, physical signs such as marked changes in body temperature or heart rate, seizures, tremors, or vomiting.

yoking An experimental procedure in which both experimental and control groups receive exactly the same physical events, but only the experimental group influences these events by its responding.

zoophilia (or bestiality) A psychosexual disorder in which the individual habitually engages in sexual relations with animals in order to be sexually aroused.

REFERENCES

Abraham, K. (1911). Notes on psychoanalytic investigation and treatment of manic-depressive insanity and applied conditions. In *Selected papers of Karl Abraham, M.D.* (D. Bryan & A. Strachey, Trans.). London: Hogarth Press, 1948.

Abrams, R., & Vedak, C. (1991). Prediction of ECT response in melancholia. *Convulsive Therapy, 7,* 81–84.

Abramson, L. Y. (1978). *Universal versus personal helplessness.* Unpublished doctoral dissertation, University of Pennsylvania.

Abramson, L. Y., Garber, J., Edwards, N., & Seligman, M. E. P. (1978). Expectancy change in depression and schizophrenia. *Journal of Abnormal Psychology, 87,* 165–79.

Abramson, L., Metalsky, G., & Alloy, L. (1989). Hopelessness depression: A theory-based subtype of depression. *Psychological Review, 96,* 358–72.

Abramson, L. Y., Seligman, M. E. P., & Teasdale, J. (1978). Learned helplessness in humans: Critique and reformulation. *Journal of Abnormal Psychology, 87,* 32–48.

ACNP-FDA Task Force. (1973). Medical intelligence—drug therapy. *New England Journal of Medicine, 130,* 20–24.

Adams, H. E., & Sturgis, E. T. (1977). Status of behavioral reorientation techniques in the modification of homosexuality: A review. *Psychological Bulletin, 84,* 1171–88.

Adams, R. D. (1989). *Principles of neurology* (3rd ed.). New York: McGraw-Hill.

Adler, T. (1989). Integrity test popularity prompts close scrutiny. *APA Monitor, 7.*

Agras, S., Sylvester, D., & Oliveau, D. (1969). The epidemiology of common fears and phobia. *Comprehensive Psychiatry, 10* (2): 151–56.

Agras, W. S. (1993). Short-term psychological treatments for binge eating. In C. G. Fairburn & G. T. Wilson (Eds.), *Binge eating: Nature, assessment, and treatment.* New York: Guilford Press.

Agras, W. S., & Kirkley, B. G. (1986). Bulimia: Theories of etiology. In K. D. Brownell & J. P. Foreyt (Eds.), *Handbook of eating disorders: Physiology, psychology and treatment of obesity, anorexia, and bulimia.* New York: Basic Books.

Agras, W. S., Rossiter, E. M., Arnow, B., Schneider, J. A., Telch, C. F., Raeburn, S. D., Bruce, B., Perl, M., & Koran, L. M. (1992). Pharmacologic and cognitive-behavioral treatment for bulimia nervosa: A controlled comparison. *American Journal of Psychiatry, 149,* 82–87.

Agras, W. S., Schneider, J. A., Arnow, B., Raeburn, S. D., & Telch, C. F. (1989a). Cognitive-behavioral and response-prevention treatments for bulimia nervosa. *Journal of Consulting and Clinical Psychology, 57*(2): 215–21.

Agras, W. S., Schneider, J. A., Arnow, B., Raeburn, S. D., & Telch, C. F. (1989b). Cognitive-behavioral treatment with and without exposure plus response prevention in the treatment of bulimia nervosa. *Journal of Consulting and Clinical Psychology, 57,* 778–79.

Aigner, T. G., & Balster, R. L. (1978). Choice behavior in rhesus monkeys: Cocaine versus food. *Science, 201,* 534–35.

Alden, L. E., & Wallace, S. T. (1995). Social phobia and social appraisal in successful and unsuccessful social interactions. *Behaviour Research and Therapy, 33*(5): 497–505.

Alexander, F. (1950). *Psychosomatic medicine.* New York: Norton.

Allen, A. J., Leonard, H. L., & Swedo, S. E. (1995). Case study: A new infection-triggered, autoimmune subtype of pediatric OCD and Tourette syndrome. *Journal of the American Academy of Child and Adolescent Psychiatry, 34,* 307–11.

Allen, K. W. (1996). Chronic nailbiting: A controlled comparison of competing response and mild aversion treatments. *Behaviour Research and Therapy, 34*(3): 269–72.

Allen, M. G. (1976). Twin studies of affective illness. *Archives of General Psychiatry, 33,* 1476–78.

Alloy, L. B., Lipman, A. J., & Abramson, L. Y. (1992). Attributional style as a vulnerability factor for depression: Validation by past history of mood disorders. *Cognitive Therapy and Research, 16*(4): 391–407.

Alterman, T., Shekelle, R. B., Vernon, S. W., & Burau, K. D. (1994). Decision latitude, psychologic demand, job strain, and coronary heart disease in the Western Electric Study. *American Journal of Epidemiology, 139*(6): 620–27.

American Psychiatric Association (1980). *Diagnostic and statistical manual of mental disorders* (3rd ed.) (DSM-III). Washington, DC: Author.

American Psychiatric Association. (1983). Guidelines for legislation on the psychiatric hospitalization of adults. *American Journal of Psychiatry, 140,* 672–79.

American Psychiatric Association (1987). *Diagnostic and statistical manual of mental disorders* (3rd ed., revised) (DSM-III-R). Washington, DC: Author.

American Psychiatric Association. (1993). Practice guidelines for major depressive disorder in adults. *American Journal of Psychiatry, 150*(Suppl. 4).

American Psychiatric Association (1994). *Diagnostic and statistical manual of mental disorders* (4th ed.) (DSM-IV). Washington, DC: Author.

Andersen, B. L. (1983). Primary orgasmic dysfunction: Diagnostic conditions and review of treatment. *Psychological Bulletin, 93,* 105–36.

Anderson, J. C., Williams, S., McGee, R., & Silva, P. A. (1987). DSM-III: Disorders in preadolescent children. *Archives of General Psychiatry, 44,* 69–76.

Anderson, J. R., & Bower, G. H. (1973). *Human associative memory.* Washington, DC: Winston.

Andreasen, N. C., Nasrallah, H. A., Dunn, V., Olson, S. C., Grove, W. M., Ehrhardt, J. C., Coffman, J. A., & Crossett, J. H. (1986). Structural abnormalities in the frontal system in schizophrenia: A magnetic resonance imaging study. *Archives of General Psychiatry, 43*(2): 136–44.

Angold, A. (1994). Unpublished data. Presentation to NIMH Workshop on Emergence of Sex Differences in Depression, Bethesda, MD, March 1994.

Angst, J. (1992). Epidemiology of depression. 2nd International Symposium on Moclobemide: RIMA (Reversible Inhibitor of Monoamine Oxidase Type A): A new concept in the treatment of depression. *Psychopharmacology, 106* (Suppl): 71–74.

Angst, J., Baastrup, P., Grof, P., Hippius, H., Poldinger, W., & Weis, P. (1973). The course of monopolar depression and bipolar psychoses. *Psykiotrika, Neurologika and Neurochirurgia, 76,* 489–500.

Angst, J., & Wicki, W. (1991). The Zurich Study: XI. Is dysthymia a separate form of depression? Results of the Zurich Cohort Study. *European Archives of Psychiatry and Clinical Neuroscience, 240* (6): 349–54.

Anisman, H. (1978). Aversively motivated behavior as a tool in psychopharmacological analysis. In H. Anisman & G. Binami (Eds.), *Psychopharmacology of aversively motivated behavior.* New York: Plenum.

Annau, Z., & Kamin, L. J. (1961). The conditional emotional response as a function of intensity of the US. *Journal of Comparative and Physiological Psychology, 54,* 428–32.

Ansbacher, H. L., & Ansbacher, R. (1956). *The individual psychology of Alfred Adler.* New York: Basic Books.

Apfelbaum, B. (1980). The diagnosis and treatment of retarded ejaculation. In S. A. Leiblum & L. A. Pervin (Eds.), *Principles and practice of sex therapy* (pp. 236–96). New York: Guilford Press.

Archibald, H. C., & Tuddenham, R. D. (1965). Persistent stress reaction after combat. *Archives of General Psychiatry, 12,* 475–81.

Arendt, H. (1978). *The life of the mind.* New York: Harcourt Brace Jovanovich.

Arieti, S. (1974). *Interpretation of schizophrenia.* New York: Basic Books.

Arieti, S., & Bemporad, J. (1978). *Severe and mild depression.* New York: Basic Books.

Aro, S., Aro, H., & Keskimaki, I. (1995). Socio-economic mobility among patients with schizophrenia or major affective disorder:

A 17-year restrospective follow-up. *British Journal of Psychiatry, 166*(6): 1759–67.

Aronow, E., & Reznikoff, M. (1976). *Rorschach content interpretation.* New York: Grune & Stratton.

Arizona Republic. (1994). Liar in drag: Rapist admits faking multiple personalities. *Arizona Republic,* April 20.

Asberg, M., Traskman, L., & Thoren, P. (1976). 5–HIAA in the cerebrospinal fluid. *Archives of General Psychiatry, 33,* 1193–97.

Asch, S. E. (1951). Effects of group pressure on the modification and distortion of judgments. In H. Guetzkow (Ed.), *Groups, leadership and men: Research in human relations.* Pittsburgh, PA: Carnegie Press.

Assad, G., & Shapiro, B. (1986). Hallucinations: Theoretical and clinical overview. *American Journal of Psychiatry, 143* (9): 1088–97.

Atkinson, J. W. (1992). Motivational determinants of thematic apperception. In C.P. Smith, J.W. Atkinson, & J. Veroff (Eds.). *Motivation and personality: Handbook of thematic content analysis* (pp. 21–48). New York: Cambridge University Press.

Ayllon, T., & Michael, J. (1959). The psychiatric nurse as a behavioral engineer. *Journal of the Experimental Analysis of Behavior, 2,* 323–34.

Babor, T. F. (1990). Social, scientific and medical issues in the definition of alcohol and drug dependence. In A. Edwards & M. Lader (Eds.), *The nature of drug dependence* (pp. 19–40). New York: Oxford University Press.

Bach, M., & Bach, D. (1995). Predictive value of alexithymia: A prospective study in somatizing patients. *Psychotherapy and Psychosomatics, 64*(1): 43–48.

Bacon, D. L. (1969). Incompetency to stand trial; commitment to an inclusive test. *Southern California Law Review, 42,* 444.

Baer, D. M., & Guess, D. (1971). Receptive training of adjectival inflections in mental retardates. *Journal of Applied Behavior Analysis, 4,* 129–39.

Bailey, J. M., Pillard, R., & Agyei, Y. (1993). A genetic study of female sexual orientation. *Archives of General Psychiatry, 50,* 217–23.

Bakker, A., Van Kesteren, P., Gooren, L., & Bezemer, P. (1993). The prevalence of transsexualism in the Netherlands. *Acta Psychiatrica Scandinavica, 87,* 237–38.

Ball, S. G., Baer, L., & Otto, M. W. (1996). Symptoms subtypes of obsessive-compulsive disorder in behavioral treatment studies: A quantitative review. *Behaviour Research and Therapy, 34*(1): 47–51.

Ball, J. C., & Ross, A. (1991). *The effectiveness of methadone maintenance treatment: Patients, programs, services, and outcome.* New York: Springer-Verlag.

Ballenger, J. C. (1986). Pharmacotherapy of the panic disorders. *Journal of Clinical Psychiatry, 47* (Suppl): 27–32.

Baltes, P. B., Reese, H. W., & Lipsitt, L. P. (1980). Life-span developmental psychology. *Annual Review of Psychology, 31,* 65–110.

Bandura, A. (1969). *Principles of behavior modification.* New York: Holt, Rinehart & Winston.

Bandura, A. (1977). Self efficacy: Toward a unifying theory of behavioral change. *Psychological Review, 84,* 191–215.

Bandura, A. (1982). Self-efficacy mechanism in human agency. *American Psychologist, 37,* 122–47.

Bandura, A. (1986). Fearful expectations and avoidant actions as coeffects of personal self-inefficacy. *American Psychologist, 41* (12): 1389–91.

Bandura, A. (1993). Perceived self-efficacy in cognitive development and functioning. *Educational Psychologist, 28,* 117–48.

Bandura, A., & Adams, N. E. (1977). Analysis of self-efficacy theory of behavioral changes. *Cognitive Therapy and Research, 1,* 287–310.

Bandura, A., Adams, N. E., & Beyer, J. (1977). Cognitive processes mediating behavioral change. *Journal of Personality and Social Psychology, 35,* 125–39.

Barefoot, J. C., Dahlstrom, W. G., & Williams, R. B. (1983). Hostility, CHD incidence, and total mortality: A 25-year follow-up study of 255 physicians. *Psychosomatic Medicine, 45* (1): 59–63.

Barefoot, J. C., Larsen, S., Von der Lieth, & Schroll, M. (1995). Hostility, incidence of acute myocardial infarction, and mortality in a sample of older Danish men and women. *American Journal of Epidemiology, 142*(5): 477–84.

Barkley, R. A. (1990). *Attention deficit hyperactivity disorder: A handbook for diagnosis and treatment.* New York: Guilford Press.

Barkley, R. A., Fischer, M., Edelbrock, C. S., & Smallish, L. (1990). The adolescent outcome of hyperactive children diagnosed by research criteria. I. An 8-year prospective follow-up. *Journal of the American Academy of Child and Adolescent Psychiatry, 29*(4): 546–57.

Barlow, D. H. (1986). The classification of anxiety disorders. In G. L. Tischler (Ed.), *Diagnoses and classification in psychiatry: A critical appraisal of DSM-III* (pp. 223–42). Cambridge: Cambridge University Press.

Barlow, D. H. (1988). *Anxiety and its disorders: The nature and treatment of anxiety and panic.* New York: Guilford Press.

Barlow, D. H., Abel, G. G., & Blanchard, E. B. (1979). Gender identity change in transsexuals. *Archives of General Psychiatry, 36,* 1001–1007.

Barnes, G. E., & Prosin, H. (1985). Parental death and depression. *Journal of Abnormal Psychology, 94,* 64–69.

Barnes, T. R. E., & Braude, W. M. (1985). Akathisia variants and tardive dyskinesia. *Archives of General Psychiatry, 42,* 874–78.

Baron, M., Gruen, R., Kane, J., & Amis, L. (1985). Modern research criteria and the genetics of schizophrenia. *American Journal of Psychiatry, 142,* 697–701.

Bartrop, R. W., Luckhurst, E., Lazarus, L., Kiloh, L. G., & Penny, R. (1977). Depressed lymphocyte function after bereavement. *The Lancet, I,* April 16, 834–36.

Bateson, G., Jackson, D. D., Haley, J., & Weakland, J. (1956). Toward a theory of schizophrenia. *Behavioral Science, 1,* 251–64.

Baum, A. (1990). Stress, intrusive imagery, and chronic distress. *Health Psychology, 9,* 653–75.

Baum, A., Cohen, L., & Hall, M. (1993). Control and intrusive memories as possible determinants of chronic stress. *Psychosomatic Medicine, 55,* 274–86.

Baum, M. (1969). Extinction of an avoidance response following response prevention: Some parametric investigations. *Canadian Journal of Psychology, 23,* 1–10.

Baxter, L., Schwartz, J., Bergman, K., Szuba, M., et al. (1992). Caudate glucose metabolic rate changes with both drug and behavior therapy for obsessive-compulsive disorder. *Archives of General Psychiatry, 49,* 681–89.

Beauvais, M. F., & Derouesne, J. (1979). Phonological alexia: The dissociations. *Journal of Neurology, Neurosurgery, and Psychiatry, 42,* 1115–24.

Beasley, C., Dornseif, B., Bosomworth, J., et al. (1992). Fluoxetine and suicide: A meta-analysis of controlled trials of treatment for depression. *International Clinical Psychopharmacology, 6* (Suppl. 6): 35–57.

Beaumont, G. (1990). Adverse effects of antidepressants. *International Clinical Psychopharmacology, 5,* 61–66.

Beck, A. T. (1967). *Depression: Clinical, experimental, and theoretical aspects.* New York: Hoeber.

Beck, A. T. (1973). *The diagnosis and management of depression.* Philadelphia: University of Pennsylvania Press.

Beck, A. T. (1976). *Cognitive therapy and the emotional disorders.* New York: International Universities Press.

Beck, A.T., & Emery, G. (1985). *Anxiety disorders and phobias: A cognitive perspective.* New York: Basic Books.

Beck, A. T., Rush, A. J., Shaw, B. F., & Emery, G. (1979). *Cognitive therapy of depression.* New York: Guilford Press.

Beck, A. T., Sokol, L., Clark, D., Berchick, B., & Wright, F. (1991). *Focussed cognitive therapy of panic disorder: A crossover design and one-year follow-up.* Manuscript.

Beck, A. T., Steer R. A., & Epstein, N. (1992). Self-concept dimensions of clinically depressed and anxious outpatients. *Journal of Clinical Psychology, 48,* 423–32.

Beck, A. T., Ward, C. H., Mendelson, M., Mock, J. E., & Erbaugh, J. K. (1962). Reliability of psychiatric diagnoses II: A study of consistency of clinical judgments and ratings. *American Journal of Psychiatry, 119,* 351–57.

Beech, H. R., & Vaughan, M. (1979). *Behavioural treatment of obsessional states.* Chichester: Wiley.

Beecher, H. K. (1959). *Measurement of subjective responses: Quantitative effects of drugs.* New York: Oxford University Press.

Beers, D. R., Henkel, J. S., Kesner, R. P., & Stroop, W. G. (1995). Spatial recognition memory deficits without notable CNS pathology in rats following herpes simplex encephalitis. *Journal of the Neurological Sciences, 131,* 119–27.

Bellack, A. S. (1992). Cognitive rehabilitation for schizophrenia: Is it really possible? Is it necessary? *Schizophrenia Bulletin, 18*(1): 43–50.

Bellak, L. and Abrams, D. M. (1993). *The Thematic Apperception Test, the Children's Apperception Test, and the Senior Apperception Technique in clinical use.* Boston: Allyn & Bacon.

Belson, R. (1975). The importance of the second interview in marriage counseling. *Counseling Psychologist, 5*(3): 27–31.

Bench, C. J., Frackowiak, R. S. J., & Dolan, R. J. (1995). Changes in regional cerebral blood flow on recovery from depression. *Psychological Medicine, 25,* 247–51.

Bench, C. J., Friston, K. J., Brown, R. G., Frackowiak, R. S. J., & Dolan, R. J. (1993). Regional cerebral blood flow in depression measured by positron emission tomography: The relationship with clinical dimensions. *Psychological Medicine, 23,* 579–90.

Benes, F. M., Davidson, J., & Bird, E. D. (1986). Quantitative cytoarchitectural studies of the cerebral cortex of schizophrenics. *Archives of General Psychiatry, 42,* 874–78.

Benet, A. E., & Melman, A. (1995). The epidemiology of erectile dysfunction. *Urologic Clinics of North America, 22*(4): 699–709.

Benjamin, H. (1966). *The transsexual phenomenon.* New York: Julian Press.

Benjamin, L. S. (1987). The use of the SASB dimensional model to develop treatment plans for personality disorders. I: Narcissism. *Journal of Personality Disorders, 1*(1): 43–70.

Berenbaum, S., & Hines, M. (1992). Early androgens are related to childhood sex-typed toy preferences. *Psychological Science, 3,* 203–6.

Berger, F. (1970). Anxiety and the discovery of tranquilizers. In F. J. Ayd & H. Blackwell (Eds.), *Discoveries in biological psychiatry.* Philadelphia: Lippincott.

Berger, P. (1977). Antidepressant medications and the treatment of depression. In J. Barchas, P. Berger, R. Ciaranello, & G. Elliot (Eds.), *Psychopharmacology.* New York: Oxford University Press.

Berkman, L. F. (1984). Assessing the physical health effects of social networks and social support. *Annual Review of Public Health, 5,* 413–32.

Berkman, L. F. (1986). Social networks, support, and health: Taking the next step forward. *American Journal of Epidemiology, 123,* 559–62.

Bernheim (1886). In J. E. Gordon (Ed.), *Handbook of clinical and experimental hypnosis.* New York: Macmillan, 1967.

Berridge, V. (1990). Dependence: Historical concepts and constructs. In A. Edwards & M. Lader (Eds.), *The nature of drug dependence* (pp. 1–18). New York: Oxford University Press.

Bexton, W. H., Heron, W., & Scott, T. H. (1954). Effects of decreased variation in the sensory environment. *Canadian Journal of Psychology, 8,* 70–76.

Bibring, E. (1953). The mechanism of depression. In P. Greenacre (Ed.), *Affective disorders.* New York: International Universities Press.

Biran, M., & Wilson, G. T. (1981). Treatment of phobic disorders using cognitive and exposure methods: A self-efficacy analysis. *Journal of Consulting and Clinical Psychology, 48,* 886–87.

Bird J. (1979). The behavioural treatment of hysteria. *British Journal of Psychiatry, 134,* 129–37.

Biver, F., Goldman, S., Delvenne, V., Luxen, A., De Maertelaer, V., Hubain, P., Mendlewicz, J., & Lotstra, F. (1994). Frontal and parietal metabolic disturbances in unipolar depression. *Biological Psychiatry, 36,* 381–88.

Black, D. W., Noyes, R., Goldstein, R. B., & Blum, N. (1992). A family study of obsessive-compulsive disorder. *Archives of General Psychiatry, 49,* 362–68.

Blair, C. D., & Lanyon, R. I. (1981). Exhibitionism: A critical review of the etiology and treatment. *Psychological Bulletin, 89,* 439–63.

Blashfield, R. K., & Draguns, J. G. (1976). Evaluative criteria for psychiatric classification. *Journal of Abnormal Psychology, 85,* 40–150.

Blashfield, R. K., & Livesley, W. J. (1991). Metaphorical analysis of psychiatric classification as a psychological test. *Journal of Abnormal Psychology, 100*(3): 262–70.

Blazer, D., Hughes, D., & George, L. (1987). Stressful life events and the onset of generalized anxiety syndrome. *American Journal of Psychiatry, 144,* 1178–83.

Bleuler, E. (1924). *Textbook of psychiatry.* New York: Macmillan.

Bliss, E. L. (1980). Multiple personalities: Report of fourteen cases with implications for schizophrenia and hysteria. *Archives of General Psychiatry, 37,* 1388–97.

Bliss, E. L., & Jeppsen, A. (1985). Prevalence of multiple personality among inpatients and outpatients. *American Journal of Psychiatry, 142,* 250–51.

Bloom, F. E., Lazerson, A., & Hofstadter, L. (1985). *Brain, mind, and behavior.* New York: Freeman.

Blumberg, S. H., & Izard, C. E. (1985). Affective and cognitive characteristics of depression in 10- and 11-year-old children. *Journal of Personality and Social Psychology, 49,* 194–202.

Bodlund, O., & Kullgren, G. (1996). Transsexualism—General outcome and prognostic factors: A five-year follow-up study of nineteen transsexuals in the process of changing sex. *Archives of Sexual Behavior, 25*(3): 303–16.

Bogerts, B. (1993). Recent advances in the neuropathology of schizophrenia. *Schizophrenia Bulletin, 19,* 431–45.

Bohman, M., & Sigvardsson, S. C. (1981). Maternal inheritance of alcohol abuse: Cross-fostering analysis of adopted women. *Archives of General Psychiatry, 38,* 965–69.

Bohn, M. J. (1993). Pharmacotherapy: Alcoholism. In D. Dunner (Ed.), *Psychopharmacology.* Volume 2: Psychiatric Clinics of North America. New York: W. B. Saunders.

Boney-McCoy, S., & Finkelhor, D. (1995). Psychosocial sequelae of violent victimization in a national youth sample. *Journal of Consulting and Clinical Psychology, 63*(5): 726–36.

Booker, J. M., & Hellekson, C. J. (1992). Prevalence of seasonal affective disorder in Alaska. *American Journal of Psychiatry, 149*(9): 1176–82.

Borkovec, T., & Costello, E. (1993). Efficacy of applied relaxation and cognitive-behavioral therapy in the treatment of generalized anxiety disorder. *Journal of Consulting and Clinical Psychology, 61,* 611–19.

Bornstein, R. F. (1992). The dependent personality: Developmental, social, and clinical perspectives. *Psychological Bulletin, 112*(1): 3–23.

Borysenko, M. (1987). The immune system: An overview. *Annals of Behavioral Medicine, 9,* 3–10.

Boscarino, J. A. (1995). Post-traumatic stress and associated disorders among Vietnam veterans: The significance of combat exposure and social support. *Journal of Traumatic Stress, 8*(2): 317–36.

Bouchard, T. J. (in press). The genetics of personality. In K. Blum & E. P. Noble (Eds.), *Handbook of Psychoneurogenetics.* Boca Raton, FL: CRC Press.

Bouchard, T., Lykken, D., McGue, M., Segal, N., & Tellegen, A. (1990). Sources of human psychological differences: The Minnesota study of twins reared apart. *Science, 250,* 223–28.

Bouchard, S., Gauthier, J., Benoit, L., French, D., Pelletier, M., & Godbout, C. (1996). Exposure versus cognitive restructuring in the treatment of panic disorder with agoraphobia. *Behaviour Research and Therapy, 34*(3): 213–24.

Boulos, C., Kutcher, S., Gardner, D., & Young, E. (1992). An open naturalistic trial of fluoxetine in adolescents and young adults with treatment-resistant major depression. *Journal of Child and Adolescent Psychopharmacology, 2,* 103–11.

Bourdon, K., Boyd, J., Rae, D., & Burns, B. (1988). Gender differences in phobias: Results of the ECA community survey. *Journal of Anxiety Disorders, 2,* 227–41.

Bourgeois, M. (1991). Serotonin, impulsivity, and suicide. *Human Psychopharmacology: Clinical and Experimental, 6,* 31–36.

Bowden, C. L. (1996). Role of newer medications for bipolar disorder. *Journal of Clinical Psychopharmacology, 16*(Suppl. 2), 48–55.

Bowlby, J. (1988). Developmental psychiatry comes of age. *American Journal of Psychiatry, 145,* 1–10.

Boyd, J., Rae, D., Thompson, J., & Burns, B. (1990). Phobia: Prevalence and risk factors. *Social Psychiatry and Psychiatric Epidemiology, 25,* 314–23.

Bradford, J. (1988). Organic treatment for the male sexual offender. *Annals of the New York Academy of Sciences, 528,* 193–202.

Bradshaw, J. (1990). *Homecoming: Reclaiming and championing your inner child.* New York: Bantam.

Brady, J. P., & Lind D. L. (1961). Experimental analysis of hysterical blindness: Operant conditioning techniques. *Archives of General Psychiatry, 4,* 331–39.

Braff, D. L., & Saccuzzo, D. P. (1985). The time course of information-processing deficits in schizophrenia. *American Journal of Psychiatry, 142*(2): 170–74.

Brandenburg N. A., Friedman, R. M., & Silver, S. E. (1990). The epidemiology of childhood psychiatric disorders: Prevalence findings from recent studies. *Journal of the American Academy of Child and Adolescent Psychiatry, 29*(1): 76–83.

Breier, A., Charney, D. S., & Heninger, G. R. (1986). Agoraphobia with panic attacks: Development, diagnostic stability, and course of illness. *Archives of General Psychiatry, 43,* 1029–36.

Brenner, H. D., Hodel, B., Roder, V., & Corrigan, P. (1992). Treatment of cognitive dysfunctions and behavioral deficits in schizophrenia. *Schizophrenia Bulletin, 18*(1): 21–26.

Breslau, N. & Davis, G. C. (1986). Chronic stress and major depression. *Archives of General Psychiatry, 43,* 309–14.

Breslau, N., & Davis, G. C. (1987). Posttraumatic stress disorder: The etiologic specificity of wartime stressors. *American Journal of Psychiatry, 144,* 578–83.

Breslin, F. C., Hayward, M., & Baum, A. (1994). Effect of stress on perceived intoxication and the Blood Alcohol Curve in men and women. *Health Psychology, 13*(6): 479–87.

Breslin, N. H. (1992). Treatment of schizophrenia: Current practice and future promise. *Hospital and Community Psychiatry, 43,* 877–85.

Brett, C. W., Burling, T. A., & Pavlik, W. B. (1981). Electroconvulsive shock and learned helplessness in rats. *Animal Learning and Behavior, 9,* 38–44.

Brew, B. J., Rosenblum, M., Cronin, K., & Price, R. W. (1995). AIDS Dementia Complex and HIV-1 brain infection: Clinical-virological correlations. *Annals of Neurology, 38*(4): 563–70.

Brickman, A. S., McManus, M., Grapentine, W. L., & Alessi, N. (1984). Neuropsychological assessment of seriously delinquent adolescents. *Journal of the American Academy of Child Psychiatry, 23,* 453–57.

Broadbent, D. E. (1958). *Perception of communication.* London: Pergamon.

Brodie, H. K. H., & Leff, M. J. (1971). Bipolar depression: A comparative study of patient characteristics. *American Journal of Psychiatry, 127,* 1086–90.

Brooks, A. D. (1974). *Law, psychiatry and the mental health system.* Boston: Little, Brown.

Brooks, N., & McKinlay, W. (1992). Mental health consequences of the Lockerbie disaster. *Journal of Traumatic Stress, 5,* 527–43.

Brown, G. W., & Harris, T. (1978). *Social origins of depression.* London: Tavistock.

Brown, R., Colter, N., Corsellis, J. A., Crow, T. J., Frith, C. D., Jagoe, R., Johnstone, E. C., & Marsh, L. (1986). Postmortem evidence of structural brain changes in schizophrenia. Differences in brain weight, temporal horn area, and parahippocampal gyrus compared with affective disorder. *Archives of General Psychiatry, 43*(1): 36–42.

Brown, T. A., Barlow, D. H., & Liebowitz, M. R. (1994). The empirical basis of generalized anxiety disorder. *American Journal of Psychiatry 151*(9): 1272–80.

Bruch, H. (1982). Anorexia nervosa: Therapy and theory. *American Journal of Psychiatry, 139,* 1531–38.

Bryant, F. B., & Yarnold, P. R. (1995). Comparing five alternative factor-models of the Student Jenkins Activity Survey: Separating the wheat from the chaff. *Journal of Personality Assessment, 64*(1), 145–58.

Bryant, R. N., & McConkey, K. M. (1989). Visual conversion disorder: A case analysis of the influence of visual information. *Journal of Abnormal Psychology, 98,* 326–29.

Buchanan, G. (1994). Explanatory style and coronary heart disease. In G. Buchanan & M. Seligman (Eds.), *Explanatory style.* Hillsdale, NJ: Erlbaum.

Buchanan, R.W. (1995). Clozapine: Efficacy and safety. *Schizophrenia Bulletin, 21*(4): 579–91.

Buchsbaum, M. S. (1990). The frontal lobes, basal ganglia, and temporal lobes as sites for schizophrenia. *Schizophrenia Bulletin, 16*(3): 379–89.

Buchsbaum, M. S., & Heier, R. J. (1987). Functional and anatomical brain imaging: Impact on schizophrenia research. *Schizophrenia Bulletin, 13,* 115–32.

Buchsbaum, M.S., Someya, T., Teng, C.Y., Abel, L., Chin, S., Najafi, A., Heier, R. J., Wu, J., and Bunney, W. E., Jr. (1996). PET and MRI of the thalamus in never-medicated patients with schizophrenia. *American Journal of Psychiatry, 151*(3), 343–50.

Buchwald, A. M., Coyne, J. C., & Cole, C. S. (1978). A critical evaluation of the learned helplessness model of depression. *Journal of Abnormal Psychology, 87,* 180–93.

Budzynski, T. H., Stoyva, J. M., Adler, C. S., & Mullaney, D. M. (1973). EMG biofeedback and tension headache: A controlled outcome study. *Psychosomatic Medicine, 35,* 484–96.

Bulik, C. M., Sullivan, P. F., & Weltzin, T. E. (1995). Temperance in eating disorders. *International Journal of Eating Disorders, 17,* 251–61.

Burgess, A., & Holmstrom, L. (1979). Adaptive strategies and recovery from rape. *American Journal of Psychiatry, 136,* 1278–82.

Burke, A. E., & Silverman, W. K. (1987). The prescriptive treatment of school refusal. Clinical Psychology Review, 7, 353–62.

Burman, A. M. (1988). Sexual assault and mental disorders in a community population. *Journal of Consulting and Clinical Psychology, 56*(6): 843–50.

Burns, B., & Reyher, J. (1976). Activating posthypnotic conflict: Emergent, uncovering, psychopathology, repression and psychopathology. *Journal of Personality Assessment, 40,* 492–501.

Burt, R. A., & Morris, N. (1972). A proposal for the abolition of the incompetency plea. *Chicago Law Review, 40,* 66–80.

Butcher, J. D., Dahlstrom, W. G., Graham, J. R., Tellegen, A., & Kraemer, B. (1989). *Minnesota Multiphasic Personality Inventory-2: Manual for administration and scoring.* Minneapolis: University of Minnesota Press.

Butcher, J. N. (1969). *MMPI: Research developments and clinical applications.* New York: McGraw-Hill.

Butler, G., Fennell, M., Robson, P., & Gelder, M. (1991). Comparison of behavior therapy and cognitive behavior therapy in the treatment of generalized anxiety disorder. *Journal of Consulting and Clinical Psychology, 59,* 167–75.

Buysse, D. J., Reynolds, C. F., Hauri, P. J., Roth, T., Stepanski, E. J., Thorpy, M. J., Bixler, E.O., Kales, A., Manfredi, R. L., Vgontsas, A. N., Stapf, D. M., Houck, P. R., and Kupfer, D. J. (1994). Diagnostic concordance for DSM-IV Sleep Disorders: A report from the APA/NIMH DSM-IV field trial. *American Journal of Psychiatry, 151*(9): 1351–60.

Bystritsky, A., Craske, M., Maidenberg, E., Vapnik, T., & Shapiro, D. (1995). Ambulatory monitoring of panic patients during regular activity: A preliminary report. *Biological Psychiatry, 38,* 684–89.

Cade, W. (1970). The story of lithium. In F. J. Ayd & H. Blackwell (Eds.), *Discoveries in biological psychiatry.* Philadelphia: Lippincott.

Cadoret, R. (1986). Epidemiology of antisocial personality. In W. H. Reid, D. Dorr, J. I. Walker, & J. W. Bonner, III (Eds.), *Unmasking the psychopath: Antisocial personality and related syndromes* (pp. 28–44). New York: Norton.

Cadoret, R. J., Yates, W. R., Troughton, E., Woodworth, G., & Stewart, M. A. (1995). Adoption study demonstrating two genetic pathways to drug abuse. *Archives of General Psychiatry, 52,* 42–52.

Cadoret, R. J., Yates, W. R., Troughton, E., Woodworth, G., & Stewart, M. A. (1996). An adoption study of drug abuse/dependency in females. *Comprehensive Psychiatry, 37*(2): 88–94.

Calingasan, N. Y., Gandy, S. E., Baker, H., Sheu, K. R., Kim, K., Wisniewski, H. M., & Gibson, G. E. (1995). Accumulation of amyloid precursor protein-like immunoreactivity in rat brain in response to thiamine deficiency. *Brain Research, 677,* 50–60.

Cameron, N. (1938). Reasoning, regression and communication in schizophrenia. *Psychological Monographs, 50* (Whole No. 221).

Cameron, N. (1947). *The psychology of behavior disorders.* Boston: Houghton Mifflin.

Campbell, M. & Cueva, J. (1995). Psychopharmacology in child and adolescent psychiatry: A review of the past seven years. Part 2. *Journal of the American Academy of Child and Adolescent Psychiatry, 34*(10).

Carey, G., & Gottesman, I. I. (1981). Twin and family studies of anxiety, phobic, and obsessive disorders. In D. F. Klein & J. Rabkin (Eds.), *Anxiety: New research and changing concepts* (pp. 117–36). New York: Raven Press.

Carlson, G. A., Kotin, J., Davenport, Y. B., & Adland, M. (1974). Follow-up of 53 bipolar manic depressive patients. *British Journal of Psychiatry, 124,* 134–39.

Carmelli, D., Dame, A., Swan, G., & Rosenman, R. (1991). Long-term changes in Type A behavior: A 27-year follow-up of the Western Collaborative Group Study. *Journal of Behavioral Medicine, 14,* 593–606.

Carroll, B. J. (1994). Brain mechanisms in manic depression. *Clinical Chemistry, 40*(2): 303–8.

Carter, A. B. (1949). The prognosis of certain hysterical symptoms. *British Medical Journal, 1,* 1076–80.

Carter, C. H. (1970). *Handbook of mental retardation syndromes.* Springfield, IL: Charles C. Thomas.

Castle, S., Wilkins, S., Heck, E., Tanzy, K., & Fahey, J. (1995). Depression in caregivers of demented patients is associated with altered immunity: Impaired proliferative capacity, increased CD8+, and a decline in lymphocytes with surface signal transduction molecules (CD38+) and a cytotoxicity marker (CD56+ CD8+). *Clinical and Experimental Immunology, 101,* 487–93.

Cautela, J. R. (1967). Covert sensitization. *Psychological Reports, 20,* 459–68.

Cegelka, W. J., & Tyler, J. L. (1970). The efficacy of special class placement for the mentally retarded in proper perspective. *Training School Bulletin, 67,* 33–68.

Centrella, M. (1994). Physician addiction and impairment—Current thinking: A review. *Journal of Addictive Diseases, 13*(1): 91–105.

Chambers, D. L. (1972). Alternatives to civil commitment of the mentally ill: Practical guides and constitutional imperatives. *Michigan Law Review, 70B,* 1107–1200.

Chandler, J., & Winokur, G. (1989). How antipsychotic are antipsychotics? A clinical study of the subjective antipsychotic effect of the antipsychotics in chronic schizophrenia. *Annals of Clinical Psychiatry, 1,* 215–20.

Chapman, L. J., & Chapman, D. T. (1969). Illusory correlations as an obstacle to the use of valid psychodiagnostic signs. *Journal of Abnormal Psychology, 74,* 271–80.

Chapman, L. J., & Chapman, J. P. (1973). *Disordered thought in schizophrenia.* New York: Appleton-Century-Crofts.

Chapman, L. J., & Taylor, J. A. (1957). Breadth of deviate concepts used by schizophrenics. *Journal of Abnormal Social Psychology, 54,* 118–23.

Charney, D. S., & Heninger, G. R. (1985). Noradrenergic function and the mechanism of action of antianxiety treatment: The effect of long-term imipramine treatment. *Archives of General Psychiatry, 42,* 473–81.

Charney, D. S., & Heninger, G. R. (1986). Abnormal regulation of noradrenergic function in panic disorders: Effects of clonidine in healthy subjects and patients with agoraphobia and panic disorder. *Archives of General Psychiatry, 43* (11): 1042–54.

Cheseldine, S., & McConkey, R. (1979). Parental speech to young Down's syndrome children: An intervention study. *American Journal of Mental Deficiency, 83,* 612–20.

Chin, J. H., & Goldstein, D. B. (1977). Drug tolerance in biomembranes: A spin label study of the effects of ethanol. *Science, 196,* 684–85.

Chodoff, P. (1974). The diagnosis of hysteria: An overview. *American Journal of Psychiatry, 131,* 1073–78.

Clark, D. A., Beck, A. T., & Beck, J. S. (1994). Symptom differences in major depression, dysthymia, panic disorder, and generalized anxiety disorder. *American Journal of Psychiatry, 151*(2): 205–9.

Clark, D. M. (1988). A cognitive model of panic attacks. In S. Rachman & J. D. Maser (Eds.), *Panic: Psychological perspectives.* Hillsdale, NJ: Erlbaum.

Clark, D. (1989). Anxiety states: Panic and generalized anxiety. In K. Hawton, P. Salkovskis, J. Kirk, & D. Clark (Eds.), *Cognitive behaviour therapy for psychiatric problems: A practical guide.* Oxford, Eng.: Oxford University Press.

Clark, D., Gelder, M., Salkovskis, P., Hackman, A., Middleton, H., & Anatasiades, A. (1990). *Cognitive therapy for panic: Comparative efficacy.* Presented at the annual meeting of the American Psychiatric Association, New York, May 15, 1990.

Clark, R. E. (1948). The relationship of schizophrenia to occupational income and occupational prestige. *American Sociological Review, 13,* 325–30.

Clausen, J. A., & Kohn, M. L. (1959). Relation of schizophrenia to the social structure of a small city. In B. Pasamanick (Ed.), *Epidemiology of mental disorder.* Washington, DC: American Association for the Advancement of Science.

Cleckley, H. (1964). *The mask of sanity.* St. Louis: Mosby.

Clementz, B. A., Sweeney, J. A., Hirt, M., & Haas, G. (1990). Pursuit gain and saccadic intrusions in first-degree relatives of probands with schizophrenia. *Journal of Abnormal Psychology, 99*(4): 327–35.

Clomipramine Collaborative Study Group. (1991). Clomipramine in the treatment of obsessive-compulsive disorder. *Archives of General Psychiatry, 48,* 730–38.

Cloninger, C. R., & Gottesman, I. I. (1987). Genetic and environmental factors in antisocial behavior disorders. In S. A. Mednick, T. E. Moffitt, & S. A. Strack (Eds.), *The causes of crime: New biological approaches.* Cambridge: Cambridge University Press.

Cloninger, C. R., Sigvardsson, S., von Knorring, A., & Bohman, M. (1984). An adoption study of somatoform disorders: II. Identification of two discrete somatoform disorders. *Archives of General Psychiatry, 41,* 863–71.

Cohen, I. (1970). The benzodiazepines. In F. J. Ayd & H. Blackwell (Eds.), *Discoveries in biological psychiatry.* Philadelphia: Lippincott.

Cohen, J. B., & Reed, D. (1985). The Type A behavior pattern and coronary heart disease among Japanese men in Hawaii. *Journal of Behavioral Medicine, 8* (4): 343–52.

Cohen, S., Tyrrell, D., & Smith, A. (1993). Negative life events, perceived stress, negative affect, and susceptibility to the common cold. *Journal of Personality and Social Psychology, 64,* 131–40.

Coie, J. D., & Kupersmidt, J. B. (1983). A behavioral analysis of emerging social status in boys' groups. *Child Development, 54,* 1400–16.

Coltheart, M. (1985). Cognitive neuropsychology and the study of reading. In M. I. Posner & O. S. M. Marin (Eds.), *Attention and Performance XI.* Hillsdale, NJ: Erlbaum.

Consumer Reports (1995). Mental health: Does therapy help? November, 734–739.

Cook, W. W., & Medley, D. M. (1954). Proposed hostility and pharisaic-virtue scales for the MMPI. *Journal of Applied Psychology, 38,* 414–18.

Coons, P. M. (1994). Confirmation of childhood abuse in child and adolescent cases of multiple personality disorder and dissociative disorder not otherwise specified. *Journal of Nervous and Mental Disease, 182*(8): 461–64.

Coons, P., Bowman, E., Pellow, T., & Schneider, P. (1989). Posttraumatic aspects of the treatment of victims of sexual abuse and incest. *Psychiatric Clinics of North America, 12,* 325–35.

Cooper, G. (1988). The safety of fluoxetine—An update. *British Journal of Psychiatry, 153,* 77–86.

Corder, E. H., Saunders, A. M., Strittmatter, W. J., et al. (1993). Gene dose of apolipoprotein E type 4 allele and the risk of Alzheimer's disease in late onset families. *Science, 261,* 921–23.

Corrigall, W. A., & Coen, K. A. (1991). Selective dopamine antagonists reduce nicotine self-administration. *Psychopharmacology, 104,* 171–76.

Costello, C. G. (1972). Depression: Loss of reinforcers or loss of reinforcer effectiveness. *Behavior Therapy, 3,* 240–47.

Costello, C. (1982). Fears and phobias in women: A community study. *Journal of Abnormal Psychology, 91,* 280–86.

Cottler, L. B., Price, R. K., Compton, W. M., & Mager, D. E. (1995). Subtypes of adult antisocial personality behavior among drug abusers. *Journal of Nervous and Mental Disease, 183*(3): 154–61.

Cotton, N. S. (1979). The familial incidence of alcoholism: A review. *Journal of Studies on Alcohol, 40,* 89–116.

Cox, P., Hallam, R., O'Connor, K., & Rachman, S. (1983). An experimental analysis of fearlessness and courage. *British Journal of Psychology, 74,* 107–17.

Coyle, J. T., Price, D. L., & DeLong, M. R. (1983). Alzheimer's disease: A disorder of cortical cholinergic innervation. *Science, 219,* 1184–90.

Craske, M. G., Maidenberg, E., & Bystritsky, A. (1995). Brief cognitive-behavioral versus nondirective therapy for panic disorder. *Journal of Behavior Therapy and Experimental Psychiatry, 26*, 113–20.

Crisp, A. H. (1980). *Anorexia nervosa—Let me be*. London: Plenum.

Critchley, M. (1966). *The parietal lobes*. New York: Hafner.

Crits-Cristoph, P. (1992). The efficacy of brief psychotherapy. A meta-analysis. *American Journal of Psychiatry, 149*(2): 151–57.

Crits-Cristoph, P. (1997). Psychological treatment for personality disorders. In P. Nathan and J. Gorman (Eds.), *Treatments that work*. New York: Oxford.

Crittenden, P. M., & Ainsworth, M. D. S. (1989). Child maltreatment and attachment theory. In D. Chichetti & V. Carlson (Eds.), *Child maltreatment* (pp. 432–63). Cambridge: Cambridge University Press.

Cromwell, R. L. (1993). Searching for the origins of schizophrenia. *Psychological Science, 4*, 276–79.

Cronbach, L. J., Gleser, G. C., Nanda, H., & Rajaratnam, N. (1972). *The dependability of behavioral measurements: Theory of generalizability for scores and profiles*. New York: Wiley.

Crow, T. J. (1980). Molecular pathology of schizophrenia: More than one disease process? *British Medical Journal*, 66–68.

Crow, T. J. (1982). Two dimensions of pathology in schizophrenia: Dopaminergic and non-dopaminergic. *Psychopharmacology Bulletin, 18*, 22–29.

Crowe, M. J., Marks, I. M., Agras, W. S., & Leitenberg, H. (1972). Time limited desensitization, implosion and shaping for phobic patients: A crossover study. *Behaviour Research and Therapy, 10*(4): 319–28.

Crowe, R. R. (1983). Antisocial personality disorders. In R. E. Tarter (Ed.), *The child at psychiatric risk*. New York: Oxford University Press.

Crowe, R. (1990). Panic disorder: Genetic considerations. *Journal of Psychiatric Research, 24*, 129–34.

Csikszentmihalyi, M. (1990). *Flow: The psychology of optimal experience*. New York: Harper & Row.

Curtis, B. A., Jacobson, S., & Marcus, E. M. (1972). *An introduction to the neurosciences*. Philadelphia: Saunders.

Cutler, S., & Nolen-Hoeksema, S. (1991). Accounting for sex differences in depression through female victimization: Childhood sexual abuse. *Sex Roles, 24*, 425–38.

Cytryn, L., & McKnew, D. H. (1972). Proposed classification of childhood depression. *American Journal of Psychiatry, 129*, 149–55.

Cytryn, L., & McKnew, D.H. (1996). *Growing up sad: Childhood depression and its treatment*. New York: Norton.

Dale, L. C., Hurt, R. D., Offord, K. P., Lawson, G. M., Croghan, I. T., & Schroeder, D. R. (1995). High-dose nicotine patch therapy: Percentage of replacement and smoking cessation. *Journal of the American Medical Association, 274*(17): 1353–58.

Damasio, A. R., Tranel, D., & Damasio, H. C. (1990). Individuals with sociopathic behavior caused by frontal damage fail to respond autonomically to social stimuli. *Behavioral Brain Research, 41*, 81–94.

Damasio, H., Grabowski, T., Frank, R., Galaburda, A. M., & Damasio, A. R. (1994). The return of Phineas Gage: Clues about the brain from the skull of a famous patient. *Science, 264*, 1102–5.

Daryanani, H. E., Santolaria, F. J., Reimers, E. G., Jorge, J. A., Lopez, N. B., Hernandez, F. M., Riera, A. M., & Rodriguez, E. R. Alcoholic withdrawal syndrome and seizures. *Alcohol and Alcoholism, 29*(3): 323–28.

Davidson, J., Kudler, H., Smith, R., et al. (1990). Treatment of PTSD with amitriptyline and placebo. *Archives of General Psychiatry, 47*, 250–60.

Davidson, R. J., Schaffer, C. E., & Saron, C. (1985). Effects of lateralized presentations of faces on self-reports of emotion and EEG asymmetry in depressed and non-depressed subjects. *Psychophysiology, 22* (3): 353–64.

Davies, J. C. V., & Maliphant, R. (1971). Autonomic responses of male adolescents exhibiting refractory behavior in school. *Journal of Child Psychology and Psychiatry, 12*, 115–27.

Davis, P. H., & Osherson, A. (1977). The current treatment of a multiple-personality woman and her son. *American Journal of Psychotherapy, 31*, 504–15.

Davis, P. J., & Schwartz, G. E. (1987). Repression and the inaccessibility of affective memories. *Journal of Personality and Social Psychology, 51* (1): 155–62.

Davison, G. C. (1976). Homosexuality: The ethical challenge. *Journal of Counseling and Clinical Psychology, 44*, 157–62.

Davison, G. C. (1978). Not can but ought: The treatment of homosexuality. *Journal of Consulting and Clinical Psychology, 46*, 170–72.

DeAngelis, T. (1990). Cambodians' sight loss tied to seeing atrocities. *APA Monitor*, July, pp. 36–37.

De Beurs, E., Van Balkom, A. J., Anton, J. L. M., Lange, A., Koele, P., & Van Dyck, R. (1995). Treatment of panic disorder with agoraphobia: Comparison of fluvoxamine, placebo, and psychological panic management combined with exposure and of exposure in vivo alone. *American Journal of Psychiatry, 152*(5): 673–82.

De Beurs, E., Van Balkom, A. J., Lange, A., Koele, P., & Van Dyck, R. (1995). Treatment of panic disorder with agoraphobia: Comparison of fluvoxamine, placebo, and psychological panic management combined with exposure and of exposure in vivo alone. *American Journal of Psychiatry, 152*(5): 683–91.

Dekker, E., Pelse, H., & Groen, J. (1957). Conditioning as a cause of asthmatic attacks: A laboratory study. *Journal of Psychosomatic Research, 2*, 97–108.

Demartino, R., Mollica, R. F., & Wilk, V. (1995). Monoamine oxidase inhibitors in posttraumatic stress disorder: Promise and problems in Indochinese survivors of trauma. *Journal of Nervous and Mental Disease, 183*(8): 510–15.

DeMeyer, M. K., Barton, S., Alpern, G. D., Kimberlin, C., Allen, J., Yang, E., & Steel, R. (1974). The measured intelligence of autistic children. *Journal of Autistic Children and Schizophrenia, 4*, 42–60.

Deneau, G., Yanagita, T., & Seevers, M. H. (1969). Self-administration of psychoactive substances by the monkey. *Psychopharmacologia (Berl.), 16*, 30–48.

Department of International Economic and Social Affairs. (1985). *Demographic Yearbook* (37th ed.). New York: United Nations.

Depue, R. (1979). *The psychobiology of the depressive disorders: Implications for the effect of stress*. New York: Academic Press.

Depue, R. H., & Monroe, S. (1978). The unipolar-bipolar distinction in depressive disorders. *Psychological Bulletin, 85*, 1001–29.

Depue, R. A., & Monroe, S. M. (1986). Conceptualization and measurement of human disorder in life stress research: The problem of chronic disturbance. *Psychological Bulletin, 99*, 36–51.

Dershowitz, A. M. (1968). Psychiatry in the legal process: "A knife that cuts both ways." *Trial, 4*, 29.

De Silva, P., Rachman, S., & Seligman, M. E. P. (1977). Prepared phobias and obsessions: Therapeutic outcome. *Behaviour Research and Therapy, 15*(1): 65–77.

Deutsch, A. (1949). *The mentally ill in America*. New York: Columbia University Press.

Devanand, D. P., Fitzsimons, L., Prudic, J., & Sackeim, H. A. (1995). Subjective side effects during electroconvulsive therapy. *Convulsive Therapy, 11*(4): 232–40.

Devanand, D., Sackeim, H., & Prudic, J. (1991). Electroconvulsive therapy in the treatment-resistant patient. *Electroconvulsive Therapy, 14*, 905–23.

Devanand, D. P., Sano, M., Tang, M., Taylor, S., Gurland, B. J., Wilder, D., Stern, Y., & Mayeux, R. (1996). Depressed mood and the incidence of Alzheimer's disease in the elderly living in the community. *Archives of General Psychiatry, 53*, 175–82.

Diamond, B. L. (1974). Psychiatric prediction of dangerousness. *University of Pennsylvania Law Review, 123*, 439–52.

Diamond, E. L. (1982). The role of anger and hostility in essential hypertension and coronary heart disease. *Psychological Bulletin, 92*, 410–33.

Diamond, R. G., & Rozin, P. (1984). Activation of existing memories in anterograde amnesia. *Journal of Abnormal Psychology, 93*, 98–105.

Diekstra, R. (1992). The prevention of suicidal behavior: Evidence for the efficacy of clinical and community-based programs. *International Journal of Mental Health, 21*, 69–87.

Dilip, J. V., Caligiuri, M. P., Paulsen, J. S., Heaton, R. K., Lacro, J. P., Harris, M. J., Bailey, A., Fell, R. L., & McAdams, L. A. (1995). Risk of tardive dyskinesia in older patients. *Archives of General Psychiatry, 52*, 756–65.

Dimsdale, J. E., Pierce, C., Schoenfeld, D., Brown, A., Zusman, R., & Graham, R. (1986). Suppressed anger and blood pressure: The effects of race, sex, social class, obesity, and age. *Psychosomatic Medicine, 48,* 430–36.

Dixon, L. B., Lehman, A. F. and Levine, J. (1995). Conventional antipsychotic medications for schizophrenia. *Schizophrenia Bulletin, 21*(4): 567–77.

Doane, J. A., Falloon, I. R. H., Goldstein, M. J., & Mintz, J. (1985). Parental affective style and the treatment of schizophrenia: Predicting the course of illness and social functioning. *Archives of General Psychiatry, 42,* 34–42.

Dodge, K. A. (1983). Behavioral antecedents of peer social status. *Child Development, 54,* 1386–99.

Dohrenwend, B. P., Levav, I., Shrout, P. E., Schwartz, S., Naveh, G., Link, B. G., Skodol, A. E., & Stueve, A. (1992). Socio-economic status and psychiatric disorders: The causation-selection issue. *Science, 255,* 946–52.

Dohrenwend, B. S., & Martin, J. L. (1978, February). *Personal vs. situational determination of anticipation and control of the occurrence of stressful life events.* Paper presented at the annual meeting of AAAS, Washington, D.C.

Dohrenwend, B. P., & Shrout, P. E. (1985). "Hassles" in the conceptualization and measurement of life stress variables. *American Psychologist, 40,* 780–85.

Doleys, D. M. (1979). Assessment and treatment of childhood enuresis. In A. J. Finch, Jr., & P. C. Kendall (Eds.), *Clinical treatment and research in child psychopathology* (pp. 207–33). New York: Spectrum.

Dominguez, R. A., & Mestre, S. M. (1994). Management of treatment-refractory obsessive compulsive patients. *Journal of Clinical Psychiatry, 55*(10): 86–92.

Donaldson, D. (1976). *Insanity inside out.* New York: Crown.

Donaldson, S. I., Graham, J. W., Piccinin, A. M., & Hansen, W.B. (1995). Resistance-skills training and onset of alcohol use: Evidence for beneficial and potentially harmful effects in public schools and in private Catholic schools. *Health Psychology, 14*(4): 291–300.

Doorn, C. D., Poortinga, J., & Verschoor, A. M. (1994). Cross-gender identity in transvestites and male transsexuals. *Archives of Sexual Behavior, 23*(2): 185–201.

Dorsey, M. F., Iwata, B. A., Ong, P., & McSween, T. (1980). Treatment of self-injurious behavior using a water mist: Initial response suppression and generalization. *Journal of Applied Behavior Analysis, 13,* 343–53.

Douglas, M. (Ed.). (1970). *Witchcraft: Confessions and accusations.* London: Tavistock.

Douglas, V. I. (1983). Attentional and cognitive problems. In M. Rutter (Ed.), *Developmental neuropsychiatry* (pp. 280–329). New York: Guilford Press.

Drake, R., & Vaillant, G. E. (1988). Predicting alcoholism and personality disorder in a 30-year longitudinal study of children of alcoholics. *British Journal of Addiction, 83,* 799–807.

Drewnowski, A., Hopkins, S. A., & Kessler, R. C. (1988). The prevalence of bulimia nervosa in the U.S. college student population. *American Journal of Public Health, 78*(10): 1322–25.

Drossman, D. A. (1982). Patients with psychogenic abdominal pain: Six years' observation in the medical setting. *American Journal of Psychiatry, 139,* 1549–57.

Droungas, A., Ehrman, R. N., Childress, A. R., & O'Brien, C. P. (1995). Effect of smoking cues and cigarette availability on craving and smoking behavior. *Addictive Behaviors, 20*(5): 657–73.

DuBois, D. L., Felner, R. D., Bartels, C. L., & Silverman, M. M. (1995). Stability of self-reported depressive symptoms in a community sample of children and adolescents. *Journal of Clinical Child Psychology, 24*(4): 386–96.

Dunner, D. L., Gershom, E. S., & Goodwin, F. K. (1976). Heritable factors in the severity of affective illness. *Biological Psychiatry, 11,* 31–42.

DuPaul, G. J., & Barkley, R. A. (1993). Behavioral contributions to pharmacotherapy: The utility of behavioral methodology in medication treatment of children with attention deficit hyperactivity disorder. *Behavior Therapy, 24,* 47–65.

Eaker, E., Haynes, S., & Feinleib, M. (1983). Spouse behavior and coronary heart disease. *Activitas Nervosa Superior, 25,* 81–90.

Edelbrock, C., Rende, R., Plomin, R., & Thompson, L. A. (1995). A twin study of competence and problem behavior in childhood and early adolescence. *Journal of Child Psychology and Psychiatry, 36*(5): 775–85.

Egeland, J. A., & Sussex, J. N. (1985). Suicide and family loading for affective disorders. *Journal of the American Medical Association, 254,* 915–18.

Eidelson, J. I. (1977). *Perceived control and psychopathology.* Unpublished doctoral dissertation, Duke University.

Ekman, P., Friesen, W. V., & Ellsworth, P. (1972). *Emotion in the human face.* New York: Pergamon.

Elkin, I., Parloff, M. B., Hadley, S. W., & Autry, J. H. (1985). NIMH Treatment of Depression Collaborative Research Program. *Archives of General Psychiatry, 42,* 305–16.

Elkin, I., Shea, T., Imber, S., Pilkonis, P., Sotsky, S., Glass, D., Watkins, J., Leber, W., & Collins, J. (1986). *NIMH treatment of depression collaborative research program: Initial outcome findings.* Paper presented at meetings of the American Association for the Advancement of Science, May 1986.

Elkin, I., Shea, M. T., Watkins, J. T., Imber, S. D., Sotsky, S. M., Collins, J. F., Glass, D. R., Pilkonis, P. A., Leber, W. R., Docherty, J. P., Fiester, S. J., & Parloff, M. B. (1989). National Institute of Mental Health Treatment of Depression Collaborative Research Program: General effectiveness of treatments. *Archives of General Psychiatry, 46*(11): 971–82.

Ellenberger, H. F. (1970). *The discovery of the unconscious: The history and evolution of dynamic psychiatry.* New York: Basic Books.

Ellickson, P. L. (1994). School-based drug prevention: What should it do? What has been done? In R. Coombs & D. Ziedonis (Eds.), *Handbook on drug abuse prevention.* Englewood Cliffs, NJ: Prentice-Hall.

Elliott, D. S., Hulzinga, D., & Ageton, S. S. (1985). *Explaining delinquency and drug use.* Beverly Hills, CA: Sage.

Ellis, A. (1962). *Reason and emotion in psychotherapy.* New York: Lyle Stuart.

Ellis, L., & Ames, M. A. (1987). Neurohormonal functioning and sexual orientation: A theory of homosexuality-heterosexuality. *Psychological Bulletin, 101*(2): 233–58.

Ellsworth, P. C., & Carlsmith, M. J. (1968). Effects of eye contact and verbal content on affective response to dyadic interactions. *Journal of Personality and Social Psychology, 10,* 15–20.

Emmelkamp, P., Hoekstra, R., & Visser, S. (1985). The behavioral treatment of obsessive-compulsive disorder: Prediction of outcome at 3.5 years follow-up. In P. Pichot, A. Brenner, R. Wolf, & K. Thau (Eds.), *Psychiatry: The state of the art* (Vol. 4). New York: Plenum.

Emmelkamp, P., & Kuipers, A. (1979). Agoraphobia: A follow-up study four years after treatment. *British Journal of Psychiatry, 134,* 352–55.

Emrick, D. C. (1982). Evaluation of alcoholism therapy methods. In E. M. Pattison & E. Kaufman (Eds.), *Encyclopedic handbook of alcoholism.* New York: Gardner Press.

Enkelmann, R. (1991). Alprazolam versus busiprone in the treatment of outpatients with generalized anxiety disorder. *Psychopharmacology, 105,* 428–32.

Ennis, B. J., & Litwack, T. R. (1974). Psychiatry and the presumption of expertise: Flipping coins in the courtroom. *California Law Review, 62,* 693.

Eppley, K., Abrams, A., & Shear, J. (1989). Differential effects of relaxation techniques on trait anxiety: A meta-analysis. *Journal of Clinical Psychology, 45,* 957–74.

Epstein, J. A., Botvin, G. J., Diaz, T., Toth, V., & Schinke, S. P. (1995). Social and personal factors in marijuana use and intentions to use drugs among inner city minority youth. *Developmental and Behavioral Pediatrics, 16*(1): 14–20.

Erickson, W. D., Walbek, N. H., & Seely, R. K. (1988). Behavior patterns of child molesters. *Archives of Sexual Behavior, 17*(1): 77–86.

Erikson, K. (1976). *Everything in its path: Destruction of community in the Buffalo Creek flood.* New York: Simon & Schuster.

Eriksson, H. (1995). Heart failure: A growing public health problem. *Journal of Internal Medicine, 237,* 135–41.

Eslinger, P. J., & Damasio, A. R. (1985). Severe disturbance of higher cognition after bilateral frontal lobe ablation: *Patient E.V.R. Neurology, 35,* 1731–41.

Esterling, B. A., Kiecolt-Glaser, J. K., & Glaser, R. (1996).

Psychosocial modulation of cytokine-induced natural killer cell activity in older adults. *Psychosomatic Medicine, 58,* 264–72.

Evans, D. L., Leserman, J., Perkins, D. O., Stern, R. A., Murphy, C., Tamul, K., Liao, D., Van der Horst, C. M., Hall, C. D., Folds, J. D., Golden, R. N., & Petitto, J. M. (1995). Stress-associated reductions of cytotoxic T lymphocytes and natural killer cells in asymptomatic HIV infection. *American Journal of Psychiatry, 152*(4): 543–50.

Exline, R., & Winters, L. C. (1965). Affective relations and mutual glances in dyads. In S. Tomkins & C. E. Izard (Eds.), *Affect, cognition and personality.* New York: Springer.

Exner, J. E. (1978). *The Rorschach: A comprehensive system: Vol. 2. Current research and advanced interpretation.* New York: Wiley.

Exner, J. E. (1993). *The Rorschach: A comprehensive system. Vol. 3: Assessment of children and adolescents.* New York: Wiley.

Exner, J. E. and Weiner, I. B. (1994). *The Rorschach: A comprehensive system. Vol. 3: Assessment of children and adolescents.* New York: Wiley.

Eysenck, H. J. (1979). The conditioning model of neurosis. *Communications in Behavioral Biology, 2,* 155–99.

Fairburn, C. G., Welch, S. L., & Hay, P. J. (1993). The classification of recurrent overeating: The "binge eating disorder" proposal. *International Journal of Eating Disorders, 13*(2): 155–59.

Fairburn, C. G., & Wilson, G. T. (1993). Binge eating: Definition and classification. In C. G. Fairburn & G. T. Wilson (Eds.), *Binge eating: Nature, assessment, and treatment.* New York: Guilford Press.

Falloon, I. R. H. (1988). Editorial: Expressed emotion: Current status. *Psychological Medicine, 18,* 269–74.

Faris, R. E. L., & Dunham, H. W. (1939). *Mental disorders in urban areas.* Chicago: University of Chicago Press.

Farmer, A. E., McGuffin, P., & Gottesman, I. I. (1987). Twin concordance for DSM-III schizophrenia: Scrutinizing the validity of the definition. *Archives of General Psychiatry, 44,* 634–41.

Farrington, D. P. (1978). The family background of aggressive youths. In L. A. Hersov & D. Shaffer (Eds.), *Aggression and antisocial behavior in childhood and adolescence.* New York: Pergamon.

Farrington, D. P., Loeber R., & Van Kammen. (1990). Long-term outcomes of hyperactivity-impulsivity-attention deficit and conduct problems in childhood. In L. N. Robbins & M. Rutter (Eds.), *Straight and devious pathways from childhood to adulthood,* (pp. 62–81). Cambridge, Eng: Cambridge University Press.

Fava, G. A., Zielezny, M., Savron, G., & Grandi, S. (1995). Long-term effects of behavioural treatment for panic disorder with agoraphobia. *British Journal of Psychiatry, 166,* 87–92.

Fawzy, F. I., Fawzy, N. W., Arndt, L. A., & Pasnau, R. O. (1995). Critical review of psychosocial interventions in cancer care. *Archives of General Psychiatry, 52,* 100–13.

Fawzy, F., Fawzy, N., Hyun, C., et al. (1993). Malignant melanoma: Effects of an early structured psychiatric intervention, coping, and affective state on recurrence and survival 6 years later. *Archives of General Psychiatry, 50,* 681–89.

Feinberg, T. E., Rifkin, A., Schaffer, C., & Walker, E. (1986). Facial discrimination and emotional recognition in schizophrenia and affective disorders. *Archives of General Psychiatry, 43,* 276–79.

Feldman, M. P., & MacCulloch, M. J. (1971). *Homosexual behaviour: Theory and assessment.* Oxford: Pergamon.

Fenichel, O. (1945). *The psychoanalytic theory of neurosis.* New York: Norton.

Fenton, W. S., & McGlashan, T. H. (1991). Natural history of schizophrenia subtypes. I. Longitudinal study of paranoid, hebephrenic, and undifferentiated schizophrenia. *Archives of General Psychiatry, 48*(11): 969–77.

Fieve, R. R. (1975). *Mood swing.* New York: Morrow.

Fine, C. G. (1991). Treatment stabilization and crisis prevention. Pacing the therapy of the multiple personality disorder patient. *Psychiatric Clinics of North America, 14,* 661–75.

Fingarette, H., & Hasse, A. (1979). *Mental disabilities and criminal responsibility.* Berkeley: University of California Press.

Fink, M. (1979). *Convulsive therapy: Therapy and practice.* New York: Raven Press.

Finkel, N. J. (1989). The Insanity Defense Reform Act of 1984: Much ado about nothing. *Behavioral Sciences and the Law, 7,* 403–19.

Finkel, N. J. (1990). De facto departures from insanity instructions: Toward the remaking of common law. *Law and Human Behavior, 14,* 105–22.

Finkel, N. J. (1991). The insanity defense: A comparison between verdict schemas. *Law and Human Behavior, 15,* 533–55.

Fiore, M. C., Novotny, T. E., Pierce, J. P., Giovino, G. A., Hatziandrev, G. A., Newcomb, E. J., Surawicz, T. S., & Davis, R. M. (1990). Methods used to quit smoking in the United States: Do cessation programs help? *Journal of the American Medical Association, 263,* 2760–65.

Fiore, M. C., Smith, S., Jorenby, D., & Baker, T. B. (1994). The effectiveness of the nicotine patch for smoking cessation: A meta-analysis. *Journal of the American Medical Association, 271*(24): 1940–47.

Fischer, M., Barkley, R. A., Fletcher, K. E., & Smallish, L. (1993). The adolescent outcome of hyperactive children: Predictors of psychiatric, academic, social, and emotional adjustment. *Journal of the American Academy of Child and Adolescent Psychiatry, 32,* 324–32.

Fisher, J., Epstein, L. J., & Harris, M. R. (1967). Validity of the psychiatric interview: Predicting the effectiveness of the first Peace Corps volunteers in Ghana. *Archives of General Psychiatry, 17,* 744–50.

Fleming, J. E., & Offord, D. R. (1990). Epidemiology of childhood depressive disorders: A critical review. *Journal of the American Academy of Child and Adolescent Psychiatry, 29*(4): 571–80.

Flood, R., & Seager, C. (1968). A retrospective examination of psychiatric case records of patients who subsequently commit suicide. *British Journal of Psychiatry, 114,* 443–50.

Foa, D. B., & Kozak, M. J. (1986). Emotional processing of fear: Exposure to corrective information. *Psychological Bulletin, 99,* 20–35.

Foa, E., & Kozak, M. (1993). Obsessive-compulsive disorder: Long-term outcome of psychological treatment. In M. Mavissakalian & R. Prien (Eds.), *Long-term treatments of anxiety disorders.* Washington, DC: American Psychiatric Press.

Foa, E. B., & Riggs, D. S. (1995). Post-traumatic stress disorder following assault: Theoretical considerations and empirical findings. *Current Directions in Psychological Science, 4*(2): 61–65.

Foa, E. B., Riggs, D. S., Massie, E. D., & Yarczower, M. (1995). The impact of fear activation and anger on the efficacy of exposure treatment for posttraumatic stress disorder. *Behavior Therapy, 26*(3): 487–99.

Foa, E., Rothbaum, B., Riggs, D., & Murdock, T. (1991). Treatment of post-traumatic stress disorder in rape victims: A comparison between cognitive-behavioral procedures and counseling. *Journal of Consulting and Clinical Psychology, 59,* 715–23.

Fogarty, F., Russell, J. M., Newman, S. C., & Bland, R. C. (1994). Mania. *Acta Psychiatrica Scandanivica, 89*(Suppl. 376): 16–23.

Folks, D. G. (1995). Munchausen's syndrome and other factitious disorders. *Neurologic Clinics, 13*(2): 267–81.

Fonagy, P., Leigh, T., Steele, M., Steele, H., Kennedy, R., Mattoon, G., Target, M., & Gerber, A. (1996). The relation of attachment status, psychiatric classification, and response to psychotherapy. *Journal of Consulting and Clinical Psychology, 64*(1): 22–31.

Ford, M. R., & Widiger, T. A. (1989). Sex bias in the diagnosis of histrionic and antisocial personality disorders. *Journal of Consulting and Clinical Psychology, 57*(2): 301–5.

Foucault, M. (1965). Madness and civilization: A history of insanity in the age of reason. New York: Random House.

Fowles, D. C., & Gersh, F. (1979). Neurotic depression: The endogenous-neurotic distinction. In R. A. Depue (Ed.), *The psychobiology of the depressive disorders: Implications for the effects of stress.* New York: Academic Press.

Frank, E., Anderson, B., Stewart, B., Dacu, C., et al. (1988). Efficacy of cognitive behavior therapy and systematic desensitization in the treatment of rape trauma. *Behavior Therapy, 19,* 403–20.

Frank, E., Anderson, C., & Rubinstein, D. (1978). Frequency of sexual dysfunction in "normal" couples. *New England Journal of Medicine, 299,* 111–15.

Frank, E., & Spanier, C. (1995). Interpersonal psychotherapy for depression: Overview, clinical efficacy, and future directions. *Clinical Psychology: Science and Practice, 2*(4): 349–69.

Frank, H., & Hoffman, N. (1986). Borderline empathy: An empirical investigation. *Comprehensive Psychiatry, 2,* 387–95.

Frank, I. M., Lessin, P. J., Tyrrell, E. D., Hahn, P. M., & Szara, S. (1976). Acute and cumulative effects of marihuana smoking on hospitalized subjects: A 36–day study. In M. C. Braude & S. Szara (Eds.), *Pharmacology of marihuana* (Vol. 2, pp. 673–80). New York: Academic Press.

Frank, J., Kosten, T., Giller, E., & Dan, E. (1988). A randomized clinical trial of phenelzine and imipramine for post-traumatic stress disorder. *American Journal of Psychiatry, 145,* 1289–91.

Frederick C. J. (1978). Current trends in suicidal behavior in the United States. *American Journal of Psychotherapy, 32,* 172–200.

Fredrikson, M., Annas, P., Fischer, H., & Wik, G. (1996). Gender and age differences in the prevalence of specific fears and phobias. *Behaviour Research and Therapy, 34*(1): 33–39.

Freeman, E. W., Schweizer, E., & Rickels, K. (1995). Personality factors in women with premenstrual syndrome. *Psychosomatic Medicine, 57,* 453–59.

Freud, A. (1936). *The ego and mechanisms of defense* (rev. ed.). New York: International Universities Press, 1967.

Freud, S. (1894). The neuro-psychoses of defense. In J. Strachey (Ed. and Trans.), *The complete psychological works* (Vol. 3). New York: Norton, 1976.

Freud, S. (1917a). Introductory lectures on psychoanalysis, Part III. In J. Strachey (Ed. and Trans.), *The complete psychological works* (Vol. 16). New York: Norton, 1976.

Freud, S. (1917b). Mourning and melancholia. In J. Strachey (Ed. and Trans.), *The complete psychological works* (Vol. 16). New York: W.W. Norton, 1976.

Friedman, M. (1988). Toward rational pharmacotherapy for post-traumatic stress disorder: An interim report. *American Journal of Psychiatry, 145,* 281–85.

Friman, P. C., & Warzak, W. J. (1990). Nocturnal enuresis: A prevalent, persistent, yet curable parasomnia. *Pediatrician, 17,* 38–45.

Frueh, B. C., Turner, S. M., & Beidel, D. C. (1995). Exposure therapy for combat-related posttraumatic stress disorder: A critical review. *Clinical Psychology Review, 15*(8): 799–817.

Gabbard, G. O. (1992). Psychodynamic psychiatry in the "Decade of the Brain." *American Journal of Psychiatry, 149*(8): 991–98.

Gabriel, T. (1994). Heroin finds a new market along the cutting edge of style. *New York Times,* May 8, p. A1.

Gagnon, J. H. (1977). *Human sexuality.* Chicago: Scott, Foresman.

Galen. In Veith, I., *Hysteria: The history of a disease.* Chicago: University of Chicago Press, 1965.

Ganaway, G. K. (1989). Historical versus narrative truth: Clarifying the role of exogenous trauma in the etiology of MPD and its variants. *Dissociation: Progress in the Dissociative Disorders, 2,* 205–20.

Garcia, E., Guess, D., & Brynes, J. (1973). Development of syntax in a retarded girl using procedures of imitation, reinforcement, and modelling. *Journal of Applied Behavior Analysis, 6,* 299–310.

Garfinkel, P. E., & Garner, D. M. (1982). *Anorexia nervosa: A multidimensional perspective.* New York: Brunner/Mazel.

Garmezy, N. (1977). The psychology and psychopathology of Allenhead. *Schizophrenia Bulletin, 3,* 360–69.

Garner, D. M. (1993). Binge eating: Definition and classification. In C. G. Fairburn, G. T. Wilson, C. G. Fairburn, & G. T. Wilson (Eds.), *Binge eating: Nature, assessment, and treatment.* New York: Guilford Press.

Garner, D., & Wooley, S. (1991). Confronting the failure of behavioral and dietary treatments for obesity. *Clinical Psychology Review, 11,* 729–80.

Garrison, C. Z., Addy, C. L., Jackson, K. L., McKeown, R. E., & Waller, J. L. (1992). Major depressive disorder and dysthymia in young adolescents. *American Journal of Epidemiology, 135*(7): 792–802.

Garrity, T. F., Somes, G. W., & Marx, M. B. (1977). Personality factors in resistance to illness after recent life changes. *Journal of Psychosomatic Research, 21,* 23–32.

Gawin, F. H., & Ellinwood, E. H. (1988). Cocaine and other stimulants. *New England Journal of Medicine, 318,* 1173–82.

Gawin, F. H., & Ellinwood, E. H. (1989). Cocaine dependence. *Annual Review of Medicine, 40,* 149–61.

Gebhard, P. H., Gagnon, J. H., Pomeroy, W. B., & Christenson, C. V. (1965). *Sex offenders.* New York: Harper & Row.

Gelenberg, A. J., & Klerman, G. L. (1978). Maintenance drug therapy in long-term treatment of depression. In J. P. Brady & H. K. H. Brodie (Eds.), *Controversy in psychiatry.* Philadelphia: Saunders.

Gelfand, D. M. (1978). Social withdrawal and negative emotional states: Behavioral treatment. In B. B. Wolman, J. Egan, & A. O. Ross (Eds.), *Handbook of treatment of mental disorders in childhood and adolescence.* Englewood Cliffs, NJ: Prentice-Hall.

George, M., Trimble, M., Ring, H., et al. (1993). Obsessions in obsessive-compulsive disorder with and without Gilles de la Tourette's syndrome. *American Journal of Psychiatry, 150,* 93–97.

George, M. S., Wasserman, E. M., Williams, W. A., Callahan, A., Ketter, T. A., Basser, P., Hallet, M., & Post, R. M. (1995). Daily repetitive transcranial magnetic stimulation (rTMS) improves mood in depression. Neuroreport, 6, 1853–56.

Gergen, K. J. (1982). *Toward transformation in social knowledge.* New York: Springer Verlag.

Gerstley, L. J., Alterman, A. I., McLellan, A. T., & Woody, G. E. (1990). Antisocial personality disorder in patients with substance abuse disorders. *American Journal of Psychiatry, 147,* 481–87.

Geschwind, N. (1975). The apraxias: Neural mechanisms of disorders of learned movement. *American Scientist, 188,* 188–95.

Gianoulakis, C. (1996). Implications of endogenous opioids and dopamine in alcoholism: Human and basic science studies. *Alcohol and Alcoholism, 31*(Suppl. 1): 33–42.

Gilberg, C. (1991). Outcome on autism and autistic-like conditions. *Journal of the American Academy of Child and Adolescent Psychiatry, 30*(3): 375–82.

Gilbert, D. G., & Hagen, R. L. (1980). The effects of nicotine and extraversion on self-report, skin conductance, electromyographic, and heart responses to emotional stimuli. *Addictive Behavior, 5,* 247–57.

Gilberstadt, H., & Duker, J. (1965). *A handbook for clinical and actuarial MMPI interpretations.* Philadelphia: Saunders.

Gillham, J., Reivich, K., Jaycox, L., & Seligman, M. (1995). Prevention of depressive symptoms in school children: Two-year follow-up. *Psychological Science, 6*(6): 343–51.

Gillum, R. F. (1994). Trends in acute myocardial infarction and coronary heart disease death in the United States. *Journal of the American College of Cardiology, 23*(6): 1273–77.

Girelli, S., Resick, P., Marhoefer-Dvorak, S., & Hutter, C. (1986). Subjective distress and violence during rape: The effects on long-term fear. *Violence and Victims, 1,* 35–46.

Gitlin, M. J. (1994). Psychotropic medications and their effects on sexual function: Diagnosis, biology, and treatment approaches. *Journal of Clinical Psychiatry, 55*(9): 406–13.

Gittelman, R., & Klein, D. F. (1984). Relationship between separation anxiety and panic and agoraphobic disorders. *Psychopathology, 17,* 56–65.

Gittleman, M., & Birch, H. G. (1967). Childhood schizophrenia: Intellect, neurologic status, perinatal risk, prognosis and family pathology. *Archives of General Psychiatry, 17,* 16–25.

Gittleson, N. L. (1966). Depressive psychosis in the obsessional neurotic. *British Journal of Psychiatry, 122,* 883–87.

Glass, D. C. (1977). *Behavior pattern stress in coronary disease.* Hillsdale, NJ: Erlbaum.

Glazer, H. I., & Weiss, J. M. (1976). Long-term interference effect: An alternative to "learned helplessness." *Journal of Experimental Psychology: Animal Behavior Processes, 2,* 202–13.

Gleitman, H. (1981). *Psychology.* New York: Norton.

Gleitman, H. (1991). *Psychology* (3rd ed.). New York: Norton.

Gold, J. M., Randolph, C., Carpenter, C. J., Goldberg, T. E., & Weinberger, D. R. (1992). Forms of memory failure in schizophrenia. *Journal of Abnormal Psychology, 101*(3): 487–94.

Gold, M. R., & Matsuuch, L. (1995). Signal transduction by the antigen receptors of B and T lymphocytes. *International Review of Cytology, 157,* 181–276.

Gold, M. S., Miller, N. S., Stennie, K., & Populla-Vardi, C. (1995).

Epidemiology of benzodiazepine use and dependence. *Psychiatric Annals, 25*(3): 146–48.

Golden, C. J. (1981). The Luria-Nebraska Children's Battery: Theory and formulation. In G. W. Hynd & J. E. Obrzut (Eds.), *Neuropsychological assessment and the school-age child: Issues and procedures.* New York: Grune & Stratton.

Golden, C. J., Hammeke, T. A., & Puriosch, A. D. (1980). *Manual for the Luria-Nebraska Neuropsychological Battery.* Los Angeles: Western Psychological Services.

Goldman, D. (1995). Identifying alcoholism vulnerability alleles. *Alcoholism: Clinical and Experimental Research, 19*(4): 824–31.

Goldman-Rakic, P. S. (1987). Circuitry of primate prefrontal cortex and regulation of behavior by representational memory. In F. Plum (Ed.), *Handbook of physiology: The nervous system* (Vol. 5, pp. 373–417). Bethesda, MD: American Physiological Society.

Goldstein, J. M. (1988). Gender differences in the course of schizophrenia. *American Journal of Psychiatry, 145,* 684–89.

Goldstein, M .J., Strachan, A. M., & Wynne, L .C. (1994). DSM-IV literature review: Relational problems with high expressed emotion. In T. A. Widiger, A. J. Frances, H. A. Pincus, W. Davis, & M. First (Eds.), *DSM-IV sourcebook.* Washington, DC: American Psychiatric Association.

Goodman, R. (1990). Technical note: Are perinatal complications causes or consequences of autism? *Journal of Child Psychology and Psychiatry, 31*(5): 809–12.

Goodwin, D. W. (1988). Alcoholism: Who gets better and who does not. In R. M. Rose & J. Barrett (Eds.), *Alcoholism: Origins and outcomes* (pp. 281–92). New York: Raven Press.

Goodwin, D. W., Schulsinger, F., Hermansen, L., Guze, S. B., & Winokur, G. (1973). Alcohol problems in adoptees raised apart from alcoholic biological parents. *Archives of General Psychiatry, 28,* 238–43.

Goodwin, D. W., Schulsinger, F., Moller, N., Hermansen, L., & Winokur, G. (1974). Drinking problems in adopted and non-adopted sons of alcoholics. *Archives of General Psychiatry, 31,* 164–69.

Gorenstein, E. E., & Newman, J. P. (1980). Disinhibitory psychopathology: A new perspective and a model for research. *Psychological Review, 87,* 301–15.

Gottesman, I. I. (1991). *Schizophrenia genesis: The origins of madness.* New York: Freeman.

Gottesman, I. I. (1993). Origins of schizophrenia: Past as prologue. In R. Plomin & G. E. McClearn (Eds.), *Nature, nurture, and psychology* (pp. 231–44). Washington, DC: American Psychological Association.

Gottesman, I. I., McGuffin, P., & Farmer, A. E. (1987). Clinical genetics as clues to the "real" genetics of schizophrenia (a decade of modest gains while playing for time). *Schizophrenia Bulletin, 13,* 23–47.

Gottesman, I. I., & Shields, J. (1972). *Schizophrenia and genetics: A twin study vantage point.* New York: Academic Press.

Gould, S. J. (1981). *The mismeasure of man.* New York: Norton.

Grace, W. J., & Graham, D. T. (1952). Relationship of specific attitudes and emotions to certain bodily disease. *Psychosomatic Medicine, 14,* 243–51.

Gram, L. F. (1994). Fluoxetine. The *New England Journal of Medicine, 331*(20): 1354–61.

Grattan, L. M., & Eslinger, P. J. (1992). Long-term psychological consequences of childhood frontal lobe lesion in patient D.T. *Brain and Cognition, 20,* 185–95.

Gray, F., Huag, H., Chimelli, L., et al. (1991). Prominent cortical atrophy with neuronal loss as correlate of human immunodeficiency virus encephalopathy. *Acta Neuropathologica, 82,* 229–33.

Green, A. R., Cross, A. J., & Goodwin, G.M. (1995). Review of the pharmacology and clinical pharmacology of 3,4- methylenedioxymethamphetamine (MDMA or "Ecstasy"). *Psychopharmacology, 119,* 247–60.

Green, B.L., Gleser, G.C., Lindy, J.D., Grace, M.C., & Leonard, A. (1996). Age-related reactions to the Buffalo Creek dam collapse: Effects in the second decade. In Ruskin, P.E., & Talbott, J.A. (Eds.), *Aging and post-traumatic stress disorder,* pp. 101–25. Washington, DC: American Psychiatric Press.

Green, B., Lindy, J., Grace, M., & Leonard, A. (1992). Chronic posttraumatic stress disorder and diagnostic comorbidity in a disaster sample. *Journal of Nervous and Mental Diseases, 180,* 760–66.

Greenberg, R.P., Bornstein, R.G., Zborowski, M.J., Fisher, S., & Greenberg, M.D. (1994). A meta-analysis of fluoxetine outcome in the treatment of depression. *Journal of Nervous and Mental Disease, 182*(10): 547–51.

Greene, R. L. (1991). *The MMPI-2/MMPI: An interpretive manual.* Boston: Allyn & Bacon.

Greenhill, L. (1997). Childhood attention-deficit hyperativity disorder: Pharmocological treatments. In P. Nathan and J. Gorman (eds.), *Treatments that work.* New York: Oxford.

Greer, S. (1964). Study of parental loss in neurotics and sociopaths. *Archives of General Psychiatry, 11,* 177–80.

Greer, S., Morris, T., & Pettingale, K. W. (1979). Psychological response to breast cancer: Effect on outcome. *The Lancet, II,* October 13, 785–87.

Gregory, I. (1958). Studies on parental deprivation in psychiatric patients. *American Journal of Psychiatry, 115,* 432–42.

Gregory, R. (Ed.). (1987). *Oxford companion to the mind.* Oxford, Eng.: Oxford University Press.

Greist, J. (1990). Treating the anxiety: Therapeutic options in obsessive-compulsive disorder. *Journal of Clinical Psychology, 51,* 29–34.

Griest, J. H. (1994). Behavior therapy for obsessive-compulsive disorder. *Journal of Clinical Psychiatry, 55*(10): 60–68.

Griest, J. H., Jefferson, J. W., Kobak, K. A., Katzelnick, D. J., & Serlin, R. C. (1995). Efficacy and tolerability of serotonin transport inhibitors in obsessive-compulsive disorder: A meta-analysis. *Archives of General Psychiatry, 52*(1): 53–60.

Grilly, D. M. (1989). *Drugs and human behavior.* Boston: Allyn & Bacon.

Grinspoon, L., & Bakalar, J. B. (1976). *Cocaine.* New York: Basic Books.

Gross, H. J., & Zimmerman, J. (1965). Experimental analysis of hysterical blindness: A follow-up report and new experimental data. *Archives of General Psychiatry, 13,* 255–60.

Grossman, H. J. (1983a). *Classification in mental retardation.* Washington, DC: American Association of Mental Deficiency.

Grossman, H. J. (Ed.). (1983b). *Manual on terminology and classification in mental retardation.* Washington, DC: American Association of Mental Deficiency.

Grove, W. M., & Andreasen, N. C. (1985). Language and thinking in psychosis. *Archives of General Psychiatry, 42,* 26–32.

Grueneich, R. (1992). The Borderline Personality Disorder Diagnosis: Reliability, diagnostic efficiency, and covariation with other personality disorder diagnoses. *Journal of Personality Disorders, 6*(3): 197–212.

Gualtieri, C. (1991). *Neuropsychiatry and behavioral pharmacology.* New York: Springer-Verlag.

Gunderson, J. G., & Mosher, L. R. (1975). The cost of schizophrenia. *American Journal of Psychiatry, 132,* 901–6.

Gur, R. E., Mozley, P. D., Shtasel, D. L., Cannon, T. D., Gallacher, F., Turetsky, B., Grossman, R., and Gur, R. C. (1994). Clinical subtypes of schizophrenia: Differences in brain and CSF volume. *American Journal of Psychiatry, 151*(3): 343–50.

Gustafsson, P.A., Bjorksten, B., & Kjellman, N. -I.M. (1994). Family dysfunction in asthma: A prospective study of illness development. *The Journal of Pediatrics, 125*(3): 493–98.

Hackmann, A., & McLean, C. (1975). A comparison of flooding and thought-stopping treatment. *Behaviour Research and Therapy, 13,* 263–69.

Haldeman, D. C. (1994). The practice and ethics of sexual orientation conversion therapy. *Journal of Consulting and Clinical Psychology, 62*(2): 221–27.

Hall, G. C. (1995). Sexual offender recidivism revisited: A meta-analysis of recent treatment studies. *Journal of Consulting and Clinical Psychology, 63*(5): 802–9.

Hall, J. (1988). Fluoxetine: Efficacy against placebo and by dose—An overview. *British Journal of Psychiatry,* 59–63.

Hall, R. V., Fox, R., Willard, D., Goldsmith, L., Emerson, M., Owen, M., Davis, T., & Porcia, E. (1971). The teacher as observer and experimenter in the modification of disputing and talking-out behaviors. *Journal of Applied Behavior Analysis, 4,* 141–49.

Halpern, J. (1977). Projection: A test of the psychoanalytic hypothesis. *Journal of Abnormal Psychology, 86,* 536–42.

Hammen, C. (1991). *Depression runs in families: The social context of risk and resilience in children of depressed mothers.* New York: Springer Verlag.

Hammen, C. L. & Glass, D. R. (1975). Expression, activity, and evaluation of reinforcement. *Journal of Abnormal Psychology, 84,* 718–21.

Hammen, D. L., & Padesky, C. A. (1977). Sex differences in the expression of depressive responses on the Beck Depression Inventory. *Journal of Abnormal Psychology, 86,* 609–14.

Hanley, J. R., & Gard, F. (1995). A dissociation between developmental surface and phonological dyslexia in two undergraduate students. *Neuropsychologia, 33*(7): 909–14.

Hannum, R. D., Rosellini, R. A., & Seligman, M. E. P. (1976). Retention of learned helplessness and immunization in the rat from weaning to adulthood. *Developmental Psychology, 12,* 449–54.

Hardy, J. A., & Higgins, G .A. (1992). Alzheimer's disease: The amyloid cascade hypothesis. *Science, 256,* 184.

Hare, R. D. (1965). Temporal gradient of fear arousal in psychopaths. *Journal of Abnormal Psychology, 70,* 442–45.

Hare, R. D. (1978). Electrodermal and cardiovascular correlates of sociopathy. In R. D. Hare & D. Schalling (Eds.), *Psychopathic behavior: Approaches to research.* New York: Wiley.

Hare, R. D. (1980). A research scale for the assessment of psychopathy in criminal populations. *Personality and Individual Differences, 1,* 111–19.

Hare, R. D. & McPherson, L. M. (1984). Violent and aggressive behavior by criminal psychopaths. *International Journal of Law and Psychiatry, 7,* 329–37.

Hare, R. D., Williamson, S. E., & Harpur, T. J. (1988). Psychopathy and language. In T. E. Moffitt & S. A. Mednick (Eds.), *Biological contributions to crime causation* (pp. 68–92). Dordecht, the Netherlands: Martinuus Nijhoff.

Hartlage, L., Asken, M., & Hornsby, J. (1987). *Essentials of neuropsychological assessment.* New York: Springer.

Harlow, J. M. (1868). Recovery from the passage of an iron bar through the head. *Publications of the Massachusetts Medical Society, 2,* 327.

Harrington, R. (1992). Annotation: The natural history and treatment of child and adolescent affective disorders. *Journal of Child Psychology and Psychiatry, 33*(8): 1287–1302.

Harris, E. L., Noyes, R., Crowe, R. R., & Chaudry, D. R. (1983). Family study of agoraphobia. *Archives of General Psychiatry, 40,* 1061–64.

Harris, G. J., Lewis, R. F., Satlin, A., English, C. D., Scott, T. M., Yurgelun-Todd, D. A., & Renshaw, P. F. (1996). Dynamic susceptibility contrast MRI of regional cerebral blood volume in Alzheimer's disease. *American Journal of Psychiatry, 153*(5): 721–24.

Harrison, R. (1965). Thematic apperceptive methods. In B. B. Wolman (Ed.), *Handbook of clinical psychology.* New York: Wiley.

Haslam, N., & Beck, A. T. (1994). Subtyping major depression: A taxometric analysis. *Journal of Abnormal Psychology, 103*(4):686–92.

Hathaway, S. R., & McKinley, J. C. (1943). *MMPI manual.* New York: Psychological Corporation.

Haynes, J. D. (1995). A critique of the possibility of genetic inheritance of homosexual orientation. *Journal of Homosexuality, 28*(1–2): 91–113.

Haynes, S. G., Feinleib, M., & Kannel, W. B. (1980). The relationship of psychosocial factors to coronary heart disease in the Framingham study: III. Eight years incidence in coronary heart disease. *American Journal of Epidemiology, 3,* 37–85.

Hawley, G. A. (1988). *Measures of psychosocial development: Professional manual.* Odessa, FL: Psychological Assessment Resources.

Hazell, P., & Lewin, T. (1993). An evaluation of postvention following adolescent suicide. *Suicide and Life-Threatening Behavior, 23,* 101–9.

Heatherton, T. F., & Baumeister, R. F. (1991). Binge eating as escape from self-awareness. *Psychological Bulletin 110*(1): 86–108.

Hecker, M., Chesney, M., Black, G., & Frautschi, N. (1988). Coronary-prone behaviors in the Western Collaborative Group Study. *Psychosomatic Medicine, 50,* 153–64.

Heebink, D. M., Sunday, S. R., and Halmi, K. A. (1995). Anorexia nervosa and Bulimia nervosa in adolescence: Effects of age and menstrual status on psychological variables. *Journal of the American Academy of Child and Adolescent Psychiatry, 34*(3): 378–82.

Heider, F. (1958). The psychology of interpersonal relationships. New York: Wiley.

Heilbrun, A. B., Jr. (1993). Hallucinations. In C. G. Costello (Ed.), *Symptoms of schizophrenia* (pp. 56–91). New York: Wiley.

Heiman, J. R., & LoPiccolo, J. (1983). Clinical outcome of sex therapy. *Archives of General Psychiatry, 40,* 443–49.

Heinz, A., Schmidt, L. G., & Reischies, F. M. (1994). Anhedonia in schizophrenic, depressed, or alcohol-dependent patients: Neurobiological correlates. *Pharmacopsychiatry, 27*(Suppl. 1), 7–10.

Hellekson, C. J., Kline, J. A., & Rosenthal, N. E. (1986). Phototherapy for seasonal affective disorder in Alaska. *American Journal of Psychiatry, 143,* 1035–37.

Hemsley, R., Howlin, P., Berger, M., Hersov, L., Holbrook, D., Rutter, M., & Yule, W. (1978). Treating autistic children in a family context. In M. Rutter & E. Schopler (Eds.), *Autism: A reappraisal of concepts and treatment.* New York: Plenum.

Hendin, H. (1969). Black suicide. *Archives of General Psychiatry, 21,* 407–22.

Hendin, H. (1974). Students on heroin. *Journal of Nervous Mental Disorders, 156,* 240–55.

Henker, B., & Whalen, C. K. (1989). Hyperactivity and attention deficits. *American Psychologist, 44*(2): 216–23.

Henningfield, J. E., & Goldberg, S. R. (1983). Nicotine as a reinforcer in human subjects and laboratory animals. *Pharmacology, Biochemistry and Behavior, 19,* 989–92.

Henningfield, J. E., & Jasinski, D. R. (1983). Human pharmacology of nicotine. *Psychopharmacological Bulletin, 19,* 413–15.

Henry, J. (1992). Toxicity of antidepressants: Comparison with fluoxetine. *International Clinical Psychopharmacology, 6* (Suppl. 6): 22–27.

Herbert, J. D., Hope, D. A., & Bellack, A. S. (1992). Validity of the distinction between generalized social phobia and avoidance personality disorder. *Journal of Abnormal Psychology, 101*(2): 332–39.

Herkenham, M., Lynn, A. B., Little, M. D., Johnson, M. R., Melvin, L. S., de Costa, B., & Rice, K. C. (1990). Cannabinoid receptor localization in brain. *Proceedings of the National Academy of Sciences U.S.A., 87,* 1932–36.

Herrmann, M., Bartels, C., Schumacher, M., & Wallesch, C. (1995). Poststroke depression: Is there a pathoanatomic correlate for depression in the postacute stage of stroke? *Stroke, 26*(5): 850–56.

Hesselbrock, V., Meyer, R., & Hesselbrock, M. (1992). Psychopathology and addictive disorders: The specific case of antisocial personality disorder. In C. P. O'Brien & J. H. Jaffe (Eds.), *Addictive states.* New York: Raven Press.

Heston, L. L. (1966). Psychiatric disorders in foster home reared children of schizophrenic mothers. *British Journal of Psychiatry, 112,* 819–25.

Hetherington, E. M., & Martin, B. (1979). Family interaction. In H. C. Quay & J. S. Werry (Eds.), *Psychopathological disorders of childhood.* New York: Wiley.

Heun, R., & Maier, W. (1995). Risk of Alzheimer's disease in first-degree relatives. [Letter to the Editor]. *Archives of General Psychiatry, 52.*

Higgins, S. T., Budney, A. J., Bickel, W. K., Hughes, J. R., Foerg, F., & Badger, G. (1993). Achieving cocaine abstinence with a behavioral approach. *American Journal of Psychiatry, 150*(5): 763–69.

Hilgard, E. R. (1977). Divided consciousness: Multiple controls in human thought and action. New York: Wiley.

Hill, P. O. (1972). Latent aggression and drug-abuse: An investigation of adolescent personality factors using an original cartoon-o-graphic aggressive tendencies test. *Dissertation Abstracts International, 33,* 1765.

Hilton, G. (1994). Behavioral and cognitive sequelae of head trauma. *Orthopaedic Nursing, 13*(4): 25–32.

Hilts, P. J. (1994a). Cigarette makers dispute reports on addictiveness. *New York Times,* April 15, p. A1.

Hilts, P. J. (1994b). Is nicotine addictive? It depends on whose criteria you use. *New York Times,* August 2, pp. C1, C3.

Hinshaw, S., Klein, R., & Abikoff, H. (1997). Childhood ADHD:

Nonpharmocologic and combination treatments. In P. Nathan and J. Gorman (Eds.), *Treatments that work*. New York: Oxford.

Hiroto, D. S. (1974). Locus of control and learned helplessness. *Journal of Experimental Psychology, 102*, 187–93.

Hiroto, D. S., & Seligman, M. E. P. (1975). Generality of learned helplessness in man. *Journal of Personality and Social Psychology, 31*, 311–27.

Hirst, W. (1982). The amnesic syndrome: Descriptions and explanations. *Psychology Bulletin, 91*, 1480–83.

Hobson, R. P. (1986). The autistic child's appraisal of expressions of emotion. *Journal of Childhood Psychology and Psychiatry, 27*, 321–42.

Hodgson, R., Rachman, S., & Marks, I. (1972). The treatment of chronic obsessive-compulsive neurosis. *Behaviour Research and Therapy, 10*, 181–89.

Hogan, R. (1969). Development of an empathy scale. *Journal of Consulting and Clinical Psychology, 33*, 307–16.

Hogarty, G. E., Anderson, C. M., Reiss, D. J., Kornblith, S. J., Greenwald, D. P., Javna, C. D., & Madonia, M. J. (1986). Family psychoeducation, social skills training and maintenance chemotherapy in the aftercare treatment of schizophrenia: I. One-year effects of a controlled study on relapse and expressed emotion. *Archives of General Psychiatry, 43*, 633–42.

Hokanson, J. E. (1961). The effects of frustration and anxiety on aggression. *Journal of Abnormal and Social Psychology, 62*, 346.

Hokanson, J. E., & Burgess, M. (1962). The effects of three types of aggression on vascular processes. *Journal of Abnormal and Social Psychology, 65*, 446–49.

Hokanson, J. E., Willers, K. R., & Koropsak, E. (1968). Modification of autonomic responses during aggressive interchange. *Journal of Personality, 36*, 386–404.

Holden, C. (1986). Youth suicide: New research focuses on a growing social problem. *Science, 233*, 839–41.

Hollander, E., Schiffman, E., Cohen, B., et al. (1990). Signs of central nervous system dysfunction in obsessive-compulsive disorder. *Archives of General Psychiatry, 47*, 27–32.

Hollingshead, A. B., & Redlich, F. C. (1958). *Social class and mental illness: A community study*. New York: Wiley.

Hollon, S. D., & Kendall, P. C. (1980). Cognitive self-statements in depression: Development of an automatic thoughts questionnaire. *Cognitive Therapy and Research, 4*, 383–95.

Hollon, S. D., Kendall, P. C., & Lumry, A. (1986). Specificity of depressotypic cognitions in clinical depression. *Journal of Abnormal Psychology, 95*, 52–59.

Holmes, D. (1990). The evidence for repression: An example of sixty years of research. In J. Singer (Ed.), *Repression and dissociation: Implications for personality theory, psychopathology, and health* (pp. 85–102). Chicago: University of Chicago Press.

Holmes, T. H., & Rahe, R. H. (1967). The social readjustment ratings scale. *Journal of Psychosomatic Research, 11*, 213–18.

Holt, C. S., Heimberg, R. G., & Hope, D. A. (1992). Avoidant personality disorder and the generalized subtype in social phobia. *Journal of Abnormal Psychology, 102*, 318–25.

Holtzman, W. H. (1961). *Inkblot perception and personality: Holtzman Inkblot Technique*. Austin: University of Texas Press.

Hooker, W. D., & Jones, R. T. (1987). Increased susceptibility to memory intrusions and the Stroop interference effect during acute marijuana intoxication. *Psychopharmacology, 91*, 20–24.

Horne, R. L., & Picard, R. S. (1979). Psychosocial risk factors for lung cancer. *Psychosomatic Medicine, 41*, 503–14.

Horney, K. (1945). *Our inner conflicts: A constructive theory of neurosis*. New York: Norton.

Horowitz, M. (1975). Intrusive and repetitive thoughts after experimental stress. *Archives of General Psychiatry, 32*, 1457–63.

Horowitz, M., Stinson, C., Curtis, D., et al. (1993). Topic and signs: Defensive control of emotional expression. *Journal of Consulting and Clinical Psychology, 61*, 421–30.

Horter, D. H. (1989). Neuropsychological status of asymptomatic individuals seropositive to HIV-1. *Annals of Neurology, 26*, 589–91.

Houts, A. C. (1991). Nocturnal enuresis as a biobehavioral problem. *Behavior Therapy, 22*, 133–51.

Howard, K., Kopta, S., Krause, M. & Orlinsky, D. (1986). The dose-effect relationship in psychotherapy. *American Psychologist, 41*, 159–164.

Hrubec, Z., & Omenn, G. S. (1981). Evidence of genetic predisposition to alcohol cirrhosis and psychosis: Twin concordances for alcoholism and its biological end points by zygosity among male veterans. *Alcoholism: Clinical and Experimental Research, 5*, 207–12.

Hudson, J. I., Pope, H. G., Jonas, J. M., & Yurgelun-Todd, D. (1987). A controlled family history study of bulimia. *Psychological Medicine, 17*(4): 883–90.

Huesmann, L. R., Eron, L. D., Lefkowitz, M. M., & Walder, L. O. (1984). Stability of aggression over time and generations. *Developmental Psychology, 20*, 1120–34.

Hugdahl, K., & Ohman, A. (1977). Effects of instruction on acquisition and extinction of electrodermal response to fear-relevant stimuli. *Journal of Experimental Psychology: Human Learning and Memory, 3*(5): 608–18.

Hung, D. W., Rotman, Z., Consentino, A., & MacMillan, M. (1983). Cost and effectiveness of an educational program for autistic children using a systems approach. *Education and Treatment of Children, 6*(1): 47–68.

Hunt, C., & Singh, M. (1991). Generalized anxiety disorder. *International Review of Psychiatry, 3*, 215–29.

Hunt, E., Browning, P., & Nave, G. (1982). A behavioral exploration of dependent and independent mildly mentally retarded adolescents and their mothers. *Applied Research in Mental Retardation, 3*, 141–50.

Hunt, W. A., Barnett, L. W., & Branch, L. G. (1971). Relapse rates in addiction programs. *Journal of Clinical Psychology, 27*, 455–56.

Huston, A. (1985). The development of sex typing: Themes from recent research. *Developmental Review, 5*, 1–17.

Hutchings, B., & Mednick, S. A. (1977). Criminality in adoptees and their adoptive and biological parents: A pilot study. In S. A. Mednick & K. O. Christiansen (Eds.), *Biosocial bases of criminal behavior* (pp. 127–41). New York: Gardner Press.

Hyler, S. E., & Spitzer, R. T. (1978). Hysteria split asunder. *American Journal of Psychiatry, 135*, 1500–1504.

Iacono, W. G., Moreau, M., Beiser, M., Fleming, J. A. E., & Lin, R. Y. (1992). Smooth-pursuit eye tracking in first-episode psychotic patients and their relatives. *Journal of Abnormal Psychology, 101*, 104–16.

Imber, S. D., Pilkonis, P. A., Sotsky, S. M., & Elkin, I. (1990). Mode-specific effects among three treatments for depression. *Journal of Consulting and Clinical Psychology 58*(3): 352–59.

Imboden, J. B., Cantor, A., & Cluff, L. E. (1961). Convalescence from influenza: The study of the psychological and clinical determinants. *Archives of Internal Medicine, 108*, 393–99.

Insel, T. R. (1992). Toward a neuroanatomy of obsessive-compulsive disorder. *Archives of General Psychiatry, 49*, 739–44.

Ironson, M., Taylor, F., Boltwood, M., et al. (1992). Effects of anger on left ventricle rejection fraction in coronary artery disease. *American Journal of Cardiology, 70*, 281–85.

Irwin, M., Daniels, M., Bloom, E. T., Smith, T. L., & Weiner, H. (1987). Life events, depressive symptoms, and immune function. *American Journal of Psychiatry, 144*, 437–41.

Jablensky, A., Sartorius, N., Ernberg, G., Anker, M., Korten, A., Cooper, J.E., Day, R., & Bertelsen, A. (1992). Schizophrenia: Manifestations, incidence, and course in different cultures. A World Health Organization ten-country study. *Psychological Medicine* (Monograph Supplement 20): 1–97.

Jacobson, N. (1992). Behavior couple therapy: A new beginning. *Behavior Therapy, 23*, 493–506.

Jacobson, N. S., & Hollon, S. D. (1996a). Cognitive-behavior therapy versus pharmacotherapy: Now that the jury's returned its verdict, it's time to present the rest of the evidence. *Journal of Consulting and Clinical Psychology, 64*(1): 74–80.

Jacobson, N. S., & Hollon, S. D. (1996b). Prospects for future comparisons between drugs and psychotherapy: Lessons from the CBT-versus-pharmacotherapy exchange. *Journal of Consulting and Clinical Psychology, 64*(1): 104–8.

Jaffe, J. H. (1985). Drug addiction and drug abuse. In A. J. Goodman & L. S. Gilman (Eds.), *The pharmacological basis of therapeutics*. New York: Macmillan.

James, R. M. (1959). Jurors' assessment of criminal responsibility. *Social Problems, 7*, 58–67.

Janssen, R. S., Saykin, A. J., Cannon, L., et al. (1989). Neurological and neuropsychological manifestation of HIV-1 infection:

Association with AIDS-related complex but not asymptomatic HIV-1 infection. *Annals of Neurology, 26,* 592–600.

Jaycox, L., Reivich, K., Gillham, J., & Seligman, M. (1994). Prevention of depressive symptoms in school children. *Behaviour Research and Therapy, 32*(8):801–16.

Jefferson, J. (1990). Lithium: The present and the future. *Journal of Clinical Psychiatry, 5,* 4–8.

Jefferson, J. W., & Griest, J. H. (1996). The pharmacotherapy of obsessive-compulsive disorder. *Psychiatric Annals, 26*(4): 202–9.

Jeffrey, R., Adlis, S., & Forster, J. (1991). Prevalence of dieting among working men and women: The healthy worker project. *Health Psychology, 10,* 274–81.

Jenike, M., Baer, L., Ballantine, T., et al. (1991). Cingulotomy for refractory obsessive-compulsive disorder. *Archives of General Psychiatry, 48,* 548–55.

Jenike, M., Baer, L., Summergrad, P., et al. (1989). Obsessive-compulsive disorder: A double-blind, placebo-controlled trial of clomipramine in 27 patients. *American Journal of Psychiatry, 146,* 1328–30.

Jenkins, C. D. (1982). Psychosocial risk factors for coronary heart disease. *Acta Medica Scandinavia Supplimentum, 660,* 123–36.

Jenkins, C. D., Rosenman, R. H., & Friedman, M. (1967). Development of an objective psychological test for the determination of the coronary prone behavior pattern in employed men. *Journal of Chronic Disease, 20,* 371–79.

Jens, K. S., & Evans, H. I. (1983). *The diagnosis and treatment of multiple personality clients.* Workshop presented at the Rocky Mountain Psychological Association, Snowbird, Utah, April 1983.

Jerome, J. (1880). Intern's syndrome. In *Three men in a boat, not to mention the dog.*

Jerome, J. (1979). Catching them before suicide. *The New York Times Magazine,* January 14.

Jeste, D. V., & Caligiuri, M. P. (1993). Tardive dyskinesia. *Schizophrenia Bulletin, 19,* 303–15.

Johnson, H., Olafsson, K., Andersen, J., Plenge, P., et al. (1989). Lithium every second day. *American Journal of Psychiatry, 146,* 557.

Jones, R. T., & Benowitz, N. (1976). The 30-day trip: Clinical studies of cannabis tolerance and dependence. In M. C. Braude & S. Szara (Eds.), *Pharmacology of marihuana* (Vol. 2, pp. 627–42). New York: Academic Press.

Jourard, S. M. (1974). *Healthy personality: An approach from the viewpoint of humanistic psychology.* New York: Macmillan.

Joyce, P., Bushnell, J., Oakley-Browne, M., & Wells, J. (1989). The epidemiology of panic symptomatology and agoraphobic avoidance. *Comprehensive Psychiatry, 30,* 303–12.

Junginger, J., Barker, S., & Coe, D. (1992). Mood themes and bizarreness of delusions in schizophrenia and mood psychosis. *Journal of Abnormal Psychology, 101*(2): 287–92.

Kabat-Zinn, J., Massion, A., Kristeller, J., et al. (1992). Effectiveness of meditation-based stress reduction program in the treatment of anxiety disorders. *American Journal of Psychiatry, 149,* 937–43.

Kaij, L. (1960). *Studies on the etiology and sequels of abuse and alcohol.* Lund, Sweden: University of Lund.

Kamen-Siegel, L., Rodin, J., Seligman, M., & Dwyer, J. (1991). Explanatory style and cell-mediated immunity in elderly men and women. *Health Psychology, 10,* 229–35.

Kamin, L. J. (1974). *The science and politics of IQ.* Potomac, MD: Erlbaum.

Kane, J. M., & Marder, S. R. (1993). Psychopharmacologic treatment of schizophrenia. *Schizophrenia Bulletin, 19,* 287–302.

Kanfer, F. H., & Karoly, P. (1972). Self-control. A behavioristic excursion into the lion's den. *Behavior Therapy, 3,* 398–416.

Kaniasty, K., & Norris, F.H. (1995). Mobilization and deterioration of social support following natural disasters. *Current Directions in Psychological Science, 4*(3), 94–98.

Kanner, A. D., Coyne, J. C., Schaefer, C., & Lazarus, R. S. (1981). Comparison of two modes of stress measurement: Minor daily hassles and uplifts vs. major life events. *Journal of Behavioral Medicine, 4,* 1–39.

Kanner, L. (1943). Autistic disturbances of affective contact. *Nervous Child, 2,* 217–50.

Kanter, R. A., Williams, B. E., & Cummings, C. (1992). Personal and parental alcohol abuse, and victimization in obese binge eaters and nonbingeing obese. *Addictive Behaviors, 17*(5): 439–45.

Kaplan, C. A. & Hussain, S. (1995). Use of drugs in child and adolescent psychiatry. *British Journal of Psychiatry, 166*(3): 291–98.

Kaplan, H. S. (1974). *The new sex therapy.* New York: Brunner/Mazel.

Kaplan, S. M., Gottschalk, L. A., Magliocco, D., Rohobit, D., & Ross, W. D. (1960). Hostility in hypnotic "dreams" of hypertensive patients. (Comparisons between hypertensive and normotensive groups and within hypertensive individuals.) *Psychosomatic Medicine, 22,* 320.

Kapur, S., & Remington, G. (1996). Serotonin-dopamine interaction and its relevance to schizophrenia. *American Journal of Psychiatry, 153*(4): 466–76.

Karasek, R., Baker, D., Marxer, F., Ahlbom, A., & Theorell, T. (1981). Job decision latitude, job demand, and cardiovascular disease: A prospective study of Swedish men. *American Journal of Public Health, 71,* 694–705.

Karbe, H., Kessler, J., Herholz, K., Fink, G.R., & Heiss, W.-D. (1995). Long-term prognosis of poststroke aphasia studied with positron emission tomography. *Archives of Neurology, 52,* 186–90.

Karlsson, J. L. (1972). An Icelandic family study of schizophrenia. In A. R. Kaplan (Ed.), *Genetic factors in schizophrenia* (pp. 246–55). Springfield, Il: Charles C. Thomas.

Kaslow, N. J., Tannenbaum, R. L., Abramson, L. Y., Peterson, C., & Seligman, M. E. P. (1983). Problem solving deficits and depressive symptoms among children. *Journal of Abnormal Child Psychology, 11*(4):497–502.

Kass, F., Spitzer, R. L., & Williams, J. B. W. (1983). An empirical study of the issue of sex bias in the diagnostic criteria of DSM-III axis II personality disorders. *American Psychologist, 38,* 799–801.

Katchadourian, H. A., & Lunde, D. T. (1972). *Fundamentals of human sexuality.* New York: Holt, Rinehart & Winston.

Katz, R. J., DeVeaugh-Geiss, J., & Landau, P. (1990a). Clinical predictors of treatment response in obsessive-compulsive disorder: Explanatory analyses from multicenter trials of clomipramine. *Psychopharmacology Bulletin, 26,* 54–59.

Katz, R. J., DeVeaugh-Geiss, J., & Landau, P. (1990b). Clomipramine in obsessive-compulsive disorder. *Biological Psychiatry, 28,* 401–14.

Kazdin, A. E. (1997). Treatments of conduct disorder in children. In P. Nathan and J. Gorman (Eds.), *Treatments that work.* New York: Oxford.

Kazdin, A. E., & Wilcoxon, L. A. (1976). Systematic desensitization and nonspecific treatment effects: A methodological evaluation. *Psychological Bulletin, 83*(5): 729–58.

Keaney, J. C., & Farley, M. (1996). Dissociation in an outpatient sample of women reporting childhood sexual abuse. *Psychological Reports, 78,* 59–65.

Keck, P., Cohen, B., Baldessarini, R., & McElroy, S. (1989). Time course of antipsychotic effects of neuroleptic drugs. *American Journal of Psychiatry, 146,* 1289–92.

Keinan, G. & Hobfoll, S. E. (1989). Stress, dependency and social support: Who benefits from husbands' presence in delivery? *Journal of Social and Clinical Psychology, 8,* 32–44.

Keith, S. J., Gunderson, J. G., Reifman, A., Buchsbaum, S., & Mosher, L. R. (1976). Special report: Schizophrenia, 1976. *Schizophrenia Bulletin, 2,* 510–65.

Keller, M. B., & Baker, C. A. (1991). Bipolar disorder: Epidemiology, course, diagnosis, and treatment. *Bulletin of the Menninger Clinic, 55*(2): 172–81.

Keller, M. B., Beardslee, W. R., Dorer, D. J., Lavori, P. W., Samuelson, H., & Klerman, G. R. (1986). Impact of severity and chronicity of parental affective illness on adaptive functioning and psychopathology in children. *Archives of General Psychiatry, 43,* 930–37.

Keller, M. B., Klein, D. N., Hirschfeld, R. M. A., Kocsis, J. H., McCullough, J. P., Miller, I., First, M. B., Holzer, C. P., Keitner, G. I., Marin, D. N., and Shea, T. (1995). Results of the DSM-IV Mood Disorders field trial. *American Journal of Psychiatry, 152*(6): 843–49.

Keller, M. B., Lavori, P. W., Mueller, T. I., Endicott, J., et al. (1992). Time to recovery, chronicity, and levels of psychopathology in major depression: A 5-year prospective follow-up of 431 subjects. *Archives of General Psychiatry, 49*(10): 809–16.

Keller, M., & Shapiro, R. (1982). "Double depression": Superimposition of acute depressive episodes on chronic depressive disorders. *American Journal of Psychiatry, 139,* 438–42.

Kelley, H. H. (1967). Attribution theory in social psychology. In D. Levine (Ed.), *Nebraska Symposium on Motivation* (pp. 192–240). Lincoln: Dot Nebraska Press.

Kendall, P. C., Haaga, D. A. F., Ellis, A., & Bernard, M. (1995). Rational-emotive therapy in the 1990's and beyond: Current status, recent revisions, and research questions. *Clinical Psychology Review, 15*(3): 169–85.

Kendler, K. S., & Gruenberg, A. M. (1982). Genetic relationship between paranoid personality disorder and the "schizophrenic spectrum" disorders. *American Journal of Psychiatry, 139,* 1185–86.

Kendler, K. S., & Gruenberg, A. M. (1984). An independent analysis of the Danish adoption study of schizophrenia: VI. The relationship between psychiatric disorders as defined by DSM-III in the relatives and adoptees. *Archives of General Psychiatry, 41,* 555–64.

Kendler, K. S., Kessler, R. C., Walters, E. E., MacLean, C., Neale, M. C., Heath, A. C., & Eaves, L. J. (1995). Stressful life events, genetic liability, and onset of an episode of major depression in women. *American Journal of Psychiatry, 152*(6): 833–42.

Kendler, K. S., Neale, M. C., Heath, A. C., Kessler, R. C., & Eaves, L. J. (1994). A twin-family study of alcoholism in women. *American Journal of Psychiatry, 151*(5): 707–15.

Kendler, K., Neale, M., Kessler, R., & Heath, A. (1992). Generalized anxiety disorder in women: A population-based twin study. *Archives of General Psychiatry, 49,* 267–72.

Kendler, K. S., Pederson, N., Johnson, L., Neale, M. C., & Mathe, A. A. (1993). A pilot Swedish twin study of affective illness, including hospital- and population-ascertained subsamples. *Archives of General Psychiatry, 50,* 699–706.

Kernberg, O. F. (1975). *Borderline conditions and pathological narcissism.* New York: Jason Aronson.

Kernberg, O. F. (1992). *Aggression in personality disorders and perversions.* New Haven: Yale University Press.

Kerr, T. A., Roth, M., Schapira, K., & Gurney, C. (1972). The assessment and prediction of outcome in affective disorders. *British Journal of Psychiatry, 121,* 167.

Kertesz, A. (1982). Two case studies: Broca's brain and Wernicke's aphasia. In M. A. Arbib, D. Caplan, & J. C. Marshall (Eds.), *Neural models of language processes.* New York: Academic Press.

Kessler, R., McGonagle, K., Zhao, S., et al. (1994). Lifetime and 12-month prevalence of DSM-III-R psychiatric disorders in the United States: Results from the National Comorbity Survey. *Archives of General Psychiatry, 51,* 8–19.

Kety, J. (1974). Biochemical and neurochemical effects of electroconvulsive shock. In M. Fink, S. Kety, & J. McGough (Eds.), *Psychology of convulsive therapy.* Washington, DC: Winston.

Kety, S., Rosenthal, D., Wender, P. H., & Schulsinger, F. (1968). The types and prevalence of mental illness in the biological and adoptive families of adopted schizophrenics. In D. Rosenthal & S. S. Kety (Eds.), *The transmission of schizophrenia.* New York: Pergamon Press.

Kiecolt-Glaser, J., Dura, J., Speicher, C., Trask, J., & Glaser, R. (1991). Spousal caregivers of dementia victims: Longitudinal changes in immunity and health. *Psychosomatic Medicine, 53,* 345–62.

Kiecolt-Glaser, J. K., Garner, W., Speicher, C., Penn, G. M., Holliday, J., & Glaser, R. (1984). Psychosocial modifiers of immunocompetence in medical students. *Psychosomatic Medicine, 46,* 7–14.

Kiecolt-Glaser, J. K., & Glaser, R. (1987). Psychosocial moderators of immune function. *Annals of Behavioral Medicine, 9,* 16–20.

Kiecolt-Glaser, J. K., & Glaser, R. (1995). Psychoneuroimmunology and health consequences: Data and shared mechanisms. *Psychosomatic Medicine, 57,* 269–74.

Kiely, J. L., Paneth, N., & Susser, M. (1981). Low birthweight, neonatal care and cerebral palsy: An epidemiological review. In P. J. Mittler & J. M. deJong (Eds.), *Frontiers in mental retardation: II: Biomedical aspects.* Baltimore, MD: University Park Press.

Kiessling, L. S., Marcotte, A. C., & Culpepper, L. (1993). Antineuronal antibodies in movement disorder. *Pediatrics, 92*(1): 39–43.

Kilpatrick, D., Resnick, P., & Veronen, L. (1981). Effects of a rape experience: A longitudinal study. *Journal of Social Issues, 37,* 105–22.

Kilpatrick, D., Saunders, B., Amick-McMullan, A., et al. (1989). Victim and crime factors associated with the development of crime-related post-traumatic stress disorder. *Behavior Therapy, 20,* 199–214.

Kilpatrick, D., Saunders, B., Veronen, L., Best, C., & Von, J. (1987). Criminal victimization: Lifetime prevalence, reporting to police, and psychological impact. *Crime and Delinquency, 33,* 479–89.

Kinsey, A. C., Pomeroy, W. D., & Martin, C. E. (1948). *Sexual behavior in the human male.* Philadelphia: Saunders.

Kirigin, K., Wolf, M. M., Braukman, C. J., Fixsen, D. L., & Phillips, E. L. (1979). Achievement Place: A preliminary outcome evaluation. In J. S. Stumphauzer (Ed.), *Progress in behavior therapy with delinquents.* Springfield, IL: Charles C. Thomas.

Kirk, S. A., & Kutchins, H. (1992). *The selling of DSM: The rhetoric of science in psychiatry.* New York: Aldine de Gruyter.

Kittel, F., Kornitzer, M., de Backer, G., & Dramaix, M. (1982). Metrological study of psychological questionnaires with reference to social variables: The Belgian Heart Disease Prevention Project (BHDPP). *Journal of Behavioral Medicine, 5*(1): 9–35.

Kleber, H. D. (1994). Our current approach to drug abuse: Progress, problems, proposals. *The New England Journal of Medicine, 330*(5): 361–64.

Klein, D. F. (1996). Preventing hung juries about therapy studies. *Journal of Consulting and Clinical Psychology, 64*(1): 81–87.

Klein, D. F., & Gittelman-Klein, R. (1975). Are behavioral and psychometric changes related in methylphenidate treated, hyperactive children? *International Journal of Mental Health, 14*(1–2): 182–98.

Klein, D. F., Ross, D. C., & Cohen, P. (1987). Panic and avoidance in agoraphobia, application of path analysis to treatment studies. *Archives of General Psychiatry, 44,* 377–85.

Kleinknecht, R. A. (1994). Acquisition of blood, injury, and needle fears and phobias. *Behaviour Research and Therapy, 32*(8): 817–23.

Kleinknecht, R., & Lenz, J. (1989). Blood/injury fear, fainting and avoidance of medically related situations: A family correspondence study. *Behaviour Research and Therapy, 27,* 537–47.

Klerman, G. L., Lavori, P. W., & Rice, J., et al. (1985). Birth cohort trends in rates of major depressive disorder among relatives of patients with affective disorder. *Archives of General Psychiatry, 42*(7): 689–93.

Klerman, G. L., Weissman, M. M., Rounsaville, N. B., & Chevron, E. (1984). *Interpersonal psychotherapy of depression.* New York: Basic Books.

Kline, N. (1970). Monoamine oxidase inhibitors: An unfinished picaresque tale. In F. J. Ayd & H. Blackwell (Eds.), *Discoveries in biological psychiatry.* Philadelphia: Lippincott.

Klosko, J., Barlow, D., Tassarini, R., & Cerny, J. (1988). Comparison of alprazolam and cognitive behavior therapy in the treatment of panic disorder: A preliminary report. In I. Hand & H. Wittchen (Eds.), *Treatment of panic and phobias: Modes of application and variables affecting outcome.* Berlin: Springer-Verlag.

Kluft, R. (1984). Treatment of multiple personality. *Psychiatric Clinics of North America, 7,* 9–29.

Kluft, R. P. (1987). An update on multiple personality disorder. *Hospital and Community Psychiatry, 38,* 363–73.

Kluft, R. P. (1991). Multiple personality disorder. In Tasman, A., & Goldfinger, S. M. (Eds.), *American Psychiatric Press Review of Psychiatry, 10,* 161–88.

Kobasa, S. C. (1979). Stressful life events, personality, and health: An inquiry into hardiness. *Journal of Personality and Social Psychology, 37,* 1–11.

Kohut, H. (1971). *The analysis of the self.* New York: International Universities Press.

Kohut, H. (1977). *The restoration of the self.* New York: International Universities Press.

Kohut, H. (1978). *The search for self.* New York: International Universities Press.

Kokkevi, A., & Stefanis, C. (1995). Drug abuse and psychiatric comorbidity. *Comprehensive Psychiatry, 36*(5): 329–37.

Koob, G. F., & Bloom, F. E. (1988). Cellular and molecular mechanisms of drug dependence. *Science, 242,* 715–23.

Kopelowicz, A., & Liberman, R. P. (1997). Psychological and behavioral treatments for schizophrenia. In P. Nathan and J. Gorman (Eds.), *Treatments that work.* New York: Oxford.

Korchin, S. J. (1976). *Modern clinical psychology: Principles of intervention in the clinic and the community.* New York: Basic Books.

Kotsopoulos, S., & Snow, B. (1986). Conversion disorders in children: A study of clinical outcome. *Psychiatric Journal of the University of Ottawa, 11,* 134–39.

Kovacs, M., & Beck, A. T. (1977). An empirical-clinical approach towards a definition of childhood depression. In J. G. Schulterbrand & A. Raven (Eds.), *Depression in childhood: Diagnosis, treatment, and conceptual models.* New York: Raven Press.

Kovacs, M., Gatsonis, C., Paulauskas, S. L., & Richards, C. (1989). Depressive disorders in childhood: I V. A longitudinal study of comorbidity with and risk for anxiety disorders. *Archives of General Psychiatry, 46*(9): 776–82.

Kovacs, M., Rush, A. J., Beck, A. T., & Hollon, S. D. (1981). Depressed outpatient treatment with cognitive therapy or pharmaco therapy: A one year follow-up. *Archives of General Psychiatry, 38,* 33–39.

Kraepelin, E. (1919). *Dementia praecox and paraphrenia.* New York: Robert E. Krieger.

Krafft-Ebing, R. von. (1931). *Psychopathia sexualis.* New York: Physicians & Surgeons Book Co.

Krantz, D., Helmers, K., Bairey, N., et al. (1991). Cardiovascular reactivity and mental stress-induced myocardial ischemia in patients with coronary artery disease. *Psychosomatic Medicine, 53,* 1–12.

Kravitz, H. M., Haywood, T. W., Kelly, J., Wahlstrom, C., Liles, S., & Cavanaugh, J. L. (1995). Medroxyprogesterone treatment for paraphiliacs. *Bulletin of the American Academy of Psychiatry and the Law, 23*(1): 19–33.

Kreek, M. J. (1992). Rationale for maintenance pharmacotherapy of opiate dependence. In C. P. O'Brien & J. H. Jaffe (Eds.), *Addictive states* (pp. 205–30). New York: Raven Press.

Krieckhaus, E., Donahoe, J., & Morgan, M. (1992). Paranoid schizophrenia may be caused by dopamine hyperactivity of CA1 hippocampus. *Biological Psychiatry, 31,* 560–70.

Krystal, H. (1968). *Massive psychic trauma.* New York: International Universities Press.

Kuch, K., & Cox, B. (1992). Symptoms of PTSD in 124 survivors of the Holocaust. *American Journal of Psychiatry, 149,* 337–40.

Kuhnle, U., Bullinger, M., & Schwarz, H.P. (1995). The quality of life in adult female patients with congenital adrenal hyperplasia: A comprehensive study of the impact of genital malformations and chronic disease on female patients' life. *European Journal of Pediatrics, 154,* 708–16.

Kupfer, D., Frank, E., Perel, J., et al. (1992). Five-year outcome for maintenance therapies in recurrent depression. *Archives of General Psychiatry, 49,* 769–73.

Kurland, H. D., Yeager, C. T., & Arthur, R. J. (1963). Psychophysiologic aspects of severe behavior disorders. *Archives of General Psychiatry, 8,* 599–604.

Lacey, J. I. (1950). Individual differences in somatic response patterns. *Journal of Comparative and Physiological Psychology, 43,* 338–50.

Lachman, S. J. (1972). *Psychosomatic disorders: Behavioristic interpretations.* New York: Wiley.

Lader, M. (1988). The psychopharmacology of addiction: Benzodiazepine tolerance and dependence. In M. Lader (Ed.), *The psychopharmacology of addiction.* New York: Oxford University Press.

Ladisich, W., & Feil, W. B. (1988). Empathy in psychiatric patients. *British Journal of Medical Psychology, 61,* 155–62.

Lahey, B. B., Loeber, R., Hart, E. L., Frick, P. J., Applegate, B., Zhang, Q., Green, S. M., and Russo, M. F. (1995). Four-year longitudinal study of conduct disorder in boys: Patterns and predictors of persistence. *Journal of Abnormal Psychology, 104*(1): 83–93.

Lahey, B. B., Piacentini, J. C., McBurnett, K., Stone, P., Hartdagen, S. and Hynd, G. (1988). Psychopathology in the parents of children with conduct disorder and hyperactivity. *Journal of the American Academy of Child and Adolescent Psychiatry, 27,* 163–70.

Laing, R. D. (1965). *The divided self.* Baltimore: Penguin.

Laing, R. D., & Esterson, A. (1964). *Sanity, madness, and the family.* London: Tavistock.

LaMontagne, Y., & LeSage, A. (1986). Private exposure and covert sensitization in the treatment of exhibitionism. *Journal of Behavior Therapy and Experimental Psychiatry, 17*(3): 197–201.

Lang, P. (1967). Fear reduction and fear behavior. In J. Schlein (Ed.), *Research in psychotherapy.* Washington DC: American Psychological Association.

Lang, P. J. (1979). A bio-informational theory of emotional imagery. *Psychophysiology, 92*(3): 276–306.

Langer, E. J., & Abelson, R. P. (1974). A patient by any other name. . . : Clinician group difference in labelling bias. *Journal of Consulting and Clinical Psychology, 42,* 4–9.

Laughlin, H. P. (1967). *The neuroses.* Washington, DC: Butterworth.

Law, W. A., Martin, A., Mapou, R. L., Roller, T. L., Salazar, A. M., Temoshack, L. R., & Rundell, J. R. (1994). Working memory in individuals with HIV infection. *Journal of Clinical and Experimental Neuropsychology, 16,* 173–82.

Lavigne, J. V., Arend, R., Rosenbaum, D., Sinacore, J., Cicchetti, C., Binns, H. J., Christoffel, K. K., Hayford, J. R., and McGuire, P. (1994). Interrater reliability of the DSM-IIIR with preschool children. *Journal of Abnormal Child Psychology, 22*(6): 679–90.

Lazarus, A. A. (1976). *Multimodal behavior therapy.* New York: Springer.

Lazarus, A. A. (1993). Tailoring the therapeutic relationship, or being an authentic chameleon. *Psychotherapy, 30*(3): 404–7.

Lazarus, A. A., & Beutler, L. E. (1993). On technical eclecticism. *Journal of Counseling and Development, 71*(4): 381–85.

Lee, D. J., Gomez-Marin, O., & Prineas, R. J. (1996). Type A behavior pattern and change in blood pressure from childhood to adolescence. *American Journal of Epidemiology, 143*(1):63–72.

Leff, J. P. (1976). Schizophrenia and sensitivity to the family environment. *Schizophrenia Bulletin, 2,* 566–74.

Leff, M. J., Roatch, J. F., & Bunney, W. E. (1970). Environmental factors preceding the onset of severe depressions. *Psychiatry, 33,* 293–311.

Lehman, D. R., Wortman, C. B., & Williams, A. F. (1987). Long-term effects of losing a spouse or child in a motor vehicle crash. *Journal of Personality and Social Psychology, 52,* 218–31.

Lehmkuhl, G., Blanz, B., Lehmkuhl, U., & Braun-Scharm, H. (1989). Conversion disorder (DSM-III 300.11): Symptomatology and course in childhood and adolescence. *European Archives of Psychiatry and Neurological Sciences, 238,* 155–60.

Leonard, H., Lenane, M., Swedo, S., et al. (1992). Tics and Tourette's disorder: A 2- to 7-year follow-up of 54 obsessive-compulsive children. *American Journal of Psychiatry, 149,* 1244–51.

Leonard, H. L., Swedo, S., Lenane, M., et al. (1991). A double-blind desipramine substitution during long-term clomipramine treatment in children and adolescents with obsessive-compulsive disorder. *Archives of General Psychiatry, 48,* 922–27.

Leonard, H., Swedo, S., Lenane, M., et al. (1993). A 2- to 7-year follow-up study of 54 obsessive-compulsive children and adolescents. *Archives of General Psychiatry, 50,* 429–39.

Lerman, C., Schwartz, M.D., Miller, S.M., Daly, M., Sands, C., & Rimer, B. K. (1996). A randomized trial of breast cancer risk counseling: Interacting effects of counseling, educational level, and coping style. *Health Psychology, 15*(2): 75–83.

Lesser, I. M. (1985). Current concepts in psychiatry: Alexithymia. *New England Journal of Medicine, 312,* 690–92.

Lester, D. (1977). Multiple personality: A review. *Psychology, 14,* 54–59.

Lester, D. (1993). The effectiveness of suicide prevention centers. *Suicide and Life-Threatening Behavior, 23,* 263–67.

LeVay, S. (1991). A difference in the hypothalamic structure between heterosexual and homosexual men. *Science, 253,* 1034–37.

Levendosky, A. A., Okun, A., & Parker, J. G. (1995). Depression and maltreatment as predictors of social competence and social problem-solving skills in school-age children. *Child Abuse and Neglect, 19*(10): 1183-95.

Levy, G. D. (1995). Recall of related and unrelated gender-typed item pairs by young children. *Sex Roles, 32*(5–6): 393–406.

Levin, A., Scheier, F., & Liebowitz, M. (1989). Social phobia: Biology and pharmacology. *Clinical Psychology Review, 9,* 129–40.

Levin, S., & Stava, L. (1987). Personality characteristics of sex offenders: A review. *Archives of Sexual Behavior, 16*, 57–79.

Lewine, R. R. J. (1981). Sex differences in schizophrenia: Timing or subtypes. *Psychological Bulletin, 90*, 432–44.

Lewinsohn, P. M. (1975). Engagement in pleasant activities and depression level. *Journal of Abnormal Psychology, 84*, 718–21.

Lewinsohn, P. M., Clarke, G. N., Hops, H., & Andrews, J. (1990). Cognitive-behavioural treatment for depressed adolescents. *Behaviour Therapy, 21*, 385–401.

Lewinsohn, P. M., Klein, D. N., & Seeley, J. R. (1995). Bipolar disorders in a community sample of older adolescents: Prevalence, phenomenology, comorbidity, and course. *Journal of the American Academy of Child and Adolescent Psychiatry, 34*(4): 454–63.

Lewis, J. M., Rodnick, E. H., & Goldstein, M. J. (1981). Interfamilial interactive behavior, parental communication deviance, and risk for schizophrenia. *Journal of Abnormal Psychology, 90*, 448–57.

Lewinsohn, P. M., Rohde, P., Seeley, J. R., & Fischer, S. A. (1993). Age-cohort changes in the lifetime occurrence of depression and other mental disorders. *Journal of Abnormal Psychology, 102*(1):110–20.

Lewy, A. J., Sack, L., Miller, S., & Hoban, T. M. (1987). Antidepressant and circadian phase-shifting effects of light. *Science, 235*, 352–54.

Liberman, R. P., & Green, M. F. (1992). Whither cognitive-behavioral therapy for schizophrenia? *Schizophrenia Bulletin, 18*(1): 27–35.

Liberman, R. P., Mueser, K. T., & Wallace, C. J. (1986). Social skills training for schizophrenic individuals at risk for relapse. *American Journal of Psychiatry, 143*(4): 523–26.

Liberman, R. P., Neuchterlein, K. H., & Wallace, C. J. (1982). Social skills training and the nature of schizophrenia. In J. P. Curran & P. M. Monti (Eds.), *Social skills training: A practical handbook* (pp. 5–56). New York: Guilford Press.

Lidz, C. W., Mulvey, E. P., & Gardner, W. (1993). The accuracy of predictions of violence to others. *Journal of the American Medical Association, 269*(8): 1007–11.

Lieberman, J. A., & Koreen, A. R. (1993). Neurochemistry and neuroendocrinology of schizophrenia. *Schizophrenia Bulletin, 19*, 371–430.

Liebowitz, M. R., Fyer, A. J., Gorman, J. M., Dillon, D., Davies, S., Stein, J. M., Cohen, B. S., & Klein, D. F. (1985). Specificity of lactate infusions in social phobia versus panic disorders. *American Journal of Psychiatry, 142*, 947–50.

Liebowitz, M. R., Gorman, J. M., Fyer, A. J., Levitt, M., Dillon, D., Levy, G., Appleby, I. L., Anderson, S., Palij, M., Davies, S. O., & Klein, D. F. (1985). Lactate provocation of panic attacks: II. Biochemical and physiological findings. *Archives of General Psychiatry, 42*, 709–19.

Liese, B. S., & Larson, M. W. (1995). Coping with life threatening illness: A cognitive therapy perspective. *Journal of Cognitive Psychotherapy, 9*(1): 19–34.

Lindemalm, G., Korlin, D., & Uddenberg, N. (1986). Long-term follow-up of "sex change" in 13 male-to-female transsexuals. *Archives of Sexual Behavior, 15*, 187–210.

Lindemann, E. (1944). The symptomatology and management of acute grief. *American Journal of Psychiatry, 101*, 141–48.

Linden, L. L., & Breed, W. (1976). The demographic epidemiology of suicide. In E. S. Shneidman (Ed.), *Suicidology: Contemporary developments*. New York: Grune & Stratton.

Link, B., Andrews, J., & Cullen, F. (1992). The violent and illegal behavior of mental patients reconsidered. *American Sociological Review, 57*, 275–92.

Linsky, A. S., Straus, M. A., & Colby, J. P. (1985). Stressful events, stressful conditions, and alcohol problems in the United States, a partial test of Bale's Theory. *Journal of Studies on Alcohol, 33*, 979–89.

Lipowski, Z. J. (1990). Chronic idiopathic pain syndrome. *Annals of Medicine, 22*, 213–17.

Lippold, S., & Claiborn, J. M. (1983). Comparison of the Wechsler Adult Intelligence Scale and the Wechsler Adult Intelligence Scale-Revised. *Journal of Consulting and Clinical Psychology, 51*, 315.

Lister, R. G. (1985). The amnesic action of benzodiazepines in man. *Neuroscience and Biobehavioral Reviews, 9*, 87–94.

Littlefield, C. H., & Rushton, J. P. (1986). When a child dies: The sociobiology of bereavement. *Journal of Personality and Social Psychology, 51*, 797–802.

Livermore, J. M., & Meehl, P. E. (1967). The virtues of M'Naghten. *Minnesota Law Review, 51*, 789–856.

Livingston, H., Livingston, M., Brooks, D., & McKinlay, W. (1992). Elderly survivors of the Lockerbie air disaster. *International Journal of Geriatric Psychiatry, 7*, 725–29.

Lochman, J. E., White, K. J., & Wayland, K. K. (1991). Cognitive-behavioral assessment and treatment with aggressive children. In P. C. Kendall (Eds.), *Child and adolescent therapy*. New York: Guilford Press.

Lockyer, L., & Rutter, M. (1969). A five-to fifteen-year follow-up study of infantile psychosis. *British Journal of Psychiatry, 115*, 865–82.

Loeber, R. (1990). Development and risk factors of juvenile antisocial behavior and delinquency. *Clinical Psychology Review, 10*, 1–41.

Loeber, R., & Dishion, T. J. (1983). Early predictors of male delinquency: A review. *Psychological Bulletin, 94*, 68–99.

Loewenstein, R. J., & Ross, D. R. (1992). Multiple personality and psychoanalysis: An introduction. *Psychoanalytic Inquiry, 12*, 3–48.

Loftus, E. (1993). The reality of repressed memories. *American Psychologist, 48*, 518–37.

Loftus, E. (1994). The repressed memory controversy. *American Psychologist, 49*, 443–45.

Loftus, E., Grant, B., Franklin, G., Parr, L., & Brown, R. (1996). Crime victims' compensation and repressed memory. Submitted to *New England Journal of Medicine*.

London, P. (1986). *The modes and morals of psychotherapy*. New York: Hemisphere.

Lonnqvist, J., Shihvo, S., Syvalahti, E., Sintonen, H., Kiviruusu, O., & Pitkanen, H. (1995). Moclobemide and fluoxetine in the prevention of relapses following acute treatment of depression. *Acta Psychiatrica Scandinavica, 91*, 189–94.

Looney, J. G., Lipp, M. G., & Spitzer R. L. (1978). A new method of classification for psychophysiological disorders. *American Journal of Psychiatry, 135*, 304–8.

Loranger, A., & Levine, P. (1978). Age of onset of bipolar affective illness. *Archives of General Psychiatry, 35*, 1345–48.

Loranger, A. W., Susman, V. L., Oldham, J. M., & Russakoff, L. M. (1987). The personality disorder examination: A preliminary report. *Journal of Personality Disorders, 1*(1): 1–13.

Losonczy, M. F., Song, I. S., Mohs, R. C., Mathe, A. A., Davidson, M., Davis, B. M., & Davis, K. L. (1986). Correlates of lateral ventricular size in chronic schizophrenia: II. Biological measures. *American Journal of Psychiatry, 143*(9): 1113–17.

Lovaas, O. I. (1966). A program for the establishment of speech in psychotic children. In J. K. Wing (Ed.), *Early childhood autism*. New York: Pergamon.

Lovaas, O. I. (1973). *Behavioral treatment of autistic children*. Morristown, NJ: General Learning Press.

Lovaas, O. I. (1987). Behavioral treatment and abnormal education and intellectual functioning in young autistic children. *Journal of Consulting and Clinical Psychology, 55*, 3–9.

Lovaas, O. I., & Simmons, J. Q. (1969). Manipulation of self-destruction in three retarded children. *Journal of Applied Behavior Analysis, 2*, 143–57.

Lovibond, S. H., & Coote, M. A. (1970). Enuresis. In C. G. Costello (Ed.), *Symptoms of psychopathology*. New York: Wiley.

Low, P. W., Jeffries, Jr., J. C., & Bonnie, R. J. (1986). *The trial of John W. Hinckley, Jr.: A case study in the insanity defense*. Mineola, NY: Foundation Press.

Luborsky, L. (1984). *Principles of psychoanalytic theory: A manual for supportive expressive treatment*. New York: Basic Books.

Luborsky, L., Popp, C., Luborsky, E., & Mark, D. (1994). The core conflictual relationship theme. *Psychotherapy Research, 4*(3–4): 172–83.

Luborsky, L., Singer, B., & Luborsky, L. (1975). Comparative studies of psychotherapies. *Archives of General Psychiatry, 32*, 995–1008.

Luckasson, R., Coulter, D.L., Polloway, E.A., Reiss, S., Schalock, R.L., Snell, M.E., Spitalnik, D.M., & Stark, J.A. (1992). *Mental retardation: Definition, classification, and systems of support*. Washington, DC: American Association on Mental Retardation.

Lykken, D. T. (1957). A study of anxiety in the sociopathic personality. *Journal of Abnormal and Social Psychology, 55,* 6–10.

Maas, J. W. (1975). Biogenic amines and depression. *Archives of General Psychiatry, 32,* 1357–61.

Mace, N., & Rabins, P. V. (1981). *The thirty-six hour day.* Baltimore: Johns Hopkins Press.

Maccoby, E., & Jacklin, C. (1974). *The psychology of sex differences.* Stanford: Stanford University Press.

MacDonald, N. (1960). Living with schizophrenia. *Canadian Medical Association Journal, 82,* 218–21.

Mackay, A. V. P. (1980). Positive and negative schizophrenic symptoms and the role of dopamine. *British Journal of Psychiatry, 137,* 379–86.

Macleod, A. K., & Cropley, M. L. (1995). Depressive future-thinking: The role of valence and specificity. *Cognitive Therapy and Research, 19*(1): 35–50.

Macleod, C., & McLaughlin, K. (1995). Implicit and explicit memory bias in anxiety: A conceptual replication. *Behaviour Research and Therapy, 33*(1): 1–14.

MacMillan, D. L., & Semmel, M. I. (1977). Evaluation of mainstreaming programs. *Focus on Exceptional Children, 6*(4): 8–14.

Madakasira, S., & O'Brien, K. (1987). Acute post-traumatic stress disorder in victims of a natural disaster. *Journal of Nervous and Mental Disease, 175,* 286–90.

Magaro, P. A. (1981). The paranoid and the schizophrenic: The case for distinct cognitive style. *Schizophrenia Bulletin, 7,* 632–61.

Magnusson, D. (1988). *Individual development from an interactional perspective: A longitudinal study.* Hillsdale, NJ: Erlbaum.

Maher, B. A. (1966). *Principles of psychopathology: An experimental approach.* New York: McGraw-Hill.

Mahler, M. (1979). *The selected papers of Margaret Mahler* (Vol. 1, 2, 3). New York: Jason Aronson.

Mahoney, M. J. (1971). The self-management of covert behavior: A case study. *Behavior Therapy, 2,* 575–78.

Mahoney, M. J. (1974). *Cognition and behavior modification.* Cambridge, MA.: Ballinger.

Mahoney, M. J., & Thoresen, C. E. (1974). *Self-control: Power to the person.* Belmont, CA: Brooks/Cole.

Maier, S. F., Laudenslager, M., & Ryan, S. M. (1985). Stressor controllability, immune function, and endogenous opiates. In F. Bush & J. B. Overmier (Eds.), *Affect, conditioning, and cognition.* Hillside, NJ: Erlbaum.

Maier, S. F., & Seligman, M. E. P. (1976). Learned helplessness: Theory and evidence. *Journal of Experimental Psychology, 105*(1): 3–46.

Maier, S. F., Watkins, L. R., & Fleshner, M. (1994). Psychoneuroimmunology: The interface between behavior, brain, and immunity. *American Psychologist, 49*(2): 1004–17.

Maier, W., Lichtermann, D., Minges, J., Delmo, C., & Heun, R. (1995). The relationship between bipolar disorder and alcoholism: A controlled family study. *Psychological Medicine, 25,* 787–96.

Mailleux, P., Verslype, M., Preud'homme, X., & Vanderhaeghen, J.J. (1994). Activation of multiple transcription factor genes by tetrahydrocannabinol in rat forebrain. *NeuroReport, 5,* 1265–68.

Main, M. (1991). Metacognitive knowledge, metacognitive monitoring, and singular (coherent) vs. Multiple (incoherent) models of attachment: Findings and directions for future research. In P. Harris, J. Stevenson-Hinde & C. Parkes (Eds.), *Attachment across the lifecycle* (pp. 127–59). New York: Routledge-Kegan Paul.

Malarkey, W., Kiecolt-Glaser, J., Pearl, D., & Glaser, R. (1994). Hostile behavior during marital conflict alters pituitary and adrenal hormones. *Psychosomatic Medicine, 56,* 41–51.

Maletzky, B. M. (1974). "Assisted" covert sensitization in the treatment of exhibitionism. *Journal of Consulting and Clinical Psychology, 42,* 34–40.

Maletzky, B. M. (1997). The paraphilias: Research and treatment. In P. Nathan & J. Gorman (Eds.), *Treatments that work.* New York: Oxford.

Malitz, S., et al. (1984). Low dosage ECT: Electrode placement and acute physiological and cognitive effects. Special Issue: Electroconvulsive therapy. *American Journal of Social Psychiatry, 4*(4): 47–53.

Malmo, R. B., & Shagass, C. (1949). Physiological study of symptom mechanism in psychiatric patients under stress. *Psychosomatic Medicine, 11,* 25–29.

Malt, U., & Weisaeth, L. (1989). Disaster psychiatry and traumatic stress studies in Norway. *Acta Psychiatrica Scandinavica, 80,* 7–12.

Manji, H. K., Potter, W. Z., & Lenox, R. H. (1995). Signal transduction pathways: Molecular targets for lithium's actions. *Archives of General Psychiatry, 52,* 531–43.

Mann, J., Arango, V., & Underwood, M. (1990). Serotonin and suicidal behavior. *Annals of the New York Academy of Sciences, 600,* 476–85.

Mannuzza, S., Fyer, A. J., Martin, L. Y., Gallops, M., S., Endicott, J., Gorman, J., Liebowitz, M. R., and Klein, D. F. (1989). Reliability of anxiety assessment. *Archives of General Psychiatry, 46,* 1093–1101.

Marciano, T. D. (1982). Four marriage and family texts: A brief (but telling) array. *Contemporary Sociology, 11,* 150–53.

Marengo, J. T., Harrow, M., & Edell, W. S. (1993). Thought disorder. In C. G. Costello (Ed.), *Symptoms of schizophrenia* (pp. 27–55). New York: Wiley.

Margraf, J., Barlow, D., Clark, D., & Telch, M. (1993). Psychological treatment of panic: Work in progress on outcome, active ingredients, and follow-up. *Behaviour Research and Therapy, 31*(1): 1–8.

Margraf, J., & Schneider, S. (1991). *Outcome and active ingredients of cognitive-behavioural treatments for panic disorder.* Paper presented at the annual meeting of the Association for the Advancement of Behavior Therapy, New York, November 26, 1991.

Mariotto, M., Paul, G. L., and Licht, M. H. (1995). Assessing the chronically mentally ill patient. In J. N. Butcher (Ed.), *Clinical personality assessment: Practical considerations.* New York: Oxford University Press.

Marks, I. M. (1969). *Fears and phobias.* New York: Academic Press.

Marks, I. (1977). Phobias and obsessions: Clinical phenomena in search of laboratory models. In J. Maser & M. E. P. Seligman (Eds.), *Psychopathology: Experimental models.* San Francisco: Freeman.

Marks, I. M. (1981). Review of behavioral psychotherapy: II. Sexual disorders. *American Journal of Psychiatry, 138,* 750–56.

Marks, I. M. (1986). Epidemiology of anxiety. *Social Psychiatry, 21,* 167–71.

Marks, I., Boulougouris, J., & Marset, P. (1971). Flooding versus desensitization in the treatment of phobic patients: A crossover study. *British Journal of Psychiatry, 119,* 353–75.

Marks, I. M., Gray, S., Cohen, D., Hill, R., Mawson, D., Ramm, E., & Stern, R. S. (1983). Imipramine and brief therapist-aided exposure in agoraphobics having self-exposure homework. *Archives of General Psychiatry, 40,* 153–62.

Marks, I. M., & Rachman, S. J. (1978). *Interim report to the Medical Research Council.*

Marks, I., & Tobena, A. (1990). Learning and unlearning fear: A clinical and evolutionary perspective. *Neuroscience* and *Biobehavioral Reviews, 14,* 365–84.

Marlatt, G. A., & Gordon, J. R. (1985). *Relapse prevention.* New York: Guilford Press.

Marshall, R. D., Stein, D. J., Liebowitz, M. R., & Yehuda, R. (1996). A pharmacotherapy algorithm in the treatment of post-traumatic stress disorder. *Psychiatric Annals, 26*(4): 217–26.

Marshall, W., Eccles, A., & Barbaree, H. (1991). The treatment of exhibitionists: A focus on sexual deviance versus cognitive and relationship features. *Behaviour Research and Therapy, 29,* 129–35.

Martin, A. (1987). Representation of semantic and spatial knowledge in Alzheimer's patients: Implications for models of preserved learning in amnesia. *Journal of Clinical and Experimental Neuropsychology, 9,* 191–224.

Martin, A., Heyes, M. P., Salazar, A. M., Law, W. A., & Williams, J. (1993). Impaired motor-skill learning, slowed reaction time, and elevated cerebro-spinal fluid guinolinic acid in a subgroup of HIV-infected individuals. *Neuropsychology, 7,* 149–57.

Martin, B. (1977). *Abnormal psychology.* New York: Holt, Rinehart & Winston.

Martin, C. L., Eisenbud, L., & Rose, H. (1995). Children's gender-based reasoning about toys. *Child Development, 66,* 1453–71.

Mason, J. W. (1971). A re-evaluation of the concept of "non-specificity" in stress theory. *Journal of Psychiatric Research, 8,* 323–33.

Mason, J. W. (1975). A historical view of the stress field, Part I. *Journal of Human Stress, 1,* 6–12.

Masters, W. H., & Johnson, V. E. (1970). *Human sexual inadequacy.* Boston: Little, Brown.

Matarazzo, J. D. (1983). The reliability of psychiatric and psychological diagnosis. *Clinical Psychology Review, 3,* 103–45.

Matthews, A., & MacLeod, C. (1986). Discrimination of threat cues without awareness in anxiety states. *Journal of Abnormal Psychology, 95,* 131–38.

Matthews, A., Mogg, K., Kentish, J., & Eysenck, M. (1995). Effect of psychological treatment on cognitive bias in generalized anxiety disorder. *Behaviour Research and Therapy, 33*(3): 293–303.

Mattes, J. A. (1997). Risperidone: How good is the evidence for efficacy? *Schizophrenia Bulletin, 23*(1): 155–62.

Matthysse, S. (1973). Antipsychotic drug actions: A clue to the neuropathology of the schizophrenias. *Federation Proceedings, 32,* 200–205.

Mattick, R., Andrews, G., Hadzi-Pavlovic, D., & Christensen, H. (1990). Treatment of panic and agoraphobia: An integrative review. *Journal of Nervous and Mental Disease, 178,* 567–78.

Mavissakalian, M., Jones, B., Olson, S., & Perel, J. (1990). Clomipramine in obsessive-compulsive disorder: Clinical response and plasma levels. *Journal of Clinical Psychopharmacology, 10,* 261–68.

Mavissakalian, M., & Michelson, L. (1986). Two-year follow-up of exposure and imipramine treatment of agoraphobia. *American Journal of Psychiatry, 143,* 1106–12.

Mavissakalian, M. R., & Perel, J. M. (1995). Imipramine treatment of panic disorder with agoraphobia: Dose ranging and plasma level-response relationships. *American Journal of Psychiatry, 152*(5): 673–82.

Mavissakalian, M., Perel, J., Bowler, K., & Dealy, R. (1987). Trazodone in the treatment of panic disorder and agoraphobia with panic attacks. *American Journal of Psychiatry, 144,* 785–91.

McArthur, J. C., Cohen, B. A., Selnes, O. A., et al. (1989). Low prevalence of neurological and neuropsychological abnormalities in otherwise healthy HIV-1–infected individuals. Results from the multicenter AIDS cohort study. *Annals of Neurology, 26,* 601–10.

McCarthy, G. W., & Craig, K. D. (1995). Flying therapy for flying phobia. *Aviation, Space, and Environmental Medicine, 66*(12): 1179–84.

McCarthy, M. (1990). The thin ideal, depression, and eating disorders in women. *Behaviour Research and Therapy, 28*(3): 205–15.

McCary, J. L. (1978). Human sexuality: Past present and future. *Journal of Marriage and Family Counseling, 4,* 3–12.

McClelland, D. C. (1979). Inhibited power motivation and high blood pressure in men. *Journal of Abnormal Psychology, 88,* 182–90.

McClelland, D. C., Atkinson, J. W., Clark, R. A., & Lowell, E. L. (1953). *The achievement motive.* New York: Appleton.

McConaghy, N. (1969). Subjective and penil plethysmograph response following aversion-relief and apomorphine aversion therapy for homosexual impulses. *British Journal of Psychiatry, 115,* 723–30.

McConaghy, N., Armstrong, M., & Blaszczynski, A. (1981). Controlled comparison of aversive therapy and covert sensitization in compulsive homosexuality. *Behaviour Research and Therapy, 19,* 425–34.

McCord, J. (1979). Some child-rearing antecedents of criminal behavior in adult men. *Journal of Personality and Social Psychology, 37,* 1477–86.

McCord, J. (1980). *Myths and realities about criminal sanctions.* Paper presented at the annual meetings of the American Society of Criminology, San Francisco, CA, November 5–8, 1980.

McDaniel, J. S., Musselman, D. L., Porter, M. R., Reed, D. A., & Nemroff, C. B. (1995). Depression in patients with cancer. *Archives of General Psychiatry, 52,* 89–99.

McDowell, F. H. (1994). Neurorehabilitation. *Western Journal of Medicine, 161,* 323–27.

McFarlane, A. (1989). The aetiology of post-traumatic morbidity: Predisposing, precipitating, and perpetuating factors. *British Journal of Psychiatry, 154,* 1221–28.

McGarry, A. L., & Bendt, R. H. (1969). Criminal vs. civil commitment of psychotic offenders: A seven year follow-up. *American Journal of Psychiatry, 125,* 1387–94.

McGhie, A., & Chapman, J. S. (1961). Disorders of attention and perception in early schizophrenia. *British Journal of Medical Psychology, 34,* 103–16.

McGlashan, T. H. (1986a). Predictors of shorter-, medium-, and longer-term outcome in schizophrenia. *American Journal of Psychiatry, 142*(10): 50–55.

McGlashan, T. H. (1986b). Schizotypal personality disorder. Chestnut Lodge follow-up study: VI. Long-term follow-up perspectives. *Archives of General Psychiatry, 43,* 329–34.

McGlashan, T. H. (1987). Testing DSM-III symptom criteria for schizoptypal and borderline personality disorders. *Archives of General Psychiatry, 44,* 143–48.

McGlashan, T. H., & Fenton, W. S. (1992). The positive-negative distinction in schizophrenia: Review of natural history validators. *Archives of General Psychiatry, 49*(1): 63–72.

McGue, M. (1992). When assessing twin concordance, use the probandwise not the pairwise rate. *Schizophrenia Bulletin, 18,* 171–76.

McGue, M., Gottesman, I. I., & Rao, D. C. (1985). Resolving genetic models for the transmission of schizophrenia. *Genetic Epidemiology, 2,* 99–110.

McGuffin, P., & Katz, R. (1989). The genetics of depression and manic-depressive disorder. *British Journal of Psychiatry, 155,* 294–304.

McGuffin, P., Katz, R., Watkins, S., & Rutherford, J. (1996). A hospital-based twin register of the heritability of DSM-IV unipolar depression. *Archives of General Psychiatry, 53,* 129–36.

McGuire, P. K., Silbersweig, D. A., Wright, I., Murray, R. M., David, A. S., Frackowiak, R. S. J., & Frith, C. D. (1995). Abnormal monitoring of inner speech: A physiological basis for auditory hallucinations. *Lancet, 346,* 596–600.

McGuire, R. J., Carlisle, J. M., & Young, B. G. (1965). Sexual deviation as conditioned behavior. *Behaviour Research and Therapy, 2,* 185–90.

McIntosh, J. (1989). Trends in racial differences in U.S. suicide statistics. *Death Studies, 13,* 275–86.

McKim, W. A. (1986). *Drugs and behavior.* Englewood Cliffs, NJ: Prentice-Hall.

McLeod, D., Hoehn-Saric, R., Zimmerli, W., & De Souza, E. (1990). Treatment effects of alprazolam and imipramine: Physiological versus subjective changes in patients with generalized anxiety disorder. *Biological Psychiatry, 28,* 849–61.

McLoughlin, D. M., Lucey, J. V., & Dinan, T. G. (1994). Central serotonergic hyperresponsivity in late-onset Alzheimer's disease. *American Journal of Psychiatry, 151*(11): 1701–1703.

McNally, R. J. (1987). Preparedness and phobias: A review. *Psychological Bulletin, 101,* 283–303.

McNally, R. (1996). Review of Eye Movement Desensitization and Reprocessing: Basic principles, protocols, and procedures. *Anxiety, 2,* 153–55.

McNeal, E. T., & Cimbolic, P. (1986). Antidepressants and biochemical theories of depression. *Psychological Bulletin, 99*(3): 361–74.

McNitt, P. C., & Thornton, D. W. (1978). Depression and perceived reinforcement: A consideration. *Journal of Abnormal Psychology, 87,* 137–40.

Mednick, B. R. (1973). Breakdown in high-risk subjects: Familial and early environmental factors. *Journal of Abnormal Psychology, 82,* 469–75.

Mednick, S. A., Cudeck, R., Griffith, J. J., Talovic, S. A., & Schulsinger, F. (1984). The Danish high-risk project: Recent methods and findings. In N. F. Watt, E. J. Anthony, L. C. Wynne, & J. E. Rolf (Eds.), *Children at risk for schizophrenia: A longitudinal perspective* (pp. 21–42). Cambridge: Cambridge University Press.

Mednick, S. A., Gabriella, W. F., & Hutchings, B. (1984). Genetic influences in criminal convictions: Evidence from an adoption cohort. *Science, 224,* 891–94.

Mednick, S. A., Gabriella, W. F., & Hutchings, B. (1987). Genetic factors and etiology of criminal behavior. In S. A. Mednick, T. E. Moffitt, & S. A. Stack (Eds.), *Causes of crime: New biological approaches* (pp. 74–91). New York: Cambridge University Press.

Mednick, S. A., Parnas, J., & Schulsinger, F. (1987). The Copenhagen high-risk project, 1962–1986. *Schizophrenic Bulletin, 13,* 485–95.

Meichenbaum, D. (1977). *Cognitive-behavior modification.* New York: Plenum.

Melton, G. B., Petrila, J., Poythress, N. G., & Slobogin, C. (1987). *Psychological evaluations for the courts.* New York: Guilford Press.

Melzack, R. (1973). *The puzzle of pain.* New York: Basic Books.

Mendels, J. (1970). *Concepts of depression.* New York: Wiley.

Mendels, J., & Cochran, C. (1968). The nosology of depression: The endogenous-reactive concept. *American Journal of Psychiatry, 124,* Supplement 1–11.

Mendelsohn, F., & Ross, M. (1959). An analysis of 133 homosexuals seen at a university health service. *Diseases of the Nervous System, 20,* 246–50.

Menzies, R. G., & Clarke, J. C. (1995). Etiology of phobias: A nonassociative account. *Psychophysiology, 32*(3): 208–14.

Merikangas, K. R., Leckman, J. F., Prusoff, B. A., Pauls, D. L., & Weissman, M. M. (1985). Familial transmission of depression and alcoholism. *Archives of General Psychiatry, 42,* 367–72.

Meyer, C. B., & Taylor, S. E. (1986). Adjustment to rape. *Journal of Personality and Social Psychology, 50,* 1226–34.

Meyer, V. (1966). Modification of expectations in cases with obsessional rituals. *Behaviour Research and Therapy, 4,* 273–80.

Meyer-Bahlburg, H., Feldman, J., Cohen, P., & Ehrhardt, A. (1988). Perinatal factors in the development of gender-related play behavior: Sex hormones versus pregnancy complications. *Psychiatry, 51,* 260–71.

Meyers, A. W., & Craighead, W. E. (Eds.) (1984). *Cognitive behavior therapy with children.* New York: Plenum Press.

Michelson, L., & Marchione, K. (1989). *Cognitive, behavioral, and physiologically based treatments of agoraphobia: A comparative outcome study.* Paper presented at the annual meeting of the American Association for the Advancement of Behavior Therapy, Washington, DC, November 1989.

Miklowitz, D. J. (1994). Family risk indicators in schizophrenia. *Schizophrenia Bulletin, 20,* 137–49.

Miller, D. J., & Kotses, H. (1995). Classical conditioning of total respiratory resistance in humans. *Psychosomatic Medicine, 57,* 148–53.

Miller, L. L., & Branconnier, R. J. (1983). Cannabis: Effects on memory and the cholinergic system. *Psychological Bulletin, 93,* 441–56.

Miller, N. E. (1985). The value of behavioral research on animals. *American Psychologist, 40,* 423–40.

Miller, N. S. (1995). Pharmacotherapy in alcoholism. *Journal of Addictive Diseases, 14*(1): 23–46.

Miller, N. S., Gold, M. S., & Stennie, K. (1995). Benzodiazepines: The dissociation of addiction from pharmacological dependence/withdrawal. *Psychiatric Annals, 25*(3): 149–52.

Miller, T. Q., Smith, T. W., Turner, C. W., Guijarro, M. L., & Hallet, A. J. (1996). A meta-analytic review of research on hostility and physical health. *Psychological Bulletin, 119*(2): 322–48.

Miller, W. R., & Seligman, M. E. P. (1975). Depression and learned helplessness in man. *Journal of Abnormal Psychology, 84,* 228–38.

Miller, W. R., & Seligman, M. E. P. (1976). Learned helplessness, depression, and the perception of reinforcement. *Behaviour Research and Therapy, 14,* 7–17.

Milner, B. (1970). Memory and the medial temporal regions of the brain. In K. H. Pribram & D. E. Broadbent (Eds.), *Biology of memory.* New York: Academic Press.

Milner, B. (1972). Disorders of learning and memory after temporal lobe lesions in man. *Clinical Neurosurgery, 19,* 421–46.

Minuchin, S., Rosman, B. L., & Baker, L. (1980). *Psychosomatic families: Anorexia nervosa in context.* Cambridge: Harvard University Press.

Mischel, W. (1973). Toward a cognitive social learning reconceptualization of personality. *Psychological Review, 80,* 252–83.

Mischel, W. (1976). *Introduction to personality* (2nd ed.). New York: Holt, Rinehart & Winston.

Mischel, W., & Peake, P. K. (1982). Beyond deja vu in the search for cross-situational consistency. *Psychological Review, 89,* 730–55.

Mishkin, M., & Appenzeller, T. (1987). The anatomy of memory. *Scientific American, 256*(6): 80–89.

Mishra, S. P., & Brown, K. H. (1983). The comparability of WAIS and WAIS-R IQs and subtest scores. *Journal of Clinical Psychology, 39,* 754–57.

Mitchell, J. E. (1986). Anorexia nervosa: Medical and psychological aspects. In K. D. Brownell & J. P. Foreyt (Eds.), *Handbook of eating disorders: Physiology, psychology, and treatment of obesity, anorexia, and bulimia.* New York: Basic Books.

Mitchell, J. E., & de Zwaan, M. (1993). Pharmacological treatments of binge eating. In C. G. Fairburn & G. T. Wilson (Eds.), *Binge eating: Nature, assessment, and treatment.* New York: Guilford Press.

Mitchell, J., Pyle, R., Eckert, E. et al. (1990). A comparison study of antidepressants and structured intensive group psychotherapy in the treatment of bulimia nervosa. *Archives of General Psychiatry, 47,* 149–57.

Mitchell, J. E., Raymond, N., & Specker, S. (1993). A review of the controlled trials of pharmacotherapy and psychotherapy in the treatment of bulimia nervosa. *International Journal of Eating Disorders, 14*(3): 229–47.

Mittler, P., Gillies, S., & Jukes, E. (1966). Prognosis in psychotic children. Report of follow-up study. *Journal of Mental Deficiency Research, 10,* 73–83.

Moffitt, T.E. (1990). Juvenile delinquency and attention-deficit disorder: Boys' developmental trajectories from age 3 to age 15. *Child Development, 61,* 893–910.

Mohs, R. D., Breitner, J. C. S., Silverman, J. M., & Davis, K. L. (1987). Alzheimer's disease: Morbid risk among first-degree relatives approximates fifty percent by ninety years of age. *Archives of General Psychiatry, 44,* 405–8.

Molin, J., Mellerup, E., Bolwig, T., Scheike, T., & Dam, H. (1996). The influence of climate on winter depression. *Journal of Affective Disorders, 37,* 151–55.

Molina-Holgado, F., Gonzalez, M. I., & Leret, M. L. (1995). Effect of delta 9-tetrahydrocannabinol on short-term memory in the rat. *Physiology and Behavior, 57*(1):177–79.

Monahan, J. (1992). Mental disorder and violent behavior. *American Psychologist, 47,* 511–21.

Monahan, J., & Shah, S. A. (1989). Dangerousness and commitment of the mentally disordered in the United States. *Schizophrenia Bulletin, 15*(4): 541–53.

Money, J., & Ambinder, R. (1978). Two-year, real-life diagnostic test: Rehabilitation vs. cure. In J. P. Brady & H. K. H. Brodie (Eds.), *Controversy in psychiatry.* Philadelphia: Saunders.

Money, J., & Ehrhardt, A. A. (1972). *Man and woman, boy and girl.* Baltimore: The John Hopkins University Press.

Montgomery, S. A. (1994). Antidepressants in long-term treatment. *Annual Review of Medicine, 45,* 447–57.

Moody, R. L. (1946). Bodily changes during abreaction. *The Lancet, 2,* 934–35.

Moore, K. E., Geffken, G. R., & Royal, G. P. (1995). Behavioral interventions to reduce child distress during self-injection. *Clinical Pediatrics, 34*(10): 530–34.

Morrison, R. L., & Bellack, A. (1984). Social skills training. In A. S. Bellack (Ed.), *Schizophrenia: Treatment, management, and rehabilitation* (pp. 247–79). Orlando, FL: Grune & Stratton.

Moscovitch, M. (1982a). Multiple dissociations of function in amnesia. In L. S. Cermak (Ed.), *Human memory and amnesia.* Hillsdale, NJ: Erlbaum.

Moscovitch, M. (1982b). A neuropsychological approach to perception and memory in normal and pathological aging. In F. I. M. Craik & S. Trehub (Eds.), *Aging and cognitive processes.* New York: Plenum.

Moscovitch, M. (1992). Memory and working-with-memory: A component process model based on modules and central systems. *Journal of Cognitive Neuroscience, 4,* 257–67.

Moscovitch, M., Vriezen, E., & Goshen-Gottstein, Y. (1994). Implicit trots of memory in patients with focal lesions and degenerative brain disorders. In F. Boller & J. Grafman (Eds.), *Handbook of neuropsychology.* Amsterdam: Elsevier.

Moscovitch, M., & Winokur, G. (1992). The neuropsychology of memory and aging. In F. I. M. Craik & T. A. Salthouse (Eds.), *The handbook of aging and cognition.* Hillsdale, NJ: Erlbaum.

Mowrer, O. H. (1948). Learning theory and the neurotic paradox. *American Journal of Orthopsychiatry, 18,* 571–610.

Mowrer, O. H., & Mowrer, W. M. (1938). Enuresis: A method for its study and treatment. *American Journal of Orthopsychiatry, 8,* 436–59.

Mueser, K. T., Bellack, A. S., Morrison, R. L., & Wade, J. H. (1990). Gender, social competence, and symptomatology in schizophrenia: A longitudinal analysis. *Journal of Abnormal Psychology, 99*(2): 138–47.

Mullaney, J. A., & Trippett, C. J. (1982). Alcohol dependence and phobias: Clinical description and relevance. *British Journal of Psychiatry, 135*, 565–73.

Munoz, R. F., Hollon, S. D., McGrath, E., Rehm, L. P., & VandenBos, G. R. (1994). On the AHCPR depression in primary care guidelines: Further considerations for practitioners. *American Psychologist, 49*(1): 42–61.

Munzinger, H. (1975). The adopted child's IQ: A critical review. *Psychological Bulletin, 80*, 623–29.

Murray, H. A. (1951). Forward. In H. H. Anderson & G. L. Anderson (Eds.), *An introduction to projective techniques.* Englewood Cliffs, NJ: Prentice-Hall.

Murray, K. T., & Sines, J. O. (1996). Parsing the genetic and nongenetic variance in children's depressive behavior. *Journal of Affective Disorders, 38*, 23–34.

Murstein, B. I. (1965). New thoughts about ambiguity and the TAT. *Journal of Projective Techniques and Personality Assessment, 29*, 219–25.

Myers, J. K., Weissman, M. M., Tischler, G. L., Holzer, C. E., Leaf, P. J., Orvaschel, H., Anthony, J. C., Boyd, J. H., Burke, J. D., Kramer, M., & Stolzman, R. (1984). Six-month prevalence of psychiatric disorders in three communities: 1980 to 1982. *Archives of General Psychiatry, 41*, 959–67.

Nagy, A. (1987). Possible reasons for a negative attitude to benzodiazepines as antianxiety drugs. *Nordisk Psykiatrisk Tidsskrift, 4*, 27–30.

Neale, M. C., Walters, E. E., Eaves, L. J., Kessler, R. C., Heath, A. C., & Kendler, K. S. (1994). Genetics of blood-injury fears and phobias: A population twin-based study. *American Journal of Medical Genetics, 54*(4): 326-34.

Nelissen, I., Muris, P., & Merckelbach, H. (1995). Computerized exposure and in vivo exposure treatments of spider fear in children: Two case reports. *Journal of Behavior Therapy and Experimental Psychiatry, 26*, 153–56.

Nelson, C., Mazure, C., & Jatlow, P. (1990). Does melancholia predict response in major depression? *Journal of Affective Disorders, 18*, 157–65.

Nesse, F. M., Cameron, O. G., Curtis, G. C., McCann, D. S., & Huber-Smith, M. J. (1984). Adrenergic function in patients with panic anxiety. *Archives of General Psychiatry, 41*, 771–76.

Nestadt, G., et al. (1990). An epidemiological study of histrionic personality disorder. *Psychological Medicine, 29*, 413–22.

Nestadt, G., et al. (1991). DSM-III compulsive personality disorder: An epidemiological survey. *Psychological Medicine, 21*(2): 461–71.

New York Times. (1994a). Albany plans house calls to monitor the mentally ill, April 24, 1994.

New York Times. (1994b). Father who fought "memory therapy" wins damage suit, May 14, 1994.

Nisbett, R., & Ross, L. (1980). *Human inference: Strategies and shortcomings of social judgment.* Englewood Cliffs, NJ: Prentice-Hall.

Nolen-Hoeksema, S. (1987). Sex differences in unipolar depression: Evidence and theory. *Psychological Bulletin, 101*(2): 259–82.

Nolen-Hoeksema, S. (1988). Life-span views on depression. In P. B. Baltes, D. L. Featherman, & R. M. Lerner (Eds.), *Life span development and behavior* (Vol. 9). New York: Erlbaum.

Nolen-Hoeksema, S. (1990). *Sex differences in depression.* Stanford: Stanford University Press.

Nolen-Hoeksema, S. (1991). Responses to depression and their effects on the duration of depressive episodes. *Journal of Abnormal Psychology, 102*, 569–82.

Nolen-Hoeksema, S., & Girgus, J.S. (1994). The emergence of gender differences in depression during adolescence. *Psychological Bulletin, 115*(3): 424–43.

Nolen-Hoeksema, S., Girgus, J., & Seligman, M. E. P. (1986). Learned helplessness in children: A longitudinal study of depression, achievement, and explanatory style. *Journal of Personality and Social Psychology, 51*, 435–42.

Nolen-Hoeksema, S., Girgus, J., & Seligman, M. (1992). Predic-

tors and consequences of childhood depressive symptoms: A 5-year longitudinal study. *Journal of Abnormal Psychology, 101*(3): 405–22.

Nolen-Hoeksema, S., Mumme, D., Wolfson, A., & Guskin, K. (1995). Helplessness in children of depressed and nondepressed mothers. *Developmental Psychology, 31*(3): 377–87.

Nopoulos, P., Torres, I., Flaum, M., Andreasen, N. C., Ehrhardt, J. C., and Yuh, W. T. C. (1995). Brain morphology in first-episode schizophrenia. *American Journal of Psychiatry, 152*(12): 1721–23.

Noyes, R., Chaudry, D., & Domingo, D. (1986). Pharmacologic treatment of phobic disorders. *Journal of Clinical Psychiatry, 47*, 445–52.

Noyes, R., Clarkson, C., Crowe, R., & Yates, W. (1987). A family study of generalized anxiety disorder. *American Journal of Psychiatry, 144*, 1019–24.

Noyes, R., & Kletti, R. (1977). Depersonalization in response to life-threatening danger. *Comprehensive Psychiatry, 18*, 375–84.

Nyman, A. K., & Jonsson, H. (1983). Differential evaluation of outcome in schizophrenia. *Acta Psychiatrica Scandinavica, 68*, 458–75.

O'Brien, C. P. (1994). Overview: The treatment of drug dependence. *Addiction, 89*, 1565–69.

O'Brien, C. P., Childress, A. R., McLellan, A. T., & Ehrman, R. (1992). A learning model of addiction. In C. P. O'Brien & J. H. Jaffe (Eds.), *Addictive states* (pp. 157–78). New York: Raven Press.

Offord, D. & Bennet, K. (1994). Conduct disorder: Long-term outcomes and intervention effectiveness. *Journal of the American Academy of Child and Adolescent Psychiatry, 33*(8).

Offord, D. R., Boyle, M. D., Racine, Y. A., Fleming, J. E., Cadman, D. T., Blum, H. M., Byrne, C., Links, P. S., Lipman, E. L., MacMillan, H. L., Grant, N. I., Rae, D., Sanford, M. N., Szatmari, P., Thomas, H., & Woodward, C. A. (1992). Outcome, prognosis, and risk in a longitudinal follow-up study. *Journal of the Academy for Child and Adolescent Psychiatry, 31*(5): 916–23.

Ogloff, J., Wong, S. & Greenwood, A. (1990). Treating criminal psychopaths in a therapeutic community program. *Behavioral Sciences and the Law, 8*, 181–90.

Ohman, A., Fredrikson, M., Hugdahl, K., & Rimmo, P. (1976). The premise of equipotentiality in human classical conditioning: Conditioned electrodermal responses to potentially phobic stimuli. *Journal of Experimental Psychology-General, 105*(4): 313–37.

Ohman, A., Nordby, H., & d'Elia, G. (1986). Orienting and schizophrenia: Stimulus significance, attention, and distraction in a signaled reaction time task. *Journal of Abnormal Psychology, 95*(4): 326–34.

Olivieri, S., Cantopher, T., & Edwards, J. (1986). Two hundred years of anxiolytic drug dependence. *Neuropharmacology, 25*, 669–70.

Oltman, J., & Friedman, S. (1967). Parental deprivation in psychiatric conditions. *Diseases of the Nervous System, 28*, 298–303.

Olweus, D. (1979). Stability of aggressive reaction patterns in males: A review. *Psychological Bulletin, 86*, 852–75.

Orengo, C.A., Kunik, M.E., Molinari, V., & Workman, R.H. (1996). The use and tolerability of fluoxetine in geropsychiatric inpatients. *Journal of Clinical Psychiatry, 57*(1): 12–16.

Orne, M. T. (1962). On the social psychology of the psychological experiment: With particular reference to demand characteristics and their implications. *American Psychologist, 17*, 776–83.

Osler, W. (1897). *Lectures on angina pectoris and allied states.* New York: D. Appleton and Company.

Öst, L.-G. (1987). Applied relaxation: Description of a coping technique and review of controlled studies. *Behaviour Research and Therapy, 25*, 397–410.

Öst, L.-G. (1991). *Cognitive therapy versus applied relaxation in the treatment of panic disorder.* Paper presented at the annual meeting of the European Association of Behavior Therapy, Oslo, September 1991.

Öst, L.-G., Fellenius, J., & Sterner, U. (1991). Applied tension, exposure *in vivo*, and tension-only in the treatment of blood phobia. *Behaviour Research and Therapy, 29*(6): 561–74.

Öst, L.-G., Sterner, U., & Fellenius, J. (1989). Applied tension, applied relaxation, and the combination in the treatment of blood phobia. *Behaviour Research and Therapy, 27,* 109–21.

O'Sullivan, G., Noshirvani, H., Marks, I., et al. (1991). Six-year follow-up after exposure and clomipramine therapy for obsessive-compulsive disorder. *Journal of Clinical Psychiatry, 52,* 150–55.

Overholser, J. C., & Beck, S. (1986). Multimethod assessment of rapists, child molesters, and three control groups on behavioral and psychological measures. *Journal of Consulting and Clinical Psychology, 54*(5): 682–87.

Overmier, J. B., & Seligman, M. E. P. (1967). Effects of inescapable shock upon subsequent escape and avoidance learning. *Journal of Comparative and Physiological Psychology, 63,* 23–33.

Pandey, G. N., Pandey, S. C., Dwivedi, Y., Sharma, R. P., Janicak, P. G., & Davis, J. M. (1995). Platelet serotonin-2A receptors: A potential biological marker for suicidal behavior. *American Journal of Psychiatry, 152*(6): 850–55.

Pandya, D. N., & Barnes, C. L. (1987). Architecture and connections of the frontal lobe. In E. Perecman (Ed.), *The frontal lobes revisited* (pp. 41–72). Hillsdale, NJ: Erlbaum.

Parada, M. A., Puig de Parada, M., & Hoebel, B. G. (1995). Rats self-inject a dopamine antagonist in the lateral hypothalamus where it acts to increase extracellular dopamine in the nucleus accumbens. *Pharmacology, Biochemistry and Behavior, 22*(1): 179–87.

Paris, J., & Zweig-Frank, H. (1992). A critical review of the role of childhood sexual abuse in the etiology of borderline personality disorder. *Candian Journal of Psychiatry, 37*(2): 125–28.

Park, L. C., Imboden, J. B., Park, T. J., Hulse, S. H., & Unger, H. T. (1992). Giftedness and psychological abuse in borderline personality disorder: Their relevance to genesis and treatment. *Journal of Personality Disorders, 6,* 226–40.

Parker, G., & Hadzi-Pavlovic, D. (1993). Prediction of response to antidepressant medication by a sign-based index of melancholia. *Australian and New Zealand Journal of Psychiatry, 27,* 56–61.

Parnas, J., Cannon, T. D., Jacobsen, B., Schulsinger, H., Schulsinger, F., & Mednick, S. A. (1993). Lifetime DSM-IIIR diagnostic outcomes in the offspring of schizophrenic mothers. Results from the Copenhagen high-risk study. *Archives of General Psychiatry, 50,* 707–14.

Pato, M., Piggott, T., Hill, J., et al. (1991). Controlled comparison of buspirone and clomipramine in obsessive-compulsive disorder. *American Journal of Psychiatry, 148,* 127–29.

Pato, M., Zohar-Kadouch, R., Zohar, J., & Murphy, D. (1988). Return of symptoms after discontinuation of clomipramine in patients with obsessive-compulsive disorder. *American Journal of Psychiatry, 145,* 1521–25.

Patrick, C. J., Bradley, M., & Cuthbert, B. N. (1990). The criminal psychopath and startle modulation. *Psychophysiology, 27*(Suppl. 4A): 87.

Patrick, C. J., Cuthbert, B. N., & Lang, P. J. (1990). Emotion in the criminal psychopath: Fear imagery. *Psychophysiology, 27*(Suppl. 4A): 55.

Patrick, M., Hobson, P., Castle, P., Howard, R., & Maughan, B. (1994). Personality disorder and the mental representation of early social experience. *Development and Psychopathology, 94,* 374–88.

Patterson, G. R. (1975). *Families: Applications of social learning theory to family life* (2nd ed.). Champaign, IL: Research Press.

Patterson, G. R., DeBaryshe, B. D., & Ramsey, E. (1989). A developmental perspective on antisocial behavior. *American Psychologist, 44,* 329–35.

Patterson, T., Spohn, H. E., Bogia, D. P., & Hayes, K. (1986). Thought disorder in schizophrenia: Cognitive and neuroscience approaches. *Schizophrenia Bulletin, 12*(3): 460–72.

Pattie, F. A. (1967). A brief history of hypnotism. In J. E. Gordon (Ed.), *Handbook of clinical and experimental hypnosis.* New York: Macmillan.

Paul, G. L. (1966). *Insight vs. desensitization in psychotherapy.* Stanford: Stanford University Press.

Paul, G. L. (1967). Insight vs. desensitization in psychotherapy two years after termination. *Journal of Consulting Psychology, 31*(4): 333–48.

Pauly, I. B. (1969). Adult manifestation of male transsexualism. In R. Green & J. Money (Eds.), *Transsexualism and sex reassignment.* Baltimore: The Johns Hopkins Press.

Pauly, I. B. (1974). Female transsexualism. *Archives of Sexual Behavior, 3,* 487–526.

Pavel, O. (1990). *How I came to know fish* (trans. J. Baclai & R. McDowell). New York: Story Line Press/New Directions.

Paykel, E. S. (1973). Life events and acute depression. In J. P. Scott & E. C. Senay (Eds.), *Separation and depression.* AAAS.

Paykel, E. S. (1974a). Recent life events and clinical depression. In E. K. E. Gunderson & R. H. Rahe (Eds.), *Life stress and illness* (pp. 150–51). Springfield, IL: Charles C. Thomas.

Paykel, E. S. (1974b). Life stress and psychiatric disorder: Application of the clinical approach. In B. P. Dohrenwend & B. S. Dohrenwend (Eds.), *Stressful life events: Their nature and effects* (pp. 135–49). New York: Wiley.

Paykel, E. S., Meyers, J. K., Dienelt, M. N., Klerman, J. L., Lindenthal, J. J., & Pfeffer, M. P. (1969). Life events and depression. *Archives of General Psychiatry, 21,* 753–60.

Payne, R. W. (1966). The measurement and significance of overinclusive thinking and retardation in schizophrenic patients. In P. H. Hoch & J. Zubin (Eds.), *Psychopathology of schizophrenia* (pp. 77–79). New York: Grune & Stratton.

Pecknold, J., Swinson, R., Kuch, K., & Lewis, C. (1988). Alprazolam in panic disorder and agoraphobia: Results from a multicenter trial: III. Discontinuation effects. *Archives of General Psychiatry, 45,* 429–36.

Pedersen, N. L., McClearn, G. E., Plomin, R., Nesselroade, J. R., Berg, S., & DeFaire, U. (1991). The Swedish Adoption Twin Study of Aging: An update. *Acta Geneticae Medicae et Gemellologiaie, 40,* 7–20.

Peele, S. (1985). *The meaning of addiction: Compulsive experience and its interpretation.* Lexington, MA: Lexington Books.

Pelham, W. E. (1989). Behavioral therapy, behavioral assessment, and psychostimulant medication in the treatment of attention deficit disorder: An interactive approach. In J. Swanson & I. Bloomingdale (Eds.), *Attention deficit disorder: IV. Current concepts and emerging trends in attentional and behavioral disorders of childhood* (pp. 169–95). New York: Pergamon.

Pennebaker, J. W. (1985). Traumatic experience and psychosomatic disease: Exploring the roles of behavioural inhibition, obsession, and confiding. *Canadian Psychology, 26,* 82–95.

Pennebaker, J. (1990). *Opening up.* New York: Morrow.

Perkins, K. A., & Reyher, J. (1971). Repression, psychopathology and drive representation: An experimental hypnotic investigation of impulse inhibition. *American Journal of Clinical Hypnosis, 13,* 249–58.

Perris, C. (1968). The course of depressive psychosis. *Acta Psychiatrica Scandinavica, 44,* 238–48.

Persons, J. B. (1986). The advantages of studying psychological phenomena rather than psychiatric diagnoses. *American Psychologist, 41,* 1252–60.

Peterson, C., Maier, S., & Seligman, M. (1993). *Learned helplessness.* New York: Oxford University Press.

Peterson, C., & Seligman, M. E. P. (1984). Causal explanations as a risk factor for depression: Theory and evidence. *Psychological Review, 91*(31):347–74.

Peterson, C., & Seligman, M. E. P. (1987). Explanatory style and illness. Special Issue: Personality and physical health. *Journal of Personality, 55*(2): 237–65.

Peterson, C., Seligman, M. E. P., & Vaillant, G. (1988). Pessimistic explanatory style as a risk factor for physical illness: A 35-year longitudinal study. *Journal of Personality and Social Psychology, 55,* 23–27.

Petersen, M. E., & Dickey, R. (1995). Surgical sex reassignment: A comparative survey of international centers. *Archives of Sexual Behavior, 24*(2): 135–56.

Petursson, H. (1994). The benzodiazepine withdrawal syndrome. *Addiction, 89,* 1455–59.

Petursson, H., & Lader, M. H. (1981). Withdrawal from long-term benzodiazepine treatment. *British Medical Journal, 283,* 643–45.

Petzel, T. P., & Johnson, J. E. (1972). Time estimation by process and reactive schizophrenics under crowded and uncrowded conditions. *Journal of Clinical Psychology, 28*(3): 345–47.

Pfohl, B. (1991). Histrionic personality disorder: A review of available data and recommendations for DSM-IV. *Journal of Personality Disorders, 5*(2): 150–66.

Philibert, R. A., Richards, L., Lynch, C. F., & Winokur, G. (1995).

Effect of ECT on mortality and clinical outcome in geriatric unipolar depression. *Journal of Clinical Psychiatry, 56*(9): 390–94.

Piggott, T., Pato, M., Bernstein, S., et al. (1990). Controlled comparisons of clomipramine and fluoxetine in the treatment of obsessive-compulsive disorder. *Archives of General Psychiatry, 47,* 926–32.

Pillard, R.C., & Bailey, J.M. (1995). A biological perspective on sexual orientation. *The Psychiatric Clinics of North America, 18*(1): 71–84.

Place, E. J. S., & Gilmore, G. C. (1980). Perceptual organization in schizophrenia. *Journal of Abnormal Psychology, 89,* 409–18.

Plomin, R., Corley, R., DeFries, J., & Fulker, D. (1990). Individual differences in television viewing in early childhood: Nature as well as nurture. *Psychological Science, 1,* 371–77.

Plomin, R., Scheier, M. F., Bergeman, C. S., Pedersen, N. L., Nesselroade, J. R., & McClearn, G. (1992). Optimism, pessimism and mental health: A twin/adoption analysis. *Personality and Individual Differences, 13*(8): 921–30.

Pokorny, A. D. (1964). Suicide rates and various psychiatric disorders. *Journal of Nervous and Mental Diseases, 139,* 499–506.

Polivy, J. (1976). Perception of calories and regulation of intake in restrained and unrestrained subjects. *Addictive Behaviors, 1,* 237–44.

Pollack, J. M. (1979). Obsessive-compulsive personality: A review. *Psychological Bulletin, 86,* 225–41.

Pope, H. G., Jonas, J. M., & Jones, B. (1982). Factitious psychosis: Phenomenology, family history, and long-term outcome of nine patients. *American Journal of Psychiatry, 139,* 1480–83.

Porsolt, R. D., Anton, G., Blavet, N., & Jalfre, M. (1978). Behavioral despair in rats: A new model sensitive to antidepressant treatments. *European Journal of Pharmacology, 47,* 379–91.

Potter, W. Z., & Manji, H. K. (1994). Catecholamines in depression: An update. *Clinical Chemistry, 40*(2): 279–87.

Pourcher, E., Baruch, P., Bouchard, R.H., Filteau, M., & Bergeron, D. (1995). Neuroleptic associated tardive dyskinesias in young people with psychoses. *British Journal of Psychiatry, 166,* 768–72.

Powell, K. E., Thompson, P. D., Caspersen, C. J., & Kendrick, J. S. (1987). Physical activity and the incidence of coronary heart disease. *Annual Review of Public Health, 8,* 253–87.

Power, K., Simpson, R., Swanson, V., & Wallace, L. (1990). A controlled comparison of cognitive-behavior therapy, diazepam, and placebo, alone or in combination, for the treatment of generalized anxiety disorder. *Journal of Anxiety Disorders, 4,* 267–92.

Premack, D. (1959). Toward empirical behavior laws: I. Positive reinforcement. *Psychological Review, 66,* 219–33.

Preskorn, S., & Jerkovich, G. (1990). Central nervous system toxicity of tricyclic antidepressants: Phenomenology, course, risk factors, and the role of drug monitoring. *Journal of Clinical Psychopharmacology, 10,* 88–95.

Price, R. W., Brew, B., Sidtis, J., et al. (1988). The brain in AIDS: Central nervous system HIV-1 infection and AIDS dementia complex. *Science, 239,* 586–92.

Prichard, J. C. (1837). *Treatise on insanity and other disorders affecting the mind.* Philadelphia: Haswell, Barrington & Haswell.

Prior, M. R. (1987). Biological and neuropsychological approaches to childhood autism. *British Journal of Psychiatry, 150,* 8–17.

Purcell, D., Brady, K., Chai, H., Muser, J., Molk, L., Gordon, N., & Means, J. (1969). The effect of asthma in children during experimental separation from the family. *Psychosomatic Medicine, 31,* 144–64.

Putnam, F. (1989). *Diagnosis and treatment of multiple personality.* New York: Guilford Press.

Putnam, F. W., Guroff, J. J., & Silberman, E. K., et al. (1986). The clinical phenomenology of multiple personality disorder: Review of 100 recent cases. *Journal of Clinical Psychiatry, 47*(6): 285–93.

Putnam, F., & Loewenstein, R. (1993). Treatment of multiple personality disorder: A survey of current practices. *American Journal of Psychiatry, 150,* 1048–52.

Putnam, F. W., Zahn, T. P., & Post, R. M. (1990). Differential autonomic nervous system activity in multiple personality disorder. *Psychiatry Research, 31,* 251–60.

Quay, H. C. (1986). Conduct disorders. In H. C. Quay & J. S. Werry (Eds.), *Psychopathological disorders of childhood* (pp. 35–62). New York: Wiley.

Quay, H. C., Routh, D. K., & Shapiro, S. K. (1987). Psychopathology of childhood: From description to validation. *Annual Review of Psychology, 38,* 491–532.

Rabavilos, A. D., Boulougouris, J. C., & Stefanis, C. (1976). Duration of flooding session in the treatment of obsessive-compulsive patients. *Behaviour Research and Therapy, 14,* 349–55.

Rachman, S. J. (1976). Therapeutic modeling. In M. Felman & A. Broadhurst (Ed.), *Theoretical and experimental bases of behavior therapy.* Chichester: Wiley.

Rachman, S. J. (1978). *Fear and courage.* New York: Freeman.

Rachman, S. (1994). Pollution of the mind. *Behaviour Research and Therapy, 32*(3): 311–14.

Rachman, S. J., Cobb, J., Grey, S., MacDonald, B., Mawson, C., Sartory, G., & Stern, R. (1979). The behavioral treatment of obsessive-compulsive disorders, with and without domipramine. *Behaviour Research and Therapy, 17,* 467–78.

Rachman, S. J., & Hodgson, R. J. (1980). *Obsessions and compulsions.* Englewood Cliffs, NJ: Prentice-Hall.

Rachman, S. J., Hodgson, R., & Marks, I. M. (1971). The treatment of chronic obsessional neurosis. *Behaviour Research and Therapy, 9,* 237–47.

Rachman, S. J., Marks, I., & Hodgson, R. (1973). The treatment of chronic obsessive-compulsive neurosis by modeling and flooding in vivo. *Behaviour Research and Therapy, 11,* 463–71.

Radloff, L. S. (1975). Sex differences in depression: The effects of occupation and marital status. *Sex Roles, 1,* 249–65.

Rado, S. (1928). Psychodynamics of depression from the etiological point of view. In W. Galen (Ed.), *The meaning of despair.* New York: Science House.

Raitakari, O. T., Leino, M., Raikkonen, K., Porkka, K. V. K., Taimela, S., Rasanen, L., & Viikari, J. S. A. (1995). Clustering of risk habits in young adults: The Cardiovascular Risk in Young Finns Study. *American Journal of Epidemiology, 142*(1): 36–44.

Rao, U., Weissman, M. M., Martin, J. A., & Hammond, R. W. (1993). Childhood depression and risk of suicide: A preliminary report of a longitudinal study. *Journal of the American Academy of Child and Adolescent Psychiatry, 32*(1): 21–27.

Rapee, R. (1991). Generalized anxiety disorder: A review of clinical features and theoretical concepts. *Clinical Psychology Review, 11,* 419–40.

Rapoport, J. L. (1988). The neurobiology of obsessive-compulsive disorder. *Journal of the American Medical Association, 260,* 2888–90.

Rapoport, J. L. (1990). *The boy who couldn't stop washing.* New York: Plume.

Rapport, M. D. (1987). Attention deficit disorder with hyperactivity. In M. Hersen & V. B. Van Hasselt (Eds.), *Behavior therapy with children and adolescents* (pp. 325–62). New York: Wiley.

Raps, C. S., Reinhard, K. E., & Seligman, M. E. P. (1980). Reversal of cognitive and affective deficits associated with depression and learned helplessness by mood elevation in patients. *Journal of Abnormal Psychology, 89,* 342–49.

Ravaja, N., Keltikangas-Jarvinen, L., & Keskivaara, P. (1996). Type A factors as predictors of changes in the metabolic syndrome precursors in adolescents and young adults—A 3-year follow-up study. *Health Psychology, 15*(1): 18–29.

Ray, O., & Ksir, C. (1987). *Drugs, society, and human behavior.* St. Louis: Times Mirror/Mosby.

Regan, M., & Howard, R. (1995). Fear conditioning, preparedness, and the contingent negative variation. *Clinical Psychology Review, 15*(1): 23–48.

Regier, D., Myers, J., Kramer, M., Robins, L., Blayer, D., Hough, R., Easton, W., & Locke, B. (1984). The NIMH Epidemiological Catchment Area program: Historical context, major objectives, and study population characteristics. *Archives of General Psychiatry, 41,* 934–41.

Regier, D. A., Narrow, W. E., & Rae, D. S. (1990). The epidemiology of anxiety disorders: The Epidemiological Catchment Area (ECA) experience. Symposium: Benzodiazepines: Therapeutic, biologic, and psychological issues. *Journal of Psychiatric Research, 24* (Suppl 2): 3–14.

Rehm, L. P. (1978). Mood pleasant events, and unpleasant events: Two pilot studies. *Journal of Consulting and Clinical Psychology, 46,* 854–59.

Rehyer, J., & Smyth, L. (1971). Suggestibility during the execution of a posthypnotic suggestion. *Journal of Abnormal Psychology, 78,* 258–65.

Reich, J. H. (1990). Comparisons of males and females in DSM-III dependent personality disorder. *Psychiatry Research, 23*(2): 207–14.

Reich, L. H., Davies, R. K., & Himmelhoch, J. M. (1974). Excessive alcohol use in manic-depressive illness. *American Journal of Psychiatry, 131*(1): 83–86.

Reiman, E., Raichle, M., Robins, E., et al. (1986). The application of positron emission tomography to the study of panic disorder. *American Journal of Psychiatry, 143,* 469–77.

Reinisch, J. (1992). Unpublished study cited in C. Gorman, Sizing up the sexes. *Time, 139,* 45–46.

Reitan, R. M., & Davison, L. A. (1974). *Clinical neuropsychology: Current status and applications.* Washington, DC: Winston and Sons.

Rescorla R. A., & Solomon, R. L. (1967). Two-process learning theory: Relationship between Pavlovian conditioning and instrumental learning. *Psychological Review, 74,* 151–82.

Resick, P., Jordan, C., Girelli, S., Hutter, C., et al. (1988). A comparative outcome study of behavioral group therapy for sexual assault victims. *Behavior Therapy, 19,* 385–401.

Reynolds, W. M., & Coats, K. I. (1986). A comparison of cognitive-behavioral therapy and relaxation training for the treatment of depression in adolescents. *Journal of Consulting and Clinical Psychology, 54,* 653–60.

Ricciardi, J. N. (1995). Depressed mood is related to obsessions, but not to compulsions, in obsessive-compulsive disorder. *Journal of Anxiety Disorders, 9*(3): 249–56.

Rice, J., Reich, T., Andreasen, N. C., Endicott, J., Van Eerdewegh, M., Fishman, R., Hirschfeld, R. M. A., & Klerman, G. L. (1987). The familial transmission of bipolar illness. *Archives of General Psychiatry, 44,* 441–47.

Rice, M. E., Harris, G. T., & Quinsey, V. L. (1990). A follow-up study of rapists assessed in a maximum security psychiatric facility. *Journal of Interpersonal Violence, 5,* 435–40.

Rie, H. E. (1966). Depression in childhood: A survey of some pertinent contributions. *Journal of the American Academy of Child Psychiatry, 5,* 653–85.

Riskind, J. H., Moore, R., & Bowley, L. (1995). The looming of spiders: The fearful perceptual distortion of movement and menace. *Behaviour Research and Therapy, 33*(2): 171–78.

Risley, T., & Wolf, M. (1967). Establishing functional speech in echolalic children. *Behaviour Research and Therapy, 5,* 73–88.

Ritvo, E. R., Freeman, B. J., Pingree, C., Mason-Brothers, A., Jorde, L., Jenson, W. R., McMahon, W. M., Petersen, P. B., Mo, A., & Ritvo, A. (1989). The UCLA-University of Utah Epidemiology Survey of Autism: Prevalence. *American Journal of Psychiatry, 146*(2): 194–99.

Roache, J. (1990). Addiction potential of benzodiazepines and non-benzodiazepine anxiolytics. *Advances in Alcohol and Substance Abuse, 9,* 103–28.

Robbins, T. W. (1990). The case of frontostriatal dysfunction in schizophrenia. *Schizophrenia Bulletin, 16*(3): 391–402.

Robertson, M., Trimble, M., & Lees, A. (1988). The psychopathology of Gilles de la Tourette syndrome. *British Journal of Psychiatry, 152,* 383–90.

Robins, E., & Guze, S. B. (1972). Classification of affective disorders: The primary-secondary, the endogenous-reactive, and the neurotic-psychotic concepts. In T. A. Williams, M. M. Katz, & J. A. Shields (Eds.), *Recent advances in the psychobiology of the depressive illnesses* (pp. 283–93). Washington, DC: U.S. Government Printing Office.

Robins, L. N. (1966). *Deviant children grow up.* Baltimore: Williams & Wilkins.

Robins, L. N. (1985). Epidemiology: Reflections on testing the validity of psychiatric interviews. *Archives of General Psychiatry, 42,* 918–24.

Robins, L. N. (1991). Conduct disorder. *Journal of Child Psychology and Psychiatry, 32,* 193–212.

Robins, L. N., & Helzer, J. E. (1986). Diagnosis and clinical assessment: The current state of psychiatric diagnosis. *Annual Review of Psychology, 37,* 409–32.

Robins, L. N., Helzer, J. E., Weissman, M. M., Orvaschel, H., Gruenberg, E., Burke, J. D., & Regier, D. A. (1984). Lifetime prevalence of specific psychiatric disorders in three sites. *Archives of General Psychiatry, 41,* 949–58.

Robinson, D. S., Davis, J., Nies, A., Ravaris, C., & Sylvester, D. (1971). Relation of sex in aging to monoamine oxidase activity in human brain, plasma, and platelets. *Archives of General Psychiatry, 24,* 536.

Robinson, D., Wu, H., Munne, R. A., Ashtari, M., Alvir, J. M. J., Lerner, G., Koreen, A., Cole, K., & Bogerts, B. (1995). Reduced caudate nucleus volume in obsessive-compulsive disorder. *Archives of General Psychiatry, 52*(5): 393–98.

Rodgers, W. M., & Brawley, L. R. (1996). The influence of outcome expectance and self-efficacy on the behavioral intentions of novice exercisers. *Journal of Applied Social Psychology, 26*(7): 618–34.

Rodnick, E. H., Goldstein, M. J., Lewis, J. M., & Doane, J. A. (1984). Parental communication style, affect, and role as precursors of offspring schizophrenia-spectrum disorders. In N. F. Watt, E. J. Anthony, L. C. Wynne, & J. E. Rolf (Eds.), *Children at risk for schizophrenia: A longitudinal perspective* (pp. 81–92). Cambridge: Cambridge University Press.

Roediger, H., Weldon, M., & Challis, B. (1989). Explaining dissociations between implicit and explicit measures of retention: A processing account. In H. Roediger & F. Craik (Eds.), *Varieties of memory and consciousness: Essays in honor of Endel Tulvin,* (pp. 3–14). Hillsdale, NJ: Erlbaum.

Roff, J. D., & Knight, R. (1981). Family characteristics, childhood symptoms, and adult outcomes in schizophrenia. *Journal of Abnormal Psychology, 90,* 510–20.

Rogers, J., Siggins, G. R., Schulman, J. R., & Bloom, F. E. (1980). Physiological correlates of ethanol intoxication tolerance, and dependence in rat cerebellar Purkinje cells. *Brain Research, 196,* 183–98.

Rogers, M. P., Weinshenker, N. J., Warshaw, M. G., Goisman, R. M., Rodriguez-Villa, F. J., Fierman, E. J., & Keller, M. B. (1996). Prevalence of somatoform disorders in a large sample of patients with anxiety disorders. *Psychosomatics, 37*(1): 17–22.

Romero, J., Garcia, L., Fernandez-Ruiz, J., Cebeira, M., & Ramos, J. A. (1995). Changes in rat brain cannabinoid binding sites after acute or chronic exposure to their endogenous agonist, anandamide, or to delta 9- tetrahydrocannabinol. *Pharmacology, Biochemistry and Behavior, 51*(4): 731–37.

Rooth, F. G., & Marks, I. M. (1974). Persistent exhibitionism: Short-term responses to aversion, self-regulation, and relaxation treatment. *Archives of Sexual Behavior, 3,* 227–48.

Roper, G., Rachman, S., & Marks, I. M. (1975). Passive and participant modeling in exposure treatment of obsessive compulsive neurotics. *Behaviour Research and Therapy, 13,* 271–79.

Rosen, J. C., & Leitenberg, H. (1982). Bulimia nervosa: Treatment with exposure and response prevention. *Behavior Therapy, 13,* 117–24.

Rosen, R. C., & Leiblum, S. R. (1995). Treatment of sexual disorders in the 1990s: An integrated approach. *Journal of Consulting and Clinical Psychology, 63*(6): 877–90.

Rosenhan, D. L. (1973). On being sane in insane places. *Science, 179,* 250–58.

Rosenhan, D. L. (1975). The contextual nature of psychiatric diagnosis. *Journal of Abnormal Psychology, 84,* 462–74.

Rosenhan, D. L. (1983). Psychological abnormality and law. In C. J. Scheirer & B. L. Hammonds (Eds.), *Psychology and the law* (pp. 89–118). Washington, DC: American Psychological Association.

Rosenman, R. H., Brand, R. J., Jenkins, C. D., Friedman, M., Straus, R., & Wurm, M. (1975). Coronary heart disease in the Western Collaborative Group study: Final follow-up experience at eight-and-a-half years. *Journal of the American Medical Association, 233,* 872–77.

Rosenstein, M. J., Milazzo-Sayre, L. J., & Manderscheid, R. W. (1990). Characteristics of persons using specialty inpatient, outpatient, and partial care programs in 1986. In R. W. Manderscheid & M. A. Sonnenschein (Eds.), *Mental health in the United States* (pp. 139–72). Washington, DC: U.S. Government Printing Office.

Rosenthal, D. (1970a). Genetic research in the schizophrenic syndrome. In R. Cancro (Ed.), *The schizophrenic reactions* (pp. 245–58). New York: Brunner/Mazel.

Rosenthal, D. (1970b). *Genetic theory and abnormal behavior.* New York: McGraw-Hill.

Rosenthal, D. (1979). Was Thomas Wolfe a borderline? *Schizophrenia Bulletin, 5,* 87–94.

Rosenthal, N. E., Carpenter, C. J., James, S. P., Parry, B. L., Rogers, S. L. B., & Wehr, T. A. (1986). Seasonal affective disorder in children and adolescents. *American Journal of Psychiatry, 143,* 356–86.

Rosenthal, N. E., Moul, D. E., Hellekson, C. J., & Oren, D. A. (1993). A multicenter study of the light visor for seasonal affective disorder: No difference in efficacy found between two different intensities. *Neuropsychopharmacology, 8*(2): 151–60.

Rosenthal, N. E., Sack, D. A., Gillin, J. C., Lewy, A. J., Goodwin, F. K., Davenport, Y., Mueller, P. S., Newsome, D. A., & Wehr, T. A. (1984). Seasonal affective disorder: A description of the syndrome and preliminary findings with light therapy. *Archives of General Psychiatry, 41,* 72–80.

Rosenthal, P. A., & Rosenthal, S. (1984). Suicidal behavior by preschool children. *American Journal of Psychiatry, 141,* 520–25.

Rosenthal, T. L., & Bandura, A. (1979). Psychological modeling: Theory and practice. In A. Bergin & S. Garfield (Eds.), *Handbook of psychotherapy and behavior change.* New York: Wiley.

Ross, C. A. (1991). Epidemiology of multiple personality disorder and dissociation. *Psychiatric Clinics of North America, 14,* 503–17.

Ross, C. A., Anderson, G., Fleisher, W. P., & Norton, G. R. (1991). The frequency of multiple personality disorder among psychiatric inpatients. *American Journal of Psychiatry, 148,* 1717–20.

Ross, C. A., Miller, S. D., Reagor, P., Bjornson, L., et al. (1990). Structured interview data on 102 cases of multiple personality disorder from four centers. *American Journal of Psychiatry, 147,* 596–601.

Ross, J. D., & Wirt, R. D. (1984). Childhood aggression and social adjustment as antecedents of delinquency. *Journal of Abnormal Child Psychology, 12*(1): 111–26.

Ross, L., Greene, D., & House, P. (1977). The false consensus phenomenon: An attributional bias in self perception and social perception processes. *Journal of Experimental Social Psychology, 13,* 279–301.

Rothbaum, B., Foa, E., Riggs, D., Murdock, T., & Walsh, W. (1992). A prospective examination of post-traumatic stress disorder in rape victims. *Journal of Traumatic Stress, 5*(3): 455–75.

Rotter, J. B. (1966). Generalized expectancies for internal versus external control of reinforcement. *Psychological Monographs, 80*(1).

Roy, M. A., Neale, M. C., Pederson, N. L., Mathe, A. A., & Kendler, K. S. (1995). A twin study of generalized anxiety disorder and major depression. *Psychological Medicine, 25,* 1037–1049.

Rozin, P. (1976). The psychobiological approach to human memory. In M. R. Rosenzweig & E. L. Bennett (Eds.), *Neural mechanisms of learning and memory* (pp. 3–46). Cambridge, MA: MIT Press.

Rubenstein, C. (1982, May). What's good. *Psychology Today, 16,* 62–72.

Rubin, R., Villanueva-Meyer, J., Ananth, J., et al. (1992). Regional xenon 133 cerebral blood flow and cerebral technetium 99m HMPAO uptake in unmedicated patients with obsessive-compulsive disorder and matched normal control subjects. *Archives of General Psychiatry, 49,* 739–44.

Rubonis, A.V., & Bickman, L. (1991). Psychological impairment in the wake of disaster: The disaster-psychopathology relationship. *Psychological Bulletin, 109*(3): 384–99.

Rush, A. J., & Weissenburger, J. E. (1994). Melancholic symptom features and DSM-IV. *American Journal of Psychiatry, 151*(4): 489–98.

Rush, H. A., Beck, A. T., Kovacs, M., & Hollon, S. (1977). Comparative efficacy of cognitive therapy and pharmacotherapy in the treatment of depressed outpatients. *Cognitive Research and Therapy, 1,* 17–37.

Russek, L., King, S., Russek, S., & Russek, H. (1990). The Harvard mastery of stress study 35-year follow-up: Prognostic significance of patterns of psychophysiological arousal and adaptation. *Psychosomatic Medicine, 52,* 271–85.

Russell, W. R. (1959). *Brain, memory, learning: A neurologist's view.* Oxford, Eng. Oxford University Press.

Rutter, M. (1975). *Helping troubled children.* New York: Plenum.

Rutter, M. (1978). Prevalence and types of dyslexia. In A. L. Benton & D. Pearl, Dyslexia: *An appraisal of current knowledge.* New York: Oxford University Press.

Rutter, M. (1985). Family and school influence on behavioural development. *Journal of Child Psychology and Psychiatry, 26,* 349–68.

Rutter, M. (1989). Isle of Wight revisited: Twenty-five years of psychiatric epidemiology. *Journal of the American Academy of Child and Adolescent Psychiatry, 28*(5): 633–53.

Rutter, M., & Garmezy, N. (1983). Developmental psychopathology. In P. H. Mussen (Ed.), *Handbook of child psychology, Vol. 4: Socialization, personality, and social development.* New York: Wiley.

Rutter, M., Macdonald, H., Le Couteur, A., Harrington, R., Bolton, P., & Bailey, A. (1990). Genetic factors in child psychiatric disorders: II. Empirical findings. *Journal of Child Psychology and Psychiatry, 31*(1): 39–83.

Rutter, M., Quinton, D., & Hill, J. (1990). Adult outcome of institution-reared children: Males. In L. Robins & M. Rutter (Eds.), *Straight and devious pathways from childhood to adulthood* (pp. 135–57). New York: Cambridge University Press.

Saccuzzo, D. P., & Braff, D. L. (1986). Information processing abnormalities: Trait- and state-dependent components. *Schizophrenia Bulletin, 12*(3): 447–59.

Sachdev, P., & Hay, P. (1995). Does neurosurgery for obsessive-compulsive disorder produce personality change? *Journal of Nervous and Mental Disease, 183*(6): 408–13.

Sack, R., & De Fraites, E. (1977). Lithium and the treatment of mania. In J. Barchas, P. Berger, R. Ciaranello, & G. Elliot (Eds.), *Psychopharmacology.* New York: Oxford University Press.

Sack, W., Clarke, G., Him, C., & Dickason, D. (1993). A 6–year follow-up study of Cambodian refugee adolescents traumatized as children. *Journal of the American Academy of Child and Adolescent Psychiatry, 32,* 431–37.

Sackeim, H. A., Greenberg, M. S., Weiman, A. L., Gur, R. C., Hunger-Buhler, J. P., & Geschwind, N. (1982). Hemispheric asymmetry in the expression of positive and negative emotions: Neurological evidence. *Archives of Neurology, 39,* 210–18.

Sackeim, H. A., Nordlie, J. W., & Gur, R. C. (1979). A model of hysterical and hypnotic blindness: Cognitions, motivation and awareness. *Journal of Abnormal Psychology, 88,* 474–89.

Sackeim, H. A., & Rush, A. J. (1995, August). Melancholia and response to ECT [Letter to the editor]. *American Journal of Psychiatry,* p. 1243.

Sacks, O. W. (1995). *An anthropologist on Mars: Seven paradoxical tales.* New York: Knopf.

Saigh, P. A., Mroueh, M., Zimmerman, B. J., & Fairbank, J. A. (1996). Self-efficacy expectation among traumatized adolescents. *Behaviour Research and Therapy, 33*(6): 701–4.

Sakai, T. (1967). Clinico-genetic study on obsessive compulsive neurosis. *Bulletin of Osaka Medical School,* Supplement XII, 323–31.

Sakamoto, K., Kamo, T., Nakadaira, S., & Tamura, A. (1993). A nationwide survey of seasonal affective disorder at 53 outpatient university clinics in Japan. *Acta Psychiatrica Scandinavica, 87*(4): 258–65.

Salamone, J. D., Kurth, P., McCullough, L. D., & Sokolowski, J. D. (1995). The effects of nucleus accumbens dopamine depletions on continuously reinforced operant responding: Contrasts with the effects of extinction. *Pharmacology, Biochemistry and Behavior, 50*(3): 437–43.

Salzman, C. (1993). Benzodiazepine treatment of panic and agoraphobic symptoms: Use, dependence, toxicity, abuse. *Journal of Psychiatric Research, 27,* 97–110.

Salzman, L., & Thaler, F. (1981). Obsessive-compulsive disorders: A review of the literature. *American Journal of Psychiatry, 138,* 286–96.

Sandler, J., & Hazari, A. (1960). The "obsessional": On the psychological classification of obsessional character traits and symptoms. *British Journal of Medical Psychology, 33,* 113–22.

Sartorius, N., Jablensky, A., Korten, A., Ernberg, G., Anker, M., Cooper, J. E., & Day, R. (1986). Early manifestations and first-contact incidence of schizophrenia in different cultures. *Psychological Medicine, 16,* 909–28.

Satterfield, J.H., Hoppe, C. & Schell, A. (1982). A prospective study of delinquency in 110 adolescent boys with attention deficit disorder and 88 normal adolescent boys. *American Journal of Psychiatry, 139,* 795–98.

Saugstad, L. F. (1989). Social class, marriage and fertility in schizophrenia. *Schizophrenia Bulletin, 15,* 9–43.

Saunders, A. M., Strittmatter, M. D., Schmechel, M. D., et al. (1993). Association of apolipoprotein E allele type 4 with late-onset familial and sporadic Alzheimer's disease. *Neurology, 43,* 1467–72.

Saver, J. L., & Damasio, A. R. (1991). Preserved access and processing of social knowledge in a patient with acquired sociopathy due to ventromedial frontal damage. *Neuropsychologia, 29,* 1241–49.

Scarr, S. (1975). Genetics and the development of intelligence. In F. D. Horowitz (Ed.), *Child development research* (Vol. 4). Chicago: University of Chicago Press.

Schacter, D. L. (1992). Priming and multiple memory systems: Perceptual mechanisms of implicit memory. *Journal of Cognitive Neuroscience, 4,* 244–56.

Scheff, T. J. (1966). *Being mentally ill: A sociological theory.* Chicago: Aldine.

Scheier, M. F., & Bridges, M. W. (1995). Person variables and health: Personality predispositions and acute psychological states as shared determinants for disease. *Psychosomatic Medicine, 57,* 255–68.

Schiavi, R. C., et al. (1984). Pituitary-gonadal function during sleep in men with erectile impotence and normal controls. *Psychosomatic Medicine, 46*(3): 239–54.

Schiavi, R. C., & Rehman, J. (1995). Sexuality and aging. *Urologic Clinics of North America, 22*(4): 711–26.

Schildkraut, J. J. (1965). The catecholamine hypothesis of affective disorders: A review of supporting evidence. *American Journal of Psychiatry, 122,* 509–22.

Schmale A., & Iker, H. (1966). The psychological setting of uterine cervical cancer. *Annals of the New York Academy of Sciences, 125,* 807–13.

Schmauk, F. J. (1970). Punishment, arousal, and avoidance learning in sociopaths. *Journal of Abnormal Psychology, 76,* 443–53.

Schneier, F., Johnson, J., Hornig, C., et al. (1992). Social phobia: Comorbidity and morbidity in an epidemiologic sample. *Archives of General Psychiatry, 49,* 282–88.

Schotte, D. E., & Stunkard, A. J. (1987). Bulimia vs. bulimic behaviors on a college campus. *Journal of the American Medical Association, 258,* 1213–15.

Schreiber, F. R. (1974). *Sybil.* New York: Warner Books.

Schreibman, L. (1975). Effects of within-stimulus and extra-stimulus prompting on discrimination learning in autistic children. *Journal of Applied Behavioral Analysis, 8,* 91–112.

Schuckit, M. A. (1984). Subjective responses to alcohol in sons of alcoholics and controls. *Archives of General Psychiatry, 41,* 879–84.

Schuckit, M. A. (1987). Biological vulnerability to alcoholism. *Journal of Consulting and Clinical Psychology, 55,* 301–9.

Schulberg, H., & Rush, A. J. (1994). Clinical practice guidelines for managing major depression in primary care practice. *American Psychologist, 49,* 34–41.

Schulsinger, F. (1972). Psychopathy, heredity and environment. *International Journal of Mental Health, 1,* 190–206.

Schulterbrand, J. G., & Raven, A. (Eds.). (1977). *Depression in childhood: Diagnosis, treatment, and conceptual models.* New York: Raven Press.

Schultes, R. E. (1987). Coca and other psychoactive plants: Magico-religious roles in primitive societies of the new world. In S. Fisher et al. (Eds.), *Cocaine: Clinical and biobehavioral aspects.* New York: Oxford University Press.

Schuyler, D. (1974). The evaluation of the suicidal patient. In J. R. Novello (Ed.), *Practical handbook of psychiatry.* Springfield, IL: Charles C. Thomas.

Schwab, J. J., Bialow, M., Holzer, C. E., Brown, J. M., & Stevenson, B. E. (1967). Socio–cultural aspects of depression in medical inpatients. *Archives of General Psychiatry, 17,* 533–43.

Schwartz, B. (1984). *Psychology of learning and behavior* (2nd ed.). New York: Norton.

Schwartz, M. F., Baron, J., & Moscovitch, M. (1990). Symptomatology of Alzheimer-type dementia: Report on a survey-by-mail. In M. F. Schwartz (Ed.), *Modular deficits in Alzheimer-type dementia.* Cambridge, MA: MIT Press/Bradford.

Schwartz, M. F., & Masters, W. H. (1984). The Masters and Johnson treatment program for dissatisfied homosexual men. *American Journal of Psychiatry, 141*(2): 173–81.

Schwartz, S., & Johnson J. H. (1985). *Psychopathology of childhood: A clinical-experimental approach.* New York: Pergamon.

Schwarz, T., Loewenstein, J., & Isenberg, K. E. (1995). Maintenance ECT: Indications and outcome. *Convulsive Therapy, 11*(1): 14–23.

Schweizer, E., Rickels, K., Csanalosi, I., & London, J. (1990). A placebo-controlled study of enciprazine in the treatment of generalized anxiety disorder. *Psychopharmacology Bulletin, 26,* 215–17.

Scoville, W. B., & Milner, B. (1957). Loss of recent memory after bilateral hippocampal lesions. *Journal of Neurology, Neurosurgery and Psychiatry, 20,* 11–21.

Searles, H. F. (1959). The effort to drive the other person crazy! An element in the aetiology and psychotherapy of schizophrenia. *British Journal of Medical Psychology, 32,* 1–18.

Sedney, M. (1987). Development of adrogyny: Parental influences. *Psychology of Women Quarterly, 11,* 321–26.

Segraves, R. & Althof, S. (1997). Psychotherapy and pharmacotherapy of sexual dysfunctions, in P. Nathan & J. Gorman (Eds.), *Treatments that work.* New York: Oxford.

Seligman, M. E. P. (1970). On the generality of the laws of learning. *Psychological Review, 77,* 406–18.

Seligman, M. E. P. (1975). *Helplessness: On depression, development, and death.* San Francisco: Freeman.

Seligman, M. E. P. (1991). *Learned optimism: The skill to conquer life's obstacles, large and small.* New York: Random House.

Seligman, M. E. P. (1993). *What you can change and what you can't: The ultimate guide to self-improvement.* New York: Knopf.

Seligman, M. (1995). The effectiveness of psychotherapy: The Consumer Reports study. *American Psychologist, 50,* 965–74.

Seligman, M. E. P. (1995). *The optimistic child.* New York: Houghton Mifflin.

Seligman, M. E. P., Abramson, L. Y., Semmel, A., & von Baeyer, C. (1979). Depressive attributional style. *Journal of Abnormal Psychology, 88,* 242–47.

Seligman, M. E. P., & Johnston, J. C. (1973). A cognitive theory of avoidance learning. In F. J. McGuigan, & D. B. Lumsden (Eds.), *Contemporary approaches to conditioning and learning.* Washington, DC: Winston.

Seligman, M. E. P., & Maier, S. F. (1967). Failure to escape traumatic shock. *Journal of Experimental Psychology, 74,* 1–9.

Seligman, M., Reivich, K., Jaycox, L., & Gillham, J. (1995). *The optimistic child.* New York: Houghton Mifflin.

Selye, H. (1956). *The stress of life.* New York: McGraw-Hill.

Selye, H. (1975). Confusion and controversy in the stress field. *Journal of Human Stress, 1,* 37–44.

Serling, R. J. (1986). Curing a fear of flying. *US AIR,* 12–19.

Shaffer, D. (1976). Enuresis. In M. Rutter & L. Hersov (Eds.), *Child psychiatry: Modern approaches.* Oxford: Blackwell.

Shaffer, H. J., & Jones, S. B. (1985). *Quitting cocaine: The struggle against impulse.* Lexington, MA: Lexington Books.

Shallice, T., & Burgess, P. W. (1991). Deficits in strategy applications following frontal-lobe damage in man. *Brain, 114,* 727–41.

Shapiro, D. (1965). *Neurotic styles.* New York: Basic Books.

Shapiro, F. (1995). *Eye Movement Desensitization and Reprocessing.* New York: Guilford.

Sharma, R., & Markar, H.R. (1994). Mortality in affective disorder. *Journal of Affective Disorders, 31,* 91–96.

Shea, M. T., Elkin, I., Imber, S. D., & Sotsky, S. M. (1992). Course of depressive symptoms over follow-up: Findings about the National Institute of Mental Health Treatment of Depression Collaborative Research Program. *Archives of General Psychiatry, 49*(10): 782–87.

Shekelle, R. B., Gale, M., Ostfeld, A. M., & Paul, O. (1983).

Hostility, risk of coronary heart disease, and mortality. *Psychosomatic Medicine, 45*(2): 109–14.

Shekelle, R. B., Hulley, S. B., Neaton, J. D., et al. (1985). The MRFIT behavior study. Type A behavior and incidence of coronary heart disease. *American Journal of Epidemiology, 122,* 559–70.

Sherif, F. M., & Ahmed, S. S. (1995). Basic aspects of GABA-transaminase in neuropsychiatric disorders. *Clinical Biochemistry, 28*(2): 145–54.

Sherman, A. D., & Petty, F. (1980). Neurochemical basis of the action of antidepressants on learned helplessness. *Behavioral and Neurological Biology, 30,* 119–34.

Shneidman, E. (1976). Suicide among the gifted. In E. S. Shneidman (Ed.), *Suicidology: Contemporary developments.* New York: Grune & Stratton.

Siever, L. J. (1990a). Adoptive and family studies of schizophrenic probands suggest that genetic factors associated with schizophrenia are expressed as a spectrum of schizophrenia-related disorders, including schizotypal personality disorder and paranoid personality disorder. *Journal of Abnormal Psychology, 103*(1).

Siever, L. J. (1990b). Increased morbid risk for schizophrenia-related disorders in relatives of schizotypal personality disordered patients. *Archives of General Psychiatry, 47*(2): 634–40.

Sifneos, P. E. (1973). The prevalence of "alexithymic" characteristics in psychosomatic patients. *Psychotherapy and Psychosomatics, 22,* 255–62.

Sigman, M., Arbelle, S., & Dissanayake, C. (1995). Current research findings on childhood autism. *Canadian Journal of Psychiatry, 40*(6): 289–94.

Silverman, J. M., Zaccario, M. L., Smith, C. J., Schmeidler, J., Mohs, R. C., & Davis, K. L. (1994). Patterns of risk in first-degree relatives of patients with Alzheimer's disease. *Archives of General Psychiatry, 51,* 577–86.

Silverman, L. H. (1976). Psychoanalytic theory: The reports of my death are greatly exaggerated. *American Psychologist, 31*(9): 621–37.

Sisoda, S. S., & Price, D. L. (1995). Role of the B-amyloid protein in Alzheimer's disease. *The PHASEB Journal, 9,* 366–70.

Smith, J. C., Glass, G. V., & Miller, T. I. (1980). *The benefits of psychotherapy.* Baltimore: The Johns Hopkins Press.

Smith, R. J. (1978). *The psychopath in society.* New York: Academic Press.

Snyder, S. H. (1974a). Catecholamines as mediators of drug effects in schizophrenia. In F. O. Schmitt & F. G. Worden (Eds.), *The neurosciences: Third study program.* Cambridge, MA: MIT Press.

Snyder, S. H. (1974b). *Madness and the brain.* New York: McGraw-Hill.

Snyder, S. H. (1981). Dopamine receptors, neuroleptics and schizophrenia. *American Journal of Psychiatry, 138,* 460–64.

Snyder, S. H. (1986). *Drugs and the brain.* New York: Scientific American Library.

Snyder, S. H., Banerjee, S. P., Yamamura, H. I., & Greenberg, D. (1974). Neurotransmitters and schizophrenia. *Science, 184,* 1243–53.

Snyder, W. D., Simpson, D. M., Nielson, S., et al., (1983). Neurological complications of Acquired Immune Deficiency Syndrome: Analysis of 50 patients. *Annals of Neurology, 14,* 403–18.

Sokol, L., Beck, A. T., Greenberg, R. L., Wright, F. D., & Berchick, R. J. (1989). Cognitive therapy of panic disorder: A nonpharmacological alternative. *Journal of Nervous and Mental Diseases, 177*(12): 711–16.

Solomon, D. A., Keitner, G. I., Miller, I. W., Shea, M. T., & Keller, M. B. (1995). Course of illness and maintenance treatments for patients with bipolar disorder. *Journal of Clinical Psychiatry, 56*(1): 5–13.

Solomon, R. L., & Corbit, J. D. (1974). An opponent process theory of motivation. *Psychological Reviews, 81*(2): 119–45.

Solomon, Z., Kotler, M., & Mikulincer, M. (1988). Combat-related post-traumatic stress disorder among second-generation Holocaust survivors: Preliminary findings. *American Journal of Psychiatry, 145,* 865–68.

Solomon, Z., Laor, N., Weiler, D., & Muller, U. (1993). The psychological impact of the Gulf War: A study of acute stress in Israeli evacuees. *Archives of General Psychiatry, 50,* 320–21.

Solomon, Z., Oppenheimer, B., Elizur, Y., & Waysman, M. (1990). Exposure to recurrent combat stress: Can successful coping in a second war heal combat-related PTSD from the past? *Journal of Anxiety Disorders, 4,* 141–45.

Southard, D. R., Coates, T. J., Kolodner, K., Parker, F. C., Padgett, N. E., & Kennedy, H. L. (1986). Relationship between mood and blood pressure in the natural environment: An adolescent population. *Health Psychology, 5,* 469–80.

Spark, R. F., White, R. A., & Connelly, P. B. (1980). Impotence is not always psychogenic. *Journal of the American Medical Association, 243,* 750–55.

Speckens, A. E. M., Hengeveld, M. W., Lycklama a Nijeholt, G., van Hemert, A. M., & Hawton, K. E. (1995). Psychosexual functioning of partners of men with presumed non-organic erectile dysfunction: Cause or consequence of the disorder? *Archives of Sexual Behavior, 24*(2): 157–72.

Spiegel, D. (1984). Multiple personality as a post-traumatic stress disorder. *Psychiatric Clinics of North America, 7,* 101–10.

Spiegel, D. (1990). Dissociating dissociation: A commentary on Dr. Garcia's article. *Dissociation: Progress in the Dissociative Disorders, 3,* 214–15.

Spiegel, D., Bloom, J., Kraemer, H., & Gottheil, E. (1989). Effect of psychosocial treatment on survival of patients with metastatic breast cancer. *The Lancet,* October 14, pp. 888–91.

Spiegel, D., & Cardena, E. (1991). Disintegrated experience: The dissociative disorders revisited. *Journal of Abnormal Psychology, 100,* 366–78.

Spiegel, R. (1989). *Psychopharmacology* (2nd ed.). New York: Wiley.

Spiletz, D. M., O'Neill, G. P., Favreau, L., Dufresne, C., Gallant, M., Gareau, Y., Guay, D., Labelle, M., & Metters, K. M. (1995). Activation of the human peripheral cannabinoid receptor results in inhibition of adenylyl cyclase. *Molecular Pharmacology, 48,* 352–61.

Spitz, R. A. (1946). Anaclitic depression. *The Psychoanalytic Study of the Child, 2,* 313–47.

Spitzer, R. L. (1975). On pseudoscience in science, logic in remission and psychiatric diagnosis: A critique of Rosenhan's "On being sane in insane places." *Journal of Abnormal Psychology, 84,* 442–52.

Spitzer, R. L. (1991). An outsider-insider's views about revising the DSMs. *Journal of Abnormal Psychology, 100*(3): 294–96.

Spitzer, R. L., & Fleiss, J. L. (1974). A reanalysis of the reliability of psychiatric diagnosis. *British Journal of Psychiatry, 125,* 341–47.

Spitzer, R., Gibbon, M., Skodol, A., Williams, J., & First, M. (1989). *DSM-III-R case book.* Washington, DC: American Psychiatric Press.

Squire, L. R. (1986). Memory functions as affected by electroconvulsive therapy. *Annals of the New York Academy of Sciences, 462,* 307–14.

Squire, L. R., (1987). *Memory and brain.* New York: Oxford University Press.

Squire, L. R. (1992). Memory and the hippocampus: A synthesis from findings with rats, monkeys, and humans. *Psychological Review, 79,* 195–231.

Squire, L. R., & Butters, N. (Eds.). (1992). *The neuropsychology of memory* (2nd ed.). New York: Guilford Press.

Srole, L., Langner, T. S., Michael, S. T., Opler, M. K., & Rennie, T. A. (1962). *Mental health in the metropolis: The midtown Manhattan study.* New York: McGraw-Hill.

Staats, A. W. (1978). *Child learning intelligence and personality* (rev. ed.). Kalamazoo, MI: Behaviordela.

Stampfl, T. G., & Levis, D. J. (1967). Essentials of implosive therapy: A learning-theory-based psychodynamic behavioral therapy. *Journal of Abnormal Psychology, 72,* 496–503.

Stangl, D., Pfohl, B., Zimmerman, M., Bowers, W., & Corenthal, R. (1985). A structured interview for the DSM-III personality disorders: A preliminary report. *Archives of General Psychiatry, 42,* 591–96.

Stapleton, J. A., Russell, M. A. H., Feyerabend, C., Wiseman, S., Gustavsson, G., Sawe, U., & Wiseman, D. (1995). Dose effects and predictors of outcome in a randomized trial of transdermal nicotine patches in general practice. *Addiction, 90,* 31–42.

Stark, K. D. (1990). *Childhood depression: School-based intervention.* New York: Guilford Press.

Steadman, H. J. (1973). Follow-up on Baxstrom patients returned to hospitals for the criminally insane. *American Journal of Psychiatry, 3*, 317–19.

Steadman, H. J. (1981). The statistical prediction of violent behavior: Measuring the costs of a public protectionist versus a civil libertarian model. *Law and Human Behavior, 5*, 263–74.

Steadman, H. J., & Keveles, G. (1972). The community adjustment and criminal activity of the Baxstrom patients: 1966–1970. *American Journal of Psychiatry, 129*, 304–10.

Steadman, H., & Keveles, C. (1978). The community adjustment and criminal activity of Baxstrom patients. *American Journal of Psychiatry, 135*, 1218–20.

Steadman, H. J., McGreevy, M. A., Morrissey, J. P., Callahan, L. A., Robbins, P. C., & Cirincione, C. (1993). *Before and after Hinckley: Evaluating insanity defense reform*. New York: Guilford Press.

Steadman, H. J., Monahan, J., Hartstone, E., Davis, S. K., & Robbins, P. C. (1982). Mentally disordered offenders: A national survey of patients and facilities. *Law and Human Behavior, 8*(1): 31–37.

Stein, J. A., Golding, J. M., Siegel, J. M., Burnam, M. A., Sorenson, S. B., & Powell, G. J. (1988). Long-term psychological sequelae of child sexual abuse: The Los Angeles epidemiologic catchment area study. In G. E. Wyatt (Ed.), *Lasting effects of child sexual abuse*. Newbury Park, CA: Sage.

Steinberg, L. (1986). Stability and instability of Type A behavior from childhood to young adulthood. *Developmental Psychology, 22*, 393–401.

Steinberg, M., Rounsaville, B., & Cicchetti, D. V. (1990). The structured clinical interview for DSM-III-R dissociative disorders: Preliminary report on a new diagnostic instrument. *American Journal of Psychiatry, 147*, 76–82.

Steptoe, A., Roy, M. P., Evans, O., & Snashall, D. (1995). Cardiovascular stress reactivity and job strain as determinants of ambulatory blood pressure at work. *Journal of Hypertension, 13*(2): 201–10.

Stern, D. (1985). *The interpersonal world of the infant*. New York: Basic Books.

Stern, J. (1981). Brain dysfunction in some hereditary disorders of amino acid metabolism. In P. J. Mittler, & J. M. deJong (Eds.), *Frontiers of knowledge in mental retardation: Vol II. Biomedical aspects*. Baltimore, MD: University Park Press.

St. George-Hyslop, P., et al., (1987). The genetic defect causing familial Alzheimer's disease maps on chromosome 21. *Science, 235*, 885–90.

St. George-Hyslop, P., Haines, J., Rogaev, E., et al. (1992). Genetic evidence for a novel familial Alzheimer's disease locus on chromosome 14. *Nature Genetics, 2*, 330–34.

Stice, E. (1994). Review of the evidence for a sociocultural model of bulimia nervosa and an exploration of the mechanisms of action. *Clinical Psychology Review, 14*(7): 633–61.

Stinnett, J. (1978). Personal communication.

Stoller, R. J. (1969). Parental influences in male transsexualism. In R. Green & J. Money (Eds.), *Transsexualism and sex reassignment*. Baltimore: The Johns Hopkins Press.

Stoller, R. J. (1976). *Sexual gender—the transsexual experiment* (Vol. II). New York: Jason Aronson.

Stone, A. A. (1975). *Mental health and law: A system in transition*. Rockville, MD.: National Institute of Mental Health, Center for Studies of Crime and Delinquency.

Stone, A. A., Neale, J. M., Cox, D. S., Napoli, A., Valdimarsdottir, H., & Kennedy-Moore, E. (1994). Daily events are associated with a secretory immune response to an oral antigen in men. *Health Psychology, 13*(5): 440–46.

Stone, D. M., Merchant, K. M., Hanson, G. R., & Gibb, J. W. (1987). Immediate and long-term effects of 3, 4-methylene-dioxymethamphetamine (MDMA) on serotonin pathways in brain of rat. *Neuropharmacology, 26*, 1677–83.

Stone, M. H. (1990). Abuse and abusiveness in borderline personality disorder. In P. S. Links (Ed.), *Family environment and borderline pesonality disorder* (pp. 131–48). Washington, DC: American Psychiatric Press.

Storms, M. D. (1981). A theory of erotic orientation development. *Psychological Review, 88*, 340–53.

Strauss, M. E., Foureman, W. C., & Parwatikar, S. D. (1974).

Schizophrenics' size estimations of thematic stimuli. *Journal of Abnormal Psychology, 83*(2): 117–23.

Streissguth, A. P., Grant, T. M., & Barr, H. M. (1991). Cocaine and the use of alcohol and other drugs during pregnancy. *American Journal of Obstetrics and Gynecology, 164*, 1239–43.

Stunkard, A. J. (1976). Anorexia nervosa. In J. P. Sanford (Ed.), *The science and practice of clinical medicine* (pp. 361–63). New York: Grune & Stratton.

Suarez, J. M., & Pittluck, A. T. (1976). Global amnesia: Organic and functional considerations. *Bulletin of the American Academy of Psychiatric Law, 3*, 17–24.

Suddath, R. L., Christison, M. D., Torrey, E. F., Casanova, M., & Weinberger, D. R. (1990). Anatomic abnormalities in the brains of monozygotic twins discordant for schizophrenia. *New England Journal of Medicine, 322*, 789–94.

Swaab, D. F., & Hofman, M. A. (1995). Sexual differentiation of the human hypothalamus in relation to gender and sexual orientation. *Trends in Neuroscience, 18*(6): 264–70.

Swaab, D. F., Gooren, L. J., & Hofman, M. A. (1995). Brain research, gender and sexual orientation. *Journal of Homosexuality, 28*(3–4): 283–301.

Svebak, S., Cameron, A., & Levander, S. (1990). Clonazepam and imipramine in the treatment of panic attacks. *Journal of Clinical Psychiatry, 51*, 14–17.

Swanson, W. C., & Breed, W. (1976). Black suicide in New Orleans. In E. S. Shneidman (Ed.), *Suicidology: Contemporary developments*. New York: Grune & Stratton.

Swedo, S. E. (1994). Sydenham's Chorea: A model for childhood autoimmune neuropsychiatric disorders. *Journal of the American Medical Association, 272*(22): 1788–91.

Swedo, S. E., & Kiessling, L. S. (1994). Speculations on antineuronal antibody-mediated neuropsychiatric disorders of childhood. *Pediatrics, 93*(2): 323–26.

Swedo, S. E., Leonard, H. L., Schapiro, M. B., Casey, B. J., Mannheim, G. B., Lenane, M. C., & Rettew, D. C. (1993). Sydenham's Chorea: Physical and psychological symptoms of St. Vitus Dance. *Pediatrics, 91*(4): 706–13.

Swedo, S., Pietrini, P., Leonard, H., et al. (1992). Cerebral glucose metabolism in childhood-onset obsessive-compulsive disorder. *Archives of General Psychiatry, 49*, 690–94.

Swedo, S. E., Rapoport, J. L., Cheslow, D. L., Leonard, H. L., Ayoub, E. M., Hosier, D. M., & Wald, E. R. (1989). High prevalence of obsessive-compulsive symptoms in patients with Sydenham's Chorea. *American Journal of Psychiatry, 146*(2): 246–49.

Sweeney, J. A., Haas, G. L., & Li, S. (1992). Neuropsychological and eye movement abnormalities in first-episode and chronic schizophrenia. *Schizophrenia Bulletin, 18*(2): 283–93.

Szasz, T. S. (1963). *Law, liberty and psychiatry: An inquiry into the social uses of mental health practices*. New York: Macmillan.

Szasz, T. S. (1970). *The manufacture of madness*. New York: Dell.

Szasz, T. S. (1974). The ethics of suicide. *Bulletin of Suicidology* (Vol. 9). Philadelphia: Charles Press.

Tagiuri, R., Bruner, J. S., & Blake, R. R. (1958). On the relation between feelings and the perception of feelings among members of small groups. In E. E. Maccoby, T. M. Newcomb, & E. L. Hartley (Eds.), *Readings in social psychology* (pp. 110–16). New York: Holt, Rinehart & Winston.

Talovic, S. A., Mednick, S. A., Schulsinger, F., & Falloon, I. R. H. (1981). Schizophrenia in high-risk subjects: Prognostic maternal characteristics. *Journal of Abnormal Psychology, 89*, 501–4.

Tamerin, J. S., & Mendelson, J. (1970). Alcoholic's expectancies and recall of experiences during intoxication. *American Journal of Psychiatry, 126*, 1697–1704.

Tangney, J. P., Wagner, P., & Gramzow, R. (1992). Proneness to shame, proneness to guilt, and psychopathology. *Journal of Abnormal Psychology, 101*(3): 469–78.

Taylor, D. P., Carter, R. B., Eison, A. S., Mullins, U. L., Smith, H. L., Torrente, J. R., Wright, R. N., & Yocca, F. D. (1995). Pharmacology and neurochemistry of Nefazodone, a novel antidepressant drug. *Journal of Clinical Psychiatry, 56*(Suppl. 6): 3–11.

Taylor, W. S., & Martin, M. F. (1944). Multiple personality. *Journal of Abnormal and Social Psychology, 39*, 281–300.

Teasdale, J. D., & Rezin, V. (1978). The effect of reducing

frequency of negative thoughts on the mood of depressed patients: Test of a cognitive model of depression. *British Journal of Social and Clinical Psychology, 17,* 65–74.

Teasdale, J. D., Segal, Z., & Williams, J. M. G. (1995). How does cognitive therapy prevent depressive relapse and why should attentional control (mindfulness) training help? *Behaviour Research and Therapy, 33*(1): 25–39.

Teicher, M., Glod, C., & Cole, J. (1990). Emergence of intense suicidal preoccupation during fluoxetine treatment. *American Journal of Psychiatry, 147,* 207–10.

Telch, M., Agras, S., Taylor, C., et al. (1985). Combined pharmacological and behavioral treatment for agoraphobia. *Behaviour Research and Therapy, 23,* 325–35.

Temerlin, M. K. (1970). Diagnostic bias in community mental health. *Community Mental Health Journal, 6,* 110–17.

Teplin, L. A., Abram, K. M., McClelland, G. M. (1994). Does psychiatric disorder predict violent crime among released jail detainees? *American Psychologist, 49,* 335–42.

Terry, R. D., & Davies, P. (1980). Dementia of the Alzheimer type. *Annual Review of Neuroscience, 3,* 77–95.

Tesar, G. (1990). High potency benzodiazepines for short-term management of panic disorder: The U.S. experience. *Journal of Clinical Psychiatry, 51,* 4–10.

Tharpar, A., & McGuffin, P. (1994). A twin study of depressive symptoms in childhood. *British Journal of Psychiatry, 165,* 259–65.

Theodor, L. H., & Mandelcorn, M. S. (1978). Hysterical blindness: A case report and study using a modern psychophysical technique. *Journal of Abnormal Psychology, 82,* 552–63.

Theorell, T., & Rahe, R. H. (1971). Psychosocial factors in myocardial infarction. I. An inpatient study in Sweden. *Journal of Psychosomatic Research, 15,* 25–31.

Thigpen C. H., & Cleckley, H. (1954). A case of multiple personality. *Journal of Abnormal and Social Psychology, 49,* 135–51.

Thompson, J., Burns, B., Bartko, J., et al. (1988). The use of ambulatory services by persons with and without phobias. *Medical Care, 26,* 183–98.

Thompson, P.M. (1996). Generalized anxiety disorder treatment algorithm. *Psychiatric Annals, 26*(4): 227–32.

Thompson, S., & Rey, J. M. (1995). Functional enuresis: Is Desmopressin the answer? *Journal of the American Academy of Child and Adolescent Psychiatry, 34*(3): 266–71.

Thorpe, S. J., & Salkovskis, P. M. (1995). Phobic beliefs: Do cognitive factors play a role in specific phobias? *Behaviour Research and Therapy, 33*(7): 805–16.

Tiefer, L., & Kring, B. (1995). Gender and the organization of sexual behavior. *The Psychiatric Clinics of North America, 18*(1): 25–37.

Tien, A., Pearlson, G., Machlin, S., et al. (1992). Oculomotor performance in obsessive-compulsive disorder. *American Journal of Psychiatry, 150,* 641–46.

Tienari, P. (1991). Interaction between genetic vulnerability and family environment: The Finnish adoptive family study of schizophrenia. *Acta Psychiatrica Scandinavica, 84,* 460–65.

Tinklenberg, J. (1977). Anti-anxiety medications and the treatment of anxiety. In J. Barchas, P. Berger, R. Ciaranello, & G. Elliot (Eds.), *Psychopharmacology.* New York: Oxford.

Tisher, M., Tonge, B. J., & Horne, D. J. DeL. (1994). Childhood depression, stressors and parental depression. *Australian and New Zealand Journal of Psychiatry, 28,* 635–41.

Tomasson, K., Kent, D., & Coryell, W. (1991). Somatization and conversion disorders: Comorbity and demographics at presentation. *Acta Psychiatrica Scandinavica, 84,* 288–93.

Tonks, C. M., Paykel, E. S., & Klerman, J. L. (1970). Clinical depressions among Negroes. *American Journal of Psychiatry, 127,* 329–35.

Torgersen, S. (1983). Genetic factors in anxiety disorders. *Archives of General Psychiatry, 40,* 1085–89.

Torgersen, S. (1986a). Genetic factors in moderately severe and mild affective disorders. *Archives of General Psychiatry, 43,* 222–26.

Torgersen, S. (1986b). Genetics of somatoform disorders. *Archives of General Psychiatry, 43,* 502–5.

Torrey, E. F. (1992). Are we overestimating the genetic contribution to schizophrenia? *Schizophrenia Bulletin, 18*(2): 159–70.

Torrey, E. F. (1997). *Out of the shadows: Confronting America's mental illness crisis.* New York: Wiley.

Traskman-Bendz, L., Alling, C., Alsen, M., et al. (1993). The role of monoamines in suicidal behavior. *Acta Psychiatrica Scandinavica, 87,* 45–47.

Trasler, G. (1973). Criminal behavior. In H. J. Eysenck (Ed.), *Handbook of abnormal psychology.* London: Pitman Medical.

Treece, C., & Khantzian, E. J. (1986). Psychodynamic factors in the development of drug dependence. *Psychiatric Clinics of North America, 9,* 399–412.

Trimble, M. (1990). Worldwide use of clomipramine. *Journal of Clinical Psychiatry, 51,* 51–58.

True, W., Rice, J., Eisen, S., et al. (1993). A twin study of genetic and environmental contributions to liability for post-traumatic stress symptoms. *Archives of General Psychiatry, 50,* 257–64.

Tryon, W. W. (1976). Models of behavior disorder. *American Psychologist, 31,* 509–18.

Tucker, D. M., Luu, P., & Pribaum, K. H. (1995). Social and emotional self-regulation. *Annals of the New York Academy of Sciences, 769,* 213–39.

Turgay, A. (1990). Treatment outcome for children and adolescents with conversion disorder. *Canadian Journal of Psychiatry, 35,* 585–89.

Turner, S. M., Beidel, D. C., Dancu, C. V., & Keys, D. J. (1986). Psychopathology of social phobia and comparison to avoidant personality disorder. *Journal of Abnormal Psychology, 95,* 389–94.

Turner, S. M., Beidel, D. C., & Jacob, R. G. (1994). Social phobia: A comparison of behavior therapy and atenolol. *Journal of Consulting and Clinical Psychology, 62*(2): 350–58.

Turner, S. M., Beidel, D. C., & Townsley, R. M. (1992). Social phobia: A comparison of specific and generalized subtypes and avoidant personality disorder. *Journal of Abnormal Psychology, 101*(2): 326–31.

Turner, W. J. (1995). Homosexuality, Type 1: An Xq28 phenomenon. *Archives of Sexual Behavior, 24*(2): 109–34.

Ullman, L. P., & Krasner, L. (1965). *Case studies in behavior modification.* New York: Holt, Rinehart & Winston.

Upham, Charles W. (1867). Salem witchcraft. Cited in A. Deutsch, *The mentally ill in America.* New York: Columbia University Press, 1949.

Urbina, S. P., Golden, C. J., & Ariel, R. N. (1982). WAIS/WAIS-R: Initial comparisons. *Clinical Neuropsychology, 4,* 145–46.

U.S. Department of Health and Human Services. (1987). *Vital Statistics of the United States, 1984. Volume II: Mortality.* National Center for Health Statistics, Hyattsville, MD.

Vaillant, G. E. (1978). Natural history of male psychological health: IV. What kinds of men do not get psychosomatic illness. *Psychosomatic Medicine, 40,* 420–31.

Vaillant, G. E. (1983). The natural history of alcoholism. Cambridge, MA: Harvard University Press.

Vaillant, G. E. (1992). Is there a natural history of addiction? In C. P. O'Brien & J. H. Jaffe (Eds.), *Addictive states.* New York: Raven Press.

Vanderlinden, J., Van Dyck, R., Vandereycken, W., & Vertommen, H. (1991). Dissociative experiences in the general population in the Netherlands and Belgium: A study with the Dissociative Questionnaire (DIS-Q). *Dissociation: Progress in the Dissociative Disorders, 4,* 180–84.

Van Dyke, C., Zilberg, N. J., & McKinnon, J. A. (1985). Post-traumatic stress disorder: A thirty-year delay in a World War II veteran. *American Journal of Psychiatry, 142,* 1070–73.

Van Goozen, S. H. M., Cohen-Kettenis, P. T., Gooren, L. J. G., Frijda, N. H., & Van de Poll, N. E. (1995). Gender differences in behaviour: Activating effects of cross-sex hormones. *Psychoneuroendocrinology, 20*(4): 343–63.

Van Kempen, G. M., Zitman, F. G., Linssen, A. C., & Edelbroek, P. M. (1992). Biochemical measures in patients with somatoform pain disorder, before, during, and after treatment with amitriptyline with or without flupentixol. *Biological Psychiatry, 31,* 670–80.

Varnik, A., & Wasserman, D. (1992). Suicides in the former Soviet republics. *Acta Psychiatrica Scandinavica, 86,* 76–78.

Vaughn, C. E., Snyder, K. S., Jones, S., Freeman, W. B., & Falloon, I. R. H. (1984). Family factors in schizophrenic relapse: Replication in California of British research on expressed emotion. *Archives of General Psychiatry, 41,* 1169–77.

Veiel, H. (1993). Detrimental effects of kin support networks on the course of depression. *Journal of Abnormal Psychology, 102,* 419–29.

Veith, I. (1965). *Hysteria: The history of a disease.* Chicago: University of Chicago Press.

Ventura, J., Neuchterlein, K. H., Lukoff, D., & Hardesty, J. P. (1989). A prospective study of stressful life events and schizophrenic relapse. *Journal of Abnormal Psychology, 98*(4): 407–11.

Versiani, M., Mundim, F., Nardi, A., et al. (1988). Tranylcypromine in social phobia. *Journal of Clinical Psychopharmacology, 8,* 279–83.

Vgontzas, A. N., Kales, A., & Bixler, E. O. (1995). Benzodiazepine side effects: Role of pharmacokinetics and pharmacodynamics. *Pharmacology, 51,* 205–23.

Victor, M., Adams, R. D., & Collins, G. H. (1971). *The Wernicke-Korsakoff syndrome. A clinical and pathological study of 245 patients, 82 with post-mortem examinations.* Philadelphia: Davis.

Videbech, T. (1975). A study of genetic factors, childhood bereavement, and premorbid personality traits in patients with anancastic endogenous depression. *Acta Psychiatrica Scandinavica, 52,* 178–222.

Vogel, G. W. (1975). A review of REM sleep deprivation. *Archives of General Psychiatry, 32,* 96–97.

Volkmar, F. R., Carter, A., Sparrow, S. S., & Cicchetti, D. V. (1993). Quantifying social development in autism. *Journal of the American Academy of Child and Adolescent Psychiatry, 32*(3): 627–32.

Volpicelli, J. R. (1989). Psychoactive substance use disorders. In D. L. Rosenhan & M. E. P. Seligman (Eds.), *Abnormal psychology.* New York: Norton.

Volpicelli, J. R., Alterman, A. I., Hayashida, M., & O'Brien, C. P. (1992). Naltrexone in the treatment of alcohol dependence. *Archives of General Psychiatry, 49,* 876–80.

Volpicelli, J. R., Clay, K. L., Watson, N. T., & O'Brien, C. P. (1995). Naltrexone in the treatment of alcoholism: Predicting response to Naltrexone. *Journal of Clinical Psychiatry, 56*(Suppl. 7): 39–44.

Wadden, T., Stunkard, A., & Smoller, J. (1986). Dieting and depression: A methodological study. *Journal of Consulting and Clinical Psychology, 54,* 869–71.

Wagner, A. W., & Linehan, M. M. (1994). Relationship between childhood sexual abuse and topography of parasuicide among women with borderline personality disorder. *Journal of Personality Disorders, 8,* 1–9.

Wakefield, J. C. (1992a). Disorder as harmful dysfunction: A conceptual critique of DSM-III-R's definition of mental disorder. *Psychological Review, 99,* 232–47.

Wakefield, J. C. (1992b). The concept of mental disorder: On the boundary between biological facts and social values. *American Psychologist, 47,* 373–88.

Wakefield, J. C. (1993). The limits of operationalization: A critique of Spitzer and Endicott's proposed operational criteria of mental disorder. *Journal of Abnormal Psychology, 102,* 160–72.

Waller, N., Kojetin, B., Bouchard, T., Lykken, D., & Tellegen, A. (1990). Genetic and environmental influences on religious interests, attitudes, and values. *Psychological Science, 1,* 138–42.

Wallerstein, J. S., & Kelly, J. B. (1980). California children of divorce. *Psychology Today, 13.*

Walinder, J. (1967). *Transsexualism.* Goteburg: Scandinavian University Books.

Warburton, D. M. (1988). The puzzle of nicotine use. In M. Lader (Ed.), *The psychopharmacology of addiction* (pp. 27–49). New York: Oxford University Press.

Warburton, D. M., & Wesnes, K. (1978). Individual differences in smoking and attentional performance. In R. E. Thornten (Ed.), *Smoking behavior: Physiological and psychological influence* (pp. 19–43). Edinburgh: Churchill-Livingstone.

Warner, R. (1978). The diagnosis of antisocial and personality disorders: An example of sex bias. *Journal of Nervous and Mental Disease, 166,* 839–45.

Warner, V., Mufson, L., & Weissman, M. M. (1995). Offspring at high and low risk for depression and anxiety: Mechanisms of psychiatric disorder. *Journal of the American Academy of Child and Adolescent Psychiatry, 34*(6): 786–97.

Warrington, E. K., & Weiskrantz, L. (1973). An analysis of short-term and long-term memory defects in man. In J. A. Deutsch (Ed.), *The physiological basis of memory* (pp. 365–96). New York: Academic Press.

Watson, C. G., & Buranen, C. (1979). The frequency of conversion reaction. *Journal of Abnormal Psychology, 88,* 209–11.

Watson, J. B., & Rayner, R. (1920). Conditioned emotional reactions. *Journal of Experimental Psychology, 3,* 1–14.

Watson, L. S., & Uzzell, R. (1981). *Handbook of behavior modification with the mentally retarded.* New York: Plenum.

Watt, N. F., Anthony, E. J., Wynne, L. C., & Rolf, J. E. (Eds.). (1984). *Children at risk for schizophrenia: A longitudinal perspective.* Cambridge: Cambridge University Press.

Weaver, T., & Clum, G. (1993). Early family environment and traumatic experiences associated with borderline personality disorders. *Journal of Consulting and Clinical Psychology, 61,* 1068–75.

Wegner, D. M., & Zanakos, S. (1994). Chronic thought suppression. *Journal of Personality, 62*(4): 615–40.

Wegner, J. T., Catalano, F., Gibralter, J., & Kane, J. M. (1985). Schizophrenics with tardive dyskinesia. *Archives of General Psychiatry, 42,* 860–65.

Weinberger, D. R. (1988). Schizophrenia and the frontal lobes. *Trends in Neuroscience, 11,* 367–70.

Weinberger, D. R., Berman, K. F., & Zec, R. F. (1986). Physiologic dysfunction of dorsolateral prefrontal cortex in schizophrenia. I. Regional cerebral blood flow evidence. *Archives of General Psychiatry, 43*(2): 114–24.

Weiner, B. (1972). *Theories of motivation: From mechanism to cognition.* Chicago: Rand McNally.

Weiner, B. (Ed.) (1974). *Achievement motivation and attribution theory.* Morristown, NJ: General Learning Press.

Weiner, H. M. (1977). *Psychology and human disease.* New York: Elsevier.

Weisaeth, L. (1989). A study of behavioural responses to industrial disaster. *Acta Psychiatrica Scandinavica, 80,* 13–24.

Weiskrantz, L., Warrington, E. K., Sanders M. D., & Marshall, J. (1974). Visual capacity of the hemianopic field following a restricted occipital ablation. *Brain, 97,* 709–28.

Weiss, F., Parsons, L. H., Schulteis, G., Hyytia, P., Lorang, M. T., Bloom, F. E., & Koob, G. F. (1996). Ethanol self-administration restores withdrawal-associated deficiencies in accumbal dopamine and 5-hydroxytryptamine release in dependent rats. *The Journal of Neuroscience, 16*(10): 3474–85.

Weiss, J. M., Glazer, H. I., & Pohoresky, L. A. (1976). Coping behavior and neurochemical change in rats: An alternative explanation for the original "learned helplessness" experiments. In G. Serban & A. King (Eds.), *Animal models in human psychobiology.* New York: Plenum.

Weiss, J. M., Simson, P. G., Ambrose, M. J., Webster, A., & Hoffman, L. J. (1985). Neurochemical basis of behavioral depression. *Advances in Behavioral Medicine, 1,* 253–75.

Weissman, M. (1990). Panic and generalized anxiety: Are they separate disorders? *Journal of Psychiatric Research, 24,* 157–62.

Weissman, M. M. (1993). The epidemiology of personality disorders: A 1990 update. *Journal of Personality Disorders, 7* (Supp., Spring): 44–62.

Weissman, M. M., Bland, R. C., Canino, G. J., Faravelli, C., Greenwald, S., Hwu, H., Joyce, P. R., Karam, E. G., Lee, C. K., Lellouch, J., Lepine, J. P., Newman, S. C., Rubio-Stipec, M., Wells, J. E., Wickramaratne, P. J., Wittchen, H. U., & Yeh, E. K. (1996). Cross-national epidemiology of major depression and bipolar disorder. *Journal of the American Medical Association, 276*(4): 293–99.

Weissman, M. M., Kidd, K. K., & Prusoff, B. A. (1982). Variability in rates of affective disorders in relatives of depressed and normal probands. *Archives of General Psychiatry, 39,* 1397–1403.

Weissman, M. M., & Olfson, M. (1995). Depression in women: Implications for health care research. *Science, 269,* 799–801.

Weissman, M. M., & Paykel, E. S. (1974). *The depressed woman: A study of social relationships.* Evanston: University of Chicago Press.

Wells, K., Burnam, M., Rogers, W., & Hays, R. (1992). The course of depression in adult outpatients: Results from the Medical Outcomes Study. *Archives of General Psychiatry, 49,* 788–94.

Wender, P. H., Kety, S. S., Rosenthal, D., Schulsinger, F., Ortmann, J., & Lunde, I. (1986). Psychiatric disorders in the biological and adoptive families of adopted individuals with affective disorders. *Archives of General Psychiatry, 43,* 923–29.

Wernicke, J. (1985). The side effect profile and safety of fluoxetine. *Journal of Clinical Psychiatry, 46,* 59–67.

Wesnes, K., & Warburton, D.M. (1984a). Effects of scopolamine and nicotine in human rapid information-processing and performance. *Psychopharmacology, 82,* 147–50.

Wesnes, K., & Warburton, D. M. (1984b). The effects of cigarettes of varying yield on rapid information processing performance. *Psychopharmacology, 82,* 338–42.

Westermeyer, J., Bouafuely, M., Neider, J., & Callies, A. (1989). Somatization among refugees: An epidemiologic study. *Psychosomatics, 30,* 34–43.

Westling, B. E., & Ost, L. G. (1995). Cognitive bias in panic disorder patients and changes after cognitive-behavioral treatments. *Behaviour Research and Therapy, 33*(5): 585–88.

White, K., Wykoff, W., Tynes, L., Schneider, L., et al. (1990). Fluvoxamine in the treatment of tricyclic-resistant depression. *Psychiatric Journal of the University of Ottawa, 15,* 156–58.

White, N. M. (1996). Addictive drugs as reinforcers: Multiple partial actions on memory systems. *Addiction, 91*(7): 921–49.

Whitehouse, W. G., Dinges, D. F., Orne, E. C., Keller, S. E., Bates, B. L., Bauer, N. K., Morahan, P., Haupt, B. A., Carlin, M. M., Bloom, P. B., Zaugg, L., & Orne, M. T. (1996). Psychosocial and immune effects of self-hypnosis training for stress management throughout the first semester of medical school. *Psychosomatic Medicine, 58,* 249–63.

Widiger, T. A. (1992). Generalized social phobia versus avoidant personality disorder: A commentary on three studies. *Journal of Abnormal Psychology, 101*(2): 340–43.

Widiger, T. A. & Corbitt, E. M. (1995). Are personality disorders well-classified in DSM-IV? In W. J. Lively (Ed.), *The DSM-IV personality disorders* (pp. 103–26). New York: Guilford.

Widiger, T. A., Frances, A J., Pincus, H. A., Davis, W. W., & First, M. B. (1991). Toward an empirical classification for the DSM-IV. *Journal of Abnormal Psychology, 100*(3): 280–88.

Wilkinson, C. (1983). Aftermath of a disaster: The collapse of the Hyatt Regency Hotel skywalks. *American Journal of Psychiatry, 140,* 1134–39.

Williams, R. B., Barefoot, J. C., & Shekelle, R. B. (1985). The health consequences of hostility. In M. Chesbney & R. Rosenman (Eds.), *Anger and hostility in cardiovascular and behavioral disorders.* New York: McGraw-Hill/Hemisphere.

Williams, R., Lane, J., Kuhn, C., et al. (1982). Type A behavior and elevated physiological and neuroendocrine responses to cognitive tasks. *Science, 218,* 483–85.

Williamson, S., Hare, R. D., & Wong, S. (1987). Violence: Criminal psychopaths and their victims. *Canadian Journal of Behavioral Science, 19,* 454–62.

Williamson, S., Harpur, T. J., & Hare, R. D. (1990). *Sensitivity to emotional valence in psychopaths.* Paper presented at the 98th Annual Convention of the American Psychological Association, Boston, MA.

Willis, M. H., & Blaney, P. H. (1978). Three tests of the learned helplessness model of depression. *Journal of Abnormal Psychology, 87,* 131–36.

Wilner, A., Reich, T., Robins, I., Fishman, R., & Van Doren, T. (1976). Obsessive-compulsive neurosis. *Comprehensive Psychiatry, 17,* 527–39.

Wilson, G. T. & Fairburn, C. (1997). Treatment of eating disorders. In P. Nathan and J. Gorman (Eds.). *Treatments that work.* New York: Oxford.

Wilson, S., Becker, L. & Tinker, R. (1996). Eye Movement Desensitization and Reprocessing (EMDR) treatment for psychologically traumatized individuals. *Journal of Consulting and Clinical Psychology.*

Winerip, M. (1994). *9 Highland Road.* New York: Pantheon.

Winnicott, D. W. (1971). *Playing and reality.* New York: International Universities Press.

Winokur, G. (1972). Family history studies VIII: Secondary depression is alive and well and . . . . *Diseases of the Nervous System, 33,* 94–99.

Winokur, G., & Coryell, W. (1992). Familial subtypes of unipolar depression: A prospective study of familial pure depressive disease compared to depression spectrum disease. *Biological Psychiatry, 32*(11): 1012–18.

Winokur, G., Scharfetter, C., & Angst, J. (1985). The diagnostic value in assessing mood congruence in delusions and hallucinations and their relationship to the affective state. *European Archives of Psychiatry and Neurological Science, 234,* 299–302.

Wirz-Justice, A., Graw, P., Krauchi, K., Sarrafzadeh, A., English, J., Arendt, J., & Sand, L. (1996). 'Natural' light treatment of seasonal affective disorder. *Journal of Affective Disorders, 37,* 109–20.

Wolf, M. M., Phillips, E. L., & Fixsen, D.C. (1975). *Achievement Place, phase II: Final report.* Kansas: Department of Human Development, University of Kansas.

Wolf, S., Cardon, P. V., Shepard, E. M., & Wolff, H. G. (1955). *Life stress and essential hypertension.* Baltimore: Williams & Wilkins.

Wolpe, J. (1969). Basic principles and practices of behavior therapy of neuroses. *American Journal of Psychiatry, 125*(5): 1242–47.

Wong, D., Horng, J., et al. (1974). A selective inhibitor of serotonin uptake: Lilly 110140, 3–(ptrifluoromethylphenoxy-N-Methyl-3-Phenylpropylamine). *Life Sciences, 15,* 471–79.

Wood, J. M., Nezworski, M. T., & Stejskal, W. J. (1996a). The Comprehensive System for the Rorschach: A critical examination. *Psychological Science, 7,* 3–10.

Wood, J. M., Nezworski, M. T., & Stejskal, W. J. (1996b). Thinking critically about the Comprehensive System for the Rorschach. A reply to Exner. *Psychological Science, 7,* 14–17.

Woodruff, R. A., Clayton, P. J., & Guze, S. B. (1971). Hysteria: Studies of diagnosis, outcome and prevalence. *Journal of the American Medical Association, 215,* 425–28.

Woodward, B., & Armstrong, A. (1979). *The brethren: Inside the Supreme Court.* New York: Simon & Schuster.

Wrobel, T. A., & Locher, D. (1982). Validity of the Wiener subtle and obvious scales for the MMPI: Another example of the importance of inventory-item content. *Journal of Consulting and Clinical Psychology, 50,* 469–70.

Yager, T., Laufer, R., & Gallops, M. (1984). Some problems associated with war experience in men of the Vietnam generation. *Archives of General Psychiatry, 41,* 327–33.

Yalom, I. D. (1980). *Existential psychotherapy.* New York: Basic Books.

Yarnold, P. R., & Bryant, F. B. (1994). A measurement model for the Type A Self-rating Inventory. *Journal of Personality Assessment, 62*(1):102–15.

Yates, A. (1966). *Theory and practice in behavior therapy* (2nd ed.). New York: Wiley.

Yates, A. (1990). Current perspectives on eating disorders: 2. Treatment, outcomes and research directions. *Journal of the American Academy of Child and Adolescent Psychiatry, 29*(1).

Yule, W., Hersov, L., & Treseder, J. (1980). Behavioral treatments of school refusal. In L. Hersov & I. Berg (Eds.), *Out of school: Modern perspectives in truancy and school refusal.* New York: Wiley.

Yule, W., & Rutter, M. (1976). Epidemiology and social implication of specific reading retardation. In R. M. Knights & D. J. Bakker (Eds.), *The neuropsychology of learning disorders.* Baltimore: University Park Press.

Zafiropoulou, M., & McPherson, F. M. (1986). "Preparedness" and the severity and outcomes of clinical phobias. *Behaviour Research and Therapy, 24,* 221–22.

Zanarini, M. C., Gunderson, J. G., Marina, M. F., Schwartz, E. O., & Frankenberg, F. R. (1989). Childhood experiences of borderline patients. *Comprehensive Psychiatry, 30,* 18–25.

Zanis, D.A., McLellan, T., Alterman, A.I., & Cnaan, R.A. (1996). Efficacy of enhanced outreach counseling to reenroll high-risk drug users 1 year after discharge from treatment. *American Journal of Psychiatry, 153*(8): 1095–96.

Zentall, S. S., & Zentall, T. R. (1983). Optimal stimulation: A model of disordered activity and performance in normal and deviant children. *Psychological Bulletin, 94,* 446–71.

Zhou, J. N., Hofman, M. A., Gooren, L. J. G., & Swaab, D. F. (1995). A sex difference in the human brain and its relation to transsexuality. [Letter to the Editor]. *Nature, 378.*

Ziegler, F. J., & Imboden, J. B. (1962). Contemporary conversion reactions: II. A conceptual model. *Archives of General Psychiatry, 6,* 279–87.

Zigler, E., & Levine, J. (1981). Age on first hospitalization of schizophrenics: A developmental approach. *Journal of Abnormal Psychology, 90,* 458–67.

Zigler, E., & Phillips, L. (1961). Psychiatric diagnosis and symptomatology. *Journal of Abnormal and Social Psychology, 63,* 69–75.

Zilbergeld, B., & Evans, M. (1980). The inadequacy of Masters and Johnson. *Psychology Today, 14,* 28–43.

Zimbardo, P. G. (1977). Shy murderers. *Psychology Today, 148,* 66–76.

Zinbarg, R. E., Barlow, D. H., Liebowitz, M., Street, L., Broadhead, E., Katon, W., Roy-Byrne, P., Lepine, J-P., Teharani, M., Richards, J., Brantley, P. J., & Kraemer, H. (1994). The DSM-IV field trial for mixed anxiety and depression. *American Journal of Psychiatry, 151*(8): 1153–62.

Zinberg, N. E. (1984). *Drugs, set, and setting.* New Haven, CT: Yale University Press.

Zisook, S., Shuchter, S. R., Irwin, M., Darko, D. F., Sledge, P., & Resovsky, K. (1994). Bereavement, depression, and immune function. *Psychiatry Research, 52,* 1–10.

Zitrin, C. M., Klein, D. F., Woerner, M. G., & Ross, D. C. (1983). Treatment of phobias I. Comparison of imipramine hydrochloride and placebo. *Archives of General Psychiatry, 40,* 125–38.

Zoccolillo, M., Pickles, A., Quinton, D., & Rutter, M. (1992). The outcome of childhood conduct disorder: Implications for defining adult personality disorder and conduct disorder. *Psychological Medicine, 22,* 971–86.

Zola-Morgan, S., Squire, L. R., & Amaral, D. (1986). Human amnesia and the medial temporal region: Enduring memory impairment following a bilateral lesion limited to the CA 1 field of the hippocampus. *Journal of Neuroscience, 6,* 2950–67.

Zorrilla, E. P., Redei, E., & DeRubeis, R. J. (1994). Reduced cytokine levels and T-cell function in healthy males: relation to individual differences in subclinical anxiety. *Brain, Behavior, and Immunity, 8*(4): 293–312.

Zubin, J. E., & Spring, B. (1977). Vulnerability: A new view of schizophrenia. *Journal of Abnormal Psychology, 86,* 103–26.

Zucker, K. J., Wilson-Smith, D. N., Kurita, J. A., & Stern, A. (1995). Children's appraisals of sex-typed behavior in their peers. *Sex Roles, 33*(11–12): 703–25.

Zullow, H., & Seligman, M. E. P. (1985). *Pessimistic ruminations predict increase in depressive symptoms: A process model and longitudinal study.* Unpublished manuscript.

ACKNOWLEDGMENTS AND COPYRIGHTS

EXCERPTS

Front and back covers: DSM-IV classification; adapted from the American Psychiatric Association, *Diagnostic and Statistical Manual of Mental Disorders,* Fourth edition. Washington, D.C.: American Psychiatric Association, 1994. Reprinted by permission. **Page 7:** Galen, cited in Veith, I., *Hysteria: The History of Disease.* Chicago: University of Chicago Press, 1965, p. 36. Copyright 1965 by the University of Chicago Press. Reprinted by permission. **Pages 15–16:** From the American Psychiatric Association, *Diagnostic and Statistical Manual of Mental Disorders,* Third edition. Washington, D.C.: American Psychiatric Association, 1981. Reprinted by permission. **Page 24:** Rapoport, J., The neurobiology of obsessive-compulsive disorder, *Journal of the American Medical Association,* 1988, *260*: 2888-90. Reprinted by permission. **Pages 70–71:** Ellis, A., *Reason and emotion in psychotherapy.* Copyright © 1962 by The Institute for Rational Living. Published by arrangement with Carol Publishing Group. **Page 92:** From the American Psychiatric Association, *Diagnostic and Statistical Manual of Mental Disorders,* Fourth edition. Washington, D.C.: American Psychiatric Association, 1994. Reprinted by permission. Pages **100–101:** Personal communication from Dr. James Stinnett, University of Pennsylvania Hospital, 1978. Used by permission. **Page 126:** From the American Psychiatric Association, *Diagnostic and Statistical Manual of Mental Disorders,* Fourth edition. Washington, D.C.: American Psychiatric Association, 1994. Reprinted by permission. **Page 129:** From the American Psychiatric Association, *Diagnostic and Statistical Manual of Mental Disorders,* Fourth edition. Washington, D.C.: American Psychiatric Association, 1994. Reprinted by permission. **Page 138:** From the American Psychiatric Association, *Diagnostic and Statistical Manual of Mental Disorders,* Fourth edition. Washington, D.C.: American Psychiatric Association, 1994. Reprinted by permission. **Pages 139–41:** From Erikson, Kai, *Everything in its path: Destruction of community in the Buffalo Creek flood.* New York: Simon & Schuster, 1976. **Pages 149, 156–57, 164, 168–69:** Laughlin, H. P., *The neuroses.* Copyright © 1967 by Butterworth Publishers, Woburn, MA. Excerpted by permission. **Pages 150, 154, 157, 164:** From the American Psychiatric Association, *Diagnostic and Statistical Manual of Mental Disorders,* Fourth edition. Washington, D.C.: American Psychiatric Association, 1994. Reprinted by permission. **Pages 152–53:** Clark, D. Anxiety states: Panic and generalized anxiety. Dr. K. Hawton, P. Salkovskis, J. Kirk, and D. Clark (Eds.), *Cognitive Behavior Therapy for Psychiatric Problems: A Practical Guide.* Oxford, Eng.: Oxford University Press. **Pages 163, 165, 166:** Rachman, S. J., and Hodgson, R. J., *Obsessions and compulsions.* Copyright © 1980 by Prentice-Hall, Inc., Englewood Cliffs, N.J. **Pages 175–76:** Personal communication from Dr. James Stinnett, University of Pennsylvania Hospital, 1978. Used by permission. **Pages 175, 176, 177:** From the American Psychiatric Association, *Diagnostic and Statistical Manual of Mental Disorders,* Fourth edition. Washington, D.C.: American Psychiatric Association, 1994. Reprinted by permission. **Pages 177, 185:** Laughlin, H. P., *The neuroses.* Copyright © 1967 by Butterworth Publishers, Woburn, MA. Excerpted by permission. **Pages 187, 188:** From the American Psychiatric Association, *Diagnostic and Statistical Manual of Mental Disorders,* Fourth edition. Washington, D.C.: American Psychiatric Association, 1994. Reprinted by permission. **Pages 189–190:** Davis, P. H., and Osherson, A., The current treatment of a multiple-personality woman and her son. *American Journal of Psychotherapy,* 1977, *31*: 504–15. Reprinted by permission of the Association for the Advancement of Psychotherapy. **Page 191:** Courtesy of Dr. Eugene L. Bliss. **Pages 199, 202, 208, 210, 211, 212, 214, 215, 216, 217:** From the American Psychiatric Association, *Diagnostic and Statistical Manual of Mental Disorders,* Fourth edition. Washington, D.C.: American Psychiatric Association, 1994. Reprinted by permission. **Pages 226, 227, 248:** Beck, A. T., Rush, A. J., Shaw, B. F., and Emery, G., *Cognitive theory of depression.* New York: Guilford Press, 1979. Reprinted by permission of

the author. **Pages 229, 235:** From the American Psychiatric Association, *Diagnostic and Statistical Manual of Mental Disorders,* Fourth edition. Washington, D.C.: American Psychiatric Association, 1994. Reprinted by permission. **Pages 254, 255, 256:** Fieve, R. R., *Mood swing.* Copyright © 1975, William Morrow & Company. **Pages 255–56:** Pavel, O., *How I came to know fish* (trans. J. Barclai and R. McDowell). New York: Story Line Press/New Directions, 1990. Reprinted with permission. **Pages 257, 261:** From the American Psychiatric Association, *Diagnostic and Statistical Manual of Mental Disorders,* Fourth edition. Washington, D.C.: American Psychiatric Association, 1994. Reprinted by permission. **Page 260:** Spitzer, R. L., Skodol, A. E., Gibbon, M., & Williams, J. B. W., *DSM-III casebook.* Washington, D.C.: American Psychiatric Association, 1989, pp. 19–21, 129–30. Reprinted by permission of the American Psychiatric Association. **Page 264:** Jerome, J., Catching them before suicide. *The New York Times Magazine,* Jan. 11, 1979. Copyright © 1979 by The New York Times Company. Reprinted by permission. **Pages 272, 310, 316, 319, 324, 325, 327, 331, 339, 344:** From the American Psychiatric Association, *Diagnostic and Statistical Manual of Mental Disorders,* Fourth edition. Washington, D.C.: American Psychiatric Association, 1994. Reprinted by permission. **Page 345:** Moody, R. L., Bodily changes during abreaction. *The Lancet,* 1946, *2*: 934–35. Reprinted by permission. **Pages 361–62:** Case history courtesy of Baycrest Hospital, Toronto, Ontario. **Page 364:** Milner, B., Memory and the medial temporal regions of the brain, in K. H. Pribram and D. E. Broadbent (Eds.), *Biology of memory.* Copyright © 1970 by Academic Press. **Page 365:** From the American Psychiatric Association, *Diagnostic and Statistical Manual of Mental Disorders,* Fourth edition. Washington, D.C.: American Psychiatric Association, 1994. Reprinted by permission. **Page 368:** Mace, N., and Rabins, P. V., *The thirty-six hour day: A family guide to caring for persons with Alzheimer's disease.* Baltimore: The Johns Hopkins University Press, 1981. Used by permission. **Pages 369, 370, 379, 380, 386, 388, 393, 394, 398, 399, 401, 402, 404, 409, 411, 412:** From the American Psychiatric Association, *Diagnostic and Statistical Manual of Mental Disorders,* Fourth edition. Washington, D.C.: American Psychiatric Association, 1994. Reprinted by permission. **Page 419:** Pauly, I. B., Adult manifestations of male transsexualism, in R. Green & J. Money (Eds.), *Transsexualism and sex reassignment.* Baltimore: Johns Hopkins University Press, 1969. Copyright © 1969 by the Johns Hopkins University Press. Adapted by permission. **Page 420:** From the American Psychiatric Association, *Diagnostic and Statistical Manual of Mental Disorders,* Fourth edition. Washington, D.C.: American Psychiatric Association, 1994. Reprinted by permission. **Page 429:** Stoller, R. J., Parental influences in male transsexualism, in R. Green & J. Money (Eds.), *Transsexualism and sex reassignment.* Baltimore: Johns Hopkins University Press, 1969. Copyright © 1969 by the Johns Hopkins University Press. Adapted by permission. **Pages 429, 430, 431, 432, 433, 440, 441, 442, 443:** From the American Psychiatric Association, *Diagnostic and Statistical Manual of Mental Disorders,* Fourth edition. Washington, D.C.: American Psychiatric Association, 1994. Reprinted by permission.

FIGURES

Figure 3–2: Adapted from Schwartz, B., *Psychology of learning and behavior,* 2nd ed. New York: W. W. Norton & Company, Inc., Copyright © 1984 by W. W. Norton and Company, Inc. Reprinted by permission. **Figure 4–1:** (A) Adapted from *Psychology* by Henry Gleitman, by permission of W. W. Norton & Company, Inc. Copyright © 1981 by W. W. Norton & Company, Inc. (B) Butcher, Dr. James, The Minnesota report. Copyright by the University of Minnesota Press. **Figure 4–2:** Reprinted from *Psychology* by Henry Gleitman, by permission of W. W. Norton & Company, Inc. Copyright © 1981 by W. W. Norton & Company, Inc. **Figure 4–3:** Reprinted from *Psychology* by Henry Gleitman, by permission of W. W. Norton & Company, Inc. Copyright © 1981 by W. W.

Norton & Company, Inc. **Figure 4–6:** Hall, R. V., Fox, R., Williard, D., Goldsmith, L., Emerson, M., Owen, M., Davis, T., & Porcia, E., The teacher as observer and experimenter in the modification of disputing and talking-out behaviors. *Journal of Applied Behavior Analysis,* 1971, *4:* 143. Adapted by permission of the Society for the Experimental Analysis of Behavior, Inc. **Figure 5–1:** Cox, P., Hallam, R., O'Connor, K., & Rachman, S., An experimental analysis of fearlessness and courage. *British Journal of Psychology,* 1983, *74:* 107–17. **Figure 5–3:** Archibald, H. C., and Tuddenham, R. D., Persistent stress reaction after combat. *Archives of General Psychiatry,* 1965, *12:* 475–81. Copyright © 1965, American Medical Association. Reprinted by permission. **Figure 8–4:** Gillham, J., Reivich, K., Jaycox, L., and Seligman, M. E. P., Prevention of depressive symptoms in school children: Two-year follow-up. *Psychological Science,* 1995, *6*(6): 343–51. Reprinted by permission. **Figure 8–5:** Rosenthal, N. E., Sack, D. A., Gillin, J. C., Lewy, A. J., Goodwin, F. K., Davenport, Y., Mueller, P. S., Newsome, D. A., & Wehr, T. A., Seasonal affective disorder: A description of the syndrome and preliminary findings with light therapy. *Archives of General Psychiatry,* 1984, *41:* 72–80. Copyright © 1984, American Medical Association. Reprinted by permission. **Figure 9–1:** From *Schizophrenia genesis: The origins of madness* by Irving Gottesman. Copyright © 1991 by Irving I. Gottesman. Used with permission of W. H. Freeman and Company. **Figure 9–2:** From *Psychology,* 3rd ed., by Henry Gleitman, by permission of W. W. Norton & Company, Inc., based on a figure from Faris and Dunham, *Mental disorders in urban areas.* Chicago: University of Chicago Press, 1939. **Figure 11–2:** Barefoot, J. C., Dahlstrom, W. G., & Williams, R. B., Hostility, CHD incidence, and total mortality: A 25-year follow-up study of 255 physicians. *Psychosomatic Medicine,* 1983, *45* (1): 59–63. Copyright © 1983 by the American Psychosomatic Society, Inc. **Figure 11–3:** Karasek, R., Baker, D., Marxer, F., Ahlbom, A., & Theorell, T., Job decision latitude, job demand, and cardiovascular disease: A prospective study of Swedish men. *American Journal of Public Health,* 1981, *71:* 694–705. Reprinted by permission. **Figure 11–4:** Greenberg, Sylvia S., *Immunity and survival: Keys to immune system health,* page 45. Copyright © 1989, Human Sciences Press. **Figure 11–5:** Kertesz, A., Two case studies: Broca's and Wernicke's aphasia, in M. A. Arbib, D. Caplan, and J. C. Marshall (Eds.), *Neural models of language processes.* Copyright © 1982 by Academic Press. **Figure 11–6:** Modified from Geschwind, N., The apraxias: Neural mechanisms of disorders of learned movement. *American Scientist,* 1975, *188:* 189. Adapted by permission. **Figure 11–7:** Modified from *Brain, mind, and behavior* by Bloom, F. E., Lazerson, A., and Hofstadter, L. Copyright © 1985 by Educational Broadcasting Corporation. Adapted by permission of W. H. Freeman and Company. **Figure 12–1:** Modified from *Drugs and the brain* by Solomon H. Snyder. Copyright © 1986 by Scientific American Books, Inc. Used with permission of W. H. Freeman and Company. **Figure 12–2:** Hunt, W. A., Barnett, L. W., and Branch, L. G., Relapse rates in addiction programs. *Journal of Clinical Psychology,* 1971, *27,* 455–56. Copyright © 1971 by the American Psychological Association. Reprinted by permission. **Figure 12–3:** Marlatt, G. A., and Gordon, J. R., *Relapse prevention: Maintenance strategies in the treatment of addictive behaviors,* Figure 1–4. New York: Guilford Press, 1985, p. 38. **Figure 12–4:** Higgins, S. T., Budney, A. J., Bickel, W. K., Hughes, J. R., Foerg, F., & Badger, G., Achieving cocaine abstinence with a behavioral approach. *American Journal of Psychiatry,* 1993, *150* (5): 763–69. Copyright © 1993 by The American Psychiatric Association. Reprinted by permission.

TABLES

Table 3–5: Abramson, L. Y., Seligman, M. E. P., & Teasdale, J., Learned helplessness in humans: Critique and reformulation. *Journal of Abnormal Psychology,* 1978, *87:* 49–74. Copyright © 1978 by the American Psychological Association. Reprinted by permission. **Table 3–6:** Adapted from Lazarus, A. A., *Multimodal behavior theory.* Copyright © 1976, Springer Publishing Company, Inc. New York, 10012. Used by permission. **Table 4–1:** Butcher, J. N., *MMPI: Research developments and clinical applications.* Copyright © 1969 by McGraw-Hill, Inc., New York. Used with permission of

the McGraw-Hill Book Company. **Table 4–2:** Robins, L. N., Helzer, J. E., Weissman, M. M., Orvaschel, H., Gruenberg, E., Burke, J. D., and Regier, D. A., Lifetime prevalence of specific psychiatric disorders in three sites. *Archives of General Psychiatry,* 1984, *41:* 949–58. Copyright © 1984, American Medical Association. Reprinted by permission. **Table 5–1:** Marks, I. M., *Fears and phobias.* New York: Academic Press, 1969. Adapted by permission. **Table 5–2:** Seligman, M. E. P., *What you can change and what you can't.* New York: Knopf, 1993, pp. 78–79. Adapted by permission. **Table 5–5:** Seligman, M. E. P., *What you can change and what you can't.* New York: Knopf, 1993, p. 67. Adapted by permission. **Table 5–7:** Seligman, M. E. P., *What you can change and what you can't.* New York: Knopf, 1993, pp. 78–79. Adapted by permission. **Table 5–9:** Seligman, M. E. P., *What you can change and what you can't.* New York: Knopf, 1993, p. 58. Adapted by permission. **Table 6–2:** Seligman, M. E. P., *What you can change and what you can't.* New York: Knopf, 1993, p. 93. Adapted by permission. **Table 6–3:** Hyler, S. E. and Spitzer, R. T., Hysteria split asunder. *American Journal of Psychiatry,* 1978, *135* (12): 1500–4. Adapted by permission. **Table 7–2:** Hutchings, B., and Mednick, S. A., Criminality in adoptees and their adoptive and biological parents: A pilot study, in S. A. Mednick and K. O. Christiansen (Eds.), *Biosocial bases of criminal behavior.* New York: Gardner Press, 1977, p. 132. **Table 8–2:** Seligman, M. E. P., *What you can change and what you can't.* Adapted by permission. New York: Knopf, 1993, p. 114. **Table 8–4:** Shneidman, E., *Suicide among the gifted,* In E. S. Shneidman (Ed.), *Suicidology: Contemporary developments.* New York: Grune and Stratton, 1976. Adapted by permission of the Psychological Corporation and Edwin Shneidman. **Table 9–2:** From *Schizophrenia genesis: The origins of madness* by Irving Gottesman. Copyright © 1991 by Irving I. Gottesman. Used with permission of W. H. Freeman and Company. **Table 10–1:** Adapted from the American Psychiatric Association, *Diagnostic and Statistical Manual of Mental Disorders,* Fourth edition. Washington, D.C.: American Psychiatric Association, 1994. Adapted by permission. **Table 11–1:** Adapted by permission of Elsevier Science Publishing Co., Inc., from Grace, W. J. and Graham, D. T., Relationship of specific attitudes and emotions to certain bodily disease. *Psychosomatic Medicine,* 1952, *14:* 243–51. Copyright © 1952 by the American Psychosomatic Society, Inc. **Table 11–2:** Holmes, T. H., and Rahe, R. H., The social readjustments ratings scale. *Journal of Psychosomatic Research,* 1967, *11:* 213–18. Elsevier Science, Ltd., Pergamon Imprint, Oxford, England. Reprinted with permission. **Table 12–1:** Kreek, M. J., Rationale for maintenance pharmacotherapy of opiate dependence, in C. P. O'Brien and J. H. Jaffe (Eds.), *Addictive states,* pp. 205–30. New York: Raven Press, 1992. **Table 12–2:** Adapted from Hilts, P. J., Is nicotine addictive? It depends on whose criteria you use. *The New York Times,* Aug. 2, 1994. Copyright © 1994 by The New York Times Company. Reprinted by permission.

BOXES

Box 1–1: Upham, 1876, cited in Deutsch, *The mentally ill in America,* New York: Columbia University Press, 1949, p. 35. **Box 4–1:** Adapted from the American Psychiatric Association, *The DSM–IV Casebook: A Learning Companion to the Diagnostic and Statistical Manual of Mental Disorders,* Fourth edition. Washington, D.C.: American Psychiatric Association, 1994. Reprinted by permission. **Box 4–3:** Seligman, M. E. P., The effectiveness of psychotherapy: The Consumer Reports study, *American Psychologist,* 1955, *50:* 965–74. Copyright © 1995 by the American Psychological Association. Adapted by permission. **Box 5–3:** Adapted by permission of Dr. Charles Spielberger. **Box 6–1:** Rachman, S. J. and Hodgson, R. J., *Obsessions and compulsions.* Copyright © 1980 by Prentice Hall, Inc., Englewood Cliffs, N.J.: **Box 6–2:** DeAngelis, T., Cambodians' sight loss tied to seeing atrocities, *APA Monitor,* July, 1990, pp. 36–37. Copyright © 1990 by the American Psychological Association. Adapted by permission. **Box 7–1:** Cleckley, H., *The mask of sanity,* Fifth edition. St. Louis: Mosby, 1976. **Box 8–2:** Seligman, M. E. P., Reivich, K., Jaycox, L. and Gillham, J., *The optimistic child,* New York: Houghton Mifflin, 1995. Adapted by permission. **Box 8–3:** Seligman, M. E. P., *Learned optimism: The skill* *to conquer life's obstacles, large and small.* New York: Random House, 1991. Adapted by permission. **Box 8–5:** Shneidman, E., Suicide among the gifted, in E. Shneidman (Ed.), *Suicidology: Contemporary developments.* New York: Grune & Stratton, 1976. Adapted by permission of The Psychological Corporation and Edwin Shneidman. **Box 9–2:** Modified from the *DSM–IV Casebook.* Washington, D.C.: American Psychiatric Association, 1994. Adapted by permission. **Box 9–3:** Adapted from Nasar, S., The lost years of a nobel laureate. *New York Times,* November 13, 1994. **Box 9–4:** Adapted from Torrey, F. F., *Out of the shadows: Confronting America's mental illness crisis.* New York: Wiley, 1997. **Box 10–2:** Modified from the *DSM–IV Casebook,* Washington, D.C.: American Psychiatric Association, 1994. Adapted by permission. **Box 10–3:** Modified from the *DSM–IV Casebook.* Washington, D.C.: American Psychiatric Association, 1994. Adapted by permission. **Box 11–3:** Adapted from Sacks, O., *An anthropologist on Mars,* New York: Knopf, 1995.

PHOTO AND CARTOON CREDITS

Chapter 1 opener (p.1): Bosch, Hieronymus, Detail from the right panel of the triptych, *The Garden of Earthly Delights: Hell,* Museo del Prado, Madrid, Spain, courtesy of Giraudon/Art Resource, NY. **p. 2:** Mantegna, Andrea, *The Sacrifice of Abraham,* monochrome painting, c. 1490, Kunsthistorisches Museum, Vienna, Austria, courtesy of Erich Lessing/Art Resource, NY. **p. 3:** Courtesy John Verano/Smithsonian Institution. **p. 4:** T.H. Matteson, *Examination of a Witch,* 1853, courtesy Peabody Essex Museum, Salem, Mass. **p. 5:** (*top*) Jan Sanders, *The Stone of Folly,* 1530, Copyright © Museo del Prado, Madrid; (*bottom*) Courtesy National Library of Medicine. **p. 8:** Wellcome Institute Library, London. **p. 9:** Bettmann. **p. 11:** (*left*) Colored-pencil drawing by Paul Duhem, courtesy Art en Marge, Brussels; (*right*) "Stressé?", illustration by Geneviève Côté. **p. 12:** Edgar Degas, *Melancholy,* c. 1874, The Phillips Collection. **p. 14:** (*top*) Photograph courtesy of Catherine Defoe and Ted Polhemus; (*bottom*) Drawing by Sempé, ©1981 The New Yorker Magazine, Inc. **p. 15:** Photofest. **Chapter 2 opener (p. 23):** Frantisek Kupka, *Red and Blue Disks,* 1911(?); oil on canvas, 39″ by 24″, The Museum of Modern Art, New York, Inter-American Fund. **p. 24:** Courtesy Dr. Henry Wagner. **p. 26:** Courtesy National Library of Medicine. **p. 28:** Bettmann. **p. 29:** ©1989 Bob Sacha. **p. 30:** Courtesy of Science Source/Photo Researchers. **p. 34:** Courtesy State of New York Office of Mental Health. **p. 35:** Cartoon by Sidney Harris. **Chapter 3 opener (p. 38):** Illustration by Eric Dinyer. **p. 39:** Courtesy National Library of Medicine. **p. 40:** ©Jonathan A. Meyers. **p. 41:** Drawing by Dana Fradon, ©1973 The New Yorker Magazine, Inc. **p. 44:** (*top*) Bettmann; (*bottom*) Courtesy Alexandra Adler. **p. 45:** (*top left*) Courtesy National Library of Medicine; (*top right*) The Warder Collection. **p. 45:** (*bottom left*) Photograph by John Erikson; (*bottom right*) AP/Wide World Photos. **p. 46:** The Warder Collection. **p. 47:** Kevin Kling. **p. 52:** (*left*) ©Marcia Weinstein; (*right*) Karen McClean. **p. 53:** AP/Wide World Photos/Kansas City Star, Joe Ledford. **p. 54:** ©British Museum. **p. 55:** AP/Wide World Photos. **p. 57:** Courtesy Sovfoto. **p. 60:** (*all*) ©1983 Erika Stone. **p. 61:** (*top*) Courtesy National Library of Medicine; (*bottom*) Photograph by Christopher S. Johnson. **p. 67:** (*both*) Suzanne Szasz. **p. 69:** Louis DeLuca. **p. 70:** Courtesy Institute for Rational Living. **Chapter 4 opener (p. 77):** Winold Reiss, mural at Cincinnati Union Terminal (detail), ©1994 Estate of Winold Reiss/VAGA, New York. **p. 78:** AP/Wide World Photos, Ruth Fremson. **p. 84:** Cartoon by Sidney Harris. **p. 86:** ©1994, B.S.I.P./Custom Medical Stock Photo. **p. 99:** James Nachtwey/Magnum. **p. 101:** Source unknown. **p. 105:** Yale Joel, Life Magazine, ©1958 Time, Inc. **p. 112:** AP/Wide World Photos, J. Pat Carter. **Chapter 5 opener (p. 120):** Marc Chagall, *Nu,* ©1994 Fundación Colección Thyssen-Bornemisza, Madrid. All rights reserved. Total or partial reproduction prohibited. **p. 121:** AP/Wide World Photos, The Clarion-Ledger, Schwalm. **p. 122:** Photofest. **p. 123:** (*left*) Charles Mason/Black Star; (*right*) James L. Amos/Corbis. **p. 127:** ©1982 Frostie/Woodfin Camp. **p. 128:** ©Chronicle Features, 1982. **p. 129:** ©Skjold Photos. **p. 130:** Rufino Tamayo, *Animals,* 1941; oil on canvas, 36″ by 28″, The Museum of Modern Art, New York.

p. 133: Courtesy Dr. Joseph Wolpe. **p. 134:** (*top*) Randy Olson; (*bottom pair*) ©Susan Rosenberg/Photo Researchers. Snake courtesy of Academy of Natural Sciences of Philadelphia. **p. 140:** (*left*) ©David Lane/The Palm Beach Post; (*right*) Agence France-Presse. **p. 141:** The Warder Collection. **p. 142:** AP/Wide World Photos, Jean-Marc Bouju. **p. 143:** Titian, *Tarquin and Lucretia,* Fitzwilliam Museum, University of Cambridge. **p. 144:** National Archives Photo 111-SC-347803. **p. 149:** Wilfredo Lam, *The Jungle,* 1943; gouache on paper mounted on canvas, 7′10″ by 7′6″, The Museum of Modern Art, New York, Inter-American Fund. **p. 151:** Courtesy David Clark. **p. 158:** Rosalyn Benjet, *The North Beach Cafes,* ©1994 Rosalyn Benjet/VAGA, New York. **Chapter 6 opener (p. 162):** Drawing by Claire Teller, courtesy Musée d'Art Brut, Neuilly-sur-Marne, France. **p. 169:** (*top*) Courtesy Dr. S. J. Rachman; (*bottom*) Drawing by W. Miller; ©1982 The New Yorker Magazine, Inc. **p. 171:** Courtesy Dr. Judith Rapoport. **p. 173:** Courtesy Dr. Edna Foa. **p. 179:** UPI/ Bettmann. **p. 186:** Photofest. **p. 189:** Jacqueline Morreau, *Divided Self I,* 1982, courtesy Jacqueline Morreau. **Chapter 7 opener (p. 198):** Painting by Jean-Marie Heyligen, courtesy Art en Marge, Brussels. **p. 200:** Courtesy The Salt Lake Tribune. **p. 204:** Photofest. **p. 210:** Drawing by Martha Grunenwaldt, courtesy Musée d'Art Brut, Neuilly-sur-Marne, France. **p. 212:** Jacqueline Morreau, *Woman Watching,* 1981, courtesy Jacqueline Morreau. **p. 217:** The Warder Collection. **Chapter 8 opener (p. 222):** Tsing-Fang Chen, *Bombardment,* Lucia Gallery, New York, Super Stock, Inc. **p. 226:** Pablo Picasso, *The Old Guitarist,* 1903, oil on panel, 48″ x 32″, photo ©1997 The Art Institute of Chicago, Helen Birch Bartlett Memorial Collection, 1926.253, ©1997, Estate of Pablo Picasso/Artists Rights Society(ARS), New York. **p. 227:** Jacqueline Morreau, *The Artist Watching,* courtesy Jacqueline Morreau. **p. 232:** ©Marcia Weinstein. **p. 233:** ©Ed Lettau/Photo Researchers. **p. 241:** (*top*) ©Will McIntyre/Photo Researchers; (*bottom*) Thomas Eakins, *Mrs. Edith Mahon,* 1904, Smith College Museum of Art, Northampton, Mass. **p. 243:** The Warder Collection. **p. 245:** (*left*) Raymond Gehman/Corbis; (*right*) Tony Arruza/Corbis. **p. 258:** Courtesy Theodore Roosevelt Birthplace, New York. **p. 262:** AP/Wide World Photos, Robert Sorbo. **p. 264:** Richard Bosman, *Witness,* 1983, courtesy Brooke Alexander. **p. 265:** UPI/Bettmann. **Chapter 9 opener (p. 269):** Adolf Wölfli, *Arnica Flower,* 1917, courtesy Adolf Wölfli Foundation, Museum of Fine Arts, Bern. **p. 271:** Drawing by Carl Lange, ©Prinzhorn-Sammlung, Universität Heidelberg/Foto Klinger Kunsthist Institute. **p. 273:** René Magritte, *The Song of the Violet,* ©1995 C. Herscovici, Brussels/Artists Rights Society, New York. **p. 275:** (*left*) Jerry Cooke/Photo Researchers; (*right*) Bill Bridges/Globe Photos. **p. 277:** Salvador Dali, *Les Eléphants,* courtesy Galerie Christine et Isy Brachot, Brussels. **p. 279:** Courtesy Prinzhorn-Sammlung, Universität Heidelberg. **p. 280:** Drawing by August Klett (Klotz), courtesy Prinzhorn-Sammlung, Universität Heidelberg/Foto Zentsch. **p. 281:** Painting by Miguel Hernandez, courtesy Musée d'Art Brut, Neuilly-sur-Marne, France. **p. 282:** ©1995 The Munch Museum/The Munch-Ellingsen Group/ARS, New York. **p. 285:** (*left*) Library of Congress; (*right*) Bethlem Royal Hospital Archives and Museum. **p. 294:** (*both*) Courtesy of Science Source/Photo Researchers. **p. 295:** (*both*) Courtesy National Institute of Mental Health. **p. 298:** Illustration by Elizabeth Wolf. **p. 299:** ©1979 Jerry Cooke/Photo Researchers. **Chapter 10 opener (p. 307):** Paul Mathey, *Woman and Child in an Interior,* Musée d'Orsay/Photo RMN. **p. 308:** Marcia Weinstein. **p. 310:** Marcia Weinstein. **p. 321:** Illustration from *Their Eyes Meeting the World* by Robert Coles, copyright ©1992 by Robert Coles. Reprinted by permission of Houghton Mifflin Co. **p. 325:** ©1982 Susan Rosenberg/Photo Researchers. **p. 332:** (*left*) Nancy Kaye/Leo de Wys; (*right*) Alan Carey/The Image Works. **p. 335:** ©Marcia Weinstein. **p. 337:** Allan Grant. **p. 338:** Alan Carey/The Image Works. **p. 340:** (*top*) Patrick Tehan; (*bottom*) Allan Grant. **Chapter 11 opener (p. 343):** Courtesy of David McGlynn. **p. 345:** Moody, R. L., Bodily changes during abreaction. *The Lancet,* 1946: 2: 934–35. Reprinted by permission. **p. 348:** Sportsphoto/Hulton Deutsch. **p. 352:** ©1986 Lennart Nilsson/National Geographic. Courtesy Bonniers Fakta, Sweden. **p. 356:** Chuck Nacke/Picture Group.

NAME INDEX

arousal *(continued)*
    and antisocial personality disorder, 205
arteriosclerosis, 345–46
assessment, *see* psychological assessment
asthma:
    and cognitions, 358
    and conditioning examples, 357
    emotionally induced, 355
at-risk studies, on schizophrenia, 290–91
attentional deficits, in schizophrenia,
    278–79
attention-deficit hyperactivity disorder
    (ADHD), 309, 314–18
    and frontal-lobe dysfunction, 371
attributional theory of helplessness,
    245–48
attributions, 68–70
autism, 335–39
    selective punishment for, 63–64
    treatment of, 339–40
automatic thoughts, 68
    and depression, 248, 250
    and stress theory, 356
Automatic Thoughts Questionnaire, 68
autonomy:
    and anorexia, 327, 328
    see also control; freedom
aversion therapy, 435–36
avoidance learning, 64–65
    and antisocial personality disorder, 204–5
avoidance responding, 123
avoidant personality disorder, 211
axes, in DSM-IV, 91–92

"bad seed," 205
barbiturates, 410–12
BASIC ID, 71, 72
Baxstrom v. *Herold*, 454
Beck Depression Inventory, 109
Bedlam, 6
behavioral assessment, 85–86
behavioral model, 21, 56–57
    and agoraphobia, 156
    avoidance learning, 64–65, 204–5
    vs. cognitive model, 71
    evaluation of, 73
    operant conditioning, 61–64, 65, 318
    and paraphilias, 434–35
    Pavlovian conditioning, 57–61, 65 (*see
        also* Pavlovian conditioning)
    of psychosomatic disorders, 357–60
    and sexual dysfunction, 444, 445
behaviorism, 56
    and change, 19
behavior management, for ADHD, 318
behavior(al) therapies:
    for autism, 339–40
    for cocaine dependence, 395
    for eating disorders, 328, 329
    for ego-dystonic homosexuality, 426–27
    for enuresis, 12
    evaluation of, 73
    for obsessive-compulsive disorder,
        172–73, 174
    operant therapy, 62–64
    optimism of, 59
    Pavlovian therapies, 60–61
    see also cognitive-behavioral therapy;
        treatment
Belgian Heart Disease Prevention Trial, 347
belief, irrational, 70
Bender Visual-Motor Gestalt Test, 87
benzedrine, 392
benzodiazepines, 35, 388, 410–12

beta blockers:
    for schizophrenia, 300
    for social phobia, 136
bias:
    in diagnoses, 96–99
    experimenter, 104
    in MMPI-2, 81
    subject, 104
biochemistry, as etiology, 30
biofeedback, 86
biogenic amines, 236, 237
biological explanation, of schizophrenias,
    291–95
biological model:
    of bipolar disorder, 259
    of depression, 236–41
biological psychiatry, 24
biological vulnerability:
    to alcoholism, 389
    to substance dependence, 383
biomedical model, 21, 23–24
    vs. behavioral view, 59
    and causes of abnormality, 24–31
    evaluation of, 36
    and obsessive-compulsive disorder, 168,
        170–72
    and panic disorder, 150–51, 153
    of psychosomatic disorders, 354–56
    and treatment, 25, 31–36
bipolar disorder (manic-depression), 223,
    224, 254–61
    cause of, 258
    course and characteristics of, 256–58
    and mania symptoms, 254–56
    and predictive validity, 96
    seasonal affective disorder, 259–61
    treatment of (lithium), 32, 34–35, 224,
        259
bisexuality, 417, 423
blindness, hysterical, 182–83
blood alcohol content (BAC), 385
blood-brain barrier, 381
blood phobia, 127, 128
    applied tension as therapy for, 135
body-mind interaction, *see* organic disor-
    ders; psychosomatic disorders
borderline personality disorder, 216–18
brain:
    and AIDS dementia, 370
    and amnesia, 365–66
    and biomedical approach, 24
    frontal lobes, 238, 294–95, 370–73
    and mental disorder, 343
    and neuropsychological tests, 86–88
    and psychopathology, 30–31
    in schizophrenics, 277, 294–95
    and sexual orientation, 424
brain imaging, 88
brain scanning, 88–89
    and depression, 238
    and obsessive-compulsive disorder, 171,
        172
brain waves, and antisocial personality dis-
    order, 207
Brawner case, 464–65
Briquet's disorder (syndrome), 176
Broca's area and aphasia, 361
bulimia, 324, 326–28
    and cultural ideals, 230

caffeine, problem-area ratings of, 408
California Alliance for the Mentally Ill
    (CAMI), 459
Cambodian regime of Pol Pot

    and PTSD, 142
    and sight loss, 179
cancer, psychological factors in, 353, 354
cannibis (marijuana), 403–5
Cardiovascular Risk in Young Finns Study,
    347
case history, *see* clinical case history
castration, 436
    chemical, 435, 436
catastrophes, *see* disasters and catastrophes
catastrophic misinterpretations, as panic-
    disorder cause, 151, 152
catatonic schizophrenia, 274–75
catecholamines, 236, 237
catharsis, 49
cathexis, 434
CAT scan, 88, 89
causality, and correlation, 110
causes, search for, *see* methodology, scientific
child abuse:
    effects of, 312
    and mental retardation, 334
    and multiple personality disorder, 188,
        192, 193
    see also sexual abuse, childhood
childhood disorders, 307–9
    and childhood sexual abuse, 312, 322–23
    depression, 230–32, 321–22
    developmental disorders, 329–40, 363
    disruptive behavior disorders, 308,
        309–18
    emotional disorders, 318–22
    frontal lobe related, 371–72
    habit disorders and eating disorders, 308,
        309, 323–29 (*see also* eating disorders)
childhood trauma:
    reliving of, 20
    see also child abuse
child molesters (pedophiles), 431, 433,
    435, 436
chlordiazepoxide (Librium), 32, 35, 410
chlorpromazine (Thorazine), 33, 89–90,
    299, 301, 302
choice:
    existentialists' stress on, 52–53
    and psychosomatic disorders, 360
    see also autonomy; voluntary behavior
chorionic villus sampling (CFS), 332
chromosomes, and sex, 417n
chronic schizophrenia, 284–85
cigarette smoking, 385, 406–10
civil commitment, 459
    see also involuntary commitment and
        treatment
civil liberties, and law-abnormality relation,
    450
    see also criminal commitment; involuntary
        commitment and treatment
clang associations, in schizophrenia, 278
classical conditioning, *see* Pavlovian condi-
    tioning
clinical case history, 99, 100–102, 116
clinical interview, 78–79
clomipramine, 172, 173–74
clonazepam, 35
clozapine, 300, 301
cocaine, 392–96
    and addiction, 379
    with heroin, 397
    problem-area ratings of, 408
    treatment of dependence on, 395–96
codeine, 396
cognition:
    in BASIC ID, 72

homeless people, and deinstitutionalization, 302
homosexuality, 417
  and "disorder," 425–26
  ego-dystonic, 416, 417, 426–27
  male, 423–25
  and marriage and children, 448
  see also sexual orientation
hopelessness, and cancer, 353
hopelessness theory of depression, 246
hospitalization:
  and deinstitutionalization, 299–300, 302, 457
  historical evolution of, 6
  and involuntary commitment, 450–59
  prior to antipsychotic drugs, 33, 299
hostility, and coronary heart disease, 347–48
Huntington's disease, and frontal-lobe dysfunction, 371
hyperactivity, impulsivity and attentional difficulties (HIA), 203
hypnotism, 8–9
  self-hypnosis, 192, 193, 194, 353
  see also suggestion
hypochondriasis, 44
  and MMPI scores, 80
hypomanic episodes, 224
hysteria, 3–4, 5, 7, 9
  and MMPI scores, 80
hysterical conversion, 175
  blindness, 182–83
  see also conversion disorders

id, 39, 40
ideal standards, violation of as abnormality criterion, 14–15, 16
idea of reference, 215, 281
identification, 42–43
identity alteration, 185
identity confusion, 185
illness and injury phobias (nosophobias), 127–28
immune system, psychological factors as affecting, 350–54
immunologic memory, 351
implicit learning, 367
impotence, *see* erectile dysfunction
imprinting, sexual, 433
incidence, of disorder, 125
independent variable, 102
index case, 287
indoleamines, 236, 238
inference, statistical, 105–6
inferred traits, 90
insane, treatment of:
  historical view on, 6
  see also hospitalization
insanity defense, 460–62
  and ALI rule, 463, 464–65
  and Durham test, 463, 464
  and "guilty but mentally ill" verdict, 466
  and Insanity Defense Reform Act, 463, 465–66
  and M'Naghten rule, 462–63
  rare use of, 460, 466
Insanity Defense Reform Act, 463, 465–66
insight, for somatoform disorder, 184
instrumental conditioning, *see* operant conditioning
intellectualization, 43
intelligence, and mental retardation, 329
intelligence tests, 83–84
interjudge reliability, 93
internal attributions, 68–70

interns' syndrome, 17
interpersonal relationships, in BASIC ID, 72
interpersonal therapy (IPT), 242–43, 252, 303
  for bulimia, 328
intersubjectivity, 46
interview, clinical, 78–79
intoxication, 382
introversion-extraversion, and MMPI scores, 80
inventory, psychological, 79–81
involuntary commitment and treatment, 450
  and commitment criteria, 453–55
  vs. criminal commitment, 459
  and due process of law, 455–56
  and patients' rights movement, 457–59
  and perceptions of abnormality, 451–53
  and right to treatment, 456–57
  and standard of proof, 456
iproniazid, 34
IQ:
  genetic factor in, 333
  and retardation, 330
irrationality, 13
irresistible impulse, 465
isolation, as defense mechanism, 43

Jackson v. *Indiana*, 467

ketamine, 402
kindling phenomenon, 322
Klinefelter's Syndrome, 331
Korsakoff's syndrome, 365

laboratory model, 114–16
language:
  and autism, 335, 336–37
  and existentialists on responsibility, 52
  for infant, 46
  localization of, 361
  and MMPI revision, 81
  see also communication
language disorders, *see* aphasias
law-abnormality relation, 450
  in criminal commitment, 459–68
  and evil-insane distinction, 431–32
  in involuntary commitment and treatment, 450–59
  and multiple personality, 468–69
  and recovered memories, 469–71
law of effect, 61
L-DOPA, 293, 373
lead exposure:
  and mental retardation, 334
  and Tay-Sachs Disease, 331
learned helplessness, 115
learned helplessness model of depression, 229, 244–48, 250, 251–52
learning:
  and antisocial personality disorder, 204–5
  avoidance, 64–65, 204–5
  implicit, 367
  see also conditioning
learning disorders, 334–35
learning models, 21
  of addiction, 396
  and drug dependence, 384–85
lesbians, 424, 425
Librium (chlordiazepoxide), 32, 35, 410
life events:
  and depression, 233–34, 236
  and immune system, 352, 353–54
  and psychosomatic disorders, 356, 358–60

lifetime prevalence, 111
limbic system, 365, 366
lipid (fat) solubility, 381
lithium, 32, 34–35, 224, 259, 300, 313
Little Albert case, 108, 130, 132
Lockerbie air disaster, and PTSD, 142
logical errors, depression produced by, 244
loneliness, and fusion with others, 53–54
longitudinal study, 114, 349
long-term beliefs, 70
long-term memories, vulnerability of, 31
loss of control, 13
LSD, 400–402
Luminal (phenobarbital), 410
Luria-Nebraska Neuropsychological Battery, 88

McDonald v. *United States*, 464n
Magnetic Resonance Imaging (MRI), 89, 295
magnification, and depression, 244
mainlining, 380
mainstreaming, of mentally retarded, 334
major depressive episode, 223, 229
maladaptiveness, 12
male sexual response, 438–39
malingering, 178
  diagnosis of, 180
mania, 223
  and MMPI scores, 80
  symptoms of, 254–56
manic-depression, 223, 254
  and biomedical model, 36
  see also bipolar disorder
manic episode, 254
  lifetime prevalence rates of, 111
MAO inhibitors:
  for agoraphobia, 32
  for depression, 32, 34, 236, 237–38, 239, 240, 247, 251
  and dreaming, 102
  for learned helplessness, 247, 251
  side effects of, 32, 136, 240
  for social phobia, 32, 136
marijuana, 403–5
  problem-area ratings of, 408
masculinity-femininity, and MMPI scores, 80
masochism, 416, 430
masturbation:
  in aversive therapy, 436
  and exhibitionism, 432
  and fetishes, 428, 429
  and pedophilia, 433
  and sexual interests, 448
  and sexual orientation, 423–24, 424, 425
  and voyeurism, 432–33
Maudsley Obsessive-Compulsive Inventory, 167
Mayock v. *Martin*, 451–52
MDMA ("Ecstasy"), 403
mean (statistical), 106
meaning, in schizophrenia, 283–84
meaning in life, and lung cancer, 353
meaning-oriented memory, 365
medical model, of alcoholism and drug addictions, 379
meditation, 159–60
megavitamins, for schizophrenia, 300
melancholic features, 223
Melancholy, Age of, 228
memory(ies):
  and Alzheimer's disease, 368–69
  and amnesia, 185–88, 195, 364–67
  false, 50, 193